STRATEGIC
MANAGEMENT

Concepts & Practices

Paul Shrivastava

Bucknell University

COLLEGE DIVISION South-Western Publishing Co.

Cincinnati Ohio

Acquisitions Editor: Randy L. Haubner
Production Editor: Sue Ellen Brown
Marketing Manager: Scott D. Person
Cover and Interior Designer: Lotus Wittkopf
Cover Photographer: Richard Hamilton Smith Photography
Production House: York Production Services

GH63AA
Copyright © 1994
by South-Western Publishing Co.
Cincinnati, Ohio

1 2 3 4 5 6 7 KI 9 8 7 6 5 4 3

Printed in the United States of America

Library of Congress Cataloging-in-Publication Data
Shrivastava, Paul.
    Strategic management : concepts and practices / Paul Shrivastava.
— 1st ed.
        p.   cm.
    Includes bibliographical references and index.
    ISBN 0-538-81749-6 (alk. paper)
    1. Strategic planning.   2. Strategic planning—Case studies.
I. Title.
HD30.28.S433   1994   93-31412
658.4'012—dc20   CIP

International Thomson Publishing

South-Western Publishing Co. is an ITP Company. The ITP trademark is used under
license.

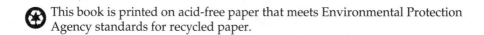

This book is printed on acid-free paper that meets Environmental Protection
Agency standards for recycled paper.

PREFACE

The field of strategic management has grown dramatically over the past three decades. In each decade we have seen companies faced with different strategic problems, and we have seen the development of new strategy concepts and theories.

In the 1960s, there were just one or two textbooks in the field of strategic management and they were based on Harvard case studies and the simple Strengths, Weaknesses, Opportunities and Threats (SWOT) model of analysis. The 1970s saw an expansion of texts: several new books appeared that expanded the SWOT model and experimented with new explanatory schema. In the 1980s, dozens of new strategy texts were published that further refined SWOT analysis. They proposed normative strategic planning models and summarized emerging research on strategic management. Despite the many incremental advances they reflect, the existing textbooks remain inadequate for the 1990s and the coming century.

The 1990s need a different textbook because the business environment of the coming decade will be very different from the past. This is the decade of change and turbulence caused by *global economic and ecological restructuring*. This change and turbulence is not only rapid, unpredictable, and complex, but also contradictory and crisis-inducing. Responding to these changes will require corporations to fundamentally rethink their strategies, structures, and performance.

The world economy is simultaneously fragmenting and integrating. Fragmentation of the former Soviet block and its reintegration into a global economy has worldwide strategic implications. Breakdown of traditional economic and political treaties, market norms, and trading and currency exchange mechanisms is inducing new uncertainties for business.

At the same time, there is integration of global economic forces. European economies are integrating into a single Common Market; the North American Free Trade Agreement (NAFTA) has created the world's largest open market; Pacific Rim economies are emerging as global competitors; new regional economic treaties are on the anvil throughout the world and ecological changes are forcing businesses to think about the future in fundamentally different terms: natural resources are limited and exhaustible; ecological crises are rampant, rooted in industrial activities; consumers want green products and reduced wastes. Environmentalism is affecting business on all sides. The rapid changes in business environments are forcing companies into numerous crises and restructurings.

Strategic management in the coming decade will need to be responsive to these and other related social, political, and cultural changes. It is from this understanding of the needs of the 1990s and the coming century that I have developed the present text.

This book examines how companies can cope and prosper in the new world. The challenge I have tried to meet is balancing the needs of the new world of the future with what we know about strategic management from the past. I have retained the core ideas from past research and practices in the field while adding a new orientation, new concepts, and new cases to reflect the changing economic and ecological order.

The book is designed with flexibility in mind. Just as companies will need to be flexible in the 1990s, so will instructors and educators. Hence, the book has four parts to it: text, Cases, Corporate Policy Documents, and Readings. The text (chapters 1-11) discusses traditional concepts of strategy formulation and implementation. It also provides new conceptual frameworks for examining global strategic management ecological crises and crisis management.

The Cases illustrate concepts and provide material for classroom discussion. There are some well-known cases and many fresh new ones written specifically for this book. The selection of cases is balanced to include international cases on American, West European, Japanese, and East European companies. Cases cover a variety of industries, different size firms, different technology sectors, and different strategic situations. There are three Industry Notes on the airlines, hospital, and tire industries. These can be coupled with company cases within the industries to study sequences of Industry Analysis followed by Company Analysis.

The Corporate Policy Documents are from actual companies and add realism and practicality to the book. This is the first strategy/policy textbook that includes actual corporate and business policy documents. They show students what real policies and strategic plans look like and offer a unique opportunity for understanding, critiquing, and improving current strategies and policies. I have experimented with these policy documents for several years, using them to illustrate strategies/policies, to explore policy implementation, to assess strategic performance, and to compare strategies/policies of different companies. In every instance, students found them valuable. The Readings, which are classics in the field and cover a broad domain, allow students to delve more deeply into selected topics.

The instructor can combine these four elements judiciously to create different versions of the Business Policy/Strategic Management courses that vary in complexity, depth, variety, and focus.

The book can also be used for special courses on Strategic Planning and Corporate Strategy, especially when the instructor wants to emphasize ecological issues. The strategic salience of ecological issues is drawn out in the chapters on environmental analysis, industry structure analysis, strategy formulation, strategy implementation, and strategic crisis management.

The Instructor's Manual contains supplementary teaching materials including case teaching notes, transparency masters, test banks, classroom exercises, and suggestions for using videos. I have tried to create a comprehensive package for both instructors and students.

This book would not have been possible without the help and support of many friends and colleagues. I want to thank all the case authors for permission to print their cases here. Several cases were written specially for this book and others are published here for the first time. For this special privilege I want to thank Jon Chilengerian, Per Jenster, Briance Mascarenhas, Susan Schneider, and Coral Snodgrass.

For permission to print corporate policy documents, I want to thank all the companies who cheerfully agreed to share this information publicly. They have set a new standard in openness which will benefit the next generation of students.

Charles Snow, Charles Hoier, Daniel Jennings, and Tim Stearns provided very valuable feedback on early drafts of this book. Their comments made me restructure the book in very fundamental ways. Thanks also to Charles Toftoy, R. Duane Ireland, Alan N. Hoffman, Ramon J. Aldag, and Jane Dutton. I am grateful for their detailed and constructive advice. I also very much appreciate the several anonymous reviewers who have helped hone the book's style, content, and topical coverage.

The production of a textbook is an ordeal no author should undertake without able editors, publishers, and secretaries. The folks at South-Western have been exemplary in their support and cooperation. Randy Haubner picked up this project midstream and tactfully guided it to completion. Sue Ellen Brown's meticulous control over production details made it possible to produce the book while I travelled incessantly. At Bucknell, Elaine Herrold held the fort, armed with *The American Heritage Dictionary*. Thanks to Luis Martins for assistance with the Instructor's Manual.

I also want to acknowledge the cooperation and support of Bucknell University and particularly the Management Department. Bucknell's commitment to teaching and students motivated me to write this book in the first place.

It is customary to thank one's spouse and family for all the support they provide during book projects. That would be patronizing and inaccurate in my case. Thanks to my wife Michelle for challenging me to think creatively about substantive issues and for actively egging me on to the end. Thanks to my children, Claudia and Kyle, for frequently disturbing my writing with their "the-world-is-ending" demands. I needed those breaks. They helped me maintain my sanity and perspective.

Despite all this help, I probably still managed to get some errors in. I seek your indulgence on them. If you catch any, do drop me a note. I hope you find this book useful and different.

Paul Shrivastava
Lewisburg, Pennsylvania

CONTENTS IN BRIEF

CONTENTS

CHAPTER 1
INTRODUCTION TO
STRATEGIC MANAGEMENT

CHAPTER OUTLINE

On August 1, 1990, one day before Iraq invaded Kuwait, Robert C. Stempel took over as the chairman and chief executive officer of General Motors (GM). GM was the world's largest industrial company. The Iraqi invasion brought with it skyrocketing oil prices. A 10,000-car order for the Chevrolet Caprice bound for Kuwait was canceled. A fresh wave of fears of economic recession threw the automobile industry into a panic.

At the end of the 1980s, the American auto industry was reeling from the devastating onslaught of foreign competition, particularly from Japan. By the end of 1990, Japanese automakers controlled 27% of the American auto market. During the previous decade, GM's share of the market had slid from a commanding 46% to a humble 35%. The company was forced to close down many plants, and it invested more than $50 billion to modernize its remaining facilities. GM offered heavy rebates to reduce inventories. It did a massive internal reorganization cutting $13 billion in costs since 1987. It upgraded the quality and reliability of its products.

The international economic and political situation at the end of 1990 was bleak. The war in the Persian Gulf caused new geopolitical uncertainty in the Middle East. Communist regimes in Eastern Europe were fast breaking down. The former Soviet Union was disintegrating. The US government budget and trade deficits were over $320 billion and $250 billion, respectively. Oil prices and financial markets fluctuated wildly. A full-scale economic recession boiled down to one thing for GM: nervous, uncertain, and reluctant car buyers.

Stempel and his top management team faced quintessential strategic problems that most American companies must deal with in the 1990s. How should GM react to the environmental changes that were battering its products, markets, technologies, and production facilities? How should GM use its scarce financial and human resources to stop its slide. How could GM become more competitive and turn around its financial performance? How could GM ensure long-term profitability? To succeed in the 1990s, GM would have to rethink its product designs and product portfolio. It would have to cut costs to be competitive with Japanese carmakers. It would have to rearrange the structure of its organization to improve efficiency and product quality. It would have to make cleaner and safer cars to comply with new environmental regulations. As it turned out these strategic challenges were not managed successfully by Mr. Stempel and his top management team. By the end of 1992 Stempel was fired and the top management team was reorganized.

GM is not the only company faced with such strategic long-term decisions. The foremost challenge facing top management of most corporations today is how to manage their companies strategically to survive and grow in the turbulent environment of the 1990s. Managing strategically is a complex task. It requires integrating knowledge from all areas of business to run the total enterprise. It requires managers to make tough economic and social choices; they must continually align their organization with its complex and changing environment. Strategic decisions involve complex internal processes. They include rational economic analysis, social interactions among managers, political considerations, and personal values of individual managers.

The subject of strategic management/business policy focuses on managerial issues that affect the organization as a whole—issues that have long-term implications and deal with **organization-environment relationships**. Strategic management/business policy teaches how to maximize the **effectiveness** of the whole organization. In a secondary way, it also teaches how to improve **efficiency** (Drucker, 1974; Hofer and Schendel, 1978). This orientation toward effectiveness, in addition to efficiency, is the hallmark of strategic management.

Efficiency refers to the ratio of inputs over outputs. An efficiency orientation attempts to maximize outputs for any given set of inputs. It involves producing goods and services in the most technologically and economically competent manner with minimum waste of resources.

Effectiveness, on the other hand, is the ratio of achieved outputs over needed outputs (goals). The output needs are determined by environmental demands. An effectiveness orientation involves understanding these demands. It requires developing organizational objectives that are consistent with the environment. It involves managing the organization's resources to be responsive to environmental changes and to meet specific objectives.

The emphasis on effectiveness does not imply that efficiency is unimportant. Efficiency is highly desirable and even necessary for success. However, alone it is not sufficient to ensure long-term success. The stories of many well-respected and mature companies illustrate the importance of effectiveness. For example, Pan American Airlines (Pan Am), Facit, and EPI Products USA failed to survive despite being large and efficient.

Pan Am was the first, and at one point the largest, US-based international airline. It went bankrupt in 1990 after nearly fifty years of operations. The company virtually created the airline industry. For decades it defined the efficiency standards in the industry. It prospered in the highly regulated airline environment up to the early 1970s. Pan Am exploited its economies of scale, excellent route structure, and efficient airplane fleet.

With the deregulation of the airline industry in 1978 came competition and radical changes in the environment. Deregulation altered the competitive structure of the industry. It lead to decontrol over routes and prices. The industry got organized along a hub-and-spoke system. Certain large cities became regional hubs. Passengers came into these hubs from smaller regional airports (spokes) and made connections to other hubs. Major trunk carriers provided connections between hubs. Smaller regional carriers connected small airports to hubs. Major airlines started tying up their flight schedules with small, regional, feeder airlines to create convenient connecting flights for travelers.

Pan Am did not anticipate these changes. It continued to do business as usual, focusing on international markets. It did not change its objectives or operations to fit industry changes. By the mid-1980s it started losing business to domestically well-connected carriers such as American Airlines and United Airlines. These competitors also expanded internationally. Pan Am found itself at a disadvantage. It did not have a good network of domestic carriers that could feed its international flights. In the 1980s other environmental changes affected Pan Am. Worldwide economic recession, aggressive competition from foreign airlines, rise in fuel prices, and labor disputes eroded its profitability. By 1985 it was losing money and started shedding assets to shore up operations. It sold some of its best international routes (New York to London) and its domestic shuttle operations. These desperate measures were insufficient to turn the company around. Finally, in January 1991, Pan Am filed for bankruptcy. By ignoring environmental changes and consequent needs for internal changes, this well-known and efficient company failed to survive. The story of Facit is even more dramatic.

Facit was the largest producer of mechanical calculators in the world. Its efficiency in production and marketing made it highly profitable. In the 1960s the electronics revolution swept through the consumer goods industry. It produced a variety of consumer electronic goods, including electronic calculators. Facit saw electronic calculators as a fad that posed a temporary threat to its operations. To meet this threat, it continued producing mechanical calculators but at higher levels of efficiency. It invested heavily in further improving production efficiency. It built bigger production plants to exploit economies of scale. It streamlined its distribution system to reduce costs to bare minimums.

Hewlett-Packard, then a small company from California, entered the calculator market with its electronic calculators. Within a few years it flooded the market with low-priced machines that out performed mechanical calculators. It did not take long before electronic calculators replaced mechanical calculators, and Facit went bankrupt.

Facit was very successful in efficiently achieving its objective of being the premier producer of mechanical calculators. Its objectives, however, were inconsistent with environmental demands. It misidentified the changing nature of the calculator market. It kept pursuing the goal of production efficiency without effectively dealing with competition. Facit efficiently pursued the wrong objectives.

The summer of 1990 was the best and the worst summer for EPI Products USA. With sales of more than $200 million, the three-year-old company was an example of quick success. It had innovative product designs, creative marketing, and a dynamic management team. Its best selling product was Epilady, a hair-removal appliance for women. This device used rotating coils to yank body hair from the roots to give the skin a smooth feel. It was priced between $60 and $89 and sold through Bloomingdale's and other fancy stores. Glamorous ads aimed at the upscale market promoted the product heavily.

The Krok sisters (Loren, Arlene, and Sharon), cofounders of the firm, became instant marketing celebrities. They appeared in photo spreads accompanying stories about their phenomenal success. Their father, a South African pharmaceuticals entrepreneur, had bought and given them rights to this hair-removal appliance. Metro, an Israeli kibbutz, manufactured the appliance. The founders did a tremendous job of making this first product highly successful in the sleepy hair-removal industry.

Although this main product had great market appeal, other products of the company were not so well received. Flush with initial success, the company rapidly expanded into many products without really studying its consumer and competitive environments. Its mini sauna, a foot bath, skateboards, expensive skin lotions, and $12 tubes of toothpaste received cool reaction from the market. The company also expanded into completely unrelated areas and lost $7 million in the production of a Broadway musical (*Meet Me in St. Louis*). The company exhibited little focus, no clear objectives, and no appreciation of its various business environments.

In a short time, EPI Products USA squandered its success from the hair remover on many losing ventures. On August 23, 1990, the company filed for bankruptcy. It had accumulated liabilities of $77 million on assets of $73 million. Lenders sued it seeking collection of $24 million in loans and cutting off credit. Its projected cash flow for the crucial month of September was a negative $2.1 million.

The failure of firms to adapt effectively to the changing global environment has lead to the decline of entire industries in the United States. During the 1970s and 1980s, we lost world leadership in the manufacture of steel, automobiles, and consumer electronics goods to Japanese firms. Japanese firms have been more effective in identifying worldwide demand for these goods and meeting it through global strategic management.

These examples illustrate the importance of managing firms for the long term and for a changing environment. It is important to be both effective and efficient. To succeed in the long term, a company must have well-formulated and consistently implemented strategic plans. Plans should be based on correct assessment of environmental demands and an appropriate set of objectives. They should help managers to monitor environmental trends and correctly align the firm's resources with these trends. Strategic plans should create an organization that achieves objectives. This is the goal of good strategic management. Strategic management involves formulating and implementing corporate and business strategies. Such strategies can propel the company to long-term growth and prosperity.

One idea that allows executives to manage for both efficiency and effectiveness is the concept of **strategy**. The management of strategy is what this book is all about. This chapter focuses on several central questions of strategic management: What is strategy? What are the tasks of strategic management? Whose responsibility is strategic management? At what levels must strategies be formulated and implemented? We will study why firms need strategies as they evolve and grow and examine the benefits of strategic management.

In commonsense terms, a strategy is simply a statement of **ends** (goals) and the **means** for achieving these ends. In corporations, strategies consist of a set of goals, strategic programs for achieving these goals, and resource allocations for implementing strategic programs. Firms choose their goals to reflect the demands of their many stakeholders. Through strategies, they align their internal resources with environmental demands to ensure long-term effectiveness (Chandler, 1962). Some authors separate goal formulation from strategy formulation as analytically separate activities. In practice, however, there is a close connection between them. Goals determine strategies, and to some extent strategic performance shapes and even limits the goals a company can pursue. In this book we include both goal formation and strategy formulation as integral elements of strategic management.

A complete statement of strategy describes the firm and its approach to doing business. It specifies what products the firm will produce and in what markets it will operate. It identifies the types of competitive advantage the firm will use. It describes how resources will be allocated. It shows how corporate objectives will be achieved (Andrews, 1970; Schendel and Hofer, 1979; Summer, 1980). For examples of strategies, see the corporate strategy of Chateau St. Michelle and of NCR Corporation in the company Policy Documents section of this book.

1.1   A PERSPECTIVE ON ORGANIZATIONS, ENVIRONMENTS, AND STRATEGIES

This book focuses on strategic management of modern, private, business firms or corporations operating in free-market economies. Most of these corporations, particularly the large ones, deal with multiple products, in multiple markets, and often in multiple countries.

There are many different ways of accomplishing strategic management activities. Each of them presumes a certain perspective on **organizations**, their **environments** and **strategies**. This book views business **organizations** as systems of production that serve multiple purposes of their stakeholders. They produce products and services for consumers, profits for investors, jobs for employees, taxes for government, and economic stability for communities. They contribute to the welfare of society by being economically productive and socially responsible. Their goals represent a synthesis of goals and demands placed on them by these stakeholders.

Although organizations primarily serve productive purposes, they also can be a source of harm if not managed well. They can harm consumers through defective products. They can harm workers by using unsafe or unhealthy work practices. They can harm the public at large by imposing technological risks and industrial accidents. They can harm the natural environment through environmental pollution and degradation of natural resources. Strategic management involves both effective management of organizational productivity and minimization of harm.

Administratively, corporations may be seen as consisting of multiple business units. Each business unit operates within specific industries and serves well-defined product markets. Business units have independent production and distribution systems and usually have profit responsibilities. For administrative convenience, several business units may be combined into a division or a group. A central office called the corporate headquarters usually coordinates activities of business units or divisions.

The **environment** of organizations consists of a continually changing competitive marketplace operating within a global economy. Many economic, social, cultural, political and technological factors influence the environment. An important part of the firm's environment is the natural environment or the ecology of planet Earth. This broad conception of the environment calls for analysis of environmental influences on firms and vice versa.

Strategies align or match the organization with its environment. This alignment requires an accurate assessment of environmental forces. It requires identifying current or potential misalignments between the firm and these forces. Sometimes this may be done through rational economic analysis. At other times it requires subjective, value-laden, personal choices of managers. The purpose of strategic management is not only maximizing the productive outputs of firms but also minimizing their harmful possibilities (Ansoff, 1987). Strategies must be viewed as much more than a means for improving a firm's competitive position. They are a means for making the firm more useful and productive to society. The strategic vision of any firm should include ways of improving financial performance, and ways of making it more socially useful.

The process of strategy implementation is both economically and socially-politically rational. Economically, it attempts to make optimal and efficient use of resources. However, optimal allocations are not always politically feasible. Strategic changes invariably involve reshuffling of the interests of internal and external stakeholders. Social and political processes intervene in formulation and implementation of strategies to maintain trade-offs and balances between competing interests. With this perspective, we now turn to the tasks of strategic management (Miller and Freisen, 1984).

1.2   STRATEGIC MANAGEMENT TASKS AND RESPONSIBILITIES

Strategic Management Tasks

Schendel and Hofer (1979) describe several tasks that constitute strategic management in organizations. Together these tasks allow firms to analyze their environment and strategically align their resources for long-term success. They are shown schematically shown in Figure 1.1. This book is structured around these central tasks and some key strategic problems facing corporations today:

1. Environmental analysis (Chapters 2 and 3)
2. Goal formulation (Chapter 4)
3. Internal resource analysis (Chapter 5)
4. Strategy formulation (Chapters 5 and 6)
5. Strategy implementation (Chapter 7)
6. Strategy evaluation (Chapter 8)
7. Strategy monitoring and control (Chapter 8)

Chapters 9, 10, and 11 discuss three critical strategic issues that corporate managers are certain to face in the coming decade. With the increasing internationalization of businesses and economies, most large companies must organize themselves for global competition and global effectiveness. Chapter 9 describes global aspects of strategic management. Today, more and more companies are facing life-threatening crises. These crises are caused by industrial accidents, environmental pollution incidents, product harm, hostile takeover, labor conflicts, and other similar events. Chapter 10 shows how to prevent and manage corporate crises. In the 1980s, mergers and acquisitions became a generic tool for strategic growth. Chapter 11 discusses strategic management of mergers and acquisitions.

Environmental Analysis. Environmental analysis is the task of examining interdependence between organizations and their environments. It involves

Figure 1.1

Strategic Management Process and Book Outline

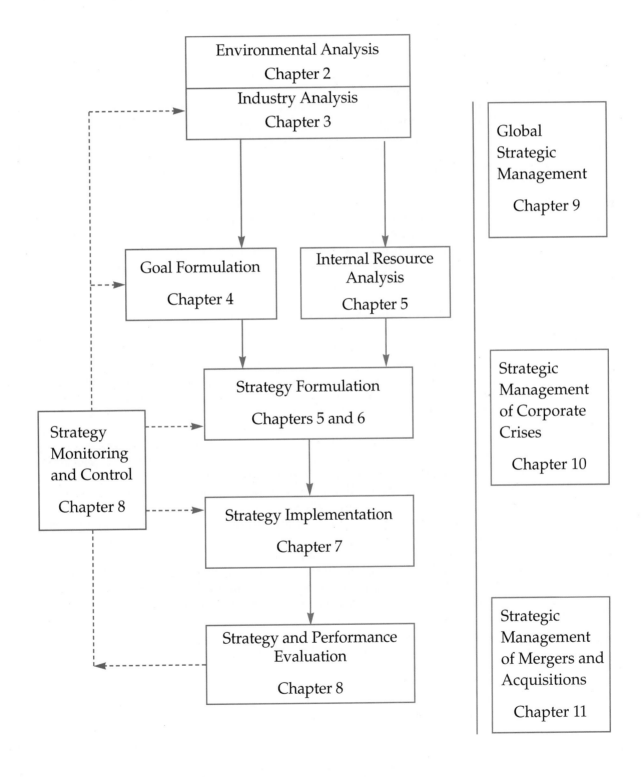

examining how forces outside the organization affect its performance and how organizational activities affect its environment. This assessment identifies opportunities and threats facing the organization. Chapter 2 describes ways of understanding the environment of companies. The environment consists of economic, technological, social, political, cultural, and physical (ecological) influences. Each segment of the environment must be studied for its history, current trends, and future prospects. Chapter 3 discusses ideas for understanding the competitive economic environment within an industry.

Goal Formulation. Goal formulation refers to setting organizational objectives and direction. Every organization must set clear and consistent objectives for the total organization and its subparts. These objectives should reflect the wants and needs of organizational stakeholders and their expectations about performance. Because organizations satisfy multiple stakeholders, demands on them are very complex and sometimes contradictory. Goal formulation, therefore, must balance the competing goals of stakeholders and set priorities on goals. Chapter 4 describes how corporations can set their general direction and formulate their missions, objectives, and goals.

Internal Resource Analysis. Internal resource analysis identifies the organization's key strengths and weaknesses. It systematically evaluates the resources available to each individual division or business unit. For each business unit, it assesses the functional area resources. It identifies strengths and weaknesses in finance, production, marketing, research and development (R&D), administration, and management capabilities. Chapter 5 discusses ideas essential for conducting internal resource analysis.

Strategy Formulation. Strategy formulation refers to development of strategies and strategic plans and programs. Strategy formulation involves matching environmental opportunities with organizational strengths and weaknesses. This must be done both at the corporate level and at the business unit level. The resulting strategic plans state the scope and objectives of the organization. They describe strategic programs for achieving objectives. Strategic programs are a set of focused action programs that make up the strategy. Chapters 5 and 6 discuss ideas and techniques for strategy formulation at the corporate and business units.

Strategy Implementation. Strategy implementation is the task of putting a strategy into action and making it work for the firm. It requires allocation of appropriate human and financial resources. To implement strategies successfully, managers may need to change organizational structures, systems, and staff. They may need to develop new skills, establish strategic leadership, and create a new culture. They may need to build a performance evaluation and compensation system that rewards behaviors that are consistent with the strategy. Chapter 7 describes means for implementing strategies.

Strategy Evaluation. Every strategy should be evaluated for feasibility and soundness. Only practically feasible strategies deserve the commitment of organizational resources. The evaluation should ensure that the strategy is consistent with corporate objectives, environmental demands, and internal resources. It should attempt to eliminate internal conflicts and contradictions between different elements of strategic plans. Any internal inconsistencies within the strategy should be identified and eliminated. Chapter 8 describes criteria and processes for strategy evaluation.

Strategy Monitoring and Control. Monitoring and control is an extension of strategy evaluation. During strategy implementation, managers must continually

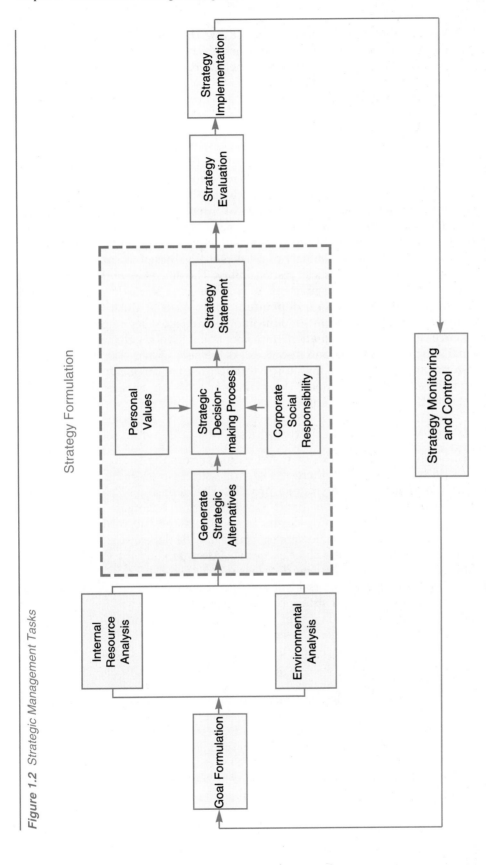

Figure 1.2 Strategic Management Tasks

evaluate the level of achievement of objectives. They must monitor performance and modify strategies if they deviate from objectives. Monitoring and control systems must provide managers with timely and actionable information on the strategy and organizational performance.

The flow chart in Figure 1.2 shows the relationships between these tasks as an idealized strategic management process. For analytical purposes, it depicts these tasks as discrete and separate. In reality, their boundaries are fuzzy and overlapping. Strategy making should begin with direction setting and goal formulation. This involves assessing current goals and determining future goals. After determining goals, two types of analyses need to be conducted simultaneously: an analysis of environmental forces to identify key opportunities and threats facing the organization and an analysis of internal resources to identify organizational strengths and weaknesses. By matching internal strengths with environmental opportunities, strategic alternatives can be generated. These alternatives should be assessed in light of the personal values of top management and the corporation's sense of social responsibility. The outcomes of this strategic decision-making process are statements of strategies and strategic plans. Strategies should be subjected to an independent evaluation of their feasibility and soundness. Evaluation permits modification of strategies before committing vast resources to their implementation. Implementation involves changes in organizational structures, systems, and resources. As the new strategy begins to influence performance, it should be monitored through regular feedback and controlled through periodic modifications. This process goes back to goal setting in the next cycle of strategic management.

Strategic Management Responsibilities

Each organization follows its own system for performing strategic management tasks. In some companies there is a separate strategic planning department in charge of facilitating the strategy process. The department has professional planners and analysts who support line managers to formulate and implement strategic plans. The planning occurs in specific steps and through analytical procedures. In other companies strategic tasks may be done informally by a group of special assistants to the chief executive. Alternatively, the Chief Executive Officer (CEO) may make strategic decisions with little consultation.

Historically, the CEO, president, or general manager of an organization had complete responsibility for strategic management. He or she was the key decision maker, leader, and coordinator of the organization. Legendary CEOs, such as Harold Geneen of International Telephone and Telegraph (ITT), Thomas Watson of International Business Machines (IBM), and Ted Turner of Turner Broadcasting System (TBS), are famous for personally directing strategic management in their respective firms.

In most large firms today, strategic problems are so complex that it is very difficult for a single individual to solve them alone. Consequently, responsibilities for strategic management tasks have become dispersed throughout the organization. The CEO or president shares strategic responsibilities with a top management team. Often an executive committee or the office of the chairman leads this function. Major companies such as General Electric, Exxon, and Shell Oil have created such special structures for strategic decision making. In addition, there are several specialized departments that help in conducting strategic analyses. These include the strategic planning department, environmental scanning department, new business planning

Figure 1.3   *Strategies and Their Functions*

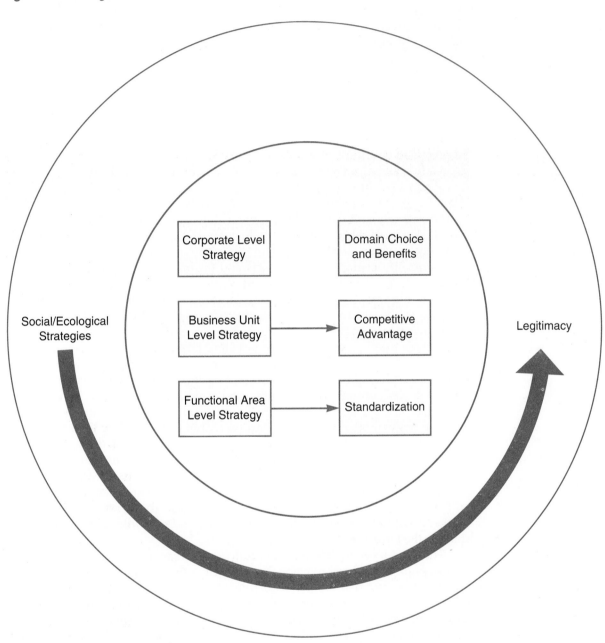

department, and mergers and acquisitions department. Staff planners serve the role of educators and process facilitators in large corporations.

Thus, the traditional strategic role of the general manager has expanded beyond a single person. The greater complexity of business environments and the large size of corporations required such expansion. These factors also require firms to make strategies at several different levels. We turn now to levels of strategy making.

1.3   LEVELS OF STRATEGY IN THE FIRM

Strategies must be developed at several levels within the organization to ensure that they cover all organizational activities. These strategies are schematically shown in Figure 1.3 and include the corporate level, business unit level, functional area level, and social and ecological.

At the **corporate level**, several strategic questions face the firm: What businesses should we compete in, given our strengths and weakness? Which new product markets should we enter? Which should we exit? This is the "domain choice" question. It delineates the product-market domain of the firm and describes the firm's scope of operations. For example, the corporate strategy of Textron is to be a multiproduct firm that manufactures industrial and consumer goods. It seeks rapid growth and an internally determined rate of return on investment. The firm acquires ongoing businesses that are sound but may need capital and management expertise to grow. It manages these businesses as financial assets and divests them when they fail to operate at an internally acceptable rate of return and growth. In contrast, GM sees itself as an automobile company. Its main product lines are different types of cars, trucks, buses, and accessories. It develops new products and businesses in this industry through internal research, acquisitions, and joint ventures.

At the **business unit level**, the strategic question is, how should we compete in the product markets in which we operate? Business unit strategy seeks to develop competitive advantage over other firms in the industry. It deals with product design, choice of the marketing mix, and establishing competitive advantage. For example, GM pursues a competitive strategy of differentiating its products through innovative product designs, strong advertising, and extensive dealer support. It will be the first American company to offer a commercial electric car in 1994. In contrast to this strategy of product differentiation is the strategy of operating at the least cost. This is the strategy Honda adopted to enter the motorcycle industry in the United States. Honda had the lowest cost in the industry because it was the largest volume manufacturer. Using automated mass production techniques, it built a sustained competitive advantage in low-cost production. It entered the United States market in the West with low-priced motorcycles. Having succeeded in the West, it expanded its market drive to the East. Within a few years it had captured the largest market share in the industry.

The third level of strategy is the **functional area** within business units. Each business unit has several functional areas such as marketing, production, finance, human resources, planning, and distribution. At this level, strategies are often called functional policies. Companies have policies that standardize and simplify tasks within each function. These policies should be consistent with each other. Functional area policies help in accomplishing functional tasks in the most efficient manner. Jointly, these policies form the basic operating system of the organization. For example, companies have standard policies for accounting, auditing, personnel hiring and retrenchment, sales order processing, production scheduling, and inventory management. For examples of functional policies, see General Electric's government transactions policy, J. P. Morgan's auditing policy, Touche Ross's human resources policy, and the records management policy of a large chemical company included in the Company Policy Documents section of this book.

In addition, companies must ensure their legitimacy through **social and ecological strategies**. These strategies aim at fulfilling demands of the community and society at large. For example, companies such as Procter & Gamble have strong social strategies involving corporate philanthropy, citizenship activities, support of public events, and environmental protection programs. These strategies aim at making the company socially desirable and legitimate. They earn the goodwill of the public, customers, government, and other stakeholders.

1.4   THE NEED FOR STRATEGIES THROUGH FIRM EVOLUTION

Advantages of Strategies

As companies evolve and grow, they need strategies to guide their behaviors. There are several advantages to having strategies and strategic plans (Figure 1.4). First, good strategic plans give the firm a sense of purpose and direction and a sense of corporate identity. They tell employees what the firm is trying to achieve and how it plans to do so. Second, they allow the firm to articulate its distinctive competences and competitive advantage. They provide the firm with a focused way of competing. Third, functional policies help to standardize operations and improve efficiency within departments. They streamline work flow and make day-to-day operations manageable. Fourth, strategic analysis helps the firm to identify strategic issues it will face in the future. This helps the firm to be ready for environmental changes.

Even if particular strategies do not lead to improved economic performance, the very process of strategic analysis and strategy formulation is useful. The strategy process instills a discipline in management. It makes managers think about the future of the firm. It provides them with a mechanism for systematically allocating discretionary resources. By engaging in strategy formulation, organizational managers develop skills of long-range planning. Detailed strategic analysis forces managers to question their own assumptions. This leads to a deeper understanding of their business. It also helps establish more trusting relationships among top managers and fosters team spirit.

An overall strategic plan may be broken down into short-term **tactical plans**. These shorter and more focused plans help companies to accomplish smaller tasks and projects without losing sight of the larger strategy. Tactics are the maneuvers, game plans, diversions, ploys, and schemes that facilitate the achievement of overall corporate goals and objectives. For example, companies pursuing the strategy of increasing market share often use tactics of price discounting for a limited period or temporarily increasing retailer margins. These short-term actions allow them to gain temporary advantage over competition.

The Strategic Evolution of Firms

Strategic management also guides the general evolution of companies. In this chapter we have repeatedly emphasized that strategic management is a function that deals with securing the long-term success of companies. In the larger context of company evolution over time, different strategic problems have to be managed at different stages of a company's growth.

As companies evolve from their birth to death, they go through several distinct stages of growth. In each stage and during transition between stages,

Figure 1.4 *Benefits of Strategies*

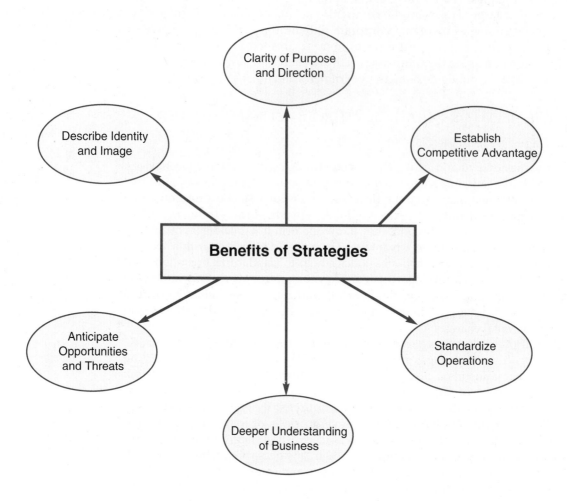

companies face some common strategic problems. Understanding stages of growth can prepare managers to cope with these problems. Greiner (1972) suggested that as firms age, they go through distinct stages of growth. The Turner Broadcasting System (case study included in this book) exemplifies growth problems.

Industry growth rate, firm size, and internal management determine the growth stages of a company. This growth occurs in sequential evolutionary and revolutionary phases. In the evolutionary phase, a dominant management style helps to achieve growth. In the revolutionary phase, a dominant management style limits growth, and the problem must be resolved before growth can continue (Greiner, 1972).

In growing industries, firms go through the five phases shown here. Each phase is both the effect of the previous phase and the cause of the following phase.

Phases	Management Style		Management Problem	
Phase 1 ──▶	Growth thru creativity	──▶	Crisis of leadership ──▶	Phase 2
Phase 2 ──▶	Growth thru direction	──▶	Crisis of autonomy ──▶	Phase 3
Phase 3 ──▶	Growth thru delegation	──▶	Crisis of control ──▶	Phase 4
Phase 4 ──▶	Growth thru coordination	──▶	Crisis of red tape ──▶	Phase 5
Phase 5 ──▶	Growth thru collaboration	──▶	??Crisis??	

The first phase begins with the entrepreneurial act of creating the firm. In this phase the primary focus of the firm is creation of products and markets. The creative entrepreneurship of company founders guides the firm. Often, the founders have technical or marketing backgrounds and personal knowledge of the business. The firm works on the emotional energy of the founders. Employees work long, hard hours and they receive modest salaries, and sometimes part ownership in the company. In the entrepreneurial phase at TBS, Ted Turner took over his father's ailing business. He immediately turned the company around by cutting costs, renegotiating bank loans, and launching new products. With a burst of entrepreneurial energy, he infused TBS with new life. Turner involved himself in all aspects of the business.

Entrepreneur-managers of start-up companies rarely focus on "management" of the firm. Instead, they work on producing and selling the product. Control over the firm is usually by one person—the owner-manager. As the firm grows, it requires specialized knowledge of various functions, such as manufacturing, marketing, and finance. A single manager cannot supply all these skills. The entrepreneur-owner is often reluctant to share responsibilities with others and thus acts as a barrier to the firm's growth. This creates a crisis of leadership. Such a crisis of leadership was apparent at TBS in that the company became an extension of Ted Turner. He resisted sharing power with his managers. He ran the company with a firm, autocratic style, thereby alienating many top managers.

Companies survive the first phase by installing capable professional managers to provide directive leadership and thus embark on a period of sustained growth. In this period of evolutionary change, the organization adopts a functional structure. Supervisory managers share authority and responsibilities. They create systems for accounting, production control, and marketing. They adopt work standards and establish formal channels of communication. TBS required this streamlining of internal operations because of its precarious financial position in its early years. Efficient operations were necessary for turning the company around. TBS hired some highly dedicated, professional managers to organize internal company operations.

Streamlining of work sustains the firm through the second phase of growth. Despite the improved efficiency of these measures, however, the firm soon outgrows their directive effects. As the firm becomes bigger, more complex, and more diverse in activities, the centralization and control by key managers becomes restrictive. Lower-level employees seek more autonomy and freedom. Moreover, problems occurring at locations remote from the central management structure need local attention. The firm faces an autonomy crisis. TBS faced such a crisis of autonomy in the early 1980s. Important top managers left because they felt highly restricted by Ted Turner's dominant management style.

Resolving this crisis requires delegating authority to a broader group of managers at lower levels. Such deepening of the management structure has a healthful effect on decision making. It decentralizes authority to operating-level managers. They can resolve problems more easily where the problems occur.

Coupling decentralization with profit center organization and bonus plans has positive effects on motivation and morale. Top management concentrates on expansion through acquisition and management of operations by exception. This sustains the organization through the next phase—growth thru delegation. In the case of TBS, such delegation occurred in the late 1980s, but only to a moderate extent. The company had by then expanded too vastly to be supervised by a single person. Ted Turner reluctantly delegated authority to his next level of management and started focusing his energies on strategic long-term issues.

Continued delegation of authority leads to the crisis of control. Too many levels of management and too many managers can lead to loss of control. This is particularly true in highly diversified firms. Moreover, autonomous field managers prefer to run their own shows. Top management attempts to regain control by establishing new coordination techniques. Coordination may involve merging product groups or business units. Procedurally, it is done by establishing formal planning and budgeting systems and companywide financial control programs. It could also involve centralizing some service and technical functions, such as data processing and R&D. Coordination improves efficiency in allocation of scarce resources. But as they get institutionalized, these procedures and systems swamp the organization and create a crisis of bureaucratic red tape. The bureaucracy stifles further growth of the company. Many large, mature companies find themselves in such a bureaucratic bind and begin to stagnate.

In the fifth phase of growth, bureaucratic stagnation may be overcome by controlling through interpersonal collaboration. This requires a focus on problem solving through team action. Cross-functional and cross-task teams are useful here. Formal systems should be simplified or integrated into a single, multipurpose system. The firm focuses on educating employees, enhancing skills, and organizational development. It encourages innovation, team performance, and use of real-time information systems.

Most companies go through these stages of growth in their lifetime. Knowing the strategic problems associated with each stage can help managers anticipate and prepare for them. They can develop strategic plans to deal with evolutionary and revolutionary changes instead of simply stumbling through them. If companies successfully evolve through these growth stages, they become large, mature international companies. However, bureaucratization often accompanies maturity and stifles individual initiative. Bureaucratic companies need to reinfuse entrepreneurship into their structures. This is the problem we turn to in the next section.

1.5   EVOLUTION AND ENTREPRENEURSHIP

Entrepreneurship is the ability of businesses to generate new businesses. This quality is essential for long-term self-renewal and regeneration of business. It is the heart of good strategic management. As firms grow into large, mature companies, their vital entrepreneurial spirit can subside. Organizational bureaucracy stifles entrepreneurial initiative. Moreover, as they age, managers themselves tend to lose their entrepreneurial drive. There are many causes of decline in entrepreneurial drive among managers. Some become satisfied with the existing situation. They lose interest in seeking new opportunities for themselves or their organization. Others may still be entrepreneurial, but they perceive no opportunity to act. Complex and overbearing organizational structures and systems stifle them. They get frustrated and stop trying.

For example, Exxon the oil giant, attempted to diversify out of the oil industry in the late 1970s. It bought several entrepreneurial companies in growth industries such as computers and electrical equipment. However, Exxon was a massive bureaucracy. Its bureaucratic procedures and "big oil culture" fostered very long-term horizons, very large deals, and elaborate formal planning. Projects required multiple levels of approval. These processes were simply too frustrating for the entrepreneurs in the newly acquired computer and electrical equipment businesses. In their own industries these entrepreneurs dealt with fast-paced environmental changes and instant strategic responses. Within three years most of the entrepreneurs quit. Exxon ended up divesting these promising businesses.

To make large organizations entrepreneurial, management must encourage internal corporate venturing and reward managers for taking calculated risks (Burgelman, 1983; Shortell and Zajac, 1988). Stevenson and Jarillo-Mossi (1986) suggest several steps for encouraging entrepreneurship, which include increasing the perception of opportunity and rewarding the pursuit of opportunity. The perception of opportunity can be increased by creating jobs that have real-time market inputs. This requires structuring jobs so that managers are in close interaction with their markets. Continuous feedback from the market should structure the managers' own objectives and tasks. Thus, market opportunities will always be visible to managers, and they will perceive more opportunities for being creative and productive. Citibank did this by making customer service the central element of managerial job descriptions, departmental goals, and training programs. Through direct contact with clients, managers began understanding customer needs and developing programs to meet them.

The perception of opportunities can be improved by making individuals responsible for broadly defined objectives. Giving managers broad responsibilities expands their field of vision and opens new areas of opportunity for them. This broadening of responsibilities may be coupled by balancing of functional needs. That means different organizational functions must be run in balance, with no one function dominating the firm's resources. Such domination by a function often demotivates and curtails opportunity for the rest of the organization. Firms can improve perception of opportunity by encouraging change and making it desirable to members. Organizational changes must not be made at the cost of individual benefits. If individuals lose personal benefits and career opportunities every time an organizational change occurs, they begin to resist changes. This discourages entrepreneurship.

Besides increasing the perception of opportunity, firms must reward the pursuit of opportunity. They can do this by (1) reducing the risk of failure, (2) accepting flexibility in implementation of ideas, (3) making short-term slack resources available to members for experimentation with new ideas, and (4) preventing premature vetoing of ideas for new projects.

Risk of failure for individuals can be reduced by encouraging risks to be taken by groups or teams instead of by individuals. Japanese companies have mastered this approach to work. They encourage group responsibility for large projects; they do not blame or penalize individual managers for failed projects. Tolerance of failure is another way of reducing the risk of failure. The organization also can keep risky new projects secret during their gestation period. This prevents news about failures from spreading widely and demoralizing other employees.

Another way of rewarding the pursuit of opportunity is by making this pursuit simpler to execute. This can be done by being flexible in implementing new projects and ideas. Projects often change as they reach the implementation phase. One of the most demoralizing occurrences is the dumping of projects in their last phase because the project does not meet original expectations. Abandoning of projects in advanced phases should be done selectively. There is nothing more demotivating than to find projects that you have nurtured over an extended period shelved at the implementation phase because they did not turn out perfectly. Clearly, this type of tolerance can be costly to the firm and must be exercised judiciously.

Texas Instruments is a good example of a system that encourages entrepreneurial behaviors. The company developed an innovative system for managing new product development projects. Their objectives, strategies, and tactics system uses product customer centers (PCC) to encourage entrepreneurship. The manager in charge of a PCC is responsible for all aspects of research, development, commercialization, and profitability of his or her specific products. These mini profit centers operate with great autonomy and freedom. Once approved by the executive committee, the PCCs do not need to seek periodic sanctions or budget approvals through cumbersome procedures. The company has hundreds of PCCs that produce thousands of products. The PCCs gave Texas Instruments unique entrepreneurial abilities by making PCC managers into entrepreneurs.

Making slack resources available to managers on a short-term basis is another effective way of encouraging experimentation with new ideas. Even though these resources can be marginal additions, they go a long way in letting managers take some risks that they otherwise would not. One way to extend the use of these resources is to let several managers share them.

Finally, preventing a single "no" vote from vetoing a project idea is important. Companies should create procedures for screening ideas that do not depend on the whim of a single manager. This gives confidence to potential entrepreneurs that their efforts cannot be killed by a single veto. A sensible procedure for selecting projects for funding may include some form of peer review by knowledgeable colleagues. Colleagues can provide thoughtful opinions on the viability of the project (MacMillan and George, 1985).

Strategic management involves managing the total business enterprise over the long term. It attempts to achieve effectiveness and meet changing environmental demands. To do this, firms need strategies. They need to articulate clearly the goals they will pursue. Strategic plans should describe programs of action and resource allocations. Strategies must be formulated for the corporations as a whole and for its various constituent business units. Each functional area within business units also needs policies to streamline its activities. Strategies must be implemented, evaluated, monitored, and controlled to achieve organizational goals.

If strategy formulation and implementation are done effectively, the firm will remain strong and competitive. It will continue to evolve as a healthy firm and be able to weather any environmental change. A corporation's ability to generate new businesses through self-sustaining growth strategy requires cultivation of entrepreneurship. Managers should be given the opportunity to act entrepreneurially and be rewarded for successes.

Summary of Chapter 1

Modern corporations operate in turbulent environments. To survive and grow, they must respond strategically to environmental changes. Strategic management makes organizations effective in meeting environmental demands and organizational objectives. This book deals with the basic tasks of strategic management.

Strategic management establishes organizational missions, objectives, and goals. It formulates corporate and business strategies for achieving goals. It allocates resources to implement strategies. Goals are established by balancing the competing demands of organizational stakeholders.

Strategy formulation requires analysis of the environmental forces. This analysis identifies key opportunities and threats facing the organization. Simultaneously, analysis of internal resources identifies organizational strengths and weaknesses. Strategies are created by matching external opportunities and threats with internal strengths and weaknesses. Strategies are divided into several strategic programs to ease implementation.

Strategies should be evaluated for their feasibility, soundness, and consistency with internal and environmental conditions. Strategy implementation requires allocating appropriate resources, creating the right organizational structure, establishing supporting administrative systems, and developing required managerial skills. Monitoring strategic performance and control of strategy are also important tasks of strategic management.

Strategic management responsibilities are dispersed throughout the organization. The CEO and top management provide leadership and overall guidance. Line managers make substantive plans. The planning staff provides analytical support to the strategic planning process.

Strategies need to be developed at three levels. **Corporate strategies** determine the company's domain of operation. They describe the products, markets, and businesses that the company wants to operate. **Business strategies** provide individual business units with a competitive advantage over other firms in the industry. **Functional area strategies** make the routine operations of business functions efficient.

Firms evolve through different stages of growth. In each stage different strategic problems become salient. By anticipating and managing these strategic problems, firms can direct their own growth trajectory. One consequence of growth in size is bureaucratization, which stifles entrepreneurship in organizations. Strategic management encourages entrepreneurship among managers by increasing managers' perceptions of opportunity and rewarding the pursuit of opportunity.

READINGS, CASES, AND POLICY DOCUMENTS

The following readings and policy documents provide additional background material for the concepts discussed in Chapter 1.

Readings

* Ansoff, H.I. "The changing shape of the strategic problem". In D. Schendel and C.W. Hofer (Eds) *Strategic Management: A New View of Business Policy and Planning*, Boston: Little Brown and Co., 1979.

Cases

   * Acme Leasing Company
   * Beverly Enterprises, Inc.
     Mud Island, Inc
   * Turner Broadcasting System Inc.

Policy Documents

   * Crain's New York Business — The Vision
     Chateau Ste. Michelle Strategic Plan
   * indicates particularly appropriate assignments

   Figures 1.1, 1.2, 1.3 & 1.4

Strategic Management Process and Book Outline

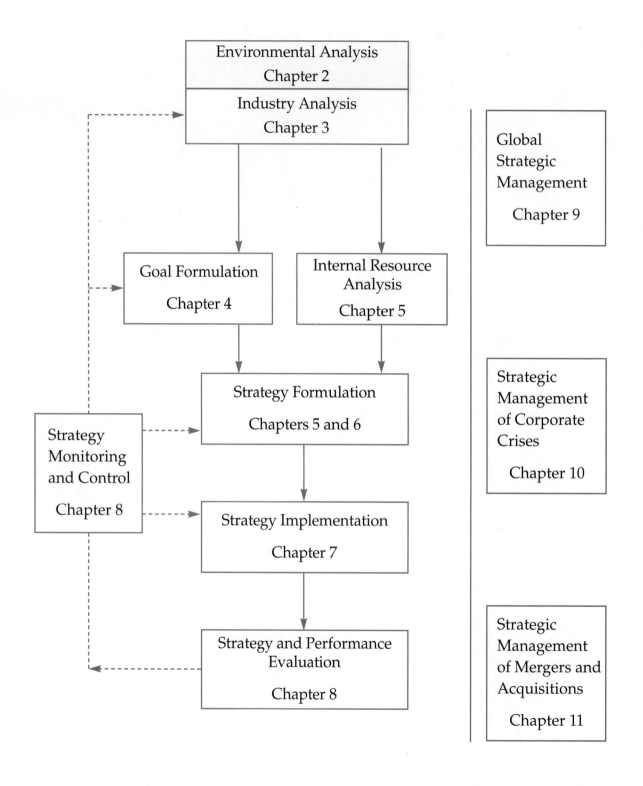

CHAPTER 2
ENVIRONMENTAL
ANALYSIS

Adapting to environmental changes is the essence of strategic management. This adaptation requires an in-depth understanding of environmental changes. In the increasingly turbulent environments that corporations face in the 1990s, adaptation will be a very challenging task. Dramatic domestic, geopolitical, and ecological changes of the past few years have grave consequences for corporations and their strategies.

The US economy headed into another recession in early 1990. The budget deficit was about $320 billion in 1990 and the trade deficit was more than $200 billion. Value of the dollar against foreign currencies fluctuated widely. Unemployment was high. The recession was deep and sustained. The early 1990s saw the downsizing of many key industries: banking, insurance, savings and loans, housing and real estate, and automobiles.

The war in the Persian Gulf had cost the United States more than $100 billion. It left little flexibility for spending on social programs needed during a recessionary period. Thus, the decade started with hardships for the public and high uncertainty for businesses. Race relations, sexual harassment, health care costs, social programs, defense spending, and environmental protection became prominent issues on the strategic agenda of corporations.

International environmental changes were even more dramatic than domestic ones. Many countries in the Eastern Block, including the former Soviet Union, started restructuring their economic and political systems. As they moved toward democratizing their political systems and deregulating their economies, they permitted private enterprise and opened up their markets to the West. In 1991 East and West Germany reunited after nearly forty years of division after World War II. The twelve major countries of Western Europe raced toward economic unification. In 1992 they created a single European Common Market. These events transformed the economic and political landscape of both Eastern and Western Europe.

In the Pacific basin, the 1990s began with resurgence of economic growth in Japan, Taiwan, South Korea, Singapore, and Malaysia. In the Middle East, the Persian Gulf War changed the economic picture of that region and of many Third World countries. Poor African countries continued to be racked by wars and famines and suffered a net decline in their real gross domestic products. In 1991 South Africa adopted sweeping reforms to dismantle its policy of apartheid and integrate itself into the world economy. South American developing nations burdened by crippling foreign debt began defaulting on interest payments. Their formal economies shrank, while their underground economies, fueled with drug trade, expanded.

The 1990s witnessed a dramatic rise in worldwide consciousness of ecological damage. The past half century of industrialization and population growth were the main sources of this damage. Industrial processes were responsible for unprecedented rise in air pollution, acid rain, global warming, and ozone depletion. The use of natural resources in industrial processes led to cutting of rain forests and reduction in biodiversity. Industrial effluents caused toxic waste. Business corporations as owners of technologies that caused these problems faced a barrage of new environmental regulations and immense public pressures to protect the environment. New competitive threats from environmentally sensitive products and technologies emerged.

Such economic, social, political, cultural, and ecological changes affect the financial performance of firms. Firms that accurately anticipate environmental changes and assess opportunities and threats created by them can strategically position themselves. Formulating strategy requires assessing the "big picture" of forces facing the company in its domestic and international contexts. It involves identifying key environmental influences and understanding their implications for organizational performance.

There are many examples of companies that have responded to current environmental changes. In the telecommunications industry, US West established a cellular telephone network in the former Soviet Union, the world's second largest telecommunications market. This venture complements the company's initiatives in Hungary and Czechoslovakia. Based in Leningrad, the venture will provide telephone services to 50,000 customers. The tobacco industry has faced declining sales and antismoking campaigns in the United States. Philip Morris and RJR Nabisco made deals to sell the 34 billion cigarettes to the former Soviet Union. The companies hope to use the increasing idle plant capacity in American plants and to satisfy the shortage of cigarettes demanded by nearly 70 million smokers in the former Soviet republics. The reunification of Germany has caused a scramble among airlines to serve Berlin. Berlin is fast becoming a major industrial, commercial, political, and transportation center in Europe. By moving quickly and early, Lufthansa took a lead over other world airlines. It aggressively acquired routes and airport gates and established a worldwide flight schedule out of Berlin. It connected Berlin to all major European cities and to New York, Tokyo, Beijing, and Dubai. These examples show that there are great payoffs to understanding a firm's general environment and responding to changes quickly.

Environmental analysis plays a central role in strategic management. Companies conduct environmental analysis to identify market opportunities and threats. It also helps them to anticipate changes in highly complex and dynamic environments. By anticipating changes accurately, companies can gain competitive advantage through quick action. Environmental analysis focuses on assessing the current environment and projecting or forecasting its future states. Based on this assessment, it is possible to identify opportunities, threats, and external constraints on the firm. Environmental analysis also helps the firm to position itself in a continually evolving environment. It examines the consequences of a firm's strategies on the environment.

This chapter provides a conceptual framework for doing environmental analysis. It describes several environmental analysis techniques and environmental information systems. The chapter also includes a discussion of organizational stakeholders and how firms can manage relationships with them.

2.1   GENERAL ENVIRONMENTAL ANALYSIS

The first step in environmental analysis is understanding *what* makes up the firm's environment. It is important to identify and map those parts of the environment that most influence the firm's performance. Generically speaking, the environment connotes conditions that surround a company. It is the locale or milieu for corporate activities.

General Environment of Corporations

Corporations are economic institutions operating in a physical world. Their relevant environment is an economic biosphere that includes both human (economic, technological, social, cultural, and political) and natural (biological and atmospheric) influences. Organizational environments thus consist of, (1) the natural environment or the ecology of the planet Earth, (2) the international world order of economic, social, and political relationships, and (3) the immediate economic, technological, social, cultural, and political context of organizations. Figure 2.1 schematically depicts these environmental levels.

The outer circle of Figure 2.1 represents the earth and its **natural environment**. This serves as the base for all human and, consequently, corporate activities. This natural environment is both a resource and a constraint for companies. The natural physical world (including atmosphere, water, and land terrain) offers resources of agriculture, mining, minerals, metals, oil, forests, marine life, and so on. Even companies that do not derive products from nature use natural resources. They use fossil fuels for energy generation. They use land for locating plants, offices, warehouses, and waste disposal sites and for housing employees. They use streams or rivers for water supply and waste disposal.

Strategic planning must acknowledge the finite and limited nature of these natural resources. It must provide for their renewal. The value of environmental sustainability is emerging at the international level. Sustainability involves slowing the pace of resource exploitation so that future generations can meet their own needs. Corporate strategic plans must aim at making companies sustainable.

The second circle in Figure 2.1 depicts the **international world order** that structures social life on earth. This world order shapes economic, social, and political relationships within and between nation states. Nation states have their own unique economic, social, cultural, and political institutions, processes, and histories that serve as the context for business. For business corporations and economic institu-

Figure 2.1 *General Environment of Corporations*

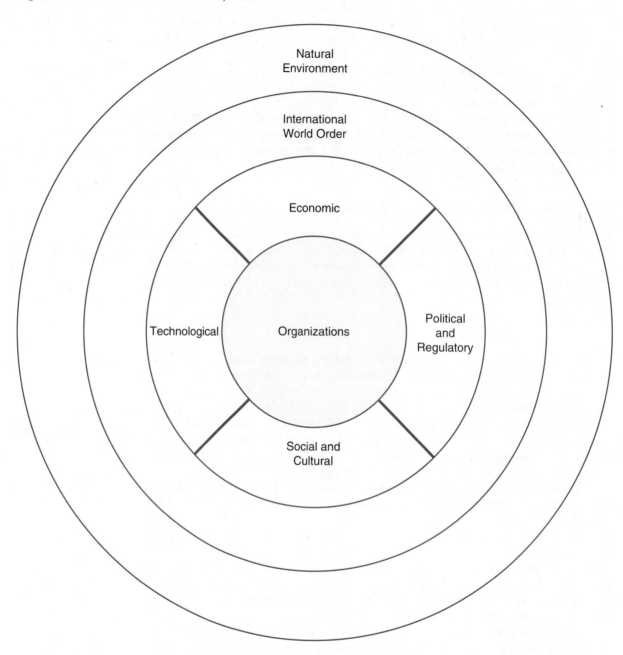

tions, processes, and relations between nation states are the most salient. Mutual treaties and international laws govern international economic relations. Despite the apparent separateness of nation states, their economies are interdependent.

Within this international world order operate organizations of various types. They pursue diverse objectives and possess different resources. The inner circle in Figure 2.1 depicts these organizations. The **immediate environment** surrounding them has the most salient influence on them. This immediate environment consists of: the general economic environment, the technological environment, the social and cultural environment, and the political and regulatory environment.

The **general economic environment** consists of the world economy, the national economy, the regional and local economies, and international trade regulations. Macroeconomic indicators, such as gross national product, interest rates, employment rates, production and consumption figures, and money supply figures, measure the health of the economy. A basic understanding of the macroeconomic structure of the domestic and international economies is essential for strategic analysis. It is also important to understand the interdependencies between the various sectors of the economy. For competitive strategies, the most relevant part of the economic environment is the **industry** in which a business competes. Industry refers to the set of firms that produce and sell similar products in competition with each other. Each industry has its own unique structure and determinants of profitability. Chapter 3 discusses this competitive structure of industries.

The **technological environment** influences firm performance through two types of changes: changes in product technologies and changes in process technologies. Product technology refers to product designs, features, and innovations. Changes in product technology can render certain products obsolete; they can reduce demand for products or shorten their life cycle. For example, the development of mechanical ballpoint pens severely reduced the demand for fountain pens and wiped out famous companies such as Waterman Pen. Similarly, the advent of refrigerators drove icebox manufacturers out of business. Electronic calculators replaced mechanical ones.

Process technology refers to the technological knowledge used in manufacturing or production processes. Changes in production processes directly influence production costs. Production process innovations can reduce the cost of manufacturing for some companies and give them a competitive advantage over others in the industry. Improvements in production process can also affect the quality and speed of production. Eventually, production technologies drive competitiveness. In the 1980s the American steel companies Bethlehem Steel and US Steel were unable to compete successfully against German and Japanese steel producers. Why? Because two decades earlier the American companies had not invested adequately in the new steel production technology that used electric arc furnaces.

The **social and cultural environment** consists of broad societal trends that affect organizations. These include demographic patterns, life-styles, social structures, social relationships, and social trends. An example of a demographic trend influencing business is the baby-boom phenomenon. There was a large increase in birthrate in the United States between 1946 and 1963. This swelled the ranks of young, educated, employed, urban-based adults in the economy in the 1980s. It increased the basic demand for housing, automobiles, and a wide range of innovative, upscale products.

The cultural environment of the firm emerges from shared beliefs, values, symbols, practices, mores, and behavioral norms of society. The United States is a multicultural society that is becoming increasingly diverse. Understanding these cultural traits and diversity is crucial for designing well-differentiated strategies aimed at culturally different client groups. For example, the retailing industry takes cultural differences into account in developing strategies for markets with culturally different customers. Urban markets in New York City, Miami, Los Angeles, and San Diego have large African-American, Hispanic, and Asian populations. Food and clothing retailers cater to these groups with appropriate choice of products, marketing strategies, packaging, and pricing. Sensitivity to cultural differences is particularly important in conducting business internationally. Managers involved in international business need to be familiar with foreign languages, business practices, and customs. They must also understand local customer needs, resource availability, legal requirements, and financial arrangements.

The **political and regulatory environment** consists of legislative and electoral politics, regulations and regulatory agencies, and interest group pressures. In the United States there are two types of regulations over business: economic and social. Economic regulation attempts to manage macroeconomic variables such as money supply, interest rates, wage rates, and inflation. The regulations seek to create a free market for goods and services by preventing anticompetitive practices. Several government departments monitor and implement economic regulations: Department of Commerce, Department of Labor, Department of Transportation, Department of the Treasury, and Office of Management and Budgets. In addition, industry-specific agencies control industry-related regulations. These include the Federal Aviation Administration, Federal Drug Administration, Interstate Commerce Commission, National Aeronautics and Space Administration, Securities and Exchange Commission, and the Nuclear Regulatory Commission. Social regulations attempt to regulate the noneconomic impacts of business on society. There are diverse laws and agencies charged with the protection of the environment, workers, consumers, and the public. Some key agencies are the Equal Employment Opportunity Commission, Consumer Products Safety Commission, Environmental Protection Agency, Occupational Safety and Health Administration, and National Transportation Safety Board.

Analysis of the General Environment

In each environmental segment, managers must analyze several issues. Figure 2.2 provides a structured approach for doing such analysis. The first two columns list the environmental segments and some common indicators for them. A first step in environmental analysis is to identify environmental segments, agencies, and actors that are most critical to the firm. The next four columns are for summarizing past, current, and future trends and the opportunities and threats in each environmental segment. For each environmental segment, strategic managers must examine past trends and their historical evolution. This analysis should aim at uncovering critical events and historical relationships that shape the environment today. Environmental analysis should include an assessment of current strategic issues in each environmental segment, and their implications for the company. Wherever possible, strategic issues and trends should be measured using objective indicators.

Another important task in environmental analysis is forecasting how strategic issues will evolve in the future. Forecasts of product demand, technological trends regulations, and competitive threats should be a part of this analysis. It is particularly important to identify sudden discontinuities in trends and their consequences for firm performance (Ansoff, 1980; Fahey and Narayanan, 1986; Filho, 1985).

One important objective of environmental analysis is to identify opportunities and threats facing the corporation. **Opportunities** represent potential for profitable action, and threats are events that represent danger and risk to the company's future. Opportunities may exist in unexploited market demand for existing products. There may be new product possibilities. It may be possible to make technological improvements in production systems that could lead to improved product quality, higher production efficiency, and reduced pollution. There may

Figure 2.2 *Framework for General Environmental Analysis*

	Some Common Indicators	Past Evolution	Current Forces	Future Forecast	Opportunities and Threats
Economic					
Industry	Sales growth rate				
International	GNP growth				
National	GDP growth, interest rate, un-employment rate				
Regional	Regional economic indicators				
Local	Tax issues				
Technological					
Product	Innovation, R&D Investments				
Process	Capital expenditure				
Social and Cultural					
Demographics	Population status				
Social relations					
Social structures	Institutions				
Social trends	Fashion, arts				
Social values and mores	Practices				
Political and Regulatory					
Legislative and electoral politics					
Laws					
Regulatory agencies					
Interest group pressures					
Natural Environment					
Environmental incidents					
Air Pollution Index					

be potential for cutting costs. In addition, there may be opportunities for acquisition of new businesses.

Environmental opportunities are both limited and temporal. There are limits to natural resources, limits to consumer demands, limits to social and cultural assimilation, limits to information, and so on. These limits should be assessed by environmental analysis. The temporal or time-dependent nature of opportunities must also be examined. Opportunities do not last forever; they may arise and fade away quickly. Managers must learn to act within the window of opportunity. They must be quick to grab opportunities while they last. The ability to act quickly and opportunistically is a strategic skill that needs to be developed.

Threats are events or conditions that can potentially harm organizational interests. They can take the form of new restrictive regulations or the arrival of new and powerful competitors. Decline in demand for products is often a major threat to business. Other threats include harm from products and production technologies, the possibility of labor strikes, consumer product boycotts, financial crunch, and disruption of critical supplies. Threatening environmental events affect firms differently. Their influence depends on company size, resources, strategic posture, and ability to weather adverse conditions. Environmental analysis should aid companies to develop contingency actions to avoid or circumvent threats.

Environmental analysis should also provide general guidance for acquiring resources from the environment. It should identify where resources may be available and how they could be obtained. It should tell managers how the firm is positioned with respect to its competitors. The following questions can help managers to assess opportunities and threats posed by the environment:

1. How do environmental issues and trends influence our current strategy?
2. How is customer demand for our products changing in quantity, quality, and style? How is the distribution system changing? What are the new market trends? How do these changes influence the way we currently do business?
3. How is our technological environment changing? What new business opportunities are likely to emerge? Which competitor in our industry is best positioned to exploit them?
4. What new social and political demands and challenges is the environment placing on our firm? How can we proactively meet these challenges?
5. How is the regulatory structure of our industry evolving? What new regulations are likely to go into effect in the next three years? What will they mean for the firm's profitability and long-term health?
6. What are the opportunities and threats facing our firm and its divisions? What are the new growth industries? How are we positioned to exploit these opportunities? How vulnerable are we to threats?

The foregoing analysis of the environment emphasizes examining the influences that environmental forces have on companies. This constitutes only half the task of environmental analysis. The other half should focus on assessing how organizational activities affect the firm's environment. Both the human and natural environments need to be considered. Concerns over environmental degradation are becoming widespread. It is essential for managers to understand the strategic implications of the harm that organizational activities can cause on the natural environment.

For example, the depletion of fossil fuels and air pollution from automobiles have many strategic implications for car manufacturers. It would be reasonable to expect more stringent regulations on auto emissions and fuel consumption in the coming years. To be competitive, automobile manufacturers may be forced into developing "lean burn" engines, improved catalytic converters, and electric cars. Thus, environmental analysis by these companies should include assessment of the potential for reducing consumption of energy and natural resources. It should identify ways of minimizing hazardous and solid wastes, recycling wastes, and minimizing pollution. It should try to reduce product and process risks and develop cleaner technologies. Ways and resources for doing these should be made a part of strategic plans.

In many small companies individual managers do environmental analysis as a part of their routine activities. Most large companies, however, have developed special analytical techniques and information systems to aid environmental analysis. Senior management receives information from this analysis as part of the strategic planning exercise. The next section describes some of these techniques.

2.2   TECHNIQUES FOR ENVIRONMENTAL ANALYSIS

Analyzing a company's environment means understanding all external influences on it. This is a daunting task that is best left in the hands of expert analysts. Environmental analysis can be structured and made more manageable by using several formal techniques for assessing current environmental trends and forecasting future trends. In most organizations, planning and staff analysts do the detailed analysis using these techniques. Strategy managers need only familiarize themselves with the techniques so that they can judge their appropriateness for different forecasting tasks.

Here, we introduce seven techniques briefly to identify their utility for environmental analysis. For each of these techniques, there is extensive literature from which to obtain a detailed understanding. For example, there are hundreds of books (and several specialized journals) available on statistical forecasting techniques. The seven techniques we discuss next are trend extrapolation, econometric forecasting, Delphi forecasting, strategic issues analysis, cross-impact matrices, scenario analysis, and system simulations.

Trend Extrapolation is a simple and versatile technique for forecasting specific environmental variables in the near-term future. It uses historical changes in a variable over time, or historical relationships between variables, to identify future trends. The assumption is that historical data accurately capture the logic of changes in the variable being forecast. The technique may use a simple linear relationship or more complex nonlinear relationships to forecast trends.

Trend extrapolation is useful for identifying time trends in single variables such as sales, productivity, demand, and cost. In a more sophisticated sense, it may be used to profile trends of several variables simultaneously, which could establish covariance patterns between variables (Martino, 1972). For example, Figure 2.3 shows sales volume over time. The trend line *AB* from 1985 to 1990 depicts a steady rise in sales from $100 million to $200 million. This trend line can be used to forecast future sales for years beyond 1990. If sales increase at the same rate as in the past, this line can be simply extended as a straight line. Line *BC* forecasts sales for 1991 and 1992. Under different assumptions about the rate of sales growth, alternative forecasts can be obtained in the trends. Thus, *BD* represents sales growth that is faster than that in previous years. Line *BE* represents sales growth slower than in previous years.

Econometric Forecasting uses large computer programs to predict major economic indicators. Macroeconomic variables such as gross national product, interest rates, employment rates, producer and consumer price indices, imports, exports, and trade balance can be predicted using econometric forecasting.

The statistical techniques most commonly used in such forecasting are multiple regression analysis and time series regression models. The statistical models consist of multiple equations. Equations represent causal relationships between key variables suggested by economic theory and empirical evidence. Models calibrated with historical data are used to forecast future trends. For example, the following equation shows a complex relationship between the dependent variable Y and three independent variables, $X1, X2, X3$. Here, $a, b, c,$ and d are the parameters to be estimated.

$$Y = a + b1X1 + b2X1 + c1X2 + c2X2 + d1X3 + d2X3$$

Figure 2.3 *Trend Extrapolation*

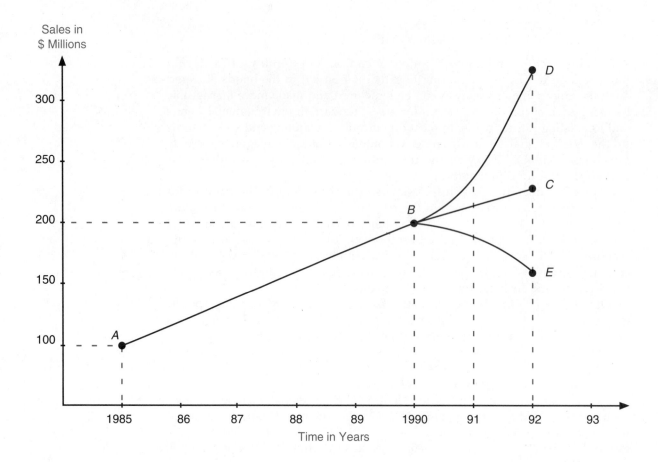

Using historical data, the model parameters can be estimated. Then Y can be forecast for different levels of $X1$, $X2$, and $X3$.

Today, professional forecasting companies do most of the econometric forecasting. Some well-known forecasters are Chase Econometric Associates, Data Resources, and Wharton Econometric Forecasting Associates. Federal government agencies (Department of Commerce, Federal Reserve Bank, and the Treasury Department) and major commercial and investment banks do their own forecasting. Instead of doing their own econometric forecasting, corporations can simply subscribe to forecasting services to receive periodic forecasts of key economic indicators. Often they subscribe to multiple services to validate forecasts and use the average forecast in their own strategic decision making.

Delphi Forecasting is a qualitative forecasting technique. It systematically elicits and consolidates the judgments of experts about the future. The technique is particularly useful when objective measures of variables to be forecast are not available. The subjective judgments of experts serve as surrogates for objective measures. Policy Delphi allows a systematic consolidation of the perceptions of experts into a consensual description of the future.

The technique begins with the selection of a panel of experts from relevant fields. These experts include economists, scientists, technologists, sociologists, experienced corporate managers and consultants. Panelists provide their opinions on relevant aspects of the future environment. A semistructured questionnaire and interviews may be used for collecting opinions. These opinions are documented, consolidated, and circulated to the panelists. Individual panelists react to opinions of their colleagues and revise their own opinions in light of other experts' opinions. This leads to a second round of opinion polling. Again the panel members share revised opinions. This process of opinion polling, sharing, and revision is repeated three or four times or until consensus emerges. This consensus view of the future serves the function of a forecast.

The Delphi technique is useful for forecasting emergence of new product and process technologies and new technological or consumer trends. The RAND Corporation pioneered the use of this technique in assessing diverse environmental issues. For example, it predicted the impact of the formation of the Organization of Petroleum Exporting Countries (OPEC) on oil supplies and oil prices. Other applications of the technique included assessing trends in terrorist activities and their influence on international businesses and prioritizing domestic social programs (Rescher, 1978).

Strategic Issues Analysis is another qualitative technique for assessing emerging strategic environmental issues. It allows broad monitoring of social, regulatory, and political changes that can affect corporate performance. The technique consists of systematically monitoring these developments and identifying their impacts on companies. For example, companies doing business in South Africa have used the technique to assess the impact of racial tensions there on their worldwide businesses. Similarly, chemical companies, such as Du Pont, Monsanto, and Stauffer Chemicals have used strategic issues analysis for assessing the impact of the environmental movement on the cost of doing business (Ansoff, 1980; Chase, 1984; Dutton, 1988).

Major corporations, including Ciba-Geigy, Dow Jones, General Electric, Polaroid, Monsanto, Stauffer Chemicals, and Sears, Roebuck have institutionalized issues analysis and management. They have permanent top management committees or specialists to perform this function.

Cross-Impact Matrices are most useful when forecasting several interrelated variables. They acknowledge that one environmental event may increase or decrease in likelihood with the occurrence of another event. The cross-impact matrix represents the influence of several related events or outcomes on each other over time. It is a simple way of keeping track of changing interactions between environmental vents. Consider the following cross-impact matrix:

Cross-Impact Matrix

Technology (probability, year)	A	B	C
(A) Permanent space station [.8, 1990]	. . .	125% impact, no time lag	must occur in 10 years
(B) Laser shield development [.9, 1995]	precluded	. . .	must occur soon
(C) Strategic defense initiative operational [.9, 2000]	precluded	25% negative impact	. . .

In this matrix the rows represent development of three technologies: (A) permanent space station, (B) laser shield, and (C) strategic defense initiative. The figures in brackets provide their probability of development and the period for development. The columns list the same technologies. The cells of the matrix represent the effects of A, B, and C on each other. The diagonal cells of the matrix are empty, (the ellipses); they represent the effect of a technology on itself.

The matrix shows that occurrence of A has a 125% positive effect and no time delays on the occurrence of B. Similarly, C has a negative 25% effect on B. C also precludes A from occurring. Creating these matrices and periodically updating them keeps the dynamically changing events within clear view of planners (Grant and King, 1982). The National Aeronautics and Space Administration and its contractors (e.g., Rockwell International, Morton Thiokol, General Dynamics) and defense contractors use cross-impact analysis. They forecast the demand for their products and services under differing assumptions about space and defense programs.

Scenario Analysis is a technique used to forecast the occurrence of complex environmental events. It is particularly useful for forecasting events in which many variables play a role. Scenarios allow the integrated consideration of these multiple variables in explaining the emergence of future conditions. A scenario is a detailed description of how certain events may occur in the future and their consequences for the organization.

Scenarios describe in detail the sequence of events that could plausibly lead to a prescribed future state. They identify factors that are likely to affect the firm, and they assess implications of future conditions for corporate objectives and performance. Strategic plans and programs that can meet environmental challenges may be explored within the scenario. Scenario analysis usually leads to the development of a best case scenario, a worst case scenario, and a most likely scenario. Each scenario represents a different set of assumptions about external and internal factors. The following steps may be used to develop scenarios:

1. Identify strategic environmental issues that are likely to affect the industry/firm. Prioritize these issues in order of their importance to the firm.
2. Select the most important issues as the focus for scenario development. List the organizational assumptions with respect to these issues and identify the possible variations in these assumptions.
3. Prepare a preliminary description of these issues and how they evolved. Include the key economic, social, political, and cultural influences that affect them. Do this with help of outside industry experts.
4. Draw out the implications of the issue for organizational performance. What has the organization done and what can it do to cope with the issues? Identify those variables shaping the issue that the management can control and partially control. Also, identify those variables over which management has no control.
5. Develop detailed descriptions of the future in the form of scenarios. Scenarios are constructed under a worst case, best case, and most likely case set of assumptions. Draw out the implications of these scenarios for future performance of the company.
6. Discuss the scenarios with top management and refine them.
7. Develop contingency action plans for each scenario.

Scenarios may serve as vehicles for discussing strategic plans and environmental trends. They are also useful for macro sociological forecasting. Kahn and Weiner (1967) used scenario analysis to predict the state of the United States and the world in the year 2000. Shell Oil and Atlantic Richfield used scenario analysis for corporate planning; they forecasted the dynamics of energy supply and demand and emergence of new industry structures. General Electric, Monsanto, and other industrial companies have also used scenario analysis for environmental analysis (Linneman and Klien, 1979; Raubitschek, 1988).

Systems Simulation is a technique for examining the structural properties of industries and economic sectors. The analysis of structure can help in forecasting trends. Forrester (1969) developed an industry forecasting model that combined endogenous and exogenous factors to predict important industry trends. Such simulations mathematically model industrial systems. Models consist of dozens of equations using many variables. Variables represent attributes of the industrial system. Equations represent relationships between variables. The simulation examines changing relationships within the industrial system. It identifies how one set of variables and relationships changes with other sets. It also describes the optimal states of the system and does sensitivity analysis.

Anheuser Busch, General Electric, and Textron have used corporate simulation models as aids in strategic planning. The models link multiple variables characterizing production, market, business, and financial parameters to simulate the total corporate system. They aim at optimizing productivity of the system under given internal and environmental constraints. Computer models also can be used to screen acquisition candidates and assess their value.

An area where simulations are becoming more popular is crisis management. Companies in chemical, pharmaceutical, nuclear, food, steel, and other hazardous industries use computerized simulations to predict industrial accidents or pollution incidents. The simulations help managers to organize emergency and rescue operations. For example, Johnson & Johnson uses the Emergency Information System (EIS-C) to simulate and manage chemical emergencies. The simulation model allows managers to predict the size and path of the chemical plume formed by a chemical release. This information is useful for organizing focused evacuation and emergency relief for high-risk populations.

2.3   ENVIRONMENTAL SCANNING AND INFORMATION SYSTEMS

Analysis of environmental forces requires many types of information. Firms have developed a variety of information systems to generate this information methodically. These systems take inputs from the firm's internal information systems in production, marketing, and financial control areas. They also use a variety of outside information sources: present and potential customers, government, industry analysts, academic researchers, and consultants. Some of these information systems are purely manual and others use computers. The systems analyze and summarize information about customers, competitors, social and cultural trends, technological developments, and regulatory changes. Strategic decision makers receive this information periodically (Aguilar, 1967; Stubbart, 1982).

Fahey and King (1977) described three types of environmental scanning systems found in organizations: irregular, regular, and continuous. Companies with **irregular environmental scanning systems** monitor the environment through *ad hoc* studies. These studies focus on critical current and imminent environmental events. Staff members in corporate headquarters or business units who are close to the issues do the studies. They focus on specific events that are important to the firm. The main objective of such studies is to keep track of important environmental issues so that surprises from drastic environmental changes can be avoided.

Companies with **regular environmental** scanning systems conduct periodic studies of selected environmental events and variables. These studies analyze how the environment will affect critical strategic decisions. Studies are oriented toward decisions or issues. A permanent strategic planning staff conducts the studies on a regular basis and updates them periodically. These systems provide a more proactive approach to tracking the environment than the irregular scanning systems.

Companies with **continuous environmental scanning systems** have institutionalized the environmental scanning activity. They have structured data collection and processing systems. These systems focus on a broad range of environmental variables that affect the firm's performance. Often the systems use computerized databases and analytical models. They analyze environmental and industry trends and forecast future ones. Long-term future forecasts often result from such analysis. Sometimes environmental scanning and strategic planning are integrated into a single program; jointly, they answer concrete questions raised by strategic planners. Organizationally, environmental scanning is part of the strategic planning department.

More recently, major companies such as GM, Eastman Kodak, and British Petroleum have developed **competitor intelligence and analysis systems**. These systems exclusively analyze competition. Their purpose is to enable the firm to use information as a strategic resource in developing competitive advantage and more effective business strategies. These competitor intelligence systems document and monitor competitor profiles, activities, and strategies. They analyze strategic changes in product lines, distribution channels, and marketing emphases, and they identify adoption of new technologies that may change the competitive balance in the industry. Information about these changes is used to develop competitive responses (Frederick and Venkatraman, 1988; Prescott and Smith, 1987).

Competitor information for these systems comes from a variety of conventional published and personal sources. These include customers, suppliers, ex-employees of competitors, governmental agencies, and public databases. More restricted governmental data may be obtained through use of the Freedom of Information Act. Some companies also invest in private intelligence investigations (Ghoshal and Westney, 1991; Prescott and Smith, 1987).

2.4   ANALYSIS OF ORGANIZATIONAL STAKEHOLDERS

Another way of conceptualizing environmental pressures on an organization is through consideration of stakeholders. Stakeholders are all individuals and organizations that influence or are influenced by the firm. Each stakeholder has different stakes in the firm. For example, stock owners seek wealth in the form of dividends and capital appreciation. Employees want good salaries and working conditions. The community expects the firm to provide jobs opportunities. The government expects tax revenues. These stakeholders influence the firm to protect and promote their own interests; these influences take the form of demands, sanctions, contractual relationships, and indirect pressures.

Nature is an important organizational stakeholder that is dramatically influenced by organizational activities. It also influences organizations by the resources it provides. Unlike other stakeholders, however, nature does not assert its demands on companies. Therefore, it is often ignored. But now nature's demands (needs) are being articulated powerfully by public interest groups and the media. Strategic managers must understand these demands and factor them into strategy formulation. The ability of a firm to operate effectively depends on support and participation of all its stakeholders (Freeman, 1984; Mitroff and Mason, 1982).

Stakeholders are both inside and outside the organization (see Figure 2.4). Some stakeholders, such as the board of directors, are on the boundary of the organization and its environment. Internal stakeholders include workers, staff, and management. External stakeholders include stockholders, customers, suppliers, competitors, communities in which the organization does business, governmental agencies, labor unions, and public interest groups.

In recent years relationships among stakeholders of the firm have changed dramatically in ways that accentuate conflicts and differences among them. For example, historically investors had been a passive stakeholder group who trusted the firm's management and let them operate without much interference. With the advent of hostile takeovers, leveraged buy-outs, and pension fund activism, investors are playing an active role in redirecting companies. Investor groups can cooperate to displace current management. They can divest parts of the firm and redeploy its assets in different ways. For example, in 1989 some disgruntled investors of United Airlines and the pilot's union joined hands. They bought out the company and restructured its management and finances. They were able to improve company performance dramatically.

Organizations can develop stakeholder-sensitive strategies by analyzing stakeholder needs and demands and adopting a broad stakeholder orientation. This requires finding a balanced way of fulfilling the demands of multiple stakeholders. It requires pursuing broad stakeholder objectives, resolving conflicts among opposing groups of stakeholders, and developing strategic programs to address stakeholders needs. Some companies, such as NCR, use stakeholder analysis for strategy formulation. For details, see the NCR statement of stakeholder strategies in the Company Policy Documents section of this book.

2.5   ORGANIZATION-ENVIRONMENT CONTACT POINTS

Organizations make contacts with their environment at several points and at several organizational levels. At each of these contact points, environmental interactions must be managed. It is through these interactions that the organization is able to get new information and resources, fulfill stakeholder demands, and build corporate image. Environmental contacts can serve as important sources of strategic information for the firm. This information can help in critical tasks by providing ideas for new products, marketing strategies, improvement in pro-duction techniques, and efficient management of materials and inventories.

Management of organization-environment interactions begins at the top. The top management and the board of directors are in contact with a broad set of organizational stakeholders: important investors, members of other corporate boards, high government officials, bankers, labor union leaders, and large customers. These stakeholders are important because they possess critical information and power that can influence the firm's performance (Vance, 1983).

These strategic contacts must be nurtured systematically. Good relationships with stakeholders ensure necessary inputs from them. YKK, the world's largest

Figure 2.4 *Organizational Stakeholders*

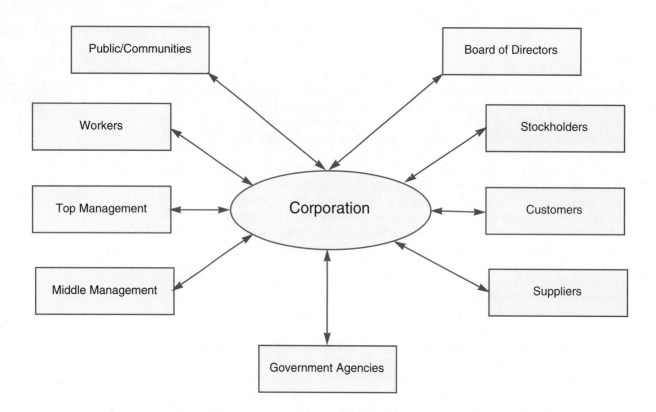

manufacturer of zippers, provides a good example. This Japanese company has institutionalized nurturing activity as an annual program. The company invites community leaders, key customers, and important business associates from its fifty international subsidiaries to visit Japan at the company's expense. They visit the company's plants, attend board meetings, and meet with the CEO and key managers—all aimed at promoting goodwill.

The purpose of strategic contacts at the board of directors level is to provide key stakeholders direct access to board members, thereby bringing stakeholders close to top management. These contacts may also be used to identify major opportunities and threats facing the organization and to verify management's perceptions about evolving trends in the environment. They can also help to bring new resources into the organization.

The board of directors serve several other important functions. Board members help in the selection and appointment of the CEO and top management team. They oversee the management function of the firm. They are trustees of stockholders and as such are responsible for ensuring that the firm's assets are managed prudently. The board of directors must provide strategic leadership to the firm in terms of the direction and identity of the company. They ratify company policies on dividends, capital expenditures, acquisitions and divestments, and strategic issues.

At the operating level, each division, business unit, and department of the firm is in contact with the environment. Boundary-spanning personnel from the company interact with their counterparts in other firms and government agencies. For example, finance personnel are in contact with bank officers, investment advisors, stockholders, and stock brokers and dealers. Marketing personnel are in contact with customers, retailers, distributors, and advertising agencies. Production personnel are in contact with equipment manufacturers, suppliers of raw materials, packagers, transporters, and sometimes with customers. At each of these contact points, the firm's image and resources should be managed in ways consistent with its strategy. General Electric's policy on employee transactions with governments is included in the Company Policy Documents section of this book. It is an example of how companies structure their relationships with key stakeholders.

The Girl Scouts of America effectively manages its environmental contacts through an annual environmental scanning report. This report describes relevant environmental trends in the economic, social, and political environment facing the organization. It forecasts how key variables are going to change over a three-year period. It also specifies what actions the organization and managers at different levels must take to maintain and nurture relationships with external stakeholders.

Summary of Chapter 2

To formulate strategies managers must have a clear picture of external opportunities and threats facing the firm. They also require accurate projections of future environmental conditions. Environmental analysis is a means by which managers can develop a detailed understanding of their company's environment.

Environmental analysis identifies key environmental influences on the company and examines their implications for organizational strategies and performance. It shows how managers can respond to environmental changes quickly and gain competitive advantage. Thus, environmental analysis plays a central role in strategic management.

The key components of a company's environment are economic, technological, social, cultural, and political environments. The economic environment consists of the world economy, national economy, regional and local economies, and international trade regulations. The technological environment includes product and process technologies. Technological changes are a major source of opportunities and threats. The social and cultural environment includes demographic trends, life-styles, social structures, and social relationships, and social trends. Social and cultural factors are particularly important for international companies. The political and regulatory environment influences firm performance and strategic choices. It is shaped by legislative and electoral politics, interest group pressures, and regulatory agencies in charge of social and economic regulations. The natural environment is an important component of the firm's environment. It sets physical and natural resource limits on a firm's strategic choices.

General environmental analysis does a systematic analysis of the aforementioned environmental segments. It identifies environmental opportunities, threats, and strategies for acquiring resources from the environment. It also assesses impacts of organizational activities on the natural environment.

Environmental analysis can be facilitated by using structured techniques. The **trend extrapolation** technique uses historical relationships among variables for forecasting specific environmental variables. It is useful for identifying time trends in single variables. **Econometric forecasting** uses regression models to forecast many related macroeconomic variables. **Delphi forecasting** is a qualitative forecasting technique that systematically elicits and consolidates the judgments of experts about future conditions of the environment. **Strategic issue analysis** is another qualitative technique. It monitors social, regulatory, and political developments and identifies their impacts on firms. The **cross-**

impact matrix technique is useful for keeping track of changing interactions among multiple environmental variables. **Scenario analysis** forecasts complex environmental events that are not under managerial control. Scenarios allow the integrated consideration of many variables. **System simulation** examines the structural properties of industries and economic sectors and uses them as a basis for forecasting trends.

Analysis of environmental forces requires many types of information. Information is provided by environmental scanning systems, which can be irregular, regular, or continuous. Irregular environmental scanning monitors important environmental trends on an *ad hoc* basis. It helps avoid crises caused by drastic environmental changes. Regular environmental scanning is done periodically. It is more oriented toward decisions or issues and is more proactive than irregular scanning. Continuous environmental scanning focuses on a broad range of environmental variables that affect the firm's performance. To develop competitive advantage and more effective business strategies, some companies use competitor intelligence systems.

Another way of understanding the company's environment is in terms of its stakeholders. Stakeholders are external agents that influence the company or are influenced by it. Their demands are critical and need to be studied systematically. Stakeholder-sensitive strategies can then be developed by adopting a broad stakeholder orientation. Firms need to proactively manage their relationships with environmental agents and forces at several levels and in several areas. General environmental analysis provides a framework for structuring these relationships. Environmental analysis sensitizes managers to the demands that external stakeholders place on the firm. *Fulfilling stakeholder demands in a balanced way is the challenge of strategy formulation.*

READINGS, CASES, AND POLICY DOCUMENTS

The following readings, cases and policy documents provide additional background and discussion material for the ideas discussed in this Chapter.

Readings

* Ansoff, H.I. "The changing shape of the strategic problem". In D. Schendel and C.W. Hofer (Eds) *Strategic Management: A New View of Business Policy and Planning*, Boston: Little Brown and Co., 1979.
  Porter, M.E. "The competitive advantage of nations". *Harvard Business Review*, March-April, 1990, pp 73-93.

Cases

  Airlines Industry—Domestic
  Airline Industry—International
* Comdisco Disaster Recovery Services International Expansion
  Copenhagen Handelsbank
  Genicom Corporation
* Greenpeace v/s Ford
* Hospital Management Industry

ISKRA Power Tools
World Tyre Industry

Policy Documents

NCR Corporation Directional Strategy
* American Express—TRS The Next Ten Years

* indicates particularly appropriate assignments

Figures 2.1, 2.2, 2.3, and 2.4.

Strategic Management Process and Book Outline

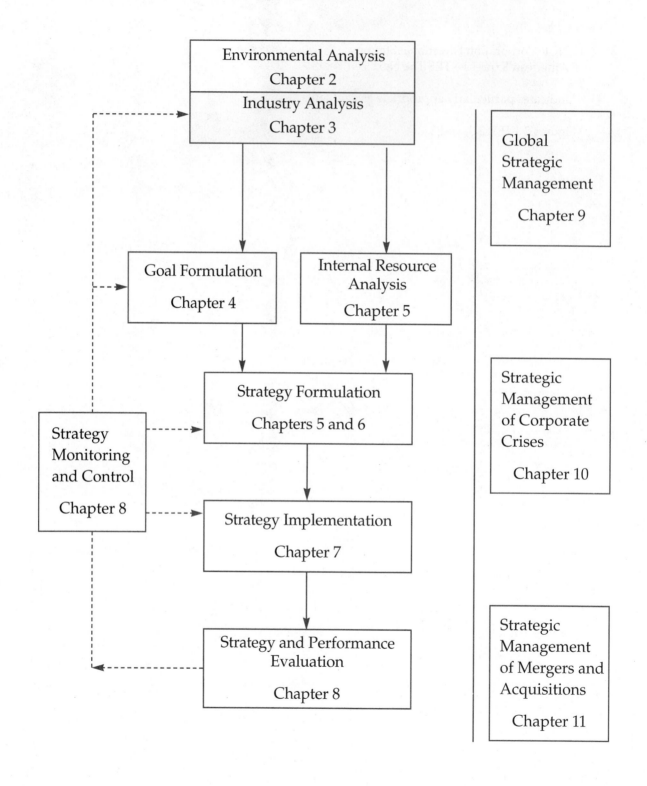

CHAPTER 3
INDUSTRY
ANALYSIS

CHAPTER OUTLINE

General environmental analysis as discussed in the previous chapter is useful for answering broad corporate strategy questions. It helps companies to choose the industries in which they should operate. Such general analysis, however, serves only as a starting point for strategy formulation. Formulating competitive strategies at the business unit level requires more detailed analysis of industry competition. Competitive strategies should be based on a detailed understanding of industry structure. The structure of competition and determinants of profitability in an industry are key to formulating good competitive strategies. They can help managers determine opportunities and threats facing their business. Then, competitive strategies can be formulated to exploit these opportunities and avoid threats.

The industry is a part of the general economic environment as discussed in Chapter 2. It refers to a set of firms producing the same, or functionally similar products/services, and vying for the same customers. An industry can include both domestic and foreign firms. For example, the automobile industry includes US firms such as GM, Ford, and Chrysler and foreign firms like Honda, Toyota, Volvo, and BMW.

Stories of excellent products that fail to become competitive successes illustrate the importance of understanding competition. Consider the case of Ultrasoft diapers. Weyerhaeuser's Personal Care Products Division launched Ultrasofts in early 1990. It used Wegman's Food Markets chain as its distributor. Much fanfare and major advertising accompanied the product launch; 50,000 customers received promotional discounts. The product was technically superior to the leading national premium brands (Pampers and Huggies). The diaper had extra cushy waistbands and cuffs to prevent leakage. It was softer than competitive products because it had a clothlike covering instead of the plastic covering typical of competitive products. Its superabsorbent pulp material woven into the pad kept babies drier than did other diaper brands. Ultrasofts cost $8.39 for a package of thirty-two diapers, about $1.60 less than competing brands. Pilot tests in the market showed that parents preferred Ultrasofts two to one over leading brands.

Despite these technological advantages and consumer support, Ultrasofts failed to become successful. Weyerhaeuser's competitive strategy was simply deficient in dealing with the fierce competition in the diapers industry. Weyerhaeuser did not have good estimates of demand for the product and market share distributions. It adopted the strategy of supplying thru a regional distributor, but regional distribution limited the demand. Suppliers of lining materials did not want to enter long-term contracts for small quantities. Weyerhaeuser's own production plant in Bowling Green, Kentucky, was too small for large-scale production, which prevented the company from exploiting economies of scale.

Weyerhaeuser also underestimated the fight for shelf space in the fiercely competitive retailing industry. Within six months of launching Ultrasofts, the company raised prices by 22% to cover extra manufacturing costs. It also cut back on promotions. Simultaneously, big national competitors Procter & Gamble and Kimberly Clark, responded to Weyerhaeuser's entry into the market by aggressively promoting their own brands. They gave special price discounts to retailers and customers. Retailers became reluctant to give shelf space to Ultrasofts. Customers switched to lower-priced alternatives. Within a year of launching Ultrasofts, Weyerhaeuser withdrew it from the market and sustained a large, unspecified loss.

This example shows that designing an excellent product is not sufficient for competitive success. Competitive strategy must be based on a broad understanding of what makes an industry profitable. Who are the most significant competitors? What are the strengths and weaknesses of these competitors? How easy or difficult is it to enter the industry? Who can enter the industry? How will competitors react to a new product entry or to new strategies? What makes consumers buy products in this industry? How can suppliers affect production schedules and costs? What economic, technological, and regulatory factors affect production scale and costs?

Such questions can be answered by analyzing the structure of competition within industries. This involves examining structural characteristics that determine industry profitability and competition. This chapter begins with a general discussion of the nature of industry competition. It describes a framework for analysis of industry structure and discusses strategic groups within an industry. Strategic groups in an industry are clusters of firms that follow similar strategies and compete with other clusters. Strategic group analysis allows us to refine industry structure analysis. These analyses are useful for identifying opportunities and threats within the industry (Porter, 1980; Karnani and Wernerfelt, 1985).

3.1   INDUSTRY COMPETITION

Competition is a complex idea that can be studied from many different perspectives. Let us begin by acknowledging several different concepts of economic competition (Barney, 1986): the Chamberlin, Schumpeterian, and industry/organization views of competition. In this chapter we briefly discuss the first two views, which historically preceded the now popular industry/organization (I/O) model of competition. The I/O model includes a comprehensive set of variables for understanding the competitive dynamics of industry.

In the 1930s, Chamberlin and his colleagues began systematic study of economic competition between firms. They viewed competition as a resource-based phenomenon. It represented attempts by firms to use their unique resources to create lasting performance benefits. The resources used by firms included finances, technology, patents, trademarks, brand awareness, marketing knowledge, and administration. For example, John Rockefeller's Standard Oil (now Exxon) gained the competitive edge by buying up oil rights. It bought exploration and extraction rights leases all across the United States and abroad. Once it had captured this unique resource, it developed exploration, drilling, refining, and marketing facilities. Soon it became the largest American oil company.

Firms in every industry have some unique and some overlapping resources. They use these resources to create three different types of market environments: monopolistic, oligopolistic, and perfect markets. In a monopolistic market, a single firm dominates the industry. Until the breakup of American Telephone and Telegraph (AT&T) in 1982, it had a monopoly in the telephone services industry. AT&T had developed the early telecommunications technology; this made it the only firm capable of operating effectively in this industry. Even today, telephone service is a monopolistic industry in many countries including Japan, Germany, and Britain.

In oligopolistic industries, a few firms control the entire industry. Each firm is of significant size and power, although some firms may be dominant. The US automobile industry, with three major firms (Chrysler, Ford, and GM), is an example of an oligopolistic industry. Together these firms control nearly 70% of the auto market. This type of competition is common in many large, mature capital-intensive industries, such as iron and steel, petroleum, and paper.

Perfect competition refers to industries in which there are many firms. No single firm dominates the industry or enjoys any unique advantages over its rivals. Although no industries are truly perfectly competitive, apparel, software, furniture, and food products are close approximations (Chamberlin, 1933; Robinson, 1933).

Chamberlin showed that industries with monopolistic markets were in competitive equilibria. Some firms in these industries were able to exploit their unique resources permanently. They got better than average financial performance on a sustained basis. Given this possibility, it made strategic sense for individual firms to search for ways of establishing monopolistic advantages. This could be done by acquiring and controlling monopoly-granting resources or by operating in niches protected by regulations. Monopolistic markets were not, however, in the best interests of consumers. Lack of competition in such industries minimized incentives to improve products, cut costs, improve efficiency, lower prices, and innovate. In brief, monopolistic markets tended to stagnate.

Since the 1930s, economic regulations have tried to eliminate monopolies. Government enacted many antitrust laws designed to reduce monopoly power of individual firms. The objective was to encourage healthful competition among multiple firms. In many industries new regulations prohibited monopolies; these industries included agriculture, the airlines, banking, construction, insurance, railways, trucking, and utilities. Over the years, as antitrust legislation made monopolies less viable, more industries became competitive. Consequently, the monopolistic way of viewing competition became less useful for understanding competitive industry structures.

In contrast to the resource-centered view of competition was the work of Schumpeter (1950). In explaining the historical process of economic development in Western industrial economies, Schumpeter focused on the role of technological revolutions and product-market shifts. These factors, he argued, were at the heart of capitalistic competition and economic change. Revolutionary innovations in products, markets, and technologies gave firms distinctive long-term competitive advantages. These revolutions could completely displace all currently competitive firms. Other factors, such as price, marketing strategies, and financial resources, were less important.

For example, Citibank used computer and telecommunications technology to automate its back office. It also used teller machines to automate some front office functions. These changes allowed the bank to increase its transaction processing capabilities enormously. They reduced labor requirements and increased processing speed. The cost of each transaction fell to a fraction of the cost of doing each manually. The bank was able to expand its retail operations in the rapidly growing money center in New York City. This technologically based competitive advantage allowed Citibank to grow rapidly so that in the 1970s and 1980s it became the largest US bank. Other banks followed its example. Bank of America, Chase Manhattan, Manufacturers Hanover, and Security Pacific also grew rapidly through use of computer and telecommunication technologies. During the deregulation of the financial services sector in the 1980s, these banks led the restructuring of the banking industry. They already had advanced automation technologies in operation, and they were able to move into other financial services quickly. When regulations allowed it, they entered securities brokerage and insurance industries.

There are many examples of industries in which technology has provided a competitive edge on an international scale. In the 1970s, German and Japanese companies beat US steel makers in international markets. They deployed advanced steel-making technologies to gain competitive cost advantages. Technological superiority was also the cause of Japan's competitive victories in the consumer electronics, personal computer, automobile, tire, and motorcycle industries (Williams, 1983).

Technological revolutions are uncertain, unpredictable, and unknown in their impacts. Firms that guess their timing and impact accurately can gain tremendous competitive advantages over rivals. But wrongly estimating the arrival of revolutions can be costly and competitively devastating. Building up resources and skills needed to exploit new technologies before the revolution is wasteful and can place the firm at a competitive disadvantage. Similarly, waiting too long after the arrival of a new technology to exploit it also misses opportunities. Such delays can lose the competitive race to other firms who have timed themselves better. In Chapter 1 we saw how Hewlett-Packard correctly identified the significance of the electronics revolution for the calculator industry. It was able to beat Facit, the world's largest manufacturer of mechanical calculators.

When technological revolutions are not restructuring competition in an industry, companies must deal with evolutionary changes in technology. Technological evolution occurs through smaller innovations and new research and development. Innovations provide improvements in product features and functions and in efficiency of production processes. They may allow substitution of materials, thereby lowering the cost of production. Innovations are also possible in the management of operations and administrative functions. These innovations can dramatically influence costs. For example, innovations such as just-in-time inventory systems, total quality management programs, and reuse/recycling of wastes allow companies to increase efficiency and lower costs.

As the example of Weyerhaeuser cited earlier shows, competition is a complex multifaceted phenomenon. Neither of the two views of competition introduced in this section captures this complexity. A third view of competition that combines elements of the two and extends them is the industry/organization model of competition (Bain, 1956, 1968; Mason, 1939).

The original model of industry/organization competition argued that financial returns in an industry are a function of two variables: the competitive structure of the industry and the conduct of firms within the industry. Several economic variables determine the structure of an industry. They include the number and relative size of competitors, barriers to entry into the industry, degree of product differentiation, and the elasticity of demand. These variables jointly determine the average level of profits of an industry. Variance from average profitability was a result of individual firm's actions. These actions affected product quality, advertising intensity, production efficiencies, costs, and profits. This basic model found empirical support in a variety of industries (Sherer, 1981). In the past decade it has served as the basis for examining competitive structures for strategy formulation (Caves, 1980; Porter, 1980).

The three views of industry competition are summarized in Table 3.1.

3.2   STRUCTURAL FORCES THAT SHAPE INDUSTRY COMPETITION

The structure of an industry can be analyzed by looking at the regulatory, technological, economic, and commercial forces that shape competition within it. This discussion draws on Porter's (1980) framework extensively. However, Porter's discussion is extended by adding two contextual elements within which all

Table 3.1 *Three View of Industry Competition*

Resource Based (Chamberlin)	Technology Based (Schumpeter)	Industry/Organization (Bain)
Competition is based on control over resources.	Competition is based on technological capability.	Competition is a function of industry structure and firm behavior.
Types of competitive markets include monopolistic, oligopolistic, and perfectly competitive.	Two main driving forces are technological revolutions and technology evolution through innovations.	

industry competition occurs. First, industry regulations form the context in which all other industry forces operate. They are a primary determinant of profitability and competition. Second, and perhaps the more crucial contextual element, is the natural environment. The natural environment acts as a source of resources and as a sink for wastes and effluents. In both these roles, it imposes limitations on firms. The natural environment is increasingly affecting costs of production, distribution, and waste management. These in turn affect profitability and competition. The rise of environmental awareness in the public has increased demands for environmental protection. Thus companies must develop environmentally responsive corporate and competitive strategies.

Figure 3.1 identifies the five major structural forces that shape competition among industries. These are threats to entry, rivalry among competitors, bargaining power of buyers, bargaining power of suppliers, and threats from substitute products. The contextual elements include industry regulations and the natural environment. This framework suggests that ground rules for competition within an industry depend on the constraints of industry regulations and the natural environment. Within this context, competition depends on who can enter the industry and compete in it profitably. Competitive rivalry depends on threats of entry into the industry, pressure from substitute products, and bargaining power of buyers and suppliers. These structural forces jointly determine the profitability of the industry. They also affect the profits of individual firms within it.

Industry profits may be conceptualized as a fixed pie. This profit pie expands or shrinks through the influence of the major structural forces. Changes in the size of the profit pie also changes the profit share of individual firms in the industry. Next examine how each structural force shapes industry profits and competition. Then we discuss the contextual elements of industry regulations and the natural environment.

Threats to Entry

An important determinant of profitability is the number of competitors within an industry who compete for a share of industry profits. This number of competitors depends on who can enter the industry and effectively compete in it. Entry barriers are economic and technological forces that prevent outside firms from entering an industry. These barriers protect competition within the industry from powerful outsiders. If entry barriers are low, threats to entry increase because outsiders can easily come into the industry and increase competition within it. This reduces the total profits available for sharing among industry participants. If entry barriers are high, outside competitors cannot enter the industry easily. This protects the industry and its profits.

Entry barriers depend on technological and commercial relationships within the industry. The most important barriers to entry are economies of scale, product differentiation, switching costs, access to distribution channels, and miscellaneous barriers.

Economies of Scale. The scale of operation of a production unit determines its economic efficiency. As the scale of operation increases, so does its economic efficiency. This is true up to a certain limit. Economic advantages of scale occur because firms can buy raw materials in large quantities at discounts. They can also distribute overhead costs over many units.

In every industry there is a minimum economic scale at which a production

Figure 3.1 *Characteristics of Industry Structure*

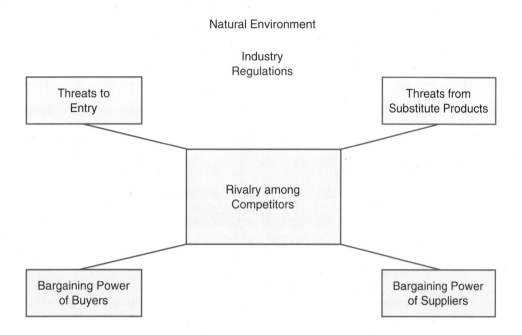

unit must operate for it to be efficient and competitive. If this minimum scale of operation is large, it requires a large amount of capital to establish. A large capital requirement acts as a barrier to entry. A larger capital requirement also imposes higher risks, which prevent smaller competitors from entering the industry.

To see how economies of scale act as barriers to entry consider two contrasting industries. The ballpoint pen industry and the automobile industry are good examples. Ballpoint pens can be assembled in a small workshop. They need a small assembly line and premolded parts. A few molding machines can mold the pen body, clips, rings, washers, and ink tubes. The cost of setting up this kind of workshop could be as low as $50,000. In contrast, the cost of establishing an economically feasible automobile assembly plant could easily run into several hundred million dollars. Thus, a small business with access to limited capital can enter the ballpoint pen industry but not the automobile industry. Capital requirements act as a barrier to entry into the automobile industry.

Product Differentiation. Product differentiation refers to how easy or difficult it is to distinguish products in an industry. Product differentiation may be based on objective features of the product or on perceived features. Perceived features include brand image, novelty, status image, and fashion appeal. Industries in which it is easy and inexpensive to differentiate products experience high product and brand proliferation. If creating product differentiation is technologically difficult and expensive, it limits the entry of new products into the industry. Creating differentiation requires creative product and package designs.

It may require heavy investments into advertising and promotion to convince consumers that the product is really different and unique.

The apparel industry is one in which it is easy and inexpensive to differentiate products. Products can be differentiated by fabric material, designs, color, size, and price. New competitors enter and exit the industry quite frequently. In contrast, the transparent adhesive tape industry produces a standardized product that is difficult to differentiate. Few new companies have entered this industry in the past decade.

Switching Costs. A switching cost is the cost that consumers must incur when they switch from one product to another. It determines how easy or difficult it is for consumers to switch. If switching costs are high, consumers continue to use the same product. They remain loyal to a familiar product and continue to buy it, despite the availability of alternative products. If switching costs are low, customers tend to experiment with new and different products. They try several products and may even substitute products from other industries to fill their needs. Thus, a high switching cost acts as a barrier to entry by discouraging consumers from moving to new products offered by new entrants.

Switching costs depend on consumer preferences, habits, and brand loyalty. Sometimes switching costs may be created by functional attributes of the product. For example, American Hospital Supply creates high switching costs through custom-tailored software. It gives its client hospitals a computer system and associated software for ordering supplies and maintaining inventory control. It also trains hospital personnel in the use of this system. Once accustomed to this system, hospitals find it difficult to switch to alternative suppliers. In this case switching suppliers would involve changes in ordering procedures, computer systems, software packages, input data, and internal record-keeping procedures.

In contrast, consumers of toothpaste have very low switching costs associated with trying different brands. Buying toothpaste from a grocery store can be almost an impulsive decision. It takes little effort by the consumer to switch from one toothpaste to another.

Access to Distribution Channels. Easy access to distribution channels lowers barriers to entry into an industry. New entrants can easily distribute their products without having to invest in the creation of a distribution network. Entry is more difficult in industries where existing participants control distribution. For example, consider the gasoline industry. Large oil companies, such as Exxon, Shell Oil, Texaco, and Mobil, control distribution outlets. New entrants into this industry cannot sell gasoline through existing outlets owned or franchised by these companies. They must create new outlets to distribute their products. In contrast, the distribution channels for hand tools are easily accessible to new entrants. New entrants can sell their hand tools through existing privately owned hardware stores or home improvement centers. They also can create new outlets by offering attractive margins to general merchandisers.

Miscellaneous Barriers. Sometimes technology patents, raw materials monopoly, and regulations can act as important barriers to entry. If a company has patents on a particular product, it can prevent other manufacturers from making that product and entering the industry. This is common in the drugs and pharmaceuticals industry. Patents provide protection from competition for a specific period.

Monopolistic control over raw materials also can act as a barrier to entry. For example, De Beers controls more than 50% of the worldwide supply of raw diamonds. This makes it very difficult for any new entrant to play an important role in the diamond industry.

All of these factors contribute to creating barriers to entry, but they do not exist evenly in all industries. In different industries, some sources of entry barriers are more important than others. More importantly, the barriers to entry change continually due to new regulations, new technologies, and new competitive strategies. For example, at one time the United States government controlled entry into the airlines industry; the government gave permission to airlines to operate particular routes. Airline deregulation in 1978 eliminated the requirement of obtaining government permission to operate routes. This opened up the industry to free competition. Regulatory changes also create uncertainty for potential new entrants into an industry and thus may discourage new entrants.

Companies in an industry can collectively create barriers to entry. They can lobby for protective legislation. They can create highly differentiated products. They can create high switching costs. And they can restrict access to distribution channels. It is important for managers to understand entry barriers in their industry. They should assess how entry barriers affect the number of new entrants and rivalry in the industry.

Rivalry among Competitors

Competition and profitability within an industry also depend on the intensity of rivalry among existing competitors. Competitive rivalry consists of dynamic moves and countermoves by competitors to attract buyers and capture a larger share of demand. Every time one firm makes a strategic move it can expect retaliation from its competitors. This retaliation may take the form of changes in product designs, promotional strategies, packaging, advertising, and prices. Price reduction is a commonly used competitive strategy. However, price wars reduce total industry profits by reducing industry revenues. Thus, fierce rivalry within an industry can be detrimental to its profitability.

Rivalry among competitors depends on several factors. They include number of competitors and their relative power, industry growth rate, fixed and storage costs, lack of switching costs, size of capacity augmentation, diversity of competitors, stakes of individual competitors, and exit barriers.

Number of Competitors and Their Relative Power. The total number of competitors is an important determinant of the nature of competitive rivalry. More competitors means more competitive interactions and more rivalry. More competitors also means smaller average shares of the profit pie for each competitor. In the early 1990s, the personal computers industry matured into a highly rivalrous, multiple-competitor industry. In this industry giant companies like IBM, Digital Equipment Corporation (DEC), and Compaq Computers are losing market share. Small but highly aggressive computer makers, such as Dell Computers, AST Research, Everex Computer Systems, Northgate, and Tandon Computers, are taking away market share from the large companies.

The relative power balance among competitors moderates competitive rivalry. If competitors are nearly equal in size and power, they may tend to avoid direct confrontation. They fear upsetting the industry balance. If they are vastly different in size, larger competitors may encroach on the turf of smaller ones to expand their markets. Industry balance can also be upset by new entrants into the industry and by large changes in the size of competing firms. When these situations occur, the industry experiences many new competitive strategies and retaliations that heighten competitive rivalry. For example, Philip Morris entered the brewing industry by buying Miller Brewing in the late 1970s. This completely upset the competitive structure of the beer industry. It triggered a series of competitive moves by existing beer companies. Smaller brewing companies were bought by larger ones and industry consolidation resulted.

Industry Growth Rate. The growth rate of an industry determines the total size of the profit pie. When the industry growth rate is high, the total profits available for sharing among competitors is also high and growing. There is low likelihood of competitors fighting with each other, because each competitor can get sufficient profits to survive. If the industry has matured, its growth rate is low. This limits the size of the total profit pie. For any one firm to do well or improve its performance, it has to take market share from other competitors. This leads to retaliation and more rivalry among competitors. Thus, pressures of rivalry are lower in high-growth industries. Current examples of such industries are biotechnology and computer software. In contrast, mature, declining, or low-growth industries, such as steel and soft drinks, experience high rivalry.

Fixed and Storage Costs. Industries in which fixed costs or storage costs are high experience intense rivalry among competitors. High fixed costs or storage costs can place significant debt burden on firms. They put pressure on firms to liquidate inventories and maintain high-capacity utilization. In such situations, it is important for firms to turn over their working capital quickly and make the best use of their fixed assets. To reduce storage costs and eliminate old model inventory, auto manufacturers routinely discount products, particularly around the end of the year. This often triggers price wars. Price wars reduce total industry profits and create higher rivalry among competitors.

Lack of Switching Costs. Industries with low switching costs have high competitive rivalry. Customers are free to choose and change their suppliers. Continuous switching between products by customers creates high uncertainty for competitors and encourages them to engage in retaliatory moves. The lack of switching costs also makes it easy for consumers to shop around for the best price. This puts the industry under continuous price pressure. Over time, the lowering of prices erodes industry profitability and increases competition.

Size of Capacity Augmentation. In some industries production capacity must be added in large sizes. These industries experience more intense competitive rivalry than industries in which capacity can be augmented in small increments. This is so because large-sized new plants are very expensive and require a great commitment of financial resources. To recoup these investments, firms charge higher prices and market their products aggressively to gain higher market share. This leads to more intense rivalry among competitors. Moreover, each round of capacity addition upsets the balance of supply and demand within the industry. Every time a new plant opens it creates a large additional capacity. So it is beneficial for one competitor (and then another) to reduce prices, sell more, and improve capacity utilization. This leads other competitors to retaliate and the whole industry gets out of balance.

Diversity of Competitors. The more diverse the competitors are in terms of their origins and operating styles, the more diverse their competitive strategies become. Diverse strategies elicit diverse responses and lead to higher competitive rivalry. Foreign competitors and competitors from other industries increase diversity. They create new competitive moves and new forms of retaliation that increase rivalry.

New competitors have different personalities and different resource bases. They can pursue new strategies in an industry, thereby creating an imbalance in the industry. Diversity among competitors also creates higher uncertainty. Existing industry participants do not know the capabilities of new competitors; they do not know what to expect from them. The presence of high uncertainty encourages rivalry. The entry of Philip Morris into the brewing industry, mentioned earlier, illustrates this point. Philip Morris entered the slow-moving and mature brewing industry with strong financial and marketing skills that it had mastered in the tobacco industry. It applied these skills to developing new strategies, new packaging, and new product design ideas for promoting Miller Beer. This upset the balance of forces, market shares, and marketing strategies within the brewing industry. Within a few years, Miller became the third largest brand in the industry.

Stakes of Individual Competitors. The willingness of individual competitors to retaliate against others also depends on their stakes within the industry. In today's environment, most large corporations operate in multiple industries. This allows them to diversify their risks. Nevertheless, if a company has unusually large stakes in any one industry, it will pay more attention to strategic changes within that industry. If there are any threats to its performance within the industry, it is likely to retaliate with much greater vigor.

For example, Coca-Cola diversified into the soft drinks, wine, and entertainment industries. It has very large stakes in the soft drinks industry and smaller stakes in wine and entertainment. It is likely to react more aggressively and immediately to any threat to its market position in soft drinks; it will be less aggressive in responding to threats in the other two industries where it has smaller stakes. In fact, even a decline in its market share in the soft drinks industry evokes a strong response from Coca-Cola.

Exit Barriers. Exit barriers refer to costs that prevent or discourage a firm from getting out of an industry. These include high unrecovered fixed costs, labor commitments, unsold inventories, and strategic interdependence among businesses. Sometimes there are emotional and psychological barriers to exit. If a company has been in an industry for a long time, its management may become committed to staying in it. The company may continue operating in an industry, even when it is not profitable to do so. In industries where exit barriers are high, competitors face higher rivalry. This is because firms unable to exit from the industry must remain in it and do the best they can. Firms thus stuck in the industry try to survive through aggressive price competition.

The most important point to remember about rivalry among competitors is that it changes continually. The entry of one or two competitors can completely change the balance of rivalry within the industry.

Bargaining Power of Buyers

Power of buyers refers to their ability to get favorable terms of trade with sellers. Powerful buyers can get attractive price discounts, better credit terms, better product quality, and more product support services from the industry. Because these concessions are costly, they have the effect of reducing industry profits. Buyers attempt to get the best value for their money, and by so doing they put downward pressure on industry profitability. The power of buyers depends on several factors: buyer concentration, degree of product differentiation, buyer switching costs, access to backward integration, impact of product on buyer's product quality, and the amount of information available to the buyer.

Buyer Concentration. Industries that have a high concentration of buyers (i.e., there are only a few large buyers) are too dependent on these buyers. Buyers in these industries can be very powerful and can extract better products, prices, and better terms of trade from the industry. For example, key buyers for diskette drives are the few large computer companies that manufacture personal and mini computer systems. Some larger buyers, such as IBM and DEC, wield enormous power over suppliers. Similarly, Sears, Roebuck brands products with its own name. It buys in large quantities and is able to exert great influence on its vendors. It virtually dictates product specifications, packaging, price, delivery terms, and payment terms.

In contrast, in industries that have a large number of buyers, each buyer tends to be small. Small individual buyers cannot exert much pressure on the industry. Such is the case in the personal products and cosmetics industry. The industry has large firms such as Avon, Mary Kay, and Estee Lauder. Buyers in this industry are individuals who buy in small quantities. They have neither the power nor the inclination to elicit attractive terms of trade from sellers.

Degree of Product Differentiation. High degree of product differentiation has the effect of limiting buyer power. In industries with highly differentiated products, most products have unique features. To obtain certain product features, buyers may have no choice but to buy from a specific manufacturer. For example, fighter airplanes are a highly differentiable product. Buyers seeking to buy planes with specific characteristics have limited choice of manufacturers. They thus have limited power to influence the terms of trade. In contrast, the degree of differentiation in luggage bags is low. Luggage buyers have the flexibility of buying from virtually any manufacturer in the industry. This increases the buyer's ability to negotiate better terms.

Buyer switching costs. Another factor that determines the bargaining power of buyers is switching costs. If switching costs are low, dissatisfied buyers can easily move from one supplier to another. Their flexibility in choosing among alternative buyers is a source of power. It gives them an advantage in negotiating better business terms from suppliers. On the other hand, if switching costs are high, buyers are locked into specific suppliers. They cannot insist on better terms of trade. Thus, higher switching costs limit the bargaining power of buyers.

Access to Backward Integration. Backward integration by a company is the strategy of manufacturing raw materials or subassemblies that go into its products. Consider automobile manufacturers. They normally buy carburetors, tires, batteries, shock absorbers, and so forth from ancillary suppliers. It is feasible, however, for automakers to backward integrate by manufacturing these supplies. If buyers of an industry can easily backward integrate to manufacture products of that industry, they gain bargaining power over the industry. The threat of backward integration is real only with powerful buyers—those that have the financial and technological capability to manufacture their supplies.

Impact of Product on Buyer's Product Quality. When a product serves as an input into other products, it can severely affect the quality of the end product. In such cases, buyers have limited power over producers. Buyers are willing to give the producing industry better terms of trade to ensure that they receive the best-quality products. For example, fuel injection systems used in automobiles are a sophisticated, precision-made product. The automobile industry buys these fuel injection systems from independent suppliers. Effective performance of these systems is critical for the performance of the expensive automobiles that use them. Automobile manufacturers have limited power over these suppliers because the quality and precision of this product is vital to them. They are willing to pay higher prices and give better terms of trade demanded to suppliers to ensure the right quality and delivery schedules.

Amount of Information Available to the Buyer. The power of buyers critically depends on the amount of information they have about product quality, cost structure, and performance characteristics. The buyer can use this information to negotiate better terms of trade with suppliers. The more information the buyer has, the more likely the buyer is to extract better terms of trade from the industry. Better terms of trade for buyers means loss of revenues and profits for the industry. In large companies, buying is now a specialized task handled by professional purchasing departments.

Bargaining Power of Suppliers

Suppliers of raw materials influence industry profitability and competition by affecting the cost of production. If suppliers are powerful, they can obtain high prices for raw materials. They may also negotiate favorable terms of trade. They can decide product features, packaging, payment schedule, credit terms, transportation, insurance, and delivery costs and schedules. The bargaining power of suppliers depends on the same variables that shape the bargaining power of buyers. These include concentration of suppliers, importance of industry to suppliers, threat of forward integration, access to other sources of supply, and the nature of labor supply.

Concentration of Suppliers. Just as the number of buyers was a determinant of buyer power, the number of suppliers is a crucial determinant of supplier power. If an industry has many suppliers, it has the option of buying from many different sources. Suppliers try to meet industry requirements, but they lack power because they are substitutable. In the opposite case where there are only a few suppliers, the industry is dependent on suppliers. Suppliers can demand and get favorable terms of trade from the industry. For example, defense contracting firms are limited in number. Each firm specializes in a narrow set of products or services. Such firms are able to charge the government premium prices for their expertise and equipment.

Importance of Industry to Suppliers. Another factor that determines the bargaining power of suppliers is how important the industry is to them as a customer. If the industry consumes a large part of the suppliers' output, it would be considered important. The suppliers would be willing to meet the industry's demands for better terms of trade. If the industry is not an important buyer, then it would have limited bargaining power. For example, the automobile industry is an important customer of the rubber tires industry. Tire manufacturers work closely with auto manufacturers and attempt to meet their requirements on product quality, delivery, and payment terms.

Threat of Forward Integration. Forward integration refers to a company entering businesses that bring its finished goods closer to customers. For example, if a steel manufacturer starts production of steel furniture, it would be considered to be forward integrating. Similarly, petroleum refining companies forward integrate into oil distribution by buying gas stations.

If industry suppliers can enter the industry through forward integration, they increase the intensity of competition. New entrants mean more competing firms, each sharing a smaller part of industry profits. The entry of suppliers into an industry jeopardizes the competitive position of existing industry participants. The new entrant has better control over supplies. Credible threats of forward integration from suppliers enhance their bargaining power. Forward integration is a threat only if suppliers have enough financial, marketing, and technological resources to enter the industry. For example, silicon chip manufacturers, such as Intel, Motorola, and Advanced Micro Devices, supply microprocessor and memory chips to the personal computer (PC) industry. They are a perennial threat to PC manufacturers because they control the development and supply of the most crucial PC components and they can assemble computers with relatively minor effort.

Access to Other Sources of Supply. Access to alternative sources of supply reduces the bargaining power of suppliers. Sometimes an industry can substitute products from current suppliers with products from other industries. Or an industry may be able to buy from foreign suppliers. Suppliers are thus pressured to give the industry good terms of trade. For example, bottlers of soft drinks can buy containers made of glass, plastic, metal, paper, or composite materials. Each of these supply industries knows it is substitutable and, therefore, vulnerable.

Labor Supply. In labor-intensive industries labor supply can be an important bargaining chip. The strength of labor unions, government regulations, and labor market conditions influence the cost of labor. In highly unionized industries, such as automobiles, steel, and construction, labor unions control the supply and price of labor. In these industries, manufacturers have little flexibility in changing the cost of labor; they have to pay high wages. This increases their cost of production and reduces profitability.

Threats from Substitute Products

The final element that affects industry competition and profitability is the pressure from substitute products. Substitute products erode into the sales and revenues of the industry. They may even eliminate demand for an industry's product. Industries with products that can be easily substituted by products from other industries are always under revenue and profit pressures. For example, we have seen that the invention of ballpoint pens in the 1950s severely cut into the sales of fountain pens. Within a few years the total demand for fountain pens declined by 80%. Similarly, mechanical pencils are a substitute for ordinary wooden pencils; they continue to erode into the demand for pencils. More recently, compact disk players have started replacing record players. In contrast, if an industry's product is unique and serves very unusual functions, it cannot be substituted easily. An example of this is the CAT (computerized axial tomography) scanner. This is such a highly specialized instrument that it cannot be easily substituted; it faces no threat of substitution by other products.

Besides product substitution, another form of substitution can create pressure on industry profitability and competition. Substitution of new raw materials, components, and subassemblies directly affects the cost of manufacture. GM substituted expensive brass and metal alloy components with cheaper but functionally equivalent plastics. This reduced GM's materials costs and the weight of its cars. It also gave GM a competitive advantage over other carmakers. Changes in production costs create wider price variation in the industry and increase competitive rivalry. We will now look more closely at competition within industries.

3.3.   CONTEXT OF INDUSTRY COMPETITION

Structural forces determine both the total level of profitability and competition in an industry. The context of the industry places important limitations on profitability and competition. This context may be viewed as a set of limits within which all industry participants must operate. Figure 3.2 depicts the context in terms of industry regulations and constraints placed by the natural environment.

Industry Regulations

The most fundamental profit characteristics of any industry are often determined by economic regulations governing the industry. A broad network of general economic regulations govern activities within each economy. These include regulations over macroeconomic variables such as interest rates, money supply, tax rates, and minimum wages. In addition, there are industry-specific regulations that determine which firms are allowed to enter an industry. Regulations can determine products and services, prices, and wages in the industry. Government regulations may also prohibit firms from exiting industries. For example, in utility industries the government mandates that companies must service all customers within specified areas. Electricity, telephone, and water utilities cannot arbitrarily stop services in areas that are allocated to them.

Besides economic regulations, industries are also regulated by social regulations. These regulations seek to protect the natural environment, worker and consumer health, and public safety. Social regulations have increased dramatically in the 1970s and 1980s, imposing new and unforeseen costs on business. A large number of regulations govern industries susceptible to technological and public health hazards. These industries include nuclear power, chemicals, food, pharmaceuticals, transportation, and hazardous waste disposal.

Regulations affect industry profits by influencing both the revenues and costs of doing business. Price controls and control over entry and exit from an industry affect industry revenues. Costs are influenced by regulation of wages and employee benefits, taxation, regulation of pollution, workplace conditions, and hazards to public health. Regulations also impose record-keeping requirements on companies, which are costly to fulfill.

Although, in theory, regulations have similar effects on all competitors within an industry, in practice this is often not true. The impact of regulations varies by size of company, diversity of its product line, its location, its access to capital markets, state and local tax provisions, and other historical factors. Regulations change frequently, thereby creating unpredictable competitive dynamics that complicate the economic sources of competition.

Figure 3.2 *Context of Industry Competition*

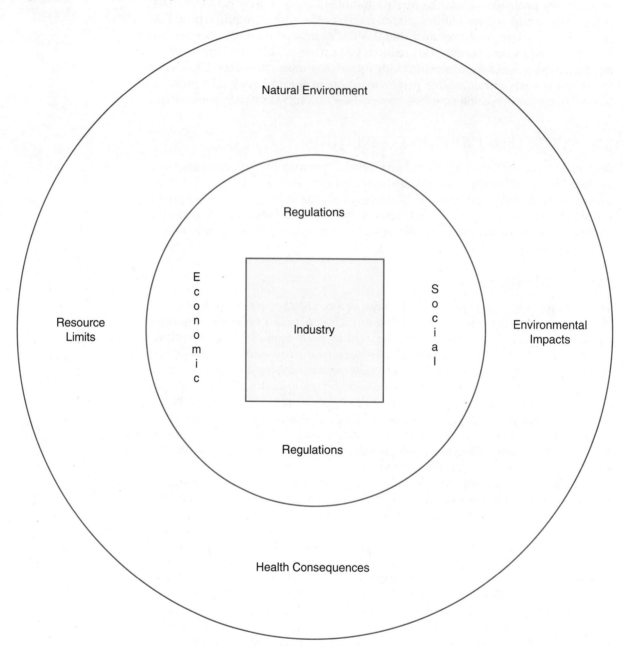

Regulations influence all of the five structural forces of competition discussed earlier. They create barriers to entry into an industry by prohibiting the entry of certain types of firms. This protects the existing firms in the industry from competitors from the outside. For example, the Glass Steagal Act effectively prohibited security brokerage firms and banks from entering each others industries. Similarly, until its deregulation in 1978, airlines needed to get permission from the Civil Aeronautics Board to operate new routes. Barriers to entry into an industry may also be created indirectly. Regulations can require companies entering an industry to have certain capital, skills, and resources that act as entry barriers. Consider the pharmaceuticals industry. The procedures for getting Federal Drug Administration (FDA) approval to market drugs are lengthy, complex, and costly. Managing the application process for a drug license requires a well-organized and well-connected administrative setup. Companies have to pursue applications to completion over several years. This complex regulatory procedure effectively prevents small, inexperienced companies from entering the drugs part of the pharmaceuticals industry.

Regulations also affect the costs of production and the power of suppliers by influencing the cost of labor, money, and materials. Labor laws provide protection to workers' rights and limit the discretion of management. They provide a framework for negotiating union contracts. These contracts determine wage and benefits costs and place limits on flexibility of work practices. In highly regulated and unionized industries, such as mining, oil, and automobiles, labor costs tend to be high.

Regulation of interest rates determine the cost of money to banks and consequently to their customers. The cost of money varies from industry to industry. For example, the cost of money for home mortgages, car loans, personal and credit card loans, commercial business loans, and export and import trade loans are all different. State and local agencies also may provide subsidized interest rates and tax subsidies to attract businesses into their areas.

Regulations affect the costs of raw materials, particularly scarce materials. Import regulations and international trade agreements affect the costs of imported materials through customs, tariffs, and transportation costs.

Regulations can affect competitive rivalry in industries. Regulating the "weapons" of competitive response (e.g., advertising, distribution practices, and pricing) sets the context for competitive rivalry. Regulations place limits on certain types of advertising. For example, cigarette manufacturers must have health warnings on cigarette packages and in commercials, and they cannot advertise on television. Advertising must conform to truth-in-advertising standards within the industry. These regulations limit a company's competitive responses to rival strategies.

Consumer protection regulations enhance the power of buyers. They give buyers certain rights and guarantees. "Lemon laws" protect buyers against fraudulent claims to quality. Consumer safety laws attempt to ensure product safety and integrity. Other laws give consumers rights to product information, hazard warning, performance warranties, user training, and disposal options. Such information makes buyers better informed and increases their power.

The Natural Environment

The natural environment is a source of material resources. It also acts as sink for emissions and wastes created by production processes in industry. As source and sink, it has limits to what it can provide and assimilate without permanent irreversible damage. The idea of the "carrying capacity" of the environment denotes these limits. Natural resources and ecosystems cannot be exploited beyond their natural carrying capacity without threat of extinction. Exceeding the environment's carrying capacity can cause permanent damage to ecosystems.

Many industries are already at the threshold of their carrying capacity. These include the energy, chemicals, automobile, steel, mining, and paper industries. Other industries involved in using, storing, or generating hazardous products and wastes are approaching these thresholds. All of these industries are the source of

Table 3.2 *Links between Production and Natural Environment*

Production Phase	Phase Content	Environmental Concerns
Inputs	Raw materials	Depletion of forests
		Harm caused by toxic material
	Fuels	Depletion of oil, coal, natural gas
		Pollution created by fossil fuel
		Hazards of using nuclear energy
Throughputs	Plant	Plant safety and accidents
		Risks to surrounding neighborhoods
	Workers	Occupational diseases and hazards
		Work-related injuries and ill health
	Wastes	Hazardous waste disposal
		Emission of pollutants
		Emission of environmentally destructive chemicals
	Transportation	Risk of spills in transporting hazardous materials
Outputs	Products	Product safety
		Health effects of products such as tobacco and liquor
	Packaging	Garbage created by packaging
	Servicing	Reliability and hazards of failure

extensive environmental devastation. They have alarmed the public at large and the communities in which the facilities operate.

Public pressures for environmental protection have mounted during the past two decades and have led to creation of thousands of laws, standards, and regulations. In addition, grass-roots community actions for environmental and health protection have created new constraints for business. The public has had a subtle but distinct impact on the competitive dynamics of industries. Today it is very difficult to make competitive strategy decisions involving hazards without participation of the public. Decisions about product safety, location of technological facilities, disposal of hazardous wastes, and release of effluents into the environment require the cooperation of external (government or public) participants. These issues, even a decade ago, were entirely a corporate competitive prerogative. Now they are controversial public issues. In response, major corporations have acknowledged the need to incorporate environmental concerns into strategy formulation and implementation. Most companies have created top management positions to address the environmental, safety, and health concerns of the public.

Table 3.2 illustrates the links between a firm's activities and its natural environment. Each phase of production, from inputs to throughputs to outputs, creates different environmental concerns. Human environmental concerns often take the form of worker, consumer, and public safety issues. These pervasive relationships call for genuine responses to environmentalism. They require transformation of all aspects of organizations. Transformation cannot be a superficial public relations response. It must address core business values, goals, strategies, products, technologies, and systems. Its aim must be the protection and conservation of nature, wildlife, and ecosystems. It must include responsible management of worker and consumer health, technological risks, and product and process hazards. Transformation includes responding to consumer demands for environmentally friendly products.

How companies react to environmental concerns affects their choice of products, production technologies, and customer loyalties. Addressing these concerns about the natural environment gives firms another basis for becoming competitive. In the past, environmental responsiveness of business was viewed as good business ethics and good public relations. Now it is becoming clear that astute environmental management can provide the basis for becoming more competitive.

The Body Shop in England, Loblaw International Merchants in Canada, and Ben & Jerry's in the United States are examples of environmentally conscious companies. They have made environmental responsiveness the cornerstone of their competitive strategies. Volvo of Sweden uses the safety of its cars and consequent protection of passengers as the basis for competing. By showing special concern for the safety and welfare of its customers, the company has created a loyal customer base. It has been successful in holding its market against technologically more sophisticated cars made by Japanese companies.

To develop competitive business strategies within an industry, managers must analyze the industry structural forces and contextual elements we have just discussed. This analysis can lead to identifying important competitors and competitive threats. Industry structural analysis must be linked to strategy formulation. It should identify specific implications of industry structure for the firm's strategy. The next chapter discusses strategy formulation.

Clearly, although all firms in an industry face the same structural forces, this does not imply that all firms will follow the same competitive strategies. In fact, each firm interprets the industry structure in light of its own objectives and resources. Each company develops its own unique competitive strategies. Thus, it is common to see many different strategic responses within an industry.

Consider the fast-food restaurants industry, which faces many problems in the 1990s. The general economic recession will curtail demand. People are becoming more health conscious and want to eat less of red meats, fats, and sugar. The changing demographics is changing demand patterns. The aging of the baby-boom population is affecting both the types of foods in demand and the location and ambiance of fast-food restaurants. Because of inflation, costs are going up. There is a shortage of labor because of declining number of teenagers.

The two major players in this industry, McDonald's and Burger King, are responding to these industry changes in different ways. McDonald's is attempting to attract adult customers and retain the baby-boom customers who are aging, more health conscious, and affluent. In many urban locations McDonald's is opening the Orchid Room—an upscale, elegant McDonald's. Some of these new rooms have a white-gloved host, fresh flowers, live piano music, Italian marble tabletops, and wood paneling. They even serve cappucino in china cups. McDonald's is also experimenting with new cuisine. In 1991 it introduced the McLean Deluxe, and it is planning entrees of pastas, seafoods, and pizzas that would attract entire families. It has abandoned the use of Styrofoam packaging for hamburgers, because Styrofoam manufacture requires ozone-destroying chloroflourocarbons.

Burger King is responding to industry pressures in a very different manner. It is not experimenting with upscale options in search of new markets as McDonald's is. Instead, it is cutting costs by streamlining its operations and management structure. The 940 company-owned stores are being made more accountable for profits and will pay rents and royalties just as the franchisees do. Burger King is also bringing out several new more healthful products. Its broiled chicken sandwich now sells more than 1 million per day. It is using 100% vegetable oil to make French fries. Instead of having salad bars, it has successfully established the prepackaged salad product line. It is also experimenting with individual-sized pizzas. It is catching the attention of customers through its aggressive and controversial marketing campaign with its saucy theme: Sometimes You've Gotta Break the Rules.

Before using industry structure analysis for strategy formulation, we need to examine industry competition more closely. This can be done by studying the similarities and differences among firms within an industry. The idea of strategic groups allows us to study competition at a more disaggregated level.

3.4   STRATEGIC GROUP ANALYSIS

The structural analysis of industries described presumes that each industry consists of a homogeneous set of firms, all competing with each other. It presumes that industry structural forces have similar effects on all firms. Although in theory these are reasonable assumptions, the reality is more complex.

All firms within an industry are not similar. They differ in size, resources, skills, products, production technologies, cultures, and many other attributes. Because of these individual differences, industry structural forces do not have the same effects on all firms. Most importantly, all firms in an industry do not compete with each other. Each industry has several clusters of closely competitive firms. For example, in the women's apparel industry, Sears, Roebuck and Kmart compete with each other and with other inexpensive brands of clothing. However, they are not in competition with high-fashion boutique stores, such as Benetton and Laura Ashley. The upscale boutiques form a separate cluster of competing firms.

A significant characteristic of industries is that different firms within it have different levels of profitability, which vary with the strategic attributes of firms (Hatten and Hatten, 1987). Figure 3.3 illustrates this. It shows the relationship between profitability and market share of brewing firms in the United States. We can interpret these data at the aggregate industry level. The rightward sloping (regression) line *AB* suggests that the industry exhibits a positive relationship between profits and market share. That means that an increase in market share will increase profits (Hatten and Schendel, 1976).

If we *disaggregate* the data in Figure 3.3, we get a contrasting interpretation. That is, we can interpret the data separately for small regional firms, large regional firms, and national firms in the industry. These three types of firms are shown in the three ellipses in the figure. For small regional and national firms, the regression line slopes toward the left. This implies a negative relationship between profits and market share. For large regional firms, the regression line is horizontal. This indicates profits do not change with market share.

Figure 3.3 thus shows that how we interpret profit characteristics of an industry depends on the level of aggregation we adopt for studying it. Greater insights can be gained into industry competition by studying industries in terms of strategic groups. Strategic groups are clusters of firms that compete with each other and are similar on some strategic dimensions. Most large and mature industries have more than one strategic group.

Firms adopt strategies that are similar or different on several basic strategic dimensions. A certain limited number of combinations of these dimensions constitute successful strategies in any industry. Firms pursuing these strategies often

Figure 3.3
Strategic Groups in the US Brewing Industry

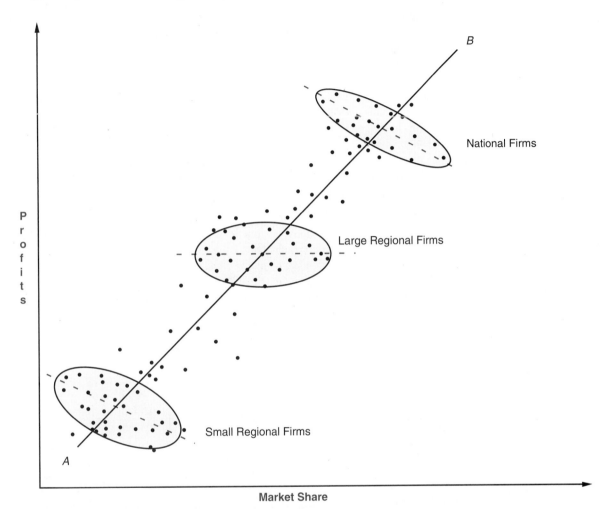

fall within a strategic group. Thus, firms within a strategic group could be similar on some or all of the following strategic dimensions:

1. Product characteristics: Firms in a strategic group may be similar in width of their product line, product features, product functions, product quality, and emphasis they place on product/brand identity.
2. Organizational characteristics: Firms within a strategic group may exhibit similarities on many organizational attributes. These include firm size, goals, scope, level of integration among divisions, and culture.
3. Production characteristics: Strategic group members may be similar on types of their production systems. They may have similar technologies, scale of operations, levels of automation, cost structures, and degree of vertical integration.
4. Market characteristics: Marketing elements of firms within a strategic group may be similar. There may be commonalties on customer segments served,

price ranges, distribution channels used, and promotion/advertising approaches. Firms also may be similar on the extent to which they support their products with ancillary services such as customer training and repair and maintenance.

5. Ownership pattern: Firms within a strategic group may serve similar functions within the business portfolio of their parent company. Business unit objectives and strategies depend on the relationship of the business unit to its parent and the expectations of the parent company. This relationship determines the resources available to the unit and limits its strategic choices.

6. Financial characteristics: Firms within a strategic group may have similarities on the degree of financial leverage, sources and costs of capital, and cash management approaches.

7. Relationship with home/host governments: For international firms, strategic group membership could be based on the relationship of the firm with the home/host government. Governmental policies can place differential strategic constraints and provide differential access to key resources.

Strategic groups are not equivalent to market segments. They are defined by broader strategic posture characterized by the seven strategic dimensions listed above. Firms within a strategic group may exhibit similarities on some but not all of these characteristics. Identification of strategic groups allows us to refine industry analysis. It allows us to examine membership within each strategic group. It identifies structural forces within each strategic group and the mobility barriers between strategic groups.

Once strategic groups are formed within an industry, they persist over time. However, membership may change over time. The persistence of strategic groups is due to inflexible fixed assets, long-term business commitments, and high exit barriers. Firms are also reluctant to make drastic changes in strategies because changes may be costly. Sometimes competitive pressures from other firms in the industry prevent a firm from changing its strategy. Firms are committed to strategies, which keeps them within a strategic group for several years.

This persistence of strategic groups does not mean that there is no movement of firms from one group to another. Many industries experience mobility of firms between strategic groups. This mobility depends on the extent of mobility barriers. The idea of mobility barriers is similar to that of entry barriers. It refers to the deterrents faced by members of one strategic group to enter and compete in another strategic group within the industry. Mobility barriers restrict the movement of firms within the industry (Harrigan, 1985; Mascarenhas and Aaker, 1989). Mobility barriers are a function of the same variables that determine entry barriers into an industry. For example, high capital requirement, large economies of scale, high switching costs, high product differentiation, and restrictions on access to distribution channels act as mobility barriers between strategic groups.

Mobility barriers act as a protection for firms within a strategic group. Thus, some firms may be consistently more profitable than others in the industry because high mobility barriers protect them from competition. Without these barriers, successful strategies would be quickly imitated by competitors. The existence of mobility barriers allows firms to enjoy persistent and continued competitive advantages.

Strategic groups in industries evolve over time based on strategic moves by

Figure 3.4 *Strategic Groups within an Industry*

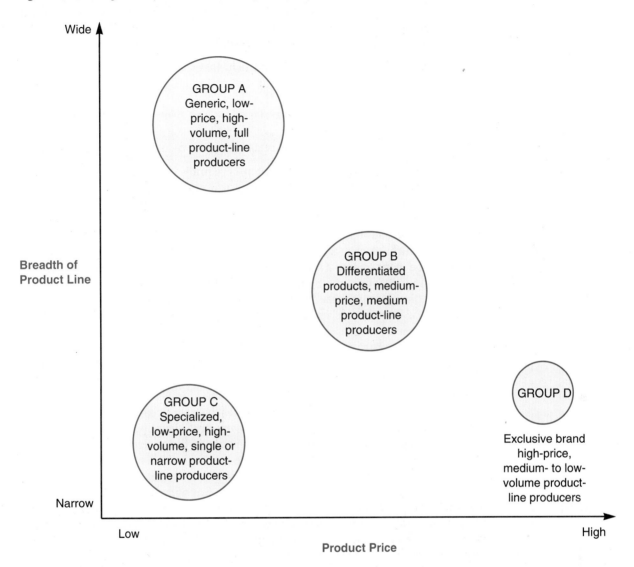

competitors. As individual firms jockey for new positions and markets, they develop new resources and skills to move from one strategic group to another. In addition, changes in the risk postures and return expectations of parent companies also can make businesses move from one strategic group to another.

Social, political, and governmental policy changes also may cause reorganization of strategic groups. For example, deregulation of the airline industry led to consolidation. Some large national airlines, such as People's Express, left the industry. Others, such as American Airlines and United Airlines, moved from the strategic group of large national carriers to that of international airlines. The strategic group of small, short-haul regional carriers was transformed by tie-ups with major national carriers. These tie-ups allowed them to feed passengers to the national carrier hubs.

3.5   STRATEGIC OPPORTUNITIES AND THREATS

The whole purpose of industry and strategic group analysis is to refine our understanding of competition. It helps us to identify more specific opportunities and threats in the industry. Analysis may be done according to four simple steps:

Step 1: Identify strategic groups within the industry.

Step 2: Analyze structural forces that determine competition within strategic groups and among groups.

Step 3: Identify strengths and weaknesses of the firm relative to competitors within its strategic group.

Step 4: Identify opportunities and threats facing the firm.

Identification of strategic groups (Step 1) requires characterizing the strategies of significant competitors in the industry according to the strategic characteristics discussed earlier. This enables identification of firms that pursue similar strategies and compete with each other. A judgment must then be made on the relative importance of the strategic characteristics to firms' performance.

Based on the two most important strategic characteristics, firms in the industry can be mapped into a few strategic groups. This is shown in Figure 3.4. This map of an industry uses the breadth of product line and product price as the two classifying dimensions; these two characteristics of each firm in the industry are plotted on the map. Four clusters of firms result. Each circle represents a cluster of firms that form a strategic group. The size of the strategic group circle reflects the collective market share of that group.

The second step of this analysis is a structural analysis of the strategic groups. Following the analytical framework of industry structure analysis presented earlier in this chapter, each strategic group can be analyzed for its structural characteristics. Thus, we can examine rivalry of firms within each strategic group. Mobility barriers among strategic groups, the power of buyers and suppliers, and the threat of substitutes from outside the industry or from outside the strategic group can also be assessed.

The third step involves identifying strengths and weaknesses of individual firms with respect to their closest competitors. Strengths are firm resources and features that build and maintain mobility barriers. These resources enhance the bargaining power of the group relative to buyers and suppliers. They insulate the firm from rivalry. Other strengths include factors that lower the cost of entry into other strategic groups or factors that allow a firm to penetrate the mobility barriers built by other groups. Similarly, greater scale of operation relative to other members in the group and an ability to implement strategies can be strengths.

Weaknesses are factors that lower the mobility barriers that protect the firm and its strategic group. These factors reduce the groups' bargaining power over buyers and suppliers. They increase rivalry among strategic group members and among groups. Other weaknesses include factors that increase the cost of entry into more desirable groups. Similarly, lower scale of operations as compared with other group members and an inability to carry out chosen strategies can be weaknesses.

The final step of identifying opportunities and threats in the industry (step 4) can be guided by the analysis of strategic groups. Firms may seek opportunities for the following:

- Creating new strategic groups within the industry: This can be done by identifying and entering ignored market niches. Firms also can create technological innovations in product design and production technologies, and they can adopt new creative marketing approaches.

- Shifting to more attractive strategic groups: Different strategic groups have different levels of profitability associated with them. If the firm has the strengths and resources to do so, it may choose to penetrate mobility barriers and enter more desirable groups. It may target those groups for entry whose members are weak or marginal and unable to resist the firm's entry.

- Strengthening the firm's competitive position within the strategic group: This may be done by improving its position on key strategic dimensions (product line, production, marketing, finance, ownership, government relations, etc.).

- Strengthening the structural position of its strategic group: This can be achieved through collaborative strategies jointly carried out with other group members. These strategies aim at increasing mobility barriers, improving position against substitute products, and increasing switching costs of customers.

Strategic group analysis allows us to refine the aggregate industry analysis by examining competition within strategically similar clusters of firms. These analyses should lead to the identification of opportunities and threats facing a business. Understanding the dynamics of competition and profitability is essential for formulating competitive strategies for business units. Competitive strategies should attempt to exploit opportunities and avoid threats.

Summary of Chapter 3

To formulate competitive business strategies, it is essential to understand the structure of competition and the determinants of industry profitability. There are many views of how competition works within industries. Chamberlin and his colleagues viewed competition as a resource-based phenomenon. They identified three basic types of competitive firms: monopolies, oligopolies, and perfectly competitive firms. In these situations, a single firm, a few large firms, or many similar-sized firms controlled the market, respectively. Schumpeter saw technological revolutions and product-market shifts as key determinants of capitalistic competition and economic change. A third view of competition is the industry/organization model. This view yields a more detailed understanding of the economic structure and the complex dynamics of competition. It holds that the competitive structure of an industry and the conduct of firms within it influence financial returns in the industry.

Many structural forces shape industry competition. **Threats to entry** into the industry, one of these forces, are a function of entry barriers. Important entry barriers include economies of scale, product differentiation, switching costs, and access to distribution channels. There may also be miscellaneous barriers such as technology patents, raw materials monopoly, and changing regulations.

A second structural force is the **intensity of rivalry** among existing competitors. Fierce rivalry within an industry is detrimental to its profitability. More competitors mean more interactions and more rivalry. Factors that influence competitive rivalry include power balance among competitors, industry growth rate, fixed and storage costs, switching costs, size of capacity augmentation, and origins and style of competitors. Higher exit barriers also tend to increase competitive rivalry.

Bargaining power of buyers is another determinant of competitive structure. The power of buyers puts downward pressure on industry profits. A high concentration of buyers makes industries dependent on a few buyers. Highly differentiated products limit buyers' power. Low switching costs increase buyers' power. If buyers of an industry can easily backward integrate to manufacture products of that industry, they gain bargaining power. Sometimes a product has an important impact on the quality of buyer's final product; this reduces the bargaining power of buyers.

Similarly the **bargaining power of suppliers** influences industry profitability and competition. It affects costs of production. The concentration of suppliers, importance of the industry to suppliers, forward integration, access to other sources of supply, and labor supply influence supplier power.

Pressure from substitute products as well as material substitution create pressure on industry profitability and competition. Cheaper substitute materials lower the cost of production for some industry participants and make them more competitive.

Industry structure is also affected by regulations and the physical limits placed by the natural environment. Regulations over wages, product and service standards, distribution, and business practices determine profitability. The natural environment is a source of resources and a sink for wastes. In both these roles it has physical limits. The costs of acquiring natural resources and disposing of waste products influence industry profits and competition.

Although all firms in an industry face the same structural forces, they interpret competitive structures in different ways. Firms view competition in light of their own objectives and resources and they develop unique competitive strategies. To examine similarities and differences between firms within an industry, the idea of strategic groups is very useful.

Each industry has several clusters of closely competing firms. Firms within a cluster have similar strategic attributes. Greater insight into industry competition can be obtained by studying these clusters or strategic groups. Strategies within a strategic group are similar or different in regard to several basic dimensions: product features, organizational attributes, production characteristics, market conditions, ownership patterns, financial resources, and relationships with home/host governments.

Because of internal and external pressures, firms are reluctant to make drastic changes in strategies. Strategic groups thus tend to persist after their formation. Mobility barriers restrict the movement of firms from one strategic group to another. Mobility barriers are similar to entry barriers; the same variables that determine entry barriers influence mobility barriers. Strategic groups in industries evolve over time based on strategic moves by competitors. Social, political, and governmental changes also may cause reorganization of strategic groups.

For a refined understanding of competition, it is important to identify strategic groups and analyze the structural forces that shape competition within them. Such analysis identifies threats and opportunities facing firms. Firms can create opportunities by creating new strategic groups. They can move to more attractive strategic groups. They can strengthen their competitive position within a strategic group. They also can cooperate to strengthen the structural position of the entire strategic group.

Strategic group analysis allows us to refine aggregate industry analysis. It examines competition within strategically similar clusters of firms. Understanding the dynamics of competition and profitability is essential for formulating competitive strategies for business units.

READINGS, CASES, AND POLICY DOCUMENTS

The following readings, cases, and policy documents provide additional background material for the concepts discussed in this Chapter.

Readings

* Porter, M.E. "The competitive advantage of nations". Harvard Business
  Review, March-April, 1990, pp 73-93.

Cases

* Airlines Industry —Domestic
* Airlines Industry —International
* Hospital Management Industry
* World Tyre Industry

Policy Documents

NCR Corporation - Directional Strategy
* American Express Travel Related Services-—The Next Ten Years

* indicates particularly appropriate assignments

Figures 3.1, 3.2, 3.3, 3.4, 3.5 and Table 3.1.

Strategic Management Process and Book Outline

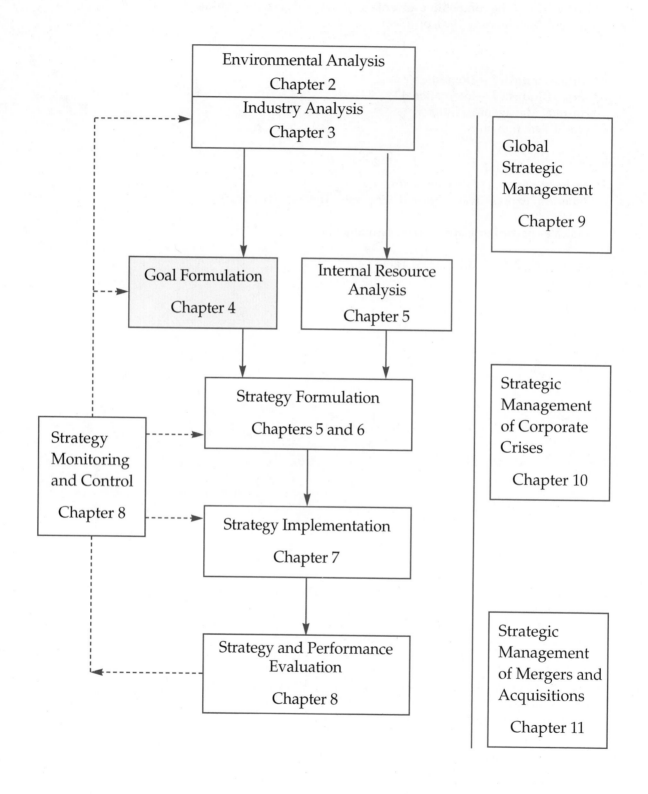

CHAPTER 4
GOAL
FORMULATION

CHAPTER OUTLINE

The starting point for strategic management is deciding corporate purpose. Without a clear purpose, a company cannot organize itself for long-term strategic success. A lack of purpose can easily distract the corporation into doing different and contradictory things. It can create confusion and diffuse company resources thinly over many areas, thereby preventing the resources from making a significant impact in any area.

Corporate purpose emerges out of a vision—a vision of what the company wants to be. The vision provides a guiding philosophy that is often articulated and codified in the form of mission statements. Having a clear vision is especially important for large, multiproduct, multinational, multicultural companies. Such companies have many seductive options and many forces pulling it in different directions. A clear vision serves as a pilot to steer the company in a chosen direction.

Corporate vision needs to be shared broadly among organizational members. A shared vision helps motivate and unite a diverse work force. It gives employees a common framework for action. Companies such as Britain's Body Shop, Japan's Sony, Italy's Benetton, Switzerland's Swatch, and the United States Wal-Mart and Merck Pharmaceuticals exhibit a visionary zeal that makes them the envy of all. Their clear vision and identity have spawned fierce employee loyalty, high productivity, and motivation. Their vision has sharply focused their strategies and is the root of their continued success.

Corporate purpose defines what the company is, what it stands for, and where it is going. It contains the company's long-term vision of itself. It provides direction and a self-identity to the company. There are many benefits of consciously deciding and explicitly stating corporate purposes:

- A clear corporate purpose serves as a beacon that provides constant guidance and direction to the firm.
- A common purpose is a unifying force that gives the company its *raison d'etre* and organizational members a spirit of camaraderie and solidarity. It is a source of personal and collective strength for members.
- A purpose gives the company an identity and public image, thereby helping external stakeholders to understand what the company stands for and what it is trying to achieve.
- A purpose provides guidance and an anchor for the tasks of strategy formulation and implementation. By keeping the company's attention focused on specific long-term targets, it can prevent the company from getting too diffused.
- The *process* of determining the corporate purpose brings to the surface many hidden conflicts that lie at the core of organizations. Managers can thus deal with these conflicts early in the strategy-making process, before they escalate into major problems.

4.1   WHOSE PURPOSES DOES THE CORPORATION SERVE?

Finding corporate purpose must answer this fundamental question: Whose purposes does a company serve? Twenty years ago, this question could be answered in simple terms: A company serves the purpose of its owners or stockholders. Stockholders' primary purpose is to increase their wealth while minimizing their level of financial risk. This corporate purpose remains legitimate for corporations today. However, the primacy or centrality of this purpose is clearly under question.

As we saw in Chapter 2, most progressive companies acknowledge that business corporations today serve many stakeholders and pursue a complex set of goals. Complexity arises because companies have to fulfill the expectations of many stakeholders simultaneously. Some of these stakeholders have conflicting demands, and none of the stakeholders have absolute power to impose their will. Corporate stakeholders include managers, the board of directors, employees, stockholders, customers, suppliers, government unions, competitors, business associates, communities, media, and the public. Although all stakeholders are not equally important for success of a company, each contributes something useful. In fact, most companies would not be able to function effectively without the cooperation of each of these stakeholders. Therefore, companies are obliged to pursue purposes that at least minimally satisfy the diverse demands of these stakeholders.

Organizational purpose should, therefore, reflect an acceptable balance between the conflicting goals of these different stakeholders. In selecting their purposes, companies should establish trade-offs between multiple demands such as rapid growth, high profitability, high dividends, low pollution, reducing harm caused by products, creating jobs, protecting the environment, providing safe working conditions, and generating tax revenues. Establishing these trade-offs is a game of compromise and appeasement. Strategy managers are responsible for creating an acceptable organizational process, for making these trade-offs, and for deciding the appropriate balance of competing demands.

The corporate purpose is articulated as several statements that jointly guide formulation and implementation of strategy. What a company wants to achieve in the future is stated in corporate missions, objectives, goals, and targets. These statements articulate the corporate purpose at different levels of specificity and for several time horizons. Corporate missions describe the complete guiding philosophy of the company. Corporate objectives provide guidance for developing corporate-wide strategic plans as well as for deciding the goals of business units. Business unit goals are chosen to satisfy corporate objectives collectively. They are based on the role that the individual business unit plays in the corporate portfolio (Richards, 1986).

Often semantic confusion exists about the terms *missions*, *objectives*, *goals*, and *targets*. To clear up this confusion, Table 4.1 describes the terminology used in this book. These terms reflect what the firm wants to achieve over different time horizons. The time horizons may vary from the averages shown in Table 4.1 depending on the nature of the industries in which a company operates.

Table 4.1 *Organizational Missions, Objectives, Goals, and Targets*

	Time Horizon	Specificity	Purpose
Missions	External	Very general	Set aspirations, symbolic
Objectives	5 to 10 years	Concrete	Set direction
Goals	2 to 3 years	Broad measure of firm performance	Evaluate performance
Targets	1 year or less	Narrow, task-oriented measures	Serve as bench marks

4.2   CORPORATE MISSIONS

Corporate missions represent the broadest statements of the company's vision and philosophy. They are general statements of what the company stands for—its core values and responsibilities toward its key stakeholders. Mission statements also may state the general domain of business operations. They describe the company's relationship to its external environment and establish the basic identity of the company for external stakeholders. Consider the mission of Apple Computers: "To make a contribution to the world by making tools for the mind that advance humankind." This broad mission statement serves as the guiding principle for all company activities; it urges the company to create innovative personal computer systems that could be used widely.

Being broad and general statements, corporate missions are only direction-setting guidelines. They serve as the conscience of the corporation and a wellspring of values. They do not provide operational guidance for strategy formulation, but they can still direct and focus corporate efforts. Consider the following mission statement developed by Honda when its leadership position in the motorcycle industry was threatened by Yamaha. Honda came up with a memorable mission: "We will crush, squash, and slaughter Yamaha."

Mission statements serve the important symbolic function of providing organizational members a vision for the future. They are a type of corporate "slogan" or "mantra" (religious code word) that can be used to evoke a focused response from members. Another symbolic function they serve is providing the cultural glue that holds the organization together as a unified entity. Mission statements are not simply static descriptions of where the company is going. They are dynamic visions of the directions in which the company hopes to move. They provide a general sense of the path the company will take in the coming years to reach a desirable state.

Missions are stated for the corporation as a whole. Consider the following example of a mission statement:

Sears, Roebuck and Co., a family of diversified businesses, is the leader in providing and distributing quality products to consumers. We will engage in those commercial opportunities that leverage the distinctive capabilities of our existing businesses.

We are committed to our most valued asset, our reputation for integrity.

We dedicate ourselves to the principle that serving the customer is of prime importance.

We strive to provide our shareholders with a foundation for consistent and profitable investment growth. . . .
(From Sears, Roebuck & Co., *Our Corporate Vision*)

This is taken from the more complete mission statement of Sears, Roebuck included in the Company Policy Documents section of this book. Other examples of mission statements of Crain's *New York Business* and the New York City Fire Department are also included.

Developing Corporate Missions

Just as our own individual philosophy evolves over time, so do corporate missions. However, corporate missions are developed in a more explicit manner than individual philosophy, and they are documented to simplify sharing among organizational members.

Missions are a function of the firm's history and its vision of the future. To develop credible and meaningful missions that actually guide the firm, and are not simply public relations statements, it is critical to meld the firm's history with its vision. Corporate missions must show how historical values and business operations are to be transformed into future values and operations. The following steps can help managers to develop useful mission statements:

Step 1: Analyze historical missions, values, and business operations and practices. Assess their adequacy and suitability in light of environmental and industry trends discussed in Chapters 2 and 3.

Step 2: Consult organizational stakeholders about directions the company should take. Identify commonalities and differences among stakeholder demands.

Step 3: Resolve conflicting demands through discussions with relevant stakeholders or by making judgments that balance competing demands. Rank demands to give them relative importance with respect to each other.

Step 4: Describe the company's values, guiding philosophy, business domains, and its role in society in a way that key stakeholder demands are fulfilled. Describe what general business directions the corporation intends to take.

Step 5: Share the draft mission statement with key managers and stakeholders; seek feedback and make modifications.

Step 6: Discuss the mission statement with all members of the organization and explain how it should be used for strategy-making and strategy-guiding operations.

If done correctly, mission statements can last the organizations many years. Occasionally, however, it may be necessary to revise mission statements or create new ones. When a mission statement loses its motivational value and becomes a rhetorical phrase, or when the mission encapsulated in a given statement is accomplished, it may be time to consider creating a new one. For example, in 1962 President John F. Kennedy defined the mission for the National Aeronautics and Space Administration (NASA) as "achieving the goal, before this decade is out, of landing a man on the moon and returning him safely to earth." Having landed a person on the moon in 1969, NASA sorely needed to revise its mission. It failed to do so and floundered without focused direction for several years. It simultaneously tried to create a space station, develop space shuttles, and dabble in a variety of other space programs for defense uses. As the Presidential Commission on the Space Shuttle Challenger accident pointed out, this floundering was partially responsible for the Challenger tragedy in 1986 in which several people died.

Revising an outdated mission can help a company regain its vitality. Reframing the mission can help it rediscover its core values, its central purpose, and the rationale for its purpose.

4.3 CORPORATE OBJECTIVES

Corporate objectives provide the foundations for developing specific corporate and business strategic plans. They concretize the general sentiments of the mission statement and convert it into guidelines for decision making. Corporate objectives are also used to improve organizational performance and as a standard to measure this performance. For example, one objective of Coca-Cola is to maintain market leadership in the soft drinks industry. This means leading in product design and packaging and capturing the largest market share among its competitors in both domestic and foreign markets. In the mature soft drinks industry, market shares have remained fairly stable for years, so even a minor gain in share implies a major challenge for the company. Textron's corporate objective is to maintain a high rate of growth by acquiring businesses in diverse industries. The "high" rate of growth is concretized in specific numbers for sales growth and profit growth that may change over the years.

Corporate objectives describe what the company wants to achieve in its various business areas. They describe the business portfolio of the company in terms of specific product markets and technologies. They explain what role different business units play in the total corporate portfolio. They show the direction in which this portfolio will change in the future: what product markets the company hopes to enter and exit, what technologies it hopes to develop, what levels of risk it will take. Corporate objectives describe the levels of technological innovation, productivity, and financial performance the company will seek. The acceptable level of corporate performance may be stated as profitability (return on investment), market penetration (market shares) standards, employee performance standards, or social performance standards.

Corporate objectives specify what the firm wants to achieve over a five- to ten-year horizon in different areas of operation. This time horizon may vary from industry to industry depending on its products and technologies. In industries where investment cycles and product life cycles are long, (e.g., oil exploration and production, forest products, and mining) objectives may be set for horizons of ten years or more. In contrast, firms in industries with short product life cycles (e.g., software and consumer electronic goods) formulate objectives for five years or less.

Wartsila OY was a large Finnish ship manufacturing company. It made arctic ice cutters and luxury liners (including the "Love Boat"). When it decided to become a global technology firm, Wartsila set several specific objectives for itself for the 1980s. It wanted to build on its existing core competencies and technologies—shipbuilding, diesel engine fabrication, security systems, sanitation, and porcelain. But in each area it would move into the high or sophisticated end of the technology. It would acquire businesses around the world to diversify and create a balanced portfolio of businesses rapidly. It would reduce its dependence on shipbuilding from more than 80% of revenues to below 50%. During the 1980s, the company bought nearly forty businesses in Europe, Asia, the Middle East, and the United States, and sold many of its losing shipbuilding operations. Having clear and concrete objectives assisted Wartsila in defining the type of businesses it wanted to buy, identifying the specific operations it would sell, and reorganizing its businesses in a new format to become competitive in its rapidly changing environment.

Besides providing specific operational guidance, objectives are also useful for evaluating strategic performance. As suggested in Chapter 1, it is effectiveness that is the hallmark of good strategic management. Effectiveness means how well a firm meets its own objectives. Judging the effectiveness of the firm and its strategy can be simplified if objectives are stated in a clear and concrete form.

Developing Corporate Objectives

The purpose of corporate objectives is to provide *operational* guidance to strategic plans, decisions, and performance evaluation. They are a step toward converting organizational missions into actions. Developing corporate objectives, therefore, is an exercise in explicating the operational implications of missions. The objectives seek to convert the values and vision embedded in mission statements into specific challenges for each business or area of operation. They place time boundaries and performance expectations on desirable ends.

One approach to generating corporate objectives involves systematically assessing the potential of business units and divisions and setting feasible performance standards for them. This can proceed by refining the environmental assessments done for generating mission statements through identifying more specific trends, opportunities, and threats. Assessment should be combined with an analysis of historical objectives to generate specific corporate objectives that reflect the core ideas of the organizational mission. Objectives should be stated in specific terms that provide directional guidance to planners and line managers.

Objectives are normally set within the context of a planning process. They are an integral part of strategic planning and the decision-making processes of the organization. Business unit and line managers are the best starting point for generating objectives for their respective business areas. It is desirable to set objectives in terms of measures (such as return on investment, sales growth rate, market share, cost per unit, etc.) that are already in use in the firm's budgeting, strategic planning, and accounting systems. Business managers' estimates of objectives must be reviewed and reconciled at the corporate level to ensure that they are mutually compatible and that they jointly meet the corporation's complete objectives.

4.4   BUSINESS GOALS AND TARGETS

The next step in concretizing and operationalizing the corporate purpose is to convert corporate objectives into statements of **business unit goals**. At the business unit level, more specific and shorter statements are preferred to provide detailed criteria for judging performance. These statements take the form of measurable *goals* and *targets*.

Goals describe what a business must achieve in the next two to three years in terms of specific performance indicators. Performance measures used to set goals vary widely with the type of business and tasks for which they are meant. General business profitability is often measured by such indicators as return on investment, return on assets, and return on sales. Goals in functional areas use function-related performance indicators. For example, in the marketing area goals may be stated in terms of growth in sales, market share, relative market share, sales volume per employee, or total sales volume. In the production area goals may be set in terms of total production volume, capacity utilization level, productivity per person, automation level, inventory holding costs, production costs, and so on. In the finance and accounting areas business goals may be stated as cash flow expectations, capital expenditure budgets, or profitability goals. In the human resource area goals may be cast as employee turnover, number of new hires, number of employees to be trained, types and scale of management development programs, establishment of new human resource programs, and so forth. Companies usually combine these measures to create composite business goals that cover all critical areas of business. For example, when Toyota launched the Lexus, its new luxury car division in the United States, it established three-year goals for its dealers. These included opening dealerships in all the states, selling a certain number of cars, and achieving the highest level of consumer satisfaction in the luxury car segment of the market.

Targets specify performance expectations in even more specific terms and for shorter terms than goals. Targets serve as bench marks against which performance can be measured weekly, monthly, quarterly, or annually. For example, IBM salespersons have targets for the number of sales calls made daily, amount of orders booked monthly, customer installations visited monthly, and payments collected on delivered orders. Salespersons who meet 100% of their annual targets consistently are rewarded with special bonuses and become members of the prestigious and exclusive 100% Club sponsored by the company.

As suggested in the beginning of this chapter, missions, goals, objectives, and targets are different expressions of the company's purpose and of what the company wants to achieve. They are stated at different levels of concreteness and for different time horizons. To illustrate the continuity of a theme across these four levels, consider the following example. In 1987 Compaq Computers adopts the *mission* of becoming a global supplier of personal computers. To achieve this mission, the company must create concrete objectives, goals, and targets as illustrated in Figure 4.1. One *objective* could be to get 50% of revenues from outside the United States by 1995. This objective could be further operationalized by the *goals* of increasing exports by 15% each year and establishing production plants in Europe by 1993 and in Asia by 1994. These goals can be further subdivided into specific *targets* such as generating $1 billion in revenues from Japan in 1990. In this example the level of detail is at a minimum. In reality, such statements are far more detailed and concrete. By creating similar statements for other mission statements, a comprehensive statement of missions, objectives, goals, and targets can be developed.

4.5   PROCESS ISSUES

Missions, objectives, and goals commit the organization to pursue certain courses of action and limit it from pursuing others. The purpose of establishing objectives and goals is to motivate members of the organization to plan systematically for and achieve progressively higher levels of performance. The motivational power of objectives and goals is increased if members of the organization believe they are realistic and achievable. Members are also motivated to fulfill performance expectations if they have participated in setting them in the first place. The entire process of formulating these statements of organizational purpose should, therefore, be designed to make these choices *realistic* and *participative*.

Realism in Goal Setting

In establishing organizational objectives and goals there is a natural tendency to either overestimate or underestimate what is feasible. The tendency to over-estimate, or push for unreasonably high goals, comes from performance pressure.

Figure 4.1 *One Firm's Mission, Objective, Goals, and Targets*

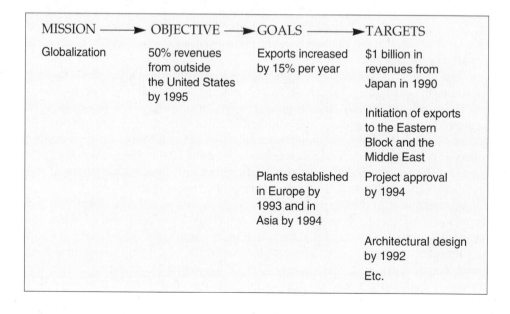

MISSION →	OBJECTIVE →	GOALS →	TARGETS
Globalization	50% revenues from outside the United States by 1995	Exports increased by 15% per year	$1 billion in revenues from Japan in 1990
			Initiation of exports to the Eastern Block and the Middle East
		Plants established in Europe by 1993 and in Asia by 1994	Project approval by 1994
			Architectural design by 1992
			Etc.

Top managers may believe that setting higher goals will make organizational members strive harder to achieve them. They may purposely set goals 20% to 30% higher than their own best estimates of what is feasible. However, line managers, who have at least as good an understanding as top management of what is feasible, may be turned off by this pressure tactic. They may view this as game playing. They may react by subtly sabotaging the whole direction-setting process, making it a meaningless ritual for the organization.

On the other hand, the tendency to underestimate goals, or set lower than feasible goals, arises from lack of good information about what is feasible. It also may be due to defensive inclinations of managers who prefer to accept lower goals and then overachieve on them. Presumably, this approach makes them look better. In this case, however, objectives and goals are easily achievable each year and fail to be challenging for performance improvements.

Both of these tendencies are dysfunctional and should be avoided. Goal formulation should aim to be realistic and fundamentally truthful. Managers must believe in the authenticity of the process. Managers realize that guessing and estimating are an integral part of setting directions, but, they should also be able to see this guessing and estimating element as an unavoidable part of the process because of our inability to predict the future. Guessing and estimating should not be a reckless and arbitrary process. The marginal benefits to be gained by underestimating or overestimating goals are not worth the risk they pose to the credibility of the entire direction-setting process.

Participation: Top-Down and Bottom-Up Processes

The process for setting objectives and goals adopted by an organization depends on the degree of centralization in decision making. The more centralized an organization is, the less participative this process is likely to be, and vice versa. Organizations that are too centralized need to make special efforts to open the process to increased participation. Participative processes have the advantage of generating objectives and goals that have a sense of "buy-in" for managers who will eventually be responsible for implementing them. A judicious combination of top-down and bottom-up processes may provide the best way to ensure broad participation and realistic goals.

Top-down goal setting refers to organizational goals being dictated by the top management or the CEO. Goals are then communicated to the rest of the organization in policy memos. When Harold Geneen was the CEO of ITT, he was known to select key organizational goals and strategies by himself without much consultation with even top managers. His autocratic style of management allowed the company to reach decisions quickly and capture fleeting market opportunities. This type of process is quick and decisive and confines organizational intentions to only a few people. On the other hand, such an autocratic, top-down process has several drawbacks. It does not consider the cumulative learning and expertise of the entire organization. It can be demotivating and disempowering to many managers who will eventually be involved in implementing goals.

Alternatively, goals may be developed through a **bottom-up process** in which lower-level managers, who are in touch with market and production realities, provide the first inputs on what is feasible. These inputs frame the agenda for setting objectives and goals and skew the process toward the narrow departmental or divisional vision of unit or functional managers.

A balanced process uses both top-down and bottom-up approaches. In such a process, top managers formulate the broad corporate philosophy and guidelines for creating objectives and specific goals. These are then used by business unit managers and middle management to come up with specific objectives, goals, and targets. Approval of these statements of purpose is done better by top management. Final ratification may be done by the board of directors.

Stakeholder Participation

An important process issue in setting missions, objectives, and goals is the involvement of the organization's stakeholders. Stakeholders have legitimate demands on the firm, and these should be incorporated in the statements of purpose. Among the issues that managers need to consider are how to generate inputs from stakeholders and how to resolve conflicts among them.

External stakeholders usually have no official part in the process of goal formulation. If their inputs are to be incorporated into organizational statements of purpose, these inputs need to be elicited through a deliberate process. Some representative inputs from key stockholders and employees or unions are desirable. Similarly, distant stakeholders, such as the public, the media, communities, or business associates, also can make valuable inputs. Informal polling of stakeholders can be a way of eliciting their opinions on the direction of the company. A more direct way of eliciting stakeholder opinions is to ask them to make presentations to the board of directors or strategic planning committee in charge of setting organizational direction. For example, a major union representative or a major investor may be invited to provide specific inputs on desirable directions for the company.

Often, different stakeholders will have conflicting demands on the firm. For example, stockholders may want the company to follow the goal of fastest growth rate and increase in wealth, despite the environmental and safety consequences. In contrast, environmentalists and the public may want the firm to pursue safer and less environmentally destructive goals. Resolving these conflicts while keeping the company moving forward on some common ground is the challenge of top management. Identifying the common ground between stakeholders is at the heart of resolving such conflicts. In most conflicts there *is* a common ground that can be identified as a basis for creating a compromise. Once this is identified, it may be expanded by developing variations and qualifying conditions. Alternative, compromise goals can be generated and discussed with stakeholders.

Ultimate responsibility for setting acceptable goals lies with top management. Even after making best efforts at reaching compromises in instances of conflicts, some goals simply cannot be pursued and others will receive low priority. By creating a priority scheme for goals, managers can accommodate more goals on the organizational agenda.

Although a deliberate and systematic approach to developing corporate objectives and goals, is beneficial, it does have disadvantages. It is time consuming; it engages top executives over long periods. If not handled well, it can raise many interdivisional conflicts and become a battleground for organizational resources. The process also opens up the discussion of objectives and goals to many organizational members; consequently, information about the company's intentions can leak out to competitors more easily. Because of such political problems, some organizations prefer to keep their objectives and goals ambiguous and unclear. They avoid making specific public commitments. By doing so, they maintain the flexibility of changing their minds at any time. They can exploit opportunities as they arise in highly dynamic environments (Quinn, 1980). This approach allows firms to be flexible and opportunistic, but it also can detract the organization from systematic formulation of strategy.

SUMMARY OF CHAPTER 4

Missions, objectives, goals, and targets provide the organization with a clear sense of direction. They guide strategy formulation.

Organizations have to satisfy the many different and competing demands of their stakeholders. Often, this creates confusion and conflict. To avoid confusion and to create an unambiguous sense of purpose and direction, a systematic direction-setting process should be adopted. Organizational direction is set at three levels—corporate, business unit, and functional area. At each level it covers different time spans.

Corporate missions provide an overall sense of purpose and direction. They broadly describe the firm's philosophy. Corporate objectives translate these missions into more concrete and actionable ideas. They interpret missions in operational terms. Goals are more specific and cover shorter time frames than objectives. They interpret objectives in terms of specific tasks that need to be performed. Goals at the business unit level specify desired business performance standards. Targets describe short-term performance expectations for a department, division, or individual employee.

Setting organizational direction and creating organizational goals and objectives is a complex process. It requires careful analysis of environmental forces and stakeholder demands. It requires managers to make rational economic choices and to assess competing demands and resolve conflicts. To be useful and motivating, goals and objectives must be both challenging and realistic. Organizations must resist from pressuring managers to adopt overly ambitious goals or too easily achievable ones. Wide participation in setting direction allows the development of realistic and implementable missions, objectives, and goals.

READINGS, CASES, AND POLICY DOCUMENTS

The following readings, cases, and policy documents provide additional background material for the concepts discussed in Chapter 4.

Cases

* Comdisco Disaster Recovery Services International Expansion
* Genicom Corporation
  Humana, Inc.
* ISKRA Power Tools
  The Southland Corporation —Formulating the Acquisition Strategy
* Turner Broadcasting System

Policy Documents

    * Crain's New York Business —The Vision
      NCR Directional Strategy
    * Sears Roebuck
    * New York City Fire Department Mission Statement

    * indicates particularly appropriate assignments

Strategic Management Process and Book Outline

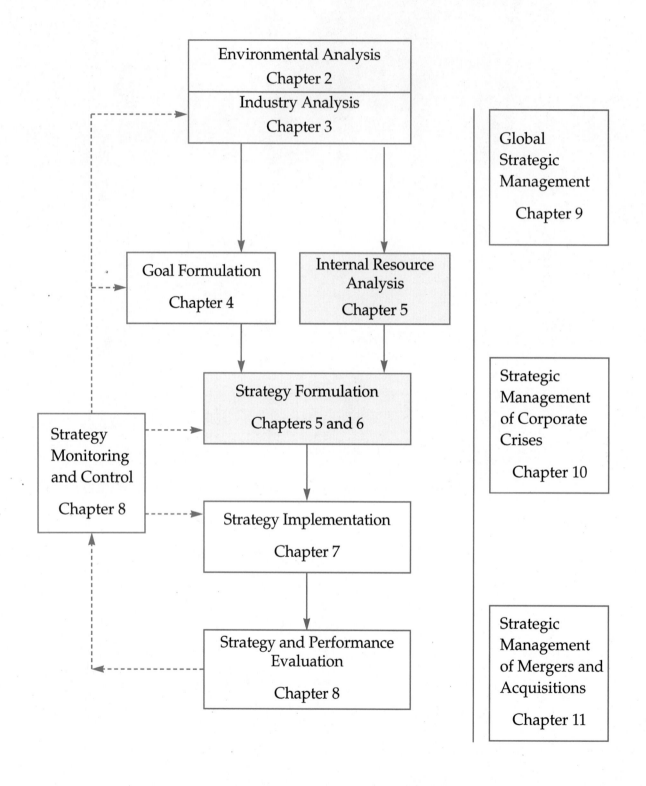

CHAPTER 5
INTERNAL
RESOURCE ANALYSIS

CHAPTER OUTLINE

In the early 1970s, when strategic planning was becoming very popular in American corporations, the CEO of a major appliance company was boasting of the first-rate strategic planning department his company had just created. He had hired a group of brilliant economists, planners, and financial experts. They were supported by sophisticated computer systems. They had excellent facilities, a generous budget, and access to top management. The expectation was that this department would create brilliant strategies that would propel the company to unprecedented growth.

At the same time, oil shocks and economic recessions battered the economy. The strategic planners had very limited success in forecasting economic changes.

They created strategic plans and contingency plans for many different scenarios and sent them down to the divisions of the company. Divisional managers, under tremendous short-term pressures for profits, simply ignored the plans. The company had several bad years of performance. Three years, and several million dollars later, the strategic planning department was disbanded.

Reflecting on this experience, the CEO said that he had learned several things about strategy making. First, in a turbulent economic environment there is no such thing as a perfect strategy. Second, having brilliant strategies is not sufficient to ensure success. Third, formulating strategies at the corporate and business unit levels requires attention to both the *content* of strategies and their development *processes*.

This distinction between strategy content and process serves as a good starting point for examining strategy formulation. Strategy content refers to the substantive economic actions the company will pursue. It answers the question what should the company do. Content must be determined for corporate, business unit, functional area, and ecological and social strategies. Strategy process refers to the internal procedures followed to develop strategies. It answers the questions how will strategies and strategic plans be developed, who will be involved, what are the time horizons, what procedures will be used, and so on. It includes the interpersonal, social, behavioral, and political processes that influence strategic choices. To create successful strategies, both strategy content and the strategy process must be managed. Chapter 6 focuses on strategy process issues.

The focus of this chapter is on determining strategy content. Strategies are created by combining internal resource analysis with environmental and industry structure analysis described in Chapters 2 and 3. This chapter describes how to conduct internal resource analysis and establish competitive advantage. The rest of the chapter deals with different types of, and techniques for, choosing strategy at the corporate, business unit, and functional area levels. The next chapter will address issues of strategy process issues. It will show the modification of economically rational strategy choices to fit ethical issues, top management's personal values, the firm's sense of social responsibility, and internal behavioral, social, and political considerations.

What strategies a firm may pursue depends on resources available to it. Therefore, it is critical to begin strategy formulation by conducting an assessment of internal resources and those that can be obtained from the outside. This internal resource analysis should identify key strengths and weaknesses of the firm. Strategy content must be designed in light of choices available to the firm. These choices are different for the three levels of strategy—corporate, business unit, and functional area. Techniques for choosing strategies at these levels are discussed in this chapter. At each level, managers must conduct internal resource analysis and environmental analysis and then match the two to generate strategies. In developing strategies at these three levels, explicit attempts must be made to integrate them into a unified strategy with minimum internal contradictions. Functional area policies must collectively support business unit competitive strategies, and business unit strategies must fit the general corporate strategy.

5.1   INTERNAL RESOURCE ANALYSIS

Managers formulate the best strategies when they know their organization's internal resources, strengths, and weaknesses. Based on that knowledge, managers

Figure 5.1 *Internal Resource Analysis*

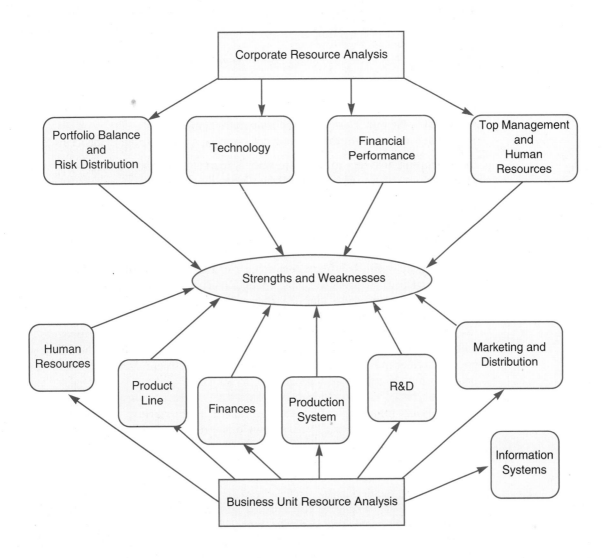

can build strategies on their strengths and avoid their weaknesses. This requires analyzing internal resources at the corporate level and the business unit level. The objective is to identify the company's strengths and weaknesses; this is depicted in Figure 5.1.

Corporate Level Analysis

At the corporate level, analysis should compare the relative performance of different businesses and identify prosperous businesses and their sources of success. The following questions may be useful for focusing this analysis:

- How well balanced is our portfolio of businesses? Do we have excessively risky businesses in the portfolio?

- Are we operating in growth industries?
- How well is each business unit performing?
- What are the strongest and weakest businesses in the portfolio? Are the strong businesses sustainable over the long term? What can be done about weak business units?
- How does our organization compare with our closest competitors in each business area?
- How can we improve the performance of each business unit?
- What is the weakest link in the value creation chain of our organization?
- What is the quality of our corporate management?
- What are our strengths in finance, technology, and human resources?

In developing answers to these questions, managers can get a sense of the complete corporate resource base and strengths and weaknesses.

Business Unit Analysis

At the business unit level, internal resource analysis should include an analysis of product lines, production systems, marketing capabilities, finances, technological and R&D capabilities, human resources and managerial skills, and information systems of individual business units. Product line assessment deals with evaluating the long-term viability of products. It should help the firm identify products with strong potential and identify the degree of fit between product characteristics and consumer demands. It should also identify products close to maturity that need to be phased out or modified. Strong products and those with good potential may be earmarked for strategic investment. Simultaneously, weak products may be identified for eventual phasing out.

Analysis of the production systems deals with assessment of production technologies, manufacturing, storage, and transportation systems. It should identify the strengths and weaknesses of manufacturing processes. It should include detailed analysis of production costs, optimal scale of operations, level of automation, capacity utilization, and labor utilization patterns. This analysis should lead to decisions about changes in technology, production scheduling, and inventory management.

Analysis of marketing capabilities should focus on assessing the appropriateness of the marketing variables—product, price, promotion, packaging, and distribution channels—to customer needs and to the firm's strategy. It should identify areas of marketing strength, which could be the sales force, distribution system, advertising strategy, or product management function.

Analysis of financial resources deals with evaluating the financial soundness of the company. It should show the financial strengths of the firm and the firm's ability to raise additional finances from the capital markets. Analytical techniques, such as ratio analysis, capital structure analysis, cash flow analysis, cost analysis, and budgetary analysis, can be used to identify financial strengths and weaknesses.

Analysis of R&D and technologies should highlight major technological strengths and weaknesses in products and production processes. It should identify new technologies in which the firm needs to invest to remain competitive. To enable the company to remain on the leading technological edge, particular attention should be paid to technological obsolescence of existing products and threats from substitute products. This analysis should also identify opportunities for improving production efficiencies and cutting costs through automation.

Analysis of human resources and managerial skills must be conducted to ensure that the firm has enough skilled workers and capable managers to carry on its work in the future. Such analysis should identify needs for management development, ways of building depth in the management structure, need for structural and cultural changes, and successors to the CEO.

Finally, information systems analysis must assess the adequacy of existing data processing systems, management information systems, and decision support systems. In information-intensive businesses and in some service industries (e.g., air travel, hotels, and banks) information systems are the basis for gaining competitive advantage. In such businesses, it is not sufficient to have information systems that are adequate for internal decision making needs. These systems must be superior in relation to competitors' capabilities.

The main purpose of internal resource analysis is to identify the firm's strengths and weaknesses, which become the basis for formulating strategies. Each strategy must build on the strengths of the firm, and avoid its weaknesses. Identification of these strengths and weakness is often a matter of the perceptions of management. What some managers consider a strength, others may consider a weakness (Stevenson, 1976). Therefore, internal resource analysis must attempt to develop managerial consensus in defining strengths and weaknesses. This consensus requires an open sharing of assumptions, information, and analysis about firm characteristics.

Strengths, Weaknesses, and Competitive Advantage

The industry analysis framework described in Chapter 3 can help identify competitive strengths and weaknesses of individual businesses. Strengths in this context are those organizational attributes that allow the business to be competitive. Weaknesses are those attributes that detract the business from being competitive.

The forces that shape competition within an industry, described in Chapter 3, can be used as a screen for determining competitive strengths. Strengths include firm attributes that raise barriers to entry into the industry, reduce the power of buyers and suppliers, reduce the threats of substitute products, and allow the firm to respond quickly and flexibly to competitive moves. For example, economies of scale in production, patented technologies, product features that raise switching costs, control over distribution channels, and capital intensity could be strengths for a business. Similarly, the firm's ability to curtail the power of buyers and suppliers because of its size, specialized skills, expertise in contracting and financing, and ability to backward and forward integrate are also strengths. Strengths that allow the firm to match rivals' competitive moves include accurate assessment of environmental trends, early information about competitors' intentions and strategies, ability to make quick decisions, and the ability to influence industry regulations.

These strengths may be used as the basis for creating competitive advantage that shelters the firm from domestic and international competition (South, 1981). Competitive advantage refers to the relative superiority of a firm over its competitors on a variety of internal and external factors. A part of competitive advantage arises from artfully selecting competitive arenas in which to do battle. Thus, a firm could create competitive advantage by operating in sheltered markets. Such sheltering is a function of government policies, import/export restrictions, differences in foreign exchange rates, and the size of market segments served.

Selecting safe havens in which to compete means abandoning the policy of blanket participation in all markets. Instead, a business must identify and operate in those enclaves that are least susceptible to abrupt technological changes, exchange rate fluctuations, business and economic cycles, and seasonality of demand. The main objective is to establish a business that is least directly vulnerable to competitive threats or major environmental changes. Remember that even the most protected markets cannot remain protected forever. Sheltered domains of operation are often temporary and dynamic and may not provide sustained competitive advantages.

More sustainable sources of competitive advantage are firm assets that provide it with unique ways of achieving efficiency, reducing costs, and capturing markets. These include relative cost and control of raw materials, a higher-skilled labor force, well-differentiated product line, control over distribution channels, brand-loyal customers, reputation of the firm, and patented technologies. Firms can use internal attributes to create competitive advantage in the following ways (MacMillan, 1983):

- Preemptive moves: Some competitive advantage may be created by being the first mover in an industry. In the productive chain there are many opportunities in the marketing, distribution, and production areas to do things first. Early entry into a market is an effective way of gaining a protected position. If done at an economic scale, it can preempt or delay the development of competition. For some time it also may provide monopolistic benefits. Early adoption of new production technologies or automation can provide competitive cost advantages. The key is to capitalize on the early entry and lack of competition, acquire prime position in the industry, build customer loyalty and brand identification, and set standards for the industry. Preemptive strategies could include establishing control over distributors, as Coca-Cola did in the soft drinks industry, or establishing early control over limited raw materials, as is common in the materials mining and oil industries.

- Product leadership: Advantage also can be established by being the first to introduce new product sizes, prices, packaging, or features into the market. At least for the time it takes for the competition to imitate, the leader enjoys the benefits of being unique. In industries where products are difficult to imitate, such as heavy machinery and mainframe computer hardware, this is an effective source of sustainable advantage. Being ahead of others in launching and producing products also allows firms to climb up the learning curve and reduce their costs. Product leadership also has reputational benefits. Once established as a leader, customers and the industry look to the firm for first moves. This gives the firm the ability to control industrywide trends.

- Patents and technology: A common way of establishing competitive advantage is through patents over new technology. For example pharmaceutical companies invest billions of dollars (often 15% to 20% of their annual revenues) to develop new drugs, which are then patented. These companies depend on a few blockbuster drugs to bring in a large proportion of their revenues. Until the product patent expires, the company has complete protection from competition in selling that drug. The key to sustaining competitive advantage in this industry is to have a continuous stream of new patented drugs.

- Cost containment: Establishing advantageous cost position and using it to gain price flexibility is an important source of competitive advantage. Focused containment of those costs that form the most significant proportion of the cost of goods is the key to successful containment. Costs can be reduced by applying scale economies in production, automation, efficient management of inventories, optimal production scheduling, vertical integration, and efficient labor contracts. Japanese automobile manufacturers have been effective in applying these techniques to keep their production costs the lowest in the world. They are now able to price their cars lower, and provide more free services to customers, than other manufacturers in most market segments.

- Financial structure: Competitive advantage also can be created by being different from the competition in financial structuring of business. Firms can gain unique advantages through judicious use of financial merchandising, credit management, and leveraging. High leverage can mean taking higher risks; but if it is done for short periods and in ways to provide cost advantages, it can be an effective source of competitive advantage. For example, in the airline industry, the main costs are for fuel, labor, and financing of the fleet of planes. Companies have limited ability to contain fuel and labor costs. American Airlines created a unique competitive advantage for itself by controlling its capital equipment financing costs. It creatively financed the purchase of its aircraft through leasing arrangements with a foreign bank. Location of the lessor and the lessee in different countries created tax advantages for both and minimized American's financing costs.

It is important to validate the internal assessment of strengths and competitive advantages. One way is through external stakeholders of the organization. Key stakeholders and business associates well acquainted with the firm should be asked for their opinions on key characteristics of the firm. This external test is particularly important in identifying strengths and weaknesses, including the image of the company, acceptance of the company's products by customers, credibility of the company with governmental agencies and public interest groups, and the ability of the company to raise capital in the financial markets. This test can provide confidence to management about its assessment of the company's strengths and weaknesses.

Earlier we distinguished three levels of strategy: corporate, business unit, and functional. At each level, companies can choose different types of strategies. Now we discuss these strategy choices and techniques for making them.

5.2   TYPES OF CORPORATE STRATEGIES

Corporate strategies describe the total objectives and goals of the firm, the firm's current and future business domains, and the firm's general approach to organizing its productive and administrative systems. They define how the product market domain of the firm is going to evolve. Top management develops corporate strategies at the corporate headquarters. Top managers create the strategic framework within which business unit strategies are developed.

A central defining feature of corporate strategies is the breadth of product market domain or the degree of diversification of the firm. Using diversification as a basis, firms can choose from among three strategies: the dominant product strategy, the related diversification strategy, and the conglomerate strategy (Montgomery and Singh, 1984; Ramanujam and Varadarajan, 1989; Rumelt, 1974).

Diversification Strategies

The **dominant product strategy** involves limiting the firm's domain to a single product or product line. Firms pursuing this strategy seek to establish themselves as the premier, most efficient, and most versatile producer in the industry. They achieve their growth objectives through product line extension and geographic expansion. Product line extensions take the form of innovations that extend the product life cycle and innovations that attract new customers. Geographic expansion takes the firm from local, to regional, to national, to international operations. Most firms start out as single or dominant product firms. The main shortcoming of this strategy is the high risk of operating in a single industry. A downturn in the industry could severely harm the company.

An example of a firm pursuing the dominant product strategy is Crown Cork and Seal. This company started as a small manufacturer of bottle crowns and corks. Soon it expanded its product line to include metal cans. For more than fifty years it has remained in the same basic product lines—metal cans and bottle crowns. During this period it has been continuously successful and has expanded internationally through its wholly owned subsidiaries. This strategy contrasts starkly with that of all other major firms in the industry, such as American Can, National Can, and Continental Can, which have diversified out of the metal cans industry.

The **related diversification strategy** refers to a domain choice that encompasses related product markets. In this strategy, a company operates in multiple businesses related to each other through common production, marketing, raw materials, or operating characteristics. As firms grow, they enter areas of business related to their original operation. This gives them an opportunity to expand quickly, diversify risks, use their existing resources more efficiently, and exploit advantages of early entry into new markets.

Examples of firms following related diversification strategy include Sears, Roebuck and Texas Instruments. Sears, Roebuck, which was historically a retail merchandising firm, expanded into retailing financial services by acquiring Dean Witter Reynolds. It also entered the real estate business by buying Caldwell Banker. In recent years Sears has reverted back to its core retail business, because it found it difficult to manage diversified operations. Texas Instruments began its operations in the electronics instruments business. In the past two decades it has diversified into a wide range of related products including calculators, computers, electronic games, software, and defense contracting. Each business division of Texas Instruments uses the core technological and marketing skills of the company to produce related products.

The related diversification strategy has been found the most profitable of the three strategies discussed here. Its main shortcoming is that it distributes organizational resources and managerial attention over multiple industries. This may make it difficult to compete with dominant product firms in the industry (Rumelt, 1974). It also may be difficult to achieve economies of large scale in many industries simultaneously.

The **conglomerate strategy** involves operating a set of diverse, unrelated businesses. Conglomerate firms treat their businesses as financial assets that are acquired and divested solely based on their financial performance. There is no consideration given to relatedness of products or markets, interdependencies between skills or facilities, or any other type of linkages between businesses. If a business unit meets the corporate financial objectives of growth and profitability, it remains part of the corporate portfolio. If it fails to meet these objectives, it is divested. This strategy aims at efficient management of financial assets by supplying business units necessary capital, general management expertise, and tight financial and planning controls.

Examples of firms using the conglomerate strategy include Textron, LTV, and Teledyne. Textron started as a textiles company and remained a dominantly textiles firm until the mid 1950s. Then, in reaction to the crisis in the textile industry, it started diversifying out of textiles by buying companies in consumer products, industrial products, and high-technology industries. Meanwhile, it downsized its textile operations. By the 1970s, Textron had fully diversified into unrelated areas such as helicopters, chain saws, light machinery, and defense contracting.

The characteristics of these three corporate strategies are summarized in Table 5.1.

Table 5.1 *Characteristics of Three Corporate Strategies*

Strategies	Characteristics	Growth	Profit	Risk
Dominant product	Operates in a single industry	Medium to high	Medium	Medium to low
Related diversification	Operates in a few related industries	Low	High	Low
Conglomerate	Operates in many unrelated industries	High	Low	Medium

This way of characterizing corporate strategy using business domain is very popular in the literature. However, it tells us little about the firm's production and administrative orientations. To comprehend corporate strategy from a production and administrative systems perspective and their fit with business domain choices, we need another way of classifying corporate strategies.

Four Patterns of Strategy

A most sophisticated description of corporate strategic orientation that captures its entrepreneurial, production, and administrative approaches is provided by Miles *et al.* (1978). They define firm strategies based on how companies solve their three key problems—the entrepreneurial, the administrative, and the engineering problems. The entrepreneurial problem deals with how the company will create businesses, what businesses it will operate, and how it will define and renew its domain of operation. The engineering problem concerns the technologies the company will use to achieve its business objectives. It involves deploying technical skills and resources to create a financially viable business. The administrative problem involves how the company will structure itself internally—how it will obtain necessary human and financial resources to make the business idea successful.

Companies resolve these problems in unique ways that characterize their corporate strategies and personalities. Their solutions involve deploying human, financial, administrative, and material resources in enduring strategic forms. Each strategy differs on many dimensions, including the scope of operations, risk propensity of firms, and activity orientation of firms (inactive or reactive to proactive). In empirical studies of several industries, Miles *et al.* (1978) found four patterns of strategy: prospectors, analyzers, defenders, and reactors.

Prospectors are firms that have a wide business scope. They operate in many diverse industries. They have risk-seeking decision makers who like to undertake high stakes business ventures. These firms actively and aggressively search for business opportunities to improve performance. They are willing to go into virtually any type of business if it provides them appropriate returns and growth. Teledyne in the 1960s is an example of a firm pursuing the prospector strategy. Teledyne was originally a consumer electronics company. In the 1960s when the stock market was booming, Teledyne embarked on an aggressive strategy of growth through acquisitions. It bought hundreds of small private companies in a diverse set of industries. Some of these companies were undervalued and good bargains, others were highly speculative ventures. Teledyne paid for these companies by issuing its own stock, which was rising in price because of its excellent growth rate.

Analyzers are firms that operate in a broad industry sector, often in related business areas in which they have accumulated experience. They do not aggressively seek risky ventures, but at the same time do not avoid risks. They try to rationally balance risks and returns by following and improving technological advances made by other firms. They actively seek out opportunities that fit their organizational capabilities. They analyze new business ventures thoroughly before embarking on them. Analysis includes assessment of financial, human, market, and product strengths. Matsushita Electronics Industries is an example of an Analyzer. As the case study included in this book shows, this company takes calculated risks in new business areas and it has succeeded in becoming a global electronics company.

Unlike prospectors, analyzers do not seek out new business opportunities; rather, they imitate successful firms. By creatively and quickly imitating high performing strategies, they are able to establish a profitable position in the market. Reactor firms thrive in certain industries. In industries such as apparel and financial services, imitation of products and strategies is easy. For firms in these industries, products or services are the key defining features of their strategies. However, all firms in the industry have wide production flexibility to produce and distribute many different types of products or services. Moreover, it is difficult to patent apparel products or financial services. Therefore, imitation is easy and frequent.

Defenders are firms that focus on a narrow domain of operations, a well-defined-industry, or even a single product. They have well-established businesses that they seek to protect and nurture. They are risk averse and invest only in proven long-term prospects. They tend to seek out opportunities only when compelled by performance pressures. Union Carbide is an example of a firm pursuing the defender strategy. Throughout its life, it has remained a chemical company, operating in many segments of this industry, including heavy industrial chemicals, specialty chemicals, agricultural chemicals, batteries, plastics, and technological services. It invests in large, safe projects in areas where it has expertise and good chances of success. Although Union Carbide is a very large company, its performance in most years is in the middle range compared with its competitors.

Reactors are firms that operate in diverse business areas without a coherent plan. They react to environmental pressures and often find themselves in crisis.

Occasionally they may get lucky and exploit emerging environmental opportunities. But their usual mode of operation is trailing behind the competition and reacting defensively to industry problems. This is not an effective strategy.

5.3   TECHNIQUES FOR CHOOSING CORPORATE STRATEGIES

The foregoing classification schemes show that companies have several choices to make. A primary choice is of **business domain**. Business domain may be defined in terms of a business portfolio. Each business unit serves a specific market with specific products. Choosing a corporate strategy involves selecting businesses that will fulfill corporate goals and create a well-balanced portfolio. In making this choice, a structured technique called **business portfolio analysis** is often used. It provides a method for systematically assessing the soundness of the company's business portfolio and the role of different business units in it (Hedley, 1977; Hofer and Schendel, 1978).

BCG's Business Portfolio Matrix

The Boston Consulting Group (BCG) originally developed the BCG business portfolio matrix as a framework for developing corporate strategies. This technique allows managers to compare and choose businesses by assessing industry growth and market strength of each business (Hedley, 1977). Figure 5.2 illustrates the BCG business portfolio matrix.

In Figure 5.2, the vertical axis represents industry growth rate. The horizontal axis represents the market share or relative market share of a business compared with its key competitors. Each of these dimensions is classified into categories of high and low, thus creating the four cells of the matrix. The high-low cutoff points are based on industry and business unit characteristics and the judgment of managers. The cell characterized by low industry growth rate and low market share is labeled Dogs. The cell characterized by low industry growth rate but high market share is labeled Cash Cows. The cell characterized by high industry growth rate and high market share is labeled Stars. And the cell characterized by a high industry growth rate but low market share is labeled Wildcats. These labels attempt to capture the central characteristic of businesses operating in each of the four cells.

Strategic analysis begins by construction of this matrix and placing the business units of a corporation into the various cells depending on their industry growth rate and market share. The size of the circle that represents each business unit indicates the relative size in either revenues or profitability of the individual business unit. The objective of portfolio analysis is to create a portfolio with a balanced net of businesses in the four cells of the matrix. Investments into businesses and cash flows from businesses can be balanced by transferring resources among business units in ways that sustain long-term profitability. Business portfolio analysis leads to strategic recommendations for business units in each cell. It also can help make investment and divestment decisions concerning specific business units.

Some general recommendations for business units in each of the four cells may now be considered. Cash Cows are businesses that have high market shares but are in low growth rate industries. Because of their high market share, these businesses generate a large amount of cash. Because they operate in low growth rate industries, it does not make sense to reinvest the cash they generate into the same industry. Some of their surplus cash can be used to finance Stars or Wildcats.

Figure 5.2 Business Portfolio Matrix

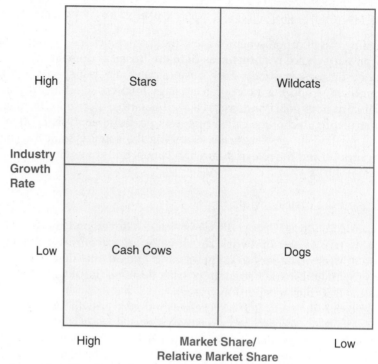

Source: Adapted from Boston Consulting Group Business Portfolio Matrix.

Over time, the objectives should be to move out of these unattractive markets by slowly phasing out Cash Cows.

Businesses in the Star category are in high growth rate industries and have a high market share. Maintaining market share in rapid growth industries is very expensive because the size of the market is continually expanding, which requires ever-increasing marketing expenditures. To maintain market share, these businesses need to reinvest cash they generate internally. They also may need additional cash infusion from outside. The objective concerning these business units should be to maintain their prominent market position until the market matures and its growth rate slows. At that point, Star businesses become Cash Cows and may be used as sources of cash.

Wildcats are businesses in high growth rate industries that have a low market share. Due to their weak market position, they may not be currently profitable, but they have good potential. They represent risky ventures that can turn in any direction. The objective for these businesses should be to increase their market share, thereby making them profitable and moving them into the Star cell. One way of doing this is by investing money in market share development. The strategy then becomes one of rapid investments that will provide good returns while the market is still attractive.

Businesses in the Dog category are characterized by low market shares and low growth rate industries. They are unlikely to be currently profitable and have few prospects. One obvious strategy is to divest these businesses; however, this strategy might not always be implementable. Sometimes Dog businesses provide crucial inputs into Star, Wildcat and Cash Cow businesses and, therefore have to be retained in the portfolio. At other times, Dog businesses provide intangible benefits such as good will, image, and legitimacy. Alternatively, it might not be possible to shut them down because of labor contracts. If these businesses cannot be divested, the strategy should be one of cutting back operations to bare minimum levels needed.

The matrix described provides a general framework for corporate strategy analysis. It is, however, a simplified framework and has several limitations. First, balancing cash flows among businesses is the basis of this approach. In many situations, however, managers are not attempting to balance cash flows as part of their corporate strategy. Instead, they may be trying to maximize growth from outside funds or maximize return on investment. Second, industry growth rate and market share (or relative market share) are imperfect measures of the attractiveness of an industry and a firm's market strength, respectively. An industry's historical growth rate may not continue into the future if the product is maturing or if new technologies can provide functional substitutes for the product. The definitions of market and market share are also ambiguous. It is not always clear how to delineate market boundaries, because often market segments overlap with each other.

A third limitation lies in categorizing the dimensions of industry growth rate and market share that vary along a continuum; having only two categories (high and low) is simplistic. Such binary division loses much information that is contained in actual market share numbers. Moreover, without huge amounts of comparative and historical statistics, the cutoff points between high and low tend to be arbitrary.

A fourth limitation is that the approach considers only two of the many factors that should be considered in formulating strategies. Other factors such as organizational size, core competencies, foreign demand and competition, and volatility of the industry, are not considered. Another limitation is that some recommendations from this type of analysis might not be practically feasible. Factors other than cash flow, market share, and industry growth considerations cause practical limitations. For example, it may not be feasible to expand or contract a particular business because of the level of technological risk involved, government regulations, patented technologies, labor conditions, and so forth. The task of the strategy analyst is to understand what role each individual unit plays in the total corporate portfolio and accordingly design strategies for those business units. Finally, this approach does not deal with strategy implementation problems (Bettis and Hall, 1983; Gray, 1986).

Despite these limitations, the BCG business portfolio matrix has great intuitive appeal, and companies use it widely (Haspeslagh, 1983). In fact, several different versions of the business portfolio matrix were subsequently developed by General Electric (GE) and McKinsey & Company as well as other strategy consulting firms. Hofer and Schendel (1978) provide a comprehensive description of these approaches. Next, let us look at GE's multifactor portfolio matrix as an example of a more refined approach.

GE's Multifactor Portfolio Matrix

The GE approach differs from the BCG matrix in the way it measures and categorizes industry attractiveness and market power, thereby overcoming some limitations of the BCG matrix. The GE multifactor portfolio matrix is shown in Figure 5.3. It uses qualitative notions of industry attractiveness and strategic position in industry, or business strength in the industry, to characterize businesses. Each dimension is a composite measure of several component factors shown in Figure 5.4. These dimensions are each classified into three categories of high (strong), medium, and low (weak), thus creating a matrix with nine cells. This is a clear refinement of the four-cell BCG matrix.

Each business unit of a corporation is plotted on this matrix. The size of the circles represents the size of the business as measured by annual revenues. The shaded area represents the estimated portion of the market served by the business. Arrows can be used to show the direction of the current business strategy.

Depending on where in the matrix a business lies, three basic strategies are possible. Along the lower left to upper right diagonal, the strategy of selective investment(s) may be appropriate. Selective investment here implies choosing businesses for investment based on their strategic potential, and within each selected business, selecting skill areas, products, and functions in which marginal investments are likely to yield the highest returns. For businesses in cells above this diagonal, investment for growth (I) strategies are appropriate. Investment should aim at building market shares, new products, technological and human resources capabilities that strengthen the competitive position of the business. Businesses below the diagonal are in unattractive markets and hold weak positions. They are possible candidates for harvesting or divesting (H). Harvesting refers to holding back new capital investment to minimal viable levels and drawing out excess cash from the business for use in other areas. Divesting, on the other hand, is a more drastic action suitable for businesses that have no potential or are a drain on existing resources.

Strategic Thrust

Corporate strategies involve more than simply choosing businesses in which to operate. Another type of domain choice question that is pertinent for corporations in mature industries is one of identifying and establishing a strategic thrust. Strategic thrust means the general direction in which a company is going to move over the long term. Here, the issue is not simply deciding which businesses to retain, acquire, or divest, but targeting and positioning the firm in a set of attractive technologies and industries.

Strategic realignment involves looking at the next five to fifteen years to identify businesses that are likely to be attractive given the strengths and weaknesses of the company. Based on this assessment, the firm develops strategic programs to move into attractive arenas. This may involve restructuring existing assets of the company or buying new ones. It also could involve buying equity in new start-up companies that use emerging technologies. Many large companies such as GE, IBM, and Eastman Kodak have set up venture capital funds to be invested in new ventures that could provide an entry into exciting industries of the future.

An example of strategic realignment is provided by Union Carbide in the mid and late 1970s. During this period, the company realigned its product portfolio and its strategic thrust. This allowed it to move away from high dependence on industrial chemicals into a more balanced set of technologies including specialty chemicals, special metals, and technology services. This realignment process occurred over a six- to eight-year period. Similarly, Shell Oil realized in the early 1970s that it was highly vulnerable to fluctuations in oil prices. Over that decade,

Figure 5.3 *GE's Multifactor Portfolio Matrix*

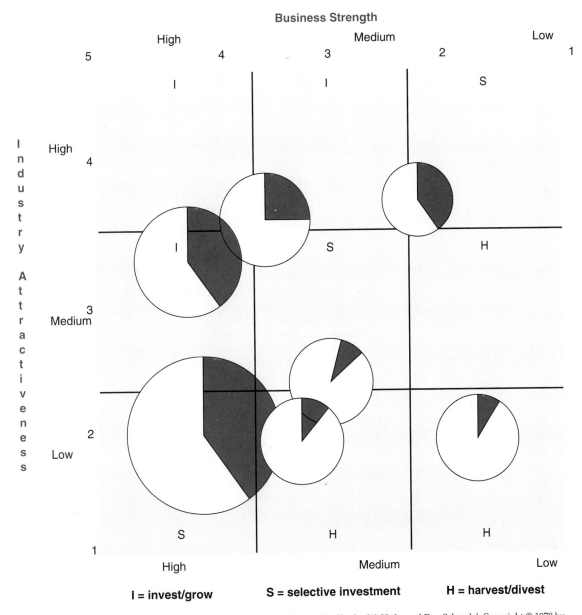

I = invest/grow   S = selective investment   H = harvest/divest

the company diversified in new high-technology industries and reduced its dependence on the energy sector.

Strategic realignment can be simplified by systematic techniques such as scenario analysis, Delphi forecasting, and structured brainstorming. Scenario analysis and the policy Delphi technique were described in Chapter 2. Structured brainstorming is an informal procedure for eliciting creative solutions to strategic

Figure 5.4 *Industry Attractiveness and Business Strength Factors*

Industry Attractiveness	Business Strength

Market Factors

Size (dollars, units, or both)	Your share (in equivalent term)
Size of key segments	Your share of key segments
Growth rate per year:	Your annual growth rate:
Total	Total
Segments	Segments
Diversity of market	Diversity of your participation
Sensitivity to price, service features, and external factors	Your influence on the market
Cyclicality	
Seasonality	Lags or leads in your sales
Bargaining power of upstream suppliers	Bargaining power of your suppliers
Bargaining power of downstream suppliers	Bargaining power of your customers

Competition

Types of competitors	Where you fit, how you compare in terms
Degree of concentration	of products marketing capability,
Changes in type and mix	service, production strength, financial
Entries and exits	strength, management
Changes in share	Segments you have entered or left
Substitution by new technology	Your relative share change
Degrees and types of integration	Your vulnerability to new technology
	Your own level of integration

Financial and Economic Factors

Contribution margins	Your margins
Leveraging factors such as economies of scale and experience	Your scale and experience
Barriers to entry or exit (both financial and nonfinancial)	Barriers to your entry or exit (both financial and nonfinancial)
Capacity utilization	Your capacity utilization

Technological Factors

Maturity and volatility	Your ability to cope with change
Complexity	Depths of your skills
Differentiation	Types of your technological skills
Patents and copyrights	Your patent protection
Manufacturing process technology required	Your manufacturing technology

Sociopolitical Factors in Your Environment

Social attitudes and trends	Your company's responsiveness and flexibility
Laws and government agency regulations	Your company's ability to cope
Influence with pressure groups and government representatives	Your company's aggressiveness
	Your company's relationships
Human factors, such as unionization and community acceptance	

Source: Derek F. Abell and John S. Hammond, *Strategic Market Planning: Problems & Analytical Approaches*. Copyright @ 1979, p. 214. Reprinted by permission of Prentice-Hall, Inc., Englewood Cliffs, New Jersey.

problems facing the firm. Managers are brought together in an informal setting and allowed to think freely about strategic problems. They have the liberty to recast the strategic problem and come up with *any* creative solution, despite its feasibility. The idea behind this technique is to give managers a completely risk-free opportunity to think creatively. Brainstorming sessions allow managers to transcend routine ways of thinking and overcome the normal pressures of organizational politics and personal insecurities to develop really creative solutions.

Once it has developed a corporate strategy, the firm knows the businesses in which it will operate and the directions in which it would like to move. In order to move individual business units into desirable directions and make them competitive within their respective industries, strategies for business units need to be developed.

5.4   TYPES OF BUSINESS UNIT STRATEGIES

At the business unit level, the key strategic issue is establishing sustainable competitive advantage within the industry in which the business unit operates. This may be done by selecting competitive arenas sheltered from competition and turbulent environmental changes, focusing marketing and advertising efforts on key product lines, cutting costs of production and distribution, and streamlining and automating operations.

At Campbell Soups ($6.2 billion sales in 1990), the new CEO, David Johnson, initiated a new business strategy for the soup division in the beginning of 1990. The objective was to increase sales of soups and improve return on equity. These were difficult objectives for a business that already controlled 65% of the domestic soup market. Campbell's old strategy had been to diversify its products away from soups and other sturdy brands such as Pepperidge Farm cookies and Le Menu and Swanson frozen foods. This led the company to spread its resources too thin.

The new "back to basics" business strategy involved selling related businesses (e.g., mushroom farms, salmon processing plants, and a refrigerated salad line) and focusing resources on the marketing of selective promising soup products. New products (e.g., more health-oriented products) replaced some poorly performing products. The soup division implemented a new cost-cutting program. Campbell's changed its advertising strategy from umbrella advertising to advertising of specific soups. Some best-seller soups such as tomato and chicken noodle and noodles, such as SpaghettiOs (which had not had brand-specific advertising since the 1960s) received their own special ads. For a special line of soups for children, the company revived the successful old rosy-cheeked Campbell Kids symbols and created ads in rap style. The company also started offering discounts on two or more cans instead of single cans.

Campbell's strategy was a judicious combination of the ways of establishing competitive advantage discussed in section 5.1. Creative new business strategies can be developed by changing product features (differentiation, product line breadth, packaging, and patents), production efficiencies (economies of scale, automation, and cost control), market positioning variables (advertising, discounting, pricing, and distribution channels), and innovative financing arrangements (leasing capital equipment and debt).

Although most firms create business strategies uniquely suited to their market conditions and internal goals and resources, there are several generic strategies that have been found to be common across many industries. Within any industry, firms follow several strategies for competing. These strategies have proven to be successful in the past and have become popularized through imitation among firms. They are tested recipes for success. These generic strategies are based on key determinants of profitability for the industry. Each industry has different determinants of profitability. For example, in the automobile and brewing industries, the lowering of production costs through large-scale operations is critical. In the fashion apparel industry, production costs are low, but creating new product designs and brand names is expensive.

Theoretically, many generic strategies for competing are possible. In practice however, there are some common strategies that are used in many industries. Based on Porter's work (1985), some of these strategies are described next. Other descriptions of generic strategies and their effectiveness are available in the literature (Chrisman, Hofer, and Boulton, 1988; Dess and Davies, 1984; Kotha and Orne, 1989; Miller, 1988; Mintzberg, 1988; White, 1986).

Least cost strategy refers to a strategy of operating at the lowest cost in the industry. Low cost can be achieved through high-volume production of standardized goods. By exploiting economies of scale in production, distribution, and raw materials purchase, and through product and process standardization, a firm can reduce its production costs to the minimum in the industry. The competitive advantage to firms following this strategy is in the flexibility they have in pricing their products lower than competition. Selling this high volume of production at small margins can be a very profitable strategy. Least-cost firms can underprice their product for long periods to gain market share and even drive competition out of the market. This strategy works best where there is a large demand for standard products.

Japanese firms in consumer electronics, steel, automobile, and motorcycle industries have used this strategy to enter new foreign markets. They produce large volumes of standard products for a collective world market. Due to economies of scale and experience effects, their cost of production is very low. They then enter new markets at prices much lower than prevailing competition. For example, Honda entered the United States market using its low-cost production facilities in Japan to serve the market for standard recreational motorcycles (Pascale, 1984).

Least-cost strategy allows a firm to participate in many market segments within the industry. It involves large investments to produce and market a broad line of products to satisfy several market segments. Firms that do not have the extensive resources required to do this can adopt a **niche strategy**. This refers to focusing on a clearly defined segment of the market and fulfilling customer expectations in that niche. Usually this means producing specialized products and marketing them through limited, focused delivery systems. Most industries have small market niches for specialized products. The total demand for the product may be low but it is constant. Therefore, firms can be strategically viable over the long run supplying only to these niches. Once established, these firms are difficult to dislodge because they possess the specialized knowledge about the customers, distribution system, product features, and production systems that gives them competitive advantage over others.

A good example of the niche strategy can be seen in the food retailing industry, where there is a market for high-quality gourmet foods. The demand for such products is low, but it is constant and widespread. Some retailers, such as Balducci's, Dean & De Luca, and Zabars in New York City, have targeted this segment as a viable business segment. Their customers are willing to pay premium prices to buy the specialized goods offered by these stores. Another example of niche retailing is Richard Meyer's Rodeo Drive (Beverly Hills, California) store that sells nothing but technically advanced makeup and shaving mirrors—some for as much as $8,400 a piece.

Even the narrowest niches can be sources of profits. For example, Swenson Stone Consultants provides consulting services to builders and architects worldwide on high-quality granite stone for building construction. These specialty stones are being used increasingly in upscale buildings such as luxury hotels, expensive residences, and office towers. The company maintains detailed and up-to-date information on granite quarries around the world. It advises builders seeking specific types of stones and matches their needs with available supplies from distant sources.

Another generic business strategy is the **differentiation strategy**. It involves creating products that have distinct and hard to imitate features and selling them widely across multiple market segments. Uniqueness can be in product features or product functions. By offering unique products, a manufacturer can lock in clients who are looking for those specific product features. This uniqueness does not have to be based on objective product characteristics. It could be based on perceived elements, such as reputation, image, or symbolic value. Once customers are convinced of the uniqueness of the product, they are willing to pay higher prices for it. The competitive advantage afforded by this strategy is that it allows a company to have higher than average prices and profits. Firms can achieve acceptable returns using this strategy even in markets with limited demand (Zajac and Shortell, 1989). The fashion apparel industry thrives on strategies of differentiation. Fashion designers attempt to create uniqueness through highly selective designs, materials, and image. Most sales in this industry are based on uniqueness and exclusivity. The upper end of this industry produces virtually one-of-a-kind, custom-tailored clothing for special clients such as entertainment performers, fashion models, and advertisers.

Strategies for entry, exit, decline, and turnaround are specialized strategies for special situations. They are useful for entering and exiting from an industry or in dealing with special situations of decline and turnaround. Entry strategies involve giving consumers competitively favorable short-term benefits. This is done to gain initial consumer acceptance for products and services during the introductory phases. The benefits include discounted prices, attractive payment or credit terms, maintenance services, and promotional giveaways. Once achieving a desirable volume of sales, the firm can revert to more competitive practices.

Exit strategies help firms to withdraw from an industry, which may be desirable in a declining industry. They involve cutbacks of product line and price discounting to reduce inventories. Production assets may be dismantled and redeployed in attempts to improve efficiency or cut costs (Harrigan, 1980; Schofield and Arnold, 1988; Woo and Cooper, 1981). Turnaround strategies attempt to revitalize businesses in a slump. They involve a combination of cost-cutting measures and revenue-enhancing strategies (Hofer, 1980).

This brief description of different types of business unit strategies shows that firms can become competitive in many different ways. Now we will discuss some concepts that can aid in the selection of competitive strategies.

5.5 TECHNIQUES FOR CHOOSING BUSINESS STRATEGIES

The choice of business unit strategies depends on structural forces governing competition and profitability in the industry and the firm's strengths and weaknesses. Business unit strategies must seek to establish sustainable competitive advantage by using strengths of the firm to exploit opportunities in the industry. Three additional considerations that should guide the choice of business unit strategies: the stage of the product life cycle of the business, the experience effect, and the market share-profitability relationship for a business.

Product Life Cycle

Most products go through a **product life cycle** (PLC) that is commonly described in the marketing literature. The PLC starts with the **introduction** of the product into the market, progresses through **growth** and **maturity** stages, and ends with the **decline** of demand. A typical life-cycle curve is shown in Figure 5.5. Each of the four stages of the PLC has distinct customer, price, profit, production, and investment characteristics as shown in the figure. Therefore, in each stage of the PLC, different business strategies are appropriate (Anderson and Zeithaml, 1984; Hayes and Wheelwright, 1979; Mascarenhas and Aaker, 1989).

In the introduction phase, demand for the product is just beginning to emerge. Customers are innovators who are willing to experiment with new products and services. The price of the product is usually high because firms prefer to skim the market. Production volumes and profits are low because of the small volume of demand. Overall, the introduction phase is perhaps the most risky stage of the product life cycle.

In the growth phase of the life cycle, demand increases very rapidly. Many early adopters enter the market. These customers use the product for its functional and efficiency-improving attributes. Producers begin to distinguish their products through product differentiation and by charging multiple and varied prices. They also improve production efficiency in anticipation of the increasing demand. Industry profits are better than in the introduction phase because of larger demand and revenues. Most of the investment is made in this phase to capture a large share of the growing market.

In the maturity stage, the demand for the product plateaus. Most users for whom the product serves some useful function are now in the market; very few new customers enter the market. The price-performance ratio for the product drops; that is, you can get better-performing products for lower prices than before. Industry profits are highest at this stage of the life cycle. Most initial investments are recovered in this stage, and the book value of capital equipment is considerably depreciated. Production is highly efficient and uses automation and mass-production techniques if applicable. Profits may be reinvested into maintaining market share or be used for developing new products.

In the decline phase, the demand for the product falls. Customers who buy the product are not adopting it for the first time; rather, they are replacing it. Prices decrease with decline in demand. Profits in this stage are low but stable. There are no new improvements in production techniques. Some manufacturers begin to divest out of the industry at this stage.

These characteristics of the product life cycle suggest that some stages of the cycle may be particularly receptive to certain generic strategies. In the introduction stage, a niche strategy aimed at innovators may be effective. The growth stage represents an expanding market in which diverse customer demands surface; at this stage, the differentiation strategy may be more effective. In the maturity stage the least-cost strategy may be feasible and lucrative to satisfy the demand of a large customer base. However, this strategy may not be feasible in the introduction phase of the cycle. Uncertainties about the development of demand may not justify

Figure 5.5 *Product Life Cycle*

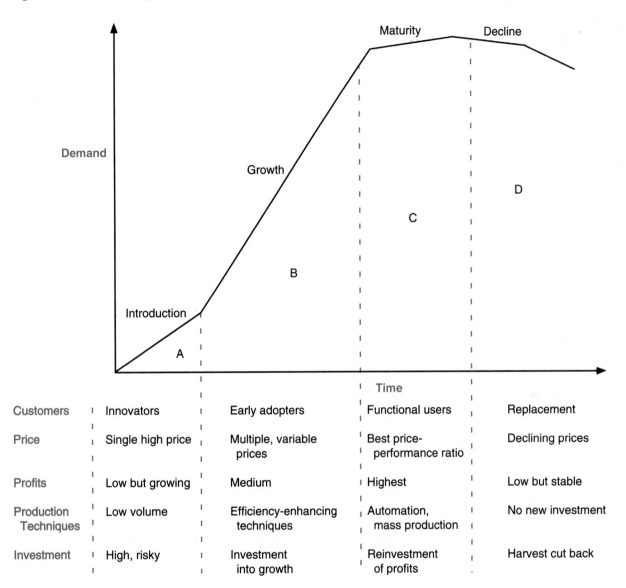

Customers	Innovators	Early adopters	Functional users	Replacement
Price	Single high price	Multiple, variable prices	Best price-performance ratio	Declining prices
Profits	Low but growing	Medium	Highest	Low but stable
Production Techniques	Low volume	Efficiency-enhancing techniques	Automation, mass production	No new investment
Investment	High, risky	Investment into growth	Reinvestment of profits	Harvest cut back

the investments required to become a low-cost producer. Similarly, the niche strategy may not be feasible in the decline phase of the product life cycle, because industry participants have already targeted all the possible niches. The niche strategy may be an option in this stage, however; if there is a proliferation of product features that make the market highly fragmented. The key idea is to keep the PLC stage of a business in mind when selecting a business strategy for it.

Experience Effect

Another important factor that should be considered in choosing business unit strategies is the effect of experience on the cost of production. The lowering of per-

Figure 5.6 *The Experience Curve*

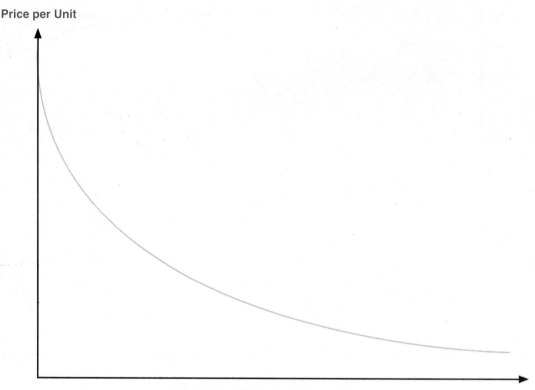

Price per Unit

Accumulated Volume of Production

unit production costs due to previous manufacturing experience is called the experience effect and is depicted in the experience curve shown in Figure 5.6. Studies show that every time the accumulated volume of production doubles in a firm, the per-unit cost of production reduces by 15%. This reduction occurs because of learning, scale economies, improvement in administrative and production techniques, and substitution of raw materials and components with less expensive alternatives. Firms that have greater accumulated experience incur lower production costs (Boston Consulting Group, 1970; Conley, 1970).

The key to a successful least-cost strategy is to exploit advantages of the experience effect. Firms can go down the experience curve quickly by having large-scale production. However, large-scale production may not be warranted given limited demand for the product in the domestic market. It may be feasible if, for example, the firm uses a single, large facility to produce for several markets around the world. At the same time, the firm can compete with other producers who supply fewer customers within a domestic market. Many Japanese firms have successfully used this approach to become low-cost producers. For example, Toyota and Nissan built automobile plants several times the size needed to satisfy the demand in Japan. The large volume of production was then used to enter foreign markets as least-cost producers.

The experience effect also provides managers with an objective basis for anticipating who in the industry can adopt the least-cost strategy. By comparing competitors on accumulated production experience, the firm can identify competitors who can sustain low costs and low prices. When faced with such competitors, it may be judicious to avoid price competition, perhaps by pursuing differentiation or niche strategies.

Market Share and Profitability Relationship

The third factor that must be considered in choosing business unit strategies is the relationship of market share to profitability in the industry. In some industries, profitability of a firm correlates highly with its market share (Buzzell and Gale, 1987; Prescott, Kohli, and Venkatraman, 1986). In such industries, companies play the game of gaining market share by expanding internally or buying market share by acquiring competitors. A good example of this is the domestic beer-brewing industry. Over the past three decades, this industry has become progressively more concentrated. In the early 1950s there were no dominant firms and the market was divided among more than 300 brewers. Today, the top few firms (Anheuser Busch, Miller, Heileman, Coors, and Stroh's) control over 90% of the market. These firms have grown in pursuit of market share to become large regional or national suppliers (Schendel and Patten, 1978).

But gaining market share is expensive. In some industries, it may be so expensive as to nullify the advantages of size. Recent research on the PIMS (Profit Impact of Marketing Strategies) database shows that not only is market share highly correlated with profitability, but that long-term profitability also depends on several other factors (Abell and Hammond, 1979; Kotler, 1988; Pfeiffer, Goodstein, and Nolan, 1989). Most important of these factors is the quality of the firm's products as compared with the competition. Quality boosts profits by allowing the firm to charge higher prices in the short term and by building growth over the long term. A second factor affecting long-term profitability is investment intensity (investment per dollar of sales). High investment intensity acts as a drag on profits. A third factor associated with long-term profitability is vertical integration. Businesses with average or above average market share stand to gain substantially by becoming vertically integrated (Buzzell and Gale, 1987).

The upshot of this discussion is that in developing business unit strategies firms must evaluate where in the product life cycle its products lie, where on the experience curve the firm stands with respect to competition, and how profits relate to market share in the industry. The full impact of business unit strategies can be achieved only if the appropriate functional area policies support them. In the next section, we turn our attention to these policies.

5.6   TYPES OF FUNCTIONAL AREA POLICIES

Strategies for organizing work within functional areas are usually called policies. Firms need two types of policies, those dealing with routine work and those dealing with nonroutine strategic issues. Work-related policies guide operating tasks. These policies usually deal with functional tasks like accounting and finance, administration, environmental protection and safety, human resource management, labor practices, marketing, operations or production, research and development, and transportation. They are developed by experts in the respective functional areas. The formulation of these policies is the subject matter for detailed courses. Our purpose here is to define their general domain and show how they may be related to corporate and business unit strategies. For further information, consult books in the respective functional areas. Policies are commonly developed in the following areas.

Accounting and Financial Policies. Accounting policies describe the accounting norms, practices, and rules that the corporation will follow. They establish organizational accounting practices, including accounting books to be maintained, accounting rules to be followed, reports to be produced, and types of accounting analyses to be performed. These practices are designed to conform with government regulations, industry practices, and business information and control needs. Financial policies describe procedures for financial forecasting and planning, evaluation of financial investments, raising capital, managing cash flows, and overall control of financial resources.

Administrative Policies. Administrative policies streamline the myriad administrative tasks in corporate offices. They cover routine tasks that nearly all offices have to do, such as record keeping, maintenance of office equipment and facilities, office planning, budgeting, coordination and control, interoffice and departmental communications, and so forth.

Environmental Protection and Safety Policies. These policies deal with minimizing the harmful effects of a corporation's activities on the natural environment, the public, and employees. They describe how the firm's plants will control hazardous emissions, manage wastes, protect workers' health, and protect the public from technological hazards emanating from its activities. They include programs for emergency management, pollution prevention, product integrity, community and government communications, and so on.

Human Resource Policies. Human resource policies aim to enhance the skills and capabilities of the organization's employees and provide them with a desirable quality of work life. They set procedures and guidelines for recruitment and training of employees, their professional development, employee benefits programs, and so on.

Labor Policies. Large corporations with multiple work locations and thousands of employees invariably have to deal with organized labor unions. To bring some degree of consistency to dealing with union demands, a firm needs clear labor relations policies. These policies describe the general corporate philosophy toward labor relations. They describe how labor negotiations will be conducted and the formats and procedures for assessing labor markets and labor productivity and establishing labor contracts.

Marketing Policies. Marketing policies deal with organization of the five P's of marketing: product, packaging, price, promotion, and point of sale. They attempt to organize marketing functions in a way that supports the overall competitive business strategy. They include development of products and product planning, segmentation of markets, organization of distribution systems, advertising strategies, pricing policies, product packaging policies, sales analysis, and management policies.

Operations and Production Policies. The production operations of a company need policies to ensure smooth and cost-effective operations. These include policies for inventory management, production scheduling, capacity utilization, automation, quality control, materials handling, substitution, energy conservation, and plant and equipment maintenance.

Research and Development Policies. Development of new products is the lifeblood of companies. To succeed in the long run, companies need to develop and launch new products continually. In some industries, such as drugs and pharmaceuticals or consumer electronics, the ability to develop new products can be a survival issue. Research and development policies guide corporate activities in product and process innovation. They set priorities for technological innovation projects, describe criteria for selection and funding of projects, and establish budgets and control procedures.

Transportation Policies. Transporting products to markets, raw materials to plants, and employees to the workplace are generic activities that all companies must perform. Transportation policies attempt to organize these activities in the most cost-efficient manner. They describe procedures for building, maintaining, and managing transportation fleets of automobiles, trucks, airplanes, and ships; cost control over transportation expenses; and coordination of transportation functions within the firm.

5.7   CHOOSING FUNCTIONAL AREA POLICIES

Functional area policies guide the performance of functional tasks in a consistent and uniform manner. These policies are usually written in voluminous policy manuals in each area. Examples of such policies are included in the Company Policy Documents section in this book.

Functional area policies are designed to meet specific organizational needs. Every organization seeks to be efficient and produce high-quality products or services. Similarly, most organizations seek to maintain consistency across various functions through integrated policies. Specific, emerging strategic issues may require separate policies. Accordingly, policies can be designed to (1) achieve efficiency and high quality, (2) to provide integrated support services to the whole company, or (3) to address specific issues.

Efficiency- and quality-oriented policies aim at executing functional area tasks in the most rational and efficient manner while achieving high-quality of products and services. This can be done by establishing quality control programs, standardizing operations and products, eliminating slack, and minimizing duplication and overlaps in operating procedures. Such policies attempt to balance organizational rules, regulations, and bureaucracy with the need for control over operations.

Companies that have been successful in developing effective functional policies do so through focused programs. For example, the IBM plant in Rochester, New York, developed highly efficient and quality-conscious operations in the manufacture of their AS/400 series computers. The output from this plant was remarkably free of the bugs and defects that frequently blemish new products. The company adopted new policies, including a participative team approach to design, modified versions of Toyota's short-cycle product development program, and Motorola's "six sigma" defect-prevention program.

Sometimes it is not possible to organize functional area tasks efficiently because of barriers that are beyond the control of management. For example, the most efficient manufacturing system may require a scale of operation that far exceeds the organization's production needs or is simply too expensive to set up. Or the most efficient marketing system may require the use of distribution channels that are not available to the firm. In such circumstances, managers can design functional area policies that provide support to all functional tasks in an integrated manner.

Integrated support-oriented policies aim at providing integrated functional area support to the business unit. Integration of policies requires designing interdependencies among functional area policies. Integration can be done by clustering policies in related functions. For example, production scheduling, plant personnel allocation, inventory management, plant maintenance, and plant safety are related functions. Policies dealing with these functions should be clustered as one set of interrelated policies. Policy integration should simplify the achievement of business unit strategies. For example, if the firm's strategy is to come out with a rapid succession of new products through internal product development, then there should be explicit new product development policies that aggressively promote this objective. On the other hand, if the firm is pursuing a least-cost strategy, production policies should reflect the requirements of this strategy.

5.8   ECOLOGICAL AND SOCIAL STRATEGIES

Ecological Strategies

Ecological strategies articulate the firm's position vis-à-vis the natural environment; they define the firm's relationship with nature. They describe strategies for use of environmental resources and acceptable environmental impacts of the company's activities. Ecological strategies try to minimize long-term environmental damages by managing the company's inputs, throughputs, and outputs. Just as "total quality management" in corporations demands attention to each stage of the design and production process, a "total environmental management" perspective can optimize the performance of the total system (Imai, 1986).

The life-cycle framework provides a holistic approach for developing ecological strategies. Identifying inputs, throughputs, and outputs helps prevent the shifting of impacts from one medium to another (e.g., from air to solid waste). Furthermore, life-cycle analysis can prevent the transfer of environmental impacts and health risks among the different stages in a product's or service's life by extending the system boundaries to include all aspects of product development, production, use, and retirement. Thus, total environmental management facilitates the integrated examination of product choice, product design, production process, and waste management practices.

Inputs. Every organization requires materials and energy as inputs to its production process. Primary industries such as mining, forest products, pulp and paper, and oil and gas are particularly oriented toward extraction and utilization of raw materials. Secondary (manufacturing) industries such as steel, construction, automobiles, and petrochemicals are important users of materials and energy. Service industries (e.g., health care, education, legal, consulting, etc.) make fewer demands for materials but use significant amounts of energy.

Environmental concerns about depletion of forests and other natural resources, loss of biodiversity, and pollution created by mining and use of fossil fuels suggest the guiding principle of **sustainable resource use**. The basis for this principle is recognition that the earth's resources are finite and that economic growth based on material consumption is limited by this fact. Organizations cannot continue indefinitely to use natural resources without providing for their renewal. *Corporations should seek to minimize the use of virgin materials and nonrenewable forms of* *energy*. This goal can be achieved by reducing the use of energy and materials through conservation measures, making greater use of recycled or renewable materials and energy, and offsetting consumption with replenishment.

The practical possibilities in resource and energy conservation are immense, and companies are already developing innovative programs to achieve them. For example, the National Audubon Society's new headquarters building in Washington, D.C. will cut the society's use of energy by 40% through solar architectural design, use of energy-efficient lighting fixtures, and conservation-oriented programs for maintainance and energy use. Herman Miller no longer uses virgin timber in its top lines of furniture, turning instead to wood grown on a sustained-yield basis. Finally, Applied Energy Services, an independent power generator, paid to plant 52 million trees to offset the 15 million tons of carbon dioxide expected to be emitted over the life of a newly constructed coal-fired power plant.

Throughputs. The production processes of goods and services often create emissions and effluents that have undesirable environmental and health consequences. In other cases, poor reliability or system malfunctions lead to spills, accidents, and or unintended consequences. Poorly designed throughput processes lead to occupational and public health risks as well as inefficient use of material and human resources.

Ecological strategies seek to eliminate emissions, effluents, and accidents. Through preventive action and continuous improvement at every step of the production process, companies can aim for zero discharge and zero risk. This preventive approach is more efficient than controlling discharges at the "end of the pipe." For example, Dow Chemical's new ethylene plant in Fort Saskatchewan, Canada, has been designed to minimize discharges. It will release only 10 gallons of waste water per minute, compared with 360 gallons for traditional plants.

Throughput process improvement makes good business sense and is a natural extension of the quality management programs installed in most companies during the past two decades. Indeed, corporations are realizing that throughput process improvement can be a cost-saving and even revenue-generating activity. Evidence of this is provided by 3M's Pollution Prevention Pays (3P) program, Dow Chemical's Waste Reduction Always Pays (WRAP) program, and Chevron's Save Money and Reduce Toxics (SMART) program. Each of these programs is a significant revenue and profit generator for its company.

Indeed, 3M saved nearly $500 million and prevented 500,000 tons of pollution between 1975 and 1989 through its 3P program. The program is based on pollution reduction at the source through product reformulation, process modification, equipment redesign, and recycling and reuse of materials. Each project undertaken by the 3P program must meet four criteria: eliminate or reduce pollution, save energy or materials and resources, demonstrate technological innovation, and save money. An example of a 3P project is an effort to redesign a resin spray booth. The previous design produced about 500,000 pounds of overspray annually, which had to be incinerated in special facilities. The new design cost an additional $45,000 in equipment, but it reduced the amount of resin used by 125,000 pounds per year. Another project in the pharmaceutical division of the company developed a water-based coating for tablets as a substitute for a solvent coating. The change cost $60,000, but it eliminated the need to install $180,000 worth of pollution control equipment. It saved $15,000 per year in material costs and prevented 24 tons per year of air pollution.

Outputs. Product choice and design also have important implications for environmental performance. Products that lack durability or are difficult to repair clearly place greater demand on the resource base for the use of new materials and energy. Furthermore, products that are difficult or expensive to reuse or recycle are destructive to the environment in that they result in unnecessary waste and disposal costs. A sustainable corporation would seek to *minimize the life cycle costs* of its products and services. Life-cycle costing attaches a monetary figure to every impact of a product—disposal costs, legal fees, liability for product harm, loss of environmental quality, and so forth. Product development decisions are then based not only on projected cash flows but also on projected future costs associated with each product design.

Some companies are now using product design and packaging as a basis for building competitive advantage (i.e, unique features of superiority over competitors). BMW, for example, has initiated a "design for disassembly" process, which the company hopes will result in the first fully recyclable car. Mazda Motors also appears committed to developing the world's first "clean" engine, using hydrogen rotary technology, in response to the growing pressure around the world for control of air pollution and reduction of carbon emissions.

Social Strategies

Social strategies deal with nonroutine social strategic issues. They describe the firm's position on specific social concerns. Thus, there may be strategies to meet the social demands of its customers, communities, the public, the environment, and other stakeholders. Other strategies state the company's position on social issues such as race, gender, age, religion, environmental pollution, or illegal drugs. For example, with the outbreak of acquired immunodeficiency syndrome (AIDS) in the early 1980s, many companies have developed policies to deal with this disease in the workplace. These policies describe how employees with AIDS will be treated, employee rights and obligations, sick leave available to employees, and confidentiality of medical records.

Strategic issues that have warranted special policies in the past deal with ethical codes of conduct for managers and social demands on companies. As exemplified by the policy documents included in this text, there are a great variety of policies that cover such issues. For example, Donaldson Lufkin & Jenrette, J. C. Penney, and Xerox have explicit ethics policies. Bankers Trust, Merrill Lynch, Salomon Brothers, and most large investment banking firms have policies dealing with employee stock transactions and insider trading. Morgan Stanley and Citibank have policies about drug use. Most companies have policies dealing with equal employment opportunities, sexual harassment, and consumer and employee safety.

In this chapter we discussed the content of corporate, business unit, functional area, and ecological and social strategies. We considered the rational economic, technological, and commercial factors that affect strategic choices. But in addition to these rational considerations, there are many behavioral, ethical, and social factors that moderate the choice of strategies. In the next chapter we turn to these issues. We will examine how behavioral processes influence the outcome of strategic decision making. We will also see how ethics and personal values of managers play a central role in strategy making.

SUMMARY OF CHAPTER 5

Strategy formulation occurs at the corporate, business unit, and functional area levels. The *content* of different types of strategies varies at each level. Corporate level strategies determine the product market domain of the firm. They determine the types of businesses and the level of diversity in the firm's business portfolio. Firms commonly pursue three types of corporate strategies. Dominant product strategy limits a firm's domain to a single product; it thus has high risk. Related diversification strategy refers to operating in several related product markets. The conglomerate strategy involves managing many, diverse, unrelated businesses. Formulating corporate strategy involves choosing businesses that will form a balanced business portfolio. The business portfolio matrix provides a useful framework for comparing the relative merits and demerits of different businesses as part of the corporate portfolio.

At the business unit level, strategies seek to establish sustained competitive advantage. They try to shelter businesses from a turbulent environment. Generic business unit strategies commonly pursued by firms include the least-cost strategy, differentiation strategy, and niche strategy. The choice of business unit strategies depends on structural forces governing industry competition and profitability and the firm's strengths and weaknesses. This choice should also take into account the stage of the product life cycle, previous experience, and the firm's market share and profitability positions. A good business strategy targets clear market opportunities. It is based on distinct competitive advantage. It places the firm in technologically and financially superior positions with respect to competition. It uses the firm's strengths and resources to create sustained superior performance. At the same time, it avoids the firm's weaknesses.

Functional area policies seek to streamline and integrate internal operations and provide guidance on strategic issues. Different policies, such as work policies, efficiency- and quality-oriented policies, and integrated support-oriented policies, guide different functional area tasks.

Ecological and social strategies establish a company's posture toward the natural environment and other societal stakeholders. They are means for making strategies ethical and for earning legitimacy.

READINGS, CASES, AND POLICY DOCUMENTS

The following readings, cases, and policy documents provide additional background material for the concepts discussed in Chapter 5.

Readings

* Hayes, R. and J. Clark, "Why some factories are more productive than others." *Harvard Business Review*, October, 1986.
* Rapaport, A. "Linking competitive strategy and shareholder value analysis." Chapter 3, in *Creating shareholder value: The new standard for business performance.* New York: Free Press, 1986.

Cases

      * Acme Leasing
        Beverly Enterprises
        Boeing Company and de Havilland Aircraft of Canada Ltd.
        Comdisco Disaster Recovery Services International Expansion
      * Genicom Corporation
      * Humana, Inc.
      * ISKRA Power Tools
      * Matshushita Electric Industries
        Mud Island
      * The Southland Corporation— Formulating the Acquisition Strategy
        World Tyre Industry and the Bridgestone Company

POLICY DOCUMENTS

        American Express TRS—The next ten years
      * Chateau Ste. Michel—Corporate Strategy and Business Plan
      * NYNEX

      * indicates particularly appropriate assignments

Strategic Management Process and Book Outline

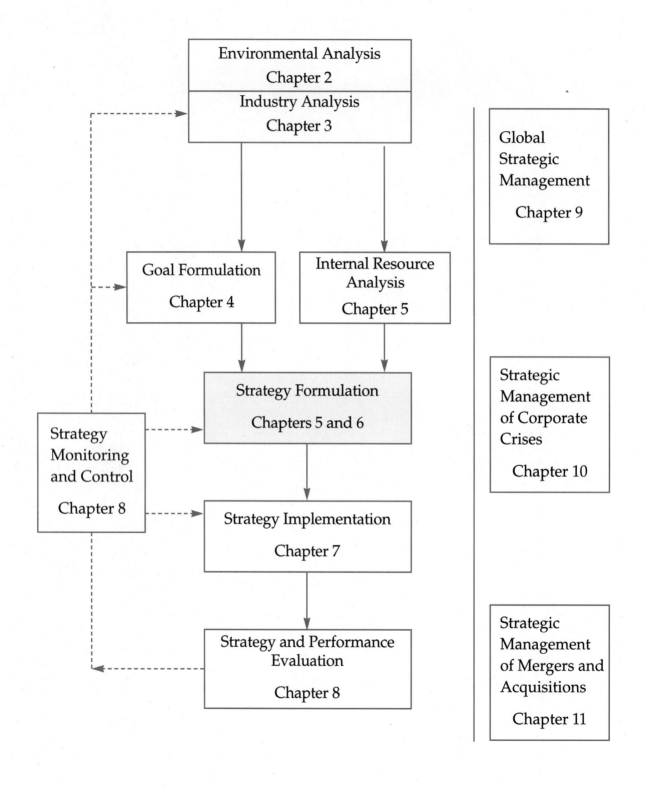

CHAPTER 6
STRATEGY
FORMULATION

CHAPTER OUTLINE

Corporations do not operate in a purely economic environment. Instead, they are influenced by and in turn influence a wider social, cultural, and political reality. Acknowledging this wider role of corporations in our lives requires a more comprehensive consideration of noneconomic variables in strategy formulation. A predominantly economic view of strategy is narrow and does not conform to current practice of strategic management.

In practice, the economically rational strategy formulation discussed in the previous chapter is tempered by noneconomic considerations of business ethics and corporate social responsibilities. In addition, the personal values of key managers and a variety of social, behavioral, and political processes within organizations influence strategy making. In this chapter, we examine ethical and social issues pertinent to strategy and discuss behavioral aspects of strategy making.

The ethical and social responsibilities of corporations arise from the simple fact that corporations serve multiple stakeholders. In Chapter 2 we discussed these stakeholders as including stockholders, employees, customers, suppliers, the public, government agencies, and the media. Each stakeholder has different stakes in the corporation and demands different outputs from it. Corporate management is responsible to these stakeholders. It has the obligation of balancing competing demands of stakeholders and providing an acceptable level of performance to each stakeholder group. In doing so, managers often run into dilemmas about ethical and social responsibilities. They must manage the behavioral and political processes that arise as a consequence. This process is depicted in Figure 6.1.

6.1   ETHICAL ISSUES IN STRATEGY FORMULATION

Several scandals involving questionable ethical practices by corporations rocked the business world in the 1980s. Examples of these include the fraudulent overcharging of government by major defense contracting firms like General Dynamics and Rockwell International. Prestigious investment banking and brokerage firms (e.g., Drexel Burnham Lambert, E. F. Hutton, and Salomon Brothers) committed insider trading and stock manipulation violations. Corporate crimes committed in the 1980s included widespread fraud in the savings and loan industry, laundering of illegal money by banks, and unsafe dumping of toxic wastes by chemical and waste disposal firms. In each of these areas, there are inadequate regulations over business activities, and corporate activities lie in the gray area between legal and illegal. Such incidents have brought to the forefront the need for corporate executives to consider the ethical aspects of their firm's decisions and strategies. Public agencies and the media have started questioning practices and scrutinizing corporations on their ethical performance.

The Realm of Ethics

Ethics, or moral philosophy, in business, deals with matters of right and wrong, good and bad. Business decisions are not simply efficient or inefficient, or effective or ineffective; they are also "good" or "bad" in a moral sense. Making ethical decisions requires that managers go beyond traditional economic, technological, and sociopolitical criteria and make evaluations based on *ethical* criteria. Decision making can be simplified if managers have a framework for understanding ethical issues. Also, the organization must have a decision-making process that allows ethical considerations to influence strategic decisions.

The examination of ethical issues can be done at three levels: individual, organizational, and societal, as shown in Figure 6.2. At the individual level, the preferences of individuals determine ethics. What is good for the individual in question is considered ethical. The ethical doctrines of Plato and the Epicureans have advocated that a person ought to act in ways to achieve the greatest good and least bad results for himself or herself. This form of ethical egoism, with its emphasis on self-interest, is at the heart of the capitalist economic system. More recently, the doctrines of individualism, libertarianism, and existentialism have suggested a similar ethic, even if in a less materialistic form. Their idea of ethics involves seeking personal freedom, self-realization, and personal virtue through authenticity and personal integrity. The self as the owner and mediator of moral values remains the key to individualistic ethics.

Conceptualized at the organizational (or group) level, ethics involves acting in ways that maximize benefits to the widest community (organization or group) affected by an action. The most complete articulation of this doctrine is utilitarianism, which was advocated by Jeremy Bentham and John Stuart Mill. Benevolence toward others is a hallmark of utilitarianism. A variety of ethical

Figure 6.1 *Ethics, Values, and Social Responsibilities in Strategy Formulation*

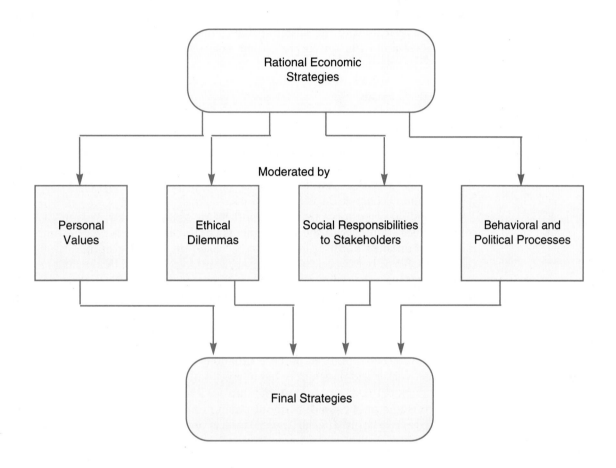

Figure 6.2 *Ethical Tensions: Individual, Organizational, and Societal*

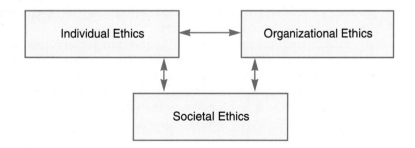

concepts, such as social justice, fairness, equity, the greater good, and altruism, originate from this collective notion of ethics.

The focuses on self and on others represent ends of a continuum of ethical orientations. Between these ends, are several dualist conceptions of ethics that attempt to relate self to the larger society. For example, the premise that individuals have a need to universalize their free will is the basis of Kant's view of ethics. Ethical acts should reflect a will that would be acceptable as universal law. Being ethical requires treating humanity (self and others) always as an end and never as just a means.

Ethical Conflicts

The dilemma of ethical decision making in business settings arises out of the tensions or conflicts between what is good for individuals, organizations, and society. These conflicts manifest themselves in rules that govern organizational behavior and in concrete decision situations.

Individual versus organizational conflicts are apparent when personal values of employees conflict with the requirements organizational tasks. For example, a junior accountant's audit opinion may be based on ethical grounds. It may be rejected by his or her superiors who do not want to relinquish the business of the client by giving a negative opinion. A salesperson may consider the company policy of giving large discounts or personal gifts to selected customers to attract their business unfair and unethical. A marketing executive may object to company advertisements on the grounds that they are not truthful. Similarly, a production worker may object, on religious grounds, to a company's work policies that require working on the Sabbath. Each of these situations raises an ethical dilemma for the individual worker and puts him or her in an ethical conflict with the organization.

Conflicts between organizational and societal interests arise when corporations consume public goods without paying for them or when they sell goods that may have harmful effects. These conflicts are most common in the areas of environmental pollution and community protection from technological and product hazards. For example, toxic waste disposal practices that are not yet regulated by law may be harmful to the natural environment. International transfer of nuclear waste to poor African countries is a case in point. Many countries, such as Benin in Africa, can more than double their annual gross national product by accepting nuclear waste from advanced industrial countries. Locating of hazardous facilities in communities and manufacturing defective products or products with harmful side effects may be other common sources of organizational-societal ethical conflicts.

Ethical conflicts between individuals and society arise when individuals acting in narrow self-interest harm collective interests. Trading stocks on privileged information is a victimless crime that is detrimental to the collective interests of stockholders and erodes confidence in the financial markets. As businesses have become international, we have seen the emergence of ethical conflicts between societies that follow different ethical standards. For example, giving bribes to officials to expedite work is ethically and legally unacceptable behavior in the United States. In many countries, however, it is an institutionalized business practice to give gifts and bribes to ease the conduct of business deals. Without such facilitation, it is impossible to conduct business. When American companies do business in these countries they face the dilemma of which country's ethical and legal standards to adopt.

Dealing with ethical conflicts requires that companies establish and communicate ethical standards to their employees. They must create decision-making procedures for resolving ethical conflicts. Conflict resolution should involve an explicit set of ethical criteria for making legitimate choices. Today, many companies are instituting ethics programs that provide information on ethical problems managers are likely to face. Some also provide procedures for resolving ethical conflicts. Broadly, the structure of such programs is as follows:

1. Identify the organizational, technological, and strategic decision areas that have important ethical dimensions. Examples of these areas include dealing with insider information, managing hazardous facilities and wastes, and avoiding job discrimination based on race, gender, ethnicity, or religion.

2. For each of these decision areas, describe a procedure for conducting a *situational analysis* of facts. Such an analysis involves studying the background and history of decisions, identifying the key stakeholders and their stakes, examining decision options and their likely consequences.

3. Analyze the ethical issues involved using an explicit and predetermined set of ethical criteria. Identify the dilemmas and tensions they pose. Examine moral conflicts, costs-benefits, and accountability-responsibility issues related to the decision.

4. Choose a *resolution strategy* for dealing with the dilemmas and conflicts. The choices available to managers are acting on personal ethical values and taking responsibility for consequences, compromising personal ethics with organizational and societal demands, and broadening participation in decision making by inviting other perspectives into the process.

5. Discuss the approach to resolution with relevant peers, superiors, and subordinates.

6. Implement the resolution strategy by bringing necessary resources to bear on the situation. These resources could take the form of personal courage, organizational resources, and new decision makers. Implementation also involves learning from the situation and codifying lessons for future use.

Examples of ethics programs at Xerox and Donaldson Lufkin Jenrette are given in the Company Policy Documents section of this book.

6.2   CORPORATE SOCIAL RESPONSIBILITY AND STRATEGY FORMULATION

The tensions between corporate and societal interests is a hot topic of debate in the business literature under the heading of corporate social responsibility. The essential question is, Do corporations have broader social responsibilities beyond their economic mandates? If they do, then how can these responsibilities be acknowledged and fulfilled through firm strategies? There are many opinions on these questions. One dominant opinion holds that corporations are primarily economic entities whose sole purpose is to increase shareholder wealth by producing and selling goods needed by customers (Friedman, 1962). This conception harbors a narrow economic view of a corporation's responsibility to society. In contrast is the view that corporations have grown to such large size and complexity that they affect many noneconomic aspects of society. These areas include health, politics, culture, and social relations. Therefore, corporations should be held responsible for these noneconomic influences on society (Davis,

1975; Drucker, 1984). These two opposing views have sparked fierce debate in recent years (Sethi and Steidlmeir, 1989; Steiner and Steiner, 1985). Table 6.1 summarizes the debate on whether corporations should have only economic responsibilities or broader social responsibilities.

There is no unambiguous resolution of this debate. On the balance, however, it seems reasonable to expect businesses to be sensitive to the new demands placed on it by society and be responsive to them. It is also clear that the resolution of this debate depends largely on individual personal values. In my view, power and responsibility have a reciprocal relationship. The scope and power of corporations to influence all aspects of social life, and their symbiotic relationship to society, impose on corporations broad social responsibilities. Understanding and fulfilling these responsibilities through strategic management of firms is the issue we turn to next.

Table 6.1 *Debate on Corporate Social Responsibility*

Position	Reasons
Corporations have broad responsibilities toward a variety of societal stakeholders.	1. It is in the long-run interest of business to be responsive to a wide range of societal demands. 2. It gives business legitimacy to operate and draw resources from society. 3. It improves the public image of business to be seen as being sensitive to societal needs. 4. By taking voluntary responsibilities to prevent harm to society, businesses can avoid governmental regulation of their activities. 5. Society expects business to provide more than just profits and products; it expects business support for important social programs. 6. Business cannot function by satisfying only stockholders because business has multiple stakeholders (government, communities, labor, public interest groups, etc.). 7. Business is the only institution that has the resources to solve many social problems. 8. Involvement in social programs may lead to new profit opportunities.
The only responsibility of business is to make profits and maximize its stockholders' wealth.	1. Assumption of social responsibilities detracts business from its primary purpose of maximizing profits. 2. Business organizations lack the skills to manage social programs and should not get involved in them. 3. Social programs are costly for business; they can make businesses noncompetitive. 4. Private business lacks accountability to the public and should not get involved in public social programs. 5. Business should be prevented from involvement in social programs, because it already wields too much power in society. 6. There is conflict of interest between the private profit goals of businesses and public-good goals of social programs.

Areas of Social Responsibility

Even though corporate responsibility for increasing the wealth of stockholders is well recognized, other social responsibilities are only beginning to be accepted. Below is a brief list of the many areas in which corporations have acknowledged their social responsibility and established programs to deal with them.

- Responsibility for *protecting the natural environment* includes judicious use of natural resources, energy conservation, limiting polluting emissions, and waste management.
- Responsibility toward *consumers* includes creating safe products and packages, educating consumers on product use and disposal, being truthful in advertising, and establishing a procedure for dealing with consumer complaints.
- Responsibility toward *employee welfare* includes providing fair compensation and benefits and safe work environments, eliminating discrimination, providing opportunities for personal and professional development, and having progressive human resource policies.
- Responsibilities toward *local, state, and federal government agencies* include fulfilling obligations under regulations and statutes of these agencies, cooperating in planning and investigations, and coordinating administrative activities with these agencies.
- Responsibilities to the *public or communities* where the corporation has operations include providing economic stability, safeguarding public safety, protecting the environment, and aiding in the development of social and cultural resources of the community through corporate philanthropy.
- Responsibilities toward the *media* include being cooperative and truthful about issues that affect public welfare.

One way to deal with these responsibilities is to establish internal procedures for forecasting strategic social issues. The company may then institutionalize social responsibility as a regular organizational function and develop socially responsible strategies.

Procedures for Dealing with Social Responsibilities

Forecasting Strategic Social Issues. In each area of social responsibility, managers need to forecast the emergence and life cycle of strategic social issues. This can be done by instituting an issues management program in the company. Issues management refers to early identification, tracking, and resolution of strategic issues that could affect the company. By considering emerging strategic issues early, firms have the opportunity to shape strategies as they become important to the firm and put them on their strategic agenda (Chase, 1984; Dutton, 1988). An example of effective management of a strategic issue was Polaroid's early assessment in the 1970s of South Africa's apartheid policy and its impact on American businesses. The company initiated internal programs to deal with apartheid and its influences on internal race relations before it became an explosive issue in the 1980s. It promoted black managers to high managerial positions in its South African business and supported black enterprises in the United States and in South Africa.

Organizing for Social Responsibility. If socially responsive behavior is to be seriously and consistently encouraged within organizations, it cannot be left up to the personal preferences of individual managers. It must be institutionalized with appropriate organizational authority and resources. Managerial roles and functions must be defined that are in charge of monitoring social performance of the firm and ensuring that it fulfills its diverse responsibilities toward its stakeholders.

Some firms have institutionalized social responsibility by creating a new position of corporate responsibility officer or a public affairs function. These positions have senior ranking officers who work full time on all social issues facing the firm. Other firms have expanded their public/external affairs, or even strategic planning, departments to include the function of monitoring social issues.

Socially Responsible Strategies. A question of central interest here is, How can corporations formulate **socially responsible strategies**? How can companies assure that corporate domain choice strategies and competitive strategies are responsive to social needs and do not harm the public interest? There are two basic approaches to dealing with these questions.

First is to evaluate the social merits of each corporate and business strategy selected based on financial, technological, and market criteria. For each strategy, one could ask these questions: What social good does the strategy contribute? Does the strategy create any public risks or harm? Does the strategy harm the interests of our stakeholders? How does the strategy affect public image and goodwill? Will the strategy lead us into social controversies? The answers to these questions can aid in modifying strategies to fit reasonable demands. The idea is not to abandon strategies that have even the slightest negative consequences, but to consider these consequences explicitly in an attempt to develop balanced strategies (McGuire, Lundgren, and Schneeweis, 1988).

A second approach to developing socially responsive strategies is adopting specific strategies toward all key stakeholders of the firm (Freeman, 1984). Such strategies pursue multiple stakeholder objectives rather than simple profitability objectives. They are sensitive and responsive to the demands of all constituencies that provide the organization with opportunities and resources for success. Conflicting demands of stakeholders are carefully balanced. While acknowledging that a primary responsibility of the company is to increase shareholder wealth, stakeholder strategies also must acknowledge responsibilities toward externalities—customers, suppliers, employees, business associates, communities, media, and government.

Specific stakeholder strategies and programs may be developed to meet stakeholder demands (e.g., see document on NCR stakeholder strategies in the Company Policy Documents section of this book). This requires listening to stakeholders, taking their needs into account, and letting their perspectives inform organizational decisions. It involves getting inputs from stakeholders, weighing them, and making decisions that are best for the whole business. It does not mean giving in to all stakeholder demands or reaching stakeholder consensus on all decisions.

Stakeholder analysis begins with identification of who they are. It involves understanding their stakes in the organization, their sources of influence, and their size and power. The history of relations with stakeholders and specific organizational decisions in which the stakeholders have the greatest interest are also important considerations. Stakeholder needs and perspectives should be sought and incorporated into strategies.

Social Responsibility Regulations. Over the past twenty years, establishment of a variety of regulations and regulatory agencies has ensured that corporations meet at least their minimal social responsibilities. Along with the various departments of the government (Commerce, Defense, Energy, Health and Human Services, Interior, etc.), the following federal agencies and their regulations address all the areas of social responsibility identified in this section:

Consumer Product Safety Commission
Environmental Protection Agency
Equal Employment Opportunity Commission
Federal Aviation Administration
Federal Communications Commission
Federal Emergency Management Agency
Federal Trade Commission
Food and Drug Administration
General Accounting Office
Interstate Commerce Commission
Mining Enforcement and Safety Commission
National Highway Safety Administration
Nuclear Regulatory Commission
Occupational Safety and Health Administration
Office of Consumer Affairs
Office of Federal Contract Compliance Programs
Office of Technology Assessment
Securities and Exchange Commission

There are literally thousands of laws at local, state, and federal levels that address public health and environmental protection concerns. Most large corporations have senior managers (or entire departments) in charge of the government relations function. Their responsibilities include ensuring compliance with all relevant regulations, confirming that all necessary information is filed with designated agencies, and participating in shaping of regulations that affect the company.

Besides issues of ethical and social responsibility, behavioral, social, and political decision-making processes profoundly influence strategy making. Social interactions among managers, departments, and divisions and the confluence of many competing internal interests shape the content of strategies. In the next section we discuss these influences on strategy formulation.

6.3   STRATEGY FORMULATION PROCESSES AND BEHAVIORS

Until now we have discussed strategy formulation as a rational, deliberately planned, intentional activity. In practice, however, there is a significant difference between intended and realized strategies. Realization of part of the intended strategy may not occur because all intentions were not clear or well articulated. Another part of the intended strategy may fail because of failures in strategy implementation. In addition, modification of intended strategies sometimes occurs to fit changed environmental and internal conditions (Mintzberg and Waters, 1985).

A host of behavioral, social, and political factors influence the strategy-making process. Instead of being a comprehensive, planned, and rational process, strategy making can sometimes be disjointed and incremental. Quinn (1980) used the term *logical incrementalism* to describe such processes. Logical incrementalism acknowledges that organizational goals are complex, changing, and unclear. It involves artfully blending formal analysis, behavioral techniques, and power politics to move organizations toward broadly conceived goals. In this process, strategy formulation and implementation are not separate; rather, they are integrated into a single-decision making process.

Indeed, this view of strategy making is consistent with reality in many corporations where the flow of decision activities often tends to be nonsequential, fragmented, and somewhat haphazard. Local exigencies interrupt decision-making interactions, which causes decisions to be designed for satisfaction rather than optimization (Fredrickson, 1986; Quinn, 1980). By acting logically and incrementally, managers can improve the quality of information used in critical decisions, overcome personal and political pressures resisting strategic changes, and deal with varying lead times and sequencing problems. They also can help build consensus and support for key decisions and create enthusiasm and psychological commitment to chosen strategies.

Quinn advocates the cautious use of logical incrementalism over the comprehensive rational planning suggested earlier in this book and in most other strategy textbooks. He believes that it is more realistic and that it allows firms to be flexible and opportunistic. It keeps sensitive strategic information within control of key decision makers. It allows managers to seek and incorporate new environmental information continually into strategic decisions.

To get a better appreciation of how strategy-making processes work, we now turn our attention to the behaviors of the managers who make strategies. Behaviors can be studied under the rubric of the **strategic decision-making process**. Figure 6.3 depicts the strategic decision-making process in terms of (1) problem familiarization activity, (2) solution development activity, and (3) decision outcome and implementation.

The process begins with identification of strategic problems. Strategic problems are ill-structured, multifaceted, and not easily apparent. Their identification or formulation is time consuming. Managers try to familiarize themselves with all facets of the problem. During this familiarization phase, several different views of the problem may be formulated (Mintzberg, Raisinghani, and Theoret, 1976). Embedded in each view of the strategic problem is an incipient solution to the problem. Over time, one view of the problem-solution (the P-S set) emerges as the dominant view. Refinement of the problem statement and solution occurs during the solution development phase of the process. During this phase, technical and financial analysis are necessary, and evaluation of several feasible alternative courses of action occurs. One acceptable alternative is chosen for implementation. Acceptability of the solution depends on rational economic criteria as well as personal, social, and political criteria. Because strategic decisions are complex, many internal and external influences affect the choice of solutions. Strategic decision making requires the involvement of both line managers from various divisions and business units and staff from the planning department. Top management performs the final ratification of the decision. The final outcomes of this process include specific decisions and policies that provide a general approach to accomplishing them.

The general process just described follows different patterns in different organizations. The patterns depend on the organization's resources, size, culture, personalities, and structure. On the one extreme, strategies may be dictated by a single top manager, such as the CEO. These strategies may reflect the CEO's personal whims and fancies. On the other extreme, strategies may evolve out of a process of negotiation among key stakeholders both inside and outside the

Figure 6.3 *Strategic Decision-making Process*

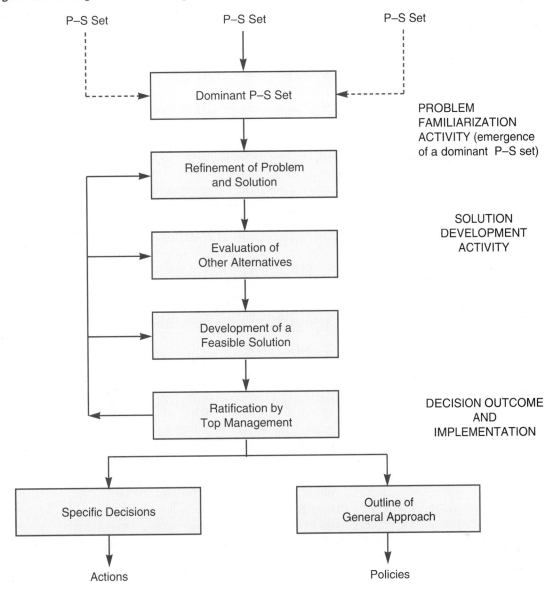

P–S = problem–solution

organization. Between these two extremes, there are many variations in which strategy formulation could occur. Several researchers have identified four common patterns of strategy formulation (Mintzberg, Raisinghani, and Theoret, 1976; Quinn, 1980; Shrivastava and Grant, 1985).

The four patterns are described here as four types of strategic decision-making processes. They represent different modes of strategy making and provide a more refined way of understanding strategic decision-making processes. It is quite possible that within an organization, different decisions follow different decision-making processes or a combination of two or more processes. These processes are the autocratic decision process, bureaucratic decision process, adaptive planning process, and political decision process.

Autocratic Decision Process

The autocratic decision process refers to situations in which a single manager is the key decision maker. His or her role and influence in every phase of decision making is significant. It is quite common to find young or small entrepreneurial firms exhibiting this mode of strategy making. In this situation, a great amount of power and authority rests with a single executive who makes all strategic decisions personally with technical assistance from subordinates. This executive usually is the entrepreneur-manager.

The key manager dominates the problem familiarization process. He or she generates and supports the problem-solution set that ultimately gains organizational acceptance. The key manager is formally in charge of the solution-building activity. Although technical and financial experts may help in evaluating alternatives by providing relevant information, they typically work under the guidance and supervision of the key manager. Due to the limited time available to the manager, and because of cognitive limitations on processing information, evaluation of alternatives lacks detail. The manager typically functions with imperfect information.

The final choice of alternatives occurs in consultation with, or at least after informing, relevant superiors, peers, and subordinates. The key decision maker channels and controls all the information used in decision making. The manager attempts to analyze all the facts available to him or her rationally and then makes a decision while maintaining full responsibility for its consequences.

The time taken under such decision-making situations is usually very short. In situations where the data involved is sensitive or secret, this model may be the only available alternative for the organization to follow. This is so because it effectively limits the distribution of sensitive information. The key manager who controls decision making is usually a member of the top-management team or a very senior middle-management person who has the confidence of the top management. Key managers are strong and influential individuals who have proven their competence in their organizations.

Organizations in which autocratic decision making commonly occurs vary in size and structure. They usually possess poorly developed management systems and management teams, so they depend heavily on individuals for making strategic decisions. The style and preferences of the decision maker in charge bias both the decision-making process and decision outcomes. Systems, procedures, or accumulated learning and experience of the organization as a whole do not influence them. Therefore, even if such an organization has previous experience in the given decision area, this knowledge does not get incorporated into the decision-making process (assuming that the decision maker does not solicit it).

Once an organization grows beyond the capacity of a single autocratic leader, its strategic decision-making process becomes more systematic and regulated. The bureaucratic decision process and the adaptive planning process present two ways in which strategy making may get systematized.

Bureaucratic Decision Process

As the name suggests, the bureaucratic decision process has an orientation that leans toward existing rules, systems, and procedures rather than toward individuals as in the autocratic decision process. Problem familiarization involves creating several alternative formal statements of the strategic problem and its solution. Individuals at different functional areas of the organization propose these. The official files of the organization document these initial problem formulations. Over time, construction of one statement of the problem occurs, and it is a combination of the original set of suggested problems. The problem formulation is often influenced by environmental forces (customers, suppliers, government agencies, and competitors) that have a stake in the decision. Environmental pressures tend to speed up the organization's problem formulation process by providing relevant information and urging decision makers to overcome bureaucratic systems that delay the decision.

After the formulation of the problem, a predetermined routine of procedures are followed in problem solving. There are well-defined and documented stepwise procedures for handling all decisions. These procedures may not be adequate or efficient ways of solving the problem, but since problems reach resolution, the organization is content with the resulting solution. Evaluation of alternatives is extensive and detailed. The company puts technically qualified persons in charge of developing feasible solutions. The evaluation procedure includes technical evaluation, financial evaluation, cost-benefit analysis, and implementation planning. At each step of the evaluation process, the decision makers attempt to fulfill the written policies of the organization. There is heavy emphasis on impersonal, rational, objective, and quantitative analysis.

Analysis leads to the selection of one specific alternative, which is presented to top management as the best available option. The ratification of this choice by top management is a critical event. It legitimizes the decision and sanctions formal authority for its implementation. In these situations, formal sanctions are the basis for initiating action. Without the written sanction of the board of directors or some such powerful body, the decision cannot be completed. Even after the sanction, the organization has to go through several months of paperwork formalities to complete the decision making.

The most conducive organizational settings for the bureaucratic decision processes are large, established, private firms or public-sector enterprises. Management systems in these organizations are highly developed, complex, and overlapping. They may not be the most sophisticated or modern systems available, but they serve functional objectives. These systems are predetermined organizational procedures for information sharing and communication. Task forces or committees are used extensively in decision making. Technically qualified personnel from all relevant functional areas of the organization compose the committees. Large, mature companies such as, Citibank, IBM, and GM exhibit some of this bureaucratic style of decision making.

One interesting characteristic of bureaucratic decision processes is that the part of the organization that has the most expertise and knowledge in the decision area receives the decision-making responsibility. Thus, organizational learning and experience easily incorporate themselves into the strategic decision.

The systematization of strategic decision as described can be made less rule driven and more adaptive to environmental demands. Organizations that have done this successfully exhibit adaptive planning processes.

Adaptive Planning Process

The adaptive planning decision-making process is the practical version of what management textbooks describe as formal planning systems. In this model, current decisions flow from previously made decisions. Formal strategic plans become a point of departure for strategic decision making.

The problem familiarization phase is almost nonexistent in such situations, because identification of strategic problems facing the firm happens at the time of formulation of strategic plans. Delegation of problem formulation goes to a specialized planning department, which develops a problem statement and systematically evaluates solution alternatives. It then recommends the planned development of solution activities. Familiarizing other parts of the organization with the problem occurs through regular management reports or annual plans.

The generation and choice of solution are conducted in a systematic manner with a consistent effort toward achieving efficient solutions to the problem. Experts are usually available to evaluate the technical merits of the proposed alternatives. They use many different evaluation procedures that consider technical, financial, and growth needs. Typically, several people from many levels of the organization involve themselves in all phases of the decision-making process.

Such a decision-making process is adaptive and incremental. Formal strategic plans, which serve as the basis for decision making, are used only as guidelines. They may be adopted, modified, or completely dropped, depending on the current analysis of issues. Organizations that exhibit adaptive planning are usually progressive public-sector enterprises or large private-sector firms with good financial performance. They are fast-growing, prosperous firms with professionally trained managers. They possess the resources and the culture required for the development of a planning system. Many Fortune 1000 companies follow this adaptive planning process (e.g., Merck Pharmaceuticals, GE, and Shell Oil).

One limitation of adaptive planning is that it does not encourage managers to seek drastically new, different, or innovative solutions. There is a tendency to follow preestablished plans broadly, with minor modifications to incorporate changing conditions. Therefore, in situations where there is a sudden and severe change in environmental conditions, these organizations are slow to respond. They may have to get permission to change their plans for capital investments from their corporate headquarters, which may be overseas. This a cumbersome and time-consuming activity, which local managers prefer to avoid.

Political Decision Process

Some strategic decisions follow a very different type of logic and process from the three discussed. In the political decision process, several key decision makers or groups of decision makers (departments, divisions, and business units) make decisions for personal or group gain. Protecting or advancing their own interest, even at the cost of organizational interests, is their primary concern (MacMillan and Jones, 1986).

Most strategic decisions made in this political mode have to be justified by the decision makers to the rest of the organization as rational and beneficial for all.

Therefore, even though a coterie of "insiders" make the actual decisions, they put up a facade of extensive rational analysis to legitimize their decision with other organizational members. Conflicts and disputes occur frequently in such situations, and negotiations among managers must settle them. The problem familiarization and solution development activities under this process could be made to look bureaucratic or planned, depending on which best fits the situation. This means that although interest-group concerns drive actual decision making, the overt actions of problem formulation, generation, evaluation, and choice of alternatives follow organizationally acceptable routines.

The decision makers are generally senior middle-management or top-management personnel with expertise in the decision area. The organization critically depends on these people for strategic activities. These managers form coalitions that orchestrate the decision process to their joint advantage. Coalitions also may be formed by organizational managers joining up with environmental agents, such as suppliers, bankers, government representatives, and labor unions. The final decision is primarily in the interest of the individuals involved in making it and only secondarily in the organization's interest. Such political decision making commonly occurs in large organizations where there is high dispersement of power among managers. Management systems and procedures exist, but managers have learned how to avoid these systems to promote their own interests. Group decision making is a norm; committees, task forces, and evaluation teams are common.

There are advantages and disadvantages to each of the four decision-making processes described in this section. The bureaucratic and adaptive planning processes are more time consuming, analytical, and expensive. The autocratic and political modes are more arbitrary, and somewhat irrational, but less time consuming. None of the four modes of decision making is inherently superior to others in terms of actual strategic performance (Gray, 1986).

The descriptions of decision-making processes can be used to diagnose and understand strategy making in firms. Managers can create facilitative information systems and administrative procedures to support decision making.

This chapter discussed the ethical, social responsibility, and behavioral considerations in strategy formulation. These considerations complement the rational, economic, and technological considerations discussed in Chapter 5. Together these two chapters give a complete description of issues relevant to strategy formulation. Strategy formulation alone, however, does not guarantee the success of companies. Strategies must be implemented effectively for them to have an economic impact. Implementation means putting strategic ideas into action. It involves changing internal structures and systems to make the strategy work. In the next chapter we turn to the task of strategy implementation.

SUMMARY OF CHAPTER 6

Strategic planning is not simply an exercise in rational economic analysis. Strategies must conform to the ethical and social expectations of the communities in which organizations operate. They must also meet the personal values of top managers. Therefore, strategies should be based on a deep understanding of an organization's ethical and social responsibilities. Ethically and socially responsible strategies earn legitimacy and goodwill for the firm.

In recent years, unethical practices in business firms have brought much negative publicity for business as an institution. Such practices have also led to the creation of many new regulations on businesses. Corporations can win the respect of their stakeholders and reduce regulatory burden by acting in a socially responsible manner through incorporating ethical and social considerations in strategy making.

The organizational processes by which strategies are formulated have profound influence on the content of strategies. These processes are influenced by many behavioral, social, political, and ethical considerations. It is useful to view strategic decision-making processes as consisting of several stages: problem familiarization, solution development, and decision outcome and implementation ratification. This stagewise development of strategies follows certain patterns that may be characterized as autocratic, bureaucratic, adaptive planning, and political. The autocratic process usually occurs in organizations possessing poorly developed management teams. A single manager, usually from top management, significantly influences decision making. These managers work with imperfect information, and outcomes are biased by their styles and preferences. The bureaucratic process is guided by organizational systems and procedures. Heavy emphasis is placed on impersonal and rational analysis and procedural integrity. This type of decision making usually occurs in large, established organizations. The adaptive planning process is less rule driven and more responsive to environmental changes. It does not encourage managers to seek drastically new, different, or innovative solutions. There is a tendency to follow preestablished strategic plans. Organizations that use this decision process react slowly to sudden environmental changes. In the political process, groups of managers make decisions for their own interest or in the interest of their department/division. They use organizationally acceptable procedures to justify their decisions. Each of these decision-making processes requires different types of information and resource support. Managers can use these descriptions of the processes as heuristic devices to identify ways of supporting and rationalizing decision processes in their own organizations.

We have now seen that strategy formulation is neither a purely rational economic process nor a purely social or political process. It combines elements of both these orientations. The resulting strategies represent the best practical choices that managers can make under their given conditions. In the next chapter we will see how these choices can be put into practice.

READINGS, CASES, AND POLICY DOCUMENTS

The following readings, cases, and policy documents provide additional background material for the concepts discussed in Chapter 6.

Readings

* Quinn, J.B. "Formulating strategy one step at a time." Journal of Business Strategy, Winter, 1981, 1(3).

Cases

Baker Medical Center

      Copenhagen Handelsbank
* Exxon Corporation
* Greenpeace v/s Ford: Catalytic converters come to the U.K.
* Manville Corporation
      Turner Broadcasting System
* Union Carbide Corporation
      YKK Inc.

Policy Documents

      American Express TRS—The next ten years
* Donaldson Lufkin Jenrette—Code of Business Ethics
      NYNEX
* indicates particularly appropriate assignment

Figures 6.1, 6.2, 6.3 & Table 6.1.

Strategic Management Process and Book Outline

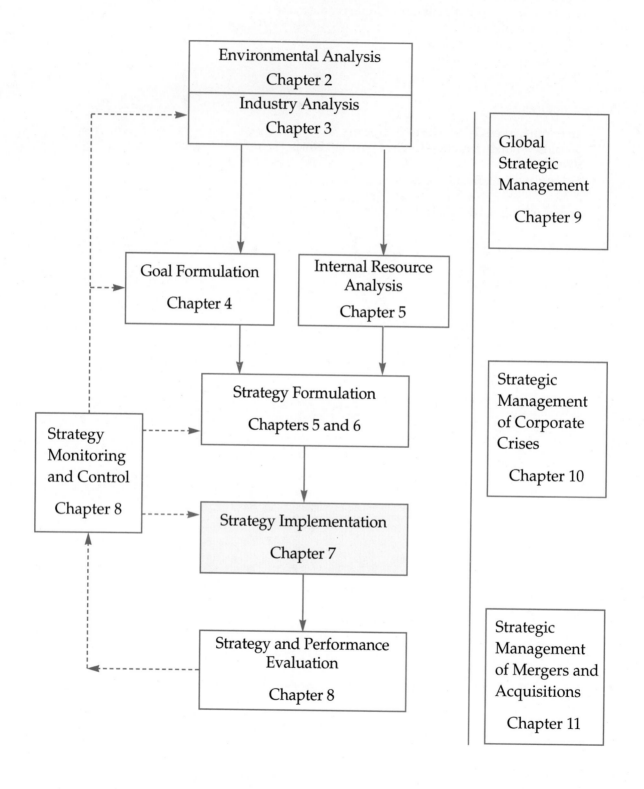

CHAPTER 7
STRATEGY
IMPLEMENTATION

Strategy implementation means putting the strategy to work, or putting it into action. It involves accomplishment of administrative tasks, allocation of necessary resources to strategic programs, and the development of appropriate organizational systems and competencies to support strategic plans.

Even brilliantly formulated strategies with grand designs can fail unless an effective implementation is made. Exxon learned this the hard way in the 1980s. The oil shocks of the 1970s convinced Exxon that the oil business was highly volatile and subject to uncontrollable geopolitical uncertainties. It needed to diversify out of the oil industry. Exxon formulated an astute diversification strategy involving entry into other energy and nonenergy but related, high-growth business areas. This diversification was to be done through acquisitions. Accordingly, it bought Reliance Electric, the manufacturer of electrical equipment. The most interesting product that Reliance produced was an asynchronous motor, which needed less than half the energy consumed by conventional motors. This motor had the potential for reducing the energy needs of many industries that use these motors (e.g., power generators, pumps, compressors, appliances, etc.). It also bought Vydec, an entrepreneurial computer company, and a small software company to enter the rapidly growing computer industry.

Exxon created a good strategy of diversification that met its long-term needs, protected it from the vagaries of foreign oil, and reduced its total risk. However, Exxon implemented its strategy poorly. Top management did not nurture the acquisitions to success. No special attention was paid to them. Exxon did not make any structural or cultural adjustments to fit the administrative and business needs of these very different businesses. Exxon had no experience in the new industries it was entering. It continued to apply the standards, scales, and time frames it used in the oil business to run electrical and computer businesses.

Although synergies in research and production areas justified the acquisition of Reliance, there was no attempt made to integrate the areas. Failure to integrate delayed the development of the asynchronous motor project. This resulted in the eventual failure of this project and consequent souring of the entire merger. A few years after the acquisition, Exxon sold Reliance at a huge loss. Vydec entrepreneurs felt stifled under the bureaucratic time-consuming procedures of Exxon. Key personnel, including the president of Vydec, left within the first year of the acquisition. Only a few years later, Vydec and the software companies were also sold. Failure at implementing its diversification strategy lead Exxon to abandon diversification altogether and revert to being an oil company.

The administrative problem of strategy implementation in firms is to reduce the uncertainty encountered in executing strategies. This is done by rationalizing and stabilizing problem-solving activities in the organization. It involves designing and implementing structures, systems, and processes that enable the organization to give a preprogrammed response to routine problems and to deal innovatively with novel problems. It may require development of new skills and recruiting new personnel. Implementation of radically different strategies might require changes in strategic leadership and corporate culture (Alexander, 1985; Galbraith and Kazanjian, 1986; Hurst, Rush, and White, 1989; Miles *et al.*, 1978).

Strategy implementation is not as well-structured, as rational, or as controlled an activity as strategy formulation is. It involves managing many intangible variables, such as structure, culture, values, motivation, commitment, organizational behavior, and power relationships. The values of the CEO and top management play a particularly important role in implementing strategies.

Good implementation is critical for strategic success. Therefore, it is important to implement strategies systematically. Several organizational variables can be used as levers for implementation. Implementation links strategies with financial performance. Systematic implementation can be accomplished by understanding the extent of strategic change implied by new strategies and the levers or variables that can facilitate change (Brodwin and Bourgeois, 1984; Drazin and Howard, 1984; Johnson, 1988).

7.1   SCOPE AND SCALE OF STRATEGIC CHANGE

New strategies invariably imply strategic changes in a host of areas. If the new strategy represents an incremental change from the past, the task of managing strategy implementation is relatively simple. It could be done through minor modifications in existing systems and structures. For example, a multinational company that already operates in many countries may decide to enter new markets (such as India, China, the former Soviet Union, etc.). It can do so within the existing framework of its internal systems by modifying its existing framework to accommodate entry into these new major markets. On the other hand, if a largely domestic (or regional) company, such as Pacific Telesis, decides to go international, it would have to make far greater strategic adjustments.

The biggest problems in strategy implementation arise when the new strategy represents a radical departure from the past. Such strategies require changes in many parts of the organization. These changes must be made simultaneously at various levels and in various divisions, business units, and functional areas. The changes must also be well coordinated. To manage these changes effectively, managers need to assess their scope and scale. The key is to identify what needs to be changed and what kinds of changes are desirable.

Large-scale organizational change is a difficult and time-consuming process. Organizations contemplating such changes must be prepared to invest time, the attention of top management and financial and human resources to it. For example, the strategic change program at AT&T after its break up into regional operating companies spanned seven years. It cost the company hundreds of millions of dollars to accomplish. The CEO personally oversaw the key strategic changes. If a company cannot make the commitment of such huge resources, it may be better off not to embark on the change rather than to leave it half done. Any large-scale program for strategic change necessarily causes unfreezing and disruption of existing patterns of work, organizational processes, and stable power relationships.

Assessing the scope of changes requires familiarity with all the levels of strategy implementation, which are described next as strategy implementation variables.

7.2 STRATEGY IMPLEMENTATION MODEL AND VARIABLES

Managers can change many organizational variables so as to implement strategies. Peters and Waterman (1980) have suggested that well-performing companies tend to have a good fit between their strategies and other organizational variables such as structures, systems, style, skills, staff, and superordinate goals. Other studies have shown the importance of resources, leadership, culture, measurement of strategic performance, and strategy monitoring (Bower, 1970; Lorange, 1986; Shrivastava and Nachman, 1989).

Figure 7.1 depicts a framework combining these variables. Strategy implementation can be accomplished by changing resource allocations, structures and systems, skills and staff, leadership and culture, and performance evaluation and reward systems. Changes must attempt to match the needs of the new strategies. Changes also must consider the relationships among these variables and their collective influences on strategic performance. The ultimate test of good strategies is in their ability to meet strategic performance goals. Strategic performance may be measured in terms of financial performance, market performance, and progress toward strategic objectives of the firm. An important aspect of implementation is continuous monitoring of the strategy. Deviations from expected performance should be identified early. These deviations should prompt modification of the original strategy.

Figure 7.1 *Strategy Implementation Model*

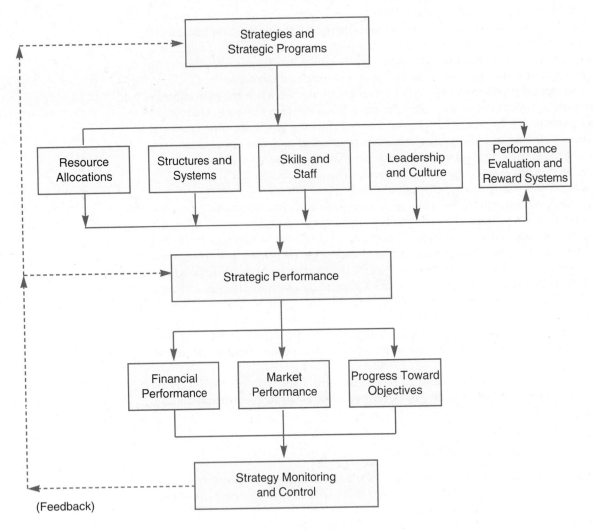

In the rest of this chapter we will examine each variable that is critical for strategy implementation. We will describe how these variables affect strategy implementation and how they may be changed in order to simplify.

7.3   RESOURCE ALLOCATION FOR STRATEGY IMPLEMENTATION

Every strategy requires the organization to undertake new strategic programs. Often, these programs involve development of new products, entry into new markets, capital investments, restructuring of production capabilities, and so forth. Setting up these programs requires allocation of appropriate financial, material, and human resources. The resources must be made available to managers who are in charge of strategy implementation. Figure 7.2 depicts the resource allocation process. Resource allocation is usually done through

Figure 7.2 *Resource Allocation*

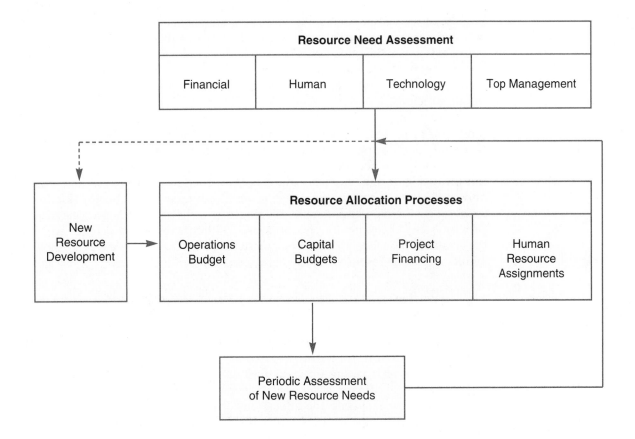

operating and capital budgeting systems, or through ad hoc allocations for projects.

Before any allocations are made, it is important to do a need assessment of strategic programs. This assessment develops accurate estimates of the amount and types of resources required for implementing strategies. Financial techniques of cost-benefit analysis, payback period analysis, discounted cash flow analysis, capital requirements analysis, and capital structure analysis may be useful at this stage. Financial resources often limit resource need assessment and estimation. Limited assessment can lead to strategic failures, because most strategic programs require specialized human, technological, and managerial competencies in addition to financial resources. Organizations must, therefore, assess and estimate the availability of these new competences. Programs for developing these competencies should be made a part of the strategy implementation process.

Unfortunately, some of these competences cannot be acquired simply by investing financial resources. For example, the Finnish company Wartsila OY decided to internationalize itself by buying nearly forty foreign businesses in the early 1980s. It suddenly faced the need to develop skills and competence in international management. It needed a cadre of 250 "international" managers who would go to the acquired unit as the controlling top-management team. Managers would have to be effective in doing business in such diverse locations as Scandinavia, Japan, India, Malaysia, Saudi Arabia, Western Europe, and the United States. These managers could not simply be hired from the market because of the extreme sensitivity of their assignments and Wartsila's corporate value of developing internal talent. Development of this competence could not be solved by just devoting financial resources to it. Instead, it took the company several years of painstaking management training and development, foreign assignments for top management, and the development of an international corporate structure.

One major problem with resource allocation is the impact of inflation on long-term programs. Many strategic programs take three to five years to implement. Inflation during this period might make earlier estimates unrealistic. This is particularly true for projects in foreign countries where inflation is higher and more variable. In many developing countries, such as Argentina, Brazil, Israel, and in Eastern European countries (Poland, Hungary, Czechoslovakia, etc.) inflation can be high and volatile, ranging between 10% to 50% per year. Some provision must be made for ensuring that additional resources, if required, will be available. For foreign projects, fluctuations in exchange rates can have a similar impact on resource requirements (Nutt, 1989).

7.4 ROLE OF STRUCTURE AND SYSTEMS IN STRATEGY IMPLEMENTATION

Organizational structure refers to the pattern of authority and responsibility relationships existing in an organization. Structural development occurs by differentiating or dividing up tasks into doable parts, grouping similar tasks together, and coordinating tasks to achieve organizational objectives. Organizational structures specify the allocation of responsibilities for specific tasks. Organizational tasks are divided based on specialization or special skill requirements. This involves defining roles and allocating responsibility for completing groups of tasks to specific roles (Hax and Majluf, 1981). Organizational charts, or at least the formal part of them, depict the company's organizational structure.

Besides the formal organizational structure, there is an informal structure that defines social relationships, work norms, and cultural practices within the organization. The informal structure supplements the formal structure in defining responsibility and authority distribution in the organization. Organizational structures determine the flow of information through the organization and the extent of centralization or decentralization in decision making. They decide who will have the authority and responsibility to implement strategic tasks. Therefore, it is critical to ensure that an organization's structures meet the needs of its corporate and competitive strategies.

Organizational Structures

There are several different types of organizational structures shown in Figure 7.3. Each is suitable under different situations.

Simple Structure. A small, owner-managed firm with a few employees often uses a simple structure in which everyone reports to the owner. This structure can work effectively if there are a limited number of employees (under

Figure 7.3 *Types of Organizational Structures*

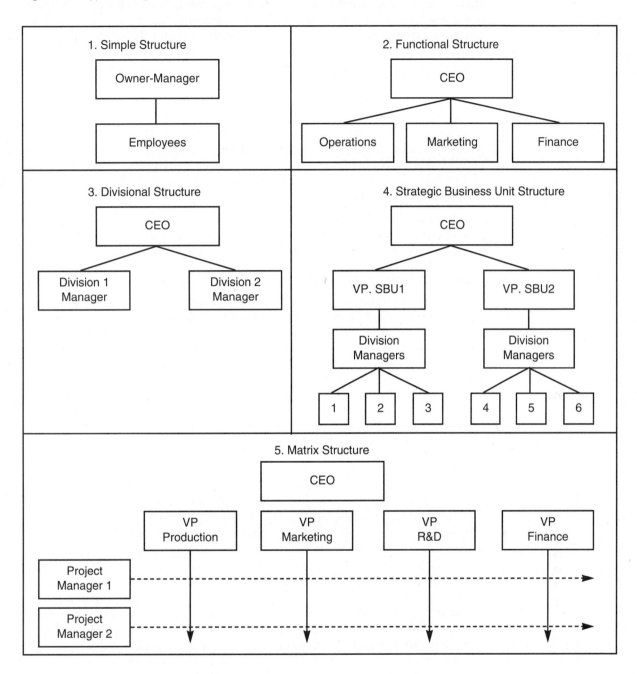

twenty). Its key advantage is that the owner can provide complete supervision over all activities, which limits the cost of supervision. On the other hand, a single person can oversee only a few employees. Even the limit of twenty suggested may be too high. The owner-manager, in such cases, is completely tied down with day-to-day activities and has little time left for doing any long-range planning.

Functional Structure. Traditionally, small businesses have been organized around **functional structures**. Here, task responsibilities are grouped by functional areas, such as production, finance, marketing, and administration. Each functional area may be headed by a vice president, and the president or chief executive (often the owner) does interfunctional coordination. This type of structure has the advantage of differentiating the organization along functional specialities, and by that, making use of specialists. It also keeps the need for coordinating personnel to a bare minimum.

Functional structures are most appropriate for small companies. But some large companies that operate in a well-defined product market in a limited geographic area also could make effective use of such a structure. For example, Weis Markets, a regional food-retailing chain in Pennsylvania, is organized along its key functions: purchasing, marketing/retailing, finance, administration, and real estate management.

Divisional or SBU Structures. Larger organizations that have multiple products and operate in multiple markets often use **divisional or SBU structures**. Divisions represent clusters of similar businesses. Each division or group has several separate and distinct operating businesses. These businesses have clearly identifiable product lines and target markets. Functional structures often make up the organization of individual business units.

Motorola, a large electronics company with $10.8 billion in sales in 1990, provides an example of divisional structure. The company is administratively divided into six divisions, sometimes called groups or sectors: communications sector, semiconductor products sector, general systems sector, information systems group, government electronics group, and automotive and industrial electronics group. Smaller business units compose each sector or group. The communications sector, for example, includes land mobile products and paging telepoint systems. When divisions have too many businesses, companies may combine several divisions into Strategic Business Units or Groups.

Matrix Structure. As firms are becoming increasingly diversified and international, they are experimenting with new structural arrangements. The **matrix structure** has become quite popular. In this structure, there are dual and sometimes triple reporting arrangements that cut across business unit, product, regional area, and subsidiary lines. Managers may report to a functional area boss for functional tasks, a business unit boss for product performance, and perhaps to a regional area boss for regional performance. For example, Union Carbide established dual control over its foreign subsidiaries through a matrix structure. Its pesticide plant in Bhopal, India, reported to the president of the Indian subsidiary, Union Carbide India. It also reported to Union Carbide's Agricultural Products Division for technical, product development, and production issues.

Matrix structures provide more comprehensive control and dual oversight over operations. They are virtually essential for running large, complex, multi-product, multimarket, global companies, and they are used widely. However, they are also susceptible to conflicts arising out of dual loyalties. To minimize these conflicts, some organizations make only one reporting relationship formal, while the others are informal or "dotted line."

Dynamic Networks. Informal, flexible, and changing reporting arrangements called **dynamic networks** also may be used to structure organizational work. They are particularly useful for organizing multiple projects in which tasks are temporary and require quick decision making. Executives organize around a project and stay involved in it until their part is done, then they move on to other projects. For example, GM used such flexible arrangements by pulling together engineers, designers, production personnel, and executives from its Asian, European, and US companies to create teams for designing new cars.

Organizational and Administrative Systems

Organizational and administrative systems support structures. These systems represent routine ways of performing organizational tasks. They provide the necessary information needed for implementing and controlling organizational strategies. Systems represent procedures, both formal and informal, that guide organizational activities. These administrative systems and processes are described next.

Management Information Systems. These are computer-based management information systems that provide a variety of marketing, production, financial, and accounting information to management. The information is used by management to judge operating performance. When performance falls below expectations or objectives, managers make changes in strategy and resource allocations. They seek to control the strategic performance of their control decisions.

Decision Support Systems. These are information systems that support a specific set of strategic decisions. Often, they combine a database with analytical modeling capabilities to allow managers to conduct strategic analysis. For example, Ebasco, a construction and architectural company, designs and constructs nuclear power plants. Each construction project costs several billion dollars and involves managing thousands of tasks and millions of parts in inventory. A computerized decision support system at Ebasco provides managers with online ability to control all parts of the construction project and keep it within time and budgetary limits.

Standard Operating Procedures. The myriad administrative tasks that all organizations perform repeatedly are made routine through standard operating procedures. For example, companies have standard procedures for purchasing, invoicing, requesting leave, issuing notifications, using transportation services, and so on.

Each functional area also has its own administrative systems to streamline and routinize functional area activities. These could include, for example, a performance evaluation and reward system in the human resource area, a financial planning and budgetary system in the accounting and finance areas, an order processing and sales analysis system in the marketing area. These systems are all vital for accomplishing strategic tasks. New strategies might require development of specialized information systems to support implementation.

Matching Strategies with Structures and Systems

Every strategy requires a compatible organizational structure to fulfill its information requirements. It is critical to match organizational structures with firm strategy to ensure effective performance. This fit can be determined by examining the task and information requirements created by strategies. Once specific tasks are identified, they can be put into logical groups. Responsibility for each group of tasks should be allocated to specific individuals. Groups of tasks must be integrated and coordinated by appointing a coordinator (Chandler, 1962).

Organizational structures may be changed by regrouping organizational divisions or units or by appointing new personnel as coordinators of different business units. Often, structures are changed by eliminating positions or adding new ones. Changing organizational systems requires redesigning work procedures. It also may be done by extending or modifying old work procedures.

There are no strict rules for matching strategies with structures. However, in implementing a strategy, managers should assess the adequacy of old structures to meet the information requirements imposed by the new strategy. For example, if a company with only domestic operations adopts a strategy of worldwide diversification, it will require differentiation on tasks as well as geographic regions. A decentralized divisional structure that allows managers in different countries to manage their own local problems without having to consult headquarters may be appropriate (Gupta and Govindarajan, 1984; Miller, 1988).

In today's rapidly changing environment, strategy and structure are in a complex and dynamic relationship. New strategies may require new structures, but structures could also constrain strategies (Hall and Saias, 1980). Effective structures need to be flexible and temporary. They must be responsive to the continuous readjustments to strategy that turbulent environments require. For example, Du Pont abolished its five-member executive committee in a bid to push more responsibility and authority to the lower ranks. For a long time, this committee, consisting of senior insiders, had signified a top-down management style. It acted as a gatekeeper; managers sought its blessing for all important projects. By abolishing the committee, coupled with changing personnel and minimizing departmental boundaries, Du Pont hopes to give much more autonomy to a broad group of executives. It also wants to facilitate a free flow of ideas.

New strategies also can create the need for new administrative and information systems. For example, banks that adopted a strategy of entering the security brokerage business and the insurance industry have had to develop entirely new administrative systems for dealing with these new operations. Similarly, security brokerage firms that have adopted a strategy of entering the banking sector have to develop information systems, reporting systems, and management systems specific to the banking business.

7.5   SKILLS AND STAFF FOR STRATEGY IMPLEMENTATION

Skills refer to the capabilities and dominant attributes of companies that allow them to assume tasks and functions with unique competence. Skills allow firms to perform strategic tasks and give firms unique competitive advantages. New strategies may be crucially dependent on certain skills that the company may not possess. Acquisition of these necessary skills should be part of strategy implementation.

Acquiring Skills

Skills may reside in individual workers employed by the firm, such as the skills of innovative design engineers or the knowledge of consultants and researchers. Alternatively, skills may be embedded in systems and procedures within firms, such as the just-in-time inventory systems and quality management programs in many Japanese companies. Skills also can reside in technological plants, equipment, and procedures. Such skills are often patented to prevent imitation by competitors.

Firms have different skills in different areas. For example, Du Pont has highly developed R&D skills, whereas IBM was known for its customer service capability and marketing prowess. Texas Instruments possesses legendary innovation skills, and ITT's financial control skills are equally well known. Skills allow firms to do specific tasks in unique and efficient ways. Each strategy requires a different set of skills. Moreover, skill requirements change with changing environmental influences. For successful implementation of strategies, the needed skills must be developed if they are not already present in the organization. For example, when AT&T broke up into regional Bell operating companies, each operating company had to develop marketing skills to function in the new, competitive, market environment. Similarly, after the deregulation of the financial services industry, banks had to develop new product management skills and new marketing capabilities to compete in a consolidated financial services industry.

Acquiring and developing skills embedded in people may involve fundamental changes in management of human resources. At the heart of skills acquisition is the process of acquiring, educating, training and retaining employees. Employees must be trained to use new operating systems, to develop new work attitudes and values, and to update their information base. Retaining these employees is critical to maintaining skill levels in the organization. We have seen that Exxon learned that it could not make its Vydec acquisition work once the entrepreneur president left the company with his key research personnel.

Management development and training programs play an important role in enhancing skill and core competencies of corporations. Unfortunately, the human resource department's operating personnel often manage these tasks routinely and inappropriately. A more effective approach to skill development is to have strategy managers articulate a *strategic human resource strategy*. It should clearly illustrate the human resource skills needed for corporate and business strategies. Then, the professionals in the human resources department could be asked to design programs for developing these skills (Fombrun, Tichy, and Devanna, 1983; Lengnick-Hall and Lengnick-Hall, 1988).

Many large American companies, such as GE, IBM, and Citibank have responded to Japanese competition by developing new business skills for doing business with Japan. By providing their managers with language training, exposing them to Japanese business practices and management techniques, and sending them on assignment to Japan, they have developed a cadre of managers who can function effectively in the Japanese environment.

Matching Strategies with Skills and Staff

Creating a fit between strategies and skills and staff involves assessing the skill requirements of the new strategy and then systematically acquiring them. At the corporate level, dominant product strategy and conglomerate strategies require very different skills. Technologically efficient and large-scale production systems, low-cost mass distribution channels, and detailed knowledge of the industry conditions best serve the dominant product strategy. The conglomerate strategy requires efficient financial controls over business subsidiaries, a large capital pool, ability to scan for and acquire businesses, ability to divest or sell assets and businesses, and strategic planning sophistication.

At the level of the business unit, attempt should be to create skills that provide the business a competitive advantage within its industry. This advantage can be in the form of novel products, lower costs, better market positioning, technological superiority, financial flexibility, efficient production and delivery system, and so forth. Usually, the business strategies of least cost, differentiation, and niche require different sets of skills. For example, business units adopting least-cost strategies will require skills in mass production and distribution, automation, efficient vendor management, and efficient management of limited working capital. A niche strategy, on the other hand, would be best served by skills of environmental scanning to identify niche demand characteristics and product design capabilities to fulfill niche requirements. For this strategy, cost efficiency and automation may not even be necessary.

Clearly, there are no fixed rules linking specific strategies to specific skills, staff, structures, and systems. The only generalization that can be made is that strategic managers should attempt to identify the skills needed to support the implementation of strategy.

7.6   ROLE OF CULTURE IN STRATEGY IMPLEMENTATION

Organizational culture refers to the system of shared values and beliefs about how the organization should be managed. It includes values, assumptions, mores, customs, and behavioral norms that guide organizational actions. Shared values act as a glue that binds organizational members together.

Organizational culture acts as a general system for guiding the actions of organizational members. Although many organizational activities have specific rules to guide their performance, not every activity can be explained through rules. Activities for which there are no rules get done in organizations through norms established by organizational culture. Culture is that unstated system of taken-for-granted practices that allows members to do things not specified by rules. For example, most companies do not have explicit dress codes, but executives and organizational members know by observing others what the accepted dress standards are in different organizational settings.

Change in strategy often requires new tasks and activities to be performed. For many of these activities, the organization does not have explicit rules. In performing these activities, members turn to the organizational culture as a source of guidance. In this sense, culture is a very valuable tool for implementation of strategies (Barney, 1986; Schwartz and Davis, 1981).

Besides simplifying strategy implementation, organizational cultures also influence performance. Several studies have found excellent companies to possess strong cultures that give their firms a competitive advantage. Excellent companies possess cultures that facilitate customer orientation, strong corporate identity, innovativeness, high quality, and cost minimization (Deal and Kennedy, 1981; Peters and Waterman, 1982). Other studies have suggested that the success of Japanese firms is attributable to their unique management cultures (Ouchi, 1981; Pascale and Athos, 1981).

For a company culture to provide competitive advantage and lead to profitability it must satisfy three conditions. The culture must (1) generate specific value for the firm; (2) it must be rare; and (3) it must not be easily imitable (Barney, 1986). The first condition means the culture must simplify the creation of some specific value. This may take the form of increasing sales, improving product quality, lowering costs, increasing production efficiency, and so on. It must have specific financial consequences. The second condition requires that the culture not be common to many firms, particularly competing firms. Rarity makes the culture an exclusive advantage for the firm. Finally, difficulty of imitation guarantees that the advantages that a culture provides will be sustainable over an extended time period. These conditions suggest that using culture as a mechanism for strategy implementation or for improving organizational performance means having a deep understanding of the concept. The following discussion provides a more detailed description of corporate cultures and suggests ways of changing them.

7.7   CORPORATE CULTURES

Most organizations do not possess a single homogeneous culture. Organizations have different cultures at different hierarchical levels and in different departments. They are multicultural entities. Strategic management must be sensitive to the multiple cultural orientations within an organization. For example, top management may have a culture that is quite distinct and different from the culture of workers at the plant level. Similarly, members of R&D departments have markedly different cultures than those of marketing or accounting departments. Cultural orientations may also vary by the national, ethnic, racial, and religious characteristics of employees. To understand different cultural patterns in a company, it is useful to view cultures as manifested in several different ways.

Manifestations of Cultures

Corporate cultures are manifested in physical objects, behavioral norms, and decision-making values, beliefs, and assumptions. **Physical objects** and use of physical spaces characterize corporate cultures. Mundane physical objects such as office decor, norms of dressing, location of key executives' offices, and reserved parking spots convey important cultural values and meanings. These objects convey the relative importance of tasks and roles within the organization and the relative power of different individuals and departments.

The special meanings attached to cultural objects within organizations allows their use as carriers of important symbolic messages to members. These objects may be used to reward and encourage certain types of behaviors and to discourage others. They also may be used to confer status and privilege on employees and to degrade and punish. One obvious way that physical objects are used to reflect status is through the use of uniforms and insignia that convey level in the hierarchy of the armed forces. Companies may give items like special ties, blazers, jackets, watches, desk accessories, or office furniture to signify status or membership in an exclusive group.

Behavioral norms are a critical aspect of corporate cultures because they act as guides to action. These norms reinforce and supplement formal rules and regulations to provide members comprehensive guidance on the proper ways to act in ambiguous situations. Behavioral norms are particularly important for guiding action where no formal rules exist. Organizations possess characteristic norms of behavior toward members, toward the environment, and toward risk taking. Some organizations encourage a tough-guy attitude. The norm is to tackle tough issues, make complex and difficult deals, and be proactive. Other companies may encourage a work hard/play hard ethos. In these companies, members work long, arduous hours and get rewarded generously for their efforts. Members may put in 200% effort and get corresponding rewards. Still other companies possess what Deal and Kennedy (1981) call the bet-the-company culture. These cultures encourage high-risk-taking behaviors.

Behavioral norms illustrate the proper ways of treating superiors, colleagues, subordinates, minority groups, visitors, and business associates. For example, at IBM norms about treatment of others encourage formality, professionalism, and polite social distance. In contrast, Marks and Spencer prides itself as a family. It encourages formation of close relationships among employees and managers and informality in interaction. Organizations have norms of conduct for business meetings, social gatherings, ceremonial events, public meetings, and so forth. Other norms may contain expectations about individual and group performance, use of language, communications behavior, and interaction behavior. Breaking norms can have negative consequences. Nonconforming members may be labeled deviant, ostracized, and even bypassed for advancement.

The most important manifestation of culture is in the **assumptions, values, and beliefs** of top managers. These values guide strategic decision making. Often, these values and beliefs are deeply embedded in the minds of the organization's members. They may be unstated, subconscious, and taken for granted, but they shape decisions by providing the framework for interpreting information, analyzing alternative courses of action, and making strategic choices. These values also influence the work attitudes of employees. They shape employees' views of themselves, of their organization, and of organization-environment relationships. These attitudes and views reflect employee commitment and motivation to the firm.

The idea of organizational frame of reference (OFOR) is useful for understanding culture as it manifests itself in the beliefs, assumptions, and values of decision makers. OFOR represents the organization's "worldview." It consists of the mental programs used to make strategic decisions. OFOR has three elements: basic data categories, cognitive maps, and reality tests. Basic data categories determine what information the organization can use in making decisions. Cognitive maps decide how the organization will interpret and make sense of the data and draw conclusions from it. Reality tests determine what is to be considered real and legitimate within the organizational framework. Different OFORs create different types of **decision cultures**, which are described next.

- Bureaucratic cultures: Organizations with bureaucratic cultures prefer to use objective and documented data. They interpret data through a battery of well-established rules and regulations. Organizational policies and rules serve as reality tests. Decision making goes according to predetermined bureaucratic rules. Standard operating procedures are ubiquitous and widely used. These cultures are often found in large governmental agencies, public-sector organizations, and even some large and old private companies.

- Entrepreneurial Cultures: The entrepreneurial culture relies on subjective and impressionistic data, often from personal sources. The cognitive maps used are the personal maps of key managers (founder, owners, CEO, etc.). Their personal biases often color data interpretation. Their personal values are broadly adopted by the rest of the organization. Decision making is centralized in the key manager or leader who makes decisions with supporting information from subordinates. These cultures are often found in small, family-type organizations or highly centralized private corporations.

- Anticipatory Cultures: Anticipatory cultures encourage the use of objective information and interpret it using scientific cognitive maps. They stress proactive, rational, technical analysis of problems. Work relationships in these organizations are informal and are guided by a shared code of professional ethics. This culture self-selects professionally trained members and encourages professionalism at work. Knowledge-based, high-tech industries such as consultant services and computer and software manufacturing often exhibit anticipatory cultures.

Changing Cultures

Each of the three decision cultures is suitable for different types of strategy. A fit or match between culture and strategy is essential for strategy implementation and good performance. Achieving this fit may require changing organizational culture. The concepts of corporate culture are summarized in Figure 7.4.

The importance of achieving a match between organizational culture and strategy is apparent from the case of AT&T. Until its breakup into regional operating companies in 1982, AT&T's corporate culture was a consequence of its corporate mission of "achieving universal service in a regulated environment." This mission guided every aspect of the company. AT&T believed that the surest way to fulfill this mission was by managing the entire telecommunications system—"end to end." This meant being a single, unified entity with complete horizontal and vertical integration and with a sense of fairness to its stakeholders.

From this philosophy emerged a culture encompassing attitudes toward employees, customers, and stockholders. Employees had lifetime careers, intense loyalty, perception of fair treatment by the company, up-from-the-ranks management succession, high level of service consciousness, and consensus management. Customer ethos was a dedication to service and high quality. Stockholder accountability was the third critical aspect of AT&T culture. It involved achieving ever higher operating efficiencies, predisposition toward operating and technical skills, and a strong focus on regulatory matters. The match between mission, strategy, and culture was sustained for decades because the environment remained unchanged.

With the arrival of deregulation in the telecommunications industry, and the breakup of AT&T into nine regional operating companies, there was a need for radical change in the culture. The new environment was more competitive and risky. The new strategies of the operating companies needed to be more aggressive and innovative. They needed to develop a market orientation (in contrast to technical orientation of the past). Management needed to become more risk oriented and entrepreneurial in search of new profit opportunities. They could no longer bank on a protected domain guaranteed by regulations.

Since its breakup, AT&T has embarked on an ambitious program of cultural readjustment. The company is now becoming more flexible and capable of coping with continuous change, in contrast to decades of stability. It is developing a customer and market orientation. It is expanding internal routes to power, which had earlier been limited to operations and technical personnel. This is encouraging development of marketing, finance, and innovation skills. Cultural adjustments at AT&T are continuing to foster new market-oriented and competition-oriented values and attitudes.

Cultural change is difficult to accomplish, and cultural interventions have ambiguous effects on organizations. Cultural changes must, therefore, be conceptualized and implemented systematically and cautiously. The following steps might be useful in implementing cultural change in organizations.

Step 1: *Gain a deep understanding of organizational cultures* in their various forms

Figure 7.4 *Corporate Culture*

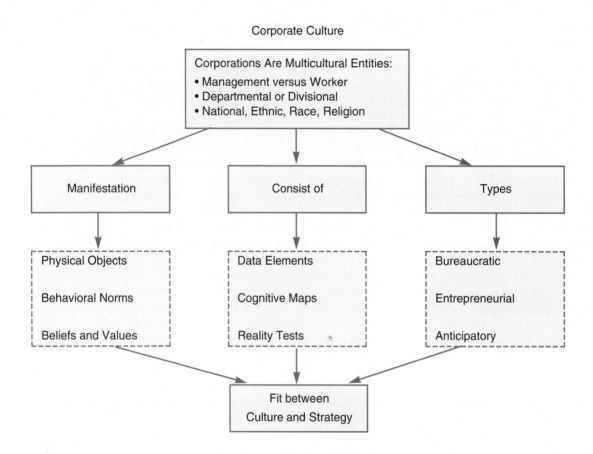

and at different levels and locations in the firm. Identify subcultures and their characteristics.

Step 2: Next, examine corporate and business unit strategies and *identify their demands* on the behavior, attitudes, and values of the organization's members. What kind of cultures do these strategies require for their success? Organizations pursuing high-risk strategies may be best served by an entrepreneurial culture. An anticipatory culture may be more appropriate for large, planning-oriented firms embarking on an expansion path.

Step 3: *Identify mismatches between the organization's corporate and business strategies and its existing culture.* State these mismatches in terms of contradictory strategic missions, values, assumptions, tasks, and responsibilities. The case of AT&T is an example of mismatch between corporate strategy and culture. Mismatch also occurs when a large firm with a bureaucratic culture attempts to pursue an aggressive prospector strategy. Such situations call for cultural change. Assess the agreement among the organization's members on the accuracy and impact of these mismatches.

Step 4: *Identify mismatches between culture and strategic decision processes.* Organizational culture constrains decision making by its limiting values, assumptions, language, data, perspectives, and analytical devices used by managers. Cultural elements that cause these constraints need to be identified. For example, the value of loyalty and trust among managers may encourage their use of subjective personal opinions in decision making and limit the use of objective impersonal analysis.

Step 5: *Bring to the surface and share the elements of culture* identified in Steps 1 and 2 that are not consistent so that those cultural elements that need to be changed are apparent. This requires collecting and sharing the data that show dysfunctional effects of cultural mismatches. Plausible explanations for mismatches and arguments for change need to be developed. Convince members of the necessity for change. Permanent changes can be accomplished only based on a true understanding of the effects of culture on strategy.

Step 6: Change cultural elements at each level by *making changes in trigger variables*. These variables include organizational values, missions, structure, key personnel, recruitment and training programs, and administrative systems and procedures. The direction of change must be guided by the strategy of the organization. It should aim at producing cultures that facilitate strategic action.

Step 7: *Institutionalize the changes* by making them explicit, coding them in organizational policies, giving them the open support of top management, and legitimizing them in practice.

Cultural changes should be assessed periodically to ensure they continue to meet the strategic needs of the organization. It is apparent from the our discussion that cultural change is a very sensitive and complex process. An equally sensitive, although more straightforward instrument of strategy implementation than corporate culture, is the performance evaluation and reward system.

7.8   ROLE OF PERFORMANCE EVALUATION AND REWARD SYSTEMS

A key success factor for strategy implementation is building motivation and commitment among managers. After allocating specific responsibilities for strategic tasks and programs, management must ensure that responsible individuals actually perform their tasks. They must be motivated and committed to the new strategy. The main difficulty in motivating employees to implement new strategies arises from the fact that new strategies invariably involve risks, imply changes in power relationships, and create uncertainties about the future. There are two ways organizations can improve employee commitment to strategies: by improving their understanding of strategies and their impact, and by rewarding them for appropriate strategic actions.

First, commitment to strategy is fostered by a clear understanding by employees of how they (and their departments or groups) fit into the organization's strategy; that is, what is their strategic role? Lack of this understanding disenfranchises employees from the strategy. It makes them feel alienated from the strategy. Under these conditions, their commitment to strategy is limited to impersonal, routine investment of their required working hours. It lacks the personal dedication or enthusiasm that makes a significant difference to strategy implementation.

The role of different divisions, departments, and top-management personnel in any strategy can be identified by showing what contributions they make to the organization's success. The success of each strategy depends to a large extent on individuals and groups giving their best performance in some specific area. For example, business units pursuing the least-cost strategy are critically dependent on efficient production systems. Manufacturing engineers, operations supervisors, inventory managers, quality control managers, and automation engineers are central to the success of such a strategy. Telling these employees and their departments the crucial role they play in strategy implementation can be a motivating factor.

It is more difficult to delineate clearly the roles of lower-level workers and staff personnel. With them, it may be useful to clarify the roles of their different functions, such as manufacturing, R&D, administration, quality control, customer service, and so forth. Show them how these functions are critical to success of the strategy. Employees within these functions can then relate to the strategy by seeing how their functional outputs affect the firm's strategy and performance.

A second means of gaining commitment involves designing appropriate performance evaluation and reward systems. The effort should be to create systems that reward performance that is consistent with the firm's strategy and that consider long-term strategic performance.

Existing reward systems in American industry have many weaknesses that must be addressed if strategic performance is to be encouraged. The first weakness is that in most companies rewards are geared toward short-term performance. Managers work under pressures of quarterly profits that are rigorously monitored by investment analysts. Often, they must abandon sensible, strategic, long-term expenditures to be able to show profits in the current quarter.

A second weakness in reward systems lies in the vast disparity in rewards between top, middle and lower levels in organizations. CEOs and top managers make multiple millions of dollars, middle managers make around 9 hundred thousand dollars, and lower-level employees make about twenty-five thousand dollars in annual income. These vast differences set up severe antagonisms between different organizational levels. With such large disparities, it is difficult to convince employees that they are a part of the same team as their top managers.

A third weakness of existing reward systems is that they do not make a balanced use of monetary and nonmonetary rewards in compensating employees. If the distribution of monetary rewards is a result of haphazard design and historical accidents, the distribution of nonmonetary rewards is largely arbitrary and unconnected to desired strategic performance.

To gain commitment to strategy, reward systems must explicitly encourage behaviors consistent with the strategy and discourage behaviors that are inconsistent. Strategy-sensitive reward systems should encourage long-term planning, and reward managers for long-term performance and for strategy implementation. This requires measurement of strategy implementation and use of specific criteria in performance evaluation.

The design of compensation systems in organizations is a complex and sensitive task, and usually it is the domain of experts in professional compensation systems. In this section we cannot cover the many legal, economic, and technical considerations that go into the design of these systems. We simply want to emphasize that beyond the traditional principles and criteria used in designing salary levels, firms must incorporate strategic performance as an additional variable (Stonich, 1981).

Strategy-sensitive Monetary Reward Systems

In 1989 Du Pont initiated a highly ambitious plan that linked business profitability to compensation of both top management and factory workers. The plan covered

20,000 employees in the fibers business, which had sales of nearly $6 billion in the United States. This "achievement-sharing" plan linked a part of each employee's compensation to company profits. By tying part of yearly pay increases to business performance, the company hoped to gain commitment to goals, give employees a greater sense of responsibility, and shape the corporate culture. Such profit-sharing plans are becoming popular in industry today. However, they are difficult to implement in cyclical industries like chemicals, where business cycles, which are beyond the control of company employees, determine profitability more than worker efforts. For example, with the onset of recession in 1990, Du Pont's fiber business suffered a 25% decline in business. Clearly, this was not related to performance of employees. The company canceled the profit-sharing plan to avoid penalizing employees for poor economic conditions.

In most organizations there is a history of compensation at each level of the organization. It is usually not possible to depart radically from historical levels of compensation without creating undue disruption. Nevertheless, when there is an opportunity to redesign compensation systems, the criteria shown in Figure 7.5 may be used for designing reward systems. These criteria can be useful in organizations undergoing restructuring or those that have been acquired.

The single biggest problem with compensation and reward systems today is their short-term orientation. They reward annual performance based on narrow accounting measures, such as return on assets (ROA), return on investments (ROI), or return on sales (ROS). This short-term orientation encourages managers to focus narrowly on variables that improve these accounting measures. They simultaneously tend to downplay strategic performance.

To make reward systems responsive to strategic long-term performance, they should measure long-term performance and reward it. One way of doing this is by the weighted-factor approach to measuring performance. Instead of evaluating performance from a single accounting measure, performance may be defined as a corporate weighted average of accounting measures (ROA, ROI, etc.), market performance measures (sales growth, market share, etc.), and strategic performance measures (expected future payoffs, progress on strategic programs, achievement of strategic objectives, etc.). Each of these measures can be assigned a weight, and a weighted average can be calculated. Weights may be determined by management based on the firm's strategy, business environment, and internal resource profile. Thus,

Strategic performance = $W_i \cdot P_i / n$

where W_i = weight assigned to individual performance measures, P_i = performance measures, and n = number of measures used. This weighted-factor method is particularly useful for rewarding strategic performance of top managers of independent business units.

A second method of rewarding long-term performance is explicitly measuring it over three- to five-year periods as a basis of deciding part of managerial compensation. Managers may be awarded deferred stock or options according to a formula that involves attaining certain preset strategic goals and earnings growth targets over successive years. With judicious choice of planning horizons and financial instruments, different types of compensation schemes can be developed. These schemes also have the benefit of sheltering income from current taxes by deferring it to later years. Under such schemes managers feel they are building future security and insurance. Their motivation is to act for the long term, and they are encouraged to remain with the firm for longer periods.

Figure 7.5 *Criteria for Establishing Rewards*

Person-related Variables
- Educational qualifications
- Work experience
- Tenure on job and in company
- Potential for growth and advancement

Job-related Variables
- Amount of skill required
- Number of people being supervised
- Special knowledge required to do the job
- Strategic importance of job

Organization-related Variables
- Salary history and triangle in the firm
- Other perks and benefits offered
- Intangible benefits
- Profitability of the company

Environment-related Variables
- Competitor's salary offerings
- Extent of job mobility in the industry

Strategy-related Variables
- Criticality for strategy
- Compensation as signals

Many organizations have devised compensation systems for top managers that are a percentage of the total profitability of their division or of the company as a whole. Only if the company achieves its objectives or targeted performance levels do managers at the top receive these incentives. By linking compensation to performance, organizations can motivate managers to achieve strategic objectives. Although these profit-sharing plans for top management are a good first step, they do not promote commitment to strategy by rank and file workers who are not included in most such plans.

A third method of measuring long-term performance is the strategic funds deferral method. This method involves separating out expenses for strategic investments from expenses required to sustain current operations (Sales, General & Administrative [SG&A] expenses in the profit and loss account). The ROI is measured by excluding these strategic investments. Below is a sample calculation of ROA that segregates strategic funds from SG&A expenses.

By treating strategic funds as part of operating SG&A, operating ROA would be $1,500,000/$5,000,000, or 30%, instead of 50% in the above calculation. Thus, managers could be tempted to cut back strategic funds to improve ROA. This method of return explicitly distinguishes between investments needed to maintain current operating revenues from those intended for the strategic health of the business. Thus, there is no incentive for managers to reduce strategic investments to improve their ROA figures. Here, managers get an incentive to invest strategic funds, whereas under conventional ROA measurement, the incentive is to hold them down in the same way as operating expenses.

Sales	10,000,000
Cost of sales	5,000,000
Gross margin	5,000,000
Operating SG&A	2,500,000
Operating margin	2,500,000
Strategic funds	1,000,000
Pretax profit	1,500,000

Assume total assets of 5,000,000

Operating ROA = 2,500,000/5,000,000 = 50%

There is no single best approach to developing strategy sensitive-compensation systems. Many companies have developed systems that combine the above approaches.

Nonmonetary Rewards

Besides the monetary rewards, motivation also can be encouraged by giving managers nonmonetary compensation—power, influence, status recognition, and perks. Nonmonetary rewards can make a manager's job more comfortable and psychologically satisfying. For example, the perk of traveling first class adds comfort and prestige. It can be a big motivating factor, especially for managers who travel extensively. Nonmonetary rewards become particularly important for managers who are receiving very high levels of compensation and are in high marginal tax brackets. For these managers, an increase of a few thousand dollars in their salaries would not make a big difference in their quality of life. But getting recognition, awards, status, or perks could be immensely gratifying.

Unfortunately, in most organizations, nonmonetary rewards are given out arbitrarily without links to strategic performance. There is no standard valuation of these awards; their value is highly symbolic and subjective. It is difficult to gauge the objective value of a corner office, an office with a view, a thick office rug, an expensive wall hanging, or any of the myriad status symbols that pervade corporate offices today. Yet, these are symbols of the worth of individuals. Highly coveted items like these have a significant motivating effect on managers.

A rational scheme for allocating nonmonetary rewards should be linked to the strategic importance of managerial roles and performance of managers. Some nonmonetary rewards may actually help managers fulfill their strategic roles. For example, for an executive who frequently deals with community and business leaders, a lavish office decor, limousine service, or club memberships could be useful for projecting the right image of the company.

The complete picture that emerges from the discussion in this chapter is that strategy implementation can be eased by matching organizational structures, systems, skills, staff, culture, and reward systems to the particular needs of the strategy. This match must be made at both corporate and business unit levels. A good match can lead to superior performance, whereas a poor match risks failure of strategy. The difficulty in creating the desirable match between strategies and these implementation variables comes from our lack of specific knowledge about the right connections among them. Strategy managers need to create a strategy implementation plan that balances these variables with respect to the needs of the strategy.

This chapter argued that it is not sufficient to formulate brilliant strategies. To affect performance, strategies must be *implemented*. Managers can orchestrate many organizational variables to implement strategies. They must change financial resources, organizational structures, administrative and information systems, corporate culture, organizational skills and staff, and performance evaluation and reward systems. The key is to match these internal elements to the needs of specific strategies. A match between strategies and internal structures and systems leads to improved performance.

A key to motivating employees for strategy implementation is the performance evaluation and reward system. Performance evaluation should focus both on long-term financial performance and performance on specific strategic objectives. To design a strategy sensitive reward system, it is essential to link the strategy explicitly with clear performance indicators and responsibilities of managers.

SUMMARY OF CHAPTER 7

Strategy implementation is the next logical step after strategy formulation. It involves putting the formulated strategy into action. It requires accomplishment of administrative tasks and allocation of necessary resources to strategic programs.

Strategy implementation involves managing many intangible variables such as motivation and commitment of people, values and culture, organizational behavior, and power relationships. In this sense it represents the "soft" side of strategic management.

Implementation of strategic programs requires allocation of appropriate financial, material, and human resources. Capital appropriations or budgeting procedures are useful for allocating financial resources. A careful estimation of financial resources can ensure that sufficient resources will be available. The human resource needs of a strategy can be met by assessing managerial and staff capabilities.

Strategy implementation may require changes in organizational structures and systems, which jointly determine the role and responsibility of managers for completing different tasks necessary for achieving objectives. Informal organizational structures also have an important influence on strategy implementation. They include social relationships, behavioral norms, and cultural practices within the organization. Different organizational structures provide a different form, type, and extent of control. Managers can use simple, functional, divisional, Strategic Business Unit, matrix, or dynamic network types of structures for strategy implementation.

Administrative systems provide support to organizational structures. They provide information needed for implementing and controlling strategy. Matching structures and systems with a firm's strategy is critical for effective performance. New strategies may require organizations to develop new skills and competencies. These new capabilities may reside in either organizational production systems or people.

Implementation of new strategies often involves performing new tasks and activities without explicit rules. Here, the organizational culture plays a vital role in implementation. It guides organizational action through shared values, assumptions, mores, customs, and behavioral norms. A rare and inimitable culture that generates specific values for the firm can provide competitive advantage and sustained profitability.

Many different organizational elements reflect an organization's culture. For example, physical objects, social norms, and abstract values reflect culture. Physical objects carry important symbolic cultural messages to members. They tell members what is important and what is acceptable. Social norms guide actions where there are no formal rules of behavior. Shared values, beliefs, and assumptions guide decision making.

Corporations exhibit several types of cultures. In bureaucratic cultures, documented rules and procedures guide activities. In contrast, key individual managers guide actions in entrepreneurial cultures. Anticipatory cultures emphasize rational, proactive, technical analysis of problems using objective information. Cultural change is difficult and can have ambiguous effects. It should be conducted cautiously and phased over time.

For successful implementation of strategies, it is important to motivate employees, and gain their commitment. Motivation and commitment of individuals can be achieved by communicating strategies effectively. It is also useful to develop appropriate performance evaluation systems and strategy-sensitive reward systems. Long-term performance and strategic performance should be assessed periodically using specific and explicit criteria. Besides monetary rewards, nonmonetary rewards such as power, influence, and status recognition also can be used to motivate managers.

READINGS, CASES, AND POLICY DOCUMENTS
The following readings and cases provide additional background and discussion material for the concepts discussed in this Chapter.

Readings

* Waterman, R.H., T. Peters, and J.R. Phillips, "Structure is not organization." Business Horizons, June, 1980, pp. 14-26.

Quinn, J.B. "Formulating strategy one step at a time." Journal of Business Strategy, Winter, 1981, 1(3).

Cases

Acme Leasing
Honeywell Europe A & B
* John Hancock Mutual Life Insurance, Inc.
Matshushita Electric Industries
Mud Island
The Southland Corporation—Implementing the Acquisition Strategy
* YKK Zippers, Inc.

Policy Documents

ABC Company—Organization and Policy Guide
* indicates particularly appropriate assignment

Figures 7.1, 7.2, 7.3, 7.4, and 7.5.

Strategic Management Process and Book Outline

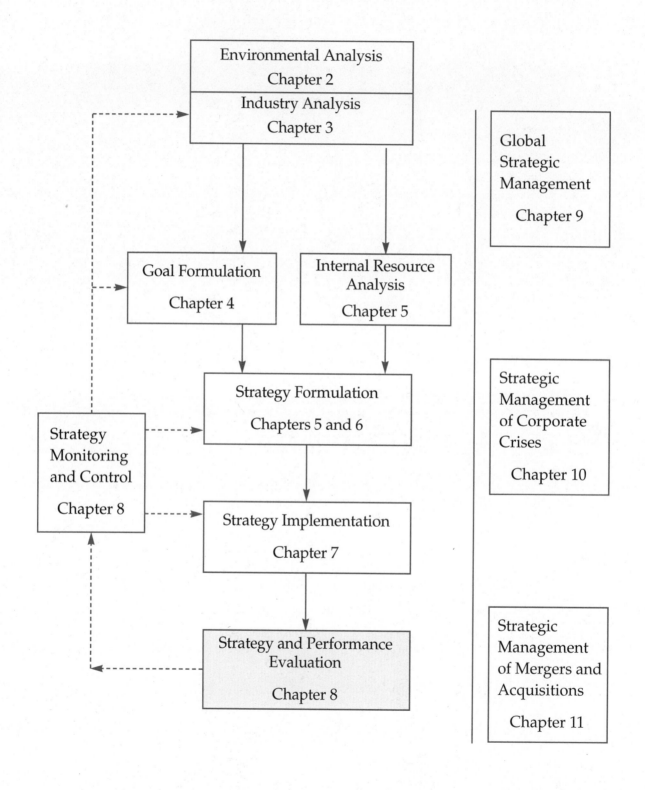

CHAPTER 8
STRATEGY AND
PERFORMANCE EVALUATION

CHAPTER OUTLINE

It is obvious from the previous chapters that strategic plans represent highly consequential, time- and resource-consuming, long-term commitments of companies. Strategic plans decide the firm's future and even its very survival. Strategic change is a high-stakes game that needs to be played with extreme caution. Major strategic changes involve change in organizational culture. They are expensive and time consuming. A company embarks on a new strategy only after it is fully convinced that the strategy is sound and has a good chance of success. How should this judgment about the goodness or worth of strategic plans be made? How should strategies be evaluated?

Once strategic plans are under implementation, progress must be evaluated periodically. This requires strategy monitoring and control. Monitoring deals with setting up an information system to track variables that will allow assessment of how well the plans are performing. Strategic control deals with providing feedback and making modifications to objectives, strategies, and implementation variables to keep the strategy on track.

Many well-conceived and generously supported strategies have gone awry because of poor evaluation, monitoring, and control. Great Northern Nekoosa had an astute strategy of growth by acquisitions. Over a twenty-year period, it bought dozens of smaller companies in the paper industry with the intention of becoming an important player in several segments of the industry. The company had a single-minded focus on making acquisitions and assimilating them into ongoing operations. On the surface, this strategy seemed to work well. No one seriously evaluated or questioned its appropriateness. Little effort was made to monitor the acquisition strategy and assess what it was doing to the business as a whole. The acquisitions created a cluster of businesses that were not well connected with each other and were difficult to control. Although individual businesses were profitable, they were not operating at peak efficiency. By the end of 1988, the company had also accumulated a large cash horde, without any clear plans for investment. Then suddenly came a hostile takeover offer from Georgia Pacific, the paper industry giant. Great Northern Nekoosa tried its best to prevent the takeover but failed.

The acquisition strategy that had helped the company to grow had blindsided the company to its own vulnerability to being acquired. Analysts cited a lack of complete control of this acquisition strategy as a main reason for this vulnerability. The surprise attack from Georgia Pacific and subsequent failure of Great Northern Nekoosa to thwart the attack showed two things: a profound failure to monitor strategic environmental trends and inability to build reliable relationships with stakeholders.

Strategy evaluation, monitoring, and control are complicated issues for which there are no simple answers. This chapter describes some basic principles for evaluating strategies and provides some questions to help structure strategy evaluation at the corporate and business unit levels. It also discusses means of monitoring and controlling strategies as they evolve over time.

The fact that a strategy succeeded in the past, or for another company, is no guarantee that it will work for your company in its present conditions. Most strategies are unique because they attempt to align unique firm resources with unique environmental conditions. Despite their uniqueness, however, there are some general principles and criteria that can be used to evaluate strategies. Strategy evaluation deals with testing the soundness and practical feasibility of formulated strategies. It involves identifying criteria for evaluation and establishing a process that structures the tasks of strategy evaluation. This process identifies who will do the evaluation, what steps will be followed, when and how often it will be done, and who will be responsible for it.

8.1   CRITERIA FOR EVALUATING STRATEGIES

The basic ideas for developing strategy evaluation criteria come from the area of military strategy. Military analysts use several principles to assess the soundness of military strategies. These include the principle of the objective, the principle of the offensive, the principle of critical mass, the principle of economy of force, the principle of maneuver, the principle of unity of command, the principle of surprise, and the principle of security. These can also be used as criteria for evaluating strategies.

Internal Validation

Quinn (1980) adapted the foregoing military principles to suggest some basic criteria for evaluating strategic plans in business contexts. A strategic plan is good if it meets these criteria:

1. It pursues a clear set of objectives and decisively moves the organization in desired directions.

2. It maintains initiative of action and a proactive posture. It anticipates environmental changes and takes preemptive actions.

3. It concentrates an organization's energy, resources, and power on critical issues and avoids dispersing them in ineffectual ways.

4. It concedes selected positions to competition as a corollary to concentration. It deflects competition from attacking its own staked position.

5. It allows the firm to be flexible enough to take advantage of fleeting opportunities. It allows the firm to maneuver, reposition resources, and change directions quickly and at short notice. It does not lock the firm on an irreversible course of action.

6. It provides responsible, committed leadership for each major goal. It coordinates goals in a unity of command and avoids confusion.

7. It uses speed, secrecy, and intelligence to create an element of surprise for competitors. This thwarts competitors from making immediate responses.

8. It provides security for all organizational resources and operating units. It does not unduly jeopardize or put at risk any part of the enterprise.

9. It is communicated to all relevant parts of the organization. It is understood by managers who will be affected by it and implement it.

These general criteria are guides for strategy evaluation. These criteria can be converted into convenient questions that managers can ask of their corporate strategies, business unit strategies, strategy implementation processes, and strategic decision-making processes.

Questions for Evaluating Corporate Strategies. The focus of these questions is on assessing how well the corporate strategy meets corporate objectives, within organizational and environmental constraints (Lauenstein, 1981; Tilles, 1963).

1. Are corporate missions, objectives, and goals clearly specified by the strategic plan? Are they consistent with the demands of external stakeholders of the firm?

2. Is the domain choice specified by the strategic plan consistent with corporate missions and objectives and with environmental trends?

3. Is the product-market portfolio balanced in terms of risk and investment requirements?

4. Does the strategic plan effectively use internal resources and skills?

Questions for Evaluating Business Unit Strategies. The following questions can help assess how good the business unit strategy is for competing in an industry.

1. Are business unit goals clearly specified in terms of revenues, profits, market shares, and budgets? Are they consistent with corporate objectives and goals?

2. Is the business unit strategy specified comprehensively in terms of functional task requirements in production, marketing, finance, and administration? Is it based on a clearly established competitive advantage?

3. Is the business unit's strategic plan based on accurate demand forecasts? Are product line composition, price structure, packaging, and distribution channels positioned competitively?

4. Are internal resources and attributes of the business in terms of technology, production systems, marketing and distribution, and finances sufficient to meet the requirements of the strategy (e.g., low-cost production, differentiation, and niche focus)? Does the business have the resources to carry out the strategic plan to its completion?

Questions for Assessing Implementability. The following questions can be used to assess whether strategies are workable.

1. Does the organization have, or can it develop, organizational structures and systems compatible with strategies, both at the corporate and business unit levels?
2. Does the organization have the financial and managerial resources necessary to implement the strategic plan fully? Does it have the necessary skills and staff to carry out the plan?
3. Is there consensus among the organization's key managers on strategic objectives and the means of achieving them? Are there any major sources of conflict that can thwart implementation of the strategic plan?
4. Are there major regulatory threats or trends that can force the firm to abandon the strategic plan in the future?
5. Does the corporation have a culture that supports its new strategy?

Questions for Assessing the Strategic Decision-making Process. The process used for strategic decision making also may be periodically assessed for its adequacy. The following questions can guide such an assessment.

1. Is the strategic decision-making process sufficiently developed and codified to be clear to all participants?
2. Does the decision process provide for the participation of technical and business experts and all important members of the top management?
3. Is the decision process adequately connected to the budgeting system, capital appropriations process, resource allocation process, and other pertinent systems of the organization?
4. Does the decision process provide opportunities for review, evaluation, feedback and monitoring of strategic decisions?

Using these questions, managers can conduct their own assessment of the soundness of strategies. Answering some of these questions may require fresh analysis of environments and organizational issues. The evaluation process gives managers an opportunity to make last-minute changes and requirements in strategies.

External Validation

Besides internally evaluating the strategic plan, it is a good idea to get a "second opinion" on it from key external stakeholders. The purpose of internal and external validation is to ensure that the strategy is acceptable to key stakeholders of the organization. Of particular importance are those stakeholders who will play a key role in implementing the strategy. These include key corporate and divisional executives, supervisory managers of plants and facilities, and department heads. Key external stakeholders could include important customers and suppliers, bankers, labor unions, and regulatory agents. Without the cooperation of these stakeholders, even the most brilliantly conceived strategic plans can fail to produce results.

One form of external validation involves using industry experts and consultants from outside the organization. A detailed review of strategic plans by these experts can provide a second opinion on the goodness of the strategy. It can lead to identification of implementation problems, which organizational managers may not see, or see but are unwilling to acknowledge. The normal political and social distortions that limit the perspective of internal managers who formulate strategies do not color an outsider's view of the organization. Moreover, industry experts possess specialized knowledge about the industry, future demand patterns, and technological and regulatory trends. External expert review can incorporate this expert knowledge into the strategy formulation process if it has not already been done.

8.2   STRATEGY REVIEW PROCESS

Review of strategic plans must be conducted periodically (usually annually) to assure that implementation is going according to the original design. The strategy review process provides an opportunity to reiterate top management's support for strategic plans, evaluate strategies, closely monitor their implementation, and assess the need for mid-course corrections. To prevent the review process from becoming an annual ritual with little real impact, it must be designed and conducted carefully.

The primary purpose of strategy review is to evaluate corporate and business unit strategic plans and do reality testing against organizational resources and environmental trends. In addition, strategy review serves several secondary purposes:

- To familiarize divisional managers and the CEO with each others' personal perspectives and assumptions about organizational strategies; to forge a psychological contract among managers and build commitment to strategic plans
- To evaluate trade-offs that top management must make in implementing strategies (These trade-offs involve balancing short-term versus long-term performance, balancing business risks and returns, and making compromises under unanticipated circumstances.)
- To negotiate strategic issues and conflicts among interdependent divisions.
- To broaden the scope of knowledge of all participants and provide them with a general view of the firm's strategy.

Both careful planning and management of the review process are essential to accomplish these purposes.

Figure 8.1 is a process flow diagram for strategy review. The first step is to ensure that all participants of the review process are familiar with strategic plans and programs to be reviewed. Preparation for a strategic review includes a careful selection of review participants. The CEO along with the top-management team must be included. In addition, experts from different business areas, strategic planning staff, and sometimes even external consultants may be included.

Preparation for the review can be simplified by circulating the plans, their implementation status, and a brief critique of them—developed by the planning department—to all participants. The critique assesses how realistic the plans are and how well they measure against the strategy evaluation criteria discussed earlier. It synthesizes five or six key issues that can serve as the focus for the review.

The review sessions are well structured with a predetermined agenda that specifies topics and time allocations. Sufficient time is provided for discussions. The agenda is developed in consultation with the chief executive and emphasizes issues that are of real concern to him or her. The session may be opened by the

Figure 8.1 *Strategy Review Process*

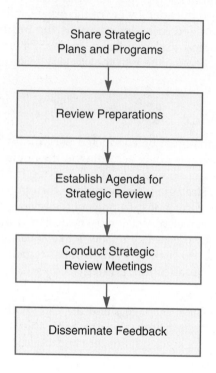

chief executive, who sets the tone for rigorous assessment and modification of strategic plans. This explicit leadership role of the chief executive gives the strategy review process credibility and seriousness and reduces the likelihood that it will become a ritual.

The review meetings provide ample time and opportunity for free and open discussions. Although most of the review will involve all participants, there may be some discussions that are too sensitive for a large audience or may be of interest to only a few members. Such issues may be separated and discussed in private by relevant executives. For example, after reviewing the capital expenditures plan, all the participants may break into smaller groups to review details of divisional capital expenditures. Similarly, ultra-sensitive strategic issues, such as strategic acquisitions under negotiation or competitive technological research projects, may be discussed in smaller, private groups.

Feedback from the strategy review process is distributed widely. A brief summary of the review process is communicated to the organization at large. Such communication could serve to legitimize changes in strategies that are to follow. It also alerts managers to impending changes and reduces the surprise associated with mid-course corrections in strategic plans.

One of the most important substantive outcomes of the review process is the modification of plans. Changes in strategic plans and programs must be communicated to managers who will implement them. They include changes in financial resources, organizational structure and systems, personnel, and time horizons for implementing changes. This facilitates broader understanding of strategic plans within the organization (Charan, 1980; Praeger and Shea, 1983).

8.3   STRATEGY MONITORING

The purpose of any strategy monitoring and control system is to ensure clear allocation of responsibilities and resources for strategy implementation. An additional purpose is to ensure that early action can be taken on strategic plans that are not performing according to expectations. Monitoring also leads to identification of special bottlenecks that can thwart the implementation of strategies and identification of emergent strategic issues.

The Monitoring Function

Figure 8.2 schematically represents the strategy monitoring function. It involves **monitoring** key variables that influence strategies and key performance indicators, **analyzing** incoming data to identify discontinuities and changes, and **deciding** about modifying strategic plans.

Strategy monitoring requires measurement of both inputs (activities performed to implement strategic plans), outputs (financial performance and performance on key objectives), and environmental trends. Input indicators may include financial costs of strategic programs, resources used, personnel allocated, and time taken to complete programs. Outputs may be measured with traditional financial measures such as return on investments, net profits, and growth rate of sales; market measures, such as market share; and measures of strategic objectives. Environmental trends include changes in industry, regulations, and social, political, and ecological environments. Strategy monitoring continually attempts to judge the evolving fit between inputs, outputs, and environmental conditions.

The monitoring function can be facilitated by clearly stating the environmental assumptions under which the strategic plans were made. Managers can compare current environmental conditions with these assumptions to identify the need for change. It is also helpful to specify dates (quarterly or biannual) as deadlines for the achievement of strategic objectives. These standards are useful for judging whether strategies need to be fine tuned or changed drastically.

Tracking these indicators requires good internal accounting, costing, and information systems, as well as appropriate environmental scanning systems. Often, existing information systems are sufficient or can be easily augmented to provide strategy-monitoring information. Information on market share changes can be obtained from industry sources. External consultants also can provide competitive intelligence and information on emergent environmental conditions.

The general responsibility for monitoring strategies often rests with corporate top management. The CEO or the executive committee is in charge of this sensitive and critical function. However, middle and lower management usually monitor the enormous function of data collection and analysis inherent in strategy. Their participation is both vital and unavoidable. It is desirable to have performance reports compiled by objective and unbiased planning staff who are not directly involved in strategy implementation. This reduces the chances of distortion of performance data, which in the early stages, is often subjective and amenable to multiple interpretations.

Critical Variables for Strategy Monitoring

The choice of what variables to monitor depends on which strategies are being pursued. Each strategy is associated with different critical inputs and outputs. For

Figure 8.2 *Strategy Monitoring*

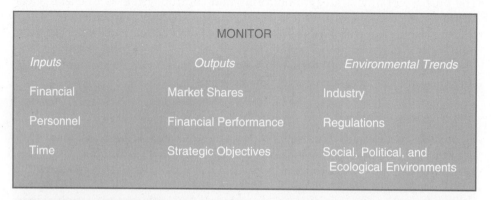

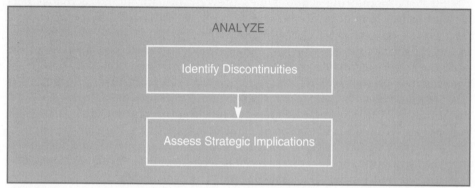

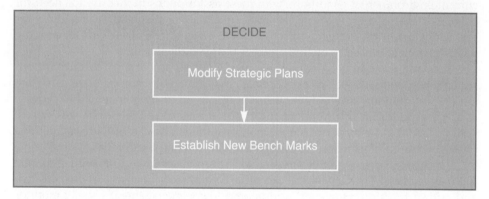

example, we discussed three types of competitive strategies in Chapter 5: least cost, differentiation, and focus or niche. The key success factor for the least-cost strategy is control over production and distribution costs. Systems for monitoring this strategy focus on all types of direct and indirect costs. They also cover secondary costs that affect factors such as changes in economies of scale, subcontracting arrangements, labor-management relations, and so on. By comparing costs of product with historical costs and competitor's costs, potential for cost reduction must be identified. An environmental variable critical for success of least-cost strategy is demand volume. Because the strategy is volume based, even minor dips in demand may be cause for concern.

Differentiation strategy, on the other hand, depends critically on the match between consumer preferences and product attributes and appropriate market segmentation. Monitoring this strategy requires continuous assessment of product characteristics, their desirability to customers, and product uniqueness with respect to competitive products. It also requires tracking the market share of the firm relative to its closest competitors in each market segment. Companies such as Levi Strauss, which follow differentiation strategies, have to cater to different consumer tastes in different countries. Levi Strauss maintains a worldwide computerized environmental scanning system. The system keeps the company abreast of fashion trends around the world and feeds critical consumer preference information to its designers and production plants.

Success of the focus or niche strategy depends on keeping the market niche protected from competitors. Here, key variables that need to be monitored are those that give competitive protection to the firm. These variables could include product features, technology patents, specialized knowledge base, unique access to raw materials or distribution channels, and long-term supply contracts.

Monitoring corporate level strategies also focuses on tracking key success factors for the firm as a whole. For example, the related diversification strategy depends on the firm's ability to exploit resource **synergies**. That implies efficient sharing of production, marketing, distribution, and financial resources across the firm. If synergies are being exploited effectively, a clear pattern of resource sharing will be visible. The monitoring system must be capable of measuring this sharing in objective terms and point out potential areas for further synergies. Specific bench marks for synergistic sharing can be created through joint sales targets among product divisions, interdivisional purchase targets, investments into joint R&D projects, and internal joint ventures among business units.

In contrast, the conglomerate strategy depends not on sharing of resources, but on the ability to manage business units with complete independence, as if they were simply financial assets. Each business unit must be monitored on comparable performance criteria, such as return on equity, return on assets, and growth rate. The monitoring system must be able to provide business unit data on returns and sales on a monthly or a quarterly basis.

Good examples of strategy monitoring in conglomerate firms can be found at Textron and Teledyne. Both these companies have developed strategic planning systems that interface well with the accounting system. The accounting system keeps close track of monthly financial performance of each subsidiary business. It reports actual versus budgeted expenditures and flags exceptional cost overruns and revenue declines. A small group of corporate staff analysts at the headquarters monitors this information. Monthly meetings with business unit managers occur to review performance and make decisions. There are clear guidelines about investment into and divestment of business units based on their quarterly profit performance.

Businesses also must be monitored on their competitive performance within their respective industries. Market share leaders are associated with profitability in many industries, so each business may be judged in comparison with the market leader. The portfolio of businesses composing the conglomerate strategy needs to be assessed for its risk profile. Single businesses that make up over 30% of the portfolio revenues represent risky situations (Dundas and Richardson, 1979).

Besides the financial health of individual business units, the success of conglomerate strategy depends on the ability of the company to acquire and divest units at the proper time. Therefore, conglomerates should monitor their acquisition policies to avoid common acquisition traps. Areas to be avoided include those in which dominant risks are uncontrollable by management, key assets are people who can leave the firm, turnaround strategies are needed to make the business viable, or businesses are concentrated in a single or a few industries. Acquisition policies should clearly state the criteria for screening acquisitions. There should be clear policies on negotiating, particularly in situations of hostile takeover.

Monitoring of strategic plans must include a continuous assessment of environmental forces, particularly those that are the basis of the strategy. Severe discontinuities that invalidate original planning assumptions must be identified when they occur. These discontinuities may warrant immediate revision of the strategy. They must be brought to the attention of the top management as well as strategy implementers. For example, between 1985 and 1988, the UNIX operating system was established as the operating system of the future. Supported by AT&T and Sun Computers, it became a virtual industry standard. Many computer companies planned products around this system. Then, in the middle of 1988, a consortium of six large firms, including IBM, DEC, Hewlett-Packard, and Apollo, announced a competing system called OS II. The industry was thrown into confusion. The strategic plans of many small companies, which were based on UNIX becoming the industry standard, became invalid virtually overnight. Sometimes discontinuities in other industries (supplier or customer industries) may affect firm strategies and therefore need to be monitored. For example, farm equipment manufacturers in the United States had to revise all estimates for product demand and production schedules because of a severe draught in the farm belt in the summer of 1988.

Another important aspect of strategy monitoring is assessing the impact of the firm's strategy on the firm's environment. The relevant environment includes both the social environment and the natural environment. Aggressive growth strategies involving new and hazardous products and technologies may have deleterious effects on customers, communities, and the physical environment. Such strategies may expose the firm to undue risks. By monitoring environmental influences on strategic programs, managers can get early warnings on issues that may cause crises in the future.

Union Carbide's Agricultural Products Division in the 1980s provides an example of how a company may be taking unwarranted risks due to lack of strategic monitoring. The company's ambitious growth strategies lead it to expand production facilities for hazardous chemicals (pesticides, heavy chemicals, fertilizers, etc.) in many developing countries. One such plant was the Bhopal pesticide plant. In terms of a strategic investment, it represented less than 0.5% of assets of the company. The company had no system for continually monitoring the strategic importance of this facility and modifying its strategies with respect to it. Being unprofitable for most of its working life, the plant was largely ignored until the 1984 industrial disaster. An accident at the plant killed and injured thousands of people and threw Union Carbide into a life-threatening crisis. A good strategy monitoring system could have identified the technological and strategic risks posed by such a hazardous facility. Even a cursory analysis could have shown that it was not reasonable to stake the company's reputation and worldwide assets by running this strategically unimportant facility.

The strategy monitoring function needs to be conceptualized and structured broadly. This will track both corporate strategy and business strategy variables, environmental changes, and the impacts of strategies on the natural environment. Monitoring serves as the "eyes and ears" of strategic management by pointing out potential bottlenecks and traps.

8.4   STRATEGIC CONTROL

The aim of strategic control is to ensure accurate implementation of strategic plans and achievement of the needed results. It attempts to maintain the integrity of strategic plans as they go through the process of implementation. It is a type of "quality control" function at the strategic level. Strategic control tries to ensure that the original intentions and outcomes of planned strategies are indeed being achieved.

Strategic control involves identifying strategy implementation bottlenecks and strategic performance deviations from designed strategies and taking steering actions to keep strategic plans on a desired path. Implementation bottlenecks could include lack of resources, skills, staff, and leadership; inappropriate organizational structures and reward systems; mismatches between strategies and organizational culture; and changed environmental conditions that make parts of the strategy impossible to implement (Guth, 1985; Roush and Ball, 1980; Simons, 1991).

Types of Control

Strategic control implies two types of control. First, it must ensure that strategies are delivering the desired financial performance. Second, firm performance should conform to the strategic objectives of stakeholders. Performance deviations from the originally intended strategies are manifested in inadequate financial performance and failure to meet strategic objectives (Eisenhardt, 1985).

Control over financial performance can be simplified by establishing performance standards and bench marks in terms of return on investments, return on assets, and other financial measures. These standards reflect both historical performance standards and needed strategic performance. By measuring current financial performance and identifying deviations from standards, managers can assess needs for control action.

The second type of control, meeting strategic objectives of organizational stakeholders, is not as concrete and measurable as financial control. This type of control requires managers to assess progress toward strategic missions and objectives that are often stated in general and nonquantifiable terms. It involves subjective assessments about the organization's general direction and long-term health.

The level of subjectivity involved in making these broad judgments can be mitigated by involving more participants. The board of directors can serve a useful function in this task. The board of directors represents different perspectives of stakeholders and is in a good position to provide diverse inputs. The board can review the financial performance of the firm, its strategic direction, and the value of the firm in the broader societal context. It can guide top management on policy issues, particularly those involving social, cultural and political concerns.

Checking performance through bench marks with respect to strategic objectives can be particularly useful in concretizing them. Bench marks provide milestones or sign posts to measure progress on strategic objectives. For example, let us say a company's strategic plan involves becoming a global supplier of its products within a four-year period. Useful bench marks for this strategy would describe what must be achieved in the first six months and first, second, third, and fourth years. The firm may want to establish its exports presence by creating dealerships in twenty countries by the end of year one. It may want to meet specific export goals by end of year two, make foreign direct investment into plants or facilities by year three, and so on. These broad bench marks can help the firm to evaluate its progress on the objective of total globalization. If by the end of year two, few foreign dealers have been appointed and exports are faltering, top management knows corrective actions need to be taken.

At the corporate level, strategic control is at best an imperfect art that requires a fair bit of managerial intuition. It is difficult to establish because strategic performance data are often not readily available, data are subjective, and corporate strategic changes are perceptible only over long periods. Changes at the corporate level, such as reorientation of the business portfolio, changing corporate culture, and corporate restructurings, are particularly time consuming. Their influences on performance may not become clear for three to five years after changes are initiated. Simultaneously, it is important to anticipate these affects.

Managerial intuition and judgment that come with experience are often the only qualities that help in anticipating the impacts of strategies. It is advisable, therefore, to have experienced managers involved in the task of strategic control. Many companies have found it useful to retain highly experienced (even retired) executives to advise them on strategic control issues.

At the business unit level, strategy control involves ensuring that the strategic plans are having the desired effect on competitive performance. It involves responding to competitor reactions. Some competitor moves may prevent the firm from continuing from its originally chosen strategy. It may call for scaling back or expanding production, readjusting marketing (advertising, promotion, sales, packaging, and pricing) strategies, making new investments, and reassigning personnel. Here, it is critical that management continue to support the original strategy cautiously, with modifications and flexibility. The mistakes often made are to react at the extremes, for example, to prematurely abandon the strategy or, conversely, to adhere stubbornly to the original plan even in the face of its infeasibility.

Strategic Control Systems

The key to maintaining strategic control is access to the right information at the right time. Routine organizational information systems are often not designed to provide strategic control information. But they can be modified to do so by expanding their scope. The financial and accounting control systems (budgetary control system, cost accounting system, production control system, etc.) can be augmented to track some strategic control variables and report exceptions on their performance. If these systems do not exist, the firm must create them. In doing so, control systems of foreign subsidiaries must be integrated with the corporate system.

Strategy monitoring and control systems also can be structured to provide control over specific projects, businesses, or brands. They can be **program or project management systems** that focus on discrete blocks of organizational activities or strategic programs. These systems use standard project management techniques, such as Gantt charts, the program evaluation and review technique (PERT), and the critical path method. They track progress on strategic programs, improve work flows, and increase productivity.

Another way of structuring strategic control is through a **profit planning system**, as used by Johnson & Johnson. The system focuses on individual business units and encompasses annual profit budgets, second-year forecasts, strategic operating and financial plans, and long-range plans. Planned and actual revenues, costs, and profits for each major cost or revenue category are tracked, and exceptions are reported. A more focused version of budgeting is **brand revenue budget systems**, which break up budgets by product lines and brand names. Alternatively, firms may structure strategic control as **intelligence or information systems** and **human development systems** (Simons, 1991).

Problems of Control

Strategy control often encounters problems of resource constraints and dealing with uncertainty. Modified strategies may require investment of more resources than those anticipated at the time of strategy formulation. The original planning estimates should provide buffers for such contingencies. If additional resources are not available, there are several options available to the firm. The first is to find creative trade-offs that reduce the need for resources by scaling-back strategies. The firm also may be able to phase out strategy implementation differently, and by that postpone less critical expenditures to a later date in the future. Another alternative is to seek new alliances with business associates (suppliers and customers) that allow the company to share the additional resource burdens (and rewards). These could include better credit terms or temporary discounts from suppliers, or longer-term supply contracts with customers that allow the firm to make strategic investments. The solution of last resort is cutting back strategies that need more resources.

Another problem in strategy control is dealing with uncertainty. Early strategy monitoring data are never clear enough to give confidence to managers about actions that need to be taken. Often managers wait too long to get a clearer picture. By the time they have confirmatory evidence that actions are needed, it is too late. With the passage of time, the strategy may be hopelessly compromised. Therefore, it is advisable to err on the safer side by taking preemptive actions or added precautions in implementation strategies. Although early action and additional precautions are expensive, they provide managers the best chance of dealing with uncertainties.

Strategy evaluation, monitoring, and control are crucial functions that provide oversight over strategic plans. Strategy evaluation seeks to ensure that the chosen strategy is economically sound, acceptable to key stakeholders, and practically feasible. This judgment must be made for corporate and business unit strategic plans and structured through a formal review process.

The strategy review process provides an opportunity for managers to get the "big picture" of the firm's strategy. It also provides for a systematic assessment of strategic plans. To be effective, it needs the support, participation, and leadership of the CEO.

Evaluation is not simply a one-time activity. Rather, strategic plans need to be assessed continually during implementation through active monitoring and control. Effective strategy monitoring requires information systems that are well integrated with the firm's internal financial control systems. They provide the information on key strategic variables needed to make strategy modifications and mid-course corrections. Strategic control can be facilitated by using budgetary and accounting systems to control financial performance and establishing clear bench marks to judge total progress on strategic objectives.

SUMMARY OF CHAPTER 8

Strategic change is a high-stakes game that needs to be played with extreme caution. To make effective strategic changes, it is necessary to evaluate, monitor, and control strategies. Although each strategy is unique, several general principles and criteria are useful for evaluating strategies. Strategies should provide a clear direction and unambiguous and operational objectives and goals to the organization. They must encourage action initiatives and a proactive posture toward the environment. They should concentrate and focus the organizations' energy, resources, and power on critical issues. Sound strategies are internally consistent. They are also consistent with environmental demands and with organizational resources. They are practically implementable and legally feasible. They are socially and ethically responsible.

Corporate strategy evaluation focuses on assessing adequacy of corporate missions, objectives, and goals. It includes evaluating the balance, cash flow requirements, and risk inherent in the corporate business portfolio. Strategy evaluation for the business unit focuses on assessing the competitive advantage and the adequacy of market shares, profits, and revenues of individual business units. Implementability of strategies can be assessed by examining compatibility of strategies with organizational resources, structures, systems, cultures, and skills.

Strategies are evaluated through a review process. This process ensures that they conform to the original strategic objectives. The review can be facilitated with proper preparation and support of top management. In preparation for the review, strategic plans and a brief critique of the plans may be circulated to all participants. Strategic review leads to modification of plans.

The purpose of a strategy monitoring and control system is to provide oversight on strategy implementation. It ensures that resources for strategy implementation are available. It also allows managers to take early action on strategies that are not performing according to expectations. The choice of what variables to monitor depends on the type of strategy. Monitoring corporate level strategies focuses on resource sharing among businesses. Business unit strategies are monitored for their competitive performance. Strategy monitoring also helps to assess environmental changes and discontinuities in original planning assumptions. It assesses the impact of these changes on the firm's strategy.

Strategic control involves taking corrective actions to steer the strategy back on its tracks. It tries to ensure that strategies lead to desired financial performance. It also makes performance conform to the strategic objectives of stakeholders. Control over financial performance can be facilitated by establishing performance standards and bench marks to measure performance. It involves taking corrective measures when performance deviates from standards. Meeting strategic objectives of stakeholders requires periodically assessing strategic direction.

At the corporate level, strategic control is a difficult task because strategic performance data are subjective and not readily available. Strategic changes are perceptible only over long periods. By the time serious shortcomings become apparent, it is often too late to do anything about them. Therefore, it is advisable to be extra cautious in conducting this task. At the business unit level, strategic control involves responding to competitive threats.

Organizationally, strategy control systems are similar to project management systems. They focus on discrete blocks of organizational activities or strategic programs. Profit planning is another way of structuring strategic control.

READINGS, CASES, AND POLICY DOCUMENTS

The following readings and cases provide additional background and discussion material for the concepts discussed in this Chapter.

Readings

Hayes, R. and J. Clark, "Why some factories are more productive than others." Harvard Business Review, October, 1986.

Cases

* Genicom
  Humana, Inc.
  John Hancock Mutual Life Insurance, Inc.
* Matshushita Electric Industries
  The Southland Corporation (both parts)

Policy Documents

US Coast Guard "Commandant's Long Range View"
* indicates particularly appropriate assignments

Figure 8.1 & 8.2.

Strategic Management Process and Book Outline

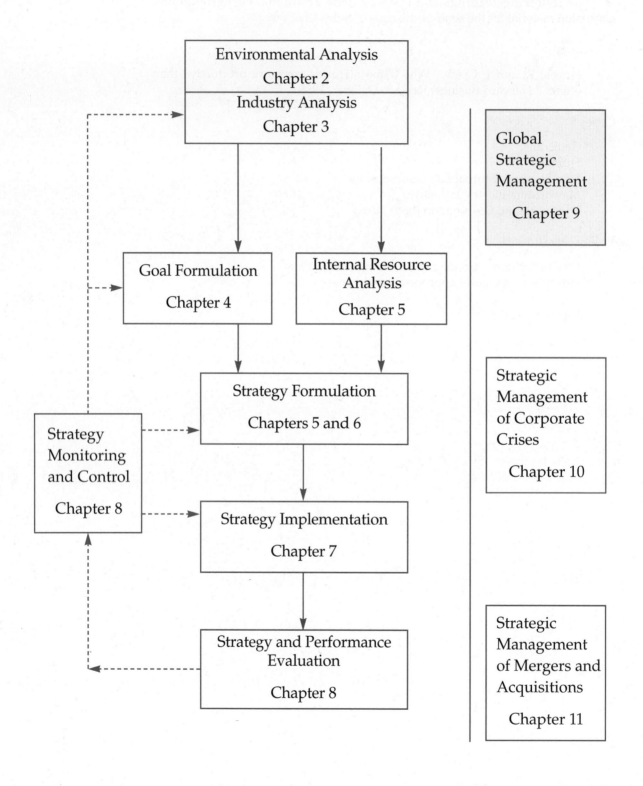

CHAPTER 9
GLOBAL STRATEGIC
MANAGEMENT

CHAPTER OUTLINE

The globalization of businesses is now an economic and competitive necessity. Most large businesses today already operate in multiple countries. Their grand designs include significant participation in foreign markets. Major corporations, such as Asea Brown Boveri, Compaq Computers, Honda, and IBM, derive larger revenues and profits from foreign markets than from their home markets. Global markets are also important from the point of view of supplies and competition. Some American industries, such as shoes, apparel, and toys, get a large part of their supplies from and have many of their production plants located in foreign countries. Foreign suppliers and collaborations provide ways of reducing costs and improving profits. As a result, companies are rushing into strategic alliances and joint ventures with foreign partners.

The trend toward globalization is intensifying with the sweeping economic reorganization in the formerly communist, Eastern Block nations and the integration of European markets in 1992. Many regional trade pacts under negotiation in the United States, Europe and the Pacific region are facilitating globalization. Today, there are signs of emergence of several distinct economic regions or **market clusters** around the world, each with more than 400 million people (see map in Figure 9.1). These market aggregations are resulting from mutual trade agreements and differential rates of economic development around the world. In the next two decades, six major market clusters are expected to emerge.

The United States and Canada signed a trade agreement (North American Foreign Trade Agreement—NAFTA) in 1988 that encourages mutual trade

Figure 9.1 World GNP and Population

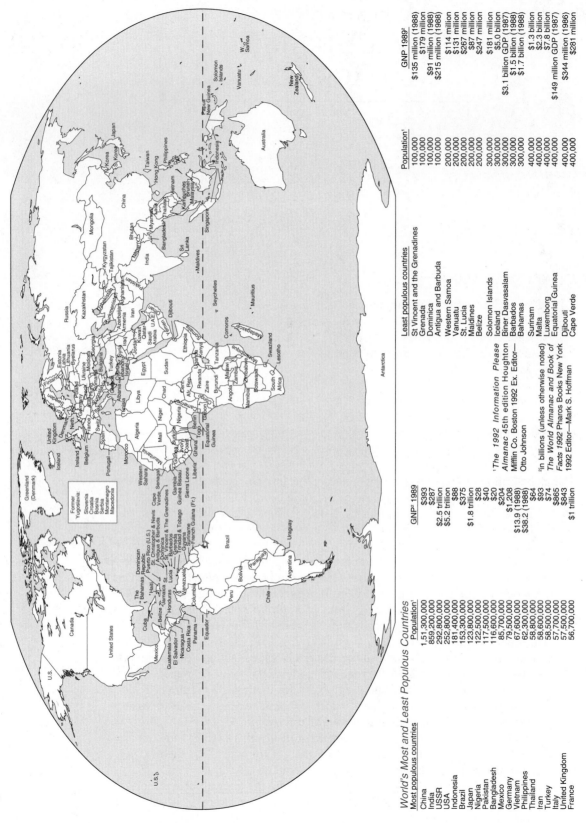

World's Most and Least Populous Countries

Most populous countries	Population[1]	GNP[2] 1989
China	1,151,300,000	$393
India	859,200,000	$287
USSR	292,800,000	$2.5 trillion
USA	252,800,000	$5.2 trillion
Indonesia	181,400,000	$88
Brazil	153,300,000	$375
Japan	123,800,000	$1.8 trillion
Nigeria	122,500,000	$28
Pakistan	117,500,000	$40
Bangladesh	116,600,000	$20
Mexico	85,700,000	$204
Germany	79,500,000	$1,208
Vietnam	67,600,000	$13.9 (1988)
Philippines	62,300,000	$38.2 (1988)
Thailand	58,800,000	$64
Iran	58,600,000	$93
Turkey	58,500,000	$74
Italy	57,700,000	$865
United Kingdom	57,500,000	$843
France	56,700,000	$1 trillion

Least populous countries	Population[1]	GNP 1989[2]
St Vincent and the Grenadines	100,000	$135 million (1988)
Grenada	100,000	$179 million (1988)
Dominica	100,000	$215 million (1988)
Antigua and Barbuda	100,000	
Western Samoa	200,000	$114 million
Vanuatu	200,000	$131 million
St. Lucia	200,000	$267 million
Maldives	200,000	$87 million
Belize	200,000	$247 million
Solomon Islands	300,000	$181 million
Iceland	300,000	$5.0 billion
Biner Dasvasalam	300,000	$3.1 billion GDP (1987)
Barbados	300,000	$1.5 billion (1988)
Bahamas	300,000	$1.7 billion (1988)
Surinam	400,000	$1.3 billion
Malta	400,000	$2.3 billion
Luxemborg	400,000	$7.8 billion
Equatorial Guinea	400,000	$149 million GDP (1987)
Djibouti	400,000	$344 million GDP (1986)
Cape Verde	400,000	$281 million

[1] *The 1992 Information Please Almanac* 45th edition Houghton Mifflin Co. Boston 1992 Ex. Editor— Otto Johnson

[2] in billions (unless otherwise noted) *The World Almanac and Book of Facts 1992* Pharos Books New York 1992 Editor—Mark S. Hoffman

Former Yugoslavia: Slovenia, Croatia, Bosnia, Serbia, Montenegro, Macedonia

through preferential treatment status and attractive trade tariff rates for each other's products. In 1990, the United States signed a similar trade pact with Mexico. These pacts create the largest regional market cluster, which consists of Canada, the United States, and Mexico.

In Western Europe, the European Economic Community, consisting of twelve countries, is integrating its markets into a single "common market." All trade barriers between these countries are being dropped. It is expected that the common market will continue to integrate its economic structures and institutions until eventually all member countries have one currency by 1999.

In Eastern Europe, the former Soviet Union and Warsaw Pact countries are deregulating their economies and encouraging the creation of private enterprise and private markets. This change offers the possibility of creating a vast new market for all kinds of goods and services.

In the past decade, the Pacific region (Japan, Korea, Malaysia, Singapore, Taiwan, and Australia) has already emerged as a potent market and a powerful producer of goods and services. Throughout the remainder of this decade, this group of economies probably will overtake Western economies, including the United States, in size and productivity.

Besides the four regions just described, China and India make up huge autonomous markets in themselves. With populations of over 1.2 billion and 880 million, respectively, they have tremendous market potential. Even marginal improvement in their economies will create tremendous market opportunities. For example, during the 1984–1989 period in India, nearly 15% of the population entered the middle class. This created a market of nearly 130 million people (larger than many European countries) for all kinds of consumer goods and services.

This regional clustering of markets provides new opportunities and poses new challenges for globalization of businesses. Firms that want to target products and production for each region need to consider similarities in markets and consolidation of demand, facilitative trade conditions, and lower transportation costs due to proximity in location. The full strategic implications of regional consolidation are still not clear. However, firms that want to succeed in this emerging global economy will need to develop strategies for globalization (Bartlett and Ghoshal, 1989; Doz and Prahalad, 1991; Schonberger, 1990).

Strategic management of global businesses is different and more complicated than that of purely domestic businesses. This chapter examines strategic issues facing global firms and the creation and management of global strategies.

Levi Strauss is one of the few US apparel makers that can be honestly called global. Thirty-nine percent of its revenues and 60% of its pretax profits came from abroad in 1990. It has successfully marketed its jeans to foreign consumers in Europe, Asia, Latin America, and even the now dismantled Soviet Union. It bases its success on a unique global strategy that refocuses attention on basic jeans instead of diluting efforts over a broad product line. It gives local managers sufficient discretion to adjust their tactics to local conditions. Meanwhile, headquarters managers tightly control product quality and finances and provide support in marketing, advertising, and computerized systems. The company's advertising has emphasized its American roots and has used such all-American images like cruising in a '57 Chevy and James Dean lore to sell "American culture" to teenagers. It has created a top-drawer image for Levi jeans. Basic jeans that sell for $30 in the United States are able to fetch $63 in Tokyo and $83 in Paris.

The company has also smartly orchestrated its production and distribution activities abroad to exploit advantageous labor rates. It has a global network of its own eleven sewing plants and contract manufacturers. It is able to supply foreign customers from nearby factories, thereby minimizing shipping times and transportation costs. It is able to respond quickly to fads in denim shading and fashion trends in local markets. An important aspect of its global strategic control is the use of the Levi Link computer system. This system allows retailers to transfer sales and inventory data from bar-coded clothing directly to Levi's central computers. The data are analyzed and used for restocking retail outlets, production scheduling, and inventory management.

By orchestrating a wide range of variables—including product design, manufacturing systems, advertising, computerized control systems, and organizational structures—Levi Strauss has established a successful global business. It developed global competitive advantage by integrating operations in many different countries. To understand how firms can create successful global strategies, we need to understand the basic determinants of global competitive advantage.

9.1   GLOBAL COMPETITIVE ADVANTAGE

Global competitive advantage refers to the sustained ability of particular industries within a country to dominate world markets through superior performance (Shanks, 1985). Good examples of globally successful industries are the Italian ceramic tile industry; the German printing press industry and high-performance automobiles industry; the US patient-monitoring equipment industry and movie industry; and the Japanese consumer electronics industry and auto industry. What makes these industries successful on a worldwide scale?

Four Attributes of Competitive Advantage

Porter (1990) provides an elegant framework for understanding the determinants of global competitive advantage. He argues that there are four broad attributes of a nation that allow its firms within particular industries to gain global competitive advantage. These attributes are depicted in Figure 9.2.

Factor Conditions. Factors of production are the input resources necessary for producing goods and services. They include raw materials, labor, land, capital, physical and institutional infrastructure, technological knowledge, and so forth. A nation's endowments of these factors offers opportunities for deriving competitive advantage. The quality and quantity of physical resources, such as land, water, mineral deposits, timber, and climactic conditions, form the base for economic development. Human resources, such as a skilled work force, good labor relations, and supportive work ethic, are necessary for converting physical resources into useful products.

Countries with low wages (e.g., Hong Kong, Taiwan, Thailand) or cheap raw materials (cotton in India, forests in Finland, iron and copper ore in Brazil) provide cost advantages to indigenous producers over foreign producers. Similarly, countries with specialized scientific, technological, and market knowledge can gain technology-based advantages through patents over product and process technologies.

Figure 9.2 *For Attributes of National Competitive Advantage*

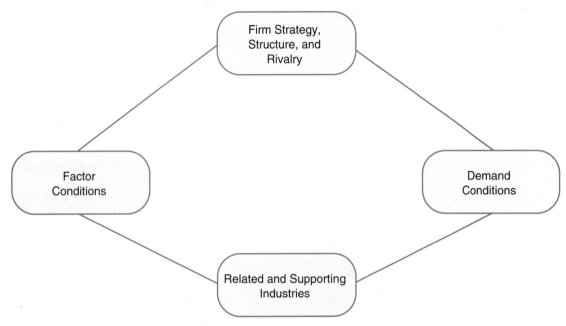

Adopted with permission from M. E. Porter, *The Competitive Advantage of Nations*, Free Press, New York, 1990.

Availability of finance capital is another source of competitive advantage for industries. Strong financial markets and other supporting financial and institutional infrastructure in a country can give its industries tremendous competitive advantage in global competition.

Demand Conditions. The nature of demand in home markets for the industry's products or services is the second broad determinant of national competitive advantage. Home demand serves as the stable base to establish businesses and hone the skills that will be needed to succeed in foreign markets. If the home market is large and differentiated, it offers local manufacturers the opportunity to develop economies of scale, differentiated products, technological innovations, and innovative distribution systems.

Some features of the home market demand increase its sophistication and place greater demands on manufacturers. These include total demand, rate of growth of demand, distribution of demand across various market segments and price ranges, sophistication, size and number of buyers, and size of export demand. These demand characteristics allow manufacturers to gain competitive advantage by achieving production efficiencies and economies of scale, gaining product design skills and packaging skills, and developing sophisticated marketing and distribution systems. The more variety that home country markets offer, the more skilled and flexible home country firms can become.

Related and Supporting Industries. The existence of related supplier industries that are themselves internationally competitive influences national competitive advantage in the global marketplace. These world-class suppliers can help manufacturers provide high-quality, innovative products, production flexibility, and price advantages. For example, the Japanese machine tool industry has gained global competitiveness entirely on the strength of Japanese producers of electronic instrumentation, motors, and numerical control devices. Similarly, the Swedish fabricated steel products (cutting tools, ball bearings) derive competitive advantage from the country's high-quality specialty steel producers.

It is not just the access to home suppliers that is of advantage. Instead, a high-quality supply industry permits ongoing *coordination*. It also allows producers and suppliers to *innovate* and *upgrade* products and processes. It gives them the flexibility to react quickly to opportunities in the global marketplace.

Firm Strategy, Structure, and Rivalry. The fourth national attribute that contributes to competitiveness in world markets is the industry context in which local firms are created, organized, and compete. The structure of the domestic industry decides the profitability of the industry as a whole and the profitability of firms in it. We discussed industry structure in Chapter 3. Here it is important to note that goals, strategies, ways of organizing firms, and firm profitability vary widely among nations. Competitive advantage for a particular nation emerges from a good match between domestic advantages and demands of the international marketplace. The more rivalrous and competitive the domestic industry is, the more likely it is to develop innovations, efficiencies, skills, technologies, and systems that will serve as the source of global competitive advantage.

Porter argues that these four attributes interact and influence each other in complex and dynamic ways to create competitive advantage for some particular national industries in international markets. Each attribute influences others and, in turn, is influenced by them to give industries unique performance capabilities.

Global Strategic Issues

The lesson from this analysis of the sources of competitive advantage of nations for global strategic management of firms is straightforward. Strategic success in the global marketplace can be ensured if firms base their international strategies on different national sources of competitive advantage. Once they have identified the basis for national competitive advantage, firms can attempt to become players by aligning internal resources to meet global market demands. In becoming global players, management must contend with several strategic issues not normally faced by purely domestic firms (Davidson, 1982):

1.   Global entry strategies and ownership policies
2.   Global production systems
3.   Global administration and control
4.   Global financial strategies

Each issue is the subject of a section in this chapter.

9.2   GLOBAL ENTRY STRATEGIES AND OWNERSHIP POLICIES

Becoming a global firm means entering several international markets and establishing international operations. Companies get involved in international operations in several ways. They usually begin the process of internationalization by exporting goods and services to foreign markets, while keeping production or operations and the administrative base in the home country. As export volumes increase, it may become more economical to set up operating subsidiaries in other countries. These subsidiaries vary from being simple liaison offices to full-fledged marketing and servicing organizations.

A successful company moves through these stages by making appropriate strategic choices about the mode of entry and form of ownership participation in foreign countries. Developing entry strategies for the global markets is a process similar to the development of competitive strategies in domestic markets, with one important difference. The firm already has an established set of standardized marketing and product policies in the home markets. Therefore, the focus now is on how to modify the existing product and market policies from the home country to fit the needs of the host countries that it plans to enter.

Mode of Entry

Strategic analysis for developing entry strategies should begin with an assessment of the size and future demand patterns in foreign markets. A general environmental analysis and competitive analysis of the industry should be conducted. This includes identifying the determinants of profitability in the targeted industry(ies) and sizing up existing competitor's buyers and suppliers. If the size of an individual country market is small, it may be meaningful to treat the combined markets in several regional countries as a single market and develop a single strategic plan for the region.

Typically, strategies for foreign markets vary from country to country and from those in the host country. This is due to different production cost structures, different distribution systems, and different economic and regulatory environments in foreign markets. These differences may dictate the need for changes in product design and marketing mix variables (price, promotion, packaging, and the distribution system). These differences also may require the development of new competitive strategies (Kobrin, 1991).

Besides these considerations, the firm may want to incorporate the concept of **international product life cycle** in deciding when to introduce new products into foreign markets. This is particularly useful in industrial and high-technology products. The idea of the international product life cycle is that each country needs products that are consistent with its stage of economic development and functional needs. Products that were useful, affordable, and popular in one country at one time may not be usable in another country later. For example, before 1940 motorcycles were used for transportation in many industrialized Western countries. In the 1950s the automobile replaced them as the dominant mode of transportation. Today, the primary use of motorcycles is for recreational purposes in most industrialized countries. In developing countries, however, motorcycles and other motorized two-wheel vehicles are becoming the dominant mode of private transportation, thereby creating huge markets. Japanese motorcycle manufacturers have used the concept of the international product life cycle to sequence their entry into markets in developing countries. They have successfully circulated their products through different countries depending on the country's needs and customer's ability to afford a vehicle.

Clearly, care must be exercised in making product choices. Host countries are sensitive to the fact that foreign firms may dump obsolete technologies into their underdeveloped economies, and by that, slow down their pace of modernization. This concern is genuine and most obvious in the computer and information technology industries. During the past two decades, international computer companies have sold obsolete, earlier-generation computers to developing countries. This practice prompted many countries to slap stringent import restrictions on the procurement of computers by local firms.

To avoid attracting unduly harsh regulation on the industry, it is reasonable to consult the regulators of host countries about the desirability of certain products in host markets. Even the most sensible product-sequencing plans may have to be abandoned if they conflict with the industrial and economic policies of a host country.

Forms of Ownership

Preferred forms of ownership of foreign ventures depend on both what is possible under the regulatory framework of the host country and the strategic objectives of the parent company. Ownership options include licensing arrangements, equity participation, and joint ventures. Each of these forms has different consequences for establishing competitive advantage.

Licensing is the easiest arrangement to establish, but it gives the parent company the least amount of control over the technology requiring licensing. It represents the mildest form of participation in foreign markets. It involves provision of technologies (product, process, and administrative) for a fee. Usually there is an up-front technical fee and a percentage royalty payment linked to volume of sales.

Equity participation is a more generic form of direct investment. In this case the parent company provides a part of the equity and raises the rest in the host country's capital markets or international capital markets. This form of participation can provide almost full control over the technology in use. Its only limitations are the foreign equity participation limits set by local laws.

Joint ventures are an intermediate form of participation in foreign markets. They involve technical and financial collaboration with companies in the host country. The parent company usually provides the technological knowledge and a part of the equity. A local partner in the host country invests the remaining equity. This arrangement allows the firm to share financial risks while maintaining strong control over technology and product quality.

Each of these forms of entry into foreign countries provides different competitive advantages, especially over the long run. The implications of each form for the future must be included in strategic analysis. For example, consider the worldwide metal containers industry in the 1960s. The US market leader, Continental Can, pursued foreign markets primarily through licensing agreements. Over time, and after many local innovations by its licensees, Continental lost nearly all control over the technology. In contrast, one of its licensees, Metal Box of the United Kingdom, went on to establish its own wholly owned subsidiaries in more than twenty countries and became a strong competitor to Continental. Another Continental competitor in the United States, Crown Cork and Seal, entered foreign markets not by licensing its technology, but with a few wholly owned subsidiaries. Twenty years later, Continental was at a competitive disadvantage in countries where it had only licensing agreements and its competitor Crown Cork and Seal had wholly owned subsidiaries.

Participation policies specify how the company will structure its ownership of foreign subsidiaries. The options range from 100% equity ownership of foreign subsidiaries, as seen at IBM and Coca-Cola, to purely technical collaboration with no equity ownership. There are many possibilities between these two extremes and the eventual choice depends on three factors:

1. *Product characteristics*: The *technology content of the product* is the most important determinant of how much control the firm should exercise over the product in foreign ventures. If the technology is very sophisticated and expensive and the product is continually updated through ongoing R&D, there is a good case for maintaining strict control over technology and its dissemination and future modifications. Other product considerations may include the ease with which the product can be copied by competitors, the strength of product patents in foreign countries, the extent of maintenance servicing the product requires, the degree of product modularity, and the length of the product life cycle. In factoring these considerations, efforts should be made to use the form of entry to establish control over the product.

2. *Production characteristics*: Another element in choosing the form of participation is the nature of the *production system*. The participation form should allow and encourage the transfer of production experience to the foreign subsidiary. If the parent is already benefiting from experience effects, these should be available to the subsidiary. This may warrant tighter control over the subsidiary through higher equity control. Technological characteristics of the production process also may influence the appropriate degree of control. These include degree of automation, need for highly skilled labor, ease of maintaining quality in production, and maintenance requirements.

3. *Host Country Characteristics*: The most important factor that decides the degree of control that the firm can establish in foreign subsidiaries is the *regulations in the host countries* and the flexibility of host country's government to accommodate the needs of the firm. Most countries have laws setting the upper limits of foreign equity participation. These upper limits may vary from 100% foreign equity in liberal, friendly, open market economies such as the United Kingdom to one third or lower in countries with mixed economies like India, China, and the Eastern Block. Although established legal limits exist, most countries are open to negotiating higher levels of foreign equity participation for new and high technologies that they need. Thus, the form of participation is often subject to negotiations between the parent company and the host country government.

Another element that should be considered in selecting the form of participation, particularly in developing countries, is the nature of environmental and product liability laws. In some countries, the parent may be held strictly liable for damages caused by operations of its subsidiary, *even if it is a minor equity participant*. In such circumstances, appropriate risk management techniques and liability insurance should be adopted (Davidson, 1982; Nohria and Garcia-Pont, 1991).

9.3   GLOBAL PRODUCTION SYSTEMS

As firms become global, they have many options about where they locate production facilities and how they organize the logistics of supplying products and services to foreign markets. Establishing a rationalized system of manufacturing facilities and organizing efficient procurement of supplies from suppliers worldwide can give a firm global competitive advantage. The key to gaining this advantage lies in the firm's ability to exploit opportunities for getting economies of large-scale production, lower labor costs in some locations, and minimizing transportation costs from production facilities to markets.

In the initial stages of establishing global markets, demand in foreign markets is often not large enough to justify a captive production facility in each country. Foreign markets may have to be supplied from distant production sources. In these situations, the most important factor to control is the cost of transportation.

As demand grows, however, each foreign market may require its own separate facility. This may create duplication of facilities and raise the costs of production. At this stage, attempts must be made to rationalize the use of distributed production facilities. This requires cost-efficient sourcing and integration of facilities. Cost-efficient sourcing means acquiring parts and components internally or externally from the lowest-cost supplier. It may require different plants of a firm to specialize in specific parts or subassemblies and to supply these to each other. For example, IBM's plants in Europe specialize and export the majority of their production to each other.

Consolidation of production units refers to eliminating duplication and costs by judicious combination of facilities. This may be required when internal costs of production are higher than the costs of obtaining from outside. Some of these costly facilities may be closed, combined, or put to alternative uses.

Once established in global markets, or even while creating competitive advantage for global marketing, a firm may choose the strategy of **world-scale manufacturing**. This refers to establishment of a central, large-scale, volume-oriented, capital-intensive, automated production facility that produces standardized products for supplying worldwide markets. Smaller regional or country units that modify, package, customize, or service the products according to local requirements support this central production facility (Harmon and Peterson, 1989; Schonberger, 1990). Examples of such operations are common in the TV, automobile, and steel industries in Japan. Nearly all the chassis for black-and-white TVs produced in Japan are produced in one plant. Similarly, Honda manufactures motorcycles and automobile engines and parts centrally in large volumes and supplies them worldwide to its assembling plants. Nike makes most of its shoes in large, world-scale plants in Taiwan and South Korea.

The location of the central plant is not required to be in the home country. It should be based on considerations of raw materials costs, labor costs, import and export regulations of the country, political stability of the country, fluctuations in exchange rates, labor problems, availability of infrastructure services, distribution of worldwide demand, and sociopolitical variables. Many US companies in the textile, consumer electronics, footwear, and home appliance industries have now established offshore production units in South America and Asia.

In planning for global production systems, firms must keep in mind the important trends toward global market clustering identified at the beginning of this chapter.

9.4   GLOBAL ADMINISTRATION AND CONTROL

Designing a global administrative structure requires dealing with three issues. The first is *how to structure* the firm by allocating appropriate authority and responsibility for performance of worldwide operations. This involves appropriately differentiating (dividing into manageable subunits) and integrating (coordinating the subunits) worldwide operations. The second issue is *how to coordinate and resolve conflicts* that are particular to global operations. These include conflicts between headquarters and foreign subsidiaries and conflicts between multinational corporations and the governments of host countries. The third issue is *how to develop effective control systems* that can monitor and control remote operations (Kim and Mauborgne, 1991).

Structuring the organization requires dividing it into manageable subunits. This may be done according to products, functions, operating units, geographic regions, or a combination of these factors. Most US firms with significant international operations initially organize themselves through an international division. The division is an autonomous unit that handles all international operations outside the normal domestic organizational structure. This arrangement is adequate only for limited-size operations (Stopford and Wells, 1972).

As international operations grow, firms tend to adopt a global structure based on product line or on geographic area. In the former, worldwide product divisions control activities related to specific product lines. In the later, geographic divisions (European Division, Asian Division, etc.) are responsible for all products for a particular geographic area. Another possibility is the hybrid structure that combines product and geographic structures, namely, the matrix structure. In this case profit responsibility rests with the foreign affiliate, which also reports to product-line managers and geographic regional managers on product and financial performance targets, respectively.

Global structures have several advantages. They allow worldwide standardization of operations. They also provide increased integration of foreign activities with domestic operations in the areas of marketing, competitive strategy, and technology transfer. They simplify communications and flow of information among domestic and foreign operations.

Coordinating global operations is a complex task usually handled by staff at the corporate headquarters. Top managers from foreign subsidiaries participate in the annual planning meeting at the headquarters to coordinate strategic plans. Plans and objectives of foreign operations are reviewed by corporate staff and integrated into the complete corporate plan of the company. Headquarters formally approves strategic plans of each foreign subsidiary.

Whereas the coordination of global planning activities is elaborate, the coordination of operations is often minimal. Foreign subsidiaries usually operate with great autonomy. They send annual, semiannual, or quarterly reports of their operation to headquarters and to other pertinent divisions of the firm. These reports allow sharing of data within the company. However, local subsidiary managers make their own decisions regarding local operating problems.

Conflict resolution between parent and subsidiary is an important aspect of coordinating a global enterprise. Conflicts arise because of several reasons. Managers in foreign affiliates operate in different environments and have different information about their problems than headquarters managers. Therefore, they often do not see things in the same way, which causes conflicts about which issues should receive priority. Conflicts also arise from miscommunications among distantly located managers. Foreign affiliates sometimes seek more autonomy and control over local resources and profits than the parent is willing to give them. Often, this leads to conflict. For example, transfer pricing between business units, which is a contentious issue even in domestic firms, is a common source of conflicts in global companies. Transfer price is the price one business unit of a firm charges another for the goods and services it provides. It is common practice for firms to have units specialize in certain components and services and supply all parts of the organization with these. Conflict arises when external, local suppliers can supply the same goods at a lower price or with better delivery and quality terms. Under such circumstances, obtaining the item from internal suppliers places unnecessary financial burden on the units. Because evaluation of all units is based on profits, the added cost of acquiring internally is resented by sister units.

Resolving conflicts requires establishment of clear policies to govern issues such as international transfer pricing, mutual sourcing of items, coordination of international sales territories, technology transfer and licensing agreements, and international labor contracts. Moreover, there must be clear-cut procedures for conflict resolution established at the regional level, so that top management is not saddled with the problem of mediating routine disputes over operating matters. Sometimes this can be done simply by designating the authority who will resolve such matters and articulating the basic principles for conflict resolution.

9.5   GLOBAL FINANCIAL STRATEGIES

Strategic management of global operations requires establishment of global financial policies that (1) guide foreign investment decisions, (2) guide ways of raising capital from world financial markets, and (3) structure the day-to-day financial management activities. Such policies represent functional area methods aimed at streamlining the global finance function. Designing the policies is the subject matter of the field of international financial management. The subject is too broad and complicated to be treated in depth in this book. The importance of establishing these policies, however, must be acknowledged. In the interest of providing a comprehensive view of global strategic management, we now briefly discuss the topics that need to be covered by global financial policies.

Making sound foreign investment decisions requires an appropriate capital budgeting system, profit repatriation policies, and international tax policies. The capital budgeting system should be linked to the total strategic planning system of the firm. It provides top management with a mechanism for controlling new investments, systematically evaluating risk-return characteristics of projects, and allocating responsibility for some investment levels to foreign affiliates.

Profit repatriation policies depend on several considerations. They establish trade-offs between the need for reinvesting profits to develop the foreign affiliate and the need for contributing profits to the corporate parent. Typically, retaining earnings for local developmental activities and reserves is a sensible policy, because it protects the firm from later having to transfer resources from the parent to the affiliate. The local laws governing repatriation of profits are another consideration. Many countries, particularly those with shortages of hard currency, place restrictions on the amount of profits that can be repatriated. Another consideration is fluctuations in exchange rates. These fluctuations may impose additional costs on repatriation transactions.

International tax planning is a critical aspect of managing global financial operations. Foreign projects are sometimes dependent on and justified based on special tax benefits. To exploit these benefits, careful tax planning is necessary. There are good reasons for leaving the tax planning of foreign affiliates to local managers. They are more familiar with local tax codes and annual changes in codes. They also know local tax authorities better than headquarters staff. However, local optimization of tax plans may not lead to global optimization for the whole company. To ensure corporate-wide optimization, affiliate tax plans should be coordinated by a central group. Expertise to coordinate tax plans centrally may not be available internally and may have to be hired from the outside. International accounting firms serve this need.

All the capital required to manage global operations need not come from the parent company or from investors in the parent's home country. In fact, global firms have the opportunity to participate in capital markets in several countries. Each country offers different forms of capital and varying rates. The variation in interest rates and rates of return on capital in different countries could be as high as 100% or 200%. For example, the central-bank interest rate in December 1991 was 3.5% in the United States, 8% in Germany, and 11% in India. By raising capital in different countries, a global firm can take advantage of these variations and reduce its total cost of capital.

Structuring day-to-day financial management activities includes establishment of cash management policies, funding of operations, managing intercompany transactions, financial reporting, and managing of exchange exposures. Except for exposure management, the activities are international extensions of domestic financial activities. In making the extension to the international sphere, domestic policies are modified to consider local and international laws, intergovernmental treaties, and local commercial practices.

To protect themselves from losing money on international transactions, international firms must manage their foreign exchange exposures. Exposure management deals with reducing two special risks associated with international businesses: transaction risk and translation risk. Every international transaction (buying or selling, payment or receipt) takes time to execute. During this time, exchange rates may change unfavorably for the company and the company loses money. Translation exposure occurs during consolidation of the financial statements of foreign affiliates. In this process, the asset and liability balances of the affiliate must be converted from local currency to dollar (or parent-company currency) amounts. Changes in exchange rates can cause these reported balances to increase or decrease, resulting in changes in the book value of the parent company.

Both these exposures can be managed through centrally coordinated financial management. This requires netting exposures in different currencies. Foreign affiliates report their payable and receivable positions denominated in local currencies to a central unit. Liabilities and assets are offset against these positions to yield net exposed positions in each currency for the corporation as a whole every day. Exposure may be further reduced by engaging in hedging activities. This involves estimating movement of foreign exchange rates and accordingly balancing receivables and payables (by postponing and hastening them to the firm's advantage).

We are now witnessing an integration of world economies. Several regional clusters of markets are forming that will eventually create truly global markets. Corporations will have to deal with this process of globalization through the rest of the 1990s. Developing strategies for global competitiveness requires that firms choose an appropriate mode of entry into foreign markets—a mode that meets the company's objectives, technological needs, and host country regulations. Firms must rationalize their production systems to take advantage of location-based materials, labor, and transportation economies.

Administratively, global coordination and control must deal with the vexing problems of interdivisional conflicts and coordination of distant operations. This calls for design of new administrative structures and systems. Finally, global strategies imply more complex financial management. Financial strategies are needed for balancing cash flows, dealing with profit repatriation, hedging fluctuations in exchange rates, and managing risk exposure in multiple financial markets.

SUMMARY OF CHAPTER 9

From economic and competitive perspectives, globalization of businesses is becoming a necessity. This is especially true in new and high-growth industries. The world economy is consolidating into several regional markets: the European Economic Community, the Pacific basin, the North American countries, the former Eastern Block nations, China, and India. New market opportunities are emerging in these regional clusters.

To exploit these emerging opportunities, it is important for firms to conduct global strategic management. Global strategic management deals with creating and managing a global enterprise. Global companies operate in global markets and have global production and distribution systems. They maintain global administrative control and do global financial management. Global competitive advantage can be gained only by considering worldwide markets and resource conditions.

To enter international markets, firms may need to modify their domestic strategies to suit the conditions of foreign markets. Changes should be based on general environmental analysis and competitive industry analysis of the foreign markets. For each foreign market, managers should analyze determinants of profitability, production-cost structure, distribution systems, and regulations.

The economic development stage of a country, its economic regulations, and its functional needs have a strong influence on demand for products. These factors also influence the type of ownership arrangement that may be feasible in foreign countries. Ownership depends on product and production characteristics and on the regulations of the host country.

Firms can gain global competitive cost advantages by exploiting the production and resource capabilities of different countries. Rationalizing production facilities for global markets can provide economies of scale.

Global administration involves allocating appropriate authority and responsibility for the performance of foreign operations. It involves coordinating international operations, resolving conflicts, and developing effective control systems.

Managing international financial strategies is another key aspect of global strategic management. It requires establishing international financial policies. These policies guide foreign investment decisions and structure day-to-day financial management activities. Appropriate capital budgeting systems, profit repatriation policies, and international tax policies ease the financial management of global companies. Routine financial management of global operations requires establishment of cash management policies, funding of operations, managing intercompany transactions, financial reporting, and managing of exchange exposures.

READINGS, CASES, AND POLICY DOCUMENTS

The following readings, cases, and policy documents provide additional background material for the concepts discussed in this Chapter.

Readings

Ansoff, H.I. "The changing shape of the strategic problem." In D. Schendel and C.W. Hofer (Eds) *Strategic Management: A New View of Business Policy and Planning*, Boston: Little Brown and Co., 1979.

* Porter, M.E. "The competitive advantage of nations." *Harvard Business Review*, March-April, 1990, pp. 73-93.

Cases

Citicorp - British National Life Assurance (U.K.)

* Comdisco Disaster Recovery Services International Expansion (Western Europe)

* Copenhagen Handelsbank (Denmark)

* Dunlop - Pirelli Union (U.K. and Italy)

Honeywell Europe (U.S.A.—Europe)

* ISKRA Power Tools (Eastern Europe)

* Matshushita Electric Industries (Japan)

Union Carbide Corporation (U.S.A. - India)

YKK Zippers, Inc. (Japan - Europe)

Policy Documents

American Express Travel Related Services—The Next Ten Years

* The NYNEX Vision

* indicates particularly appropriate assignments

Figures 9.1 & 9.2.

Strategic Management Process and Book Outline

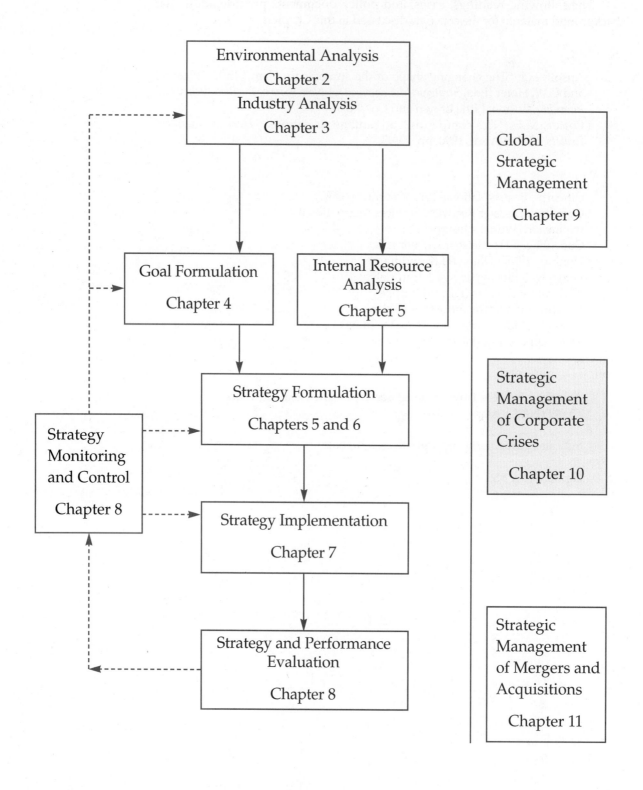

CHAPTER 10
MANAGEMENT OF
CORPORATE CRISES

CHAPTER OUTLINE

Corporate crises threaten the company's most important goals and its survival. They represent an important strategic problem for companies today. Increasingly, top management is having to deal with unplanned situations that threaten the very existence of their companies. Consider the following examples.

For many years Tylenol had been the leading over-the-counter pain killer in the United States. In October 1982, six people in a Chicago suburb who had just taken Tylenol capsules died of cyanide poisoning. A quick investigation by the company revealed that the Tylenol these victims had ingested was contaminated with the deadly poison cyanide. The contamination was not caused by a manufacturing defect, but by tampering with the product, probably after it had reached retail outlets. As news reports of these deaths started coming in, Johnson & Johnson, the parent company, realized what a major risk to public health this incident posed. There were millions of capsules in the distribution system and on store shelves across the United States. It was not known if the tampering was an isolated incident in Chicago or if it was more widespread. Consultations with local police and the FBI suggested that the tampering was the work of a psychopath. The extent of tampering was not determinable. McNeil Labs, the manufacturer of Tylenol, and its parent Johnson & Johnson found themselves in the throes of a major crisis.

In the late 1960s, Occidental Petroleum embarked on an aggressive strategy of expanding market share by acquiring specialty chemical companies. One company it bought was Hooker Chemicals, a company with plants in upstate New York (Niagara Falls). During the 1952–1956 period, Hooker Chemicals had buried hazardous chemical wastes in an abandoned canal called Love Canal. After the canal was filled, it was covered with mud and dirt and forgotten. Later, it was sold for the price of $1 to local municipal authorities and became the site of a school playground and residential housing. In 1974 residents of the area noticed a foul smell emanating from the site and chemicals leaching from the ground. This started a process of media and governmental investigations and heightening public concerns about health and safety of area residents. Before long, Occidental Petroleum found itself in the middle of a major crisis that threatened its finances, tarnished its image, and tied it up in lawsuits for several years.

Johnson & Johnson and Occidental Petroleum are not isolated cases. Corporate crises are becoming increasingly frequent and devastating. How can corporations prepare for, prevent, and manage these crises? These issues form the focus of this chapter. The chapter begins by describing characteristics and types of crises faced by companies. It discusses corporate and business unit strategies for preventing and preparing for crises. It shows how crises can be prevented by making a corporation's business portfolio inherently safe through screening out technologies that pose unduly high risks. The chapter argues that companies must prepare for crises by conducting periodic crisis audits and establishing a trained crisis-management team. Finally, it discusses the basic tasks of crisis management: structuring a crisis, rescue and emergency management, stakeholder communications, conflict resolution, and business recovery.

Corporate crises are harmful events that threaten the survival and long-term health of the company. A variety of internal and external environmental failures are the causes of crises. Internal failures that can cause crises include labor strikes, cash flow shortages, industrial accidents, environmental pollution incidents, product injuries, and occupational hazards. Crises from environmental forces include hostile takeover attempts, decline in market demand, foreign competition, attacks from public interest groups, terrorism, and regulatory changes.

Crisis-triggering events cause extensive damage to human life, to property, to company image and reputation, and to the natural environment. They threaten the survival of corporations in which they originate because of the withdrawal of support from customers and the financial community. They place corporations under media and government scrutiny. Once a crisis occurs, investigations into company affairs proliferate, whether they relate to the crisis or not. Crises create major financial liabilities for firms. In some cases in the recent past, these liabilities lead to bankruptcy of the company.

Some examples of crises related to product harm include the Dalkon shield crisis of A. H. Robins, the Tylenol crisis of Johnson & Johnson, and the infant formula crisis of Nestle. Union Carbide at Bhopal, Metropolitan Edison at Three Mile Island, and Hooker Chemicals at Love Canal all experienced crises caused by industrial accidents and incidents of environmental pollution. An example of crisis caused by labor dispute was the International Harvester strike in 1976–1978. The strike lead to a 40% drop in the company's market share and drove the company to the brink of bankruptcy. Foreign competition has been the source of crises in several US steel companies. Competition from Japanese and German companies has forced a complete restructuring of the entire steel industry. Figure 10.1 indicates the range of events that can cause crises in companies.

Corporate crises represent a corporate strategic problem that is receiving increasing attention from the media, the public, and government. Top management of corporations has had to devote increasing amounts of time and energy to it. In many companies, more than 50% of top management's time is spent dealing with such events. Some crises are caused by multiple sources; all organizations and strategic managers need to be prepared for dealing with them.

10.1   CHARACTERISTICS OF CORPORATE CRISES

The first important characteristic of crises is **surprise**. No matter how well managers understand the normal operations of their business, they are never fully prepared to deal with crises. In spite of experiencing a previous crisis or multiple near-misses, the onset of a real crisis is always a surprise. Thus, crises represent novel situations for which managers are not. For example, the *second* incident of Tylenol poisoning in 1986 took Johnson & Johnson by surprise. By then the company had disbanded its 1982 crisis-management team under the presumption that such an event could not occur to them again.

A second characteristic is **time pressure to act**. Crises often occur suddenly and involve events that managers have not analyzed previously. They require managers to make many decisions in a very short time. This creates a tremendous pressure to act quickly. An escalating flow of events exacerbates time pressures. Even before any remedial actions are taken, many different things go wrong. Like falling dominoes, the events cumulatively build up the seriousness of damages and the scope of their effects. For example, in the Union Carbide crisis in Bhopal,

---

Figure 10.1 *List of Corporate Crises*

- Major Product Defects (e.g., Dalkon shield of A. H. Robins)
- Major Plant and Equipment Failure (e.g., Three Mile Island of Metropolitan Edison)
- Major Industrial Accident (e.g., Bhopal disaster of Union Carbide)
- Hostile Takeover (e.g., Nestle's infant-formula crisis)
- Securities Fraud (e.g., insider trading at Drexel Burnham Lambert)
- Illegal Financial Transactions (e.g., money laundering by First Boston)
- Onsite Sabotage (e.g., polluting meat products at Hormel)
- Offsite Sabotage (e.g., Tylenol poisonings at Johnson & Johnson)
- Attacks by Activists (e.g., Operation PUSH attack on Coca-Cola)
- Terrorism (e.g., bomb threat at Gulf Oil)
- Executive Kidnapping (e.g., hostages in Electronic Data System's Iran office)
- Natural Disasters (e.g., hurricanes, floods, and earthquakes)
- Counterfeiting (e.g., computer and apparel industries)

before the company could even assess damages or causes of the accident, local authorities impounded the plant from the company. As the company sought to gain back control over the plant, its CEO Warren Anderson was arrested when he arrived in Bhopal. Before the end of the week, the company was under siege by victims, government agencies, and the media. Soon after that, thousands of victims sued the company.

A third characteristic of crisis is **imperfect information for decision making**. Information available for making decisions in the immediate aftermath of crisis is incomplete, contradictory, subjective, undocumented, and in the form of opinions. Managers have little time available to verify the correctness of information or to analyze it. In the Bhopal crisis, Union Carbide managers and medical doctors in Bhopal did not have basic toxicological information on the poisonous methyl isocyanate that had caused injuries. This made it impossible for them to treat victims, and they had to resort to simple symptomatic treatments.

The fourth characteristic of crisis is the **critical scrutiny** that corporations receive from the outside. The media, regulatory agencies, politicians, and community leaders seek information on the crisis and investigate the company's role in causing it. The interesting thing about this scrutiny is that it is mostly negative. The media is usually critical. Even friendly politicians and community leaders distance themselves from the company. Regulatory agencies start investigating everything related or unrelated to the crisis. For example, an infant formula produced by Gerber was found to contain glass pieces. The company denied any error on its part and claimed that the glass pieces were caused by chipping away of the glass jars during transportation. Nevertheless, the media jumped on this incident and i andnvestigated Gerber's safety performance on many products. The FDA conducted its own investigations. The company received much negative publicity over the incident.

During a crisis, the **board of directors and top management are often thrown into confusion**. The board members represent different constituencies and stakeholders and pull the company in different directions. Confusion occurs in top management because its responsibilities in a crisis are not always clear, because typically, firms are not organized to deal with crises. They are organized for steady-state operations. Employees feel insecure and upset because crises involve large-scale damages and threats to organizational survival. Crises threaten jobs and stigmatize the company name. Its resources are under siege.

Another important characteristic of some crises is a **sudden decline in stock prices**. Financial markets often overreact to bad news, and stable investors tend to abandon companies in crisis. They are uncertain about the financial consequences of the crisis. This increased uncertainty invites speculators and arbitragers to acquire the company stock. Speculative trading of stocks may put the troubled company "in play" and in the market for corporate takeovers (Meyers and Holusha, 1986; Reilly, 1987; Smart and Vertinsky, 1984). The case of Union Carbide exemplifies this characteristic. The Bhopal crisis depressed the company's stock price by nearly 40% for several months. During this time, GAF Corporation and several Wall Street specialists acquired a large stake in the company. In August 1985, GAF announced its plans to takeover the company. This forced Union Carbide to divest 20% of its most profitable assets to ward off the takeover attack.

When companies are not prepared for dealing with crises, they respond in characteristic ways that exacerbate damages. They lose control of the situation. Managers panic and a feeling of helplessness overcomes them. They exhibit a siege mentality. They try to protect resources at all costs and stonewall the media. They downplay effects of the event, even when they do not know all of the effects. They try to blame a single individual or people outside the firm for causing the crisis. Decisions are focused on the short term and deal with symptoms instead of causes. These unprepared responses deepen the crisis for the firm (Mitroff and Pauchant, 1990). All these responses were apparent in the *Exxon Valdez* oil spill. Exxon tried to assign blame for the accident to the ship's captain. It blamed its own failure to respond to the oil spill on delays caused in getting permissions from state and federal regulatory agencies. It minimized the environmental damage caused by the spill. And, after a few months of cleanup effort, it claimed that most of the environmental damage had been rectified. Throughout the crisis, Exxon reluctantly gave out information to the media and public interest groups.

To deal with corporate crises, managers need to understand their causes and develop strategies for preventing them. Our discussion suggests that there are many different types of crises, each having different causes. Therefore, a first step in understanding the cause of corporate crises is to develop a scheme for characterizing different types of crises—a typology.

10.2   A TYPOLOGY OF CORPORATE CRISES

The typology of crises suggested here was derived from a compilation of different crises that corporations have faced in the past decade. Each crisis resulted from organization-environment interactions of sociotechnical factors. The main causes of crises were either internal or external to the organization, and they dealt with either technical and economic or human, organizational, and social factors. Crises can, therefore, be classified along these dimensions, as shown in Figure 10.2 (Shrivastava and Mitroff, 1987). Using these dimensions to classify different types of corporate crises, we have the four cells shown in Figure 10.2.

Cell 1 represents technological or economic failures in internal organizational systems. Crises occur because of failures in the core technology of firms or in organizational policies and procedures. Defective plant equipment, design, or supplies are the primary causes of these crises. Major industrial accidents, such as Bhopal, Three Mile Island, and Chernobyl, are examples of crises that fit in this cell.

Crises in Cell 2 result primarily from technological and economic failures in the firm's environment, which cause crisis within the organization. For example, hostile takeover attempts prompted by restructuring of industries, changes in exchange rates, other macroeconomic forces, or attacks by corporate raiders can create crises for corporations.

Cell 3 represents failures in internal human, organizational, and social processes and systems. Operator or managerial errors, intentional harm by saboteurs or psychopaths, faulty control systems, inadequate safety policies, unhealthy working conditions, miscommunications, and failure in decision-making systems are the primary causes of these failures. Unsafe decisions and deliberate harm result from these failures. The explosion of the space shuttle Challenger, which created a crisis for NASA and many of its subcontractors, could be attributed to this type of failure.

Cell 4 represents failures in the external human or social environment of corporations. These crises happen when human agents or social institutions in the company's environment react adversely to the corporation. Incidents of sabotage, terrorism, or offsite product tampering are examples of such failures. The Tylenol

Figure 10.2 *Different Types of Corporate Crisis Triggers*

Technical/Economic

CELL 1 Major Industrial Accidents Defective Products Computer Breakdowns Undisclosed Information	**CELL 2** Widespread Environmental Destruction Hostile Takeovers Societal Crises (Civil or Political) Large-scale System Failure
CELL 3 Sabotage by Insiders Communications Breakdown Illegal Activities of Employees Occupational Health Diseases	**CELL 4** Sabotage by Outsiders Terrorism, Kidnappings Counterfeiting Symbolic Projection

Internal (left side) — **External** (right side)

Human/Organizational/Social

poisonings, presumably done by an outsider, would fall in this category. Similarly, the illegal detention by local authorities of two executives of Electronic Data Systems during the tumultuous Iranian revolution created a crisis for the company. The company financed an attempt to rescue the executives from a prison in Tehran.

Industrial Crises

Industrial crises represent a special type of corporate crisis. Their causes cut across the four cells depicted in Figure 10.2. In the recent past they have played havoc with human lives, the natural environment, and organizational resources. These crises *involve industrial facilities and products*. They are triggered either by sudden and discrete harmful events or by chronic harmful conditions. Examples of the former are industrial accidents and incidents of environmental pollution. These typically occur in hazardous industrial facilities, such as nuclear power plants and chemical plants, and hazardous storage facilities and transportation systems.

An example of a chronic-harm triggering event for crisis was the aggressive marketing of infant formula in developing countries. Harm caused by infant formula use in the 1970s led to a crisis for Nestle and other manufacturers of infant formula. Customers mixed the formula in polluted water and diluted it to levels where infants suffered from malnutrition. Large-scale misuse of the product led to a whole generation of malnourished children. It created major conflicts among Nestle, other producers of infant formula, and public interest groups. The public interest groups along with United Nations agencies and the World Council of Churches organized a worldwide boycott of Nestle products, which created a crisis for the company.

Environmental pollution and toxic waste disposal are other examples of slow, chronic harm that can create crises for companies. Recall the Love Canal incident, which caused a crisis for Hooker Chemicals and its parent, Occidental Petroleum. Similarly, Chisso, a chemical company in Japan, faced a crisis as a result of mercury poisoning of Minamata Bay. Tons of mercury-based toxic waste from the company's plant were released into Minamata Bay in the 1940s and 1950s. This waste poisoned the fish in the bay. Over the years, about 500 people who consumed the fish died of mercury poisoning, and illness and mental retardation occurred in thousands of people.

Unhealthy occupational and work conditions are another source of slow, continuous crisis. Companies manufacturing or using asbestos have had major health problems among their workers. Johns Manville, the largest producer of asbestos, went bankrupt because of the damages it had to pay to injured workers and consumers (see the John Mansville case study in this book).

To prepare for and prevent industrial crises, managers must understand their causes. Crises are caused by many simultaneous failures. Figure 10.3 depicts the causes of crises in terms of internal and external failures. **Internal failures** occur in the technological core, in the organizational context, and in human interactions with the technology. The technological core includes hardware, software, and operations of industrial facilities. An organizational context surrounds this technological core. It is made up of an organization's structure, culture, systems, policies, and procedures. Human interactions with the technology take the form of operator and managerial judgments and decisions.

External failures also contribute to crises. Failures in the external environment consist of poor or inadequate regulations, poor safety infrastructure, and lack of community preparedness to deal with crises.

Crises are the result of *simultaneous and interacting failures* in these elements (Perrow, 1984). Crisis-triggering events usually, though not always, occur within the technological core. The seriousness of the accident escalates if the organization's systems, policies, and management are unable to stop the event. Harm caused by the accident may be exacerbated by conditions in the external environment. Failures in regulatory systems, infrastructure, and the level of preparedness of communities living around hazardous facilities vastly increase the level of harm. Infrastructure refers to basic services that make industries safe: transportation, communications, water supply, electrical supply, housing, hygiene, sewage systems, and so on. When these are inadequate, the affected community is not able to cope with the accident; crisis is the result.

The key point is to recognize that crises are rooted in *multiple causes inside and outside* the organization. Therefore, preventing and managing them requires addressing issues of both internal organization and external environment.

10.3   STRATEGIC MANAGEMENT OF CORPORATE CRISES

Strategic management of corporate crises must focus on both preventing crises from occurring and developing corporate capabilities for managing crises if they do occur. Figure 10.4 is a simplified model for organizing corporate crisis management.

Figure 10.3 *Crisis Causes*

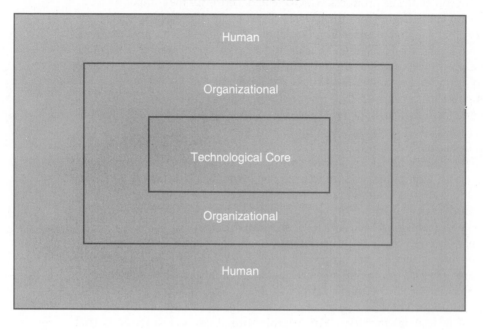

INTERNAL FAILURES

EXTERNAL FAILURES

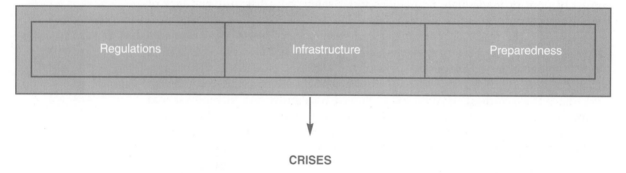

CRISES

    The first step in crisis management is **early detection of error signals**. The organization must establish early warning systems both in technical plants and facilities and in administrative systems. These systems serve as the eyes and ears of the organization and should identify potential sources of crises in advance. Warnings must reach top management so that they can be incorporated into strategic decisions.

    The next step of crisis management is the organization's **preparation for crises and prevention planning.** Preparation involves ensuring that adequate safety policies and equipment are in place in the organization. Planning for crisis

Figure 10.4 *A Model of Corporate Crisis Management*

prevention begins with the assumption that any type of crisis can affect the corporation. However, all corporations are not equally susceptible to all types of crises. The crisis potential of corporations varies with the types of technologies they use, the nature of their products and customers, and their external environment. To understand their own crisis potential, firms need to evaluate carefully hazards posed by each product or process technology in their business portfolio.

The next step is to establish **crisis-management and damage control systems** at both the corporate and business unit levels. These systems include emergency management, stakeholder communications programs, and conflict resolution mechanisms. After the hot phase of a crisis has passed, the organization still needs to plan for **business recovery** (Mitroff and Pauchant, 1990; Meyers and Holusha, 1986; Shrivastava, 1987). In the next sections, we discuss how these crisis management tasks can be accomplished.

Corporate Strategies

Crisis-management efforts at the corporate level should aim at reducing the complete crisis potential of the corporation. This can be accomplished through designing safer technology portfolios, identifying likely sources of crises through regular crisis audits, and enhancing corporate capacity to deal with crises by establishing crisis-management teams.

Corporate Technology Portfolio Matrix. A primary concern of corporate strategy is the choice of product-market portfolios. Traditionally, financial and market criteria determine this choice. In Chapter 5 we saw how a portfolio of business is created to achieve a needed rate of return on investment and to ensure a steady rate of growth. Inherent in the design of business portfolios is the choice of technologies and consequent levels of technological risk. This risk can be reduced by designing portfolios with safer technological choices.

In Chapter 5 we also described the traditional criteria for choosing product-market portfolios based on the BCG matrix or the GE multifactor portfolio matrix. These portfolio models used market power and industry growth as criteria for choosing businesses. Besides these criteria, companies should screen businesses based on their **crisis potential**. One scheme for such screening is the **technology portfolio matrix**. Figure 10.5 shows a simple form of this matrix that can enable

Figure 10.5 Technology Portfolio Matrix

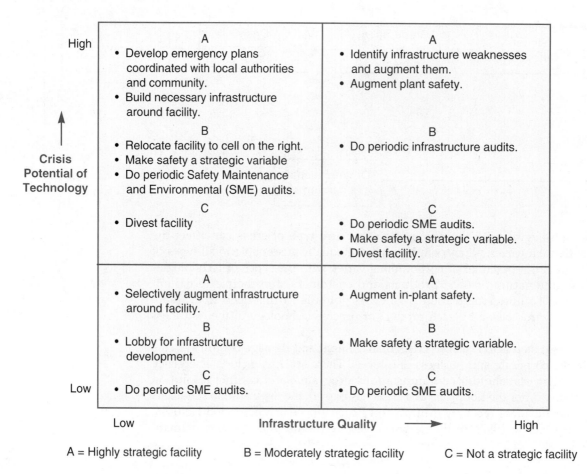

A = Highly strategic facility   B = Moderately strategic facility   C = Not a strategic facility

firms to make safe technological choices. The vertical axis represents the crisis potential of technologies used by the business. The horizontal axis represents the quality of the environmental infrastructure supporting the business. Using these two dimensions, a four-cell matrix is created.

Evaluative criteria for assessing the crisis potential of technological facilities are listed in Figure 10.6. These criteria should be used to assess each business facility for its susceptibility to crises. Assessment should lead to categorization of the facility as having high or low crisis potential. A similar kind of assessment can be made about the quality of environmental infrastructure in which the facility is located. The environment may be assessed on variables such as quality of infrastructural services, strength and implementation of regulations, and level of community preparedness to handle emergencies.

Business units of the corporations can be plotted on the matrix as circles whose size is proportional to their strategic importance to corporate objectives. Strategic importance may be measured by the proportion of the business unit's profit to the total profit of the company. Or, another composite measure of strategic importance may be developed. Businesses of more strategic importance are represented by larger circles. Figure 10.5 lists recommendations for businesses

Figure 10.6 *Evaluative Criteria for Measuring Crisis Potential of Technologies*

1. Intentionality of Harm (high, moderate, and low)

2. Spatial Reach of Harm (square miles or radius around facility)

3. Concentration of Releasable Energy (catastrophic, high, . . . low)

4. Persistence of Harm (days, weeks, . . . years)

5. Population at Risk (number, concentrations)

6. Delay Time Between Exposure and Harm (minutes, hours, days)

7. Human Mortality and Morbidity Caused by Technology (average and maximum)

8. Nonhuman Mortality Caused by Technology (average and maximum)

9. Environmental Destruction ($ cleanup costs)

10. Transgenerational Risk (% affected in next generation)

in each cell of the matrix. This matrix provides a simple vehicle for incorporating considerations of crisis potential into the task of corporate portfolio design. It is only a first step toward developing a safer technology portfolio.

Corporate Crisis Audits. Even the safest possible technology portfolios do not guarantee complete immunity from crises. It is prudent, therefore, for corporations to be prepared to deal with a diverse range of crises. A periodic audit of hazards associated with products, production systems, safety systems, management systems, and environmental sources of crises can identify trouble spots and give early warning. The audit may be patterned on existing safety or operations audits, but with two major differences. First, whereas safety audits attempt to establish reliable protection against common types of technological failures and most likely failures, a crisis audit should cover worst-case contingencies. Worst-case scenarios should be developed as aids for analyzing crisis effects and recovery needs. Second, crisis audits, unlike safety audits, should not be limited to technological systems. They should examine potential for failure in human, organizational, technological, and economic factors in the firm as well as failures in the social, political, and economic environment of the firm. Particular note should be made of possible interactions among failures in these domains.

Crisis audits can be effective only if they are comprehensive, periodic, and linked to the strategic planning and reward systems of firms. The output of crisis audits should be a set of early warning signals conveyed to the top management for strategic monitoring of safety, health, and environmental problems and to line managers for immediate remedial action. These warnings also should be systematically incorporated into emergency planning procedures.

Crisis-Management Teams. Another task at the corporate level is the development of crisis-management teams. A professional and trained team of crisis managers can prevent mistakes in the immediate aftermath of the crisis and enable quicker recovery. The team should be interdisciplinary, that is, it should consist of managers from public relations, legal, environmental, safety and health, and finance functional areas and external experts. The involvement and support of the chief executive is virtually indispensable for a successful crisis-management team. Such a team can enhance a corporation's ability to respond to crisis. It brings together diverse technical, social, organizational, and environmental information that is needed urgently in crisis decision making. In addition, other line managers from the headquarters and business units may be included. The design may include a core group of managers who possess general crisis-management skills and responsibilities. It should be coupled with a set of specialists who possess expertise about specific business units and their crises. Different sets of specialists could be called in to manage different types of crises.

Members of the crisis-management team must be skilled in understanding different stakeholders' perspectives, and the dynamics of internal and external communications. They should be able to maintain emotional stability under stress and to deal with intense and multiple conflicts. Finally, the team should have sufficient authority to make critical decisions and commit organizational resources.

It is essential that the crisis-management team be established as a permanent, flexible structure within the firm and that it receive the legitimacy and resources necessary for it to be effective. Internal and external stakeholders should be encouraged to develop interfaces with the crisis-management team so that they can work together smoothly in times of crisis.

To maintain readiness for action, crisis teams conduct periodic crisis audits. They also do simulations of crisis decision making and emergency management drills. These simulations put employees through likely crises. Participants get the opportunity to make the decisions they would have to make in an actual crisis in realistic settings. Participants may include company employees, community members, and relevant government agencies, such as the police and fire departments, department of environmental resources, and so on. After the simulation, participants and facilitators analyze the team's decisions, behaviors, interactions, communications, coordination, and leadership.

Business Unit Strategies

Business unit efforts in dealing with crises should be aimed at reducing vulnerability to failure of plants or facilities through increased vigilance. Business units should follow, support, and encourage industry-wide safety efforts and improve community relations that enhance the capacity of individual business units to cope with crises.

Reducing Vulnerability Through Increased Vigilance. Vigilance is the quality of being aware and watchful of hazards. It implies that the firm places a high value on safety, health, and environmental protection. Vigilance also calls for proactive and anticipatory actions to prevent crises. Businesses can be made more vigilant by instituting systematic studies of hazards such as safety and maintenance audits of plants, storage facilities, and product distribution systems. Assessment of environmental impact can identify potential hazards from new projects.

Studies should lead to the institutionalization of safety by developing a **culture of safety and vigilance**. Vigilance may be institutionalized through a continuous process of inspection, modification, and reinspection. It can be supported by developing performance evaluations and reward systems that explicitly measure and monitor vigilance.

Attention also must be paid to the development of vigilance skills in operating personnel within plants. Extreme specialization and differentiation of tasks give operators tunnel vision. They don't see the bigger picture of how the whole organization fits together. They are unable to see where their job fits into the total manufacturing process. They are unable to identify the interactive failures that can be triggered by a minor mistake on their part. Often, workers with long tenure in hazardous facilities simply get accustomed and desensitized to hazards, which reduces their level of vigilance.

Vigilance skills can be enhanced by rotating workers through different jobs and departments in the plant, thereby giving them a first-hand understanding of the entire system. Workers become more appreciative of the interconnectedness of the system and able to anticipate effects of failures in different parts of the system. Vigilance also can be enhanced by providing human backups in critical subsystems. Redundancy in personnel can be used selectively to enhance reliability, especially in systems that depend on manual interventions.

It is more difficult to develop vigilance over external threats such as product sabotage from external sources (terrorists, psychopaths, etc.). Some companies have found it useful to engage in systematic exercises to develop profiles of likely saboteurs or terrorists, identify likely modes of sabotage, and understand the response capabilities of their organizations to such events. Environmental scanning may be another way of identifying specific groups or individuals who may have grudges or other motives to hurt a company's interests. These groups may be monitored or studied intensively to understand their behavior and to anticipate their attacks on a company. Based on this analysis, blocking actions such as the following may be developed: preemptive product and package designs, customer education, warning labels, increased security at facilities and establishment of security over distribution channels.

Industrywide Safety Efforts. The threat of certain types of crises, such as product sabotage of ingestible products by outsiders or industrial terrorism in politically troubled areas, may be pertinent to entire industries or to particular geographic regions. In such situations, it is useful to seek cooperative solutions at the industry level.

Two specific types of cooperative efforts are suggested as examples of the opportunities that exist to reduce the likelihood of crises. First, joint R&D may be feasible. Product and process safety, development of safer industry-wide distribution systems, siting of hazards, and environmental protection measures could be undertaken as R&D projects by firms within an industry. By sharing technological expertise and costs of research, firms can raise the total safety level in the industry.

Second, joint efforts also may be feasible in the area of **infrastructure development**. Many hazardous plants and facilities suffer from increased risk of disaster because the physical and social infrastructure supporting them is simply inadequate. This is particularly true in developing countries where even industrial parks do not possess basic amenities such as water, electricity, sewage transportation, and communications facilities. In such situations, businesses affected by weak infrastructure can jointly invest in upgrading the basic facilities to a level that makes their operation safe. They also could jointly lobby with local authorities to provide them these support services.

Community Relations. The ability of a plant to cope with a crisis that originates within it is significantly improved if the affected community, local authorities, government agencies, and media cooperate with plant officials. If **cooperative relationships** are not developed before the onset of a crisis, they rarely come spontaneously during crisis. Cooperation must be cultivated through joint emergency planning that includes participation of external stakeholders and establishment of open communications with external groups.

An informed public deals with emergencies more effectively, and by such actions it can mitigate the effects of disasters. In most states, right-to-know laws mandate that the *public be provided with information needed to protect itself.* New Jersey and Delaware have passed more elaborate laws to cover emergency planning for extremely hazardous or toxic catastrophes. Keeping the community informed of hazards and emergency procedures for dealing with them need not compromise competitive information or alarm the public. Community information programs are more effective when the corporation, government, and public interest organizations design and implement them cooperatively.

10.4   THE TASKS OF CRISIS MANAGEMENT

Despite the best efforts at preventing crises, some crises will occur. Coping with crises after their onset requires different managerial decisions and tasks than those needed for running normal business operations. Managing corporate crises involves structuring the crisis, rescue and emergency management, stakeholder communications, conflict resolution, and business recovery and learning.

Structuring the Crisis

Structuring the crisis means making full sense of it and developing a structured set of activities to deal with it. This entails several tasks. Managers must *assess damages* caused by the crisis triggering event and *examine their implications* for the firm. They also must *identify all parties affected* by the crisis, that is, the stakeholders of the crisis. Stakeholders may be inside the firm (e.g., local employees, foreign subsidiary employees, top management, etc.), or outside the firm (e.g., suppliers, customers, bankers, business associates, etc.). All crisis-management actions should be geared toward dealing with stakeholder concerns. Define the stakes and damages to these stakeholders in financial, social, political, medical, environmental, organizational, and symbolic terms. Damages escalate with time. Therefore, it is necessary to document initial damages and periodically update them as the crisis progresses.

Another aspect of structuring the crisis is to *focus efforts* on activities that provide the most leverage in resolving the crisis in the shortest period of time. Many variables that are normally under management's control pass out of their control during a crisis. Managers should avoid wasting time trying to regain control over these variables and concentrate on those variables that they *can* do something about. For example, in the Bhopal crisis, the local plant manager lost control over the plant immediately after the accident because local police took over the plant. This restricted the manager's ability to set up damage-control procedures within the plant. He immediately turned his attention to things he could still do, such as switching on the warning siren, evacuating people from the neighborhood, and providing medical help.

In dealing with crises, managers have to make hundreds, even thousands, of decisions every week. However, all decisions do not have to be made immediately. In structuring the crisis it is useful to *prioritize decisions* by their level of urgency.

This enables management to identify and focus on urgent decisions immediately and deal with less urgent ones later.

Perhaps the most critical task in structuring crisis activities is the allocation of responsibilities for the tasks that must be accomplished. As the Johnson & Johnson case illustrated, the *CEO should assume primary responsibility* for complete management of the crisis. His or her authority and leadership can key assets in the tense and trying period that follows a crisis.

In addition, it is good practice to *form an interdisciplinary crisis-management team* consisting of representatives of key departments (production, marketing, legal, public relations, environment, safety and health, specialists, etc.). Each member of the team should have clearly delineated responsibilities for technical damage control, emergency management, governmental relations, stakeholder communications, and conflict management. A separate backup and monitoring team also may be created to follow up on the work of the crisis-management team. This ensures that some tasks do not fall between the cracks in the heat of the crisis.

Rescue and Emergency Management

Crisis-triggering events often injure people and place large populations at risk of damage. The objective of the rescue and emergency management phase of crisis management is to *rescue the injured and minimize the damage potential* of the triggering event. The first task is damage control of technical factors. Depending on the nature of the triggering event and its technical characteristics, different procedures for damage control need to be adopted. These include shutting down plants or production processes, reducing or neutralizing inventories of hazardous materials, recalling products that caused harm, cordoning off dangerous areas, and evacuating immediately endangered people.

Rescue and emergency management can be made more effective by following several simple heuristics. First, it is helpful to *remember that 90% of the damage usually occurs to 10% of affected populations*. By sharply concentrating rescue efforts on this 10% of most severely affected people, firms can prevent maximum damage.

Second, *seek or take help from external agencies*. The reluctance of companies to involve outsiders in crisis management stems from several motivations. Companies prefer to be viewed as adequate to handle the job themselves. They also prefer to keep information about the event and its causes from getting to outsiders, who may later be able to use it against the company in liability litigation. In any major crisis, time is of essence. Outside help can make a difference in mitigating the effects of the crisis. There are many government agencies (Federal Emergency Management Agency, Occupational Safety and Health Administration, Environmental Protection Agency, Nuclear Regulatory Commission, Consumer Product Safety Commission, Coast Guard, FBI), voluntary social service organizations (Red Cross, Caritas), international organizations (United Nations Disaster Relief Organization, United Nations Environment Program, World Council of Churches), and industry associations and their affiliates (Chemical Manufacturers Association, Edison Electric Institute) that can provide helpful information and resources to counter the crisis. The use of external resources must be well coordinated with a company's crisis plans, otherwise they can act as an impediment to effective relief for victims.

Third, *take timely action*: the importance of timely action in controlling the escalating effects of crises cannot be overemphasized. There is a small and fleeting window of opportunity in every crisis during which timely action can dramatically reduce damages. Acting within this window may require rescue workers to avoid standard operating procedures and permissions and to take action at their own discretion. If these circumventions do not create more hazard, the organization must be willing to tolerate them. Giving employees such discretionary power is not a simple matter. Such discretion can be misused easily, and more likely, it can cause harm unwittingly. Therefore, it cannot be formalized in any organization. However, the company's culture can promote the values of courageous actions, valor, and helping the needy even at personal costs. Culture can symbolically support the use of abnormal discretion under emergencies.

The Bhopal crisis illustrates the dramatic impact of timely action. Two passenger trains carrying thousands of people were scheduled to arrive at the Bhopal railway station located less than two miles from the Union Carbide plant. The trains would have to pass by the plant and contaminated area to arrive at the railway station. An off-duty station clerk had gone to the station to meet a friend who was on one of these trains. When he saw the devastation that was occurring at the station, he immediately rushed to the signal room. Abandoning all rules and regulations and in contravention of railway policy, he signaled the trains to stop at the outskirts of town. By taking this timely action he single handedly saved the lives of thousands of people. Had he waited to get permissions and approvals from relevant authorities the scope of this tragedy might have been doubled.

Fourth, *be guided by a humanistic attitude* in rescue and emergency work and not by a legalistic one. The work should show concern for affected victims and endangered populations. It should not reflect an overly zealous concern for establishing legal liability for damages or a staunchly defensive posture. Management's initial attitude sets the tone for complete crisis management. It moderates the relationships that emerge between the firm and the media and government agencies. A legalistic attitude antagonizes external stakeholders and makes the company look heartless. Johnson & Johnson's initial reaction to the Tylenol poisonings was a good example of a humanistic approach to managing the crisis. The company's pronouncements, decisions, and actions reflected a profound concern for their affected customers and those potentially at risk. The initial reaction of Gerber to the discovery of glass fragments in its baby food packages was starkly different. The company first minimized the seriousness of the event. Then it argued that the glass fragments were not introduced into the package at their plants; therefore, the company was not to blame. The company suggested that the glass fragments were pieces of the container bottles broken by bumpy transportation in trucks. Although the event turned out to be not very serious, the company's defensive attitude attracted much criticism (Bussey, 1986).

Rescue efforts must be followed up by longer-term relief and rehabilitation activities. These could include providing medical help, financial compensation, and other social services to victims.

Stakeholder Communications

Crises invariably create the need to communicate with multiple internal and external stakeholders. It is a good idea to prepare for such communications by identifying the most likely stakeholders even before a crisis occurs. Internally, these include the board of directors, top management, local employees, and employees at remote locations such as plants, sales offices, and foreign subsidiaries. External stakeholders include the following: customers; suppliers; investors; government regulatory agencies; offices of local, state, and federal government; media; the local civil defense infrastructure such as the police, fire department, hospitals, and port authority; and the public at large. A directory with names, address, and phone and fax numbers can be a valuable asset during a crisis.

The task of accurately communicating large amounts of information to many people in a short time can be simplified by the following practices:

1. *Establish communications professionals as the company's spokespersons* for the crisis. It also may be necessary to establish a spokesperson at each location where media are likely to seek information from the company. The spokespersons should be articulate, convincing, and well informed about the company and the crisis event. It is not a good idea to use the CEO as the spokesperson, despite his or her high credibility with the outside world. The CEO's time should be preserved for the myriad decisions that will need to be made in overcoming the crisis. The CEO should be used initially to communicate the company's crisis-management strategy. After that, the CEO should be available to key outside persons, such as the city mayor, state governor, or high federal government officials (Lukaszewski, 1986; Mitroff and Kilmann, 1984).

2. *Provide as much information as possible in written form* to avoid misinterpretation and distortions due to memory lapses. The information should be clear and precise. A good example of this was the retailer advisory memo sent by Johnson & Johnson to its retailers after the Tylenol incident. The message was in writing, it specified exactly which batch numbers of Tylenol bottles were suspect, and it described the procedure for recalling the product. Companies often use press kits, press releases, videos, newsletters, and advertisements as part of their communication program.

3. *Do not use incomplete information about the crisis as an excuse for stonewalling the media.* In any crisis, there is never complete information available on all its causes or consequences. The seriousness of the event requires that companies share the little information that they have with other societal agents that may be affected by the event or may be able to mitigate its effects. Sometimes, open communications can exonerate the company from blame. At other times, open communications can create goodwill and public support that simplify crisis management. Communication also opens up channels through which the company can receive information that can be helpful in its crisis-management efforts.

4. *Communicate the most critical pieces of information to the public.* Critical information includes company background, description of crisis-triggering event and damages, known safety and health consequences, known remedial procedures, precautionary measures to be taken, actions taken by the company, and the role external agencies can play to help. Do not minimize the extent of damages; do not speculate about causes; and do not make unprepared public statements.

Technical, toxicological, epidemiological, and medical information can be found in the existing databases in these disciplines. In addition, unconventional sources of information should be used to gain a multiperspective understanding of the crisis; these include systematic polling of customers, the public opinion, and independent investigations.

If a company mismanages stakeholder communications, it invites bad publicity and a hobbled crisis-management effort. Exxon's efforts at managing the crisis after the *Exxon Valdez* oil spill were hampered by its inept communications.

Exxon's CEO did not come out to face the press for five days after the accident. The company had no systematic procedure for getting information out to the media or the public. In the first few days of the crisis, it stonewalled the media. When it did come out to talk about the accident it blamed the ship's captain for the accident and the Alaska Department of Environment for delaying its emergency efforts. This defensive behavior set a negative tone for the company's crisis-management effort. And, although the company spent more than $2.5 billion in the cleanup effort, it received extensive negative publicity on its crisis-management effort.

Conflict Resolution

Corporate crises invariably lead to multiple conflicts with stakeholders. These conflicts result in litigation over liability for damages. They may be overlaid with social, political, and ideological conflicts. Most crises result from multiple, complex causes. They are associated with high technological uncertainty and incomplete information about causes. As a result, it is not easy to determine the liability for damages. Moreover, due to lack of knowledge about all the consequences of crises, it is difficult to determine the appropriate size of damage awards.

Litigation is usually costly, time consuming, and unable to resolve all conflicts. Legal systems in most countries have not been exposed to conflicts created by industrial crises. There is lack of legal doctrines and legal precedents for judicial resolution of the conflicts. It is necessary, therefore, to explore nonconfrontational alternatives to conflict resolution. Third-party mediation, arbitration, and joint conciliation are possible in many situations. Companies may seek the involvement of international organizations (e.g., United Nations, World Council of Churches, International Red Cross) to resolve international conflicts. For large-scale conflicts, special mediating agencies or tribunals may be set up. For example, the Nestle crisis over marketing infant formula in developing countries was resolved through the involvement of the World Council of Churches. The Council provided activists and organizations involved in the crisis a legitimate and trustworthy forum for discussing their differences. Today, environmental mediators involve themselves in resolving hundreds of disputes between communities and corporations. They consider diverse issues such as location of hazardous waste incinerators, cleanup of polluted rivers, land zoning, protection of wetlands and wildlife, and conservation of forests.

Business Recovery and Learning

Once the hot phase of the crisis is over and immediate victims are taken care of, the company must embark on the task of business recovery. Crises present unique opportunities for radical change. Organizational resistance to change is small because survival is at stake.

Recovering from a crisis may require radical internal organizational changes and technological changes. The company may need to divest itself of some hazardous technologies completely. Hazardous systems and products need to be redesigned. Operating policies and procedures need to be improved. To prevent future product crises, firms may redesign the products and packaging. They may redesign the production system and quality control procedures. They may embark on a continuous search for innovations. Attention must be paid to managing the morale of employees, who invariably experience severe stress during crisis.

Internal changes must be complemented by renewed efforts to regain markets and lost public image. This calls for revised forecasts for product demand and a new approach to promoting and merchandising. The company also needs to reaffirm and renew relationships with business associates, particularly those who have experienced discontinuities. Recovery from crises must institutionalize lessons learned from the crisis. These lessons must be reflected in the written policies and the unwritten culture of the firm.

Johnson & Johnson and Perrier provide good examples of successful business recovery after crises. Johnson & Johnson lost 80% of its market share after the second Tylenol poisonings in 1986. Perrier did a 100% recall of its premium bottled spring water after traces of benzene were found in it in 1990. The product remained off the market for several months. In both these cases, the companies made a strong business recovery. They made extensive changes in their products, production system, advertising, and consumer education to gain back their preeminent position in the market.

Johnson & Johnson abandoned the capsule form of Tylenol and created a caplet (capsule-shaped hard tablet) that was difficult to tamper with. It also created tamper-resistant packaging. It retooled its production facilities at the cost of more than $100 million. It launched a massive advertising campaign to inform customers of the new Tylenol and its safety features. It offered to refund the cost of the old packages of Tylenol capsules or replace them. Before the end of the year, Johnson & Johnson had recovered all of its lost market share.

Perrier did a thorough study of the causes of its benzene disaster and found that a faulty production process that had defective filtering equipment caused it. The company changed the filtering system and quality control procedures. It brought out a new version of the product under the label Perrier Nouvelle. It expanded its distribution system by appointing new dealers and launched a $60 million advertising campaign to attract back its customers.

This chapter indicates clearly that corporate crises are proliferating and are a strategic problem for companies. In today's turbulent business environment, most companies are vulnerable to one form of crisis or another. Every company must develop strategies for preventing crises and internal capabilities for coping with them if they occur.

Crisis prevention planning and management must be done at the strategic level; the task cannot be relegated to operating facilities. Companies can reduce the risk of crises by selecting an inherently safe business portfolio. Business facilities can be made less prone to crisis by developing early warning systems and a vigilant culture. Management of crisis can be facilitated by being prepared for it. Companies can prepare for crisis by establishing a professionally trained crisis-management team that can move into action at the very onset of a crisis.

In the event of a crisis, managers need to handle several basic tasks. They should begin by gaining a comprehensive understanding of the impacts of the crisis and structuring tasks to take care of all key issues. The most urgent task is to minimize the potential damage from the crisis-triggering event and rescue persons at risk of harm. Companies also must manage communications with all stakeholders, including victims, employees, customers, suppliers, government, community, and the media. Every crisis causes multiple conflicts that must be resolved. It is advisable to seek out all possibilities for resolving conflicts, short of litigation. Finally, crisis management should include business recovery. This may require new products, new production systems, and new marketing strategies.

SUMMARY OF CHAPTER 10

Corporate crises represent threats to organizational survival. They can be triggered by a variety of events. For example, major industrial accidents, incidents of environmental pollution, product injuries, sabotage, labor strikes, hostile takeovers, and product boycotts have been the source of crises. This chapter discusses ways of preparing for, preventing, and managing corporate crises.

Corporate crises often come without warning. After the onset of a crisis, damages escalate very rapidly. There is tremendous pressure to act fast. Information available to make decisions in a crisis is limited. Corporations receive critical scrutiny from outside. Top management and the board of directors are pulled in conflicting directions. Unprepared handling of a crisis makes damages more pronounced.

Most crises have complex causes. Several simultaneous and interacting failures lead to a crisis. Failures occur within the technological core of the organization: plants, warehouses, waste facilities, and transportation systems. Failure of organizational systems, policies, and processes compound technological failures. Organizational failures include failures in communications, maintenance, and safety practices. Inappropriate cutbacks that erode safety and lack of training or low levels of supervision over hazards also contribute to crises. Organizational failures create preconditions for technological accidents. Outside the corporation, failures in the physical and social infrastructure contribute to crises.

Prevention of crises and development of corporate capabilities for managing crisis are two important objectives of strategic management. Prevention and preparation for crisis should begin by assessing the potential for crisis. Careful evaluation of hazards posed by each product or process technology in a company's business portfolio can identify potential sources of crises.

The overall crisis potential of the corporation can be reduced at the corporate level. It requires designing safer technology portfolios and enhancing corporate capacity to deal with crisis. This can be done by establishing crisis-management teams, developing emergency plans, and training workers to be vigilant about hazards. A trained professional crisis-management team can prevent mistakes in the immediate aftermath of the crisis. It can also enable quicker recovery.

Chapter 5 noted that the choice of business portfolios should be made on financial and market criteria. In addition, corporations should screen businesses based on their crisis potential. A periodic corporate crisis audit can identify trouble spots and provide early warnings. This audit should include products, production systems, safety systems, management systems, and environmental sources of crisis.

At the business unit level, vigilance over hazards can be increased by doing a vulnerability analysis of each product and facility. By sharing technological expertise and costs of research, it is possible to raise overall safety levels in an industry. A company's ability to cope with a crisis can be significantly improved by building better relationships with the media and communities.

Coping with crises after their onset involves five tasks. First, managers need to structure the crisis. This requires understanding the crisis and assigning responsibilities to deal with various crisis-management activities. Crisis-management efforts should focus on activities that provide the most leverage. Managers should set decision priorities and allocate necessary resources.

The second important task of crisis management is rescuing victims and emergency management. By acting quickly within a short window of opportunity, managers can minimize damages. Rescue and emergency management can be made more effective by getting help from external sources. Help is often available from government agencies, industry associations, volunteer organizations, and international organizations.

The third key task of crisis management is communicating with multiple internal and external stakeholders. Usually it is necessary to communicate accurately large amounts of information. Communications must reach many people in a short time. A company in crisis should design a communications program that uses press kits, press releases, video messages, and other suitable communication vehicles. It should also appoint spokespersons and make its top management available for discussions with key external stakeholders. Open and frequent communications with the media and injured victims can help avoid many misperceptions during a crisis.

A fourth important task of crisis management is dealing with conflicts arising from the crisis. Determining liability for damages is a major cause of conflicts. Companies should explore nonconfrontational methods of resolving conflicts. Using third-party mediation, arbitration, or joint conciliation is often less expensive and quicker than litigation.

After the hot phase of the crisis, management must embark on the fifth task: business recovery. This involves internal organizational changes, technological improvements, financial restructuring, and changes in market focus. Companies may develop new forecasts, design new products, change production systems, and modify transportation systems. These changes aim at regaining lost customers and lost public image. Even though a crisis threatens the life of a company, it offers unique opportunities for radical transformation.

READINGS, CASES, AND POLICY DOCUMENTS

The following cases and policy documents provide additional background and discussion material for the concepts discussed in this Chapter.

Cases

Baker Medical Center (A, B, & C)
Greenpeace v/s Ford: Catalytic converters come to the U.K.
* Manville Corporation
* Union Carbide Corporation
* Exxon Corporation

POLICY DOCUMENTS

J.C. Penny's —The Penny Idea and Statement of Ethics

* indicates particularly appropriate assignments.

Figures 10.1, 10.2, 10.3, 10.4, 10.5, & 10.6.

Strategic Management Process and Book Outline

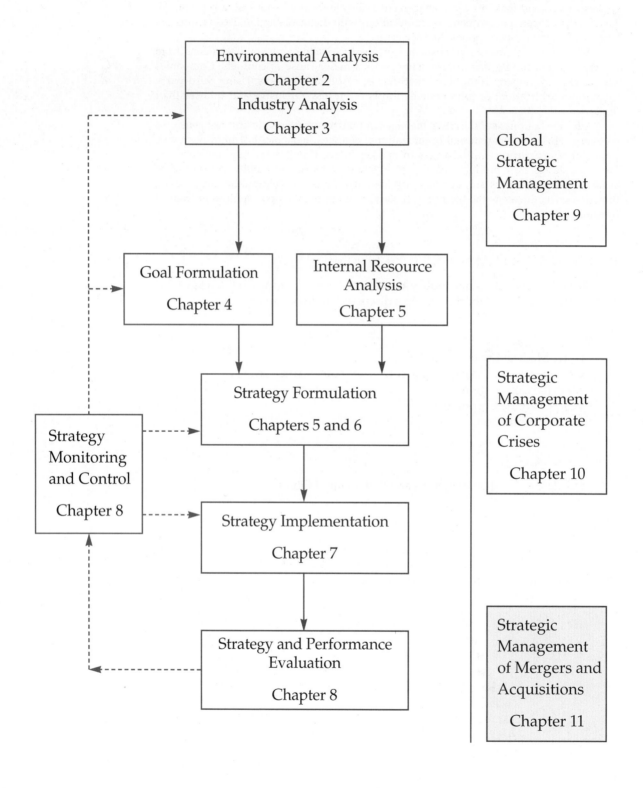

CHAPTER 11
STRATEGIC MANAGEMENT OF
MERGERS AND ACQUISITIONS

CHAPTER OUTLINE

Acquisitions and divestitures have become a common way of restructuring corporate assets. In this chapter the terms "merger" and "acquisition" are used synonymously. Although the term merger is sometimes used to describe creation of a new entity by combining two companies. In the twentieth century, American business has witnessed several waves of mergers. The first wave of mergers occurred in the first quarter of this century. It involved consolidation of basic industries such as automobile manufacturing, railroads, iron and steel, and oil production. Economies of scale in these industries, coupled with intense competition, drove firms to merge and become more competitive.

During the past twenty-five years, there have been more than 75,000 mergers in the United States. Just in the past five years, acquisition transactions of more than $35 million in sizes increased from $186.4 billion in 1984 to $234.1 in 1989. These mergers were quite different from early consolidations. They responded to a diverse set of objectives, involved international partners, and involved very large firms. An additional basis of their rationale was creating value through combined synergies (Haspeslagh and Jemison, 1991).

An example of modern megamerger is the 1990 acquisition of MCA by Matsushita Electronics Industries of Japan. The giant American entertainment company (1989 revenues of $3.4 billion) was purchased for $7 billion. Also, in 1988 Sony bought CBS Records for $2 billion and in 1989 it bought Columbia Pictures for $3.4 billion. These megamergers created strong global entertainment companies with American entertainment knowledge and Japanese financial and technological backing out of what were essentially successful American film studios.

Mergers and acquisitions have become a permanent feature of our corporate economy. Many corporate strategies use mergers and divestitures to achieve different strategic objectives. To do this, mergers should be able to create value for the firm. New value can be created only by choosing the right partner for merger and managing the merger to deliver good business performance. This requires carefully managing both the acquisition decision-making process and the postmerger integration processes that affect business performance.

Different types of mergers and acquisitions create different types of value for companies. Mergers based on "strategic" rationale add value by allowing the combined firm to make more productive use of its assets. The real value in such mergers occurs in the period following the merger, when complementary assets of the merging firms are used to create new value. For example, Electrolux of Sweden acquired Zanussi of Italy so that it could use Zanussi's extensive marketing network in southern Europe to market Electrolux's technologically sophisticated products. It also improved capacity utilization and production efficiency of Zanussi's plants by transferring production technologies and product orders to them.

In contrast, mergers that are simply financial deals capture hidden asset value by bringing undervalued assets to the market. In such mergers, the deal itself creates value, and little attempt is made to enhance value after the merger. Sometimes the acquired firm's assets are unbundled and sold piecemeal. For example, in the 1960s Textron built itself into a conglomerate by buying up undervalued, privately held companies in several industries. Textron's rapidly rising stock paid for the companies.

In strategic mergers, the focus of this chapter, clear links between the acquired business and the corporate strategy of the acquiring firm must ensure two things: first, that the acquisition will receive the managerial attention it needs to become successful and second, that resources needed for the acquisition's long-term development will be available. The acquiring firm must have the finances to pay the acquisition price and make necessary investments into the new business. Ensuring these things involves careful selection of merger candidates and managing postmerger integration, as depicted in Figure 11.1.

11.1   STRATEGIC CONSIDERATIONS IN MERGERS AND ACQUISITIONS

It is important for managers to give their merger and acquisition efforts a true strategic focus rather than making them short-term financial deals. A strategic focus and clear strategic fit for mergers can ensure long-term success and avoid the many pitfalls associated with mergers of recent past. Strategic assessment should include evaluation of how the merger or acquisition helps the company to achieve its long-term objectives and strategies.

Figure 11.1 *Strategic Management of Mergers and Acquisitions*

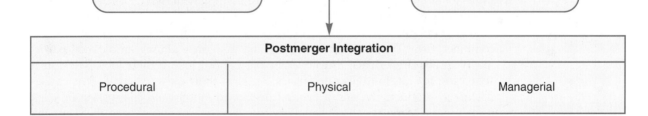

The Downside of Mergers and Acquisitions

Many of the negative consequences of mergers are often forgotten in the hustle and excitement of acquisition. The unfortunate fact about mergers is that, in the long term, most of them fail financially. Even if they make sense as financial deals at the time of the merger, they can still fail to meet strategic objectives of the acquiring firm. There are many downside risks or pitfalls in mergers and acquisitions that can be avoided by careful strategic assessment.

A common source of failure of mergers is overpayment. It is hard to estimate the true value of companies, particularly of multiproduct, multinational companies. The best methods we have available for valuing companies make many assumptions about the company, specifically, about the potential of the company, remaining life of its assets, value of its goodwill, its ability to perform in the future, and future economic and industry conditions. Managers make reasoned guesses about these uncertain conditions and sometimes they are wrong. If careful evaluation of the acquisition candidate does not occur, the buying company may end up paying too much for it. Overpriced acquisitions can become financial burdens for years to come.

The means of financing mergers and acquisitions is another source of failure. Throughout the 1980s, it was popular to finance acquisitions with debt using "junk bonds." These high-yield bonds required the issuer to pay 15% to 20% interest, which created an enormous interest payment burden on the combined firm. If the merged firm ran into a few bad years of financial performance, the interest burden became unbearable. Many companies had to resort to bankruptcy because they could not meet interest payments.

Mergers also may turn sour due to hidden liabilities or financial needs of the acquired unit. Hidden liabilities may be in product injury liabilities for hazardous products or toxic waste cleanup liabilities at sites of the acquired firm. For example, when Occidental Petroleum bought Hooker Chemicals, it did not fully realize the liability associated with Hooker's Love Canal waste site. Within a few years, Love Canal became the source of a major environmental crisis, saddling Occidental with millions of dollars in liability.

Hidden financial needs such as a future capital expenditure requirement also can lead to failure of mergers and acquisitions. Misjudgments on this issue are common when acquiring managers are not familiar with the technologies of the firm being acquired. They may grossly underestimate what it will cost to keep the acquired unit in good productive shape.

Asset rationalization, downsizing, and cost cuts often follow a merger. This may involve the sale of some assets, closing down of facilities, reductions in the work force, and general tightening of budgets. Invariably, these actions have negative effects on communities. In some communities, mergers have been the cause for shutting down the main source of employment, which throws the entire community into a crisis.

Mergers and acquisitions often create many human problems within the combined firm. They create uncertainty and insecurity among employees, particularly in acquired firms. Employees worry about losing their jobs. They start searching for alternatives and lose interest in their current work. This causes decline in productivity, and a general decline in morale and motivation of work force occurs. Mergers can cause labor strife. Some employees leave the company and join the competition, carrying with them valuable information and customer contacts (Buono and Bowditch, 1989; Walsh, 1988).

Because of such failures, acquisitions often flounder for years, loosing money and demotivating employees. When they fail to meet organizational objectives, acquisitions are divested, causing disruption of business and financial losses (Duhaime and Grant, 1984). Failure to manage an acquisition effectively has led to the decline of even stellar companies. The acquisition of Telerate by Dow Jones is an example. Telerate was a fast-growing global supplier of financial information and transactional services when Dow Jones bought a 32% stake in it in 1985. For the next four years, Telerate was a market leader and earning star, with earnings growth of a stunning 45% compound annual rate. In October 1989, Dow Jones bought 100% of Telerate. From then on, Telerate went into a steady and rapid slide. Its entrepreneurial freewheeling ways clashed with Dow Jones's more deliberate and bureaucratic style. Dow Jones could not respond quickly to dramatic changes in the financial services industry and onslaught of competition. It was slow to exert control and mold Telerate because it had acquired it piecemeal over a period of five years. Meanwhile, Telerate lost many key executives and downsized its work force. The competition left it behind in product offerings, particularly in the area of financial analytical software. By 1990, Telerate's revenue growth fell to 6%, less than half the projected rate, and operating earnings fell 44% for the Dow Jones information services unit.

To avoid the downside effects, it is valuable to think of mergers and acquisitions in strategic terms. Some important strategic considerations on which mergers should be assessed are discussed next.

Strategic Considerations

The most important considerations in acquiring businesses are the strategy and objectives of the acquiring firm, synergies between merger partners, financial considerations, and opportunism.

Corporations can achieve a staggering variety of strategic objectives through mergers. This fact, along with the relative ease of accomplishing mergers, explains their popularity. Companies use mergers to create new stockholder wealth quickly, invest excess cash, avert being takeover targets, diversify risks, and enter new markets. They also use mergers to acquire new technologies, skills, and personnel, minimize competition, achieve higher growth rates, and buy market share.

Most firms pursue multiple objectives through their merger strategy. In fact, motives behind individual mergers are highly complex. They range from purely financial gains to altruistic "white knight" gestures in which a company buys another to save it from an acquisition by an undesirable firm. The strategic objectives pursued through acquisitions are part of the total corporate or business strategy of the acquiring firm. For an acquisition to deliver long-term strategic benefits, it must fit well with the firm's objectives and strategies.

The second strategic consideration deals with the notion of synergy. Synergy, as an abstract idea, says that the whole is more than the sum of its parts. Mathematically it may be represented as $2 + 2 = 5$. In business, it refers to the use of a set of resources or attributes of the combined firm. These assets generate more value than the individual, constituent firms could have generated with them separately. When merging firms have complementary assets, the merged assets can be used to create new value that the component firms could not create individually.

Premerger analysis must establish exactly what synergies can be exploited through a merger. These synergies could be in marketing, production, or finance functions. Philip Morris's acquisition of Miller Brewing provides an example of using synergies. Philip Morris used its very strong marketing and financial capabilities to build Miller into a formidable brewing company. Philip Morris used the marketing, promotion, advertising, and brand management strategies learned in its core tobacco businesses to create a unique brand image for Miller Brewing products.

Synergies can be complementary in nature; that is, they create additional value by bringing together complementary resources or capabilities. Or they may be supplementary; that is, they create value by strengthening or supplementing existing resources or capabilities to new and higher levels of productivity. Although incipient synergies justify many mergers, in most cases exploit synergies fail to be exploited after the merger occurs. Part of the failure is because managers perform vague and casual analysis of synergies. The existence of synergies are often presumed rather than proved through specific, objective analysis. This trap can be avoided by conducting a detailed and specific analysis of the different synergies expected from the merger. For example, if the firm expects to gain marketing synergies, analysis must establish the possibility of these synergies. Specifically, exactly which products or product lines can be combined fruitfully? Which customer segments can be exploited jointly? Which distribution channels can be used jointly? What price levels can be supported in each new product-market segment? Which marketing services can be used to serve the new product line? This level of detail in analysis, although cumbersome and expensive, is the only way of ensuring that presumed synergies can be actualized.

A third strategic consideration in mergers is long-term financial implications. In other words, how well does the acquisition fit with the long-term plans of the company? This issue is different from simply determining a good price for the acquisition. It deals with how the acquisition affects the total financial ability of the combined firm. High-yield, high-risk junk bonds have financed many recent mergers. Such highly leveraged acquisitions impose large financial risks in the future. For example, high-yielding bonds (returning 16% to 19% interest) of the combined RJR Nabisco financed the 1980 merger of RJ Reynolds and Nabisco Food. Soon after the merger, the economy went soft and growth in the food sector leveled off. The company did not get the anticipated cash flows from its business units. The interest burden imposed by the high-yield bonds virtually ran the company into the ground within two years. The prices of these bonds plummeted, as did the company's shares. In assessing the financial feasibility of acquisitions, managers must examine long-term financial consequences.

Finally, opportunism plays an important role in acquisitions, because opportunities for buying companies at attractive prices emerge randomly. The stock market, regulatory, and industry forces outside the control of acquiring managers create these acquisitions. Therefore, to be successful in doing acquisitions, companies must be flexible enough to seize opportunities as and when they arise. It is critical, however, that opportunism be balanced and moderated by a careful analysis of the strategic value of the acquisition candidate (Salter and Weinhold, 1979; Singh and Montgomery, 1987). The next section describes some key attributes for valuing acquisition candidates.

11.2   EVALUATING ACQUISITION CANDIDATES

Strategic considerations provide only a broad framework for assessing mergers; they serve as general guidelines for developing merger strategies. The evaluation of specific attributes of merger candidates must be the basis of the actual task of choosing the right partners. Although assessing the strategic fit between the acquiring firm's strategy and the merger candidate must occur, more must happen before any merger takes place. The following strategic characteristics of the merger candidate should be evaluated before the merger decision.

Earnings Performance. Earnings ability is a basic evaluation criterion for any business operation. It can be judged by assessing the past five years of earnings performance. Earnings may be measured by net income, return on assets, or return on investment. Three to four years of steady profits and sales is an indication of a healthy earnings record. This variable is particularly important for highly leveraged mergers, because traditional credit theories place great importance on it. In leverage situations, earnings potential should at least be sufficient to cover interest and principal payments over the entire period of the proposed debt package.

Value of Assets. Price of the acquisition is critically dependent on the value of assets. Assets include both real assets and goodwill. Real assets can be assessed from the company's balance sheet. Note that book value of assets may be very different from the market value. The market value of publicly traded companies can be assessed from their stock price and price-earnings ratio. Usually, the balance sheet should suggest sufficient and high-quality assets. "Hard," "clean" assets, such as accounts receivables, inventories, equipment and machinery, and real property unencumbered by pledges to lenders or other third-party are desirable. Another characteristic of a strong balance sheet is limited liabilities.

All assets should be assessed for their resalability for two reasons. First, some assets of the acquired company may not be needed because they duplicate existing facilities or are not valuable to the acquiring firm. The acquirer may wish to sell them to recover part of the acquisition cost. There also may be "excess," or hidden, assets not factored into the price of the acquisition; these also can be sold. Second, it is now quite common for acquired units to be divested within a few years. Divestiture is easy if the assets are inherently more salable.

Market Position. Strong market position is a desirable characteristic of acquisition candidates. This variable, often measured by market share, is an indicator of the market power of the company. The top two or three position holders in any industry are less susceptible to market downturns than other participants. This is particularly true in mature industries where market share correlates to profitability. Clearly, this is a rather stringent requirement for screening merger candidates, because only two or three firms can have market leadership in any industry. Moreover, industry leaders are often not for sale because of their superior performance.

Product Line. Strength of the existing product line and ability to develop new products are important characteristics of acquisition candidates. Strong products are those that are well accepted by consumers and have been on the market for several years. They also have a strong brand image and are expected to have strong demand in the coming years.

Buyers should be particularly careful about companies dealing in high-technology products. High-tech products may have great potential, but they usually have more volatile earnings, more technological uncertainty, quicker obsolescence, and high mobility of management. These features make them highly risky acquisitions. This is an important consideration if the acquisition requires loans. Lending institutions prefer more mundane, easily understood products to high-technology products.

Quality of Management Team. All mergers depend heavily on the existing management team for continued success, at least in the period immediately following the merger. These managers possess industry-specific knowledge, experience, and contacts necessary for the business. A good management team is one that has a proven track record in financial performance. It should have experience in profit center management, asset management, and professional planning, budgeting, and management control functions.

Even if the acquiring company brings in its own trusted persons to head the acquired business, the existing management is still instrumental in postmerger management. It can be a valuable asset that should be maintained at least through the period of ownership transition. It can help in the smooth transfer of responsibility and power to the new set of managers. To retain the services of the management team, merger contracts should include employment guarantees for the team members.

Capital Intensity. Capital expenditure requirement is an important consideration in assessing merger candidates. After paying the purchase price up front, acquirers are often reluctant or unable to infuse large amounts of capital into the acquired business. An excessive capital expenditure requirement in early phases of the merger often creates major problems. This also could happen in seasonal businesses that require significant working capital increases for inventory buildup.

Merger analysis begins with a preliminary assessment of the preceding six factors. If the acquisition candidate looks attractive, a detailed financial analysis must be conducted on the past, present, and future operations of the business. This may be done by merger analysts within the firm or by an outside consulting firm. Even if internal analysts do most of the analysis, it is necessary to get a "fair price" opinion on the price of the acquisition from an independent outside evaluator.

The financial analysis and pro forma statements should provide a true picture of the financial strengths of the acquisition candidate. Projections should be made for expected earnings and cash flow and their affects on the company's financial position. Projections should be subjected to sensitivity analysis with varying assumptions. For example, the impact on earnings of an increase in unit labor costs or interest rates should be determined through sensitivity analysis. These what-if analyses can help quantify risks of a business and determine its price. Several spreadsheet software packages allow these types of analyses on personal computers.

Once a prospective merger candidate passes all the financial and strategic screens, the actual merger deal must be structured and operationalized. This involves several routine steps:

1. Negotiating the price and terms of contract
2. Obtaining all regulatory clearances
3. Determining the legal and accounting aspects of the merger
4. Arranging finances
5. Signing the contract and making payments

11.3   MANAGING THE ACQUISITION DECISION PROCESS

Until very recently, companies left acquisition decision making in the hands of financial and legal departments. Managing the acquisition decision process itself did not receive much attention. This led to several problems. Acquisition decisions lacked participation from operating business managers who had to manage the acquired business later. They were not very enthusiastic about managing a business bought by someone else. Often, financial and legal issues were the only justifications for the acquisition. Strategic and organizational synergies were not clear.

Lack of attention to the acquisition decision-making process also allowed irrelevant factors to affect the choice of acquiring a company. These included multiple and ambiguous motives, lack of a broad search for acquisition candidates, personal biases of key players, escalating momentum to acquire, and unclear expectations from acquired businesses. Moreover, such acquisitions occurred with little analysis of cultural fit between merging partners, and with managerial disagreements about time horizons for planning and competitive strategies. These problems eventually contributed to the failure of mergers.

Now, acquisitions often occur using the existing resource allocation process in the acquiring firm. This is problematic because it allows all the shortcomings of the routine resource allocation process to affect the acquisition. These shortcomings include short-term horizons, limited involvement of top management, an orientation toward quick financial results, organizational politics, and a single-champion approach to investing. It is necessary, therefore, to develop a separate decision process for making acquisition decisions.

Acquisition decision making must start with the articulation of a total acquisition strategy in which individual acquisitions can be assessed. Acquisitions should be clearly linked to business plans and corporate strategies. The acquisition decision process should be organized to accomplish several tasks. First, it must ensure the quality of the acquisition justification. The rationale for the acquisition must be illustrated in terms of its links to the acquiring firm's strategy, nature of synergies, and financial investment justification. Second, the decision process must ensure a broad-based search for acquisition candidates with speed and confidentiality. Third, it should ensure participation of all relevant managers who can jointly bring organizational expertise and learning to bear on the decision. This eases the transfer of expertise between firms and eventual integration of the merging firms (Haspeslagh and Jemison, 1991).

The acquisition analysis should not be limited to financial and strategic concerns. It should include the human resource aspects of the merger. It is essential to answer and be prepared for questions such as these: What does the merger mean to employees of the two companies? How many jobs will be eliminated? What will it do to the morale of employees? How will merger details be communicated to employees? These questions become legitimate only if the analytical scope of acquisitions analysis expands beyond its traditional boundaries (Buono and Bowditch, 1989).

Organizing for acquisition decision making should begin at the corporate level. It is here that understanding of corporate strategies is at its clearest. A separate acquisitions cell can be established to give the acquisition activity an identity and to coordinate decision making both within the corporate headquarters and with business unit managers. This coordination should incorporate acquisition decisions into ongoing strategic planning and budgeting procedures. It should usher the decision process forward and prevent it from stalling by managing the decision process through its many steps.

This approach has worked well for the British chemical giant ICI. In 1984 the company responded to years of stagnation by embarking on an aggressive acquisition strategy aimed at a broad restructuring of its business portfolio. It created a small corporate acquisition team to guide it through this period of strategic change. The objectives of the acquisition team were to make ICI more proactive in searching for acquisition candidates and capable of handling multiple acquisitions simultaneously. The team acted as an internal clearinghouse for acquisition leads coming from industry intermediaries, investment bankers, and business brokers. As a central repository of all acquisition-related experience, the team was able to provide the benefits of its learning to all acquisitions made by ICI. Using this approach, ICI bought dozens of businesses and sold many existing businesses. It bought Beatrice Chemicals and Stauffer Chemicals. The Beatrice businesses went to existing divisions of ICI. Similarly, the Agro Chemicals division managers of ICI managed the relevant parts of Stauffer. Meanwhile, the acquisition team turned around and sold the remaining two thirds of Stauffer businesses to Akzo and Rhone Poulenc. Without a centralized corporate team, management of complex buying, unbundling, and selling operations could not have happened.

Besides the corporate team, it is advisable to organize an acquisition task force around specific acquisitions. The main role of the task force is to organize and coordinate actual investigations for business managers. It does the detailed search and analysis necessary to determine price and purchase terms. The task force should include members of different functional areas (marketing, finance, etc.) and business managers who will be in charge of the business after its acqustion. Additionally, industry experts who can provide the task force comparative data on other acquisitions in the industry may be included (Hunt, 1990).

11.4   POSTMERGER INTEGRATION OF ACQUIRED BUSINESSES

Completion of a merger does not occur upon the signing of the contract between buyer and seller. In one sense, it is just beginning. It must be nurtured and managed carefully, particularly in the immediate postmerger period. Integration of the merged business with existing operations is necessary for deriving the strategic synergies that are the basis of the merger. Without integration, the long-term benefits of the merger simply do not appear.

External Integration

Estimates state that nearly two thirds of all mergers simply do not work out in the long term. A third of these failures are due to inadequate postmerger integration. Exxon's acquisitions of Vydec and Reliance Electric are examples of postmerger integration failures. Both these mergers represented attempts by Exxon to add new technologies to a portfolio dominated by oil businesses. Vydec was a small, high-spirited, entrepreneurial manufacturer of word processing systems. The two companies' cultures, processes, and systems were so different that there was continual conflict between Exxon and Vydec executives. They disagreed about product design, marketing strategy, financial plans, and even day-to-day operations. Exxon's big-company culture stifled the entrepreneurial zeal at Vydec and finally led to its divestment. The Reliance Electric acquisition by Exxon in 1981 met with a similar fate. Reliance was acquired with the objective of entering the asynchronous motor business. These energy-efficient motors promised to revolutionize the electric motor industry. However, lack of integration led to poor management of the product, slow development of the market, and multiple conflicts among executives of the two companies. Finally, Exxon got out of the business by selling Reliance.

Besides the financial implications of failed mergers, managers need to consider the human and social implications. Mergers can be traumatic events in the lives of employees. Many mergers call for rationalization of assets, which often results in elimination of jobs. These jobs include factory workers and middle managers. In hostile acquisitions, even top management personnel may find themselves jobless after the acquisition.

Even if actual job elimination is small, acquisitions create many uncertainties about individual careers and foster anxiety and insecurity. Rumors, partial information, and misinterpretation of events distract employees. To play it safe, they desist from making serious decisions. This leads to loss in productivity during merger negotiations and during the postmerger phase.

Mergers also can result in plant closings, transfer of facilities, or opening of new facilities in communities. Influences on the community can elicit social and political responses that adversely affect the company. All these human and community side effects of mergers must be managed during the postmerger integration phase.

Internal Integration

Internally, postmerger integration should be aimed at dealing with three problems: coordination, control, and conflict resolution. The problem of coordination of diverse activities performed within a firm gets further exacerbated with acquisitions. Coordination of activities must be done within the acquired unit and between the acquired unit and the parent company. Old coordination mechanisms may need to be modified and new ones established. Coordination of procedures involves design and implementation of new administrative systems. Coordination of physical assets and facilities involves evaluating and redeploying assets, assuring their availability where needed, and documenting their usage. Coordination of personnel involves reallocating responsibility for groups of tasks to individual managers.

Control is the counterpart of coordination. It involves selecting the use of organizational resources and establishing new mechanisms for wielding authority. Implementing new legal and financial control systems establishes control. Authority and responsibility allocations, and managing the reward system, maintain control over human resources.

Conflict resolution deals with preventing and resolving conflicts among competing departmental, divisional, and personal interests in the organization. It is also necessary to deal with conflicts with external stakeholders affected by mergers.

Degree of Integration

The seriousness of these problems varies from situation to situation. Therefore, each merger requires different degrees of integration. Nonintegration of the acquired business may be satisfactory in some situations. Some mergers, such as conglomerate acquisitions, are not for synergistic gains but for purely financial reasons. These require minimal integration. Overintegration can be expensive, and underintegration can be unproductive. It is important, therefore, to determine the optimal degree of integration for each situation. The prime determinants of the extent of integration needed are merger objectives and size of the acquisition.

The motives and objectives of the merger primarily determine the need for integration. Mergers are a part of a general strategy of diversification or growth. For example, consider a merger that forms part of a strategy of related diversification. In this case, an acquired business is expected to provide important new marketing resources, product line extensions, and sales expertise. On the other hand, consider another merger in which the acquired business does not relate to existing businesses in a conglomerate firm. The motivation of this merger is the need to improve the price-earnings ratio and the growth in sales; there is no intention of sharing resources. In these two cases, postmerger integration needs are very different. For the first merger to be successful, extensive integration is necessary so that the firm can exploit marketing synergies. It requires rationalizing the product line and integrating the sales forces. The second merger could actually fail in its objective if integration is forced on it. In this case, the acquired business should be allowed to run as a separate, autonomous unit that is evaluated periodically on sales growth and earnings contribution.

The size of merging companies is a key influence on postmerger integration needs. The larger the size, the more diverse and intensive integration problems tend to be. The Du Pont-Conoco merger in 1984 is a classic example of the integration problems faced when both merging partners are very large. Each individual partner has its own problems of internal integration because of its large size. These problems become compounded geometrically during mergers. The merged company is so large that it is virtually impossible for individual managers to even fathom all the areas where integration is necessary. Therefore, the tendency is to react when encountering problems rather than to preplan integration (Datta, 1991).

To achieve successful integration of merged business, it is necessary to do three types of postmerger integration: procedural integration, physical integration, and managerial and sociocultural integration. The next three sections detail these types of integration.

11.5   PROCEDURAL INTEGRATION

Procedural integration involves combining systems and procedures of the merged companies at the operating, management control, and strategic planning levels. The objective of integration is to homogenize and standardize work procedures and administrative systems. Standardization of procedures simplifies communications between acquiring and acquired companies. It also improves productivity and reduces the cost of processing information. It involves integrating the legal entities, accounting systems, functional areas, and strategic business units.

Legal and Accounting Integration. The most basic integration is of the legal entities of the merging partners through transfer of ownership title. This is often a part of the merger contract. Integrating the companies' accounting systems follows. Two optional procedures, the pooling method and the purchase method, are available for integrating the balance sheet and the profit and loss accounts of merging firms. Many factors guide the choice of procedures: objectives of the merger, terms of merger, nature of financing arrangements, and the need for restructuring the balance sheet and the profit and loss accounts of the merged firm. The pooling method evaluates assets of the acquired business on book value. This method can be useful when the objectives of the merger include unbundling some acquired assets and divesting them at higher market value. The purchase method assesses value of the acquired business on market value of its common stock. Another important aspect of accounting integration is the establishment of financial control systems in the acquired business. A good control system enables corporate management to monitor and keep track of the acquisition.

Functional Integration. Besides the accounting systems, other functional area control systems and procedures also may be transferred from one firm to the other. If one of the merging firms possess highly developed, effective, and transferable systems for performing functional tasks, these systems can be implemented in the partner firm. These systems include inventory control, production scheduling, material requirements planning, sales analysis, order processing, and costing.

Transferring systems at the functional level is sometimes disruptive. It may require the collection of new data changes in report format, redesign of work procedures, structural adjustments, and even changes in personnel. After Texas Instruments acquired Metals and Controls (M & C), it imposed its sophisticated planning and budgeting systems to the rather loosely run M & C organization. Managers in the acquired unit experienced tremendous problems. The problems included a drop in performance, resistance from M & C personnel to adopt new procedures, lack of input data and bench marks to make the budgeting system work in the new setting, and a tendency to subvert long-term goals of the organization to show improvements in the short term. Texas Instruments had to restructure several departments at M & C, implement a new information and reward system, change motivation techniques, and change key personnel to initiate the new system. It took several years for the new system to stabilize, and even when it did, its performance was far from optimal.

Strategic Business Unit Integration. Strategic business unit (SBU) integration involves converting the acquired business into an autonomous profit center with appropriate administrative controls and integrating it into the corporatewide strategic planning system. This involves providing the acquired SBU broad guidelines for its role in the corporate portfolio and its goals for the coming years. Expectations are for the new SBU to develop strategic plans and propose specific strategic programs to achieve goals. Corporate management approves these plans and allocates resources for their implementation. SBU integration does not warrant changes at the operating level. Most production and marketing operations may continue as they did before the merger.

11.6   PHYSICAL INTEGRATION

Physical integration of resources and assets usually accompanies procedural integration. It involves the consolidation of product lines, production technologies, R&D projects, plants and equipment, and real estate assets. Physical integration of assets is a laborious and time-consuming task. For example, consolidation of the equipment and maintenance functions after merger of the Pennsylvania and New York Central Railroads required more than 400 steps.

A problem commonly encountered during physical integration is redeployment of assets in the process of resource sharing. Mergers often occur between firms that possess some common assets and some mutually exclusive assets. Asset integration ensures that the firms have enough in common to be able to use each other's resources. The mutually exclusive assets form the basis for synergistic operations if used jointly to benefit the combined firm. Some common assets, on the other hand, become redundant and need to be redeployed. These assets include physical assets like product lines, production systems, R&D facilities, and inventories or reserves of raw materials. Non-material financial assets include tax credits, cash flows and reserves, and human assets (skilled workers, management personnel, and technical staff). Plant closures and layoffs of workers often accompany asset redeployment. They are a source of tremendous anxiety among workers. To minimize demoralization of the work force and conflicts over employment issues, managers should work cooperatively with representatives of the work force to reach an acceptable solution.

Another problem typical of postmerger situations deals with achieving the synergy objectives of the merger. Sharing and mutual exploitation of joint resources does not occur without concerted effort. A long-term strategy for exploiting synergies must be communicated to all relevant organizational members. This strategy should describe specific programs such as consolidating product lines and raw materials inventories, cooperating in marketing efforts, coordinating production schedules, and combining financial power. These programs need to be supported by adequate resources.

Product Line. Integration of product line involves assessment of whether the products of the acquired business fit with the strategy of the combined firm. Two types of product lines may be discarded based on this evaluation. First, those products that are already being produced in sufficient quantities at lower cost by the acquiring firm may become redundant and, therefore, eliminated from the consolidated product line. Second, product lines or divisions that do not fit the acquiring firm's strategic needs may be divested. This unbundling of the acquired firm's product lines often enhances the value of the acquisition. For example, Texaco acquired Getty Oil which owned ESPN. It sold ESPN to ABC within a year of the acquisition, thereby improving the value of its acquisition.

Product line integration is not always a simple task. The basis of the Du Pont-Conoco oil merger was the fact that the two companies had a natural fit between their product lines. Du Pont's chairman claimed that even before 1979 the company's strategic planners had identified Conoco as a merger candidate because of its oil and coal reserves. Du Pont maintained that its future supply of petrochemical raw materials could be virtually assured if it acquired a suitable oil company. At the time of the merger, Du Pont had four major product groups: chemical (15% of sales), plastics (20% of sales), specialty products (30% of sales), and fibers (35% of sales). The chemical group was the most competitive, the slowest growing, and the most dependent on readily available, low-cost feedstock. The commodity sector of the chemicals group (7% of sales) included such products as ethylene, methanol formaldehyde, aromatic intermediaries, aniline, and methylamines. It was the major user of natural gas and gas-liquid feedstock. The plastics and fibers groups were the other major consumers of natural gas and petroleum feedstocks. Conoco, on the other hand, had three main businesses at the time of the merger. Petroleum was the largest (49.5% of sales), with coal, chemicals, plastics, and other businesses forming the rest.

Du Pont was unable to integrate its product lines with Conoco's. First, it could not economically break its existing contracts for supply of raw materials like ethylene and natural gas. Second, it was uneconomical for Du Pont to use Conoco oil and gas reserves due to high transportation costs between their distantly located plants. Third, it was uneconomical to use Conoco's ethylene production because Du Pont already had too much of this product. The only integration occurred in joint oil and gas explorations.

Production Technologies. Integration of production technologies is more complex than product line integration. A simple type of production integration may involve screening and divesting redundant production facilities. A more difficult type of integration involves the transferring of production systems across divisional and business unit boundaries. Failure to integrate technological systems can be an anathema to the entire acquisition, as illustrated by Exxon's acquisition of Reliance Electric. Exxon purchased Reliance to diversify out of the oil business and enter the electrical equipment manufacturing business. Reliance was a reputable (and sufficiently large) electrical equipment company. However, it also possessed a new electronic technology for synthesizing alternate current to direct current using the alternating current synthesizer (ACS). Exxon recognized the market potential of the revolutionary ACS. It became the central argument in favor of acquiring Reliance. After the merger, however, Exxon was unable to integrate Reliance's production systems and technology into its own operations. Deeper analysis of the ACS's potential suggested that Exxon would have only a narrow market advantage over competition because the product could be imitated easily. This meant that Exxon would have to enter the market on a very large scale to achieve a sustainable market advantage. The ACS technology itself was not completely proven, and its production systems were experimental. So Exxon executives became reluctant to attempt a full-scale effort toward mobilizing the technology through complete integration into Exxon operations. Their failure to integrate Reliance into Exxon made the acquisition useless for Exxon. Eventually, Reliance was divested.

Plants and Equipment. Related to the integration of new production technologies is the issue of integrating existing plants and equipment. Because of mergers, relocation of plants and equipment may be necessary to reduce production costs, inventory holding costs, and the costs of transporting goods to markets. If these variables are key determinants of profitability in the industry, then a rationalized reallocation of plants and equipment becomes crucial for a successful merger. In fact, the geographic distribution of plants becomes an initial criterion for acquiring businesses, as reflected in Heileman's acquisition strategy over the past several years. Heileman has now become a national brewer by expanding into the South and the West and competes with such giants as Miller and Anheuser Busch.

Real Estate Assets. The integration of real estate assets primarily involves revaluation of properties and their allocation to appropriate functions. Premerger analysis and valuation of real estate assets often do not consider the rapid escalation of property prices, especially properties located in urban areas. The undervaluation of acquired property could be substantial enough to make a significant depressive impact on the stock prices of the merged company. Current market valuation of real estate assets is necessary before these assets may be assigned for productive uses.

11.7   MANAGERIAL AND SOCIOCULTURAL INTEGRATION

Managerial and sociocultural integration are perhaps the most difficult and least examined problems of postmerger integration. They involve a complex combination of issues related to selection or transfer of managers and changes in organizational structure and development of a consistent corporate culture including a frame of reference to guide strategic decision making. Commitment and motivation of personnel and the establishment of new leadership are also important issues.

Personnel Transfers and Organizational Structure. At the most basic level, managerial integration involves appointment of a trusted top manager from the acquiring company or from outside as the chief executive of the acquired company. The executive may bring along a team of trusted managers to ensure smooth operations and to facilitate the transfer of systems and procedures to the new business. The objective is to ensure control of the acquired business. It may involve appointing new members to the board of directors. This approach of bringing in a new management team has the disadvantage of alienating the existing managers in the acquired business. They do not feel trusted and feel limited in their upward mobility. Often, they leave the company for other jobs. If an existing management team is critical for the success of the business, then bringing in a new management team from the outside should be avoided. Instead, a single, trusted manager should be placed in a key position from where he or she can monitor the entire operation.

The Du Pont acquisition of Conoco led to important changes in the top management and board of directors. Richard Heckert, formerly president of Du Pont, was appointed vice chairperson and took on responsibilities for all of Du Pont's operations except Conoco. Conoco's CEO, Ralph Bailey, was also made vice chairperson of Du Pont, but he was given operating responsibilities for Conoco. Du Pont appointed Bailey to the Du Pont executive and finance committees, and Bailey and two other Conoco board members also joined Du Pont's board of directors. Edward Jefferson headed the office of the chairperson, and the office included both Heckert and Bailey. Conoco retained its old board and management as if it were actually a subsidiary of Du Pont, but it added several new managers.

If the intention is to integrate the merging firms fully, then the transfer of personnel should extend to middle management, line, and staff personnel. Transfer of personnel between the acquired and acquiring firms help in cross-fertilizing the two firms. Managerial transfers across firms and departments are not always easy, because many managerial skills and experiences are not transferable. Sometimes retrenchment is required, and this creates insecurities among all employees.

Under conditions of change and uncertainty, retaining good technical personnel is a major problem. Retention can be simplified by clear communications to avoid misunderstandings about job stability. In addition, granting reasonable autonomy to managers of the acquired firms and avoiding unnecessary interference in operational affairs encourages people to continue working in their current jobs.

The transfer of key managers alone does not ensure complete managerial integration for strategic decision making in the acquired business. Transfers must be supplemented by integration of the social norms and cultures of the merging organizations.

Sociocultural Integration. Strategic decision making involves managers from several levels and sometimes includes operational personnel. The basic assumptions that managers hold about their organization and its environment guide the decision making. The general cognitive framework that guides strategic decisions has been described earlier (see Chapter 4) as the organizational frame of reference (OFOR). The OFOR consists of assumptions, information, and mental maps that managers use in decision making. Assumptions are the taken-for-granted beliefs about the organization and its environment. Often, managers are not fully aware of all the assumptions they make.

The OFOR represents the cognitive framework within which decision making occurs. It simultaneously reflects and shapes sociocultural and interpersonal relationships such as trust among managers, degree of cohesiveness in small groups, and level of understanding and communication among managers. OFOR subtly shapes decision-making processes. It should be made a critical focus of postmerger sociocultural integration.

Merging firms usually possess different and even conflicting frames of references. Sociocultural integration unifies the organizational frames of reference of merging firms. It eases communications between managers by ensuring that they have the same assumptions and consistent mental maps. It helps in developing a new corporate culture with compatible value systems that reduces conflicts among personnel of the merging firms. Conflicting corporate cultures have been the undoing of many mergers (e.g., the mergers of Fluor with St. Joe Minerals and Westinghouse with Teleprompter).

Sociocultural integration takes a long time to achieve, and often it does not occur at all. When it does happen, it occurs through processes of socialization and mental readjustment among managers. Managers of merging firms must learn each others' perspectives and assumptions until they start seeing and appreciating each others' perspectives. Simplifying this task can be done in several ways: transferring managers among the acquiring and acquired firms, developing homogeneous decision-making procedures, building trust among managers, and providing consistent information to all managers through new information systems (Nahavandi and Malekzadeh, 1988).

Gaining Commitment and Motivating Personnel. Achieving complete corporate objectives through the newly acquired business requires maintaining morale and gaining the commitment of people to new corporate objectives and strategies. Motivation may be improved by new incentives and compensation schemes, new opportunities for personal development, career opportunities, and improvements in the quality of work life.

The impact of mergers on morale and productivity is generally negative. Employees feel uncertain about their jobs and prospects and view mergers as occasions of major personal decisions and changes. They may become emotional about losing their identity and affiliation. New political and social alliances emerge and often disrupt old patterns of social accommodation. The anger, resentment, and hostility that build up may be expressed in subversive behavior and a drop in productivity. Many of these negative consequences can be minimized by encouraging open communications and allowing key employees to participate in the merger decision making.

Establishing New Strategic Leadership. Change in personnel, for the most part, occurs at the level of top management. The new top management may not be widely accepted by existing members of the acquired business. Therefore, a crucial task in postmerger integration is to reestablish a new strategic leadership in the organization. Strategic leadership refers to the creation of a set of conditions in the organization that gives it direction and purpose and guides integrated strategy formulation and implementation. It also involves strategic control of the firm's growth. The establishment of leadership requires well-respected and flexible leaders. It can be simplified by organizational restructuring, development of participative strategy-making procedures, open communications, and establishment of professional norms.

Immediate failures in postmerger leadership occur because managers do not resolve integration problems. Often, the lines of authority between functional groups of the acquired firm and the parent company are unclear. Managers from the acquiring firm are often unfamiliar with the work culture of the acquired firm. They do not have trusting relationships established with their new colleagues and subordinates. They do not have the necessary information to make decisions, and so they drag their feet over even simple issues.

Postmerger problems become compounded by the resistance to change exhibited by employees. There are two challenges in establishing new strategic leadership: new leadership must be immediate and it must seek to control all critical variables that influence performance. ConAgra acted effectively with the Banquet Foods acquisition. By installing a top-notch management team, ConAgra was able to turn around an ailing company.

11.8   STRATEGIES FOR INTEGRATION

Actions for achieving integration should begin even before the merger is complete. Merger integration should be conducted over time to avoid sudden disruptive changes. In the premerger phase, it is advisable to "seed" integration ideas. This can be done by making those managers who will be responsible for running the acquired business participate in acquisition analysis and decision making. These managers should participate in the acquisition screening process. Some companies that are frequently involved in mergers and acquisitions provide merger-management training to all key managers. Thereby, they create a cadre of managers well equipped to deal with mergers. In friendly mergers managers may be asked to work along with managers of the to-be-acquired business. Together, they develop operating plans for the postacquisition period.

Facilitative Merger Terms and Conditions. The terms and conditions of acquisitions can be formulated in ways to simplify postmerger integration. Legal provisions can be made in the merger contract for the following purposes:

- To smoothly transfer power and authority to the acquiring firm
- To grant security of employment to existing employees, thereby reducing anxieties and trauma over change of ownership
- To include details of physical and managerial integration (The acquired firm's managers can provide valuable information at this stage that can be used later to implement the acquisition.)
- To assist contested takeovers, which are the most difficult to integrate and control. (If contested takeovers cannot be avoided, the contestant parties should at least be identified and dealt with separately as a group of special stakeholders.)

Merger terms and conditions should include a comprehensive share-purchase agreement. It must ensure the acquirer gets appropriate relief if the acquired business does not reflect its original representation. Recourse to misrepresentation or material omission should be built into the agreement by necessary warranties, covenants, agreements, conditions to closing, indemnification clauses, and non-competition covenants. Often, agreements include a general warranty clause. They protect the acquirer against unforeseen developments and uncontrollable acts of nature (e.g., floods or earthquakes).

Another activity that facilitates integration is communicating with key stakeholders about the impact of the acquisition on their interests in the firm. These stakeholders include stockholders, suppliers, major customers, employees, labor unions, government agencies, the media, and the financial community. A report sent to relevant audiences should include some general information. It should discuss the likely impact of the merger on future prospects, employment policies, and supplier and market relationships. Such communications could alleviate fears about abrupt policy changes.

The bulk of merger integration must occur after the merger is complete, and it lasts for several years. A phased, evolutionary approach to integration is likely to reduce shocks of ownership changes.

Creation of Value Through Integration. The realization of synergies and creation of value in the combined firm requires transfer of strategic capabilities, skills, and assets between the two merging firms. For this transfer to occur, the firms must try to understand each other's organizational context and must be motivated to exchange capabilities.

There are no proven methods of easing such mutual understanding and motivation in a merger. Experience suggests, however, that eliminating barriers to change and hurdles to meaningful interaction between firms is essential. There are three common barriers encountered in merger integration: lack of vision and leadership after the merger, inflexibility of managers to do things differently, and loss of value for employees of the acquired company, which makes them feel insecure and diminished.

These three barriers demotivate employees from learning from each other and each barrier should be addressed systematically. The vision and leadership issue should be addressed by officially designating a specific individual to head the acquired unit. This person should be an experienced manager who has the trust of top management and has or can gain the respect of employees in the acquired unit. Some companies have found it useful to have the CEO of the parent company visit the acquired unit personally. The CEO can describe the strategic role that the business must play and provide a vision for the future.

The inflexibility of managers to change is both a behavioral problem and an information problem. Managers persist in past behaviors because they can avoid the effort of learning new ones and because they do not know new, desirable behaviors. They must be motivated to make changes by showing them the benefits offered by the new behaviors. In transferring strategic capabilities, such as sophisticated information systems, high-technology resources, and financial investments, these benefits should be easy to identify. It may be necessary to provide reluctant managers with structured information about transferred strategic capabilities. Companies do this by organizing formal educational and training programs.

The loss of value for employees stems from two sources. First, there are real changes in power and income associated with mergers. Many careers are affected, some adversely. This fosters uncertainty, fear, and demoralization. Second, a psychological diminishment occurs among employees of the acquired firm. They feel "bought," disempowered, unimportant, and helpless. This feeling of disempowerment reduces their self-confidence and motivation. There are limitations on what a firm can do about the real changes in power and income required by mergers. It may be able to minimize the negative effects of these changes by being open and forthcoming about them. It can give managers enough advance notice about changes. It can help employees who wish to leave the organization by assisting them in finding appropriate alternative jobs. The psychological pain and anxiety involved in mergers and acquisitions can be minimized through an organized counseling program. Many companies have used psychological consultants to advise the organization's members on how to deal with the trauma and stress created by mergers. Such help touches some intensely personal issues, so it is important to provide it with the utmost sensitivity and confidentiality.

To manage a successful strategic mergers program, firms should develop complete merger strategies that are consistent with their corporate and business strategies. The choice of individual acquisitions should be moderated by the firm strategy, potential for synergies, and financial considerations. A well-managed acquisitions decision-making process can be instrumental in making the right choice of acquisitions.

Mergers are not complete at the signing of the merger contract. An acquired business must be integrated into the firm's ongoing operations to derive synergies and generate value from the combination. Postmerger integration should be done at the level of organizational systems and procedures, physical assets and facilities, and managerial and sociocultural systems. Integration can be eased by providing clear and directive leadership. The company also must systematically educate managers about changes to be made and help them to overcome anxieties and stresses caused by the merger.

SUMMARY OF CHAPTER 11

Firms are increasingly choosing mergers and acquisitions as means for restructuring corporate assets. They allow companies to achieve many different objectives and create value for their stockholders. Value creation occurs by exploiting latent synergies between merging partners. This chapter discusses strategic considerations in selecting acquisitions and postmerger integration of acquired companies.

An acquisition can be a strategic merger or simply a financial deal. Strategic mergers create value by an efficient and rationalized combination of assets. On the other hand, financial deals try to capture hidden asset value. The focus of this chapter is on strategic mergers.

Strategic mergers are guided by several considerations: strategies and objectives of the acquiring firm, potential synergies between merger partners, and price of the acquisition. Other related considerations are the availability of finances and the opportunity to buy. Many firms fail to achieve synergies after the merger. To avoid this failure, a detailed and specific analysis of potential synergies is necessary. In assessing the financial feasibility of the acquisition, managers must examine the long-term financial health of the acquisition. This can be done by examining past earning performance, value of assets, market position, product line, quality of management team, and capital expenditure requirements.

Lack of attention to the acquisition decision-making process allows irrelevant criteria to affect the choice of merger partner. Failure of the merger results. It is useful to develop a separate decision-making process to make acquisition decisions with speed and confidentiality. This process should be guided by an overall acquisition strategy, which can guide the selection of individual acquisitions by assessing their fit with the corporate strategy.

Merger analysis should also include the human resource aspects of the merger. By planning for smooth transition of ownership, many personnel problems and demoralization of the work force can be avoided. Establishing a special acquisition task force can simplify management of a newly acquired business.

Integration of the merged business with existing operations is necessary for deriving strategic synergies. Postmerger integration deals with three problems: coordination, control, and conflict resolution. The extent of integration necessary depends on the seriousness of these problems. It also depends on the motives and objectives of the merger and the size of merging companies.

Three types of postmerger integration are common. Procedural integration involves combining systems and procedures of the merged companies at the operating, management control, and strategic planning levels. It involves integrating the legal entities, accounting systems, functional areas and strategic business units.

Physical integration means combining resources and assets. It involves consolidating product lines, production technologies, R&D projects, plants and equipment, and real estate assets. Product line integration rationalizes and matches products of the combined businesses and is the basis for a new product strategy.

Managerial and sociocultural integration involve selection and transfer of managers and changes in organizational structure and development of a consistent corporate culture. Commitment and motivation of personnel and establishment of new leadership are also involved.

Ideally, postmerger integration should begin before completion of the merger deal. At this stage, managers can communicate with key relevant stakeholders and identify potential integration problems. They also can accomplish the integration over time and avoid sudden disruptive changes.

READINGS, CASES, AND POLICY DOCUMENTS

The following readings and cases provide additional background material for the concepts discussed in this Chapter 11.

Readings

* Rapaport, A. "Linking competitive strategy and shareholder value analysis." In creating shareholder value: The new standard for business performance. Chapter 3. New York: Free Press, 1986.

Cases

* Boeing Company and de Havilland Aircraft of Canada Ltd.
* Citicorp—British National Life Assurance
* Dunlop-Pirelli Union
* The Southland Corporation—Formulating the Acquisition Strategy
* The Southland Corporation—Implementing the Acquisition Strategy
  World Tyre Industry and the Bridgestone Company

Policy Documents

Ernst and Whinney—Statement of Firm Philosophy
Touche Ross—Human Resource Initiatives

* indicates particularly appropriate assignments

Figure 11.1

REFERENCES

REFERENCES

Abell, Derek F., and John S. Hammond. 1979. *Strategic Market Planning: Problems & Analytical Approaches*. Englewood Cliffs, N.J.: Prentice-Hall.

Aguilar, Francis Joseph. 1967. *Scanning the Business Environment*. New York: Macmillan.

Alexander, Larry D. 1985. Successfully implementing strategic decisions. *Long Range Planning* 18(3):

Anderson, C.R., and C.P. Zeithaml. 1984. Stages of the product life cycle, business strategy, and business performance. *Academy of Management Journal* 27:5–24.

Andrews, K.R. 1970. *The Concept of Corporate Strategy*. Homewood, Ill.: Dow-Jones-Irwin.

Ansoff, H.I. 1979. The changing shape of the strategic problem. In D. Schendel and C. W. Hofer, eds. *Strategic Management: A New View of Business Policy and Planning*. Boston: Little, Brown.

Ansoff, H.I. 1980. Strategic issue management. *Strategic Management Journal* 1:133.

Ansoff, H.I. 1987. The emerging paradigm of strategic behavior. *Strategic Management Journal* 8(4):501-515.

Bain, J.S. *Barriers to New Competition*. 1956. Cambridge, Mass.: Harvard University Press.

Bain, J.S. 1968. *Industrial Organization*. 2nd ed. New York: John Wiley & Sons.

Barney, J.B. 1987. Types of competition and the theory of strategy: toward an integrative framework. *Academy of Management Review* 11(4):791-800.

Barney, J.B. 1986. Organizational culture: can it be a source of sustained competitive advantage? *Academy of Management Review* 2(3):656-665.

Bartlett, C. and S. Ghoshal. 1989. *Beyond global management: Transnational Solutions* Harvard Business School Press, Boston, MA.

Bettis, R.A., and W.K. Hall. 1983. The business portfolio approach: where it falls down in practice. *Long Range Planning* 16:95-105.

Biggadike, E.R. 1979. The risky business of diversification. *Harvard Business Review* 57 (May-June):103-111.

Bower, J.L. 1970. *Managing the resource allocation process: A study of corporate planning and investment*. Boston: Divn of Research,

Graduate School of Business Admin. Harvard University, Boston.

Boston Consulting Group. 1970. *Effects of Experience*. Boston: Boston Consulting Group.

Brodwin, David R., and L. J. Bourgeois III. 1984. Five steps to strategic action. *California Management Review*. Spring:176-190.

Buono, A.F., and J.L. Bowditch. 1989. *The Human Side of Mergers and Acquisitions*. San Francisco: Jossey Bass.

Burgelman, R.A. 1983. A process model of internal corporate venturing in the diversified major field. *Administrative Science Quarterly* 28:223-244.

Bussey, John. 1986. Gerber takes risky stance as fears spread about glass in baby food. *The Wall Street Journal*, March 6:19.

Buzzell, R.D., and B.T. Gale. 1987. *The PIMS Principles: Linking Strategy to Performance*. New York: Free Press.

Caves, R.E. 1980. Industrial organization, corporate strategy, and structure: a survey. *Journal of Economic Literature* 18(1):64-92.

Chamberlin, E.H. 1933. *The Theory of Monopolistic Competition*. Cambridge, Mass.: Harvard University Press.

Chandler, Alfred. 1962. *Strategy and Structure: Chapters in the History of the American Enterprise*. Cambridge, Mass.: MIT Press.

Chase, W.H. 1984. *Issue Management: Origins of the Future*. Stamford, Conn.: Issue Action Publications.

Chatterjee, S., and M. Lubatkin. 1990. Corporate mergers, stockholder diversification, and changes in systematic risk. *Strategic Management Journal* 11(4):255-268.

Chrisman, James J., Charles W. Hofer, and William R. Boulton. 1988. Toward a system for classifying business strategies. *Academy of Management Review* 13(3):413-428.

Conley, Patrick. 1970. Experience curves as a planning tool. *IEEE Spectrum* 7(6):63-68.

Daft, Richard L., Juhani Sormunen, and Don Parks. 1988. Chief executive scanning, environmental characteristics, and company performance: an empirical study. *Strategic Management Journal* 9:123-139.

Datta, S.K. 1991. Organizational fit and acquisition performance: effects of post-acquisition integration. *Strategic Management Journal* 12(4):271-280.

Davidson, W.H. 1982. *Global Strategic Management*. New York: John Wiley & Sons.

Davis, Keith. 1975. Five propositions for social responsibility. *Business Horizons* June:19-24.

Deal, T., and A. Kennedy. 1981. *Corporate Cultures*. New York: Harper & Row.

Dess, G., and P. Davies. 1984. Porter's (1980) generic strategies as determinants of strategic group membership and organizational performance. *Academy of Management Journal* 27:467-488.

Doz, Y., and C.K. Prahalad. 1991. "Managing MNCs: A search for a new paradigm." *Strategic Management Journal* 12:145–164.

Drazin, Robert, and Peter Howard. 1984. Strategy implementation: a technique for organizational design. *Columbia Journal of World Business* Summer:40-46.

Drazin, Robert, and Peter Howard. 1986. Tactics of implementation. *Academy of Management Journal* 29(2):230-261.

Drucker, Peter. 1984. The new meaning of corporate social responsibility. *California Management Review* Winter: 53-63.

Duhaime, Irene M., and John M. Grant. 1984. Factors influencing divestment decision-making: evidence from a field study. *Strategic Management Journal* 5(4):301-318.

Dundas, K.N.M., and P.R. Richardson. 1979. Business policy and the concept of market failure. Working paper, Queens University. Ontario, Canada.

Dundas, K.N.M., and P.R. Richardson. 1982. Implementing the unrelated product strategy. *Strategic Management Journal* 3:287-301.

Dutton, J.E. 1988. Perspectives on strategic issue processing: insights from a case study. In R. Lamb and P. Shrivastava, eds. *Advances in Strategic Management*, vol. 5:223-244.

Dutton, J.E. and Robert B. Duncan. 1987. The creation of momentum for change through the process of strategic issue diagnosis. *Strategic Management Journal* 8(3):279-295.

Eisenhardt, K.M. 1985. Control: organizational and economic approaches. *Management Science* 16:134-148.

Fahey, L., and W.R. King. 1977. Environmental scanning for corporate planning. *Business Horizons* 61-71.

Fahey, Liam, and V.K. Narayanan. 1986. *Macroeconomic Analysis for Strategic Management*. St. Paul: West Publishing.

Fiegenbaum, A., and H. Thomas. 1990. Strategic groups and performance: the U.S. insurance industry. *Strategic Management Journal* 11(3):197-216.

Filho, Paulo De Vasconcellos. 1985. Environmental analysis for strategic planning. *Managerial Planning* January-February:24.

Fombrun, C., N. Tichy, and M.A. Devanna. 1983. *Strategic Human Resource Management*. New York: John Wiley & Sons.

Forrester, J.W. 1961. *Industrial dynamics*. Cambridge, MA: MIT Press.

Frederick, Peter, and N. Venkatraman. 1988. The rise of strategy support systems. *Sloan Management Review* Spring:47-54.

Frederickson, James W. 1986. The strategic decision process and organizational structure. *Academy of Management Review* 11(2):280-296.

Freeman, R.E. 1984. *Strategic Management: A Stakeholder Approach*. Marshfield, Mass.: Pitman.

Friedman, Milton. 1962. *Capitalism and Freedom*. Chicago: University of Chicago Press.

Galbraith, J.R., and R.K. Kazanjian. 1986. *Strategic implementation: The role of structure and process*. 2nd ed. St. Paul: West Publishing.

Ghoshal, S., and D.E. Westney. 1991. Organizing competitor analysis systems. *Strategic Management Journal* 12(1):1-16.

Grant, J.H., and W.R. King. 1982. *The Logic of Strategic Planning*, Boston: Little, Brown.

Gray, Daniel H. 1986. Uses and misuses of strategic planning. *Harvard Business Review* February:89-97.

Greiner, L. 1972. Evolution and revolution as organizations grow. *Harvard Business Review* July-August:37-42.

Gupta, A., and V. Govindarajan. 1984. Business unit strategy, managerial characteristics, and business unit effectiveness at strategy implementation. *Academy of Management Journal* 27:25-41.

Guth, William D. 1985. *Handbook of Business Strategy*. Boston: Warren, Gorham & Larmont.

Hall, David J., and Maurice A. Saias. 1980. Strategy follows structure! *Strategic Management Journal* 1(2):149-163.

Hambrick, D., and C.C. Snow. 1989. Strategic reward systems. In C.C. Snow, ed. *Strategy, Organizational Design, and Human Resource Management*. Greenwich, Conn.: JAI Press.

Harmon, Roy L., and Leroy D. Peterson. 1989. *Reinventing the Factory: Productivity Breakthroughs in Manufacturing Today*. New York: Free Press.

Harrigan, K.R. 1980. *Strategies for declining industries*, Lexington, Mass.: Lexington Books.

Harrigan, Kathryn Rudie. 1985. An application of clustering for strategic group analysis. *Strategic Management Journal* 6(1):55-73.

Haspeslagh, P. 1983. Portfolio planning: uses and limits, *Harvard Business Review* January-February:58-73.

Haspeslagh, P.C., and D. B. Jemison. 1991. *Managing Acquisitions: Creating Value Through Corporate Renewal*. New York: Free Press.

Hatten, K.J., and Schendel, D.E. 1976. *Heterogeneity within an Industry: Firm Conduct in the U.S. Brewing Industry, 1952-1971*. West Lafayette, Ind.: Institute for Research in the Behavioral Economics.

Hatten, K.J., and Mary Louise Hatten. 1987. Strategic groups, asymmetrical mobility barriers and contestability. *Strategic Management Journal* 8(4):329-342.

Hax, Arnoldo, and Nicholas S. Majluf. 1981. Organization design: a case on matching strategy and structure. *Journal of Business Strategy* 4(2):

Hayes, R., and J. Clark. 1986. Why some factories are more productive than others. *Harvard Business Review* October:

Hayes, Robert H., and Steven G. Wheelwright. 1979. Link manufacturing process and product life cycles. *Harvard Business Review* January-February:133-153.

Hedley, B. 1977. Strategy and the business portfolio. *Long Range Planning* 10:9-15.

Helmer, O. 1983. *Looking Forward: Guide to Futures Research*. Beverly Hills, Calif.: Sage Publications.

Hill, Charles W.L., and Gareth R. Jones. 1989. *Strategic Management: An Integrated Approach*. Boston: Houghton Mifflin.

Hofer, C.W. 1975. Towards a contingency theory of business strategy. *Academy of Management Journal* 18:784-810.

Hofer, C.W. 1980. Turaround strategies. *Journal of Business Strategy* 1:19-31.

Hofer, C.W., and D. Schendel. 1978. *Strategy Formulation: Analytical Concepts*. Minneapolis: West Publishing.

Hunt, J.W. 1990. Changing pattern of acquisition behaviour in takeovers and the consequences for acquisition processes. *Strategic Management Journal* 11(1):69-78.

Hurst, David K., James C. Rush, and Roderick E. White. 1989. Top management teams and organizational renewal. *Strategic Management Journal* 10 (Summer):87-105.

Imai, M. 1986. Kaizen. New York: Random House.

Jemison, David B. 1981. Organizational versus environmental sources of influence in strategic decision making. *Strategic Management Journal* 2(1):77-89.

Johnson, Gerry. 1988. Rethinking incrementalism. *Strategic Management Journal* 9(1):75-91.

Kahn, A., and A. Weiner. 1967. *The Year 2000.* New York: Macmillan.

Karnani, Aneel, and Birger Wernerfelt. 1989. Multiple point competition. *Strategic Management Journal* 10(1):157-170.

Kim, W.C., and R. A. Mauborgne. 1991. Implementing global strategies: the role of procedural justice. *Strategic Management Journal* 12 (Summer):125-144.

Kobrin, S. 1991. (?????)

Kotha, Suresh, and Daniel Orne. 1989. Generic manufacturing strategies: a conceptual synthesis. *Strategic Management Journal* 10(3):211-231.

Kotler, Philip. 1988. *Marketing Management: Analysis, Planning, and Control.* 6th ed. Englewood Cliffs, N.J.: Prentice-Hall.

Kriger, Mark P. 1988. The increasing role of subsidiary boards in MNCs: an empirical study. *Strategic Management Journal* 9(4):347-360.

Lauenstein, Milton. 1981. Keeping your corporate strategy on track. *Journal of Business Strategy* 2(1):64.

Lengnick-Hall, Cynthia A., and Mark L. Lengnick-Hall. 1988. Strategic human resources management. *Academy of Management Review* 13(3):454-470.

Lenz, R.T. 1981. Determinants of organizational performance: an interdisciplinary review. *Strategic Management Journal* 2:131-154.

Linneman, R., and H.E. Klein. 1979. The use of multiple scenarios by U.S. industrial corporations. *Long Range Planning* 12:

Lorange, P.G., Scott Morton, and S. Ghoshal. 1986. *Strategic Control.* St. Paul: West Educational Publishing.

Lukaszewski, J. 1986. "Tactical ingenuity: new technique for surviving industrial crisis." *Industrial Crisis Quarterly* 2(3&4):309–322.

MacMillan, I. 1983. Preemptive strategies. *Journal of Business Strategy* 4(2):

MacMillan, Ian C., and R. George. 1985. Corporate venturing: challenges for senior managers. *Journal of Business Strategy* 5:34-43.

MacMillian, Ian C., and Patricia E. Jones. 1986. *Strategy Formulation: Power and Politics.* St. Paul: West Publishing.

Martino, J. 1972. *Technological Forecasting for Decision-making.* New York: Elsevier North-Holland.

Mascarenhas, Briance, and David A. Aaker. 1989. "Strategy over the business cycle," *Strategic Management Journal* 10(3):199-210.

Mascarenhas, Briance, and David A. Aaker. 1989. Mobility barriers and strategic groups. *Strategic Management Journal* 10(5):475-485.

Mason, E.S. 1939. Price and production policies of large scale enterprises. *American Economic Review* 29:61-74.

McGuire, Jean B., Alison Lundgren, and Thomas Schneeweis. 1988. Corporate social responsibility and firm financial performance. *Academy of Management Journal* 31 (December):854-872.

Meyers, Gerald C., with John Holusha. 1986. *When It Hits the Fan: Managing the Nine Crises of Business.* Boston: Houghton Mifflin.

Miles, R.E., Charles C. Snow, Alan D. Meyer, and Henry J. Coleman, Jr. 1978. Organizational strategy, structure, and Process. *Academy of Management Review* July:546-562.

Miller, D., and P.H. Freisen. 1984. *Organizations: A Quantum View.* Englewood Cliffs, N.J.: Prentice-Hall.

Miller, Danny. 1988. Relating Porter's business strategies to environment and structure: analysis and performance implications. *Academy of Management Journal* 31(2):280-308.

Mintzberg, H. 1988. Generic strategies: toward a comprehensive framework. In P. Shrivastava and R. Lamb, eds. *Advances in Strategic Management.* vol. 5. Greenwich, Conn.: JAI Press:1-67.

Mintzberg, H., and J.A. Waters. 1985. Of strategies, deliberate and emergent. *Strategic Management Journal* 6:257-272.

Mintzberg, H., D. Raisinghani, and A. Theoret. 1976. The structure of unstructures decision processes. *Administrative Science Quarterly* 21:246-276.

Mitroff, I., and J. Emshoff. 1979. On strategic assumption making: a methodology for strategic problem solving. *Academy of Management Review* 4(1):1-12.

Mitroff, I.I., and R. Kilmann. 1984. *Corporate Tragedies: Product Tampering, Sabotage and Other Catastrophes.* New York: Praeger Books.

Mitroff, I.I., and R.O. Mason. 1982. Business policy and metaphysics: some philosophical considerations. *Academy of Management Review* 3:361-371.

Mitroff, I.I., and T. Pauchant. 1990. *We Are So Big And Powerful Nothing Bad Can Happen to Us.* New York: Caroll Publishing.

Montgomery, Cynthia A., and Harbir Singh. 1984. Diversification strategy and systematic risk. *Strategic Management Journal* 5(2):181-191.

Montgomery, Cynthia A., and Ann R. Thomas. 1988. Divestment: motives and gains. *Strategic Management Journal* 9(1):93-97.

Nahavandi, Afsaneh, and Ali R. Malekzadeh. 1988. Acculturation in mergers and acquisitions. *Academy of Management Journal* 31(2):79-90.

Nielsen, Richard P. 1988. Cooperative strategy. *Strategic Management Journal* 9(5):476-492.

Nohria and Garcia-Pont, 1991.

Nutt, Paul C. 1989. Selecting tactics to implement strategic plans. *Strategic Management Journal* 10:145-161.

Ouchi, W. 1981. *Theory Z: How American Business Can Meet the Japanese Challenge.* Reading, Mass.: Addison-Wesley.

Pascale, R.T. 1984. Perspectives on strategy: the real strategy behind Honda's success. *California Management Review* 26:47-72.

Pascale, R.T., and A. Athos. 1981. *The Art of Japanese Management.* New York: Warner Books.

Perrow, C. 1984. *Normal Accidents.* New York: Basic Books.

Peters, Tom J., and Robert H. Waterman. 1982. *In Search of Excellence.* New York: Harper & Row.

Pfeiffer, William J., Leonard D. Goodstein, and Timothy M. Nolan. 1989. *Shaping Strategic Planning.* Glenview, Ill.: Scott, Foresman.

Porter, Michael E. 1980. *Competitive Strategy.* New York: Free Press.

Porter, Michael E. 1985. *Competitive Advantage: Creating and Sustaining Superior Performance.* New York: Free Press.

Porter, Michael E. 1986. *Competition in Global Industries*. Boston: Harvard Business School Press.

Porter, Michael E. 1990. *The Competitive Advantage of Nations*. New York: Free Press.

Prager, A.J., and M.B. Shea. 1983. *The strategic audit*. In K. J. Albert, ed. *The Strategic Management Handbook*. New York: McGraw-Hill.

Prescott, John E. 1986. Environments as moderators of the relationship between strategy and performance. *Academy of Management Journal* 29(2):329-346.

Prescott, John E., and Daniel C. Smith. 1987. A project-based approach to competitive analysis. *Strategic Management Journal* 8:411-423.

Prescott, John E., Ajay K. Kohli, and N. Venkatraman. 1986. The market share-profitability relationship: an empirical assessment of major assertions and contradictions. *Strategic Management Journal* 7(4):377-394.

Quinn, James B. 1980. *Strategies for Change: Logical Incrementalism*. Homewood, Ill.: Richard D. Irwin.

Quinn, James B. 1981. Formulating strategy one step at a time. *Journal of Business Strategy* 2 (Winter):1(3).

Ramanujam, Vasudevan, and P. Varadarajan. 1989. Research on corporate diversification: a synthesis. *Strategic Management Journal* 10(6):523-551.

Rapaport, A. 1981. Selecting strategies that create stakeholder value. *Harvard Business Review* May-June:

Rapaport, A. 1986. *Creating Shareholder Value: The New Standard for Business Performance*. New York: Free Press.

Raubitschek, Ruth S. 1988. Multiple scenario analysis and business planning. In R. Lamb and P. Shrivastava, eds. *Advances in Strategic Management*. vol. 5. Greenwich, Conn.: JAI Press: 181-205.

Reilly, Ann. 1987. Are organizations ready for crisis? A managerial scorecard. *Columbia Journal of World Business* 22:79-88.

Richards, Max D. 1986. *Setting Strategic Goals and Objectives*. St. Paul: West Publishing.

Rescher, N. 1978.

Robinson, J. 1933. *The Economics of Imperfect Competition*. London: Macmillan.

Roush, Charles H., Jr., and Ben C. Ball, Jr. 1980. Controlling the implementation of strategy. *Managerial Planning* November-December:3-12.

Rumelt, Richard P. 1974. *Strategy Structure and Economic Performance*. Cambridge, Mass.: Graduate School of Business Administration, Division of Research, Harvard University.

Salter, M.S., and W.A. Weinhold. 1979. *Diversification Through Acquisition: Strategies for Creating Economic Value*. New York: Free Press.

Schendel, Dan, and C. Hofer. 1979. *Strategic Management: A New View of Business Planning and Policy*. Boston: Little, Brown. 1979.

Schendel, Dan, and G.R. Patton. 1978. A simultaneous equation model of corporate strategy. *Management Science* 24(5):1611-1621.

Scherer, F.M. 1981. *Industrial Market Structure and Economic Performance*. Chicago: Rand McNally.

Schofield, Malcolm, and David Arnold. 1988. Strategies for mature businesses. *Long Range Planning* 21(3):69-76.

Schonberger, Richard J. 1990. *The World Class Company*. New York: Free Press.

Schumpeter, J.A. 1950. *Capitalism, Socialism, and Democracy*. 3rd ed. New York: Harper.

Schwartz, Howard, and Stanley M. Davis. 1981. Matching corporate culture and business strategy. *Organizational Dynamics* Summer: 30-48.

Schwenk, Charles R. 1984. Cognitive simplification processes in strategic decision making. *Strategic Management Journal* 5(2):111-128.

Sethi, S. P., and P. Steidlmeir. 1989. *Up Against the Corporate Wall*. Englewood Cliffs, N.J.: Prentice-Hall.

Shanks, David C. 1985. Strategic planning for global competition. *Journal of Business* 5(3):80-89.

Shortell, Stephen M., and Edward J. Zajac. 1988. Internal corporate joint ventures: development processes and performance outcomes. *Strategic Management Journal* 9(6):527-542.

Shrivastava, Paul. 1987. *Bhopal: Anatomy of Crisis*. Cambridge, Mass.: Ballinger Publishing.

Shrivastava, Paul. 1987. Rigor and practical usefulness of research in strategic management. *Strategic Management Journal* 8(1):77-92.

Shrivastava, Paul, and J.H. Grant. 1985. Empirically derived models of strategic decision-making processes. *Strategic Management Journal* 6:97-113.

Shrivastava, Paul, and I.I. Mitroff. 1987. Strategic management of corporate crises. *Columbia Journal of World Business* 22(1):5-11.

Shrivastava, Paul, and Sidney Nachman. 1989. Strategic leadership patterns. *Strategic Management Journal* 10 (Summer):51-66.

Simons, R. 1991. Strategic orientation and top management attention to control systems. *Strategic Management Journal* 12(1):33-48.

Singh, Harbir, and Cynthia A. Montgomery. 1987. Corporate acquisition strategies and economic performance. *Strategic Management Journal* 8(4):377-386.

Smart, Carolyne, and Ilan Vertinsky. 1984. Strategy and the environment: a study of corporate responses to crises. *Strategic Management Journal* 5(3):199-213.

South, Steven F. 1981. Competitive advantage: the cornerstone of strategic thinking. *Journal of Business Strategy* 1(4):

Steiner, George A., and John F. Steiner. 1985. *Business, Government, and Society*. New York: Random House.

Stevenson, Howard H. 1976. Defining corporate strengths and weaknesses. *Sloan Management Review* 17(3):51-68.

Stevenson, H.H., and Jose Carlos Jarillo-Mossi. 1986. Preserving entrepreneurship as companies grow. *Journal of Business Strategy* Summer:

Stonich, Paul J. 1981. Using rewards in implementing strategy. *Strategic Management Journal* 2(4):345-352.

Stopford, John, and Louis Wells. 1972. *Managing the Multinational Enterprise*. London: Longmans.

Stubbart, Charles. 1982. Are environmental scanning units effective? *Long Range Planning* 15 (June):139-145.

Summer, Charles E. 1980. *Strategic Behavior in Business and Government*. Boston: Little, Brown.

Tilles, Seymour. 1963. How to evaluate corporate strategy. *Harvard Business Review* July-August: 111-121.

Vance, S.C. 1983. *Corporate Leadership: Boards, Directors, and Strategy*. New York: McGraw-Hill.

Walsh, James P. 1988. Top management turnover following mergers and acquisitions. *Strategic Management Journal* 9(2):173-183.

Waterman, Robert H., Tom Peters, and J.R. Phillips. 1980. Structure is not organization. *Business Horizons* June:14-26.

White, Roderick E. 1986. Generic business strategies, organizational context and performance: an empirical investigation. *Strategic Management Journal* 7(3):217-231.

Williams, Jeffery R. 1983. Technological evolution and competitive response. *Strategic Management Journal* 4(1):55-65.

Williamson, Oliver E. 1975. *Markets and Hierarchies: Analysis and Antitrust Implications*. New York: Free Press.

Woo, Carolyn Y. Y., and Arnold Cooper. 1981. Strategies of effective low share businesses. *Strategic Management Journal* 2(3):301-318.

Yip, George S. 1982. Diversification entry: development versus acquisition. *Strategic Management Journal* 3(4):331-345.

Zajac, Edward J., and Stephen M. Shortell. 1989. Changing generic strategies: likelihood, direction, and performance implications. *Strategic Management Journal* 10(5):413-430.

CASES

ACME LEASING COMPANY

Fresno Truck Sales Corporation

Phillip H. Phan, York University, Toronto
and
John E. Butler, University of Washington at Seattle

Our goal is to add value to the franchise regardless of the size. The leasing company often becomes the number one or two customer for the dealership in parts, service and new truck sales. We seem to forget that sometimes and it is important.

Frank Fuller
President, Truck Leasing Corporation

Fresno Truck Sales Corporation,[1] in business for 20 years, is a highly successful retailer of class 7 and 8 commercial trucks. The firm is located in a company owned office building along Highway 99 in the San Joaquim Valley.

Currently, it operates a 16-bay service shop with 23 full time mechanics, and a 200,000 square foot sales, parts, and service facility. Fresno Truck Sales had grown from a small independent dealer of trucks to a $15 million a year operation specializing in the sale of U.S. manufactured commercial trucks, parts, and service. Ten years ago, David Krose, its current owner, took over active management from his father, who had started the firm.

OPPORTUNITIES FOR DIVERSIFICATION

In 1985, Dave Krose was approached by John Russo, Area Manager for Truck Leasing Corporation, and asked to consider entering the LeaseCorp full service truck rental and leasing network as a franchise. At the time, full service rental/leasing was a relatively new concept in the Fresno area. It entailed the rental/leasing and maintenance of medium, and heavy-duty trucks for commercial use. In addition to maintenance and other transportation services, the LeaseCorp franchise also provided truck financing, fuel and mileage tax reporting services, state license applications, substitute rental vehicles, insurance, and driver safety programs for its customers.

After considering the pros and cons of the offer, Dave decided it was a logical extension to his current business. Always one to take the lead in his marketplace, he saw full service leasing as the most viable transportation alternative to owning for private carriers. It relieved these carriers of having to deal with the administrative and maintenance headaches associated with owning a fleet of trucks. He also felt that some companies currently using common carriers could be converted to full service maintenance leasing. These customers would have to be shown that the services offered with leasing were comprehensive enough to relieve them of the administrative burdens and costs incurred through dealing with a second party common carrier.

Coincidentally, at the time he spoke with John, Dave was already looking for opportunities to diversify. In 1985 the economy was recovering from a slight recession, competition was becoming more

---

[1]Acme Leasing Company is a fictitious franchise built up from interviews with actual truck lease/rental franchises. Financial data has been disguised, and names have been changed.

intense, and profit margins in the dealership were shrinking. Dave saw starting the leasing company as a way to build and preserve the customer base of the dealership. This could create a steady stream of income that would help reduce extreme revenue fluctuations that are common in this business.

Dave had also spoken with Frank Fuller, president of Truck Leasing Corporation before considering a franchise arrangement. Frank told him,

> *Current trends indicate that 40% of all new Class 8 trucks sold in the next few years will end up in truck leasing/rental companies. Sixty-four percent (64%) of the projected growth in the truck leasing industry will come from existing customers. Ninety-four percent (94%) of customers who lease become attached to the leasing concept and will continue to remain full service lease customers. This means that, one, your leasing company will become your dealership's biggest and most loyal customer in the years to come. Two, if you treat your leasing customers right, you are almost guaranteed of a strong repeat business base, and three, you can participate in 100% of your market. If you follow the LeaseCorp system, and adhere to our guidelines, you'll make a good profit—competitive to what you are earning in your dealership now.*

Further assurances were given by John,

> *LeaseCorp will provide all the necessary administrative and operational support through our various programs. You must keep in mind that this is a management intensive business—you cannot forget that.*

After consulting with his lawyer, Dave agreed to join the LeaseCorp network.

ACME LEASING COMPANY ORGANIZATION

David Krose selected Thomas Kelley, his son-in-law, as general manager in charge of the new operation, now known as Acme Leasing. Acme Leasing was structured as an autonomous subsidiary of Fresno Truck Sales (see the Organization Chart depicted in Figure 1). Associated with the leasing company was a dedicated service department, originally staffed by a mechanic transferred from the dealership. Eager to get the new venture off to a running start, Dave selected his best mechanic for the job. As the fleet size increased, more

mechanics were added and by 1989, Acme Leasing had a total of 4 mechanics assigned to it. Major engine repair, and warranty jobs were subcontracted to the dealership's service department because they possessed the equipment necessary to do the work. The dealership service manager, Ted Ketch, was in overall charge of both service departments, and reported directly to Dave.

The leasing service department started with a service bay and added another after the fleet size exceeded 40 units. The facilities, including capital equipment, were rented from the dealership. Thus, as part of its housing overheads, Acme paid a monthly rental fee to the dealership.

Tom, a recent master's degree graduate in history from the University of California at Irvine, had a short work history with the firm and no experience in the leasing business. After graduating in 1983, Dave hired him as a salesman for the dealership. Tom, a personable young man, demonstrated a natural flair for selling. He rose to be top performer in the company after only 18 months. He was extremely enthusiastic, a good conversationalist, and was good at motivating the other salesmen. Tom seemed a logical choice for the position when the LeaseCorp franchise was started. Dave saw an opportunity to groom Tom for a future senior management position, and decided this was a good place to start. He also knew that Tom felt himself to be over-qualified for the sales job. Dave, inclined towards keeping the business a family affair, welcomed the chance to nurture a future leader for the business.

Tom Kelley, eager to establish himself in the company, was glad for the opportunity to be his own boss. In this capacity, Tom was responsible for the day to day running of the leasing operation, soliciting new business and, with the help of the dealership's credit manager, making decisions on credit matters. In addition, he was provided administrative and operational support from Truck Leasing Corporation, such as licensing and reporting services, training programs, operating manuals, and frequent on-site visitations by experienced field personnel. Working for Tom was a secretary to handle the daily paperwork, and a rental salesman.

COMPENSATION SCHEMES

As a manager, Tom was paid a base salary. In addition, because he was also responsible for lease

Figure 1 *Acme Leasing Company: A Subsidiary of Fresno Truck Sales Corporation*

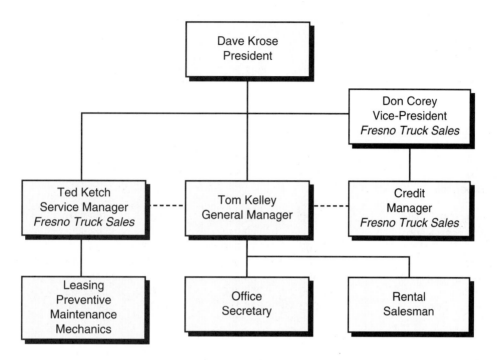

sales, he was given a commission for each truck lease he sold. The rental manager was compensated on a base salary plus bonus basis. The bonus was tied directly into the amount of rental business he generated. Tom's secretary was paid a salary. All personnel in the leasing company were given medical and dental insurance benefits, paid annual leave, and participated in incentive travel programs related to their job performances.

OPERATING HISTORY

The first two years of the new venture passed uneventfully. Revenue increased steadily during the second year (see Table 1) as more agricultural produce packing companies in the area became aware of LeaseCorp. In the third and forth years, however, revenues increased dramatically, reaching $1.6 million in 1989. The economy moved toward another recessionary trend in early 1989, and more agricultural companies turned to the leasing alternative in order to ease their capital commitments and improve their cash flows.

An additional side effect, which seemed fortuitous at the time, was the increase in business with common carriers during the seasonal highs. In order to reduce the cash commitment required for owning sufficient specialized trucks to meet the seasonal demands, the trucking companies in the area turned to signing 3-year leases and to renting heavily from LeaseCorp. In addition, because Acme Leasing also offered a contract maintenance package and rental of additional trucks to leasing customers, these companies were able to save substantially on operational costs and, at the same time, reduce revenue lost due to truck downtime. It seemed the perfect marriage because the common carriers needed additional vehicles during seasonal peaks, and Acme Leasing found a substantial additional source of revenue. During the seasonal peak periods, rental utilization typically ran 90% to 100%. This was reduced to 40% during the lows; but with a steady base of lease business, overall utilization did not fall below 70% throughout the year.

THE ISSUE OF FUTURE GROWTH

Currently, in 1990, Acme Leasing is facing the prospect of another surge of growth. Two weeks ago, Tom approached Dave for capital to expand their service facilities, and acquire 10 trucks. He

Table 1 *Acme Leasing Company Income Statement**

	1985	1986	1987	1988	1989
Revenues					
Fixed					
Full service lease—fixed	166,400	287,200	645,000	840,800	998,800
Rental—fixed	68,279	128,720	152,899	197,485	279,985
Total fixed	234,679	415,920	797,899	1,038,285	1,278,785
Variable					
Full service lease—variable	36,600	78,150	196,150	207,500	222,700
Rental—variable	38,943	44,550	55,048	80,659	99,789
Total variable revenue	75,543	122,700	251,198	288,159	322,489
Total Revenues	310,222	538,620	1,049,097	1,326,444	1,601,273
Expenses					
Fixed					
License, permits, PPT, FHUT	23,805	40,380	80,960	105,510	128,455
Outside vehicle costs—subs.		9,917	16,840	28,222	36,218
Insurance	6,000	11,040	22,560	29,520	36,240
Interest Expense	3,968	8,080	14,760	17,280	22,280
Deprec.—vehicles in service	21,450	38,350	42,200	45,860	47,970
Vehicles—sub-lease	121,800	208,400	442,580	577,530	714,000
Total Fixed Costs	177,023	316,167	619,900	803,922	985,163
Variable					
Fuel use taxes	0	389	0	841	888
State mileage taxes	0	432	0	423	536
Oil, antifreeze, and lubricants	3,591	6,910	15,379	21,905	28,493
Repair labor	14,590	30,835	70,990	90,898	104,898
Repair parts	10,780	23,632	57,954	81,579	85,388
Outside repairs	817	14,991	32,549	45,820	88,778
Damage repairs	0	735	0	449	525
Tires	14,012	25,062	49,118	64,906	80,838
Warranty (credit)		−1,389	−1,955	−1,203	−1,383
Total Variable Costs	43,790	101,599	224,036	305,617	388,961
Total Fixed & Variable Exp	220,813	417,766	843,936	1,109,540	1,374,124
Gross Profit	89,409	120,854	205,161	216,904	227,149
Overheads					
Maintenance Overhead					
Mechanics labor and fringe	24,876	24,928	53,785	72,789	95,782
Shop supplies	966	1,432	1,696	2,325	3,643
Service vehicle exp	986	1,358	2,664	2,890	2,523
Shop Equip Exp	1,638	2,699	3,103	3,991	4,175
Total Maintenance Overhead	28,466	30,417	61,249	81,995	106,123
Personnel Overhead	57,410	67,389	78,800	79,745	77,700
Housing Cost Overhead	16,000	22,000	37,728	37,846	38,174
Administrative Overhead	9,674	10,573	12,902	13,515	17,130
Total Overhead Expenses	111,551	130,379	190,679	213,101	239,127
Total Expenses	332,364	548,145	1,034,615	1,322,641	1,613,251
Total Operating Profit	−22,142	−9,525	14,482	3,803	−11,978
Adjustments					
Gain/loss on sale of vehicles			−1,057	−4,120	−6,067
Misc other income/(expense)**	1,303	1,281	985	1,604	1,435
Income Before Taxes	−20,839	−8,244	14,410	1,287	−16,610
Provision for Income Tax	0	0	0	0	0
Net Income	−20,839	−8,244	14,410	1,287	−16,610

*Abbreviated and disguised statement.
**Includes transfers to dealership.

Table 2 *Acme Leasing Company Balance Sheet**

	1985	1986	1987	1988	1989
Assets					
Cash	1,603	2,074	3,125	1,118	1,437
Receivables					
Lease receivables	38,462	80,101	202,214	318,689	452,966
Other receivables	3,127	5,156	8,137	14,127	16,127
Total Receivables	41,589	85,257	210,351	332,816	469,093
Total Inventory	10,305	11,615	14,725	15,239	12,256
Other Assets					
Prepaid Expenses	19,917	10,795	13,633	15,647	15,001
Misc. other assets	4,955	9,611	10,529	15,327	17,278
Total Other Assets	24,872	20,406	24,162	30,974	32,279
Fixed Assets					
Units for leasing	165,000	295,000	240,000	345,000	345,000
<Accumulated deprec.>	−21,450	−59,800	−91,000	−135,850	−180,700
Other fixed assets	35,596	31,945	32,895	35,493	37,710
<Accumulated deprec.>	−8,862	−5,974	−13,478	−15,896	−16,726
Total Fixed Assets	170,284	261,171	168,417	228,747	185,284
Total Assets	248,653	380,521	420,780	608,894	700,349
Liabilities & Capital					
Acct Payable & Accrued Exp					
Accounts Payable—Trade	167,427	291,189	293,286	419,031	494,460
Accounts Payable—Misc	55,485	59,931	45,634	72,264	95,346
Intercompany Payable	7,820	7,600	8,112	8,934	10,685
Other accrued expenses	8,920	6,964	22,421	29,889	30,652
Total Accts Pay & Accrued Exp	239,651	365,684	369,453	530,119	631,143
Long Term Debt					
Notes payable lease equip	4,840	8,920	21,000	27,160	34,200
Total Long Term Debt	4,840	8,920	21,000	27,160	34,200
Total Liabilities	244,491	374,604	390,453	557,279	665,343
Capital					
Capital Stock Par value	25,000	35,000	45,000	65,000	65,000
Retained earnings					
Beginning Balance		−20,839	−29,083	−14,672	−13,385
YTD earnings	−20,839	−8,244	14,410	1,287	−16,610
Net Retained Earnings	−20,839	−29,083	−14,672	−13,385	−29,995
Total Capital	4,161	5,917	30,328	51,615	35,005
Total Liability & Capital	248,653	380,521	420,780	608,894	700,349

*Abbreviated and disguised statement.

said he needed 5 trucks to replace those Acme was planning to retire during the current year. In addition, he needed 5 more because the rental business was taking off and he could not keep up with demand given the current size of their rental fleet. This was the third time in 5 years that Acme would be expanding its operation. Growth, Dave admitted to himself, had been spectacular. From a 4 truck operation at startup, the fleet now consisted of 84 units. In addition to an increasing number of regular renters, they were currently servicing 15 leasing customers. As further proof, Tom submitted a 5 year income statement and balance sheet, showing the growth in lease and rental revenues, and total assets (see Tables 1 and 2).

> *The pace of growth in the leasing business continues to be unrelenting. This is particularly pronounced in the Valley because transportation happens to be a very important component of production in the agriculture industry,*

he said. To drive his point home, he cited a recent special report in *Successful Dealer* (July/August 1990) which indicated that

> *lease/rental is becoming increasingly popular. As dealership customers try to concentrate on their main business, they are looking to turn their transportation needs over to a professional.*

Tom said,

> *You don't see many trucks parked out in the yard do you? It has been like this for the last year and a half. Already, Ryder is moving in on the Fresno market, and if we don't do something about increasing our capacity, our potential customers will be lost to competitors who will have the capacity to handle them. We are sitting on a gold mine, but if we wait, we'll lose it for sure.*

Dave was inclined to agree with Tom's general assessment. However, because Tom was requesting so many additional trucks Dave wanted to be sure. Besides, there was the question of where the money was going to come from. The dealership side of the business had not been doing well recently. Last year, the dealership took several large credit losses after two fleet customers filed for Chapter 11 bankruptcy. Furthermore, owner-operators have been scaling back on new truck purchases in order to weather the continuing economic downturn. Realistically, there was no way for expansion funds to be generated from the dealership at this time.

However, Dave could not ignore the need for growth. He reasoned that in this business, stagnation was fatal. Then, he turned his attention to the financial statements Tom submitted. In doing so, he realized that this was the first time since startup he had seriously looked at Acme Leasing's financial structure. In general, he received informal feedback from Tom and his service manager, Ted, during the weekly operations meetings. In addition, he usually received a consolidated profit and loss statement at the end of each quarter, and as long as he did not see a negative bottom line, Dave did not question Tom's management.

> *If you can't trust your managers, then you shouldn't hire them,*

was his operating philosophy.

HISTORIC FINANCIAL PERFORMANCE

As Dave examined the financial and sales data for the past 5 years, he began to realize that things were not going as well as his general manager had been projecting in his verbal reports (see the Statement of Income and Balance Sheet in Tables 1 and 2). In particular, operating profits in the current year had declined dramatically (see Figure 2). Further, even though total revenue had been growing in previous years, it became evident that its rate of growth had started to slow three years ago. Dave was concerned because the signs of slowing growth had not been detected and brought to his attention at the time. Although the recessionary trend had weakened by late 1989, promising a stronger economy for the future, Dave Krose did not see this improved economy reflected in Acme's income statement. This was especially disturbing because general economic forecasts, provided by various trade journals and industry experts, indicated an accelerating increase in the use of the leasing alternative over the next five years. As more agricultural and transportation companies, concerned with maintaining a healthy cash flow, began to realize the benefits of leasing, this upward trend was also expected to continue in the Fresno area.

A possible explanation for the reduced rate of growth in revenues could be the recently estab-

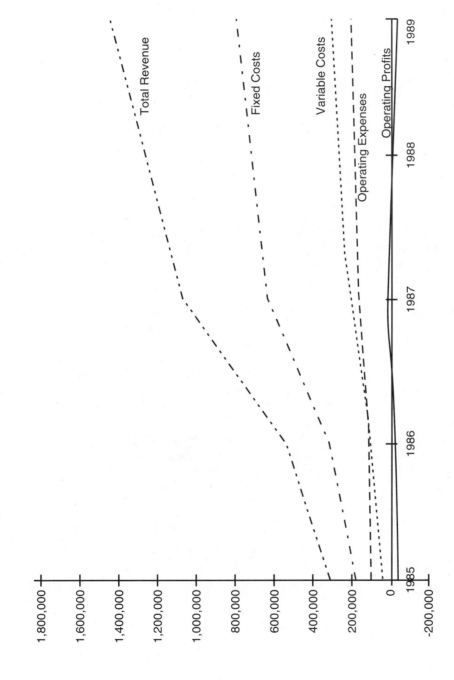

Figure 2 Acme Leasing Income Statement

Table 3 *LeaseCorp Standard Ratios Summary*

Fixed Expenses

Sub-lease Expense/Revenue	<46%
License + Permits + FHUT)/Total Revenue	< 8%
Outside Subs/Total Revenue	< 1.5%
Total Fixed Expense/Total Revenue	< 58%

Variable Expense

(Oil, Lube + Labor + Parts + Outside)/Total Revenue	<17%
Tires/Total Revenue	< 4%
Warranty/Total Revenue	> 2%
Total Maintenance/Total Revenue	< 21%

Gross Profit

20–28% of Total Revenue

Overhead

Total Overhead < Gross Profit

Net Profit

5–10%

Source: LeaseCorp Operations Handbook.

lished Ryder truck leasing outlet, which heated up competition in the Fresno area. However, Fresno was a growing market for leasing, so it stood to reason that a loss of market share did not provide all the answers. Other possible causes of decreasing growth in revenues could be the increase in rentals in the rental/lease mix. Subject to seasonal demand, increases in rental units may have sometimes resulted in more trucks parked for longer periods of time.

Comparing the *LeaseCorp Standard Operations Handbook* key ratios summary (see the LeaseCorp Standard Ratios in Table 3) with Acme's operating ratios, Dave found that certain components of his cost structure had also increased dramatically (see the Summary of Operating Ratios in Table 4). Both of those factors, declining rate of growth in sales, and increasing growth in costs, contributed to an overall decline in profits.

Dave Krose wanted to reverse these trends and insure a strong position for his business in the future. The leasing company has been making positive profits, and there still exists a lot of upside potential. Thus, no thought was being given to abandoning the business.

In order to identify the issues he must address, and then to correctly deal with them, Dave assigned Donald Corey, his vice-president, to determine the causes for the decline in profit growth. Dave had never taken an accounting course, and found financial statements to be of

little assistance as a decision making aid. However, he needed to know why the rate of growth in revenues has declined, despite the upward industry trend for leasing, and secondly, why certain cost components have risen so rapidly.

Don was also recently promoted from his general manager's position with the dealership. Eager to prove his worth, he attacked the project with enthusiasm. In order to make sure he covered all aspects of the business, he requested additional help from Frank Fuller. Frank assigned John Russo as the LeaseCorp representative, and operations troubleshooter. Together, Don and John went over the entire operation with a fine-tooth comb. In two weeks, Don submitted a memo that summarized his findings, with general comments and personal observations about the various issues (see Exhibit 1).

Exhibit 1 *Fresno Truck Sales Corporation*

<u>Memorandum</u>

TO: David Krose, President, Fresno Truck Sales

FROM: Donald Corey, Vice-President, Fresno Truck Sales

RE: Report on Acme Leasing Company's 5 year financial performance

Following your request dated August 6th, 1990, I have tried to discover, with the help of John Russo, the origins of the problems you highlighted in Acme's 5 year income statement. During the course of my analyses I have also come across other additional problems. As I originally suggested, much of the fluctuation in revenues has come from rentals to private carriers who currently own part of their fleets. About 31% of our fleet is currently designated rental. Operating margins tend to be higher in the short run for this segment due to customers' price insensitivity to short term rentals, but the market is highly seasonal. In particular, our periods of high demand tend to start in July and run through to September during the fresh produce peak seasons. There is less demand between March and June, and almost no demand at all between October and February.

As I see it, the first issue to address is the optimal rental/lease mix for our fleet. A related issue is our dependence on a single industry for the major portion of our business. The private carriers we are dealing with are mostly in the agricultural produce industry. The trucking companies that we deal with are divisions of companies servicing the agricultural sector in this area.

Another feature I noticed in our operation is that, of the 15 lease customers we are currently servicing, 4 are trucking companies. In analyzing the individual truck profit and loss statements, it seemed apparent that the vehicles belonging to the trucking companies consistently produced lower returns than those of the other companies. Conversations with Ted Ketch revealed that trucking companies run on very tight schedules in order to maximize their revenues per truck. Thus, they are not as conscientious in keeping to their P.M. schedules. On the revenue side, other problems with this customer segment were also evident. It is undeniable that trucking companies constitute a large portion of the market, but we need to reassess our leasing policy for them.

I noticed that our lease and rental rates are extremely competitive with Ryder's. While staying competitive is important to maintaining our presence in the marketplace, it is possible that in the bid to remain ahead, we may have under-priced some of our contracts.

The operative word, I believe, has been 'volume' rather than 'margin'. I have been told, *If we are able to get volume, then sacrificing margin is justified.*" In addition, because many of our contracts with trucking companies are for only 3 years, the cost accel-erator clauses in several of them, especially with our high volume customers, have been waived. We really need to define some parameters with respect to the kinds of contracts we are willing to pursue.

In connection with the contract writing issue, I have discovered a large number of high mileage trucks with high residual values. High mileage used trucks with high residual values cause two things to happen. High mileage lowers their resale values, while high residuals require their resale prices to be high. This incongruity has forced Acme to absorb some losses resulting from the sales of such vehicles. In addition, most of our vehicles are specialized to service the agricultural transport industry.

A tour of our leasing company's service shop impressed on me the short amount of time it took to turn a truck around during a preventive maintenance service. This did not seem to be the case with lease trucks in the dealership's shop. John pointed out the difference is in the nature of the work done during preventive maintenance versus repair maintenance. John also suggested that the dealership mechanics have been trained to sell labor to the customer, whereas the leasing company's mechanics are supposed to repair at minimum cost. Coupled with this problem, you will notice that most of our fleet is at the point where lease variable revenue rates will not cover our actual variable maintenance costs (see Attachment 1).

Excluding the trucking companies, a quick telephone survey of our remaining customers indicated that 40% do not plan to renew their leases. Some preferred to rent during the short, peak seasons. One indicated that Ryder offered them better terms, and the rest cited poor maintenance and maintenance scheduling as major reasons. To verify the last reason, I found that our use of substitute trucks was unusually high. Six of our vehicles have to be put on standby rental just to deal with the need for substitutes when they are required. We need to look into this problem because it will affect our repeat customer base in the long run.

In the area of operational support from Truck Leasing Corporation, I found that while much information was provided by LeaseCorp's regular company visitation reports, they did not seem to translate into positive action by Acme Leasing. The most common complaint I received from various personnel in the company hinted at the lack of time available to implement many of the suggestions. I feel we need to address these issues because they affect how the company sees its relationship with Truck Leasing Corporation.

Finally, an analysis of the receivables revealed that they are growing at a faster rate than sales. Credit granting, while important for garnering business, is a sensitive issue. On the other hand, collecting is just as important for maintaining current receivable accounts. We should review our policies with respect to this matter as soon as possible. I have investigated the possibility of using our credit department at the dealership to do the collections. We have the capacity to take on the extra work and can simply charge the leasing company for services rendered.

Please contact me if you have any questions, or wish to discuss this report further.

Attachment.

STRATEGIC CONCERNS

Dave had not anticipated that Tom's simple request for more funds would snowball into an operations audit of this nature. However, he reasoned, it was better that the problems got caught now, rather than later. In general, some of the problems the memo highlights seemed to indicate a fundamental conflict between the needs of a retail dealership and those of a leasing franchise. It appears that certain strategies adopted by the company, although appropriate at the time of startup, might now need some modifications. Finally, it is apparent that Dave Krose has to rethink the philosophy of the leasing operation. Specifically, while initially seen as an adjunct to the main business of selling trucks, it has grown too large to be treated as such. Using the leasing company simply as a customer for the dealership was a good idea, but for the operation to grow and prosper, a basic realignment of its strategic goals and objectives appeared necessary. Tom Kelley's and Dave's own roles in the business also have to be resolved. Time, attention, and resources have to be committed in order to ensure that the leasing company succeeds and adds value to the entire business. Otherwise, continuing on this course will end up hurting the entire corporation instead.

David Krose believed that timely decision making is critical to the long term growth of the firm. On one count, at least, Tom was right. They were sitting on a gold mine, and if they did not act quickly, opportunities would be lost. Given the competitiveness of the dealership business, it is foreseeable that leasing will become as competitive in the future. Opportunities lost will not be easily regained. If they want to get in on the ground floor of what will prove to be a growing market, they need to make plans now. Dave feels he cannot afford to wait another year and adopt a "wait and see" attitude. In addition to all this, Dave has to think about where the funds for the expansion are going to come from should he decide to pursue growth.

Due to the rising costs of doing business, Dave is already cash strapped in his dealership—no money can come from there. The cash situation in the leasing company is just as poor. Thus, he would have to look elsewhere in order to obtain funds.

As a matter of policy, LeaseCorp will overfinance the purchase price of a new vehicle.[2] However, Dave has always felt that in the interest of minimizing the costs of keeping liquid assets, the excess cash had to be used rather than kept idle as reserves. Thus, he was in the habit of redirecting these funds into his dealership to meet his cash flow needs or for capitalization purposes. Currently, these cash reserves are unavailable, because they are locked up in capital equipment and inventory.

Dave forwarded a copy of Don's memo to Tom Kelley, John Russo, and Ted Ketch. He called a meeting with Tom, Don, John, and Ted for Friday of the following week to discuss the issues raised. He also requested that all of them attend with suggestions for the next step.

Thomas Kelley

Tom was uncertain what the memo meant, but he had once said to Dave,

> *You can't really tell if you've made any money until the contract runs its full course. What with constantly changing costs, and with competition from Ryder, you may get to the end of the lease period and find you haven't made any money at all.*

---

[2]Actually, the overfinancing is intended to be used to help the lease franchises offset vehicle startup costs, i.e., licensing, sales commissions, pre-delivery and inspection, etc.

Attachment 1 *Acme Leasing Company: Analysis of Truck Variable Cost per Mile*

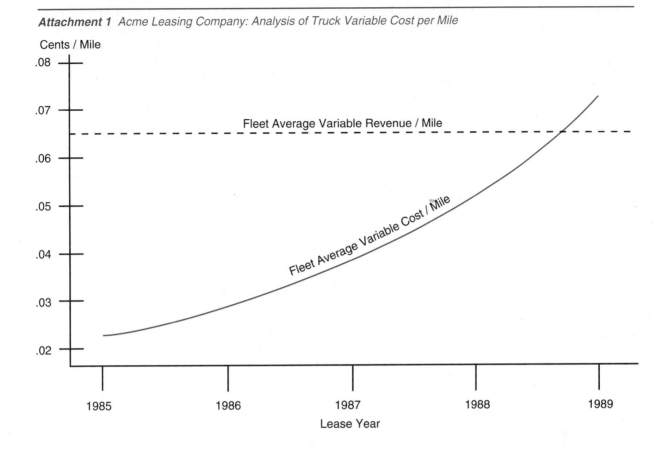

Tom believed that was what they were now witnessing. Several contracts had expired and, on reflection, they probably came out just breaking even. It was a real problem because he was trying to predict events over a 5 year time horizon with rates that cover all contingencies, yet having to remain competitive.

The way he got around that problem was to do more rental business. During the seasonal highs, he could rent tractors at $575 a week and 14 cents a mile with no loss in business. The extra 5 tractors targeted for rental will bring in even more revenue. He was uncertain as to the reasons why Don felt rental business was overemphasized. He was confident there was nothing wrong with his marketing.

Tom decided that cost was the cause of the problems. The leasing company was made to pay full retail prices for the services and parts used during repair maintenance work by the dealership's service department. He reasoned to himself,

It's close to impossible to compete with Ryder, who gets the best fleet rates from their suppliers, when I have to bear full retail cost for parts and service from my own dealer's service shop.

Tom couldn't understand why Dave allowed this practice to continue. He had previously said to Dave,

After all, LeaseCorp is your best customer. We are 100% loyal, come to you for everything, even though we can sometimes get better prices outside. With an 84 unit fleet, we are now your largest single customer! Good treatment is not too much to ask for is it?

This has been the focus of a running battle he conducts with Ted Ketch, the service manager. Ted's reluctance to give him any price breaks is why Tom felt the most important thing was to get the customer signed to a contract, whether lease or rental. Often, this meant that he had to cut rates in order to be competitive, but as a salesman, he knew that high volumes *did* justify lower margins.

Ted Ketch

Ted had his own thoughts on the matter. If Tom had built the right cost per mile allowances into the contracts he sold, he wouldn't be in this bind. There's no way that he will service a truck for the kind of rates Tom wants,

> *Why should I sacrifice my bottom line for the leasing company so that they can give away the house? I can't see myself wasting resources to work on a lease truck for $35 an hour when I can be increasing my margins with customer work at $45 an hour. It just doesn't make sense,*

Frank Fuller

Frank was thinking about the phone conversation he had with Dave in which Dave had asked for more funds to acquire the 10 trucks. In looking at the income statement, Frank was in agreement that revenues were good. But Dave's balance sheet did not seem to reflect the same story. He was over leveraged, cash poor, and had major loan commitments that were coming due in the near future. Technically, Dave should have had additional equity in his leasing company if he had not been transferring the excesses from the 6% overfinancing to the dealership. With the additional equity, Truck Leasing would be more willing to finance his trucks. As it stood, expansion seemed a poor idea at this stage.

From what Frank gathered through their conversation, Acme Leasing had a lot of "shop cleaning" to do before taking the next step. Frank was always willing to lend a hand, but was hesitant to commit any funds at this point. On hearing Dave's complaints about his cash position, Frank had informed him over the phone,

> *Do you realize the excesses from the overfinancing is really a low interest loan for you to take care of your future expansion needs? Dave, you know that Truck has always backed you. Almost all your trucks are now being financed by us. We have never turned you down before, but you have to realize that the first thing any finance officer looks for is equity in a company before considering a loan. Truck Leasing Corp. has to see some equity in Acme.*

Frank felt it wasn't up to him to dictate how the franchises ran their businesses, but it was in Truck Leasing's interest that the franchises all did well for themselves, and he was glad Dave called on him at the time he did.

Before sending John out, Frank expressed his concern over Acme's poor record of used truck sales,

> *Find out why Acme's used truck sales have been so poor. This is an area where they can easily pick up extra cash. I want us to help them sort this out because the impact on their bottom line will be immediate. Find out what they have been doing and see what can be done to change things.*

Despite his concerns, Frank was confident that with John's expertise, and Dave's willingness to improve his operations, Acme Leasing would get through this slump in good shape.

John Russo

John, on receiving the memo, was pleased that some action was being taken. To his mind, there were two major issues with which Dave had to deal. One was the question of growth. Sure, timing was important, but, if asked, he would advise strongly against growing now. The simple reason was that Acme Leasing did not have the managerial capabilities to handle growth at this point in time. Yet, he agreed that Dave must move quickly if he wanted to capitalize on the current growth in the area. This led to the second issue. The relationship between Dave and Tom. This was a sensitive issue, and though it was not like him to express unsolicited opinions, he felt that using the leasing company as a training ground for Tom was proving to be too expensive. John felt a sense of urgency in the kind of danger signs he was witnessing. Lack of cash flow, receivable build ups, increasing costs, decreasing revenue growth, and the lack of cooperation between the leasing company and dealership service department on basic policy issues. Issues such as the disagreement over intercompany charges make for an inflated cost burden that can potentially lead to collapse. Yet, he feels, these are merely the superficial symptoms of a deeper, more subtle problem.

> *There appears to be a lack of appreciation for the finer aspects of managing a leasing business. The business is different, radically different, from that of a dealership. In fact, about*

the only thing they have in common are the trucks,

he once said to Don Corey during the operations analysis they conducted.

URGENT NEED FOR ACTION

Dave was anxious to get something going. The agriculture peak season was 2 months away. With that, business from the trucking companies was expected to increase. He knew that Ryder in Fresno had already put in an order for more trucks to handle the extremely profitable peak season rentals. Acme could use the additional revenue, and he had no wish to be short changed on any business he could get out of the harvest season. But at this point, it seemed that everything hinged on the outcome of the next meeting.

Glossary of Terms

Common Carrier
Generally a generic term that refers to companies engaged in the business of selling commercial transportation. In this case, we are dealing with trucking companies.

FHUT
Federal Highway Utilization Tax—imposed on class 8 heavy trucks

Fixed and Variable Revenues
Fixed revenues are the base lease rate charged for the truck. Variable revenues refer to the additional cents per mile and other mileage or time related charges. Akin to the base rate plus mileage charges imposed by car rental companies.

Fleet Customers
Leasing customers with leases on more than two trucks

Full Service Leasing
A truck leasing contract that includes regular preventive maintenance, normal wear spare parts (such as tires, hoses, oil, lubrication, etc.), and other administrative services (such as fuel tax reporting, substitute truck rentals, 24 hour emergency service, etc.) as part of the package. The price of the contract should take into account all these expenses to arrive at the profit margin. Thus, once the contract is signed, the leasing company must try to protect that predetermined margin.

Inter Company Pricing
Most leasing companies are set up as units autonomous from the dealership or holding company. Thus, work done by the dealership service department is usually charged back to the leasing company as expense items. This may take two forms: full retail rates or special intra-company preferred rates.

Sub-lease
A financing program offered by the franchisor in which the franchisee leases the trucks it needs from the parent in order to sub-lease them to customers. The lease arrangements are usually on a case by case basis. In general, leases run anywhere from 5 to 6 years with a certain residual value built into the truck at the end of the contract. The residual is determined by considering the type of vehicle, the number of miles per year, and the expected wear on the truck. By using this type of arrangement, the franchisee does not have to put up vast amounts of capital up front. In a sense, it is a "pay as you earn" scheme; devised to allow franchisees to expand quickly as demand grows. At the end of the lease period, the trucks are usually bought over from the parent at the residual price and then resold in the used trucks market, ideally at the residual or a higher price.

National Account
In which a leasing customer is serviced by more than one LeaseCorp franchise over a wide geographical area.

P.M.
Preventive maintenance

LeaseCorp
The name of the Truck Leasing Corporation franchising system. The franchise system consists of privately owned truck sales dealerships that add truck leasing/rental to their service options by becoming a LeaseCorp franchise, stand alone truck leasing/rental companies that join the system, and Truck Leasing Corporation owned leasing outlets. The franchisor provides various administration and operational reporting services including truck financing, training, operations analysis, etc.

PPT
Personal Property Taxes—imposed by county governments for the ownership of trucks

Private Carrier   A goods manufacturing company that transports its own products. Transportation is an essential but not primary component of its business.

Rebillable Line Items   Some expenses incurred by the leasing company are chargeable to the customer as extraordinary items. Such as taxes, outside repairs for damages that are caused by abuse of the equipment, etc.

Specialized Trucks   Generally trucks that have been custom designed to meet the specific needs of certain industries. Thus, the most common specialized trucks used in the agriculture transport industry are the refer straight trucks (refrigerated trucks) and stake body (box) straight trucks.

AIRLINE INDUSTRY—DOMESTIC

Paul Shrivastava
Bucknell University

Major airlines are part of the "scheduled" US airline industry, defined as carriers which provide scheduled flights and which are authorized to operate on interstate routes with large aircraft, that is, 60 seats or more. In 1985 there were 106 scheduled carriers with total revenues of $47 billion. They accounted for 99% of all industry revenue. The majority of these revenues 84%, came from passenger service. The geographic breakdown of traffic volume was 78% domestic and 22% international.

Scheduled airlines have enjoyed strong growth in recent years. The industry measures volume in terms of revenue passenger miles (RPMs), that is, one paying passenger transported one mile. Total RPMs have doubled since 1975 to 336 million, representing 8% average annual growth.

Historically, demand for airline service has consistently followed macroeconomic trends. Revenue passenger miles closely tracked growth in both corporate earnings and personal disposable income from 1966 to 1986. In some years, during the recession of 1980 and 1981 for example, it even outpaced these indicators.

In view of recent predictions for gross national product (GNP) growth, these trends suggest a favorable outlook for airline traffic. For 1987 to 1997, the "consensus forecast" of the Office of Management and Budget and four econometric research firms is 3.2% average annual growth. Based on these estimates, the Federal Aviation Administration (FAA) is predicting 5% average traffic growth from 1987 to 1997.

There are 12 "major" airlines in the United States each with annual revenues of $1 billion or more. They operate on the nation's principal high-density routes, and compared with other types of carriers, have a higher percentage of long-distance flights. Other main groups in the airline industry are national carriers, regionals, and commuters. The nationals have revenue ranging from $100 million to $1 billion. Their routes tend to be shorter than the majors, and most of them specialize in a particular region of the country. Large and medium regionals have revenues from $10 million to $100 million. Small regionals and commuters earn less than $10 million a year.

The distribution of revenue and passenger traffic among these four groups is given in Exhibit 1. The data show that the industry is highly concentrated, with the majors dominating by a wide margin. Majors accounted for 82% of all traffic and 80% of all revenues. Majors also dwarfed other groups in terms of individual firm size. As can be seen in Exhibit 2, the five largest majors had average revenues of $5 billion each in 1985 vs. only $600 million for the five largest nationals.

Despite their weaker market position, some nationals have become significant competitors in recent years. Among them are Piedmont and People's Express for example, both of which graduated to major status in 1986. The regionals and commuters on the other hand posed less of a threat. There were 218 carriers in these groups, but their market share was only 4%. Moreover, only 38 regionals were classified as "scheduled interstate carriers," and thus legally qualified to compete on the majors' nationwide routes. The remaining 180 were restricted to operating small planes (60-seat maximum) within a single state.

Exhibit 1 *Composition of US Airline Industry*

	Number of Carriers	Market Share (pass traffic)	Revenue[a] Share
Majors	12	82%	80%
Nationals	16	14%	. . .
Large and medium regionals	40	3%	20%
Small regionals and commuters	178	1%	. . .
Total	246	100%	100%

[a]Majors: revenues of $1 billion plus. Nationals: revenues between $100 and $999.9 million. Large and medium regionals: revenues between $10 and 99.9 million. Small regionals and commuters: revenues between $0 and $9.9 million.

Source: FAA Aviation forecasts fiscal years 1986-1997, Airline Deregulation. S & P industry surveys.

Exhibit 2 *Major Players, Year 1985*

Category	Revenue (million $)	Average Revenues (million $)	% of Industry Revenue
Majors			
American	5,858	13%	
Delta	5,738	12%	
United	4,919	11%	
Eastern	4,813	10%	
Northwest/Republic	4,384	9%	
Total	25,712	5,140	59%
Nationals			
People's Express	928		
Southwest	606		
Pacific Southwest	583		
Frontier	558		
Ozark	494		
Total	3,169	634	7%

Source: Aviation Week and Space Technology, June 1986.

THE REGULATORY ENVIRONMENT

Historically regulation has played a very important role in determining all aspects of competition and profitability in the airline industry. Formal regulation of passenger service began in 1938 with the formation of the Civil Aeronautics Authority. In 1940 this body was reorganized into the Civil Aeronautics Board (CAB), an entity designed to function as an independent regulatory agency of the federal government. The CAB was able to control the operations of the industry's participants through its authority to (1) issue Certificates of Public Conve-

nience, a requirement before any airline could offer scheduled route service; (2) grant permission to service particular routes, which were then noted on the certificate; and (3) influence the fares charged by the airlines, either by its rulings on filed requests for fare changes or by actually setting exact fares or a narrow band of acceptable fares. In 1938, 16 carriers had been granted certificates for trunk operations of scheduled routes, however, several mergers had reduced the number to ten by the mid-1970s.

Pressure for the establishment of air service for smaller communities arose in the early 1940s. The CAB had misgivings that these feeder routes would face stiffer competition from the various forms of ground transport than the longer trunks routes. It felt that these proposed communities (typically with under 50,000 residents) would be unable to generate sufficient daily passenger traffic to support profitable operations, and that the industry's primary passenger aircraft, the DC-3, was unsuitable for short-haul service.

However, new carrier proposals stressing economy and less luxurious service ultimately convinced the CAB to establish feeder service on an experimental basis in 1945. Between 1945 and 1951, nineteen additional airlines were certificated as "local service carriers." Their status as certificated airlines brought them under the watch of the CAB, but also entitled them to receive subsidization on unprofitable routes. These carriers comprised the ranks of the "national" airlines in the 1980s.

The small commuter carriers evolved from the on-demand non-scheduled (air taxi service) operators of the mid-1940s. In the post World War II era, the combination of surplus transport planes and a large number of former military pilots led to the rapid expansion of service in the short-haul low-density markets lacking scheduled service. Most of the operators soon faded, with the number dwindling from 2,730 in 1946 to less than 50 in 1951 due to insufficient management skills and competition from the local service airlines. Unsubsidized air taxi operators soon found that their best markets were those smaller communities without local service airline competition.

The enactment of the Deregulation Act of 1978 was a watershed event for the airlines industry. It was the inevitable outcome of mounting pressures towards deregulation, in particular the phasing out of the CAB. As early as 1975, various individuals and groups (Congress, the FTC, and consumer groups) started to pressure the CAB for regulatory reform. Their argument was that the impact of the CAB's regulatory policies was inequitable, inefficient, and uneconomical. Fares were higher on average than necessary, while carriers were forced to fly with excessive frequency and to buy unnecessary aircraft. Studies conducted on the largely unregulated intrastate markets of California and Texas confirmed these premises. These studies showed that actual fares in these markets tended to be 30% to 50% less than those awarded by the CAB for similar routes and distances. In support of this movement towards deregulation, President Ford proposed a legislation

which would "remove most of the Federal Government's control over determining the price of airline tickets and in designating which companies may enter the airline business and what routes they may fly." This legislation, titled "The Aviation Act of 1975," was made public in October 1975. Under the Carter Administration, barriers to entry and fare discounting restrictions were further relaxed.

The two major changes that created a number of market opportunities for airlines were the elimination of most rate and entry regulations. On the one hand, entry into new routes was granted with minimal delay, provided the applicant was found "fit, willing, and able to perform air transportation properly." On the other hand, airline operators were allowed to set their own fares within a given range (from 5% to 10% above to as much as 50% below the standard level established by the CAB). As a result of these rulings, the established trunk and local service carriers withdrew from the short- to medium-haul markets that they were forced to serve under CAB regulation. These routes were unprofitable to large airlines due to the size of the aircraft, which were more efficient in long-haul service. Commuters were better equipped to serve these shorter-haul and low-density markets. Their smaller aircraft (more fuel-efficient per passenger carried on shorter-haul flights) and their cost advantage (less overhead and lower—nonunion—labor costs for example) allowed them to charge lower fares while offering cheaper service with fewer on-board amenities, for a profit.

The liberalization of the exit restrictions on certificated carriers, accompanied by the eligibility of commuters to provide subsidized small community service, further intensified competition and prompted a number of trends that continue to evolve even today. The more important trends included price wars, mergers, and consolidations, and route restructuring.

INDUSTRY TRENDS

Industry profits have been poor despite impressive gains in volume. In the past 10 years there was 8% compound annual traffic growth and 12% annual revenue growth. However, due to intense price competition since deregulation, profits have stagnated as shown in Exhibit 3. Historically, airlines have had low profit margins, only 1.79% from 1967 to 1977, vs. 4.8% for US manufacturing companies. Since the advent of deregulation in

Exhibit 3 *Total Net Income of US Scheduled Airlines*

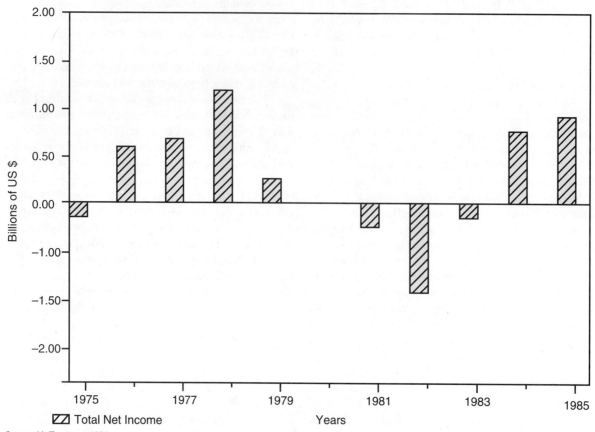

Source: *Air Transport*, 1986.

1978, performance has been even worse. Beginning in 1981 there were three straight years of losses and margins have declined to 0.2%.

The industry returned to profitability in 1983, with particularly strong earnings in 1984 and 1985 (approximately $1.5 billion per year). The outlook for continued recovery is uncertain however, at least for the near term. Some problems such as rising fuel costs no longer exist, but the operating environment remains difficult, due largely to the effects of deregulation.

PRICE WARS

An airline's profitability depends on the balance between its cost per seat mile, yield (revenue per passenger mile) and load factor (percent of seats occupied). The load factor can be increased significantly by offering discounted fares. This fact has prompted price wars in the industry. The damaging effect of price wars can be seen in the relationship of these factors from 1979 to 1983, during which period the first round of price cutting occurred. The trouble began in 1979 when costs increased by 15% primarily due to fuel price increases. The fares rose only 5%. For the next three years, the gap between cost and yield persisted, averaging seven percentage points per year. In this environment an airline could stay profitable only by achieving a higher load factor. Whereas 55% was sufficient prior to deregulation, the breakeven load factor climbed to about 60% by 1980. Unfortunately, the air travel is price inelastic, in the sense that new passengers attracted by lower fares did not make up for the lost revenues. Actual load factors fell short of breakeven by about 1% between 1980 and 1982, causing the large losses in those years.

Airlines recognized the hazards of unrestricted price wars and abated them for a while beginning in 1983. However, fare discounting was not abandoned. Ninety-one percent of all tickets are now discounted vs. only 81% in 1984 and 50% prior to deregulation. The size of discounts has also moved up slightly, from 51% off full fare in 1984 to 56% in 1985. Although few analysts believe that all-out fare wars will return any time soon, many airlines remain wary and ready to respond aggressively to any price challenge. Continental Airlines is a case in point. Ignored by majors when it first began to introduce low fares, it soon made significant inroads in important market niches. As a result, a common attitude toward discounters today is to "match them no matter at what cost."

Price wars were also related to the fluctuating price of oil. After a drastic price rise of 153% between 1978 and 1981, the airlines have enjoyed steady declines in jet fuel prices. From a peak of $1.05 per gallon in May 1981, prices have fallen to 43.8 cents per gallon as of August 1986 (see Exhibit 4). As a result, fuel now makes up less than 20% of total operating costs, vs. 31% in 1981.

Although supply and demand for oil is highly unpredictable, the FAA was moderately optimistic about future trends. It forecasted a continuing price decline through 1989 and a moderate increase of 2.5% per year from 1990 to 1997. By recent estimates, total industry profitability increased $100 million with every 1 cent drop in fuel costs.

NEW ENTRY CONSOLIDATIONS AND MERGERS

It was hoped that with deregulation, free market forces would foster greater competition and efficiency in air transportation. However, the size of four industry subgroups has not changed significantly since deregulation, as Exhibit 5 shows. There were 10 majors in 1978 vs. 12 in 1985. Nationals numbered 16 in 1985 vs. 19 in 1978, while regionals and commuters declined slightly from 245 to 218.

These numbers tend to mask the way the industry's structure has been altered. A more significant pattern of change emerges by just looking at the number of scheduled interstate carriers. These are airlines authorized to operate large aircraft nationwide, and thus legally capable of competing with the older, established carriers. Scheduled interstate airlines have increased dramatically since deregulation, from 36 in 1978 to 106 in 1985. Among these new interstate carriers

have been some remarkably successful new entrants. Until its recent takeover, People's Express had a 3% market share. New entrants as a group now have 10% of all traffic.

Statistics on traffic shares also point out how the market has grown more competitive. The majors did poorly in the first five years after deregulation, growing only 2% a year while overall traffic growth was 8%. In contrast, the 10 largest nationals and top 50 regionals grew 19% a year in the same period. A decline in the majors' market share was the inevitable result, from 91% in 1978 to 82% currently.

High merger and takeover activity is another new characteristic of the industry. The Department of Transportation must approve all mergers, while the Justice Department enforces any anti-trust concerns. To date, all merger and takeover requests have been approved by the current Administration, and a permissive environment is expected to continue at least through 1988.

Some experts believe that this new freedom will trigger repeated consolidations until the long-distance market is completely dominated by five or six large carriers. Although economies of scale in the industry are limited, it's easy to see why an airline might be motivated to expand via acquisition. Given strong price competition, it has become harder to build customer loyalty. With a larger system, it is possible that an airline can improve scheduling and other services so that the effect of price competition is reduced.

Acquiring other lines is a defensive strategy. It is common for airlines to exert sustained competitive pressure on particular routes in an effort to penetrate them or eliminate rivals. Often the challengers have been nationals or regionals trying to expand onto major's routes. To eliminate such threats, airlines resort to acquiring rivals.

Opportunities presented by financially weak carriers may also have fueled the consolidation trend. Examples of airlines weakened by competition and thus attractive as takeover candidates can be found in every carrier class—majors, nationals, and regionals.

Finally, a shortage of airport capacity has become an important factor. Airport gate and landing slots were once controlled by the CAB and allocated to an airline based on its approved route structure. With deregulation, this slot control passed to the carriers themselves, according to whatever allocation existed at the time. In many

Exhibit 4 *Total Domestic Fuel Prices, 1981–1986*

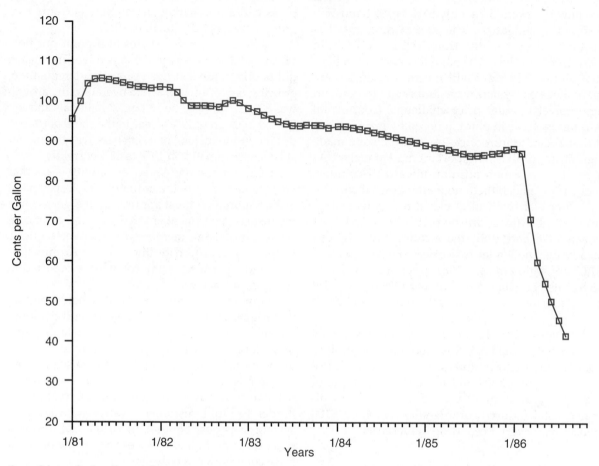

Source: Salomon Brothers Research Reports.

Exhibit 5 *Airline Growth, 1950–-1985 (Number of Carriers)*

	1950	1978	1985
Entire Industry			
Majors	16	10	12
Nationals	19	19	16
Regionals and commuters	50	245	218
Total	85	275	246
Scheduled Interstate Carriers	16	36	106

Source: FAA aviation forecasts fiscal years 1986–1997, airline deregulation. S & P industry surveys.

Exhibit 6 *Major Players—1985: Principal Hub and Marketing Strategies*

Category	Principal Hub	New Markets/ Strategy	Number of Commuter Affiliates
Majors			
American	Dallas	Nashville, Durham	4
Delta	Atlanta	Houston, Eastern's routes	4
United	Chicago	Washington, D.C., Pacific region	9
Eastern	Miami	Cut back, acquired	2
Northwest/Republic	Minneapolis	Phoenix, West	4
Nationals			
People's Express	Newark	Acquired Frontier	
Southwest	Dallas	Acquired Muse, Mid-West	
Pacific SouthWest	San Francisco, Los Angeles	Restructured	
Frontier	Denver	Acquired (People's Express)	
Ozark	St. Louis	Acquired (TWA)	

Source: S & P industry surveys.

markets, the shortage is so severe that the only way to grow is by acquiring new slots by acquiring airlines that control them. This situation is likely to persist moreover, since the FAA currently has no major plans to expand capacity.

While there is no predicting how far consolidation will go, it's clear that few important airlines have been unaffected by the trend. Exhibit 6 lists the five largest majors and nationals as of 1985. Among the nationals, People's Express and Southwest made significant acquisitions in late 1985, taking over Ozark and Frontier respectively. Among the majors, United expanded by acquiring Pan Am's pacific routes, and a key development in 1986 was the formation of the new Texas Air—out of Eastern, Continental, People's Express/Frontier, and New York Air. Texas Air now has a 20% market share, more than any existing major. The potential for more takeovers and restructuring also seems high in 1987. American for example, is actively considering acquisition of troubled Pan Am, there is speculation that Delta is looking for candidates, and Allegis is in the midst of a troubled restructuring.

ROUTE RESTRUCTURING/HUB-OR-SPOKE SYSTEM

The complete freedom to choose routes has prompted airlines to develop an effective route structure as an essential part of their marketing strategy. Prior to deregulation, the CAB tried to guarantee service to all communities based on need, providing subsidies on routes that did not yield sufficient profit. The elimination of subsidies is one reason airlines have moved to restructure their routes. Even more important, however, are the new competitive pressures that made it crucial to use capacity efficiently.

Since deregulation, there's been increased use of a hub-and-spoke format, as opposed to point-to-point non-stop service. Under a hub-and-spoke system, carriers try to merge as many routes (spokes) as possible into a single hub, from which traffic can then be routed on a connecting basis with a wide variety of origins and destinations.

Numerous changes under deregulation make this system advantageous. First, with open competition on all routes, carriers can no longer take "backup" markets for granted. In other words, localities that could once be counted on as a source of traffic for long-distance flights can now be easily tapped by competitors. Second, local-service airlines that once served as feeders for the majors' non-stops increasingly retain those passengers, because they've started long-haul flights of their own. Finally, discount offers often divert passengers to other carriers, increasing the risk of low utilization on non-stop flights.

Exhibit 7 *Concentration of Carrier Operations at Their Principal Hubs, 1978 and 1983*

Carrier	Hub	*Percent of Carrier's Total Domestic Departures Flown from Specified Hub*	
		1978 (2nd quarter)	1983 (2nd quarter)
American	Dallas	11.2	28.6
US Air	Pittsburgh	16.0	23.2
Continental[a]	Houston	12.8	22.9
Delta	Atlanta	18.3	21.4
Eastern	Atlanta	18.3	21.0
Frontier	Denver	18.0	33.8
Northwest	Minneapolis	16.1	20.7
Ozark	St. Louis	15.5	35.6
Pan American[a]	New York	12.3	24.0
Piedmont	Charlotte	3.7	19.6
Republic[a]	Minneapolis	3.4	7.7
TWA	St. Louis	11.9	33.0
United	Chicago	13.8	18.9
Western	Salt Lake City	10.3	16.9

[a] Reflects combined data for then-independent carriers which later merged into these carriers systems.

Source: Civil Aeronautics Board, Annual Report, 1984.

Under these conditions, hub-and-spoke operations are preferable because they make a carrier less vulnerable to diversions that might occur on any particular route. They also make it possible to retain passengers in the system longer and to avoid lightly traveled routes.

Hub-and-spoke systems have been adopted by all large airlines. The extent of the shift can be seen in Exhibit 7, which shows the percent of an airline's traffic that is concentrated at its principal hub (i.e., main airport and its surrounding metropolitan area). Concentration averaged about 15% in 1978, but has moved up to about 25%.

Unfortunately, use of a hub strategy by itself does not guarantee good traffic. One reason is that so many airlines are implementing ambitious plans to expand at particular hubs or move onto new ones. Another common strategy is to form affiliations with regionals or commuters, in which the latter agree to feed passengers onto majors' flights. As of 1985, the five largest majors had an average of five affiliates each. Most carriers are still engaged in major programs to rationalize and/or expand their routes. Their efforts further illustrate how much more complex and challenging the operating environment has become.

LABOR

Labor has emerged as one of the most difficult issues in the new environment. Labor averages about 35% of total operating costs for the majors, but exact figures range from a low of 22% at Continental to a high of 43% at Delta.

Continental achieved its low costs by declaring bankruptcy and abrogating its labor contracts, a strategy that few others can copy. Use of a two-tiered pay-scale is at least a partial solution many others have adopted. American introduced this concept in 1984, when it negotiated contracts that maintained pay and benefit levels for existing employees, but cut them for new workers by as much as 30% to 50%. Eight majors now use some form of the two-tier system. Industrywide, 35% of all labor contracts include such provisions.

Although helpful in cutting costs, these contracts have served to polarize labor and management. Unions have become more militant in fighting wage and other concessions, as evidenced by two costly strikes in 1985—at Pan Am and United. Besides fighting two-tier scales, unions also want greater protection in merger situations. They are lobbying for legislation, for example, that will require the new management to honor existing contracts and seniority rights after a takeover.

TECHNOLOGICAL AND OPERATING ENVIRONMENT FLEET STRUCTURE

An airline's fleet composition can have an important effect on profitability. Planes represent a huge capital investment, have a long life (20 years or more), and due to long lead-times on new purchases, cannot be replaced quickly. These factors mean that an airline has limited flexibility in adapting its fleet to market changes.

Deregulation has begun to force some adjustments in fleet structure. When non-stop long-distance flights were more common, large planes were most efficient. With the shift to hub-and-spoke operations, flights are now shorter and more frequent. Smaller planes are considered most efficient for this kind of traffic, and orders for new aircraft are beginning to reflect the new preference. In recent years, only 14% of new plane orders were for very large aircraft—200 seats or more. Based on this trend, the FAA predicts that narrow-body, two-engine planes will make up 56% of the total US fleet by 1997, compared with 37% in 1985.

Airlines that are able to scale down their fleet are likely to have an edge over competitors. Unfortunately, the loss of the investment tax credit under the new tax law makes fleet changes even more costly. Carriers with low cash reserves or poor financing prospects thus have particular disadvantages.

COMPUTER RESERVATION AND YIELD MANAGEMENT SYSTEMS

Computer reservation systems (CRS) represent the most important new use of technology in the industry. Airline fare and flight schedules have become very complex, and a CRS is the most practical solution. Sixty-five percent of all domestic bookings are done through CRSs, including 90% of tickets sold by travel agents. American's SABRE system and United's APPOLLO dominate the market. Counting time-share customers, they book 45% of all tickets.

CRS systems can be valuable as a direct source of income. It's estimated that American will earn $100 million from SABRE in 1986, out of $340 million total income. Equally crucial is their role as the foundation of a comprehensive yield management system. It is known that due to lack of information, airlines often sell more discount tickets than necessary to fill their planes. Only a CRS/yield-management system can provide up-to-the-minute data on passenger loads, as well as the historical information needed to make better pricing decisions.

Given these benefits, airlines are pushing hard either to buy CRS services or develop their own. Airlines with a headstart in this effort are in the strongest position, as the investment of time and money required is huge. SABRE and APPOLLO, for example, each cost about $500 million to build and took 10 years of research and development.

AIRPORT CAPACITY AND SAFETY

Because they require a higher frequency of flights, hub-and-spoke operations have caused a sharp increase in the number of aircraft landings and takeoffs. Per the FAA, carrier departures will be 20% higher in 1986 than in 1982. Due to the resulting congestion, average flight delays are expected to climb 22%.

Since the FAA is not planning to expand airport capacity significantly, congestion will persist as a serious problem. A shortage of air traffic controllers aggravates the problem. The number of controllers is down 28% from 1981, and their experience and training level is also lower due to President Reagan's action against them.

Thus far, there has been no significant increase in the number of fatal accidents since deregulation. With the new stress on cost-cutting however, the FAA has found some evidence that maintenance standards are being compromised. It has increased its inspection staff by 30% in order to deal with the problem and has also levied fines higher than any previously collected. Pan Am paid $1.95 million for example, while Eastern paid $9.5 million.

As yet, none of the established majors has suffered a noticeable loss of public confidence due to safety concerns. And at least among this group, it seems that congestion has reduced on-time performance across the board. Nevertheless, safety and congestion have become issues as never before, further complicating the job of airline managements.

THE COMPETITIVE ENVIRONMENT

Post-deregulation competition has been intense and continues to grow. Elements that fuel competition are briefly described below.

The Rivalry Among Existing Competitors

The intense rivalry observed among airlines stems from four structural characteristics of the industry:

- high fixed costs
- chronic overcapacity
- commodity-like nature of the product
- absence of switching costs to users

Airlines' fixed costs are high due to their substantial investments in planes, ground support services, and computer reservation systems. Since there's little difference in expense between flying a plane at 90% capacity vs. 60%, there's a strong incentive to fill planes, which leads to aggressive price competition. This need not be the case if demand were in good balance with total industry capacity. Unfortunately, this has not been true of the airlines, as average load factors have rarely exceeded 60%.

The fact that air transportation is akin to a commodity also fuels competition. Airlines constantly struggle to differentiate themselves, but with little success, as most worthwhile innovations can be easily copied by others. The absence of switching costs also makes it hard to build "brand" loyalty. Airlines have tried to impose such costs through frequent-flyer programs and other types of bonuses. These tend to be ineffective however, as repeat travelers often join several airlines' programs and still tend to consider price as the deciding factor.

Bargaining Power of Buyers

Business and leisure travelers are the airlines' two main buyer groups. Both have characteristics that weaken their bargaining power. Neither group is concentrated and no single customer makes large purchases relative to an airline's total sales. Similarly, air transportation rarely makes up a significant percent of buyer's total purchases, and there's clearly no threat of backward integration between the two groups.

Despite these weaknesses, other factors prevent carriers from gaining a dominant position, for example, lack of switching costs and product differentiation, and the fact that buyers get full price information via travel agents. We believe that these strengths more than offset buyers' weaknesses and have characterized their position as moderate to strong.

Bargaining Power of Suppliers

The industry's main suppliers are aircraft manufacturers, oil companies, and labor. Aircraft manufacturers are relatively concentrated and have a product that is very important to users, highly differentiated, and lacking in substitutes. We believe that their position is only moderately strong, however, as their strengths are offset by the chronic overcapacity among airlines and the fact that individual airlines can be very important to particular suppliers.

Although a commodity, oil is a very important input which lacks substitutes. Its importance could increase significantly if OPEC becomes strong again. The industry has no control over oil prices, which fluctuate with changes in the global economy. While labor is well-organized and has been aggressive recently, its power has been reduced by the industry's erratic profitability.

Threat of New Entrants

Although there have been many new entrants in the regional and commuter class, there's very little threat of new entrants among majors. The large capital investment required is one strong barrier, particularly as financing has become scarce for start-up firms, due to the high risk associated with attempts to enter a mature industry. Once favored by lenders when the CAB virtually guaranteed profits, many airlines are now thought to be poor credit risks.

Lack of airport capacity, particularly during peak hours, is another barrier. On most major routes, landing slots and gates are already fully utilized and controlled by existing carriers. Additional capacity is available at off-peak times, but these slots alone would be insufficient for building an effective, major-size airline. Demonstrating this fact is the recent experience of Delta and United Airlines. Both failed to expand capacity in recent years, lost scheduling flexibility, and then lost significant market share as a result.

Threat of Substitutes

Where fast, long-distance transportation is needed, there's no viable substitute for air travel. Teleconferencing may eventually reduce the need for business travel, but this alternative is yet to become popular. However, for shorter distance travel or for trips in which travel time is not critical, there are several substitutes to air travel. Automobile and train transportation have served as substitutes for vacation travel and short distance travel.

BOOK BIBLIOGRAPHY

Cowes, Richard E. *Air Transport & Its Regulators*. Cambridge: Harvard, 1962.

Douglas, George W. and James C. Miller III. *Economic Regulation of Domestic Air Transport: Theory & Policy*. Washington, D.C.: Brookings, 1974.

Federal Aviation Administration. *Statistical Hand Book of Aviation*. Washington, D.C.: Dept. of Transportation, 1979–1982.

James, George W., ed. *Airline Economics*. Toronto: D. C. Heath (Lexington Books), 1982.

MacAvoy, Paul W. and John W. Snow, eds. *Regulation of Passenger Fares and Competition Among the Airlines*. Washington, D.C.: American Enterprise Institute for Public Policy Research, 1977.

Mandell, Robert W. *Financing the Capital Requirements of the U.S. Airline Industry in the 1980's*. Toronto: D. C. Heath (Lexington Books), 1979.

Meyer, John R. and Oster, Morgan, Berman, and Strassman. *Airline Deregulation—The Early Experience.*: Auburn House, 1981.

Meyer, John R. and Clinton V. Oster, Jr., contrib. eds. *Deregulation and the New Airline Entrepreneurs*. Cambridge: MIT, 1984.

National Bureau of Economic Research. Airline Costs and Managerial Efficiency, in *Transportation Economics, a Conference of the Universities*. New York: Columbia, 1965.

Norling, Alfred H. *Industry Follow-up: The Airline Industry*. New York: Kidder Peabody Research Dept., Oct. 1983.

Regional Air Line Association. *1983 Annual Report*. Washington D.C.: Regional Airline Assoc., 1984.

Taneja, Narval K. *Airline Planning: Corporate, Financial and Marketing*. Toronto: D. C. Heath (Lexington Books), 1982.

U.S. Civil Aeronautics Board. *Handbook of Airline Statistics*. Washington, D.C.: U.S. Department of Transportation, 1983.

MAGAZINE BIBLIOGRAPHY

Bailey, Elizabeth. The growing complexity of aircraft financing. *Euromoney* (October 1981):289–295.

McHugh, Jim. Opec's loss is the economy's gain. *Business Week* (November 5, 1984):28–31.

Miller, Gregory. The wooing of the yuppie. *Institutional Investor* (December 1984):151–156.

Ott, James. Future growth in cargo forecast. *Aviation Week & Space Technology* 14 (May 1984):27–30.

Shifrin, Carole. Further regional traffic gains in 1984. *Aviation Week & Space Technology* 12 (March 1984):191–193.

Spencer, Charles. The financiers check out the regional airlines. *Commuter Air* 6 (November 1984):37–38.

Welling, Brenton. The airlines' dilemma: no cash to buy fuel-efficient jets. *Business Week* (September 27, 1982):65.

Witte, Michael. Baby boomers rush for power. *Business Week* (July 2, 1984):52–62.

ACI offers commuter study. *Airfinance Journal* (October 1984):37.

Congestion defied by smaller is better. *Airfinance Journal* (November 1984):1, 28–30.

Airline woes catch up with Delta. *Business Week* (November 8, 1982):131–134.

Fuel cost rise is forecast in late 1980's. *Aviation Week & Space Technology* 12 (March 1984):209.

The sky's the limit in luring the frequency flier. *Business Week* (October 18, 1982):152.

The year things changed. *The Economist* (December 22, 1984):50–51.

AIRLINE INDUSTRY—INTERNATIONAL

Briance Mascarenhas
Rutgers University

Air transportation freed travellers from the slowness of oceans, rail, bus, and highway travel but initially involved a newly emerging, possibly dangerous technology also used by the military. The support structure for air transportation also had to be built: airports, navigation aids, air traffic control systems. Air travel was a powerful earner of foreign exchange, as well an indicator "progress." So governments have dominated and subsidized the airline industry from the early days.

OWNERSHIP, REGULATION, AND OPERATING PATTERNS

Only in the United States are scheduled airlines 100 percent privately owned. Most private ownership outside the United States involves charter airlines where entrepreneurs seized opportunities presented by high fares charged by scheduled airline services. In most of the world, despite some private ownership in the pioneer days, governments own their international scheduled airlines, particularly in developing countries with insufficient traffic or investment capital. Even where private investment is allowed, governments may limit foreign investment in airlines. Last year, the United Kingdom (UK) government made it clear that SAS would not be allowed to "control" a British carrier, British Caledonian. And a 25 percent limit exists on foreign investment in US airlines.

In 1945, airlines gave a new role to the International Air Transport Association (IATA). Previously IATA had served strictly as a trade organization. The new idea was that airlines would fix fares jointly and submit them to governments for approval, instead of either multilateral or unilateral governmental imposition of fares on airlines.

US carriers went along with the idea of IATA fares, since the alternative was to let other governments control US carrier fares. Besides, US carriers wanted joint fare setting too. All fares had to be submitted to governments involved for approval. In countries where governments owned their airlines, the fare submission procedure was mostly a formality. The US case was another story.

For approximately 30 years, until the mid-1970s, most nations adhered to international rate-setting rules. But the US government was never comfortable with the cartel-like arrangement, frequently disapproving of IATA. Ultimately, the US administration said US carriers could remain within IATA and foreign lines serving the United States could continue to meet jointly as well.

What the US government did not ban officially, the marketplace is accomplishing unofficially. While still reviewing international fares, the US government ignores enforcement of rates that undercut official filings. It has negotiated several types of bilateral agreements with trading partners such as the Netherlands, Belgium, West Germany, Switzerland, Singapore, and Israel that permit marketplace fare setting.

Even with governments that still support tight fare regulation, international competition has intervened. Across the Pacific, for example, many airlines of developing nations do not belong to IATA. Companies such as China Airlines, Singapore Airlines, Thai Airways, and Cathay Pacific, representing countries with developing economies or entrepots, want to be free to compete. Airlines of the USSR and China also do not belong to IATA's tariff-setting conferences. So conservative carriers plying the same routes—Japan Airlines, Qantas—must meet marketplace competition.

IATA members' share of traffic is shown in Table 1. In 1971, IATA members carried 65.5 percent of world traffic. By 1986 that had fallen to 54.2 percent.

When the US government deregulated its own industry, it did not stop at the borders. Instead, in 1977, it began an aggressive campaign to expand the number of US airlines able to fly abroad, the number of foreign airlines able to serve the United States, and the number of cities within the United States and abroad tied directly to the international air service system. As a result, several carriers now have widely expanded international route systems, as Table 2 suggests.

Airport Constraints

The long-term outlook for capacity increase is limited. In the United States the last new airport to open was at Dallas/Fort Worth in 1974. Only two more airports are planned—in Austin, Texas, and Denver, Colorado—and neither will be completed until well into the 1990s. Even with modernization of the air traffic control system, the problem of space on the ground will get worse.

In Europe, capacity constraints are even worse. Traffic reached levels predicted for 1992 by the end of 1987. The Association of European Airlines (AEA) predicts a doubling of traffic in 13 years. Large carriers are creating commuter links to build

guaranteed feeder traffic just as their US counterparts did. That means more flights in Europe. Other than modernization of current terminals and a replacement terminal at Munich, no capacity increases are planned in Europe, however.

European liberalization will bring demand for more space from the new or smaller carriers with loosening of route restrictions. Simultaneously, Europeans are moving faster than the Americans toward tougher aircraft noise restrictions. As in the United States, if airlines want to continue with expansion plans—or authorities want to maintain a semblance of competitive entry—bigger planes will have to be acquired to accommodate more passengers.

The situation is repeated in Japan, the key market for Pacific operations. Tokyo's adjacent Haneda Airport does not even have enough space for domestic/international flights. At Narita International, 70 miles away, expansion has been stalled by environmental protests. Passengers are sometimes unloaded at Narita's cargo terminal. Because of limited capacity, neither domestic nor international competitors can easily threaten Japan Air Lines.

Elsewhere, Singapore's Chiangi International Airport is new and looking for business but is underutilized because of its small traffic base. Hong Kong is attractive as a possible alternative to Tokyo, particularly with the ability to tap China's traffic, but the airport is old, limited in space, and beset by environmental problems. Environmental disputes have held up airport development in Australia, too.

How to alleviate the shortage of airport space? As US carriers found, all hubs do not have to be located in major traffic generating areas. Hubs such as Salt Lake City and Dayton, neither of which

---

Table 1 World Air Traffic: IATA Share of the Total, 1971–1986
(millions of passengers per kilometer)

	1971	1977	1986
Total world commercial traffic (including USSR), scheduled and charter[a]	586,200	941,000	1,588,130
IATA members' commercial traffic, scheduled and charter	383,882	599,994	861,130
IATA members' share (%)	65.5	63.8	54.2

[a]The International Air Transport Association (IATA) statistics historically have made its members' share look larger because it did not include the Soviet Union traffic, which the International Civil Aviation Organization (ICAO) does.

Sources: ICAO, IATA.

Table 2 Major US Carriers: International Traffic and Revenue Growth, 1979 and 1986

Airline	International RPMs[a] (millions)	System RPMs (millions)	International share of system (%)	International revenue (million $)	System revenue (million $)	International share of system (%)
1979						
American	4,425	33,892	13.1	381	3,253	11.7
Braniff	4,124	13,687	30.1	330	1,338	24.7
Continental	650	9,501	6.8	65	922	7.0
Delta	1,564	26,440	5.9	103	2,672	3.9
Eastern	4,873	28,918	16.9	401	2,882	13.9
National	1,495	8,326	18.0	102	693	14.8
Northwest	4,579	13,546	33.8	398	1,297	30.7
Pan Am	22,537	25,082	89.9	2,125	2,574	82.6
TWA	10,511	31,081	33.8	827	2,892	28.6
United	. . .	38,248	. . .	. . .	3,224	. . .
Western	957	10,495	9.1	64	932	6.9
1986						
American	4,927	48,792	10.1	510	5,857	8.7
Braniff	. . .	2,542	. . .	. . .	234	. . .
Continental	1,171	20,949	5.6	363	2,052	17.7
Delta	2,390	31,373	7.6	248	4,496	5.5
Eastern	3,063	34,921	8.8	426	4,522	9.4
National	. . .	. . .	. . .	. . .	. . .	. . .
Northwest	12,623	27,892	45.3	1,405	3,535	39.8
Pan Am	17,776	22,363	79.5	2,063	2,733	75.5
TWA	9,773	27,386	35.7	985	3,181	31.0
United	7,692	59,312	13.0	924	6,688	13.8
Western	596	10,977	5.4	58	1,235	4.7

[a]RPM = revenue passenger miles.

Source: US Department of Transportation.

produces significant originating traffic are appealing (Table 3). So Singapore need not create its own demand. Airlines seeking additional European hubs do not have to locate in Frankfurt, Paris, or London. Small package carriers have used Brussels as a hub because it is centrally located and politically liberal in transportation policy, even though originating traffic does not compare with that of other capitals.

Airlines may also reduce airport congestion by improving passenger and baggage processing through automation with innovations such as machine-readable tickets, boarding passes, and baggage tags. Governments can ease international travel congestion, too, through immigration pre-clearance and speedier customs clearance, such as those used between the United States and Canada.

Many cities around the world may take inspiration from Atlanta. Atlanta historically was

not a great transportation hub; it had no great seaport. It served mainly as an artificial domestic hub for Delta Airlines and had far less originating traffic than connecting passengers. To attract international investment, developers used their political leverage during the Carter administration so that their city could obtain more international air service. Between 1975 and 1986, 966 foreign-based companies set up facilities in the metropolitan area after start-up of new international air links.

With domestic deregulation, the US government in 1977 began signing liberal airline operating agreements with its trading partners. Several countries took advantage of the opportunity to gain better access to the lucrative US market. Singapore, with only a small domestic travel market, wanted to boost its attractiveness as an entrepot. The Netherlands, which gets four fifths of its traffic

Table 3 Major US Operating Hubs and Hubs Where One or Two Carriers Dominate, June, 1987

Airport	Dominant Hub Carrier (% enplanements)[a]	Second Hub Carrier, If Any (% enplanements)[a]
Atlanta	Delta (53.8)	Eastern (40.9)
Baltimore	Piedmont (51.5)	
Boston	Northwest (8.8)	
Charlotte, NC	Piedmont (88.0)	
Chicago O'Hare	United (49.4)	American (29.0)
Cincinnati	Delta (69.5)	
Dallas Love Field	Southwest (93.5)	
Dallas/Ft. Worth	American (63.3)	Delta (25.5)
Dayton	Piedmont (69.5)	
Denver	United (44.9)	Continental (43.3)
Detroit	Northwest (65.1)	
Houston Intercontinental	Continental (73.1)	
Houston Hobby	Southwest (46.5)	
Kansas City	Eastern (40.4)	Braniff (17.2)
John Wayne/Orange County	American (60.7)	PSA (23.7)
Memphis	Northwest (85.8)	
Miami	Eastern (50.5)	Pan Am (17.0)
Minneapolis	Northwest (83.0)	
Nashville	American (60.7)	
Newark	Continental (39.2)	
New York Kennedy	TWA (28.5)	Pan Am (26.8)
Philadelphia	USAir (36.2)	
Phoenix	American West (42.4)	Southwest (14.8)
Pittsburgh	USAir (82.8)	
Raleigh/Durham, NC	American (18.3)	
Salt Lake City	Delta (73.7)	
San Francisco	United (37.1)	PSA (16.5)
San Juan, Puerto Rico	Eastern (46.4)	American (43.0)
Seattle	United (27.3)	Alaska (18.6)
St. Louis	TWA (82.7)	
Syracuse	Piedmont (40.5)	
Washington Dulles	United (37.6)	Continental (32.3)

[a]Carriers' enplanement figures include those of their code-sharing partners.

Sources: Airline Economics, Aviation Daily.

from outside its home market, saw new access as a competitive advantage to offer passengers. Newly emerging countries such as Thailand and South Korea saw that, if they helped the United States promote competition abroad, they could aid their own export economies. Even a mature, tightly controlled West Germany could not turn down the chance. In return for 13 US destinations, US airlines provide a variety of services to and within West Germany.

In 1987, after years of prodding by the European Commission, a timid plan to loosen fare and entry rules emerged in Europe. Small airlines were able to compete with the national flag carriers, but primarily between small and hub airports, not from one hub airport to another. And airports in several countries—Greece, Spain, Denmark, and Italy—are exempted, in part or totally. The previously accepted 50-50 split of traffic between two flag airlines on trunk routes connecting capital cities has been loosened. But no opportunity exists for small airlines to try to beat out the bigger, nor for one flag airline to take over all the traffic from the other on a given route.

EQUIPMENT

Economics

When fuel prices were high—but capital costs could be passed on with regulated fares—airlines bought new wide-body aircraft with three and four engines and flew them infrequently. The more people in one plane, the less spent on the direct costs of fuel. When fuel prices plummeted—and the cost of new aircraft soared—airlines started hanging on to their old planes, acquired smaller new ones, and flew them more frequently into hubs. Not so coincidentally, this switch in equipment deployment occurred at about the same time as the reduction in regulation.

Airlines are becoming less able to afford improvements in aircraft technology. Private airlines are spending their money on computers and marketing. Nationalized airlines no longer have free access to government money. Thus, without inducement of much higher fuel prices or definite deadlines to reduce aircraft noise, or major reductions in acquisition cost, investment in new equipment is less justified.

Airlines have asked manufacturers to build them cheaper planes. But aircraft production is not a high-volume business. The most successful Boeing plane (excluding the current B-737 still in production) was the B-727 which sold 1,831 units over a 21-year life. Few economies of scale—certainly not the same degree as in other industries—and few standard products exist.

One can get an idea of how much customized requirements cost by the man-hours required in production. Production of Boeing's original B-737 model required approximately 120,000 engineering man-hours. Changes made to the plane between sale and delivery to various customers added 30,000 man-hours. Manufacturers make a profit on customization and therefore do not encourage a standardization.

Airlines could reduce costs if they ordered standard aircraft. American Airlines tried several years ago to convince competitors to create a pool of planes, from which they would lease as needed. To work, the pooled planes would have had to have been standard issue, rather than versions with specific paint colors, interior design, seat upholstery, cockpit configuration, and other items that add tremendously to the cost. A variety of problems doomed the project. One was the inability of airlines to agree on a common design.

Twin Engines

Manufacturers of large twin engine aircraft are now offering a variety of models whose original versions could not be flown across oceans but whose derivatives, with more powerful engines, can. The new high-bypass engines have so much power that large twin engine aircraft can carry more than 200 passengers, burn less fuel, have lower operating costs, and can fly as far as most four-engine and three-engine models.

These twins are being used on routes not busy enough at the outset to justify jumbo jet or trijet operations. Many twinjet routes were served previously as part of multistop services or had no direct international service at all. Now millions of travellers have non-stop international services available from local airports.

Even for those markets that are obvious jumbo jet points—New York to London, for example—twinjets offer intriguing possibilities. Airline marketeers believe that frequency builds traffic. Twinjets can also be developmental tools, permitting off-peak as well as peak-day and peak-hour flights or providing year-round service at points that previously only supported seasonal flights.

So far, relatively short international hauls, like transatlantic routes or routes within the Pacific or Europe-Africa, are the principal use for extended range twinjets. But the future holds the same possibilities for long hauls. The B-767-300ER and the proposed A-330 (available in the 1990s) offer the same seat-mile costs as the not yet delivered new version of Boeing's B-747, permitting marketing freedom on long haul routes that they have had on short haul ones.

Rules required that twin engine aircraft follow routes no further than 60 minutes away from an airport, designed to protect against potential loss of one engine. The "60 minute" rule is inappropriate in light of modern technology. Boeing has applied for an exemption that would permit large twins to fly routes that are 180 minutes of one engine flight from the nearest airport, opening up trans-Pacific routes. The company thinks that large twins now in service will one day be used on all routes flown by four-engine and three-engine aircraft.

New High-speed Aircraft

Time and physiological factors are major disincentives to significant amounts of travel to and from the Pacific. High-speed flight shrinks distance and makes trade and travel easier. Airlines will want to buy these planes because of long distance business travel. Frequent travellers will want it, because it will expand the length of the working day on a business trip.

The new Boeing jumbo B-747-400 is designed to improve conditions. The new plane (first delivery is in late 1988) can fly 7,400 nautical miles with almost 450 passengers. It will no longer incur weight penalties to fly non-stop between Singapore and European capitals in either direction: Los Angeles and San Francisco to Sydney; San Francisco to Hong Kong and Seoul; Chicago and New York to Seoul; Los Angeles and Taipei. Boeing based its decision to go ahead with the B-747 derivative based primarily on traffic potential in the Pacific.

Pacific countries and carriers dream of commercial aircraft that will fly 100,000 feet high at a speed of 3,400 miles per hour and eliminate the formidable time and physiological barriers to Pacific travel. That aircraft is now informally called the Orient Express and could permit travellers to eat breakfast in New York, lunch in Beijing, and dinner back in New York.

But that aircraft has yet to be designed. The level of investment requires military funding, followed by joint commercial production. The French and British, who built the Concorde, do not want to repeat the same economic failure no matter how many jobs the project might produce. To have a chance of success, airlines around the world would have to rethink traditional operating and marketing concepts.

Northwest is enthusiastic about a hypersonic transport (HST). It poses a hypothetical route pattern by which a plane would leave Tokyo, a Northwest hub, at 9 AM on a Monday, fly to Los Angeles and back to Tokyo; continue to New York and London and back to New York; then fly to Tokyo, arriving at 7 AM on Tuesday. Flying time would be 22 hours. The route pattern presupposes having the necessary operating licenses to perform the flights and also that sonic booms from flights over land will not create barriers to obtaining licenses. The planes may need to fly in pool, through multi-national airlines, a challenge to anti-trust authorities. Airlines would alternate routes to maximize utilization and guarantee enough passengers.

Because HST depends on huge sums of money, a somewhat slower, more conventional supersonic transport be built before. Boeing continues to study the possibility of an SST that could fly at up to 3.2 times the speed of sound (compared with 6 times for the HST), use a variation of conventional fuel, and be available in the mid-to-late 1990s.

MERGERS

Around the world, the airline industry has been consolidating for the past 20 years. Most mergers have been within national borders. Whether airlines are private or nationalized, many countries had too many companies trying to serve the same market. The process continues, through outright purchase, exchanges of equity shares among airlines, and feeder agreements that are the same as consolidations in operating terms.

Even under regulation, the US government permitted many mergers of local service airlines during the 1960s and 1970s. The Japanese domestic airline industry still has many participants, but they are far fewer in number.

In the United Kingdom, British Overseas Airways Corporation (BOAC), the long haul international airline, and British European Airways (BEA), which flew shorter haul routes, merged to reduce losses. British Airways (BA), the result of that merger, purchased British Caledonian (BCal) in 1987 to eliminate competition and to grow to compete with the major US carriers.

Thai International was nurtured from infancy by SAS. Now SAS is counting on Thai to be its low-cost and high-quality Asian partner in a multinational marketing alliance. That alliance in Asia will only work well if the two international carriers can feed one another traffic to beat the competition. To ensure maximum Thai traffic flows on to SAS-Thai, a domestic carrier's loyalty had to be assured by merging it into the international company.

Another format is Lufthansa's partnership in a charter airline with Iberia. The new airline, Viva, is 48 percent owned by the West German company, while 52 percent is in Spanish hands. Lufthansa already has a charter airline, Condor. But it wants to tap Europe-wide charter business to the Mediterranean coast. The Spanish partner also gives Lufthansa a much needed opportunity to cut costs. Lufthansa's high labor cost makes it difficult to compete in fare discounting.

The new airline combinations are intended to avoid restrictions on transborder ownership or operations and permit expanded market share outside traditional Third and Fourth Freedoms of the Air (see Figure 1). Several companies want to strengthen themselves not only within their own country but within regions, which are gradually beginning to supplant a single country as the base for business. Airlines are also picking their partners based on the strategic importance of hubs they could bring, having seen how the US hub-and-spoke concept has enhanced US major carrier dominance.

MARKETING

The Single European Act will not help airlines that want to buy an airline in another community member state. The act eliminates certain barriers to free trade still remaining under the Treaty of Rome, but air transport is treated under special provisions of the treaty. Even though the European Court has ruled that the treaty's competition rules apply to air transport, members are giving themselves as much time as possible to conform to the rules supposed to apply in 1992.

For the foreseeable future, marketing is mostly shaped by computerized reservation systems (CRS) and their travel agent networks. The principal movers in this worldwide development are airlines in the three major traffic generating areas: Europe, North America, and Asia-Pacific. If things work out the way the parties to these worldwide systems plan, they will use CRS to tap one another's seat inventory and pricing systems to sell to increasing numbers of travellers.

Of considerable importance to the CRS links is the extent to which code sharing will spread beyond the United States. Foreign airlines see it as a way to gain additional access to US markets that they are precluded from obtaining because of the ban of foreign ownership and cabotage. These carriers have observed the restructuring of the domestic US commuter airline business as a result of code-sharing with major airlines. US government policy already permits foreign lines to share codes with US airlines at points that are on the former's licenses. What foreign airlines really want are code-sharing deals to points not on their route certificates.

United Airlines and British Airways announced the first major code sharing deal between a big US airline and a foreign carrier. Since United has no European routes and BA's Pacific operations are limited, the potential is significant. The two airlines blanket the globe. They started modestly, with the Seattle-Chicago-London route. The two companies want to expand the arrangement. The sharing of facilities at four airports in the United States helps give United the possibility of taking away domestic business from other US airlines that do have European operations. BA's London hub, which is a center for service to more than 70 European cities, expands United's marketing potential and that of its Apollo CRS.

Very little effort is being made to find CRS subscribers among Third World airlines. The Third World does not generate enough revenue passengers to make the investment worthwhile. Yet to survive economically, the airlines of smaller nations must find a way to become part of the system used to sell and distribute tickets. Even with free access, Third World countries still will have problems connecting to a CRS. The lack of basic telecommunications networks and the shortages of skilled personnel may discourage vendors.

FINANCE

US airlines' finance departments became internationally minded long before their marketing departments. They wanted to spread the risk in sources of capital, reducing dependence on the home market. American Airlines and other US carriers have tapped European capital sources and, increasingly, Japan, since the 1970s. That was before many of them acquired route rights in capital source countries. Last year American was listed on the Zurich, Geneva, and Basel exchanges. It was the first US transportation company to be listed on a foreign exchange. Recently, about a third of American's financing has come from abroad, even though its international revenue is only about 9 percent of total revenues. Newly privatized British Airways figured that its partial US ownership would increase its exposure and expand awareness of its services and international network—in addition to raising capital in a major market.

Figure 1 *The Six Freedoms of the Air*

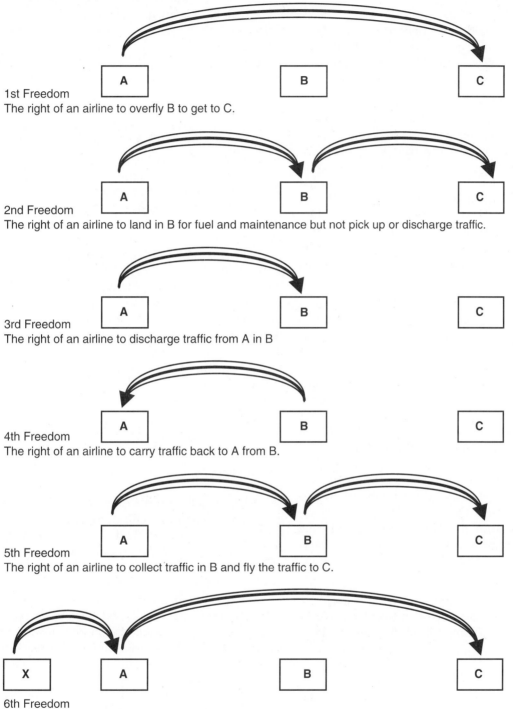

1st Freedom
The right of an airline to overfly B to get to C.

2nd Freedom
The right of an airline to land in B for fuel and maintenance but not pick up or discharge traffic.

3rd Freedom
The right of an airline to discharge traffic from A in B

4th Freedom
The right of an airline to carry traffic back to A from B.

5th Freedom
The right of an airline to collect traffic in B and fly the traffic to C.

6th Freedom
The right of an airline to pick up in X, traffic that is bound for C and
route it through A. This traffic normally belongs to the airlines of X and C.

Source: Airline Pilots' Association. *Airline Pilot* May 1986

THE NEW REALITIES

Growth Prospects

Airlines have recently experienced a particularly good period of traffic growth (see Table 4). But the economic structure and political conditions that have pertained since World War II are changing.

Organization for Economic Cooperation and Development countries. Travel organizations continue to issue optimistic projections about future prospects in the industrial world. But economic growth in the 24 member countries of the OECD is slowing down. Even Japan's average annual growth of 10.4 percent in 1960–1968 was less than half that by 1979–1985 (4 percent). As a result, the growth in disposable income that has buoyed travel in the past will not continue as rapidly and not necessarily in the same countries as before.

Eastern Europe. The Soviet Union's drive to improve its citizens' economic position could produce world economic stimulus and have implications for the Eastern Bloc. The USSR could not long force its neighbors to follow one path if it chooses to follow another. The two Germanys are slowly strengthening economic ties. The poor financial condition of the Comecon countries could be reversed if introduction of market economies were allowed to replace their managed economies.

As a result, Western airlines are lining up to take advantage of the changing picture. Pan Am and Aeroflot have renewed their services to one another's countries. Others have begun establishing themselves in the Berlin corridor to take advantage of improved relations between East and West Germany.

Asia and Pacific Basin. The Asian and the Pacific markets will outperform what historically were the top three markets—United States, North Atlantic, and intra-Europe. Table 5 shows Boeing's forecasts of the growth potential of the different regions.

In 1950, visitor arrivals in the Pacific were 1 percent of all international trips; in 1985 the total was 11 percent and growing. Australian tourism grew 25 percent in 1986; for South Korea, the figure was 16.1 percent; India, 17 percent; Thailand, 15.6 percent. The tourism industry calls the trend

"The Age of Pacific Tourism." In 1960, 75 percent of arrivals in the Pacific Rim were in Hong Kong, Japan, and Hawaii. Today, travel in the region is more widely dispersed. Singapore, Thailand, and China had more than 2 million visitors each in 1986, and South Korea, Taiwan, Australia, and Malaysia were growing substantially. Table 6 shows forecasted airline market shares by region.

Some companies are disappointed at the rate of development in China. Nevertheless, many are investing for the long term. Lufthansa, for example, established a joint venture with CAAC, designed at the outset to cover technical functions such as aircraft and engine overhaul. Lufthansa and other West German partners are also paving the way for future travel, through agreements to build a hotel, catering service, apartments, and shopping and trade facilities.

The projections look good, but the established strength of the Asia-Pacific airlines means that Western airlines will have to fight hard to establish a position. The airlines in the region will account for and expect to take a large share of the rewards. As they mature, their costs will increase, meaning their labor advantage will not be as great in the future as it has been in the past. They will be looking to build traffic, to reduce unit costs, outside their own traffic base.

Other Regions. The economy of the Middle East depends on oil, which is in oversupply, and peace, which is elusive. Air services will not be attractive to any carriers except flag airlines of the region.

Africa is falling further behind in growth generally as well as in its ability to join the international air services network. It is ordering a smaller share of new aircraft than it did eleven years ago (Table 7). The continent contains most of the world's lowest-income economies. The prospects for airlines in the region are poor.

Latin America, Brazil, and Mexico, in particular, represent potential that is sure to attract more airline interest in the future. The World Bank classifies the region in its middle-income category (economies with significant potential). The region's labor force is projected to grow to almost 200 million by the year 2000, from 54.7 million in 1950. The burden of debt in several countries of the region has produced a protectionist approach that makes tourism and travel development difficult. High

Table 4 Development of World Scheduled Revenue Air Traffic, 1978–1987[a]

Year	Passengers Carried (millions)	Freight Tons Carried (millions)	Passenger/ kilometer Performed (billions)	Seat/ kilometer Available (billions)	Passenger Load Factor (%)
1978	679	10.6	936	1,451	65
1979	754	11.0	1,060	1,607	66
1980	748	11.1	1,089	1,724	63
1981	752	10.9	1,119	1,757	64
1982	766	11.6	1,142	1,795	64
1983	798	12.3	1,190	1,852	64
1984	847	13.4	1,277	1,971	65
1985	898	13.7	1,366	2,079	66
1986	955	15.1	1,454	2,236	65
1987[b]	1,040	16.6	1,603	2,376	67

Year	Ton/kilometer Performed		Total (passengers + baggage freight, mail) (millions)
	Freight (millions)	Mail (millions)	
1978	25,940	3,270	113,540
1979	28,010	3,430	126,870
1980	29,380	3,680	130,980
1981	30,880	3,790	135,490
1982	31,540	3,870	138,460
1983	35,110	4,000	146,390
1984	39,640	4,300	159,090
1985	39,810	4,390	167,530
1986	43,220	4,530	178,770
1987[b]	48,070	4,670	197,440

[a]Excluding states that were not members of the International Civil Aviation Organization in 1987.
[b]Preliminary estimates.

Source: International Civil Aviation Organization, December 1987.

Table 5 Boeing Forecasts of Air Traffic Growth by Region, 1985–2000

	Average Annual Growth (%)	
	1970–1985	1985–2000
Europe-Asia	13.1	7.4
Intra-Orient	10.8	7.1
Trans-Pacific	9.7	7.4
Total	11.0	7.3
US domestic	6.3	4.3
North Atlantic	6.1	4.2
Intra-Europe	5.8	3.8
Total	6.2	4.1

Table 6 *Airline Market Shares by Region: 1985 Actuals Compared with Forecasts for 2000*

	1985 (%)	2000 (%)
United States	42.4	35.9
Canada	3.5	3.1
Europe	25.4	23.9
Japan	4.7	6.3
Other Asia	9.8	15.1
Latin America	5.1	2.6
Africa	3.0	2.6
Middle East	3.3	3.6
Australia/New Zealand	2.8	3.0
Total revenue passenger miles	828 billion	1,800 billion
OECD countries[a]	78.8	72.2
World domestic passenger traffic	46.6	44.9
World international passenger traffic	53.4	55.1

[a]OCED = Organization for Economic Cooperation & Development

Source: Boeing Commercial Airplane Company.

inflation, currency controls, and lack of a middle class mean that airlines are, temporarily, biding their time. But SAS has already said it would like a Rio hub, American wants to reenter the Brazilian market, and others are keeping tabs on developments.

Management Skills Needed

Countries will not give up their sovereignty over airlines. Yet governments are partly withdrawing subsidies and protection from airline competition. They are sometimes encouraging surface competition to their air carriers. That means surviving airlines, while still waving their nation's flag, will have to make more marketplace decisions.

Some European carriers, like KLM and Swissair, have had to develop sophisticated management skills for operations abroad because of their small traffic base. SAS is working hard to understand economic factors influencing business outside Europe as well as it understands them inside Europe. Lufthansa has a long history of understanding international management. And the European airlines for years have cooperated in several transborder aircraft maintenance and purchasing projects that have honed these skills.

In the United States, American Airlines years ago began assembling managerial staff from outside the airline industry, staff with skills that could be applied in a domestic or international business.

It still needs to develop a management and staff oriented to its international operations. The company's aggressive business style bothered some airlines outside the United States. American's problems in establishing the SABRE CRS abroad even caused it to file a lawsuit in the United Kingdom (American's legal costs, along with Texas Air's, are the highest in the industry). American is expanding rapidly in Europe. American's habit of controlling operations from the chairman's office may have to change with the company's goal of a 50-50 split between its domestic and international operations.

British Airways has been strengthening its international competitive skills too. It has hired new, younger outsiders who understand business, not simply the airline business. The company has reduced staff by several thousands, been privatized, and bought a competitor—all in the space of three or four years.

United Airlines acknowledges how unsophisticated and unprepared it was to provide international service when it bought Pan Am's Pacific Division in 1985. Prior to the purchase, United was as Yankee as apple pie: service to all 50 states, folksy advertising, and a friendly spirit that reflected its Midwestern base. The purchase gave United an Asian network of 13 cities in ten countries. For one of its inaugural flights to celebrate the takeover, this one from Hong Kong, United

Table 7 *The Third World Falls Further Behind: Announced World Airliner Orders, All Manufacturers, By Region, 1977–1987*

Region	North America	Europe	Far East	Africa	South America	Middle East	World Total
1977							
No.	161	87	46	12	13	26	345
%	46.6	25.2	13.3	3.5	3.8	7.5	
1978							
No.	348	181	96	13	26	18	682
%	51.0	26.5	14.1	1.9	3.8	2.6	
1979							
No.	172	141	118	27	39	31	528
%	32.6	26.7	22.3	5.1	7.4	5.9	
1980							
No.	198	73	70	10	32	25	408
%	48.5	17.9	17.2	2.5	7.8	6.1	
1981							
No.	149	43	37	23	13	19	284
%	52.5	15.1	13.0	8.1	4.6	6.7	
1982							
No.	145	67	21	8	8	2	251
%	5.8	26.7	8.4	3.2	3.2	0.8	
1983							
No.	118	33	70	9	2	17	249
%	47.4	13.3	28.1	3.6	0.8	6.8	
1984							
No.	213	129	28	8	4	19	401
%	58.1	32.2	7.0	2.0	1.0	4.7	
1985							
No.	375	132	159	4	2	. . .	672
%	55.8	19.6	23.7	0.6	0.3	. . .	
1986							
No.	319	277	108	4	17	17	742
%	43.0	37.3	14.6	0.5	2.3	2.3	
1987							
No.	234	230	81	10	1	1	557
%	42.0	41.3	14.5	1.8	0.2	0.2	
11-year total							
No.	2,432	1,393	834	128	157	175	5,119
%	47.5	27.2	16.3	2.5	3.1	3.4	

Source: Boeing Commercial Airplane Company.

ordered white carnations for some of its personnel. The flower is a Chinese symbol of bad luck. United has begun to lose some of its reputation for arrogance and is learning how to get along internationally.

Alliances

As a result of political constraints and capital shortages, airlines may have to rely on others as business partners. One vehicle could be an interna-tional holding company with local affiliates. Or the links could be through cooperative alliances, consortia, joint ventures, depending on the funds available and attitudes of governments.

International airlines may obtain lower costs and some additional aircraft operating flexibility through partnerships. Airlines may mix and match equipment, depending on the type of flight. They would not have to sign operating leases to do so, either. Rather, partners could develop loosely based agreements that would permit reassessment of equipment utilization depending on loads, markets, and other factors that change operating conditions.

A company with primarily business passengers may want to spread risk by linking with an airline whose leisure traffic was higher. An airline from a cold country may want access to beach resorts. Old-line airlines in the industrial world are bound by high-cost contracts written at a time when costs could easily be passed on in regulated fares. In countries where deregulation has yet to happen, airlines must compete with America's deregulated companies while simultaneously adhering to national labor laws that may make such competition costly. Wages and work rules, whether negotiated through private contracts or as a result of national laws, together form a barrier to flexibility. The need to circumvent rigidities, however, provides even more impetus to striking deals that can lower costs.

How far US carriers might be able to go in participating in such deals remains to be tested. The United States has long-standing restrictions on pooling routes, revenues, profits of its own airlines, although it permitted BCal and Sabena to do so on the Atlanta route. The European Community is supposed to be getting rid of pools too. The United States has allowed less extensive combinations abroad such as aircraft interchanges, where crews of participating airlines replace one another at common points, and blocked space agreements, where one airline buys the space on another carrier's aircraft. American and Qantas only recently received approval for just such a blocked space arrangement.

Whether temporary or permanent, partners are not just an inexpensive way of serving a wider market. They will ease cultural sensitivities and shortages of managers knowledgeable in local business practices.

The low-labor cost advantage is one that airlines have already experienced, when competing with low(er)-cost and high-quality Singapore Airlines. In Europe and Australia, the traditional, protectionist way of fighting Singapore's fare discounts was to keep them out. There are more low-cost companies on the way, and from countries with a traffic base worth fighting for. High-cost countries cannot keep out Air India or CAAC if they want to participate in those countries' traf-

fic. Such competition, plus that from the more efficient US carriers, means that airlines have to find better ways to compete. High-cost operators might want to create worldwide alliances with an eye to saving money, not just buying market share.

Reconfiguring and Dispersing Airline Functions

Decentralization of functions, whether based on labor cost or other factors, has already occurred in some instances. American set up a data processing center in Barbados to take advantage of lower wages from tasks that do not require skilled labor. When national institutional rigidities make it difficult to lower wages or make staff redundant, the incentive exists to go overseas. Other lower-cost countries such as the Irish Republic, Portugal, and Greece might become focal points for more airline functions.

The question also arises of how many jobs will be available to export. The airline task known as revenue accounting (sorting tickets) is becoming almost entirely automated. American used to have 1,000 accounting personnel, now has 600, and expects to be down to 100 in less than ten years. As travel agents become less central to the distribution function (through increased use of personal computers, for example), users will communicate more with their terminals, not airline reservation agents.

Providing New Services

Airlines are not just transporters of passengers and cargo; sometimes they act as their own retailers, even though most tickets are sold by travel agents; as wholesalers of groups of seats that then are sold at markup; as packages of travel rather than providers only of transportation; as creditors, through industry charge cards; as their own risk arbitragers through investment in foreign currency; as processors of information such as reservations, visa, and currency information; and as engineering and maintenance firms. They may increase the services they offer.

Service businesses require customer contact and quality control assurance. A basic requirement for success is satisfied employees. Airlines around the world are tied into labor contracts that sometimes impede satisfactory customer relations and quality assurance. Union leaders sometimes interpose themselves between corporate management and employees. Long periods of government regulation permitted labor costs to be passed on through fares to the customers.

One competitor feared in the area of quality service is Singapore Airlines. Singapore's lower costs allowed it to compete easily with high-cost firms whose route systems were more extensive, who were better known, and whose resources exceeded its own. Over the years, Singapore's services have become a world standard. It was ranked top, with Swissair, in a 1987 passenger survey.

SAS has selected quality service as its niche, too. But it has gone beyond air transportation to offer a variety of ground and information services. SAS began offering a high-quality business-class service on its European and intercontinental routes in 1981. These passengers who pay full fare receive extra services: check in at SAS-affiliated hotels, baggage transfer from hotel to airport, limousine arrangements, access to airport lounges, and office and communications centers at hotels and airports where travellers can continue to conduct business.

Airlines have found one way to increase revenues without increasing financial risk greatly is by "affinity card" arrangements with bank card issuers. Cardholders receive frequent-flyer points every time they use affinity cards, whether for air transportation or other purchases. The card issuers pay the airlines a fixed amount, transaction fees, and/or for frequent-flyer miles, and in return obtain access to airlines' customer information.

The airlines do not take the credit risk for this arrangement. Citibank claims its American Airlines affinity card offer produced the largest promotional response it has received.

Europeans have not yet used credit cards as extensively as Americans. European airlines must compete with already established credit cards. The increased fee-earning potential plus the extension of marketing possibilities look good in the planning stage. But penetrating a market occupied by such established names as Diners, Mastercard, Visa, and American Express for third-party services will not be easy.

In summary, the outlook for world air transportation is promising but challenging. Boeing's projections show a doubling (since 1986–1987) of passenger traffic to 1,800 billion revenue passenger miles by the end of the century. Air freight traffic could more than double by the year 2000. But international airlines must select an appropriate strategy in this complex dynamic setting if they are going to capitalize on those projections and differentiate themselves from competitors.

REFERENCES

The Economist, several issues.
The Financial Times, several issues.
"The World Airline Industry," *The Economist Intelligence Unit*.

AMERICAN AIRLINES

Briance Mascarenhas
Rutgers University

In 1991, Robert Crandall, chief executive officer and president of AMR, had reason to feel satisfied with how American Airlines, its major subsidiary, had grown and prospered since domestic airline deregulation in 1978.

American's performance was tied to its numerous innovations. It won union approval for an innovative cost-cutting pay structure that had become the industry's model. It introduced a frequent-flyer program. It led the way in putting together imaginative financial deals to acquire aircraft. And it pioneered the airline computerized reservation system, SABRE, which dominates the industry and recently accounted for 85% of its earnings.

"These sons of bitches are the best there are," claims Crandall of his top management team. The executive officers of AMR are described in Table 1.

Name-calling has not always been so friendly at American, particularly in respect to Crandall, a former marketing and financial manager at Eastman Kodak, Hallmark Cards, TWA, and the Bloomingdale's department store chain. He joined American as head of the finance department in 1973 and became president and chief operating officer seven years later. Crandall struts like a street fighter and hunches at a conference table like a gambler who has just raised the ante. He lopped some 7,000 people off the payroll in his ferocious drive to cut costs and became widely known among employees as Atilla the Hun or Darth Vader. The Justice Department continues to call Crandall names such as would-be monopolist.

The change stems from the belief—shared by insiders and outsiders—that Crandall's tough, impatient, and often bullying ways helped save American. Few airlines that went into deregulation in at least as good a shape as American have emerged as well. Braniff and Eastern went broke. Pan Am and Continental are limping along in Chapter 11. And TWA's survival is in jeopardy.

Crandall thinks the competitive battles ahead will be even more intense than in the past. Moreover, he says, "if a lot of people lose their jobs, politicians will take note," and may be tempted to meddle in the industry, deregulated or not.

American was not always flying on course. Under Chairman George A. Spater, the handpicked successor of pioneer C. R. Smith, it had jettisoned its sure-fire strategy—catering to businesspeople—in favor of trying to lure vacationers. Businesspeople deserted to United and TWA. The vacation market never took off the way Spater envisioned; instead it began to fade. American was also rocked by the revelation that Spater had approved an illegal $55,000 contribution to President Nixon's 1972 reelection campaign. Spater quit, and the crusty Smith, who had ruled American for more than three decades, came out of retirement until a new chief executive, Casey, could be found.

American faced trouble in its subsidiaries. The Americana hotel subsidiary was draining as much as $12 million a year. United's parent, UAL, makes money in its Westin Hotels, but American could not run hotels well. So they were divested, together with other businesses such as carpet cleaning.

A holding company was set up, AMR Corp., to own both American Airlines and a handful of other businesses. As its cash hoard grew, AMR

Table 1 AMR Executive Officers, 1989

Name[a]	Title	Age
Robert L. Crandall	Chairman of the board, president, and chief executive officer	54
Robert W. Baker	Executive vice president	45
Donald J. Carty	Executive vice president and chief financial officer	43
Michael J. Durham	Senior vice president and treasurer	39
Max D. Hopper	Senior vice president	55
Anne H. McNamara	Senior vice president and general counsel	42
Charles D. MarLett	Corporate secretary	35

[a]The business experience over the past five years of the executives mentioned is as follows:

Mr. Robert L. Crandall assumed the responsibilities of chairman and chief executive officer of AMR and American in March 1985. Prior to that, he served as president and chief operating officer of American since 1980 and of AMR since its formation in 1982.

Mr. Robert W. Baker was elected an executive vice president of AMR in September 1989. He was elected a senior vice president of AMR in July 1987 and, prior to that, he had served as senior vice president—operations of American since November 1985. From April 1985 to October 1985, he served as senior vice president—information systems. From 1982 to March 1985, he served as vice president—marketing automation systems of American.

Mr. Donald J. Carty was elected an executive vice president and chief financial officer of AMR in September 1989. Prior to that, he served as senior vice president and chief financial officer of AMR and senior vice president—finance and planning of American since January 1988. Prior to that, he served as senior vice president—planning of American since April 1987. From March 1985 until March 1987, he was president of Canadian Pacific Air. Prior to that, he served as senior vice president and controller of both AMR and American since March 1983.

Mr. Michael J. Durham was elected senior vice president and treasurer of AMR in September 1989 as well as senior vice president and chief financial officer of American. Prior to that, he served as vice president and treasurer of American from March 1989 to September 1989, vice president financial planning and development of American from 1987 to 1989, and vice president financial analysis and corporate development of American from 1985 through 1987.

Mr. Max D. Hopper was elected senior vice president—information systems of American on November 20, 1985 and was elected a senior vice president of AMR on May 21, 1986. From September 1982 until November 1985, he was an executive vice president of the Bank of America.

Mrs. Anne H. McNamara was elected senior vice president and general counsel in June 1988. Prior to that, she served as vice president—personnel since January 1988. She served as corporate secretary during the preceding five years for American and held the same position with AMR since its inception in 1982.

Mr. Charles D. MarLett was elected as corporate secretary in January 1988. He served as an attorney with American beginning June 1984 and prior to that was associated with the law firm of Drinker, Biddle & Reath, Philadelphia, Pennsylvania, from 1982 to 1984.

There is no family relationship (blood, marriage, or adoption, not more remote than first cousin) between any of the above named officers.

There have been no events under any bankruptcy act, no criminal proceedings, and no judgments or injunctions material to the evaluation of the ability and integrity of any director or executive officer during the past five years.

Source: AMR, *10-K Report*, 1989.

began to invest in onshore US oil and gas reserves— as a hedge. Other AMR ventures include Sky Chefs, a food-service operation, training schools for pilots and flight attendants from other airlines as well as American, and an investment services subsidiary which sells cash management and pension fund management services to outside companies. Ameri- can is also attempting to increase its air cargo services, an industry that is expected to triple in sales by 1995 but which is now dominated by integrated door-to-door overnight courier companies.

Deregulation was in the wind when Casey came to American, and he spent much of his time testifying before congressional committees and calling in many of the political IOUs he had in his pocket in a vain effort to kill it. The government restricted price competition and allocated markets. If costs, particularly for labor, went up the government agreeably approved fare increases. Since routes were set, airlines were spared painful choices between one aircraft and another: American, with its long hauls, stocked up on Boeing 707s, 727s, and 747s.

Deregulation opened everything—airports, routes, fares—to competition. But as the industry was trying to cope with the confusing new environment, it got slugged from several other directions almost simultaneously. Fuel prices zoomed, doubling in a year. The air traffic controllers who struck were promptly fired by President Reagan. The government rustled up replacements, but not enough to handle traffic increases at the busier airports. Thus, the ripest markets under deregulation could not grow and were, therefore, off limits to newcomers trying to crack them. Then came the recession, which slashed passenger volume. The established airlines flew fewer and fewer passengers on huge planes that were more and more expensive to operate. Meanwhile, new airlines equipped with used aircraft—bought at bargain prices and staffed with non-union personnel willing to work for far less than their union counterparts—were springing up all over the United States. The fare wars were on.

Like other pre-deregulation carriers, American joined, and along with other established airlines, it was clobbered. American had too many big airplanes, because under regulation the government dictated it fly long hauls. When the government shackles came off, executives knew they would need a flexible fleet but could not replace the fleet without profits. Capital was unavailable. A second deficiency was high cost.

In 1979, Chairman Casey decided to move American's headquarters out of Manhattan to Dallas/Fort Worth. Since airline employees can fly at huge discounts, the move was less wrenching, Casey says the move saved American $500,000 a month in real estate and labor costs. The relocation made its executives' travel to outlying points easier. He also thinks it shook the company out of its lethargy. "The company had to get repotted, replanted," he says. "When you move you rethink lots of opportunities. American had to get off the dime."

LABOR

This cost disadvantage led to American's so-called two-tier wage contracts, which are the envy of other airlines as well as many other industries. American's three main unions (representing flight attendants, mechanics and ground crews, and pilots) agreed that new employees would be paid as little as 50% of what current workers earned for the same jobs, saving American on average $10,000 per year for each new employee. Currently the pilots American is hiring are coming from the ranks of the 450 furloughed in early 1982; they are being rehired at 85% of their old salaries. But as the airline starts to hire new pilots over the next five years, it expects to save an additional $150 million a year.

The agreement was sweetened by a guarantee of job security and the introduction of profit sharing, but not everybody is happy. Captain Henry A. Duffy, president of the 34,000-member Air Line Pilots Association (ALPA), which does not represent American's pilots, thinks that "to create a second level of employee who does the same work is bound to lead to instant unhappiness." The ALPA is currently wrangling with United and other airlines. So too is the Transport Workers of America. TWA's International President William G. Linder is also unhappy. But he blames deregulation itself: "I suspect the whole purpose of the law was to undermine the whole collective bargaining process."

Crandall and other executives conducted a seemingly endless series of meetings, seminars, and conferences with union members. The message, says Crandall, was simple: "We all have to accept the world as it is, not as it was."

Lately, American has been trying to revise its internal systems to tap into the expertise of front-line employees who are in daily contact with and understand customers. It wants to develop a system that gives employees greater responsibility and power in dealing with customer problems. The goal is to solve every complaint at the first point of contact.

OPERATIONS

To build its market, American uncharacteristically became a copycat, adopting—as did the rest of the industry—the hub-and-spoke route system that Delta pioneered in Atlanta. The system replaces direct but often low-volume nonstop flights between low-density airports with a series of short-distance feeder flights (the spokes) into a major airport (hub) where passengers can make connections. American implemented just such a plan at Dallas/Fort Worth and then in Chicago, a direct challenge to United's home base where it has increased flights by 27%. In another challenge to United, American has built a hub in Denver, a market now dominated by United. American's new hubs at Raleigh/Durham and Nashville facilitate north-south traffic. The hubs operated by American and other major carriers are shown in Table 2.

During the next five years, Robert Crandall expects American to continue expansion into Latin America, Western Europe, Eastern Europe economies, and the Pacific Rim. Crandall expected American's route system to be as much as 25% to 30% international by the year 2000. One of the reasons for this international expansion is that air traffic in the United States is expected to grow more slowly than abroad. A critical factor for the company is to gain experience as quickly as possible in these very different political, cultural, and economic markets. While American has succeeded in a cost-price competitive domestic market, the international market may call for higher service and more comfort in longer-range planes. International expansion will also expose American to new competitors. The major airlines of the noncommunist world are described in Table 3.

American's recent foray into the Latin American market was propelled by the purchase of Eastern Airlines' extensive South and Central American route system. American's newly inherited hub in Miami will quickly expand to over 70 departures per day by early 1991. American's initial plans are to serve the old Eastern destinations using 16 rerouted aircraft and then over the next 10 to 20 years to exploit more fully the additional route authority included with the Eastern purchase. Initial traffic flow over the Latin American routes will be north-south between North America and South America, but American wants to find ways of linking the Latin American segment with the European and Pacific segments, requiring additional hubs in the United States that will be efficient. The large number of governments involved will also mean substantial regulatory complexity to be overcome.

The plan calls for aggressive expansion into Europe before the European Community consol-

idates at the end of 1992, when new routes into the area are expected to become more difficult to obtain, and the acquisition of new routes in other parts of the world—which are currently more restricted than Europe—as they become available. Crandall asserts, and most industry executives agree, that entry into foreign markets will become harder as time goes by.

In Europe, American has tried to fragment traffic flows between Europe and the United States by using smaller airplanes and overflying the coastal gateways. This strategy has not been possible in the Pacific for a number of reasons, one of them being the range of aircraft and the other one being the strength of alternative points in the Pacific vis-à-vis Tokyo. As other points in the Pacific become stronger and as aircraft configurations become closer to optimum, American's fragmentation strategy could become a viable alternative here.

Another potential international destination is the Soviet Union: the company has applied for a Chicago-Moscow route. Many airline executives believe that Western airlines will get the right to fly over Russia, perhaps even in the near term. Traffic between North America and the Pacific may then move via Europe, changing flight paths and aircraft needed. Companies will be able to do more with their airplanes out of North America than currently.

Along with other major carriers, American has aspirations to expand in the Pacific. American has been operating a Dallas/Fort Worth–Tokyo route for almost three years and in early 1990 began one-stop service to Australia and New Zealand through Honolulu. Specific markets being targeted by American in Asia include Korea, Taiwan, and the Peoples Republic of China. Bangkok, Thailand, is also being given a very close look by American because the company expects it to become increasingly important. American blundered when it did not pursue Pan Am's Asian division several years ago. United, which bought the routes for $750 million, has enjoyed double-digit growth in these markets every year since. In fact, United's Tokyo and UK routes and beyond enable it to dominate two large, fast growing regions of the world.

AIRCRAFT FLEET

American is changing the mix of its fleet. Table 3 shows American's fleet composition and planes on order. It has sold off its entire collection of fuel-

Table 2 *Principal Hub Cities for the Major Airlines (as of April 1990)*

Carrier	Hub cities
American Airlines	Dallas/Fort Worth, Chicago, San Juan, Nashville, Raleigh/Durham, San Jose
America West	Phoenix, Las Vegas
Continental Airlines	Houston, Denver, Newark
Delta Air Lines	Atlanta, Dallas/Fort Worth, Salt Lake City, Los Angeles, Cincinnati
Eastern Air Lines	Atlanta
Northwest Airlines	Minneapolis/St. Paul, Detroit, Memphis
Pan Am	New York, Miami
TWA	St. Louis, New York
United	Chicago, Denver, Washington, D.C., San Francisco
USAir	Pittsburgh, Philadelphia, Charlotte, Baltimore, Dayton

Source: *Standard and Poors' Industry Surveys,* June 21, 1990.

Table 3 *Existing and Planned Aircraft Fleet in 1990 (Excluding American Eagle)*

Make/Model	Passenger Capacity	Maximum Range (miles)	In Service	On Order	Options
Airbus					
A300-600R	267	4784	25	7	5
Boeing					
727-100	118	NA	39	...	...
727-200	NA	NA	125	...	...
737-200	120	2650	11	...	...
737-300	150	2830	8	...	...
747SP	440	7658	2	...	...
757-200	186	4474	9	66	55*
767-200	216	3639	13	...	...
767-200ER	174	6633	17	...	...
767-300ER	210	6978	15	10	30*
British Aerospace					
146-200	122	1355	6	...	...
Fokker					
100	122	1543	...	75	75
McDonnell Douglas					
DC10-10	278	NA	49	...	...
DC10-30	270	7490	10	...	...
Super 80	172	3431	180	80	90
MD-11	323	5760	...	8	42
Aircraft Totals			509	246	297

*85 convertible 757/767 options placed.

guzzling, 707s, which have been grounded since 1981, and is relying largely on less thirsty 727s. In a swap with Pan Am, American gave up eight 747 passenger planes and some cash for 15 DC-10s that Pan Am had acquired in its merger with National. The DC-10s are being used to beef up American's coast-to-coast service. But American's big bet is on McDonnell Douglas's narrow-bodied MD-80s, some of which are already in service. These aircraft have two big cost-saving virtues: a two-person cockpit crew (vs. three for larger planes) and high fuel efficiency.

To obtain the MD-80s, American persuaded the manufacturer to let it try 20 planes, to test-drive them, in effect. If unsatisfied, American had the right to return them, paying only a small penalty. A security analyst says American "bludgeoned" McDonnell Douglas into the deal. Apart from individual sales here and there, even though it was an excellent plane, nobody was buying it.

American did like the planes, however, and ordered 13 more through an elaborate leasing deal that required hardly any cash. A syndicate headed by Bankers Trust bought seven planes, and Orient Leasing and Japan Leasing, both of Tokyo, bought the other six.

The average age of major US carrier's fleets ranges from almost 16 years at TWA and Pan Am to under 10 years for American, USAir, and Delta, with United in the middle at 13 years. United, American, and Delta have placed the largest orders for new aircraft, with United heading the pack with a $50 billion order to be delivered in the next decade; Delta and American have placed orders of about half that amount.

One of American's biggest problems is its insufficient number of aircraft for its intended international expansion. The company has been alleviating this problem through "creative rerouting," using the help of its SABRE online management information system. The acquisition of the South and Central American routes, however, will force American to slow its move into Europe somewhat as the company will have to devote many of its international-capable aircraft to them. American has sufficient aircraft on order but deliveries of long-range, wide-bodied aircraft will not catch up to the airline's needs until 1992. American will take delivery of 8 long-range MD-11s in 1991–1992, and has options on 42 more. The company believes, and is betting, that with the delivery of the MD-11s it will have the airplanes with the appropriate range and cargo space for the Pacific market.

MARKETING

Finding passengers to fill these planes will be the long-term challenge. But American's marketing may be the strongest in the industry. In addition to its popular frequent-flyer discount program, its

SABRE computer reservations system dominates the travel agent business and generates 85% of the airline business earnings. The CAB and many travel agents are critical of the built-in bias of such systems. SABRE screens, for example, list American flights and connections before anybody else's. But travel agents using the system stick with it because they can not only give their customers boarding passes with assigned seats, but also book Broadway plays, line up housing for the summer Olympics, and send flowers to passengers on planes.

American is using a limited number of marketing alliances with other carriers to establish itself overseas early and at a low cost. It has code-sharing agreements with Cathay Pacific of Hong Kong, Qantas of Australia, and Malev of Hungary, and is negotiating more. American also used its 7.5% ownership of Air New Zealand to help introduce its SABRE reservation system in the Pacific.

American's chief rival, United, has sold 49% ownership in its reservations system, APOLLO, to four European carriers: British Airways, Swissair, KLM, and Alitalia. Furthermore, APOLLO has been recently integrated with another European-developed reservation system, GALILEO. United and British Airways also have a marketing agreement that includes connecting operations on some transatlantic routes, as well as a code-sharing agreement. And Delta has a marketing alliance with Swissair and Singapore Airlines.

FINANCE

The financial condition of American Airlines and its major competitors is detailed in Table 4. Crandall has committed $11 billion, more than half of American's capital spending budget, to expanding and upgrading international operations over the next five years. In 1990, management stated publicly that it would use any opportunity to acquire international assets. It took advantage of weak airlines to do just that as shown in Table 5.

Future asset purchases were uncertain, however. In June of 1989, US Transportation Secretary Samuel K. Skinner specifically warned US airlines that international routes they operated should not be considered property which could be bought and sold without serious consideration of the national and public interest.

Table 4 *Composite Statistics: Air Transport Industry*

1987	1988	1989	1990	1991	1992		94–96
25417	32240	36697	40011.9	**43115**	**48075**	Revenues ($ million)	**64865**
58.1%	57.8%	60.4%	62.6%	**60.0%**	**61.5%**	Load Factor	**62.0%**
12.0%	13.5%	11.0%	**7.0%**	**6.0%**	**9.5%**	Operating Margin	**11.5%**
1548.1	1768.7	1901.1	2145	**2490**	**2740**	Depreciation ($ million)	**3585**
694.9	1432.1	1318.8	383.9	**d270**	**970**	Net Profit ($ million)	**2235**
39.2%	35.7%	37.8%	37.1%	**NMF**	**32.5%**	Income Tax Rate	**37.5%**
2.7%	4.4%	3.6%	1.0%	**NMF**	**2.0%**	Net Profit Margin	**3.5%**
7562.8	7502.8	6504.2	**9215**	**10830**	**12020**	Long-term Debt ($ million)	**14615**
10460	9770.5	11240	**10865**	**11390**	**12455**	Net Worth ($ million)	**15400**
5.5%	10.2%	9.3%	**3.5%**	**1.5%**	**5.5%**	% Earned Total Capital	**9.0%**
6.6%	14.7%	11.7%	**3.5%**	**NMF**	**8.0%**	% Earned Net Worth	**14.5%**
5.8%	14.0%	11.2%	2.0%	**NMF**	**7.5%**	% Retained to Common Equity	**14.0%**
15%	6%	8%	43%	**NMF**	**13%**	% All Dividends to Net Profit	**6%**
18.6	6.6	10.6	28.5			Average Annual Price/Earnings ratio	**12.5**
1.24	.55	.80	2.15			Relative Price/Earnings Ratio	**1.05**
.8%	.8%	.6%	.9%			Average Annual Dividend Yield	**2.0%**

Source: Value Line, March 29, 1991.
Bold figures are Value Line estimates.

Table 5 *Recent AMR Purchases from Other Airlines*

Selling Airline	Asset(s) Purchased	Amount* (millions)
Eastern	NY/Newark-Montreal/Ottawa route Terminal facilities in Montreal, Nashville, Orlando, and Hartford 10 La Guardia slots	$10.0
Eastern	Additional La Guardia slots	10.0
	Miami/Tampa-Toronto route	10.0
	Latin American routes	310.0
Continental	Seattle-Tokyo route	150.0
TWA	Chicago slots, facilities	85.0
	Chicago-London route	110.0
TWA	London route authorities from a number of other cities	445.0
TWA	Certain other facilities in O'Hare, Philadelphia, Nashville, Orlando, and Fort Lauderdale	70.0
	Total	$1,200.0

*Does not include aircraft.

REFERENCES

AMR Corporation annual reports and 10-K statements, several years.

Brown, David A. 1990. American Airlines' external growth keyed to internal development. *Aviation Week and Space Technology*, March 12.

Brown, David A. 1990. American uses marketing alliances to establish presence in new areas. *Aviation Week and Space Technology*, November 26.

Labich, Kenneth. 1990. American takes on the world. *Fortune*, September 24.

Leinster, Colin. 1984. How American mastered deregulation. *Fortune*, June 11.

Shifrin, Carole A. 1990. American chief outlines international route plans. *Aviation Week and Space Technology*, March 12.

Tait, Nikki. 1990. Painful predicament of the high-fliers, *Financial Times*, November 19, p. 16.

BAKER MEDICAL CENTER (A)

Jon Chilingerian
Brandeis University

March 5, 1985 was a typical Tuesday morning after a day away from the hospital. Dr. Timothy Hunt (M.D.), president and chief executive officer at Baker Medical Center (BMC), strolled into his office at 7:00 AM and smiled when he saw the number of phone calls he had received on Monday and the stack of mail on his desk waiting for his attention. Knowing how desk work accumulates when he travels out of town, he was looking forward to pouring a cup of coffee, doing some desk work, and organizing his activities for the week.

He was not prepared for the call at 7:05 AM from Alice Semenza, assistant vice president of public affairs. She wanted Tim to know that a reporter for a nationally circulated newspaper had called requesting a "telephone interview this afternoon with the director of the hospital, regarding the nurse who had died of AIDS." Alice explained that the reporter had been researching a story on AIDS for the Science and Technology Section of the Sunday paper. While talking to people with the Community AIDS Project, the reporter learned that a nurse at BMC had been diagnosed as having AIDS. The reporter wanted more details about the case, including the name of the nurse.

"Alice," Hunt asked, "How much does the reporter appear to know?"

"Very little," she said, "beyond three basic facts. First, the reporter knows that the nurse with AIDS told his supervisor and the supervisor consulted with the chief of infectious diseases. The chief and the supervisor both agreed that as long as the nurse felt well he should continue in his reg-ular job assignments as long as everyone followed the usual infection precautions. Second, the reporter knows that the nurse became too ill to continue working and resigned voluntarily. Finally, the reporter knows that the nurse recently died. I believe that the reporter does not know that the nurse had worked in the surgical intensive care unit."

"Tim," added Semenza, "he was a good nurse who cared a great deal about his patients, and he was highly regarded by his colleagues. He wanted his colleagues to know that he had AIDS and after they were informed no one objected to continuing to work with him."

"Thanks, Alice, for alerting me. I'll do some thinking and let you know what to tell the reporter about interviewing me. Keep me up-to-date on this one."

A STRATEGIC ISSUE FOR THE CEO

Hunt pondered the phone call. Between 1980 and 1985, AIDS had been transformed from a medical curiosity into a deepening national and global crisis. Because of its deadly nature, it was a disease shrouded in myths and half-truths. Since there were no precedents around the issue of health workers with AIDS, there was a potential for public hysteria and patient lawsuits.

This could be the first story published about a person with AIDS working directly with patients. In hospital circles, inquiries about the health of nurses, physicians, and other personnel could cause panic.

"The name of a new piece of equipment is something to tell the public about," Hunt mused, "but the name of a sick employee should be confidential. On the other hand, we are proud of our personnel policies. . . . Depending on how this gets reported, thousands of Sunday readers will be questioning our judgment."

He glanced one more time at his schedule to determine how many of the people he needed to acquire information from and/or put on alert (see Exhibit 1). Some of the people he wanted to alert—his top managers and the legal counsel—were scheduled to see him today before the interview on Tuesday. His chiefs, and the trustees, were on his schedule this week. Glancing again at the subject matter of these scheduled meetings, he noticed that they were loaded with other important matters.

In thinking about next steps, he considered cancelling all meetings that morning. If he freed his calendar he might call a special meeting of the important chiefs of service and the two or three top vice presidents. That would put a lot of important hospital decision makers into one room. On the other hand, would it be a signal that something extraordinary was happening—a crisis that Hunt couldn't handle. Hunt thought carefully and concluded this was really just another "routine crisis" for him. One that he could handle with subtle scripting, creative choreography, and some luck.

The big questions in his mind were what would be the reporter's angle. How could he help to guide the way the story was told? With a sigh, Tim took another look at his schedule. He was tempted to delegate the reporter's request to Harvey Hopkins, his vice president of operations. "If AIDS wasn't becoming such a 'hot' topic, I might do just that."

BACKGROUND: PLANNING FOR AIDS IN 1985

As Hunt browsed through some notes in his office files on AIDS, the scope of the problem became clearer to him. There were three aspects of acquired immunodeficiency syndrome (AIDS) that challenged hospital managers' planning and policy-making capacities. First, and most important seemed to be the lack of information and rapidly changing information about the nature of the disease, its cause(s), its amelioration, and its cure.

Second, the enormous uncertainty produced an almost irrational fear among health care employees as well as the general public. Third, the uneven geographical distribution of AIDS cases and the way it gradually insinuated itself as an issue had led to a lack of preparation.

Lack of Information

When the first cases of AIDS were described in the *New England Journal of Medicine* in 1981, the causative agent was not known. When HTLV-III (now called HIV) was isolated, tests were developed to determine if a person or a supply of donated blood had antibodies. Researchers thought that humans would develop antibodies within six months of infection. But some reports suggested that the antibodies might develop more slowly. Even if a patient or hospital employee suspected of carrying AIDS was tested for HIV, and the test was negative, the person still might be infectious. Thus, at any point in time a community has an unknown prevalence and incidence of HIV infection.

Fear, Prejudice, and Public Hysteria

In general, health care providers were trained to treat patients with infectious diseases and treat people who will die. Rarely did the same patient fall into both of those groups. Since the probability of a person with AIDS dying seems almost guaranteed, AIDS was such a disease.

With the exception of hemophiliacs or newborns whose mothers were infected, people hospitalized with HIV probably became infected through sexual activity or intravenous drug use. In fact, most of the early cases of AIDS were diagnosed in homosexual men. AIDS was the first sexually transmitted disease that seemed only to affect people whose behavior was scorned by some people and/or illegal in many communities.

How can hospital employees who are socialized by their communities' standards overcome homophobia and loathing for those who engage in illegal drug activities. Can hospital policies change life-long learning? Furthermore, since drug use (and in some cases, homosexual behavior) was illegal in most states, there was a danger of subjecting people who test positively for AIDS to prosecution, firing, or harassment. If testing identified and stigmatized the patient not only in the hospital but also in the community, then public disclosure would become a devastating event. Patient along with employee confidentiality issues became very salient.

Between 1981 and 1985, 57% of the people diagnosed with AIDS have died. The lack of a cure for AIDS enhanced the anxiety of the caregivers by adding a layer of frustration to the fear of infection.

Uneven Geographic Distributions

By 1985, all of the states in the United States, and all of the territories, had reported at least one case of AIDS. However, the incidence varied from fewer than 20 cases to more than 5,000 cases. Some of the hospital CEOs in low-incidence areas reached the conclusion that AIDS was not going to have an impact on their hospital. These hospitals were not prepared when the first patient with AIDS was admitted to the hospital, nor when their first employee was HIV positive.

Other Factors

Other factors were contributing to the policy dilemma for hospitals. If hospitals offered to test for HIV, they could help determine the prevalence of HIV. But even if the more socially minded hospitals participate, there was no guarantee that the majority of hospitals would participate. Some hospitals that were testing did so to notify staff and modify care procedures. Here the issue of stigma was salient; confidentiality and informed consent rules were needed.

Finally there were the patient care issues. The obligation of caregivers to treat AIDS patients placed an unfair burden on a minority of physicians at hospitals like BMC. Hunt believed that in some of the competing hospitals, physicians were viewed as profit maximizers, patients as customers, and health care as a "marketplace product-line." In those hospitals physicians would have no special obligation to treat patients with AIDS, no more obligation than that of an any ordinary citizen. On the other hand, in hospitals like BMC where medicine was viewed as a profession, and the caregivers were morally bound by an obligation to healing and curing the sick, there would be a stronger commitment to selfless caring. At Baker, caregivers were not free to choose whom they would serve.

Even at Baker, however, many nurses and physicians would not be affected because care-

givers were not required to care for patients with illnesses that were beyond the caregiver's expertise. Therefore, the AIDS problem would be managed by a few physicians, which seemed unfair to Hunt.

Hunt realized that anticipating how other hospitals would respond was difficult. Eventually that problem would affect the public interest. But more important to him today was to be sure that Baker was positioned internally for a potential crisis.

THE EXECUTIVE RESPONDS

After returning several phone calls, reading six memos, skimming the Center for Disease Control's (CDC's) report on AIDS, and looking at the agendas for the board meeting, the weekly luncheon with the chiefs, and the middle-managers meetings, Tim left his office to go to the building committee meeting. On the way back from that meeting he thought about the way he got people "on board" by "privately" negotiating new ideas with key individuals before going "public" in a group meeting. For this issue, he did not have the time to spend occasioning private meetings. He thought he knew how most of the hospital leadership would respond to the way they handled the nurse with AIDS. But Hunt must orchestrate it well. On the other hand, in the long run a more detailed policy was needed.

The Meeting with Legal Counsel

At the ten o'clock meeting on Tuesday morning Hunt waited until Brian James, the legal counsel, had discussed the current legal matters on his agenda. After those issues were addressed, Hunt interjected that he had also had a few issues, one of which was the AIDS case.

The legal counsel said he was familiar with the case and informed the CEO that he had heard in the streets that the reporter might use an anecdote in the story about another hospital that hadn't treated an employee with AIDS as humanely as BMC. He suggested that perhaps the reporter would set the other hospital up as the "bad guy." He also suggested that Hunt admit to the facts and get it over with.

Hunt responded, "That's all very interesting, Brian, but it's how the "Yellow Press" picks up this story that I'm concerned with. This is only one of a variety of infectious diseases that people get. In each case the hospital makes a decision. Although athlete's foot is an infectious disease, you don't throw those employees out; you have them wear shoes!"

Added Hunt, "Brian, my position is not to indulge the emotional responses if there are no data to support it. Knowing what we now know about this disease, its hard to prevent a nurse or physician from exercising normal patient care duties, even if the patient population demanded an AIDS-free environment. What of the legal implications of dismissing a competent professional on the basis of an antibody test? What about discrimination suits? We can't forget that a person's livelihood is at stake. Our policy must consider the basic fact that to let go of one's professional work is to let go of hope."

Brian responded, "There is no real case law on this yet. Look Tim, do you want us to go to the front and raise the banner on this issue? Test it?"

Hunt replied, "Possibly, but I'm nervous about being personally set-up by every aggressive plaintiff's attorney in the state."

The Ten O'Clock Managers Meeting

At 10:30 that morning, Hunt met with all the top managers in the hospital (see Exhibit 1). At that meeting Hunt told the managers that the public affairs department had received an inquiry which could present more problems than usual. He explained, "We are going to have some publicity you should know about. We had an employee on our nursing staff who had AIDS. After he was given the diagnosis, he was evaluated by our staff and it was decided that he could continue caring for patients. The nurses he worked with agreed. He was a very caring and compassionate nurse. It was a good decision, very rational, and in accordance with the CDC guidelines. A newspaper reporter has picked up the story and has pursued it with some of our staff. I understand that another local hospital had a similar situation but handled it in a more medieval way. We did not fall prey to any unfounded fear, given the media's interest in this sort of thing."

The director of nursing interrupted and said, "I would just like to make a comment. When I found out about this employee, I called a nursing friend of mine in San Francisco to see how they dealt with AIDS. Their policy for employees with AIDS is similar to ours, but they have encountered problems with how the press responds to that policy."

Hunt continued, "Well there are two issues: Did Baker have an employee who had AIDS? The answer is 'Yes.' The second question is what is our policy?"

Hunt informed the managers that the decision to allow the nurse to continue treating patients was consistent with CDC guidelines. Although people might be unhappy with the decision, it was in his opinion an impeccable decision. Hunt went on to say that it would be counterproductive to stonewall the story. He reminded them that historically, on controversial issues, Baker has had the courage to be the first hospital to take a stand. But he assured everyone that the fundamental issue of employee privacy was not being violated.

He concluded, "If I'm in the position of spokesperson, the worst scenario is that Tim Hunt ends up being interviewed by someone like Ted Koppel. In any case, I assure you that no confidential information about hospital workers will be available to the press. But we have to make our information consistent." The moment Hunt spoke those words, he realized a possible action. He asked, "Is there any utility in putting this information in the employees' newsletter?"

There was a consensus that informing the employees was a good idea. Especially given everyone's concern that the confidentiality of employee information was at stake. Hunt added, "I would like all of our 3,000 employees armed with some information. . . . Alice, this evening I will write a draft of an article for the employee and the physician's newsletters."

The Chief of Infectious Disease Comments

After the managers meeting, a brief phone conversation with Dr. James Stanford, the chief of infectious diseases at Baker, revealed how the chief felt about the matter. He told Hunt, "AIDS doesn't raise any issues that haven't been raised 50,000 times by hepatitis-B virus. . . . The likelihood of transmission is very low. I believe we acted responsibly and put no one at risk, because AIDS is not easily transmitted."

"Jim, queried Hunt, "What precautions were taken?" Stanford replied, "While he was working, if he came into contact with patient's bloodstream or mucous-lined tissue or when he handled any catheters, he wore gloves. Look, HIV should not disqualify a caregiver from caring for patients. The precautions recommended for nurses or doctors with AIDS are much less austere than with chicken pox. The rules are as follows. First, wear gloves when likely to come into contact with blood or body fluids, and second, wear additional attire such as masks and protective eyewear in surgery or whenever splashing of blood or body fluids is likely to occur." He added that in the San Francisco hospitals, the criterion for letting infected employees work was whether or not the employee had symptoms of infection that placed the other employees or patients at risk of illness. While the nurse with AIDS was working in Baker's surgical intensive care unit, there was no risk of infecting either co-workers or patients.

Operational Issues

Later that day, informal conversations with Harvey Hopkins, the executive vice president (of operations) and John Michelian, the vice president of financial planning and issues management brought some of the implications of the policy into sharper relief. Harvey said, "Look, I had a conversation with our competitors at Alberta Medical Center. I was told that if they had an employee with AIDS, they would immediately eliminate all direct patient contact. Tim, this battle may be fought in the marketplace and end up a matter of competitive advantage. What if we become the preferred hospital of people with AIDS? We have to think about the impact on operations."

John Michelian, the vice president of financial planning and issues management played the devil's advocate. He said, "I know that what I'm about to say is not what BMC is all about, but as CFO I think we have to confront it. If the word gets out that we are 'soft' on AIDS, we could be overrun with people with AIDS who are indigent. What if occupancy drops to 70% or 75%? Worse, if community physicians and their patients think we have workers with AIDS, they will stay away. . . ."

"Look Tim," Michelian blurted out, "the chiefs of service will not have any problems with this. They are a rational group. But some of the fee-for-service physicians are already disagreeing with each other on this policy." "If I can speak frankly," continued Michelian, "this morning, a physician, who wants to remain anonymous, approached me and he said he had spoke with the chief of surgery about AIDS. Intellectually, he thinks we did the right thing, but emotionally, he said he has serious problems accepting treatment from a nurse with AIDS. He said, 'Sure, we can try to be as rational and medically honest as possible about this, but the issue is not the scientific discussion of medical risk or infection control. It boils down to public hysteria, ignorance, and prejudice.' He went on to say, 'For many of us with admitting privileges here, this hospital is our livelihood. If patients are scared off, everyone suffers."

Harvey agreed. He said, "Look Tim, I know the fear doesn't make any sense. I know you don't have sex with a nurse with AIDS, but what about cuts on the hands or a runny nose? What if the research is wrong about the mode of transmission? It's the lack of a cure that I think about. I wouldn't mind so much working with people with other diseases if we knew what to do. But this one's a killer!"

THE REPORTER INTERVIEWS HUNT BY TELEPHONE ON TUESDAY

By Tuesday evening, Hunt had met with and alerted all the important managers. He was ready to speak with David Fort, who was a nationally noted journalist and medical reporter. The interview went as follows.

Fort began the interview with these questions: Did you have an employee with AIDS? What was his name? Was he working in the operating room? What is Baker's policy? Did his co-workers know?

Hunt said that although he did not have all the details, they certainly did have an employee with AIDS. He did not work in the operating room, nor did he do any procedures that would put him or his patients at risk. Hunt refused to give the name of the employee. He repeated that while he would cooperate with the interview, he would not do anything that violated the confidentiality of any BMC employee.

Hunt explained that BMC's AIDS policy was similar to its basic policy regarding any communicable disease. The experts would evaluate the potential threat of an illness to the employee with the illness, the co-workers, and the patients. "Precautions are always taken," remarked Hunt, "but the hospital is not bound to terminate the individual." Hunt emphasized that "in each case, we have an expert—the chief of infectious diseases—who brings to every decision situation the best available information."

Hunt explained to David Fort that since the nurse with AIDS wanted his co-workers to know, each of them had been informed. Hunt said to the reporter, "David, you must understand that the nurse in question was regarded very highly by everyone. The nurse's co-workers were very supportive. Moreover, the chief of infectious diseases and the vice president of nursing never received a single complaint from the other employees."

When Fort asked if he could speak with the co-workers, Hunt said through the Office of Community Relations he could have access to any employee. Hunt suggested that while polling employees today will result in a "spectrum of responses," he believed that Baker employees would basically support how AIDS had been handled in this case.

"I know you and trust you, David," said Hunt. "I know that you will not go searching till you find someone, you know, an outlier, who makes a "yellow press" headline." Hunt quickly added,

"But as long as a patient is at no risk, judgments must be based strictly on the epidemiology. We can't go back to the middle ages and start persecuting people for their illnesses. We are just getting over our prejudices about cancer. The history of medicine chronicles terrible behavior toward sick people. Take leprosy for example. . . . When I was an intern, David, people had active polio. There was no better place to catch that disease than a hospital. . . . I believe that it's important that one not give in to fear and prejudice, otherwise we lose the civilization that we are trying to build. . . ."

Fort again asked if the nurse with AIDS had worked in the operating room. Hunt quickly said, "No. Nor was he doing any procedure that would place patients at risk. Look David, there is a very important issue here. I think the tone and thoughtfulness with which you approach the article will be critical."

WEDNESDAY: A MEETING WITH THE DIRECTOR OF NURSING AND THE WEEKLY LUNCH WITH THE CHIEFS OF MEDICINE

Wednesday morning Hunt called Alice Semenza and told her that he had written the article for the employee and physician's newsletter. He said, "Our responsibility to the 'Baker family' [Baker's employees] is sufficiently great that we have to release information about this incident this week via our newsletters. Call David Fort and tell him that we will publish our own version of this story on Friday of this week. Tell him our intention is not to scoop him, but to inform our employees."

Prior to the long-term care meeting, Hunt spoke informally with the director of nursing who was a member of that committee. Hunt conveyed his ideas about their policy and the need to keep the story consistent if and when she was interviewed by David Fort, the reporter.

Later that day Hunt attended the weekly lunch meeting with the chiefs where "matters of mutual interest were discussed." The agenda for Wednesday's meeting included: developments in cardiac surgery, the need for microbiology funds, how to do a critical incident report on a physician-subordinate, and a variety of interesting but low-priority items. About halfway through the meeting, Hunt casually brought up the forthcoming newspaper article on the nurse with AIDS and how it was handled. Virtually the same information was given to the chiefs as the middle managers. He added, "To reinforce my feelings—we did not fall prey to unfounded fears. You might take note of this story in the employee newsletter. . . . I know that hospitals in San Francisco have handled AIDS that way, too. . . ."

After Hunt spoke, the chiefs appeared to be satisfied with the information provided. There were neither questions nor further discussion about this AIDS issue. Hunt believed his arguments had convinced the chiefs that allowing the nurse with AIDS to continue working was the only rational and responsible action to take.

THURSDAY AFTERNOON: THE TRUSTEES MEETING

Prior to the trustees' meeting, on Wednesday and Thursday, Hunt "telegraphed" the AIDS issue to three or four trustees (including the chairman of the board) by talking to them on the telephone. In these discussions, Dr. Hunt argued that Baker's actions represented the "right and responsible" position to take. He declared that "no rational person could criticize what we did. I would, without reservation, recommend that we do it again if the situation arose." As Hunt later recalled, "When I told the chairman that the issue might result in some poor publicity, he was not pleased, but he more or less accepted it."

At the trustees meeting, Hunt calmly mentioned the fact that BMC had had a nurse with AIDS and that a reporter had been interviewing employees in order to fashion a story to educate the public about AIDS. He then provided the trustees with the facts about AIDS. He explained that it was not a very infectious disease—casual contact would not transmit it, therefore there was no reason to restrict the individual with AIDS. The following two questions were raised by Trustees.

"Dr. Hunt did you say that AIDS is not communicable?" Hunt responded that it was transmitted only through intense sexual contact, blood transfusion, or frequent oral and genital contact.

Another trustee asked, "Dr. Hunt what is our personnel policy? I guess I am thinking about the bank fiasco a few years ago where an employees confidentiality was violated." Hunt's response was, "The way we handled the reporter's inquiry was, 'Yes, we had an employee with AIDS. But no, we will not reveal his name.'"

HUNT REVIEWS THE CURRENT SITUATION

After the trustees meeting, Hunt rubbed his forehead and thought about what happened during the past three days. Hunt had met with the legal counsel, the chiefs of service, and several key trustees. All the top managers are aware of the situation. By tomorrow, the hospital employees would be empowered with the information through the employee newsletter.

Today he had alerted the trustees to the fact that a story would be breaking. Although the chairman of the board was not very happy about the news story, the chiefs were supportive. What about the other stakeholders, both inside and outside? Irrespective of how responsibly the story is told, Hunt was convinced that more planning and policy-making around this issue of AIDS was desperately needed.

APPENDIX

Baker Medical Center

Baker Medical Center was a voluntary, non-profit, non-sectarian, short-term, acute care hospital serving a large geographical area on the eastern coast of the United States. The hospital was licensed by the state to operate approximately 450 beds and was fully accredited by the Joint Commission on Accreditation of Hospitals.

Mission and Goals

During Hunt's tenure as CEO, Baker moved from being a second-rate institution to the enviable position of one of the nation's leading hospitals. Baker had always focused on three activities: patient care, teaching, and research. The medical staff had always maintained a delicate balance between innovative research, new technology, and responsiveness to patients' needs. A statement issued a few years earlier exemplified a consensus that had been reached by the hospital chiefs and administration regarding the mission of Baker Medical Center.

The major mission of Baker Medical Center is to deliver patient care of the highest quality, in both scientific and human terms. This mission is to be carried out within a framework of financially responsible administration. . . . Patient care at Baker is to be provided in a context of clinical teaching via participation and teamwork of clinicians, teachers, research scientists, and others who jointly become the sources of innovation and progress for future improvement in care capabilities. . . .

Baker could be differentiated from other hospitals not only by its emphasis on quality care to patients but also by its "strong humanist tradition" and policies regarding its employees. For example, long before other hospitals, it had instituted a patient "bill of rights," which was a statement of the patient's right to quality care at Baker Medical Center.

Organizational Structure

In a 1982 memo to the board, Hunt argued that the old and limited concept of the hospital would fail as they moved toward the 1990s and beyond. In that memo he argued for a reorganization that would change his title from hospital general director to chief executive officer and president, and the titles of his top administrators to vice presidents (see Exhibit 2 for the latest organization chart).

The board of trustees had ultimate authority for all policy decisions of the medical center. When the board hired the CEO, it delegated the management of policy formulation and implementation to

Exhibit 2 *Baker Medical Center Organization Chart*

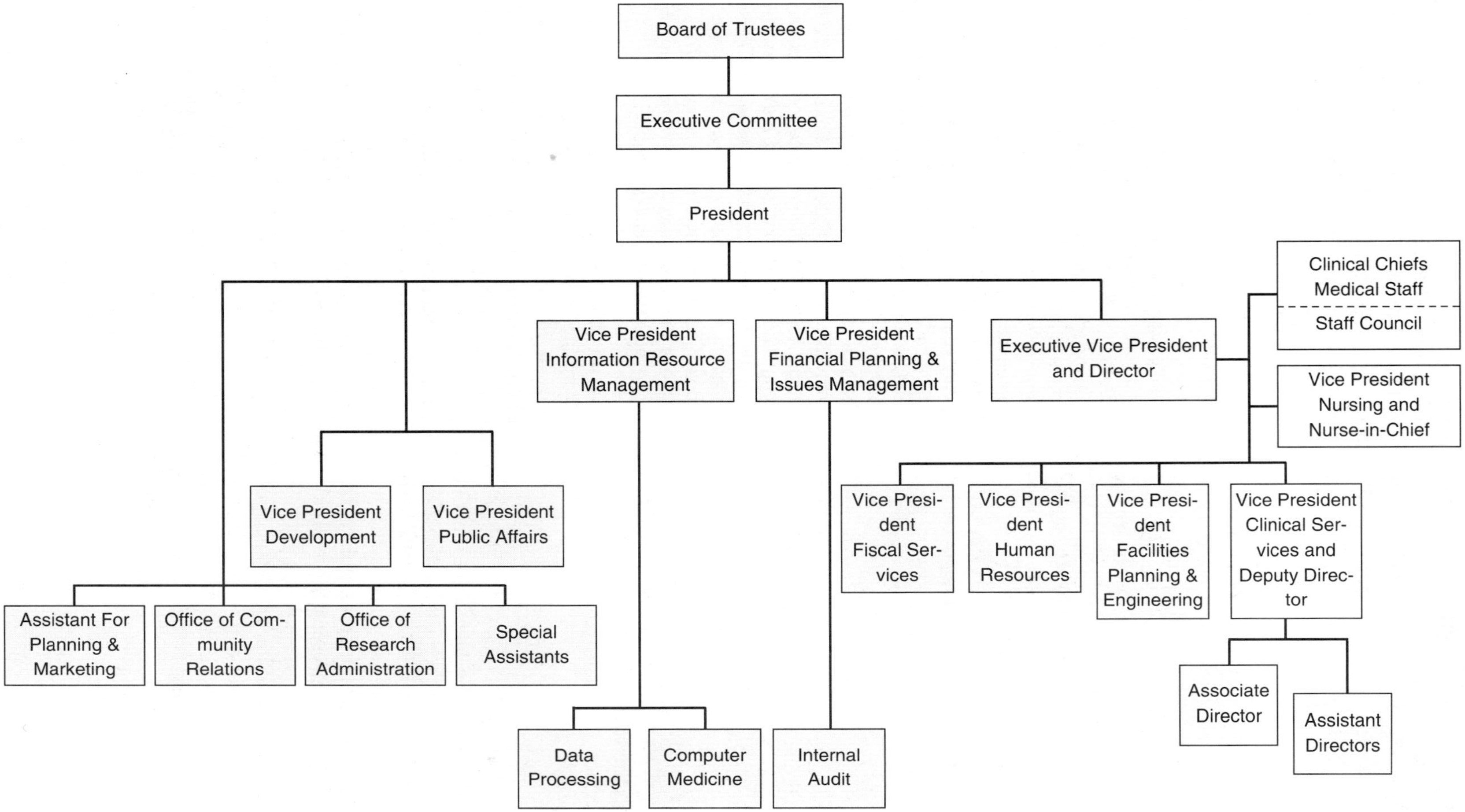

that individual. While the board also has ultimate authority and responsibility for clinical outcomes, it does not have the professional expertise in matters of clinical decision making, teaching, and research. In these matters, the board delegates its responsibility to the chiefs of service.

Medical Staff

The medical staff at BMC consisted of a large full-time staff who admitted and practiced only at BMC and an associate staff with admitting privileges. The medical staff all belonged to a separate physician corporation; however, administratively they reported to the CEO through the chiefs of service. The chiefs of service were, in effect, general managers of their departments. The two most powerful and influential physicians were the chief of surgery and the chief of medicine. At the time, Hunt considered both of these people to be his close, personal friends.

Timothy Hunt, M.D.

Timothy Hunt, M.D., age 50, had been president of the hospital since the late 1960s. He held B.A. and M.D. degrees from Yale University. He was trained in internal medicine and endocrinology at Johns Hopkins Medical Center.

Exhibit 1 reveals Hunt's schedule of appointments the week of March 5, 1985. Every week Hunt met with all the top and middle managers, all the chiefs of service, the chairman of the board, and the top vice presidents.

Policy Process

Hunt bemoaned, "During the last 20 years, I've become very concerned with the process of policymaking. You know, I've learned some very hard lessons." For example, Hunt has learned that he not only must include the chiefs in all policy discussions, but "they must represent the embodiment of our strategy."

In general, Hunt described his job as chief policymaker as co-aligning the chiefs of service, trustees, and administrators. Until a consensus had been reached, there would be no policy. Since it was the task of the CEO to develop long-range planning for the institution and to serve as "managing partner" for the medical center in its relations with the medical school, the CEO sought the advice and counsel of the chiefs concerning clinical and academic matters. His goal is to provide communication in both directions.

Hunt involved the board, the medical staff, and the top managers in the policy-making process. In order to move policy forward, he carefully channeled information about important issues to key people. To explain how he raised strategic ideas with the board, he said:

> *I might introduce an idea anywhere, but an idea is introduced as an intellectual concept rather than a proposal—let's do dum de dum de dum. . . . [After I became the general director of Baker], I developed a style that defined the boundaries in the following way. Twice a month there is an early morning meeting with the chairman of the board, and on alternate weeks there is an early morning meeting with the officers of the board. These are informal meetings. In part, they are for me to convey the news of what's going on, but in part they're also for me to educate them so they are better informed when decision time comes. They're also a time to raise a flag and see whether anybody deems that maybe when we shape that flag up a little bit, it might be worth saluting. Those meetings are not only educational for the board, the chairman, and myself, but I also am testing the waters. I test the waters in two ways: not only substance of the policy issues, but also on the process. They say, "Have you discussed this with the dean? Have you talked it out with this group?" . . .*

These meetings enabled Hunt to test ideas and elicit suggestions from an attentive constituency group. If Hunt wins their support, cooperation, and enthusiasm, he can expect acquiescence from the rest of the organization. Hunt is careful to control the process by defining the problems, the approach, and possible solutions.

Hunt claimed that contacts with people aimed toward policy discussions were carefully planned activities intended to negotiate new ideas and build coalitions:

> *What I did was evolve a style, where rather than spring full-blown requests or directives on people, I'd first acquaint them with an issue and at the same time, by virtue of their response, get new insights on the issue because things that require my attention are often multifaceted. It's a dual process.*
>
> *On the one hand, I am educating managers about a dissatisfaction of mine—that is,*

Exhibit 1 *Hunt's Scheduled Meetings*

Time	Subject Matter	Place	Size	Group*
AM: Tuesday March 5th				
08:30–10:00	Building committee	Inside	9	S
10:00–10:30	Legal issues	Inside	2	C
10:30–11:30	Middle-managers meeting	Inside	25	S
11:30–12:00	Tour of hospital	Inside	1	
12:00–01:00	Lunch w/chief surgery	Inside	2	M
01:30–02:00	Career counseling	Inside	2	S
02:15–03:30	Executive VP	Inside	2	S
03:30–04:00	Asst. clinical director	Inside	2	S
04:00–04:30	Interview with reporter	Inside	2	O
05:00–07:00	Talk at local university	Outside	40	O
AM: Wednesday March 6th				
08:00–10:00	Long-term care issues	Inside	9	B/S
11:30–12:30	Women's auxiliary	Inside	2	O
12:30–02:30	Chiefs of service	Inside	10	M
03:00–05:00	MBA course	Outside	30	O
AM: Thursday March 7th				
08:00–09:00	Medical school deans	Outside	15	O
09:00–10:00	Department heads	Inside	50	S
10:00–10:30	Problem in nursing	Inside	4	S
10:30–11:30	Asst. planning/marketing	Inside	2	S
11:30–12:30	Dir. community relations	Inside	2	S
01:00–03:00	Ceremony at city hall	Outside	100	O
04:00–06:00	Monthly board meeting	Inside	26	B
07:00–10:00	Visiting committee	Outside	25	O
AM: Friday March 8th				
08:00–10:00	Strategic planning	Inside	5	S
10:00–01:00	VP information resources	Inside	2	S
11:30–01:00	MIS joint venture issue	Inside	4	S
02:30–04:30	Assoc. teaching hospital	Outside	12	O

*Group: S = subordinate; C = consultant; M = medical staff; O = outsider; B = board.

when something requires a change. However, I am also getting educated by that manager—that is, how the problem looks to others, what it means to them, and how they might be impacted by a change that I might mandate. That doesn't mean I need their assent before I go ahead and do something. But if it comes to the [decision] point, it won't come as a surprise. . . .

In one sense the process is educational— educating those on whom the policy will fall— but it is also being educated. In a sense it's eliciting information and trying to telegraph the situation that has to be dealt with, and trying to expose the various alternatives before they get finalized. . . .

Decisions tended to emerge at Baker Medical Center. Prior to any policy decisions, the basic requirements for policy have already been considered by many of these individuals separately: in informal meetings with Hunt, in a weekly strategy meeting on Friday mornings (involving the top vice presidents), in the weekly meeting with the officers of the board, and in the chiefs of service "kitchen cabinet" meeting. While Hunt may not have controlled the final outcome, he personally orchestrated it by controlling the attention of these participants as well as their effort.

Personnel Policies

The vice president of human services was in charge of all personnel policies for the nearly 3,000 full-time equivalent employees working at the medical center.

Their salaries and fringe benefits represented nearly 65% of the total operating costs of the hospital. At the time, statewide wage and benefit surveys indicated that the hospital provided a very competitive wage along with a comprehensive fringe benefit package that included medical insurance, a pension plan, tuition reimbursement, tax-deferred annuity, and life insurance for all full-time employees. The fact that no hospital employee was represented by any labor union indicated that employees were basically satisfied with personnel policies.

There was an interpreter/translation service available to provide caregivers with an increased ability to care for non-English-speaking hospital patients. It also served non-English-speaking employees in the area of benefits communication, job information, disciplinary actions, and performance reviews. As one official claimed, "Baker cares almost as much about its employees—whom we all refer to as the 'Baker Family'—as its patients."

This was reflected in their policy never to violate the confidentiality of an employee. In general, the identity of employees with medical problems was not disclosed to the public or the press. When inquiries were made the following policy was used:

> *A knowledgeable and authoritative representative of the hospital from the Office of Community Relations staff will be the designated representative to the press. All other hospital staff members are required to coordinate all press communications through this representative.*

Financial Matters

Between 1979 and 1984, the hospital had an operating surplus. The excess of revenue over operating expenses for fiscal 1984 was over 1 million dollars, and in 1985 the excess is projected to be $1.8 million. As a result, the hospital had been able to fund an increasing amount of depreciation. Regarding the balance sheet, every financial indicator suggested that Baker was not only financially healthy, but it was a thriving medical enterprise (see Exhibits 3–5).

Although BMC competed directly with six other hospitals, the occupancy rates were well over 86%. In 1985, admissions and outpatient visits had been forecast to increase over the next five years. Hunt believed that the institution's success was based on successfully differentiating the hospital on the quality of services it delivers.

The hospital took its budgetary process very seriously. The process involves the board, all levels of management, and each clinical chief. A financial forecast is developed by senior management to guide the process, and programming decisions are considered in conjunction with the forecast. The annual budget is adopted, which meets the annual excess of revenues over the expenses goal established by the board. During the year variances are always questioned and action is taken (see Exhibit 4).

The hospital's management control system had been instrumental in achieving the financial objectives. In 1985, the operating budget was in very good shape. Key volume statistics were slightly overbudget and key expenses were slightly underbudget. The occupancy rates were consistently about 85%. At the time, hospital management and medical staff believed that 85% occupancy and the more than 14,000 discharges would continue throughout the 1980s. From a financial viewpoint, the auditors believed that Baker Medical Center was among the best-managed institutions in the United States.

Facilities

The main hospital complex consisted of 15 buildings, built in the past 60 years. The complex was situated on nearly 10 acres of land. Nearly 75% of the facilities had been renovated, replaced, or updated between 1975 and 1985.

Exhibit 3 *Baker Medical Center Current Operating Summary Through Five Periods
(2/10/85–Year to Date, in 000s)*

	Actual	Budget Variance	% Change from Last Year
Gross patient service revenue	$60,000	$1,500	3.8
Deductions	11,000	(2,200)	(30.5)
Other operating	2,577	(70)	6.6
Net	51,577	(770)	15.7
Salaries	25,300	1,100	9.3
Supplies	19,200	170	13.8
Interest and depreciation	6,010	111	79.0
Total expenses	50,510	1,381	16.5
Excess of revenues over expenses	978	611	14.6
Nonoperating	2,180	142	31.8
Surplus	$3,158	$753	12.8

Exhibit 4 *Baker Medical Center Statement of Revenue and Expenses (in 000s)*

	1983	1984
Revenues from services to patients	$94,433	$112,543
Deductions from revenue	23,124	27,509
Net Revenue from service to patient	71,309	85,034
Other operating revenue	12,996	14,844
Total Revenue	95,305	99,878
Operating expenses	84,054	97,941
Excess of operating revenue over expense	11,251	1,937
Nonoperating revenue	2,601	2,748
Excess of revenue over expense	13,852	4,685

Exhibit 5 *Baker Medical Center Balance Sheet—Unrestricted Funds*

	Sept. 26, 1983	Sept. 25, 1984
Assets		
Funded depreciation	$3,928	$4,620
Investments	3,954	1,791
Property, plant, and equipment	39,309	60,708
Other	3,204	58,665
	74,595	152,404
Liabilities and Fund Balance		
Current liabilities	13,590	15,491
Other liabilities	2,986	10,263
Long-term debt	23,622	77,487
Fund Balance	34,397	49,163
	74,595	152,404

[1]The information in this case is based on an actual incident. The names, data, and organizational relationships have been changed to protect the confidentiality of those involved.

BAKER MEDICAL CENTER (B)

Jon Chilingerian
Brandeis University

On Friday morning, March 8, 1985, the story broke. The story was on page 20 and had the following headline: "Case of Nurse with AIDS Poses Difficult Issues: Despite Fears, No Risk, Specialists Say."

The article emphasized the rational side of the argument and suggested that Baker Medical Center made a very sound choice—one that was safe for patients, for co-workers, and for the nurse involved. The article ended with quotes from physicians deriding the emotional arguments when there is no data to support them and a powerful quote from the interview with Dr. Hunt:

In these instances there are two choices: one is more hysterical and emotional, and the other is more rational. In the last analysis, if the hospital does not choose the more rational option, it will not fulfill its responsibility. We can't go back to the middle ages and start persecuting people who have diseases of one kind or another. The hospital has to take the most rational viewpoint that it possibly can. . . ."

The story came out on Friday. No other newspapers picked up the story. No lawsuits ever arose.

———

The information in this case is based on an actual incident. The names, data, and organizational relationships have been changed to protect the confidentiality of those involved.

BAKER MEDICAL CENTER (C)

Jon Chilingerian
Brandeis University

FRIDAY MORNING

At 7:40 AM Dr. Tim Hunt arrived in his office, picked up his dictating machine, and dictated a letter to David Fort. As he spoke into the microphone he said,

> Dear David,
>
> I want to compliment you on your article. It was masterfully done in a professional sense. It was both normative and educational. That represents one of the highest functions of the press. I am sorry that your timing was upset. . . ."

The employee newsletter came out on Friday. Hunt had written an article explaining the situation as a very rational and responsible action taken by the hospital. He reassured the employees that the hospital did not and would not violate fundamental issues of privacy. He ended the article with the following sentence:

> I am proud that the people with whom this individual worked, while saddened at the illness of a respected colleague, were careful to act on the basis of medical fact in exercise of their professional responsibilities. . . .

A DISCUSSION ABOUT AIDS WITH THE STRATEGIC PLANNING COMMITTEE

At 8:03 AM the strategic planning meeting began. Attending the meeting was Harvey Hopkins, executive vice president, John Michelian, vice president of financial planning and issues management, and Richard Carter, vice president of information resource management. The major topic for discussion was the intention to acquire another hospital so they could lower their average costs. The meeting began with a discussion of the AIDS article.

Harvey Hopkins spoke first, "Tim, the AIDS article was great, if you get past the first paragraph."

Hunt interjected, "I think the article was very normative. What do you want? For me to ghost write for Fort?"

"No, no!" Hopkins argued, "I just think interjecting certain words like 'the nurse's lover of seven years' made it sound like a human interest story. Writers should not interpose personal views and perspectives."

Hunt responded, "Hey, I am surprised at you, Harvey. I think we were very lucky. Our Community Affairs Office handled it well."

John Michelian spoke: "I would like to update everyone on the Medicare reimbursement issues."

"Wait a minute, John," Hunt interjected, "Maybe we should think a little about our AIDS policy."

Based on his knowledge of the disease and after reading the CDC's guidelines on AIDS, Dr. Hunt opened the discussion by reviewing several important facts about the disease. He reminded them that AIDS is a fatal disease that is primarily transmitted by direct contact with mucousal surfaces. The virus that causes AIDS—human immunodeficiency virus (HIV)—is extremely fragile and does not survive outside body cells. Consequently, AIDS cannot be transmitted through

303

casual contact such as shaking hands, hugging, kissing, or touching an infected person. Furthermore, people with AIDS present no danger to those with whom they work, share bathrooms, eat, or sit.

Harvey asked, "Is it prudent just to write a policy that advises hospital personnel to take the same precautions when caring for patients with AIDS as those used for patients with hepatitis B virus infection, in which blood and body fluids are considered infective?"

"It is a bit more complicated, Harvey," Hunt replied. He continued: "First, we all know that the hepatitis policy has been poorly implemented in most hospitals. Aside from that, what makes the AIDS issue even more intractable is the uncertainty. We just don't know who is carrying this disease. What about the patient or employee with 'suspected' AIDS. What if a patient's mucous membrane is exposed to the bodily fluids of a caregiver with AIDS (or suspected of AIDS)?"

"Since you put it that way," replied Harvey, "perhaps the blood and bodily fluids of every patient should be handled as contaminated. Although this changes the way we currently do business, the confidentiality of people with AIDS is guaranteed."

John Michelian spoke: "Or what should be done when patients with a known or suspected case of AIDS are admitted? Should they be treated on a separate floor, or throughout the hospital? Can we do that without placing other patients at risk? Where are the economies of scale?"

Harvey added, "Since a single AIDS patient may be served by many hospital departments, personnel should be informed that the patient's blood or bodily fluids may transmit the HIV virus. If we don't identify the AIDS patients to our staff, I am concerned about our personnel. Our policy must balance disclosure (to ensure that appropriate precautions are taken) with confidentiality."

Hunt responded to Harvey's first question: "Let's talk about approaches. So far two generic approaches have been taken by hospitals in these situations. First, give an AIDS patient a private room, or isolate these patients in special intensive care facilities, if they need such care. Precaution signs are either posted on the door of the AIDS patient's room and/or all of their bodily fluids taken to the labs are marked with red stickers. As you might have guessed, I dislike that approach.

"The other approach is more humane, and it may have its own economies of scale in terms of quality of care. It would place patients with AIDS throughout the hospital so they can obtain the expertise they need while protecting their confidentiality. I believe that private rooms are unnecessary unless a patient's hygiene is poor. While I favor the second option, I realize it must be done without placing other patients at increased risk.

"There is another idea that might work here. One model would create a specialist—an AIDS physician—who in a few years may be swamped with thousands of cases and burned out. Let's consider an alternative model whereby all of our primary care physicians care for people with AIDS from the outset, and only call upon specialists as necessary."

Harvey continued, "What about caregivers who refuse to perform duties in relation to caring for an AIDS or suspected AIDS patient? Is this a disciplinary problem? What about caregivers who are also parents? Children cannot give informed consent about the hazards of their parents' occupation. What about pregnant caregivers?"

While Hunt felt strongly that "medieval" behavior should be avoided, he advocated taking a tough stand against caregivers who refuse to treat people with AIDS.

At that point, Richard Carter jumped into the discussion: "If we fire surgeons who refuse to perform surgery on AIDS patients, to what extent does this become a matter of competitive advantage? We might lose some physicians who admit Blue Cross paying patients"

Hunt retook control of the discussion again by saying: "I am keeping notes on this discussion, so let's not try to answer the questions but identify the needs and the constraints. For now, let's combine a discussion of patients with AIDS with the issue of our employees with AIDS. In the future, how should the decision to allow an employee with AIDS to have direct patient contact be made? The employees who have AIDS become more susceptible to infections, hence they also need to be protected from the acquisition of nosocomial pathogens. When should caregivers with symptoms automatically be reassigned to non-patient-care duties to protect them from patients and vice versa? How should their health status be monitored if they are not being treated here? Who ought to have responsibility? I suppose our chief of infectious diseases, Jim Stafford. And what about public inquiries? For example, what if a famous "rock" musician with AIDS is admitted here? Our policy now is that a knowledgeable person from the office of public affairs will centralize communications. Is that who should be responsible for every inquiry?"

HUNT DECIDES TO DELEGATE

On Friday afternoon, March 8, 1985, Hunt reviewed the events of the past week. He decided that a task force was needed to plan for AIDS. He called John Dorn, an associate vice president, and asked him to stop by his office that afternoon.

When Dorn walked in, he congratulated Hunt on how the AIDS story was reported. They spoke briefly about the events leading up to the article in the paper. While Dorn agreed with Hunt that their current policy in the workplace was rational, more detailed planning for AIDS was needed. Hunt then asked Dorn to chair an AIDS task force, made up of trustees, nurses, physicians, and top administrators, which Dorn accepted.

Hunt handed over his notes from the 8:00 AM strategic planning meeting (see above) along with some articles and materials on AIDS and said, "Before the task force meets, John, I would like you to find a way to frame the critical issues. Perhaps you can get together with Jim Stafford [chief of infectious diseases] over the weekend. Whatever you decide to do, think about all of the issues that AIDS raises for BMC. Perhaps over the weekend you can draft a memo to me that analyzes the issue strategically and recommends a process."

Discussing Hospitalwide Policy Requirements for AIDS

While Hunt kept the discussion very general, he talked about an approach for BMC and some solutions. Hunt remarked that AIDS raised a number of clinical, financial, managerial, and ethical issues for the hospital. He listed seven areas of concern:

1. Preservation of the dignity of the patient as well as confidentiality of the patient, avoiding stigmatizing patients in the hospital and community. A related concern is the need for informed consent and post-test counseling when patients suspected of AIDS are tested.

2. The need to take another look at the hospital's policy on caregivers with AIDS or suspected of AIDS

3. Patient care guidelines and employee safety. Given the poor implementation of hepatitis B precautions in many institutions, there is a need for something other than rules and regulations. Perhaps widespread education is needed for surgeons as well as other caregivers.

4. Precautions for laboratory personnel

5. The projected cost of bad debt, free and uncompensated care to AIDS patients

6. Some sense of the competitive responses from other hospitals

7. How the prejudice and fear that may be generated in the community may be played out; Educational activities undertaken by Baker to allay those fears

"Most of all I want to be sure that AIDS patients are treated with efficiency, expertise and human dignity," said Hunt, "AIDS is just another disease that Baker must treat. I don't want people with AIDS stigmatized and tyrannized by our health system. Plus, it's important for us not to fear being the first hospital with a humane policy."

"Well, Tim, anyone who has a sense of what this institution stands for can anticipate our policy on AIDS," remarked Dorn.

A Worried Associate Vice President

As John Dorn walked out of Hunt's office his head was spinning. He began to think about all of the issues he would take to the task force—next week he hoped.

SATURDAY MORNING

On Saturday morning, John decided to work in his office at Baker Medical Center. He dug out several articles on AIDS and began to read. He listed seven facts about AIDS on a piece of paper:

1. The number of AIDS patients had been doubling every 10 to 12 months; without adequate planning, the financial impact could be tremendous. To date, Baker has had 43 patients with AIDS—amounting to just under 700 patient days. No newborns with AIDS have been reported at BMC, but those costs could be very expensive.

2. The average daily cost for a patient with AIDS at Baker Medical Center is $1,621; however, the state is reimbursing only $515 of that amount. Of 43 patients, 12 had Blue Cross, 9 had private insurance, 7 were on Medicare, and 15 became eligible for Medicaid. Since some had private insurance, on average, Baker is losing only $105 a day per AIDS patient.

3. Blue Cross/Blue Shield is still claiming that it will insure people with AIDS; however, in other states, most patients have been covered by Medicaid and Medicare. The state currently allows people with AIDS to by-pass the one- to two-year waiting period for Supplemental Income and Medicaid Benefits.

4. According to the CDC, the national cost per day for a patient with AIDS is $830. While this is double the national average cost for treating other patients, since BMC is an academic medical center, its average costs per day are much higher—about $1,100.

5. As Hunt had outlined to him, there are two basic choices: spreading patients with AIDS around or isolating them. Isolating patients to centralize resources and caregiver expertise may also relieve public hysteria about sharing a room with a person with AIDS. On the other hand, it might get a "death ward" reputation which would certainly fatigue the caregivers and create a very unpleasant specialty; furthermore, it might open the hospital up to discrimination suits.

   By spreading the AIDS patients throughout the hospital, it might be possible to save on routine nursing costs and improve quality of care. But one of the major advantages of spreading the patients out is to maintain their anonymity. It requires taking precautions that amount to treating all patients and employees as if they had AIDS.

6. One interesting alternative is treating patients with AIDS either on an outpatient basis or at their homes. Baker has recently begun providing home health care services. Since the cost for home care is about $100 per day, hospital costs could be cut by as much as 90%. In order to treat patients at home, an aggressive discharge planning policy is needed.

7. Although hospital workers are undoubtedly afraid of AIDS, while the risk of contracting the disease is low, several factors influence the risk of HIV infection among caregivers. The first is the frequency of needle (and other instrument) puncture injuries, and the proportion of patients treated who are HIV positive. The risk of becoming HIV positive after one needle stick is about 1%. Among surgeons who operate on many patients with AIDS, the risk is very high because they may get stuck 40 times a year. To date, fewer than a half of 1% of the patient population at Baker have tested positively for AIDS. There may, of course, be more patients (or employees) carrying AIDS.

   According to recent CDC evidence, of 1,500 health care workers who had been exposed to AIDS through direct bodily fluid contact or a needle stick, 26 tested positive for AIDS and only 3 of the 26 were not members of a high-risk group.

   As John walked toward his car, he wasn't thinking about what was left of the weekend. His thoughts were focused on the time bomb that Dr. Hunt had entrusted to him.

[1]The information in this case is based on an actual incident. The names, data, and organizational relationships have been changed to protect the confidentiality of those involved.

BEVERLY ENTERPRISES

Positioning for Growth in Long-term Care

Per V. Jenster
International Institute for Management Development
Lausanne, Switzerland

As the 1985 fiscal year was coming to a close, increasing interest focused on the future of Beverly Enterprises, in particular the prospects for diversification into alternative forms of long-term care. Upon examining environmental factors such as labor issues, government regulation, increased competition, and increased change in market demand, management realized the need for a strategic plan effective over the next five years. Rapid change in the factors effecting Beverly required immediate action by top management.

HISTORICAL INFORMATION

In the past, Beverly Enterprises had experienced tremendous growth financially and geographically. The firm had expanded into forty-four states, limiting its markets to the traditional long-term care facility. It became a national leader in the health industry developing the market of long-term care. Historically, its direction remained closely tied with nursing homes, and its growth was due mainly to geographic expansion versus product expansion. Based on the belief that local managers were more sensitive and thus better informed of the needs of the market, the firm developed a decentralized style of management. This philosophy allowed the nursing home facilities to better incorporate themselves into the community and thus gain more support from the local region.

While Beverly Enterprises had become one of the most recognized and successful companies in the health care industry, changing environmental conditions were initiating a drastic change in the characteristics and requirements of the long-term care customer. Beverly's ultimate goal had been defined as "striving to become the nursing home of choice, not necessity." With this goal in mind, Beverly had to correctly interpret the market and enact a strategic policy which would incorporate the changing structure of the industry.

REGULATION AND LEGISLATION

Medicaid

One of the overriding factors affecting the success or failure of nursing homes had been their ability to adapt and adjust to the changing regulatory environment. Recently, long-term care facilities had been forced to deal with the tenuous future of Medicaid. In 1981 Congress passed the Omnibus Act. Such legislation enabled individual states to determine the number of Medicaid patients and the amount of tax dollars allocated to long-term health care. This had placed an incentive on long-term care facilities to reevaluate their patient mixes and reduce the number of Medicaid-dependent customers. The issue dominated the concerns of this consulting team due to Beverly's patient mix where historically and presently Medicaid recipients comprised 60 percent of the customer base.

Due to the increased pressure on state-paying agencies to limit the allocations for Medicaid, many states adopted screening policies which were legislated in 1972. In brief, the screening process had required that the recipient be qualified for aid, the nursing home be qualified to meet the patient's need, and finally, the care the patient received be what the patient really needed. In conjunction with the above, nursing homes were required by participating states to perform reviews on all patients, dismissing those who did not fall within the realm defined by licensure. The situation thus defined had limited long-term care facilities in their ability to select the most profitable patient mix.

MORATORIUMS

While screening regulations controlled, to a certain extent, the ability for facilities to target a more profitable customer mix, some proposed measures had provided companies like Beverly with a potential advantage. In an attempt to limit the number of patients and lower costs, states had begun to consider enforcing moratoriums on the number of new construction starts on nursing homes. The rationale was that if one limited the available space, in effect one limited the number of qualified recipients and thus cost. Such proposed legislature had opened an opportunity for Beverly and similar institutions in two ways. Primarily such legislation had further limited supply in an industry where demand has already exceeded the available space. Thus, Beverly had been handed a legislative barrier to entry. Secondly, by prohibiting new constructions, states had given an advantage to large chains by placing them in a better situation to buy up existing independent facilities due to their more flexible financing alternatives.

Financial Legislation

Traditionally, the long-term care industry financed its growth through debt, equity, or a combination of both. Of the debt alternatives tax-exempt industrial development bonds (IDBs) were always less expensive than conventional debt. This allowed smaller interests to enter the long-term market by providing easy financing terms. There had been discussion in Congress to enact a bill which would limit or extinguish the IDB financing alternative. The results of such legislation would give the larger chains a distinct advantage since very few firms would have the financial capacity for growth without the easier credit terms of IDBs.

Medicare

Like the Medicaid system, Medicare experienced a major shift in its present definition, and it, too, was placed in a precarious position with respect to its future. In 2983, Congress implemented Prospective Payment Systems (PPS) and Diagnostic Related Groups (DRG) plans. These plans were to be phased in over a three-year period and were to encourage hospitals to lower costs and increase profits by paying a fixed fee for different categories of treatment. Originally, these systems made Medicare patients less attractive to hospitals and forced hospitals to cooperate with nursing homes—a relationship that was tenuous at best. The migration of patients from hospitals to long-term care facilities effectively placed a further limitation on the supply of long-term care facilities as it increased the demand for their services.

Prospective Payment Systems and Diagnostic Related Groups

In answer to the PPS/DRG legislation, hospitals began to investigate the possibility of converting wings within the hospital to accommodate long-term care and acute-care patients. The idea was based on two factors: the aging population and increasing space utilization. Provided the patient received three medically required hospital days, Medicare covered 100 days of skilled nursing care at a long-term care facility. Thus, it was obvious that such a market invoked further investigation on the part of hospitals. However, what this meant to long-term care facilities was the possible entry of a new and potentially dangerous competitor. Complicating the situation even further was the relationship between long-term care facilities and Medicare. Historically, Medicare maintained an unfavorable position in the eyes of nursing homes due to the inadequate reimbursement system, the burdensome paperwork, and the inconsistent coverage of the Medicare system. Success, however, required that long-term care facilities reevaluate their present position and determine a strategy against potential hospital movements.

Industry Analysis

The industry was undergoing numerous changes in supply and demand. While demand for long-term care services had been increasing at a 5 percent annual rate, supply had been increasing at an annual rate of only 1 percent. The long-term care industry was transforming from a state of near decline to rapid growth. This situation put increasing pressure on competitors to formulate strategic plans that would accommodate for the changing conditions.

OPPORTUNITY

Increasing demand was providing opportunities for growth. There were three factors influencing demand. Demographics was the most immediate influence on demand. In 1986 it was estimated that the elderly (those over 65 years of age) represented 11 percent of the population; by the year 2000 the percentage was forecasted to increase to 15 percent; by 2025 it was projected to be 19 percent. This trend was further supported by the statistic that through the rest of the decade, the 75-and-over segment was predicted to expand at four times the rate of persons under 65.

Another factor affecting demand was the restructuring of the family unit. Couples' desire to have fewer children was resulting in fewer offspring to care for their parents. This has been compounded by more women entering the work force instead of staying home to take care of parents or relatives. Family tendencies toward geographic dispersion had made it more difficult to take care of elderly relatives in their homes. A further factor influencing demand was the high rate of divorce, which left spouses alone without someone to care for them. A survey reported that one-third of the nations householders were not living with someone who could care for them should they need continuous care.

The third factor which influenced demand was the heightened cost consciousness in the health care field. The government and third-party payers had been concerned about costs for patients with extended stays in hospitals and acute-care facilities. In particular, Diagnostic Related Group's implementation of Prospective Payment Schedules limited hospitals' Medicare/Medicaid receipts. When feasible, many patients had been moved to nursing homes where it was more economical for them to stay for an extended period of time.

The above paragraphs demonstrated the expanding demand in the long-term care industry. On the supply side, the long-term care industry also had a number of opportunities for expansion and diversification. In 1985, 90 to 95 percent of nursing home beds were filled. This limitation in supply presented an opportunity for firms currently in the industry to expand to fill future gaps in capacity. Also, existing competitors had the chance to merge or acquire smaller firms exiting the industry. These small firms were being pushed out by the need for economies of scale.

Existing competitors had further opportunities for horizontal integration through diversification. A diversification strategy offered the chance to include everything from traditional nursing homes to new services. In the nursing home market, some firms had started offering sub-acute-care so older people with less serious problems were moving out of hospitals. Other nursing homes built child care centers in the facility which integrated residents, children, and working parents. A further expansion was building nursing homes which tried to re-create life outside the home. This was accomplished through activities such as cocktail hour and community involvement projects. Another home placed a village shopping center in the nursing home which allowed the residents to shop, get hair cuts, etc.

Alongside nursing homes, the industry had started to diversify into other services in order to meet the changing demands of the elderly. Services already created include adult day care centers which took older people out of their homes for recreational activities. Another service offered was home health agencies which provided short-term and long-term care. This service offered older people a variety of things, such as taking blood pressure, providing therapy, light housekeeping, or cooking.

The most integrated concept was continuum of care which provided a level of health and medical services to meet the specific needs of the individual. The concept was put into operation by offering levels of health care on a single campus, where patients were easily shifted form one level of service to another. An example of a retirement village was one which consisted of four levels: (1) garden apartments, (2) efficiencies with central dining facilities, (3) nursing homes for patients requiring professional care, and (4) homes providing a high level of medical attention. Continuum of care provided flexibility to the consumer by offering a spectrum of services which met many of the consumers' needs.

The future for long-term care has great potential for better facilities that supply the diversification desired by the elderly. The demand was secure, so the task of firms was to provide a quality service at a fair price. Firms that succeeded were sure to be rewarded by good profits and satisfied consumers.

Threats

While future demand was insulated from economic factors, supply was not. Government regulation and high internal costs threatened supply. Concern over Medicare/Medicaid payments had forced many state governments to impose restrictions in the form of moratoriums on the number of nursing home facilities being constructed. More specifically, cutbacks on Medicare/Medicaid receipts had initiated the vertical integration of hospitals into alternative long-term care services. Two-thirds of the nation's hospitals provided long-term care. In 1986 alone, over 30 percent planned to convert empty acute-care wings into nursing home facilities. In addition, the potential threat of expansion of hospital services extended to include the home health care market as well as the adult day care market. In 1985, hospital involvement in the home health care market had totaled 47 percent; adult day care involvement had totaled 10 percent.

The growing popularity of Health Maintenance Organizations (HMOs) provided the next largest threat to profitability of the nursing home industry. With over 385 organizations in existence, HMOs provided individuals who paid a fixed monthly fee any medical service which they may have needed. A drawback as a member seeking service was that individuals were required to see only member physicians and hospital organizations. Yet, pending legislation that involved new regulations was predicted to permit the country's 28 million elderly on Medicare to join HMOs. Thus, strategic planners in the health care industry had been paying close attention to the progress of the above-mentioned new entrants to the market.

In view of current operating costs, industry insiders had also voiced great concern over the potential threat of increasing costs. In 1985 alone, expenditures within the health services industry totaled 10.5 percent of gross national product or roughly $423.8 billion. More specifically, 1985 expenditures totaled $35.2 billion. Consequently,

despite prospects for increased profit potential, increased operating costs were necessitating the need for reevaluation of competitive positions within the industry. In addition, pressure toward unionization of the nursing home industry's laborers had resulted in the threat of increased labor costs. As a result, many smaller long-term care facilities unable to finance unavoidable fixed costs were being forced to exit the industry. Only larger firms able to maintain economies of scale were able to remain a competitive force within the industry.

Along with increasing costs, the industry was concerned with methods of financing. As already mentioned, industrial development bonds were some of the most popular financing methods because of their tax exempt status. However, in 1985, new tax legislation was proposed which would limit or eliminate IDBs. This legislation had a good chance of passing due to the federal government's desire to shift industrial policy into the state's hands. This change in IDBs would have a twofold effect on the industry. First, it would close a cheap method of financing to company balance sheets, specifically smaller firms who were the major users of IDBs. Second, without other financing methods available, smaller firms would be more susceptible to being acquired by larger firms.

COMPETITIVE ANALYSIS—BEVERLY

Strengths

The following discussion of strengths focuses on Beverly's resources, skills, and other advantages relative to its competitors. The most influential factor had been Beverly's large market share. In 1985, Beverly led the industry in terms of number of beds provided with a total of 106,000 beds in 946 facilities across the country. Most recently, Beverly's acquisition of Southern Medical Services, Inc. at $25,000 per bed tripled Beverly's bed capacity and increased Beverly's industry share to a record 6.57 percent. As Beverly's most immediate competitor, National Medical Enterprises ranked second in terms of total capacity, supplied with 39,642 beds operating in 323 facilities nationwide. In terms of overall, profitability performance however, after its acquisition of Four Seasons nursing centers, Manor Care provided Beverly's largest source of competition with approximately 19,500 beds in 150 facilities located across the United States. See Exhibit 1 for a more detailed account of industry capacity in terms of individual chains.

Another important strength of Beverly was its strategy of geographic dispersion. As a result of moratoriums limiting construction of new facilities, Beverly's management had responded with an aggressive acquisition program which had enabled the corporation to expand operations to cover 41 states. Complementing the above-mentioned acquisition strategy, Beverly developed a concentration strategy centralizing operations in three key markets: Texas (17 facilities), California (82 facilities), and Arizona (48 facilities).

As a consequence of the size of Beverly's operations, the company had strategically positioned itself in such a manner as to allow for future expansion in new market areas. As of November 1985, Beverly had entered a cooperative agreement with Sun Health, a multihospital system based in Charlotte, NC, to provide home health care services to the hospitals' patrons through a Beverly affiliate, Shared Home Care of St. David's, Pennsylvania. This example has been only one illustration of Beverly's entrance into the home health care market. Similarly, in 1984, Beverly's joint venture with Leisure and Technology, a major developer of retirement communities enabled the company's entrance into the retirement village market. This retirement village concept was facilitated through the development of a life-care housing program.

Weaknesses

Although Beverly had many strengths, two major weaknesses existed. Beverly's key weakness centered in the concentration of its patient mix. While many larger chains in the industry had been repo-

sitioning target markets toward private-pay patients who contributed 42 percent of nursing home receipts, Beverly's patient mix still included 63 percent Medicaid, which was well over the industry average of 50 percent. Manor Care, one of Beverly's most immediate competitors, had reversed its patient mix strategy as early as 1983 with 56 percent private-pay patients as opposed to 31 percent Medicaid patients. Resulting from their repositioning strategy, Manor Care had succeeded in producing a gross profit of 19 percent or twice the industry average. Consequently, strategic planners had been concerned Beverly had been failing to adequately target the private-pay market and as a result was failing to maximize corporate profits.

Despite the profit potential resulting from Beverly's joint venture with Leisure and Technology, strategic planners still believed the company's second largest weakness centered on the large number of entrants already existing within the retirement village market. Beverly's second largest competitor, National Medical Enterprises, Inc., had already incurred $150 million in expenditures to build seven retirement villages in an effort to offer private-pay patients an alternative to long-term care. Similarly, as of 1985, Forum Group had proven the market leader in terms of capitalizing on the private-pay alternative retirement community concept operating 11 such retirement centers with a total capacity of 2,204 beds. Both Summit Health Limited and Basic American Medical had also diversified into this market, operating six retirement villages each, with a total capacity of 903 and 682 beds, respectively. For a more detailed account of chains that had pursued this market, see Exhibits 1 and 2. Exhibits 3 and 4 contain Beverly's financial information.

Exhibit 1 *Capacity of Long-term Care Facilities*

Chain	No. of Nursing Home Facilities	Capacity (# beds)	Location	Alternative Services*	Capacity
Basic American	8	359		6 ret. comm.	903
				22 hospitals	1,800 b
Beverly	946	106,000	41 states: TX = 117 CA = 82 AZ = 48	26 mentally dis. fac.	
Manor Care	146	19,047	24 states: Four Seasons Acquisition	hotel chain (4th lgst)	
National Medical Enterprises	323	39,642		112 acute care 35 psychiatric	
Geriatric & Medical Services	17		NJ, PA	basic acute care	
National Health Corp.	50		9 SE states	18 home health agencies 1 retirement comm. (FL)	
Mediplex	26	1,340	NE		
Forum Group	77	4,539		11 ret. ctrs.	2,204
Summit Health Ltd.	33	4,225	CA, TX, AZ South, West, Midwest	6 ret. hotels 10 hospitals	682 1,057

*ret. = retirement; comm. = communities; ctr. = center; dis. = disabled; fac. = facilities.

Exhibit 2 *Industry Comparisons of Ratios**

	Beverly	Community Psychiatric Centers, Inc.	Hospital Corp.	Manor Care	Humana
Price	34	25	33	18	27
Earnings Per Share	2.15	1.50	3.50	.76	2.19
Dividend	.32	.26	.58	.11	.68
Price-earning	15.81	16.67	9.43	23.68	12.33
Yield	.94%	1.04%	1.76%	.61%	2.52%
Payout	14.88%	17.33%	16.57%	14.47%	27.40%

*Ratios based on information obtained from Value Line.

Exhibit 3 *Beverly Enterprises Consolidated Statements of Income for the Years Ended December 31, 1981–1985 (figures in millions except EPS)*

	1981	1982	1983	1984	1985
Revenues	$486.2	$816.2	$1,091.5	$1,420.1	$1,690.7
Expenses					
Operating	422.7	689.2	935.7	1,197.9	1,426.2
Operating margin	13.1%	15.6%	14.3%	15.6%	16.0%
Depreciation and amortization	15.33	27.54	39.50	57.72	70.00
Total expenses	$438.0	$716.8	$975.2	$1,255.6	$1,496.2
Net	48.21	99.43	116.30	164.46	194.51
Interest	13.24	40.80	54.81	82.04	97.03
Taxes	13.52	22.19	26.05	35.43	35.43
Net Profit Margin	3.3%	3.2%	3.2%	3.3%	3.5%
Net Income	$16.04	$26.12	$34.93	$46.86	$59.17
EPS	1.8	1.33	1.45	1.8	2.14
# at shares*	14,895	19,571	24,387	26,135	27,650

*Weighted average number of shares of common stock and dilutive common stock equivalents.

Exhibit 4 *Internal Comparisons of Ratios**

	1981	1982	1983	1984	1985
Internal Liquidity					
Current	1.0974	1.6169	1.6233	1.2592	1.5614
Quick	.9871	1.5008	1.5117	1.1492	NA
Operating Performance					
Gross profit	.1306	.1556	.1427	.1564	.1500
Operating profit	.0608	.0591	.0563	.0580	.0581
Net operating profit	.0330	.0323	.0324	.0331	.0325
Leverage					
Debt-equity	1.5563	2.1746	2.1107	2.2795	2.2686
Interest coverage	2.5904	1.9422	2.1212	2.0044	NA
Growth					
Return on equity	.1121	.1031	.0917	.1081	.1121

*Ratios based on information obtained from Beverly Enterprise's annual reports (1982–1985).

BOEING COMPANY AND DE HAVILLAND AIRCRAFT OF CANADA, LTD.

Per V. Jenster
International Institute for Management Development
Lauzanne, Switzerland

On November 21, 1985, T. A. Wilson, chief executive officer of the Boeing Company, and its board of directors sat down to make the final decision on the proposed acquisition of de Havilland Aircraft of Canada. This small, Canadian-owned manufacturer of twin-engine turboprop aircraft had been put up for sale by the Canadian government after losing money every year since 1980. Boeing was in competition with two European companies and one Canadian company for the rights to de Havilland. Wilson knew that a decision had to be made that week whether to continue or withdraw from the bidding.

THE BOEING COMPANY

Since 1916, Boeing had built over 30,000 aircraft in its numerous factories and had produced more commercial jetliners than any other company in the nation. Boeing's reputation in commercial aviation had begun with the Stratoliners and Model 314 Flying Boats of the 1930s and had continued with the post-World War II Stratocruisers. The company had continued to grow with its family of 707, 727, 737, and 747 jets (see Exhibit 1). Boeing's 727 had been the world's largest selling aircraft.

Boeing's 747 superjet, the first wide-bodied jetliner, had built an impressive performance record. The company's product improvement efforts on the 747 included the 747 convertible, the 747 freighter, the 747 short-range version, and other versions. This was a typical pattern of product development in the industry, with one model being constantly improved and enhanced.

The descendants of the 707 dominated the commercial airways. By 1985, Boeing had manufactured 55 percent of all the passenger jets ever built in the free world. Due to a dedicated work force, smart management, attention to quality, and a willingness to risk billions on research and development, Boeing showed no signs of losing altitude. Its sales were expected to climb 32 percent to $13.6 billion in 1985, with profits expected to climb by 45 percent to $566 billion. At a time when the United States suffered from a record trade deficit, Boeing was the country's number one exporter of manufactured products, with foreign sales of $5.8 billion (see Exhibit 2). The total employment of the company, excluding foreign nationals, was 104,000 on January 31, 1985. During 1985, total employment was expected to increase by 11,000 people.

Boeing had developed a new family of jetliners, beginning with the 757 and 767. The 757 was an advanced, standard-body airplane; the 767 was wide-bodied for greater passenger convenience and for more efficient freight handling. Both aircraft contained advanced-technology wings and engines to provide much quieter operation and improved fuel efficiency. Boeing designed these new airplanes to meet the needs of the world's airlines for the remainder of the twentieth century. There were no plans to develop smaller non-jet aircraft.

Boeing was also a major developer and producer of defense hardware. It was heavily involved in electronics, information systems, and logistics, and it held research contracts in a broad range of high-technology areas. It had also received many contracts in other areas of the government. The

Exhibit 1 *Jet Transport Deliveries by Model*

Model	1985	1984	1983
707*	3	8	8
727**		8	11
737–200	32	60	82
737–300	83	7	0
747	24	16	23
757	36	18	25
767	25	29	55
Total	203	146	204

Exhibit 2 *Sales by Type of Consumer*

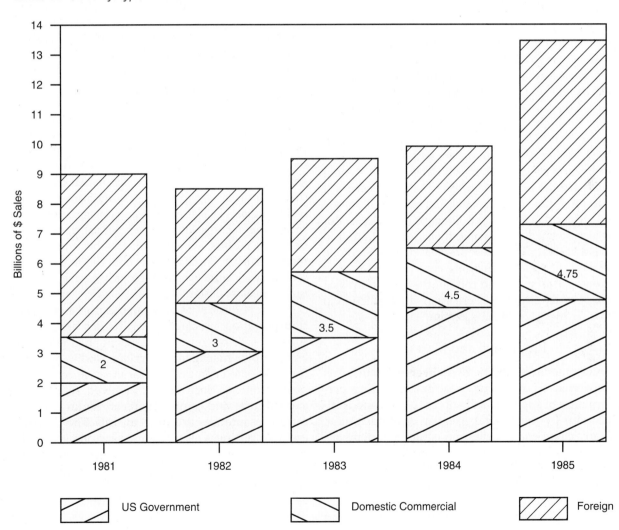

company divided itself into four main divisions: military production, computer services, aerospace development, and aircraft manufacturing. Exhibit 3 shows breakup of sales by customers.

Boeing's Success

A vital ingredient in Boeing's success was its willingness to bet billions of dollars, and sometimes the whole company, on new types of planes. In the late 1960s Boeing executives risked more than $1 billion on the first jumbo jet, the 747, and nearly drove the firm into bankruptcy. Ten years later, Boeing gambled again and invested $3 billion in the simultaneous development of two fuel-efficient, twin-engine jets: the trim 757 and the wide-bodied 767. The success of these programs had allowed Boeing to stay at the forefront of technology and to gain a reputation for leadership throughout the industry.

Supreme as Boeing's reputation was, it was also fragile. On those rare occasions when a Boeing jet crashed, a shudder of sympathy and concern ran through Seattle, the company's corporate home. When a Japan Air Lines 747 went down in 1984, killing 520, the company sent a twelve-member team of investigators to the scene. Boeing accepted the blame, admitting that repair work it had once done on the plane's tail had been faulty.

The tragedy shocked Boeing's employees. But it also seemed to redouble their determination to build the best and safest possible planes. Said one worker, "I watch something come in one door as thousands of parts and roll out the other door as a ready-to-fly airplane. There's a great satisfaction to that. I can say, 'that baby is mine'".

Factors in Production and Marketing

The company's ability to deliver jet transports depended on a variety of factors, including performance of suppliers and subcontractors and certifications by the Federal Aviation Administration. Many major components and equipment items for the company's products were produced from, or subcontracted to, various domestic and foreign companies. Although Boeing had periodically experienced certain problems with supplier and subcontractor performance, these situations have been manageable.

The introduction of new commercial jets and major design changes also involved increased risks

associated with meeting development, production, and certification schedules. The company was highly dependent on its suppliers and subcontractors in order to meet commitments to its customers.

While Boeing owned numerous patents, and had licenses under patents owned by others, relating to its products and their manufacture, it did not believe that its business would be materially affected by the expiration or termination of any patents or any patent license agreements. The company had no trademarks, franchises, or concessions considered to be of material importance to the conduct of its business. Because of long lead times and production cycles in the aerospace industry, the amount of backlog of unfilled orders was highly significant (see Exhibit 4). If backlog became too great, the delivery delays could cause potential buyers to look to other aircraft manufacturers to fill orders. Of the total firm order backlog at year end 1985, approximately 49 percent would not be filled in the coming year.

The commercial transportation segment was highly competitive. All of the company's commercial jet transport sales were subject to intense competition from both foreign and domestic companies; including companies with substantial resources and companies which were nationally owned or subsidized. Domestic competition, mainly from McDonnell Douglas's DC jet series, was constant. Boeing's main foreign competitor in commercial transportation was Airbus, which competes head-on in jet manufacturing. Some analysts believed that Airbus would soon launch a technological attack with a radical new jet design.

Competition was also intense in the military transportation products and missiles and space segments. To be competitive, Boeing had to establish complex management systems and to prepare for anticipated competition far in advance of proposal requests. Such efforts involved substantial expenditures and commitments of resources without any assurance of contract awards. The US government business environment was one in which continued intense competition among potential suppliers for defense and space procurement could be expected.

Boeing had been successful in marketing its planes through a sales and customer representative force which submitted bids to potential buyers. Boeing then remained in contact with the airlines that had purchased aircraft, periodically

Exhibit 3 *Sales by Type of Consumer*

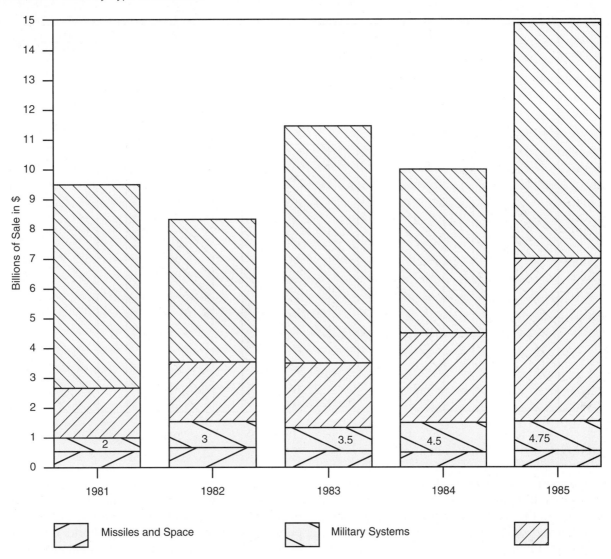

servicing their planes. This promise of high-quality service was considered integral to the sales package.

Current Financial Summary

The company would end 1985 with cash and short-term investment of $3,209 million, stockholders' equity of $4,364 million, and total borrowings of $34 million. As in the past two years, internally generated funds were more than sufficient to meet the company's working capital and its developmental and new plant and equipment requirements, resulting in a significant increase in cash and short-term investments of $1,614 million in 1985. This followed increases of $500 million and $801 million in 1984 and 1983. During 1985, stockholders' equity was estimated to increase $669 million from $3,695 million at the end of 1984. Total borrowings would decrease $265 million to a balance of $34 million, or less than 1 percent of stockholders' equity.

Principal factors affecting the company's liquidity position were the timing of new commercial jet design programs (resulting in both high developmental expenditures and inventory buildup),

Exhibit 4 *Firm Backlog*

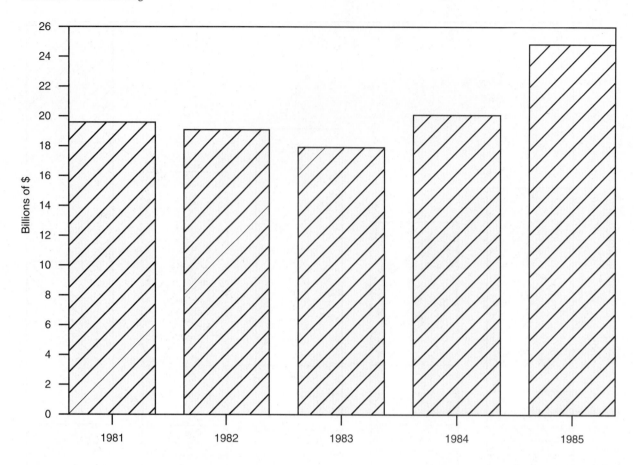

the airline industry's cyclical equipment require-ments (resulting in varying inventory investment levels), and the level of new plant and equipment investment. Exhibits 5 to 11 contain relevant finan-cial information.

DE HAVILLAND AIRCRAFT OF CANADA, LTD.

Company History

Geoffrey de Havilland, widely regarded as one of aviation's true pioneers, began de Havilland Air-craft in 1928. First gaining prominence during World War I, he produced over 70 new aircraft designs in a span of 50 years. Many of these designs were recognized as being well ahead of their time.

A Canadian company, de Havilland Aircraft was founded in response to a demand for aircraft

that could operate on the short runways and harsh weather conditions of the Canadian north. At first the company only sold and assembled planes im-ported from England, but during World War II it expanded its operations into a substantial manu-facturing concern. During the 1940s and 1950s, de Havilland produced original-design aircraft aimed at the "bush" market—planes that were rugged, could carry heavy payloads, and could land on very short airstrips.

In 1960, de Havilland was absorbed by Hawker Siddeley, a large British aircraft company. De Havilland tried to maintain its own identity within the larger company and this resulted in many conflicts. The main problem was competing for resources against projects within the Hawker Siddeley group. De Havilland often found itself short-changed of company funds for development allocations or of support from the British-based upper management.

Exhibit 5 *The Boeing Company and Subsidiaries Consolidated Statement of Financial Position (Dollars in Millions)*

	December 31,	
	1985	1984
Assets		
Cash and certificates of deposit	$3160	$1067
Short-term investments	49	528
Accounts receivable	822	639
Current portion of customer financing	63	138
Inventories	6592	7107
Less advanes and progress billing	−3920	−3309
Total current assets	6766	6170
Customer financing	514	541
Property, plant and equipment, at cost	4381	3916
Less accumulated depreciation	−2515	−2245
Investments and other assets	100	103
	$9246	$8485
Liabilities and Stockholders' Equity		
Accounts payable and accrued liabilities	$2699	$2528
Advances and progress billings in excess of related costs	571	644
Federal taxes on income, principally deferred	1129	853
Current portion of long-term debt	18	15
Total current liabilities	4417	4040
Long-term debt	16	284
Deferred taxes on income	326	322
Deferred investment credit	123	144
Stockholders equity:		
Common shares, issued at stated value— 1985—155,245,862; 1984—146,429,678	1347	843
Retained earnings	3018	2854
Less treasury shares, at cost— 1985—57,205; 1984—592,184	−1	−2
Total Stockholders' Equity	4364	3695
	$9246	$8485

In 1974, the Canadian government exercised the option it had retained to buy back de Havilland were it to meet financial trouble. The government wished to ensure the financial strength of de Havilland because of the large export potential of the firm and the number of people it employed. Under the terms of the purchase, the Canadian government became substantially the only shareholder, though the company was allowed to continue operating basically as a private enterprise. From this point, de Havilland had produced only turboprop airplanes.

The Current Situation at de Havilland

The driving force behind de Havilland was president and CEO William Benton Boggs. He first ran the company in 1965, but he left in 1970 because of the problems Hawker Siddeley management was creating. Boggs, a skilled and experienced manager, was brought back to run the company in January 1985.

The Canada Development Investment Corporation (CDIC), a government-owned holding company, was responsible for looking out for the government's interest in de Havilland. Although it had no direct managerial control, the CDIC could put considerable pressure on management to take the actions the government desired. In

1985, the CDIC was exploring ways to improve de Havilland's profit situation and to lower costs. Many observers felt the only way to run de Havilland efficiently was to return it entirely to the private sector.

Before any bid was accepted, the CDIC required guarantees that the manufacturing operations would remain in Canada and that jobs and technology would not be transferred to Europe and thus to de Havilland's main competitors. The CDIC was having similar troubles with Canadair, another Canadian aircraft manufacturer of which it was trying to divest itself. The Canadian government was internally split between liberals and conservatives. The conservatives, who were in power, wanted to go through with the sale of de Havilland to a foreign firm or government, while the liberals wanted to help the company and try and turn it around. The administration had made it easier than in the past for a foreign firm to acquire a Canadian company by eliminating the Foreign Investment Review Agency, which had been responsible for stringently reviewing all sales of Canadian firms to foreigners.

One of the government's main concerns was the loss of Canadian jobs. During 1985, de Havilland employed 4,980 workers, up from more recent years when employment fell to under 3,000 employees. This improvement was the result of increased sales activity. The firm sold its aircraft

Exhibit 6 *The Boeing Company and Subsidiaries Consolidated Statement of Net Earnings (Dollars in Millions Except Per Share Data)*

	Year ended December 31,		
	1985	1984	1983
Sales	$13,636	$10,854	$11,129
Cost and expenses	13,053	9,998	10,797
Earnings from operations	583	356	332
Federal taxes on income before			
DISC adjustment	297	241	179
	566	390	355
Adjustment of prior years' federal tax			
provisions on DISC earnings		397	
Net earnings	566	787	355
Net earnings per share*			
Primary	3.75	5.39	2.44
Fully Diluted	3.68	5.16	
Cash dividends per share	1.04	0.93	0.93

*Per share data restated for 1985 three-for-two stock split.

Exhibit 7 *Net Sales*

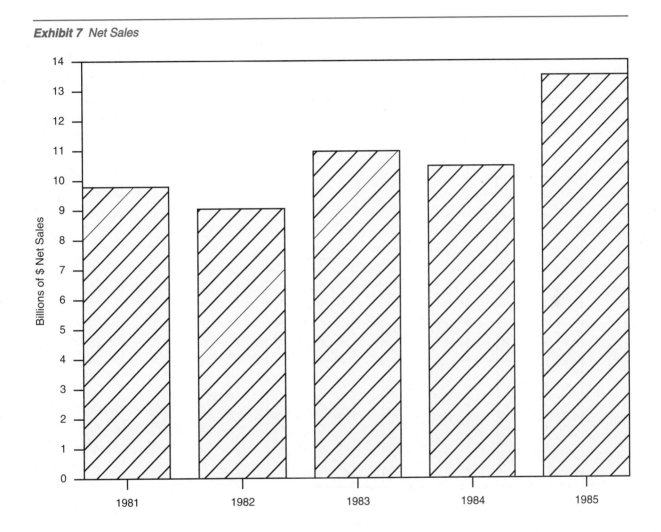

Exhibit 8 *Net Earnings*

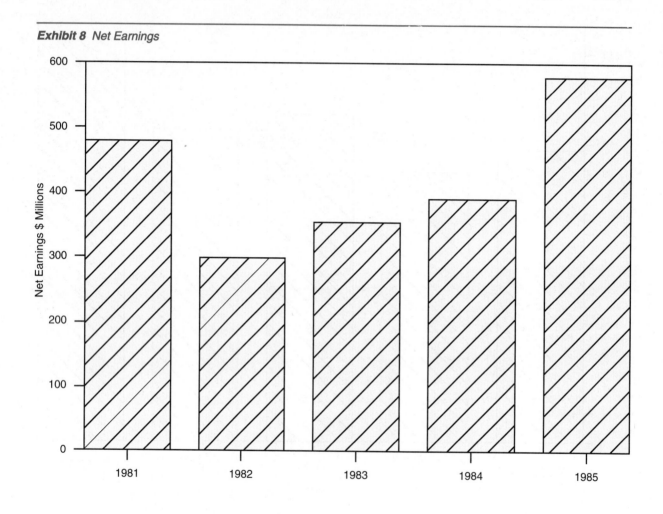

Exhibit 9 *Net Earnings per Share Resulted for 1985 Stock Split*

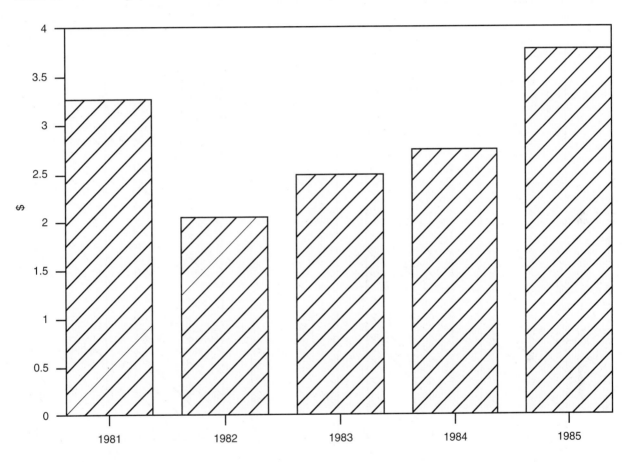

Exhibit 10　Stockholders' Equity

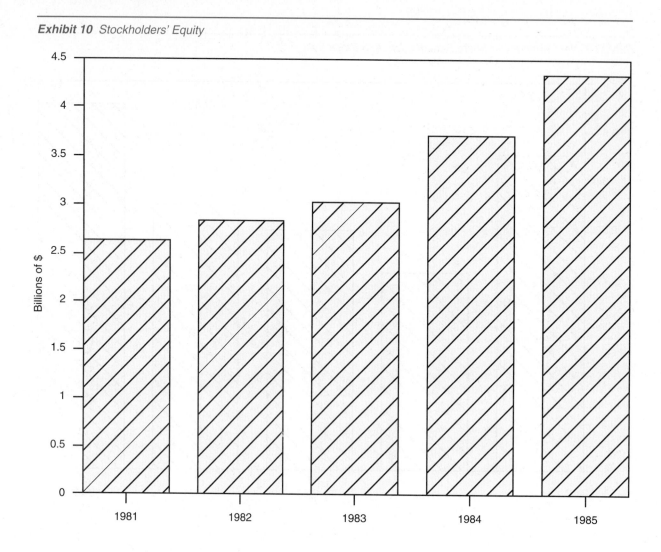

Exhibit 11 *The Boeing Company and Subsidiaries—Five Year Summary (Dollars in Millions Except per Share Data)*

	1985	1984	1983	1982	1981
Operations					
Sales:					
Commercial	$8893	$6026	$7618	$5829	$7620
US government	4743	4328	3511	3206	2168
Total	12636	10354	11129	9035	9788
Net earnings					
Per primary share	566	390	355	292	473
Percent of Sales	4.2%	3.8%	3.2%	3.2%	4.8%
Cash dividends paid	157	136	136	135	135
Per share	1.04	.93	.93	.93	.93
Other income	293	241	179	171	285
R and D expenses	409	506	429	691	844
G and A expenses	477	420	374	348	330
Additions to plant and equipment	551	337	223	331	545
Depreciation of plant and equipment	356	337	337	324	271
Salaries and wages	3442	3011	2825	2983	3020
Average employment	98700	86600	84600	95700	105300
Financial position at Dec. 31					
Total assets	9246	8485	7471	7593	6954
Working capital	2349	2130	1957	1800	1471
Long-term customer financing	514	541	539	339	390
Cash and short-term investments	3209	1595	1095	294	920
Total borrowings	34	299	383	473	344
Long-term debt	16	284	301	315	327
Long-term deferred taxes	326	322	743	666	499
Stockholder's equity	4364	3695	3033	2813	2655
Per share	2812	25.34	20.89	19.42	18.34
Common shares outstanding (000s)	155189	145837	145442	144244	144741
Firm backlog					
Commercial	18637	15949	12845	14913	15664
US Government	6087	5562	5198	4112	3725
Total	24724	21511	18043	19025	19389

through a network of representatives in Canada, Europe, and the United States.

Since de Havilland was a quasi-public firm, communication between top management and the organization was good. Every report made to the government was widely printed and distributed; good news and bad news were known by everyone in the firm. Many considered this one of the structural strengths of the organization.

In the past few years, due to operating losses, the firm had not been able to spend money on expanding its marketing efforts. This had obviously led to a further deterioration in the firm's revenues. Any money provided to de Havilland by the Canadian government that was not used for working capital went into research and development of new airplanes. This was understandable, since de Havilland's main strength was its engineers.

The company's plant facilities were badly in need of modernization. Some of the equipment was more than 30 years old. It would cost an estimated $100 million to $125 million to make the plant competitive with other producers.

In the past several years de Havilland had suffered from a problem with credibility. Much of this image problem stemmed from government indecision about what to do with the company and the government's periodic unwillingness to provide cash infusions for plant modernization improvements needed to keep it a viable producer. In the aircraft industry a lack of credibility of the manufacturer usually results in diminished sales and profits, as buyers do not want to risk placing an order with an insolvent supplier.

In 1980 de Havilland's sales started to drop. Sales bottomed out in 1983 when the company sold only 12 airplanes. Financial results and company employment plunged to their lowest levels since Canada bought the firm in 1974. After employing 5,415 people in 1981, staff levels fell to 2,864 employees in 1983. Net profits also fell during this time from C$6.3 million (US = $5.10 million; C$ = Canadian dollars) in 1981 to a loss of C$265 million (US $215 million) in 1982 and C$236 million (US = $182.2 million) in 1983 (see Exhibits 12, 13, and 14). The Canadian government pumped over $5 million US dollars into the company in 1984–1985 to keep it afloat as sales and working capital levels dropped. In the first three quarters of 1985, de Havilland had lost an additional $55 million. Due to the political controversy

these infusions of money caused and the conflicting attitudes of the Canadian administration, it was not believed the government would continue to invest at this level in the future. This was one of the reasons the government was looking for a buyer.

De Havilland's Product Line

De Havilland offered three types of twin turbo-prop, short-takeoff and landing (STOL) planes, all marketed as short-haul commuter aircraft:

1. DHC-6 Twin Otter. This small plane was a return to the bush/utility market that had made de Havilland initially successful. Seating 20 passengers, the plane was most attractive to those who flew very lightly traveled routes because of its low-maintenance and operating costs.

2. DHC-7 Dash 7. This plane was very specialized. Its four-engine, low-payload design offered commuters more comfort than other planes in the short-haul market. Seating 50 passengers, the Dash 7 was primarily marketed to those customers who flew high-volume routes. The increased seating capacity and high-technology features of the plane also made it more expensive to maintain and fly than other planes in the market.

3. DHC-8 Dash 8. This new de Havilland aircraft, designed to accommodate 32 to 36 passengers, was intermediate in size between the Twin Otter and the Dash 7. The Dash 8 was marketed to a similar market as the Dash 7 except that it offered more competitive maintenance and flying costs and appealed to those who flew moderately traveled routes. Few other aircraft in the market offered the size and cost advantages of the Dash 8.

In addition to these products, de Havilland was working on a "stretch" version of the DHC-8 that would seat as many people as the Dash 7 while operating at a much more competitive cost.

THE INDUSTRY AND COMPETITORS

The aircraft market was split into two main categories: the commercial market and the general aviation market, both of which were profoundly changing due to the deregulation of airlines and

Exhibit 12 *Revenues & Net Income of De Havilland*

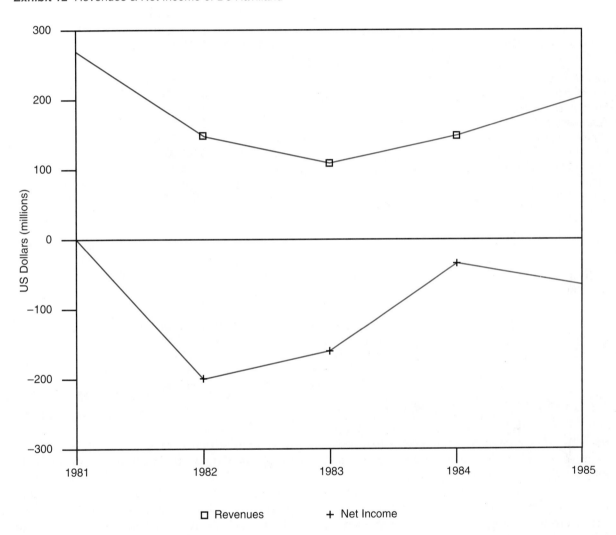

Exhibit 13 *De Havilland Aircraft of Canada, Ltd. Financial Statements**

	Fiscal year ended Dec. 31	
	1985	1984
	$000	
Revenue	$220,006	$157,550
Interest Income	$ 595	0
Deprec. & Amort., etc.	$ 3,331	$ 3,390
Interest Charges	0	$ 7,629
Income Tax Provision	$ (129)	$ (158)
Net Income from Operations	$ (69,337)	$ (31,183)
	$000	
Cash & Equivalent	$ 28,879	$ 16,334
Inventories	$174,044	$111,976
Fixed Assets (net)	$ 31,212	$ 34,567
Total Assets	$253,930	$174,949
Current Liabilities	$147,418	$116,689
Long-term Debt (net)	$ 13,496	$ 41,961
Shareholder's Equity	$ 93,004	$ 16,282
Working Capital	$ 75,300	$ 23,693
Cash Flow	$ (66,006)	$ (24,839)

*U.S. Dollars

Exhibit 14 *De Havilland Aircraft of Canada, Ltd. Revenues vs. Net Income**

Fiscal Year		Revenues	Net Income
85	_____	$220,005,000	($ 69,337,000)
84	_____	$157,549,000	($ 31,183,000)
83	_____	$ 93,980,000	($182,257,000)
82	_____	$145,506,000	($215,116,000)
81		$279,809,000	($ 5,105,000)

*In U.S. Dollars

the 1980–1982 recession. These events had forced many competitors in the industry to reevaluate their product lines and production processes.

Sales of all the industry players were multinational in scope. Foreign sales of American products were increasing in importance, representing approximately 60 percent of large commercial transport sales and 25 percent of general aviation sales. US exports of large transports represented approximately two-thirds of total sales in the rest of the world (see Exhibit 15).

In the previous 20 years, industry progress had been enormous due to rapid technology advances in aircraft design and productivity, US

government support for small airports, and the willingness of domestic aviation manufacturers to accept the risk of applying new technology in new products. This meant that market segment technological leaders, such as Boeing and de Havilland, had had the advantage when their research and development could be put to quick use.

THE PRESENT ENVIRONMENT OF REGIONAL TRANSPORT

Regional transport planes (commercial transport aircraft with less than 60-passenger capacity) had historically presented a bleak profit picture for US

Exhibit 15 *US Civil Aircraft Shipments and Exports, 1978–1985*

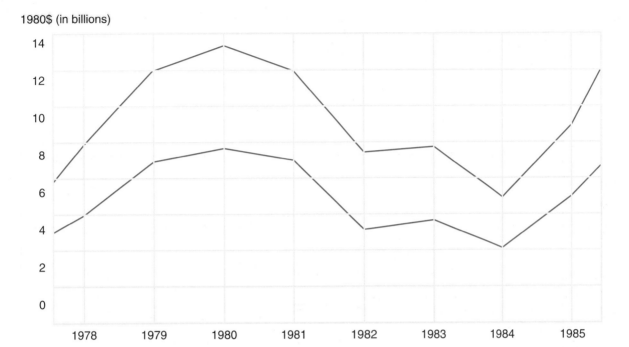

1980$ (in billions)

manufacturers. The financial, technological, and managerial requirements of producing these aircraft were less severe than those of producing of large transports; however, the investment needed was still beyond the capabilities of many US companies in this industry. Investment for the development of small commuter aircraft was normally only available within very large conglomerates or through government backing in a nation where the huge technological and start-up funds could be raised. In addition to Canada, England, France, Holland, and Sweden, smaller countries as well perceived this segment as a means of participating in air transport design and manufacture. Some of the programs in these countries were even being undertaken as international partnerships.

Regional airlines and air travel in general were projected to grow significantly over the coming years (see exhibits 16, 17, and 18). Growth in regional traffic was largely attributable to the deregulation of the airline industry, which had allowed more competition and expanded routes. Major airlines were shifting to smaller planes on regional routes to save on fuel and operating costs.

The airlines were also better able to match aircraft size to passenger demand with smaller commuter planes. In addition, the small planes allowed more frequent flights, improving scheduling ability.

The European commuter aircraft market was also expected to grow significantly in the near term. If deregulation occurred in the European airline markets, as some expected, the same forces that were at work in the United States could be expected to appear there.

For foreign manufacturers, the US market had the attraction of not having many strong US competitors. Most large aircraft producers, Boeing included, did not make small planes. Sales in the United States were essential to commuter/regional aircraft producers because the United States comprised over half of the potential market. Most foreign manufacturing competitors were backed by governments whose goals were full employment, technological development, healthy trade, and commercial gain. These competitors were likely to stay in selected market sectors even if large expenditures were required to sustain extended product development. Such actions could be unsound for a

Exhibit 16 *World Revenue Passenger Miles, All Services*

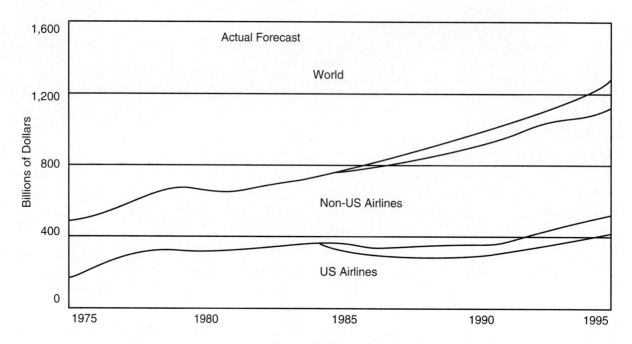

Note: Excludes USSR and non-ICAO nations, but includes Taiwan.
Shaded area = non-US Airlines.

Exhibit 17 *Projected Growth in Air Travel*

	Share of Traffic (percent)		
	1970	*1982*	*1995*
United States	55	40	36
Europe and Canada	29	31	31
Rest of the world	16	29	33
Total	100	100	100
Revenue—passenger miles (billions)	288	678	1,413

Source: Presentation before US Civil Aviation Manufacturing Industry Panel, July 7, 1983.

Exhibit 18 *US Large Regional Airlines: Financial Performance—1985 VS. 1984*

Airline	Operating Profit or Loss (000)		Net Income or Loss (000)	
	1985	1984	1985	1984
Airlift Int.	524	*	466	*
Air Midwest	(3237)	4383	(3677)	1625
Arrow	*	*	229914	*
Aspen	*	*	*	*
Atlantic S.E.	15218	10739	10325	5301
Big Sky	178	339	(132)	21
Buffalo	(1098)	(219)	25	385
Comair	4001	2707	4004	2836
Flamenco	46	19	*	*
Florida Express	5235	(1740)	4420	(1897)
Horizon	*	*	(9100)	293
Markair	10936	*	(2956)	*
Mesaba	1059	440	361	202
Midstate	(1388)	*	(701)	(1436)
Midwest Express	(3489)	(2139)	1768	(1133)
Presidential	(9831)	*	(9482)	*
Reeve	712	(1518)	445	(213)
Rich	1283	(609)	1064	(1102)
Rocky Mountain	*	*	(956)	(637)
Royale	3657	2353	1712	1307
Simmons	5393	2550	1950	1376
Skybus	(568)	*	(684)	*
Skystar	(2257)	*	(2236)	*
Skywest	4743	*	2474	*
South Pacific	376	2944	(82)	2529
Suburban	797	1526	*	*
Sunworld	2518	(560)	2464	(533)
Tower	2042	(973)	1607	(800)
Total	36,750	20,242	232,973	7,357

*No data available.

private manufacturing company, but made long-term economic sense for a country.

FINANCIAL PERFORMANCE OF THE INDUSTRY

The financial record of commercial aircraft manufacturing was below the average manufacturing performance in the United States (Exhibit 19). The industry was subject to major swings in sales, employment, and earnings due to its cyclical nature. This made building and maintaining competitive development, design, and production teams very difficult.

In 1985, while the commuter aircraft segment was growing, deliveries of general aviation aircraft dropped in aggregate to an estimated 2,050 units, down from 2,438 units in 1984. This was the lowest level of shipments ever recorded by the General Aviation Manufacturers Association.

THE INTERNATIONAL POLITICS OF AIRCRAFT SALES

In the previous 10 years there had been an increasing trend of internationalization among aerospace companies, including domestic airframe producers.

Access to foreign markets and capital had been a prime motivation for internationalization in the industry. Since foreign airlines were, for the most part, state owned, selection of aircraft for purchase was often subject to political review. Governments could demand certain arrangements as a part of the transaction. Consequently, a strong foreign marketing advantage could be achieved by forming foreign partnerships.

Internationalization of aircraft manufacturing had a number of other important implications. One was the evolution of a new skill in managing transnational technological development among partner firms. Multinational development programs in any industry had previously been considered very poor risks. This attitude was slowly changing, but domestic manufacturers would need to demonstrate sensitivity to the positions and attitudes of their potential partners.

MANAGING IN THE NEW ENVIRONMENT

The top managers of aircraft manufacturing companies faced an array of threatening changes, including weakened domestic customers, increased foreign competition, pressure to internationalize manufacturing, and escalating financial

---

Exhibit 19 *Aerospace Industry Earnings Compared with Earnings of All Manufacturing Industries, 1970–1985*

	Profits after Taxes as Percent of Sales	
Year	Aerospace Industry	All Manufacturing
1970	2.0	4.0
1971	1.8	4.1
1972	2.4	4.4
1973	2.9	4.7
1974	2.9	5.5
1975	3.0	4.6
1976	3.4	5.4
1977	4.2	5.3
1978	4.4	5.4
1979	5.1	5.7
1980	4.3	4.9
1981	4.4	4.7
1982	3.2	3.5
1983	3.5	4.1
1984	4.1	4.6
1985 (6 months)	4.0	4.1

risks. It is crucial to manage technological innovation to retain product leadership in the face of escalating costs for developing new technology and growing uncertainty over market requirements and customer liability. Also, managers needed to recognize that they must move from a position of global dominance to one of partnership with foreign competition.

The deteriorating balance sheets and uncertain fate of domestic airlines were leading to increasing caution by those who provided financial support for aircraft production. The United States would no longer be able to maintain leadership in every design and production technology. Many governments in developed and developing countries had identified their civil aircraft sectors for special support.

The growing importance of international markets increased the likelihood that control of access to markets would be used as a lever against domestic producers. Since the US manufacturers did not start from a position of global dominance in the market for smaller transport aircrafts, they would have to be selective in their decisions to enter foreign markets or to join with foreign competition.

DE HAVILLAND'S DIRECT COMPETITION

De Havilland competed in a portion of the broad general aviation market, which included commuter, business, utility, and specialty aircraft of various sizes. De Havilland specialized in the commuter/regional market, specifically in twin turboprop aircraft with fewer than 60 seats. These planes were primarily used by regional airlines or by major airlines as shuttles from smaller cities to the airline's hub.

As mentioned earlier, this segment of the aircraft manufacturing industry was characterized by multinational sellers, which were usually subsidiaries of larger corporations or were partially government owned. The trend in recent years had been for the larger commuter aircraft producers to acquire small independent manufacturers in the same way that large national airlines were buying small regional carriers. This had made competition intense as the small aircraft builders had been given access to large amounts of capital from their parent companies.

The industry's main competitors are listed in Exhibit 20, along with their respective product models, 1984 deliveries, and 1985 orders as of

December 1. All of these competitors sold internationally, and no one manufacturer had a dominant position in the industry. The number of planes in service built by each competitor is given in Exhibit 21.

Though there was no true leader in the turboprop industry, there were "favorite" planes from year to year. In 1985, the hardest-to-get products were the British Aerospace Jetstream 31s, Embraer Brasilias, Fairchild Metro IIIs, Saab-Fairchild SF-340s, and de Havilland Dash 8s.

The Four Major Competitors

British Aerospace competed in this segment primarily with its 19-seat Jetstream 31. At that time, the company had a backlog of orders which equaled a year of production. It was gradually trying to increase production capacity to decrease delivery time to its customers. British Aerospace also offered slightly larger planes (up to 50 passengers) in its 146 and Super 748 lines. It was also developing a 64-passenger craft to be delivered in late 1986.

Embraer Aircraft, a Brazilian company, had recently unveiled a new airplane, the EMB-120 Brasilia, to replace its very successful Bandeirante. This new 30-seat craft was becoming popular with US regional airlines and was also being aimed to the corporate buyer as a private business propjet. The company expected total demand of 250 to 300 planes before the design became obsolescent.

Fairchild Industries was one of the strongest competitors in the turboprop market. There were more Metros in service, by far, than representative from any other turboprop aircraft line. Orders for the 19-seat Metro III in 1985 were almost twice those received in 1984. This increase had prompted Fairchild to increase production to avoid lengthy customer delays. In 1985 its backlog stood at nearly a year's worth of production.

Saab-Fairchild, a partnership between two companies that was planned to be disbanded in early 1986, had produced one of the most popular planes. The SF-340, which Saab had announced that they alone would continue to make after the partnership was dissolved, was the first new generation 30- to 50-passenger aircraft to be put into service. These new planes had pressurized cabins, state-of-the-art interiors, and advanced engine designs. The plane had had a rough introduction, however, as several inflight

Exhibit 20 *Competitors in Commuter/Regional Aircraft Manufacturing*

Manufacturer	Parent Company	Models	1984 Deliveries	1985 Orders
British Aerospace	NA	146	10	20
		Super 748	7	10
		Jetstream 31	14	30
Beech Aircraft	Raytheon	C99	12	0
		1900	30	20
Fairchild	NA	Metro III	29	46
Fokker	NA	F27	11	17
		F28	16	16
		Fokker 50	. . .	38
		Fokker 100	. . .	30
Shorts Brothers	NA	330	4	1
		360	29	25
Embraer	NA	Bandeirante	29	. . .
		EMB-120	. . .	20
de Havilland	NA	Twin Otter	11	14
		Dash 7	10	5
		Dash 8	2	30
Saab-Fairchild	Partnership	SF-340	6	28
Dornier	NA	228	5	21
Cessna	General Dynamics	402	12	12
Piper	Lear Siegler	T-1020	8	. . .
		T-1040	6	. . .
Aerospatiale	NA	ATR 42	. . .	10
Aeritalia	NA	ATR 72	. . .	10
Casa	NA	C-212	. . .	8

Exhibit 21 *Turboprops in Use—Selected Major Manufacturers, 1985*

Model	Manufacturer	Number
Metro	Fairchild	204
F27	Fokker	163
DHC-6	de Havilland	137
Bandeirante	Embraer	115
Beech 99	Beech	102
Shorts 330	Shorts Brothers	65
Shorts 360	Shorts Brothers	61
Jetstream 31	British Aero	56
DHC-7	de Havilland	45
Beech 1900	Beech	35
Caravan	Cessna	30
SF-340	Saab-Fairchild	29
DHC-8	de Havilland	16

engine shutdowns forced the grounding of the aircraft in fall 1984. Production of this plane had been slower than the company desired because of modifications needed to the engine and the delayed set-up of the assembly line in Sweden. Saab hoped to achieve a 50-per-year production rate by the end of 1987. It was also planning to release a stretch 44-seat version of the plane in 1987.

The other competitors listed in Exhibit 20 had models that generally followed one of the above designs. None of the planes was particularly better than any other. The key to success, many industry analysts recognized, was to deliver the aircraft to the customer as soon after the order was received as possible. To appease customers, some manufacturers had been giving price concessions to buyers who were willing to be placed further back on the waiting list.

The Near-term Competitive Environment

The near future would be a telling one for the small competitors, but even yearly losses did not mean a manufacturer would drop out of the market because many foreign firms were government subsidized. The recent turmoil in the US airline industry, however, should have made or broken many of the small US aircraft producers. The 30- to 50-passenger turboprop market was considered too small to support all the players.

One trend that seemed to be emerging was the "package deal" in which a large aircraft manufacturer with a small aircraft division would sell an airline a package consisting of one or more large jets and several smaller planes. This was mainly seen in the European market, as no US manufacturers were in the position to offer this kind of service.

Government subsidization gave foreign firms a distinct advantage in the market. In addition to providing infusions of equity, governments often helped firms finance their buyers' purchases. This allowed foreign manufacturers to offer very attractive interest rates. Governments were motivated to provide this assistance because of technological benefits derived from the aerospace industry and the jobs provided in the factories.

THE DECISION

At Boeing's 1985 board meeting, CEO T. A. Wilson called de Havilland an odd acquisition target. He stated this with good reason. Financially, the company was a mess. On sales of $185 million US dol-

lars (C$250 million), de Havilland was expected to lose more than $55 million US dollars, following a loss of $30 million US dollars in 1984 and earlier losses of $210 million US dollars in 1983 and $215 million US dollars in 1982. The company had been kept alive by $585 million US dollars in equity injections from the Canadian government in the previous four years.

While keeping de Havilland's financial problems in mind, Boeing's board needed to consider the synergies that the merger between the two firms might create. Boeing was developing a new type of fan engine for use on its smaller planes. These types of engines required engineers familiar with the use of propellers, and de Havilland's engineers were better with this type of work than were Boeing's. In addition, Boeing's engineers acknowledged that the Dash 8 was a good design and that de Havilland's 350 engineers achieved technically what it would have taken many more Boeing engineers to do.

Furthermore, Boeing wanted to be able to offer a full line of aircraft. The commuter airlines had become more numerous and more important since deregulation.

Wilson reminded the board it would be dealing with a state-owned company in de Havilland and that government objectives differed from those of private industry. The Canadian government wanted assurance that the workers from Seattle wouldn't replace Canadian engineers and that plant operations would remain in their present location. The state also wanted de Havilland to remain a viable company, not just a tax write-off for its acquisitor. In addition, the government insisted that Canadian technology not be transferred to foreign nations.

Boeing officials were concerned with the legal liability associated with de Havilland planes. If Boeing made the acquisition, it would be liable for the thousands of de Havilland planes already flying. Also, Boeing officials estimated that high modernization costs would be needed to sustain de Havilland.

Boeing knew that it needed to be on good terms with foreign governments if it were to sell its present line of aircraft outside the United States. For example, when Boeing was trying to sell its aircraft to England's air force, it made an agreement with the English government to use Rolls Royce engines. This guaranteed a large number of new English jobs, and the government decided to buy the planes from Boeing. Similarly, most countries tried to save for its own factories, part of the work associated with an order from its airlines or its air force.

With all of these issues in mind, Boeing and the Canadian government had worked out an offer whereby Boeing would pay C$155 million for de Havilland. In addition, the Canadians had offered an incentive: for each new order Boeing placed with manufacturers located in Canada, the government would trim C$1 million from the purchase price to a minimum of C$90 million. Boeing's board would now have to decide what to do.

CITICORP–BRITISH NATIONAL LIFE ASSURANCE

Per V. Jenster
International Institute for Management Development
Lausanne, Switzerland
John M. Gwin
William K. Carter
University of Virginia

Ira Rimerman, group executive, Consumer Services Group, International, Citicorp, was in his third-floor office at Citicorp's headquarters in New York City on January 16, 1986 when he received notice from the board of Citicorp that his major expenditure proposal (MEP) to acquire the British National Life Assurance Company, Ltd. (BNLA) in England had been approved. For a total investment of $33.3 million, Citicorp was now in the life underwriting business.[1]

Although pleased with the board's approval, there were several issues on Rimerman's mind as he thought back over the past few months when his staff analyzed and developed suggestions for a business strategy for BNLA, including key policies, tactics, and organizational changes.

CITICORP'S HISTORY

Citicorp's corporate history spanned 175 years, from its early inception as a small commercial bank in New York City in 1812 through its growth into one of the world's largest financial services intermediaries. A recurring historical theme seemed to be the firm's ability to correctly identify the developing trends in the marketplace and to devise appropriate strategies for taking advantage of them.

The firm first emerged as a significant bank in the latter part of the nineteenth century by responding successfully to the transition of the United States from an agricultural to an industrial economy. Since the mid-1960s, the firm had transcended the corporate treasurer and the metropolitan New Yorker as its sole funding sources and found ways to attract the more than $1.5 trillion consumer savings market in the United States.

During the 1960s and 1970s, Citicorp completed two separate but integral strategic efforts that revolutionized the company and influenced the whole financial service industry. First, in 1967, the firm formed a bank holding company, which permitted it to broaden its geographic and product bases. Second, in the early 1970s, it redefined its business from a US commercial bank with branches abroad to a global financial services enterprise with the United States as its home base. By 1980, the firm had further broadened its scope by defining its business as that of providing services and information to solve financial needs. Exhibits 1 and 2 provide a summary of the firm's financial profile.

CITICORP'S STRATEGY

The firm's strategic plan called for three separate kinds of world-class banks, all of which could leverage off an unrivaled global network. By the mid-1980s, the Investment Bank, also known as the Capital Markets Group, enabled the firm to fully

---

[1]All financial information related to BNLA has been changed for proprietary reasons.

Exhibit 1 *Citicorp and Subsidiaries: Revenues Earned and Rates of Return Achieved*

	Revenues (billions)	ROA[a]	ROE[b]
1981	$4.0	.46%	13%
1982	$5.1	.59%	16%
1983	$5.8	.67%	16%
1984	$6.6	.62%	15%
1985	$8.5	.62%	15%

Source: 1985 Annual Report of Citicorp.
[a]ROE = (net income – preferred dividends) / average common equity;
[b]ROA = net income / average total assets.

Exhibit 2A *Consolidated Balance Sheet: Citicorp and Subsidiaries (Billions of Dollars)*

	December 31, 1985	December 31, 1984
Assets		
Cash, deposits with banks, and securities	$ 40	$ 31
Commercial loans	$ 58	$ 59
Consumer loans	55	43
Lease financing	3	2
Allowance for credit losses	1	1
Net	$115	$103
Premises and other assets	18	17
Total	$173	$151
Liabilities		
Deposits	$105	$ 90
Borrowings and other liabilities	42	39
Long-term debt	16	13
Capital notes and redeemable preferred	2	2
	$165	$144
Stockholders' Equity		
Preferred stock	1	1
Common stock	1	1
Additional paid-in capital	1	1
Retained earnings	5	4
	$8	$7
Total	$173	$151

Source: 1985 Annual Report of Citicorp.

Exhibit 2B *Consolidated Income Statement: Citicorp and Subsidiaries (Billions of Dollars, Except per Share Amounts)*

	1985	1984	1983
Interest revenue	$19.5	$18.2	$15.2
Less: Interest expense	14.0	13.9	11.2
Provision for credit losses	1.3	.6	.5
Net	$ 4.2	$ 3.7	$ 3.5
Other revenues	3.0	2.3	1.8
	$ 7.2	$ 6.0	$ 5.3
Operating expenses	5.5	4.5	3.7
Income before income taxes	$ 1.7	$ 1.5	$ 1.6
Income taxes	.7	.6	.7
Net income	$ 1	$ .9	$ .9
Earnings per share:			
Common and equivalent	$7.12	$6.45	$6.48
Fully diluted	7.11	6.36	6.15

Source: 1985 Annual Report of Citicorp.

Exhibit 2C *Consolidated Balance Sheet: Citibank and Subsidiaries (Billions of Dollars)*

	December 13, 1985	December 31, 1984
Assets		
Cash, deposits with banks, and securities	$ 40	$ 28
Loans and lease financing, net	75	69
Premises and other assets	16	15
Total	$131	$112
Liabilities		
Deposits	$ 92	$ 78
Borrowings and other liabilities	29	26
Long-term debt	3	2
Stockholders' Equity		
Capital stock	1	1
Additional paid-in capital	1	1
Retained earnings	5	4
Total	$131	$112

Source: 1985 Annual Report of Citicorp.

intermediate the capital flows of the world, with over $6 billion in transactions in the swap market. The Institutional Bank was the principal supplier of financial service mechanisms to corporations and governments worldwide. Finally, the Individual Bank served the individual consumer on a worldwide basis.

Walter B. Wriston, former chairman of Citicorp/Citibank, explained the firm's strategy:

> *Over time, it seemed to us, the institution without access to the consumer would slowly become an institution without adequate funding. In addition, consumer-led economic recoveries are becoming more the rule than the exception and we looked for ways to participate. For all of these reasons, you have often heard about this consumer transition and the identification of the consumer as a key to our strategy in the middle '70s. It was usually described as risky but there are also risks in doing nothing.[2]*

The holding company structure was used to overcome the geographic constraints of the domestic businesses. It also allowed for a few acquisitions and for the creation of de novo units to build a global network which, among other things, featured a unique competitive franchise for bank cards within the Individual Bank. Wriston also remarked:

> *It costs about $150 per year to service an individual through a branch system. That number plummets to $20 if we use the credit card as our primary delivery vehicle. In short, through fees and merchant discounts, the card as a stand-alone product is a profitable endeavor. By the 1990s, it may well become the core delivery mechanism when augmented by automatic teller machines and home banking. . . . We envision a world of 35 million Citicorp customers producing earnings of $30 per customer. . . . We had big plans for this group when it started and we can now see a time by which it will become a billion dollar business.*

The 1980s also dictated a new philosophy which differed from traditional bank practice and from the media's bias for focusing on size as a measure of success. Commercial asset growth on the books of Citicorp was discouraged. In fact, management stretched its imagination to take assets off the firm's books, not to put them on. In 1983, more than $2 billion in loans generated in the United States by the Institutional Bank was sold to others by the Investment Bank. That number was expected to reach $20 billion by 1989. Wriston further explained:

> *Our stockholders benefit, since we keep part of the spread while someone else keeps the assets (and the risk). But in order to make this a viable business, you must have both the asset generating capability and the distribution capability nationwide and worldwide.*

The worldwide orientation was further encouraged as cross-border lending started to slow down. Citicorp predicted that individual countries would be forced to develop their own indigenous capital markets. Thus, there was an opportunity to develop a "multidomestic" strategy that would enable Citicorp to offer full financial services in 60–80 countries before 1990.

The Five I's

In the early 1980s, Citicorp added two more "I's" to the strategic thrust which had initially included development of the Investment Bank, the Individual Bank, and the Institutional Bank. The two embryonic "I's" were the Information and Insurance businesses. According to Wriston:

> *We want to be in the information business simply because we are in the information business. Information about money has become almost as important as money itself. As bankers, we are familiar with the time value of money. As investors, we must think of the time value of information. The cental core of any decision making process is information. The fact that you know something relevant before, or more clearly than, your competitors may lead you to act sooner, to your advantage. Herein lies the problem, determining what is relevant. Hence, the packaging of information and its distribution will be critical. . . . We eventually intend to become a main competitor, as a preeminent distributor of financial database services worldwide. This is only possible*

---

[2]The Citi of Tomorrow: Today, Walter B. Wriston's address to the Bank and Financial Analysts Association, New York, March 7, 1984.

with a truly global system, one through which information is distributed with electrons rather than the mail.[3]

The rationale for entering the insurance business was simple: insurance services accounted for fully 40% of all financial services in 1985. Citicorp would therefore not be a truly effective financial services enterprise without offering these products. Insurance was also a natural adjunct to the consumer business, considering the outmoded and expensive agency method of distribution that dominated the industry. Moreover, the firm was already a major factor in credit insurance. For example, one-third of its second-mortgage customers bought credit life insurance.

The Banking Holding Company Act of 1956, and specifically Regulation Y, Section 4(c)-8 for the Board of Governors of the Federal Reserve System, prohibited banks from engaging in life insurance underwriting (with certain exceptions). Thus, the firm's insurance strategy was primarily aimed at an overseas expansion. This expansion was made possible by the Federal Reserve Board's ruling, requested by Citicorp, which enabled the firm to establish a fully competitive insurance operation in the United Kingdom (UK). The board concluded:

> *The general activity of underwriting life insurance in the United Kingdom can be considered usual in connection with banking or other financial operations in the United Kingdom.*

This shift in the board's attitude enabled Citicorp to consider expansion into insurance, to identify UK as a potential country in which to do so, and ultimately to pursue BNLA for acquisition.

Citicorp's goals for the five I's as of 1986 can be summarized as follows[4]:

Institutional

- Trim work force from 20,000 to 17,000.
- Pull back from middle markets overseas.
- Push investment banking products more.
- Clean up loan portfolio; reduce write-offs.

Investment

- Build credible corporate finance group, especially in mergers and acquisitions.

- Hold on to investment banking talent.
- Wire 90 trading rooms around the globe.
- Improve coordination between London, Tokyo, and New York.

Individual

- Continue to grow fast in retail banking.
- Make all acquired S&Ls profitable.
- Push international consumer business.

Information

- Leave Quotron alone to calm customers.
- Develop new products.

Insurance

- Push for easing limits on banks.
- Grow overseas.
- Cross-sell more insurance products through customer base.

The 1985 sector performance is displayed in Exhibit 3.

CITICORP'S STRUCTURE AND OBJECTIVES

The Investment Bank, the Institutional Bank, and the Individual Bank were each organized into a sector and headed by a sector executive. Activities related to insurance and information were under the auspices of group executives within the three sectors, until such time as they justified the creation of their own sectors.

Each of the three sectors was composed of several groups, divisions, and business families headed by a group executive, with business managers reporting to him or her. The organization of the Individual Bank, which is of particular interest in this case, was somewhat different from the others. As dictated in John S. Reed's (chairman of Citicorp since 1985) memorandum of March 9, 1976 (internally known as the "Memo from the Beach"), the business manager was responsible for the day-to-day operation, whereas a division executive's responsibility was strategic in nature.

This meant that a branch manager in, say Hong Kong, would report to an area manager, then

---

[3]Consistent with these plans, Citicorp acquired Quotron, a firm specializing in informational databases.

[4]*Source*: *Citicorp* and *Business Week*, December 8, 1986.

Exhibit 3 *Sector Performance: Citicorp and Subsidiaries (Millions of Dollars)*

	1985	1984	% change
Individual Bank			
Net revenue	$4,120	$3,107	33
Operating expenses	3,614	2,735	32
Other income and expense	102	(12)	NA
Income before taxes	608	360	69
Net income	$ 340	$ 222	53
ROA	.61%	.51%	
ROE	15.3 %	12.7 %	
Institutional Bank			
Net revenue	$2,168	$2,068	5
Operating expenses	1,500	1,275	18
Income before taxes	668	793	(16)
Net income	$ 392	$ 454	(14)
ROA	.54%	.64%	
ROE	13.6 %	15.9 %	
Investment Bank			
Net revenue	$1,589	$1,241	28
Operating expenses	803	587	37
Income before taxes	786	654	20
Net income	$ 425	$ 343	24
ROA	1.34%	1.33%	
ROE	33.5 %	33.2 %	
Unallocated			
(Certain corporate-level items which are not allocated among sectors)			
Revenue	$ 28	$ (79)	NA
Operating expenses	148	116	28
Additional provision for credit losses	226	68	132
Income before taxes	(346)	(263)	(32)
Net income	(159)	(129)	(23)

Source: 1985 Annual Report of Citicorp.

a country manager, a division manager, a group executive, a vice chairman or sector executive, and then the chairman. In effect, the flat structure placed only three layers of management between the most junior branch manager and the Policy Committee (thirty senior executives) of Citicorp.

In January 1986 Reed issued a set of guidelines developed by the Policy Committee, which included Citicorp's objectives for the next ten years (Exhibit 4) and its values (Exhibit 5).

The International Opportunity

In the 1985 Annual Report, the board stated:

> We recognize that, ultimately, our success will be directly attributable to our ability to offer our consumers worldwide preeminent service for each of their relationships with us. Our view is that by pursuing service excellence across all of our efforts, we enhance our standing with our customers and thereby the likelihood that they will choose us for a growing share of their financial needs.[5]

Internationally, Citicorp expanded its presence in a number of markets during 1985, while maintaining returns well in excess of corporate standards. In that year, Citicorp completed significant acquisitions in Italy (Banca Centro Sud), Belgium (Banque Sud Belge), and Chile (Corporacion Financiera Atlas), as well as consumer businesses in Colombia, Guam, and India. Richard S. Braddock, sector executive of the Individual Bank and director of Citicorp and Citibank, explained:

> We view our opportunities in the international marketplace as substantial, not only because our share tends to be relatively small in most places, but also because we have the opportunity to apply lessons learned from market to market and to expand attractive and proven product packages. . . .[6]

The Consumer Service Group, International (CSGI)

The Consumer Service Group, International, within the Individual Bank, was organized in separate divisions: the Asia-Pacific division had its headquarters in Tokyo; Europe-Middle East-Africa

(EMEA) division, in London; the Western division, in Rio de Janeiro; Payment Products Division (Diners Club), in Chicago; and Systems Division, in New York. The group employed 26,000 people in 70 businesses located in 40 countries.

John Liu, senior human resource officer, Consumer Services Group, International, summarized how Citicorp's culture was reflected by the group:

> We want to be part of the largest low-cost provider of financial service in the world. As such we don't focus only on banks such as Chase Manhattan. Rather, we look also at Sears, AMEX, and others who provide financial services. This is the stretch we hold in front of us.
>
> In order to help achieve this, we have to find new ways of doing things. Taking insurance as an example, Citicorp practices its decentralized operational mode, sometimes referred to as the "thousand flowers" approach.
>
> In insurance, to use a metaphor, we want to have a thousand flowers bloom. Over time, we'll put the flowers together in a bouquet, and if we don't like the shape of it, we'll take this or that flower away. However, today we just started our picking and that is why you'll find insurance activities in the Institutional Bank (commercial insurance), the Investment Bank (brokerage insurance activities), and with us in the Individual Bank (life underwriting, mortgage insurance, etc.). It's all emerging slowly out of our philosophy, and the BNLA acquisition is the first major life underwriting acquisition we have ever had.
>
> As part of this stretch, the corporation applies certain hurdle rates to guide this vision. We have a stated hurdle rate, internally, such as a ROE of no less than 20%. Additionally, we also have a ROA hurdle rate of 90 basis points. In our group, we use our own internal hurdle rates as a way of managing our businesses. One such hurdle rate which comes to mind is to target a ratio of 1.5 between consumer net revenue and delivery expenses.
>
> Within the Group, we want to more than double our earnings over the next five years. We want to do this partly through acquisitions, of which we must have done at least 10 over the past three years and added more than

---

[5]Citicorp *1985 Annual Report*, p. 11.
[6]Ibid.

Exhibit 4 *Citicorp Objectives*

Citicorp's objective is to continue to build the world's leading financial services organization by creating value for our stockholders, customers, staff members, and the communities where we live and work. Creation of value is dependent on building an internal environment based on integrity, innovation, teamwork, and a commitment to unquestioned financial strength.

Value for the Shareholder

- 12% to 18% compound growth in earnings per share
- Improving return on equity to 17%/18% (maintaining the internal hurdle at 20%)
- A strong balance sheet including a 10% capital position and a AA+ credit rating
- Performance profile (earnings, market position, returns) improving within the top 30 companies in the world
- Improving market position for our businesses, defined by explicit market share reporting
- Well-diversified geographic and business earnings, assets, and liabilities

Value for Our Customer

Maintain and build our two customer sets, institutional and individual, through customer service excellence, professionalism, product innovation, and the energy of our response to customer needs. Regularly monitor progress through external and internal surveys.

Value for Our Staff

Maintain an open, challenging, rewarding, and healthy working environment characterized by excellence and fairness in dealing with our employees. Business unit management is responsible for maintaining this working environment and will support and adhere to the People Management beliefs outlined [Exhibit 5]. We will regularly monitor such support and adherence with specific, measurable, goals.

Value for the Communities in Which We Operate

Management of each business unit and/or geographic location is part of the community within which we operate and has an obligation

- to contribute to community values.
- to participate in appropriate ways.
- to work to change the legal and regulatory environment to enhance our "opportunity space."
- to deal with our communities in an open, straightforward manner.

January 29, 1986

Exhibit 5 *Citicorp—Excellence in People Management: What We Believe*

The Basics

While people management is a part of our business, there are certain nonnegotiable assumptions we make about how we will deal with the people who make up Citicorp. These basics must take precedence in everything we do.

- Respect for individuals
- Treating people with dignity, openness, honesty, and fairness

Citicorp Values

In addition to our other specific Citicorp values (innovation, integrity, and service excellence), we have a set of values related to people management. These are things we feel strongly about and which are driven by the needs of our business.

- Meritocracy: Emphasizing excellence of performance, professionalism, and effectiveness as the determining factors for selection, retention, rewards, and advancement. Recognizing good performance wherever and whenever it occurs. Appropriately exiting consistent nonperformers.
- Independent initiative: Promoting personal freedom to act and allowing people to succeed and to learn from failure.
- Listening: Creating an environment where we really hear what people say. Working together so that people throughout the organization have an impact.
- Development: Consciously building experience and talent of our people with the goal of professional growth. Creating a balance between developmental experiences and current contribution.

Working Style

Our working styles will vary in different business situations and environments. The following describe the ways in which we approach people management, each applied as appropriate to individual business conditions.

- Teamwork: Building effective business driven partnerships within the organization. Achieving a balance between cooperation and entrepreneurial spirit.
- Integration: Helping new people and new businesses to effectively and appropriately become part of the Citicorp culture.

6,000 people. Although we still will make acquisitions, we clearly must slow down and develop these new businesses.

The acquisitions have not been hostile and for the most part have been either "hospitalized" or unprofitable businesses. This has given us certain advantages, but also created challenges when it comes to integrating a new business into our organization.[7]

The unique culture and reward system of CSGI is reflected in Exhibit 6, which summarizes the results of an organizational survey of its senior managers.

The Search for an Acquisition

Liu further explained how the BNLA acquisition came about:

About three years ago, we started a drive to get into insurance and encouraged our people in the UK, Australia, Germany, and Belgium to start to look into insurance. As you know, there are three ways you can get into a new business: You can (a) acquire, (b) start a de novo unit, or (c) do a joint venture.

In England, which was one of the largest and most profitable markets (relatively) for life insurance, we initially identified Excelsior Life Assurance[8] as a possibility in early 1984. As an insurance company of substantial size in the UK, the acquisition would immediately bring us into this market on a large scale. However, the more we analyzed the numbers, the more concerned we got. This was a significant investment, and we had little knowledge about life insurance. So when our joint-venture partner (a large US insurance company) withdrew, we reconsidered our options.

Then Citicorp's UK country manager and the European division manager of the United Kingdom sponsored (identified) BNLA as a potential candidate for our move into life underwriting insurance. After the identification of the candidate, an acquisition team was put together. The team consisted of people from across our UK businesses as well as outside consultants and were all selected for their specific skills as they related to this opportunity.

One of the important issues for us is now to decide how to integrate the business—

should we fully integrate, keep it at an arm's-length distance, or somewhere in between, and how should we do it. With this decision also comes the question of what type of person to put into the driver's seat.

THE UNITED KINGDOM

The UK economy is the sixth-largest in the world and is in transition, as is the US economy, from an industrial to a service orientation. By 1985, UK had the lowest level of legal/regulatory control for domestic and international financial activity of any developed country. However, UK regulation of life insurance underwriting, particularly with regard to reserves, was among the most stringent in the world. The government was considered politically stable, and the conservatives in power were committed to controlling inflation and government spending to provide a platform for economic growth. Even though 12% of the work force was unemployed, there was little social unrest.

The UK was expected to remain self-sufficient in oil for the remainder of the century. Inflation was expected to be controlled in the 5%–7% range, and there were expected to be no major changes in either the political system or the regulatory environment. Expected growth figures for UK GNP for 1986 and 1987 were 1.5% and 2.6%, respectively. Inflation was expected to be around 5.0% for the same two periods.

The UK Life Assurance Market

The UK life assurance market was considered large and growing. Growth in new premiums went from $1.9 billion in 1980 to $4.7 billion in 1983. During the same period average growth of premium income, rose from $7.8 billion to $13.2 billion, and total sums insured grew an average of 17% to $295 billion. There were 289 licensed underwriters in the UK. The relative size of the top twelve companies is presented in Exhibit 7.

Analyses showed that life assurance in the UK was seen as both a protection instrument and a consumer investment. The policies accumulated cash value and also yield dividends to policyholders.

---

[7]Interview with John Liu.

[8]The name has been changed to protect confidentiality.

Exhibit 6 *Summary of Organizational Surveys Conducted by the Case Writers*

	Low degree/extent				High degree/extent		
	1	2	3	4	5	6	7

1. Loyalty
2. Promotion from within
3. Extent managers are free to take independent actions
4. Degree to which goals are venturesome
5. Degree of accountability for individual managers
6. Encouragement of risk taking
7. Goals used as context
8. Lateral communications
9. Clear measures to judge managerial performance
10. Organization successful in developing talent from within
11. Extent to which conflicts are discussed openly
12. Encouragement to innovate
13. Clarity of goals
14. Overall communication
15. Opportunities for individual growth and development
16a. Formality of planning
16b. Completeness of planning
17. Clarity of organizational roles
18. Performance demands
19. Departmental understanding of goals
20a. Innovativeness in decision making
20b. Timeliness in decision making
21. Fit between compensation and performance
22. Encouragement of constructive criticism
23. Downward communication
24. Support received to carry out job responsibilities
25. Clear expectations
26. Degree of cooperation
27. Degree of coordination
28. Extent of clear plans
29. Matching of managerial talents and jobs
30. Organization's ability to cope with urgent matters
31. Extent to which middle managers' jobs urgent matters are defined in qualitative terms
32. Extent to which superiors depend on own judgment vs. quantitative performance data when evaluating subordinates
33. Extent to which managers obtain feedback from performance data vs. get it from superior
34. Extent of promotion from within
35. Use of merit pay
36. Use of stocks to award performance
37. Extent to which superior's judgment determines subordinates' raises vs. company policies
38. Use of status symbols and perquisites as rewards
39. Extent to which above are distributed according to strict company policies

Citicorp*_ _ _ _ _ _ _   BNLA*_____

*Questionnaires were completed by managers and outside observers. Items of the questionnaire are summarized and labeled because of proprietary reasons; values indicate average scores.

Exhibit 7 *Major Players in the Life Market*

Worldwide Premium Income

| Company | Classification | Ranking | *Premium Income* | | | | Size of Life Fund (END 1982; $ billion) |
			$ Million Value	% of Total	% Increase on 1982/1981	% Increase on 1981/1980	
Prudential	Stock	1	1656	13	12	16	9.4
Legal and General	Stock	2	775	6	15	10	6.6
Standard Life	Mutual	3	630	5	13	20	6.3
Norwich Union	Mutual	4	565	4	19	13	3.8
Hambro Life	Stock	5	464	4	20	32	2.1
Commercial Union	Stock	6	444	4	12	15	3.8
Eagle Star	Stock/sub	7	414	3	21	28	2.2
Abbey Life	Stock/sub	8	353	3	8	63	1.4
Sun Life	Stock	9	328	3	2	25	2.1
Scottish Amicable	Mutual	10	319	3	24	38	2.5
G.R.E.	Stock	11	318	3	14	27	2.8
Pearl	Stock	12	311	2	8	10	1.9
Subtotal			6577	53	13	21	44.9 (56%)
Others	13/48		4924	40	15	21	
Balance			823	7	5	15	36.1 (44%)
			12324	100	15	21	81.0

$1.20 = £1.

There were basically three types of underwriters in the marketplace: industrial, orthodox, and linked life.

The industrial companies offered small-value policies which were targeted at the lower socio-economic groups. The premiums were collected in person, usually monthly, by employed agents, who did little actual "selling." The policies carried high administrative overheads and were, therefore, relatively poor values for the customer. This sector of the market was dominated by Prudential, which wrote 65% of the new policies issued each year. This type of insurance had a vast customer base, with over 70 million policies in existence. At the same time, this type of policy had a declining market share, and smaller companies were retrenching because of overhead inefficiencies.

The orthodox life companies offered larger value policies which catered to the more affluent customer. This type of policy was distributed through "independent" professionals who usually had some other relationship with the customer. These independent agents could be insurance brokers, solicitors (attorneys), accountants, banks, or estate agents. It was fairly common in the UK for all of these groups to offer insurance as a part of their service portfolio to their clients. These independent agents typically offered policies from three to six different underwriters. The firms which offered orthodox policies had traditionally not "marketed" to their consumer base for fear of offending the professional intermediary. There were different "classes" of agents who covered specific market segments.

The linked-life policy was relatively new, and was introduced in the 1960s as an alternative to the orthodox life policy. It targeted the same consumer as the orthodox policy, but was sold normally by a commission-paid, self-employed sales force, much like insurance representatives in the United States. Policyholders of linked-life insurance did not "participate" in the profits of the underwriter through dividends, but their investments were placed in a number of funds (similar to mutual funds) managed by the underwriter. Thus, the linked-life policyholder took investment risk/return, and the underwriter provided a death guarantee. The range of products offered by the three types of underwriters is depicted in Exhibit 8.

Trends in the UK market indicated that the role of single-premium life assurance was expanding. This type policy was one in which a single payment was made to the underwriter at the beginning of the policy life, and no further premiums were due. Before the creation of the single-premium policy, most life policy premiums were paid yearly over the life of the policy. Logically, there was no single-premium industrial underwriting, given the socio-economic status of most policyholders. The target for the single-premium policies was the "banked homeowner"—a person who had a relationship with a bank and owned his or her home.

In addition to the expansion of the single-premium policy, there had been a decline in share of the industrial policy from 13% of total insurance in 1980 to 6% in 1983. The growth sectors of the market were linked life and personal pensions (which were similar to the Individual Retirement Account in the United States).

Premium income had generally become increasingly volatile, because single-premium income had grown from 12% of total premium income in 1980 to 22% in 1983. Since 1968, the growth segments for premium income were linked life, personal pensions, and mortgage endowment. In 1983, the government introduced Mortgage Interest Relief at Source (MIRAS), which caused mortgage repayments on insurance—linked mortgages to appear more competitive than conventional mortgages, and thus causing an increase in the mortgage endowment business. In March 1984, the British government abolished Life Assurance Premium Relief (LAPR).

In their attempt to expand their share of the market, traditional companies had begun moving into the linked-life segment. Major growth was expected in pension-related policies as the most efficient (from a tax perspective) savings medium. Allied Dunbar and Guardian Royal Exchange exemplified a movement to "full financial services."

For the future, the desire of the government to increase the "portability" of pensions could open a major new market. At this time, personal pensions were sold only by life assurance companies (by law). The removal of this restriction was under consideration and would bring new banks into the market. There was some concern that the government policy of "fiscal neutrality" between savings mediums could cause further amendment to tax laws, but this was not expected in the short term.

In the future marketplace, it would be possible for banks to exploit their customer bases and "sell" insurance instead of being passive pro-

Exhibit 8 *Product Range*

	Non-profit/ Participating	Relative Importance (low/medium/high)	Industrial	Traditional	Linked
Protection					
Whole life	NP	L	—	✓	—
	P	L	✓	✓	✓
Term	NP	H	✓	✓	✓
Permanent health	NP	M	—	✓	—
Savings					
Endowment	NP	L	—	✓	—
	P	H	✓	✓	✓
Pensions	NP	L	—	✓	—
	P	H	✓	✓	✓
Annuities	NP	M	—	✓	✓
Single-premium bonds	P	H	—	✓	✓
Group Schemes					
Pension	NA	H	—	✓	✓
(can include term and permanent health insurance)					

viders. Building Societies (very similar to US savings and loan institutions, and responsible for writing most home mortgages in the UK) did not currently have legislative permission to function as insurance brokers as did the banks. It was expected that the Societies would request that power in 1986–1987, which would bring more new players to the market. There would be an increase in the pensions business to reach the large self-employed group in the UK. Exhibit 9 offers a view of the current and future importance of key segments in the UK market.

In summary, the UK life underwriting market was the seventh largest in the world and was growing. Life assurance in the UK filled a dual role for the consumer—protection and savings/investment. The market was led by large and well-established players, but there were major market opportunities for other well-managed companies. The market was differentiated by distribution methods, and the long-term profit stream generated by most firms led to high investor confidence and high share prices. UK premium income in 1982 totaled $28 billion, of which $12 billion was in life assurance underwriting. The market was predominantly UK-owned, as were the major players, though a company did not necessarily need to be a general insurance firm to compete successfully in either market. Each market involved different legislative bases, different distri-

bution channels, and different skills. UK firms were significant in world markets, particularly non-life, where they received over 50% of the premium income.

The UK Financial Services Market

There were five major categories of financial services in the UK: transaction accounts, savings, shelter (home) financing, lending, and protection. Exhibit 10 is a chart of the major players and other entrants in these markets. The total savings market had grown from $124 billion in 1980 to $193.6 billion in 1983. The relative share figures for the major institutions in the savings market are shown in Exhibit 11. Shelter finance had grown from $62.8 billion to $108.8 billion in the same period. A synopsis of the growth and change in the unsecured loan market is shown in Exhibit 12.

Banks were leading the expansion into the related areas of mortgage financing, estate agency (trust), stock brokering, and life assurance underwriting. Building Societies now offered checkbook access to savings and ATM networks. Legislation intended to equalize competitive roles in the market had been passed. Technological advancements were expected at this point, but were not yet in place. The market would continue to change rapidly due to continuing deregulation and increasing technological sophistication. Traditional

Exhibit 9 *Intermediaries View of Key Market Segments*

	Currently Important % polled	Likely to Increase in Importance % polled
Self-employed	90	65
People on medium incomes	82	46
Owners/directors of small companies	80	57
People on high incomes	79	53
Young couples	78	57
Middle-aged couples	72	43
Women	68	51
People with free capital	66	39
Retired couples	46	38

Exhibit 10 *Elements of the Market*

	Major Players	Other Entrants
Transaction accounts	Clearing banks	. . .
Savings	Building societies Life assurance companies	Banks
Shelter finance	Building Society	Banks Finance houses
Lending	Banks	Finance houses In-store credit
Protection	Life assurance companies General insurance companies	. . .

Exhibit 11 *Market Movements—Savings ("50% of Deposits with Insurance Companies")*

	1980	1983
Insurance funds	45%	50%
Building Society	28%	28%
Banks	13%	7$\frac{1}{2}$%
National savings	7%	7%
Shares, etc.	7%	7$\frac{1}{2}$%
Total market	$124 billion	$193.6 billion

$1.20 = £1 for all years.
Compound growth 16% per annum (RPI 8.3% compound).
Insurance funds ($97 million at end 1983) are not accessible.

Exhibit 12 *Market Movements—Unsecured Loans ("Not Participating as a Principal, but Providing Cover to Repay")*

	1980	1983
Finance houses	34%	29%
Bank loans	29%	37%
Bank credit cards	18%	21%
In-store cards	11%	9%
Other	8%	4%
Total market	$7.1 billion	$13.2 billion

Compound growth 23%. An estimated 30% of bank and finance house loans are covered by life/disability insurance to cover repayments. New developments from 1982 on larger loans gives bullet repayments covered by endowment insurance. Statistics exclude "loan backs" from long-term savings under an insurance policy.

barriers were falling, and banks were leading the way into other sectors of the economy to satisfy consumer demand. Insurance was an integral part of the market and was supported by past and present government and fiscal policy.

Citicorp in the UK

The Consumer Services Group (UK) was dominated by Citibank Savings, a mature business operating in four specific markets:

1. Finance housing: indirect financing for autos and home improvement.
2. Mortgage banking: consumer mortgages through association with insurance firm partners.
3. Retail cards: private label card operation for London's High Street retailers, as well as the European Banking Centre, Travellers Checks, and Diners Club.
4. Consumer banking: cross-selling a portfolio of products to consumers, such as personal loans, checking (transaction) accounts, mortgages, and insurance.

Citibank Savings had 39 branches in the UK, 19 of which were recognized as direct branches within the consumer bank.

UK Life Assurance Consumers

UK life assurance consumers were underinsured relative to those of other developed nations. The total life coverage as a percent of yearly average wage as compared for seven industrialized nations was

UK	88%
France	147%
Sweden	148%
Australia	178%
US	183%
Canada	184%
Japan	325%

The product was seen by UK consumers as intangible and offering no present benefit. The contracts were viewed as a "mass of small print" and were inflexible once purchased. The purchase pattern was characterized as infrequent and having a high unit cost, and the consumer had a "low knowledge base" about the product. The benefits perceived were "peace of mind," a response to issues of social responsibility, and investment/tax avoidance. Seventy-four percent of UK households had life coverage, which included 45% of all adults (predominantly men). A chart of UK consumer behavior regarding purchase by product type is presented as Exhibit 13. The major reasons for purchase were "protection" and "house purchase." In general, no major alternatives were considered, and the decision to buy insurance coverage was a joint one in the family. The amount of coverage was generally based on affordability rather than need, and shopping among companies was minimal. Exhibit 14 characterizes the major segments of the market; required company attributes from the consumers' view are shown in Exhibit 15.

The life assurance market was not as mature as its size might indicate. Most consumers were underinsured, and over half the adult population had no coverage at all. There was a key role to be played for protection products (distinct from investment products). Linked-life companies

Exhibit 13 *UK Consumer Behavior*

Key Product Groups	Holding %	Recent Purchase %[a]	Future Purchase %[b]
Endowment mortgage	9	17	9
Mortgage protection	16	24	16
Protection cover	35	42	19
Endowment cover	42	63	39
Total (including multipurchase)	74	100	57

[a]Purchased in the past 12 months.
[b]Expected purchase in the next 12 months.

Exhibit 14 *Consumer "Types"*

	Medium	Purchase	Timing	Knowledge	Mind Set
Thinking young couple	Broker, direct to company	Buys	Regular	Sophisticated	Protection
Young family man	Agent, salesman	Sold	Spasmodic	Low—trusting	Protection/savings
Middle-aged man	Any	Sold	Spasmodic	Low—wants known company	Protection/savings
Self-employed	Salesman, broker	Sold	Spasmodic	Learns quickly, decision maker	Savings
Late arrivals	Direct (coupon response)	Indirectly sold	Once	Low	Protection (burial policy)

Exhibit 15 *Required Company Attributes: What to Look for in a Company (Excl. Industrial)*

	Spontaneous	Prompted
Well known	33%	60%
Good reputation	27%	51%
Good investment performance	23%	30%
Good salespeople	15%	56%
Long established	8%	43%

concentrated on "investment policies," and the benefits to the policyholder were neither fixed nor guaranteed by the company, but were invested in a separate range of funds (at the risk/return of the consumer). In this sense, linked-life firms worked very much like mutual fund companies in the US. Their sources of income were profits from insurance underwriting, a 5% bid/offer differential on investments in the funds and a 3/4% fund management fee. The products were sold through a direct sales force, which was normally paid only by commission.

In the UK market, 15% of adults had a linked-life policy (33% of adults with life assurance coverage). The policies were most popular in the under-55 age range, and in London and the southeast of England.

BRITISH NATIONAL LIFE ASSURANCE

History

British National Life Assurance was a spinoff company from the British National Insurance Society. It was created in 1982 by Sir William Baltimore[9] as a subsidiary of EXCO Corporation[9] (a large US company), when EXCO Corporation had decided to diversify into financial services. British National Insurance remained a property and casualty life underwriter, while BNLA became the life underwriting business of EXCO Corporation. The managing director of the new firm was Ernest Smith,[9] a true English gentleman and skilled manager. The sales director was Frank Jones,[9] a charismatic and skilled salesman with considerable experience in the insurance business.

EXCO Corporation took very little interest in the performance of BNLA and allowed Smith and Jones to manage the company as they saw fit. In essence, Jones controlled sales and marketing, and Smith controlled public relations and administration.

In the interim, Sir William Baltimore retired from EXCO Corporation. He subsequently became director of insurance development (on a consulting basis) for Citicorp's Consumer Services Group International EMEA Division, headquartered in London.

The consumers' view of the Citicorp/BNLA merger was that it offered wider financial services as a result, and a bank-owned insurance company was seen positively. Negative reaction to the fact that it was American-owned could be foreseen.

In January 1986, BNLA employed 392 people, 101 at its headquarters and 250 comprising the sales force from 22 branches. Each branch had a branch manager and an administrative assistant. A staff analysis is provided in Exhibit 16.

There were 47,600 policyholders and $305 million in life insurance in force. However, BNLA policy lapses and salesperson turnover were twice the industry average. The commission-only sales force was the major distribution method for BNLA products, and its productivity was some 75% below average. The sales force was inappropriately trained, and the commission structure resulted in low pay relative to the competition.

BNLA spent considerable sums of money training a sales force that was paid poorly relative to industry averages. Jones subscribed to the philosophy that a high-quality product would essentially sell itself, and that, therefore, high commissions were unnecessary. His view was that sales goals would be achieved, in the long run, as a result of high training levels and high-quality products. This became known in the organization as "Frank's philosophy." This philosophy also constrained promotional activities to direct selling only. The marketing department was, therefore, mostly engaged in arranging flashy conventions and gimmicks for the sales force.

Communication between top management and the organization was generally considered poor or nonexisting. Bad news, such as the lack of profits, the low sales-force performance, and information about the negative cash flows was never passed along to the management team. Although annual budgets were compiled, their content was never shared with departments. Conversely, no formal system existed for monthly reporting on departmental activities.

Smith believed that financial reporting should be kept to a minimum, although all requiried disclosures were always filed on time. The financial officer had a small minicomputer at his disposal. Moreover, the firm had taken steps to automate

---

[9]The name has been changed to protect confidentiality.

Exhibit 16 *British National Life Staff Analysis*

Department	January 1986
Actuarial	5
Administration	21
) Operations	
Office services)	10
Data processing	21
Finance	16
Investment	3
Personnel and training	–
Legal	1
Marketing	13
Sales	9
Credit insurance (from Nov 86)	–
Managing director	2
Subtotal	101
Branch managers	22
Branch administrators	19
Subtotal	142
Salaried sales force	NA
Total	142
Sales associates	250

the office environment at its headquarters by establishing a word processing pool.

Toward the end of 1984, EXCO Corporation decided that it was not going to make a go of BNLA (or of financial services generally) and put the company up for sale. The company knew that it was "on the block," and employee morale took a nose-dive. This enhanced the "rudderless" sense of the company, as performance became even less of an issue and "Frank's philosophy" became the guiding force in the firm. A culture-reward system profile of BNLA is shown in Exhibit 6.

Product/Market Posture

At the time of the Citicorp acquisition, BNLA was a linked-life firm that offered six basic products to the market:

1. Plan-for-Life—a highly flexible policy offering the consumer control over the content of his or her plan. The consumer decided what proportion of the premium to devote to savings or protection, and this could be changed as needs and circumstances warranted.

2. Plan-for-Capital—a regular savings plan with high investment content and minimum life coverage. It was ideal for someone who

wanted to save dynamically for eight to ten years. The proceeds were free from basic rate income tax (the "off the top" rate in the UK), from personal capital gains tax, and, after ten years, from higher-rate tax as well. This product was quite similar to the US Individual Retirement Account in its tax treatment. It differed in its small insurance cover.

3. Plan-for-Investment—a lump-sum plan to invest in the company's different funds. The capital invested was allocated a set number of units, depending on the current value of the fund. At any time, the plan had a value equivalent to the bid (sell) value of the price of units multiplied by the number of units held. This fund was very similar to the mutual funds offered through brokerage houses in the United States, except there were certain tax advantages not offered in US mutual funds.

4. Plan-for-Retirement—a retirement annuity policy which was suitable for the self-employed and those who had no private pension scheme, unit-linked but had outstanding tax advantages. This plan was similar to the US Keogh plans but was free of investment limits.

5. Plan-for-Executive—an individual pension plan suitable for senior members of a trading

company (brokerage house) who wished to add to their retirement benefits. This was a very specialized policy and was, once again, similar to the IRA, except that both the executive and his or her employer could contribute.

6. Plan-for-Pension Preservation—a specialized plan conforming to legislation passed in 1970 which allowed the transfer of vested pension funds from a previous employer into this plan without tax penalties.

In addition to these plans, a brokerage provided access to general insurance such as motor, house contents (homeowners), and building insurance (UK insurance companies are not permitted to act as insurance brokers). The BNLA product line was generally complete and well rounded and fulfilled the all-around needs of the consumer, from protection and investment to retirement planning.

A Financial Perspective

Accounting standards in the US required earnings on a life insurance policy to be recognized evenly over the years of premium payments. UK life insurance regulations, in contrast, required maintenance of prudent reserves that resulted in a new life assurance company's generating losses or very low profits during its early years. The function of the regulations was to severely restrict dividend payments and thereby protect policyholders. US accounting was significantly less conservative; when the balance sheet of a UK life firm was recast to comply with US accounting, the reported equity generally increased considerably.

Citicorp's customary financial goals and targets were designed for traditional banking businesses and did not lend themselves to evaluating an investment in a life insurance company. For that reason, Citicorp measured BNLA performance against a hurdle rate of 20% ROE on BNLA's recorded equity. Based on Citicorp's projections at the time of the acquisition, BNLA was expected to produce negative ROEs in 1985 and 1986 (see Exhibit 17) and to achieve the 20% hurdle rate for the first time in 1991. To comply with US accounting, BNLA's recorded equity at the time of the acquisition was adjusted as follows (in millions; please note that all BNLA financial data have been changed for proprietary reasons):

Book values of assets	$77.1	
Book amount of liabilities	66.9	
Book value of equity	$10.2	
Adjustments to comply with US accounting:		
Write-downs of assets	−3.5	
	$ 6.7	
Reduction of reserves	+6.5	
Adjusted equity	$13.2	
Portion acquired	100%	
Purchased equity	$13.2	
Purchase price	$13.7	$13.7
Goodwill	$0.5	
Additional capital infusion		19.6
Total investment[10]		$33.3

Exhibit 17 presents summary financial data on BNLA, including forecasts. For 1985, production of new life policies was 40% below forecast. Operating expenses were 50% higher than forecast and about 50% higher than the industry norms for a firm at this stage of development. This is fairly consistent with expense levels of previous years.

THE ACQUISITION

During the time when Citicorp UK was actively seeking an insurance company to acquire, Bob Selander was the new country manager of Citicorp's UK business. The acquisition of an insurance company was a part of the strategic plan he inherited from his predecessor. Sir William Baltimore had previously developed a list of potential acquisitions for consideration.

The first possibility which came to light was Excelsior Life Assurance—one of the largest life assurance firms in the UK. Sir William Baltimore had been a director of Excelsior Life Assurance and knew its inner workings very well. Upon his recommendations and with the joint-venture participation of another life assurance firm, an acquisition plan was put together. Late in the process, the joint-venture partner withdrew from the deal, and Citicorp decided that Excelsior Life Assurance was too large to acquire alone. The search was reopened.

---

[10]Investment was made in pounds sterling and was fully hedged via the forward market.

Exhibit 17A *BNLA Operating Forecast, Including Required Synergies—Restated According to US Accounting Principles (Millions)*

	1985	1986	1987	1988	1989
Premiums, net	$19.9	$47.0	$74.5	$109.9	$153.1
Reinsurance	0	2.7	8.5	12.5	15.0
Investment income	3.2	8.4	12.9	19.8	30.4
Total revenues	$23.1	$58.1	$95.9	$142.2	$198.5
Benefits paid	$ 3.1	$ 4.2	$ 7.2	$ 13.3	$ 34.1
Increase in reserves	12.0	40.5	66.4	96.4	119.3
Commissions	2.9	6.7	11.6	17.2	23.4
Operating expenses	5.5	7.8	7.4	9.1	12.5
Total expenses	$23.5	$59.2	$92.6	$136.0	$189.3
Income before taxes*	$ (0.4)	$ (1.1)	$ 3.3	$ 6.2	$ 9.2
Income taxes	0	0	0.8	2.8	4.3
Net income	$ (0.4)	$ (1.1)	$ 2.5	$ 3.4	$ 4.9
ROE					
On BNLA equity	(7%)	(5%)	7%	9%	12%
By Citicorp formulas	(30%)	(40%)	6%	11%	16%

Source: Citicorp MEP; the data have been altered for proprietary reasons.
*Reconciled with BNLA's stand-alone forecast, under UK accounting principles, as follows:

	1985	1986	1987	1988	1989
UK pretax income, without synergies	$(0.7)	$(3.9)	$(2.4)	$(0.6)	$1.5
Adjustment for US accounting rules		(0.1)	(0.1)	(0.1)	(0.1)
Impact of synergies		1.1	4.0	4.9	5.6
Impact of capital infusion	0.3	1.8	1.8	2.0	2.2
Income before taxes, as reported above	$(0.4)	$(1.1)	$ 3.3	$ 6.2	$9.2

Exhibit 17B *BNLA Forecast Balance Sheets, Including Required Synergies—Restated According to US Accounting Principles (Millions, as of December 31 of Each Year)*

	1985	1986	1987	1988	1989
Securities	$91	$126	$177	$257	$363
Reinsurance receivable	0	1	7	13	15
Other assets	4	8	21	38	59
Total assets	$95	$135	$205	$308	$436
Insurance reserves	$62	$103	$169	$266	$385
Other liabilities	1	1	3	6	10
Common stock	32	32	32	32	32
Retained earnings	0	(1)	1	4	10
Total	$95	$137	$205	$308	$437

Source: Citicorp MEP; the data have been altered for proprietary reasons.

Exhibit 17C *BNLA Historical Balance Sheets —According to UK Accounting Principles (Millions, as of December 31 of Each Year; All Balances Restated at an Exchange Rate of 1 Pound Sterling = $1.4)*

	1984	1983
Securities	$56	$38
Other assets	4	1
Total assets	$60	$39
Insurance reserves	$56	$31
Other liabilities	1	5
Capital	3	3
Total	$60	$39

Source: Citicorp MEP; the data have been altered for proprietary reasons.

Exhibit 17D *BNLA Historical Income Statements —According to UK Accounting Principles (Millions; All Balances Restated at an Exchange Rate of 1 Pound Sterling = $1.4)*

	1984	1983
Premiums, net	$31	$5
Investment income	4	3
Total revenues	$35	$8
Benefits paid	$3	$3
Increase in reserves	25	7
Commissions	1	1
Operating expenses	9	1
Total expenses	$38	$12
Income before taxes	($3)	($4)
Income taxes	0	0
Net income	($3)	($4)

Source: Citicorp MEP; the data have been altered for proprietary reasons.

Note: Caution should be exercised in comparing BNLA financial data with that of Citicorp, or even with that of other UK life assurance companies. This is because, first, there were some significant differences between traditional banking businesses and a UK life insurance operation, especially in rules governing the accounting recognition of earnings and in UK tax and regulatory requirements. Second, these differences were exaggerated in the case of a relatively new, rapidly growing UK life assurance company, where the reported amount of equity may have been as large as 60% of reported assets because of the conservatism inherent in regulatory requirements. Third, it was also difficult to make meaningful financial comparisons among different UK life companies. An immature firm had a financial picture bearing little resemblance to that of an older, established competitor, which may have reported equity as low as 2% of total assets.

After considering several moderately sized firms, it was decided that the goodwill portion of the purchase price for a moderately sized firm would never allow such an acquisition to make Citicorp's internal hurdle rates. The search was moved to smaller firms. From a list of 12 life assurance firms, BNLA emerged as the most desirable candidate. Exhibits 18 and 19 discuss Citicorp's rationale for the acquisition. Not only was BNLA of a size that permitted the acquisition to be managed, but there was fairly little to be paid for the goodwill of the company. In short, the price was right and the potential was there. Negotiations with EXCO Corporation and with Ernest Smith continued for some time, and finally, the purchase price was agreed upon. Citicorp had its UK life assurance company.

Exhibit 18 *Memorandum*

Memorandum

TO: Group Executive

FROM: Divisional Executive

RE: UK Insurance Acquisition MEP

DATE: 14th August 1985

As you know, in 1981 Citibank submitted an application to the Fed seeking permission to expand its line of insurance activities in the UK to write whole life in addition to its traditional base of credit life. This action was felt appropriate given that in the UK expanded insurance activities are considered a normal part of the banking sector with most large UK banks engaged in such activities through wholly owned insurance subsidiaries. Therefore for Citibank to enjoy equal footing with the competition, approval would be necessary since these activities are not otherwise permitted under Citibank's US charter.

Upon receiving permission from the Fed in early '84 we were then confronted with the business decision of how best to tackle this new opportunity. A team from within Citibank Savings was formed to evaluate the market place and make a recommendation on how to proceed. In this effort they were assisted by a senior insurance consultant from the UK who had a prior relationship with Citibank. A broad range of companies were evaluated as possible acquisition candidates and several points became clear. A direct sales force (versus mass solicitation) was considered key as well as the company's ownership structure (i.e., if publicly owned how could a takeover be affected).

Considerations of size became important because additional Fed approval would be required for any takeover. A unique opportunity confronted us to acquire a major UK insurer, PQ Life Assurance, but the cost of such an acquisition was put at a figure several hundred million dollars higher than the desired size of investment. This acquisition which would have been a joint venture was approved internally within Citibank but closure with our proposed partners failed.

We then shifted our thinking back to internal "de novo" growth and in so doing have reevaluated several smaller acquisition candidates which had surfaced previously. Acquiring a smaller company may be regarded as "accelerated de novo" and we are actively pursuing the acquisition of British National Life Assurance Company at a cost of $13.7MM (goodwill of $0.5MM) with a further capital increase of $19.6MM bringing the total investment to $33.3MM. If we were to pursue the internal de novo growth route we would also require additional capital of about $19.6MM as our current capitalization of $3MM supports the credit life business only. These capital levels are prescribed by the UK insurance regulatory bodies in order to meet minimum solvency margins.

The following analysis compares forecasted earnings through acquisition versus internal growth. On a cumulative basis through 1990 the acquisition route produces over $17MM in incremental earnings.

It is important to note that there is a lag in profitability in an emerging life assurance business due to the slow build up of premium income (net of commissions) which in the earlier years is not sufficient to cover the fixed costs of the distribution system. The difference in profitability between the two alternatives below is simply a reflection of this curve and that once a steady state is achieved both propositions would yield the same results.

PCE $MM	DE NOVO	ACQUISITION	B/(W)
1985	$(.5)	$ (1.3)	$ (.6)
1986	(1.3)	(2.9)	(1.6)
1987	(3.6)	.4	4.0
1988	(3.5)	1.3	4.8
1989	(2.5)	2.5	5.0
1990	(1.3)	4.9	6.2
	(12.7)	4.9	17.8

This MEP assumes no tax credit against the operating losses in 1985 and 1986. In 1987, the first full year of profitability, the loss carryforward is absorbed. In any event, no current UK taxes will likely be payable at least until 1990 and the tax expense is therefore all US deferred.

Your approval of the attached MEP is recommended.

Note: All numbers in this document have been changed for proprietary reasons.

Exhibit 19 *Interoffice Communication*

Memorandum

TO:	*Office Person*	Kensington Divisional Executive
FROM:	*Office Person*	Hammersmith UK Country Business Managers

SUBJECT: British National Life Acquisition

REFERENCE: AAA/dcb

DATE: 13th August 1985

Attached is an MEP covering the proposed acquisition of 100% of British National Life Assurance Company Limited (BNL) for a price not to exceed US$13.7MM. We have also included a $19.6MM capital injection in this MEP as we anticipate this being the incremental requirement under UK statutory provisions prior to adequate earnings levels being achieved. Injection of this capital will also improve the companies earnings performance allowing earlier consolidation for tax purposes.

RATIONALE

Life insurance continues to be viewed as a key element to our Individual Bank strategy in the UK. Consumers view life insurance not only as protection, but also as a tax planning and investment opportunity. 50% of total UK consumer savings are invested in insurance company managed funds. In order to meet the full financial needs of the UK consumer, we must offer life insurance related services. In order to do so, we filed in 1981 and received US Federal Reserve Board approval in 1984 to sell and underwrite life insurance through our UK subsidiaries. To date these have been involved only in the credit life related areas complementary to our Citibank Savings lending activities.

We have been pursuing a full service life insurance sales and underwriting firm to broaden our presence in the UK consumer market. Due to extremely high premiums, the acquisition of a large company giving us an immediate and substantial presence has been eliminated as an option. Instead, we have decided to develop our existing insurance operations and look at BNL as an opportunity to accelerate our de novo expansion. BNL gives us an existing infrastructure, including systems, investment management, and a direct sales force, a reasonably capable management team; and an appropriate product line. Utilizing BNL and our existing customer base we anticipate substantial sales/revenue synergies which could not otherwise be realized by a de novo development in less than two years.

Based on our projections, a de novo development of a direct sales insurance business involving the hiring of management, systems and product development and branch/sales force recruitment and training would require 18–24 months and US$3.5MM in expenses before any sales occur. Cumulative, after tax losses through 1990 on a start-up would be US$12.7MM. This compares with the BNL acquisition cumulative profits of US$4.9MM through 1990.

The success of the acquisition is dependent on our providing BNL with sales prospects from our existing UK customer portfolio. This will enhance sales force performance by increasing new policy sales per salesperson by 50% in 1986 and up to 100% in 1990. The resultant sales per salesperson in 1990 are expected to be at the level currently achieved by mature direct sales forces in the life insurance industry.

COMPANY BACKGROUND

The origins of BNL date back to 1920, but true development started with the relaunch of the company as a direct selling unit linking life company in January 1983, and today has 34M policyholders with $218MM insurance in force. 1984 premiums were $4.2MM generated through a direct sales force of 247 operating out of 22 branch offices. Its premium income in 1984 was $17.2MM single and $3.2MM regular.

A wholly owned subsidiary of XYZ Corporation [this company's identity is altered to protect confidentiality], the firm is now being sold as part of XYZ's efforts to refocus on its non-financial business activities.

FINANCIAL EXPECTATIONS

BNL presently looses approximately $3.1MM pre-tax due to start-up expenses and the higher costs in the growth phase of a life insurance company. With our purchase of BNL, the company will be able to offer insurance to the 1MM consumers with whom we have an established relationship in the UK. We expect this to nearly double sales and lead to a fifth year achievement of our corporate hurdle rates. Cumulative losses prior to breakeven in year three will amount to US$4MM. Of the $1.3MM premium, goodwill is anticipated to $.5MM after allowing for a $.8MM adjustment to revalue policyholder liabilities.

REGULATORY AND OTHER CONSIDERATIONS

Any agreement will be subject to UK/US regulatory approvals where we do not anticipate any objections to the acquisition given the small size and our existing permissions.

The purchase will be subject to our audit and acceptance of

- BNL's operating system, controls and procedures
- a review of contracts, leases, and other documentation
- personnel, legal, and regulatory compliance
- a review of their investment portfolio
- the financial statements and tax returns (Peat Marwick will handle)
- current policyholder portfolio (we will retain an outside actuarial consultant for valuation purposes)

Additionally, we will require management continuity and will negotiate employment contracts with several key managers to ensure continuity after our acquisition.

The companies headquarters are approximately one hour's drive from our Hammersmith offices, so I envision no management complications due to location.

The company will initially be managed independently from our other Individual Bank activities focusing on the necessary adjustments to ensure Citicorp standards are met. The building of sales momentum is the next priority with further synergies to be explored at a later date. Given the apparent strength of the BNL management team, minimal personnel moves into BNL are anticipated. The existing managing director will report to me and I will retain the insurance expertise currently on my staff.

I recommend your approval.

Note: All numbers in this document have been changed for proprietary reasons.

COMDISCO DISASTER RECOVERY SERVICES' INTER-NATIONAL EXPANSION

Coral R. Snodgrass
Canisius College

In the summer of 1987, the management of Comdisco Disaster Recovery Services (CDRS) decided to study the question of whether or not they should expand their operations into Western Europe. Although they were already kept quite busy with their US operations and they believed the US market was not yet exhausted, they also believed the time was right to consider an international move. They thought they should move into Western Europe. But they did not know precisely where they should go or how they should get there.

In order to start the ball rolling on this project, Ray Hipp, the president of CDRS, called an all-day strategy session for July 7. At the session were Ray, Bob Barrett and Rich Zane of CDRS sales and marketing, John Jackson and Rick Wargo of CDRS product development, Mitch Levine from finance at the parent company, and a professor of business strategy from a local university. This group was given the task of answering the following questions:

1. Should CDRS enter the Western European market?
2. If yes, what should the market entry look like?

They believed that answering these questions would best proceed by addressing the issues of the relationship between CDRS and its parent company, the nature of CDRS business, the keys to success for CDRS, and the nature of the Western European market.

CDRS AND ITS PARENT COMPANY

CDRS is a fully owned subsidiary of Comdisco, Inc. (CDO). CDO is a computer services firm located in Rosemont, Illinois. It is the largest and most profitable independent computer leasing and remarketing company in the world. Its largest line of business is the leasing and remarketing of IBM computer equipment. It also leases and remarkets other high-technology equipment. Disaster recovery is the third of its three basic businesses, accounting for approximately 3% of revenues in 1987. A number of other subsidiaries ranging from oil and gas exploration to financial services contribute 2% of revenues (see Exhibit 1 for the consolidated financial statements of CDO).

CDO History

CDO was founded in 1969 by Kenneth N. Pontikes. At that time the concept of leasing and remarketing used computer equipment was unheard of. Pontikes parlayed six years of experience as an IBM salesman and $5,000.00 of borrowed capital into a company with nearly $1.2 billion of revenues on $3 billion of sales in 1987. He also made himself one of the 400 richest persons in America.

Comdisco (a name derived from the company's original name of Computer Discount Corporation) started out as a "marriage broker," getting buyers and sellers of used equipment together. Eventually, it began to accumulate its own computer equipment for leasing. As of 1987, it controlled in excess of $8 billion worth of IBM equipment (calculated at IBM list price). CDO had also begun to expand its inventory of non-IBM computer equipment and of other types of high-technology equipment. Throughout the 1980s, CDO

Exhibit 1A *Selected Financial Data: Comdisco, Inc. and Consolidated Subsidiaries*

	Years ended September 30,				
	1987	1986	1985	1984	1983
Consolidated Summary of Earnings					
Revenue					
Leasing	$ 871	$ 728	$ 587	$ 499	$ 430
Sales	243	232	95	112	147
Disaster recovery	39	28	18	12	6
Other	22	18	14	19	14
Total revenue	1,175	1,006	714	642	597
Costs and expenses					
Leasing	470	386	295	286	248
Sales	211	200	79	88	119
Disaster recovery	18	14	11	7	6
Other	9	5	3	—	—
Selling, general and administrative	118	99	78	69	58
Interest	226	221	198	156	107
Total costs and expenses	1,052	925	664	606	538
Earnings from continuing operations before income taxes and extraordinary gain	123	81	50	36	59
Income taxes	46	17	1	7	—
Earnings from continuing operations before extraordinary gain	77	64	49	29	52
Earnings from discontinued risk arbitrage activities (net of income taxes)	17	15	8	1	–
Earnings before extraordinary gain	94	79	57	30	52
Extraordinary gain (net of income taxes of $30)	—	—	30	—	—
Net earnings	$ 94	$ 79	$ 87	$ 30	$ 52

	1987	1986	1985	1984	1983
Common and Common Equivalent Share Data					
Earnings from continuing operations before extraordinary gain	$ 1.85	$ 1.55	$ 1.21	$ .68	$ 1.19
Earnings from discontinued risk arbitrage activities	.41	.36	.20	.02	—
Extraordinary gain	—	—	.74	—	—
Net earnings	2.26	1.91	2.15	.70	1.19
Stockholders' equity (per share outstanding)	11.22	8.65	6.75	4.67	4.43
Cash dividends paid	.19	.15	.13	.13	.10
Average common and common equivalent shares (in thousands)	41,537	41,224	40,616	42,320	44,253
Stock splits	—	3 for 2	—	—	2 for 1

	1987	1986	1985	1984	1983
Financial Position					
Total assets	$3,023	$2,855	$2,111	$1,811	$1,517
Total long term debt	366	425	204	270	276
Discounted lease rentals	1,734	1,759	1,440	1,239	899
Stockholders' equity	466	351	272	188	191

	1987	1986	1985	1984	1983
Leasing Data					
Total firm rents of new leases	$1,400	$1,700	$1,200	$1,300	$1,055

In millions except per share data.

Exhibit 1B *Consolidated Balance Sheets: Comdisco, Inc. and Consolidated Subsidiaries*

	September 30,	
	1987	1986
Assets		
Cash	$ 41	$ 109
Marketable securities, at cost which approximates market	60	57
Receivables (net of allowance for doubtful accounts of $3 in 1987 and 1986)	129	98
Inventory of equipment	68	58
Net investment in sales-type and direct financing leases	1,496	1,454
Leased equipment	1,492	1,367
Less: accumulated depreciation and amortization	665	580
Net	827	787
Buildings, furniture and other, net	53	37
Net assets of discontinued risk arbitrage activities	148	105
Oil and gas properties	75	69
Other assets	126	81
	$3,023	$2,855
Liabilities and Stockholders' Equity		
Notes payable	$ 101	$ 11
Senior notes	225	225
Subordinated debentures	140	196
Accounts payable	84	83
Income taxes:		
Current	10	5
Deferred	48	43
Other liabilities	215	182
Discounted lease rentals (nonrecourse)	1,734	1,759
	2,557	2,504
Stockholders' equity:		
Common stock $.10 par value. Authorized 100,000,000 shares;		
issued 46,499,489 shares (44,366,832 in 1986)	5	4
Additional paid-in capital	121	76
Deferred translation adjustment	6	3
Retained earnings	384	298
Treasury stock at cost; 5,022,005 shares (3,818,505 in 1986)	(50)	(30)
Total stockholders' equity	466	351
	$3,023	$2,855

In millions except number of shares.

Exhibit 1C *Consolidated Statements of Earnings: Comdisco, Inc. and Consolidated Subsidiaries*

	Years ended September 30,		
	1987	1986	1985
Revenue			
Leasing	$ 871	$ 728	$ 587
Sales	243	232	95
Disaster recovery	39	28	18
Other	22	18	14
Total revenue	1,175	1,006	714
Costs and Expenses			
Leasing	470	386	295
Sales	211	200	79
Disaster recovery	18	14	11
Other	9	5	3
Selling, general and administrative	118	99	78
Interest	226	221	198
Total costs and expenses	1,052	925	664
Earnings from continuing operations before income taxes and extraordinary gain	123	81	50
Income taxes	46	17	1
Earnings from continuing operations before extraordinary gain	77	64	49
Earnings from discontinued risk arbitrage activities (net of income taxes)	17	15	8
Earnings before extraordinary gain	94	79	57
Extraordinary gain (net of income taxes of $30)	—	—	30
Net earnings	$ 94	$ 79	$ 87
Net earnings per common and common equivalent share:			
Earnings from continuing operations before extraordinary gain	$ 1.85	$ 1.55	$ 1.21
Earnings from discontinued risk arbitrage activities	.41	.36	.20
Extraordinary gain	—	—	.74
Net earnings	$ 2.26	$ 1.91	$ 2.15

In millions except per share data.

Exhibit 1D *Consolidated Statements of Stockholders' Equity: Comdisco, Inc. and Consolidated Subsidiaries*

Years ended September 30, 1987, 1986, and 1985	Common stock $.10 par value	Additional paid-in capital	Deferred translation adjustment	Retained earnings	Treasury stock
Balance at September 30, 1984	$3	$ 71	$(2)	$144	$ 28
Net earnings	—	—	—	87	—
Dividends paid	—	—	—	(5)	—
Stock options exercised	—	1	—	—	—
Translation adjustment	—	—	1	—	—
Purchase of treasury stock	—	—	—	—	(2)
Income tax benefits resulting from exercise of non-qualified stock options	—	2	—	—	—
Balance at September 30, 1985	3	74	(1)	226	(30)
Net earnings	—	—	—	79	—
Dividends paid	—	—	—	(7)	—
Stock split	1	(1)	—	—	—
Stock options exercised	—	3	—	—	—
Translation adjustment	—	—	4	—	—
Balance at September 30, 1986	4	76	3	298	(30)
Net earnings	—	—	—	94	—
Dividends paid	—	—	—	(8)	—
Issuance of common stock upon conversion of 8% convertible debentures	1	44	—	—	—
Stock options exercised	—	1	—	—	—
Translation adjustment	—	—	3	—	—
Purchase of treasury stock	—	—	—	—	(20)
Balance at September 30, 1987	$5	$121	$ 6	$384	$(50)

In millions.

Exhibit 1E *Consolidated Statements of Cash Flows: Comdisco, Inc. and Consolidated Subsidiaries*

	Years ended September 30,		
	1987	1986	1985
Increase (Decrease) in Cash:			
Cash flows from operating activities:			
Leasing receipts, primarily rentals	$ 522	$ 462	$ 301
Leasing costs	(150)	(119)	(60)
Sales	32	31	16
Disaster recovery	27	15	8
Other revenue	22	22	17
Selling, general and administrative expenses	(114)	(93)	(74)
Interest	(60)	(51)	(36)
Income taxes	(77)	(10)	15
Net cash provided by continuing operations	202	257	187
Discontinued risk arbitrage activities	28	18	8
Net cash provided by operating activities	230	275	195
Cash flows from investing activities:			
Equipment purchased for leasing	(1,130)	(1,320)	(986)
Investment in:			
Discontinued risk arbitrage activities	(43)	(69)	(8)
Oil and gas	(15)	(19)	(19)
Marketable securities	(3)	(55)	1
Other	(23)	(16)	(6)
Net cash used in investing activities	(1,214)	(1,479)	(1,018)
Cash flows from financing activities:			
Discounted lease proceeds	869	1,057	844
Increase in notes payable	90	9	—
Issuance of senior notes	—	225	—
Purchase of treasury stock	(20)	—	(2)
Redemption of subordinated debentures	(12)	—	—
Dividends	(8)	(7)	(5)
Other	(3)	—	—
Net cash provided by financing activities	916	1,284	837
Increase (decrease) in cash	$ (68)	$ 80	$ 14
Reconciliation of earnings before extraordinary gain to cash provided by operating activities:			
Earnings before extraordinary gain	$ 94	$ 79	$ 57
Adjustments to reconcile earnings before extraordinary gain to net cash provided by operating activities:			
Depreciation and amortization	362	297	279
Leasing revenue—principally rentals discounted with financial institutions	(488)	(431)	(399)
Principal portion of sales-type and direct financing rentals received	109	91	49
Interest	166	170	161
Income taxes	(21)	6	15
Decrease (increase) in other assets	(19)	(40)	4
Increase in other liabilities	3	55	19
Other—net	24	48	10
Total adjustments	136	196	138
Net cash provided by operating activities	$ 230	$ 275	$ 195

Exhibit 1E, *continued*

	Years ended September 30,		
	1987	1986	1985
Supplemental schedule of noncash financing activities:			
Principal portion of discounted lease rentals collected by financial institutions	$ (894)	$ (737)	$ (644)
Exchange of 8% convertible debentures for 9.65% subordinated debentures	$ —	$ —	$ 192
Common stock issued upon conversion of 8% convertible subordinated debentures	$ 45	$ —	$ —

In millions.

expanded into international operations all over the world. It also expanded into other related computer services, such as the disaster recovery business.

CDO Goals and Objectives

The corporate goals of CDO, as expressed by the founder and president, are increased earnings, growth, and innovation. In support of these goals, CDO has three financial objectives. The first is to provide stockholders with superior returns on their investment through stock price appreciation. This is an objective the company has been achieving with remarkable success ever since it went public in 1972. In the 16 years between 1972 and 1988, the market value of CDO stock appreciated at a compound annual rate of 40% (making $1.00 invested in 1972 worth $216.00 in 1988). Earnings per share grew at a compound rate of 24% between 1982 and 1987.

The second financial goal is to maintain return on equity (ROE) at 20%. Throughout the 1980s, ROE averaged 25%. The third financial goal is to maintain financial flexibility and to increase the company's bond ratings from BBB to BBB+ and from Baa – 2 to Baa – 1.

In early 1987 Pontikes predicted that CDO would double its revenues and earnings by the end of the decade. In fact, by the end of 1987 revenues were up 17% and earnings were up 19% over the previous year. Such continued growth was to come from the basic leasing business and disaster recovery (see Exhibit 2 for expected future revenues and expenses). The fact that CDO's current volume of leasing represents less than 10% of IBM's domestic sales volume of computer equipment indicates that there is room for significant

expansion in this business segment. Pontikes believes that the disaster recovery market is young and vital enough that a 40% growth rate is achievable, at least for the short term.

CDO Customer Service

Pontikes also emphasizes quality customer service, which he believes is the basis of the company's continuing leadership. CDO does not provide the cheapest service in the business, but it does believe it provides the best. In order to best serve the customer, CDO management has built an organization characterized by a high degree of expertise in the leasing and remarketing area, flexibility in meeting customer needs, financial strength, and a very knowledgeable sales team. CDO is proud of the fact that it was the first service firm ever to win Sears' Partners in Progress award, an award given annually to 75 of Sears' 10,000 vendors. In order to enhance customer service, CDO plans to increase the size and the expertise of its sales force. The sales force increased 17% in 1987 and was predicted to increase 20% in 1988. In addition, CDO intensified its sales training program.

CDO is also dedicated to adding value to its customers, who include 800 of the Fortune 1000 firms as well as many middle- and small-sized firms, representing 5,000 of the 10,000 data centers in the United States. Adding value can take many forms such as analyzing customer needs and counseling them on the best data processing configuration for their needs. An example of how this concept operates in the remarketing business occurred in 1982. At that time, IBM introduced its new 3081 mainframe with a lease costing $90,000 per month.

Exhibit 2 *Expected Future Revenues and Expenses*

	Years ending September 30,					
	1988	1989	1990	1991	1992 and After	Total
Expected future revenue and expense from existing contracts:						
Leasing revenue						
Operating leases						
Discounted, on equipment owned	$299.8	$220.1	$116.7	$ 27.1	$ .3	$ 664.0
Not discounted, on equipment owned	99.3	52.6	16.4	7.4	3.3	179.0
Not discounted, on equipment leased from others	82.5	57.6	26.7	7.5	3.2	177.5
Sales-type and direct financing lease revenue						
after lease inception	110.7	78.0	54.3	30.1	8.4	281.5
	592.3	408.3	214.1	72.1	15.2	1,302.0
Leasing costs						
Operating leases						
Depreciation and amortization	313.3	218.3	109.6	27.8	2.8	671.8
Rentals paid to others	85.7	35.9	15.3	5.3	3.0	145.2
	399.0	254.2	124.9	33.1	5.8	817.0
Disaster recovery revenue	41.3	33.0	24.4	15.3	6.3	120.3
Disaster recovery costs	10.6	10.0	9.2	7.7	6.3	43.8
Interest expense from discounted lease rentals	126.5	69.1	30.1	7.7	1.7	235.1
Expected earnings contribution from existing contracts	$ 97.5	$108.0	$ 74.3	$ 38.9	$ 7.7	$ 326.4
Estimated earnings contribution from remarketing residuals:						
Realization of excess of estimated fair market value						
of residuals over book value at lease termination	$ 21.2	$ 55.2	$ 77.1	$51.6	$ 54.1	$ 259.2
Expected cash to be provided from existing contracts:						
Leasing receipts						
Operating leases						
Not discounted, on equipment owned	$ 99.3	$ 52.6	$ 16.4	$ 7.4	$ 3.3	$ 179.0
Not discounted, on equipment leased	82.5	57.6	26.7	7.5	3.2	177.5
Sales-type and direct financing lease						
receipts (not discounted)	124.0	78.0	52.3	39.5	26.6	320.4
	305.8	188.2	95.4	54.4	33.1	676.9
Leasing payments						
Operating leases-rentals paid to others	82.4	33.5	13.8	4.5	3.0	137.2
Disaster recovery receipts	41.3	33.0	24.4	15.3	6.3	120.3
Disaster recovery payments	4.5	4.5	4.5	4.5	4.5	22.5
Expected cash to be provided from existing contracts	$260.2	$183.2	$101.5	$ 60.7	$ 31.9	$ 637.5
Estimated cash from remarketing residuals:						
Realization of estimated book value of residuals	$ 15.2	$ 46.9	$ 81.4	$81.4	$ 97.6	$ 322.5
Realization of excess of estimated fair market value of						
residuals over book value at lease termination	21.2	55.2	77.1	51.6	54.1	259.2
Estimated cash to be provided from						
remarketing residuals	$ 36.4	$102.1	$158.5	$133.0	$151.7	$ 581.7

In millions.

CDO customers who require state-of-the-art computing capabilities were counseled to lease the new equipment immediately. Other customers, however, were analyzed by CDO and their needs were determined to be such that they were counseled against installing the new equipment until 1985. CDO reasoned that within two years IBM would have made such improvements that a large number of 3081s would be available for remarketing. At that time the lease costs would be substantially lower. In the meantime, more appropriate equipment would be found for the customers.

As it happened, in 1984 IBM introduced the 3084. Customers who had leased the 3081 in 1982 (on four- or five-year leases) required the upgrade. CDO was able to remarket these used 3081s to the customers who had waited at $40,000 per month (saving them more than $1 million over the two years). They leased new 3084s to the customers who needed them. Such flexibility, knowledge, and willingness to work with its customers has made CDO the recognized leader in its field.

CDO Services

By far the largest part of CDO's services is the leasing and remarketing of IBM equipment. This service may take many forms: leasing original equipment, lease extensions or reworking of original leases, remarketing used equipment to new users, and selling equipment. The bulk of its business takes the form of CDO leasing equipment to customers under the following scenario: CDO works with the customer to determine computing needs; the equipment is ordered for the customer; CDO pays for the equipment and leases it back to the customer.

Starting in 1983, CDO began to lease equipment made by manufacturers other than IBM. In addition, it began to deal in equipment other than mainframe computers. Consequently, as of 1987, it was dealing in equipment made by manufacturers such as Digital Equipment, NCR, Wang, and Xerox in support of such industries as telecommunications, microcomputers, and office automation. By 1987 this business had grown to half the size of the IBM leasing business.

CDO moved into the international market offering similar leasing and remarketing services as in the United States. The company operates mostly in Canada and Western Europe, with some business in South America, Japan, and Australia. CDO has subsidiaries in Australia, Austria, Belgium, Canada, Denmark, Finland, France, Germany, Italy, Japan, the Netherlands, Spain, Sweden, Switzerland, and the United Kingdom.

In Canada, CDO does business much as in the United States. In Europe prior to 1984, most of its business was in the form of selling computer equipment. Since then, it has been trying to expand its leasing business. To support this, CDO has been working to develop increasing lines of financial support. CDO does business in Japan through joint ventures with Japanese leasing companies. Total international investment represents about 25% of total CDO revenues (see Exhibit 3).

COMDISCO DISASTER RECOVERY SERVICES

CDRS was formed in 1980 to provide CDO customers with backup data center facilities in the event of a "disaster" at their own facilities. A disaster is any event such as a flood or fire that renders the customer's computer facilities inoperative. CDRS has 13 recovery centers located throughout the United States and Canada. These centers, called "hot sites," are fully equipped with a full range of state-of-the-art IBM central processing units, peripherals, and communications equipment. These centers are high-security areas which provide full telecommunications support. In addition to IBM equipment, CDRS also provides backup for Tandem and DEC users. CDRS also maintains 14 "cold sites," which have all the support for a large computer facility, such as power and telecommunications capabilities, but no computer equipment. CDRS does not build any new recovery centers until it has enough long-term contracts to justify construction. This minimizes its financial exposure while maximizing profit margins. The president of CDRS is Ray Hipp who was hired to be president at the company's inception, bringing with him 15 years of experience in sales and marketing at IBM.

CDRS Services

In the event of a disaster, the customer brings its data and personnel to the hot site and sets up operations. Each customer goes through extensive planning and mock drills with CDRS in order to be certain it will be able to make the smooth transition to the hot site if necessary. As an example of

Exhibit 3 *International Segment Information*

	United States	Europe	Canada	Japan	Export sales	Elimin- ations	Consol- idated
1987							
Revenue from unaffiliated customers	$ 885.4	$ 204.1	$ 59.1	$ 25.0	$ 1.4	$ —	$ 1,175.0
Transfers between geographic areas	13.7	4.3	11.4	6.0	8.6	(44.0)	$ —
Total revenue	$ 899.1	$ 208.4	$ 70.5	$ 31.0	$ 10.0	$ (44.0)	$ 1,175.0
Earnings (loss) from continuing operations before income taxes	$ 121.0	$ (5.2)	$ 7.2	$ .5	$ 1.8	$ (2.3)	$ 123.0
Total assets (end of period)	$2,640.3	$ 238.1	$ 171.2	$ 7.7	$ 5.8	$ (40.1)	$ 3,023.0
1986							
Revenue from unaffiliated customers	$ 755.8	$ 179.5	$ 56.8	$ 8.6	$ 5.3	$ —	$ 1,006.0
Transfers between geographic areas	5.0	9.5	16.1	9.0	5.5	(45.1)	—
Total revenue	$ 760.8	$ 189.0	$ 72.9	$ 17.6	$ 10.8	$ (45.1)	$1, 006.0
Earnings from continuing operations before income taxes	$ 67.1	$ 4.7	$ 7.9	$ .5	$ 1.7	$ (0.9)	$ 81.0
Total assets (end of period)	$2,597.2	$ 159.7	$ 157.6	$ 4.2	$ 3.1	$ (66.8)	$ 2,855.0
1985							
Revenue from unaffiliated customers	$ 619.9	$ 60.6	$ 31.5	$ —	$ 2.0	$ —	$ 714.0
Transfers between geographic areas	3.5	37.8	6.8	—	—	(48.1)	—
Total revenue	$ 623.4	$ 98.4	$ 38.3	$ —	$ 2.0	$ (48.1)	$ 714.0
Earnings (loss) from continuing operations before income taxes	$ 45.0	$ (0.3)	$ 4.6	$ —	$ 1.0	$ (0.3)	$ 50.0
Total assets (end of period)	$1,939.9	$ 77.1	$ 107.9	$ —	$ 2.3	$ (16.3)	$ 2,110.9

In millions.

how this works, take the case of a large Canadian retailer who had a fire on October 26, 1986. Between the fire, the water damage, and the power and telecommunications loss, the company's entire data processing center was inoperative. The company flew its data recovery team to a CDRS hot site in New Jersey. There they worked with a CDRS team to set up the required data processing facilities using backup data tapes that had been shipped in. In the meantime, a data processing team was established in a cold site in Montreal where they set up remote data communications with the hot site. Within 48 hours after the fire and within 28 hours of declaring the disaster, all sales and distribution networks were operational. By October 29, business as usual was resumed including the processing of weekly payroll checks to 28,000 employees.

CDRS Growth

Established in 1980, CDRS grew consistently yet lost money until 1985. Since 1985, growth has been nothing short of phenomenal. From 1985 to 1986,

revenues increased 50% and earnings nearly quadrupled (see Exhibit 4). In 1987 CDRS earned $10 million on $40 million of revenues. Considering that the market is still quite young and firms are becoming increasingly dependent on their computer facilities, the future looks quite optimistic. In an article published in *The Wall Street Journal*, of the companies responding, 19.6% said they were totally dependent on their computing facilities and 65.8% said they were highly dependent. Only 13.9% were moderately dependent and a mere 0.7% were slightly dependent.

Nature of CDRS Services

The service that CDRS offers is a unique one. On the one hand, it is a computer service offering state-of-the-art hardware and software support. On the other hand, it is an insurance policy offering protection against the loss of business in the unlikely event of a disaster. Consequently, the customer subscribing to the service is one who values both the technology and the protection. CDRS esti-

Exhibit 4 *CDRS Growth 1984–1986*

	1984	1985	1986
Shells	10	11	14
Hot sites	6	7	11
Employees	43	65	91
Revenues	$11,602	$19,417	$29,214
Pretax earnings	$(1,996)	$ 1,657	$ 6,309

mates that less than 10% of its revenue is generated through actual disaster recovery. In excess of 90% comes from retainer fees and costs of designing and testing recovery plans.

The unique character of the services offered by CDRS makes its competitive position unique also. Because it owns the sites and the equipment, it is highly capital intensive. Because it sells "insurance," it must deal with the long sell cycle associated with this. These two characteristics present imposing barriers to entry into this market. At present, there are only two serious competitors in this business: CDRS and SunGard Recovery Services, a unit of SunGard Data Systems, Inc. There are approximately 2,000 subscribers to disaster recovery services in North America. CDRS counts approximately one-half of them as clients. SunGard counts approximately one-quarter. The potential market is a total of 14,000 data centers. CDRS considers 70% of them to be fair game.

The service offered by CDRS is expensive. However, considering the costs of a "disaster," the money is well spent. As an example, one of CDRS' customers has spent nearly $1 million each year since 1982 on preparations for a disaster, including $25,000 per month to CDRS for its retainer. In May 1988, while conducting its semi-annual test of the backup plan, the company discovered a problem. It called CDRS, declared a disaster, and set the recovery plan into action. Within hours, the recovery team and the data tapes were in a CDRS hot site, setting up business. The customer remained in the hot site for two weeks. The costs to the customer were $600,000, which included the costs of supporting the 31-person recovery team and a $40,000 fee to CDRS. The customer estimates it saved in excess of $30 million in sales while also saving the confidence of its own customers.

In addition to the cost considerations, there are a number of regulatory pressures on customers which provide motivation for them to subscribe to CDRS. First of all, both internal and external auditors are increasing their pressure on companies, especially those in computer-dependent industries such as banking and retailing, to provide protection for their data. Secondly, Congress, through the Foreign Corrupt Practices Act of 1977, and the Comptroller of the Currency have mandated that steps be taken to insure the integrity of a firm's data.

Consequently, the service can be described as one which

1. is intangible.
2. the customer has never bought before.
3. the customer probably will never use.
4. has the potential to save the customer time and money.
5. can protect the client company and management.
6. can enhance company and personal status.
7. shows technological sophistication.

FACTORS SUPPORTING CDRS SUCCESS

Customer Values

The customer who would subscribe to a service such as CDRS would be one who values

1. protection.
2. status.
3. time saving.
4. money.
5. things that are new.
6. technology.

These values have been present in the US market and have supported the continued growth of CDRS since its establishment in 1980.

Sales Force

The sales force must be knowledgeable enough to understand both CDRS' capabilities and the customers' needs so they can be most effectively matched. CDRS believes it has hired and trained a sales force uniquely qualified to do this. It estimates it requires one full year of daily training for the new salesperson to become productive.

Operational Support

The technical personnel must also have a vast array of expertise. A typical recovery center will provide complete facilities for users of IBM 370 and 370 XA processors with 3090-400E, 308X, and 43XX central processing units (CPUs); 3725 and 3705 communications controllers; 3890 item processors; 3480 tape drives; 3800 laser printers; and 3380E, 3375, 3370, and 3350 direct access storage devices (DASD). In addition, CDRS provides specialized facilities for unique customers such as banks which must comply with extensive regulatory requirements. CDRS also provides equipment for Tandem and DEC users and networking and telecommunications support.

In addition to technical expertise to handle all of this, the operations staff also must have the ability to interact with the clients during the planning and drill stages, as well as during the very stressful transition in the event a disaster does occur.

Management

Managing a firm such as CDRS requires almost constant interaction between management and the sales force, the technical staff, and the customers. Because both the technical capabilities in the market and the technical requirements of the customers are in a state of constant change, management cannot stand back and manage by exception. There is a continuous need to update the hot sites, develop new and retrain existing sales and technical personnel, develop new hot site locations, and cater to the changes in customer requirements, while all the time staying within the budget. CDRS managers must understand technology, people, and business.

CDO

CDRS has benefited greatly from the success of CDO itself. CDO does business with half of the data centers in the United States. Of CDO's existing customers, many were CDRS' initial customers. In addition to the initial entree, CDO supplies CDRS with the total hardware package it needs to satisfy its customers' needs at the hot sites. CDO also supplies financial, technical, design, construction, and transportation services. This synergistic relationship provides CDRS with unique advantages in its markets.

THE EUROPEAN MARKET

Prior to the July meeting, some initial research had been carried out to determine the feasibility of the expansion into Western Europe. A number of factors supported the decision to move into Western Europe. The number of mainframes in operation indicated sufficient number of potential customers to warrant further study (see Exhibit 5). It was also determined that there are at least two "disasters" each month in France alone and virtually no French firms carried insurance against losses associated with such disasters. There was also adequate reason to expect continued disasters from both natural causes such as the weather and unnatural causes such as terrorism. Further, the rising costs of downtime had begun to make disaster recovery an attractive service. In addition, there appeared to be little competition in the market at the time.

However, there were also some negative indicators. The European market is very heterogeneous in terms of language, political systems, telecommunications capabilities, technological sophistication, and the reliability of power sources. There are also restrictions on the movement of data across political boundaries. In addition, there is not a uniform perceived need for a disaster recovery service. As an example, one CDRS manager spent some time discussing disaster recovery with representatives of 13 firms from Northern Italy. They all responded favorably to the technology. However, they said they didn't believe they needed the service.

CDRS also asked some of its existing US customers about the possibilities of using a disaster recovery service in their European operations. Of the 29 responses,

- 20 had no European data centers.
- 4 said their European centers were not under their control.
- 1 was not interested in a hot site in Europe.
- 4 indicated interest.

THE STRATEGY SESSION

As they sat down to the meeting to discuss the international expansion, the managers of CDRS also brought with them a value for flexibility and a willingness to adapt to the market which had always been a characteristic of both CDO and CDRS. They wanted to remain completely open to any ideas that would help them grow. They were willing to reorganize the company to reflect the realities of the global marketplace. They were willing to look at any type of entry strategy that would help them to achieve the same type of market success they had become used to. With this willingness to explore the issue from any and all perspectives, they sat down to work.

Exhibit 5 *Estimated Number of European Mainframes*

Country	Quantity of Mainframes
France	2,249
West Germany	1,888
Italy	1,402
Great Britain	870
Sweden	347
Netherlands	338
Switzerland	334
Spain	322
Denmark	272
Austria	210
Norway	185
Finland	155
Belgium	112
Portugal	17
Luxembourg	10

COPENHAGEN HANDELSBANK

Flemming Ornskov and Susan C. Schneider
INSEAD, Fontainebleau Cedex, France

1992 AND THE EUROPEAN BANKING INDUSTRY[1-4]

The European Economic Community (EEC) was established in 1957 with the Treaty of Rome to promote the economic and political integration of its member states (now 12) and 320 million citizens. The essential objective of the EEC is to establish a common market enabling the free movement of goods, persons, services, and capital in order to maintain fair competition and coordinate national economic policies. Although initiated over 30 years ago, this objective has yet to be achieved.

The EEC Commission's first initiatives in the banking arena, which date back to the early 1960s (see Exhibit 1), broadly defined categories of capital movements among the EEC member states. In June 1973, the Commission initiated action on the more specific subject of the freedom to establish credit institutions across EEC borders. The First Banking Directive followed in 1977 to coordinate national legal, regulatory, and administrative issues.

In its White Paper on the Completion of the Internal Market, published in 1985, the Commission identified some 300 measures needed in order to remove existing obstacles to establishing a gen-uine Internal Market within the Community by the end of 1992. The White Paper was dedicated to the free movement of capital, goods, and services. Open capital markets would be a further incentive for member states to adopt sound economic policies conducive to price and exchange rate stability, two major preconditions for achieving economic and monetary union in Europe. Furthermore, the opening of the capital markets would increase the freedom of investors, leading to more efficient allocation of savings and to greater general welfare. Also included in the White Paper were proposals for the harmonization of basic rules governing the banking industry, i.e., calling for prudential supervision of banking establishments (in terms of size and composition of own funds, solvency and liquidity coefficients, concentration of credit risks) and setting common standards for investor protection. Furthermore, it called for mutual recognition of each member country's supervisory criteria and home country responsibility in the supervision of foreign branches.

The Single European Act in 1986 called for majority voting, which facilitated adoption of directives by the Council of Ministers, the legislative body of the EEC. One of the most complicated

---

[1]The discussion and information provided in this case is relevant to the time period July 1989 when the interviews were conducted.

[2]Zavvos, George S. "1992—One Market," *International Financial Law Review*, March 1988, pp. 7–11.

[3]Bellanger, Serge. "Toward an Integrated European Banking System 1992 and Beyond," *Bankers Magazine*, July/August 1988, pp. 54–59.

[4]Wilson-Smith, Peter. "Banking Proposal Would Give European Firms New Freedoms," *Europe*, June 1988, pp. 24–26.

Exhibit 1 *EEC Banking Timetable*

1957	Treaty of Rome
1972	United Kingdom, Denmark, and Ireland join the EEC
1973	Commission's First Report on Freedom of Establishment of Credit Institutions
1977	First Banking Directive
1985	White Paper on Completion of the Internal Market
1987	Danish referendum about Single Act International Bank of Settlements: Cooke Committee Report
1988	Second Banking Directive Solvency Directive proposed, passed in 1989 Own Capital Directive Directive about Free Capital Movements
1989	All 12 EEC members participate in ECU

steps towards realizing the Internal Market was accomplished without major problems when the Free Capital Movement Directive was passed in June 1988. The Directive sets the deadline for full liberalization on July 1, 1990, with separate rules, allowing for some capital movements for Greece, Spain, Portugal, and Ireland until 1992.

In 1988, the Second Banking Directive established the principles of mutual recognition and harmonization. It sets minimum requirements regarding the size of own funds of credit institutions, contains the requirement of disclosure of the bank's more important shareholders, eliminates the need for separate endowment capital for foreign branches, and regulates the flow of information between home and host-country supervisory authorities. Most importantly, the Second Directive proposes a single banking licence valid across all member states under home country supervision. By June 1989 it became clear that this directive would be approved.

Two other directives—the Solvency Directive and the Own Capital Directive—were passed in April 1989 by the EEC. The Own Capital Directive calculates core capital and supplementary capital as a percentage of the risk adjusted value of the credit institution's active and passive engagements in order to specify precise guidelines for determining

"capital adequacy." The Solvency Directive proposes 8 percent of weighted actives for "de minimus" capital backing as suggested by the Cooke Committee for the International Bank of Settlements.

In addition to these directives, there are rules in the area of insurance and in the areas of collaboration between stock exchanges and foreign exchange. For example, in the Free Capital Movements Directive it is mentioned that each country can suspend free movements for shorter periods if there is major speculation taking place. These directives are called "minimal directives" in that they allow even more restrictive national rules. However, competitive pressures will likely encourage each country's government to bring its policy into line with the minimum requirements.

In the progression towards the Internal Market, the Free Capital Movements Directive is very tied in with the European Monetary System (EMS). As of September 20, 1989, the 12 member states will be taking part in the European Currency Unit (ECU) cooperation. From July 1990 onwards, in accordance with the first phase of the Delors report, the United Kingdom, Greece, and Portugal are supposed to join the ERM (European Exchange Rate Mechanism) which limits the fluctuation of currency. The next proposed step is for cooperation among the 12 central banks, e.g., in a sort of federal bank system.

THE DANISH BANKING ENVIRONMENT [5,6]

Economic Context[7,8]

Key economic indicators for the year 1988 are shown in Exhibit 2. After two years of recession, with a decline of real GNP of 1 percent in 1987 and about 0.4 percent in 1988, the Danish economy entered its recovery phase in 1989. The annual survey by the Economy Ministry forecasts gross domestic product growth of 2 percent for 1989 and 1.5 percent in 1990. But it is predicted to be a weak recovery and not enough to prevent a rise in unemployment, which is now about 9 percent. Inflation is moderate, about 3.5 percent. Denmark's membership of the European Monetary System links the krone to the D-Mark. In spite of this, the Danish krone is considered to be, and historically has always been, a relatively weak currency in the EMS.

Denmark has had 25 consecutive years with current account deficits and a net foreign debt that equals 40 percent of GNP. The minority-ruled government has tried to stop the increase in private consumption, to reduce public spending in real terms, and to implement policies that encourage household savings. Attempts are being made by the government to achieve a compromise with the opposition, the Social Democratic Party, in order to pass a tax reform including reductions in corporate tax rate and marginal income tax rates.

Recently there has been significant merger activity in the Danish industrial sector as companies try to gain economies of scale and scope prior to 1992. As Danish companies become larger and more international, they will be seeking new sources of finance, both in Denmark and elsewhere. As they are likely to reduce their use of traditional bank loans and turn to capital markets for their financing requirements, this will put pressure on Danish banks to increase their capital base or establish international alliances.

Political Context

The Danish political scene is quite confusing. There are eight parties in the Folketing (Parliament). The government, elected in May 1988, is headed by Conservative party member, Poul Schluter, and consists of a three-party minority coalition (including Conservative, Liberal, and Radical parties). This fragile coalition rests on supporting cuts in taxes and public spending, and "nationalist" ideologies. The main opposition party is the Social Democratic Party, the largest party (genuine cousins to the German and Swedish Social Democratic parties and the British Labour Party), which represents labor and general welfare concerns. This complexity often leads to a locked-in political situation. For example, the often promised tax cuts for the business sector get postponed again and again. The corporate income tax of 50 percent, high salary levels, and high personal taxation has tended to discourage foreign investment.

Since the 1972 referendum approving Denmark's entry to the EEC, little attention had been paid to the implications of realizing a common market. However, a referendum to adopt the 1986 Single European Act was passed by a large majority. Still, much of the political debate centers on VAT (value-added tax) and the price of cars and liquor rather than explicitly on issues of national sovereignty. According to one political scientist, "Nobody believed that this Brussels thing would really happen."

Regulatory Context[9–11]

Danish banks have some of the toughest capital requirements in the world, i.e., 8 percent measured on liabilities rather than the EEC proposed 8 percent measured on risk-weighted assets. All three major banks just exceed this minimum capital ratio. To establish insurance or mortgage credit activities in addition to banking activities, a hold-

---

[5]Laurie, S. "Shoot-out in Danish City." *The Banker*, May 1989, pp. 38–43.
[6]Fairlamb, D. "The Nordic Countries Play-It-Safe Strategy for 1992," *Institutional Investor*, August 1989, pp. 99–106.
[7]Barnes, Hilary. "A Long Hard Road to Eliminate Deficit," *Financial Times*, April 5, 1989.
[8]Barnes, Hilary. "Down Goes the See-Saw in Denmark," *Banker*, December 1986, pp. 27–31.
[9]French, Martin. "Denmark Where Foreigners Are Free to Show a Loss," *Euromoney*, February 1989, pp. 113–116.
[10]Barnes, Hilary. "All Change in Danish Banking," *Banker*, December 1985, pp. 41–43.
[11]Knudsen, Niels Chr. "Danish Banking: The New Competition and Its Consequences," *Technovation*, October 1986, Vol 5, no. 1–3, pp. 61–71.

Exhibit 2 *Denmark Economic Context: Key Facts*

Population	5.1 m
Area	43,069 sq km
GDP (1988 prov)	DKr729 (billion)
per capita (at av 1988 $ exchange rate)	$21,090
Merchandise exports (1988)	DKr187.3 (billion)
Imports	DKr178.2 (billion)
Current balance of payments	DKr–12. (billion)
Debt service ratio	13%
Exports: (billion DKr)	
Agriculture, animal	21.32
Vegetable	7.65
Canned meat, milk	5.29
Manufactures	128.17
Ships	4.68
Fish, fresh, frozen	8.92
Pelts	3.49
Energy	4.50
Crude oil, natural gas	1.86
Other	3.30
Imports	
Agricultural inputs	6.91
Building industry inputs	13.22
Manufacturing inputs	69.67
Energy	10.89
Crude oil	3.24
Machinery	19.70
Transport equipment	10.27
Consumer goods	42.97
Other	4.61
Consumer price change (Dec–Dec 1987–1988)	4.6%
GDP growth rate	
1981–1986 average: 3.3%; 1986: 4.2%; 1987: –0.7%; 1988: –0.4%	
Exchange rate	
£1=12.5550 Danish kroner (29.3.89)	

Source: Financial Times, April 15, 1989.

ing company must be created at a cost of 2 percent of own capital plus the afore mentioned tough capital requirements. Also, Danish banks pay 50 percent tax on their profits before allocating dividends, and then the shareholder is taxed by 50 to 68 percent on the dividend as personal income. This is effectively double taxation, although it is partially offset by some form of dividend tax credits. There is little point in passing out high dividends to shareholders in light of this. Bankers hope for some fiscal changes, but are still waiting.

On the legislative front, Denmark partially lifted capital controls in the years 1983–1984, enabling companies, but not individuals, to make loans on foreign currencies. In June 1988 Denmark adopted EEC directives allowing free flow of capital, and in October 1988 lifted all foreign exchange controls, two years ahead of the 1990 target set by the EEC. The New Banking Act, scheduled for July 1989 but postponed until spring 1990, loosens restrictions on banks' industrial holdings (from 50 to 75 percent) and allows for a more liberal definition of banking activities (e.g., insurance).

The Danish Banking Association has had to lobby the government in order to get the Danish legislation in line with existing and forthcoming EEC directives. Banks have been waiting for the implementation of the solvency ratios established in the Second Banking Directive in order to become more competitive with foreign banks. An implementation commission has been set up by the government to decide how to implement the second directive and to resolve tensions between the banking associations and the regulators (the central bank and industry ministry) over stricter supervision and tougher rules. The collapse of two small banks in 1987 (and the desire to constrict the supply of money) led to the immediate move to curb the right of banks and savings banks to meet their cash requirements through loans from the National Bank. Until January 1988, they were able to borrow the equivalent of 40 percent of their equity capital without providing collateral. This has been reduced to 25 percent. Legislation implementing the EEC directives is expected to take place at the beginning of 1990.

Market Context[12,13]

Denmark is heavily overbanked and the fragmentation of the Danish banking scene is considerable: 70 commercial banks and 140 savings banks serve 5.1 million people (see Exhibit 3). A handful of large banks with national networks, about 15 to 20 regional banks and many small-town banks fight for survival. The top four banks together have a market share of less than 50 percent (see Exhibit 4).

At the top of the Danish banking layer one finds the three big commercial banks: Den Danske Bank, Copenhagen Handelsbank, and Privatbanken; two savings banks: Bikuben and Sparekassen SDS; three or four large regional banks; the two biggest insurance companies: Baltica and Hafnia; and the three major mortgage credit institutions: Kreditforeningen Danmark, Nykredit, and Byggeriets Realkreditfond. The largest of the banks are medium-sized in comparison to European banks (see Exhibit 5). In the 1988 rankings of the top 500 banks, Den Danske Bank rates 43 and Copenhagen Handelsbank rates 72 based on assets. Danish banks, however, are more profitable when measured on return on assets than equity (see Exhibit 6).

Danish companies, small by European standards, are encouraged by the EEC to build networks, to cooperate, and to establish joint research activities (e.g., EUREKA projects). Some Danish multinationals have outgrown the Danish banks as their equity requirements have grown too large for the banks to handle. Although Denmark has been open to foreign banks for many years, foreign banks still account for only 1 percent of the market. High taxation, high labor costs, high net capital requirements, and a significant lack of sizable corporations kept most away. In October 1988 Denmark lifted practically all exchange controls, two years before the date stipulated in the European Commission directive; but there is still no significant inflow of foreign banks.

Competitive Context

The three largest commercial banks together represent only 40 percent of the market share. Den Danske Bank (number 1) and Copenhagen Handelsbank (number 2) are arch rivals, even though they occupy adjoining eighteenth-century mansions on Holmens Kanal. Den Danske Bank already holds 30 percent shares of Provinsbanken. The savings banks, Bikuben and Sparekassen SDS, are about to be converted into public limited companies, thus removing the last formal distinction between commercial and savings banks. So mergers between savings banks and commercial banks are now possible.

Another potential source of competition comes from the expected move of the three largest insurance companies towards banking, allowed for by their holding company structure. This may lead to banks moving towards the insurance area. The three big mortgage credit institutions will soon be offered the possibility of converting from their present mutual structure to joint stock, leading to a breakup of their monopoly on mortgage credit. So the mortgage credit institutions might also be looking at ways of expanding towards financial services.

A restructuring of the industry—some form of shake-out and consolidation—on the home front is expected. The question is who is going to take the first step. Rumors indicate a merger between the biggest insurance company, Baltica, which has already gone into banking, and a mortgage credit institution. Other possible combinations are also fueling speculation. According to one senior bank-

---

[12]Stoehr, Isabella. "Strange Options for Danish Banks," *Euromoney*, April 1989, pp. 67–68.
[13]Kanji, Shireen. "Denmark Slow Dancing in the Big City," *Banker*, May 1988, pp. 67–70.

Exhibit 3 *Number of Inhabitants per Bank Branch, End of 1986 (Letters represent countries; e.g., B = Belgium.)*

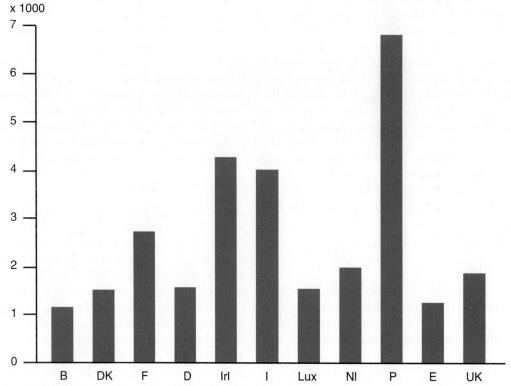

Source: OECD 1987.

Exhibit 4 *Market Concentration and Share of Foreign Institutions[1] (As of the End of 1987—Figures in % of Total Assets)*

	Market Share Absorbed by the Largest Four Banks[2]	Market Share Absorbed by Foreign Institutions[3]
Belgium	42	46
Denmark	47	1
France	42	16
Germany	15	4
Greece	64	NA
Ireland	74	11
Italy	25	3
Luxembourg	24	91
Netherlands	69	10
Portugal	57	3
Spain	21	11
United Kingdom	27	60

Source: OECD, European Central Banks and National Banking Associations, 1987.
[1]Foreign institutions include branches of foreign banks and establishments totally or majority owned by foreign banks.
[2]End 1986 for Belgium, Denmark, France, Germany, and Spain. Figures based on unconsolidated balance sheets.
[3]End 1986 for Ireland.

Exhibit 5 *Comparative Size of Banks*

Rank		Bank and Head Office	Strength Capital ($million)		Soundness Capital Assets Ratio (%)		(Rank)		Profitability Profits ($million)		Profits on Capital (%)		(Rank)		Performance Real Profits Growth (%)		(Rank)	
Capital	Assets		1988	Change	1988	1987	1988	1987	1988	Change (%)	1988	1987	1988	1987	1988	1987	1988	1987
51	63	Banco di Sicilia, Palermo	1,480	13	4.75	4.49	280	269	109	37.8	7.8	12.1	282	233	31.6	NA	76	NA
52	67	Banco Hispano Am, Madrid	1,451	15	5.22	5.00	242	216	454	667.5	33.5	5.2	21	290	632.3	−71.3	5	133
53	72	Bank of Scotland, Edinburgh	1,446	27	5.90	5.94	197	153	311	36.0	24.0	21.6	80	149	36.0	10.8	70	47
54	60	Kansallis-Osake-Pankki	1,439	38	4.15	3.71	343	339	159	54.0	12.8	8.4	217	270	46.5	−6.3	58	91
55	113	Caja de Madrid, Madrid	1,406	19	9.18	8.94	81	66	182	28.8	14.1	NA	201	NA	22.9	18.4	94	37
56	43	NMB Bank, Amsterdam	1,390	9	3.21	3.14	422	384	203	36.7	15.3	12.2	183	228	35.6	21.6	72	31
57	32	Nordeutsche Lbank, Hanover	1,381	14	2.28	2.16	472	437	104	1.7	8.0	8.5	279	269	0.4	72.8	220	13
58	80	Swiss Volksbank, Berne	1,318	5	5.73	5.86	209	158	104	3.3	8.1	8.1	275	274	1.4	−4.5	213	87
59	55	Credit Comm de France	1,310	23	3.40	3.16	409	382	134	23.3	11.3	12.3	235	226	20.1	6.4	103	57
60	58	BFG Bank, Frankfurt	1,304	0	3.48	3.45	403	358	113	−0.8	8.7	17.5	262	175	−1.1	NA	229	NA
61	95	Crediop, Rome	1,283	13	6.86	6.44	146	119	NA	NA	NA	NA	NA	NA	NA	NA	NA	NA
62	36	Banco di Roma, Rome	1,263	0	2.31	2.50	471	415	61	NA	4.9	−68.0	319	320	NA	−608.9	NA	146
63	111	Bank of Ireland, Dublin	1,254	20	8.02	8.40	109	79	181	17.8	15.8	18.0	173	169	14.9	30.3	127	21
64	99	Postipankki, Helsinki	1,237	111	6.89	3.85	144	331	131	98.2	14.4	11.7	197	237	88.6	−32.8	35	120
65	48	ASLK-CGER Bank	1,233	19	3.07	2.80	432	400	223	176.2	19.6	9.4	120	260	172.9	NA	19	NA
66	61	Postbank, Amsterdam	1,176	8	3.45	3.52	407	352	210	17.3	18.5	17.1	133	180	16.4	−17.3	121	109
67	79	Banca Popolare di Novara	1,169	4	5.08	6.57	250	114	379	37.7	33.1	NA	22	NA	31.0	NA	78	NA
68	101	Banco Pop Espanol, Madrid	1,120	24	6.26	5.72	178	172	423	26.1	41.8	74.4	12	13	20.3	7.6	102	53
69	53	Kredietbank, Brussels	1,108	16	2.85	2.81	445	399	184	18.2	17.9	17.0	141	181	18.2	−12.0	115	100
70	74	LB Baden-Wurttemberg	1,101	7	4.59	4.92	292	224	2	192.9	0.2	0.1	335	309	189.4	NA	17	NA
71	83	SG Warburg Group, London	1,098	53	5.03	3.13	256	385	209	13.4	23.0	32.1	90	88	13.4	NA	137	NA
72	96	Copenhagen Handelsbank	1,056	12	5.87	5.74	199	169	186	494.9	18.6	3.5	131	300	468.7	NA	8	NA
73	143	Mediobanca, Milan	1,034	10	10.44	10.04	63	52	126	−13.5	12.8	16.8	218	182	−13.5	−33.8	269	122
74	66	La Caixa, Barcelona	1,022	6	3.63	4.39	387	278	196	43.7	19.8	13.4	117	216	37.1	2.3	67	69
75	90	Banco Popolare di Milano	963	12	4.83	4.84	271	236	204	9.3	22.4	23.1	96	136	4.0	−19.1	191	110

Source: The Banker, October 1989.

Exhibit 6A *Indexes of Bank Profitability**

	Rate of Return on Equity (before tax)	Rate of Return on Assets (before tax)	Average Rate of Inflation
Belgium	14.25	0.39	4.87
Denmark	10.83	1.07	5.20
France	12.93	0.33	5.83
Germany	19.06	0.72	2.27
Greece	14.61	0.40	19.60
Ireland	12.84	1.08	6.27
Italy	19.27	1.09	9.53
Luxembourg	9.06	0.32	6.10
Netherlands	17.12	0.67	1.60
Portugal	5.06	0.33	21.67
Spain	9.95	0.83	10.60
United Kingdom	22.78	1.15	4.70

Source: OECD, Financial statements of banks and EC Commission, 1987.

*Figures in percentages. Averages for the period 1984–1986. The inflation rate has been approximated with the GDP deflator at market prices.

Exhibit 6B *Return on Equity Before Tax, Average 1984–1986*

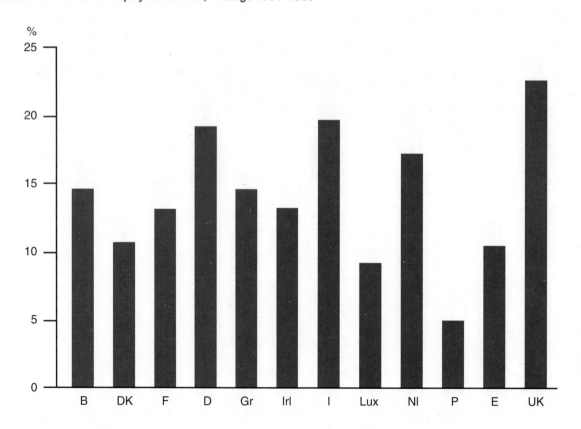

ing executive, "This is like a shoot-out in Dodge City. We're walking around in the shadows with our guns holstered, waiting for the first shot."[14]

Danish banks have had a good history of collaboration, e.g., common credit cards (Dan Kortet).[15] The pressure for home mergers does not come from an inability to serve clients or from the advantage of running data processing systems together—Danish banks have been doing this for years—but from the belief that a strong home base in Denmark is necessary in order to continue expanding abroad. Other initiatives have been to search for European partners. Privatbanken A/S, for example, is part of the Scandinavian Banking Partners (together with Bergen Bank, Skandinaviska Enskilda Banken and Union Bank of Finland). Privatbanken is also the most international of the three big banks with 50 percent of its earnings and assets coming from outside Denmark.

Sociocultural Context[16]

Danish society places less emphasis on hierarchy, avoiding show of power and status. "Jantelov"[17] in Danish refers to keeping a low profile, i.e., the wish not to stick out or try to look better than anyone else. As egalitarianism is stressed, consensus is sought in decision making and committees are often formed to manage tasks. Some say that poor decisions where there is agreement are preferred to good decisions which may cause conflict.

There is more concern for the collective than for the individual, for social welfare than for business opportunity, and for quality of life and relationships rather than task achievement and material benefits. Informality is encouraged and there is generally less reliance on written documents, e.g., policies and procedures. People are mostly motivated in the workplace by job security, interesting work, and time off (vacations). Given the tax structure, it makes little sense to work hard or to be entrepreneurial in order to make more money.

COPENHAGEN HANDELSBANK A/S

Nature of Activities

Copenhagen Handelsbank A/S (CHB) was established in 1873. By 1988, CHB was ranked second in size and seventh in profitability in Denmark (see Exhibit 7). CHB is ranked 98th in terms of assets (72nd in terms of capital) in Europe.[18] By global rankings, CHB rated 185th in June 1988, but was no longer among the top 200 by 1989.[19] As of December 1988, the bank has 6,319 employees and a domestic network of almost 300 branches.

The principal activity of the bank is offering full banking services to the corporate as well as the household sectors in Denmark. The activities of the Copenhagen Handelsbank Group are, however, quite widespread (see Exhibit 8). The financing of Danish trade and industry takes place through the provision of overdraft facilities, short- and medium-term loans, acceptance credits, and the discounting of trade bills. The bank's lending is funded from the current accounts of both its individual and corporate customers, not one of which accounts for a significant proportion of total loans and deposits.

International operations consist of branches in London, New York, Singapore, and the Cayman Islands, a wholly owned subsidiary in Luxembourg, and representative offices in Fuengirola and Madrid (Spain), Nice (France), Hong Kong, Stockholm, and Tokyo. CHB's international business consists of foreign exchange operations, international payments, and financial arrangements. Foreign exchange operations are extensive, accounting for approximately 30 percent of the total Danish foreign exchange business at present. In the Eurocurrency markets, the bank deals in short-term funds both for its own account and for the account of its customers and negotiates medium-term financing through syndicated loans.

[14]Laurie, S. (1989).

[15]Ladegaard, Per. "Overcoming Resistance and Achieving Success with a National Payment Card—Dan Kortet," *World of Banking*, March/April 1986, pp. 21–25.

[16]This discussion is based on findings of Hofstede, G. *Cultures Consequences*. Berkeley, Calif: Sage Publications (1980).

Laurent, A. "The Cultural Diversity of Western Conceptions of Management," *International Studies of Management and Organization*. (1983), Vol. XIII, no. 1–2, pp. 75–96.

[17]Sandemose, A. *En Flykting Krysser Sitt Spor*. Oslo, Norway (1933).

[18]"International Banking Survey," *The Banker*, October 1989.

[19]*Business Week*, June 1988; *Business Week*, June 1989.

Exhibit 7 *Size and Profitability of Danish Banks (Figures for 1987)*

Denmark	Size	Profitability
Den Danske Bank	1	1
Copenhagen Handelsbank	2	7
Privatbanken	3	6
Sparekassen SDS	4	4
Provinsbanken	5	3
Bikuben	6	8
Andelsbanken Denmark	7	2
Jyske Bank	8	5

Source: OECD, 1987.
Spearman correlation index = 0.0151.

Copenhagen Handelsbank A/S is owned by approximately 160,000 shareholders. It is estimated that about 85 percent of the share capital is owned by Danish shareholders while about 15 per cent is in foreign hands. Copenhagen Handelsbank A/S are bearer shares, but the shareholders may have their shares registered. At the end of 1988, the bank's register of shareholders numbered 139,800. No shareholder holds more than 10 percent of the share capital. According to the "Danish Companies Act," shareholders holding more than 10 percent of the share capital must notify the bank. At the end of 1988 no shareholder had given such notice.

Recent History and Change

For many years CHB was ranked number one in Denmark, earning good margins in a not very competitive market. In 1986 the bank lost Dkr821 million, primarily due to losses on foreign exchange, huge bond losses, a downturn in the economy, and mismanagement.[20] It was then that Den Danske Bank, arch rival and next door neighbor, took over the number one position in Denmark. This situation was described by one senior manager as "definitely not a crisis" but as "slightly going in the wrong direction"; concern seemed primarily for loss of image than loss of profitability. Others attributed it to a lack of understanding of the changes in the Danish macroeconomy and to internal political concerns.

The CEO Bendt Hansen, a traditional banker who had been with CHB for all of his working life and who was a long-standing chairman of the Danish Banking Association, brought in a service-oriented consultant "as a mental exercise"; no great changes were expected. From 1986–1987 the bank was redesigned by an ad hoc organization composed of committees and teams supervised by a steering committee. The previous functional structure was replaced by a divisional structure defined by customer segments—four independent customer organizations or delivery systems (i.e., corporate, retail, international and support)—and was crossed with product-oriented departments in a "matrix-like" manner. All product development was placed in one division. The support function, previously seen as powerful, was split into four departments EDP, logistics, safety and education. In 1987 a strategic planning unit was created reporting directly to the CEO. In November 1988, a new strategic plan was developed.

Over 200 people at headquarters and one-third of the branch network changed jobs within the company. Profit responsibility was pushed down the hierarchy and decision making became more decentralized. Information flows were directed more vertically, with coordination and control at the top. "Before, everyone needed to know everything." Afterwards, less information was exchanged laterally as the different divisions were now more independent; "now everyone has their own shop . . . and competes." The culture became less traditional: the dress code less formal, with more use of first names, i.e., it became more typically "Danish" and less typically "banking." Profitability became the raison d'être; the focus was on the bottom line.

[20]Laurie, S. (1989).

Exhibit 8 *The Copenhagen Handelsbank Group*

Subsidiaries

Customer Areas

Copenhagen HandelsBank
International S.A.
Retail banking
Luxembourg
Share capital LUF 1,000 million

Corporate mid-market

Nordania Holding A/S
Share capital Kr. 72,000,000

Corporate large clients

COCO Securities A/S
Stockbroking company
Institutional banking
Share capital Kr. 50,000,000

CHB International
Holger Morville
Holdingaktieselskab
Share capital Kr. 75,000,000

Divisions
Investment Bank

Investor Venture A/S
Share capital Kr. 300,000,000
Copenhagen HandelsBank owns 50%

Investment Service

Handels Finans A/S
Trade Finance Center
Share capital Kr. 40,000,000

Money Market and Foreign Exchange
ErhvervsParmer A/S
(Corporate Partner)
Share capital Kr. 20,000,000

Staff and Supply Departments
Service Center
  Supply and support
  EDP/organization
KHB Ejendomsadministration A/S
  Training
and 5 property companies
Total share capital Kr. 16,550,000

Group staff and secretariats

7 finance and
leasing companies
Internal audit
Total share capital Kr. 11,778,740

Source: Copenhagen Handelsbank report and accounts, 1988.

Exhibit 9 Annual Report (Three-year Summaries)

Copenhagen Handelsbank   **Copenhagen Handelsbank Group**

1986	1987	1988	Profit and Loss Account (million kroner)	1988	1987	1986
2,145	2,442	2,551	Net income from interest and commission	2,971	2,759	2,425
238	62	187	Profit on foreign exchange	192	8	208
528	489	535	Other ordinary income	614	526	534
2,911	2,993	3,273	Profit before expenses, etc.	3,777	3,293	3,167
1,952	2,133	2,225	Expenses	2,398	2,238	2,012
959	860	1,048	Primary operating profit	1,379	1,055	1,155
421	433	855	Provisions and depreciation	998	561	514
538	427	193	Profit before extraordinary income and expenses, etc.	381	494	641
238	−8	−211	Extraordinary income and expenses (including revaluation of Combi-pension portfolios)	−206	3	242
−1,612	−165	1,275	Revaluation of portfolio of bonds and shares, etc.	1,104	−282	−1,669
−836	254	1,257	Profit before taxes	1,279	215	−786
−15	−13	149	Paid/estimated taxes	169	−39	34
			Profit including minority shareholders	1,110	254	−820
			Minority shareholders	2	−13	1
−821	267	1,108	Net profit for the year	1,108	267	−821

1986	1987	1988	Balance Sheet as of December 31st (million kroner, assets cash in hand, and assets held in domestic and foreign banks)	1988	1987	1986
19,640	28,254	29,691		33,878	30,591	22,920
22,754	20,803	24,008	Bonds, shares and mortgage deeds, etc.	24,257	20,470	22,622
39,979	44,178	44,897	Total advances	−57,544	55,346	48,760
11,056	12,050	14,928	Customers' liability for guarantees	8,827	8,530	7,768
6,036	5,054	7,534	Other assets	8,018	6,313	6,376
99,465	110,339	121,058	Total assets	132,524	121,250	108,446

Liabilities

1986	1987	1988		1988	1987	1986
47,696	50,403	52,710	Total deposits	55,154	51,255	48,108
27,472	34,429	35,863	Debt to domestic and foreign banks	50,616	46,309	38,534
11,056	12,050	14,928	Liability on guarantees	8,827	8,530	7,768
4,500	4,156	7,054	Other liabilities	7,273	5,708	5,185
2,746	2,829	3,242	Subordinated loan capital	3,242	2,829	2,746
			Shareholders' funds:			
			Of which: Minority shareholders	151	147	110`
5,995	6,472	7,261	Copenhagen Handelsbank	7,261	6,472	5,995
99,465	110,339	121,058	Total liabilities	132,524	121,250	108,446

Exhibit 9 *continued*

Copenhagen Handelsbank				**Copenhagen Handelsbank Group**		
1986	1987	1988	Key Figures Primary operating profit in percent of average shareholders' funds)	1988	1987	1986
15.0	13.9	15.3		20.1	17.0	18.1
			Net profit in per cent of average			
−12.8	4.3	16.1	shareholders' funds	16.1	4.3	−12.8
9.34	9.09	9.30	Capital ratio	8.37	8.26	8.48
15.0	15.0	15.0	Dividend			
414	384	430	Book value per share			
260	228	351	Share price at year-end			
6,224	6,277	5,988	Number of employees at year-end	6,319	6,532	6,350
			(in terms of full-time employees)			

Source: Copenhagen Handelsbank report and accounts, 1988.

Exhibit 10 *Copenhagen Handelsbank's Share Price*

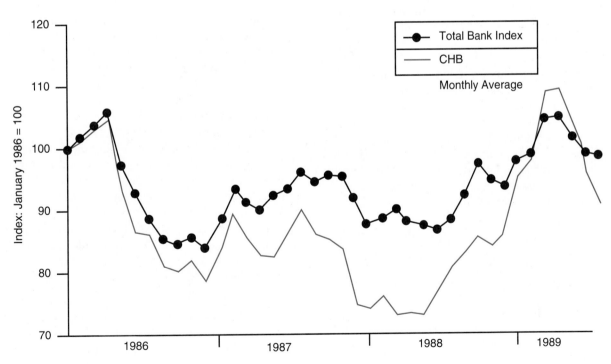

Throughout the last two years (1987–1989) "drastic" changes have taken place. These changes were triggered mostly by concern for survival and profitability. CHB had moderate profits in 1987 of Dkr267 million. The results of 1988 were better, namely Dkr1,108 million. Exhibit 9 provides the three-year summary. CHB's share price has improved as well (see Exhibit 10).

New Directions

In September 1987 Hans Ejvind Hansen (HEH) was brought in to assist in implementing the changes. He was appointed chairman in March 1989, the first non-banker in the history of CHB to become CEO. An economist by education, former CEO of a major mortgage credit institution (Nykredit), and an assistant director in the Danish Banking Association, HEH was chosen by the board, according to him, for his "experience in mergers" and for "being a team player." HEH prefers to maintain a low profile and is seen as informal, even humble—he reportedly drives a "deux chevaux" and is often seen in shirt-sleeves. He is described as "undogmatic and friendly, but tough when decisions have to be implemented."

The new CEO brings a new vision (even recorded on video tape): "To be the first organization that springs to mind when money is the essence for the translation of ideas into reality." HEH sees the overriding mission of CHB to be the leading, although not necessarily biggest, financial service organization. The strategy, clearly articulated in speeches (as shown in Exhibit 11), is threefold: (1) self-development; (2) to be an active player; and (3) to become European. Nine Principles of Banking (see Exhibit 12) spell out goals (e.g., profitability) and the necessary attitudes (e.g., international, customer close, and credible).

COPENHAGEN HANDELSBANK A/S AND 1992

Views of 1992

"1992" evokes a wide range of views within CHB. For some, 1992 seemed to be considered "business as usual." This is seen in the following remarks: "1992 is not special, it is an ongoing process." "1992 is not a major change." "All this talk about 1992 may speed up some already ongoing processes."

From this view point, 1992 is seen as just one step further in the development of the Common Market.

Others are optimistic and see 1992 as something positive: "1992 is equal to a lot of potential." CHB is secure and confident about 1992. One reason given for being confident is the effective personal networks of the bank's key personnel. Another reason given is that, having managed the recent changes, CHB feels prepared to manage the changes induced by the Internal Market. It is, according to one senior manager, "pretty cocksure that we can manage it."

Some within the bank express "difficulties in getting to grips with 1992." They find it rather "diffuse" and find that expectations may fuel some changes but may also lead to disappointment. Others are more concerned and see 1992 as "very emotional and ill defined. . . . Hidden within the issue are a lot of more or less well understood processes." Some felt that the implications were farreaching and were doubtful about whether senior management was really aware of the implications of 1992.

Many emphasized that 1992 was more of a concern for their customers. According to HEH, 1992 is "not that important to us [but] is important primarily because it is important to the bank's customers." Another senior manager also acknowledged that customers although "not terribly sophisticated," are the most affected. The position of the bank, however, was, "It's not our business to educate customers." A one- to two-person unit existed, however, to advise customers regarding the EEC and functioned as a referral service— "basically a telephone number."

Others also saw 1992 as having more external than internal relevance: "1992 is very political"; "a power field between European and national law making." Nevertheless, it was felt that the bank had to keep close to public opinion on the EEC in general and on 1992 in particular. The bank was considered, by some, to be "ahead of the political scene."

Awareness of 1992

Although Denmark joined the EEC in 1972, the issue became more salient to the general public when the referendum on the single European Act was passed in 1986. Within the bank, however, it was acknowledged that attention to 1992 had only begun within the past 6 to 12 months. According to the chairman, "By July 1988 it became a neces-

Exhibit 11 CHB Strategy

- Self-development
- Active role in structural development of the Danish financial sector
- Becoming a European regional bank and having an open and active attitude to European cooperation

Exhibit 12 Nine Principles of Banking

Goals
1. Financial service organization
2. Leadership
3. Profitability

Attitudes
4. Openness
5. Credibility
6. Danish and international
7. Closeness to customers
8. Visible and consistent management
9. Professional, creative, and flexible colleagues

sity to take 1992 into account."[21] This was confirmed by one senior manager who was asked to give a seminar regarding 1992 in May 1988 when 150 managers "were forced to attend." However, by November 1988, another seminar was organized on the request of the legal department; 300 interested participants attended. There was seemingly little interest in the issue before actual legislative measures forced the bank to act.

In contrast, Per Bendix, head of strategic planning, stated that CHB has always been aware of 1992 and had been tracking the development towards the Internal Market very closely: "Since the appearance of the First Banking Directive in 1977 information has been coming in a steady stream." He also stated, however, that he would be surprised if more than ten people knew about the Second Directive. One senior manager acknowl-

edged that although there was "a lot of talk in the papers and the TV [about 1992], very few really knew anything." Another said that little information was provided by the bank—"You have to get it for yourself." There was, apparently, "no dialogue" within the bank on this issue.

Time and Money Spent in 1992

No specific funds have been allocated per se to deal with 1992. The time allotted by head office to this issue is estimated at between 5 to 10 percent maximum. However, several top managers, the CEO, and the chiefs of strategic planning and accounting and control are actively involved in committee work within the Danish Banking Association. In the summer of 1989 a standing committee of 20 members, two from each of the three major banks,

---

[21]In June 1988 the ECOFIN (European Council of Finance and Economic Ministers) decided to scrap foreign exchange controls by July 1990. Also, the Free Capital Movement Directive was passed in July 1988.

was formed from the EEC committee to "upgrade 1992." This committee, which included the CHB head of planning, met "a couple of times a month."

Lobbying in Brussels on an individual basis was not considered worth the hours or kroner for the bank, but was done at a national level, primarily through the banking association, and at the European level, through the Federation Bancaire. "In Denmark, we have a virgin-like approach to lobbying. Perhaps this stems from a national inferiority complex." Denmark is considered to be too small to exert any real influence, and the bank did not have the resources to do so. "Here we can chat with the Prime Minister and the Finance Minister; it's a more casual approach."

One senior manager spent considerable time and effort on the issue and wrote a book about 1992, but this effort was based on personal interest rather than on any interest on the part of the organization. The bank's attitude seemed to be, "Well, it's not your job, but go ahead if it doesn't interfere with doing your job."

Sources of Information about 1992

At first, information regarding 1992 was obtained mainly via the Federation Bancaire (The European Banking Association) of which the former CEO was a member, and then later—increasing "dramatically over the last few years"—from the Danish Banking Association. There is a considerable exchange of information between the different major financial institutions. The Danish Banking Association has recently established a permanent committee which meets regularly to discuss special financial sector problems concerning the Common Market. It is not clear, however, to what extent senior managers feel that they receive or provide information to these sources. Several indicated that they can't wait or rely on official channels.

Most senior managers rely on personal experience and contacts. Many have personal friends in the government where they have held positions in the past. The CEO refers to his experience as head of a credit mortgage institution as having been a useful source of information. Another senior manager gets useful information by tracking competitors and by listening to his people "out there in the field."

According to Per Bendix, "most of the information comes from networking, travelling to Brus-

sels several times a year and speaking with people." He estimated that 10 percent of information came from written reports. The Price Waterhouse and Cecchini reports are "good as they give comparative data which we can't afford to collect ourselves." These reports (which do not include Denmark) are "not believed as truth but are used to see trends." CHB also has access to certain databases on the EEC, developed by the ministry, but has rarely used them.

Per Bendix feels confident that his department can manage to prepare the bank for change. Other senior managers state that little information about 1992 is available from the planning department, leaving them to get information on their own initiative. No external consultants have been used specifically with regard to 1992. One senior manager, Hans Martens, has been used quite regularly on an informal, ad hoc basis as an internal source of information on 1992 since he has written a book on the subject of the Internal Market. Senior management is aware of this, but has not delegated any specific task to him along these lines. The bank accepts that he is used as an expert by other institutions and only asks that he uses the CHB name.

Mechanisms Used for Gathering Information about 1992

Historically, the responsibility for tracking 1992 has been gradually shifted from the economics department to the planning department (even before the reorganization). Within the planning department, one to two persons have followed Common Market issues and have served as consultants to some customers. Now the responsibility of keeping track of the 1992 development is seen to lie primarily in the 12-person planning department, particularly with Per Bendix. This is one of his tasks along with the recently acquired (past three months) responsibility for the group's corporate marketing and information (communication and image, i.e., public relations)—25 people in all. The planning department is responsible for tracking 1992 until a directive has been issued at which point it is followed by the legal and accounting departments according to their field of interest.

No new structures—special units, task forces, or committees—have been created to manage 1992. They prefer to manage it on an "ad hoc basis, with no extra set-up . . . as committees tend to grow bureaucratic." 1992 is considered part of the daily routine: "Everyone should have this in their backbone." While a few seminars about 1992 have been held within the bank, they have been primarily for general information purposes.

According to Per Bendix, 1992 will be treated in the formal framework; i.e., the planning department will provide input to the top management who in turn will provide information to the board of directors. However, some feel that there is no coordination of the effort to understand the implications of 1992. According to one senior manager, "planning shouldn't plan, it's too important . . . it needs to put inputs together, to coordinate." The International Division, for example, has apparently not been integrated into these discussions despite the fact that one-third of the balance sheet is generated outside Denmark. And, very few managers, particularly at the top, have any international experience or knowledge.

Models and Methods for Evaluation

The bank uses no formal or sophisticated methods to evaluate information regarding 1992. Informal models based on profitability and cost concerns were used in general. The balance sheet was considered to be the best model. Klaus Monsted Pedersen, head of budget, has developed online reporting systems linking all branches, foreign and domestic, to the accounting and control department. He also reports that efforts have been made towards linking the budget with the business plan. According to some, "There is still a long way to go on the business plan level." The last one (which was based on Porter models) was described as "weak, vague, and diffuse" and as having had problems with implementation. Strategy in the past is described as having sometimes been based on "muddling about"; concern was expressed that they were "not systematic in our approach."

No formal scenarios have been used. Some quite broad scenarios were used not as a model but led to the idea of an international regional bank. Specific scenarios were constructed regarding economic situations/country and the structure of formal markets, but there was "little use made of it finally."

According to Per Bendix, "Simulation models can be created or bought but do not provide meaning":

What 1992 means can't be described in just two overheads. This doesn't provide competitive advantage for very long. Intellectual mechanisms are needed. We have to bring people around the table and make them work, make the organization and its different parts work together. It depends on organizational capability, not capital and technology.

Hans Ejvind Hansen prefers "to have a vision, or goals, which are more robust and free of external changes and influences. . . . In this way, we can be more open to events, and can adapt more readily." A vision has been formulated, not to address Common Market issues per se, but the broader expected changes in domestic and foreign competition given the increasing internationalization and deregulation. A video of the CEO explaining the new strategy and the new vision of the bank has been created.

Decision Rules Used

An often expressed view was that past experience or procedures cannot be used in the present situation. For example, the international "strategy" of the early eighties setting up foreign branches was considered to have been "quite unclear" and "done in bits and pieces," whereas "1992" needed "clear strategic reasoning."

It was acknowledged that decisions regarding 1992 would be made at the top—by HEH and the board of directors—based on input from the planning department as well as the top management team. As different perspectives result in different scenarios, "the core of the process is political bargaining and trade-offs." One senior manager compared the process to that of the Communist Party as "there can be wild debate before the decision is made, but after this people stay loyal to the conclusion."

Although the organizational hierarchy has been flattened and decision making has been decentralized following the reorganization, the top management group (composed of three people) is perceived as taking all the major decisions. In fact, some feel that decision making has become more political now that the structure is more flat and as there are more trade-offs involved. Information flows less easily as different units have become more independent and more competitive. Strategic plans are now "secret." Of course, some information and decisions have become more sensitive, e.g., those concerning merger and acquisition proposals.

Criteria Determining Priorities about 1992

Profitability has become the number one criteria for determining priorities. "Profitability is the main issue in deciding, and has been more and more stressed in the last five years. Everyone is very aware now, whereas ten years ago they didn't bother." Before, image was more important. Now, "the prospect of being hanged concentrates the mind wonderfully."

According to HEH, decisions would be based on "business not people" criteria. For example, while it might be easier for the bank to collaborate with other Scandinavian banks, from business criteria it is more important to look for alliances with "continental" European banks.

Decisions would be driven less by a need for certainty or "security" and more by the need to take the right decisions earlier, even if the risks are greater. Others felt it was important not to rush; i.e., time was needed to think so that "if we jump on the wagon, we jump on the right wagon." Some hoped that the bank would be proactive in its approach: "If it would be reactive it would be a pity."

Manageability was also seen as an important criteria for setting priorities. Some within the bank are very confident about the bank's capability to deal with 1992: "We are very cocksure that we can manage it." The recent changes in the bank were thought to have prepared it to deal with the changes to be brought about by 1992 "with joy not with fear." However, one senior manager stated that he would like to get used to the changes only just implemented without having to worry about what happens next.

Another senior manager felt that the implications of 1992 need to be understood and accepted by the organization and that it is "a long process to communicate and to educate." For example, one must educate the organization to consider credit risks not only in the short-term but more in the light of long-term implications and commitment. Another senior manager expressed the need for the bank to learn that there are no differences between domestic and foreign risk or between domestic and foreign assets. While a senior personnel manager acknowledged the need for management to become more international in thinking and in experience, with regard to management training and development, "we have enough to do without 1992."

Most decisions would be taken without a sense of urgency. Urgency, however, would clearly be felt in the event of a possible takeover. It was Per Bendix who was quoted as saying, "This is like a shoot-out in Dodge city. We're all walking around in the shadow with our guns holstered to our legs, waiting for the first shot."

THE DUNLOP-PIRELLI UNION

Sumantra Ghoshal
INSEAD, Fontainebleau Cedex, France

In the first week of March 1979, the management of Pirelli, the Italian tire, cable, and rubber group, received a request to contribute £25 million to the restructuring plan of Dunlop, its UK-based partner of over 10 years in a Union that had originally been conceived as a "total integration of the operations of the two leading European rubber and tire companies." In essence, the restructuring plan officially confirmed what was widely known within the industry: that Dunlop's competitive position in the tire business had eroded and it was facing severe financial difficulties. Dunlop's request for Pirelli's contribution to its restructuring plan was based on the provision in the union agreement that should additional investments be required for any business, each of the two parties to the Union would provide finance in proportion to its share of the particular operation.

Opinions within Pirelli were divided on how to respond to Dunlop's request. Broadly, there were two views and most senior managers appeared to support the first:

1. *Pirelli should turn down the request, just as Dunlop had turned down a similar request from Pirelli in 1972 for contributing to the investments necessary for restructuring Industrie Pirelli (IP), the Italian company's most important subsidiary controlling all its operations in Italy and within the European Economic Community (EEC). Despite a 49% share in IP, Dunlop had distanced itself from the restructuring plan for it did not believe that IP had a future. The situation now was exactly the reverse: as one Pirelli manager*

described, *"all of Dunlop was sinking and nothing could save the company any more."*

Those who supported this view acknowledged that a negative response to Dunlop would be the final straw that would break the back of the Union. However, they felt that the Union had never worked, anyway, and had only constrained Pirelli's development, serving as a massive drain of management time and energy. "We had to focus our attention on rationalizing and integrating our own operations," said one manager who supported dissolution of the Union. "Our approach to the business was to ride the tiger—to improve factories and develop new products—while Dunlop believed in a defensive 'keep the system going' strategy. It was clear that the Union was already dead, and I felt we should stop dragging along the corpse."

2. *There were others within Pirelli who felt that while the Union had so far not provided the advantages that were expected, the strategic problems it had been intended to solve still remained. "The Union was based on very sound logic, and nothing had changed to alter that logic." Both companies were undersized, individually, to compete with the global giants in the tire business. Yet, because of the almost perfect complimentarity of their operations, their combined force was formidable. Despite the obvious strategic potential, the Union had not been effective because of defective systems and, particularly, because of an inadequate management structure. These managers, therefore, advocated that Pirelli should seriously*

consider Dunlop's proposal and use it as an appropriate context to make some basic changes in systems and management processes so as to make the Union function as had been originally foreseen. While some of these managers also considered the possibility of acquiring Dunlop, that option was quickly ruled out since it was obvious that Pirelli did not have the requisite resources.

For Leopoldo Pirelli, the elegant, soft-spoken, and publicity-shy chairman of the family-held company, the decision posed a basic dilemma. Even beyond the obvious strategic potential for both companies, the Union was a statement of the faith that he shared with Sir Reay Geddes, the recently retired chairman of Dunlop, that European companies could and must cooperate to mount an effective European challenge to the American global competitors. Apart from the specific consequences for his own company, dissolution of the Union would amount to a public confirmation of the failure of the first and most visible venture on the part of two large European companies to mount such a European challenge. Yet, it was also clear that the Union had not served its purpose and efforts to save it might lead to his company going down with the sinking Dunlop. Besides, he did not share the same personal rapport with Sir Campbell Fraser, the new chairman of Dunlop since 1978, as he did with Sir Reay. Perhaps the two companies had far more in common in 1969, when the Union was formed, than they had 10 years later. Changes in the environment, in relative performance, and in people might have destroyed too many bridges. If the vision had not worked so far, could anything make it work now, he wondered.

A decision had to be made soon. The next meeting of the Central Committee of the Union was scheduled for the third week of March and Sir Campbell Fraser would expect to have an answer from Pirelli during that meeting. In two weeks, Pirelli had either to say 'no' to Sir Campbell, and think through its own strategy for competing in a business in which stagnant demand, technological change, and intense worldwide competition among a few large and resource-rich rivals made the survival of a relatively small company like Pirelli both difficult and uncertain. Alternatively, it had to have a detailed set of proposals to make to Sir Campbell about changes in the structure and management of

the Union as a pre-condition for the company's continuance in the hitherto unsuccessful partnership.

PRIOR TO THE UNION

Tire Industry Trends

In the 1960s, the rubber and tire industry was still growing at an average yearly growth rate of 8%, down from 15% during the 1950s. At the end of the decade the five large US rubber groups (Goodyear, Firestone, Uniroyal, General Tire and Rubber, B. F. Goodrich) dominated the industry, followed by four European companies (Dunlop, Pirelli, Michelin, and Continental) and Bridgestone from Japan. Dunlop and Pirelli were respectively number one and two in size outside the US. The following table shows consolidated turnovers of world players: in 1969, however, Pirelli's revenue from tires was 45% of total sales, vis-à-vis 65% for Dunlop and nearly 100% for Michelin. US producers showed varying degrees of diversification: tire divisions accounted for over 80% of turnover for Goodyear and Firestone, and roughly 50% of turnover for Uniroyal and General T&R.

Although growth in Europe had exceeded that of the US in the 1960s, the size gap—which had originated from the earlier development of the US auto industry—had not closed significantly. This was due in good measure to the expansion of the large American rubber groups into Europe. As a Pirelli manager emphasized, "while in 1965 their presence had been marginal, by 1970 US companies had 25% of the European tire market." This trend, which was noticeable in other industries as well, led many observers to comment on the growing hegemony of the big US multinationals as a major threat to European business. The American tire firms had increased their overseas investments in the wake of the large US automotive manufacturers. Indeed, by the end of the 1960s, most key OEMs (original equipment manufacturers) operated in several countries. Also, tariff barriers in Europe were dropping as the EEC became operational. These trends meant that the international interdependence of markets was increasing.

It was also during the sixties that Michelin, the third-largest rubber/tire company outside the US, followed an aggressive strategy to introduce the radial, a new type of tire which the company had invented in 1948. This product offered significant

	Turnover	(M£)	Net Profit	(M£)	Employees	(000)
	1961	1969	1961	1969	1961	1969
Goodyear	1473	3215	76.2	156.2	91.3	133.5
Firestone	1183	2279	63.6	116.7	82.6	109.1
Uniroyal	940	1554	27.1	46.6	58	67.0
General T&R	809	1078	27.3	89.9	46.3	36.3
B. F. Goodrich	758	1229	31.0	37.8	39	48.9
Dunlop	742	1188	16.5	26.3	95	108.0
Pirelli	552	1067	19.7	8.9	55	76.0
Michelin	405	1062	4.2	9.9	35	75.0
Bridgestone	—	363	—	20.0	—	16.3
Continental	—	361	—	11.0	—	31.7

advantages over both the traditional bias-ply and the newer bias-belted American tires. Total life doubled from 20,000 to 40,000 miles with an added cost of only 25%. Road holding and load characteristics of the radial were also markedly better. However, it had the disadvantage of requiring extensive redesign of the vehicle's suspension system, which entailed significant R&D costs on the part of the automotive manufacturers. For this reason, the industry outside France had been reluctant to convert to the new tire. Michelin had made massive investments in new plants and manufacturing technology development and was marketing the radial aggressively, stimulating demand for the new tire. The spread of cars using front wheel drive and the improvements of vehicle performance supported Michelin's efforts and by 1970, the radial tire accounted for over 50% of the original equipment market for automobiles in Western Europe, up from about 38% in 1965 (see Exhibit 1). By contrast, in the US and Japan radials were virtually unknown in 1970. Thus, the technology was exclusively European, with Michelin the clear leader, offering the only steel-belted radial commercially available. Pirelli was in the number two position, offering the CN53 tire, a textile-belted radial particularly suited for luxury and sports cars because of its ride and handling characteristics. In 1968, Michelin scored a marketing coup by offering to supply radials to Fiat (Italy's largest automotive manufacturer and Pirelli's largest single customer) at conventional tire prices: Fiat announced its intention to "radialize" car production within six months. Pirelli launched a major investment program to expand production of its radials.

"G. B. Pirelli & C" had been founded in 1872 to manufacture and process rubber goods and had diversified into tires and cables by the end of the century. Its policy of expansion and internationalization had continued all along, so that the group, in 1969, operated in 13 different countries including all the major European and South American nations and Canada. Since its foundation, several changes had been made to its legal structure: Pirelli & C was now a holding company controlling Pirelli Spa (PSPA), the Italian and European industrial concern based in Milan, and Societe Internationale Pirelli (SIP), a holding company based in Basel, Switzerland, which had overall responsibility for the group's overseas operations. PSPA and SIP had been originally separated for legal and financial reasons only. SIP dated back to the early 1920s, when it was created to meet the group's needs for access to international money markets.

Until 1969 the Pirelli group had been developing steadily: the turnover of the Italian company, PSPA, had increased 44% since 1964 to a total of 353 billion Lit. (Italian currency) and the turnover of the Swiss holding company, SIP, had reached 335 billion Lit., with a growth of over 80% since 1964 (in 1969, 1$ = 625 Lit.). The aggregated turnover of almost 700 billion Lit. came 45% from tires, 40% from cables and 15% from diversified consumer and industrial products. The group operated 82 plants worldwide, employed 76,000 people, half of whom worked in Italy with a concentration of 13,000 employees at the Bicocca factory in Milan. The company's operating results for the 1965–1969 period are summarized in Exhibit 2.

Leopoldo Pirelli exercised control through the holdings of his family and friends in Pirelli & C and, through a complex ownership structure, on the whole group (see Exhibit 3). In 1969, the Milan-based PSPA had an organization structure headed by three managing directors in charge of electric goods, rubber

Exhibit 1 *Sales of Car Tires: France, Germany, Italy, and the UK*

Year	Sales (Million Units)			% Radials	
	OEM[a]	Replacement	Total	OEM	Replacement
1965	33	32	65	37	34
1966	34	35	69	40	36
1967	33	40	73	44	39
1968	39	45	84	49	43
1969	41	48	89	56	48
1970	44	52	96	64	53
1971	46	56	102	74	61
1972	47	61	108	82	70
1973	48	58	106	88	77
1974	40	52	92	92	82
1975	37	53	90	93	83
1976	42	55	97	94	85
1977	44	54	98	95	87
1978	45	56	101	96	89

[a]OEM = original equipment manufacturers.

Exhibit 2 *Pirelli's Operating Results: 1965–1969 (All Figures in £000)*

	1965	1966	1967	1968	1969
Sales	239,940	275,362	316,210	351,429	392,896
Operating profits before depreciation, interests, and taxes	35,937	47,342	45,825	46,999	41,597
Income from other sources	767	871	1,046	1,266	1,472
Gross income	36,704	48,213	46,871	48,265	43,069
Depreciation	10,695	11,690	14,156	15,228	16,791
Interest	5,533	6,785	7,082	7,823	10,339
Taxation	8,075	11,859	11,094	8,336	4,187
Net income	12,401	17,879	14,539	16,878	11,752
Minority shareholders' interests	2,853	3,067	1,736	4,945	5,533
Attributable income	9,548	14,812	12,803	11,933	6,219

goods, and finance and administration, who reported to the president, Pirelli himself. At the time, observers remarked that company loyalty was perhaps the most important criterion to enter top management of Pirelli. Indeed, there was a strict rule of promoting managers only from within as part of a distinct company culture which permeated the corporation. Considering the firm as a family, a low-profile attitude towards the public and the press and a propensity to understatement were some of the key ingredients of what was referred to, both inside and outside the company, as the "Pirelli style." These strong values, together with the group's international presence, characterized Pirelli on the Italian industrial scene.

PSPA stood at the center of the Pirelli group. It represented the real "casa madre" (parent company), where worldwide strategies for tires originated, including decisions on products as well as on key functions like raw-material purchasing. R&D on new products and on manufacturing process technology was conducted in Milan. Directors of overseas subsidiaries were fully responsible for the local operations in all three sectors and reported to SIP in Basel on a country-by-country basis. This meant that the group as a whole lacked a coordinated worldwide business sector approach: PSPA's strategic decisions influenced directly each business of the foreign subsidiaries,

Exhibit 3   *Organization Chart: Pirelli Group, 1969*

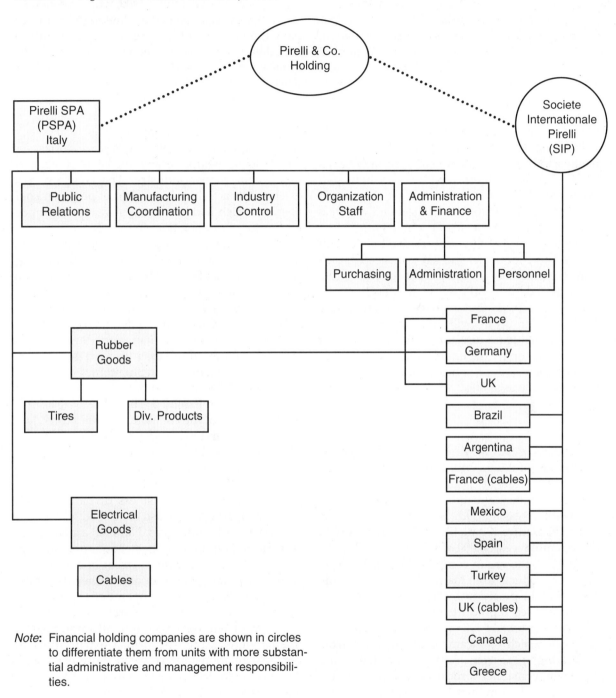

Note: Financial holding companies are shown in circles
to differentiate them from units with more substantial administrative and management responsibilities.

which, however, answered to SIP. The lines that tied the whole structure together were mainly functional across all three business sectors: for example, even though the cable businesses were run nationally by the subsidiaries, the technical direction for cables woldwide came from the director general of cables in Italy. Training and personnel development was another PSPA function: a typical top manager's career path would include an initial position in PSPA, some international experience, and possibly the direction of a subsidiary within SIP, and subsequently a return to the upper management of PSPA. SIP, based in a small office with a very light staff was, in the words of a Pirelli manager, "separated by isolation rather than decentralization," as it had no role in defining strategies. "It would limit its task to the monitoring of financial results. PSPA's culture was more industrial and top management took a direct interest in the business." Leopoldo Pirelli sat on the board of SIP, which was traditionally chaired by a Swiss, but managed by an Italian. "Pirelli is a group by will, not [an] institutional [one]" commented a director, "a loose group, but united at the top by the understanding of the four top managers." Indeed, cohesion at the upper management level was strong.

Dunlop

"It was destiny that we would both be at the same point in our thinking," said Leopoldo Pirelli, referring to the strategic issues that Dunlop management was facing at the end of the sixties. By then, Dunlop was the 39th largest concern outside the US, operating 130 plants in 22 countries with 108,000 employees, 56,000 of whom worked in the UK. In 1969, the group comprised of 14 divisions spanning products from foam rubber to tires, from wheel rims to precision mechanical goods, from sporting articles to products for the aviation industry. Turnover totaled 495 million Lst (in 1969 1 Lst = 2.4\$) of which 65% came from tires, 7% from engineering, 12% from industrial products, and 14% from consumer products. Profit after tax amounted to 14.6 million Lst, with the tire business contributing 61%. Exhibit 4 provides a summary of Dunlop's operating results during the 1965–1969 period.

The company had its origins in 1888 with the invention of the first practicable pneumatic tire by John Boyd Dunlop. The Pneumatic Tire & Booth Cycle Agency was formed a year later to market Dunlop's invention and by 1900, when the name of the company was changed to Dunlop Rubber Company Limited, manufacturing or selling operations had already been established in Australia, Canada, France, Germany, and South Africa. Between the wars, the base of the company's operations was progressively broadened both geographically and by the addition of a wide range of consumer rubber products including "Dunlopillo" latex foam, which was invented in the company's laboratories and which subsequently became the basis of a worldwide foam rubber industry. The company also extended its activities in the field of precision engineering which had become a growing and important sector of its operations in the UK.

Over time, the company had emerged as the market leader in many Commonwealth countries such as Nigeria, South Africa, Malaysia, Zambia, Uganda, Australia, New Zealand, and India, in addition to its dominance in the UK and considerable strengths in the United States, Germany, France, and Ireland. It had also developed an important foothold in Japan through 44% ownership of a joint venture with Sumitomo.

A simplified organization chart of Dunlop in 1969 is shown in Exhibit 5. The heads of the different businesses of the company reported directly to the chairman and managing director, and many of these divisional directors were also responsible for particular staff groups as shown in the exhibit. The company's tire business within Europe was managed separately, as a business division under a director-in-charge who also controlled all R&D for tires on a worldwide basis. National affiliates outside Europe reported to the headquarters through a director responsible for overseas operations and were thus managed on an area rather than business basis. The entire US operations of the company were controlled by a separate director.

Almost without exception, all foreign subsidiaries were headed by British expatriates, and personal relationships between those expatriates and managers in the headquarters were the key element of Dunlop's international coordination and control systems. Typically, the foreign affiliates enjoyed fairly extensive autonomy for developing and implementing their own strategies and policies within the broad guidelines on plant design, product specifications, and manufacturing processes that were established by the parent com-

Exhibit 4 *Dunlop's Operating Results: 1965–1969 (All Figures in £000)*

	1965	1966	1967	1968	1969
Sales	330,053	338,648	378,335	435,762	479,364
Operating profits before depreciation, interest, and taxes	33,919	34,837	38,791	46,374	46,803
Income from other sources	560	401	509	746	1,158
Gross income	34,479	35,238	39,300	47,120	47,961
Interest	4,775	5,590	5,274	5,925	8,248
Taxation	7,491	7,178	8,847	12,846	11,454
Net income	10,464	9,932	11,687	13,810	12,909
Minority shareholders' interests	1,785	1,844	2,167	2,607	3,603
Attributable income	8,679	8,088	9,520	11,203	9,306

Exhibit 5 *Organization Chart: Dunlop, 1969*

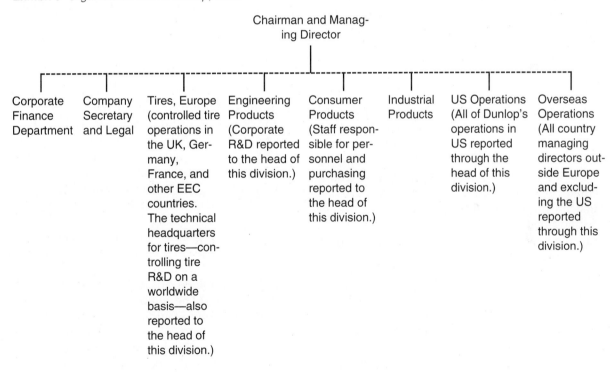

Chairman and Managing Director

Corporate Finance Department

Company Secretary and Legal

Tires, Europe (controlled tire operations in the UK, Germany, France, and other EEC countries. The technical headquarters for tires—controlling tire R&D on a worldwide basis—also reported to the head of this division.)

Engineering Products (Corporate R&D reported to the head of this division.)

Consumer Products (Staff responsible for personnel and purchasing reported to the head of this division.)

Industrial Products

US Operations (All of Dunlop's operations in US reported through the head of this division.)

Overseas Operations (All country managing directors outside Europe and excluding the US reported through this division.)

pany. Besides, major investment decisions required approval from London even when they were financed through the subsidiary's retained earnings or local borrowing—as was typically the case.

By the end of the 1960s, however, Dunlop was facing some serious problems in the tire business. Some of the problems were similar to those confronting Pirelli: size disadvantage in comparison to the American giants and a technology lag vis-à-vis Michelin in the rapidly growing market for radial tires. In addition, the company's dependence on the UK market was proving to be a disadvantage. Dunlop's 30% local market share was supported by a strong OEM relationship with the British automakers who were losing market share to their American and European competitors. These multinational automakers typically sourced their tire requirements from local subsidiaries of the American and continental producers based on relationships developed in their home countries. Furthermore, Dunlop's other businesses in engineering, industrial products, sporting goods, etc. were performing very well and they provided opportunities for large and profitable investments that were far more attractive compared to the returns from the tire business.

THE UNION

It is not clear as to where and how the idea emerged for organizing a combined European challenge in the tire industry. By mid-1969, however, a proposal was already afoot for creating the CDMP Union, combining the operations of Continental, Dunlop, Pirelli, and Michelin. When Michelin turned down the proposal, the concept was modified to CDP. Finally, the German banks prevented Continental from joining the Union leaving Dunlop and Pirelli as the only two remaining parties.

The Announcement

The official announcement of the Union came in the wake of considerable speculation, in business circles and in the press, of some sort of imminent accord between the two groups. In recent history there were several instances of collaboration. A reciprocal production agreement, whereby Dunlop manufactured Pirelli tires sold in France and Pirelli produced all Dunlop tires for the Italian

market, had been in existence for a few years; in Brazil, Dunlop had sold its tire facilities to Pirelli in a move to rationalize the somewhat limited market. In February 1970, a joint venture had been formed in Germany between Dunlop, Pirelli, and Continental for the production of steel cord reinforcement, an important tire input.

On the second of March 1970, the boards of the parent companies of the Pirelli and Dunlop tire and rubber groups declared their intention to integrate the industrial activities of their respective operating companies. The announcement was made simultaneously by PSPA in Milan, by SIP in Basel, and by Dunlop in London.

Strategic Objectives

After declaring that an "agreement in principle" had been reached on the integration of the two companies' operations, Leopoldo Pirelli and Sir Reay Geddes called attention in their statements to the friendly relations between the two groups, to the complementarity of their operations, and to the similarity in turnover, assets, and profitability. This facilitated the establishment of an alliance on an equal footing.

The motives for the alliance, as stated in an internal Pirelli memo, included the following benefits:

1. In the tire sector, increased speed, efficiency, and economy would be obtained in the field of research and development. The benefits of R&D would double for each party with no increase in costs; in fact, through rationalization of the research effort, a lowering of costs could be achieved. Furthermore, production would be rationalized in certain countries through reciprocal production and other agreements, leading to economies of scale and better use of facilities.
2. In the diversified products sector, similar advantages could be gained.
3. The new group would match the market leaders in size, becoming number three in the world, and deriving significant benefits from the greater total market share; the geographic spread would be very wide, while the technology would remain European.
4. Geographic risk would be better spread, as Pirelli investments were more concentrated in Italy, in certain European countries, and in

South America, while Dunlop's activities were more concentrated in the UK, in two other European countries, in North America, Africa, and Australasia (see Exhibit 6).

5. Risk would also be spread across a more diversified product range, with Pirelli bringing in cable production, and Dunlop contributing specialized engineering work, growing businesses in consumer products such as sporting goods and various other products not produced by Pirelli.

6. The greater common financial resources would facilitate investments in new initiatives and in new countries.

7. Joint development and implementation of new marketing techniques would increase the new group's ability and efficiency in bringing products to the market.

8. Greater purchasing power would be achieved through sharing of experience and through leverage due to the Union's larger size.

9. Commonly used services would be rationalized and possibly unified, reducing duplication of efforts and cutting down overheads.

10. Exchange of experience would be sought in all areas of management and organization including possible exchanges of executives and increased training opportunities.

11. Collectively, these advantages would lead to higher efficiency, faster technological development, and lower costs. Competitive advantage and growth opportunities for each partner's operations at home and abroad would be enhanced.

The Financial Structure

Over the months following the March 1970 announcement of the Union, representatives of the two groups carried out an in-depth study to work out the financial and legal details of the alliance. The starting point was the establishment, on the part of the two firms' auditors, of "Common Accounting Principles" to be used in evaluating their financial positions. Data from the previous five years were reconstructed accordingly, and a comparison of the profits over this period was used to arrive at a formula that assured exact parity between the two parties. The analysis was further complicated by the fact that not two but three parent companies were involved: Pirelli SPA, SIP, and Dunlop Co. Ltd. The complex financial analysis and the subsequent discussions lasted nearly eight months, and led to the reconstructed operating results shown in Exhibits 2 and 4, and to an assessment of the assets contributed by the two parties (see Exhibit 7). These analyses showed an unusual degree of parity in the financial contributions of the two partners and supported the firm principle of "uniting as equals." Finally, on December 31, 1970, shareholders of the three companies approved the new structure for the Union that had been devised to ensure this equality.

To begin with, the two groups were remolded into symmetric organizations: Pirelli Spa (PSPA) was changed into a holding and nearly all of its industrial and commercial activities and subsidiaries were transferred to a new company, called Industrie Pirelli Spa (referred to hereafter as IP). IP would have administrative control over the operations of all Pirelli subsidiaries in Italy and in the EEC (i.e., France, Germany, and Belgium), even though PSPA, which would own 100% of IP, would also continue to own directly 100% of the manufacturing subsidiaries in EEC countries excluding Italy. This distinction between financial ownership and administrative control would prove to be crucial during the early phase of the Union.

The Dunlop Co. Ltd. was transformed into a holding named Dunlop Holdings Ltd. It owned two new companies: Dunlop Ltd., which had jurisdiction over all subsidiaries in the UK, Ireland, and the EEC, and Dunlop International Ltd., which was responsible for the overseas subsidiaries and affiliates. The separate interests were then traded between the two groups. Dunlop Holdings Ltd. gave 49% of Dunlop Ltd. and 20% of Dunlop International Ltd. to PSPA in exchange for 49% of IP and of PSPA's EEC manufacturing subsidiaries outside of Italy, and for 20% of PSPA's holdings in SIP's overseas subsidiaries. SIP then traded 20% of its own shares in Pirelli's overseas subsidiaries to Dunlop Holdings Ltd. for 20% of Dunlop International Ltd. In this way each group would have a minority interest of 49% in the other's operations in Europe and of 40% in the other's overseas subsidiaries. This particular structure emphasized the underlying concept of equal partnership: the equality of financial interest so as to reap equal benefits from the Union.

Exhibit 8 shows the structure of the Union. One notable exception to the arrangement described is Pirelli's UK subsidiary, Pirelli Ltd., in

Exhibit 6 Manufacturing Locations of Union

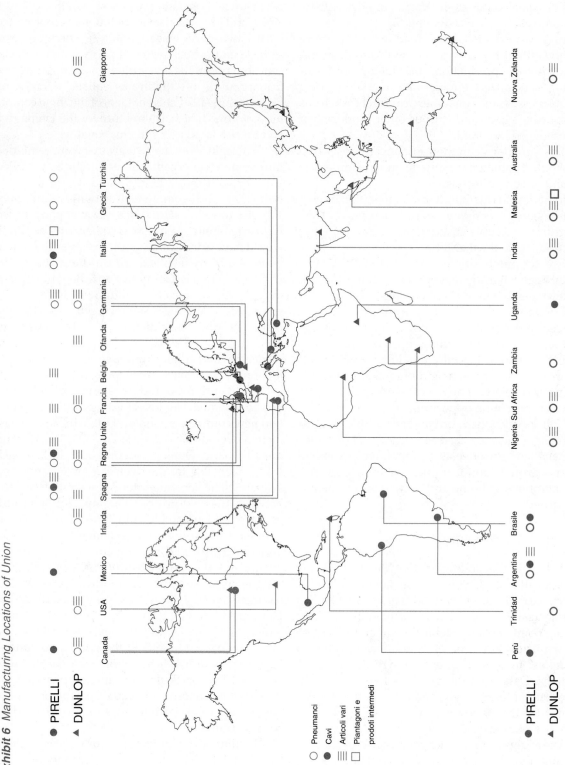

Exhibit 7 *Net Assets Contributed to the Union (All Figures in £000)*

	Dunlop		Pirelli	
1. Fixed Assets				
Properties (cost or valuation)	81,996		89,565	
Plant and equipment (cost or valuation)	212,529		235,424	
Less depreciation	148,797		117,344	
Net Fixed assets		145,728		207,645
2. Good will		32,463		–
3. Investments		11,591		16,264
4. Current Assets				
Inventories	115,802		121,858	
Debtors	117,417		133,665	
Cash and bank balances	5,868		10,216	
Total	239,087		265,739	
5. Current Liabilities				
Creditors and Provisions	82,092		80,383	
Taxation	9,594		5,006	
Total	91,686		85,389	
Net current assets		147,401		180,350
6. Other liabilities (bank overdrafts, loans, debentures, minority investments, etc.)		164,164		234,019
7. Net assets contributed to the Union		173,019		170,240

which Dunlop took a 51% stake and direct management control to satisfy British legal requirements. In order to ensure perfect parity of interests, which was considered a basic premise for a working alliance, some minor activities of the two groups were left out of the Union, although an option was retained to include them at a later date.

The Management Structure

The top management of both companies firmly believed that the Union must ultimately be managed through a single and fully integrated management structure. However, they also felt that such integration could not be achieved in one fell swoop, given the enormous differences in the cultures, histories, and management styles of the two companies and the great differences in the backgrounds and attitudes of their managers. "We were clear that ultimately we would have a single line management for the joint operations but that it would take time," said Sir John Dent, then director of the Engineering Products division of Dunlop and a member of its board. "Doing it immediately, we felt, could lead to confusion, conflict, and much heart-burn among managers on both sides." As a

result, a temporary transition structure was created to oversee different aspects of the Union's operations. As the Union evolved, however, the expected "full integration of management" could not be achieved, and the original "transition structure" remained unchanged throughout its history.

To underline top management's commitment to an effective integration, Sir Reay Geddes joined the boards of PSPA and SIP, while Leopoldo Pirelli accepted a seat on the board of Dunlop Holdings Ltd. In addition, a number of coordination committees were formed, each consisting of an equal number of members from both companies (see Exhibit 9).

The overall task of coordination was entrusted to the central committee, which consisted of the chairman and three top managers each from both partners. The objectives of this committee were to elaborate strategies of the Union, to oversee implementation of those strategies, to resolve those differences that could not be resolved by the other committees, and to be responsible to the boards of Pirelli and Dunlop regarding all aspects of the Union's functioning. While supported by the mutual admiration and respect between the chair-

Exhibit 8 *Structure of the Union*

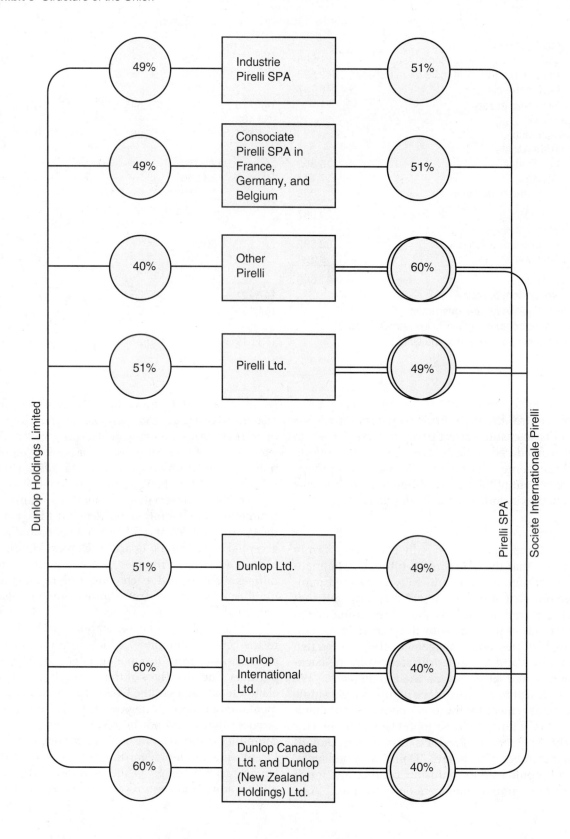

Exhibit 9   *Committees and Subcommittees Formed to Coordinate the Union's Activities*

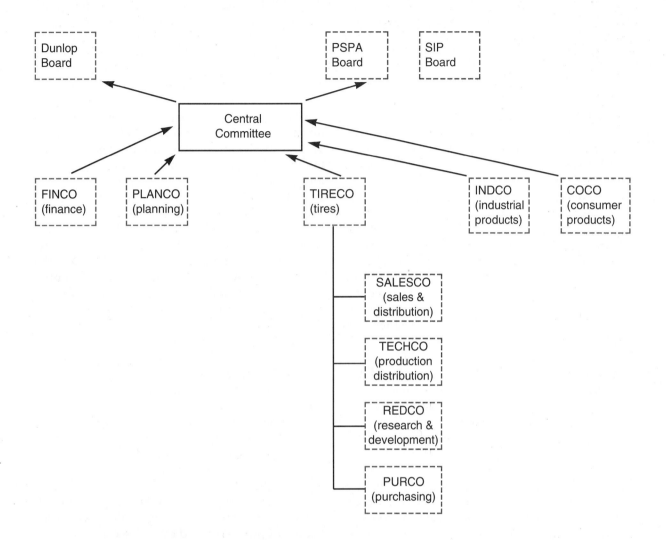

men of the two companies, the committee also reflected some of the main differences between the partners. For example, of the four Dunlop representatives, three were accountants by training and had significant exposure to the finance function, and one was an engineer. On Pirelli's side, the situation was exactly the opposite: three of its representatives on the committee were engineers and only one was an accountant.

The Finance Committee (FINCO) was responsible for yearly review of the three-year management plan, which required ultimate approval by the Central Committee. Another function of the Finance Committee was the coordination of the financial

workings of the Union, including such issues as the exchanges of dividends, joint approaches to the raising of capital and to its allocation. The Strategic Planning Committee (PLANCO) was created to "assist [. . .] in (a) establishing Group objectives, (b) developing long-range growth plans for the Group and its constituent elements, and (c) ensuring the most effective utilization of resources in achieving these objectives." According to a senior Pirelli executive, both companies expected PLANCO to play an important role for the Union, given its mandate of "identifying the two groups' resources in areas of possible synergy," and developing guidelines for their joint allocation.

The Tire Committee was the key to the functioning of the Union, as it dealt with its most crucial business sector. Its operational objective was the exploitation of synergies to rationalize the tire sector and to integrate as much as possible the two groups' businesses towards a common strategy. However, its scope of activities was largely limited to the two companies' operations within Europe and no specific coordination structure was built for the Union's operations outside Europe. The Tire Committee, as well as the industrial and consumer products committees, were structured in a similar way and oversaw subcommittees which examined various functional areas: the Sales Committee, which would study benefits in distribution deriving from the increased geographic spread of the Union; the Technical Committee, to study joint production processes; the Purchasing Committee to exploit sourcing synergies; and the R&D Committee to develop a common approach to new products and to ensure an unconstrained flow of technical information and knowledge between the two companies so as to maximally leverage their individual technological capabilities.

All committees were formed with an equal number of members from each group. As a Pirelli manager recounted, "the idea of an equal partnership was the cardinal principle on which the Union was based [. . .] There was an obsession with equality which led to dissenting opinions within each group [. . .] However, Mr. Pirelli and Sir Reay Geddes felt it was an essential condition for the first step—essential in order not to betray the trust of their respective managers." Indeed, this principle of equality in management was intended to go all the way down the organizational structure of the Union, as a consequence of the equality of ownership reflected by the financial exchanges.

UNION IN OPERATION

Between 1971, when the Union was formed, and 1979, when Dunlop's restructuring plan was received by Pirelli, the operating environment changed quite dramatically. From a situation of low growth, the market deteriorated to a situation of actual and significant contraction. Within Europe, for most companies the problem of a declining market was compounded by the growing strength of Michelin which expanded its share of the Western European market from 22% in 1970 to 34% in 1979 (see Exhibit 10 for companywise performance over the decade). The oil shocks of 1973 and 1978 had a twofold effect on the entire market: prices of raw materials drove up costs (synthetic rubber went from 22 cents/oz in 1973 to over 50 cents/oz in 1980), and demand slowed sharply. This was partly a result of lower output of cars and partly of the cutback in motoring caused by higher fuel costs and lower speed limits. These traumatic events coincided with a period of rapid increase in market share for the radial tire (Exhibit 1). The success of the new tire implied a further lowering of replacement demand due to its much longer life. For example, although the car population in the UK grew from 15 million to 16 million between 1973 and 1980, replacement tire sales dropped by 2.5 million units per year to less than 19 million; in the US, total yearly tire shipments dropped from 200 million to 166 million in the same period. Also, the changeover had required massive investments in new production facilities and in manufacturing process R&D. An important consequence of this situation was severe overcapacity, which put pressure on prices and led to a further erosion of profits. The tire industry became, in the words of Charles Pilliod, president of Goodyear, "an environment of intense competition in weak markets."

Within Italy, the first half of the 1970s proved to be a particularly difficult period, but the position improved considerably in the second half. By 1972, the economic boom of the 1960s had turned into what the *Economist* factitiously described as an "incomplete miracle." The country's lack of a modern infrastructure was brought into focus by a decade of prosperity and caused social and political unrest and a widespread loss of confidence accompanied by huge capital outflows. As productivity and investment dropped, the country suffered through five years of extremely low growth. Car tire production, reflecting the performance of the economy, saw a consistent drop until it hit bottom level in 1975, and only in 1979 could it bounce back to the 1972 level.

The 1970s also saw a major new center of power emerge within the country: the trade unions were now a group that exercised considerable influence on the country's political and economic life. The government, political parties, and private and public enterprises found themselves unprepared to cope with the new situation.

Exhibit 10 *Sales and Market Shares of Major Producers in the Car Tire Market (OEM + Replacement) in Western Europe[a]*

Company	1970	1971	1972	1973	1974	1975	1976	1977	1978	1979
Michelin	29,727	32,507	36,167	40,422	38,124	38,949	42,685	45,881	47,647	47,929
	(22.1)	(23.2)	(24.3)	(26.9)	(28.3)	(29.5)	(30.6)	(33.0)	(34.0)	(33.8)
Dunlop/Pirelli	28,831	28,051	29,757	27,757	23,117	21,864	23,916	23,831	—	—
	(21.4)	(20.1)	(20.0)	(18.4)	(17.2)	(16.6)	(17.1)	(17.1)		
Dunlop	16,982	16,892	17,453	15,599	13,222	12,783	13,288	13,393	12,759	12,268
	(12.6)	(12.1)	(11.8)	(10.4)	(9.8)	(9.7)	(9.5)	(9.6)	(9.1)	(8.6)
Pirelli	11,849	11,159	12,304	12,158	9,895	9,081	10,628	10,438	11,252	11,774
	(8.8)	(8.0)	(8.3)	(8.1)	(7.3)	(6.9)	(7.6)	(7.5)	(8.0)	(8.3)
Goodyear	16,083	17,741	17,153	16,435	14,298	13,594	15,071	14,200	15,598	16,207
	(11.9)	(12.7)	(11.6)	(10.9)	(10.6)	(10.3)	(10.8)	(10.2)	(11.1)	(11.4)
Firestone	11,108	11,373	9,834	10,315	9,520	8,303	8,834	8,678	7,687	7,497
	(8.2)	(8.1)	(6.6)	(6.9)	(7.1)	(6.3)	(6.3)	(6.2)	(5.5)	(5.3)
Uniroyal	6,540	7,018	7,965	8,542	8,267	8,510	9,579	9,701	8,795	8,981
	(4.8)	(5.0)	(5.4)	(5.7)	(6.1)	(6.4)	(6.9)	(7.0)	(6.3)	(6.3)
Kleber Colombes	7,837	8,816	9,152	9,027	8,161	6,950	7,949	6,937	7,045	7,114
	(5.8)	(6.3)	(6.2)	(6.0)	(6.1)	(5.3)	(5.7)	(5.0)	(5.0)	(5.0)
Continental	10,937	11,246	10,867	10,220	7,662	7,369	7,103	7,579	7,868	7,809
	(8.1)	(8.0)	(7.3)	(6.8)	(5.7)	(5.6)	(5.1)	(5.4)	(5.6)	(5.5)
Semperit	3,051	3,214	3,107	3,310	3,009	3,106	3,347	3,360	2,871	2,707
	(2.3)	(2.3)	(2.1)	(2.2)	(2.2)	(2.2)	(2.4)	(2.4)	(2.1)	(1.9)
Ceat	3,737	2,884	3,370	3,389	2,803	2,742	3,127	2,590	2,626	2,596
	(2.8)	(2.1)	(2.3)	(2.3)	(2.1)	(2.1)	(2.2)	(1.9)	(1.9)	(1.8)
Others	16,958	17,014	21,107	20,908	19,716	20,755	18,081	16,482	15,923	16,986
	(12.6)	(12.2)	(14.2)	(13.9)	(15.5)	(15.5)	(12.9)	(11.8)	(11.4)	(12.1)
Total	134,878	139,864	148,479	150,325	134,677	132,142	139,692	139,239	140,071	141,868
	(100.0)	(100.0)	(100.0)	(100.0)	(100.0)	(100.0)	(100.0)	(100.0)	(100.0)	(100.0)

Source: Company data.

[a]Sales in '000 units (% market share).

The rigidities of the labor market, on the one hand, and the structure and dynamics of labor costs, on the other, collectively had a devastating impact on the industrial sector. By 1975, wages were linked to inflation, which was galloping, and non-wage labor costs and contributions had become higher in Italy compared to every other country in the EC. As companies tried to restructure their operations to respond to these changes, labor-management conflicts became increasingly frequent.

The situation in the UK was broadly similar with one exception: while the 1975–1979 period was generally better in Italy compared to the 1970–1975 period, exactly the reverse was true in the UK. In the first half of the decade, expansionist policies of the government provided some support to demand and modest growth was maintained. In the second half, these policies came home to roost, plunging demand while pushing inflation to almost 20%. Dunlop's performance reflected these changes in the economy: it did moderately well in the first half but faced increasing difficulties in the second, as its home market shrank and its own sales fell even more because of large volume, low-cost imports from Japan and increasing penetration of Michelin's radials. As Sir John Dent described, "the Union was formed to respond to the challenge of the American multinationals. For us, what proved to be far more damaging were the Japanese exports and Michelin."

Industrie Pirelli's losses

"No sooner were we married, than the bride, namely us, caught smallpox." With these words Leopoldo Pirelli referred to the problems experienced by IP from 1971 onwards. The company was born under the heavy burden of the investments to complete the "radialization" process forced on the industry by Michelin's success: IP's capital investment increased from 27 billion Lit. in 1969 to over 94 billion Lit. in the two year period 1970–1971, and its total debt to total equity ratio increased progressively from 2.4 in 1971 to 8 in 1975. By 1972, the radial tire had conquered 65% of the automobile original equipment market in Western Europe (Exhibit 1). Michelin was number one in car tires in Europe with 22.1% of the market (see Exhibit 10 for market share evolution in the 1970s). Pirelli's CN53 textile belt radial proved no match in the marketplace and hopes for a successful counterattack were

dashed. Between 1971 and 1975, Pirelli's Italian tire production decreased 20% and its home market share diminished on average by 5.5%. As a result, IP's plants were operating at 70% of capacity.

Exhibit 11 shows IP's income statements for the 1970s. According to the financial statements, the Italian operating company's losses in 1971 and 1972 were mainly due to the recession, to the dramatic rise in labor costs and to the tense industrial relations: between 1969 and 1971 Pirelli's work force in Italy was on strike for nearly 6 million hours. From 1969 to 1972, spiraling wage rates caused labor costs to increase 75%. Italian labor expense was thus 7% higher than that of Pirelli's German factories, which were more productive.

Dunlop's results for the period from 1971 to 1975 were satisfactory (Exhibit 11): turnover grew by 74%, and profits were steady. The tire division developed the Denovo, or "Total Mobility Tire," which could be driven on for 100 km after a puncture, and which won an important safety award. The prestige of the engineering division was boosted by the award of the contract for supplying wheels and carbon fiber brakes for the Concorde project. However, a major preoccupation for Dunlop's management in 1971 and 1972 was the performance of IP. There was severe criticism in the UK over the choice of partner in the Union: it was considered unthinkable that a firm that had been in the tire business for 90 years did not realize that the CN53 was a "dud." Also, investors did not have faith in the Italian economy and considered IP as a burden: Dunlop's share price fell from $4.78 to $2.50 in 1972. A Dunlop manager later wrote: "By Anglo-Saxon accounting, the business [IP] was bankrupt."

"Dunlop was under the impression that they had been misled about future expectations: their reaction was very hard," recalled a Pirelli manager. "Pirelli announced its 1969 results in the mid-1970s, after the decision to form the Union had already been announced. They never talked about it in all our discussions till then," described a senior manager of Dunlop who was a member of the Tire Committee of the Union: "some within Dunlop believed that Pirelli knew that the 1969 figures would be disastrous; others were willing to give them the benefit of doubt. But nobody expected the results to be so bad and all of us were shocked!"

After four months of negotiations in the Central Committee, Dunlop took the following three steps: (1) Dunlop's shares in IP were given preferred

Exhibit 11 *Sales and Net Income of SIP, IP, Dunlop Holdings and Union for the period 1971–1980*[a]

	1971	1972	1973	1974	1975	1976	1977	1978	1979	1980
SIP[b]										
Sales	354	386	501	610	720	986	1,241	1,395	1,646	2,317
Net income	4	4	5	7	8	11	11	13	14	16
PSPA										
Holding Co.										
Revenues	NA	15	34	16	18	18	25	22	25	24
Net income	NA	4	—	4	—	11	10	7	7	8
IP										
Sales	308	278	320	455	405	556	622	696	867	1191
Net income	(15)	(35)	(17)	(11)	(27)	(2)	(5)	(2)	(19)	4
Dunlop										
Sales	883	928	1,071	1,338	1,471	1,916	2,095	2,402	2,793	2,760
Net income	30	32	23	30	35	38	31	18	4	(30)
Union										
	1,470	1,501	1,884	2,423	2,478	3,437	4,046			
Sales										
By country										
EEC	65%	62	59	60	60	64	60			
Rest of Europe	5%	6	7	7	7	8	6			
North America	9%	9	9	7	8	9	8			
South America	10%	11	14	13	14	15	15			
Africa	5%	4	5	4	5	5	6			
Asia	6%	6	6	7	6	7	6			
Australasia	1%	1	1	1	1	1	1			
By product										
Tires	53%	53	52	50	53	53	53			
Cables and Eng.	22%	21	23	24	22	22	21			
Div. Prod.	25%	25	24	25	24	24	25			
Other	1%	1	1	1	1	1	1			
Net Income	15	21	52	38	37	127	94			
By country										
EEC	34%	30	30	36	30	36	36			
Rest of Europe	6%	8	10	6	4	3	6			
North America	13%	13	10	9	8	9	9			
South America	23%	32	34	35	40	37	35			
Africa	8%	6	7	6	6	5	6			
Asia	12%	7	9	2	10	8	2			
Australasia	2%	2	2	1	1	1	1			
By product										
Tires	46%	36	33	31	40	36	31			
Cables and Eng.	42%	44	47	36	38	40	36			
Div. Prod.	7%	16	18	22	17	20	22			
Other	3%	2	3	6	3	4	6			

Source: Financial statements.

[a]Union figures are broken down by product and by country (average period exchange rates have been used).

[b]Billion Lit.

status to protect their nominal value; (2) Dunlop declared that it would not participate in any future losses on the part of IP, nor invest additional capital until losses were covered and profits achieved; (3) Dunlop wrote the entire 41.5 million Lst investment in IP off its books to avoid having to report any future losses. Dunlop, separating itself from IP, believed that recovery could be achieved only in the very long term, and did not wish to commit to it. For the managers in Pirelli, who considered IP as the "heart of the tire group," this was a traumatic event: "we felt abandoned by our ally in time of need."

After 1972, the withdrawal of Dunlop from IP added a disturbing element by creating an imbalance and undermining the basic trust within the Union. However, the event had a strong cohesive effect on IP management: "we felt mad as hell, and said to ourselves: now we'll do it on our own." Pirelli's top management turned itself towards the problems of IP with a significant effort to develop new products: "At no time, even in the moments of greatest difficulty, did we consider divesting from tires; on the contrary, we knew that new products were our way out." This meant continuing large-scale investments in the tire business. In September 1973, IP presented a restructuring plan after two months of negotiations with the trade unions. The plan called for investment in cables R&D, further investment into tires, rationalization of unprofitable product lines, and tightening of cost control. A total 128 billion Lit. would have to be invested over a five-year period. In 1973, the CN54, a textile radial improvement on the CN53, was launched. More significantly, in 1974 Pirelli produced their first steel-belted radial, the P3.

The cables sector performed positively with a spurt in demand in 1973, which could not be entirely met due to insufficient capacity. In 1974, demand from the telecommunications industry slackened, but by 1975, thanks to large foreign contracts, IP was exporting 30% of its cables turnover. Diversified products reported losses in 1971, 1972, and 1975: further diversification proved unsuccessful, and new investment in the attractive market of industrial components did not entail greater revenues since "it was difficult to sell the product because of the lack of knowledge of the market."

In 1973, IP's management was undergoing organizational changes as a new generation of managers moved up from within. Business sectors became more distinct and each became staffed with its own key functions, with the objective of delegating operational control down the management structure.

SIP's role in the period 1970–1975 was crucial to the survival of the group. Mainly operating in developing countries—a high-growth, low-cost environment—meant high profits and an almost constant dividend payment to the Union. Indeed, the Union's overall results for the period 1970–1975 were satisfactory (Exhibit 11), and the percentage breakdowns of sales and profits by country and products showed that the risk diversification objective of the Union had been achieved.

The Committees in Action

"There was considerable enthusiasm at first about the idea of building a common management," recalled a Pirelli manager. However, in carrying out their tasks, the committees found that the obstacles to integration were often greater than had been thought. For example, it was discovered that larger than expected technological differences existed in tire production processes. Also, although the agreements called for free access to tire R&D information within Europe, both parties were reluctant to share all their technology and, even when they were shared, NIH barriers prevented cross-fertilization of ideas. In general, the choice of keeping two separate brands had a limiting effect on the cooperation of the two groups. The distribution networks, for example, were often in direct competition. In the words of a Pirelli director: "There was some help in selling our tires in the US, but in Western Europe, which was the large natural market for the Union, we achieved very little."

The Central Committee met on a monthly basis. Both Pirelli and Dunlop engaged in time-consuming preparation, which included separate preliminary reunions. Efforts to fuse these preliminary meetings were not successful. Gradually, the Central Committee became more of a forum for briefings on unilateral decisions than for elaborating joint strategies. Furthermore, according to a Pirelli manager, the Central Committee "answered to three different boards, elected by the shareholders of three parent companies, whose authority could not be overruled."

It was in the functional and operational areas where attempts were made, in the second half of the decade, to improve cooperation. A system of "pairs" was instituted whereby the two heads of the respective departments met to decide on issues of common interest. A Pirelli manager recalled: "Where there is no structure [for decision making], one tries to rely on the goodwill of individual managers." Indeed, personal rapport between Italian and British managers had generally been excellent, but the emphasis on equality, it was slowly realized, was paralyzing decision making. A significant attempt to improve this situation was made in the Tire Committee, where a top Pirelli manager was elevated to the position of joint director of tires in 1975. However, he had no effective powers and found himself in a difficult negotiating position: the psychological pressures of IP's continuing losses were strong. "It lasted one morning," said a Pirelli man later, "Industrie Pirelli was our original sin."

These difficulties in reaching joint decisions posed a major obstacle to exploiting the Union's potential advantages. In the mid-1970s, large American car manufacturers adopted a new approach to the European market by introducing new models to be produced in different countries at the same time. In 1976, Ford started manufacturing their Fiesta in Spain, Germany, and the UK. This presented an excellent occasion for the Union to deal directly with a single buyer in several countries and to present a coordinated supplier front able to offer the required product development, technical assistance, and distribution. The Tire Committee, however, did not manage to reconcile the interests of the different players. The problem lay with the fundamental differences between the OEM and the replacement markets (RM) and with the final destination of the cars being built in any given country. This meant that one company would have to provide OEM tires essentially at cost and without benefitting from the higher replacement market margins if the cars were exported. In Spain, for example, Pirelli was to supply the original tires, but 70% of local Fiesta production was destined for export. Who would then have benefitted from RM sales? "A possible solution," recalled a manager, "would have been to shoe Fiestas directed to the UK market with Dunlop tires and those directed to Germany and Italy with Pirelli tires." The Tire Committee could not agree on a unified strategy that assigned responsibilities to the various operating units, because a single profitability objective for the Union could not overrule the interests of the two participants.

Thus, the original strategy to increase market power through the union proved difficult to implement. In the field of purchasing, however, the joint effort achieved some positive results. Through a common approach to suppliers of raw materials, better conditions were secured and costs were lowered. In R&D, good results were obtained in research on raw materials and the study of new tire compounds. Some synergy was achieved in development of a few new products (for example, van and light truck tires), where the group leading in the relevant area took over responsibility for the project. Opinions in the R&D managers in both companies were reflected in the summary comment of Pirelli's head of tire research: "Whereas we worked well on basic research, we stopped short at the product development stage." To overcome the obstacle posed by the differences in processes, joint research on automation of tire production was launched in the late 1970s. However, in the fields that were specific to each group—cables for Pirelli and engineering products for Dunlop—no dialogue was ever established as neither group took a particular interest in the other's business.

At a different level, the managers involved realized that the cultural gap that had to be bridged was wider than expected. English had naturally been chosen as the common language, and, while technical discussions usually posed no difficulties, interpretation problems sometimes arose when discussing sensitive business issues. Beyond the subtleties of language, differences in mentality and in approach emerged: "We were dazzled by their ability to collect information, to elaborate it numerically, and tabulate it," said a Pirelli director referring to Dunlop. "We were more messy. This was our first shock; our second surprise was to find that [on Dunlop's side] there was a lack of sufficient interpretation of what was behind the numbers. Ours was an industrial culture and theirs was more a culture of financiers."

On the Dunlop side, feelings were quite different. "Our controls were superior, but Dunlop managers were not financiers," said Geoffrey Wheater, who was a member of the Dunlop board during the 1970s. "As a privately held company in Italy, they did not quite understand our constraints as a public company in the UK. We were making profits and yet our share prices were going down. We simply had to try our best to improve the overall financial performance of the Union. Another big difference lay in the roles of the two national governments. Whenever Pirelli was in real trouble, it could expect supportive government action—a right law would fall on its lap. We could expect no such help from the British government. Our actions were influenced by our industrial system—our relations with our government, the banks, and the city—and their actions were based on the norms of their industrial system. These differences in the industrial systems led to a lot of misunderstanding between the two companies."

IP Regains Momentum

In 1976, Dunlop did not participate in IP's recapitalization and its minority interest dropped from 49% to 30%. A British financial analyst commented dryly at the time: "30% of nothing is just as good, if not better, than 49% of nothing. If it ever becomes profitable, which is doubted here, [Dunlop] can always increase their holding by putting in more cash."

The investments in tire development were beginning to pay off for IP as the low-profile, wide-series radials were successfully introduced into all segments of the car market with the P6 tire in 1977 and the P8 "energy-saving" tire in 1979. Developed through the experience gained in world rally championship victories, this tire was characterized by an increased area of tread against the road. Some of the initial ideas about the wide tires came from Dunlop though most of the actual development work was done by Pirelli. The tires' major advantages were braking efficiency, better control on wet surfaces, and longer life.

The cables sector experienced a fluctuating demand, much dependent on foreign contracts. Other multinationals were increasing their presence in the booming telecommunications market through joint ventures or other alliances, thus jeopardizing the Pirelli group's world leadership position in cables. SIP, however, expanded its power cables operation by acquiring two companies in the US and France and starting a new manufacturing unit in Australia. The diversified sector slowly returned to profitability by the end of the 1970s, as a different business approach was implemented by bringing in new managers at senior levels and by developing a new high-technology product mix. Opportunities to sell engineering know-how, especially to the Soviet Union,

grew considerably and were coordinated by the newly formed diversified products division.

Despite these favorable developments, IP continued to accumulate losses, which totaled 28 billion Lit. from 1976 to 1979. IP presented a second restructuring plan to the trade unions in May 1976 with new ideas to improve productivity, and a proposal to invest 270 billion Lit. in the following five years, directed at the rationalization of manufacturing lines and new product introductions. In 1978, the Pirelli skyscraper in the center of Milan, a nationwide symbol of the economic boom of the 1960s, was sold to bring in extra cash. By 1979, however, it was manifest that IP would show a profit in the following year, its first in nine years. Its financial structure remained, nevertheless, an area of concern. This problem was tackled by exploiting new industrial policy measures, which were adopted in Italy after 1977, specifically to allow firms "to breathe some oxygen" during the economic crisis. Under new laws, IP was able to revalue some fixed assets, consolidate the outstanding debt by transforming burdensome ST liabilities into longer-term finance at a low interest rate, and issue new shares underwritten by a bank consortium with a deal that PSPA would buy them back at the end of a five-year period.

Dunlop Faces Problems

Dunlop's tire business was showing signs of weakness by the middle of the decade, and, although management called 1976 "the best year in the company's history, [. . .] the main customer [for tires], British Leyland, was losing its share of the market." The Denovo tire had been a technical success, but did not achieve wide commercial acceptance. The added expense, the extra weight entailing higher fuel consumption, and the complicated installation procedure discouraged the auto industry from adopting it on a large scale. Within Dunlop, there was a feeling that the Denovo might have succeeded if Pirelli had put its weight behind that tire. "Pirelli had developed DIP—another run-flat tire—which was never introduced in the market. However, because of DIP they stayed away from the Denovo," said Geoffrey Wheater. As a result of the drop in demand and the lack of a competitive product, Dunlop's market share in the UK peaked in 1977 and declined thereafter (see Exhibit 10). In Italy, on the other hand, the automobile industry showed signs of growth. Also, while Italian industry benefited from supportive government policies, the British carmakers claimed that shifts in government policy caused irreparable harm to the domestic automobile industry, laying the seeds of British "de-industrialization."

The problems of Dunlop's UK tire business were extended to Pirelli Ltd., PSPA's UK subsidiary which operated under Dunlop management. This situation, whereby Dunlop ran a company with the Pirelli name, had caused friction since the beginning of the Union. Lord Thornycroft, the chairman of Pirelli Ltd., was married to an Italian and held close friendships with a number of senior managers of Pirelli. Many Dunlop managers felt that he reported to Dunlop only in name and had actually much closer ties with the Pirelli management. Pirelli's view of the situation was quite different: as described by one manager, "Pirelli Ltd. suffered in Dunlop's hands. When Dunlop management took over one or two years into the Union, they let the company slide by taking a short-term perspective and cutting back investment." For Pirelli management, this was symptomatic of the Dunlop approach to business. They believed that Dunlop did not invest sufficiently in modernizing production facilities, with the result that, in the late 1970s, the company's plants were "dramatically obsolete." In 1977, operating profits of Dunlop were down 13%, with tire divisions in the UK, France, Germany, and the US reporting heavy losses, due primarily to low productivity and weak demand. Dunlop shut down two factories and reduced the tire work force from 51,000 to 32,000 in three years. In 1978, Sir Reay Geddes retired as chairman of Dunlop and was replaced by his CEO, Sir Campbell Fraser.

THE SITUATION IN 1979

In 1979, the problems and concerns of the two partners to the Union had become very different. In Pirelli, the main concern of managers was to develop the organizational capability necessary to leverage the strategic strengths of the company. In Dunlop, the top management was worried about the rapidly deteriorating financial performance of the company, caused largely by the tire business and despite strong showing in some of the other activities, and they focused on ways to stop the impending hemorrhage.

Pirelli had adopted the Dunlop-instituted management control systems of the Union for its own internal working too. As a result, the company's internal analysis had improved significantly providing far greater clarity to its own problems and shortcomings. In the process, the company had come to believe that its underlying strategic strengths were considerable and the key task for managers was to build an appropriate organization that could effectively exploit those strengths.

The historical split between PSPA and SIP was seen to be the obstacle in implementing an unified strategy for the company as a whole. Interestingly, it was the problems of coordinating its activities with Dunlop at the Union level that perhaps helped most in focusing management attention to the problems created by the duality within the Pirelli organization. It had become manifest to the company that the traditional country-based structure of its organization was inconsistent with the increasingly global structure of its businesses. In the absence of a unified management structure, the major foreign operations that reported to SIP continued to operate as a portfolio of independent businesses, with no strategic and only limited operational integration with the company's businesses in Europe. "Internally, the problem was even worse, because the foreign operations were profitable while the European operations were losing money," said a senior manager of the company. "This was so because they faced far less competition and benefited from PSPA's services for which there was no accounting and they paid no money. Brazil, for example, had grown into a billion dollar operation—comparable in size to IP—and was becoming more and more independent, setting up its own R&D, and often competing with other units for exports. Because of SIP's light structure and financial rather than business focus, our main difficulty was that we did not have adequate central coordination and control to manage our worldwide businesses."

In 1978, PSPA and SIP had begun to take action by unifying all of Pirelli's cables R&D under one manager and by establishing joint coordination of product strategies in tires. The results were most encouraging and, to give momentum to the process of management integration, Leopoldo Pirelli had decided to focus his own role and activities "on the holding companies, on the coordination of their activities and on their representation within the Union." To this end, he had decided to resign from the chairmanship of IP, remaining as chairman of PSPA, and had been nominated as the vice chairman of SIP.

In the context of this organizational transition, many Pirelli managers saw the Union as an obstacle that prevented Pirelli from focusing attention on the key task at hand and, in fact, impeded the internal integration within Pirelli because of the structure of the coordination committees. As one manager described, "We did not need external synergies. We could be competitive if we could achieve the potential synergies within our company. And we had to first integrate our own organization and learn to exploit our own strengths before we could benefit from others."

In Dunlop, on the other hand, the problems in 1979 were seen to be primarily strategic. "Our position in 1979 was the mirror image of Pirelli's position in the early 1970s," said Sir John Dent. "Falling markets, sharply reduced OEM demands, imported cars, imported tires, radialization, and serious labor problems hit us as they had hit IP in 1971. Furthermore, we were affected badly by the 'petro-pound.' With the sterling overvalued on the basis of North Sea oil, our exports had become unprofitable." The company believed that with the help of Pirelli, it could pull itself out of its problems. "We had invested in the 1970s—our new plants in Washington, in the UK, and in Germany were at least as productive as those of Pirelli. However, we needed a large investment in the UK and in France to reduce costs and rationalize our production system." He also expected Pirelli to stand by the Union, despite Dunlop's earlier refusal to finance IP's restructuring. "We had contributed all the positive cash flows of the Union and certainly hoped that Pirelli would support us in our time of need."

EXXON CORPORATION

Paul Shrivastava
Bucknell University

In the early morning of March 24, 1989, the *Exxon Valdez* oil tanker struck Bligh reef and spilled 11 million gallons of oil into Prince William Sound in Alaska. The oil pollution had devastating effects on the delicately balanced ecology of this area. Approximately 2,600 miles of beaches were blackened by the oil that drifted ashore. Nearly a year later, fewer than 10 miles of the polluted beaches had been cleaned up.

Estimated damages from the accident included deaths of 1,000 sea otters, 148 bald eagles, and 34,000 birds. The damage to the natural environment and its ability to recover are still not fully known. Officials now claim that the known damages could represent as little as 10% to 30% of actual damages.

Within the first year after the spill, the Exxon Corporation had already spent nearly $2 billion in cleanup operations. In addition, the federal government spent several hundred million dollars. By the time this crisis is fully resolved, it is expected to cost several billion dollars more. As of September 1989, there were 153 lawsuits against Exxon Corporation, including 58 class action suits dealing with the crisis. These were expected to go up to 1,500 within a year.

This crisis was caused by multiple, simultaneous, and interacting failures within and outside Exxon. Failures within Exxon included these:

- A lax security system that allowed a captain under the influence of alcohol to command the ship
- Breach of operating procedures in manning the tanker, allowing an unqualified third mate to be in control of the vessel
- Sharp cuts in the size of the tanker crew (20 men on duty) leaving it short handed.
- Supply of low-alcohol beer to crew on board in contravention of company policy
- Inadequate substance-abuse treatment programs
- Inadequate organizational follow-up of the ship captain's ten-year drinking problem
- Inadequate preparedness to contain the spill.

Societal failures outside Exxon Corporation included the following:

- Failure of five separate government emergency plans to contain the spill. These included The National Contingency Plan, Regional Contingency Plan, On-Site Coordination Plan, State Emergency Response Commission Plan under SARA Title III, and The Spill Prevention, Control, & Counter Measures Program under the Clean Water Act.
- Failure of the Alyeska Pipeline Company, the oil industry consortium, to have adequate emergency plans and equipment to deal with the spill as mandated by state law.
- Failure of the state of Alaska to mobilize permissions, equipment, and personnel that could abate the impacts of the spill during the first 12 hours.
- Failure of the US Coast Guard to monitor the erratic behavior of the *Exxon Valdez* as it veered outside the shipping lanes.

To fully understand the causes and management of this disaster, we begin by examining the company in detail.

HISTORY OF EXXON CORPORATION

Exxon was founded in Cleveland, Ohio, by John D. Rockefeller in 1870 as Standard Oil Company. The Exxon name was adopted on November 1, 1972. Within ten years of organization, the Standard Oil Company had control of 95% of all the oil reserves in the nation, which some allege was done through secret rebates and kickbacks. From this start, the company grew into a trust which controlled oil reserves in the United States and abroad. In 1911, the Supreme Court broke up the trust through a "Dissolution Decree" (Gifford, 1989). The Standard Oil Company distributed to its several thousand shareholders the shares it held in 33 constituent companies. Each company became publicly held, completely separate, and diversely owned.

In 1919 the company purchased 50% of Humble Oil and Refining Company, an important oil producer in Texas. Exxon acquired its first foreign subsidiary in 1898 when it acquired Imperial Oil Limited in Canada. Its first South American affiliate was established in 1921 in Venezuela. Further foreign expansion was achieved through exploration or reorganization of affiliates in Japan, Turkey, Iraq, Saudi Arabia, and Lybia.

Today, Exxon is a large, integrated petroleum company with substantial investments in exploration and production of crude oil and natural gas, manufacturing of petroleum products, transportation and sale of crude oil, natural gas, and petroleum products, and exploration for mining and sale of coal. The corporation is organized around its basic products; the major division is the petroleum and natural gas division which is further subdivided into exploration and production and refining and marketing subunits. Other divisions include the chemicals and coal and minerals divisions.

Exxon operates in the United States and 79 other countries. In 1990 it had sales of $117 billion and earnings of $5 billion. It ranked second on the nation's list of industrial corporations by assets and first by profits.

MAJOR BUSINESS LINES OF EXXON

A financial summary and business profile of Exxon are presented in Exhibits 1 and 2. The production of crude and natural gas is by far the largest contributor of revenues. The company also gets significant revenues from chemicals, coal and minerals, and energy generation businesses.

Exhibits 3 and 4 provide the consolidated balance sheet and income statements. Exhibit 5 provides consolidated cash flows.

Exploration and Production of Crude and Natural Gas

The operating summary for Exxon is provided in Exhibit 6. Oil and gas are commodities that require a high level of technology and capital investment. The payback period for new investments in this area is longer than that for most commodities. Oil exploration is a highly risky business and has high political visibility. Oil prices are sensitive to even modest supply-demand changes. Exxon had the experience and capital needed for the oil business and has managed to keep operations profitable. The competition in oil production is low because the market is relatively closed, and smaller firms do not survive the swings in oil prices. For Exxon, oil production earnings accounted for more than half of the total consolidated earnings until 1988. Since then, Exxon has considerably diminished its upstream processing in view of declining oil prices.

Exxon's strategy for upstream operations involved these three factors:

1. Improving exploration efficiency and reducing production costs through research and development

2. Improving the cost-effectiveness of developing reserves by buying attractively priced acquisitions and high-quality exploration ventures

    Exxon has large amounts in static reserves (total = 7.4 billion barrels), which are too expensive to develop now but could be viable at higher oil prices predicted in the 1990s (Grigsby, 1988). The Canadian Texaco acquisition in 1989 was an excellent strategic fit for Imperial (70% owned by Exxon) and will result in better balanced oil and natural gas operations, lower unit costs, and improved marketing distribution. In addition, this will provide attractive growth opportunities in all phases of the business (D'Arcy, 1989).

3. Increasing efficiency through corporate restructuring throughout the 1980s. The reorganization was comprehensive. It eliminated jobs, paperwork, and bureaucracy. Reduced bureaucracy made decision making and budget approvals more efficient and straightforward.

Exhibit 1 *Financial Summary: Exxon Corporation*

	1986	1987	1988	1989	1990
	(millions of dollars, except per share amounts)				
Sales and other operating revenue					
Petroleum and natural gas	$65,477	73,197	76,625	83,934	104,102
Chemicals	6,079	7,177	8,797	9,210	9,591
Coal and minerals	542	594	823	948	1,003
Hong Kong power generation	637	699	745	838	875
Other and eliminations	2,252	416	262	243	223
Total sales and other operating revenue	74,987	82,083	87,252	95,173	115,794
Earnings from equity interests and other revenue	1,568	1,252	1,311	1,112	1,146
Revenue	$76,555	83,335	88,563	96,285	116,940
Earnings					
Petroleum and natural gas					
Exploration and production	$ 3,060	3,767	2,591	3,058	4,038
Refining and marketing	1,934	509	1,812	1,098	1,315
Total petroleum and natural gas	4,994	4,276	4,403	4,156	5,353
Chemicals	470	750	1,306	1,082	522
Coal and minerals	12	(11)	55	75	8
Hong Kong power generation	132	162	173	167	181
Other operations	70	56	53	48	55
Corporate and financing	(551)	(393)	(730)	(873)	(1,109)
Restructuring	233	—	—	—	—
Earnings before special charges and cumulative effect of accounting change	5,360	4,840	5,260	4,655	5,010
Valdez provision	—	—	—	(1,680)	—
Cumulative effect of accounting change	—	—	—	535	—
Net income	$ 5,360	4,840	5,260	3,510	5,010
Net income per common share	$ 3.71	3.43	3.95	2.74	3.96
—before cumulative effect of accounting change	$ 3.71	3.43	3.95	2.32	3.96
Cash dividends per common share	$ 1.80	1.90	2.15	2.30	2.47
Net income to average shareholders' equity (percent)	17.5	14.7	16.1	11.3	15.8
Net income to total revenue (percent)	7.0	5.8	5.9	3.6	4.3
Working capital	$ 1,100	95	(2,633)	(5,408)	(5,689)
Ratio of current assets to current liabilities	1.07	1.01	0.85	0.75	0.76
Property, plant and equipment, less allowances	$49,289	53,434	54,059	60,425	62,688
Total additions to property, plant and equipment	$ 5,402	5,787	5,927	12,002	6,474
Total assets	$69,484	74,042	74,293	83,219	87,707
Exploration expenses, including dry holes	$ 1,231	818	979	872	957
Research and development costs	$ 616	524	551	592	637
Long-term debt	$ 4,294	5,021	4,689	9,275	7,687
Total debt	$ 7,878	7,885	9,638	16,032	13,777
Fixed charge coverage ratio	8.8	8.5	8.9	3.9	6.0
—before Valdez provision	8.8	8.5	8.9	5.3	6.0
Debt to capital (percent)	19.0	18.2	22.1	32.6	27.7
Shareholders' equity at year-end	$32,012	33,626	31,767	30,244	33,055
Shareholders' equity per common share	$ 22.30	24.38	24.65	24.19	26.54
Average number of common shares outstanding (millions)	1,445	1,412	1,333	1,264	1,248
Number of registered shareholders at year-end (thousands)	740	732	713	671	639
Wages, salaries and employee benefits	$ 5,553	4,646	4,979	5,131	5,881
Number of employees at year-end (thousands)	102	100	101	104	104

Exhibit 2 *Business Profile: Exxon Corporation*

	Earnings after Income Taxes		Average Capital Employed		Return on Average Capital Employed		Capital and Exploration Expenditures	
Financial	1989	1990	1989	1990	1989	1990	1989	1990
	(millions of dollars)				(percent)		(millions of dollars)	
Petroleum and natural gas								
Exploration and production								
United States	$1,133	1,259	12,218	12,257	9.3	10.3	$ 2,139	1,635
Foreign	1,925	2,779	10,331	10,992	18.6	25.3	5,028	3,109
Total	3,058	4,038	22,549	23,249	13.6	17.4	7,167	4,744
Refining and marketing								
United States	370	78	3,207	3,411	11.5	2.3	498	428
Foreign	728	1,237	9,464	11,057	7.7	11.2	2,619	1,385
Total	1,098	1,315	12,671	14,468	8.7	9.1	3,117	1,813
Total petroleum and natural gas	4,156	5,353	35,220	37,717	11.8	14.2	10,284	6, 557
Chemicals								
United States	682	354	2,235	2,592	30.5	13.7	416	571
Foreign	400	168	2,602	3,025	15.4	5.6	350	534
Total	1,082	522	4,837	5,617	22.4	9.3	766	1,105
Coal	(50)	(49)	1,613	1,547	—	—	279	81
Minerals	125	57	455	566	27.5	10.1	131	188
Hong Kong power generation	167	181	1,279	1,243	13.1	14.6	93	133
Other operations	48	55	977	1,056	4.9	5.2	213	193
Corporate and financing	(873)	(1,109)	(438)	(1,150)	—	—	18	76
Earnings before Valdez provision and cumulative effect of accounting change	4,655	5,010	43,943	46,596	12.3	12.8	11,784	8,333
Valdez provision	(1,680)	—	—	—	—	—	—	—
Cumulative effect of accounting change	535	—	—	—	—	—	—	—
Net Income/Total	$3,510	5,010	43,943	46,596	9.7	12.8	$11,784	8,333

Operating	1989	1990		1989	1990
Net liquids production	*thousands of barrels daily*		Petroleum product sales	*thousands of barrels daily*	
United States	693	640	United States	1,147	1,109
Foreign	1,008	962	Foreign	3,478	3,549
Proportional interest in production of:			Total	4,625	4,658
Equity companies	39	34			
Other non-consolidated companies	27	37	Refinery crude oil runs	*thousands of barrels daily*	
Oil sands production—Canada	37	39	United States	999	868
Total	1,804	1,712	Foreign	2,300	2,408
			Total	3,299	3,276
Natural gas production available for sale	*millions of cubic feet daily*				
United States	1,827	1,778	Coal production	*millions of metric tons*	
Foreign	1,872	1,787	United States	26	28
Proportional interest in production of:			Foreign	10	12
			Total	36	40
Equity companies	1,686	1,753			
Total	5,385	5,318			
			Minerals production	*thousands of metric tons*	
			Copper	119	112
			Zinc	13	5

Exhibit 3 *Consolidated Balance Sheet: Exxon Corporation*

	Dec. 31, 1986	Dec. 31, 1987	Dec. 31, 1988	Dec. 31 1989	Dec. 31 1990
					(millions of dollars)
Assets					
Current assets					
Cash and cash equivalents	$ 2,908	$ 1,911	$ 2,333	$ 1,865	$ 1,332
Other marketable securities	908	620	76	151	47
Notes and accounts receivable, less estimated doubtful amounts	6,784	6,278	6,094	7,787	9,574
Inventories					
Crude oil, products and merchandise	3,603	4,200	4,158	4,639	5,367
Materials and supplies	948	972	993	983	1,019
Prepaid taxes and expenses	1,169	1,410	1,192	1,151	997
Total current assets	16,320	15,391	14,846	16,576	18,336
Investments and advances	2,778	3,822	4,123	4,277	4,385
Property, plant and equipment, at cost, less accumulated depreciation and depletion	49,289	53,434	54,059	60,425	62,688
Other assets, including intangibles, net	1,097	1,395	1,265	1,941	2,298
Total assets	$69,484	$74,042	$74,293	$ 83,219	$87,707
Liabilities					
Current liabilities					
Notes and loans payable	$ 3,584	$ 2,864	$ 4,949	$ 6,757	$ 6,090
Accounts payable and accrued liabilities	9,515	10,248	10,535	13,581	15,611
Income taxes payable	2,121	2,184	1,995	1,646	2,324
Total current liabilities	15,220	15,296	17,479	21,984	24,025
Long-term debt	4,294	5,021	4,689	9,275	7,687
Annuity reserves and accrued liabilities	5,121	5,902	5,684	5,928	6,810
Deferred income tax liabilities	10,828	11,863	11,849	12,353	12,568
Deferred income	466	560	547	572	612
Equity of minority and preferred shareholders in affiliated companies	1,543	1,774	2,278	2,863	2,950
Total liabilities	37,472	40,416	42,526	52,975	54,652
Shareholders' equity					
Preferred stock without par value (authorized 200 million shares, 16 million issued)	—	—	—	1,006	955
Guaranteed LESOP obligation	—	—	—	(1,000)	(925)
Common stock without par value (authorized 2 billion shares, 1,813 million issued)	2,822	2,822	2,822	2,822	2,822
Earnings reinvested	37,322	39,476	41,865	42,433	44,286
Cumulative foreign exchange translation adjustment	(196)	1,750	1,554	1,207	2,426
Common stock held in treasury, at cost (563 million shares in 1989, 568 million shares in 1990)	(7,936)	(10,422)	(14,474)	(16,224)	(16,509)
Total shareholders' equity	32,012	33,626	31,767	30,244	33,055
Total liabilities and shareholders' equity	$69,484	$74,042	$74,293	$83,219	$87,707

Exhibit 4 *Consolidated Statement of Income: Exxon Corporation*

	1986	1987	1988	1989	1990
			(millions of dollars)		
Revenue					
Sales and other operating revenue, including excise taxes	$74,987	$82,083	$87,252	$95,173	$115,7
Earnings from equity interests and other revenue	1,568	1,252	1,311	1,112	1,1
	76,555	83,335	88,563	96,285	116,9
Costs and other deductions					
Crude oil and product purchases	28,876	34,331	33,558	39,268	50,7
Operating expenses	9,209	9,315	9,968	10,535	11,9
Selling, general and administrative expenses	5,230	5,621	5,824	6,398	7,7
Depreciation and depletion	4,415	4,239	4,790	5,002	5,5
Exploration expenses, including dry holes	1,231	818	979	872	9
Interest expense	614	451	944	1,265	1,3
Valdez provision	—	—	—	2,545	
Income taxes	3,196	2,703	3,124	2,028	3,1
Excise taxes	5,099	5,667	7,695	8,517	10,2
Other taxes and duties	13,076	15,084	16,151	16,617	19,8
Income applicable to minority and preferred interests	249	266	270	263	2
	71,195	78,495	83,303	93,310	111,9
Income before cumulative effect of accounting change	$ 5,360	4,840	5,260	2,975	5,0
Cumulative effect of change in accounting for income taxes	—	—	—	535	
Net Income	$ 5,360	$ 4,840	$ 5,260	$ 3,510	$ 5,0
Per common share—Before cumulative effect of accounting change (dollars)	$ 3.71	$ 3.43	$ 3.95	$ 2.32	$ 3.
—Cumulative effect of accounting change (dollars)	—	—	—	$ .42	
—Net income (dollars)	$ 3.71	$ 3.43	$ 3.95	$ 2.74	$ 3.

Exhibit 5 *Consolidated Statement of Cash Flows: Exxon Corporation*

	1987	1988	1989	1990
	(millions of dollars)			
Cash flows from operating activities				
Net income				
Accruing to Exxon shareholders	$ 4,840	$5,260	$3,510	$5,010
Accruing to minority and preferred interests	266	270	263	272
Adjustments for non-cash transactions				
Depreciation and depletion	4,239	4,790	5,002	5,545
Deferred income tax charges/(credits)	110	(2)	(668)	(90)
Annuity and accrued liability provisions	353	(76)	192	523
Dividends received which were in excess of/(less than) equity in current earnings of equity companies	18	(230)	(63)	(22)
Changes in operational working capital, excluding cash and debt, net of effects from capital stock acquisitions				
Reduction/(increase)—Notes and accounts receivable	(218)	87	(1,341)	(1,347)
—Inventories	(95)	(162)	(181)	(399)
—Prepaid taxes and expenses	(130)	211	(245)	72
Increase/(reduction)—Accounts and other payables	(223)	302	1,729	1,763
All other items—net	165	104	(283)	(681)
Net cash provided by operating activities	9,325	10,554	7,915	10,646
Cash flows from investing activities				
Capital stock acquisitions, net of cash acquired and non-cash financing	(1,432)	—	(4,158)	—
Additions to property, plant and equipment	(4,443)	(5,918)	(6,313)	(6,548)
Sales of subsidiaries and property, plant and equipment	1,586	639	522	854
Additional investments and advances	(580)	(518)	(153)	(409)
Sales of investments and collection of advances	144	112	169	830
Other marketable securities sales/(additions)—net	(162)	235	(23)	104
Net cash used in investing activities	(4,887)	(5,450)	(9,956)	(5,169)
Net cash generation/(usage) before financing activities	4,438	5,104	(2,041)	5,477
Cash flows from financing activities				
Additions to long-term debt	1,352	336	4,105	477
Reductions in long-term debt	(329)	(49)	(155)	(1,427)
Additions/(reductions) in short-term debt—net	(1,509)	1,549	1,242	(1,387)
Cash dividends to Exxon shareholders	(2,686)	(2,871)	(2,942)	(3,157)
Cash dividends to minority interests	(159)	(176)	(228)	(240)
Additions to minority interests and sales of affiliate preferred stock	28	315	374	37
Common stock acquired—net	(2,486)	(4,052)	(1,750)	(336)
Preferred stock issued	—	—	1,006	—
Net cash provided/(used) in financing activities	(5,789)	(4,948)	1,652	(6,033)
Effects of exchange rate changes on cash	60	(52)	(79)	23
Increase/(decrease) in cash and cash equivalents	(1,291)	104	(468)	(533)
Cash and cash equivalents at beginning of year	−3,520	2,229	2,333	1,865
Cash and cash equivalents at end of year	$ 2,229	$ 2,333	$1,865	$1,332

Exhibit 6 *Operating Summary: Exxon Corporation*

	1981	1982	1983	1984	1985	1986	1987	1988	1989	1990
	(thousands of barrels daily)									
Net production of crude oil and natural gas liquids										
Net production										
United States	752	740	781	778	768	761	756	760	693	640
Canada	94	95	90	93	116	164	188	206	269	260
Other Western Hemisphere	11	10	14	16	18	18	19	18	18	18
Europe	194	289	370	412	417	458	441	429	338	298
Middle East and Africa	39	5	5	4	3	9	16	67	74	71
Australia and Far East	230	228	267	310	330	304	326	326	309	315
Total consolidated affiliates	1,320	1,367	1,527	1,613	1,652	1,714	1,746	1,806	1,701	1,602
Proportional interest in production of equity companies	32	33	32	21	20	25	27	39	39	34
Proportional interest in production of other non-consolidated companies	27	21	25	23	19	25	28	36	27	37
Oil sands production—Canada	26	18	23	21	29	32	34	38	37	39
Worldwide	1,405	1,439	1,607	1,678	1,720	1,796	1,835	1,919	1,804	1,712
Refinery crude oil runs										
United States	1,111	989	958	1,021	1,054	1,080	1,026	968	999	868
Canada	430	366	378	365	344	332	351	350	487	489
Other Western Hemisphere	401	375	341	295	98	87	86	88	87	88
Europe	1,472	1,324	1,135	1,111	1,003	1,112	1,116	1,200	1,257	1,327
Middle East and Africa	12	8	5	4	5	6	5	6	6	6
Australia and Far East	452	434	449	424	399	415	397	430	463	498
Worldwide	3,878	3,496	3,266	3,220	2,903	3,032	2,981	3,042	3,299	3,276
Petroleum product sales										
Aviation fuels	323	330	316	312	326	317	338	344	381	381
Gasoline, naphthas	1,369	1,346	1,344	1,380	1,397	1,434	1,460	1,541	1,678	1,709
Home heating oils, kerosene, diesel oils	1,324	1,299	1,280	1,349	1,343	1,340	1,316	1,396	1,467	1,461
Heavy fuels	1,051	849	681	685	539	447	405	451	490	527
Specialty products	534	486	464	466	477	505	524	574	609	580
Total	4,601	4,310	4,085	4,192	4,082	4,043	4,043	4,306	4,625	4,658
United States	1,295	1,174	1,146	1,149	1,123	1,106	1,057	1,113	1,147	1,109
Canada	439	408	393	407	404	396	430	433	625	597
Other Western Hemisphere	459	453	436	400	377	380	388	386	383	384
Europe	1,807	1,704	1,566	1,684	1,629	1,636	1,634	1,680	1,718	1,796
Other Eastern Hemisphere	601	571	544	552	549	525	534	694	752	772
Worldwide	4,601	4,310	4,085	4,192	4,082	4,043	4,043	4,306	4,625	4,658

Exhibit 6 *continued*

Natural gas production available for sale · *(millions of cubic feet daily)*

Net production										
United States	3,065	2,594	2,345	2,485	2,085	1,919	1,698	1,805	1,827	1,778
Canada	186	186	181	168	141	142	128	189	389	397
Other Western Hemisphere	82	72	70	70	69	54	61	58	59	63
Europe	799	773	851	1,069	1,086	1,058	1,179	1,225	1,068	977
Middle East and Africa	46	—	—	—	1	1	1	1	—	1
Australia and Far East	251	264	225	215	231	246	289	314	356	349
Total consolidated affiliates	4,429	3,889	3,672	4,007	3,613	3,420	3,356	3,592	3,699	3,565
Proportional interest in production of equity companies	2,191	1,860	1,956	1,911	2,048	1,909	1,871	1,600	1,686	1,753
Worldwide	6,620	5,749	5,628	5,918	5,661	5,329	5,227	5,192	5,385	5,318

(thousands of deadweight tons, daily average)

Tanker capacity, owned and chartered	21,880	18,930	15,820	13,540	12,720	10,152	9,218	8,997	8,844	8,383

Operating statistics include 100 percent of operations of majority-owned affiliates; for other companies, gas and crude production include Exxon's ownership percentage, and crude runs include quantities processed for Exxon. Net production excludes royalties and quantities due others when produced, whether payment is made in kind or cash.

Refining and Marketing of Oil

These operations are concerned with manufacturing final products for sale to the public. Using superior refining methods like flexicoking and hydrotreating, Exxon is able to manufacture gasoline and chemicals from cheaper crude. It sells its higher-quality, more expensive crude to other firms.

The market for refined petrochemical products is highly competitive and has overcapacity. Exxon is able to remain profitable in this business in three ways:

1. By improving product quality and customizing products for various geographic areas. Special products introduced included lead-free, low-temperature fuel and odorless fuel.
2. By enhancing gasoline marketing, improved customer billing, and added services at Exxon gas stations
3. By consolidating operations by acquiring gas stations near Exxon's refineries to reduce transportation costs.

Chemicals

Exxon Chemicals is the world's tenth largest chemical company, and the third largest chemical company in the United States behind DuPont and Dow. In 1988 it achieved record earnings of $1.3 billion; this was achieved by introducing innovative products, geographic expansion both in the United States and in Europe, and joint ventures with Dow. In 1990 its net income was $522 million, down $560 million from its 1989 net income of $1,082 million. The decrease in earnings was due to an increase in industry production capacity and higher feedstock costs.

Exxon Chemicals' products are organized into three main lines: Basic Chemicals, Polymers, and Performance Products. Basic Chemicals is the industry's lowest-cost supplier of petrochemical raw materials. It is currently growing through low-cost expansion of its existing facilities. Polymers is highly marketing oriented, focusing on key industry sectors like packaging and textiles. Performance Products is well positioned in many specialty chemical businesses and offers innovative products.

Coal and Minerals

Exxon diversified into coal and minerals to decrease its reliance on crude oil production operations. After a few initial years of losses, this business has grown steadily and now provides significant profits. The production of coal has increased from 22.8 million metric tons in 1984 to 40 million metric tons in 1990, due mainly to an increase in demand for electricity and steam.

Exxon plans to decrease capital and exploration expenditures in its coal and minerals segments in the United States while increasing spending on foreign projects. Growth of operations in foreign countries is achieved through a combination of acquisitions and expansion of existing facilities.

Hong Kong Electric Power

Exxon holds a majority interest (60%) in the Hong Kong Power Plant, which is operated by China Power and Light. The plant has shown significant growth in earnings, which have doubled in the last five years (from $88 million in 1984 to $173 million in 1988). New construction, expected to be completed in 1990, will make the facility the largest coal-fired power plant in Asia, with a capacity of 4,350 megawatts (*Exxon Annual Report*, 1990). Profits from the operations of this plant help offset some of the losses due to currently low prices of coal.

Tanker Fleet

Exxon owns a shipping business in the name of Exxon Shipping Corp. This business had losses from 1984 to 1986 and was under constant pressure to cut costs. Losses were sharply reduced in 1986 due to increased shipment triggered by lower oil prices. Improved charter rates also made it profitable to operate large vessels like the *Exxon Valdez*, which went into operation in 1986. Restructuring of the fleet and an increase in demand for short-haul and long-haul tonnage have improved the utilization of Exxon's marine fleet, which in 1988 was operating its 28 tankers at full utilization levels.

Exxon's past diversification attempts outside the oil business have proven unsuccessful. Its unsuccessful diversification into the office systems business indicated its inability to survive in highly dynamic markets requiring instantaneous decisions. Similarly, diversifications into electric equipment (Reliance Electric) and nuclear power were failures. Now Exxon is bullish about energy and spends $25 million a year on research on synthetic fuels, thus reinforcing its strategy to expand within the energy business (Byrne, 1988).

EXXON IN THE EIGHTIES

In the early 1980s, Exxon recognized that it had overextended capital spending plans with the expectation of strong oil demand and increased prices. When oil prices remained weak and demand declined, Exxon found itself with excess supplies and capacity. Its strategic response was to slow down capital spending, increase production efficiency, replace oil reserves with lower priced reserves, and repurchase its stock.

Exxon significantly decreased the amount of money spent on capital expenditures and exploration costs by 32% from 1981 to 1988, as shown below in millions of dollars (*Exxon Annual Reports*):

1981	11,092
1982	11,412
1983	9,030
1984	9,755
1985	10,793
1986	7,219
1987	7,136
1988	7,508
1989	11,784
1990	8,333

It realigned its operations to the new environment by downsizing. Between 1980 and 1982, the number of personnel was reduced by 100,000 through elimination or reassignment. To reduce operating expenses and increase efficiency, Exxon continued to trim its personnel ranks, decreased its number of stations by 20%, reduced refining capacity by 24%, and decreased its tanker fleet tonnage by 34% (Byrne, 1988). The company sold its Sixth Avenue (New York) headquarters building which it co-owned with the Rockefeller Group and moved its headquarters to Irving, Texas.

To increase efficiency and improve communications between headquarters and operating units, an international communications network connecting foreign affiliates to company headquarters was installed. Also, the Administrative Computer System (ACS) was installed in the United Kingdom.

Exxon also developed an investment program in new exploration and development to replace its expensive oil and gas reserves with lower priced ones. This it did by acquisitions rather than exploration.

Exxon invested its significant cash reserves in a profitable investment program. It bought back its own shares. The buy back provided a higher rate of return than any other investment and also showed its commitment to profitability. Since 1983–1984 Exxon has purchased 10% of the corporation's outstanding shares (Grigsby, 1988).

EXXON'S RESTRUCTURING

Soon after he took over as chairman and chief executive officer in early 1987, Lawrence G. Rawl began a huge downsizing at Exxon, eliminating unnecessary bureaucracy that existed in the 20-year-old former structure. Six separate international subsidiaries were restructured into one. Unprofitable subsidiaries were divested. Numerous regional subsidiaries were folded together, and other operations were consolidated. Thirty percent of the work force was eliminated and the net annual income per employee increased to $52,100, one of the highest in American industry. At company headquarters in New York alone, the staff was reduced from 1,362 in 1985 to 330 in 1986.

As a result of the restructuring, red tape was reduced and decision making speeded up, enabling the corporation to react faster to any situation. The restructuring also resulted in a change of company culture. Previously, Exxon was a bureaucracy, attracting quality people to high-paying, secure jobs. Now, with decisions more clearly associated with individuals, executives sensed that their careers were on the line more than ever before (Bryne, 1989). Company strategy was to concentrate on the business it knew best: energy and chemicals.

The primary effect of the reorganization was to decentralize the operations of the company, which in theory would allow for prompt response to situations facing the company. However, this was not the case, as was evidenced by Exxon's slow response when word of the *Valdez* oil spill reached headquarters in New York. Cleanup crews were late in arriving on the scene, early public relations efforts were uninformed, and it was a week before the CEO publicly acknowledged the incident.

Reorganization left Exxon short handed to deal with a crisis. Nine oil spill experts left the company during the downsizing, leaving Exxon without the top talent that it once possessed. The entire responsibility for organizing the public relations effort fell to the US operations public relations staff—one man and an answering machine in Houston. That staff was beefed up after the *Valdez* accident, to support enquiries, but it was unable to field all questions and referred many callers to Exxon's Alaska office. Even company executives complained that they could not get necessary information and had to rely on the news media for information. In the early stages of the crisis, even the president of Exxon USA had to rely on second-hand information, which he subsequently relayed to Rawls. This fact alone may have contributed to the delayed public response of Rawls.

EXXON'S RESPONSES TO THE *VALDEZ* ACCIDENT

Soon after Exxon was informed about the *Valdez* accident, it announced that it would assume responsibility for the cleanup. Exxon-wide spill response teams were activated and the president of Exxon Shipping Company, accompanied by his staff, arrived at the site of the accident the same afternoon to direct cleanup efforts.

The negative publicity resulting from the spill presented Exxon with a major public relations challenge. Exxon held daily open-door press conferences to provide information about the spill. While Exxon's cleanup crews battled the oil spill, the corporation's executives managed the response at the national level. However, top corporate executives remained emotionally distant from the spill, treating it instead as a PR exercise.

Exxon CEO Lawrence Rawl did not visit the site of the accident immediately after the spill. Instead, Rawl focused on communicating to the public and shareholders that Exxon was doing all it could to minimize the damage from the spill. He presented a video production that stated that 75% of the oil that had spilled had already been cleaned up or dissipated in other ways. Rawl also ran newspaper ads across the country in which he apologized for the spill and expressed a belief that Exxon had handled the spill efficiently. In a shareholders meeting in April, Rawl assured shareholders that Exxon was committed to cleaning the affected shorelines.

The cleanup was expected to cost Exxon $2 billion, and even then the beaches would not be as clean as they were before the accident. Exxon executives saw the cleanup effort as a severe financial drain and wanted to stop the operation as soon as they could. There were no clear state or federal guidelines that specified the degree of cleanliness that was to be achieved, and under the existing law, it was entirely up to the spiller's sense of moral obligation.

Over the summer of 1989, it became clear that Exxon took clean to mean "treated" and would continue its cleanup efforts only until the environment of Prince William Sound was "environmentally stable" and not fatal to wildlife. This drew severe criticism and attacks by environmentalists and legislators, who advocated a zero-tolerance policy.

The size of the work force and the resources committed to the cleanup effort in 1990 was much smaller than in the previous year. Exxon's *1990 Annual Report* stated that "scientific studies and field observations conducted in association with cleanup operations provide compelling evidence of the environmental vitality of the [Prince William] sound and the Gulf [of Alaska]. . . . Exxon has responded to the *Valdez* accident with all appropriate resources to undertake an unprecedented, state-of-the-art cleanup effort."

THE OIL INDUSTRY

World oil reserves are concentrated in the Middle East, the former Soviet Union, North America, South America, China, Europe's North Sea region, Africa, and the Far East. With an estimated 660.3 billion barrels, the Middle East has 65.3% of the total world oil reserves of 1,011.8 billion barrels of proven oil reserves. The major consumers of oil are North America, Japan, the former Soviet Union, and Western Europe. This imbalance in production and consumption levels has made control of sources of oil very important.

The Middle East is the world's largest producer of oil. In 1960, in response to declining oil prices, several Middle Eastern countries along with Venezuela formed the Organization of Petroleum Exporting Countries (OPEC), thus dividing the industry into OPEC and non-OPEC producers. In 1989, OPEC producers pumped out 23,215 thousand barrels a day, while non-OPEC producers produced 40,345 thousand barrels per day. Since its founding, other countries have joined OPEC and today the organization is the most important player in the world oil industry.

The main function of OPEC is to control oil prices. In the 1970s, oil prices rose by about 1,000%, peaking at $39.80 per barrel in 1980. This tremendous increase was due to the Arab oil embargo that lasted from October 1973 to January 1974, and the 1979 Iranian revolution. However, OPEC has been plagued by numerous disagreements among members, over oil prices, production quotas, etc. and has been unable to maintain a unified oil strategy. In 1985, Saudi Arabia began producing large amounts of crude oil in an attempt to regain its slipping market share, and other countries followed suit, driving the price per barrel down to $10. The industry has shown a slow recovery in the 1980s but still suffers from overcapacity.

The major companies operating in the oil industry are British Petroleum (1989 revenues $48.611 billion), Chevron (1989 renenues $32.785 billion), Exxon (1989 revenues $96.285 billion), Royal Dutch/Shell (1989 revenues $85.412 billion), and Texaco (1989 revenues $35.656 billion). Major companies in the domestic market are Amerada Hess, Amoco, Atlantic Richfield, Occidental Petroleum, Phillips Petroleum, Sun, and Unocal.

The oil industry can be functionally divided into exploration, production, refining, and transportation. Exploration for oil is conducted both on land and off shore. Drilling technology has shown tremendous improvement in recent decades. One new method is the use of tension leg platforms (TLPs). The tension leg platform uses cables by anchoring them to the ocean floor and enables access to much deeper waters than fixed structures. TLPs also cost less than fixed structures and provide greater production flexibility. Another innovation being developed is the floating production, storage, and offloading system (FPSO). FPSOs are removable and are designed to withstand adverse environmental and climatic conditions. Another important technological development includes horizontal or directional drilling, for geological reservoir formations that are vertical. In this method, one well can access a multitude of reservoirs. Computer imaging and seismic analysis provide a computer-enhanced three-dimensional image of the reservoir and the drill, thus enabling the driller to maintain a specific direction.

Refining is the process of breaking down crude oil into a wide range of final products. Some of the methods used for refining are coking, catalytic cracking, hydrocracking, hydrofining, reforming, and alkylation. Various technological innovations have been developed that enable refineries to operate on lower-quality crude, thus reducing overall costs.

One of the major concerns facing refineries is the increase in environmental regulations. The Environmental Protection Agency (EPA) phased out lead in motor gasoline, forcing refiners to change their refining procedures to meet environmental requirements. There is considerable concern among environmentalists about the depletion of global oil reserves. Environmental groups in several countries are lobbying lawmakers for stricter regulation of reserves and measures for conservation of oil and natural gas.

Economic barriers to entry into the industry include government regulation of production, cost of equipment, and overcapacity in the industry. In most oil-producing countries, the production of oil is controlled by the government. The industry has to deal with increasing environmental and conservation regulations. This forces firms in the industry to develop higher quality products, which in turn drives up production costs.

The oil industry is highly capital intensive due to the high cost of equipment. The payback periods for investments in equipment are long, and firms face barriers to exit due to high unrecoverable costs. Competition within the industry is intense and there is significant overcapacity. The situation is worsened by the continual squabbling among OPEC nations regarding their production quotas, which leads to some of them secretly selling more than their alloted quota, thus increasing supply.

Following increasing concerns of environmentalists and conservationists, several nations are decreasing their dependence on oil as a source of energy. Some of the substitute energy sources being used are nuclear energy, coal, and solar energy. France has moved toward nuclear energy as the main source of electricity and other nations are following suit. Though considerable research is being conducted on substitutes to oil as an energy source, the oil industry does not face any significant threat of substitute products in the near future.

Oil is transported primarily through pipelines, by tankers, and to a lesser extent, by trucks and rail tank cars. The most widely used transportation method is tankers. Tankers require significantly lower investments than pipelines. Also, tankers can transport heavy crude, which cannot be transported through pipelines. Tankers, however, pose greater threats to the environment since marine oil spills are more difficult to control and spread faster than spills on land. Increased marine oil transportation activity in response to increasing demand for oil has environmentalists concerned. Stringent rules and controls are being instituted in several nations to reduce risks of oil discharge into oceans and inland waterways, thereby increasing tanker operating costs.

HISTORICAL DATA ON MARINE OIL SPILLS (1989)

A continual growth in the world energy demands coupled with concentrated deposits of petroleum has led to increases in production facilities and maritime transport. Over 2.2 billion tons of crude are consumed each year and roughly half is carried by tankers (Tippie and Lester, 1982). However, only 3.27% of all oil spills are traceable to tanker accidents.

Besides tanker accidents, several other factors contribute to oil discharge into oceans and inland waterways. According to US Coast Guard data, in 1983, 1.7% of all pollution was due to tanker ships, while 53.8% was due to other ships or facilities. In 1984, 11.9% of all pollution came from tankers, while other ships and facilities were responsible for 41%. Refineries are responsible for an estimated 300,000 metric tons per year of oil introduced into oceans from their operations (Johnston, 1976). Oil wells off the coast, of which the United States has 26,000, also contribute to the oil discharged into the oceans. According to a 1983 US geological survey, a single platform could endure one to three major spills (1,000+ barrels); up to 25 medium spills; and over 2,000 small incidents (less than 50 barrels) (Simon, 1984). An MIT study of the United Kingdom's largest terminal in Milford Haven in 1973 concluded that terminal losses contribute the least of all petroleum-handling operations.

Another source of oil in oceans is normal tanker cleaning operations. Tankers fill their empty cargo tanks with seawater to "ballast" their return voyage (for vessel stability and proper propeller immersion). This ballast mixes with the remaining oil (.35%–1%) and must be removed before entering port. Crew also wash down tanks for arrival ballast to ensure compatibility in the tank, and to prevent sludge build-up. The resultant oily water must be removed before loading the new cargo. Until recently, tankers discharged this oily water ballast and tank cleanings directly into the ocean.

However, new oil tankers of 70,000 dwt and above must now be fitted with segregated ballast tanks (SBTs). These tanks are piped and pumped separately and are dedicated to saltwater use only for ballast purposes. In addition, the SBTs are to be built into protective locations around cargo tanks so as not to allow a break or rupture in the event of a collision (Mankubady, 1986). These changes along with other recommendations of separators, collision bulkheads, forepeak tank dismantlement, and minimum damage standards should help to lessen oil pollution from operational discharges.

TANKER ACCIDENTS

Worldwide tanker accidents account for .2 million metric tons (9.4% of total) of oil discharges per year. Most tanker mishaps occur close to shore, near to ports, and off recreational shorelines, making them painfully visible and drawing the attention of the public and media. According to oil industry calculations, an accident will happen on a statistical average of every thousandth harbor approach or after fifty years of regular tanker service (Gerlach, 1976).

The *Torrey Canyon* grounded off the British coast on March 18, 1967, spilling 29.4 million gallons. On December 15, 1976, the *Argo Merchant* ran aground off the coast of Massachusetts, spilling 63 million gallons of oil into the Atlantic. On December 29, 1976, the *Grand Zenith* sank near Nova Scotia, causing an 8.2-million-gallon spill. On March 6, 1978, the *Amoco Cadiz* broke apart off the Brittany coast, resulting in a 68-million-gallon crude oil spill that washed up on 130 miles of coast line. On October 31, 1984, the oil tanker *Puerto Rican* caught fire and exploded, resulting in North California's worst oil spill.

The causes of tanker accidents are very complex. Usually, there are several simultaneous and interacting failures that cause accidents. These failures include human error, unqualified captains, poorly maintained vessels, poor vessel design, incorrect operating procedures, miscommunication with vehicle traffic control systems, and aging fleets. Moreover, countries such as Cyprus, Greece, Lebanon, Liberia, Panama, Singapore, Bahamas, and Oman permit operations without major safety inspections, little or no insurance requirements, little or no taxes, and lower crew wages.

Vessel size is an important determinant of the scope of accidents. Larger vessels provide better economies of scale and less traffic, therefore, less chance of collision. However, when accidents do occur, the possibility of catastrophic spills increases. Larger vessels are longer and deeper, stand increased chances of grounding, are harder to maneuver, and require longer distances to stop, thus increasing their susceptibility to accidents. When damaged, vessels must be towed long distances to ports capable of recieving large vessels, thereby increasing spillage and damage to the environment. Longer vessels may ride two-wave crests on the bow and the stern during rough seas. This leaves the center unsupported and subject to stresses that can "break the vessel in two" (Ross, 1978).

REFERENCES

Browne, Malcolm W. Radar could have tracked tanker. *The New York Times* April 5, 1989: A24.

Byrne, John A. The rebel shaking up Exxon. *Business Week* July 18, 1988: 104–111.

Church, George J. The big spill. *Time* April 10, 1989: 38–41.

Cook, James. Exxon proves that big doesn't mean rigid. *Forbes* April 29, 1989: 66–74.

Crude drama. *Time* April 18, 1988: 57.

D'Arcy, Jenish, John Daly, and Bruce Wallace. Takeover fever hits Canada. *Macleans* January 30, 1989: 30–33.

Day, Charles R. Jr. Corporate strategies: the year's gutsiest decisions. *Industry Week* February 23, 1987: 28–30.

Deutsch, Claudia H. The giant with the black eye. *The New York Times* April 2, 1989: F1,8.

Environmental Conservation. Washington, D.C.: Kauffmann Graphics, 1972.

Exxon Annual Reports: 1985, 1986, 1987, 1988, 1989, 1990.

Exxon Chemical says it will expand unit at Baton Rouge. *New York Times* June 14, 1988: D3.

Exxon reduced its staff of oil spill experts. *The New York Times* March 30, 1989: A20.

Exxon News Letter to Shareholders: First quarter and second quarter, 1989.

Gerlach, Sebastian A. *Marine Pollution*. Hiedelberg, Germany: Springer-Verlag, 1976.

Gifford, Bill. The original octopus. *Village Voice* April 18, 1989: 18.

Gifford, Bill. How it got away: an account of the fumbling in Washington and Alaska. *Village Voice* April 18, 1989: 17–18.

Good Year may buy Exxon film business. *Chicago Tribune* December 21, 1988.

Gregory, K. J., and D. E. Walling. *Human Activity and Environmental Processes*. Great Britain: John Wiley & Sons Ltd., 1987.

Grigsby, Jefferson. Treening the tiger. *Financial World* October 18, 1988: 20–21.

Johnston, R. *Marine Pollution*. London: Academic Press, 1976.

Lazo, Shirley A. "Speaking of dividends. *Barrons* May 2, 1988: 59.

Leinster, Colin. Exxon's axman cometh. *Fortune* April 14, 1986: 92–96.

M'Gonigle, R. M., and M. W. Zacher. *Pollution, Politics, and International Law*. Berkeley Calif.: University of California Press, 1979.

Mankubady, S. *The International Maritime Organization* Beckenham, England: Crown Helm Ltd., 1986.

The Ocean Yearbook 7. Chicago: University of Chicago Press, 1988.

Oil and dirty hands. *New York Times* April 5, 1989: A28.

Petroleum in the Marine Environment. Washington, D.C.: National Academy of Sciences, 1973.

Powell, William J. Jr. Exxon: a drive to disaster in the office. *Business Week* June 3, 1985: 94.

The Pulse of the Planet. New York: Crown Publishers, 1972.

Ross, D. A. *Opportunities and Uses of the Ocean*. New York: Springer-Verlag, 1978.

Saxon, Wolfgang. Ousted tanker captain still in hiding. *New York Times* April 5, 1989: A24.

Standard & Poor's Industrial Surveys.

Sullivan, Allanna, and Amanda Bennett. Critics fault chief executive of Exxon on handling of recent Alaskan oil spill. *Wall Street Journal* March 31, 1989: B1.

Tippie, V. K., and D. R. Lester. *Impact of Marine Pollution on Society.* South Hadley: J. F. Bergin Publishers, 1982.

US Department of Transportation, US Coast Guard. *Polluting Incidents In and Around US Waters.* Washington, D.C.: US Government Printing Office, 1986.

US Environmental Protection Agency. *1980 Environmental Outlook.* Washington, D.C.: US Government Printing Office, 1980.

US Industrial Outlook, 1989. Washington D.C.: US Government Printing Office, 1990.

Value line Investment Survey Ratings and Reports, April 1989: 140.

Walsh, John. Oil industry R&D takes a fall. *Science* June 27, 1986: 1593–1594.

Witteman, Paul A. The stain will remain on Alaska. *Time* September 25, 1989: 58–59.

GENICOM CORPORATION

Per V. Jenster,
International Institute for Management Development
Lausanne, Switzerland
John M. Gwin
David B. Croll
Univeristy of Virginia

Curtis W. Powell, president of GENICOM, faced the morning of June 18, 1985 with uncertainty. His upcoming meeting with the labor union at the firm's Waynesboro, Virginia, facility was one that raised some disturbing questions about the company's future, and even its past.

Prior to today's meeting, GENICOM had proposed wage and benefit reductions, which resulted in increasing confrontation with union representatives. Powell pondered what strategic alternatives the company should pursue if the union did not accept the proposed reductions. And even if the union did make the concessions needed, what strategy should GENICOM follow in the competitive computer printer market over the next three to five years?

BACKGROUND

GENICOM was founded in June 1983 as a result of a leveraged buy-out of General Electric's (GE) Data Communication Products Business Department in Waynesboro, a relatively self-contained entity that produced computer printers and relay components. The department had operated as one of GE's strategic business units.

GE came to Waynesboro, a small town in central Virginia, in 1954 as part of a major decentralization effort, which also included establishing facilities nearby in Lynchburg and Salem, Virginia. Between 1954 and 1974, the Waynesboro plant produced a wide variety of highly sophisticated electromechanical devices such as process controls, numerical controls, and aircraft controls, many of which are now produced by other GE divisions. Products once manufactured in the Waynesboro facility accounted for several hundred million dollars in annual sales revenues for GE. As a result, the Waynesboro factory had a long-standing reputation for skill in electromechanical design and engineering and for ability to solve difficult design tasks in its highly vertically integrated facilities.

The first electromechanical printer was created by GE in Waynesboro as a result of the firm's own dissatisfaction with the performance of the Teletype 33 printers. The new GE printer was three times faster than the Teletype 33 and quickly gained popularity. In 1969, a send-receive printer was introduced with such success that it evolved into one of GE's fastest-growing product lines. Other products were added using the same technology, and by 1977 the business in Waynesboro had attained annual revenues of $100 million while being very profitable.

In 1980, GE changed corporate leadership. The new GE chairman, John F. Welch, initiated a major review of the corporation's businesses to determine which ones were critical to GE's future strategies. Businesses with products that did not rank number one or number two in their served industries or did not have the technological leadership to become first or second required special review. The Waynesboro products did not rank number one or number two in their industry, nor were these products deemed critical to GE's long-term strategies. In 1981, the firm's strategic planning process investigated the possibility of divestiture as an alternative course of action.

During 1981, the then current general manager resigned and Curtis Powell, the financial manager and long-time GE employee, was appointed the new general manager.[1]

During the same time frame, the line of reporting in the printer business was in disarray; the general manager, the division manager, and his superior, the group vice president, left GE and the executive vice president and sector executive retired. As a result, there were no persons at the administrative levels between the Waynesboro facility and a newly appointed sector executive. Powell received the dual task of (1) positioning the business for divestiture and (2) making it viable if no acceptable buyers could be found. To accomplish these two objectives, Powell implemented programs to improve the competitiveness of the department's printer products and productivity programs to reduce the cost of operations. To support aggressive new product design efforts, funding of research and development activities were increased by $1 million per year. The first product, the new 3000 series printer, was introduced in the latter part of 1981. By 1982, the 3000 series product had received an excellent reception in the marketplace. Variable cost had been reduced by 28%, primarily as a result of the relocation of 300 jobs from Waynesboro to the department's Mexican facility; fixed costs had been reduced by 25%; and net assets in the business had been reduced by $14 million. Despite the successful introduction of the new printer product and rapidly increasing orders, GE was still interested in divesting the business.

After several months of meetings with potential acquirers, GE did not received an acceptable offer. During the fourth quarter of 1982, Powell and a group of plant managers (the management team) offered to purchase the Waynesboro based business from GE.

THE BUY OUT OF GENICOM

During early 1983, GE agreed to sell the business as a leveraged buy-out, but required a substantial cash payment. In order to complete the transaction, the management team was joined by two New-York-based venture capital firms that provided the cash needed to purchase the business.

The price agreed on for the business was net depreciated value plus $8 million (the business had been in Waynesboro since 1954 and the net depreciated value was significantly less than the appraised value). The purchase price amounted to less than six months of sales revenue.

The assets purchased included every printer design developed by the Waynesboro facility, all customers and contracts, all patents and cross licenses, tools, and buildings, as well as the crystal relay business. The purchase agreement was signed October 23, 1983, at which time GE received approximately 75% of the purchase price in cash and subordinated notes for the balance. The purchase amount was financed through sale of shares to the venture capital firms and to local management (approximately 45 of the top managers received stock or stock options). Twelve million dollars was borrowed against fixed assets in the business, and a revolving credit line was secured against equipment leases, receivables, and selected inventory. Given the assessed value of the firm, GENICOM had not exceeded 65% of its borrowing capacity.

The allocation of ownership of GENICOM gave the management team a small but significant interest in the business after the buy-out. The majority ownership was held as security against the debt to the venture capital firms.

THE GENICOM CORPORATION

By 1983, GENICOM was one of the larger independent computer printer companies that manufactured teleprinters (i.e., keyboard send/receive units), dot-matrix printers, and line printers. These printers were primarily industrial grade and thus were not widely used for personal computer output. They served a wide variety of data processing and telecommunications needs, with printing speeds ranging from 60 characters per second (CPS) in the teleprinter version to 400 lines per minute (lpm) in

---

[1] In this respect, it is important to understand GE's organizational structure. GE was organized as follows: The chairman, three vice chairmen, seven industry sectors, numerous groups and divisions, each containing many departments. The Waynesboro factory was a department.

the line printer series. GENICOM was also the industry leader in crystal relays sold to defense, space, and other industries where there was a need for highly reliable electrical switches.

GENICOM continued to be a multinational company with production facilities in Waynesboro (1,300 employees) and Mexico (700 employees). Approximately 20% of the 1984 sales revenue of $140 million was derived from international customers, primarily original equipment manufacturers (OEMs). GENICOM was in the process of establishing its own sales affiliates in the United Kingdom, France, Germany, and Sweden in order to further serve its foreign customers.

In the process of buying the company, GENICOM's management negotiated a comprehensive benefits package, which was essentially the same as GE's, a new agreement with the union was signed, and customers and suppliers were briefed. All but fifteen employees had been offered positions with GENICOM at the same salary and similar benefits as provided by GE and all accepted.

According to Powell: "Everything considered, the buy-out went extremely well. 1984 was an excellent year, a very successful year for GENICOM. We are still trying to change the culture we inherited from GE, where people feel they have unlimited resources to a small company climate, a climate in which costs must be contained. Some of our people in Waynesboro believe that the successful business year we had in 1984 will continue forever. They don't realize that in our industry product life-cycles are short and even if your products are doing well today, you need to prepare for tomorrow. This transition from GE to GENICOM has been difficult.

"When we were a part of GE all employees were paid GE wages and salaries. Other firms in our industry and other firms in Waynesboro paid considerably less than GE rates." As one of the two largest employers in Waynesboro, GENICOM's actions when dealing with its employees became public very soon. "We have a very quality-conscious work force in Waynesboro and quality has always been extremely important to us. But in our competitive market quality is not enough, we must be cost competitive also."

Management and Structure

Genicom's management inherited a vertical structure and a control system that reflected GE's philosophies and procedures. As a result of GE's capital budgeting and performance evaluation system, GENICOM was probably the most vertically integrated printer company in the world, making almost everything in-house from tools to printer ribbons to sales brochures. This high degree of vertical integration enabled GENICOM to respond quickly to specific requests for redesign of products to suit individual customer needs.

The firm's information system was also aligned with GE's reporting system, which led one outside observer to conclude that he "had never seen an organization with such a sophisticated information system which used it so little." As an illustration, Exhibit 1 shows GENICOM's management information systems (MIS) budget vis-à-vis industry averages. Exhibit 2 compares GENICOM's data processing department with a similar organization in the industry. According to Coopers & Lybrand, a consulting firm retained by GENICOM, the cost problem, highlighted in these two exhibits, could also be found in other areas: finance, materials, shop operations, manufacturing engineering, quality control, marketing, product engineering, and relays.

The management team of GENICOM (April 1985) consists of the following members:

- Curtis W. Powell, president/chief executive officer: Powell graduated from Lynchburg College, Lynchburg, Virginia in 1961 with a BA degree in business administration—Economics. Prior to the purchase of the Waynesboro business by GENICOM, Powell had served 22 years in various GE assignments, the last two as department general manager of the Waynesboro business.
- John V. Harker, executive vice president: Harker was responsible for the sales and marketing functions, including product planning, market and new business development, marketing administration, customer service, domestic sales, and international operations. He formerly held positions as senior vice president for marketing and corporate development at dataproducts; vice president of Booz, Allen, and Hamilton, a management consulting firm; and with IBM in various marketing capacities. Upon joining GENICOM, he initiated the hiring of six new marketing and sales executives from the computer peripherals industry.
- Robert C. Bowen, vice president and chief financial officer: Bowen served in various financial

Exhibit 1 *Comparison with Industry Averages*

	Manufacturing (Electronics, Electrical)		GENICOM	
	Amount	Percent	Amount	Percent
Total revenue	$75,790	NA	$165,000	
MIS Operating budget	723	100	2,567.4[a]	100
Personnel	308	42.5	1,271.0	49.5
Hardware	208	28.4	400.6[b]	15.6
System software	21	3.1	27.5	1.1
Application software	36	4.9	76.5	3.0
Supplies	57	7.8	110.3	4.2
Outside services	36	7.8	559.0	21.8
Communications	21	3.3	19.8	0.8
Other	36	5.0	102.7[c]	4.0

Sources: Infosystems 25th and 26th annual salary surveys, June 1984 and June, 1983.

Survey of 642 firms conducted for Datamation and published March 15, 1985 shows that firms averaging $200 million in revenue employ an average of 20.1 people in data processing (equivalent to IS&S at GENICOM without office services). This provides an index of average revenue of $9,950,200 per data processing employee.

[a]GENICOM's IS&S actual expenses January–May 1985 have been annualized and have been modified to remove office services expenses and to add estimated hardware depreciation expense and estimated occupancy expense in order to correlate to survey figures.

[b]This category includes equipment rental, maintenance, and depreciation expense. Depreciation expense is drawn from GENICOM's fixed asset register and includes annual depreciation (book) for all assets acquired through December 1984.

[c]This category includes occupancy expense estimated at 4% of total MIS expense budget.

Exhibit 2 *Comparison of a Data Processing Department with Some Similarities to GENICOM's*

	GENICOM	Other Firm
Hardware	5 Hewlett-Packard 3000s	4 Hewlett-Packard 3000s
Number of data centers	1 current 1 planned	2
Annual revenues of organization	$165,000,000 (1985 budget)	$500,000,000 (1985 budget)
Type of business	Manufacturing	Manufacturing
Number of employees in MIS	34 (includes staff at one data center)	44 (includes staff at both data centers)
Salary expense	$1,051,300	$1,075,200 (1984 + 5%)
Processing characteristics	In-house plus heavy use of remote computing service	In-house plus heavy use of remote computing service
Company revenues per MIS employee	$4,852,900	$12,500,000

capacities with GE since 1964 and with GENI-COM's predecessor for the past ten years.

- W. Douglas Drumheller, vice president of manufacturing: Drumheller joined GE's manufacturing management program in 1970 and was appointed vice president at GENICOM in 1983.
- Dennie J. Shadrick, vice president of engineering: Shadrick recently joined GENICOM after seventeen years with Texas Instruments, where he served in a variety of engineering and management positions in the terminal and printer business unit.
- Charles A. Ford, vice president of relay operations: Ford has had a long career with GE and GENICOM serving in the areas of manufacturing, engineering, and general management.
- Robert B. Chapman, treasurer: Chapman has been with GENICOM since 1984, after holding positions with Centronics Data Computer Corporation, Honeywell, and Datapoint where he was assistant treasurer.

Part of GE heritage was a strong engineering and manufacturing orientation and this was a valuable asset. However, as a new and independent company, Genicom needed to establish a marketing presence. It needed a new and aggressive approach to marketing and sales activities. One of its first actions was to recruit the best marketing and sales executives. GENICOM's strategy for developing marketing strengths was to bring experienced and capable people from other firms in the computer peripherals industry.

Financial Status

The 1984 financial statements are included in Exhibits 3–6. Eleven footnotes followed the statements. Although each provided some additional information only footnote number 11 affects the issues addressed in this case. That footnote states:

> Subsequent Event
> *On January 3, 1985, through a private placement, the Company sold 353,000 shares of its unissued common stock for $5 per share. If these shares had been issued at December 30, 1984, unaudited pro forma stockholders' equity would have been $16,993,000.*

The financial statements including the eleven footnotes received an unqualified (clean) opinion from their auditors the accounting firm of Coopers & Lybrand.

Costs

A major issue was that GENICOM's product costs were well above those of its competitors. GENICOM's willingness to customize many of its products to meet its customers' individual needs allowed it to charge a premium price, which helped overcome its cost disadvantage. The costs that seemed disproportionately high were salary and hourly wages. GENICOM's salary and wage structures were established over many years while it was a part of GE. General Electric traditionally provided its employees with both a generous base salary and a generous fringe package. As wages and benefits were negotiated with the union on an overall corporate basis, the Waynesboro printer manufacturing operation had avoided serious conflicts with the union.

Consultants from Coopers & Lybrand were hired by GENICOM to evaluate the firm's cost structure. Although the study was not completed, preliminary research had focused on this labor cost problem. The preliminary findings suggested that most areas of the firm seemed overstaffed and salary and wage levels exceeded both industry norms and local community standards. (e.g., see Exhibits 1 and 2).

An interesting point was that GENICOM's wage and salary differential over other local companies was so great that it had proved detrimental to some laid-off employees. Other companies in the region had reported that they were hesitant to hire a laid-off GENICOM employee knowing that, as soon as an opening existed, the employee would be lost back to GENICOM.

Union Negotiations

Negotiations with Local 124 of the United Electrical Radio and Machine Workers (UE) of America started on April 23, 1985. Management's primary goal was to reduce the average costs of an applied direct labor hour by four dollars. Included in the employee benefit package were vacation (five weeks maximum), holidays (ten days), comprehensive medical benefits, life insurance, temporary disability, overtime premium, pension, breaks, night-shift bonus, paid sick days/personal time, and job structures that included seventeen pay grades. The appendices

Exhibit 3 *GENICOM Corporation and Subsidiaries: Consolidated Balance Sheet*

	December 30, 1984	January 1, 1984
Assets	*(amount in thousands)*	
Current assets		
Cash	$ 451	$ 3,023
Accounts receivable, less		
allowance for doubtful accounts of $958 and $483	21,224	22,459
Inventories	26,917	24,343
Prepaid expenses and other assets	1,368	356
Total Current assets	49,960	50,181
Property, plant and equipment	27,821	27,314
Other assets	239	180
	$78,020	$77,675
Liabilities and Capital		
Current liabilities		
Current portion of long-term debt	1,600	11,841
Accounts payable and accrued expenses	16,104	15,682
Deferred income	1,519	1,359
Income taxes	5,579	
Total current liabilities	$24,802	$28,882
Long-term debt, less current		
portion	36,400	44,500
Deferred income taxes	1,590	504
Redeemable preferred stock, $1 par value;		
32,000 shares issued and outstanding at		
January 1, 1984; stated at liquidation value of $100/share		3,200
Stockholders' equity		
Common stock, $.01 par value; 20,000,000		
shares authorized; shares outstanding:		
12/30/84-10,995,500 & 1/1/84-8,575,000	110	86
Additional paid-in capital	9,297	772
Retained earnings (deficit)	5,821	(269)
	15,228	589
	$78,020	$77,675

Exhibit 4 *GENICOM Corporation and Subsidiaries: Consolidated Statement of Income*

	Year Ended December 30, 1984	October 21, 1983 to January 1, 1984
	(amount in thousands)	
Net sales	$136,661	$ 26,752
Cost of goods sold	90,647	20,403
Gross profit	46,014	6,349
Expenses		
Selling, general & administration	22,442	3,965
Engineering, research, and product development	4,795	890
Interest	6,900	1,386
	34,137	6,241
Income before income taxes	11,877	108
Income tax expense	5,787	377
Net income (loss)	$ 6,090	$ (269)
Net income (loss) per common share and common share equivalent		
Primary	$ .61	$ (.03)
Fully diluted	$ .59	$ (.03)
Weighted average number of common shares and common share equivalents		
Primary	$ 9,967	$ 8,753
Fully diluted	10,292	8,892

Exhibit 5 *GENICOM Corporation and subsidiaries: Consolidated Statement of Changes in Capital Accounts for the Year Ended 12/30/84 and the Period from 10/21/83 (Commencement of Operations) to 1/1/84*

	Redeemable Preferred Stock	Common Stock	Additional Paid-in Capital	Retained Earnings
	(dollar amounts in thousands)			
Issued in connection with acquisition				
32,000 shares of redeemable preferred stock	$3,200			
8,000,000 shares of common stock		$80	$721	
Issuance of 525,000 shares of common stock		5	47	
Exercise of stock options		1	4	
Net Loss				$ (269)
Balance, January 1, 1984	3,200	86	772	(269)
Issuance of 1,297,000 shares of common stock		13	5,288	
Redemption of preferred stock	(3,200)	6	3,194	
Exercise of stock options		5	43	
Net income				$ 6,090
Balance, December 30, 1984		$110	$9,297	$ 5,821

Exhibit 6 *GENICOM Corporation and Subsidiaries: Consolidated Statement of Changes in Financial Position*

	Year ended December 30, 1984	October 21, 1983 to January 1, 1989
	(amounts in thousands)	
Sources of Working Capital		
From operations		
Net income (loss)	$ 6,090	$ (269)
Changes to income not affecting working capital		
Depreciation	4,664	630
Amortization	49	
Deferred income taxes	1,086	504
Working capital from operations	11,889	865
Issued or assumed in connection with acquisition		
Redeemable preferred stock		3,200
Common stock		801
Long-term debt		57,841
Proceeds from issuance of common stock	8,501	52
Exercise of options	48	5
Other, net	357	(189)
Total sources	$20,795	$62,575
Applications of Working Capital		
Additions to property, plant and equipment	5,636	918
Noncurrent assets purchased in acquisition		27,017
Reduction of long-term debt	8,100	13,341
Redemption of preferred stock	3,200	
Total applications	$16,936	$41,276
Analysis of Working Capital Components		
Increase (decrease) in current assets		
Cash	(2,572)	3,023
Accounts receivable	(1,235)	22,459
Inventories	2,574	24,343
Prepaid expenses and other assets	1,012	356
Totals	221	50,181
Increase (decrease) in current liabilities		
Current portion of long-term debt	(10,241)	11,841
Accounts payable and accrued expenses	422	15,682
Deferred income	160	1,359
Income taxes	5,579	
Totals	(4,080)	28,882
Increase in working capital	3,859	21,299
Working capital, beginning of period	21,299	
Working capital, end of period	$25,158	$21,299

to this case provide a picture of the negotiations as the confrontation grew from both interim reports and company communications.

Earlier in April, a different local of the UE in a nearby Virginia town had been involved in an almost identical situation. A former department of Westinghouse that had been sold to outside interests, confronted with wage and benefit structures originally negotiated at the national level, attempted to win major financial concessions from its work force in order to become cost competitive in its market. The local refused to accept any cutbacks in its package and, after several months of negotiation, went on strike. Two days later the company announced it would begin hiring permanent replacements for the striking workers on the following Monday and placed help wanted ads in the local newspapers. On Sunday afternoon, in a close vote, the union members voted to end the strike and accept management's proposals.

The Printer Industry

The demand for printer hardware is derived from the demand for computing machinery. As the demand for computing capability shifted from mainframe computers to minicomputers to microcomputers, so did the demand for printing capacity shift from output capability to output quality. Similarly, the attributes of printers that determined their success in the marketplace changed from reliability and performance when dealing with mainframe applications to price and capability when dealing with microcomputer applications. At the same time, as business applications of microcomputers moved into networking situations, where a number of microcomputers are linked to a central database and a single printer, the demands placed on the printer hardware changed from the demands of a stand-alone microcomputer.

The Market. The total market for printers of all types was predicted to be $10.44 billion in 1986. The breakdown of sales by printer type is shown in Exhibit 7. The market was segmented by impact printers (which use a print head that actually strikes the paper) and nonimpact printers (which do not strike the paper, but apply ink in some other fashion). Within the impact market, printers were also segmented by dot-matrix printers (which use dots to form the characters printed) and fully formed printers (which print an entire character at once,

such as a daisywheel printer). This market was further segmented according to whether a printer was a serial printer (one that prints character by character in a serial fashion) or a line printer (one that prints an entire line at a time—in general, line printers are called high speed and print faster than serial printers, but often at a lower quality). Finally, the impact market segment was subdivided according to speed of printing. The nonimpact segment was divided further according to printer technology (electrostatic, ink jet, laser) and by speed (in characters per second). Certain nonimpact printers were also segmented as page printers (those which print a complete page at a time). All nonimpact printers were considered to have fully formed characters. A schematic representation of the complete market for printers is shown in Exhibit 8.

Besides print quality, different classes of printers had advantages and disadvantages for end users. Fully formed character printers, whether daisywheel or band line, offered no graphics capability since they were limited to alphanumeric characters. These printers also were very noisy while printing, unless special quieting enclosures were used to surround them. Additionally, daisywheel printers, which were found almost exclusively in offices for word processing applications, were extremely slow.

The primary drawback to dot-matrix printers was perceived print quality, although a number of technological developments had improved their performance. These printers, however, supplied excellent adaptability to applications needs—graphics, spreadsheets, data and word processing, for instance—and prices had been dropping very rapidly in this market segment.

Nonimpact printers offered many of the best aspects of performance—quiet operation, flexible application, and outstanding print quality—but drawbacks included high prices, inability to print multiple copies simultaneously (i.e., continuous multipart forms printing), higher cost of operation because of their utilization of consumable supplies such as toner, and some perception on the part of users that nonimpact printers, like the copiers their technology was derived from, were less reliable.

As advances in technology decreased the cost of nonimpact printers, the growth of sales in these segments was expected to increase. The prices of nonimpact printers were still high relative to impact offerings, and the impact printers still enjoyed a

Exhibit 7 *US Printer Market*

	1983				1986			
	# of units	(% share)	$ value	(% share)	# of units	(% share)	$ value	(% share)
Serial daisywheel	712,000	25	1.37 billion	25	2,000,000	24	2.4 billion	23
Serial dot-matrix	1,857,000	66	2.28 billion	41	4,600,000	54	4.14 billion	40
Serial nonimpact[a]	132,000	5	162 million	3	1,600,000	19	990 million	9
Nonimpact page printers[b]	5,200	0	222 million	4	150,000	2	1 billion	10
Fully formed line printers	86,000	3	1.13 billion	21	100,000	1	1.4 billion	13
Dot-matrix line printers	31,000	1	318 million	6	55,000	0	510 million	5
Total	2,823,000		5,482 billion		8,505,000		10.44 billion	

Source: Datek Information Services Inc.
[a]Inkjet and thermal transfer printers.
[b]Laser and similar printers.

Exhibit 8 *Electronic Printer Market Breakdown*

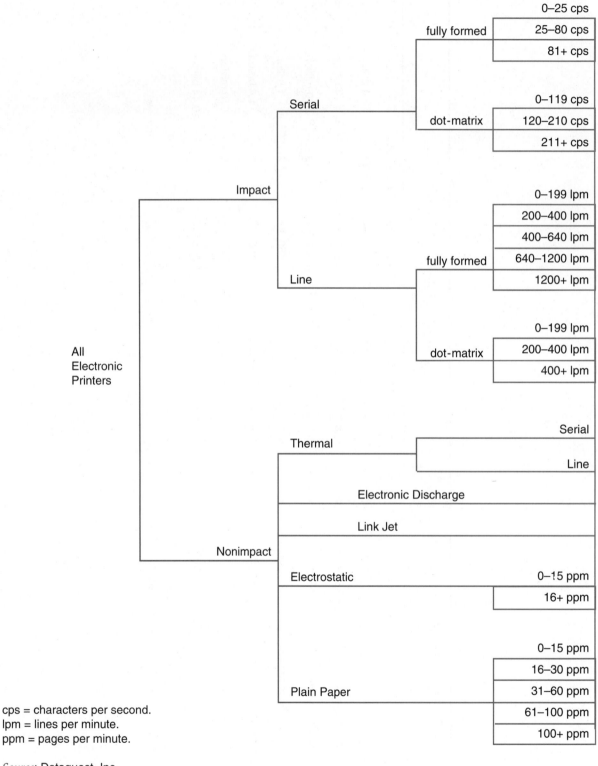

cps = characters per second.
lpm = lines per minute.
ppm = pages per minute.

Source: Dataquest, Inc.

speed advantage. However, the nonimpact printers were much quieter than their impact counterparts, and the quality of their output was at least as high as the best fully-formed impact output.

End User. The end user for GENICOM products was faced with a complex decision process in the choice of a printer. The current products operated faster, printed more legibly, and cost less than those of a few years ago. However, there were more machines to choose from, so the choice needed to be made carefully.

GENICOM Product Line. By April 1985, GENICOM primarily produced dot-matrix impact printers, though $6 million in 1984 revenue was derived from a 300-lpm fully formed character line printer. The company produced line and serial printers which could print from 60 cps in an office environment to 600 lpm in a high-speed line printer used for volume production. Most of the GENICOM product line also offered letter-quality printing at slower speeds, so the machines were flexible. GENICOM offered branded printers as peripheral devices and produced OEM printers for a number of major

customers. GENICOM's products generally were more expensive than those of their major competitors, but had higher performance capabilities and greater durability. GENICOM sales by product for 1984 are shown in Exhibit 9.

GENICOM Competitors. GENICOM had a number of major competitors in each of the market segments it served. Its two major US competitors were Centronics and Dataproducts, both competing essentially head on with GENICOM in almost every market segment. There were other, smaller US competitors for special applications and certain of GENICOM's market segments. In addition to the changes that took place in the printer industry as a result of changes in the computer industry, there was change in the competitive structure of the marketplace.

The presence of the Japanese manufacturers had altered the competitive nature of the industry. As had been the strategy in other industries, Japanese manufacturers entered the market at the bottom of the price structure. Because of lower labor rates and efficient production capability, the Japanese prod-

---

Exhibit 9 *GENICOM 1984 Sales*

Printers	$(000)	Units
340/510	5,980	1,749
200	8,564	4,016
2030	6,131	}
		} 9,623
2120	5,011	}
3000	30,924	20,495
3014/3024	3,879	5,036
4000	—	—
Other	399	—
Subtotal	60,888	31,296
Parts	16,962	
Ribbons	7,846	
Lease	18,140	
Service	9,380	
Printer business total	113,216	
Relays	23,426	
Company total	136,642	

Exhibit 10 *US Serial Impact Printer Market—1984: Market Share (Units)*

Country of Manufacture	Manufacturer	% Share	Fully Formed	Dot-matrix
Japan	Epson	20.1		X
	C. Itoh (TBC)	13.9	X	X
	Okidata	11.4		X
	Star	3.2		X
	NEC	2.4	X	X
	Brother	2.0	X	X
	Ricoh	2.0	X	
	Toshiba	1.1		X
	Canon	0.9		X
	Juki	0.9	X	
	Fujitsu	0.6	X	X
	Subtotal	58.5		
United States	Xerox	3.2	X	
	IBM	3.0	X	
	Texas Instruments	2.2		X
	DBC	2.2		X
	Teletype	2.0		X
	Qume	2.0	X	
	Centronics	1.6		X
	GEMICON	1.1		X
	Anadom	0.6		X
	Datasouth	0.4		X
	Dataproducts	1.6	X	X
	Subtotal	19.9		
Europe	Mannemaron	0.9		X
	Facit	0.5	X	X
	Philips	0.3		X
	Hermes	0.2		X
	Subtotal	1.9		
Other		19.7		

US Nonimpact Printer Market—1984: Market Share (Units)

Country of Manufacture	Manufacturer	% Share	Page	Thermal	Ink Jet
Japan	Canon	17.3	X		X
	Okidata	17.0		X	X
	Star	12.8		X	
	Sharp	8.5		X	X
	Brother	4.5		X	
	Subtotal	60.1			
United States	IBM	8.0	X	X	X
	Hewlett-Packard	4.5		X	X
	Xerox	3.6	X	X	X
	Texas Instruments	2.5		X	
	Subtotal	18.6			

continued

Exhibit 10 *continued*

Country of Manufacture	Manufacturer	% Share		Page	Thermal	Ink Jet
Europe	Siemens	3.5		X		X
	Honeywell	1.0		X		
	Subtotal		4.5			
Other			16.8			

US Line Impact Printer Market—1984: Market Share (Units)

Country of Manufacture	Manufacturer	% Share		Fully Formed	Dot-matrix
United States	Dataproducts	31.0		X	
	IBM	23.0		X	X
	Teletype	8.0		X	
	Centronics	7.0		X	
	Hewlett-Packard	6.0			X
	Printronix	6.0		X	X
	GEMICOM	1.5		X	
	Subtotal		82.5		
Japan	NEC	4.1		X	
	Fujitsu	1.6		X	
	Hitachi	0.7		X	X
	Subtotal		6.4		
Europe	Mannermann	2.1		X	
Other		8.0			

ucts forced extreme price pressure into the market. Once established, the Japanese manufacturers then began to "trade up" through product improvement and brand extension. As a result, the Japanese printer manufacturers became a formidable force in the marketplace, particularly in the microprinter (for personal computer use) segment. This set of competitors was a force all US manufacturers of printers must have accounted for in the formulation of new product introductions and pricing strategies. A number of US manufacturers had licensed offshore (Mexican, Korean, Taiwanese, and Japanese) manufacturers to produce price competitive products under the US manufacturer brand names as a means of competing with the Japanese manufacturers. Exhibit 10 offers market share estimates for major competitors in each major segment.

GENICOM MARKETING STRATEGY

GENICOM's general marketing strategy had been one of improving current products and expanding product lines rather than developing entirely new products or diversifying into new technologies. The strategy could have been characterized as evolutionary rather than revolutionary. GENICOM's main distinctive competencies in the market had been flexibility in production and the quality of its products. It had traditionally been on the upper end of price points for similar products and had sought to gain market share by stressing the advantages its machines offered relative to the competition. Each of GENICOM's products offered some distinct advantage—speed, print quality, quietness, or flexibility—that was thought to offset price disadvantages.

GENICOM had an important presence in the OEM market, offering those customers a wide variety of choices regarding specifications for products. The GENICOM presence in the branded printer market was not so strong, though efforts were underway to increase the importance of that market.

The product positioning of the GENICOM line had been for the professional user. Both for data processing and for word processing, the strength of GENICOM's product line had been in the commercial rather than the personal segments. The current product line was more durable, had more capability, and was more expensive than the bulk of the personal printer market. The GENICOM products could be compared to IBM office typewriters:

they were generally considered "overengineered" for the home market. GENICOM was giving some consideration to the personal printer market to compete with Epson, Okidata, Toshiba, and others. It recognized that among other factors, a new product line, rather than modification of an existing product, would be necessary to compete in this highly price-competitive market.

DISTRIBUTION

In early 1985, GENICOM products were distributed through a distributor network that focused on industrial users and on wholesale/retail distributors who serviced end-user needs. Consideration was given to entering retail distributorship relations with large companies or with independently owned and franchised chains.

The GENICOM distribution system was not vertically integrated at that time. Although GENICOM had been contemplating expanding the distributor network slightly to effect better geographic coverage of markets, other plans suggested that it develop recognition of authorized dealers through the current distributor network. A schematic representation of the GENICOM distribution system is presented in Exhibit 11.

Although prices and margins for dot-matrix impact printers had been dropping as market pressures grew, the future could be said to be nothing but certain. Curtis Powell considered the union negotiations a critical turning point in the firm's history.

APPENDIX 1: UNION MEMO TO ITS MEMBERS

THE MEMBERS DECIDE

At the end of the second session of negotiations management still insists on demanding a $4.00 an hour wage and benefit concession from you. They set the record straight so there would be no mistake in anyone's mind; we were told "we are taking it." We asked time and time again what they would do with the $4.00 if they can take it and we were told rather matter of factly, "we are going to put it in our pockets." It's not that GENICOM didn't make a profit last year; its just plain and simple they just want to add an additional $3,200.00 an hour to their

Exhibit 11 *GENICOM Domestic Multi tier Distribution Channels*

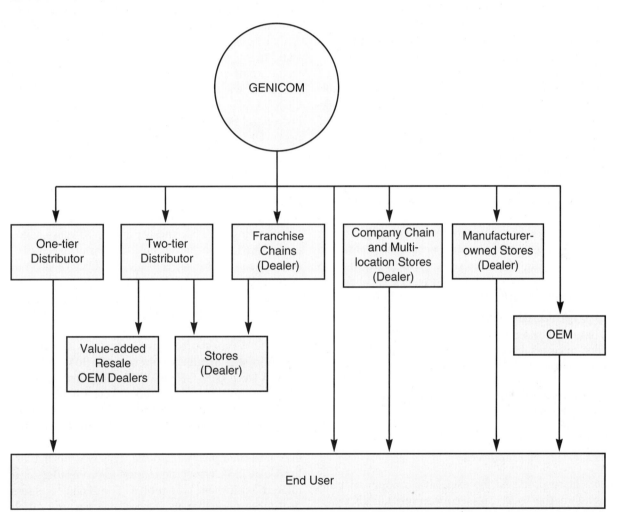

pockets (300 employees x $4.00 per hr. = $3,200.00 an hour) at your expense.

At a full-house special membership meeting, 1st and 2nd shift, the committee was instructed to take a secret ballot strike vote. We normally keep the meetings to one hour but due to the number of members who wanted to speak, the meeting lasted well over the normal length of time and then a vote was taken, which was in favor of a strike action. As we have said before, this local doesn't have a history of strike action but the workers at GENICOM feel they have no choice but to fight on the issues of wages and working conditions in this plant. Management sometime ago decided to cut the rate of the mold machine operators from R13 to R9 and it seems this only wet their appetite to want to take even more. We filed a grievance and processed it through the required steps of the grievance procedure and we will be taking action on that grievance at the proper time of which you will be notified.

We don't need to tell you how important it is for everyone to support the strike action. The issue is over a rate cut on one job but remember the bigger issue is now management is saying they are going to cut $4.00 off of everyone in wages and benefits. Whether they can get away with it or not depends on you and everyone in the plant. The stakes are high and it's up to you to decide. Do you just fork over the $4.00 in wages and benefits or do you join your fellow workers and fight?

SHOP STEWARD ELECTION

There will be a meeting at Jim Durcin's desk today, five minutes before the end of lunch break, to nominate and elect a shop steward.

APPENDIX 2: GENICOM MEMO TO EMPLOYEES

Date: May 31, 1985
TO: All Employees

In response to the excessive amount of publicity in the local press concerning GENICOM's negotiations with the UE Local 124, the following advertisement will appear in tomorrow's *Waynesboro News-Virginian* and Sunday's *Staunton News Leader*. We felt you, as GENICOM employees, should be the first to have this information.

WHAT'S REALLY HAPPENING AT GENICOM

GENICOM and its negotiations with Local 124 have been the subject of much discussion in our community and among GENICOM employees in recent weeks. All the information to this point has come from the Union. Since so much is at stake for GENICOM, its employees, and our community, we believe management should do its best to assure that the people who may be affected understand what is happening—and why.

GENICOM is a Waynesboro company that is dedicated to remaining a Waynesboro company. That dedication is reflected in GENICOM's proposals to UE Local 124 to establish a wage and benefit program that will allow GENICOM to meet competition while providing GENICOM workers with wages and benefits in line with community standards.

As part of the negotiations process, GENICOM provided wage survey data to Local 124 on both GENICOM's national competition and its Waynesboro neighbors. Reflecting that data, GENICOM's proposal includes job rates from $6.50 to $12 per hour, three weeks paid vacation, eight holidays, medical and dental insurance at a cost of $4 per week to employees, a defined benefit pension plan with limited contributions by employees, as well as company paid-life and disability programs.

Starting in 1954, and for nearly 30 years, General Electric Company conducted manufacturing operations at the current GENICOM facility in Waynesboro. Under General Electric, wages were negotiated on a national basis. As a result, Waynesboro wage and salary costs reached levels which were out of line with the electronics industry and with the Waynesboro community. GENICOM Corporation was formed to operate the Business purchased from G.E. GENICOM is now managed by people who are committed to establishing and maintaining a successful and profitable business— because it is our only business. In the 19 months since GENICOM acquired its business, it has been operated on a profitable basis. This was particularly true in 1984, when the market for computers and related equipment was robust. The Business is less profitable now that its market has become much softer and competition for sales of electronic products such as GENICOM's has become very intense. GENICOM management is determined and committed to reducing costs and competing.

These costs reductions can be accomplished either by moving operations to GENICOM's existing lower cost locations or by lowering costs in Waynesboro. GENICOM has decided to stay in Waynesboro.

The wage and benefit concessions requested will make Waynesboro a competitive manufacturing location—a manufacturing location with a future. These concessions will not be easy or insignificant for GENICOM workers to accept, but they are not unreasonable. Competitive wages will make operations in Waynesboro much more economically attractive for GENICOM and increase GENICOM's incentive to maintain and expand those operations, thus offering more job security to Waynesboro workers and greater stability to the Waynesboro community.

C. W. Powell
President and chief executive officer
GENICOM Corporation

APPENDIX 3: UNION MEMO TO ITS MEMBERS

GENICOM SHOULD TELL IT LIKE IT IS INSTEAD OF WANTING TO POCKET 6 ½ MILLION DOLLARS OF ITS EMPLOYEES AND THE COMMUNITY

That's what GENICOM wants in concessions from the hourly workers. GENICOM said that's all. They are going to get a like amount from the lower paid salary workers and supervisors. Not once have they said they are going to cut top-paid GENICOM employees such as Mr. Powell.

GENICOM says they are dedicated to remaining in Waynesboro. If that is so, why have they moved over 600 jobs to Mexico and continue to move jobs out of Waynesboro. They say they need concessions from their employees to do this. But they refuse to put in writing to the Union that these concessions will keep jobs in Waynesboro.

Instead, the company tells us they want to "put the money in their pockets." They go on to say they will use some of this money to buy other plants in other states. This will not bring jobs to Waynesboro. The company is going to run the plants where they buy them. Not once has the company said they would brings jobs back from Mexico with the $4 per hour concessions that they want.

THE TRUTH IS!

The company proposal to the Union means 2 less paid holidays per year; it means that employees would lose 2 weeks paid vacation per year. All employees would take pay cuts. GENICOM families would take cuts of $12,000 per year. As for the pensions and the insurance, the proposal is to leave it as it is now. The company proposal would take away all of the night-shift bonus, the few sick days workers have now, and would do away with rest breaks.

If the company really means that they will bring more jobs to Waynesboro, they should be willing to put it in writing.

If the Company really means to have greater stability for the community, they should reinvest the extra profits in the GENICOM Waynesboro plant, not take the money and buy plants in other states.

GENICOM would like the community to believe that GE negotiated the last Union contract. THAT IS NOT SO. GENICOM NEGOTIATED THE LAST CONTRACT. Mr. Stoner of Genicom Management was part of the last negotiations and he is part of these negotiations. Mr. Stoner plays a big part in negotiations.

The company admits in their paid ad that they made money with the last Union contract. They could make money with the new contract that has no cuts.

It's time for GENICOM to put in writing to its employees that the company will keep jobs in Waynesboro. GENICOM is making a profit. They should let the employees keep what they have. There should be NO CUTS. Workers should keep their 6½ million dollars. This would keep the money in the community, not take it to other states and Mexico.

If GENICOM takes this money and "puts it in their pockets," merchants will lose, taxes for other people in the community will go up, and everyone in the community will lose.

Only top management like Mr. Powell will gain when they line their pockets with our money at community expense.

APPENDIX 5

June 13, 1985

This letter was mailed to all hourly employees on 6/14/85. This copy is for your information.

TO: OUR GENICOM EMPLOYEES AND
     THEIR FAMILIES

I would like to take this opportunity to express my appreciation for the patience being displayed by the majority of our employees during a very diffi-cult time in which we are negotiating a new labor agreement.

GENICOM and its Management team remain dedicated to the resolution of differences with UE Local 124 and the adoption of a new collective bargaining agreement through the negotiation process. Nevertheless, in reflecting on Local 124's recent newsletter concerning strike preparations, we feel compelled to offer our thoughts on some questions and other appropriate subjects that should be addressed by the Union's lawyer at Sunday's meeting.

QUESTION: Is the Company required to pay wages to strikers during an economic strike?

ANSWER: No, the Company is not required to pay wages to economic strikers.

QUESTION: Is the Company required to pay the premiums to continue health insurance, life insurance and other benefits for strikers during an economic strike?

ANSWER: No, the Company is not required to continue payments for benefits to economic strikers.

QUESTION: Are economic strikers eligible for Virginia unemployment benefits during an economic strike?

ANSWER: No, state law disqualifies employees involved in a "labor dispute."

QUESTION: Is it possible for the UE to guarantee that GENICOM will change its proposals because of strike action?

ANSWER: No, negotiations are a give and take process that may remain unchanged in the face of employee strikes or Company lockouts.

QUESTION: If there is no agreement for a new contract by June 23rd, is the company required to keep the current contract in effect?

ANSWER: No, at that time the company may unilaterally implement its final proposal.

QUESTION: Can economic strikers be permanently replaced by new workers if the company decides to continue operations without them?

ANSWER: Yes, federal law allows a company to continue operations with new employees. The law also does not require the company to discharge these employees to allow returning strikers to resume their jobs. Replaced strikers who indicate they wish to return to work on the company's terms may fill open positions if any exist or be placed on a hiring list ahead of nonemployees.

Once again let me say we, as GENICOM's management team, remain dedicated to reaching agreement with UE Local 124 *without* any strike action. However, we are also dedicated to continue the growth of a viable business in Waynesboro. In order to accomplish this, we *must* reduce our cost structure to a level that will allow GENICOM to meet our competition.

Currently, the demand for our printers is poor due to a downturn in the computer market and foreign competition. This market situation, and GENICOM's decision to maintain Waynesboro as our primary production location, demand the changes we have proposed to the UE.

We have furnished wage data on Waynesboro and our national competition to the Union negotiating committee establishing that our proposals are competitive with both Waynesboro and national rates.

Under one proposal, wages would run between $6.00 per hour and $11.50 per hour and benefits would remain at current levels or slightly better. In recognition of the economic impact that such concessions may have, we have offered alternative proposals such as eliminating sick days, night-shift differential and afternoon breaks. These reductions would increase the wage proposal to between $6.50 and $12.00 per hour. All other benefits would remain the same or slightly better.

We hope that our employees, their families, and their collective bargaining representatives will consider all these factors before taking any action that could be injurous to both the employees and the company.

Sincerely,
C. W. Powell
President, Chief Executive Officer
Genicom Corporation

GREENPEACE VS FORD

Catalytic Converters Come to the United Kingdom

H. Landis Gabel, Graham Wrigley, and Hanna Nolan
INSEAD, Fontainebleau Cedex, France

On the afternoon of Tuesday, April 14, 1989, the London office of Greenpeace had a party. Ford UK had just issued a press release stating that it would offer a range of cars fitted with three-way catalytic converters within the next 12 months. Only 6 months earlier, Ford had opposed catalytic converters, arguing that "to make catalyst-equipped cars available to the general public in the UK . . . might not be the best course of action for either the environment or the consumer." As a result, Ford had become the object of an abusive Greenpeace campaign.

"It was a great day for us," recalled Steve Elsworth, unit head of Greenpeace's Air Pollution Division. "Ford will probably say that its decision had nothing to do with our campaign. I don't believe that for a second, but, anyway, it's not relevant. The important thing is that now our air will be cleaner."

HISTORY OF GREENPEACE

Greenpeace is dedicated to the protection of the world's environment. It began in 1971 when a group of American and Canadian environmentalists chartered a boat, which they christened "Greenpeace," to stage a protest against a planned US nuclear test on the Alaskan island of Amchitka. The protest proved a success and was followed by others through the 1970s. Targets included French nuclear testing in the Pacific, the killing of whales and seals, and the dumping of nuclear waste at sea. The protest campaigns had increased in scale and scope in the 1980s, and Greenpeace achieved worldwide name recognition in 1985 when one of its ships, the *Rainbow War-rior*, on a mission to oppose French nuclear testing, was bombed and sunk by the French secret service. In 1988, more than 40 separate campaigns were in progress around the world.

Greenpeace had 35 offices in 20 countries throughout the world that year, with 375 paid employees. Its membership of 80,000 in 1988 had spread across the world. They claimed not to be awed by authority. "In the spectrum of environmental groups, Greenpeace is on the radical edge because of the uncompromising stands it takes," said one of its campaigners. Furthermore, Greenpeace's campaigns sometimes caused controversy within the organization itself. An anti-fur apparel campaign in 1984 displayed a fashion model carrying a fur coat which left a trail of blood as it was dragged along the floor. Below was the caption, "It takes up to forty dumb animals to make a fur coat but only one to wear it." Because the Greenpeace offices in Denmark and Canada had built up a relationship with the Inuit Eskimos, who depended on the fur trade for their livelihood, Greenpeace's International Council voted to end the campaign.

Direct Action. Greenpeace continually sought innovative and dramatic ways to bring its campaigns to public attention. It developed close ties with the media and had become expert in staging spectacular protests. While Greenpeace was a nonviolent organization, its protests sometimes broke the law and often involved physical danger to the protesters. Examples include hanging banners from smokestacks and swimming in the path of toxic waste ships.

Independent. Greenpeace's money came mainly from public donations and merchandising. It had a policy of independence from political parties (including Green parties), businesses, or any other organizations. On some occasions, however, Greenpeace had cooperated with other environmental groups, for example, when international petitions were being signed.

Group Process. Although there had been charismatic campaign leaders, individuals kept a low profile. Greenpeace preferred collective strength to reliance on a few particular individuals.

THE LONDON OFFICE

Greenpeace UK began when four people established an office in London in 1977. The office grew very quickly and by 1988 there were 45 paid employees plus an average of 10 volunteers who helped out with administrative tasks such as replying to letters. The office's 1988 budget was about £5 million (see Exhibit 1 for an organization chart).

The office occupied three floors above a small shopping arcade in the fashionably scruffy area of Islington, North London. The atmosphere was informal, relaxed, and personal. Cardboard boxes with leaflets and stationery seemed to be everywhere, and the walls were covered with colorful posters and pictures. For example, the Save the Whales campaign unit was indicated by a large sign reading Big Critter Department. The photocopiers used recycled paper and were set to make double-sided copies in order to save paper. The balcony on the first floor was crowded with employees' bikes.

The employees dressed casually with many sporting Greenpeace T-shirts. Most were under 35 years old. What sort of people were they? "It is very hard to generalize," said Alison Reynolds, head of personnel. "A lot of people still think that we all fit the 'open-toed sandals, bicycle to work, muesli for breakfast' stereotype. There is no doubt that the office is unconventional. But people don't realize how professional our approach is. We have a traditional management structure. We also have many experts working for us, both our own employees and outside consultants. People are very efficient—much more so than in many businesses."

Since the issues with which it was involved were often technical, as well as controversial, Green-

peace was aware of how important the scientific accuracy of its work was. It had recently formed a Science Division headed by Jeremy Leggett, who for 11 years had held the post of Reader in Earth Sciences at Imperial College, London. His role was to provide "quality control" for the campaign documents and reports using both a process of peer review and reviews by independent consultants. "The issues are getting more complicated, and the level of detail is becoming more sophisticated," he explained. He also hoped "to encourage more people in the science world to become established in controversial issues of the day." Greenpeace intended to continue to emphasize the scientific validity of its claims. For example, in one campaign it bought full-page advertisements in national newspapers to dispute the idea that an expansion of nuclear power would help solve the greenhouse effect. Headed, "Scientifically Speaking, It Is Just a Lot of Hot Air," the advertisements bore the signatures of 40 well-known scientists including two Nobel prize winners.

Despite its growing size, those in the office were confident that operations would not become too bureaucratic. To the contrary, they prided themselves on how quickly they could move. For example, one Tuesday afternoon the office heard of a toxic Canadian PCB shipment being delivered by a Russian ship to the London docks. A meeting was immediately called for 4:00 in the afternoon, Greenpeace's power boat operation was called to action, and the Media Department alerted the press. At 4:00 the following morning, Greenpeace staged its protest in full view of more than 40 journalists.

Elsworth was in his late 30s and had just joined Greenpeace. He had earned his degree in English literature and worked as a teacher before writing a number of books including a dictionary of the environment. The experience was sufficient to convince him to spend all his time on environmental issues. Elsworth did not fit the "open-toed sandals" stereotype. With short blond hair, gold-rimmed glasses, white shirt and jeans, Elsworth looked like an MBA student and spoke with the same apparent command of technical detail.

Greenpeace had started the Global Air Pollution campaign in 1986. As head of the Air Pollution Unit, Elsworth was in charge of a £30,000 budget, two campaigners, and an occasional supplement of volunteers and outside consultants. His job covered all the issues involved with acid rain

Exhibit 1 *Greenpeace UK Organization Chart*

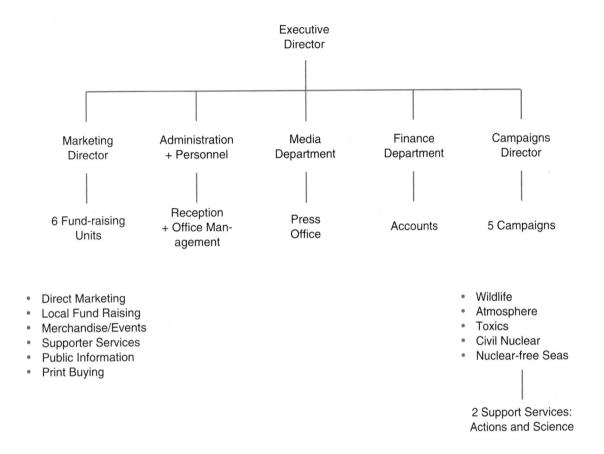

and the greenhouse effect. However, having done 2 years of research on the subject, Elsworth had become particularly interested in automobile emissions. He persuaded the senior campaign directors that a campaign against automobile pollution should be a Greenpeace priority.

AIR POLLUTION AND THE AUTOMOBILE

Air pollution was not new to the UK in the 1970s and 1980s. Winter smog had polluted London and other UK cities for over a century. A combination of sulphur dioxide and particulates from coal burning regularly produced "pea soup fogs"—fogs so thick that visibility was reduced to only a few meters. The infamous London smog of 1952 killed an estimated 4,000 people in one month.

In response, the UK government passed the 1956 Clean Air Act which raised chimney heights and established smoke-free zones. Smoke emis-

sions were reduced nationally by 85 percent over the next 30 years. Consequent in part to this success, air pollution receded for a time as a public policy issue and the government became complacent. It stated in 1987, for example, that "the effects of pollution by motor vehicles can be summarized as follows: there is no evidence that this type of air pollution has any adverse effect on health."

But the UK government was behind the times. During the 1980s, environmentalists, scientists, policymakers in other countries, and the general public had all seized upon the issue of air pollution. If any factor may be said to have brought this about, it was the phenomenon now referred to as *Waldsterben* (dying forest), which was caused by acid rain. But other global air pollution problems like the depletion of the ozone layer and global warming had drawn attention as well. In short, air pollution was once more an area of intense public interest and the automobile was implicated as a major cause.

Public policy attention focused on six air pollutants: sulphur dioxide (SO_2), airborne particulates, carbon monoxide (CO), ozone, nitrogen oxides (NO_x), and carbon dioxide (CO_2). Alone or in combination, these pollutants were primarily responsible for the environmental problems of acid rain and global warming.

Acid rain is formed when a variety of compounds including sulphur dioxide, ammonia, NO_x, and hydrocarbons (HC) are mixed in the atmosphere to form a "pollution cocktail" of sulphuric acid, sulphates, nitric acid, ozone, and other compounds which then return to earth. Acid rain has severely damaged lakes, soil, buildings, wildlife, and vegetation, and the public has been horrified by stories of rainfall with the acidity of lemon juice. More than 7 million hectares[1] of forest in the European Community (EC) have been damaged, and more than 50 percent of the trees in West Germany showed some degree of acid rain damage in 1986.

The UK was a major net exporter of acid rain—mostly to the Continent. The UK Department of the Environment estimated that 77 percent of the UK's emissions went abroad, while 80 percent of the acid rain falling on the UK was "home-made." The UK was one of the four biggest SO_2 polluters in Europe, and its pollution contributed a greater NO_x deposition in Belgium, Denmark, the Netherlands, and Norway than the emissions from those countries themselves—a fact that earned the UK the sobriquet of "dirty man of Europe."

Acid rain, ozone depletion, and global warming were not the only consequences of air pollution. Hydrocarbons hindered oxygen transport from blood into tissues, causing chronic respiratory and cardiac disorders in susceptible individuals. NO_x caused lung problems for people with chronic bronchitis or emphysema. There was some evidence that HC caused cancer, and lead (from burning leaded gasoline) retarded children's mental development.

Most of the public's concern over air pollution focused on the automobile. Automobiles produce a number of different pollutants, but the most serious are CO, NO_x, HC, lead, and CO_2. In 1985, the UK Department of the Environment estimated that 5.8 million tons of these pollutants were emitted from cars in the UK every year. About 40 percent of NO_x emissions were caused by autos, as were 90 percent of urban CO and 40 percent of HC. Twenty percent of the UK's CO_2 emissions originated with road transport (each car producing nearly four times its own weight in CO_2 each year). Diesel engines accounted for 80 percent of urban UK particulate pollution.

Every year additional cars circulated on the UK's motorways. If the trend were to continue, the present 20 million cars in the UK would reach 30 million by the end of the century. A graphic forecast by a transport consultant estimated that these extra vehicles would fill a 306-lane motorway from London to Edinburgh!

AUTOMOBILE EMISSION CONTROL TECHNOLOGIES

Catalytic Converters

Of the various ways in which the emissions from automobiles can be reduced, the three-way catalytic converter is the best known. A catalytic converter looks like a muffler and is connected to the exhaust pipe of a car. Exhaust gases are passed through an elaborate honeycomb coated with heavy metal catalysts—often rare metals including rhodium, platinum, and palladium. Inside the converter, hydrocarbons are converted into CO_2 and water, and NO_x emissions are reduced. Tests on a 1.6-liter Volkswagen equipped with a three-way catalytic converter had shown reduced emission of CO by 97 percent, HC by 90 percent, and NO_x by 84 percent.

Although the best known, a catalytic converter is not the only way to reduce air pollution from cars. Others methods include these:

- Using unleaded gasoline: The availability of unleaded gasoline had been slowly increasing in the UK. This was in part a result of relative tax reductions for unleaded gasoline in three consecutive budgets which ultimately dropped the price of unleaded 5 percent below that of leaded. And it was also due in part to a campaign by a voluntary organization called CLEAR (Campaign for Lead-free Air). While in 1986 only one service station in ten provided unleaded gasoline, it was expected that by the end of 1989 nearly half of the UK's 20,000 stations would provide unleaded.

[1]Over 17 million acres.

- Driving at reduced speeds: Vehicle emissions rise significantly when a car is operating at high speeds. For example, NO_x emissions are six times greater at 130 kph than at 50 kph. In 1988, legislation was proposed in Sweden to reduce the speed limit to 90 kph. Even in West Germany, where the absence of any speed limit on the *autobahns* is a cherished tradition, one could hear occasional voices urging slower driving to reduce air pollution.

- Changing driving patterns: In the Black Forest of Western Germany, badly damaged by acid rain, road signs encouraged drivers to switch off their engines at traffic lights.

- Use of lower carbon fuels: The use of lower carbon fuels, such as methanol, would reduce the amount of CO produced. These fuels were still very expensive in 1988 compared with gasoline.

- Adoption of what was called the "lean-burn" engine: Some car manufacturers like Ford and Peugeot had invested heavily in the development of "lean-burn" engines, which they said would provide an attractive alternative to catalytic converters. These engines operate at higher air/fuel ratios than regular engines (20/1 as opposed to 14/1). Combustion occurs at higher temperatures, less fuel is consumed, and harmful emissions are significantly reduced. But, although emission reductions were impressive, they were not adequate to meet the US 1983 emission standards which had come to represent a worldwide reference point and a possible new standard for Europe. In particular, the combined HC-NO_x levels of a lean-burn engine could not be cut below six grams per cycle—a level well above the US limit of 4.6 grams per cycle.

Catalytic Converters vs Lean-burn Engines

Catalytic converters and lean-burn engines were essentially alternative technologies in the late 1980s. It was not possible to fit a truly lean-burn engine with a three-way catalytic converter because of the high oxygen content of the lean-burn engine's exhaust. The choice of which technology was to be the focus of anticipated EC standards was clearly critical for the European manufacturers. Each of the two alternatives had advantages and disadvantages compared with the other, and each had its proponents and opponents.

Catalytic converter technology was effective and well tested, especially in the US where it had been required for years as the only technology able to meet automobile environmental standards. The same was true for European Free Trade Association (EFTA) countries, Canada, and Japan. Virtually all manufacturers worldwide had experience with the technology, especially those with large exports to the US.

Catalytic converters did have disadvantages, however. Although there was some disagreement on the point, they seemed to raise fuel consumption (estimates of the increase run in the range of 4–10 percent). They required rare metals supplied by South Africa, which was offensive to those who advocated a boycott of that country. The converters lost efficiency over time and had to be regularly checked to assure they worked. Some car manufacturers argued that if the catalysts were damaged, possibly by leaded gasoline, the converters would not work efficiently and emissions might even increase. Yet, periodic obligatory auto inspection was not a common policy in Europe. Another problem was that a catalytic converter only functioned at temperatures above 300°C, but cars release enormous amounts of pollution before their engines heat to that temperature.

Catalytic converters require unleaded gasoline—one tank of leaded gasoline alone can poison the converter and render it useless. Thus, widespread adoption of catalytic converters had as a prerequisite widespread availability of unleaded fuel. In 1988, however, unleaded gasoline was rare in the UK. To prevent accidental use of leaded gasoline (or purposeful use were leaded gasoline cheaper than unleaded), cars equipped with catalytic converters were fitted with narrower inlets to their gasoline tanks, which would only admit the nozzle of an unleaded gasoline pump.

Because of the precision required in metering fuel for the catalytic process, traditional carburetors had to be replaced by sophisticated electronic fuel injection systems. The cost of the three-way catalytic converter and the fuel injection system was expected to raise the price of large cars (generally defined as those with engines larger than 2 liters) 2 to 3 percent, that of medium-sized cars (1.4–2 liters) 6 to 8 percent, and that of small cars (below 1.4 liters) 10 to 15 percent. The fact that large cars frequently had fuel injection systems as standard equipment anyway magnified the already disproportionate impact that catalytic converters would have on small car prices.

The increased cost of cars equipped with catalytic converters meant that consumers had no financial incentive to buy them. Either consumers would have to be required to do so or else subsidies or tax concessions would be needed. Altruism might prompt some to buy catalysts, but a study done in the Netherlands in 1988 showed that, without some financial incentives from the government, virtually no one would buy a car with a catalytic converter. This opinion was echoed by Robert Stempel, president of General Motors, who observed, "I haven't seen one guy buy a car because it's got the cleanest tailpipe."

Even supporters of catalytic converter technology admitted that it was not a suitable long-term solution to automobile-caused air pollution. In their opinion, it was simply better than any other alternative.

Supporters of lean-burn technology felt, in contrast, that they had the long-term solution close at hand. That solution, in simple terms, was to build lower pollution into the engine with improved combustion, ignition, and fuel economy rather than clean up the pollution once it was created. Forced adoption of catalytic converters would kill lean-burn technology just when the investment was due to pay dividends.

One potentially significant advantage of lean-burn engines, many people thought, was improved fuel economy. By the end of the century, fuel economy standards could well be obligatory in Western Europe just as they were in the US. Even if they were not, improved fuel economy provided an inducement for consumers to adopt lean-burn engines without the necessity of government compulsion.

Not only was improved fuel economy directly beneficial, but it also implied reduced CO_2 emissions. This might be significant should the European Commission add CO_2 to the auto pollutants that were already the object of its regulations.

Another potentially significant advantage of lean-burn engines was that they were robust and more reliable than catalytic converters. It was possible—and a study by the US Environmental Protection Agency supported the view—that they might cause lower pollution over the full life-cycle of an engine.

Yet to opponents, lean-burn engines that could match the environmental performance of catalytic converters were just a promise—a "phantom technology" in the words of Laurens-Jan Brinkhorst, European Commission Director General for the Environment. Current lean-burn engines could only reduce harmful emissions by about 50 percent, and they were especially ineffective for NO_x emissions. Unlike catalytic converters, few lean-burn engines were actually available, and those few that were ran on just slightly leaner mixtures of 16/1 or 18/1. While some Japanese manufacturers had developed "true" lean-burn engines operating on an air/fuel ratio of 20/1, the engines had proven unsatisfactory because of ignition problems and rough running.

Unfortunately, most of the "facts" of the debate were purely speculative. Performance figures were controversial and varied with different testing procedures and driving cycles. All were theoretical results rather than concrete ones. To give one example of the differences of opinion that existed, an unpublished 1987 United Nations report estimated that the manufacturing cost difference between a lean-burn engine and an engine fitted with a catalytic converter was very small, with little difference in fuel consumption between the two.

Despite or because of all the uncertainties, Greenpeace gave catalytic converters its de facto support. Elsworth argues, however, that Greenpeace never formally campaigned for catalytic converters per se. "If the 1983 US emissions standards could have been met by lean burn, we would have accepted the technology. Unfortunately, the manufacturers of lean burn could never deliver in practice what they believed to be possible in theory."

AUTOMOBILE ENVIRONMENTAL STANDARDS INTERNATIONALLY

The United States

The United States has one of the longest legislative records regarding automobile pollution control. As early as the 1950s, the federal government provided administrative grants to states that adopted air pollution control measures. Congressional legislation in 1965 and 1967 established federal controls on new-automobile emissions and far-reaching programs for state adoption and enforcement of ambient air quality standards. The new decade saw passage of the landmark 1970 Clean Air Act which, among other things, required a 90 percent reduction of three major pollutants emitted from cars—NO_x, HC, and CO_2. This was an early example of what came to be called "technology-forcing" legislation in that the means for achieving the target were not known at the time. Yet it was believed that catalytic systems could meet the target (in fact, the target and testing methods were set specifically with catalytic converters in mind), and catalytic converters were required on all new cars in 1975.

Although the 1970 Clean Air Act resulted in a substantial reduction in automobile exhaust pollution, the US automobile industry failed for many years to meet the required 90 percent reductions, and legislation had to be amended repeatedly to extend the standards' deadlines.

Japan, Canada, and the EFTA Countries

The US was not alone. Japan also passed exhaust standards legislation in 1968, and in 1988 it had legislation similar to that of the US. So did Canada. All of the EFTA countries likewise required catalytic converters.

The European Community

The European Community adopted its first Directive on motor vehicle exhaust in 1970, and some reduction in emissions was achieved, but not on the scale of that achieved in the US. Contributing to the relative lack of accomplishment in Europe was disagreement among member states over the extent and speed of implementation of auto pollution standards. Some countries, notably West Germany, Denmark, and the Netherlands, were pushing for quick implementation of legislation similar to that in the US, Japan, and EFTA. Others, including France, the UK, Italy, and Spain wanted more gradual adoption of less-strict standards. Consequently, environmental laws for autos in the 1980s differed widely among member states. Significantly, emission standards for small cars had yet to be defined even though they constituted about half of the 10 million cars sold annually in the EC.

In 1984, the European Commission presented a proposal for a Community-wide reduction in vehicle emissions and a proposal on lead-free gasoline. The latter proposal was adopted in 1985. The emission standards proposal provoked a major battle with those countries predominantly manufacturing small cars on one side and those predominantly manufacturing large cars on the other. In essence, the battle was over whether small and medium-sized cars would have to use catalytic converters or whether they could use lean-burn engines instead.

In 1985, a compromise was accepted by all countries except Denmark and Greece, which wanted tighter standards. The Luxembourg Compromise, as it was called, set standards for large cars that required three-way catalytic converters, standards for medium-sized cars that could be met by lean-burn engines (with a simpler oxidation catalyst), and standards for small cars that necessitated neither (see Exhibit 2). However, there was a provision for a future review of the small car standards. The standards for large and medium-sized cars, to be phased in from 1988 to 1993, were adopted in 1987 following the introduction of the Single European Act. This act permitted legislation to be passed by majority vote (rather than unanimously as was the case before the act); thus, Danish and Greek objections were overruled. The standards were expected to cut emissions of CO, HC, and NO_x by 30 to 50 percent.

The European Commission returned to the issue of small-car standards in 1988 with a proposal for tightening those standards to require lean-burn engines. The Council of Ministers agreed to the proposal in June 1988, but less than a month later France withdrew its support and joined the opposition. The result was that there was no longer had a majority behind the tightened standards. French support was rewon and the proposal adopted by the Council of Ministers in November 1988. (The price of the French vote was a Commission agreement to challenge the Dutch in the European Court of Justice on the grounds that their plans to provide tax incentives for cars meeting the higher US standards constituted an unfair trade practice.)

Under the new procedure of the Single European Act, however, the directive still had to be accepted by the European Parliament.

The United Kingdom

The UK had long had a relatively poor record on environmental legislation. In 1953, Harold Macmillan, the future prime minister, set the tone when

---

[2]It also established the Environmental Protection Agency.

Exhibit 2 *The Regulations*

- In 1970, the US authorities established a 90% reduction target for pollutant emissions from cars. This was achieved in thirteen years by a series of regulatory restrictions, of which the most modern is the US 1983 standard.
- In Europe, car emissions are subject to United Nations Economic Commission for Europe (ECE) Regulation 15 and subsequent amendments, which also began implementation in the 1970s. ECE regulations have achieved emission reductions, but they are much more lenient than US standards. UK cars are currently sold under ECE regulation 15:04.
- US equivalence to ECE 15:04 regulations is listed below. This describes how many grams of carbon monoxide, and the combined amount of hydrocarbons and nitrogen oxides, are permitted under each system.

Permitted amount of pollutants (grams per test cycle)

	CO	$HC + NO_x$	NO_x alone
US 83	16	4.6	2.4
ECE 15:04	67	20.5	NA

It can be seen that ECE 15:04 is four times as lenient as the US 83 standard. The regulation is, in fact, similar to 1973 limits implemented in other areas.

- The EEC plans to implement new car standards. Because of lobbying by car manufacturers, different standards will apply according to the engine size of the car: and small cars will have regulations applied in two stages.

EC petrol vehicle emission standards (grams per test)

Vehicle engine size	CO	$HC + NO_x$	NO_x alone	% of UK car fleet
over 2 litres	25	6.5	3.5	8%
1.4 to 2 litres	30	8.0	NA	42%
under 1.4 litres (Stage I)	45	15.0	6.0	50%

The planned EEC limits, to be implemented in the UK between 1990 and 1993, allow between 50% and 300% more pollution than emission standards enforced in the US since 1983. Stage II of the small cars regulation is to be negotiated.

Source: Greenpeace briefing on air pollution from cars, 1988.

he said in Cabinet that "we cannot do very much, but we can seem very busy—and that is half the battle nowadays." Yet this attitude was changing in the later 1980s as the power of the "green vote" grew in the UK just as it did elsewhere. Margaret Thatcher made a major environment speech in 1987 after her election victory. The success of the campaign for lead-free gasoline was another sign of changing times. Even the Queen had supported the campaign by converting the royal fleet to unleaded gasoline! The UK government, like the others in the EC, was aware of the EC elections due in June 1989 and was anxious not to alienate itself from the green vote.

Yet the government still opposed EC adoption of the US 1983 standards. It accepted the arguments it heard advocating lean-burn technology. The minister of the environment stated in July 1988 in the UK Parliament that lean-burn engines offered substantial environmental benefits compared with catalytic converters because lean-burn engines were inherently cleaner and more fuel efficient. At a meeting of the European Council of Environmental Ministers in November 1988, the UK minister argued that to force three-way catalytic converters on the industry would sabotage further development of what were superior technologies.

THE AUTOMOBILE MANUFACTURERS

The political positions taken by the EC member governments were heavily dependent upon the competitive positions of their domestic automobile manufacturers, competitive positions that varied widely among manufacturers and even among their subsidiaries.

Companies that earned a large percentage of their revenues in the North American, Japanese, or EFTA markets were generally better prepared to provide catalysts since they were required in those markets. Companies with a relatively high dependence on sales of large cars were likewise able to provide catalytic converters easily, since EC law already required them for large cars and they made little difference in the final price of an expensive car.

Of the major firms selling in the UK market, the Japanese (Toyota, Honda, Nissan, Mitsubishi, and Mazda) were well positioned—all offered catalytic converters in Japan and the US. The same was true for Ford and General Motors. Mercedes-Benz, BMW, Volvo, Saab, and Jaguar were also

well positioned given the preponderance of large luxury cars in their sales.

In greatest jeopardy were companies like Fiat, Peugeot, and Renault, which made small cars and exported relatively few of them to countries requiring catalytic converters. Exacerbating their problem was the fact that their domestic customers were overwhelmingly buyers of small cars whose demand was likely to prove sensitive to the price increase that catalytic converters would cause.

FORD UK

Ford Motor Company's 1988 worldwide revenues were $92.5 billion with net profits of $5.3 billion. Ford UK is a wholly-owned subsidiary of Ford US whose UK's 1988 revenues and after-tax income were £5.9 billion and £436 million, respectively. Since the recession of the early 1980s when Ford UK lost £103 million, its financial performance had improved steadily. And, although Ford's share of the UK passenger-car market had been gradually declining (by 1988 it stood at 26 percent), the company still maintained its long time position as the UK market leader and had a strong presence in most segments.

Ford of Europe, with headquarters in Essex, England, was set up in 1967 to coordinate Ford's 15 national companies. With the establishment of Ford of Europe, new models were developed to meet European rather than strictly national requirements, thus affording substantial economies of scale. Ford of Europe had no direct authority over the national companies, however, and Ford UK had considerable discretion in introducing models with or without catalytic converters as it preferred.

During 1988, Ford UK managers' attention was focused on several major threats. One was the possibility that with the "1992" trade liberalization in Europe, competition between Japanese imports and UK-manufactured cars would intensify. The existing system of bilateral export agreements between individual European countries and Japan was coming apart, and no one knew what, if anything, would replace it. Another threat was the recent rejuvenation of both Peugeot and General Motors.

A further threat was that standards comparable with those in the US would be required in the EC. In Ford UK's judgment, adoption of such standards would de facto mandate catalytic converters and render lean-burn engines worthless. Ford had spent over £90 million on research and development of lean-burn technology at its research and engineering center at Dunton; it had invested £175 million in its Dagenham plant to produce a lean-burn, 2-liter engine; and it had been selling lean-burn engines in the UK market on its Escort, Orion, and Fiesta models since 1986. Yet, the engines were not capable of meeting the NO_x levels of the US standards, and, although research was continuing, it was nevertheless unlikely that the US standards could be met in the near future. Ford's engine emissions were significantly lower than existing UK legislation required, however, and met the CO limit of 30 grams per cycle and the combined $HC-NO_x$ limit of eight grams agreed to by the EC Council of Ministers in June 1988.

Ford lobbied its case for lean-burn engines with the UK government and with the EC via the UK Department of Trade and Industry. Furthermore, the Society of Motor Manufacturers and Traders, an umbrella organization of UK auto manufacturers, similarly advocated lean-burn technology.

The UK government sided with lean-burn engines when it and the others comprising the majority of the European Council of Ministers decided on small car standards in June 1988. Criticizing the minority group of countries which were in favor of tighter standards, the UK minister for the environment said that such standards would effectively terminate development of the lean-burn engine in return for only modest improvement to the environment and that at great additional cost.

GREENPEACE VS. FORD UK

In March 1988 Toyota launched the Celica GT-Four, which was the first car to be sold in the UK with a catalytic converter as standard equipment. Three months later, Volkswagen announced that three of its models (the Golf, Passat, and Jetta) would be offered with converters. Volkswagen said its decision was motivated by respect for the environment rather than by any expected UK legislation.

The announcements were enthusiastically received at Greenpeace's offices in London. "With the Germans and the Japanese now offering converters in the UK, we felt we really had something on which to build our campaign," explained Elsworth.

Elsworth persuaded his senior colleagues that

a campaign for catalytic converters now had a realistic chance for success. He described the process. "A campaign is very much like a product launch. We always look for three things. First, there must be clear scientific evidence of major environmental harm. Second, there must be a visible polluter so that we can target somebody easily and focus public attention on that specific body. Third, we must have a strong moral argument in order to win the support of the public in the face of potentially strong opposition."

Greenpeace was already convinced of the harm caused by auto emissions from work it had done on acid rain. But what especially attracted Elsworth's attention was the difference in the international policies of the auto manufacturers. "I found it very interesting, to say the least, that a manufacturer was supplying to different standards throughout the world. If we can find an area were we can see differences of opinion between governments or businesses, we can leverage this disunity. It makes our job an awful lot easier."

For the next two weeks, Elsworth and one of his campaigners lay out the guidelines for the campaign. They wanted to "start on a level playing field" by giving the manufacturers a chance to reply to Greenpeace's demands. Assuming some would rebuff them, they next decided to target one manufacturer. This, they reasoned, would increase the chance that the particular manufacturer would change its policy; and it would reduce the likelihood of an industrywide defense.

"Whereas the objective of the campaign was to change the entire accepted norm for vehicle pollution around the world, we considered that Ford was a good target because it was the biggest manufacturer in the UK which formed an obstacle to that process. If the outcome of the campaign had been a change in the legal standards requiring catalytic converters we would, of course, have been satisfied too," explained Elsworth. "A further objective of the campaign was to destabilize the friendly image of the family car which had been the result of years of careful advertising by the manufacturers."

Ford is Targeted

On July 25, 1988, Greenpeace sent letters to the public relations directors of the 18 car manufacturers that had more than 1 percent of the UK market (Elsworth's letter to John Southgate, Ford's director of public and governmental affairs is shown in Exhibit 3). Eleven of the companies replied that catalysts either were supplied or would be in the near future. Greenpeace categorized these as favorable replies (an example of such a reply was Honda's, shown as Exhibit 4). Greenpeace regarded another four of the replies as unsatisfactory but not entirely negative. Three manufacturers' replies—those of Ford, Mercedes-Benz, and Peugeot-Citroen—were "extremely negative."

Ford's "extremely negative" reply came in an eight-page letter from John Southgate. The letter gave no indication of when Ford would make catalyst-equipped cars available in the UK, but it did attempt a detailed defense of Ford's support for lean-burn engines. Southgate argued that Ford shared Greenpeace's concern for the environment but that it believed that lean burn was the best long-term technical solution (Southgate's arguments repeated those outlined above).

Pressure in favor of catalytic converters increased in mid-August when Volkswagen announced that it would supply catalysts on all its models by September 1989. The following month the Greenpeace team concluded that Ford would be its target.

"We had several reasons for choosing Ford," explained Elsworth. "First, Ford was the market leader in the UK. If you can 'judo throw' the leader, there will always be a follow-on effect from the others. If you target the number-two firm, it can then reply, 'Why me? Why not number one?' Tackling the leader fits with our style, anyway. We don't mind confrontation. Secondly, Ford was a prime example of double standards. In the US, Ford boasts about its achievements in reducing emissions 90 percent through converters. Ford supplies cars in the rest of Europe equipped with converters. We had received a reply from Ford Austria saying it was 'proud its cars passed the strict Austrian emission tests.' And, finally, we did not accept Southgate's arguments about lean burn. In our view, lean burn was 'jam tomorrow.' We have evidence that shows it was promised back in 1984, but today, even under the best possible conditions, lean burn can only reduce emissions by a maximum of 60 percent. We know that converters are not the ultimate solution, but we support the principle of the best available technology, and lean burn was simply not good enough."

Greenpeace then began to prepare the detailed plans for the campaign. It commissioned nine advertising agencies to draft briefs and allocated £25,000 from the contingency fund to pay for the campaign.

A small London advertising agency called SPD was selected. Elsworth and the others had been impressed with its aggressiveness. The agency pointed out that Ford had several strengths. It complied with the existing law, it was no worse than most of the competition, unleaded gasoline was still not widely available, and the public would have to pay more for fuel for catalytic-converter-equipped cars (it was only later that tax rate changes reduced the price of unleaded gasoline below that of leaded). The agency felt that the campaign message should emphasize the fact that Ford was a US company and one that offered its American customers a cleaner car than it offered to the British. The campaign theme that was finally agreed upon was:

In Britain a Ford Pumps out 100 percent more toxic fumes than a Ford back home in America.

Greenpeace had consulted with Michael Walsh, widely recognized as a world authority on auto emissions, to ensure the technical accuracy of its indictment.

SPD and Greenpeace agreed on two advertisements. One was a US license plate reading, F-U-GB. The other had a skull at the end of a Ford exhaust pipe with the slogan Ford Gives You More—a slogan Ford had used in its ads for a number of years. The advertisements were consciously abusive and they attracted considerable criticism, some from Greenpeace's own members. Yet Elsworth defended them. "They *were* offensive. The campaign was designed to catch attention and create emotion. But the advertisements are less offensive than destroying the environment."

On October 6, 12 days before the launch of the campaign, Elsworth wrote again to Ford and the other two companies on Greenpeace's short list of targets. Ford was informed that it was a "possible candidate," and that, although Greenpeace regretted the necessity of campaigning against any car manufacturer, "our duty is to speak on behalf of the environment" (see Exhibit 5). Southgate replied a week later. "I am particularly saddened

Exhibit 3 *First Greenpeace Letter to Ford (July 25, 1988)*

I am writing to you as a result of Volkswagen's announcement that three cars in their range—the Golf, Jetta, and Passat—will from September 1988 be available with catalytic converters.

Greenpeace welcomes this announcement, as we are extremely concerned about forest dieback in the UK. The damage to Britain's forests is as severe as that in West Germany and Switzerland, where the widespread decline in tree health is treated as a national emergency: The British decline is identical in extent and character.

Forest dieback is associated with air pollution from power stations and cars. In Switzerland and Austria, catalytic converters are mandatory for all new cars. This is also the case in the USA, Canada, and Japan. In the FRG, a substantial number of vehicles are being sold with catalysts fitted. This contrasts with the UK, where car manufacturers have been slow to limit the air pollution caused by their products.

Greenpeace UK are about to launch a major campaign against air pollution from cars. This will be targetted on a single manufacturer: the campaign will be directed against a company that sells clean cars in the European and American markets, but chooses not to do so in the UK. We would expect to run an advertising campaign, and adopt some high profile actions to attract publicity.

As an organisation, we do not launch campaigns before they are thoroughly researched: so I am writing to all large car manufacturers in the UK, to ascertain their plans for air pollution reduction. Could you tell me when Ford plan to make catalyst-equipped cars available to the general public in the UK, as they are in North America and Europe?

Thank you for your assistance.

Exhibit 4 *A Favorable Reply to Greenpeace (August 26, 1988)*

Thank you for your letter regarding availability of cars fitted with catalytic converters in the U.K.

Honda (UK) is extremely supportive of any efforts to improve the environment. Honda has led work in anti-pollution technology dating back to 1973 when the C.V.C.C. engine was introduced (Compound Vortex Controlled Combustion). Also in 1975 when further developments were made to comply with Exhaust Emission Standards.

Since then development has continued, and we have been one of the few car manufacturers in the U.K. who have had models which run on lead free petrol, since 1980.

Therefore, catalytic converters which we use in other markets will be available here in the U.K. long before the Government's requirements for such emission control. We envisage that our 1990 specification models will be fitted with catalytic converters.

We also have a company policy that we use lead-free petrol.

If you need any further information please do not hesitate to contact me.

that, despite the trouble taken to explain the complexity of the subject, you have chosen to disregard our careful reasoning and refuse to recognize that Ford shares your concern about the environment." Neither party contacted the other again until the end of the Greenpeace campaign.

The Campaign Begins

Greenpeace's campaign was launched at the London Motor Show on October 18. This prestigious annual event is always given wide coverage by the press. Greenpeace hired a large truck draped with the Ford Gives You More advertisement and drove it around the parking lot in front of the show. It also displayed on the same lot a catalytic-converter-equipped Ford Escort from the Continent. It was, Greenpeace's publicity explained, "the only clean Ford in the UK."

Greenpeace had booked 20 billboards for its campaign, most from a poster company, Mills & Allen. Mills & Allen later refused to display the posters, due, Greenpeace believed, to fear of losing its Ford account. Greenpeace also felt that the newspapers were slow to pick up the story for fear of possible Ford commercial reprisal. *The Guardian* covered the story well, however, and the campaign was featured on a few television and radio programs. Ford refused invitations to participate in any of them.

On February 2, 1989, Ford unveiled its new Fiesta range, due to go on sale in April. The range had cost £550 million to develop, had lean-burn engines, and could run on either leaded or unleaded gasoline. Ford announced that the new cars would emit only half the CO of present models and were more economical to operate as well.

The Ford Dealer Mail Shot

By February, Greenpeace felt that its campaign was failing. "It looked like Ford was shrugging it off. Although CLEAR's lead-free gasoline campaign had really taken off, with our small budget we were not getting very far," Elsworth recalled. "But then the fund raising team had a great idea."

The idea was to write to Greenpeace's members to enlist their help. Greenpeace printed a F-U-GB postcard for members to send to Ford's local dealers. "If they wouldn't listen to us, perhaps they would listen to their consumers and dealers," said Elsworth. On February 23, 150,000 of the postcards, each with an information pack, were

mailed. More than 5,000 postcards were remailed by the Greenpeace members to Ford's dealers. "Our morale picked up when all the letters poured in. Members sent us copies of the dealers' replies. The dealers were obviously contacting head office, because we started seeing standard replies from the dealers," recounted Elsworth. "They came in three stages. The early ones said that Ford supported lead-free gasoline. This had nothing to do with our campaign. Then they argued that there are significant costs in equipping right-hand drive cars with converters. (While the converter itself goes under the car, the required piping for the fuel injection system would have to go on the right side of the engine where it would obstruct the steering equipment). But the third-stage letters said that Ford would progressively introduce converters over the next 12 months."

The End of the Campaign

On March 28, Elsworth called Kenneth Cannell, who had replaced John Southgate as director of public and governmental affairs, to ask about Ford's current position. Cannell stated that Ford would, in fact, be introducing converters within the next 12 months. This was the first contact between the two adversaries since the campaign had begun. Cannell wrote to Greenpeace on April 14 to confirm Ford's decision (see Exhibit 6). Ford's change of position was covered, with specific reference to Greenpeace's campaign, in all the major UK newspapers. "We were fairly confident that Ford would carry out its promise, although a campaign is never really over until action has been seen to have been done. I have no bitterness towards Mr. Cannell or Mr. Southgate. I try not to get personal. We are all professionals, just on different sides of the divide. After our celebration, we decided to turn away from Ford for the time being," Elsworth said.

Elsworth's call to Ford on March 28, and the end of Ford's resistance, came only 3 weeks after the European Commission proposed adoption of the 1983 US standards and catalytic converters for all cars. And just 2 weeks after Elsworth's call, the European Parliament overturned the Council of Ministers' compromise of November 1988 which had sanctioned lean-burn engines for small cars. The Parliament voted by an overwhelming 309 to 5 in favor of more stringent measures based on the 1983 US standards. This meant that the ultimate decision on the issue of automobile emission

---

Exhibit 5 *Last Warning Letter to Ford from Greenpeace (October 6, 1988)*

Thank you for your letter of 12 August. Greenpeace UK is extremely disappointed that you are unable to supply cars in the UK with comparable emission standards to those which you sell in the US.

We are currently planning our car campaign and I have to inform you that your company is a possible candidate. We very much regret the necessity of campaigning against any car manufacturers: it is a disappointment that only part of the industry has perceived the gains, both financial and environmental, that can be made from cleaning up the emissions from their cars. Our duty is to speak on behalf of the environment, which involves pointing out to the public the consequences of polluting practices when carried out by a manufacturer such as yourself.

Exhibit 6 *Ford's Letter Confirming Introduction of Catalytic Converters (April 14, 1989)*

Thank you for your letter of March 30th.

I think the easiest way of responding to the points you raised is to send you a copy of a press statement we have just issued announcing that with the increasing availability of unleaded fuel following the budget, we are proposing to bring forward our plans for the introduction of catalysts. You will see that as a first step our intention is to make catalysts available on selected models across each car range within the next 12 months. This is the time we need to complete the necessary engineering work.

I am not able at this stage to respond to specific questions you raised about cost and publicity. These are matters that will be decided as we develop our manufacturing and marketing programmes in preparation for the launch of each catalyst equipped model.

standards would have to be made by the European Council of Ministers.

"We always have to assess the effectiveness of our efforts. There are virtually unlimited campaign possibilities. We try not to get lost on marginal areas, and campaigns always go through peaks and troughs," explained Elsworth. "In this case, we turned to the situation at the EC. We wanted to be sure that the UK government would not block the measures the European Parliament had just proposed." Greenpeace then contacted all the supporters of the Ford campaign to urge them to write their local members of Parliament to support the European Parliament's position.

History proved Ford's efforts on behalf of lean burn futile. US-based standards for all cars are now the law in the European Community and will take effect in 1993. Yet Ford's Cannell defends his company's strategy and its handling of Greenpeace. "We still believe that our position was justified. Lean burn satisfied all the current and planned emission requirements. Catalysts do involve substantial extra costs, and it is difficult for any manufacturer facing normal commercial pressures to take actions beyond those required in the countries in which it operates and which could add to its costs or the prices charged."

Ford did not feel that Greenpeace's campaign had damaged it. There had been no evident impact on market share, and memories of the campaign, from Ford's perspective at least, soon faded away.

"I don't think it caused us any real damage," Cannell continued. "Of course, a campaign of the kind Greenpeace conducted cannot be ignored. We were aware of their advertisements, and we had all the correspondence from the dealers. Every company wants to be loved, and the Greenpeace campaign was one of the factors that had to be considered when we were reviewing our policy. But it was only one issue. No single factor led to our introduction of catalytic converters in the UK. European Commission regulations became tougher than we had anticipated. The biggest single factor was the government's decision to reduce the tax on unleaded fuel (in April 1989) and the speed with which unleaded petrol became available. There was no simple cause and effect between Greenpeace's campaign and our decision."

HUMANA, INC.

George S. Vozikis and
Timothy S. Mescon
The Citadel and
Kennesaw State College

Michael M. LeConey, security analyst for Merrill Lynch, Pierce, Fenner and Smith, has said, "With Humana, investors are dealing with what I believe may be the most aggressive and smartest major company in the US. That's a lot to say about any company, but Humana's success, and the absolutely uncanny accuracy of its corporate strategy, make it a supportable statement" (*Wall Street Transcript*, June 9, 1980).

HISTORY

Humana, Inc. was begun in 1961, when David A. Jones and Wendell Cherry, two young lawyers, built their first nursing home. Humana, Inc. was incorporated in Delaware, on July 28, 1964, as Extendicare Inc. It became the successor to Heritage House of America Inc., which commenced operations in 1961.

By 1967, government health programs such as Medicaid and Medicare had been implemented by Congress, and Humana, Inc. was running eight nursing homes. In 1968, a flu epidemic struck New Haven, Connecticut, and a hospital placed its overflow in Humana's local nursing home.

The "Gold Dust Twins," as business associates sometimes call Jones and Cherry, discovered that hospitals earned six times as much from Medicare and Medicaid as nursing homes did.

In 1968, a boom year for nursing home stocks, they took their company public. Humana began to buy up existing private hospitals at a rate of one per month, and by selling their nursing homes and mobile home parks (and by borrowing heavily), in 1972 and 1973 embarked on a $300 million dollar hospital construction program, completing some 39 hospitals in the South and Southwest by 1976. The National Health Planning and Resources Development Act was passed in 1974, which prohibited the renovation, construction, or purchase of equipment costing more than $100,000, unless state and local health planning agencies approved it as necessary. Humana, Inc. was convinced that this law would practically halt new construction, and it began to supplement hospital purchases by buying out competitors such as American Medicorp, number two in the industry in 1978 when it was purchased by Humana.

Little cash was used. The acquisitions were accomplished by exchanging stock with doctor-owners. Success in acquisition efforts precipitated an internal growth strategy of construction of additional hospitals, coupled with a divestment of the nursing homes. By 1977, this strategy increased revenues to $316 million from $85 million in 1971, and long-term debt to $224.3 million from $87.8 million.

In 1980, Humana's revenues increased to $1.1 billion from 1977's $316 million, and profits from $11.8 million to $64.6 million. Significantly, Humana's 10-year compounded growth rate of 32% exceeded all but eight companies in *Financial World* magazine's annual ranking of 10-year performance by companies with revenues above $500 million.

Humana views the pursuit of medical excellence as its most important task. The company's Mission Statement is the focal point of its commitment: "The mission of Humana is to maintain an unequaled level of measurable quality and productivity in the delivery of health services that are responsive to the needs and values of patients, physicians, employers, and employees."

In an era where the continued demand for quality health care is matched by the need to control costs, Humana provides an integrated system of high-quality, cost-efficient health care services through its three operating divisions: Hospital Division, Health Services Division, and Group Health Division.

Hospital Division

Humana owns and operates 86 hospitals containing approximately 17,700 beds in 21 states, England, Switzerland, and Mexico. (See Exhibit 1.)

As a reflection of Humana's commitment to medical excellence, the Centers of Excellence program was established at Humana hospitals in 1982 to support practicing physicians who excel in their specialty so that they can undertake clinical

Exhibit 1 *Existing Hospital Locations, Their Capacity, and Hospitals under Construction (as of August 1985)*

State	No. of Hospitals	Total Bed Capacity	Hospitals or Additions under Construction	Additional Beds
Alabama	6	983	—	
Alaska	1	199	1	39
Arizona	2	434	—	—
California	5	938	—	—
Colorado	2	450	—	—
Florida	17	3,820	5	138
Georgia	4	718	—	—
Illinois	2	556	—	—
Indiana	1	150	—	—
Kansas	2	510	—	—
Kentucky	7	1,861	1	61
Louisiana	8	833	—	—
Mississippi	1	101	—	—
Nevada	1	670	—	—
North Carolina	2	196	—	—
Tennessee	4	472	—	—
Texas	11	2,990	2	35
Utah	1	110	—	—
Virginia	3	650	—	—
Washington	1	155	—	—
West Virginia	2	201	—	—
England	2	265	—	—
Mexico	1	200	—	—
Switzerland	1	242	—	—
Total	87	17,706	9	273

research and medical education programs in conjunction with their private practices. A Center of Excellence is a medical referral and consultation center at a Humana hospital that provides the surrounding region with the highest quality of care in a given clinical specialty. Currently, 15 Centers of Excellence have been designated in the clinical specialties of burn care, cardiovascular disease, diabetes, neurosciences, women's medicine, orthopedics, spinal injury, pulmonary medicine, and ophthalmology.

Humana is recognized as a leader in the hospital industry in providing high-quality, cost-efficient health care services. Through centralized purchasing, computer services, and flexible staffing techniques, the cost per admission at Humana's hospitals averages 19.4% less than other hospitals in the same communities with the same types of patients according to the *1985 U.S. Industrial Outlook*.

Health Services Division

In 1981 Humana began developing a network of freestanding, extended-hour, medical treatment centers called MedFirst. More than 147 MedFirst units provide consumers with primary medical care at least 12 hours a day, 7 days a week. The number of Humana MedFirst offices is expected to grow to approximately 260 by September 1986, according to George Atkins, vice president of public affairs.

MedFirst is a cooperative effort between independent physicians in a given community and a Humana subsidiary. Humana builds an office, provides equipment and supplies, and hires, trains, and employs the support staff. The physicians control all medical aspects of their private practice.

In addition to the continued expansion of the Humana MedFirst office network, the company's Health Services Division is exploring new health care services including freestanding breast diagnostic centers and home health care services.

Group Health Division

In September 1983, Humana introduced Humana Care Plus, an innovative group health benefit plan that gives employers, for the first time, the controls they need to keep the cost of employee health care in line with other normal costs of doing business. Humana can offer guaranteed caps on an employer's health care costs because of its ability to control hospital costs.

Humana Care Plus offers employers a variety of flexible benefit plans to meet the individual needs of companies. All plans allow employees to keep their own doctors. If hospital care is required, plan members are given economic incentives to use Humana Care Plus participating hospitals. Humana has added a number of participating hospitals from outside the Humana system in order to ensure comprehensive coverage in its service areas. In addition members receive benefits at non-participating hospitals when emergency services are needed, or if an elective service is not available at a participating hospital.

During its first year, approximately 65,000 Humana Care Plus members were enrolled in 11 metropolitan areas. By August, 1985 Humana health plans were available in approximately 53 metropolitan areas across the United States and total plan members numbered more than 359,000.

INDUSTRY TRENDS

The health care industry is a complex one. There are many distinct categories of products and services and a corresponding range of company types in business to provide them. In most references the industry is defined as those companies/institutions which directly interface with patients and those which supply medical products/services to the directly interfacing companies.

The major categories of companies/institutions involved are hospitals, physicians, dentists, drug manufacturers, medical device manufacturers, medical supplies manufacturers, nursing homes, and miscellaneous services (professional, cleaning, management, etc.).

Health care expenditures have grown dramatically, both in absolute dollars and as a percent of the GNP over the past 20 years and will continue to do so through 1990. (See Exhibit 2.) The sources and uses of health care funds are shown in Exhibit 3.

Several factors accounted for the quantum leaps in health care expenditures over the years:

- General inflation in the economy, especially over the seventies
- Enactment of Medicare and Medicaid by Congress. A key ingredient of this legislation was its cost plus reimbursement scheme, which encouraged increased expenditures by all providers. (See Exhibit 4.)

Exhibit 2 *Total Health Care Expenditures 1965–1990*

Year	Total Health Care Dollars (in billions)	Percent of GNP
1965	$ 41.7	6.0
1970	74.7	7.8
1975	132.7	8.6
1980	249.0	9.3
1984	392.7 E[a]	10.9 E
1987	529.8 E	11.8 E
1990	690.4 E	12.3 E

Source: Standard & Poor's Industry Surveys, Health Care, January 17, 1985, p. H13.
[a]E = estimate.

Exhibit 3 *National Health Expenditures by Sources and Uses of Funds*

	1970	1984 E	1990 E
Sources			
Patients	34.8%	28.8%	27.8%
Federal government	23.7%	29.0%	30.4%
Health insurers	22.9%	27.8%	28.8%
State and local	13.5%	12.7%	11.5%
Other	5.1%	1.5%	1.5%
Uses			
Hospital care	37.2%	42.2%	43.8%
Physician's services	18.1%	19.4%	19.3%
Drugs and medical sundries	10.7%	6.8%	6.3%
Nursing home care	6.3%	8.3%	8.5%
Administration, prepayment, public health activity, research, and construction	12.7%	11.0%	10.4%
Dentist's services	6.3%	6.0%	5.8%
Other personal health care	7.7%	6.3%	5.9%

Source: Standard & Poor's Industry Surveys, Health Care, January 17, 1985, pp. H14–H15.
E = estimate.

Exhibit 4 *Medicare Expenditure for Hospitals*

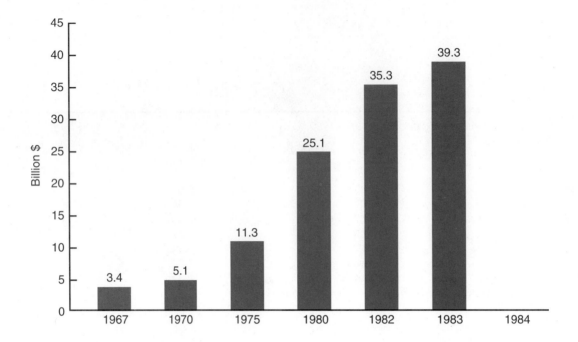

- Growth in the use and per capita expenditures of third-party insurers (Ford Motor Company spent $22 per car for health insurance in 1965 and $275 in 1985.)
- A general aging of the population, especially in the over 65 age group (See Exhibit 5.)
- Development and expanded use of expensive medical equipment and procedures (CAT scan, kidney dialysis, organ transplants, etc.)

The tremendous growth in health care costs has alarmed all those parties who must pay for it. For all levels of government these costs are budget busters (especially for the federal government) at a time when deficits are a major national issue. For the insurance and general business sectors these cost increases mean significant increases in the cost of doing business, tending to make them raise prices and become, thereby, less competitive. Members of the general public who have to pay some or all of their health care bills are also concerned.

In 1984 hospitals accounted for $17.2 billion in revenues. Within the industry, Humana had revenues of $2.6 billion, or 15.1% of the total hospital revenues for the year. Increase for the industry from 1983 was 8.3%.

On April 20, 1983, President Reagan signed P.L. 98-21 (the "Act") into law. Title VI of the Act substantially changed Medicare payments to acute care hospitals for inpatient hospital service by creating a prospective form of payment based on 470 diagnostic related groups (DRGs) whereby hospitals are paid a fixed amount per patient for operating costs regardless of their actual operating costs attributable to such patient. DRGs are a system of classifying illnesses according to the estimated intensity of hospital resources necessary to furnish care for each diagnosis. If the hospital's costs to treat the patient exceed the DRG payment, the hospital will generally not be entitled to any additional amount. Furthermore, the hospital is precluded from charging the patient any costs beyond the co-insurance and deductible required under Medicare. The method of payment provided for in the Act became effective for most of Humana's hospitals on September 1, 1984. Although it would appear that this newly imposed payment system would have an adverse effect on Humana's revenue, it did not. In fact, the company experienced a significant increase in net revenue per Medicare admission compared to the amount it would have received under the prior cost-based reimbursement system.

Exhibit 5 *Elderly Population Projections, 1980–2000*

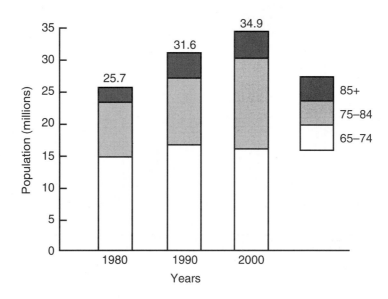

Source: US Census Bureau, "*Projections of the Population in the US*," Series P-25, No. 952, May 1984.

This increase is primarily attributed to the fact that the DRG payment is a fixed amount rather than a reimbursement of cost. Humana's operating costs and annual increases in operating costs are, on the average, generally lower than those of most other hospitals. This type of cost containment measure has finally slowed down the dramatic rise in health care costs whose annual rate of increase has abated, as Exhibit 6 shows.

COMPETITIVE STRUCTURE

In many areas served by Humana's hospitals, there are other hospitals, some of which are larger and more established than the hospitals operated by Humana. In addition, certain hospitals located in the areas served by Humana are special service hospitals that provide medical, surgical and psychiatric services not available at Humana or other general hospitals. Certain hospitals which compete with Humana's hospitals are operated by not-for-profit, non-taxpaying or governmental agencies, which can finance capital expenditures on a tax-exempt basis, and which receive funds and charitable contributions unavailable to Humana's hospitals.

The competitive position of a hospital is to a large degree dependent on the number and quality of its staff physicians. Although a physician may at any time terminate his or her connection with a hospital, Humana seeks to retain physicians of varied specializations on its hospital staffs and to attract and maintain high ethical and professional standards. Humana's competitive position and hospital pricing policies are increasingly affected by the development of facilities which provide, on an outpatient basis, services that have traditionally been provided in hospitals. Health care delivery and financing systems such as health maintenance organizations (HMOs), which attempt to direct and control utilization of hospital services and obtain discounts from hospitals' established charges, also affect the competitive position of a hospital.

The occupancy rate of a hospital is affected by a number of factors, including the number of physicians using the hospital, the composition and size of the population, general economic conditions of the area serviced by the hospital, variations in medical and surgical practices in local communities, the degree of outpatient use of hospital services, the length of patient stay (Exhibit 7), the number, type,

Exhibit 6 *Health Care Cost Increases Are Slowing Down*

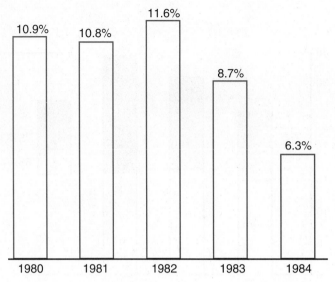

Source: Bureau of Labor Statistics.

Exhibit 7 *Average Length of Hospital Stays (All Patients)*

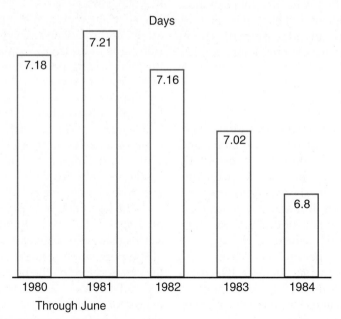

Source: American Hospital Association.

and quality of other hospitals in the area and its competitive position. The decrease in occupancy rates during the past four fiscal years (as well as the decreasing rate of increase in the number of hospitals in general) was caused primarily by cost-containment efforts by federal and state governments, third-party payers, and private industry, whose efforts resulted in fewer admissions and shorter lengths of stay. These efforts include pre-hospital admission authorization, increased deductibles and copayments in employee health benefit plans, and incentives that encourage increased use of outpatient services. The decline in occupancy rates in 1983 and 1984 at certain hospitals was also influenced by general economic conditions.

It is estimated that investor-owned hospitals account for approximately 13% of the total number of community hospital beds in the country. Approximately 52% of those investor-owned beds are owned by four hospital companies. Humana ranks third in number of hospital beds owned.

GENERAL ORGANIZATION AND MANAGEMENT

By the end of 1984, the CEO, David A. Jones, and the president, Wendell Cherry, had put together a management team "second-to-none." The top levels of management are young and energetic executives that bring together many years of experience in marketing, management, and innovation (Exhibit 8).

The day-to-day administrative operation of each hospital is under the supervision and direction of a full-time professional administrator. Three regional executive vice presidents and one senior vice president are responsible for operations in their designated geographic areas.

Centralized management services are supplied to each hospital by the company's headquarters. These services include financing, recruiting, personnel development, accounting, data processing, legal advice, public relations, marketing, insurance, and purchasing. Each hospital is responsible for devel-

---

Exhibit 8 *Humana, Inc. Organization and Management*

Directors

William C. Ballard, Jr., Executive Vice President— Finance and Administration, Humana, Inc.

Hilary J. Boone, Jr., Owner-Operator, Wimbledon Farm, Thoroughbred horse farm, Lexington, Ky

Wendell Cherry, President and Chief Operating Officer, Humana, Inc.

Michael E. Gellert, Executive Director, Drexel Burnham Lambert Incorporated, Investment bankers, New York, NY

J. David Grissom, Chairman of the Board and Chief Executive Officer, Citizens Fidelity Corporation, Bank holding company, Louisville, Ky

David A. Jones, Chairman of the Board and Chief Executive Officer, Humana, Inc.

Antonie T. Knoppers, MD, Business Consultant, Summit, NJ

John W. Landrum, Owner, Executive Flight Service, Harrodsburg, Ky

Carl F. Pollard, Senior Executive Vice President, Humana, Inc.

David C. Scott, Chairman of the Board, Allis-Chalmers Corporation, Manufacturer of processing, agricultural and electrical equipment, Milwaukee, Wisc

Charles L. Weisberg, Chairman of the Board, Bass & Weisberg Realtors, Real estate and property management, and President, Charmar Galleries Limited, Antiques and art gallery, Louisville, Ky

William T. Young, Chairman of the Board, W. T. Young, Inc., Public warehousing, Lexington, Ky

continued

Exhibit 8 *continued*

Executive Committee

| William T. Young, Chairman | Wendell Cherry
David A. Jones | Carl F. Pollard |

Audit Committee

| David C. Scott, Chairman | J. David Grissom
Antonie T. Knoppers, M.D. | Charles L. Weisberg
William T. Young |

Compensation Committee

| Michael E. Gellert, Chairman | Hilary J. Boone, Jr.
Charles L. Weisberg | William T. Young |

Officers

| David A. Jones, Chairman of
the Board and Chief
Executive Officer | Wendell Cherry, President
and Chief Operating Officer |

Staff Management

William C. Ballard Jr.,
  Executive Vice President,
  Finance and Administration
Thomas J. Flynn,
  Executive Vice President and
  General Counsel
H. Linden McLellan,
  Senior Vice President,
  Facility Management
H. Herbert Phillips,
  Senior Vice President,
  Administration
Fred Pirman Jr.,
  Senior Vice President,
  Information Systems
David G. Anderson,
  Vice President and Treasurer
George L. Atkins,
  Vice President, Public Affairs

W. Roger Drury, Vice
  President, Finance and Control
Michael A. Hendricks,
  Vice President,
  Real Estate
John V. Kessler,
  Vice President,
  Insurance
Gail H. Knopf,
  Vice President,
  Information Systems
Patrick B. McGinnis,
  Vice President,
  Finance and Planning
Paul B. Powell,
  Vice President, Purchasing
Richard A. Schweinhart,
  Vice President
  and Controller

Michael R. Smith,
  Vice President,
  Human Resources
Kenneth E. Snyder,
  Vice President,
  Information Systems
Robert B. Steele,
  Vice President, Taxes
Charles E. Teeple,
  Vice President,
  Investor Relations
James J. Walters,
  Vice President,
  Design and Construction
Tyree G. Wilburn,
  Vice President,
  Internal Audit
Alice F. Newton,
  Secretary

Operating Management

Carl F. Pollard,
  Senior Executive
  Vice President

EXHIBIT 8 *continued*

Hospital division

Paul A. Gross,
Executive Vice President and
Division President
Jack Clark, Executive
Vice President,
Mid-South Region
Lee R. Ledbetter,
Executive Vice President,
Florida Region
Wayne T. Smith,
Executive Vice President,
Central Region
James D. Bohanon,
Senior Vice President,
Pacific Region

Gary W. Metcalf,
Senior Vice President
and Controller
F. David Rollo, MD,
PhD, Senior Vice President,
Medical Affairs
Philip B. Garmon,
Vice President,
Central Region
Donald L. Maloney II,
Vice President, Florida Region
Kathryn M. Mershon,
Vice President,
Nursing

Larry H. Montgomery,
Vice President,
Mid-South Region
Thomas D. Moore,
MD, Vice President,
Medical Affairs
George G. Schneider,
Vice President,
Pacific Region

Group Health Division

Henry J. Werronen,
Senior Vice President
W. Larry Cash, Vice
President, Finance,
and Controller

Richard M. Mastaler,
Vice President,
Sales and
Marketing

John H. Morse,
Vice President,
Operations

Joseph E. Shiprek,
Vice President,
Group Administration

Health Services Division

Randolph G. Brown,
Senior Vice President

Savas G. Mallos,
Vice President

Donald L. Stewart,
Vice President

oping its own competitive strategy within the area it is located. However, the company operations have enough autonomy within the regions to have a voice in the corporate and regional decision-making process.

MARKETING

Humana ranked second in the amount of revenue generated for fiscal year 1985 among the major hospitals. It accounted for 17.3% of the revenue generated by all hospitals during that period.

With the clampdown on health care spending by both the employers and the government, marketing among hospitals has become big business. With occupancy rates at an average of 66% for the industry, the lowest in two decades, hospitals are fighting for patients. Traditionally, hospitals have been unable to use the word "marketing." Those days are gone. Humana Hospital Phoenix recently took out ads promoting "special rates" in local newspapers to drum up business.

Kenneth Abramowitz, an analyst at Sanford C. Bernstein & Co., emphasized in an interview with *USA Today*, February 26, 1986, that "health care is moving from a provider-controlled industry to a consumer-controlled industry. That means companies are going to have to start appealing to the needs of consumers." Humana threw the first punch in early 1986 when it opened a $20 million advertising campaign featuring Olympic gymnast Mary Lou Retton in order to establish a national brand image. Retton underwent arthroscopic surgery performed on her knee at a Humana hospital six weeks before the 1984 Olympic Games. "Instead of saying 'take me to the hospital,' we want consumers to say 'take me to a *Humana* hospital,'" says George Atkins, spokesman for Humana.

Humana has also placed increased emphasis on promoting its Humana MedFirst medical centers, which maintain extended hours, including evenings and weekends, with independent physicians providing medical care to their ambulatory patients. Humana is also promoting Humana Care Plus, which offers an indemnity type health insurance and prepaid health care. These products generally permit individuals the freedom to choose any physician or hospital facility, but provide incentives to use the company's hospitals.

Marketing and advertising as a whole have been expensive for Humana since the summer of 1983, with the promotion of Humana Care Plus and Humana MedFirst. However, MedFirst and Care Plus have been industry trendsetters since their inception. Humana has also made its name a household word since Dr. William DeVries implanted the first successful artificial heart into William Schroeder in 1984.

OPERATIONS

Humana enjoys a strong position in its three operating divisions. The three operating divisions include the Hospital Division, Group Health Division, and Health Services Division. The principal source of the company's revenues (approximately 96% in fiscal 1985) is provided by the Hospital Division, which as of August 31, 1985, operated 87 hospitals containing 17,706 licensed beds. The company's hospitals are located in 21 states, two hospitals in England, one in Mexico, and one in Switzerland.

[Note: As used in Exhibit 9, the term "licensed beds" is the maximum number of beds permitted in the facility under its license regardless of whether the beds are actually available for patient care. The term "weighted licensed beds" is the number of licensed beds after giving effect to the length of time the beds have been licensed during the period. "Patient days" is the total number of days of patient care provided by the company's hospitals. Occupancy rates are calculated by dividing average patient days (total patient days divided by total number of days for the period) by weighted licensed beds.]

The day-to-day fiscal and administrative operation of each hospital is under the supervision and direction of a full-time professional administrator. Three regional executive vice presidents and one senior vice president are responsible for operations in their designated geographic areas.

Centralized management services are supplied to each hospital by the company's headquarters. These services include financing, recruiting, personnel development, accounting, data processing, legal advice, public relations, marketing, insurance, and purchasing. As of August 31, 1985, Humana had under construction the major projects shown in Exhibit 10, nearly $230 billion in new construction for fiscal 1985.

Exhibit 9 *Humana, Inc.—Operative Data*

	1985	1984	1983	1982	1981
Hospitals:					
Revenues	$2,785,435	$2,578,106	$2,284,151	$1,920,130	$1,702,077
Number of hospitals in operation at end of period	87	91	90	89	89
Licensed beds at end of period	17,706	18,242	17,248	16,286	16,431
Weighted average licensed beds	17,853	17,360	16,767	16,165	16,655
Patient days	3,142,400	3,454,900	3,579,300	3,548,600	3,723,300
Humana Care Plus patient days	44,500	3,400	—	—	—
Admissions	525,400	549,500	566,700	561,300	579,500
Humana Care Plus admissions	9,300	700	—	—	—
Occupancy	48.2%	54.4%	58.5%	60.1%	61.3%
Length of stay	6.0	6.3	6.3	6.3	6.4
Humana Care Plus:					
Revenues	$ 89,126	$ 7,893	—	—	—
Number of operational markets at end of period	50	10	—	—	—
Number of members enrolled and committed at end of period	359,200	40,900	—	—	—
Humana MedFirst					
Revenues	$ 37,960	$ 23,128	$ 14,457	$ 3,398	$ 1,520
Number of operational units at end of period	148	68	65	45	5
Hospital revenues paid by Humana Care Plus (eliminated in consolidation)	$ 37,381	$ 2,712			

Exhibit 10 *Humana, Inc.—Description of Projects under Construction*

2 new hospitals (138 beds)	$ 14,402,000
Replacement of 1 hospital (net reduction of 78 beds) and renovation and expansion of 2 hospitals (47 net additional beds)	61,144,000
Renovation of 24 hospitals	68,174,000
12 new medical office buildings, 14 condominium office buildings	77,383,000
12 medical care centers	7,952,000
Total	$229,055,000

PERSONNEL

One of the company's major strengths is in the capability, experience, and leadership of the executive and management team personnel. On August 31, 1985, Humana hospitals had approximately 32,500 full-time and 11,300 part-time employees, including approximately 16,800 registered nurses and licensed practical nurses. Approximately 28,000 licensed physicians are members of the medical staffs of the hospitals, approximately one-half of whom are members of the active staffs. With minor exceptions, physicians are not employees of the hospitals. However, some staff physicians provide ancillary services in Humana hospitals under contract. Any licensed physician or dentist may apply to be admitted to the medical staff of any of the Humana hospitals, but admission to the staff must be approved by the medical staff and the board of trustees or the board of directors. Members of the medical staffs of Humana hospitals may also serve on the medical staffs of other hospitals.

All hospitals have generally experienced satisfactory labor relations. Approximately 560 employees at four hospitals are represented by labor unions. The company experiences union organizational activity in its hospitals from time to time. Humana promotes from within whenever feasible. Several of the personnel now occupying executive and managerial positions came in at lower levels out of college. Their maturity and growth in their job performance has been rewarded through promotions and other recognition. This in turn provides incentives for the new and lower-level employees to recognize that they too will be rewarded for their diligent and loyal services to Humana, Inc.

FINANCE

Exhibits 11 through 14 present the consolidated financial statements for Humana, Inc.

Exhibit 11 *Humana, Inc.—Consolidated Statement of Income for the Years Ended August 31, 1985, 1984, and 1983 (Dollars in Thousands Except per Share Results)*

	1985	1984	1983
Revenues	$2,875,140	$2,606,415	$2,298,608
Provisions for contractual allowances and doubtful accounts	686,750	645,226	533,485
Net revenues	2,188,390	1,961,189	1,765,123
Operating expenses	1,546,128	1,420,429	1,310,424
Depreciation and amortization	147,337	120,560	94,665
Interest	118,825	87,950	71,252
	1,812,290	1,628,939	1,476,341
Income before income taxes	376,100	332,250	288,782
Provision for income taxes	159,880	138,909	128,133
Net income	$ 216,220	$ 193,341	$ 160,649
Earnings per common share	$2.19	$1.96	$1.63

Exhibit 12 *Humana, Inc.—Consolidated Balance Sheet August 31, 1985 and 1984 (Dollars in Thousands except per Share Amounts)*

	1985	1984
Assets		
Current assets:		
Cash and cash equivalents	$ 82,255	$ 260,954
Accounts receivable less allowance for loss of		
$63,415—1985 and $59,215—1984	365,851	257,675
Inventories	50,904	45,249
Other current assets	39,501	41,428
	538,511	605,306
Property and equipment, at cost		
Land	181,160	165,413
Buildings	1,449,565	1,228,701
Equipment	791,669	681,756
Construction in progress (estimated		
cost to complete and equip after		
August 31, 1985—$132,000)	91,177	160,079
	2,513,571	2,235,949
Accumulated depreciation	562,300	452,641
	1,951,271	1,783,308
Other assets	230,112	189,233
	$2,719,894	$2,577,847
Liabilities and Stockholders' Equity		
Current liabilities:		
Trade accounts payable	$ 85,261	$ 88,323
Salaries, wages and other compensation	55,001	52,292
Other accrued expenses	117,945	97,936
Income taxes	48,972	59,956
Long-term debt due within one year	57,817	53,720
	364,996	352,227
Long-term debt	1,205,559	1,286,526
Deferred credits and other liabilities	246,489	195,909
Common stockholders' equity		
Common stock, 16⅔¢ par; authorized 200,000,000		
shares; issued and outstanding 97,299,419		
shares—1985 and 96,848,643 shares—1984	16,217	16,141
Capital in excess of par value	223,392	219,218
Translation adjustments	(16,076)	(19,340)
Retained earnings	679,317	527,166
	902,850	743,185
	$2,719,894	$2,577,847

Exhibit 13 *Humana, Inc.—Consolidated Statement of Changes in Financial Position for the Years Ended August 31, 1985, 1984, and 1983 (Dollars in Thousands)*

	1985	1984	1983
Funds provided:			
From operations:			
Net income	$ 216,220	$193,341	$160,649
Items which did not require working capital:			
Depreciation and amortization	147,337	120,560	94,665
Deferred income taxes	39,785	7,404	21,876
Other	1,281	3,593	(16,374)
	404,623	324,898	260,816
Additions to long-term debt	207,198	358,811	316,795
Issuances of common stock	4,236	9,695	116,967
Increase in allowance for professional liability risks	23,707	22,032	18,808
Disposition of properties	97,233	55,442	72,183
Other	19,959	22,869	13,553
	756,956	793,747	799,122
Funds applied:			
Additions to property and equipment	400,855	445,741	514,776
Reduction of long-term debt	285,216	137,067	108,094
Redemption of preferred stock	—	62,277	188
Payment of cash dividends	64,055	60,217	50,609
Insurance subsidiary's investments	30,769	23,566	22,621
Additions to goodwill	18,066	1,017	—
Additions to deferred charges	18,276	7,862	10,965
Other	19,283	19,989	27,526
	836,520	757,736	734,779
Increase (decrease) in working capital	$ (79,564)	$ 36,011	$ 64,343
Increase (decrease) in working capital consists of:			
Cash and cash equivalents	$(178,699)	$ 10,906	$ 40,530
Accounts receivable	108,176	57,222	32,671
Inventories	5,655	3,735	7,152
Other current assets	(1,927)	11,884	14,686
Trade accounts payable	3,062	(5,938)	(14,842)
Salaries, wages and other compensation	(2,709)	2,890	(8,666)
Other accrued expenses	(20,009)	(16,577)	(22,923)
Income taxes	10,984	(25,094)	26,569
Long-term debt due within one year	(4,097)	(3,017)	(10,834)
	$ (79,564)	$ 36,011	$ 64,343

Exhibit 14 *Humana, Inc.—Consolidated Statement of Common Stockholders' Equity for the Years Ended August 31, 1985, 1984, and 1983 (Dollars in Thousands Except per Share Amounts)*

	Common Stock		Capital in Excess of Par Value	Translation Adjustments	Retained Earnings	Total
	Shares	Amount				
Balances, August 31, 1982	90,630,107	$15,105	$ 93,474	$ (9,424)	$286,057	$385,212
Net income					160,649	160,649
Cash dividends on common stock ($.46⅞ per share)					(44,364)	(44,364)
Cash dividends on preferred stock ($2.50 per share), and $216 provision for redemption value					(6,461)	(6,461)
Unrealized translation losses				(3,369)		(3,369)
Public offering of common stock, net of expenses of $3,891	4,800,000	800	112,684			113,484
Stock options exercised and related tax benefits, net of 11,562 shares tendered in partial payment therefor	315,095	52	3,113			3,165
Other	69,847	12	306			318
Balances, August 31, 1983	95,815,049	15,969	209,577	(12,793)	395,881	608,634
Net income					193,341	193,341
Cash dividends on common stock ($.57½ per share)					(55,541)	(55,541)
Cash dividends on preferred stock ($1.875 per share), and $162 provision for redemption value					(4,838)	(4,838)
Unrealized translation losses				(6,547)		(6,547)
Stock options exercised and related tax benefits, net of 16,280 shares tendered in partial payment therefor	1,008,644	168	9,551			9,719
Redemption of preferred stock					(1,559)	(1,559)
Other	24,950	4	90		(118)	(24)
Balances, August 31, 1984	96,848,643	16,141	219,218	(19,340)	527,166	743,185
Net income					216,220	216,220
Cash dividends on common stock ($.66 per share)					(64,055)	(64,055)
Unrealized translation gains				3,264		3,264
Stock options exercised and related tax benefits, net of 71,071 shares tendered in partial payment therefor	281,398	47	3,514			3,561
Other	169,378	29	660		(14)	675
Balances, August 31, 1985	97,299,419	$16,217	$223,392	$(16,076)	$679,317	$902,850

HONEYWELL EUROPE (A)

Susan C. Schneider, Lenny Hansen, and Avivah Wittenberg-Cox
INSEAD, France

"1986. What a year!" Mike Bonsignore settled into his seat for the seven-hour plane ride from Brussels to Minneapolis. He was leaving his job as president of Honeywell Europe. Tomorrow, he'd settle into his office of executive vice president of International at Minneapolis headquarters. He thought back over his three years in Brussels with some pleasure and some worries. So much had been accomplished in Europe and the region had been doing so well. But Bonsignore wondered what would be the impact of the major strategic reorientation recently decided by US corporate headquarters.

Bonsignore remembered arriving in Brussels early 1983, from Honeywell's Marine Systems Division in Seattle, Washington. In Brussels, as president of Honeywell Europe, he found himself facing a multibusiness, multicultural operation. Given the breadth and diversity of the national organizations, each with its own management, product lines, and national cultures, Bonsignore's mission had been to improve the coordination of the highly decentralized structure, to promote "togetherness" while preserving local autonomy, and to emphasize the *one* in Honeywell.

Reviewing in his mind all the programs implemented to strengthen and integrate Europe, Bonsignore tried to draw some lessons for his new mission—to transform Honeywell into a global company.

HONEYWELL, INC.

Company History

Honeywell, Inc. celebrated its centennial in 1983. One hundred years ago, an unassuming inventor, Albert Butz, applied the principle of feedback to an apparatus that opened and closed the damper on home furnaces. This was the start of automatic temperature control. The promising gadget, known as the "damper flapper," however, was not a commercial success. And Al Butz was "no fireball of a salesman." Leaving for a job in Chicago, Butz sold his business, complete with two patents. They were the first application of the feedback principle which would become the basis for automated control technology.

W. R. Sweatt of North Dakota bought Butz's company and merged it with his own in 1902. Meanwhile, Mark Honeywell, in Indiana, was developing his own Heating Specialty Company. After a couple of decades of fierce competition, the rival firms, "staid and proper" Honeywell and "aggressive and blunt" Sweatt, realized that each had patents that blocked the other from growing and decided to merge in the 1920s.

With Sweatt as chairman of the new company, and Honeywell as president, Sweatt's son, Harold, was named vice president, becoming president of the company in 1934. Harold remained president for 40 years, shaping the company into a major corporation. By pushing technology development and by focused mergers and acquisitions, the company became specialized in manufacturing automatic temperature controls for industrial processes and heating regulation in office buildings.

In the early 1940s, Honeywell entered the electronics field. Production of the first successful autopilot introduced the company to aviation and in 1955, a joint venture opened the door to the large-scale computer systems market. By 1967, sales exceeded the $1 billion mark. Three years later, Honeywell, after merging with General Electric's computer business, became the second largest computer company in the world.

Honeywell was split into two divisions in 1972—Honeywell Information Systems (HIS) and Honeywell Control Systems. Each division had very different management approaches, particularly in their overseas operations. HIS had one major product, computers. It had the same competitors throughout the world: IBM and the rest of "The Bunch".* This meant that policies, strategies, pricing, and management decisions could be highly centralized, operating as one business with branches in Italy, France, Britain and the United States.

Honeywell Control Systems, however, had multiple products. It designed, manufactured and marketed systems, components, and products for the automatic control of equipment and processes. The many small businesses involved had varying amounts of business abroad. The aerospace and defense business, for example, was primarily a domestic market, while the industrial business had a large international market.

The Control Systems division generated about twice HIS's revenue and operating profit with almost twice the number of people. By the early 1980s, Control Systems was organized into four divisions:

1. Aerospace and Defense was strong in military avionic subsystems, marine and ordinance products, space shuttle controls, and subsystems for space and strategic military applications. It was largely dependent on government contracts.

2. Control Products included residential controls and industrial components (microswitch and semiconductor products). These high unit-volume products were distributed through reseller channels.

3. Control Systems engineered and installed commercial building and industrial systems. It had several service businesses and generally sold directly to end users and contractors.

4. International was responsible for all non-US operations across the various lines of business (shown in Exhibit 1).

INTEGRATING HONEYWELL, EUROPE

Honeywell became "international" as early as 1915, with its first distributors in Canada. Companies were established in Europe in the 1930s and agreements were signed in Tokyo. When Europe and Japan began rebuilding after the war, Honeywell established subsidiaries throughout Europe and Asia. In the 1960s and 1970s, Honeywell continued to expand by building or acquiring production units, subsidiaries, and distributors around the world.

European activities, until the early 1970s, consisted largely of the sale of imported products and services, mostly from the United States. National affiliates reported directly to Honeywell, Inc. But by 1971, Europe was producing 50% of its own products and, in response, a regional headquarters, referred to as HESA, was created in Brussels. HESA's role was to direct activities in Europe, the Middle East, Africa, and the Mediterranean basin.

HESA was responsible for 14 national affiliates. These units had always been fairly autonomous, more so than their American counterparts, and each integrated all of the company's business in a given country. National managers appreciated the lack of interference in local problems, but headquarters staff found that implementing policies was sometimes frustrating. According to one general manager,

You had all these fiefdoms. . . . It was like everybody had a castle with a moat around it and the affiliate general managers spent about 80% of their time pumping water in the moat to

---

*The Bunch: Burroughs, Unisys, NCR, Control Data Corporation, and Honeywell.

Exhibit 1 *Review of Major Lines of Business*

	Aerospace & Defense			*Control Products*	
	1985	1984		1985	1984
Revenue	$1,899	$1,608	Revenue	$1,016	$1,025
Operating profit	$ 125	$ 116	Operating profit	$ 114	$ 141
Margin	6.6%	7.2%	Margin	11.2%	13.8%

In 1985, revenue increased 18 percent to $1,899 billion. Operating profit was up 7 percent to $125 million and included a loss on a military contract that is costing more to complete than originally anticipated; the contract ends in 1986. Other parts of the business performed well in 1985. Total orders were at an all-time high and included major contracts from the US Air Force for inertial navigation systems and electronic-warfare test systems. Backlogs entering 1986 were up significantly over 1985.

Approximately 80 percent of the Aerospace & Defense business depends on spending by the US Department of Defense. Honeywell's growth has resulted from concentrating on defense markets that are growing faster than defense spending as a whole.

Honeywell also serves commercial aviation, space and marine markets, all of which are expected to grow in 1986. The commercial aviation business, which had required significant investment over several years, achieved market leadership and profitability in 1985 and is expected to produce excellent long-term results.

US defense spending will not increase in the next few years at the rate it has recently. However, growth in Honeywell's target markets is expected to approximate an average annual rate of 8 percent over the next five years. Aerospace & Defense will continue to be one of the company's fastest growing businesses, but is likely to slow from the 14-percent compound growth rate of the last five years. Expansion of core businesses, where Honeywell enjoys market and technological leadership, and selective emphasis on new opportunities, particularly in space and strategic defense, are key strategies. Operating profit and margins should benefit from earlier investments in the business and are expected to improve.

Control Products revenue of $1,016 billion was about even with 1984, primarily because of softness in industrial component and keyboard markets. Domestic revenue was flat; in international markets, which represent about one-third of Control Products, revenue was up in local currency but flat in dollars. Total orders declined, and backlogs entering 1986 were even with a year ago.

The 19-percent decline in operating profit to $114 million resulted from weak industrial and computer markets, along with increased competition and pricing pressure from foreign suppliers. In spite of this, Control Products remains the company's highest-margin business.

The primary economic factors affecting Control Products are housing starts and modernization, durable goods spending, non-defense capital spending and non-residential fixed investment. In 1985, lower interest rates and strength in housing markets were major positives in Control Products' performance. Residential Division maintained its position as the leading supplier of controls for the home in both US and international markets, and posted a profit increase over 1984.

In 1986, housing starts are projected to be flat, with non-residential fixed investment up modestly. Durable goods spending in markets served by Micro Switch Division is likely to increase, with capital spending declining somewhat. International markets should benefit from a weaker dollar and stronger economies, especially in Europe. Control Products looks for modest revenue growth in 1986.

Operating profit in the near term may be under pressure from a commitment to maintain market share in the face of increased pricing pressure, as well as heavy investment in Control Products factories to reduce costs and increase productivity. These actions are necessary to maintain market leadership and to improve future performance.

continued

Exhibit 1 *continued*

	Control Systems			*Information Systems*	
	1985	1984		1985	1984
Revenue	$1,758	$1,616	Revenue	$1,952	$1,825
Operating profit	$ 140	$ 136	Operating profit	$ 200	$ 180
Margin	8.0%	8.4%	Margin	10.2%	9.9%

Revenue increased 9 percent to $1,758 billion. Growth occurred in every sector of the business and was especially strong in industrial systems. Revenue was higher for both the domestic and international business, with the latter accounting for about one-third of the total. Orders increased over 1984, and backlogs entering 1986 were up moderately.

Operating profit of $140 million was up 3 percent from 1984, in spite of a difficult pricing environment in a flat commercial buildings market. This was more than offset by improvements in commercial services and industrial systems. Volume shipments of TDC 3000 systems began midyear, with 100 systems installed by year end.

Capital spending is the major economic indicator for Control Systems. In 1986, the worldwide outlook for large building construction remains flat, with some growth projected for buildings of 50–200,000 square feet—a market of increased emphasis for Honeywell. In addition, pricing pressure in the long-lead-time commercial systems business began to ease gradually late in 1985. Demand for building services will continue to grow.

The outlook for industrial capital spending in 1986 is mixed, although interest in manufacturing automation is expected to remain high. Oil refining and petrochemicals, one of Control Systems' principal industrial markets, will remain soft although modernization is expected to continue. Pulp and paper and chemicals, markets of increasing importance to the business, are expected to grow. While competitive pressure will remain strong, Honeywell's industrial business should benefit from a favorable product cycle with a full year of TDC 3000 shipments in 1986 and the added advantage of better exchange rates. Control Systems is positioned to achieve improvement in operating profit and margins.

Revenue in the computer business was $1,952 billion, up 7 percent, with growth in both the domestic and international sectors of the business. International operations represented over one-third of the total, with major operations in the United Kingdom, Italy, Canada, Mexico and Australia. Large-systems revenue increased significantly, while the small-systems business in the United States reflected the industry-wide softness in that segment of the computer market in 1985. Rental and service revenue declined slightly. Orders were higher in total, with a substantial increase in large-systems orders. Backlogs were down moderately from a year ago.

Operating profit increased 11 percent to $200 million, reflecting the strength of the large-systems business in 1985 as well as efforts to control costs and expenses. Research and development spending was $210 million, with approximately half for software development.

Relationships with Bull in France and NEC in Japan grew closer during the year. Our three companies concentrate on selling in our respective markets, share product planning and development, and buy from each other to take advantage of manufacturing efficiencies.

Information Systems will continue serving its base of 10,000 customers, with 1986 the first full year of volume shipments of the very large DPS 90 computers and the second year for DPS 88. To capture a greater share of the small systems market, 40 percent of the sales force is dedicated to selling small computers in the office and departmental systems markets.

This year will include a number of major new product introductions. Research and development expenditures are expected to increase to support new hardware, software and systems offerings. Attention to costs and operating efficiencies will continue. Thus, while operating profit may be under pressure in 1986, these actions continue the strategy to position Information Systems for future growth and improving returns.

Source: Annual Report 1986.

*keep everybody else out so you'd have peo-
ple developing the same systems, the same
products.*

By the end of 1983 Honeywell Europe had over
11,200 people (almost all local nationals), over 2
million square feet of factory space, and 33 major
locations across 14 countries. Revenues from Euro-
pean-made products accounted for 77% of European sales in 1984. The company was

*at that adolescent stage in a transition from
being a distributor of US goods and services to
a whole cloth European business for Europe.*

In order to facilitate the implementation of corporate policies at the national level and to develop
European integration, two decisions were taken.
First, regional vice presidents were added to the
HESA organization (see Exhibit 2). National affiliates reported directly to the new position which
was responsible for regional coordination and for
"buffering, filtering and sheltering" company policy for the affiliates. The VP rank was meant to give
them more "clout" with headquarters. Secondly,
the European Policy Committee was formed. The
EPC consisted of the HESA president, regional
VPs, HESA VPs and other senior staff. It met to
address European issues, coordinate policy, and
mediate among the different regions.

In 1983, the EPC studied the European organization and found that an increasingly competitive
external environment demanded a more responsive
organization. This meant that Honeywell needed to
increase coordination between units and focus on
economies of scale. The study stressed three issues:

1. Improving responsiveness to customers
2. Focusing internal decision making and short-
    ening lines of communication
3. Pushing profit responsibility as far down as
    possible

In Bonsignore's words, "we looked for a new
approach to the business that would emphasize
the central guidance from headquarters as the
'what' and the decentralized implementation by
the affiliates as the 'how.'" With this in mind, the
Centers of Excellence were created.

Centers of Excellence

Six self-standing businesses with reputations for
quality were designated Centers of Excellence in

1984. Each had profit and loss responsibility and
managed its own marketing, engineering, manufacturing, finance, and administration. Each Center would be the European focal point for its
business as well as the point of the contact for corresponding US divisions.

*Setting up wall to wall responsibility for the
business allowed us to say "Now we know
what's happening to the whole industrial business in Europe," not just what's happening in
France, in Britain, or in Italy.*

The Centers had three key links with the rest of the
company (see Exhibit 3): the national affiliates,
HESA marketing directors, and Honeywell, Inc.
Center managers and the heads of national affiliates shared information and performance objectives for the business on a pan-European basis. In
essence, the centers were the producing locations,
while the affiliates were "the selling locations and
the 'customers' of the Centers."

Advisory committees were set up to bring together the people most affected by the Center's
activities. This included the group director, certain
national affiliate general managers, and technical
experts. The committee advised and promoted the
Center while members served as bridges of communication to the rest of the company. It was considered important

*to put affiliate managers on the advisory board
because they were the customers. It was a
wonderful check and balance so that these
Centers of Excellence wouldn't run off and do
their own thing at the expense of their clients.*

Business unit success measurements were designed to avoid inter-country competition and to
keep the Centers from becoming the property
of the national affiliates. Paul Dick, the European
Factory Automation Center general manager, commented,

*There's a certain level of autonomy and yet at
the same time a certain level of reporting accountability. . . . Honeywell has strong financial
controls. You don't get too far out of line before
you get a lot of help in a hurry because the
alarm bells go off.*

In addition to structural changes, Europe started
to look at corporate culture as a potential tool of
integration.

Exhibit 2 *Honeywell Europe—Organization Chart—General Management January 1986*

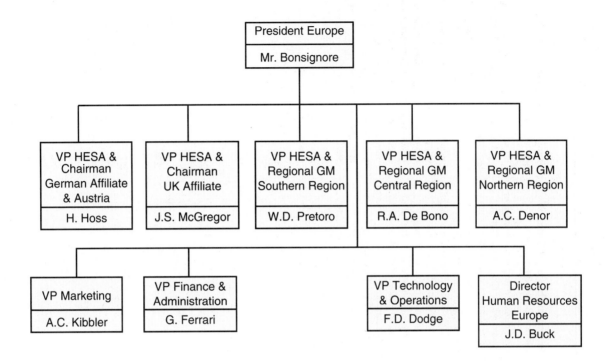

Exhibit 3 Centers of Excellence

The new Honeywell Europe organization linkage

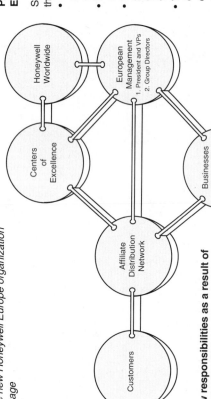

New responsibilities as a result of reorganization

As can be seen above, the Centers of Excellence complement the other businesses in satisfying customer needs through the existing affiliate structure.

The Centers of Excellence have 3 key linkages:

1. with the Affiliate Network,
2. with HESA Group Directors, and
3. with Honeywell worldwide.

In order to facilitate correct operation of these linkages, five Advisory Councils have been created—one for each Center of Excellence.

Advisory Councils

Each Advisory Council comprises a group of upper level managers representing the organizations who most affect or are most affected by the Center: the Group Director; selected Affiliate General Managers; and people with critical skills in marketing, design and manufacturing from outside the Center.

The Advisory Councils will help in identifying strategic business needs and opportunities; advise on the development and implementation of strategies to meet these business needs; provide input on formulating and implementing an Operational Plan consistent with long-range business strategies; advise on how the activities of the Center can be internationalized to make it more effective within Honeywell worldwide; and promote the Center through Honeywell worldwide.

Prime responsibilities of Center of Excellence General Managers

Strategic direction and management of their business for Europe as a whole.

- Product strategy which includes planning, development and manufacture of the products to be supplied.
- Marketing strategy: selection of target segments and customer groups.
- With affiliate support, determining types of distribution channels; promotion; pricing policy; and customer/distribution support.
- Wall-to-wall P&L. This comprises two elements: P&L operation under direct control; and P&L contribution of products and services sold through the Affiliate Distribution Network.

Prime responsibilities of Affiliate General Managers

The strategic and operational management of each Center's business in their territory. This will include:

- Strategic management of the distribution system—selection of distributors, local pricing variations and distributor support strategy.
- Operational management of the distribution system—distributor control and support, control of selling costs, implementation of pricing policies and local promotion. (Where an existing distribution system has been acquired, cooperation with that system to ensure cost-effective integration into the affiliate structure).
- P & L responsibility for achieving objectives and targets negotiated with the Center General Managers.

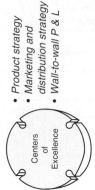

- *Product strategy*
- *Marketing and distribution strategy*
- *Wall-to-wall P & L*

- *Strategic and operational management of each center's business within each affiliate's territory*

Source: Honeywell documentation.

Exhibit 4 *Honeywell Principles*

Honeywell is an international corporation whose goal is to work together with customers to develop and apply advanced technologies through products, systems and services, which in turn serve primarily to improve productivity, conserve resources, and meet aerospace and defense needs. Honeywell adheres to the following principles.

Profits - Profitable operations are necessary to assure the continued health and growth of the company. Honeywell expects profits which equal or exceed those of leading international companies.

Integrity - Honeywell believes in the highest level of integrity and ethical behavior in relationships with customers, employees, shareholders, vendors, neighbors, and governments.

Customers - Honeywell is dedicated to serving customers through excellence of product systems, and service, and through working together with customers to find the answers to their problems.

People - People are key to Honeywell's success. The company actively and affirmatively attracts and promotes the best people without regard to age, race, sex, creed, disability, or nationality, and rewards them on their performance. Honeywell provides an environment for open, timely communications, safe working conditions, and opportunities for personal growth and accomplishment. Honeywell respects the dignity and privacy of individuals and believes in a climate of trust, cooperation and employee involvement.

Quality - Quality of product, application, and service is essential to continue Honeywell's success. Quality improvement should pervade every job within the company. Honeywell believes quality results from an environment in which people work together to sustain excellence.

Decision-making - Honeywell believes sound growth is necessary to successful company performance. This is achieved through well-managed risk taking, innovation, and entrepreneurship. Honeywell is committed to a decentralized structure in which business decisions are made at the lowest appropriate level.

Citizenship - Honeywell operates in compliance with all applicable laws and in ways that build a lasting reputation for integrity and good citizenship in all countries where it does business. The company encourages employees to become involved in community and national affairs. Honeywell manages its business in ways that are sensitive to the environment and that conserve natural resources.

Source: Honeywell documentation.

Corporate Culture

Honeywell's culture is based on a set of principles which can be traced back to W. R. and Harold Sweatt although only put in writing in 1974. Each Honeywell business has these principles hanging on the wall, presenting Honeywell's approach to profits, integrity, customers, people, quality, decision making, and citizenship (see Exhibit 4).

> *"These seven items," explains Bonsignore, "are the formula responsible for the special chemistry that brings Honeywellers together as a family. People power, is the sine qua non of our business success as modern day corporations. . . . We are doing business in fast moving markets that are people intensive. . . . Our challenge is to overcome the cultural and communication differences that divide us, and ensure that every one of our employees knows how he or she can participate in the growth and prosperity of the corporation.*

This "people" principle is the driving force behind a variety of programs: Honeywell's active recruiting of minorities and "hire the handicapped" policies; an award given each year to good "people developers"; the adoption, during 1983 centennial celebrations, of Honeywell's theme "Together, we can find the answers"; programs to increase employee participation; and a stock plan to reward outstanding performance.

Employees are encouraged to demonstrate good citizenship by participating in charities and local volunteer activities. Honeywell prides itself on its social responsibility in designing products to regulate energy consumption, which help conserve natural resources. The integrity principle emphasizes the ethical conduct of business worldwide.

The culture, steeped in history and heritage, was expressed in a simple, one page declaration of values. Could these values provide the cohesiveness that Mike Bonsignore was looking for?

Corporate Culture, Europe-style

Bill George, Bonsignore's predecessor, described Honeywell's strategy for managing cultural diversity in the following terms:

> *. . . rather than try to force our foreign managers into an American mold, we attempt to draw upon the unique characteristics of managers in different parts of the world to strengthen our market position and our world*

organization. In the UK, the managers excel in interpersonal relationships and have led even the parent company in creating and effectively implementing progressive people programs. Consequently, we have begun to use our British affiliate as a creator and as a "test bed" for new human resource programs.

> *Our Italian management is known for its flexibility and its ability to respond rapidly to environmental changes. For this reason management responsibility for the Middle East, Mediterranean countries, and Africa has been given to a small regional office based in Milan. We have used the discipline and creativity of our German and Swiss organizations as a basis for major new product developments. Due to the international skills of our Belgian and Dutch organizations, we have located our European headquarters, our European distribution center, and our process automation center for Europe in these countries. . . . Finally, we continue to look to the US organization for strategic guidance, marketing skills, and basic technology.*

Mike Bonsignore, inspired by the popularity of corporate culture campaigns in the United States, began to think how corporate culture could create a "sense of togetherness" across the 14 countries, 11 languages, and more than 150 locations of Honeywell Europe. The Human Resource Advisory Board, created in 1984 under the direction of Dr. Hoss, the general manager of Austria and Germany, identified the key beliefs, values, and practices which it thought represented Honeywell. These beliefs echoed the original principles, but the board tried to show what they actually meant to people. A brochure was created which described each principle in detail, with specific examples (see Exhibit 5). It was translated into 8 languages and distributed worldwide. Only the United States kept the original one-page list of principles.

The European view of Honeywell's corporate culture was that it embodied solid midwestern American values—great concern and emphasis on people and family and a strong sense of moral values. One manager noted "a deep spiritual belief in people." Others used phrases such as "people person" in describing admired managers. Honeywell was seen as "a good honest company," "very straight," and "clean" in its business dealings.

Some of the negative aspects of the culture were considered to be its perceived paternalism and its reluctance to fire people. Honeywell was

Exhibit 5A *Honeywell Principles*

People are key to Honeywell's success. The company actively and affirmatively attracts and promotes the best people without regard to age, race, sex, creed, disability, or nationality, and rewards them on their performance.

Honeywell provides an environment for open, timely communications, safe working conditions, and opportunities for personal growth and accomplishment. Honeywell respects the dignity and privacy of individuals and believes in a climate of trust, cooperation and employee involvement.

Because people are Honeywell's greatest asset their interests are inseparable from the interests of the organization. Whether they are managers responsible for the direction, motivation and control of their staff; field personnel who build lasting relationships with their customers; or warehouse staff responsible for the control of goods—each and every person in Honeywell has a vital role to play in ensuring the company meets its objectives and remains profitable.

This people-orientation means that Honeywell personnel practices are based upon the importance of the individual, through whose efforts and abilities new ideas, solutions and working methods are developed. Our policies on promotion, training, career development, appraisal and compensation lead back to offering employees the opportunities for personal growth.

The fast-changing nature of our business means we have a much more informal operating style than many traditional companies. Employees are encouraged to work together across divisional and departmental boundaries, to contribute to decision-making and to suggest new ideas and better methods. In fact, many of our best results are achieved through team work. Also, significant efforts are being made, both through line managers and in-house publications, to give everyone more information about the company business and his or her own part in it. This increased communication will lead to more co-operation and greater involvement of employees at all levels.

Honeywell strives to attract the best people and to develop their talents to their full potential. A great deal of time and effort is spent in training and educating employees at all levels to ensure they have the correct technical and interpersonal skills for their work.

"If we don't provide a specific course internally, we arrange it outside and some 15-20% of our people attend. One man we sent was a designer. After the course he became a product manager, and now he's a supervisor. These training programmes can work."

Engineering Manager

"What motivates our people? The freedom to do what they want . . . it helps achieve some of our best results."

Information Management Manager

continued

Exhibit 5A continued

"The co-operative and informal feeling is apparent in locations throughout the world. One reason why we have been able to manage technology and develop customer confidence is that we can talk to each other quickly, informally and directly."

Ed Spencer

"Honeywell has always treated me fairly. As I've demonstrated what I would like, and was capable of, increased responsibility and challenge, management has made every effort to help me meet my individual goals. At the same time, because of their responsiveness, I've felt an increased desire to do everything I could to help make Honeywell successful."

Employee Relations Employee

Our appraisal systems are designed to develop the entire staff and encourage them in their personal advancement. Honeywell has an excellent record for internal promotion; and, although our approach to compensation and benefits is firmly rooted in a continuous and close assessment of the marketplace, our policies encourage and reward individual ability, skills and effort. Many of the divisions and operations have special programes and awards which recognize outstanding performance by their employees.

It is Honeywell's policy to respect the privacy of its employees and applicants. The dignity of the individual is important too—whether it's listening to a worker with a personal problem; devising a fair retirement plan; or securing a new position for a worker who, for health reasons, cannot continue in his or her present job.

The People Principle affirms the significance of people to the Honeywell enterprise at all times. Good employee relations are only achieved through the involvement and commitment of every individual. Our objective is to provide an environment that enables and rewards people for giving their best—both individually and on a team basis. Our low turnover of staff shows that Honeywell is a good company to work for and that the People Principle works.

Q. How can the People Principle help me to advance my career?

A. As a company, we provide you with the opportunities for personal growth through challenging job assignments and training, and the right atmosphere of communication and team work in which to develop your skills. However, in the end, it's up to each individual to put in the effort, to want to succeed.

Q. Why are there so few women in senior positions in the company?

A. Because of increased social awareness, more opportunities are being given to women and other minorities today than existed in the past. As more women enter the business world, Honeywell is responding by taking the appropriate steps to ensure that women have an equal chance to compete with other qualified candidates for advancement and success within the company. Today, women hold positions within Honeywell ranging from Regional Personnel Manager, to Director, Public Relations, and to Assistant Legal Advisor. This progression will continue as more and more candidates become qualified for advancement.

Source: Honeywell documentation.

ExhibitT 5B *Honeywell Principles*

Honeywell believes in the highest level of integrity and ethical behavior in relationships with customers, employees, shareholders, vendors, neighbours, and governments.

Business integrity has always been a keystone in Honeywell's dealings both inside and outside the company. By integrity we mean a code of conduct which requires honest, decent behavior. Honeywell has a reputation for trading in an ethical way and for providing top quality products and services. Whether at work or representing the company, Honeywell employees act in accordance with the high standards which have been set, even though, as individuals, they represent a considerable cross-section of people with different ideas, interests and values.

The Integrity Principle underlies the way we operate on a day-to-day basis. It forms the basis of our overall commitment to working together and dealing with each other fairly. Outside the company Honeywell has a lasting reputation for integrity and good citizenship which helps generate a positive company image. For example, if there's a problem or fault with one of our products, we take the necessary steps to examine all the products and make repairs wherever required. In dealing with customers, salespeople will often give impartial advice in an effort to match the customers' needs exactly.

Integrity does not make us less dynamic as a company. Indeed, knowing what is ethical and what is unacceptable makes us better equipped to form lasting relationships with the various groups with whom we transact business. Thus, our success and profit are achieved through responsible, well-considered policies.

Integrity is vital not only in dealing with our customers, but also in dealing with ourselves. Honeywell tries to treat its employees fairly, and its employees have responded in kind. From top management on down, Honeywell employees have maintained the highest ethical standards. This has been a continuing source of pride for Honeywell.

continued

Exhibit 5B continued

"In the late 1960s we discovered a fault in one of our gas valves which could have produced a dangerous leak. With 30,000 products already sold, we took our salesmen off the road to find these valves and repair them. We had to work closely with organisations like the British Gas Council which meant there was a lot of outside publicity. However, we received many letters from various people saying Honeywell had done a fabulous job, and sales increased accordingly."

Control Products Manager

"Honeywell imposes a code of conduct, a set of standards that is above the norm. There's a high level of integrity to be seen in Honeywell's top management."

Residential Employee

"Honeywell is a loyal employer. We always treat our people fairly. We always try to find an equitable solution."

Information Management Manager

"We are able to deal with each other in direct, open and honest ways which make our work more enjoyable as well as successful."

Ed Spencer

In accordance with the Integrity Principle, Honeywell would rather give up business opportunities than lower its ethical standards. As a result, Honeywell's record remains untarnished, and its reputation for integrity is still valued as highly today as it was a century ago.

Q. I know Honeywell is an honest company, but how does that affect me as an individual?

A. Honeywell has a reputation for trading in an ethical way, so it has certain high standards in which it operates. It is because of these standards that everyone who works for Honeywell knows what is expected of him or her in this regard. We expect that when any employee is either at work or representing Honeywell he or she will act within the standards the company has set. The integrity for which Honeywell is known is a direct result of the high standards its employees have maintained.

Q. I understand integrity when it comes to dealing with customers, shareholders and governments, but how does it apply to me inside the company?

A. It is important that we are all honest with each other in our work. If you expect your manager to be straight and fair with you, then it's obvious he expects the same from you. And that applies equally to anyone who works with you. Think of those you serve as customers—people to whom you're responsible for providing a service, and you'll see why employees are included as a key group within the Integrity Principle.

Source: Honeywell documentation.

"not a company that focused very much on performance" and it was "slow to change, slow to get moving . . . and not much of a risk taker."

Although there were fewer than ever American expats in Europe, some complained that the culture was "very American," which meant "not listening," being too concerned with the short term, making decisions with too few facts or numbers only, neglecting local input, and standardizing based on US practices. These concerns needed to be taken into account in adapting strategies and policies to Europe, particularly the human resource programs which had been quite successful in the States.

HUMAN RESOURCE (HR) PROGRAMS

The Human Resources Advisory Board met quarterly to align human resource policies across Europe and to support strategic HR initiatives. Three developments were identified as priorities: upgrading the quality of the work force, leadership development, and performance management.

Upgrading the Work Force

Changing technology and marketing requirements were pushing Honeywell to focus on integrating systems rather than concentrating on products. But Honeywell was a "high-tech company with a low tech work force." The push to upgrade the work force was also driven by perceptions that the average age of employees was too high and the educational level too low. In one Center of Excellence's engineering group only 10 of its 40 employees were engineers. The rest had worked their way "up from the floor" and were unable to cope with advanced software and micro-digital technology. The Center reacted by doubling the number of engineers within a year and a half. It sent non-engineers to manufacturing and hired young graduates.

Leadership Development

Leadership development focused on identifying and preparing leaders through succession and career path planning. In the United Kingdom, a sudden void was created by the early retirement of the general manager and the unexpected death of the number 2 man who was very charismatic. Toby Warson, an American from the Aerospace and Defense division, was told to "strap on his gun and go and fix it." He considered as his primary objective "to turn this company back to the Brits."

Performance Management

The performance management program was set up to improve productivity. John Buck, the human resource director in Brussels, described it as

> *an integrated approach that requires having a culture that is performance driven . . . it's looking at all the practices ranging from recruitment to selection, to setting objectives, to setting standards, to giving feedback, praising people, paying people, management style, all those practices.*

Focusing on quality, two-day quality colleges were set up to teach the Crosby philosophy—"getting the job done right the first time, and understanding the cost of failing to do so." A semi-annual quality awareness day was also introduced. Quality policy statements were placed behind the reception desk of all sales offices. However, Bonsignore reiterated that "the quality-through-people theme allows each national environment to implement the process in its own way."

European Reactions to the HR Programs

Some of these programs provoked unexpected reactions. "The title, 'upgrading the quality of the work force,' was interpreted as insulting to our current work force. Today we call it upgrading work force skills." Lammert Hielema, Holland's general manager, considered the policy as "a gross misunderstanding of the European educational system." He pointed out that although many people did not hold university degrees, his affiliate was the most successful.

The career pathing system developed by Brussels was described as unrealistic by one HR manager. Since there was little room for upward mobility, he preferred not to raise false hopes. He thought that Europeans were more "realistic" as they did not consider success to depend on reaching a certain level at a certain point in time. The UK HR manager added that "we're certainly not going to write things down about people . . . we're nervous about doing that, feeling that it is too sensitive."

The quality program was also seen as an American preoccupation. "Americans see quality improvement as a program and not as a process."

Some national subsidiaries had already taken measures to assure quality. Others saw it as another example of Honeywell starting a project and then not following it through far enough to get results. One HR manager deplored,

> the time and money that has been wasted in trying to operate programs like that without really understanding what it was about. . . . Nobody really knew how to take that into their work place and put it into practice.

Management by objectives (MBO) was used throughout the company to reinforce performance management. But one general manager felt that the MBO system encouraged short-term thinking and profit and contributed to lowering objectives. Unachieved goals "looked lousy and affected one's personal income . . . [as a result] over the last 7 years we downgraded our goals."

But Europe was soon to face more fundamental challenges than implementing human resource policies: 1986 was to be a year of radical change for Honeywell, both in the United States and in Europe.

1986: RESTRUCTURING HONEYWELL, INC.

By 1986, Honeywell was doing worldwide business in five technology segments—Industrial Controls, Commercial Building Controls, Residential Energy Management, Business Computers, and Aerospace and Defense. Sales in 1985 reached $6,624 million. International revenues represented 25% of total sales (see Exhibit 6) of which Europe, Honeywell's largest overseas market, generated two-thirds. Trouble, however, was brewing at corporate headquarters in Minneapolis. Honeywell lost $398 million in 1986 (see Exhibit 7) and takeover rumors began to circulate.

In response, Honeywell redefined its strategy and undertook major changes. The goals were clear: (1) streamline—have all business units be a number one or a strong number two in their mar-

kets; and (2) lead in volume with broader and stronger distribution than competitors. Three short-term targets were set: improving margins, making major acquisitions to strengthen core businesses, and resolving the future of the HIS division.

Extensive cost-cutting began. The worldwide work force was reduced by 4,000 people (4%), factories were consolidated, and some ventures were terminated. Only marketing and engineering, thought essential for the long term, were left untouched.

Honeywell next sold a majority interest in HIS, which had been losing money, through a joint venture with France's Compagnie des Machines Bull and Japan's NEC Corporation.

Sperry Aerospace Group was bought for $1,029 billion, giving Honeywell a solid position in the avionics instrument market. The Aerospace and Defense division, which absorbed the Sperry acquisition, had doubled its share of Honeywell's total business, from 25% to 50%.

Emphasis shifted from technology to marketing. Businesses were aligned by market, leaving the new organization with four divisions: Aerospace and Defense, Home and Building Automation and Control, Industrial Automation and Control, and International.

Bonsignore realized that he was leaving at a crucial time. So much had been accomplished to integrate Honeywell, Europe: the regional vice presidents; the European Policy Committee; the Centers of Excellence; and the Human Resource Advisory Board. These mechanisms had created the coordinated and cohesive organization he left as his legacy in Europe. He wondered what the impact of restructuring would be, just when everything had been going so well. Would efforts to unify Europe withstand the pressures of change? Would they facilitate or impede his vision of a global approach? What challenges awaited his successor, J. P. Rosso, former executive VP of HIS and the first European to be appointed president of Honeywell, Europe?

Exhibit 6 *Revenue by Geographic Region (Dollars in Millions)*

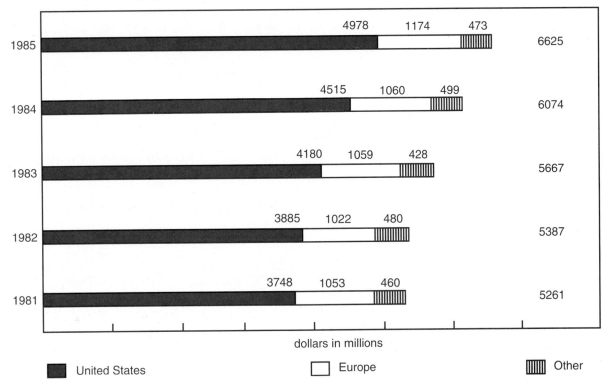

dollars in millions

■ United States   □ Europe   ▥ Other

Exhibit 7A *Financial Highlights, Annual Report 1986, Honeywell, Inc. and Consolidated Subsidiaries*

	1986	1985
	(Dollars in millions except per share amounts)	
Sales	$5,378.2	$4,992.8
Income before income taxes	39.8	336.9
Income from continuing operations[1]	12.9	219.6
Net income (loss)	(398.1)	281.6
Earnings per common share		
continuing operations[1]	.28	4.80
Net income (loss)	(8.83)	6.16
Cash dividends per common share	2.00	1.95
Stockholders' equity per common share	48.67	56.08

Source: Annual Report 1986.

[1]Income from continuing operations for 1986 was reduced by $134.4 ($2.98 per share) as a result of nonrecurring items (see Note 6 to financial statements) and by $42.3 ($0.94 per share) as a result of the write-down of certain inventories to net realizable value, equipment write-offs and the accrual for anticipated nonrecoverable costs related to contracts.

Exhibit 7B *Income Statement, Honeywell, Inc. and Consolidated Subsidiaries*

		For the Years Ended December 31		
		1986	1985	1984
		(dollars and shares in millions except per share amounts)		
Sales		$5,378.2	$4,992.8	$4,537.0
Costs and expenses	Cost of sales	3,848.1	3,497.3	3,146.6
	Research and development	246.7	242.1	218.7
	Selling, general and administrative	972.5	865.6	768.6
	Nonrecurring items	219.4		
		5,286.7	4,605.0	4,133.9
Interest	Interest expense	79.7	82.5	73.0
	Interest income	28.0	31.6	45.5
		51.7	50.9	27.5
Income from continuing Operations before income taxes		39.8	336.9	375.6
Income taxes	Provision	26.9	117.3	131.3
	Adjustment related to DISC			(40.0)
Income from continuing operations		12.9	219.6	284.3
Discontinued operations	Income (loss) from discontinued operations net of income taxes	(3.3)	55.8	25.3
	Recovery (loss) on disposal of discontinued operations net of income taxes	(407.7)	6.2	(70.6)
Net income (loss)		$ (398.1)	$ 281.6	$ 239.0
Earnings (loss) per common share	Continuing operations	$ .28	$ 4.80	$ 6.06
	Discontinued operations	(.07)	1.22	.54
	Recovery (loss) on disposal of discontinued operations	(9.04)	.14	(1.50)
	Net income (loss)	$ (8.83)	$ 6.16	$ 5.10
Average number of common shares outstanding		45.1	45.7	46.9

Source: Annual Report 1986.

Exhibit 7C *Balance Sheet, Honeywell, Inc. and Consolidated Subsidiaries*

Assets		1986	1985
		(dollars in millions)	
Current assets	Cash and temporary cash investments	$ 119.5	$ 446.9
	Receivables	918.0	922.3
	Inventories	949.0	801.2
		1,986.5	2,170.4
Investments and advances	Finance subsidiaries	140.4	143.2
	Other companies	250.8	187.3
		391.2	330.5
Property, plant, and equipment	Property, plant, and equipment	2,178.2	1,811.5
	Less accumulated depreciation	843.5	723.9
		1,334.7	1,087.6
Other assets	Long-term receivables	35.2	13.7
	Goodwill	81.7	124.1
	Patents, licenses, and trademarks	234.2	
	Software and other intangibles	338.4	
	Other	98.3	94.2
	Net assets of discontinued operations	638.8	681.0
Total assets		$5,139.0	$4,501.5

Source: Annual Report 1986.

HONEYWELL EUROPE (B)

Susan C. Schneider, Lenny Hansen, and Avivah Wittenberg-Cox
INSEAD, France

Honeywell's restructuring took Europe by surprise. The region had been doing very well. Profits and performance were up and Europe felt that it was gaining clout in the worldwide organization. In 1987, sales passed the $1 billion mark (on Honeywell sales of $5½ billion) of which 80% came from products designed, produced, and sold in Europe (see Exhibit 1). Of the 18,000 employees working outside of the United States, only 150 were American.

The sudden shift in priorities, the image change, and the layoffs were felt to be "traumatic" and largely incomprehensible to European eyes. Europe's role in a restructured Honeywell was not clear and adapting to new strategies was often difficult. Honeywell was seen as an "entirely different company than it was a year ago."

REACTIONS TO STRATEGIC REORIENTATION

Europe's image of Honeywell was confused by the sale of the computer business. The Honeywell Information Systems (HIS) divestiture was "particularly difficult for the Europeans to digest. It was a very successful business in Europe . . . which exported to the US." Particularly in the United Kingdom, customers and employees had identified Honeywell with the prestigious computer industry—not with thermostats. The Sperry acquisition and increased importance of Aerospace and Defense (A&D) "changed the face of the company." National affiliates were concerned that their own activities would be less valued, because A&D, primarily an American market, represented less than 10% of European operations. Important positions had been filled with people from A&D and people began referring to the "A&D Mafia."

FROM TECHNOLOGY TO MARKETING

The reorganization pushed Honeywell to become more marketing driven and less focused on technology. "Honeywell is typically an expensive product, high in quality and reliability . . . but sometimes it's not too related to what the market wants." The campaign to make the company more market driven was seen as "unnatural" and "painful." One manager said that he was "fighting the environment, which is strongly product oriented." He wanted the customer to be happy, but was unable to know what would make him so because his marketing people tended to be product planners and designers.

Some said that understanding the local market was difficult because marketing had traditionally been a US responsibility. HESA marketing directors were Americans who "tended to extrapolate from . . . a US marketing sales environment, when the European market is absolutely different . . . not only in style but also in competition." The problem was exacerbated by the rapid rotation of people in the position.

CORPORATE CULTURE CHANGES

Honeywell's "family" corporate culture was badly hit by the layoffs. European reactions reflected attitudes to changes in the company's overall culture. Perceptions of how "nice the company was"

Exhibit 1 *Honeywell and the European Community*

This document reflects Honeywell's wish to extend its role as a partner in the development of the technological and economic resources of the European Community. Honeywell is a strong supporter of the Community's program for the creation of an open internal market. The company is actively participating in progress toward 1992 and is committed to continuing its contribution to the future.

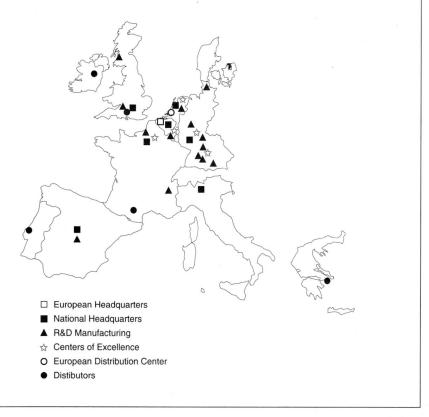

□ European Headquarters
■ National Headquarters
▲ R&D Manufacturing
☆ Centers of Excellence
○ European Distribution Center
● Distibutors

continued

Exhibit 1 continued

LOCATIONS AND PRINCIPAL ACTIVITIES
(Employees—November 1988)
Belgium/Luxembourg:
Brussels   • national headquarters (278)
                  • Center of Excellence: Honeywell Process Automation
                    Centre (PACE) (155)
                  • European headquarters (106)
Denmark:
Copenhagen   • national headquarters (123)
France:
Paris   • national headquarters (378)
Amiens   • Center of Excellence: Honeywell European Factory
                    Application Center (EFAC) (flame safeguard controls,
                    factory automation controls and systems) (243)
Grenoble   • photo-electric switches, automatic lighting controls,
                    safety floors and safety barriers (63)
Toulouse   • commercial aviation service center (70)
Germany:
Offenbach   • national headquarters (779)
                  • head office of Honeywell Regelsysteme
Gammertingen   • mechanical control products for heating systems (60)
Kiel   • marine systems and sonar equipment (300)
Maintal   • Center of Excellence: Building Automation and Con-
                    trols (heating, ventilating, and air conditioning con-
                    trols and systems) (1233)
                  • industrial process control valves, ultrasonic sensors,
                    proximity switches, laser gyros, components and sub-
                    systems for aerospace and defense
Mosbach   • Center of Excellence: Water Products (518)
Munich   • optoelectronics (5)
Schoenaich   • electronic and electromechanical energy management
                    and comfort control products (659)
Wiehl   • programmable controls and automation systems (180)
Greece:
Athens   • distributor
Ireland:
Dublin   • distributor
Italy:
Milan   • national headquarters (329)
Netherlands:
Amsterdam   • national headquarters (404)
Hoofddorp   • Honeywell European Distribution Center (119)
Emmen   • Center of Excellence: Combustion Controls (home
                    heating and flame safeguard controls) (654)

Portugal:

Lisbon   • distributor

Spain:

Madrid   • national headquarters (204)
                 • industrial process control instruments, power supply
                   units, and building automation data-gathering panels

United Kingdom:

Bracknell   • national headquarters (1954)

Corsham   • components and sub-systems for aerospace and
                   defense (310)

Newhouse   • precision switches, solid-state sensors, heating/venti-
                   lation controls, air-cleaning equipment, integrated
                   process plant information and control systems, micro-
                   processor-based process control systems (940)

Basingstoke   • commercial aviation service center (71)

Honeywell Europe is a controls company: the corporation ceded its business computer interests in 1987, in line with a strategic decision to concentrate on the controls and automation business. It is rated by industry observers as the world's leading specialist in controls technology.

Honeywell Europe provides products, systems, and services to a variety of market sectors:

In **Residential and Commercial buildings**, the company's activities contribute to providing environmental comfort, reducing energy consumption and operating costs, and improving security.

In the **Industrial sector**, the company provides systems used in the control and optimization of manufacturing processes in refineries, petrochemical and fine chemicals plants, pulp and paper and food processing industries. Industrial components are used to sense and control the handling and packaging of products, and to command and control functions in appliances, automobiles, computers.

In **Aerospace and Defense**, the company's technologies are used in aircraft flight control and navigation systems, in training systems, as well as in Western Europe's defense programs.

Honeywell's arrival in Europe dates back to 1934: from a single sales company established that year in the Netherlands, Honeywell Europe has since grown into an organization present in all European countries.

With a total turnover well over one billion ECUs, Honeywell Europe makes an important contribution to the economies and technologies of member states of the European Community.

Eighty percent of Honeywell's revenue in Europe is derived from European-based design, manufacturing, and service activities.

Employment: Honeywell Europe employs 11,000 people in Western Europe, 90 percent of them in Community member states.

continued

Exhibit 1 continued

Manufacturing: the company operates 14 manufacturing units in Belgium, France, Germany, the Netherlands, Spain, and the United Kingdom.

Assets: Honeywell currently has assets in Europe valued at over 800 million ECUs.

R&D: Honeywell has five research and development centers within the European Community—in Belgium, France, Germany, the Netherlands, and the United Kingdom. Honeywell Europe's annual R&D budget, including customer-funded projects, is estimated at over 50 million ECUs (5% of revenue). Current high-technology projects include energy management and building management systems, "smart" ultrasonic and optical sensors, distributed process control systems, and optical "safety curtains" for use in factory automation.

Centers of Excellence: an integral part of the company's development strategy is to create Centers of Excellence, which assume European or worldwide responsibility for progress in specific aspects of the company's technologies. To date, of the six Centers of Excellence in Europe, five are established within the Community (Belgium, France, Germany (2), and the Netherlands).

Distribution: in anticipation of the Single Market, Honeywell operates a European Distribution Center at Hoofddorp in the Netherlands. It is the central warehouse and expediting facility serving all Honeywell Europe sales offices, factories and Centers of Excellence. All intercompany trading is conducted in ECUs.

Education and Training: Honeywell is committed to offering outstanding educational opportunities to its employees and customers through a network of Technical Training Centers in Italy, Germany, Belgium, and the UK and a centralized Management Development Center in Brussels.

The Honeywell "Futurist" Competition: this annual contest, introduced by Honeywell Europe in 1985, invites young people from Europe's universities to give their views on the technological trends of the future. Awards are adjudicated by a distinguished panel of European academics and industrialists.

The company has a record of participation in major European research projects: these include a joint study into the development of a European Language System (ELS), a contract from the European Space Agency to supply systems to the European Space Research and Technology Center (ESTEC) and to the European Space Operations Center (ESOC), and a participation in association with other European companies in the ESPRIT II Home Systems Project for the development of communication standards in the home of the future.

Source: Honeywell documentation.

had been affected, as had management performance. One manager described his major task during the restructuring as one of protecting his people from the disorientation and low morale felt in the United States. He considered that the company had violated its own people principle.

Other managers, however, thought the redundancies were "normal housecleaning" and necessary because in the past, Honeywell had been "too nice." The social context in Europe had also evolved so that layoffs, which would have been very difficult 10 years earlier, were now considered acceptable.

HESA'S ROLE

HESA's role had also been questioned. According to Mr. Ferrari, VP of Finance and Administration,

> the one that really made the difference in the relationship between headquarters and the affiliates was Mike (Bonsignore). He was the one who cut the headquarters by 30 people . . . he wanted to have this office more strategically oriented.

National affiliates took over some of HESA's functions and Brussels emphasized coordination and policy rather than operations. The marketing director retired and was not replaced and most of the marketing staff, many of whom were Americans, were relocated to Centers of Excellence.

> "No longer an ivory tower," headquarters had evolved from playing referee to being "one of the players."

But some managers complained that Brussels wanted to be more deeply involved in decisions now and that while affiliates still made decisions locally, the approval process was heavier. Some people thought HESA had no role at all and one general manager gave it another five years to live.

> People have wondered for years why we have this expensive European headquarters? What do they add to the business?

GLOBALIZATION

Bonsignore, as executive VP of Honeywell's International Division, has a slightly different view now. From Minneapolis, he sees International consisting of five divisions: Europe, Asia Pacific, Latin America, Canada, and the United States. His ambition is to make Honeywell a truly global company.

> We are a midwestern, US-based, conservative company and this globalization process is tending to raise the awareness level that we're not a US business anymore.

He considers that the company's global distribution network and worldwide revenue base give Honeywell globalized competitive leverage.

> We went from a domestic US company to an international US company to a multinational company and now we're trying to make this final move to a really global company . . .

Yet the meaning of "global" is far from clear. The following definitions reflect some of the diverse meanings that the word holds across Honeywell.

> What is really meant by globalization . . . putting all your manufacturing resources together?

> Global means providing consistent products and services wherever a customer comes in contact with the company around the world.

> Global strategy doesn't mean anything . . . some products could have a global strategy, others not.

> Unless all customers are the same, which is not the case for the time being, a global solution is certainly not the way that we are going to solve all the customer problems.

What does the future hold for Honeywell as it attempts to consolidate the lessons of its European integration and apply them to even broader, global boundaries? Opinions again diverge but reveal some of what has been learned, and some of what has not. Some are pessimistic:

> "We are more American than ever before. We are a US company and we've got exports . . . the change from a computer company to A&D is going to reinforce that . . . 50% of the business is now A&D which is principally a US market. The newly acquired Sperry is very American. And computers, which is a global business, disappeared. Chances are that we will have difficulty in becoming a global company.

Others are hopeful:

> "The only way we're going to be able to [go global] is to have sensitive people who are willing to be mobile and really have international careers . . . it's very important that global strategies are formulated by people who can understand the driving forces.

NOTE ON THE HOSPITAL MANAGEMENT INDUSTRY

Paul Shrivastava
Bucknell University

The American Hospital Association defines a hospital as "an establishment that provides—through an organized medical or professional staff, permanent facilities that include in-patient beds, medical services, and continuous nursing services—diagnosis and treatment, both surgical and non-surgical, for patients who have any of a variety of medical conditions." There are basically two types of hospitals: Investor owned, for-profit hospitals and not-for-profit hospitals owned by charitable and religious institutions.

Historically, for-profit hospitals were owned and operated by the physicians who staffed them. In the past two decades, the trend is toward hospital ownership by publicly held companies. Unlike not-for-profit hospitals, the for-profit hospitals are subject to federal and state income taxes. The focus of this note is for-profit hospitals.

The hospital industry is an exciting part of the overall health care industry. Until the end of this century, health care is expected to experience rapid growth. It will continue to be fundamentally changed by radical technological innovations in biotechnology and medical instrumentation. Evolving regulations and progressive privatization are other significant forces that make this industry one of the most dynamic in the 1990s.

Several strategic issues facing participants in the hospital management industry need to be analyzed.

1. What is the competitive structure of this industry? How is it changing? What are the key determinants of profitability in the industry? How can industry participants cope with the changing competitive structure of the industry?
2. When and in what form will consolidation occur in this industry? Is privatization likely to increase? How will regulations affect profitability?
3. What sources of competitive advantage are available to firms in this industry? What competitive strategies should key firms, such as Hospital Corporation of America, Community Psychiatric Inc., and National Medical Enterprises, adopt to succeed in this industry?
4. What are the most viable organizational structures for prospering in this industry? How can internal conflicts between clinical professionals (doctors) and hospital administrators be managed to improve efficiency?

Background information for examining these issues is provided in this note.

In 1987, there were 6,366 hospitals in the United States, distributed as follows:

US Hospitals by ownership:	Number	Percentage	% Inpatient Bed Capacity
Government/State	2,112	33.2%	38.2%
Non-governmental	. . .	. . .	. . .
Not-for-profit	3,323	52.2%	53.9%
For profit	931	14.6%	7.9%
	6,366	100%	100%

Exhibit 1 shows the largest hospital management companies.

A HISTORICAL PERSPECTIVE ON THE HOSPITAL MANAGEMENT INDUSTRY

Organized hospitals are a twentieth century phenomenon. They emerged in early 1900s to meet the requirements of large-scale scientific medical practice. The development of surgery and radiology, and the need for antiseptic conditions, necessitated establishment of large hospital institutions that could economically provide support services to doctors. Prior to this time, most medical care was administered in private homes and doctors' offices. The efficiency and usefulness of these large-scale institutions was also demonstrated during the two World Wars. After the wars, hospitals became the most effective means for delivering high-quality health care on a mass scale.

By mid-1950, a large hospital capacity had been built by state and voluntary organizations. The package of Medicare and Medicaid legislation in 1965 led to a revival of investor-owned hospitals. Most important in sparking this renewed interest was the creation of a potentially large government-paid demand and legislative provisions that allowed investor-owned hospitals to achieve a reasonable return on equity on government-reimbursed services. Most of the investor-owned hospitals were owned by small groups of physicians or entrepreneurs, and thus they were not in a position to capitalize on the new boom. Many were also short of capital, inefficiently operated, unable to control the inflationary increases in expenses, and incapable of dealing effectively with increasingly complex government regulations.

This situation created an opportunity for new firms to enter the industry. In the late 1960s, more than 30 hospital management companies were organized. The fledgling companies built some new hospitals themselves, but nearly all of the growth came from acquisitions. By 1970, hospital management firms had acquired 246 investor-owned hospitals with 25,135 beds. This represented 24% and 39%, respectively, of the investor-owned hospitals and beds.

Stock prices of hospital management companies collapsed in the general economic recession in 1972, thereby making the acquisition route for growth more difficult. Most hospital management companies shifted their emphasis in two directions. First, they moved increasingly toward construction activities, which were financed with internal cash flow and unused debt capacity. By 1975 however, industry debt ratios had risen as high as 75% of capitalizations and construction slowed in the industry. The second major thrust of the management firms was into management contracts. They sought contracts to manage existing facilities for a share in the profits. This trend was prompted by financial constraints that prompted hospital management firms to seek ways of achieving growth that were less capital intensive than ownership.

GENERAL ENVIRONMENT OF THE HOSPITAL MANAGEMENT INDUSTRY

The hospital management industry is a part of the complex overall health care system in the United States, as shown in Exhibit 2. Health services are available in several formats (hospitals, health maintainence organizations, home health services, etc.), which creates several health care markets. A unique feature of this industry is that payment for

Exhibit 1 *Hospital Management Companies: Number and Size of US Hospitals Owned (1985)*

	Hospitals	Beds
Hospital Corporation of America	230	37,409
American Medical International	116	17,751
Humana, Inc.	83	16,939
Charter Medical Corporation	58	5,962
National Medical Enterprises, Inc.	50	8,053
Community Psychiatric Centers, Inc.	22	1,990
Total	559	80,051
Percentage of total investor-owned	52.9%	69.1%

Source: Statistical Profile, Federation of American Health Systems, 1986.

over two thirds of all health services consumed in the United States comes from private insurance companies or from government third-party payment systems. These markets and their respective business associates interact in complex ways to shape intramarket and intermarket competition among health care providers. To understand the general environment of this industry, we must examine some basic demographic trends and government policies on health care.

Demographic Trends in Health Care

Demand for health care services is directly related to the size and age of the population. Exhibit 3 shows the growth and aging of the US population. There is an unmistakable trend toward a "graying America" in the estimates to the year 2000. While total population will grow at .8% per year, the above-65-year segment will grow at 2.8% per year. Exhibits 4 and 5 show the implications of this aging on health care services—longer and more intensive services, more expensive services, and more frequent services than for younger populations.

These demographics have resulted in ever-increasing expenditures on health care services, as shown in Exhibit 6. These expenditures as a percentage of the gross national product (GNP) have also grown dramatically in the past decade, as shown in Exhibit 7.

Increases in health care expenditures have routinely outstripped inflation, and they reached a staggering 11.8% of GNP in 1987. About 28% of the money spent on health care in 1985 came directly from patients, about 30% came from private insurance companies, and the rest came through the third-party payment system established by the government over the past three decades. Government policy has been a prime force in shaping the health care industry.

Government Regulation of Health Care Costs

Hospitals operate in an environment where a large portion of their costs are borne by the federal government. The government traditionally reimbursed a hospital for 100% of costs incurred while treating Medicare patients. For the average hospital, this program provided no incentive for cost controls because 42% of its patient base was made up of Medicare patients.

The rapid escalation of health care costs prompted the federal government to change its method of Medicare reimbursement. It instituted the Prospective Payment System (PPS) in October 1983, creating perhaps the largest change in the industry since the 1940s. Under the PPS, a hospital recieves a predetermined fee for each patient admitted. This fee is based on a complex calculation that takes into account such factors as the patient's diagnosis, historical cost structure of the admitting hospital, and hospital location. Each type of treatment and illness has now been categorized into a Diagnostic Related Group (DRG). Each DRG has a fixed predetermined fee set by the government. A hospital must collect any fees over and above this predetermined rate directly from the patient. Due to the difficulty in assigning mental illness to DRG categories, all psychiatric services are presently exempt from the PPS.

Exhibit 2 *Competitive Forces in the Health Care Industry*

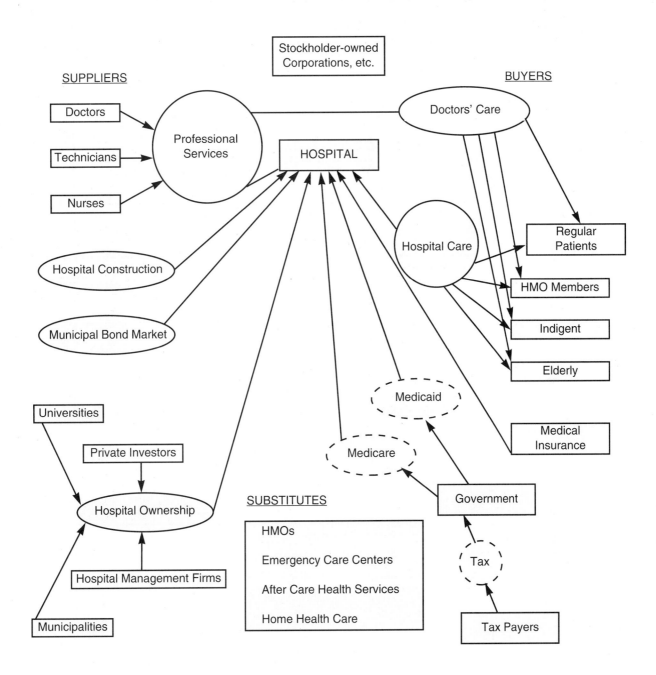

POTENTIAL ENTRANTS

Stockholder-owned Corporations, etc.

SUPPLIERS

BUYERS

Doctors

Technicians

Nurses

Professional Services

Doctors' Care

HOSPITAL

Hospital Care

Regular Patients

HMO Members

Indigent

Elderly

Medical Insurance

Hospital Construction

Municipal Bond Market

Medicaid

Medicare

Universities

Private Investors

Hospital Ownership

Hospital Management Firms

Municipalities

SUBSTITUTES

HMOs

Emergency Care Centers

After Care Health Services

Home Health Care

Government

Tax

Tax Payers

Exhibit 3 Population Trends (Millions)

	1965	1970	1975	1980	1981	1982	1983	1984	1985	1990E	1995E	2000E
Total Population	196.7	207.5	217.5	227.7	230.0	232.3	234.5	236.7	238.6	249.7	259.6	268.0
Population 65+	18.5	20.1	22.7	25.1	26.3	26.9	27.5	28.0	28.7	31.8	34.0	35.0

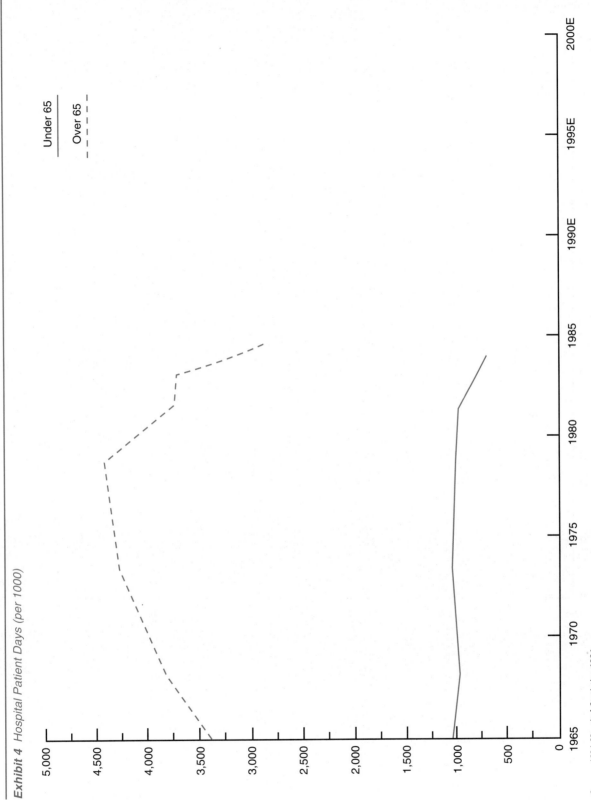

Exhibit 4 *Hospital Patient Days (per 1000)*

Under 65

Over 65

5,000

4,500

4,000

3,500

3,000

2,500

2,000

1,500

1,000

500

0

1965   1970   1975   1980   1985   1990E   1995E   2000E

Source: AHA Hospital Statistics, 1986.

Exhibit 5 *Hospital Admissions (per 1000)*

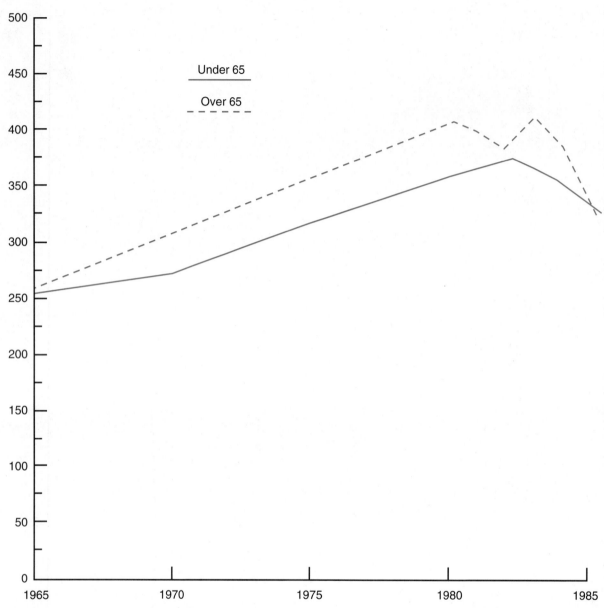

Source: *AHA Hospital Statistics*, 1986.

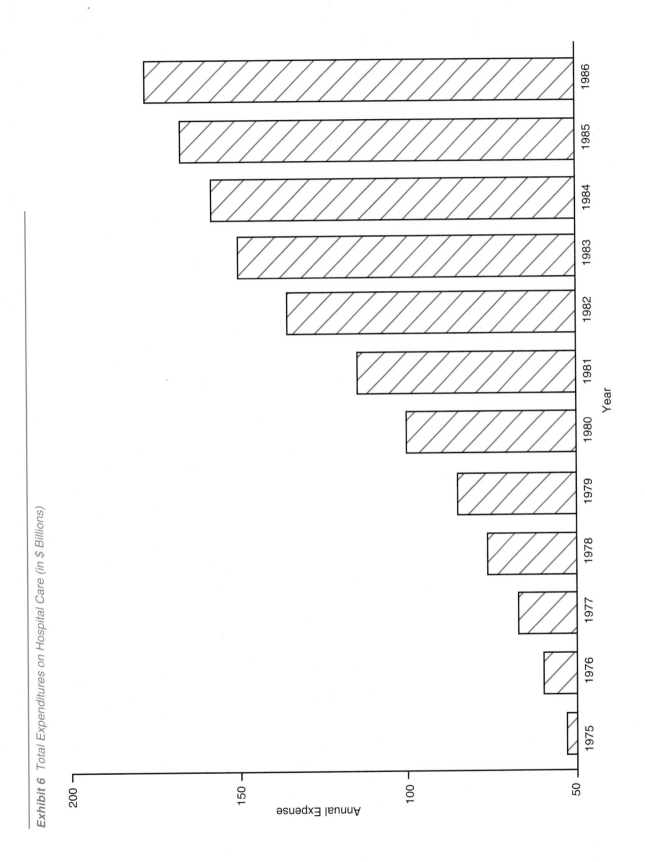

Exhibit 6 Total Expenditures on Hospital Care (in $ Billions)

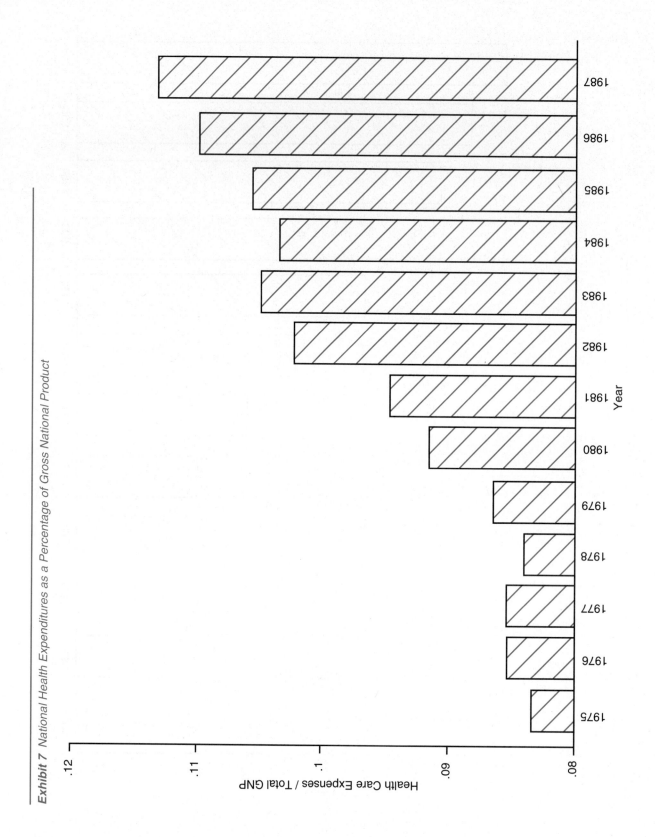

Exhibit 7 *National Health Expenditures as a Percentage of Gross National Product*

Over the three-year phase-in period, the PPS has forced hospitals to begin to control and reduce their operating costs in order to survive. It has also prompted private insurers to study the implementation of similar programs to reduce their health insurance costs. Although the PPS currently includes only the operating costs of a hospital, it is anticipated that capital costs, which are now 100% reimbursed, will one day be part of the PPS reimbursement restrictions.

The PPS has also injected a new level of uncertainty into a hospital's operating environment. The DRG reimbursement formula changes annually and must be approved by Congress. The primary change each year is in the updating factor that is used to adjust for inflation.

The result of the advent of the PPS has been a reorientation of hospitals toward controlling costs and watching the bottom line. The large for-profit chains have generally fared better under the PPS because their costs were lower, whereas many of the small community hospitals have closed their doors because of continual losses. No one, however, has come through the past three years unscathed. The six leading for-profit hospital chains posted average earnings growth of 39% in 1983 versus 16% in 1985. Thus, all health care entities must reevaluate their current operations in order to survive in this new environment.

COMPETITION IN THE HOSPITAL MANAGEMENT INDUSTRY

Competition in the hospital management industry is a curious combination of dynamic technological and regulatory changes coupled with rather slow-changing management and institutional customers who pay for individual consumers of services.

Customers

The three major groups of customers of hospital care are the government, employers through insurance companies, and individual consumers. In 1985, $170.6 billion, or 4.7% of that year's GNP, was spent for hospital care in the United States. Of this amount, the federal government spent $75.1 billion (44%); state and local governments, $18.8 billion (11%); private health insurance companies, $63.1 billion (37%); individuals, $11.9 billion (7%);

and other private sources, mainly through philanthropy, $1.7 billion (1%).

Since the 1965 establishment of Medicaid and Medicare, the federal, state, and local governments have been, by far, the largest customers for hospital services. In 1982, the Tax Equity and Fiscal Responsibility Act (TEFRA) established the DRGs, which dramatically changed the cost structure of the hospital industry.

Employers, through insurance companies, are the second largest purchasers of hospital care. Employee insurance premiums can be a significant cost to corporations. For example, Goodyear estimates that $2 of a $57 tire is used to pay for employee health care.

Industry is responding to this cost pressure in three ways: (1) by forming industry coalitions, (2) by bargaining individually with the health care providers, and (3) by encouraging their employees to reduce health care costs. Currently, there are at least 130 private business coalitions formed with the specific purpose of reducing health care costs. Some companies are bargaining individually with the health care providers. Insurance companies and employers are forming Preferred Provider Organizations (PPOs), which negotiate volume discounts from doctors and hospitals. Currently 330 PPOs exist, but this number is expected to increase dramatically.

Finally, firms are encouraging their employees to reduce health care costs (1) by requiring second opinions for surgical procedures, (2) by encouraging the use of substitute serves such as health maintenance organizations (HMOs), (3) by requiring larger copayments, and (4) by encouraging disease prevention.

Individual consumers' power in this industry is linked to their ability to switch between suppliers. Individuals have become more selective in choosing hospitals. Their choice is based on their changing family requirements, insurance coverage, location, and need for different types of services. However, switching between facilities is often constrained by insurance contracts, which usually require the insured person to stay with their choice for at least one year.

Cost of Services and Supplies

The cost of operating hospitals depends on the cost of labor, consumable goods, and equipment.

Suppliers to the industry fall into three groups: labor, consumable goods and equipment, and capital. Each group has multiple small- and medium-sized suppliers. Individually, their products have little importance to hospital services. In some areas such as labor (particularly physicians, nurses, and technicians), an oversupply and regional imbalances exist. Regional imbalances are caused by a preference of doctors and nurses to work in urban areas over rural areas. Moreover, hospitals are reducing their need for labor by concentrating on efficiency.

Labor. At present growth rates and utilization levels, a projected 70,000 excess physicians will exist by 1990. For the period 1984 through 1990, the government expects a 2.5% growth rate in the number of practicing physicians. This growth rate is almost three times the expected growth rate of the general population. Currently, there are 2.1 doctors per 1,000 people, which is at par with standards in European countries. At these growth rates, by 1990, there will be 2.25 doctors per 1,000.

In addition, with the trend toward higher efficiency in the hospital industry, the need for nurses and other medical support personnel should drop. Technological develoments are also reducing the need for some forms of nursing services. For example, Abbott Laboratories has developed a medication delivery system in which patients can self-administer pain-relieving drugs. Smith Kline Beckman developed Monocid, an antibiotic that can be injected just once daily instead of the typical three to four times a day, thus reducing the need for nursing care and increasing hospital fficiency.

Union activity increased only moderately in the 1980s. This can be traced to (1) downsizing of the hospital industry and employee fear of replacement, (2) the fact that the "easy" places have been unionized, and (3) less effort by unions to unionize. In addition, Reagan's pro management stance made unionizing activities more difficult. In 1980, 27% of hospitals and 21% of hospital employees were unionized. Experts predict that in the 1990s, 45% to 65% of all hospitals will be unionized. Indeed, the entry of the Union of Auto Workers and the American Federation of Teachers into the industry should increase union activity. The consolidation trend and the movement of physicians into salaried positions will facilitate future union activities.

Consumable Goods and Equipment. Overall, the hospital industry uses about 130,000 products produced by 3,000 manufacturers, and the eight largest producers generate about 40% of industry shipments. Suppliers fall into two groups: consumable goods (such as pharmaceuticals and housewares) and diagnostic equipment. One study identified 50 product segments representing more than 1,500 items from over 300 separate companies and totaling nearly $100 billion.

Declining occupancy and surgery rates imply reduced use of hospital products. And uncertainty about reimbursement schedules and policies, as well as uncertainty about financial stability, has induced many hospitals to delay capital equipment orders. In addition, the new multi-hospital groups are exercising their purchasing power to reduce costs.

Consumable goods suppliers are not fragmented, but multiple sources are available to hospitals. Similarly, diagnostic equipment suppliers are also neither fragmented nor consolidated, but they command fewer average hospital dollars than consumable good suppliers.

Capital. Traditional sources of capital to the industry are municipal bonds, government loans, philanthropy, and internally generated funds. Today the equity markets are a new source of funds. Until 1983, capital acquired in the financial markets was chiefly used to finance construction and renovation of hospital facilities. Now it is also used as a source of working capital and for refinancing debt. During the early 1980s when interest rates declined sharply, the industry's reliance on the capital markets increased as hospitals sought to refinance their debt at more favorable rates. This trend was made possible largely because of the availability of tax-exempt financing.

The dollar volume accounted for by health issues in the tax-exempt market increased from 5.7% in 1974 to 12.3% in 1982. Total tax-exempt volume went from $22 to $75 billion during this same period. Non-profit hospitals were the primary users of this financing, because they were barred from equity markets. However, as a result of the more restrictive use of tax-exempt financing legislated by the Tax Reform Act of 1986, industry experts expect the volume of tax-exempt financings to decrease sharply, including hospital financings.

Since 1983, the long-term debt per hospital has declined, on average, from $235 million to $191 million. Since 1983 the average fixed asset base has contracted from $285 million to $200 million, a reduction of about 30%. Indeed, hospital construction is predicted to come to a virtual standstill by 1990. Thus, the industry is reducing its need for external funding sources due to both a downsizing in hospital assets and a reduction in hospital building.

Competitive Threats to the Industry

Medical technology today is so flexible that economically viable health service facilities can be established at virtually *any* scale of operation—ranging from individual and group practices to full-service hospitals. Only in specialized sectors are there economies of scale. For example, to be able to afford expensive specialized capital equipment, such as a CAT scanner, the hospital needs to be of a certain size and serve a certain minimum population base.

Lack of economies of scale has led to low barriers to entry into the industry. Captial requirements for entry into the industry are not significant. Moreover, existing hospitals are available for purchase at relatively low prices. Nearly 500 hospital closings (or 8.7% of all hospitals currently operating) are predicted to occur before 1990. Many public and voluntary hospitals, unable to raise capital funds, are seeking to be acquired. An estimate of the average price paid per hospital in 1986 is $6.03 million. This figure is based on representative data and will vary depending on factors such as number of beds, location, facility age, and facility profitability.

Large consumers have shown the ability and inclination to enter the industry. For example, Goodyear established a medical clinic for its 1,700 employees by buying a small medical practice. This facility could easily be upgraded to a full-service hospital.

The main governmental barrier to entry into the hospital industry was the requirement of a Certificate of Need (CON). Obtaining a CON was primarily a political process controlled by existing hospitals. The CON process was ineffective in controlling the growth of hospital beds in existing

hospitals, but it served as a strong barrier to new entrants. For this reason, CONs are being phased out, or modified, in a number of states. For example, in 1986 twelve states had weak CON programs and seven had no program to control the number of hospital beds.

Another threat from outside the industry is from substitutes for hospitals, which can be grouped into three categories: long-term care facilities, ambulatory care facilities, and HMOs. Long-term care facilities include nursing homes, psychiatric hospitals, and hospices. The services offered by these facilities overlap only slightly with those of acute-care facilities, which accept patients whose course of treatment is expected to be less than 30 days.

Ambulatory care facilities include birthing centers, emergency centers, and dialysis units. Ambulatory care has increased in importance over the past ten years. For example, in 1984, 330 emergency surgery centers existed. This was a 59% increase over 1983. Other ambulatory care services, such as renal dialysis units, are experiencing similar growth. These centers perform services that would otherwise be obtained through a hospital; therefore, their growth is a significant threat to the hospital industry.

Technological developments are enabling treatment on an outpatient basis which would otherwise require hosptial care. For example, laser surgery has made possible the removal of cataracts, and lithiotripters have made possible the removal of kidney stones, on an outpatient basis. Many experts predict that by 1990, 40% to 50% of all surgery will be performed away from the hospital.

HMOs are an important substitute for hospital services. In August 1985, 431 HMOs existed; they covered 16 million members. HMOs have blossomed over the past few years as the subscriber base increased from 9 million in 1984. Industry sources predict 47 million people will be enrolled in HMOs by 1990.

Though HMOs cannot provide all the services of a hospital, they dramatically affect hospital admissions and revenue. HMO members are only 60% as likely as non-HMO members to be admitted to a hospital because of the stress HMOs place on preventive medicine and their close monitoring of hospitalized patients. Once admitted, the revenue attributable to HMO patients is are 25%

lower than their non-HMO counterparts. Therefore, HMO members generate only 45% of the revenue that non-HMO members generate. This,
coupled with high expected growth rate projected
for HMOs over the next five years, make HMOs a
serious threat to the hospital industry.

Existing Competition

Hospitals are now operating within an intensely
competitive environment. Indeed, many hospital
chains are aggressively trying to increase their
market shares. The industry has numerous competitors (profiled later in this note). Competition is
fueled by low growth of the industry, high fixed
costs, and a lack of differentiation among competitors. Furthermore, individual hospitals operate
under different ownership patterns, financial constraints, and demand assumptions.

Symptoms of the new highly competitive
environment include hospital underutilization,
industry overcapacity, new substitute services,
and advertising.

Underutilization. Hospitals have reacted to
the government's switch to a fixed payment system from a cost-plus system by reducing lengths
of stay in hospitals. Average industry length of
stay fell from 7.6 days in 1982 to 7.3 days in 1985.

Overcapacity in the Industry. Industry occupancy rates have declined from about 75% in 1982
to about 69% in 1984. Experts estimate that the US
hospital industry has at least 25% too many beds,
and *Standard and Poor's Industry Review* reports
that the industry has about 25% to 33% more
capacity than required.

Development of New Substitute Services.
Substitute products are increasingly available and
popular. As discussed previously, hospitals face
considerable threats from emergency care centers,
outpatients surgery centers, diagnostic centers,
outpatient birthing centers, HMOs, and PPOs—all
of which have shown dramatic increases over the
past few years.

Marketing and Advertising. Marketing as a
dedicated function within hospitals is on the
increase. At present, about 60% of the hospitals
use some type of marketing. Surveys of consumer
satisfaction with hospital services are becoming more common. Marketing efforts have also
focused on managing the information sources
(reference system) consumers use to select a hospital. Major hospital chains are mounting extensive and expensive advertising campaigns. For
example, Humana spent $20 millon and AMI
spent $15 million on advertising during the spring
of 1986.

HORIZONTAL CONSOLIDATION AND VERTICAL INTEGRATION

Despite some recent slowing, the movement
toward horizontal consolidation and vertical integration within the hospital industry is still under
way and likely to persist. Increased financial pressure has been a major impetus for growth in multi-
hospital systems and the diversification of
services. This has resulted from recent payment
reforms, compounded by declining utilization.
These factors have prompted hospital mergers and
acquisitions, affiliations, and shared service
arrangements. They have also encouraged formation of joint ventures among hospitals and collaborative arrangements with physicians, ambulatory
and long-term care providers, and insurers.

In theory, the consolidation of hospitals and
other health care providers into horizontally or
vertically integrated delivery systems should permit the realization of productive efficiencies. These
efficiencies are presumably derived from the centralization of management, volume purchasing
discounts, diversification of revenues, and other
economies of scale and scope. In reality, the economic benefits of administration, purchasing, and
production promised by horizontal consolidation
have not been significant. The major benefits of
system affiliation are capturing of additional
patients and enhanced access to capital, especially
of the debt-financed type. Larger organizations
and systems generally enjoy lower costs of capital
than smaller, free-standing facilities.

COMPANY PROFILES AND STRATEGIES

Case 17A provides profiles of four major companies in this industry. These profiles give a brief
assessment of individual company performance,
key attributes, and recent strategies. Companies
profiled are the Hospital Corporation of America,
Humana, Inc., National Medical Enterprises, Inc.,
and Community Psychiatric Centers, Inc.

HOSPITAL COMPANY PROFILES

Paul Shrivastava
Bucknell University

COMPANY A: HOSPITAL CORPORATION OF AMERICA

Hospital Corporation of America (HCA) is the world's largest hospital management firm; it operates more than 450 acute-care and psychiatric hospitals in the United States and abroad. HCA began in 1960 as a single hospital in Nashville and did not begin to expand until 1968 when Jack Masey, founder of the Kentucky Fried Chicken chain, assumed the position of president.

In 1970, HCA initiated its first management contract. Until the mid 1970s, HCA used management contracts as a means of achieving ownership of a hospital. Typically, HCA would agree to an interim management arrangement while purchase negotiations were being finalized. However, in 1976 HCA created a separate management contract subsidiary, which today accounts for just under 1% of revenues.

Prior to 1981, the thrust of the company's development effort was by way of acquisition of well-run, profitable hospitals. Since that time, HCA has embarked on an aggressive growth strategy whereby new bed additions have been result of construction rather than acquisition. HCA's capital spending program included (1) the acquisition of older, not-for-profit institutions in good locations that needed extensive renovation or complete replacement to avoid loss of market share; (2) de novo construction of new hospitals; and (3) the expansion of existing facilities. The majority of HCA's hospitals are located in the south and southeastern United States, especially Texas,

Florida, and Tennessee. Exhibits A1 through A3 provide basic operating and financial characteristics of the firm.

HCA has traditionally been known in the industry for its expertise in the design and development of new hospitals. HCA hospitals became standardized in their design and equipment specifications, which led to shorter construction times, lower construction costs and interest charges, and a reduction in the time for a new facility to achieve profitability. When the company completes a new hospital or renovates one if its existing units, it generally has the newest and most sophisticated facility in the area. This has traditionally enabled HCA to attract doctors and patients from older, not as well-run institutions.

HCA has also attempted to build hospitals in clusters: a large central facility surrounded by smaller satellite hospitals (usually within a 50-mile radius). HCA has created eight regional/local systems for its facilities that account for 50% of hospital division earnings, with seven more planned for 1986. These cluster markets enable cost sharing and greater coordination of marketing.

The company's ranking as the largest hospital management firm put it in a premier position to negotiate a joint venture with a large insurance company. In October 1986, HCA and Equitable Life Assurance Society of the United States formed "Equicor," the first joint venture between a hospital management firm and health care insurer. The size and scope of the combined entities make HCA a prime contender in bidding for CHAMPUS contracts. CHAMPUS, a health insurance program

Exhibit A1 *Hospital Corporation of America: 1985 Sales by Division ($ Millions)*

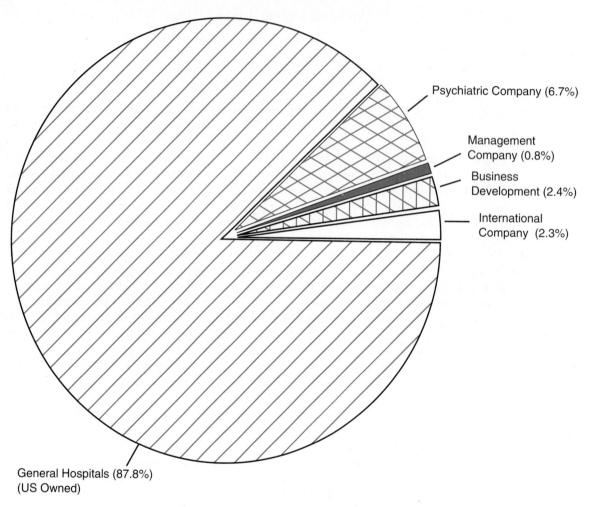

Psychiatric Company (6.7%)

Management Company (0.8%)

Business Development (2.4%)

International Company (2.3%)

General Hospitals (87.8%)
(US Owned)

Total Company = $4,998

Exhibit A2 *Hospital Corporation of America: 1985 Operating Profit by Division ($ MIlions)*

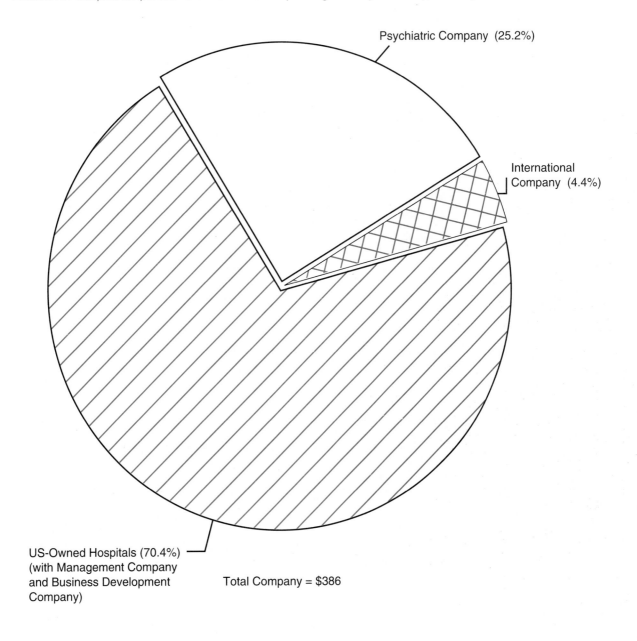

Psychiatric Company (25.2%)

International Company (4.4%)

US-Owned Hospitals (70.4%)
(with Management Company
and Business Development
Company)

Total Company = $386

Exhibit A3 Hospital Corporation of America: Income Statement—Base Case (Projections Given Present Strategy)

Fiscal Year Ended December 31,

	1983 (Actual)		1984 (Actual)		1985 (Actual)		1986		1987		1988		1989		1990	
Operating revenues	$3,917.1	122.3%	$4,178.0	119.4%	$4,997.9	120.4%	$5,795.5	121.1%	$6,231.3	121.2%	$6,865.8	122.5%	$7,656.2	124.0%	$8,601.7	125.5%
Less: prov. for contract. and doubtful accts.	$714.1	22.3%	$679.3	19.4%	$846.3	20.4%	$1,010.0	21.1%	$1,090.0	21.2%	$1,260.0	22.5%	$1,480.0	24.0%	$1,750.0	25.5%
Net operating rev.	$3,203.0	100.0%	$3,498.7	100.0%	$4,151.6	100.0%	$4,785.5	100.0%	$5,141.3	100.0%	$5,605.8	100.0%	$6,176.2	100.0%	$6,851.7	100.0%
Costs and expenses:																
Operating exp.	$2,535.3	79.2%	$2,663.1	76.1%	$3,292.7	79.3%	$3,780.0	79.0%	$4,061.6	79.0%	$4,428.6	79.0%	$4,825.0	78.1%	$5,350.0	78.1%
Depr. & amort.	$156.0	4.9%	$192.2	5.5%	$240.7	5.8%	$295.0	6.2%	$348.1	6.8%	$403.8	7.2%	$460.3	7.5%	$515.6	7.5%
Interest	$162.5	5.1%	$187.8	5.4%	$232.0	5.6%	$250.0	5.2%	$245.0	4.8%	$240.0	4.3%	$225.0	3.6%	$225.0	3.3%
Total	$2,853.8	89.1%	$3,043.1	87.0%	$3,765.4	90.7%	$4,325.0	90.4%	$4,654.7	90.5%	$5,072.4	90.5%	$5,510.3	89.2%	$6,090.6	88.9%
Income from operations	$349.2	10.9%	$455.6	13.0%	$386.2	9.3%	$460.5	9.6%	$486.6	9.5%	$533.4	9.5%	$665.9	10.8%	$761.1	11.1%
Invest. & other income	$42.5	1.3%	$50.4	1.4%	$81.3	2.0%	$55	1.1%	$55	1.1%	$60	1.1%	$60	1.0%	$65.9	1.0%
Joint venture participation											4		7.5		10	
Income before taxes & extra. items	$391.7	12.2%	$506.0	14.5%	$467.5	11.3%	$515.5	10.8%	$541.6	10.5%	$597.4	10.7%	$733.4	11.9%	$837.0	12.2%
Prov. for income taxes	$148.5	4.6%	$209.2	6.0%	$183.8	4.4%	$231.9	4.8%	$232.9	4.5%	$256.9	4.6%	$315.4	5.1%	$359.9	5.3%
Income before extra. items	$243.2	ERR	$296.8	7.6%	$283.7	6.8%	$283.6	5.9%	$308.7	6.0%	$340.5	6.1%	$418.0	6.8%	$477.1	7.0%
Extraordinary items:																
Gain-term. of merger					$65.4	1.6%										
Loss-extinguish. of debt					($10.5)	-0.3%										
Net income	$243.2	7.6%	$296.8	7.6%	$338.6	8.2%	$283.6	5.9%	$308.7	6.0%	$340.5	6.1%	$418.0	6.8%	$477.1	7.0%
Depreciation	$156.0		$192.2		$240.7		$295.0		$348.1		$403.8		$460.3		$515.6	
Funds from divestitures	$199.0		$25.6		$116.1		$116.0		$100.0		$10.0		$10.0		$10.0	
Maintenance capital	$200.0		$200.0		$220.0		$250.0		$250.0		$250.0		$275.0		$275.0	
Expansion capital	$650.0		$575.0		$1,110.0		$450.0		$250.0		$250.0		$325.0		$325.0	
Debt repayment	$71.8		$25.7		$111.2		$40.3		$242.2		$326.7		$337.3		$391.9	
Stock repurchase	$0.0		$0.0		$3.6		$225.0		$0.0		$0.0		$0.0		$0.0	
Dividends	$34.1		$43.6		$53.2		$53.9		$58.7		$64.5		$79.4		$90.6	
Cash flow	($357.7)		($329.7)		($802.6)		($324.6)		($44.1)		($136.9)		($128.4)		($79.8)	
Discounted @ 9.8%							($324.6)		($40.1)		($113.6)		($97.0)		($53.3)	
Total							$2,082.2									
Terminal value							$628.6								$3,323.0	
Net present value							$1,453.6									
Total assets	$4,083.4		$4,829.1		$6,259.1		$6,947.6		$7,781.3		$8,715.1		$10,022.0		11224.9	
Total equity	$1,570.9		$1,869.6		$2,092.1		$2,162.8		$2,400.7		$2,664.8		$2,957.9		$3,283.3	
ROA	5.96%		6.15%		5.41%		4.08%		3.97%		3.91%		4.17%		4.25%	

continued

	1	2	3	4	5	6	7	8
ROE	15.48%	15.88%	16.18%	13.11%	12.86%	12.78%	14.13%	14.53%
Net rev. growth	7.59%	9.23%	18.66%	15.27%	7.43%	9.03%	10.18%	10.94%
Net earnings growth	41.48%	22.04%	14.08%	-16.24%	8.85%	10.30%	22.76%	14.14%
Earnings per share	$ 2.80	$ 3.35	$ 3.75	$ 3.38	$ 3.68	$ 4.05	$ 4.98	$ 5.68
Shares outstanding	87.6	88.6	90.4	84	84	84	84	84
LTD/equity								
Interest coverage ratio	3.41	3.69	3.02	3.06	3.21	3.49	4.26	4.72
Maturities LTD	71.8	25.7	111.2	40.3	242.2	326.7	337.3	391.9
Debt service coverage	1.7	2.14	2.36	2.85	1.85	1.74	1.96	1.97
Total hospitals	391	414	458	474	474	466	467	469
Domestic hospitals	334	355	386	393	383	371	366	363
Licensed beds	28231	28960	32687	31487	30187	28987	28407	28123
Length of stay (days)	6.4	6.04	5.92	5.8	5.9	5.9	5.95	6
Admissions (000's)	974	934	930	942	905	989	1096	1224
Total patient days	6237.2	5643.5	5501.5	5466.6	5338.8	5251.2	5287.7	5372.7
Occupancy rate	63.4%	55.4%	49.5%	47.6%	48.5%	49. 6%	51.0%	52.3%
Total corporate revenue	$3,917.1	$4,178.0	$4,997.9	$5,795.5	$6,231.3	$6,865.8	$7,656.2	$8,601.7
Total inpatient revenue	$3,188.8	$3,305.9	$3,669.6	$4,067.1	$4,329.6	$4,620.5	$5,001.5	$5,463.1
Outpatient as % inpatient	9.0%	12.0%	16.9%	20.0%	23.0%	26.0%	29.0%	32.0%
Domestic hospital revenue	$3,545.9	$3,744.6	$4,388.3	$4,990.5	$5,444.2	$5,950.1	$6,590.5	$7,360.9
As % total revenue	90.5%	89.6%	87.8%	86.1%	87.4%	86.7%	86.1%	85.6%
Psychiatric hospitals	25	27	40	44	54	58	62	66
Total psychiatric revenue	$ 192.5	$ 231.4	$ 335.3	$ 425.0	$ 501.5	$ 591.8	$ 698.3	$ 824.0
As % total revenue	4.91%	5.54%	6.71%	7.33%	8.05%	8.62%	9.12%	9.58%
Operating expenses	$ 123.1	$ 145.6	$ 211.2	$ 263.5	$ 310.9	$ 361.0	$ 425.9	$ 502.6
As % psych. rev.	63.9%	62.9%	63.0%	62.0%	62.0%	61.0%	61.0%	61.0%
Operating profit	$ 53.2	$ 66.7	$ 97.2	$ 127.5	$ 150.4	$ 185.3	$ 216.5	$ 255.4
As % psych. rev.	27.6%	28.8%	29.0%	30.0%	30.0%	31.3%	31.0%	31.0%
Pretax profit	$ 29.0	$ 34.7	$ 49.3	$ 61.2	$ 78.2	$ 94.7	$ 118.7	$ 144.2
Margin	15.1%	15.0%	14.7%	14.4%	15.6%	16.0%	17.0%	17.5%
International hospitals	32	32	32	37	37	37	39	40
Total international revenue	$ 108.2	$ 113.3	$ 114.9	$ 135.0	$ 151.2	$ 169.3	$ 189.7	$ 212.4
As % total revenue	2.8%	2.7%	2.3%	2.3%	2.4%	2.5%	2.5%	2.5%
Operating expenses	$ 81.9	$ 84.3	$ 85.0	$ 101.3	$ 113.4	$ 126.9	$ 142.3	$ 159.3
As % int. rev.	75.7%	74.4%	74.0%	75.0%	75.0%	75.0%	75.0%	75.0%
Operating profit	$ 15.0	$ 17.7	$ 17.0	$ 20.3	$ 22.7	$ 25.4	$ 29.4	$ 32.9
As % int. rev.	13.9%	15.6%	14.8%	15.0%	15.0%	15.0%	15.5%	15.5%
Pretax profit	$ 6.2	$ 7.4	$ 6.9	$ 6.1	$ 9.8	$ 12.7	$ 14.2	$ 15.9
Margin	5.7%	6.5%	6.0%	4.5%	6.5%	7.5%	7.5%	7.5%

Assumptions: (1) 12% asset growth 1986–1990

(2) 11% growth in equity after 1986

run by the Defense Department, wants to turn over the government's health care of military personnel and their dependents to preferred providers. CHAMPUS covers 6 million individuals and generates fees of approximately $1.6 billion annually.

HCA has developed a reputation for good relationships with physicians. This reputation stems from several factors, the most obvious of which is that Thomas Frist, Jr., MD, is chairman. His father, also a doctor, preceded him as chairman before stepping down to become the company's chief medical director. The presence of physicians in top management leads one to believe that HCA is more in touch with doctor's concerns and thus better able to develop its marketing strategies vis-à-vis the group accordingly.

Physicians have a significant interest in approximately 8% of all hospitals in the HCA system. The company also operates a physicians services company that offers such services as purchase of supplies through HCA contracts with preferred vendors, malparactice insurance, and joint ventures is ownership of medical office buildings as well as diagnostic business.

Current Strategy

HCA has taken several concrete steps to improve it's position and combat the negative trends in the health care industry. A single vendor (Baxtor Travenol) is being emphasized to reduce costs. Labor expenses have been put under tight control, and decreased capital spending should result in lower interest and depreciation expenses. Although discounts (health maintenance organizations, etc.) are expected to rise slightly over the next five years; bad debts, labor, supplies, interest, depreciation, and "other expenses" are all expected to remain the same or decline slightly as a percentage of revenues due to the cost policy.

After $1.4 billion in capital expenditures in 1985, HCA targeted negative acute-care bed growth. In addition to halting its aggressive construction program, the company has been selling marginal capacity. In early 1986, plans were announced to sell upward of 10% of operating capacity. To date, 20 hospitals with 1,800 beds have been sold. These facilities were primarily outside urban areas and did not fit HCA's revised strategic plan.

In November 1985, HCA announced a $350 million stock repurchase program. By June 30, 1986, 8.3 million shares had been repurchased at a cost of $302 million. In addition, the company has retired $200 million of high-interest debt as well as refinancing debentures at substantially lower interest rates.

HCA has taken itself from a backseat position behind Humana in health insurance to a leadership stance by joining forces with Equitable. The joint venture, Equicor, will be accounted for by HCA using equity accounting with earnings recorded on the income statement. The venture was originally seen as the answer to HCA's declining acute-care admissions. However, analysts have recently scaled back their expectations of Equicor's impact on admissions and thus potential earnings.

HCA is shifting from decentralized to centralized management. Staffing will now be set by corporate rather than local hospital planners. Information systems will become more centralized as well as part of an attempt to streamline operations.

The company's plans for further development in the psychiatric area have been tempered by declines in general hospital utilization. While psychiatric admissions will remain doctor driven, the firm feels that utilization will drop off in the future. Thus, management has become more conservative in site development and is placing limits on its willingness to pay inflated prices for acquisitions. In addition, HCA is developing psychiatric residential treatment centers. This area is not doctor driven, so HCA can affect its markets. These centers are also less expensive to develop than traditional psychiatric hospitals and do not require a certificate of need.

HCA plans to continue investing only in premium facilities abroad, which will allow the company to differentiate itself from the common local hospital. With regard to consulting, the company will concentrate on large-fee contracts with government, major teaching hospitals, and other large organizations.

COMPANY B: HUMANA, INC.

Humana, Inc. is a 23-year-old health services company that provides an integrated national brand of hospital care through prepaid health plans and medical care centers where independent physicians deliver primary medical care. It operates 88 acute-care hospitals with 17,625 licensed beds spread in 22 states; most of the hospitals are concentrated in the southeastern United States. It also operates two hospitals in Europe. In 1987, it was the second largest for-profit hospital chain in the United States with net revenues of $2.9 billion. Exhibits B1 through B5 show its operating and financial characteristics.

Humana has managed its portfolio by selling its small and rural hospitals, replacing aging equipment, and adding beds to existing hospitals. Simultaneously, it has increased productivity to emerge as a low-cost provider of high-quality health care. It has also integrated vertically into insurance. Its present portfolio comprises Humana Care Plus (a group insurance plan), Humana Medfirst, and Hospitals Services.

Humana Care Plus

Humana Care Plus is a prepaid health benefits program that is used to replace an employer's group insurance plan. It competes against large insurance companies and Blue Cross plans. Although the plan permits the clients to choose their own physicians, it encourages use of Humana facilities through financial incentives like lower deductibles. In addition, initially the plan guaranteed premiums with rate increases limited to the cost of living index for two to three years. It also allows preauthorized elective hospitalization and retrospective claims reviews.

The prepaid health scheme was launched to improve utilization of Humana's facilities. So far, this aggressively priced plan has been most successful with small employers, although Humana also plans to market it to large employers in the future. Similarly, Humana also acquired the largest health maintenance organization in Florida in 1986, which brought in additional 110,800 Medicare patients and improved utilization of Humana's facilities. However, even though the utilization of Humana's facilities is improving, the losses are increasing. As a result, Humana increased its premium rates, reduced the contracts to a one-year period, improved controls, limited its exposure, and withdrew from those markets where it did not have its own hospitals. It also introduced a new policy: Medi-Gap. This policy covered the $540 deductible Medicare patients had to pay for each hospital admission.

In spite of recent rate increases, however, Humana continues to be priced below the competitors. This is because of the advantages Humana enjoys as a result of its vertical integration.

Medfirst

Medfirst was designed to provide non-emergency primary physician care to walk-in patients. The centers were designed to treat minor injuries that did not require hospitalization.

Humana had planned to further expand this service to achieve greater economies of scale. However, although Medfirst performed successfully in markets with heavy concentration of people, the overall Medfirst scheme turned out to be uneconomical. Humana often had to pay its physicians and other staff for non-productive hours, thereby reducing productivity levels. In 1987, most of the Medfirst clinics were sold off, eliminating a $6 to $8 million pre-tax loss.

Hospitals Services: Centers of Excellence

The stated mission of Humana is to achieve an unequaled level of measurable quality and productivity in the delivery of health services that are responsive to the needs and values of patients, physicians, employers, and employees. It has evolved four strategies to achieve the above mission: reduce its costs by achieving economies of scale; increase revenues by focusing on younger, private-pay patients; provide excellent quality care in selected areas; and maintain a well-qualified physician staff.

For years, Humana shied away from Medicare and Medicaid patients because only a part of their costs were reimbursed. However, even though payments for Medicare and Medicaid patients are less than those for private-pay patients, they are greater than variable costs involved. Thus, hospitals with less than a 100% bed utilization rate can reduce their fixed expenses per patient by filling up their surplus capacity with Medicare and Medicaid patients. Faced with spare bed capacity, Humana also began attracting such patients to reduce its average fixed costs.

Secondly, Humana located its facilities in growing affluent areas to attract young working families covered by insurance. Such patients are also less likely to suffer from multi-system or chronic diseases or require long stays. Shorter

Exhibit B1 *Humana, Inc.: Revenues per Business Group for 1987*

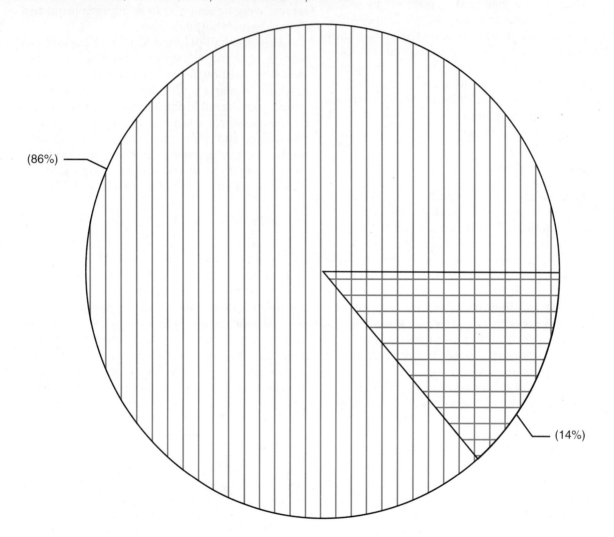

Revenues = 86% Hospitals, 14% Group Health

Exhibit B2 *Humana, Inc.: Financial Highlights*

| | *For the year ended August 31,* | | |
	1988	1987	Change
Earnings			
Revenues[a]	$3,435,397,000	$2,973,643,000	+15.5%
Income before income taxes	$353,642,000	$330,035,000	+7.2%
Net income	$227,121,000[b]	$182,839,000	+24.2%
Earnings per common share	$2.30	$1.86	+23.7%
Financial Position			
Assets	$3,421,962,000	$3,208,765,000	+6.6%
Working capital	$294,673,000	$271,801,000	+8.4%
Property and equipment	$1,987,759,000	$1,967,366,000	+1.0%
Common stockholders' equity	$1,154,617,000	$1,012,042,000	+14.1%
Per share	$11.80	$10.36	+13.9%
Return on average common stockholders' equity	21.0%	19.2%	
Other Data			
Shares outstanding	97,886,147	97,660,445	+0.2%
Number of hospitals	83	85	−2.4%
Number of licensed beds	17,323	17,598	−1.6%
Weighted average licensed beds	17,573	17,617	−0.2%
Number of days of patient care	2,987,900	2,995,300	−0.2%
Number of admissions	492,400	498,200	−1.2%
Number of health insurance members	790,700	554,500	+42.6%
Number of employees[c]	49,400	46,500	+6.2%
Number of holders of common stock[d]	36,900	37,800	−2.4%

[a]Revenues are reported net of contractual allowances.
[b]Includes extraordinary loss of $16,133,000 ($.16 per share) on early extinguishment of debt and gain of $16,214,000 ($.16 per share) resulting from a change in accounting principle for retirement plan actuarial gains.
[c]Includes both full-time and part-time employees.
[d]Includes 24,200 employees in 1988 and 23,700 employees in 1987 who are indirect owners through participation in the Humana Thrift Plan.

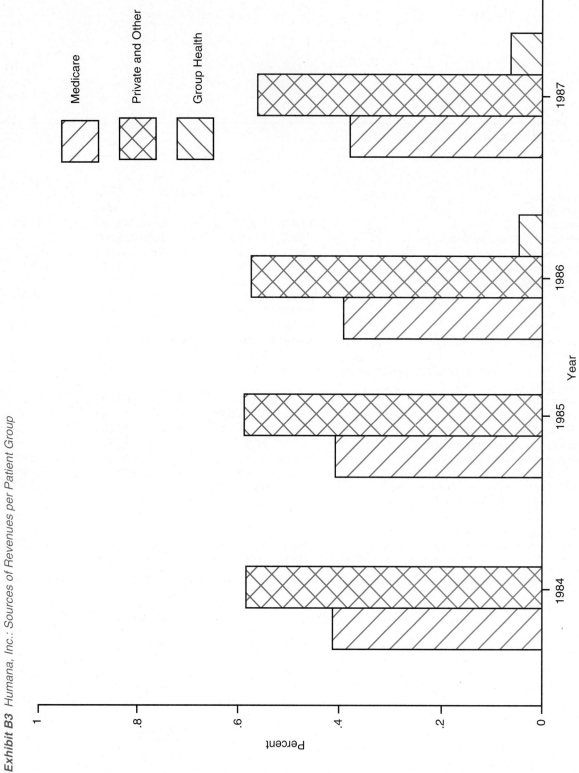

Exhibit B3 *Humana, Inc.: Sources of Revenues per Patient Group*

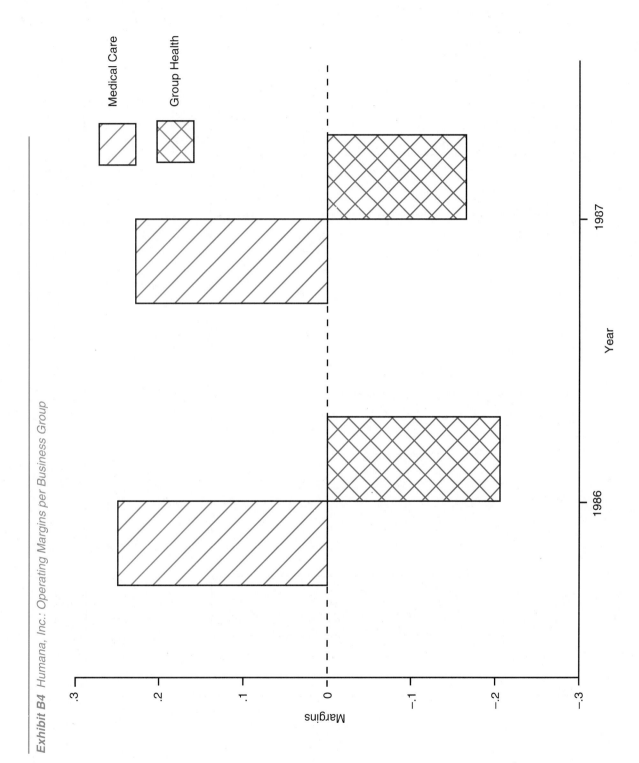

Exhibit B4 Humana, Inc.: Operating Margins per Business Group

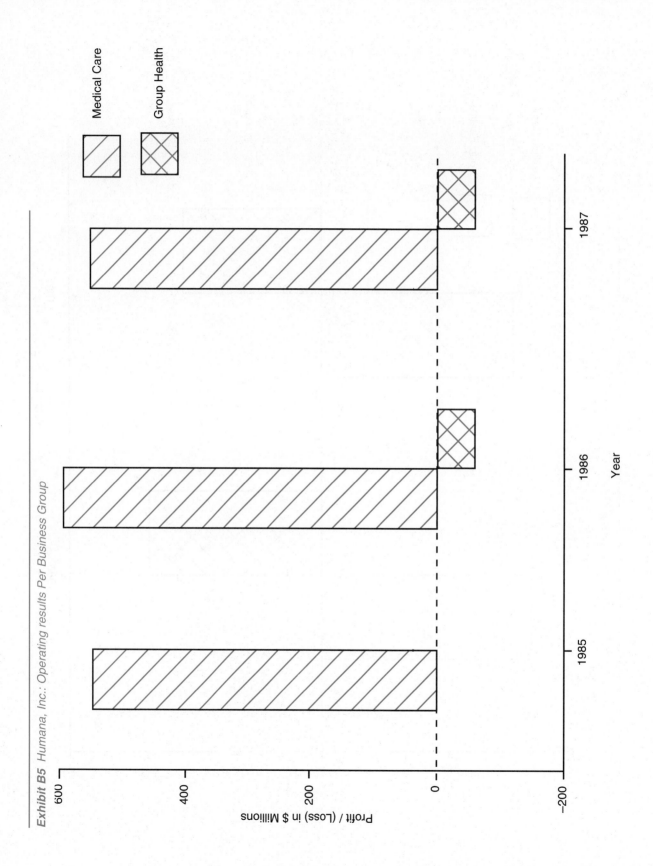

Exhibit B5 *Humana, Inc.: Operating results Per Business Group*

Medical Care

Group Health

Profit / (Loss) in $ Millions

600

400

200

0

−200

1985   1986   1987

Year

patient stays are more profitable for hospitals because most diagnostic tests, operating room services, and intensive care facilities are required only during the initial few days. During the remaining days, patients are charged primarily for room and board.

Humana also tries to attract the "right" kind of patients by influencing doctors. It focuses on recruiting and influencing those specialists whose customers are primarily younger, private-pay patients.

The Centers of Excellence can be viewed as sub-businesses within Humana serving specific customer segments. For example, the Spinal Injury Center of Excellence is a 35-bed unit dedicated to spinal cord injuries; it is located within a 267-bed acute-care hospital. Humana's most famous center perhaps is the Heart Institute where artificial heart transplants have been performed.

The three essential elements of a Center of Excellence are a physician group, a medical education and clinical research program, and a Humana hospital. A physician group is selected that has exceptional diagnostic and treatment skills in a given specialty, practices state-of-the-art medicine, and participates in continuing education and research. Also, the physicians should have a productive professional relationship with referring physicians in the specialty and be recognized by their peers for their professional expertise.

A medical education and clinical research program is a program with clearly defined plans, directed by an independent advisory board. The program should have a productive relationship with academia.

The Humana hospital involved should have a committment to achieving excellence in medical care and have comprehensive diagnostic and therapeutic services that feature state-of-the-art facilities. It should also have adequately qualified administrative and nursing staffs.

The Centers of Excellence improve the standard of medical service provided by Humana in selected areas and also provide an avenue for attracting grants and funds for research and education from external sources. The following table shows the funds received by Humana for research and education in 1987.

Specialty	Medical Education	Clinical Research	Total
Burns	. . .	$ 93,333	$ 93,333
Cardiovascular	$ 17,850		$ 17,850
Diabetes	$ 98,470	$ 74,737	$173,207
Neuroscience and perinatal	$ 41,466	$ 15,187	$ 56,653
Ophthalmology	$145,481	$ 24,051	$169,532
Orthopedic	$ 39,191	$ 21,629	$ 60,820
Total	$387,971	$240,017	$627,988

Humana tries to retain existing physicians and attract new ones by improving facilities and maintaining high ethical and professional standards. Humana believes that such a multi-pronged approach will help it maintain a competitive position in the industry.

Joint Strategy with University of Louisville for Providing Indigent Care

In 1983, Humana entered into a unique lease arrangement with the University of Louisville and the city of Louisville for a new 404-bed hospital. The arrangement called for Humana to guarantee hospital admission to all indigent and medically needy local residents in return for a fixed annual payment by the government to cover the expenses.

This arrangement was, in effect, similar to any other "prepaid group." The additional patients admitted under the scheme increased the volume for Humana, thereby decreasing its average fixed cost per patient. This resulted in a win-win situation for all involved. The needy got the medical attention. The government provided care for the needy while putting a cap on its financial obligations. And Humana reduced its average costs while at the same time discharging its social responsibility and creating a favorable public image.

Cost-control Strategies at Humana

As a part of the overall cost-reduction strategy, Humana has standardized all its products and uses a common nomenclature system for them. This has simplified record keeping and has resulted in a saving of about 17%. It also has an integrated inventory control system (PICS) that uses standardized procedures and has streamlined the materials management function at Humana. PICS automatically recommends orders, which must simply be reviewed and approved by the materials manager. The orders are then transmitted to the vendor directly—computer to computer. This reduces costs for both Humana as well as the vendors, who pass on a discount of 1% to 2% to Humana. The invoicing and the payment procedures between the vendors and Humana are also standardized and computerized, which results in more efficient cash management.

COMPANY C: NATIONAL MEDICAL ENTERPRISES

These are dynamic times at National Medical Enterprises (NME). Management has been actively restructuring its business portfolio since 1986 to position itself better for long-term growth and profitability. It wants to position the firm as a leader in providing highest quality service in specialty niche markets. It is, therefore, refocusing on institutional care while withdrawing from all other aspects of the health care industry.

Peripheral health care was attractive during late 1970s. NME grew into several divergent areas that required a variety of skills. NME was successful at first, but the environmental changes in the past few years (emergence of Diagnostic Related Groups [DRGs], health maintenance organizations [HMOs], and the Prospective Payment System [PPS]) made it difficult for NME to manage a wide variety of businesses. In 1986, management decided to restructure the firm and sell off peripheral health care businesses, including retail services, home health care agencies, construction and leasing businesses, and small, unprofitable hospitals with low occupancy rates. Although NME took a loss of $77 million on these divestments, management was confident of the long-term advantages. The remaining businesses of NME were organized into three operating divisions: the hospital group, the specialty group, and the long-term care group. Exhibits C1 through C3 show operating and financial characteristics.

The Hospital Group

Of all the divisions, the hospital group is undergoing the greatest transformation. Its goal is to be a smaller but stronger and better managed group. Management believes that the public will pay for quality health care and services. Such a business will also be less cyclical. Therefore, it is divesting or converting to specialty hospitals any units that do not meet NME's profitability and market share standards. It is also investing in upgrading its facilities rather than in expansion or new acquisitions. Acute-care facilities are being located so that they can be used as hubs for providing related services.

Also, realizing that health care is a distinctly regional business, the group is decentralizing its

Exhibit C1 *National Medical Enterprises, Inc.: Five-year Summary*

Year	Sales	Net Income	EPS[a]
1990	3,935,000,000	242,000,000	3.03
1989	3,676,000,000	192,000,000	2.58
1988	3,202,000,000	170,000,000	2.29
1987	2,881,000,000	140,000,000	1.84
1986	2,577,000,000	116,000,000	1.48
Five-year growth rate (%)	11.1	20.1	19.6

[a]EPS =

Exhibit C2 *National Medical Enterprises, Inc.: Financial Ratios*

	Fiscal Year Ending May 31,		
	1990	1989	1988
Quick ratio	1.16	1.51	1.38
Current ratio	1.36	1.81	1.57
Sales/cash	23.15	33.72	33.71
SG&A/sales	0.83	0.84	0.84
Receivables: turnover	6.30	5.06	4.78
Receivables: days' sales	57.18	71.10	75.33
Inventories: turnover	89.43	60.26	57.18
Inventories: days' sales	4.03	5.97	6.30
Net sales? working capital	15.80	8.24	10.10
Net sales/net plant and equipment	1.71	1.59	1.53
Net sales/current assets	4.21	3.68	3.68
Net sales/total assets	1.03	0.95	0.91
Net sales/employees	86,865	49,276	44,721
Total liability/total assets	0.67	0.72	0.73
Total liability/invested capital	1.26	1.45	1.32
Total liability/common equity	2.03	2.52	2.65
Times interest earned	3.93	3.31	3.27
Current debt/equity	0.17	0.02	0.04
Long-term debt/equity	0.61	0.74	1.01

Exhibit C3 *National Medical Enterprises, Inc.: Financial Ratios*

	Fiscal Year Ending May 31,		
	1990	1989	1988
Total debt/equity	0.77	0.76	1.05
Total assets/equity	3.03	3.52	3.65
Pretax income/net sales	0.10	0.09	0.09
Pretax income/total assets	0.11	0.08	0.08
Pretax income/invested capital	0.20	0.17	0.15
Pretax income/common equity	0.32	0.29	0.30
Net income/net sales	0.06	0.04	0.05
Net income/total assets	0.06	0.04	0.04
Net income/invested capital	0.12	0.07	0.08

operations. Hospitals are being given greater autonomy to make them more responsive to local needs. This decision has started to be reflected in the bottom line.

NME is faced with five strategic issues: occupancy rates, revenue problems, labor relations, physician recruitment, and cost control. Occupancy rates have declined in the entire industry due to the general trend toward greater outpatient care. To combat this, NME has started adding specialty units and is also actively soliciting critical-care business where the occupancy rates are highest.

The revenue problems of the industry have been adversely affected due to discounting by private payers and the discrepancy between what hospitals charge and what the government and private health care plans pay. While NME is trying to seek better rates from various health plans, it also has to improve its productivity and cost control. To combat these problems, NME is trying to improve its patient mix (more private patients than Medicare and Medicaid patients) and is entering new venture agreements (acute-care and long-term care) to stabilize the flow of patients.

Quality of employees is crucial to the success of any service business—including the health care business. Apart from physicians, these employees consist of nurses, technical staff, management, and nurse's aides.

Recently, the industry faced a shortage of nurses, especially in the northeastern region. Nurses are crucial to the long-term care group, a highly labor-intensive business. NME has launched innovative programs, including providing transportation and child care services, to attract and retain workers. NME has also experienced high turnover among senior executives as a result of a shakeup in 1987. Things have, however, stabilized.

Physicians have a unique relationship with hospitals in the industry in general and in NME in particular. They are not employed by NME but are affiliated with them. This affiliation can be terminated by the physicians any time. In addition, they may also work with competing hospitals.

Physicians have a powerful role because they attract and refer patients to the hospitals. These referrals are generally based on quality of care available at the hospital, its location, reliability and availability of modern equipment, quality of support facilities, and quality of staff and other physicians. To ensure continued referrals by physicians, hospitals have to satisfy their expectations. On its part, NME has initiated several steps to improve its standing with physicians. It has located medical office buildings adjacent to certain of its general hospitals and is encouraging physicians to locate their practices near the NME hospitals.

Although it is focusing on providing high-quality care, NME also realizes that cost controls are required in the long run due to the steadily decreasing patient population (3% per year) in acute-care hospitals, increasing expenses per patient (10%), and increasing third-party scrutiny (DRGs, HMOs, and the PPS). As a result, NME has taken several steps to control its costs. Nurses are being provided with aides to perform less skillful activities, overheads are being reduced, management reporting systems have been strengthened, medical records coding has been improved, and so on.

Research and Development Policy. In accord with its overall policy, NME recently refocused its R&D policy to concentrate on a limited number of areas, including treatment of head trauma, spinal cord injuries, ventilator-assisted breathing, and Alzheimer's disease. This would prevent diffusion of resources in many directions.

Product	Market	NME
Acute care	1,007	36%
Long-term care	993	35%

Specialty Hospital Group

The specialty hospital group, which includes psychiatric care, substance abuse care, and rehabilitation, is the rising star at NME. Demand for these services is strong and is expected to grow in the future. This is due to the increased awareness among the public of various mental illnesses like anxiety, schizophrenia, acute depression, and alcohol and substance abuse.

In the recent past the payers, as in the case of physical illnesses, have been pushing for outpatient therapy. However, the hospitals, with the support of psychiatrists who direct the therapy, have managed to thwart the movement toward outpatient care. In this environment, NME has been able to increase both its bed capacity as well as its occupancy rates. It has outpaced its competition by its focus on providing specialized services for teenage drug dependency, depression evaluation, head trauma, spinal cord injuries, and ventilator-assisted breathing.

NME has been successful in this business due, in part, to its reputation as a provider of high-quality care. This image has also enabled it to recruit highly qualified physicians from major universities. NME is also trying to create synergies among its various businesses by locating its specialty units in acute-care facilities.

Long-term Care Group

In the field of long-term care, NME faces competition from home health agencies, other long-term care facilities, and hospitals that convert empty beds for long-term care patients. However, the demand for long-term care is expected to increase significantly in the coming years due to the growth in the number of elderly people in the United States. Presently this care is being provided by about 20,500 facilities with a total of 1.6 million beds, but the demand is expected to go up to about 2.1 million beds in 1990 and about 2.7 million beds by 2000. In addition to providing traditional services, hospitals can also diversify into related services like rehabilitation services, specialty units for inpatient treatment of people with terminal diseases like Alzheimer's disease, AIDS, and cancer.

The key issue for the industry, however, is whether adequate financing will be available to cover the increasing costs of providing such care. In light of the long-term prospects for this business, NME has taken several steps. First, it is expanding and promoting special care units (SCUs) for Alzheimer's disease patients. Presently, it operates 36 SCUs and it plans to open another 12. NME is also expanding its rehabilitation services division. This group assesses the needs of each long-term care facility. It provides physical, occupational, and speech therapists for their staffs and ensures quality care at NME facilities. These therapists are also marketed to non-competing hospitals and clinics

on a private contracting basis with a view to attract more patients to NME.

Finally, NME is also attempting to attract private-pay patients by providing attractive private rooms, alternative food plans, and non-essential services at extra charges.

COMPANY D: COMMUNITY PSYCHIATRIC, INC.

Community Psychiatric, Inc. (CPI), was established in 1962 in the form of one psychiatric hospital near San Francisco. Since that time, CPI has grown to include 25 psychiatric facilities in the United States and Britain. Historically, CPI has capitalized on its ability to enter favorable geographic locations before its competitors. It was the first stand-alone psychiatric chain to establish a presence in California where the stigma of mental illness has disappeared more rapidly than in other parts of the country.

For the past several decades, the majority of the states in the United States have regulated the number of hospitals in a geographic locations. These Certificate of Need (CON) regulations have served to protect CPI's preeminent locations. The CON regulations are currently being phased out by many states, which will result in increased competition in several of CPI's primary markets. However, CPI should continue to benefit from having an established presence and relationships with psychiatrists in some of the best markets.

CPI has also diversified into home health care and dialysis centers. It is currently the largest independent psychiatric hospital chain in the country. Although the company is still small compared to HCA and Humana, it has been one of the fastest-growing health care companies in terms of earnings. From 1965 to 1985, CPI posted average revenue growth of 32% and average net income growth of 39%. Exhibits D1 through D3 show its operating and financial characteristics.

CPI has consistently obtained higher operating margins than many of its competitors (34% in 1985 versus 24% and 21% for Charter Medical and National Medical Enterprises, respectively). In addition to strict cost control of its everyday operations, the company has achieved its cost advantage through utilizing the same simple design for all of its facilities and through innovative measures such as cafeteria service for patients. In an environment where increasing pressure is being exerted by the government and private insurers to keep health care costs down, this low-cost position gives CPI added flexibility in responding to future changes in the industry.

Corporate Strategy

To date, a central part of CPI's strategy has been to locate its facilities in the growth areas of the nation. The company's 25 psychiatric facilities, 54 dialysis centers, and 11 home health offices are currently concentrated in California and the southeast. The higher margins that are attainable on psychiatric services result from this sector of health care being exempt from the Medicare Prospective Payment System (PPS). Both the home health and dialysis centers are subject to reimbursement under PPS and, therefore, have experienced increasing revenue pressure in recent years.

The major weakness of CPI is the high vulnerability of its main product line, psychiatric services, to increased competition. The decline is acute-care admissions and the pressure from cost-containment programs in recent years have caused the large health care management chains to diversify out of acute-care services. The tremendous untapped market for psychiatric services and their exemption from the Diagnostic Related Group program have made psychiatric services one of the most attractive areas in health care. CPI has already felt the effects of this competition. Since 1981, CPI has moved from first to fourth place—behind HCA, Charter Medical, and National Medical Enterprises—in terms of psychiatric revenues. The competition in this sector is expected to continue as other players attempt to move away from the mature acute-care segment.

This limited national presence is expected to dampen the company's revenue growth as new competitors enter the market and deregulation opens up states to new psychiatric hospitals. Because all hospital services tend to be largely doctor driven, the first competitors to enter a geographic area have an advantage in developing relationships with the local psychiatrists. If other chains expand more rapidly than CPI, the company's ultimate growth potential will be inhibited. Traditionally, there has never been an emphasis on marketing health care services. Both acute-care and specialty hospitals relied in the past on their location and doctor referrals for admissions. As the industry has become more competitive, however, many of the large health care chains have significantly increased their marketing efforts. CPI has been very slow to improve the degree of name recognition that it has in its markets. This is an area that it will have to improve on if it is to compete effectively with corporations such as HCA and Humana.

Exhibit D1 *Community Psychiatric, Inc.: Operating Revenue by Division, Fiscal 1985*

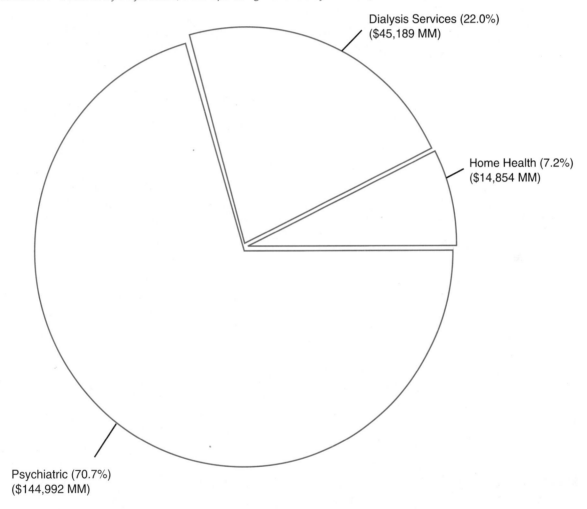

Dialysis Services (22.0%)
($45,189 MM)

Home Health (7.2%)
($14,854 MM)

Psychiatric (70.7%)
($144,992 MM)

Exhibit D2 *Community Psychiatric, Inc.: Operating Profit by Division, Fiscal 1985*

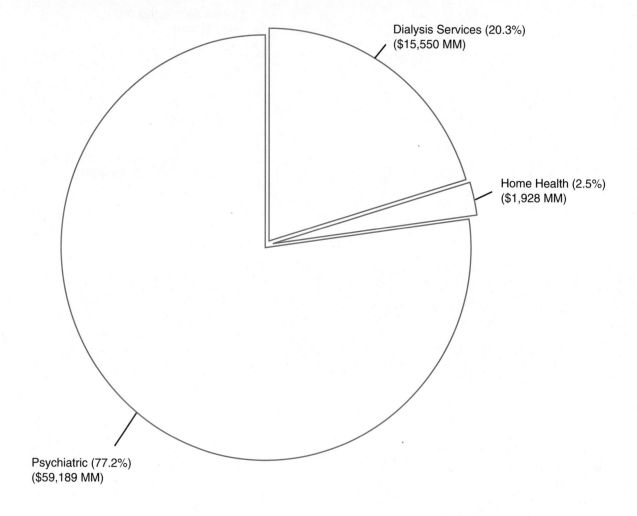

Dialysis Services (20.3%)
($15,550 MM)

Home Health (2.5%)
($1,928 MM)

Psychiatric (77.2%)
($59,189 MM)

Exhibit D3 Community Psychiatric, Inc.: Current Strategy—Income Statement (Dollars in 000)

Fiscal Year Ended November 30,

	1983		1984 (Actual)		1985		1986		1987		1988		1989		1990	
Operating revenue	$162.6	117.7%	$207.8	119.7%	$250.4	122.1%	$281.5	122.0%	$358.4	122.0%	$414.7	122.0%	$454.5	122.0%	$492.0	122.0%
Less: contractuals	24.4	17.7%	34.2	19.7%	45.4	22.1%	50.8	22.0%	64.6	22.0%	74.8	22.0%	82.0	22.0%	88.7	22.0%
Net op. rev.	138.2	100.0%	173.6	100.0%	205.0	100.0%	230.7	100.0%	293.8	100.0%	339.9	100.0%	372.6	100.0%	403.3	100.0%
Costs & exp:																
Operating exp.	61.0	44.1%	74.3	42.8%	90.0	43.9%	99.2	43.0%	129.3	44.0%	152.9	45.0%	167.7	45.0%	181.5	45.0%
Gen. & admin.	30.0	21.7%	34.5	19.9%	38.7	18.9%	42.0	18.2%	53.8	18.3%	61.2	18.0%	67.1	18.0%	72.6	18.0%
Depr. & amort.	3.7	2.7%	4.5	2.6%	5.4	2.6%	6.5	2.8%	8.2	2.8%	9.2	2.7%	10.1	2.7%	10.9	2.7%
Interest	3.3	2.4%	1.8	1.0%	1.1	0.5%	0.5	0.2%	0.5	0.2%	0.5	0.1%	0.5	0.1%	0.5	0.1%
Total	98.0	70.9%	115.1	66.3%	135.2	66.0%	148.1	64.2%	191.8	65.3%	223.8	65.8%	245.3	65.8%	265.5	65.8%
Operating income	40.2	29.1%	58.5	33.7%	69.8	34.0%	82.6	35.8%	102.0	34.7%	116.1	34.2%	127.3	34.2%	137.8	34.2%
Other income	8.5	6.2%	9.0	5.2%	12.9	6.3%	13.8	6.0%	17.6	6.0%	20.4	6.0%	22.4	6.0%	24.2	6.0%
Income before taxes	48.7	35.2%	67.5	38.9%	82.7	40.3%	96.4	41.8%	119.7	40.7%	136.5	40.2%	149.6	40.2%	162.0	40.2%
Prov. for taxes	21.8	15.8%	31.4	18.1%	37.9	18.5%	43.4	18.8%	53.8	18.3%	61.4	18.1%	67.3	18.1%	72.9	18.1%
Net income	26.9	19.5%	36.1	20.8%	44.8	21.9%	53.0	23.0%	65.8	22.4%	75.1	22.1%	82.3	22.1%	89.1	22.1%
EPS	$ 0.95		$ 1.22		$ 1.51		$ 1.76		$ 2.19		$ 2.49		$ 2.73		$ 2.96	
Shares outst.	20.2		29.9		30.1		30.1		30.1		30.1		30.1		30.1	
Dividends	$ 5.3		$6.8		$ 8.1		$9.5		$ 11.8		$ 13.5		$ 14.8		$ 16.0	
Capital expend.	$ 16.6		$ 21.2		$ 42.4		$ 45.0		$ 53.4		$ 24.2		$ 25.5		$ 27.0	
ROA	13.0%		15.2%		16.1%		16.6%		17.9%		18.1%		17.6%		16.8%	
ROE	17.1%		19.4%		19.6%		19.5%		20.2%		19.4%		18.1%		16.9%	
Net rev. growth	18.2%		25.6%		18.1%		12.5%		27.3%		15.7%		9.6%		8.2%	
Net income growth	47.8%		34.2%		24.1%		18.4%		24.1%		14.0%		9.7%		8.3%	
Total assets	$206.9		$237.3		$277.7		$319.4		$367.3		$415.0		$469.0		$529.9	
	$157.3		$186.5		$228.1		$271.6		$325.6		$387.1		$454.6		$527.7	
Cash flow	$ 6.7		$10.9		($2.0)		($5.3)		$7.1		$44.8		$50.4		$55.3	
Principal pmts.	$ 2.0		$1.7		$1.7		$10.3		$1.7		$1.7		$1.7		$1.7	
Hospitals (no.)	20		22		25		33		41		43		45		47	
Number of beds	1,834		2,005		2,231		2,801		3,401		3,541		3,681		3,821	
Length of stay (days)	29.7		26.9		25.1		24.6		23		22.5		22.5		22.5	
Admissions	11,912		14,985		18,255		20,993		27,291		31,749		33,563		34,840	
Patient days	354,034		403,443		458,029		516,428		627,693		714,353		755,168		783,900	
Occupancy	57.4%		59.1%		59.2%		52.8%		52.8%		59.0%		60.0%		60.0%	
Inpatient rev./day	$ 259		$285		$303		$307		$325		$341		$358		$376	
Psychiatric rev.	$ 91.8		$115.0		$138.6		$158.5		$204.0		$243.8		$270.6		$294.9	
Total hosp. rev.	$ 96.8		$121.0		$145.0		$164.0		$214.0		$253.8		$280.6		$304.9	
Dialysis centers	44		49		54		66		73		76		79		82	
Dialysis stations	547		636		750		925		1022		1064		1106		1148	

Exhibit D3 Community Psychiatric, Inc.: Current Strategy—Income Statement (Dollars in 000)

Fiscal Year Ended November 30,

	Actual				1987	1988	1989	1990
	1983	1984	1985	1986				
Treatments(#)	242,143	289,323	323,316	362,114	459,900	489,440	508,760	528,080
Treatment/station	443	455	431	438	450	460	460	460
Rev. per treat.	$148	$142	$140	$137	$131	$130	$130	$130
Dialysis revenues	$35.8	$41.1	$45.3	$49.6	$60.2	$63.6	$66.1	$68.7
Home health care rev.	$5.4	$11.5	$14.8	$17.0	$19.6	$22.5	$25.9	$29.7
Total op. rev.	$138.0	$173.6	$205.1	$230.7	$293.8	$339.9	$372.6	$403.3

Assumptions:
Growth: Additional two psychiatric hospitals per year, 1987–1990, with 70 avg. beds
         Additional three dialysis centers per year, 1987–1990, with 14 avg. stations
Psychiatric rev./day: increases 5% 1987–1990
Dialysis rev./treatment: constant at $130 1988–1990
Home health care revenues: increases 15% 1987–1990
Length of stay: stable at 22.5 days 1988–1990
Tax rate 45%
Total asset growth of 15% in 1986 and 1987, 13% in 1988–1990
Non-operating hospital revenue of $10 million
Capital expenditures for a psychiatric hospital are $70,000 per bed and $500,000 for a dialysis center.

Net present value analysis (Dollars in 000)

	1986	1987	1988	1989	1990
Net income	53.0	65.8	75.1	82.3	89.1
Less dividends	9.5	11.8	13.5	14.8	16.0
Add-back depreciation	6.5	8.2	9.2	10.1	10.9
Capital expenditures:					
Maintenance	7.5	9.9	12.7	13.7	14.8
Expansion	37.5	43.5	11.5	11.8	12.2
Debt repayment	10.3	1.7	1.7	1.7	1.7
Net cash flow	($ 5.3)	$ 7.1	$44.8	$50.4	$55.3
Discounted at 11.04%	1.000	0.901	0.811	0.730	0.658
Years	0	1	2	3	4

Present value of cash flows	$110.5
Plus terminal value[a]	$174.0
Total net present value	$284.5 $ 9.45 per share

[a]Assumes a constant growth rate of 8.3% after 1990.

ISKRA POWER TOOLS

Robert C. Howard, William A. Fischer, and Per V. Jenster
International Institute for Management Development
Lausanne, Switzerland

As he walked through his factory one frigid winter morning in January 1991, Miro Krek, general manager of Iskra Industrija za Elektricna Orodja in Kranj, Yugoslavia, commented to his visitors, "There are certain things we need to do in aligning our marketing and manufacturing. As you walk through here, you can see that our efficiency could easily be improved by 10% to 15%. For example, we could put in longer lines and plan larger volume runs to get better efficiency. At the same time, we are considering concentrating our manufacturing on certain parts such as motors." Placing his hand on his chest, he said with considerable emotion, "Motors are at the heart of any power tool—we need to manufacture them!"

For Iskra's management, the situation in Yugoslavia was tumultuous. Krek explained, "Over the last three months, Yugoslavia has undergone incredible political change towards adapting a Western-style market economy. As this change has touched all aspects of our society, so it has forced us to rethink our entire power tool business. The question for me is, 'Should we try to become a major player in the West and East European power tool markets or, should we only focus on a few select markets or customers? Then, too, what would be the consequences for the Iskra organization?'"

Soon after the government approved several free enterprise laws in Yugoslavia in January 1989, revolutions occurred in many of the neighboring countries in Eastern Europe. Prior to those events, Iskra had concentrated its sales primarily on Western power tool markets, where the management believed its competitive advantages were low labor costs and, to a lesser extent, a few niche products. In fact, until January 1991, these two dimensions had formed the basis of Krek's plans for leading the Iskra Power Tool Division into the 1990s. Now, however, with Europe's political landscape in upheaval, new markets were emerging, and old advantages were threatened. Consequently, it was necessary to review the interrelated issues of manufacturing and marketing power tools.

As Krek saw it, there were at least three options available for Iskra Power Tools. First, continue to capitalize on Yugoslavia's low labor costs and compete on price in Western markets. Alternatively, Iskra could build on the two major successes that it had enjoyed, and manufacture and market a select few power tools in Western niche markets. Third, the management of Iskra Power Tools could try to build on Yugoslavia's tradition as a commercial link between East and West, and develop the power tool markets of Eastern Europe.

Along with the above, Miro also had the continuing worry of how to preserve Iskra's domestic position at a time when the firm was under direct attack from a Black & Decker assembly operation in Yugoslavia. With less than two weeks to prepare for his final presentation to senior management of the Iskra Group, Krek knew a full review of the options for the 1990s was necessary.

THE ISKRA GROUP OF COMPANIES

The Iskra Group of Companies was founded in Ljubjana in 1961 through the merger of four major electrical companies in Slovenia, Yugoslavia's northernmost republic. The group based its name on the oldest of these companies—Iskra—which also meant "spark" in Slovenian and symbolized the electronic nature of the group's products. By 1991, Iskra had become the leading electronic and electrical manufacturer in Yugoslavia, manufacturing and marketing a broad range of products through 14 domestic subsidiaries and 18 foreign offices. Moreover, in Slovenia, Iskra was home to roughly 25,000 employees, making the Iskra Group of Companies the largest Slovenian employer.

Iskra Power Tools

Although the Iskra Group was founded in 1961, the origins of some of its companies could be traced to the end of World War II or earlier. What became Iskra Power Tools, for example, had begun as a textile company in Kranj during the 1930s when Czechoslovakian textile manufacturers moved their operations to Northern Yugoslavia to take advantage of the low-cost labor force. During World War II, the Nazis gained control of Yugoslavia and transformed the textile facility into a military factory for aircraft engine parts; in the process, they transferred substantial metal working and engineering skills into the Iskra factories.

Throughout the postwar era, the mechanical expertise brought to Iskra by the Germans grew increasingly intertwined with electronics, supported by the expertise in Iskra's electronics companies. Until the early 1950s, Iskra's employees had channeled that expertise into industrial and consumer products for rebuilding the Yugoslavian infrastructure and meeting the needs of the domestic market, respectively. Included among the group's industrial products were electric power meters, transformers, capacitors, and electric motors. In the consumer area, typical products included automotive electronics such as starters, alternators, and voltage regulators, and household appliances such as vacuum cleaners, toasters, and power tools.

In time, the Kranj production facility became too constrained to continue manufacturing the entire Iskra product offering, and several products were transferred to other sites in the area. Power tool production, however, along with kilowatt meters and telecommunications switching equipment remained in Kranj. (See Exhibit 1 for the Iskra Power Tools organization chart.)

Iskra Commerce

As was typical in many centrally planned economies, the production and distribution of Iskra Group's products were partitioned into separate responsibilities. While the factories concentrated on production, a separate sales organization, Iskra Commerce, was founded in 1961 to handle the marketing and distribution responsibilities of the organization. Originally, Iskra Commerce had served as a central commercial organization, conducting all purchasing and selling for the Iskra Group of Companies—both inside and outside Yugoslavia. In the early 1970s, following marked growth in size and responsibility, Iskra's domestic companies began to purchase and sell directly in Yugoslavia. However, Iskra Commerce retained responsibility for foreign commercial intercourse.

In foreign markets, Iskra Commerce continued purchasing and selling for all companies within the Iskra Group until the late 1980s. Thereafter, Iskra's foreign companies, like the ones in Yugoslavia, began to establish direct commercial links with suppliers and buyers. Mitja Taucher, former senior advisor of Iskra Commerce, recalled the organization's mission, "When Yugoslavia had strong regulations regarding imports, it made a lot of sense to channel all the group's purchases and sales through one organization; the group was stronger as a whole than as individual companies. Now, however, with the changes in Yugoslavia concerning imports and the strength of our individual companies, it makes sense for Iskra Commerce to serve in a different capacity."

THE POWER TOOL INDUSTRY

Generally speaking, power tools included any tool containing a motor that was capable of being guided and supported manually by an operator. Thus, power tools played an intermediary role between traditional hand tools and sophisticated machine tools. Typical products in the power tool family included the household drill, circular saw, jigsaw, router, angle grinder, hedge trimmer, chain saw, and less familiar and more specialized products such as nut runners and impact wrenches used in assembly-line manufacture. The wide availability of electrical energy and the relatively low cost of electric tools facilitated their use in small workshops, the building and construction industries, and in households.

Exhibit 1 *Iskra Power Tool Organization Chart*

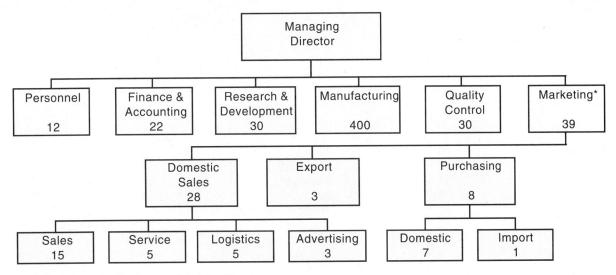

*Includes 10 people who also work in Iskra Commerce.
Source: Company records.

Analysts and participants classified the industry into two broad segments according to end usage: professional and hobby. In the professional category, users worked in industries such as assembly-line manufacture, foundries, shipbuilding, and woodworking. The building and construction trade, on the other hand, covered both user segments; that is, tools dedicated to the professional builder as well as tools designed for the home enthusiast or do-it-yourself (DIY) market. Worldwide, power tool purchase behavior varied as a function of labor costs and disposable income. Generally, the professional power tool sector was most developed in high-labor-cost countries; the DIY market tended to be more pronounced in countries with higher personal disposable incomes.

In 1989, the worldwide electric power tool industry was valued at just over DM10 billion,[1] with sales concentrated in three major markets: North America, 28%; Europe, 47%; and the Far East, 18%. Although the industry had grown an average of 3% per annum on a worldwide basis since 1980, market growth rates varied considerably among individual countries (as indicated in Exhibit 2). Within Europe, where the industrial segment had traditionally

dominated, Germany, France, Great Britain and Italy represented 75% of the region's sales (as summarized in Exhibit 3).

Segments and Channels

Professional tools were traditionally bought in hardware stores, from wholesalers, large tool specialists, or from a manufacturer's or distributor's direct sales force. Quality products suited to specific tasks, durability, and after-sales service were viewed as important buying criteria. In addition, some manufacturers of high-end tools viewed education and problem solving as part of the sales effort, with trained sales people needed to meet the technical requirements of the user.

In the hobby segment, customers bought from wholesalers, hardware stores, department stores, home centers, mail order houses, and hypermarkets. In this segment, manufacturers considered image, product quality, and price as important purchase factors. Also in this segment, competition was becoming increasingly like that of other consumer products, namely, brand name and packaging were gaining in importance relative to other product fea-

---

[1]In 1989, average exchange rates were 1 European Currency Unit (ECU) = deutsche mark (DM) 2.02, and US$1 = DM1.88.

Exhibit 2 *% Growth of European Power Tool Markets in 1989 and 1990*

Country	% Growth 1989	Country	% Growth 1990
Portugal	20	Greece	35
Spain	18	Germany	18
Italy	15	Portugal	18
Greece	15	Italy	12
Finland	12	Netherlands	10
Austria	12	Sweden	10
Sweden	10	Ireland	8
Great Britain	8	Belgium	6
Germany	8	Spain	6
France	8	Austria	4
Belgium	8	Denmark	3
Switzerland	8	Switzerland	3
Netherlands	5	France	0
Ireland	5	Great Britain	0
Denmark	−5	Norway	0
Norway	−5	Finland	−3

Source: 1989—Databank; 1990—Bosch.

Exhibit 3 *1989 Unit Sales in Europe's Four Largest Markets*

Country	Thousands of Pieces	%European Sales
Germany	7,000	28
France	5,000	20
Great Britain	4,300	17
Italy	2,500	10
Other countries	6,200	25
Total	25,000	100

Source: Bosch.

tures. At the low end of the market, products were designed to meet an expected lifetime use of 25 hours. At the high end, on the other hand, which tended to enlarge as the market matured, there was more emphasis on durability and ergonomic characteristics, similar to professional products.

In Europe, a shift in purchasing patterns had led to a shift in the distribution of power tools. In the professional sector, direct sales had begun to play a more significant role in the distribution process, particularly in the more mature and structured markets. And, in the consumer segment, the volume of tools sold through mass merchandisers was growing at the expense of conventional tool sellers. In short, increased specialization in power tool usage, combined with a proliferation of applications, was leading manufacturers to establish more direct links to professional users and more visible links to the DIY segment. The volume of power tools sold through any one of these channels varied as a function of country. Generally speaking, the markets in Northern Europe were more mature and more structured than those in the Mediterranean countries. Likewise, mass merchandisers and direct sales played a more significant role in the North than in the South. (Exhibit 4 contains comparative data on power tools sold through different channels in Germany vs Italy.)

Manufacturing

Power tools embodied a range of technologies including a motor shaft around which copper wire was wound to form an armature, gears, plastic or metal housing, switches, and cables. In conjunction with a trend in production specialization in the post-war era, power tool manufacturers relied heavily on subcontractors to produce many of these components. Generally speaking, the major competitors only made components that were central to the performance of the final product, such as the motor. The following summarizes the key elements in a typical power tool:

Portable Electric Power Tool

- Outer shell
- Electric motor
- Screw machine parts
- Switches and attachments
- Packaging

Typically, power tools were mass produced, although the extent of mechanization varied with the volume of production, nature of the product, and the efficiency of the individual manufacturer. According to one industry analyst, purchased materials accounted for 50% of a power tool firm's manufacturing costs, machining 15%, diecasting/molding 9%, motor winding and assembly 12%, and final assembly 14%.

Trends

By the late 1980s, a number of trends began to influence the level and nature of competition in the worldwide power tool industry. Among these were a growing preference for battery-powered tools, globalization of the industry, and the opening up of Eastern Europe.

Exhibit 4 % of Country Sales by Distribution Channel—1990

Channel\Country	Germany	Italy
DIY Segment		
Wholesalers	5	25
Hardware stores	55	45
Department stores (mass merchandisers)	15	11
Home centers	21	—
Others (cash and carry, mail order)	4	19
Professional Segment		
Direct	10	—
Hardware	50	55
Wholesalers	40	25
Large-tool specialists (mass merchandisers)	—	20

Source: Black & Decker, Iskra Company records.

Battery-powered Tools. During the 1980s, battery-powered (also known as cordless) tools benefited significantly from advances in technology. Because of their low energy storage, initial battery-driven products were limited to the smaller jobs of the DIY market. However, the combination of superior power storage and lighter materials that was developed during the 1980s permitted battery-operated tools to be used in more demanding applications, thus facilitating their penetration of the professional market. At the end of the 1980s, cordless tools represented 20% of all power tool production worldwide; and, like many products using electronics, the Japanese were particularly adept at developing cordless power tools. During the 1990s, advances in materials science and battery technology were expected to increase both the usage life between recharges and the number of applications cordless tools could handle.

Globalization. Throughout the 1980s, the electric power tool industry became increasingly globalized, enabling larger players to have an operational flexibility unavailable to smaller companies. By decreasing a firm's reliance on a single market, multinational power tool companies were able to leverage their positions worldwide. That is, firms with manufacturing as well as sales in many markets were able to exploit uncertainties in exchange rates, competitive moves, or government policies far better than their smaller rivals.

Eastern Europe and the USSR. During 1989, communist dictatorships across Eastern Europe were replaced by a variety of governments which, in general, expressed their commitment to develop market economies. Analysts believed that these developments would influence the power tool business in two ways. First, these newly opened markets and their power tool manufacturers were expected to be the targets of firms already established in the West. Secondly, once the legal issues surrounding privatization became clear, the surviving power tool manufacturers in Eastern Europe could begin to restructure their own operations and market their products at home and abroad.

Competition

In 1989, there were approximately 75 power tool manufacturers worldwide. Generally speaking, these competitors could be grouped into two categories: large multinationals and, primarily, domestic manufacturers. Typically, the large players offered a full range of power tools to both the professional and the DIY segments, as well as a complete line of accessories such as drill bits, saw blades, battery packs and after-sales service. Smaller power tool manufacturers, on the other hand, tended to concentrate production on a limited line of tools, augmented by original equipment manufacturer (OEM) products to one or a few segments of the market. Although these small firms lacked the product offering of their larger rivals, they were well known and respected for their expertise in their chosen fields.

Black & Decker. Black & Decker was the largest power tool maker in the world. With manufacturing plants in 10 countries and sales in nearly 100, the company reported 1989 power tool sales of $1,077 million. With approximately 25% of the total market, Black & Decker commanded a worldwide share more than twice that of its next biggest rival. Like most of its competitors, the company segmented the industry into professional and DIY sectors; between the two, Black & Decker derived two-thirds of its revenue from consumers and one-third from professional users.

In addition to its sheer size, Black & Decker enjoyed a number of competitive advantages. New product introduction, for example, was a high priority; the company launched 77 products in 1989 alone and, in the same year, new and redesigned products accounted for 25% of revenues. By 1991, the company expected new entries to represent more than half its sales.

In Europe, where Black & Decker pioneered the introduction of products to the DIY segment, its name was virtually synonymous with power tools. In Britain, for example, it was not uncommon for DIY remodelers to "Black & Decker" their homes. And, in France, individuals "plugged in" to the social scene were said to be "*très Black & Decker.*"

One company spokesman attributed his company's success to proper market segmentation and a restructuring that had begun in the mid-1980s. Thus, when the market for power tools as a whole was growing at a rate of only 5% to 6%, Black & Decker achieved 11% growth in 1989, twice the rate of the markets served, due in part to its concentrated focus on accessories and cordless products. Although the latter grew 30% in 1989, Black & Decker's successful identification of the trend toward cordless products allowed its sales in this segment to grow by 70%, reaching $100 million in 1989.

From the mid-1980s onward, the management of Black & Decker devoted significant attention to "globalizing" its worldwide operations and, by the beginning of the 1990s, design centers, manufacturing plants, and marketing programs were adept at making and selling products to a worldwide market. As early as 1978, Black & Decker had undertaken the standardization of its motors and armature shafts, and it had, over the years, consistently pursued manufacturing approaches that combined product variety with volume output such as dedicated lines and facilities for specific items (focused factories and group technology); flexible manufacturing systems (FMS),[2] just-in-time manufacturing (JIT),[3] and significant vertical integration of the fabrication and assembly process. In addition, Black & Decker achieved substantial cost savings through global purchasing programs and saved millions of dollars by restructuring its manufacturing facilities. In one facility, for example, the company standardized production around a limited number of motors. In another case, the company consolidated production of drills from five different plants to two.

To strengthen its presence in Eastern Europe, Black & Decker had recently established an assembly operation via a joint venture in Kranj. Although the company owned only 49%, its proximity to Iskra was seen as a serious challenge to the latter's position in Yugoslavia. And, in May 1989 in Czechoslovakia, Black & Decker entered into a joint venture to produce DIY tools and lawnmowers for the Czechoslovakian and West European markets. Once the joint venture reached full capacity, planned for the start of 1990, Black & Decker intended to cease production at its French and Italian facilities, and rely on its new Eastern European manufacturing platform.

Makita. Based in Japan, the Makita Electric Works had entered the power tool market in the 1950s. In the mid-1970s and the 1980s, Makita established itself in a number of foreign markets by emphasizing its price competitiveness. At one point

in the mid-1970s, for example, Makita products were selling at price levels that were 20% to 30% lower than the industry average. Nonetheless, by the beginning of the 1990s, Makita had established a solid reputation for quality and after-sales service, supported by a three-day repair policy. And, through engaging a large number of distribution outlets in target markets to promote and service its products, Makita had climbed to number two in the industry by 1991.

In contrast to Black & Decker, Makita concentrated only on the professional segment of the market, with a broad range of tools for professionals. The company attributed its success in overseas markets to superior after-sales service and a close working relationship with well-informed retailers who kept in touch with consumers regarding the latest in product development. Beginning with two factories in Japan in the mid-1970s, Makita had decided to globalize its operations during the 1980s, establishing factory operations in the United States, Canada, and Brazil.

In Europe, Makita's 1989 sales increased by 15% and, in the same year, a company spokesman stated that Makita intended to become the largest power tool supplier in the region. In a step toward fulfilling that vision and meeting the company's expressed goal of supplying 25% of European sales with locally manufactured products, Makita began constructing a new power tool plant in the United Kingdom in March 1990. Scheduled to begin operating in early 1991, the plant would initially make cordless and percussion drills, angle grinders, and circular saws for the professional sector. Ultimately, however, the plant was to produce only electric motors. As of January 1991, Makita had not begun to compete in any of Iskra's markets.

Robert Bosch. Robert Bosch was the third largest power tool producer in the world and had manufacturing plants in Germany, the United States, Brazil, and Switzerland. Like Black & Decker, Bosch produced a variety of power tools for both the professional and the DIY segments, buying the portable tool division of Stanley Tools in the United States in 1979. The company was particularly strong in Europe where it distributed through all channels.

---

[2]Flexible manufacturing systems consisted of sophisticated computer-driven lines, with relatively independent routing and intelligent machining centers.

[3]JIT referred to the Japanese-inspired approach to manufacturing which had originated with the philosophy of continuous improvement, superior quality, low changeover costs, and greatly reduced work-in-process inventories.

In 1990, despite an unfavorable trend in the $/DM exchange rate, Bosch's sales increased 14% to over DM2.2 billion.

Following the unification of East and West Germany, Bosch management announced plans for a joint venture with VEB Elektrowerkzeuge Sebnitz to assemble power tools in Dresden (formerly East Germany) to be distributed through the latter's network of 1,400 hardware outlets. By the end of 1990, the Sebnitz facility was a fully owned subsidiary and earmarked for DM50 million in investment, initially for producing one-handed angle grinders and small drills. In the longer term, the management of Bosch planned to concentrate all export production in Sebnitz.

Skil. Skil was a major manufacturer of power tools based in the United States, where the company was originally known as a professional tool supplier. More recently, however, Skil had concentrated on developing tools that fulfilled needs somewhere between the professional and consumer levels. In Europe, Skil had positioned itself in the Nordic markets as a professional tool company. It approached the rest of Europe, on the other hand, in the DIY market with a strong price emphasis, and was particularly strong in Germany and France.

Niche Players. Aside from the larger multinational power tool companies, there were a host of successful, albeit smaller, players in Europe which pursued niche strategies. In Germany, for example, Festo and ELU were well known for their fine-crafted woodworking tools, especially circular saws. Likewise, Kango, a British company, was renowned for its percussion drills. Generally speaking, niche players in the European power tool business charged premium prices and earned the majority of their sales in their home markets. (See Exhibits 5 and 6 respectively, for a summary of Iskra's competition according to category, and a competitor positioning diagram prepared by a team of Iskra management.)

ISKRA POWER TOOLS' COMPETITIVE POSITION

Market Development

From its beginning in the early 1950s, the Iskra Power Tool division concentrated its sales in the Yugoslavian market. Ventures into Western Europe did not begin until the 1960s when the management sought to expand its product offering, consisting primarily of electric drills, based on the company's expertise in small electric motors. The cornerstone of this expansion strategy was exchange programs with other power tool manufacturers.

In 1966, Iskra entered into a cooperation agreement with Perles, a small power tool manufacturer in Switzerland. In exchange for Perles' angle grinders sold under the Iskra name in Yugoslavia, Perles received Iskra's drills, which it distributed through its own network under the Perles label. In 1971, Iskra management sought to build on the Perles name and distribution network by acquiring the Swiss-based manufacturer. Mitja Taucher commented that, in the early 1970s, Iskra management realized they would have difficulties with an unknown name in Europe and, thus, decided to acquire Perles. "Perles is still in existence mostly for its name, not its manufacturing capacity, which is small," recalled Mitja. He added, "It was a good name across Europe for large angle grinders and some drills."

Bolstered by its first co-marketing arrangement with Perles, in 1972 the management of Iskra entered into an agreement with Skil Europe. In exchange for Iskra's small drills, sold under Skil's name through its European distribution network, Skil supplied Iskra with percussion drills, belt sanders, and circular saws, sold in Yugoslavia under the Iskra name.

Eastern European Ventures

Following the first of a series of oil crises that began in 1973, it was difficult for Iskra to continue its expansion plans into Western markets. As an alternative, the management of Iskra Power Tools began to strengthen business ties with its socialist neighbors in Eastern Europe.

Czechoslovakia. Iskra's Eastern European experience began in 1978 with Naradi, a power tool manufacturer, and with Merkuria, a trading company, both based in Czechoslovakia. Due to a lack of convertible currency in Czechoslovakia, Iskra devised a three-way trading agreement: Perles shipped drills from Switzerland to Naradi, which marketed the products under the Naradi name, and to Merkuria, which sold products under the Iskra name. In turn, both Czech firms delivered products to Iskra; the process was completed when Iskra sent its power

Exhibit 5 *Iskra's Main Competitors in Europe*

Competitor	Location of Corporate Headquarters[a]	Specialist (S) or Generalist (G)	Perceived Successful by Iskra
AEG	D	G	
Black & Decker	US	G	+
Bosch	D	G	+
Casals	E	G	
ELU	D	S, woodworking tools, especially circular saws	
Fein	D	S, metal working tools, especially drills, and angle grinders	
Festo	D	S, same as ELU	+
Hilti	D	S, drills	+
Hitachi	J	G	
Impex	D	S, drills	
Kango	UK	S, percussion drills	
Kress	D	G	
Makita	J	G	
Metabo	D	G	
Peugeot	F	G	
Rockwell	US	G	
Rupes	I	S, table saws	
Ryobi	J	G	+
Skil	US,NL	G	
Stayer	I	G	+
Wegoma	D	S, same as ELU	

Source: Company records.
[a]D = Germany; US = United States; E = Spain; J = Japan; UK = United Kingdom; F = France; I = Italy; and NL = Netherlands.

tools to Perles in Switzerland. Although Iskra achieved nearly a 10% market share through these two agreements in Czechoslovakia, its success was not without problems.

One executive stated that the weak point in the process was the power tools from Czechoslovakia; tools made by Naradi did not measure up to the quality standards demanded by Yugoslavian consumers. Moreover, after a few years, Naradi's products were out of date in comparison to competitors' offerings. Finally, because of the difficulties posed by the lack of real distribution channels or a service network in Czechoslovakia, Iskra management terminated the agreement in 1988.

Poland. Iskra had also participated in a cooperative arrangement to exchange power tools with

Celma, a Polish power tool manufacturer. Like the agreement with Naradi in Czechoslovakia, Iskra marketed Celma's products under the Iskra name in Yugoslavia. However, Celma's products were of such low quality that Iskra soon found itself inundated with repair requests. Consequently, the management of Iskra devised a new agreement for close cooperation on specialty tools such as shears, steel cutters, and die grinders.

USSR. More recently, Iskra Power Tools had tried manufacturing in the USSR. After five years of negotiating with the Institute for Power Tools in Moscow, in 1984, the first 100 power tools were brought to Yugoslavia. Unfortunately, due to the length of the negotiating period, the products were out of date on arrival. Like the previous efforts in

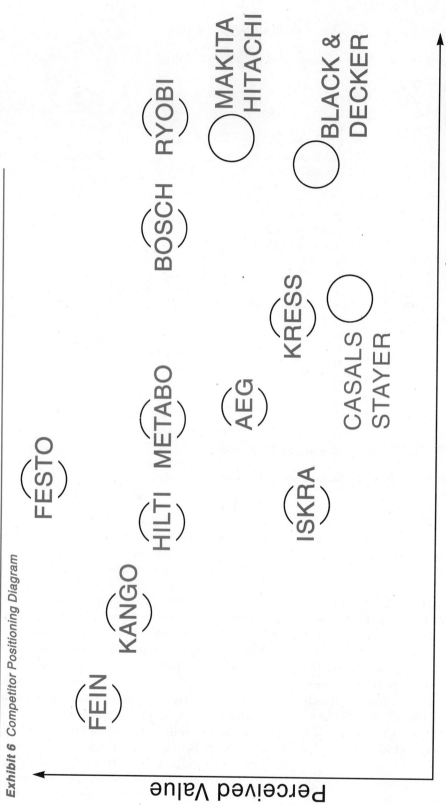

Exhibit 6   Competitor Positioning Diagram

Czechoslovakia and Poland, Iskra brought its Russian efforts to a halt.

Refocus on Western Europe

Like many firms that manufactured in and exported from Yugoslavia, Iskra earned a certain level of income from the domestic market. Although that income was not guaranteed, limited competition in the Yugoslavian power tool market had almost always provided Iskra with a source of funding to manufacture tools sold outside the country. By the beginning of the 1980s, however, the management of Iskra Power Tools grew concerned about becoming too dependent on the domestic market. Moreover, when it combined the uncertainties of the domestic market with its unsuccessful ventures in Eastern Europe, the management concluded it was time to resume strengthening ties with Western power tool producers.

Iskra as OEM Supplier

ELU. In 1980, Iskra signed a cooperation agreement with ELU, a German manufacturer of woodworking tools. Despite Iskra's successful development and initial manufacture of a small circular saw for sale under the ELU label, the management of ELU canceled the agreement after two years. According to Branko Suhadolnik, export manager for Iskra Power Tools, Iskra was simply unable to supply the quantity of saws specified in the contract because of delays in starting production.

Kango. Iskra also began manufacturing for Kango, a UK company specializing in drills. In exchange for Kango's rotary hammer, sold under the Iskra name in Yugoslavia, Iskra provided Kango with circular saws sold under the Kango name in the United Kingdom.

Iskra as Volume OEM

Skil. In the mid-1980s, Iskra management expanded its cooperation with Skil. In addition to supplying Skil with a small drill, Iskra provided a small angle grinder, a circular saw, and orbital sander. These items were sold under the Skil name in support of Skil's low-price strategy. In November 1990, the management of Iskra approached Skil to discuss strengthening their partnership still further. However, as of January 1991, no additional cooperation had been agreed to.

Ryobi. In 1990, Miro Krek and Branko Suhadolnik began negotiating a joint venture agreement with Ryobi from Japan. Suhadolnik explained that Ryobi was considering Yugoslavia as an entry point into the European Economic Community and wanted to capitalize on Yugoslavia's comparative advantage in labor costs. In return for supplying angle grinders to Ryobi, Iskra was to market Ryobi's battery-operated power tools in Yugoslavia. Although the management of Ryobi was impressed with Iskra's products, they said that the manufacturing costs were too high; in order to meet Ryobi's terms, Iskra had to invest in more equipment. Shortly thereafter, the management of Ryobi decided to postpone further dealings in Eastern Europe until the political environment stabilized.

Bosch. In its most recent effort to supply a foreign manufacturer, Iskra approached Bosch concerning a router that complemented Bosch's offering. This deal, too, nearly succeeded, but was contingent on Iskra's dissolving its independent sales network in Germany and elsewhere. Because Bosch was not willing to purchase what Iskra management believed was the required volume necessary to compensate for the loss of its sales network, Iskra declined the offer.

In summary, the management of Iskra had made several attempts over the years to increase its attractiveness to foreign firms. With Skil, a generalist in the power tool industry, Iskra's competitive advantage was being a low-cost supplier; with ELU, Kango, and Bosch, on the other hand, Iskra's success was based on the high perceived value of a niche product. With Ryobi, price competitiveness and market presence in Eastern Europe were important.

Iskra's Products and Channels

At the beginning of 1991, Iskra marketed a range of 200 products; 10 of these were obtained from other manufacturers via exchange agreements, while the balance were designed and produced by Iskra alone. Roughly speaking, accessories accounted for 20% of Iskra Power Tools' turnover, while drills and angle grinders accounted for approximately 50% and 30%, respectively, of tool sales. Outside Yugoslavia, Iskra distributed its own products under the Perles name, almost exclusively through specialist hardware outlets in both the DIY and professional segments. In addition, Iskra Commerce marketed Iskra's power tools through its own offices. Although the influence of the latter was declining, Suhadolnik commented that, until the late 1980s, Iskra Commerce's foreign companies often made policies to survive for the short term, with little attention to the long term. For example, in those markets where the two organizations overlapped, prices sometimes differed between Iskra Power Tools and Iskra Commerce for the same products. More recently, he added, Iskra management had succeeded in changing this policy but, Suhadolnik commented, "To change something with a life of its own is not so easy."

In Yugoslavia, where Iskra had a market share of 50% in 1989, the company sold its power tools through Iskra Commerce with its own network of shops in each republic. However, the company had a significantly larger market share in Serbia than in Slovenia or Croatia. According to Branko, natives of the latter two provinces, because of their proximity to Italy and Austria, were not only better informed as to Western power tool alternatives, but could more easily access these alternative products. Power tools were also sold through the Iskra Power Tools sales organization, and directly from the factory in Kranj.

Design

In 1990, the design group at Iskra consisted of six people, all working primarily with pencil and paper. By contrast, their Western counterparts worked with computer-aided design (CAD) systems. Despite the lack of modern design equipment, the Iskra design team possessed strong artistic talents and lacked the engineering bias of Western designers. In describing the evolution of the relationship between design and manufacturing at Iskra, one manager commented that, until the early 1980s, there was a "we draw, you make" attitude. A few years thereafter, employees in the two functions began taking a more interdisciplinary approach to designing and making Iskra's power tools. Designers, for example, began asking those in manufacturing about the costs associated with individual parts; those in manufacturing, on the other hand, asked designers for new technological solutions. "Yet," recalled one designer, "new solutions were not possible because they required too much investment in new technology."

As of January 1991, there were two ways of concentrating on new product development at Iskra Power Tools. One was via direct cooperation with manufacturing on existing product lines, a process which tended to focus on minor changes and had been practiced for at least 15 years. The second pertained to new products and was primarily concerned with shortening product development time, through interdisciplinary teams, to a level comparable to Iskra's competition.

Not unlike the design-manufacturing relationship, the interaction between design and marketing was based on a philosophy of "we design, you sell". Beginning in the mid-1980s, however, this relationship also began to change as collaboration with Iskra's partners—Skil and Perles—on new designs began to increase, and greater and earlier cooperation between the two functions began to evolve.

Iskra was receptive to ideas from the marketplace, communicated to the design team via Iskra's customers and foreign distributors. In 1988, for example, Iskra formed a multidisciplinary team to determine which products had to be produced in the subsequent five years, at what price and what quantity. In the export market, ideas were solicited from Iskra's agents and distributors via an annual conference. As for feedback from end users, Iskra conducted market research for both its professional and its DIY customers, albeit only in Yugoslavia. (See Exhibit 7 for design information at Iskra Power Tools.)

Manufacturing

Despite Iskra's product offering of 200 power tools, most were variations of a common manufacturing mix of 10 to 15 models, all made in one factory using traditional batch production. Depending on the model, the array of products was manufactured on a monthly, quarterly, or annual basis. For example, Iskra had 70 variations of its drill, which was produced throughout the year in the same way as its angle grinders and circular saws. On the other hand, smaller volume products such as sanders and routers were made only on a quarterly basis.

Planning. At Iskra, batch sizes and sequencing were developed by a central planning department located in the Kranj factory. Typically, the planning department estimated the year's production and adjusted their forecast quarterly. In addition, three planners prioritized the work at each factory work-

Exhibit 7 Information on Iskra Power Tools' Design Function

	1982	1983	1984	1985	1986	1987	1988	1989	1990
No. designers	5	5	5	5	5	3	6	6	5
Average age	40	41	42	42	43	35	37	40	41
Years of experience (absolute)	38	43	48	49	54	20	26	28	33
Reconstructed products[a]	6				7				3
Modifications	148				208				190
Commercial variants	717				1,802				827
New products	0	1	3	1	2	1	0	1	0

Source: Company records.

[a]A reconstructed product was one that had been developed and produced, but corrected for flaws. A modification, on the other hand, corresponded to a product with an incremental innovation such as a new spindle, a different type of handle, or an additional speed. As the name implied, commercial variants were simply the number of variations possible for Iskra's products needed to meet the different demands of Iskra's many markets and customers.

station, based on the assembly plan which, in turn, was based on delivery promises. Prior to final assembly, the manufacturing department received figures for specific markets and attached the correct labels to the final package.

Differences between the batches produced and the amounts needed for assembly at any point in time (due to lead time varations) were stored in inventories until needed. In other words, purchasing of components and product fabrication at Iskra were always begun before the ultimate destination of a power tool was known, thereby limiting the ability to use dedicated machining in the first and last stages of the production process. From 1987 to 1989, Iskra Power Tools' inventory turnovers averaged 4.4, with the biggest inventories occurring at the beginning of the assembly process. By comparison, one manager estimated that Bosch's inventory turnover was in the range of 5 to 10 per year.

Milan Bavec, manufacturing manager, believed that parts inventories were too high because of difficulties in linking purchasing more closely to assembly. As an example, he explained that, on August 1, he might begin a series of 3,000 sanders, for which he ordered parts three months in advance. However, he said, when some parts took six months to arrive, one simply had to maintain the necessary inventory. All parts, he continued, were moved in and out of inventory. That is, whether Iskra produced or purchased its parts, all parts were stored in a warehouse until the full range was available to make a particular product. As an aside, Igor Poljsak, financial and accounting department manager, mentioned that the constant shifting of parts between Iskra's many

buildings added 10% to 15% to production costs. Then, too, at 40% to 50% per year to borrow money, he estimated that the interest on working capital was 10% to 12%. Within manufacturing, some believed that if the individual market demands could be better coordinated with the manufacturing function, inventories could be reduced and more dedicated assembly implemented, thereby raising productivity.

Productivity. In terms of performance, productivity at Iskra Power Tools was somewhere between that of Eastern and Western power tool makers, with direct labor estimated at 10% to 12% of the cost of goods sold. (See Exhibit 8 for productivity figures, Exhibit 9 for a breakdown of the manufacturing costs associated with a typical product, and Exhibits 10 and 11 for the Iskra income statement and balance sheets, respectively.)

In discussing productivity, the management of Iskra acknowledged that labor costs were a serious burden and that the company probably had three times as many people as necessary. "And," commented one executive, "indirect costs are always too high, and we think that we have extremely high indirect costs for our production volume. For example, we have data indicating that Skil, with approximately the same number of people as Iskra, produces nearly 1 million pieces. Kress employs 400 to 500 people and produces around 1 million pieces. We have around 550 people, recently reduced from 760 without any strikes; however, I don't believe that will hold if we try to reduce further."

In addition to too many employees, Iskra's productivity was influenced by significant differences

Exhibit 8 *Productivity Figures for Selected Power Tool Firms*

Company or Location	No. Workers	Output(Units/Year)
Iskra	550	600,000
Bulgarian	5,000	40,000
Czechoslovakian	2,000	150,000
Western firm	250	600,000

Source: Company records.

Exhibit 9 *Breakdown of Manufacturing Costs for Angle Grinders (%)*

Purchased materials	65.1
Machining and diecasting and molding	15.9
Motor assembly	9.1
Final assembly	9.9
Total	100.0

Source: Company records.

in production. Specifically, work was performed both in batch and in sequence, and, because all parts (except motors) were continually moved in and out of physical inventory, the flow of goods through the factory was complicated. (See Exhibit 12 for the flowpath of a typical item.) On the third floor of the factory, where a dedicated motor assembly line was located, the situation was even more chaotic; there was little apparent continuity among workstations and, although the production machinery was only about 10 years old, the manufacturing process appeared much older. Lastly, the final assembly of tools was like a rabbit warren, with lots of discontinuities. As an example, newly finished goods often sat for several days waiting for complementary parts, such as chuck-keys, which had become stocked out.

Quality. The management of Iskra Power Tools was well aware that it needed to establish, improve, and maintain quality in products and processes. In fact, the manager responsible for quality had organized statistical process control (SPC) procedures within the factory but, to date, had had only mixed success. Specifically, the level of quality was no-

where near that required to move to a production process—like JIT which could significantly reduce work-in-process inventories.

As of early 1991, incoming goods continued to be checked on arrival, according to prearranged contractual standards, using a standard acceptance sampling (Acceptable Quality Level—AQL) system. In fact, acceptance sampling was done at final production and final assembly, as well as with incoming items. In all cases, quality control (QC) was based on the first five pieces in a batch, followed by statistical sampling.

For the future, the quality manager hoped to integrate a quality attitude throughout the company. As part of the process, management had prepared a book containing quality standards, based on the International Standards Organization (ISO) 9000 series set of standards.[4] As of January 1991, management had not had much success implementing quality improvement. To do so, management believed, would require reshaping the attitudes of Iskra's workers.

The Production Workers. Iskra Power Tools' production process was characterized by low employee involvement, poor changeover perfor-

---

[4]ISO 9000 was a technical standard that required the establishment of a complete system for monitoring quality standards.

Exhibit 10 *Income Statement for Iskra Power Tools*

Sales Revenue	*Fiscal Year Ending December 31*				
	1986	1987	1988	1989	1990
	($US '000)				
Domestic	25,362.9	4,842.5	18,196.4	20,658.6	24,886.9
Exports	7,559.2	12,311.6	11,882.3	10,204.6	12,815.1
Others	1,932.5	1,852.7	486.0	406.2	548.5
Total sales	34,854.6	39,006.8	30,564.7	31,269.4	38,250.5
Cost of sales	18,753.8	27,596.4	22,948.2	23,676.4	27,425.9
Gross income	16,100.8	11,410.4	7,616.5	7,593.0	10,824.6
Selling and administrative expenses	10,065.4	8,226.5	5,032.3	5,191.8	6,020.4
Operating income	6,035.4	3,183.9	2,584.2	2,401.2	4,804.2
Other Income:					
Interest	58.3	3.3	36.6	14,928.1	797.5
Sundry income	1,049.6	269.3	152.8	406.2	2,320.8
Total other income	1,107.9	272.6	189.4	15,334.3	3,118.3
Other expenses:					
Interest	3,611.4	907.9	1,753.9	12,201.8	4,558.6
Sundry expenses	1,380.5	583.0	482.5	13,664.8	4,781.7
Total other expenses	4,991.9	1,490.9	2,236.4	25,866.6	9,340.3
Obligatory contributions to community funds	1,090.7	1521.9	507.6		
Net income (loss)	1,060.7	443.7	29.6	(8,131.1)	(1,417.8)
Allocation of net income (loss):					
Business fund	140.6				
Reserve fund	269.7	292.8	26.6		
Collective consumption fund	557.2	128.6			
Joint venture partners	93.2	22.3	3.0		
Depreciation	1,109.7	1,402.7	1,269.9	1470.2	2,591.5
Net income	1,060.7	443.7	29.6	(8,131.1)	(1,417.8)
Cash generation	2,170.4	1,846.4	1,299.5	(6,660.9)	(1,173.7)

Source: Company records.

Exhibit 11 *Iskra Power Tools Balance Sheets*

	Fiscal Year Ending December 31				
	1986	*1987*	*1988*	*1989*	*1990*
Assets					
Current assets:					
Bank balances and cash	68.2	71.9	13.7	29.0	24.3
Bills and trade receivables	6,068.1	6,815.3	4,954.3	5,791.2	10,257.3
Prepayments and other receivables	1,734.9	1,497.4	4,931.1	520.8	137.3
Current portion of long-term receivables	29.1	1.8	0.5	408.6	184.1
Inventories:					
Raw materials	4,104.0	3,506.8	2,289.7	856.8	3,367.0
Work-in-process	1,538.8	1,367.4	957.8	245.9	1,148.0
Finished products	1,367.9	1,211.4	640.9	802.2	1,750.0
Subtotal	7,010.7	6,085.6	3,888.4	1,904.9	6,265.0
Total current assets	14,911.0	14,472.0	13,788.0	8,654.5	16,868.0
Long-term receivables	106.3	67.8	56.6	2,503.3	3,500.0
Investments	1,187.9	1,324.7	1,289.1	34.1	
Deposits for capital expenditure	147.4	16.9	201.8	28.9	998.4
Fixed assets:					
Land and building	1,635.0	1,343.1	1,199.8	1,453.9	2,611.6
Equipment	12,571.4	12,804.9	11,697.2	17,554.8	32,520.9
Deferred expenditure	0.2	15.8	14.0	188.0	
Construction in progress	241.3	24.9	70.5	107.5	191.9
Total gross fixed assets	14,447.9	14,188.7	12,981.5	19,304.2	35,324.5
Less: accumulated depreciation	7,238.1	7,495.2	7,542.2	12,363.5	25,093.6
Net fixed assets	7,209.8	6,693.5	5,439.3	6,940.7	10,230.9
Intangible assets			125.9		
Net assets allocated to funds					
Reserve fund	501.7	338.6	94.1	69.6	137.4
Collective consumption fund	1328.1	847.3	466.1	169.6	380.6
Other funds	43.9	21.4	9.6	21.3	168.5
Subtotal	1,873.7	1,207.3	569.8	260.5	686.5
Total assets	25,436.1	23,782.2	21,470.5	21,089.8	35,987.9
Liabilities and Funds					
Current liabilities:					
Bills and trade payables	2,859.0	2,945.6	2,581.5	7,656.1	4,282.7
Payables for fixed assets	2.6	6.5	1.3		
Customers deposits and other					
Current liabilities	4,231.5	2,648.2	2,689.5	0.9	3,836.9
Short-term loans	3,224.9	5,381.4	5,981.1	4,325.3	7,188.4
Current portion of long-term loans	1,503.3	889.5	511.1	502.7	263.2
Amounts due to reserve and					
collective consumption funds	91.2	309.3	17.3		
Deferred sales	2,158.8	1,355.9	1,111.5	172.1	4,207.3
Total current liabilities	14,071.3	13,536.4	12,893.3	12,657.1	19,778.5
Long-term loans	3,024.2	3,362.5	3,345.4	2,788.3	5,001.0

Exhibit 11 *continued*

	Fiscal Year Ending December 31				
	1986	*1987*	*1988*	*1989*	*1990*
Joint venture partner investments:					
Domestic partners	107.9	17.8	22.1	0.7	
Foreign JV partners					
Business funds	6,476.4	5,668.0	4,659.5	5,368.9	10,541.4
Other funds:					
Reserve fund	501.7	338.6	94.1	160.2	137.4
Collective consumption fund	1,236.9	847.2	448.8	69.6	380.6
Other funds	17.7	11.7	7.3	35.2	149.0
Subtotal	1,756.3	1,197.5	550.2	265.0	667.0
Total liabilities and funds	25,436.1	23,782.2	21,470.5	21,080.0	35,987.9

Source: Company records.

mance between different models, and relatively poor maintenance performance. The assembly-line workers were analyzed using modern time and methods analysis (Work Factor), and the analysis used to allocate labor staffing. However, since assembly was performed on a paced line, it was not possible for the employees to work faster. Thus, no pay incentives existed for higher output and workers were paid as a group. On occasion, quality bonuses were paid within the factory, despite the fact that some of the production being "rewarded" was not actually perfect.

Jakob Sink, quality assurance manager, commented on the difficulties met in transforming the mindset of Iskra employees. "It is a new idea to send back a QC approval form within a few weeks. 'Why not do it in a couple of months?' is still very much the attitude of those working in production." Then, too, Sink added, workers were concerned that identifying poor quality could cause either himself or a co-worker to be fired. Also, he mentioned that some employees might resist altering manufacturing processes, discussed by management in an attempt to deal with high-variety manufacturing in a more efficient format. In defense of the work force, Sink said that incoming materials played a key role in the quality problem and that, although Iskra controlled what it bought, it sometimes cost as much to control incoming materials as to produce a finished product.

The Supply Situation. Given that all major players in the power tool industry relied on suppli-

ers for major components, it was not surprising that Iskra was also involved in such relationships. However, in Iskra's case, there was widespread agreement among the management team that the supply relationships were a competitive disadvantage. In fact, some thought that Iskra's manufacturing costs were 20% to 25% more expensive than for Bosch, for example, because of the supply situation. Then too, the company faced the added complication that one of its major suppliers was based in Serbia, a republic with which political tensions had been growing.

Within Yugoslavia, the manufacturing director distinguished suppliers according to raw materials or finished components such as gears and cables. He commented that, aside from having a lower quality, raw materials were also more expensive in Yugoslavia than in Western Europe. Furthermore, there were few finished component suppliers to choose from in Yugoslavia, and those that did exist did not possess a high quality standard. To use domestic components, Iskra would have to take what was available from several firms and remachine those components before assembling its power tools. In other words, the absence of quality suppliers and subcontractors added yet another step to Iskra's manufacturing.

As one remedy, Iskra forged close working relationships with its local suppliers. Generally speaking, these suppliers were able to respond to major design changes without any real problem, but efforts to upgrade the quality of the finished components had been unsuccessful. Despite the close relationships, it was highly unlikely that Iskra could

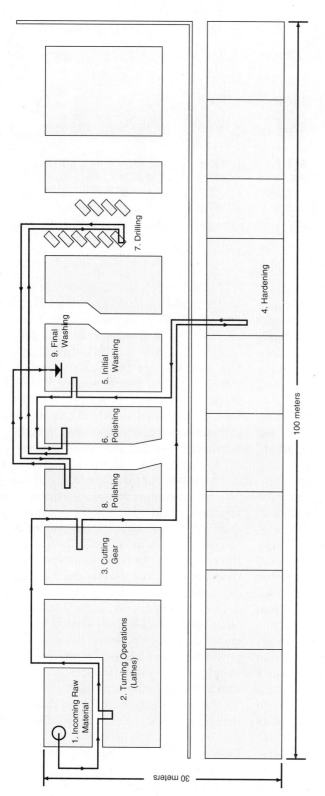

Exhibit 12 Flowpath for Iskra Power Tool Gear Manufacturing

1. Incoming Raw Material

2. Turning Operations (Lathes)

3. Cutting Gear

8. Polishing

6. Polishing

5. Initial Washing

9. Final Washing

7. Drilling

4. Hardening

30 meters

100 meters

Source: Company records.

put SPC into a supplier facility. According to Milan Bavec, "SPC is still too new, and even though we've held seminars, run films and the like, our results are still poor. At present, the real problem is getting the suppliers to comply with Iskra's own quality check-lists. And that will take at least another two to three years."

Foreign Suppliers. Another manager pointed out that an obvious remedy to the problems encountered with domestic suppliers was to source from foreign firms. In general, sourcing at Iskra began after Iskra Power Tools had identified a potential supplier and negotiated the contract. Iskra Commerce then handled the commercial issues, such as invoicing and foreign exchange, for which it charged a fee of 4% to 6%. In addition, Iskra Power Tools paid an import duty of 4% to 5% on all items which it reexported. For items sold on the domestic market, however, the import tax was 45%.

Another sourcing disadvantage for Iskra was customs delays. Typically, it took the company up to one month to obtain import clearance. To counter such delays, Iskra was obliged to order large stocks in advance. Additional factors that complicated Iskra's sourcing arrangements were premium prices because of small order volumes, payment problems due to foreign exchange availability, and the problem of Yugoslavia's external political image.

To summarize, one Iskra executive prepared a business system depicting the company's contribution to added value. For a customer paying a price of 100 (without VAT), distribution accounted for 50%, while parts, fabrication and assembly represented the balance (as summarized below):

FORMULATING A STRATEGY

In formulating Iskra's future strategy, Branko Suhadolnik believed the company should concentrate on less mature and less structured markets such as France and Italy. He reinforced his point by stating that the only way to succeed in these markets was to establish the Perles brand name and structure the distribution. Revamped manufacturing facilities, Branko added, would play a primary role in associating the company's image with quality products. Although he also supported the idea of serving as an OEM, he favored serving the niche players, provided Iskra could overcome what he believed was the company's inability to supply a requested volume of product at a competitive price.

On the other hand, Miro Krek believed the company's future lay in concentrating on becoming an OEM supplier to high volume producers, not trading under the Perles brand or worrying about distribution. As an OEM supplier, Krek felt that Iskra's inability to attract outside cooperation was due to a lack of price competitiveness, quality, and supply reliability. Consequently, special attention should be devoted to developing its price competitiveness and strengthening its ties with volume players such as Skil.

Then, too, a third group of Iskra executives believed that now was the time to attack Eastern Europe and the USSR. Specifically, these executives believed that Western suitors saw Iskra as a possible entryway into the Soviet Union.

Western Markets with Perles Branding

Based on the company's experiences through January 1991, Branko Suhadolnik felt that any activity in

The Iskra Business System

Parts	Fabrication	Assembly	Distribution	Customer
32.5	8.0	9.5	50.0	100.0

———————————————► Value Added ————————————————►

Source: Company records.

Western Europe required a concentrated focus on France, the second biggest market in Europe. Branko emphasized that with more than 8% growth in 1989 and 5 million power tools sold, France represented 20% of the total European market and warranted further attention.

He went on to say that in France, there was no strong national producer of power tools. Secondly, the market was not nearly as developed as in Germany or the Netherlands and, therefore, customers bought more on price, less on quality and tradition. Third, the distribution channels in France were not well defined. "Then too," he added, "we believe the Latin way of life in France is closer to our way of life than the Germans, who are more formal and direct."

Like France, Suhadolnik also stressed the need for Iskra to target the Italian market. "Italy has a small power tool producer, but most of its production is exported, almost 60%. In value, almost 70% of the Italian market is imported. Bosch is number one, and Black & Decker number two with its own production through Star, a local company. Moreover, all the Japanese and other companies are minor, the market is close to Yugoslavia and, therefore, transport costs are low. Finally, Yugoslavia and Italy have a clearing agreement that allows unlimited import and export." One of Suhadolnik's colleagues added that the clearing agreement was one reason why Iskra entered the Italian market in the first place; Italy was the cheapest source of raw materials for cables, switches, plastic, and blades—almost half of Iskra Power Tools' raw materials.

In developing a strategy for the Italian market, Suhadolnik proposed to concentrate on that half of the professional segment which catered to specialty repair shops. "In Italy," one manager commented, "where the first thing for an Italian man is his car, there are an abundance of repair shops to service those cars." The manager then referred to a market research survey stating that Italy had about 100,000 known repair shops of all kinds; the unknown number was anyone's guess. The study also mentioned a trend in these shops toward building maintenance. "That's why," the manager concluded, "we believe Iskra can reach a 3% market share in Italy within two years, up from our present 1.3% to 1.5% share of market."

Western Markets as Volume OEM

It was no secret that one of Iskra's competitive advantages in foreign markets was low price. In Germany, for example, Metabo sold one of its drills for DM299, AEG sold a comparable drill for DM199, and Iskra, under the Perles name, sold its drill for DM139. A number of Iskra managers believed that a low price should be vigorously pursued. In their opinion, bolstered by favorable comments from foreign power tool manufacturers, Iskra's products possessed good value for money. Therefore, one executive added, he saw no reason why Iskra could not continue to use its low-labor cost advantage and underprice the competition.

Western Markets as Niche OEM

During one meeting, Suhadolnik emphasized that Iskra was simply too small and had too few resources to offer a full range of products the way Bosch did. On the contrary, he added, Iskra should concentrate on angle grinders and drills, beginning with a new focus on R&D and production. In other words, focus on those products that represent Iskra's distinctive competence, beginning with design, followed by component sourcing and new manufacturing technology.

Taucher added, "Our output is 600,000 pieces per year. All our large European competitors are in the order of 1.5 to 2 million pieces per year. That is probably the threshold; we are much too small to compete on their terms. We are too small and we don't have a name like Bosch or AEG. That's the problem and, to be a niche manufacturer, you still need the name. We are not a Formula 1, but a Yugo on which we have put a Maserati label."

Eastern Europe

In Eastern Europe, Iskra management knew about power tool manufacturers in Poland, East Germany, Bulgaria, Czechoslovakia, and the Soviet Union. In three of these countries—Poland, Czechoslovakia, and the Soviet Union—Iskra had had some experience. In general, Suhadolnik explained that all these markets were virtually untapped and thus presented a tremendous opportunity for Iskra. Nonetheless, with the exception of the East Germany, which was now part of Germany and where the one power tool manufacturer had been purchased by Bosch, none of the remaining countries could pay hard currency for Iskra's products. Therefore, Iskra was required to sell its products via counterpurchase agreements as it had done with Naradi in Czechoslovakia. Despite these countries' hard currency shortages, an executive pointed out that some of Iskra's competitors had not been discouraged from taking a further look at these markets. In particular, both Bosch and Black & Decker had planned to start manufacturing in the Soviet Union and were actively looking for personnel to run these facilities and market their products.

JOHNS-MANVILLE AND RIVERWOOD-SCHULLER

Arthur Sharplin
McNeese State University

Blood and bones are more important than bricks and mortar.
US Bankruptcy Judge Burton R. Lifland

In 1898, Henry Ward Johns, inventor of many asbestos products and founder of Johns-Manville Corporation (J-M), died of scarring of the lungs, presumably asbestosis.[1] But his company survived, and for most of the next century it would be the world leader in mining and distributing the deadly fiber and developing, manufacturing, and marketing asbestos goods. Exhibit 1 discusses asbestos applications and health issues.

By 1930, the second generation of J-M managers had taken over. They would remain with the company into the 1960s, accumulating profits, opposing victims' claims for compensation, and suppressing research and publicity. The trickle of asbestos-health (A-H) lawsuits in the 1920s and 1930s would become a flood in the 1970s. As use of the mineral was restricted in the United States, the industry shifted sales overseas.

A third generation of J-M managers and directors took office about 1970 and started to diversify the company and change its image. Four events made the strategy more urgent: J-M lost its first major A-H case in 1973; a short, steep recession in 1974–1975 cut profits in half; in 1976, the former medical director confessed the company's 1940s and 1950s knowledge of asbestos dangers; and in 1977, A-H attorneys discovered a batch of incriminating correspondence among industry officials of the 1930s and 1940s.

J-M installed lawyer John A. McKinney as chief executive in 1976. He arranged the firm's acquisition of Olinkraft Corporation, a large wood products firm, paying half in cash and half in preferred stock. J-M was reorganized into several incorporated divisions and renamed Manville Corporation in 1981. By August 1982, A-H claims totaled 20,000, and several juries had awarded victims punitive damages. Also, the operating businesses had begun to lose money.

On August 26 that year, the company filed for bankruptcy reorganization. This stayed the A-H claims, and none would be paid for over six years. Commercial debt was stayed too, but those creditors were soon assured of full payment.

The managers and directors also did even better than commercial creditors. All got improved pay and benefits, continued indemnity against the A-H claims, and added tenure to retirement. Some set up groups to buy assets out of the bankruptcy, including the main asbestos mine and factories. Soon thereafter, remaining third-generation executives chose successors and retired, several with large severance checks as well as pensions.

The fourth-generation managers set about sorting Manville's $2.7 billion in assets and cash into divisions to be renamed Riverwood International and Schuller International. They began a public relations campaign, which produced a barrage of inspirational metaphors. For example, chief executive W. Thomas Stephens surrounded himself with loaves and fishes and mimicked Jesus Christ for the cover of *Corporate Finance*. The article inside expressed wonder at

---

[1]David Ozonoff, "Failed warnings: asbestos-related disease and industrial medicine," in Ronald Bayer, ed., *The Health and Safety of Workers: Case Studies in the Politics of Professional Responsibility* (Oxford: Oxford University Press, 1988), 151.

Exhibit 1 *Asbestos Applications and Health Issues*

Asbestos is a mineral fiber, obtained by crushing asbestos-containing rock, mainly from open-pit mines, and sifting and blowing away the unwanted material. The fine strands are fireproof and almost impervious to most acids, to body fluids, and to oxygen. Before about 1978 (and afterwards in many countries), asbestos cloth was used to make such household items as drapes, rugs, pot holders, and ironing board covers. Asbestos was mixed into slurry and sprayed onto building walls and ceilings. It was used in most industrial insulations, in roofing and floor tiles and wallboards, in a wide range of putties and sealants, and in automobile brakes, clutches, and mufflers. The substance was present in practically every ship, automobile, airplane, home, factory, and school completed before the mid 1970s, and many completed afterwards.

As asbestos products are worked or disturbed, they exude dust containing microscopic pieces of fiber. Ingested, the fibers cut and penetrate moving tissue, especially in the lungs. Intense or prolonged exposure leads to asbestosis, a progressive and irreversible scarring, thickening, and calcification of the lungs and their linings (the pleura). Mesothelioma, a rare and fatal cancer of the pleura (sometimes also affects the peritoneum, the lining of the abdomen), is strongly connected with prolonged occupational exposure to asbestos, as are increased incidence and severity of lung cancer and many other respiratory ailments. The first symptoms of asbestos disease typically appear ten to thirty years after exposure begins. But early damage is easily detectable by X rays and some cancers and respiratory deficiencies show up after only a year or two. Cigarette smokers are several times more susceptible to respiratory diseases, especially those related to asbestos, than are non-smokers. It is widely agreed that as long as asbestos is "encapsulated"—as in floor tiles or painted insulating blocks—the danger of disturbing it in the process of removal exceeds that of leaving it in place.

Stephens' "miracle."[2] *Fortune* featured him as one of 1988's "25 most fascinating business people" and proclaimed the company "free at last." And chief financial officer John Roach appeared under the caption "redeeming Manville" on the cover of *CFO*. Inside, was a recurrent theme: "Manville is out to redress past wrongs—by growing big enough to repay its victims." Soon Stephens and his men would be confident of escaping the asbestos mess altogether and taking their new divisions with them.

Meanwhile, bankruptcy judge Burton R. Lifland issued an injunction shunting the A-H claims to a trust. This procedure was the brainchild of New York attorney Leon Silverman, the representative of future A-H claimants in the bankruptcy. It was ardently supported by the present victims' representatives, a committee of 19 contingent-fee attorneys and one victim. The trust was to be funded with $150 million from the company and $695 million from its insurers. It also received common and preferred stock but could not trade or vote the shares for several years.

The trust paid its first claim in 1989 and ran short of funds three months later. By late 1991, the chief executive of the trust and all but one trustee had resigned. Sixteen thousand A-H claimants had gotten an average of about $20,000 each, about one percent of Silverman's compensation.[3] Payment of another 12,000 claims was promised by the year 2020. But 160,000 still waited to be processed. And new claimants were told they could expect their first payment in 23 years.[4]

Despite victims' urgent pleas for more money, Lifland reaffirmed the injunction, which shielded Manville; its past, present, and future managers and directors; its insurers; and even its codefendants from billions in claims. Manville legal chief Richard B. Von Wald exulted, "That's the kind of certainty we were after. Manville is a company which has put the asbestos risk questions behind us." But many victims faced a less exultant certainty—the one Johns had confronted nearly a century before.

THE EVIL IS VERY INSIDIOUS

The year Johns died, a British factory inspector had described a common fate of asbestos textile workers: "In the majority of cases the evil is very insidious. . . . The worker falls into ill-health and sinks away out of sight in no sudden or sensational manner."[5] And in 1918, Prudential Insurance Company's chief actuary wrote, "[I]n the practice of American and Canadian life insurance companies asbestos workers are generally declined on account of the assumed health injurious conditions of the industry."[6]

Studies reported in the medical literature in 1924, 1928, and 1930 began to show the nature of the A-H problem. The 1930 research revealed 26.3 percent of the workers studied had fairly serious asbestosis, a name given the disease in 1927.[7]

A PRINCIPAL DEFENSES

By 1929, J-M was defending lawsuits for asbestos deaths. In court, the company claimed employees assumed the risks of employment, knew or should have known the dangers, and were contributorily negligent. Legal documents in these cases bore the signatures of senior J-M officials who would remain with the company until the late 1960s. Through the 1950s, most A-H claimants were present and former J-M employees who had been exposed in the company's mines and factories; later ones were mainly asbestos insulation workers employed by others.

Prominent among J-M's insurers was Metropolitan Life Insurance Company. In 1930, Dr. A. J. Lanza, of Metropolitan, began a four-year study called the "Effects of Inhalation of Asbestos Dust upon the Lungs of Asbestos Workers."[8] His pre-

---

[2]Stephen W. Quickel, "Miracle at Manville: how Tom Stephens raised the bread to overcome bankruptcy," *Corporate Finance*, November 1987 (no page numbers; reprint of article provided by Manville Corporation). Jesus' miracle of the loaves and fishes is described in Matthew 14:15–21.

[3]The average payment per claim was $43,902 (from the A-H trust 1991 annual report). Standard contingent-fee contracts gave the attorney one-third, or $14,634, plus expenses. The remainder, perhaps $20,000, went to the claimant. Lifland directed the trust to pay Silverman's firm double his billings, $2.3 million, for his "services."

[4]Claims statistics are from the A-H trust's 1991 annual report. The 23-year estimate was reported in, "Your check is not in the mail," *Time*, September 17, 1990, 65.

[5]Quoted in Ozonoff, 155–156.

[6]Quoted in Ozonoff, 157.

[7]Ozonoff, 155, 167.

[8]Vandiver Brown to A. J. Lanza, December 10, 1934.

liminary report, written the next year, showed 87 percent of the workers with over 15 years of exposure and 43 percent with under five had X-ray-visible fibrosis.[9] J-M vice president Vandiver Brown reviewed a draft of Lanza's report and wrote him,

All we ask is that all of the favorable aspects of the survey be included and that none of the unfavorable be unintentionally pictured in darker terms than the circumstances justify. I feel confident that we can depend upon you and Dr. McConnel to give us this "break."[10]

Although the insurers had liability—and growing culpability—J-M remained primary defendant in the lawsuits. In 1934, J-M's chief outside attorney, George Hobart, wrote Brown:

It is only within a comparatively recent time that asbestosis has been recognized by the medical and scientific professions as a disease—in fact one of our principal defenses in actions against the company on the common law theory of negligence has been that the scientific and medical knowledge has been insufficient until a very recent period to place on the owners of plants or factories the burden or duty of taking special precautions against the possible onset of the disease in their employees.[11]

A half century later, Brown successor John A. McKinney would be claiming to have just recently learned that asbestos "can sometimes cause certain lung diseases."[12] And McKinney would hire Hobart's firm, then called Davis Polk Wardwell, to defend his veracity.

THE MINIMUM OF PUBLICITY

In October 1935, Brown wrote Raybestos-Manhattan Corporation president Sumner Simpson, "I quite agree that our interests are best served by having asbestosis receive the minimum of publicity."[13] He was commenting on Simpson's response to the editor of the industry journal *Asbestos*, who had written,

You may recall that we have written you on several occasions concerning the publishing of information, or discussion of, asbestosis. . . . Always you have requested that for certain obvious reasons, we publish nothing, and, naturally your wishes have been respected.[14]

Brown and Simpson convinced nine other asbestos companies to provide an average of $450 each per year for the industry's own three-year study of the effects of asbestos dust on guinea pigs and rabbits. Brown wrote the researcher, Dr. LeRoy U. Gardner, "In the event it is deemed desirable that the results be made public, the manuscript of your study will be submitted to us for approval prior to publication."[15] Gardner later advised the companies of "significant changes in guinea pigs' lungs within a period of one year" and "fibrosis" produced by long fibers and "chronic inflammation" caused by short fibers.[16] He made several requests for funding but died in 1946 without reporting final results.

LET THEM LIVE AND WORK IN PEACE

World War II brought J-M spiraling sales, as thousands of tons of asbestos were used in building war machines, mainly ships, thus exposing hundreds of thousands of shipyard workers and seamen, many of whom would die of asbestos diseases decades later.

In 1947, a study by the Industrial Hygiene Foundation of America found that from 3 to 20 percent of asbestos plant workers had asbestosis. A J-M plant employing 300 was reportedly producing "5 or 6 cases annually that the physician believes show early changes due to asbestos."[17]

In 1950, J-M chief physician Dr. Kenneth W. Smith gave superiors a report showing that of 708 workers he studied only four had "essentially nor-

---

[9]Ozonoff, 167.

[10]Vandiver Brown to A. J. Lanza, December 21, 1934.

[11]George S. Hobart to Vandiver Brown, December 15, 1934.

[12]Manville Corporation, "Beleaguered by asbestos lawsuits Manville files for reorganization," news release, August 27, 1982.

[13]Vandiver Brown to S. Simpson, October 3, 1935.

[14]Anne Rossiter to Sumner Simpson, September 25, 1935.

[15]Vandiver Brown to LeRoy U. Gardner, November 20, 1936.

[16]LeRoy U. Gardner, MD, "Interim report on experimental asbestosis at the Saranac Laboratory," enclosure to letter from Vandiver Brown to Sumner Simpson, December 26, 1939.

[17]W. C. L. Henderson, "Industrial Hygiene Foundation of America, Inc.: report of preliminary dust investigation for Asbestos Textile Institute," June 18, 1947, 2, 15.

mal and healthy lungs" and 534 had "fibrosis extending beyond the lung roots," "advanced fibrosis," or "early asbestosis."[18] Concerning the more serious cases he wrote,

> *The fibrosis of this disease is irreversible and permanent so that eventually compensation will be paid to each of these men but as long as the man is not disabled it is felt that he should not be told of his condition so that he can live and work in peace and the company can benefit from his many years of experience.[19]*

Smith later said he tried to convince senior J-M managers to put caution labels on the bags of asbestos in 1953. In a 1976 deposition, he characterized their response: "We recognize the potential hazard that you mentioned, the suggested use of a caution label. We will discuss it among ourselves and make a decision." Asked why he was overruled, Smith said, "Application of a caution label identifying a product as hazardous would cut out sales."[20]

By 1952, John A. McKinney, Fred L. Pundsack, Chester E. Shepperly, Monroe Harris, and Chester J. Sulewski had all joined the company in various capacities. They would be the firm's top five officers as it prepared for bankruptcy thirty years later.

DISASSOCIATE THIS RELATIONSHIP

In 1956, the board of governors of the Asbestos Textile Institute (made up of J-M and other asbestos companies) met to discuss the increasing publicity about asbestos and cancer and agreed that "every effort should be made to disassociate this relationship until such a time that there is sufficient and authoritative information to substantiate such to be a fact."

The next year, the Asbestos Textile Institute rejected a proposal by the Industrial Health Foundation that asbestos companies fund a study on asbestos and cancer. Institute minutes reported, "There is a feeling among certain members that such an investigation would stir up a hornet's nest and put the whole industry under suspicion."[21]

NOT UNTIL 1964 WAS IT KNOWN

An increasing number of articles connecting asbestos with various diseases appeared in medical journals over the next few years. And in 1963 Dr. I. J. Selikoff, of Mt. Sinai Medical Center in New York, presented his study of asbestos insulation workers to the American Medical Association. Like the earlier research, the Selikoff study implicated asbestos in many thousands of deaths and injuries. Selikoff would soon estimate that at least 100,000 more Americans would die of asbestos diseases before the year 2000.

In later congressional testimony, Selikoff told of a group of 632 insulation workers he had followed from 1942 through 1962:

> *During these years, 27 men have died of asbestosis, of a total of 367 deaths. . . . [In addition,] while we would have expected approximately six or seven deaths due to lung cancer among these men, there were 45. While we would have expected nine or ten cancers of the stomach or colon, there were 29. . . . Incidentally, since 1963 the figures have been, if anything, even worse. While we would have expected approximately 50 of the remainder of these men to have died in the past five years, there have been 113 deaths. And while we would have expected 3 to have died of cancer of the lungs or pleura, 28 have died of this disease.[22]*

Incredibly, J-M officials claimed Selikoff's 1964 report was their first knowledge of the danger, a fabrication they would persistently repeat over the next two decades. For example, on August 27, 1982, McKinney would write,

---

[18]Kenneth W. Smith, "Industrial hygiene—survey of men in dusty areas," enclosure to memorandum marked *Confidential* from A. R. Fisher (Manville president) to Vandiver Brown, February 3, 1949, 2.
[19]Ibid, 3.
[20]Dr. Kenneth W. Smith, discovery deposition, Louisville Trust Company, Administrator of the estate of William Virgil Sampson v. Johns-Manville Corporation, File no. 164–122, (Court of Common Pleas, Jefferson County, Kentucky, April 21, 1976).
[21]David A. Shaw, "Memorandum in opposition to motions for summary judgment filed by the Wellington defendants and defendant Raymark Industries," reprinted in *Asbestos Litigation Reporter*, November 18, 1988, 18051.
[22]Irving J. Selikoff, testimony before House of Representatives, Select Committee on Labor, Committee on Education and Labor, US Congress, March 7, 1968.

Here's the bottom line. Not until 1964 was it known that excessive exposure to asbestos fiber released from asbestos-containing insulation products can sometimes cause certain lung diseases.[23]

And the *1982 Annual Report and Form 10-K* would state, "The company has maintained that there was no basis for product warnings or hazard controls until the results of scientific studies linking pulmonary disease in asbestos insulation workers with asbestos exposure were made public in 1964."[24]

In 1964, J-M placed its first caution labels on certain asbestos products. The labels read, "Inhalation of asbestos in excessive quantities over long periods of time may be harmful" and suggested that users avoid breathing the dust and wear masks if "adequate ventilation control is not possible." The company's most profitable—and deadly—product, bags of asbestos fiber for distribution to other manufacturers and insulators throughout the world, would not be caution labeled for another five years.

Use of asbestos in the United States had risen from around 200,000 metric tons a year in the 1930s to about 700,000 during the 1950s, 1960s, and early 1970s. Then it dropped sharply, to just over 100,000 in the 1980s.[25] Worldwide, production plateaued at about 4.6 million metric tons a year in the mid 1970s. This would drop only a little in the 1980s, as increased shipments to developing countries offset declining usage elsewhere.[26] Canada, the world's dominant marketer of asbestos in the 1980s and early 1990s, sold an estimated 42 percent of its output to Asia in 1988, up from just 16 percent in 1979. Other leading producers were Russia, Zimbabwe, and Brazil.[27]

THE SMOKING GUN

Always lucrative, the asbestos trade became even more so as the industry came under suspicion during the 1960s and 1970s. For example, sales of the raw fiber alone produced 41 percent of J-M's operating profit in 1976, though it accounted for just 12 percent of revenues. J-M had accumulated about $2.8 billion (1991 dollars) in assets and $1.6 billion in book value net worth, practically all from asbestos and asbestos products.[28]

Like R. J. Reynolds and American Tobacco, J-M had already begun to invest its wealth in "clean" businesses, first fiberglass, then a variety of unrelated enterprises. A prestigious new slate of directors had taken over in the late 1960s. Among them were college deans at Princeton and New York universities, the chief executive of Ideal Basic Industries and former three-time governor of Colorado, the head of Phelps-Dodge Corporation, and the top managers of three other firms.

The directors installed psychologist-consultant Richard Goodwin as president in 1970. Goodwin promised to diversify the company and change its image. He moved J-M headquarters from its old Madison Avenue brick building to a new, modern structure in the Denver countryside and arranged twenty or more small, diverse acquisitions. But he would not have time to finish his program.

In 1972, J-M and its codefendants lost their first big A-H case, which, according to a later news report, "triggered the greatest avalanche of toxic tort litigation in the history of American jurisprudence."[29] A short, steep recession in 1974–1975 cut J-M profits in half. It made matters worse when, in

---

[23]Manville Corporation, "Beleaguered by asbestos lawsuits Manville files for reorganization," news release, August 27, 1982.

[24]Manville Corporation, *1982 Annual Report* and *Form 10-K*, December 31, 1982, 49.

[25]Barry I. Castleman, *Asbestos: Medical* and *Legal Aspects* (Clifton, NJ: Prentice-Hall Law and Business, 1987), 614.

[26]Ibid, 636–637.

[27]Alan Freeman, "Canadian asbestos mining enjoys a modest recovery," *Wall Street Journal*, March 10, 1989, B2.

[28]Conversion to 1991 dollars, here and elsewhere, employs the Consumer Price Index for All Urban Consumers (CPI-U), not seasonally adjusted, as reported in Ibbotson Associates, *Stocks, Bonds, Bills, and Inflation: 1992 Yearbook* (Chicago: Ibbotson Associates, 1992), esp. 84.

[29]"Arkansas plane crash kills Marlin Thompson, Robin Steele, Four Others," *Asbestos Litigation Reporter*, December 2, 1988, 18086–18087.

1976, former J-M medical director Smith told of his earlier knowledge and research on asbestos and health. Later that year, the directors fired Goodwin and replaced him with long-time J-M lawyer John A. McKinney. A later chief executive would claim Goodwin had been a womanizer and an alcoholic,[30] but Goodwin would deny that and say he was not given a reason for his firing.[31]

Then, in April 1977, A-H attorneys found J-M's "smoking gun," the Raybestos-Manhattan Correspondence. Included were many letters and memoranda among Manville officials and other asbestos industry executives. Most were written during the 1930s. A South Carolina judge reviewed the material and wrote,

> *The Raybestos-Manhattan Correspondence very arguably shows a pattern of denial of disease and attempts at suppression of information which is highly probative [and] reflects a conscious effort by the industry in the 1930s to downplay, or arguably suppress, the dissemination of information to employees and the public.[32]*

By April 1978, J-M would be defendant in 623 A-H lawsuits asking as much as $4 million for each plaintiff[33]—but no suggestion of that appeared in the company's annual report.

Relief was in sight. A liberal new bankruptcy code would be passed by Congress that October. Chapter 11 of the law so favored big debtors that public-company assets in bankruptcy would soon increase more than tenfold.[34] Exhibit 2 describes bankruptcy reorganization under the new law.

AGGRESSIVE DEFENSE AND A SUBSTANTIAL ACQUISITION

Upon taking office, McKinney had vowed "aggressive defense" of the A-H lawsuits and a "substantial acquisition." J-M purchased Olinkraft Corporation in late 1978. The price was $595 million ($1.2 billion in 1991 dollars), over twice recent market value. But only half was to be cash; the remainder was debt-like preferred stock, required to be repurchased at par starting in 1987.[35] Olinkraft's main assets were several paper mills and 600,000 acres of prime timberland, with many trees over fifty years old.[36]

J-M changed its name to Manville Corporation in 1981 and reorganized itself, segregating its various businesses in separate divisions. Also that year, juries began awarding Manville A-H claimants punitive damages, over $1 million each in some cases. Actually, J-M paid few A-H claims—such expenses never amounted to even a half percent of sales—but the operating businesses were in trouble. In real terms, the company's sales fell 20 percent from 1978 to 1982 and profits disappeared. Manville's auditor, Coopers & Lybrand, qualified its opinion on the company's 1980 and 1981 annual reports.[37] Of course, Standard and Poor's and Moody's downgraded the debt.[38] Exhibit 3 provides J-M and Manville financial data for 1976–1982.

And Manville's insurers gave the executives little solace; they stopped paying for most of the asbestos claims by 1981[39] and generally could not pay punitive damages anyway. The firm's insurers of the 1970s and 1980s, when many asbestos-health problems manifested, argued the claims should be paid

---

[30]W. Thomas Stephens, conversation with author, October 16, 1987.

[31]Richard Goodwin, conversation with author, January 21, 1988.

[32]Amended Order (Survival and Wrongful Death Actions), Bennie M. Barnett, Administrator, for Gordon Luther Barnett, deceased, v. Owens-Corning Fiberglass Corp., et al, (Court of Common Pleas, Greenville County, South Carolina, August 23, 1978), 10 and 5.

[33]Manville Corporation, Form 10K, 31 December 1977, 26–27.

[34]Christopher McHugh, ed., *The 1992 Bankruptcy Yearbook and Almanac* (Boston: New Generation Research, 1992), 40.

[35]The repurchase requirement would be canceled by the bankruptcy filing in 1982. W. Thomas Stephens, who would later become Manville chief executive, was Olinkraft's chief financial officer at the time and was an early advocate of the sale.

[36]This made Olinkraft an ideal "cash cow," especially after J-M doubled the division's plywood capacity and adopted a 32-year life for the tree farms.

[37]Manville Corporation, *1980 Annual Report, 21,* and *1981 Annual Report, 15.*

[38]See, for example, "Manville ratings cut by Standard and Poor's," *Wall Street Journal,* June 11, 1982, p. 36.

[39]Manville Corporation, *US Securities and Exchange Commission Form 10-Q,* June 30, 1982, II-11 through II-14.

Exhibit 2 *Chapter 11 Bankruptcy Reorganization*

A voluntary Chapter 11 petition acts as an order to stay all legal and administrative proceedings against the debtor, which becomes Debtor in Possession (DIP). Neither good faith nor insolvency is required. Unless removed for cause, the DIP may pursue the ordinary course of business and has the powers and duties of a trustee. Except as modified by the court, the stay remains in effect throughout the proceeding. Often, a secured creditor requests the stay be lifted with respect to its claim. The DIP can usually prevent this by showing the liened asset is needed and providing "adequate protection" of the secured claim.

Reorganization is accomplished through implementation of a written plan. At first, only the DIP may file a plan. But if a plan is not submitted within 120 days and accepted in 180 days, any party in interest may file one. Both time limits may be extended or shortened for cause. A committee is appointed to represent unsecured creditors. A stockholders committee and other representatives may also be appointed.

A confirmed plan binds all parties. Here are the main requirements for confirmation: (1) The plan must be proposed in good faith and disclose "adequate information" (done by means of a written "disclosure statement"). (2) Each holder of a claim or interest who has not accepted the plan must receive at least as much value, as of the plan's effective date, as Chapter 7 liquidation on that date would provide. (3) Each class of claims or interests which is "impaired" under the plan must have "accepted" the plan unless the judge rules the plan "does not discriminate unfairly and is fair and equitable with respect to the class." The DIP, or the trustee if one is assigned, sorts claims and interests into classes, usually when a plan and disclosure statement are filed. A class of claims or interests is unimpaired if reinstated and the holders compensated for damages or if paid in cash. Acceptance of a plan by a creditor class requires approval by over half the claims representing at least two-thirds in amount of allowed claims in the class which are voted. For classes of interests, such as shareholders, the requirement is two-thirds in amount of interests which are voted. Imposition of a plan on a class of impaired claimants which has not accepted it is called "cramdown," and is only allowed if at least one class of claimants (equity is an "interest," not a "claim") has accepted the plan. (4) Confirmation must not be deemed likely to be followed by the need for further financial reorganization or liquidation.

Executory contracts, except financial accommodations (e.g., agreements by banks to extend additional borrowing), may be assigned, assumed, or rejected by the debtor at any time before plan confirmation— or in an approved plan. "Executory" means neither party has completed its legal obligations under the contract. The rejection of executory contracts may create allowable claims, which are usually treated as prefiling,

continued

Exhibit 2 continued

unsecured claims. While collective bargaining agreements are executory contracts, Code Section 1113 sets special requirements for their assumption or rejection.

Ideally, the company will remain viable and will propose to pay its creditors more than they could get through liquidation. The first claim to payment goes to administrative costs of the proceeding and any post-filing obligations, especially any assigned "superpriority" status by the judge. It is generally believed that any remaining value should be distributed to the claimant and interest groups in order of their prebankruptcy entitlements: (1) secured debt (up to the value of respective collateral as of the effective date of the plan), (2) unsecured debt (including nominally secured debt above the value of respective collateral), and (3) equity interests in order of preference (e.g., preferred, then common). Claimants within each group, again ideally, share pro rata according to the value of their respective claims. The value may be distributed as cash, securities, or other real or personal property. Negotiation among stakeholder representatives and court intervention often result in departures from such an "ideal" distribution. In general, claims not provided for in the plan or the order confirming it are discharged. But unlike debt forgiveness, the discharge of debts in bankruptcy does not create income.

Exhibit 3 J-M and Manville Financial Data, 1976–1982 (Dollars in Millions)

Year	Net sales	Operating Income	Net Income	Year Ending Net Worth	Year Ending Total Assets
1976	$1,309	$135	$ 73	$ 672	$1,188
1977	$1,461	$193	$ 86	$ 742	$1,334
1978	$1,649	$232	$122	$1,134	$2,217
1979	$2,276	$259	$115	$1,196	$2,324
1980	$2,267	$197	$ 81	$1,222	$2,328
1981	$2,186	$151	$ 60	$1,203	$2,298
1982	$1,685	$104	($ 98)	$1,066	$2,236

by those from decades earlier, when most of the claimants were exposed. The insurers from the earlier period took the reverse position. This "manifestations versus exposure" debate gave the insurers a rationale for refusing to pay claims, without confronting the issue of Manville's culpability, which some of the insurers clearly shared.[40]

Recording the A-H liabilities would justify a bankruptcy filing, but accounting rules required they be reasonably estimable to be recorded. A committee of directors assessed the liabilities with the help of consultants. In mid 1982, the committee reported the A-H liabilities would total "at least $1.9 billion." Selikoff's associates said that was "a serious underestimate." The directors suggested as much by saying the estimate involved "conservative assumptions favorable to Manville."[41] Of course, a lower number might not have justified the soon-to-come bankruptcy filing and a higher number would have substantiated calls for liquidation. By mid-August 1982, Manville's stock dropped below $8, less than one-fourth its 1977 high.

IN FULL READINESS FOR CHAPTER 11

There were five main reasons to consider the company well prepared for bankruptcy.[42] First, assets were dispersed in separately incorporated divisions. The divisions could file joint or separate petitions and reorganization plans.

Second, a large part of Manville, the former Olinkraft, had never been in the asbestos business.[43] And the company had other nonasbestos divisions, such as fiberglass. This would be a public relations advantage, at least. At best, these divisions could become safe havens for executives who might manage or buy them.

Third, management was cohesive: tough, long-tenured, laced with lawyers, and bound together by potential culpability as well as by attacks from without. The company had opposed often pitiable opponents since the 1920s and had a reputation for ruthlessness and guile which struck fear into the hearts of adversaries.[44] Eight of the eleven prefiling directors had been with the firm since the 1950s and 1960s. They were distinguished in business, government, and academe, so could hardly claim naivete. McKinney and four others were attorneys. The top five officers in 1982 each had at least thirty years tenure. Only one, President Fred Pundsack, voiced dissent, and he resigned. The A-H lawsuits were out of control. The claims totaled 20,000, and new ones were arriving at the rate of three per business hour.[45]

Fourth, the firm had competent counsel, resolute leadership, and access to the nation's preeminent pro-debtor bankruptcy judge. McKinney retained top bankruptcy lawyer Michael Crames as well as New York law firm Davis Polk Wardwell and investment banker Morgan Stanley and Company. The latter two firms had been Manville allies since the 1930s. McKinney insisted on one fundamental principle: the reorganized Manville must not have asbestos liabilities. McKinney later wrote that his resistance to compromise was considered stubbornness, adding, "In this context, I am proud

---

[40]An excellent argument for the conspiracy theory is found in David A. Shaw, "Memorandum in opposition to motions for summary judgment filed by the Wellington defendants and defendant Raymark Industries," reprinted in *Asbestos Litigation Reporter*, November 18, 1988, 18048-18053.

[41]Manville Corporation, *1982 Annual Report* and *Form 10-K*, 9.

[42]See, Arthur Sharplin, "Chapter 11: A Machiavellian analysis," in Samuel M. Natale and John B. Wilson, ed., *The Ethical Contexts for Business Conflicts* (Lanham, Md: University Press of America, 1989), 23–28.

[43]Of course, it had been purchased mainly with asbestos profits.

[44]The company's Machiavellian culture affected the author directly after he wrote a short "Open letter to Manville stakeholders" in 1983. A Manville division vice president confronted the author's college dean, demanding the research be stopped and threatening various repercussions. And the division president, well-known "ax man" Albert Dunlop (Dunlop had been brought in to pare down the Olinkraft operation and later performed a similar function at Lily-Tulip Corporation), spoke to the author's university president about the letter. The author continued the research. But the dean was so shaken by the events he later confiscated and shredded 2,000 copies of the *Northeast Louisiana Business Review*, in which the author's first academic article on Manville appeared. The issue was then reprinted without the offending article.

[45]G. Earl Parker, "The Manville decision," paper presented at the symposium "Bankruptcy Proceedings—The Effect on Product Liability," conducted by Andrews Publications, Inc., Miami, March 1983, 3.

to be called stubborn."[46] The company met require-ments for filing in the Southern District of New York, where Burton R. Lifland was chief bankrupt-cy judge.[47]

Finally, the firm's debt was practically all un-secured and the debt-like preferred stock would not have to be repurchased, assuring plenty of cash and borrowing capacity. McKinney would soon boast of "nearly $2 billion in unencumbered assets." The company's "cash portfolio" would increase to $760 million during bankruptcy. And cash would exceed $300 million even after implementation of the reor-ganization plan.[48]

THE BANKRUPTCY REORGANIZATION

On the evening of August 25, 1982, the directors met in New York and were briefed on bankruptcy. A Chapter 11 petition had been prepared and was filed the next day. The required committee of unsecured creditors was formed. The usual, but optional, com-mittee was set up for shareholders. A committee of nineteen contingent-fee attorneys and one victim represented present A-H claimants. New York lawyer Leon Silverman was appointed to represent future ones.

Shareholders would shortly lose their represen-tation. Certain ones would demand a special meeting, at which they might elect new directors. In response, Lifland would disband the shareholders committee and eject shareholders from the proceedings.

Some A-H attorneys called for liquidation, which Manville later said would yield $2 to $2.4 billion ($2.8 to $3.4 billion in 1991 dollars).[49] But the directors and officers understandably opposed that: they depended on the company for indemnification, not to mention jobs, pensions, and perquisites. It would be years before breaking up the team or allowing an outsider in would be prudent, let alone expeditious.[50]

Shortly after the filing, many "property-dam-age" (PD) claims—soon totalling $90 billion—poured in. These were mostly for asbestos removal and abatement in buildings. McKinney successor W. Thomas Stephens later said the PD claims had been his main reason for opposing liquidation.[51] But a trust set up to pay them would run out of money and soon cease operating. Lifland would rationalize the limited funding for PD claims as compared to A-H ones: "Blood and bones are more important than bricks and mortar."

The largest division, Manville Forest Products Corporation (MFP—formerly Olinkraft), emerged from Chapter 11 March 26, 1984. MFP paid its com-mercial debt, but was ordered immune from asbestos claims.[52] Various other units, notably the main asbestos fiber subsidiaries and certain asbestos-cement pipe operations, were sold that year, also shielded from asbestos liabilities.[53]

A reorganization plan for the remaining divi-sions was filed in 1986. It promised commercial creditors full payment with 12 percent interest, guar-anteeing their approval. A trust was to be set up to pay A-H claims and Lifland issued an injunction prohibiting such claims against any other entity. Morgan Stanley affirmed Manville's plan was feasi-ble—but added elsewhere in its report, "No repre-sentations can be made with respect to the accuracy of the projections. . . . Morgan Stanley did not inde-pendently verify the information considered in its reviews."[54]

---

[46]John A. McKinney to editor, *Business Month*, February 1989, 5.

[47]Lifland administered more big cases than any other bankruptcy judge and was known for favor-ing debtors. See, for example, Beth Lubove, "A bankrupt's best friend," *Forbes*, April 1, 1991, 99–102.

[48]John D. C. Roach, "Reshaping corporate America: Chapter 11 forced Manville to reexamine the way it did business," *Management Accounting*, March 1990, 22.

[49]Manville Corporation, *First Amended Disclosure Statement, Second Amended and Restated Plan of Reorganization,* and *Related Documents*, August 22, 1986, M-399.

[50]Many of the A-H suits named the officers and directors, of course, and leading A-H attorney Ronald Motley had even spoken of criminal prosecution of the company or its executives.

[51]Private conversation with author.

[52]Manville Corporation, *1983 Annual Report* and *Form 10K*, 13.

[53]Ibid, 15. The author reminded Lifland and certain A-H attorneys that these transactions shielded hundreds of millions in assets from the A-H claimants, but he was told that Manville still con-trolled its divisions and the claimants had access to Manville.

[54]The author attempted to explain the plan—in Arthur Sharplin, "Liquidation versus 'The Plan,'" *The Asbestos Litigation Reporter*, November 21, 1986, 13636–13640—but the effort received little attention.

To explain its plan to the mostly blue-collar, high-school-educated A-H claimants, Manville distributed 100,000 copies of its 550-page *Information Packet*. Accompanying the packet were brief, glossy, vote-yes fliers provided by the A-H committee and emphasizing its members' trustworthiness. Later, the A-H attorneys voted claimant proxies overwhelmingly for the plan. Lifland confirmed the plan just before Christmas 1986. It survived two appeals and became effective two years later.

RESULTS OF THE REORGANIZATION

The plan was intricate and subtle. For example, it promised the A-H trust a "$1.65 billion bond." But that number was the sum of forty-four semiannual payments which would start six years later.[55] Discounted at 16 percent, the forty-four bond payments were worth just over $200 million. In 1987, Stephens would admit the fallacy, but still claim the bond was worth $350 million.[56]

The trust was to own 50 percent of Manville's common stock. But only the managers could vote the shares before November 1992. And the stock could not be traded until a year later.[57] The trust would also get 7.2 million preferred shares convertible to bring common stock ownership to 80 percent. But a description of the stock would say it "does not pay a dividend; has no maturity or mandatory sinking fund; has restrictions on convertibility, transferability, and voting rights; is nonredeemable by Manville; and has a liquidation preference of $89 per share."[58] Such subtlety notwithstanding, bankruptcy's practical results for Manville's main stakeholders were becoming clear by 1992.

Benefits of Bankruptcy for the Managers and Directors

The third generation of Manville executives and directors retired in the mid 1980s, some with bonuses in addition to their pensions.[59] For example, McKinney left in 1986 with $1.3 million in severance pay. His annual cash compensation had gone from $408,750 in 1982 to $638,005 in 1985, his last full year of employment. And legal chief G. Earl Parker got $1.2 million after he stepped down. McKinney was replaced by his protege W. Thomas Stephens and Parker by his, Richard B. Von Wald.

Other managers got good deals on company assets. A group headed by the chief of J-M Canada, which owned the world's largest asbestos mine, bought that division in 1983.[60] All but a small, borrowed down payment was to be paid "out of 85.5% of available future cash flows."[61] Payment took less than four years, prompting division president Peter Kyle to remark, "As far as leveraged buy-outs go, I don't think there are any as good as this one."[62] John Hulce, Manville president for a short while in 1986, could challenge Kyle for bragging rights. He retired and paid $7 million for Manville plants with annual sales of $17.5 million.[63]

Staying behind with the fourth-generation managers was long-time board chairman and Stephens advocate George C. Dillon. Dillon signed a consulting agreement with Manville and stepped down to director and chairman of the executive committee. He later compared Manville to such companies as Johnson & Johnson, whose handling of the Tylenol scare made it the nation's most respected firm; to Union Carbide, whose chief executive risked his own life by rushing to India after a disastrous gas leak at a subsidiary's plant there; and

---

[55]On that basis, a $100,000, 30-year, 13 percent mortgage loan would be worth $829,100.

[56]Speech at National Conference on Business Ethics, October 1987.

[57]A-H trust, 1991 annual report.

[58]Ibid.

[59]A sympathetic story of several of the departing executives is told in Greg Barman, "Life after Manville," *Colorado Business Magazine*, November 1989, 15–23.

[60]"Hearing on sale of J-M Canada scheduled for August 30," *Stockholders and Creditors News Service*, August 15, 1983, 1315.

[61]Ibid.

[62]Alan Freeman, "Canadian asbestos mining enjoys a modest recovery," *Wall Street Journal*, March 10, 1989, B2.

[63]"3 Manville manufacturing plants sold to former president Hulce," *The Denver Post*, January 5, 1988, 2C, and "Manville sells three plants for $7 million," *Stockholders and Creditors News Service*, January 11, 1988, 7, 261–262.

to Perrier, which discovered a trace of benzene in its mineral water and soon corrected the problem. Dillon ended as ironically as he had begun, by quoting his "granddaddy," who allegedly said, "If you ain't got a choice, be brave."[64]

The fifteen executive officers hiked their cash pay to an average $423,726 during 1990 and 1991—that of Stephens went from $330,000 in 1985 to over $1 million in the later two years. And they sorted Manville's $2.7 billion in assets into divisions to be renamed Riverwood International and Schuller International. The divisions would have $1 to $1.4 billion in tax benefits,[65] created by nuances of the bankruptcy code and a large special charge in 1988.

The managers were confident they would be free of the A-H trust before it could vote its shares. Stephens remarked,

> We know the change in ownership is going to happen. What we've tried to do is have the maximum flexibility, in case the market puts more value on the pieces than the whole.[66]

"Change of ownership" was interpreted to mean a sale of Manville stock or of one or both divisions by the A-H trust. But a management-led buy-out was an obvious possibility. Stephens himself had reason to covet Riverwood.[67] Plans were made in April 1992 to restructure that division and for it to buy another company for $220 million in debt or equity.[68] This would further shield Riverwood from possible A-H trust control.[69] Exhibit 4 shows Manville financial data for 1983–1991.

Benefits of the Bankruptcy for Unsecured Creditors and Insurers

The unsecured creditors, who had cooperated with management, were paid in full, with 12 percent interest. The secured debt was variously paid or reinstated. And Manville's insurers, with assets totaling hundreds of billions, settled billions in contingent liabilities by contributing about $695 million for the A-H trust.

Exhibit 4 *Manville Financial Data, 1983–1991 (Dollars in Millions)*

Year	Net Sales	Operating Income	Net Income	Year Ending Net Worth	Year Ending Total Assets
1983	$1,729	$161	$ 67	$1,131	$2,253
1984	$1,814	$200	$ 77	$1,197	$2,339
1985	$1,880	$ 36	($ 45)	$1,178	$2,393
1986	$1,803	$180	$ 81	$1,275	$2,513
1987	$1,935	$310	$ 73	$1,370	$2,753
1988	$2,062	$157	($1,299)	$ 798	$2,393
1989	$2,192	$328	$ 197	$ 994	$2,645
1990	$2,245	$250	$ 111	$1,141	$2,796
1991	$2,025	$ 76	$ 35	$ 780	$3,003

[64]George C. Dillon, "Does it pay to do the right thing? Not necessarily. But for Manville Corporation, that's the wrong question to ask," *Across the Board*, July 1991, 15–17.

[65]Andy Zipser, "The asbestos curse," *Barron's*, October 14, 1991, 13.

[66]Marj Charlier, "For Manville, a sale or breakup appears imminent," *Wall Street Journal*, March 3, 1992, B4.

[67]Riverwood's main plant was in Stephen's former hometown of West Monroe, La. He had been Olinkraft's chief financial officer at the time of the Manville buy-out of that firm. Throughout his tenure with Manville, he had maintained contacts in Louisiana. For example, he accepted an invitation to speak as a distinguished lecturer at Louisiana Tech University in March 1992.

[68]The announcement resulted in downgrading of the preferred stock held by the A-H trust. See Marj Charlier, "Manville's rating on debt and stock is Cut by Moody's," *Wall Street Journal*, April 13, 1992, C15.

[69]At the time, Manville owned all the stock of Riverwood, and the trust was to gain control of Manville, and therefore Riverwood, in November 1992—if it resisted pressures to sell its interest. After the restructuring, outsiders might own a significant share of Riverwood stock and could thus prevent operation of Riverwood for the primary benefit of the A-H trust.

Results of the Bankruptcy for Asbestos Victims

The asbestos claimants were often painted as opportunists, even charlatans—represented by "ambulance chasing lawyers."[70] Perhaps 2,000 of the 1982 claimants died before 1989,[71] when the A-H trust made its first payments. Many surviving plaintiffs were old and sick. Smokers among them knew smoking had multiplied their chances of getting asbestos diseases. And few were sure who their main malefactors were, since most had been exposed to asbestos from several companies.

But most were accustomed to adversity. They had generally discovered their diseases after years of declining health. They had fared poorly in state courts. Manville had usually been able to delay A–H lawsuits if not to win them. The company had employed top law firms and had certain valid defenses, as suggested above. So few large judgments against the company had come down, and fewer yet had been paid.

Finding the Raybestos-Manhattan papers had promised to change that. But it had taken A-H attorneys several years to get them before juries. The first big awards were not even funded before Manville filed its bankruptcy petition—which

McKinney said "preserved the position of the victims as equal creditors (virtually all unsecured) in the event of a financial calamity."[72] And prefiling A-H claimants were soon joined in line by thousands of new ones. Many of these had been recruited by Manville, which in 1986 had advertised nationally for potential claimants.[73]

Representatives of both present and future victims were preempted in the bankruptcy court. In the five months ending January 1984, the A-H committee tried to dismiss the bankruptcy,[74] rejected Manville's plan,[75] requested management be replaced with a trustee,[76] and asked the court to cut executive pay.[77] But in November 1983, Manville pronounced the contingent-fee contracts "completely unconscionable."[78] And in January 1984 a hearing was set on its motion to void them.[79] In March 1984, Motley's group withdrew its motion to cut management salaries.[80] And Manville stopped questioning the fees. For the ensuing two years, the committee filed no action to contest management power or benefits or to eject Manville from bankruptcy.[81] In fact, the committee became a management ally, providing glossy brochures to promote the company's plan.[82] In defense of his committee, chairman Ronald Motley wrote, "[The] intimation that there is some rela-

---

[70]Of course, this may have been a fair characterization in a few cases.

[71]Estimate by Heather Maurer, executive director of the Asbestos Victims of America.

[72]McKinney to Arthur Sharplin, May 11, 1987.

[73]The A-H committee assisted with the advertising program. Whatever the committee's purposes, this assured its 19 lawyer members thousands of potential new clients—and as many proxies, which would be voted for Manville's plan.

[74]"Committee of Asbestos-Related Litigants again asks bankruptcy court to dismiss Johns-Manville bankruptcy," *Asbestos Litigation Reporter*, September 23, 1983, 7148.

[75]"Asbestos claimants committee rejects plan," *Asbestos Litigation Reporter*, November 25, 1983, 7416.

[76]"Asbestos-related litigants move to have bankruptcy court appoint trustee," *Asbestos Litigation Reporter*, January 6, 1984, 7625.

[77]"Committee of Asbestos-Related Litigants and/or Creditors withdraws its motion to reduce salaries of Manville officers," *Asbestos Litigation Reporter*, March 16, 1984, 7999.

[78]"Johns-Manville asks court to void asbestos-claimants attorney fees," *Asbestos Litigation Reporter*, November 25, 1983, 7411. In general, such contracts give attorneys a third of gross receipts. The attorneys' expenses are reimbursed out of the other two-thirds, with the remainder going to clients.

[79]"Hearing set on replacement for plaintiff contingency fee arrangements," *Asbestos Litigation Reporter*, February 3, 1984, 7785. Lifland later made it clear that he would have cut the fees. For example, see "Judge Lifland refuses to stop trust payments to claimants," *Stockholders and Creditors News Re. Johns-Manville Corp., et al.*, May 8, 1989, 8799, which reports that Lifland complained that the victims were not told how to contest the fees.

[80]"Committee of Asbestos-Related Litigants and/or Creditors withdraws its Motion to reduce salaries of Manville officers," *Asbestos Litigation Reporter*, March 16, 1984, 7999.

[81]"In re Johns-Manville Corp.," *Asbestos Litigation Reporter: Eight-Year Cumulative Index*, February 1979–July 1987, August 1987, 37–38.

[82]The Committee of Asbestos-Related Litigants and/or Creditors representing asbestos-health claimants of Manville Corporation, "Questions and answers on asbestos-health claims and the Manville reorganization plan" and "A very important message for people with asbestos-related diseases," undated, distributed in August–October 1986.

tionship between Manville's withdrawal of its objection to contingency fees in exchange for the A-H Committee's not opposing certain management decisions is both false and insulting."[83] As to future claimants, their representative, Leon Silverman, got $2.3 million and accolades from Lifland for helping design a plan which essentially disenfranchised his constituents.

Even the A-H trust seemed to lose sight of its objectives, spending millions on salaries, luxuriant offices, and expert help. Lifland had appointed the executive director of the US Trial Lawyers Association, Marianna S. Smith, to head the trust, at $250,000 a year. She hired three assistants, at salaries above $150,000 each. The six lifetime-tenured trustees' received $30,000 each per year, plus expenses, and plus $1,000 a day for meetings. The trustees got a total of $440,555 not including expenses before any A-H claim was paid[84] and Smith got at least $500,000. In addition to directors and officers insurance, $30 million of trust funds was set aside to indemnify the trustees and others. The trust leased 32,038 square feet of Washington, DC office space for $849,007 a year, $26.50 annually per square foot. During 1990 and 1991 trust expenses would average $3.5 million a month—about 50 percent more than would be paid to A-H claimants in those years.[85]

The trust ran short of money three months after paying its first claim. Silverman remarked, "This recent flurry of publicity should not lead to disquiet. All of these problems were anticipated in the original plan and should not result in diminution of payments to claimants."[86] And Smith told a reporter, "Based on current projections over the life of the trust, there will be enough money to pay all the claimants, although there will be temporary cash shortfalls."[87]

By the end of 1991, the trust had received over $900 million. It had dispensed $696 million for 15,864 A-H claims, an average $43,902 each. A-H attorneys presumably got a third, $232 million, plus estimated expenses of $140 million. This left perhaps $325 million for claimants, an average of $20,487 each for the one in ten who got paid.[88] "Settled" but unpaid claims totaled $523 million—to be paid by the year 2020. Over 160,000 claims were waiting to be processed.[89] And prospective new claimants had been told they might expect their first payment twenty-three years after filing a claim.[90]

By March 1992, the A-H trust was in chaos. The directors and officers insurance had not been renewed. Smith and all but one trustee had resigned.[91] New trustees were hired in early 1992. But Smith's job remained vacant. Lifland's superior, district judge Jack B. Weinstein, had ordered claims processing suspended until the existing "first-come, first-served" waiting line could be rearranged and payments cut further. Under the new system, the "most urgent" claims would be paid first. Initial payments would be 12 percent of *settlement* value and payments could never total more than 45 percent of that amount.[92] The new chief trustee said, "That could create a lot of heat and fire. But I'd rather it come to the surface now."[93]

---

[83]Ronald L. Motley to Arthur Sharplin, April 1, 1988. He later said the author, who made the offending suggestion, might soon be "so far out on a limb [he] can neither see the ground nor the tree."

[84]"Manville Personal Injury Settlement Trust financial statements," *Stockholders and Creditors News Re. Johns-Manville, et al.*, March 6, 1989, 8639–8655.

[85]A-H trust annual report for 1991. Claims payments would average $4.7 million a month, of which perhaps $2.2 million a month would go to claimants. Again, the calculations assume standard contingent fees and expenses totaling 20 percent of gross payments.

[86]Stacy Adler, "Payouts do not imperil Manville trust: director," *Business Insurance*, February 13, 1989, 2.

[87]Ibid.

[88]This assumes standard contingent-fee contracts and expenses totaling 20 percent of settlement amounts.

[89]Ibid.

[90]"Your check is not in the mail," *Time*, September 17, 1990, 65.

[91]"Marianna S. Smith resigns as executive director of trust," *Stockholders and Creditors News Re. Johns-Manville Corp., et al,*" December 9, 1991, 12279. Smith said she was resigning because the directors and officers insurance was not being renewed.

[92]This limit was to be relaxed if *all* claims were ever resolved.

[93]"Manville Trust to hold regional meetings on claims process," *Stockholders & Creditors News Re. Johns-Manville Corp., et al.*, March 25, 1992, 12638.

MATSUSHITA ELECTRIC INDUSTRIAL CO., LTD.

Sumantra Ghoshal, Christopher A. Bartlett, and Raymond Ouellet
INSEAD, Fontainebleau, Cedex, France

They (Matsushita) believe in peace, brotherhood, and market share.
Fortune, October 31, 1933

In 1977, when Toshihiko Yamashita took over as its president, *Fortune* had described Matsushita Electric (MEI) as the "most dazzling corporate success in Japan." Almost a decade of his leadership had only enhanced that reputation. Compounded annual sales growth of 11.6% between 1980 and 1985 had helped MEI move ahead of Philips, Siemens, and Hitachi and emerge as the world's largest producer of customer electronics products, and the fourth largest electrical and electronics firm in the world, behind IBM, AT&T, and GE. By 1985, Matsushita ranked twentieth on *Fortune's* list of the world's largest companies—up 26 positions from the 1980 list.

Financially too, MEI had done extremely well. The company's 14.6% annual growth in net profits between 1980 and 1985 had been well above those of its domestic rivals (see Exhibit 1), and had helped it accumulate a cash mountain of over $6.8 billion by the end of 1985. Its equity ratio of 47% was unusually high for Japanese companies and "qualified it as an international blue-chip company," according to Yamaichi Securities.

Yet, as Yamashita recognized, a new and different era had arrived. The dramatic rise in the value of the yen from 239 to the dollar in the fourth quarter of 1985 to 159 a year later led to a 20% decline in Matsushita's 1986 international sales compared with 1985. The company's highly centralized production system left it particularly vulnerable. The financial impact of the exchange rate changes was cushioned by the effect of what many observers called "The Matsushita Bank." In 1986,

over 67 billion yen in dividend and interest income from its cash hoard contributed almost 10% of pre-tax profits, obscuring the fact that operating margins of the company had steadily declined from the second quarter of 1985 (Exhibit 2). Of particular concern were the sales declines of 30% in color TV and 19% in VCR, since these had been the products that had fueled the company's dramatic growth in sales and profits in earlier years.

Yamashita was fighting hard to prevent decline in MEI and had tied a great deal of importance to two programs he had initiated to spearhead the necessary change. Operation Localization was a program to shift more activities to Matsushita's vast overseas operations, and ACTION 86 was a broad-based effort to revitalize the company and shift its business emphasis. Were they appropriate responses? Would they work? Were they enough? These were the questions that filled Yamashita's mind in 1986.

BACKGROUND HISTORY OF MEI

Humble Beginning

In 1918, very few houses in Japan had electricity, and in those that did, the only source was usually a single ceiling outlet in one room. Electricity was distributed to other rooms by attaching a large and cumbersome cord to the outlet. That same year, Konosuke Matsushita, a 23-year-old inspector with the Osaka Electric Light Company, saw an opportunity to start his own business by solving that problem. Investing $100, he set up shop in his modest

Exhibit 1 *Comparison among Leading Manufacturers of Electrical and Electronic Products: 1985*

Corporation	Matsushita	Hitachi	Sony	IBM	GE	Philips
Sales ($million)	20,749	29,473	5,777	50,056	28,285	18,079
Net profits ($million)	1,012	884	297	6,555	2,336	277
Net assets ($million)	10,130	10,251	2,832	31,990	13,094	5,865
Total assets ($million)	21,452	30,378	6,841	52,634	26,432	19,202
Equity ratio (%)	47.2	33.7	32.3	60.8	52.6	30.5
Average annual growth: 1980–1985 (%)						
Sales	11.6	8.3	10.0	13.8	2.5	10.4
Net profits	14.6	9.1	1.2	13.0	9.1	21.6

Source: *Yamaichi Company Report 86-14*, September 1986.

Exhibit 2 *Net Profit Margin of MEI on a Quarterly Basis: 1983*

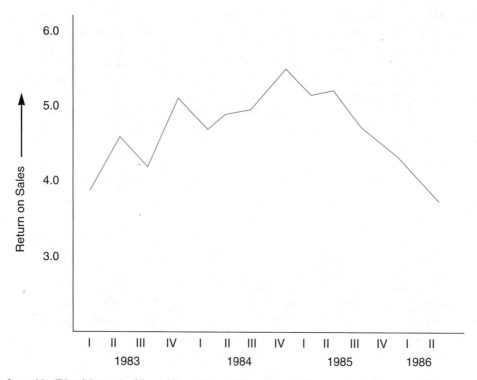

Source: Merrill Lynch International Research Report, May 4, 1983 and *Yamaichi Company Report*, September, 1986.

home to produce a double-ended socket that would make the extension cord easier to use. By 1922 the company had 50 employees and KM, as the founder came to be called, was ready for bigger and better things.

Strategic Foundation: Product Diversification and Domestic Dominance

Between 1923 and 1929, the company grew rapidly, primarily on the strength of a battery-powered bicycle lamp and an electric iron which established a 50% market share despite its 30% price premium. In 1931, the company made its first radio.

In 1935, a public offering gave the company a total capital base of $2.9 million and allowed rapid proliferation of high-volume products. Domestic fans and light bulbs were the next additions, followed by small motors for domestic appliances, then the appliances themselves. Production of black and white TV sets commenced in 1952, leading an avalanche of new product introductions: transistor radios in 1957; stereos, tape recorders, and air conditioners in 1958; driers and disposal units in 1959; color TVs, dishwashers, and electric ovens in 1960. By 1968, Matsushita had 5,000 products compared to about 80 at Sony.

Based on the strength of its large product portfolio, and wanting to bypass the highly fragmented Japanese distribution system that provided little service and no customer education, Matsushita established a retail chain throughout Japan. By the late 1960s, a chain of 25,000 "National Shops," about 40% of all electric appliance stores in Japan, was providing the company's full product line with a strong leadership position in domestic distribution (Sony, Matsushita's archrival in the consumer electronics business, had only 4,000 exclusive shops). These shops also became the company's primary source for competitive and market intelligence and an important training ground for new employees.

But even its rapidly expanding product line and its excellent distribution system could not protect the company from the eventual slow down in the phenomenal postwar expansion of the Japanese consumer electronics market. Exhibiting its normal flexibility, the company resorted to many different tactics to deal with the slowing growth—including sending assembly line workers out into the markets as door-to-door salesmen—but eventually recognized that continued rapid expansion would be hard to achieve at home.

Cultural Foundation: Company Creed and the 250-Year Plan

As important as the product market evolution was the development of a unique culture and set of values that also shaped the company's subsequent growth and strategies. On the fifth of May 1932, the fourteenth anniversary of the company's founding, Konosuke Matsushita assembled his 162 employees and announced his business philosophy and a 250-year corporate plan, broken up into ten 25-year sections. "I, myself and you assembled here are to carry out the first 25 years. Our successors will carry on exactly the same for another 25 years, and so on." The business philosophy KM described that day has since been codified in the form of a company "creed" and in the "seven precepts or spirits of Matsushita" (see Exhibit 3). Typically, the creed, the seven principles, and the company song are woven into morning assemblies held in Matsushita facilities worldwide.

The values are deeply ingrained in the organization, however, and involve far more than rote repetition of principles as a morning ritual. During the first seven months on the job, all white-collar employees spend a good portion of their time in "cultural and spiritual training." They study the fuller philosophy of Konosuke Matsushita that underlies the creed and the seven spirits, much of which evolved as KM struggled to understand the role of business in society. (Some examples of his conclusions are presented in Exhibit 3). At the conclusion of the formal program, employees are grouped under a leader to continue discussions on how the philosophy translates into their daily responsibilities in the company. Furthermore, the personnel department in each of the company's different units conducts on-going "spiritual training" to further reinforce and embed the corporate values.

To most Westerners and even some Japanese, the values and philosophies appeared so idealized as to be gimmicky. Yet, within the company, managers remained convinced of their importance. They were referred to frequently at all levels within the company and often became the basis for deciding on even the most operational issues.

Exhibit 3 *Matsushita Creed and Philosophy: Selected Excerpts*

Matsushita Company Creed

Through our industrial activities, we strive to foster progress, to promote the general welfare of society, and to devote ourselves to furthering the development of world culture.

Seven Spirits of Matsushita

- Service through Industry
- Fairness
- Harmony and cooperation
- Struggle for progress
- Courtesy and humility
- Adjustment and assimilation
- Gratitude

Konosuke Matsushita's Business Philosophy (Selected Quotations)

"The purpose of an enterprise is to contribute to society by supplying goods of high quality at low prices in ample quantity."

"Profit comes in compensation for contribution to society . . . (it) is a result rather than a goal."

"The responsibility of the manufacturer cannot be relieved until its product is disposed of by the end user."

"Unsuccessful business employs a wrong management. You should not find its causes in bad fortune, unfavorable surroundings, or wrong timing."

"Business appetite has no self-restraining mechanism. . . . When you notice you have gone too far, you must have the courage to come back."

Organizational Foundation: The Divisional Structure

In 1933, one year after he formulated the company's business philosophy, Konosuke Matsushita introduced the divisional structure in MEI, making it not only the first company in Japan to adopt this organizational form, but also an international pioneer. Plagued with poor health, KM felt he needed the ability to delegate more than was normal in traditional Japanese companies. He wanted to create an organization that would develop managers able to lead the company into the first phase of its ambitious long-term mission. The division structure he implemented was designed to allow easy identification of the performance of each division through unambiguously defined profit responsibilities while creating a "small business" environment necessary to maintain its growth and flexibility.

Under his "one product-one division" system, each product line was managed by a separate autonomous division which was expected to operate as if it was an independent corporation. When a new division was created, corporate management provided it with initial funds for establishing new assets and this was credited to the divisional balance sheet as internal capital. In assessing the initial capital needs, working capital requirements were deliberately underestimated to motivate the division to work hard to retain and accumulate its earnings. Divisional profitability, measured after management fees to cover corporate overheads, direct charges for central services such as R&D, and interest on internal borrowings, was made public within the company. Performance expectations were uniform across the 36 business divisions regardless of the maturity of the market or the company's competitive position, and divisions in which operating profits fell below 4% of sales for two successive years had the division manager replaced.

The corporate treasury operated essentially like a commercial bank. Divisions were required to deposit their excess funds and received normal market interest. All inter-divisional sales, the prices for which were set at market rates, were payable within 30 days and were settled by transfers of the relevant divisions' corporate deposits. Each division paid about 60% of its net earnings as dividends to the headquarters and was expected to finance all additional working capital and fixed asset requirements from the retained 40%. Requests for additional corporate funds to meet expansion plans were submitted as loan applications to the central finance department, which reviewed the proposals like a bank. Approved loans carried interest rates slightly higher than commercial bank rates and had to be repaid on first priority from subsequent division earnings.

This organizational system generated a high level of internal competition among divisions and helped drive new product development, which managers saw as their best way to maintain long-term growth and profitability. For example, the radio and the tape recorder divisions competed for the right to introduce a radio-cassette recorder. When corporate managers decided to allow the radio division to develop this product to compensate for its declining sales and earnings in a saturated world market, the tape recorder division was forced to find a new product to secure its own future. The result was the "Karoake," a dual-track recorder that allowed amateurs to sing with pre-recorded music accompaniment, that became enormously popular in Japan. Similarly, the black and white TV division developed CATV and computer display products to compensate for its maturing market. The need to fund new product development also drove managers to maximize performance of existing products. For example, the funds required to support the development of VTR made the video division extremely aggressive in maximizing sales of color TV sets. To maintain this "hungry spirit" in all divisions, whenever a new product established any significant volume potential, company policy was to create a separate division.

THE INTERNATIONALIZATION OF MATSUSHITA

On May 5th, 1981, 50 years after the company's "spiritual foundation day," 100,000 employees worldwide celebrated the beginning of the third section of the 250-year plan. Although the central theme of the third plan was to achieve "true internationalization" of the company, the seed of overseas expansion had been sown much earlier.

Establishing the Base: Expanding through Color TV

In 1951, Konosuke Matsushita made his first trip to the United States and was extremely impressed with the sophistication and dynamism of the US market. In meetings with American manufacturers, he sought collaborations but found no takers. Returning to Japan via Europe he visited Philips where he met with a more positive response. On his first day back in Kodama City, he told his managers: "To survive and to grow we have to become international not only in our operations but also in our outlook."

The first task was to upgrade technology and in 1952 MEI entered into a technology exchange and licensing agreement with Philips, which led to the formation of a joint venture producing electronic components in Japan. In 1953, the company opened a branch office in New York, and six years later, upgraded it to become MEI's first overseas company—Matsushita Electric Corporation of America (MECA). In following years, similar sales companies were established in Canada, Central and South America, and a number of nearby countries in Southeast Asia.

The international environment in which this expansion was taking place was in flux. Successive rounds of GATT negotiations continued to reduce trade barriers, while the introduction of containerization and supercargo ships were bringing down transportation costs. From its modest start exporting three black and white models, Matsushita made export of TV sets the base of its international expansion. With neither the contacts and past relationships necessary to get distribution through small specialty electrical stores where personal selling was the norm, nor the reputation or brand image to gain access to the traditional chains and retailers, Matsushita was forced to establish its products through different outlets and on the basis of aggressive pricing. Capitalizing on emerging changes in the distribution system in the United States and other Western countries, it sold primarily through the new mass merchandisers and discount chains, often private-branding its products specifically for these retailers.

In 1961, the company established its first overseas manufacturing facility in Thailand and over the next decade opened many other such operations, primarily in the developing countries of East-Asia and Central and South America. Top management explained that these affiliates were not established as part of a well defined worldwide strategy (as they perceived subsidiaries of US and European Multi National Corporations (MNCs) as

being), but were set up solely to comply with requests of host governments or local distributors. Most were simple assembly operations that imported knockdown kits of components and subassemblies from the company's efficient Japanese plants. Later, as manufacturing costs rose in Japan, more and more production was transferred to efficient plants in low-wage countries like Singapore, Puerto Rico, and Mexico.

By the early 1970s, Matsushita found that its historically successful international strategy and the manufacturing infrastructure supporting it were being threatened by rising protectionist sentiments in the West. The first warnings came from the United States, where local manufacturers became concerned with the rapidly increasing sales of imported Japanese color TVs, which had risen from 350,000 sets in 1967 to 880,000 (or 20% of the market) the following year. Through their association, they filed an antidumping suit with the US Treasury Department. Although its worldscale plants in Singapore, Taiwan, and other low-cost sources offered a means of circumventing the quotas that were subsequently established on Japanese exports, Matsushita felt obliged to respond to the political pressures more directly. In 1972 it established a color TV plant in Canada; two years later it acquired Motorola's TV business and started manufacturing its Quasar sets in the United States; and in 1976 it built a plant in Cardiff, Wales, to supply the Common Market.

To build even broader ties with the national environments in which it operated, the company began making overtures to overseas capital markets. In 1971, Matsushita was listed on the New York Stock Exchange, and within two years listings had been secured in six more international financial centers, mostly in Europe. In 1975, its $100 million convertible bond float was rated AA by both Standard and Poor's and Moody's. Reflecting Matsushita's financial strength, the rating was subsequently upgraded to AAA by both companies.

Building Global Leadership: Dominating through VCRs

More than anything else, it was the birth of the video cassette recorder (VCR) that propelled MEI into its mid 1980s position as the world's number one consumer electronics company. The first commercially viable videotape recorder was launched in 1956 by Ampex, a California-based company that focused on broadcast applications. Engineers at Matsushita (as well as others at its own 50% owned subsidiary JVC, and Sony) recognized the potential consumer application of this technology and, with some funding from MITI and the Japanese National Broadcasting Corporation (NHK), began modifying a prototype built on the Ampex design. Under the leadership of Hiroshi Sugaya, a young physicist in the central research laboratory, the company developed a video head that became its key VCR development, and within six years Matsushita launched its commercial broadcast video recorder just in time for the Tokyo Olympics.

Following close on the heels of Sony, Matsushita introduced a consumer market version in 1966. Over the next seven years, the company developed several major technological breakthroughs, which it incorporated in successive new consumer VCR models, but again market acceptance was poor. The 1,400 workers in the new Okanyama plant—the first in the world dedicated solely to VCR production—were operating at well below the plant's 120,000-unit annual capacity, and corporate pressure was increasing to get this product out of the red.

In 1975, Sony introduced its new Betamax system and the following year JVC launched the VHS format. In 1977, with the urging of MITI, which was concerned about the internally competing formats, Matsushita agreed to adopt the VHS standard, and the Okanyama plant was finally able to begin mass production of a successful VCR. Although the 20 years of losses created pressures within the profit-driven Matsushita system, the company's commitment to the product never flagged. The losses were "tuition fees" as one manager described them, helping Matsushita refine its development and manufacturing capabilities, by responding to market feedback.

As was the practice in Matsushita, various members of the research team that had remained under Sugaya's leadership had moved from the central labs to the product division and finally out to the plant as the task evolved from basic research to product development and finally to production engineering. Even when the new Okanyama plant was lying almost idle, the cadre of manufacturing engineers was kept together and assigned to "research projects." Expertise was continually sought from Matsushita engineers in other divisions working on related technologies or applica-

tions, such as solid-state circuit design or tape cassette manufacture.

Having finally developed a commercially viable product, Matsushita and its subsidiary company JVC adopted a very aggressive policy in licensing the VHS technology to other manufacturers, signing up such leaders as Hitachi, Sharp, Mitsubishi, and later, Philips. An aggressive original equipment manufacturer (OEM) policy ensured that companies like GE, RCA, and later, Zenith, were also locked into the VHS format on units they sourced from Japan to market under their own brands. By building "format volume" Matushita hoped to make VHS the industry standard and lock in future sales (see Exhibit 4 for a history of format market shares).

The company quickly built production volumes to ensure it could accommodate the fast-growing worldwide demand. Capacity, which was only 205,000 units in 1977, was increased 33-fold to 6.8 million units by 1984—a scale-up effort five times greater than the increases necessary in the boom days of color TV production. Distribution channels that had been opened with TV products were now loaded up with the new product lines, and brand names and images that had been established to introduce the earlier consumer electronics products were used to sell the VCRs. The boom was reflected in the company's overseas sales growth of the early 1980s, which increased a remarkable 52% in 1980 (from 764 billion to 1,164 billion) then by a further 35% in 1981 (to 1575 billion), with most of the growth being attributable to VCR exports. By 1985, VCR sales comprised an estimated 43% of the company's total overseas volume (see Exhibit 5).

By concentrating all of the tremendous growth on its focused factories and its network of established suppliers in Japan, Matsushita was able to reap scale and experience benefits that allowed prices to drop by 50% within five years of the product launch (see Exhibit 6). Meanwhile, product quality and reliability as measured by carefully monitored consumer return rates continued to rise as plant engineers constantly refined production processes and worked with the company's numerous internal and external suppliers to improve sourced components and sub-assemblies. As a result, by the mid-1980s, VCRs were contributing almost 30% of the company's total sales, and an estimated 45% of its profits (see Exhibits 7 and 8).

Exhibit 4 *VCR Production and Market Shares: 1981–1984*

Company	Production Shares (%)				Market Shares (%)			
	1981	1982	1983	1984	1981	1982	1983	1984
VHS Group								
Matsushita (including JVC)	36.8	36.5	45.1	41.7	25.2	25.3	24.6	24.0
Hitachi	9.5	9.9	11.1	14.5	2.0	3.4	4.0	3.8
Sharp	6.8	7.2	8.5	9.1	1.2	1.5	3.0	3.5
Mitsubishi	3.2	3.0	3.4	4.4	1.0	1.0	2.0	2.0
RCA	—	—	—	—	28.0	22.0	16.0	16.0
GE	—	—	—	—	3.3	5.0	5.5	5.0
Others*	11.9	15.1	6.8	10.7	11.2	12.6	16.5	24.3
Total VHS	68.2	71.7	74.9	80.4	71.9	70.8	71.6	78.6
Betamax Group								
Sony	17.9	14.1	11.8	9.1	14.2	13.0	7.0	6.5
Sanyo	9.2	9.5	7.7	5.5	2.6	4.0	5.0	5.0
Toshiba	4.2	4.1	3.6	3.3	1.5	1.0	1.2	1.5
Others**	0.5	0.6	2.0	1.7	6.0	4.1	2.6	—
Total Betamax	31.8	28.3	25.1	19.6	24.3	22.1	15.8	13.0

Source: Michael Cusumano, "Note on the VTR industry and market development: Japan, the US, and Europe, Ca 1975–1985." Unpublished paper, Harvard Business School, May 1985.

*Includes Fisher, Philips (Magnavox, Sylvania, Philco), Zenith (from 1984), Montgomery Ward, J. C. Penney, Emerson, Akai, Tatung, Kenwood, etc.

**Contributed almost exclusively by Zenith, before switching to VHS in 1984.

Exhibit 5 *Percentage Contribution to Total Sales by Product and Region*

	Domestic (%)	Foreign (%)
Video equipment		
VCR	13	43
Color TV	8	11
Black and white TV	1	2
Total video	22	56
Audio equipment	7	19
Home appliances	24	6
Information/industrial equipment	19	6
Energy/kitchen appliances	8	2
Electrical components	12	4
Others	8	7
	100	100

Source: Author's estimates based on company balance sheet.

MANAGEMENT OF INTERNATIONAL OPERATIONS

Organizational Evolution

As much as anything else, it was Matsushita's strong tradition of profit center responsibility that drove product divisions to leverage the capabilities of their efficient domestic plants through exports. Matsushita Electric Trading Company (METC), a separate corporate entity formed in 1935, provided the distribution contacts and logistical infrastructure that facilitated this export process. The formation of a branch sales office in New York in 1954 led to the creation of the Overseas Department in MEI headquarters. With the opening of more overseas offices, this department became the company's Overseas Division.

The existence of these two separate international management groups at MEI and METC created some confusion about the reporting relationship of the overseas companies. This became even more complex as offshore sourcing plants were established and began to link back to MEI's product divisions. In general, the company thought about its overseas companies in three groups. The A group were the wholly-owned, single-product global sourcing plants such as the Singapore audio plant or the Hong Kong fan factory that reported primarily to the relevant product divisions of MEI and were tightly controlled by them. The B group were the multiproduct sales and manufacturing subsidiaries like MELCOM, the Malaysian company, or National do Brazil, many of which were joint ventures, often producing a broad product line for their local markets. These companies reported to Corporate Overseas Management (COM), the MEI corporate group that had replaced the Overseas Division. The third group of offshore companies were the sales and marketing subsidiaries like the Argentinian and French companies that imported their products from Japan and from the global production centers. These reported to METC, the Trading Company (with the notable exception of the US sales companies which reported to COM, the corporate group).

In 1985, in an attempt to rationalize and clarify this situation, the 120 staff of COM were merged in to the 1,500-person METC organization (Exhibit 9). In addition to uniting Matsushita's overseas strategy, the purpose of the change was to speed up decision making, decrease overall corporate costs, and better integrate overseas sales and marketing operations.

Changing Systems

The tight division level systems and controls that were at the center of Matsushita's domestic operations had not been transferred to the overseas companies with the same rigor. The return-on-investment (ROI) measures were rendered meaningless by the fact that the overseas companies were financed by the parent company, and the profit center concept was undermined by the fact that the divisions received only a cost-based transfer price, and a modest 3 % royalty.

Increasingly, however, sales and profit numbers were consolidated and reviewed on a worldwide basis, and by the early 1980s, product

---

Exhibit 6 *Matsushita's Production and Selling Prices of VTRs: 1977–1984*

Year	Production (in '000 units)	Average Price in Japan (in thousand yen)	Relative Production (1977 as base)	Relative Price (1977 as base)
1977	205	172	1.00	100
1978	526	144	2.56	82
1979	624	135	3.04	68
1980	1,273	127	6.21	64
1981	2,701	114	13.18	60
1982	3,520	98	17.17	54
1983	5,228	83	25.50	46
1984	6,860	73	33.46	39

Exhibit 7 Sales Breakdown by Divisions: 1981–1985

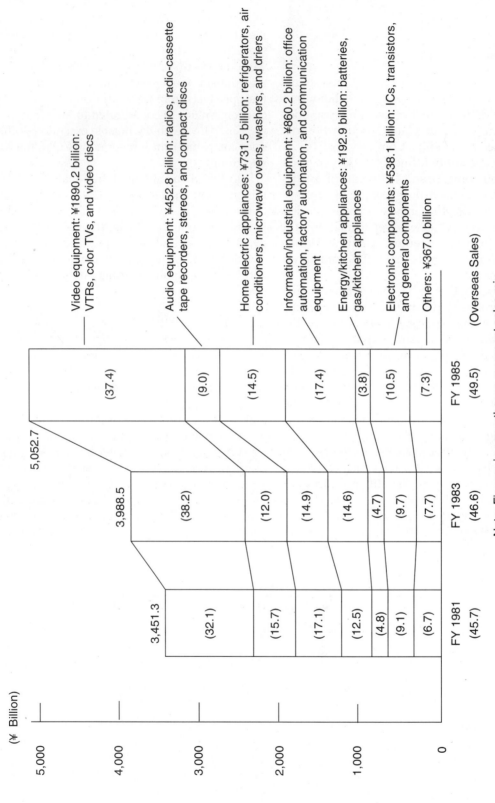

Video equipment: ¥1890.2 billion: VTRs, color TVs, and video discs

Audio equipment: ¥452.8 billion: radios, radio-cassette tape recorders, stereos, and compact discs

Home electric appliances: ¥731.5 billion: refrigerators, air conditioners, microwave ovens, washers, and driers

Information/industrial equipment: ¥860.2 billion: office automation, factory automation, and communication equipment

Energy/kitchen appliances: ¥192.9 billion: batteries, gas/kitchen appliances

Electronic components: ¥538.1 billion: ICs, transistors, and general components

Others: ¥367.0 billion

(Overseas Sales)

Note: Figures in parentheses represent sales mix.

(¥ Billion)

	FY 1981	FY 1983	FY 1985
Total	3,451.3	3,988.5	5,052.7
Video equipment	(32.1)	(38.2)	(37.4)
Audio equipment	(15.7)	(12.0)	(9.0)
Home electric appliances	(17.1)	(14.9)	(14.5)
Information/industrial equipment	(12.5)	(14.6)	(17.4)
Energy/kitchen appliances	(4.8)	(4.7)	(3.8)
Electronic components	(9.1)	(9.7)	(10.5)
Others	(6.7)	(7.7)	(7.3)
(Overseas Sales)	(45.7)	(46.6)	(49.5)

Source: Company balance sheets and summary in *Yamaichi Company Report 86-14*, September 1986.

Exhibit 8 *Percentage of Total Profits Contributed by Various Products (All Figures in %)*

% of Total Profits Contributed by	1977	1978	1979	1980	1981	1982	1983	1984
Video division								
VCR	4	9	16	26	39	44	44	45
Color TV	22	20	17	16	11	10	10	9
Black and white TV	1	1	1	1	1	1	1	1
Total video	27	30	34	43	51	55	55	55
Audio division	17	14	10	11	10	8	7	7
Home appliances	18	18	16	9	9	8	9	8
Information/industrial equipment	14	16	16	14	12	12	13	13
Energy/kitchen appliances	8	8	9	8	5	6	6	6
Electronic components	9	8	8	8	7	6	6	6
Others	8	7	7	7	6	5	5	5
Total	100	100	100	100	100	100	100	100

Source: Merrill Lynch International Research Report, May 4, 1983.

divisions were receiving globally consolidated return on sales reports for their businesses. Formally, the financial statements of all foreign subsidiaries were consolidated in the accounts of METC whose performance, like that of other Matsushita units, was evaluated primarily on the basis of growth in sales and market share. The financial plans of newly established overseas companies normally required that they recover accumulated operating deficits and begin to make profits by the end of their third year of existence.

In addition to these administrative systems, the international operating controls were also changing. In the late 1960s and early 1970s, the ability of central product divisions to control overseas operations was greatly facilitated by the fact that offshore plants had equipment designed by the parent company, followed manufacturing procedures dictated by the center, and used materials supplied from Matsushita's domestic plants. With increasing pressures for more local sourcing and independence, however, the divisions' overseas operations departments were unable to continue managing as directly or simply. Instead of controlling the inputs, they were forced to monitor output on a variety of dimensions (quality, productivity, inventory levels, etc.), tailoring the nature and number of such reporting systems to the size and maturity of the particular subsidiary.

Finally, the company began adding greater sophistication to its strategic planning systems. Upon assuming control in 1977, President Yamashita began introducing medium-term planning as a means of counterbalancing the short-term perspective created by the company's financial systems. At first these three-year plans were largely financially oriented and domestic in focus, but gradually Yamashita began asking for more qualitative data and began suggesting that plans be prepared for the worldwide business. By the mid-1980s, global product strategies began to appear in the three-year plans. The final strategy for a given business in a particular country was the outcome of negotiations between the MEI product division representing the global business strategy and the appropriate METC regional division that had prepared geographic strategies.

Headquarters-Subsidiary Relations

Tomio Koide, the managing director of Matsushita's subsidiary in Singapore described the way foreign subsidiaries are managed in the company:

> *Headquarters-subsidiary relations in Matsushita is a process of "hands-off" management: Japan gives a sales and a profit target and the subsidiary must achieve them. That is the only basis. As long as these targets are achieved, local management has complete autonomy on*

Exhibit 9 *Changes in Matsushita's Headquarters Organization for International Companies*

1984 Organization

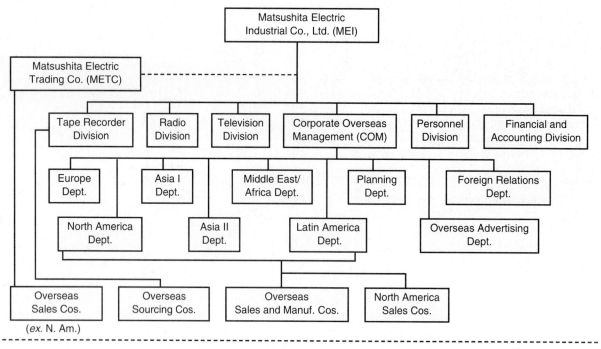

1985 Organization

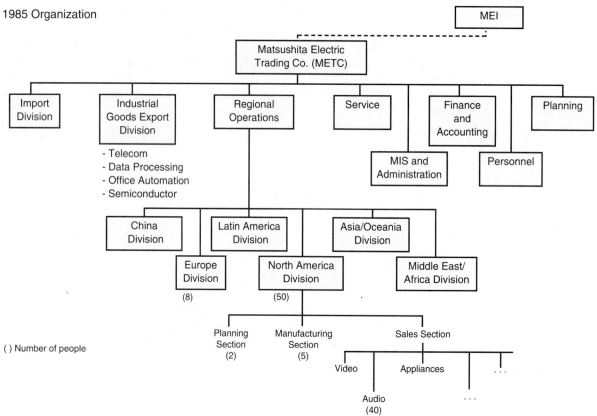

( ) Number of people

everything else. How many people are required, how much they should be paid, what other expenses should be incurred—they are all subsidiary decisions and nothing is told by Japan.

However, 'Mike' Matsuoka, the president of MELAC, the company's largest European production subsidiary in Cardiff, Wales emphasized that failure to meet targets forfeits the freedom:

Losses show bad health and invite many doctors from Japan who provide advice and support.

There were many linkages between headquarters and subsidiaries, extending across all levels of the organization. For example, in the video department of MECA, the North American sales subsidiary, the vice president was a veteran of Matsushita Electric Trading Company and remained a member of its top management team that decided overall strategy for the North American market. As the VP of MECA, he implemented the strategy that he had helped to form. The department general manager was also an expatriate who had spent over 10 years in the video product division of MEI and maintained close contacts with his former colleagues. Finally, the assistant manager in the department, the junior-most expatriate in the subsidiary, had worked for five years in the central production plant in Japan and acted as the key link between the factory and the subsidiary.

The general managers of all foreign subsidiaries visited the company headquarters at least two to three times each year, and the heads of the larger subsidiaries travelled to Japan almost every month. Other key managers went to Japan at least annually. Each subsidiary also received numerous visits from senior corporate managers each year and major operations hosted at least one headquarters manager almost each day of the year. One headquarters manager estimated there were 5,500 trips from the parent company to overseas operations during 1985. Face-to-face meetings were a vital part of the company's style of operation. "Figures are important, but the meetings are necessary to develop judgment" said one senior manager. Telephone, telex, and fax communication between headquarters and overseas subsidiaries was intensive. In particular, regular after-hours telephone calls between headquarters managers and their expatriate colleagues abroad represented a vital management link.

Foreign production subsidiaries were required to buy key components from within the company but could choose their internal source. In recent years, they gained more freedom to purchase minor and less critical parts from local vendors as long as quality standards could be assured. While they were expected to carry out all routine production tasks independently, corporate technical personnel became intimately involved when plans called for major expansion or change.

Sales subsidiaries, similarly, had some choice with regard to the products they sold. Each year the company held a two-week merchandising and product planning meeting, essentially a large internal trade show, in which all product divisions displayed the items that would be available during the following model year. Three to five managers from each sales subsidiary attended these week-long meetings to "buy" the specific products they wanted for their local markets and also to suggest changes in product design. The ultimate decision on product choice, however, rested with corporate managers who could overrule the subsidiary if introduction of a particular item in a particular market was thought to be of strategic importance to the company.

Transfer prices for products supplied from Japan were negotiated annually and increasingly took into account not only production costs but also the conditions prevailing in the subsidiary's market. In general, the plant was expected to absorb the effect of any changes in its costs during the year, while the subsidiary was expected to deal with changes in market conditions without modifying the transfer price.

Role of Expatriates

Matsushita had over 700 expatriate managers and technicians in its overseas operations but defended that relatively high number by describing the complexity of their task. Not only did these managers have to transmit a complex and subtle philosophy, they also had to act as the communication links translating information about the overseas environment to headquarters and transferring the company's strategies and technologies to the local companies. In the words of one manager,

This communication role almost always requires a manager from the parent company. Even if a local manager speaks Japanese, he

would not have the long experience that is needed to build relationships and understand our management processes.

For this reason, there were a few senior positions that were typically reserved for expatriates, the most visible being that of the subsidiary general manager. "The key task of the general manager," according to the general manager of a major international production center, "is to translate the Matsushita philosophy to the local environment. To do that, you really have to have experienced the philosophy as it is practiced in Japan." Indeed, all headquarters employees assigned to foreign companies received additional training in the company's impressive Overseas Training Center (OTC) before departing. A central focus of OTC was to ensure that expatriates had a deep understanding of the company's philosophy so they could adapt it appropriately to the culture to which they were transferring the philosophy.

Another position usually reserved for an expatriate was that of accounting manager. These individuals reported directly to the corporate accounting division at the headquarters, and were expected to "mercilessly expose the truth" so that problems could be identified and acted on quickly. These accounting managers formed a very well-defined cadre within the company and received intensive on-the-job training at the headquarters for about nine years before taking up foreign assignments.

Technical managers were the third common expatriate roles and were responsible for transferring product and process technologies. They also served as the product division's eyes and ears, translating local market needs to the engineering and development groups for development of new products and enhancement of existing models.

Most expatriate managers were posted abroad only once in their careers and spent between four and eight years in the same subsidiary. When assigned, each Japanese manager identified a senior colleague as his headquarters contact and counselor, to keep him in touch with company changes, provide him with advice on official and personal matters, and arrange for an appropriate reentry position. This mentor role supplemented the formal developmental responsibilities that rested with a senior manager in the employees' parent division, who evaluated and rewarded the expatriate, with the input of his local manager.

Socially, the expatriate groups spent much of their time together, and some local managers felt that key decisions were often taken off-hours in these informal gatherings. However, considerable effort was made to keep local nationals in the foreign subsidiaries informed and involved. Key decisions would be taken at regular weekly management meetings, usually after lengthy discussion. Senior managers admitted that the impression that local managers could not achieve top-level decision-making positions had impeded recruitment in the past, but felt this problem was diminishing.

NEW CHALLENGES, NEW RESPONSES

Although he took charge at a time of unprecedented growth and profitability, by the mid 1980s, Yamashita had become increasingly concerned about Matsushita's long-term prosperity. In particular, he feared that the two growth engines of the company—international exports and the VCR product line—had both become vulnerable. He reminded his managers that despite the company's strong situation, leadership positions could be lost quickly.

"In 1956, Matsushita's sales were about half Hitachi's," he said, "But Hitachi failed to adjust to the times, and by 1973 Matsushita had overtaken it. Today, NEC's sales are about half of ours, but if we do not take action, we will be overtaken by NEC within ten years for sure."

In Yamashita's view, in order to continue to grow, Matsushita first had to respond to the growing protectionist pressures that threatened the 50% of sales that came from abroad. Second, it had to reduce its dependence on consumer electronics, which also represented about half the volume and over 75% of international sales. To reduce these risks and prepare for the future, Yamashita set in motion a variety of different programs and activities, but central to his plans were two core initiatives—Operation Localization and the ACTION programs.

Operation Localization

From his earliest days as president of Matsushita, Yamashita had been aware of rising protectionist sentiment in the world and had urged his company to seek a better balance between exports from Japan, overseas local production, and exports from overseas companies to other countries. Despite his internal urgings and external statements, however, the company's foreign sales grew as fast as its transfer of production to offshore plants, and as it entered the 1980s with 50% of its sales volume coming from abroad, it seemed unable to increase its offshore production levels beyond 10%.

But pressure continued to mount and the flood of VCRs into Europe in the early 1980s triggered a response similar to the reaction in the United States to color TV imports a decade earlier.[1] In the United States, rising trade deficits were being hotly debated in Congress and a strong protectionist sentiment was gaining broad political support. Realizing he had to take a stronger stand, in 1982 Yamashita launched Operation Localization, which set an ambitious target of increasing overseas production to 25%, or half overseas sales, by 1990. As a means to achieve this target, he set out a program of four localizations that he expected his overseas operations to follow—localization of personnel, technology, material, and capital.

In personnel appointments, the objective was to increase the number of local nationals in key positions. For example, in the United States, while the chief executive of MECA was still Japanese, three of the six company presidents reporting to him were Americans; halfway around the world a similar pattern existed in Matsushita Electric (Taiwan) where the majority of production divisions were now headed by local Chinese managers. In each case, however, the local managers were supported by senior Japanese advisors who maintained a direct link with the parent company.

To localize technology and material, the company had tried to help its national companies to evolve from what the manager of the Overseas Operations Department of the TV Division termed "Phase I and Phase II" operations to become "Phase III" facilities. In contrast to the Phase I plant that is almost completely dependent on the parent for equipment, supplies, and manufacturing technology, the Phase III company is one which has developed the expertise to source equipment locally, modify designs to meet local market needs and incorporate local components, and adapt corporate

processes and technologies to accommodate these changes while maintaining the company's quality standards.

By transferring more assets and responsibilities abroad, by upgrading local management and technological capabilities, and by giving national units more independence and autonomy, Yamashita hoped that Matsushita's overseas companies would develop more of the innovative capability and entrepreneurship that he had long admired in the national organizations of arch-rival Philips. These subsidiaries of the giant Dutch multinational not only adapted central products and strategies to meet their local needs, but also used the technical and other resources available in their host countries to create new products that the company could use worldwide. In contrast, Matsushita subsidiaries historically had played the role of efficient implementers, adopting central products and strategies instead of taking the lead to create their own. Past efforts to develop technological capabilities abroad had failed due to the company's highly centralized R&D structure in Japan. For example, when it acquired the Motorola's TV business in the United States, the local R&D group had been responsible for a number of major innovations both before the acquisition and also immediately afterwards. But this important local capability was lost when most of the American engineers resigned in response to what they felt to be excessive functional control from Japan. Yamashita was determined that the localization program would solve such problems in the future.

But, despite important achievements in raising the local content of many of its overseas products, replacing expatriates with local nationals, and linking its overseas companies into their local financial markets, Matsushita was having difficulty evolving into the kind of truly international company it aspired to be. In an unusual move for a Japanese executive, Yamashita showed his frustration in an interview with the London *Financial Times* when he expressed his unhappiness with the company's TV plant in Cardiff, Wales. The basic problem was, despite the transfer of substantial resources and the delegation of many responsibilities to the plant, it

---

[1]European imports of VCRs from Japan in the period 1978 to 1982 rose as follows: 1978: 275,000; 1979: 555,000; 1980: 1,499,000; 1981: 2,855,000; 1982: 5,250,000. Strong pressure from Philips, trying to establish its own technology standard and its own European manufacturing base, caused several governments to impose limits on the Japanese imports.

remained too dependent on the center. He wanted to see it become more innovative and self-sufficient.

To support the localization thrust structurally, the foreign production subsidiaries, which were earlier controlled by the product divisions of MEI, were brought under the control of METC, thereby consolidating the company's international operations within one central administrative unit. Because MEI's product divisions received only 3% royalties for foreign production against at least 10% return on sales for exports from Japan, separating the foreign subsidiaries from MEI was considered important to prevent this factor from impeding the development of manufacturing capacity outside Japan. But opinions on the implementation of the localization program were divided. Some subsidiary managers felt that localization could weaken their relationships with headquarters managers and reduce their access to central resources and expertise. If export income began contributing less, the central product division managers could give priority to domestic needs over foreign operations. A senior manager in one of the company's largest foreign subsidiaries voiced his concerns quite explicitly,

> *Our main strengths lie in MEI's product divisions in Japan and we have to use those strengths to grow. Without them, we do not have a chance.*

A senior headquarters manager raised another critical question,

> *Given the low-growth environment, foreign production must come at the cost of domestic production. What will that mean for employment in Japan? Protecting the interests of employees is one of our greatest moral commitments. We cannot sacrifice that for any reason.*

Others voiced concerns about whether the company could maintain its innovative product development record and cost and quality advantages if control over R&D and production became more decentralized.

ACTION 1986: Strategic Redirection at Home

In 1979, soon after taking over as president of MEI, Yamashita had initiated the first ACTION program aimed at revitalizing the company. *ACTION* was an acronym of six major thrusts envisaged in the program: *A*ct immediately, *C*ost reduction, *T*opical products, *I*maginative marketing, *O*rganization revi-

talization, *N*ew management strength. By drawing attention to the fact that over 65% of Matsushita's revenues came from traditional consumer products most of which were entering the mature phase, the ACTION program was aimed at refocusing the company in new and growing sectors such as semiconductors, robots, computers, and other instruments for automated offices and factory floors. The company planned to build these new lines without dismantling the traditional ones. So large was this refocusing task that the program had to be renewed in 1983 and again in 1986.

In 1986, Matsushita was already Japan's largest robot manufacturer and the domestic leader in office automation products like the facsimile machines and push-button telephones. Besides producing its own personal computers under the Panfacon brand name in a joint venture with Fujitsu, the company also supplied IBM's 5550 personal computers on OEM basis. It had also begun to move aggressively into the area it called the "new media": studio equipment for cable TV stations, big-screen TV sets for stadium use, and telecommunications systems for home automation.

In the area of technology, Yamashita saw the central challenge this way:

> *Life cycles of products have become shorter and technological innovations more rapid. For example, the product costs of LSI becomes half in six months. If we cannot lead to develop products at the beginning, we will never catch up. R&D has become the key to success.*

The company was strong in linear semiconductor technology, but not in digital technology, which was essential in the new businesses. It also lagged behind such domestic competitors as Hitachi, NEC, Sharp, Fujitsu, Ricoh, and Canon in technologies for computers and copiers, the two products that played key roles in office automation. To overcome these deficiencies, management had substantially increased the research budget from 200 billion yen (4.2% of sales) in 1984 to 260 billion yen (5.7% of sales) in 1986. Semiconductors, optical technology, computer and software, and new materials had been defined as the focal points for future research, and in all four areas the company planned to become the technology leader rather than a mere application engineering specialist—shrugging off the "Maneshita" (copycat) nickname its earlier strategy of technology followership had created. To make this technological leapfrog possible, MEI had joined Kyoto University in the development of high-speed supercomputers that were expected to be 100 times larger than those available from Cray Research, Fujitisu, and IBM. It had also created four new research laboratories at a total cost of over Y40 billion. And, in a symbolic gesture to emphasize the importance of R&D, President Yamashita had taken on the additional post of head of the central research laboratory.

But, according to Yamashita, by far the biggest challenge lay in revitalizing the Matsushita organization. In his view, the divisionalized organization had developed "structural weaknesses." In a period of low growth, the profitability oriented responsibility accounting system was causing division managers to emphasize short-term results and to avoid risky development investments. Furthermore, competition among divisions impeded transfers of information, resources, and people across different parts of the organization. A large number of trained engineers were needed for the growing information equipment business and the company was facing difficulties in recruiting an adequate number of people at the entry level. The problem was particularly acute for software engineers, the demand for whom in Japan far exceeded domestic supply. However, despite huge difficulties in recruiting scarce software engineers for the new information and communication businesses, internal competition made it difficult to transfer specialists from one division to another. Besides, with the integration of information technologies, new products were increasingly taking the form of multifunctional "systems" rather than stand-alone equipment, and joint action on the part of multiple divisions was becoming more and more essential. Under these circumstances, the invigorating force of divisional autonomy and interdivisional competition had become less important than the need for internal transfers, sharing, and synergies.

Although there was strong organizational commitment for the ACTION program, privately some managers expressed some doubts about such a major technological and strategic redirection. While supporting the need for acquiring new technologies, they feared that by deemphasizing traditional products, the company might lose its competitiveness in its existing markets. They expected the consumer electronics business to reemerge as a high-growth sector in the 1990s with the advent of integrated home entertainment systems and feared that unless Matsushita maintained its technologi-

cal and market leadership in this business, it might be overtaken by companies like Sony and Philips, which continued to invest heavily for the development of such systems. Others believed that the autonomy and responsibility emphasized by the "one product-one division" logic had allowed the company to respond quickly and flexibly to market changes, while motivating managers to work hard to increase revenues and reduce costs, and any significant change in the divisional structure might compromise Matsushita's culture and philosophy, undermining its source of strength.

The Situation in 1986

Many of Yamashita's fears seemed to be justified in 1986 when sales declined 10% and profits dropped by over 30% compared to 1985. While domestic sales had remained flat, international sales had collapsed (Exhibit 10). The rising yen, deteriorating trade relations with China, and increasing competition in the video market (particularly with the new Korean entrants) all contributed to the problem.

Meanwhile, overseas production levels were still stuck at about 10% (although geographic mix was also shifting as shown in Exhibit 11) and the boom in VCR sales had kept the company dependent on that single product for a quarter of its sales. What the company was attempting was, to borrow *Fortune*'s colorful metaphor, "to get the new giant to perch on the old giant's shoulders without both of them toppling over." In early 1987, there were many who were wondering if the company could pull off such an astounding feat of strength, skill, and balance.

REFERENCES

1. Fushimi, T. *Matsushita Electric Industrial Co. Ltd.—Divisional Management Control.* Keio Business School, Japan, February 1987.
2. Kraar, L. A Japanese champion fights to stay on top. *Fortune,* December 1972, pp. 94–103.
3. Noda, Y., and K. Yoshida. *Matsushita Electric Industrial Co. Ltd.* Company Report 86-14, Yamichi Securities Co. Ltd., Tokyo, Japan, September 1986.
4. Rapoport, C. Matsushita sits atop an $11 billion cash mountain. *Boston Globe,* July 13, 1986.
5. Rosenbloom, R., and M. Cusumano. Technological pioneering and competitive advantage: birth of the VCR industry. *California Management Review,* Vol. 29, no. 4, (Summer 1987), pp. 51–76.
6. Sloane, L. Panasonic's president pursues growth goals. *Wall Street Journal,* March 17, 1982.

7. Smith, L. Matsushita looks beyond consumer electronics. *Fortune*, October 31, 1983, pp. 96–104.

8. Snodday, R. Matsushita warns over Welsh TV plant. *Financial Times*, June 7, 1985.

9. Matsushita tunes up its marketing machine. *The Economist*, August 3, 1985, pp. 66–67.

10. Matsushita Electric Industrial Company. *International Herald Tribune*, May 26, 1987.

11. Matsushita electric Industrial Company. *International Research Report*, Merrill Lynch, May 4, 1983.

12. Matsushita to shift more output to foreign plants. *Financial Times*, June 18, 1981.

13. *Matsushita*. Company publication, Matsushita Electric Industrial Co. Ltd., Osaka, Japan, 1983.

14. Takahashi, K., and H. Ishida. *The Matsushita Electric Industrial Co. Ltd.—Management Control Systems*. Keio University, Japan. Distributed by Intercollegiate Case Clearing House, Soldier's Field, Boston (case no. 9-378-922), undated.

Exhibit 10 *Operating Results: 1986: Y Billion (% change from 1985)*

	1st half: Fiscal 1986	2nd half: Fiscal 1986	Fiscal 1986
Video division			
VCR	586.8 (−18)*	533.2 (−20)	1120.0 (−19)
Color TV	170.4 (−21)	139.6 (−38)	310.0 (−30)
Total Video	793.2 (−18)	684.0 (−26)	1477.0 (−22)
Audio division	200.0 (−11)	195.0 (−15)	395.0 (−13)
Home appliances	338.5 (4)	406.5 (0)	745.0 (2)
Information/industrial equipment	416.0 (−2)	444.0 (−3)	860.0 (−2)
Energy/kitchen appliances	99.0 (6)	99.0 (−10)	198.0 (−2)
Electronic components	257.2 (−7)	248.0 (−5)	505.0 (−6)
Others	190.0 (2)	180.0 (−1)	370.0 (.5)
Total	2,293.9 (−8)	2,256.0 (−12)	4,550.0 (−10)
Domestic sales	1,254.8 (0)	1,304.0 (0)	2,550.0 (0)
International sales	1,048.1 (−16)	952.0 (−24)	2,000.0 (−20)

Source: Yamaichi Company Report 86-14, September 1986.

*Figures in parentheses represent growth rate over the same period of the previous year.

Exhibit 11 *Percentage of Overseas Production in Different Regions: 1985 Actuals and 1988 Plans*

	North America	Latin America	Europe	Asia Oceania	Middle East/ Africa	China
Fiscal 1985	21	11	10	37	7	14
Fiscal 1988	19	11	11	30	7	22

Source: Yamaichi Company Report 86-14, September 1986.

MUD ISLAND

George S. Vozikis, Timothy S. Mescon, and Ernst P. Goss
The Citadel, Kennesaw State College,
and University of Southern Mississippi

The city of Memphis park director, Bob Brame, pondered the future of Mud Island, the city's river park on the banks of the Mississippi River. Things did not look upbeat, especially since the sixth person to serve as general manager of Mud Island in as many years had just resigned the month before. Brame realized that Mud Island is a seasonal attraction. During 1987, it drew the second highest number of tourists in Memphis, attracting almost 33,000 more tourists than Elvis Presley's Graceland during the season of April 15 to August 31. However, the cold weather months especially after Thanksgiving, caused the number of visitors to drop dramatically. The facility was closed from January 1 to March 12 during 1988, and Brame thought that a plan to stretch the closing for seven weeks longer during the cold off-season made sense and would save the city about $233,000, reducing the island's budget to about $1.5 million. Memphis mayor, Dick Hackett, however, had already rejected a 1987 Park Commission proposal to close Mud Island for five months during the fall and winter. Brame decided to try once again and resubmit his request to the City Council Operating Budget committee in May 1988.

HISTORY

Mud Island, a 53-acre island offshore from downtown Memphis in the middle of the Mississippi River, was built up from mud and silt carried down river after the Civil War and deposited around a sunken Union gunboat. The island has been used as farmland, a racetrack, and even an airstrip, but because of flooding it was never considered to be a particularly valuable piece of property until recently. The Corps of Engineers in Memphis tried different ways of destroying it in the early 1900s, but the island just kept growing. In 1923, E. H. Crump, the mayor of Memphis, finally said, "Well, if we can't get rid of this thing, we'd better make a park out of it" (Mud Island press release, 1987, p. 5). Fifty short years later, Roy Harrover and Associates was selected to design the park. Construction of what was to become known as Mud Island, America's only Mississippi River museum and park, began in 1974. The city of Memphis raised the money for the entire project with general obligation bonds, except for federal funds used for dredging to raise the island above flood level. Total costs for the project had come to $63 million by the time Mud Island opened on July 3, 1982.

The money for the project was partially spent on construction of a monorail/walkway connecting the island with the Memphis mainland. Visitors can also get to the island on a riverboat, the *Memphis Queen II*. The main attraction is a scale model of the Mississippi River, the only one of its kind on public display anywhere and only the second one ever built. The other scale model, a 40-acre-long hydraulic model of the entire Mississippi River, was built by German laborers during World War II in Clinton, Mississippi, for American engineers. The scale model at Mud Island, known as the River Walk, is five city blocks long and illustrates the bends and curves of the Mississippi

River, as well as the major riverside cities and watersheds from Cairo, Illinois, to the Gulf of Mexico.

The other main attraction, the Mississippi River Museum, includes a three-story reproduction of an 1870s paddlewheeler "afloat" within the museum, reconstruction of a Civil War battle, memorabilia tracing the development of river music, and other exhibits featuring historical depictions of the Civil War era and river history. Three restaurants on Mud Island offer foods and snacks ranging from sandwiches at Paddy Meagher's, seafood at Crawdaddy's on the Gulf, and Creole specialties at the River Terrace Restaurant. Retail stores offering souvenirs and handicrafts are River Mercantile, the Delta Drummer, River Crafters, and a shop known as the Just for Fun Store.

The most recent addition to Mud Island's permanent exhibits took place in May 1987. The *Memphis Belle*, a B-17F World War II bomber, was restored in 1986 through public fundraising and corporate contributions, then dedicated at the Memphis Belle Pavillion on May 17, 1987 where it will remain on permanent display. Another outdoor attraction, thought by some to have the greatest money-making potential of any attraction on Mud Island, is the amphitheater which seats 5,000 and has featured in the past the Beach Boys and Chicago as well as Broadway performances.

Plans for the future of Mud Island under the most recent general manager's tenure had included European-style open-air cafes and beer gardens on the promenade-level terrace of the River Center, the removal of a hillock that blocked the view of the river behind the main stage in front of the River Center, and more events to attract black Memphians.

THE LEISURE TIME/RECREATION INDUSTRY

Leisure time spells big business. During 1986, a US population of about 240 million spent more than $11 billion to attend movies and/or watch home video, another $4 billion on pre-recorded music, and lots more than $20 billion in various gaming activities. Hundreds of billions more were expended on hotels, restaurants, sporting equipment, reading material, toys, and other diversions. (Graves, 1987)

The gross national product has risen from $3.132 billion in 1980 to $3.548 billion in 1985 (as measured in constant 1980 dollars). Overall recreational spending for 1985 came to $176.3 billion. Recreational spending was basically in line with overall personal consumption expenditures during the ten-year period between 1975 and 1985 and rose about 165% during that time period, largely because of inflation (Graves, 1987). Of this amount, the *Statistical Abstract of the United States* reports that $13.7 billion was spent on amusement and recreational services in 1980, increasing to $17.4 billion in 1985 (in constant 1980 dollars).

According to *Forbes*, earnings per share for the group of leisure and recreation stocks were up 7.7% in 1986, compared with only 2.8% for all of American industry. Average revenues for the group more than doubled the all-industry median, reaching 10.4% (Frank, 1987).

The forecast for further growth of leisure-time and recreational spending is generally good, because of rising growth in consumer disposable income, lower unemployment, and more favorable federal income tax laws for American consumers' disposable income (Graves, 1987). Because of the recent stock market upheaval, however, some analysts are predicting slower growth in leisure and recreational spending because of the possibility of a recession (Zweig, 1987). *Forbes* analysts also comment on a different reason for a slowdown in the leisure and recreational spending market. They feel that the large gains in this particular market have already been made because of the growth in recent years of mergers and acquisitions that have saturated the market (Frank, 1987).

The types of establishments making up the leisure-time/recreational industry are more varied, perhaps, than any other service industry. They may include billiard parlors, bowling alleys, skating rinks, amusement parks, golf courses, motion picture theaters, sight-seeing tours, museums, and so on. Almost anything that can be done in one's leisure time that money can buy can be classified as belonging to the leisure-time/recreational industry (Exhibit 1).

Exhibit 1 *Share By Type of Recreational Services (In Millions of 1980 Dollars)*

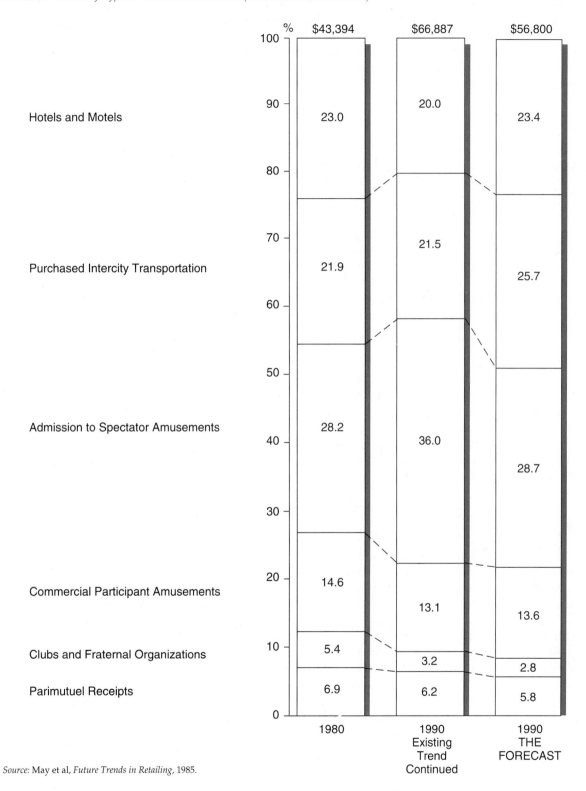

Source: May et al, *Future Trends in Retailing*, 1985.

Amusement parks are now attracting more people than ever. "Last year, theme parks had at least 215 million visitors, up from more than 170 million a decade ago (Jeffrey, 1987, p. 21).

A *Public Participation of the Arts Survey* reports that the following numbers of adults attended the following forms of recreational activities at least once in the previous 12 months:

Jazz performances	14.8–16.3 million
Classical music performances	20.5–22.5 million
Opera performance	4.7–5.5 million
Musical plays	29.6–31.4 million
Plays (nonmusical)	18.7–20.3 million
Ballet performances	6.7–7.2 million
Art museums or galleries	35.2–37.3 million

The survey also found that 61% of adults surveyed did not participate at all in any of the above activities. Level of education achieved by those surveyed was the most important factor involved in an analysis of which adults participated in which activities (National Endorsement for the Arts, 1984).

The diversity of activities involved in the leisure-time/recreational industry makes it difficult to generalize about competing companies and pricing policies. Each recreational-type organization is basically in competition with other local and/or national organizations offering leisure/recreational-type services. Their pricing policies are determined by these factors, as well as the locale and the particular type of consumers within the locale (Exhibit 2).

INDUSTRY ISSUES

One factor that has had a definite impact on the attendance at museums and parks in recent years has been the phenomenal growth of in-home electronics and videocassette recorders. VCRs, now present in 40% of American homes, have created a $7 billion cassette business. Home video and pay television now generate more revenue for the movie industry than theaters do (Graves, 1987). Some surveys report that the average household has a television set going about seven hours a day.

> *Masses of Americans are now living in electronic cocoons, and there are indications that this passive leisure style may become even more popular in the future. (Cornish, 1986, p. 58)*

Nevertheless, tourism will probably become the world's biggest industry by the year 2000. Constant improvements in all forms of transportation make traveling more enjoyable and increasingly less expensive for tourists to travel greater distances. More advanced communications systems will also make it easier to transfer money and confirm hotel reservations (Cornish, 1986).

One major issue facing the leisure-time/recreational industry, which has only recently been recognized as a major problem, is the lack of long-range strategic planning. Tindell (1986, p. 33) states:

> *Long range planning—a process sometimes called "futuring"—is a methodology completely accessible to the leisure industry, yet rarely applied at the operational level in most of its organizations. While academics, researchers, and state or federal parks and recreation planners do trends analysis and recreation participation projections, few local municipalities have formally adopted "5-year strategic business plans" or "20-year comprehensive long range plans" to guide their daily work. They are without the anchor of having articulated a creative, inspiring vision of the future they dream of and prefer for their communities, with their services and facilities cornerstone contributions to the quality of life there.*

"Quality of life" has to be understood by recreation and park officials as a 24-hour a day process, where all aspects of an individual's life come into focus during the fairly brief impact on that life of leisure activities.

GENERAL ORGANIZATION AND MANAGEMENT OF MUD ISLAND

Mud Island is owned by the city of Memphis and operated by the Memphis Park Commission. The city of Memphis was incorporated in 1826 and operated under a commission form of government until January 1, 1968. Since that time, the city has functioned under a strong mayor-council form of government and is organized into the following divisions: executive, finance and administration, fire, police, parks, sanitation, public works, personnel, public service, general service, community development, and legislative and community affairs.

Exhibit 2 *Participation in Outdoor Recreation Activities, by Selected Characteristics: 1983*[a]

Activity	All Persons	Male	Female	White	Black	12–24 yr	25–39 yr	40–50 yr	60 yr and over	Did not finish high school	High school but not 4 yr college	4 yr college	Under 5,000	5,000–14,999	15,000–24,999	25,000–49,999	50,000 and over
Walking for pleasure	53	45	61	54	49	57	58	53	42	35	56	67	45	46	54	61	62
Swimming	53	56	51	56	32	79	65	41	16	19	52	66	34	39	57	68	72
Visiting zoos, fairs, amusement parks	50	50	51	51	40	65	62	41	26	26	51	61	32	40	55	62	62
Picnics	48	45	51	49	42	52	59	46	29	29	51	61	36	41	53	56	58
Driving for pleasure	48	47	49	50	35	48	59	46	35	31	54	59	29	43	53	55	60
Sightseeing	46	45	47	47	36	46	54	47	31	27	50	63	27	38	48	57	67
Attending sports events	40	44	38	41	33	55	44	36	16	15	39	51	24	30	43	51	61
Fishing	34	47	23	35	27	43	40	31	17	26	35	30	24	30	38	38	35
Bicycling	32	33	32	33	29	55	37	22	7	11	28	37	23	24	35	41	42
Boating	28	32	24	31	6	38	35	25	9	11	28	41	16	20	27	39	43
Canoeing or kayaking	8	10	7	9	1	14	9	6	1	1	7	13	6	5	8	12	10
Sailing	6	7	5	7	1	9	7	5	2	1	4	14	4	3	5	9	14
Motorboating	19	22	16	21	3	25	23	17	7	8	19	25	10	13	18	27	32
Running or jogging	26	30	23	26	30	51	31	13	2	6	20	34	21	20	27	33	37
Attending concerts, plays, etc.	25	25	26	26	21	34	29	22	12	10	24	40	17	21	24	32	38
Camping	24	28	22	27	6	36	30	19	6	10	25	27	15	19	29	31	25
Backpacking	5	6	3	5	1	9	5	2	(z)	(z)	4	7	3	3	5	7	5
Outdoor team sports	24	30	18	24	27	50	26	11	2	7	19	23	22	20	25	29	28
Tennis	17	18	16	17	13	32	20	10	1	2	13	31	12	11	18	22	37
Day hiking	14	15	13	15	3	19	17	12	5	3	13	25	10	10	13	18	25
Golfing	13	20	7	14	1	16	13	13	7	4	12	24	6	6	13	20	27
Birdwatching, nature study	12	11	12	13	5	10	12	12	13	6	13	17	9	10	12	14	19
Hunting	12	22	3	12	7	15	13	13	5	10	13	7	8	12	14	14	8
Off-road vehicle driving[1]	11	14	8	12	3	20	11	6	2	3	10	10	9	8	10	15	13
Sledding	10	12	9	12	2	22	11	5	(z)	1	7	11	9	6	12	13	15
Waterskiing	9	11	7	11	(z)	17	12	4	(z)	2	8	12	5	6	10	13	14
Snow skiing	9	10	7	10	1	15	11	5	1	1	6	18	5	5	7	13	21
Horseback riding	9	8	10	10	4	18	10	5	2	2	8	9	7	6	9	11	15
Ice skating	6	6	6	7	1	15	6	3	(z)	1	4	8	5	3	7	10	11
Other activities	4	4	3	4	1	3	4	4	3	2	4	5	4	3	4	4	9
No participation	11	8	14	8	18	3	5	13	30	29	9	5	28	18	6	4	3

Source: National Park Service, and US Bureau of the Census, *1982–1983 National Recreation Survey,* 1985

z Less than 5 percent

[1] Includes motorcycles, excludes snowmobiles

[a] Represents percent of respondents who said they participated once or more during 12 months prior to interview. Covers persons 12 years old and over and period from September 1982 to June 1983. Based on a sample survey of 5,757 conducted by the Bureau of the Census.

The mayor of the city of Memphis is an elected chief executive who prepares the budget, approves and removes department heads and other principal officials, and is responsible for both the political and the administrative functioning of the city.

The city council is an elected body that performs the legislative functions of the city. The council reviews and approves the proposed budget as well as the administrative appointees of the mayor. In addition, the council passes all ordinances and laws affecting the area of the city.

A centralized organizational structure exists in all city of Memphis government entities. The decision making at Mud Island moves from the bottom up, all the way to the mayor. Bob Brame, director of the Park Commission and interim general manager of Mud Island, reports directly to Jim Broughton, chief administrative officer of the city of Memphis, who reports directly to Mayor Hackett. The city council approves the budget and other capital improvements designated for Mud Island (Exhibit 3).

The general manager of Mud Island has authority over all the island employees and is responsible for their performance appraisals. He is the communication link between Mud Island and the city of Memphis government. The general manager's degree of control is narrow and limited, largely because of the restrictions of city of Memphis policies, particularly in relation to the Mud Island budget and capital improvement plans for the future.

MARKETING

The marketing function of Mud Island could be considered to be the most important. The budget for the marketing function is $639,000 per year, with $365,000 of that budget contracted out to a local independent advertising agency. Mud Island is now doing more advertising in-house than it did previously. Services offered by Mud Island are extremely diverse in nature. The park is billed as the only attraction in the world to showcase a river from all aspects—recreational, educational, cultural, historic, and scientific. The services offered by Mud Island include:

- River Center—housing the monorail terminal, Mississippi River Museum, and gift shops

- Restaurants—The River Terrace, Crawdaddy's on the Gulf, Paddy Meagher's, and Harbor Landing (a catering facility)
- Outdoor attractions—River Walk, observation deck, 70-boat public marina and picnic areas, *Memphis Belle* pavillion, river boat tours, amphitheater

Because Mud Island features such diversified types of entertainment, it is difficult to classify Mud Island's current or potential visitors.

To find out what types of people visited Mud Island during a special occasion (dedication of the *Memphis Belle*) and during a typical weekday, a survey was conducted by the American Marketing Association during a Sunday in May 1987. It was found that on the special occasion, 52% of the respondents received their information about the dedication of the *Memphis Belle* from newspaper advertising and 25% from friends. Only 3% were notified of the dedication from street banners and only 1% from billboards. Eighty percent of those surveyed had visited Mud Island before (32% of those within the last six to twelve months, 24% within the last one to two years, and 12% within the last month.) The majority of respondents were from Tennessee (73%), and 90% of the Tennesseeans were from Shelby County, where the city of Memphis is located. The adjacent counties of Lauderdale and Gibson, as well as Nashville's Davidson county, were the other most represented counties (2.3%, 1.7%, and 1.3%, respectively). The most prevalent age groups at the time of the *Memphis Belle* dedication were 25 to 34 years of age (166 individuals of a total of 230 surveyed) and 35 to 44 years of age.

Information about the regular weekday visitors was obtained on three separate occasions during different weeks in the month of June 1987. Of approximately 1,440 visitors to the island on these three days, 420 people participated in the surveys.

It was found that only 29% of the respondents were from Tennessee. Shelby County was still the most represented county with 18%, and Nashville's Davidson County was next with 5% representation. Out-of-state representation accounted for 71% of the visitors: 11% coming from Arkansas, 7% Texas, 6% Missouri, 5% Mississippi, and 5% California. Thirty-five states and foreign countries were represented including

Exhibit 3 *City of Memphis Administrative Structure*

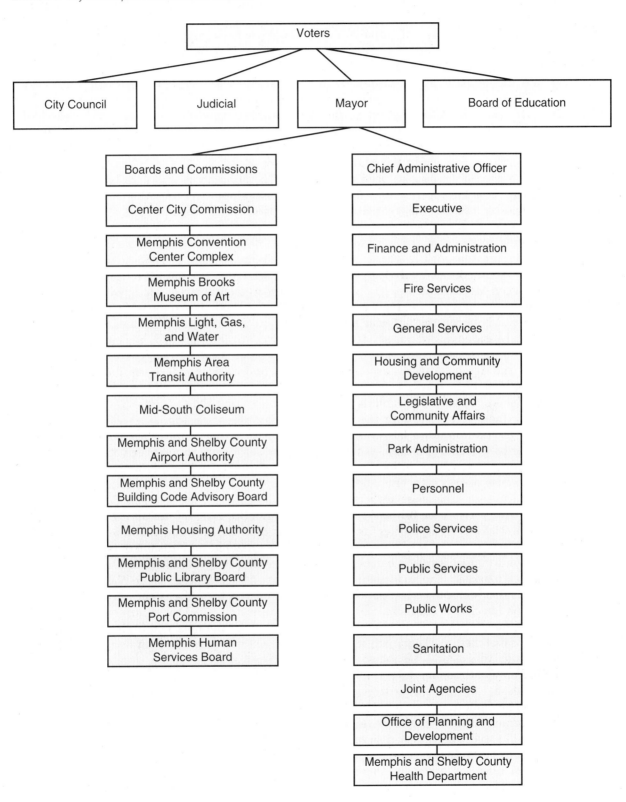

Canada, Mexico, the Grand Cayman Islands, Germany, England, Switzerland, Finland, and the Netherlands.

Forty-four percent of these individuals came to Mud Island because of word of mouth; 12% because of television advertising; 10% because of newspaper advertising; and 5% because of radio advertising. Billboards and street banners were still the least effective method of promotion, with only 4% and 1% effectiveness, respectively. Seventy percent of the respondents to the average weekday interviews were visiting the island for the first time. Of the 30% who had been to the island previously, 50% had been within the last year and 60% had been within the last two years. Twenty-one percent of respondents were back at Mud Island after more than three years had elapsed since their previous visit.

This survey indicated that a very large difference exists between Mud Island's special events and/or weekend customer and the regular weekday customer, and between the national tourist market and local residents. Special services for local residents include festivals and special events, lectures and demonstrations, as well as a changing exhibit gallery in the River Gallery, so that local residents can see new exhibits for a reduced price without having to tour the entire museum again. In addition, Mud Island officials now lead field trips for schoolchildren, as well as summer day camps. Attendance of local tourists has gone up because of special events and festivals like the Budweiser Challenge Cup (a boat race held in September 1987), the British Car Festival, and special Halloween festivities for local children.

The advertising budget is split in half between these two target markets. The management of Mud Island feels that Memphis is a pass-through city, not a destination city for tourism. If a tourist visits Memphis and does not visit Mud Island, then they believe that their marketing efforts have failed. As a result, Mud Island has joined forces with other Memphis attractions to promote the city of Memphis as an entire tourist package. When visitors to Memphis tour the city, it is hoped by the newly formed Attractions Association that these tourists will explore all the local sights, not just one attraction. Additionally, the new Crowne Plaza Hotel will offer discounts in conjunction with a visit to Mud Island.

By teaming up with other local businesses such as the Crowne Plaza, Mud Island hopes to gain an edge over other local attractions. The island's major competitors for the local market are other local attractions such as Graceland, the Pink Palace Museum, Libertyland, and the Memphis Zoo. It also is in competition with these attractions for the tourist and convention business. In addition, other leisure-time activities such as shopping, going to the movies, and eating out are diversions that rob Mud Island of a possible customer market.

Operating hours for the restaurants as well as the Mississippi River Museum may vary according to season (peak season: April 11–October 31, 10 am–10 pm; off season: November 1–April 10, 10 am–5 pm; closed from January 1–March 5). Though the weather has a lot to do with the operating schedule, the multilevel programming and the broad target market, along with the contracted businesses, help determine when the island will be open and for how long it remains in operation. The major controlling factor is the city. Although the Park Commission does not like to think of itself in terms of organizational charts, the city owns Mud Island and, therefore, the city has the final say about operational decisions.

Pay-one-price admission was adopted only two years ago in order to resolve long-term consumer confusion about overly complex pricing. The comprehensive admission price includes the 18-gallery River Museum (including the changing exhibits gallery), the *Memphis Belle*, River Walk, and monorail travel to and from the island. Admission is $4 for adults and $2.50 for children, senior citizens, and disabled persons. Regular park admission includes the changing exhibits gallery, *Memphis Belle*, River Walk and monorail travel to and from the island. Admission is $1.50 for adults and $1.00 for children, senior citizens, and disabled persons. Children under four years of age get in free under both pricing policies, and group rates are available for groups of 25 or more.

OPERATIONS

Mud Island, as mentioned earlier, is a non-profit organization owned by the city of Memphis. It is maintained and operated under the direction of the Memphis Park Commission, which is chiefly funded through property taxes. This organization is a service operation; its primary mission is to provide intangible services (leisure and recreation) instead of physical products for the city of Memphis. These services are intended to be available to all people from all walks of life. In the words of Bob Brame, Park Commission director, "we try to be all things to all people."

The goal of all non-profit organizations in the city of Memphis is to try to cut costs by reducing expenditures and generate enough funds to cover expenses. Therefore, the operational budget policy set for Mud Island by the city is that of cost minimization rather than profit maximization.

The number one priority of Mud Island is customer satisfaction, closely followed by cost efficiency. The city, and in particular the Park Commission, striving to ensure customer satisfaction and quality of services, encourage the collection of customer feedback. Any complaints, which are few in number, are monitored, examined, and acted on immediately to alleviate problems.

On the other hand, cost-efficiency measures necessary to reduce expenditures have already been implemented. Many of the services needed to maintain the operations of the island were previously contracted out. Management has begun, in efforts to reduce costs, a preventive maintenance program. Mud Island workers are now better able to perform many of these maintenance tasks themselves.

Another cost-reduction tactic considered by Mud Island is additional dependence on the private sector. An example of this is the island's attempt to reduce the advertising budget by suggesting to TV Channel 3 (the Memphis CBS affiliate) that Mud Island should not buy advertising but instead co-op with Channel 3 to help promote an event intended to be a public service. The management officials of Mud Island are trying to stress to the community that they have a social responsibility, because they provide a recreational facility for the public to enjoy that without community support would not otherwise exist.

The construction budget is an important part of the city's capital improvement program. A ten-year plan is drafted, yet the city council approves the individual items on a yearly basis. For the next ten years, the Park Commission has a ranking of 46

projects. Three of these projects pertain to Mud Island. Ranked 18th is Mud Island improvements, covering fiscal years 1988 through 1992.

The state is presently funding the construction of the Auction Street bridge over to the area just north of the Mud Island boundaries. To capitalize on this, funds are presently being used to add a parking lot, turnstiles, ticket booths, and eventually a new retail facility. In 1989 there are plans to recaulk the River Walk and construct sheltered and non-sheltered picnic areas to replace existing areas currently covered by tents. Finally, 1992 may bring an expansion of office space and the creation of a storage facility at the east terminal.

Project improvements to the Mud Island River Center from 1990 to 1993 include enclosing the entire west terminal. At present, only a few of the floors are enclosed and a great deal of heat/cool escapes at great cost to the island. Also, due to exposure to the elements, the escalators need to be replaced. Finally, another elevator needs to be added, since two shafts were built but only one elevator was installed in an effort to cut costs during the initial phase of construction of the island.

The chief purpose of a proposed retail warehouse would be for the storage of purchased merchandise and display fixtures. This would eliminate the high costs of storage and split storage, and better security would be provided for the merchandise.

The three major sources of revenue for Mud Island are admissions, retail sales, and promenade lot parking (54%, 20%, and 17%, respectively, for the period ending 10-31-87). Each of these areas is expected to increase in the future. As more people learn about Mud Island through local and national publicity, more people are expected to visit the park. The new retail stores that are planned in the near future—one at the new north gate and one at the east end of the tram—are an effort to "catch" visitors just before they leave the park. Parking revenues will also increase, as the new lot will be built at the north gate with room for between two and three thousand more parking spaces. In addition, existing parking spaces are now being leased to downtown businesses, and the continuous influx of new development will ensure maximum parking usage.

PERSONNEL

The director of personnel for the city of Memphis is responsible for administering the employment and promotional procedures for all divisions of the city government, including Mud Island employees, as set forth in the city of Memphis Charter and Code of Ordinance. The director of personnel is also responsible for the development and maintenance of all policies related to employment, wages and salaries, benefits, records, and other employee services. The personnel policies of the city of Memphis provide a uniform system of discipline and work rule expectations so that all city employees, their supervisors, department heads, and division directors know exactly what is expected of them in the performance of their duties. The Compensation Bureau, located within the city personnel, is responsible for the design and maintenance of the city's pay plan, providing uniform salary guidelines and related policies and procedures.

Permanent full-time employees in the divisions of city of Memphis government are subject to a performance appraisal review during the initial and/or administrative probationary period. The employee's appointing authority or designee is responsible for monitoring the employee's performance during the critical and/or administrative probationary period. Written documentation is maintained that records the employee's ability and willingness to competently perform the assigned job duties as well as the employee's adaptability, dependability, and attitude.

Finally, centralization of employment and promotional procedures in the office of city personnel is required in order to monitor necessary and pertinent documentation in compliance with Equal Employment Guidelines and to reduce the amount of time expended by the separate city divisions in the processing and screening of applicants for positions that are to be filled. The personnel division serves the various divisions and agencies of the city by establishing registers and providing initial screening of applicants.

The critical strength of the personnel policies of the city of Memphis is the uniformity in the interpretation and the administration of the provisions of the city Charter, the Code of Ordinances, and the policies, decisions, and directions of the city administration. The personnel policies pro-

vide guidance to supervisory personnel on issues such as leave, pay and benefits, retirement, disciplinary procedures, and the employee termination process. This ensures consistency in employee-manager relations across the divisions of the city government.

This strength may, however, prove to be a weakness to those given the responsibility to manage Mud Island. The general manager and staff must utilize recruitment and employee compensation procedures that make no distinction for the nature of Mud Island. The island's management does not have the flexibility to hire employees with the unique skills necessary to market the park as an entertainment or theme park. Job descriptions and classifications, although tailored to the needs of the island, still resemble those within the current Park Commission organizational structure. Since few, if any, of the current positions within the Park Commission are engaged in profit-generating activities, it is doubtful that the recruitment and selection of employees for Mud Island will identify those traits necessary for the employees of a profit-making enterprise. (Exhibit 4).

In addition, once employees are in place, the general manager of the island is limited as to the incentives that can be provided to reward performance. It is doubtful that the island could attract the caliber of employees needed to transform the park into a profit-making facility, when those employees would receive the same pay raise and benefit package voted to all regular city employees.

FINANCE

Mud Island was cited as an "economic catalyst" upon its opening five years ago. In addition to possibly further downtown revitalization, it was also expected to change Memphians' perception of their city. Among the major economic impacts expected of Mud Island were these four:

1. Creation of about 5,000 jobs—both full-time and part-time
2. Infusion of new money into the city. The Convention and Visitors Bureau estimated that a visitor spends about $50 per day. If each out-of-town visitor spends one night in Memphis, $25 million in revenue could be generated,

Exhibit 4 *Parks and Recreation Authorized Positions: Staffing—FY 1986—FY 1988*

Bureau	FY 1986 Actual	FY 1987 Original	FY 1987 Amended	FY 1988 Proposed
Administration	18	20	20	20
Recreation	134	134	134	134
Mud Island	68	63	63	63
Maintenance	134	132	132	132
Special Services	156	156	156	156
Rangers	6	6	6	6
Mallory Neeley	0	0	0	1
Total Division	516	511	511	512

changing hands three to four times within the community

3. Purchases of local goods and services—paper goods, retail store items, gasoline, restaurant foods, and beverages

4. Marketing strategies that would promote the entire city of Memphis while selling the sponsoring attraction (Clubb, 1982)

Mud Island is a line item of the Memphis Park Commission's budget, which falls under the jurisdiction of the city of Memphis' budget for parks and recreation. The Park Commission received 5.5% of budgeted expenditures for fiscal year 1988, an amount just over $21 million (Exhibit 5). Whereas the city budget for parks and recreation proposed expenditures of $21,044,916 and net expenditures of $14,663,891 (Exhibit 6), Mud Island received a budget of $3,478,517, a 16.5% share of the Park Commission budget (Exhibit 7).

Even though Mud Island is subsidized by property taxes, the majority of its resources are supplied through admission, parking, and retail sales. There are other functions on the island which generate funds, as can be evidenced by the financial data presented in Exhibit 8. It should be mentioned, however, that during the 1985–1986 fiscal year when the city subsidy peaked at $1.9 million, the land budget was trimmed and revenue increased, resulting in a decrease from 66% to less than 50% of the current $3.4 million budget (Gaither, 1987).

The most solid hope for the future of Mud Island is probably its amphitheater, a 5,000-seat auditorium. Another source of revenue for the island is Midland Food (a division of Coca-Cola),

an independent company that has exclusive catering rights and pays 5% of its on-land gross sales to Mud Island. Revenues derived from contracts through restaurant sales are computed on a progressive scale. The more the restaurants earn, the larger the percentage of their revenues that go to the island.

The four retail shops contribute a small portion of the revenue of the island (3.3% for the 1987 fiscal year). Mud Island does the purchasing for these retail shops. In an effort to reduce additional operational costs, management has budgeted the building of a warehouse to store their inventory, thereby reducing inventory costs.

Other items necessary for the operation of Mud Island are supplied by the city through City Hall. A request is made by the general manager of Mud Island and works its way up the organizational ladder until it is approved by City Hall.

The finances of the city are reported under a modified accrual basis of accounting. This method records revenues in the accounting period in which they may become susceptible to accrual, that is, when they are both measurable and available (*City of Memphis Annual Report*, 1986). The Mud Island accounting reporting also falls under fund accounting, with the general fund being the most important. These funds are entirely or predominantly supported by user charges. Mud Island was originally classified as an Enterprise Fund. "Effective June 30, 1986, the City determined that the activity of this fund was more properly accounted for in the General Fund due to the inability of user charges to cover the majority of the operating expenses of Mud Island. As a result, the city finances the majority of these expenses" (*City of Memphis Annual Report*, 1986).

Exhibit 5 1987–1988 City of Memphis Budget

Where the Money Comes from—FY 1988 Budget

Property taxes	$ 95,329,232	24.8%
Other local taxes	78,032,996	20.3%
Charges for services	56,335,665	14.6%
State shared	49,027,000	12.7%
Intergovernmental	45,659,432	11.9%
License and priveleges	31,110,000	8.1%
Federal grants	12,425,038	3.2%
Investment interest	9,646,150	2.5%
Fines and forfeitures	3,950,000	1.0%
Other	3,126,286	0.8%
Total operating revenues	$384,641,799	100.0%

Where the Money Goes—FY 1988 Budget

Police services	$ 60,131,329	15.6%
Fire services	53,905,975	14.0%
Special accounts	53,110,811	13.8%
Debt service	51,582,144	13.4%
Public works/sewer	50,409,932	13.1%
Sanitation	24,793,220	6.4%
Park commission	21,044,916	5.5%
Other funds	20,992,889	5.5%
General services	16,336,738	4.2%
Community development	13,131,156	3.4%
Executive services	7,113,385	1.8%
Finance and administration	3,711,575	1.0%
Public services	3,484,400	0.9%
Judicial and legislative	2,868,040	0.7%
Personnel	2,025,239	0.5%
Total operating expenditures	$384,641,799	100.0%

Exhibit 6 *City of Memphis Budget Summary: Parks and Recreation*

	Actual Expenditures FY 1986	Budgeted Expenditures FY 1987	Forecasted Expenditures FY 1987	Proposed Expenditures FY 1988
Full-time salaries	$ 8,587,972	8,869,267	9,073,000	8,859,598
Other salaries	459,841	481,352	389,430	457,017
Fringe benefits	1,884,683	1,939,641	1,928,419	1,873,507
Full-time subtotal	10,932,496	11,290,260	11,390,849	11,190,122
Part-time/temporary	2,945,224	3,267,085	3,196,367	2,910,320
TOTAL PERSONNEL	13,877,720	14,557,345	14,587,216	14,100,442
Intragovernmental	482,533	496,880	390,249	490,954
Telephone	212,836	209,186	213,496	201,574
Data processing	11,480	11,800	11,145	10,658
Operating supplies	1,576,856	1,715,965	1,628,824	1,379,424
Repairs/maintenance	183,108	222,874	169,029	169,600
Professional services	1,569,848	1,378,817	1,157,428	1,284,414
Travel	24,743	24,200	25,569	24,199
Transportation	57,263	77,900	59,284	58,097
Utilities	2,316,081	2,529,459	2,629,146	2,793,524
Misc srvc/chg/contr	307,666	579,305	497,488	504,230
Total material/supplies	6,742,414	7,246,386	6,781,658	6,916,674
Capital outlay	0	0	0	0
Lump sums	522,739	93,966	29,249	0
Goods purchased for resale	25,114	109,725	155,600	150,000
Contingency	0	0	0	0
Gross expenditures	21,167,987	22,007,422	21,553,723	21,167,116
Expense recovery	190,615	113,600	142,655	122,200
Total city expenditures	20,977,372	21,893,822	21,411,068	21,044,916
Departmental revenue	6,727,096	6,396,936	6,136,883	6,331,808
Grant revenue	768,310	995,302	957,490	49,217
Net city expenditures	13,481,966	14,501,584	14,316,695	14,663,891

Exhibit 7 Mud Island Budget Summary, 1986–1989

	Actual FY 1986	Budgeted FY 1987	Forecast FY 1987	Actual FY 1987	Budgeted FY 1988	Forecast FY 1988	Actual October 31 (YTD)	Annualized FY 1988	Forecast FY 1989
Full-time salaries	$1,044,589	1,133,695	1,135,411	1,168,823	1,102,105	1,212,889	420,444	1,681,776	1,192,972
Other salaries	20,132	45,426	31,304	46,959	44,083	61,183	25,507	102,028	59,759
Fringe benefits	238,531	272,928	256,830	267,527	256,259	286,855	100,339	401,356	292,548
Full-time subtotal	1,303,252	1,452,109	1,423,545	1,483,309	1,402,547	1,560,927	546,290	2,185,160	1,545,259
Part-time/temporary	589,017	557,155	550,600	563,238	557,155	580,433	286,714	1,146,856	585,000
Total personnel	1,892,269	2,009,264	1,974,145	2,046,547	1,959,702	2,141,360	833,004	3,332,016	2,130,259
Intragovernmental	44,229	47,461	51,571	58,542	46,130	48,352	24,377	97,508	48,000
Telephone	42,472	38,782	40,072	925	35,155	33,306	313	1,252	33,300
Data processing	0	0	0	0	0	0	0	0	0
Operating supplies	213,443	196,783	199,394	186,041	193,710	183,098	51,007	204,028	184,950
Repairs/maintenance	103,333	112,850	73,564	68,324	67,600	68,001	23,595	94,380	69,000
Professional services	884,583	703,183	516,631	536,973	533,035	530,830	106,060	424,240	530,000
Travel	11,369	11,350	6,566	4,388	0	0	2,949	11,796	0
Transportation	3,366	10,950	5,935	7,208	4,831	4,735	1,264	5,056	4,900
Utilities	452,506	501,400	486,709	475,962	510,779	510,211	168,946	675,784	545,000
Misc srvc/chg/contr	124,110	183,500	113,757	86,981	21,575	19,965	7,835	31,340	19,700
Total material/supplies	1,879,411	1,806,259	1,494,200	1,425,344	1,412,815	1,398,498	386,346	1,545,384	1,434,850
Capital outlay	0	0	0	0	0	0	0	0	0
Lump sums	0	0	0	0	0	0	0	0	0
Goods purchased for resale	25,114	109,725	155,600	160,397	150,000	186,549	74,899	299,596	170,000
Contingency	0	0	0	0	0	0	0	0	0
Gross expenditures	3,796,794	3,925,248	3,623,945	3,632,288	3,522,517	3,726,407	1,294,249	5,176,996	3,735,109
Expense recovery	44,216	53,000	58,297	60,586	44,000	38,885	9,444	37,776	39,000
Total city expenditures	3,752,578	3,872,248	3,565,648	3,571,702	3,478,517	3,687,522	1,284,805	5,139,220	3,696,109
Departmental revenue	1,761,671	2,054,500	1,789,122	1,819,969	1,881,124	1,909,060	945,979	3,783,916	1,888,000
Grant revenue	13,368	3,550	7,527	6,480	0	19,908	3,480	13,920	0
Net city expenditures	$1,977,539	1,814,198	1,768,999	1,745,253	1,597,393	1,758,554	335,346	1,341,384	1,808,109

Source: City of Memphis FY 1988 Proposed Operating Budget and Appropriation Statements FY 1986 thru 1989.

Exhibit 8 Mud Island Revenue Summary, 1986–1989

	Actual FY 1986	Budgeted FY 1987	Forecast FY 1987	Actual FY 1987	Budgeted FY 1988	Forecast FY 1988	Actual October 31 (YTD)	Annualized FY 1988	Forecast FY 1989
Summer day care				6,237	8,299	7,732	5,652	22,608	8,000
Mud Island admission				855,573	935,000	945,048	510,147	2,040,588	930,000
Amphitheatre admission				89,835	86,600	80,570	39,976	159,904	81,500
Mud Island retail				364,599	339,666	356,551	185,722	742,888	354,000
Restaurant revenue				60,994	59,500	61,029	24,680	98,720	56,500
Amusement revenue				4,356	5,285	3,178	1,810	7,240	3,000
Excursion boat revenue				8,996	8,746	9,333	7,789	31,156	10,000
Sponsorships				59,000	60,000	55,750	42,750	171,000	55,000
Marina income				9,582	0	14,769	5,669	22,676	14,500
Promenade lot parking				354,306	370,028	368,737	160,852	643,408	370,000
Camp fees				0	6,000	0	225	900	0
Folkfest rentals				3,226	0	0	0	0	0
Miscellaneous revenues				4,212	2,000	6,781	5,635	22,540	5,500
Sales tax commission				1,038	0	(417)	(266)	(1,064)	
Overage/shortage				(1,985)	0	(1)	(566)	(2,264)	
Accts rec and prior yr collections				0	0	0	(44,096)	0	
Total departmental revenues	1,761,671	2,054,500	1,789,122	1,819,969	1,881,124	1,909,060	945,979	3,960,300	1,888,000
MAC grant				3,000	0	0	0	0	0
Local other revenues				3,480	0	19,908	3,480	13,920	0
Grant revenues	13,368	3,550	7,527	6,480	0	19,908	3,480	13,920	0
Total revenues	$1,775,039	2,058,050	1,796,649	1,826,449	1,821,124	1,928,968	949,459	3,974,220	1,888,000

Source: City of Memphis FY 1988 Proposed Operating Budget and Appropriation Statements FY 1986 thru 1989.

Consequently, the general fixed assets of the city now include a $53.9 million reclassification of Mud Island's fixed assets from enterprise assets. This represents the original or estimated original cost. (Exhibit 9) This figure consists of mostly land and buildings, with a smaller portion allocated for furniture and equipment. These assets comprise just over 8% of the city's total investment in general fixed assets. No depreciation is taken on these assets.

In addition to reclassifying fixed assets, long-term debt of $32,221 was reclassified to the General Long-Term Debt Account Group. This is much less than 1% of outstanding long-term debt, which is funded through general obligation debt and revenue bonds.

EPILOGUE

As is common with most other "attractions," both local (Memphis Zoo, the Pink Palace Museum, etc.) and nationwide, Mud Island operates at a deficit, even though the deficit has been decreasing. Annualizing from October 1987 figures, the deficit for 1987 will be $600,000 less than that for 1986. Part of the reason for the decrease was the presence of complementary local attractions during 1987, such as the Ramesses exhibit and the Zoo's panda bear exhibit, as well as the addition of the *Memphis Belle* to the island. While nothing of this magnitude is planned for fiscal years 1988 or 1989, park officials do hope that they can maintain the increased level of admissions and revenues.

BIBLIOGRAPHY

American Marketing Association. *Dedication of the Permanent Home for the Memphis Belle: Survey Results.* Memphis: Memphis State University, 1987.

Beifus, J. Cottam quits as Mud Island chief. *The Commercial Appeal.* April 13, 1988, p. B1.

Brame, B. Assistant director, Memphis Park Commission and interim general manager, Mud Island. Personal interview, November 20, 1987.

City of Memphis Fiscal Year Proposed Operating Budget and Fiscal Year 1988–1997 Capital Improvements Program. Memphis: City of Memphis.

Clubb, D. Model shows a mile of river for a step. *The Commercial Appeal.* June 27, 1982, p. J3.

Comprehensive Annual Financial Report/Year Ended June 30, 1986. Division of Finance and Administration. Memphis: City of Memphis.

Cornish, E. Free time. *Parks and Recreation.* May, 1986 pp. 57–60.

Frank, A.D. Leisure and recreation. *Forbes.* January 12, 1987, pp. 158–159.

Gaither, S. Island's lure of residents increasing, Ogle says. *The Commercial Appeal.* October 11, 1987, p. B4.

Graves, T. Leisure-time: current analysis. *Standard and Poor's Industry Surveys,* July 30, 1987, pp. L1–L60.

Humphrey, F. The future of leisure services: will we be architects or reactors? *Parks and Recreation.* May 1986, pp. 38–39.

Jabbour, C. Financial manager, Memphis Park Commission. Personal Interview, November 19, 1987.

Jeffrey, N. Joy rides: theme parks introduce more high-tech thrills and chills. *Wall Street Journal.* July 2, 1987, p. 21.

Jordan, T. Seasonal closing of island urged. *The Commercial Appeal.* May 5, 1988, p. B1.

Kotler, P. *Marketing Management: Analysis, Planning, and Control.* 5th ed. Englewood Cliffs, NJ: Prentice-Hall, 1984.

Lollar, M. Opening day at Mud Island. *The Commercial Appeal.* March 11, 1988, pp. E12–E13.

May, E.G., Ress, C.W., and Salmon, W.J. *Future Trends in Retailing.* Cambridge, Mass: Marketing Science Institute, 1985.

Mud turns to millions. Mud Island press release, 1987.

National Endowment for the Arts. *Five-year Planning Document: 1986–1990.* Washington, DC: US Government Printing Office, 1984.

Nave, M. Park officials seek way to market Mud Island. *Memphis Press Scimitar.* February 22, 1984, p. D1.

Obermark, J. Economic catalyst cited among island's benefits. *The Commercial Appeal.* June 27, 1982, p. J4.

Personnel, Policies, and Procedures for the City of Memphis. Memphis: City of Memphis, 1987.

Roberts, N. Marketing director, Mud Island. Personal interview, November 18, 1987.

Tindell, J.P. The art and science of futuring. *Parks and Recreation.* May 1986, pp. 32–35.

Zweig, P.L. Panic/industry analysis. *Financial World.* December 1, 1987, pp. 21–26.

Exhibit 9 City of Memphis, Schedule of Changes in General Fixed Assets—by Source (For the Fiscal Year Ended June 30, 1986)

	Land and Buildings	Improvements Other Than Buildings	Equipment and Furniture	Construction Work in Progress	Totals 1986	Totals 1985
Total investment in general fixed assets—July 1	$352,387,979	48,029,090	122,009,326	38,512,109	560,938,504	517,706,407
Add						
Net equipment and furniture increases from operating fund:						
General city government	—	—	7,486,664	—	7,486,664	3,803,681
Board of education	8,300,287	—	8,590,380	—	16,890,667	16,997,996
Expenditures from capital projects fund:						
General city government	—	—	—	14,952,418	14,952,418	20,566,780
Board of education	—	—	—	12,805,306	12,805,306	7,162,884
Transfer capital projects fund projects to general fixed assets						
General city government	5,909,198	908,070	668,756	(7,486,024)	—	—
Board of education	1,280,759	—	—	(1,280,759)	—	—
Reclassification of assets of Mud Island	50,852,684	—	3,050,589	—	53,903,273	—
Less disposal of general fixed assets						
General city government	—	—	(4,863,633)	—	(4,863,633)	—
Board of education	(763,193)	—	(3,141,818)	—	(3,905,011)	(5,299,194)
Total investment in general fixed assets—June 30	$417,967,714	48,937,160	133,800,264	57,503,050	658,208,188	560,938,504

THE JOHN HANCOCK MUTUAL LIFE INSURANCE COMPANY

Raymond M. Kinnunen and L. Jake Katz
Northeastern University

John G. McElwee, chairman of the board and chief executive officer of the John Hancock Mutual Life Insurance Company, asked himself three questions in the spring of 1984 as he prepared the company for the 1990s and beyond: What is it you want the institution to be? What do you think the world will be like? How do we prepare for that in terms of what business the company will be in and what it will need in terms of talent? A move to financial services came out of that analysis and, more specifically, an analysis of what McElwee saw as his six criteria: economy, demographics, attitudes and lifestyles, competition, technology, and government action. In McElwee's view, however:

> Nobody really knows what the financial services industry will be. We all admit to that. We are all trying to be flexible. We know we all are not doing everything right, and the jury is still out as to which companies will have the right combination and the wisdom and courage to remedy the situation as it evolves. When will this happen? When will the paradigm of the new FSI be in place? In my view it won't be before 1990.

The John Hancock Mutual Life Insurance Company began its move into financial services in 1968. This case offers some background on the financial services industry (FSI), the insurance industry, and the nature of the issues and problems facing the company in 1984.

TRENDS IN THE INDUSTRY

The late 1970s and early 1980s saw a significant trend toward the provision of fuller financial services being offered by institutions:

> The FSI is a huge amalgam of firms ranging in size from the CitiCorp with well over $130 billion in assets to many small credit unions with a few hundred thousand dollars of assets. In 1980, there were over 40,000 individual firms competing in the FSI with a mix of products including savings accounts, life insurance policies, pension management services, and stock brokering. The size of the FSI as measured by financial assets under control was nearly $4 trillion in 1980 and was experiencing nearly 11% annual growth.
>
> Historically, the various segments of the FSI have been primarily defined by government regulation. In fact, this is the reason many firms in the FSI are considered institutions rather than firms in the economic sense. The institutional segments of the FSI have been controlled and defined by their relationships to regulatory agencies. For example, banks are regulated at the federal, state, and local levels by various agencies. Securities firms are regulated only at the federal level by the Securities and Exchange Commission (SEC). Insurance companies, since 1946, have been regulated by state agencies. The result is an industry where products have been defined

by regulation and customer markets have been given access to those products only through specific institutions. Until fairly recently, a customer went to a bank for a loan, to an insurance company for an insurance policy, and to a securities firm to trade stock. In this regulated environment, which defined the channels between customers and the financial products, the FSI was on average, very profitable. Between 1975 and 1980, the banking industry reported annual profit growth of 18%, the life insurance industry reported 30% annual profit growth, and the securities industry reported 7% profit growth (for a scale of measurement, all US industry reported 12% profit growth during that time). . . .

Competition in the FSI has not been very intense compared to other industries; in fact, the common view of many financial institutions has been that the main objective is not to compete, but to provide public services. This view has been allowed and reinforced by: (a) the regulatory environment, (b) the web of relationships among financial institutions which required a large degree of coordination and cooperation, and (c) the historical values and culture which preside in most financial institutions. (The "lean and mean" operation has not been the role model for most financial organizations.) Regulations, severely limiting the dimensions of competition, have sought to create a sort of economic DMZ (demilitarized zone) between the customers and the financial markets, reasoning that unlimited competition, by nature, causes behavior and results which are not in the best interest of the customer. The regulatory thinking assumed that unbridled competition would certainly mean more failures of weak and poorly run institutions. This would, over time, create a more efficient marketplace, but the result on the customer of a failing institution could be devastating. Also, it was expected that competition would drive institutions to more predatory and less benign behavior towards their customers and competitors as the scramble for profits intensified.

Traditionally, different types of institutions offered different types of products and services. Banks have concentrated on offering transaction products and many kinds of loan products to individuals and corporations. Savings and loans (thrifts) have provided savings products and specialized mortgage lending to individuals. Securities firms have tended to specialize to a degree with different firms offering "wholesale" products to corporations such as underwriting and other investment banking activities (e.g., Goldman Sachs and Salomon Brothers) and other firms specializing in "retail" brokerage and trading for consumers (e.g., Merrill Lynch, Shearson and E. F. Hutton). Insurance companies have generally specialized in either life insurance products (e.g., Prudential, Metropolitan, and New York Life) or property and casualty insurance (e.g., State Farm, Allstate, INA). To a degree they have also been involved in mortgage and commercial lending. Traditionally, most insurance companies have served both individual and corporate customers. Finance companies have concentrated on consumer lending and mortgage lending primarily to individuals. As noted above, a dominant reason in the traditional product/institution relationship has been regulation but institutional thinking has also greatly influenced how the industry has defined itself.[1]

While the level of merger and acquisition activity within the financial services industry over the last decade seemed to suggest an inevitable fusion of services under one roof, companies found that sales personnel trained to move one service were not necessarily well suited at uncovering client needs for another. For example, Merrill Lynch, the largest marketer of securities, found it inefficient to have their stockbrokers selling insurance policies. "Meanwhile, Merrill has begun experimenting with a more specialized approach to selling. Convinced that the average broker is unable to sell insurance, Merrill last June began installing life insurance specialists in 32 branches. It plans to hire 100 more this year."[2]

David Koehler, president of Financial Learning Systems, a firm training both securities and insurance personnel to sell new products and to prepare for licensing exams, cites five major barriers insurance agents face when selling noninsurance products. These barriers include (1) licensing (state licensing exams are relatively easy for the insurance industry but fairly rigorous exams for securities); (2) product knowledge (the level necessary for life

---

[1]"The Evolving Financial Services Industry: Competition and Technology for the '80's," copyright 1983, by the President and Fellows of Harvard College, 9-183-007, pp. 1-3.
[2]"Merrill Lynch's Big Dilemma," *Business Week,* 16 January 1984, p. 62.

agents to be comfortable selling securities may be underestimated); (3) skills to sell the product (different skills are required to sell a life insurance policy than a mutual fund); (4) commissions (to get a similar dollar-for-dollar commission, an agent has to sell a fund possibly fifty times the "value" of a life policy); and (5) attitude (life agents are accustomed to selling "guaranteed" products).[3]

Others in the industry acknowledge these barriers but conclude that the lines between agents and brokers are becoming blurred. Because of competition, the agent has diversified his or her product line while the broker has added more service through financial planning.[4]

To make matters more complex, some feel that both agents and brokers will be competing with other brokers selling products based more on price than on service.[5] The vast majority of consumers' liquid assets are held in depository institutions, which gives the banking industry an advantage. One way for insurance companies to compete with banks is to offer transaction accounts. To do this, however, they must acquire a bank image.[6]

Standard and Poor's Industry Surveys note the following in regard to the trend toward full service:

> The emergence of alternative products, along with general deregulation of the financial industry, has intensified competition in the life insurance industry. The successful life insurance company will be one that adapts quickly to the changing environment. The competitiveness of life insurance will increasingly depend not only on innovations in products and services, but also importantly on the quality of marketing and distribution systems.
>
> Insurers are aware of the need for more effective marketing strategies and some already are making changes. One approach that is taking hold is the combination of insurers and other major financial institutions to form broad-based financial services conglomerates.

> The goal here is to bring together a variety of financial products and services, provide one stop access to the consumer, and allow cross-marketing of product and service combinations as financial services packages. This approach to market expansion is evidenced by such recent acquisitions as Bache Group Inc. by Prudential Insurance Co. of America and Shearson Loeb Rhoades by American Express (which owns Fireman's Funds Insurance Co.) among others.[7]

Theodore Gordon, president of the Futures Group, summed it up this way:

> The whole marketplace for insurance is becoming very dynamic. It will be increasingly difficult in the future to tell the difference between a brokerage house, an insurance company, a bank, and a large-scale credit card company. To some degree, the functions of these institutions already overlap.[8]

A May 1982 article in *Institutional Investor* questions the effects of mergers that result in extended financial services:

> While it is too early for a verdict on that, however, there's another critical question at stake here. These firms have also been trumpeting the synergistic benefits that are supposed to flow from these mergers. American Express, for example, hopes to sell a wide variety of financial services through its credit cards, opening up vast new vistas for Shearson. Sears can envision its millions of customers buying Dean Witter products at its stores. And the Pru can look forward to its agents selling Bache products nationwide. Bache chairman Harry Jacobs, Jr. perhaps best sums it up when he says, "We expect the merger to extend the range of services both firms provide."
>
> Yet, amid all the euphoric talk, no one has really stopped to ask whether these future synergistic wonders will actually come to pass,

---

[3]Stephen Piontek, "Securities Products Face Agents with Problems," *National Underwriter, Life and Health Insurance Edition*, 17 July 1982, pp. 28-36.

[4]Ibid., p. 3.

[5]Ibid., p. 43.

[6]Barbara E. Casey, "Customer is Key to Insurance-Banking Rivalry," *National Underwriter, Life and Health Edition*, 17 July 1982, pp. 8-9, 36.

[7]*Standard & Poor's Industry Surveys*, 7 July 1983 (Vol. 151, no. 27, sec. 1), *Insurance & Investments Basic Analysis*, p. 155.

[8]Theodore J. Gordon, "Life Insurance Companies in the 80's: A Quiet Revolution," *Resources*, July/August 1981, p. 3.

whether synergy on such a grand scale can really work in the financial services business. Will the vaunted synergy ever materialize to any significant extent? Will the diverse parts of these financial services conglomerates truly mesh and spur each other on to new heights—boosting sales, cutting costs and adding up to more than the sum of the parts?

Actually, there's plenty of evidence to suggest these companies may be in for a tougher time of it than most people suspect. For one thing, there's the nagging fact that dozens of previous attempts to create synergy in the financial services industry have, at best, been somewhat disappointing. It was fashionable in the early 1970s, for example, to suppose that retail brokers could sell life insurance as a sideline, thereby increasing their earnings and those of their firms. As it turned out, however, these brokers either lacked the skills to sell insurance or were too busy with stocks to bother with it. No precise figures are available, but Securities Industry Association statistics indicate that Wall Street firms gathered revenues of less than $500 million from insurance in 1980, compared with their total revenues of $16 billion.[9]

The article goes on to detail the experience of Continental Insurance:

Continental Insurance made little progress toward the synergy that was supposed to accrue from its consumer finance subsidiary and its Diners Club credit card operations—both of which have since been sold. Other than the relatively minor business of travel life insurance, Continental found it difficult to sell policies via the credit card. It was hard, says one Continental official, to design a home insurance application form to mail out with bills because it entailed asking so many detailed questions. Nor was it really feasible to sell insurance through consumer finance outlets—local Continental agents would have been annoyed by the competition—Continental feared. Reports Continental chairman John Ricker sadly: "One-stop financial shopping is a

buzzword returning to our vocabulary. I am skeptical, not by nature, but by experience. Continental has tried the full financial services approach, and it didn't work.[10]

Robert Beck of Prudential is quoted later in the same article with this view:

"I don't think previous attempts have all been failures," is the way Prudential chairman Beck shrugs it off. Or perhaps a better way of putting it is that they're persuaded that times have changed dramatically since their previous efforts to achieve financial services synergy were made. Notes American Express chairman Robinson, "The environment today is 100 percent different than it was when those [previous] relationships were formed." For one thing, he notes, "there's a trend toward constructing hybrid financial products," begun by Merrill Lynch's CMA account—a trend Robinson thinks multifaceted houses may be able to exploit.[11]

The customer base is also an important factor when it comes to offering financial services.

Sears, Roebuck and Company, American Express Company and Prudential Life Insurance Company currently sell their services to some 50 million Americans. The three companies intend to bombard these clients with new financial services products. But according to conventional wisdom in the financial services business, it's not really the quantity of customer that counts, but the quality—how rich the customers are. . . . it's generally assumed that servicing well-heeled folk will be more profitable in years to come than pushing financial products at people of moderate means.[12]

"Well-heeled" is typically defined as meaning an annual family income of $50,000 or more; there are an estimated 3.2 million households in this group. Some experts fear that, with a large number of big as well as small institutions competing, few will make a profit. Given those estimates "the supercompanies plan to concentrate on the vast middle market of families earning $20,000 to $50,000 a year.[13]

---

[9]Neil Osborn, "What Synergy," *Institutional Investor*, May 1982, p. 50.

[10]Ibid, p. 52.

[11]Ibid, p. 52

[12]Ibid, p. 54.

[13]Arlene Hershman, "The Supercompanies Emerge," *Dunn's Business Month*, April 1983, p. 46.

The supercompanies (Sears, Roebuck and Company, Prudential-Bache Securities, Bank America Corp., American Express, Citicorp, and Merrill Lynch and Co.) continue to expand into new businesses as fast as the law and technology permit (Table 1 compares some financial and product data on the supercompanies with those of the John Hancock). Some large insurers are acquiring small securities firms, money managers, and mortgage bankers. Alexander Clash, president at New York's John Alden Insurance Company, expressed one view that acquisitions are a cheap form of R&D and added, "Buying a foothold in every conceivable financial service is a way of participating in every business because no one is sure what the hot areas will be in 1990."[14]

Obviously, there are considerable mixed feelings in the financial services community concerning recent changes. Movement continues to take place even in light of the questionable results companies may achieve when they offer one-stop financial services, in effect becoming financial supermarkets (see Exhibit 1). Part of the reason for this trend may be the estimated $200 billion that Americans spent on financial services in 1982, reportedly earning suppliers of those services $42 billion.[15]

The decade of the 1980s promises to be an exciting one for the huge American financial services industry, which has, until now, been fragmented. Some uncontrollable factors, such as interest rates, the economic climate, the regulatory climate, and the role of technology, will also affect the industry. Many experts believe that technology (especially computers and telephones), with its costs and unpredictable product breakthroughs, will play such a large part in product cost and delivery that the big competition to worry about may be not other companies in the financial services industry but AT&T and IBM.[16]

THE JOHN HANCOCK MUTUAL LIFE INSURANCE COMPANY[17]

The John Hancock Company began in 1862 when John Hancock started selling life insurance. By 1864 the company had over half a million dollars of insurance in force. In less than ten years, the company's insurance in force grew to nearly $20 million. In the early part of the twentieth century, the company pioneered a number of products, including group life insurance. The John Hancock Company prospered during the boom years following World War I and continued to grow through the Depression. As late as the mid 1960s the company was still primarily a seller of insurance. A hundred years after its founding, the company's pool of capital had been invested in nearly every imaginable sector of the economy, both private and public.

In December 1983, in an internal bulletin to all home office employees, the John Hancock Mutual Life Insurance Company announced a definitive merger agreement with the Buckeye Financial Corporation of Columbus, Ohio. The merger agreement provided for the acquisition of Buckeye by the John Hancock subsidiary for approximately $28 million in cash, equal to $13.50 per share of Buckeye common shares on a fully diluted basis. Buckeye, a savings and loan holding company in Columbus, Ohio, is the parent of Buckeye Federal Savings and Loan Association. Buckeye Federal, a federally chartered savings and loan association, conducts its business through nineteen offices located throughout central Ohio. With assets of approximately $1.2 billion as of September 30, 1983, Buckeye Federal is one of the largest savings and loan associations in Ohio and is the largest mortgage lender in central Ohio. In April 1982, less than two years prior to this merger, the Hancock had acquired Tucker

---

[14]Ibid, p. 47.

[15]Ibid, p. 44.

[16]Ibid, p. 50.

[17]Historical facts on the company were taken from *A Bridge to the Future; One Hundreth Anniversary 1862-1962,* copyright 1962, John Hancock Mutual Life Insurance Company, Boston, Mass.

Table 1 The Supercompanies and John Hancock: Financial and Product Data (All Figures in Millions of Dollars)

	American Express	Bank America	Citicorp	Merrill Lynch	Prudential	Sears	John Hancock[a]
Financial Data							
Revenues	7,800	13,112	18,258	4,590	13,200	29,180	4,422
Net Income	559	425	774	220	NC[c]	735	NC
Assets	27,700	120,496	128,430	20,940	62,500	34,200	23,714[b]
Customers' deposits	5,700	93,208	77,359	3,930	—	2,300	—
Customers' credit balances	1,200	—	—	2,700	740	200	—
Money market funds	17,200[d]	—	—	48,900	5,000	9,000	1,125
Commercial loans	4,200	48,800	60,411	400	1,560	—	2,000
Consumer loans	1,000	25,100	22,029	5,000	3,900	4,250	1,900
What They Do							
Securities brokerage	•			•	•	•	•
Securities trading	•	•	•	•	•		
Cash management services	•			•		•	•
Investment management	•	•	•	•	•	•	
Commodities brokerage	•			•	•		
US corporate underwriting	•			•	•		
International corporate underwriting	•	•	•	•	•		
US commercial banking		•	•				
International commercial banking	•	•	•	•			
Savings and loan operations			•			•	
Small-loans offices		•	•			•	
Credit card, charge cards	•	•	•			•	
What They Do							
Traveler's checks	•	•	•				
Foreign exchange trading	•	•	•	•	•	•	
Leasing	•	•	•	•	•		•
Data processing services	•	•	•	•			•
Property-casualty insurance	•				•	•	•
Life health insurance	•				•	•	•
Mortgage insurance						•	•
Mortgage banking	•	•	•	•		•	•
Real estate development	•				•	•	•
Commercial real estate brokerage				•		•	
Residential real estate brokerage				•		•	
Executive relocation services				•		•	

Source: The New Financial Services, Schaumburg, Ill: Alliance of American Insurers, 1983 (reprinted with permission of Prudential-Bache Securities).

[a]*Source:* John Hancock internal documents.
[b]Not including subsidiary assets.
[c]NC = not comparable.
[d]Total assets under management, $37 million.

Exhibit 1 *Financial Services Announcements: The First Half of 1983*

- Travelers owns Securities Development Corporation (securities clearing subsidiary).
- President of American Express joins Travelers (hiring said to be influenced by his financial services background).
- Equitable Life and First National Bank of Chicago to market cash management services.
- Prudential to buy Capital City Bank of Hopeville, Georgia.
- Sears to have Dean Witter offices in 100 stores by the end of 1983, 150 by end of 1984, and eventually 400.
- CIGNA buys automatic Business Centers, commercial payroll processing centers.
- Kemper's regional brokerage houses earned $8.3 million in 1982.
- Nationwide to offer insurance in offices of Banc One.
- John Hancock's Independent Investment Associates to offer financial services for corporations and institutions.
- Prudential to have 30 joint offices with Bache by the end of 1983.
- Travelers to offer insured cash management services through its trust company.
- Hartford to buy 24% of Minneapolis brokerage firm.
- Aetna Life & Casualty buys majority interest in Federal Investors.
- Mutual of Omaha plans to acquire investment banking and brokerage firm of Kilpatrick, Pettis, Smith, Polian, Inc.
- J. C. Penney to buy First National Bank of Harrington, Delaware.
- Merrill Lynch to buy Raritan Valley Financial Corporation, a New Jersey savings and loan.
- Kemper announces intention to buy a savings and loan.
- Chairman of Manufacturers Hanover says much of the euphoria about financial supermarkets may be exaggerated.

Source: Robert A. Bull, Insurance and the financial services industry, *United States Banker*, August 1983, p. 118.

Anthony Holding Corporation, the parent of Tucker Anthony and R. L. Day Inc., a regional brokerage house with thirty offices in the Northeast.[18] These two announcements were the latest of a number of financial services subsidiaries (most developed internally) that had been added since 1968. In a letter dated December 23, 1968, and addressed to home office associates, then President Robert E. Slater discussed the concept of subsidiaries:

We think of them (the subsidiaries) as a device through which we can develop markets and new products and, as a corollary, other new avenues toward increased compensation for our sales forces. They also provide investment vehicles to enhance the return on total investable funds. Life insurance is still our main business—by a very wide margin—but in the larger view we can use these subsidiaries to augment or supplement our life insurance sales with the marketing of a wide array of financial services.

BACKGROUND ON THE INSURANCE INDUSTRY

Today in the United States the insurance industry is divided into three major categories: life, health, and property and casualty. The life and health areas further divide into group and individual categories. In 1981 new purchases of life insurance in the United States amounted $812.3 billion.[19]

Commercial life insurance companies are divided into two categories: stock and mutual companies.[20] A company that has stockholders is a stock company, whereas a mutual company is owned by its policyholders. Just over 2,000 life insurance companies were doing business in the United States in 1982; 135 were mutual companies, while 1,900 were stock companies. Although mutual companies represent only 7 percent of the total they own 57 percent of the assets of all life insurance companies in the United States and accounted for 43 percent of the life insurance in force in 1982.

Stock companies seek to earn the highest possible profits for their shareholders. Policy owners do not benefit from any gains the stock company enjoys nor are they hurt by any losses the company suffers. Because they are not directly affected by the company's financial experience, their policies are called nonparticipating. Because no dividend is expected the premium paid by a stock company must meet capital and surplus requirements as well as other requirements established by its home state. Having met these requirements and having had its stock subscribed, a stock company may begin doing business. Because a stock company is owned by its shareholders, the first responsibility of the directors is to those shareholders. Because stockholders can vote on major issues and elect the board of directors, control of the company rests with the owners of a majority of the stock. Shareholders may sell their stock or buy more shares at prevailing market prices.

Mutual insurance companies are owned by policyholders. Management's first obligation is to create profit for policyholders, who have the right to vote for directors. When funds available exceed solvency requirements, the directors may pay policyholders a dividend, although such payment is not mandatory. The cost of a policyholder's premium less the dividend paid determines the final cost of the insurance coverage. Because the policyholder may benefit from the favorable financial experience of a mutual company, that policy is called participating. Owners of mutual companies are numerous and scattered and have proportionately small ownership positions. For these reasons, control of a mutual company remains largely with management.

By the end of the 1960s, the rising inflation rate caused a number of people to seek new investment vehicles that offered higher returns than life insurance. The public's attention turned to the stock market. Many viewed life insurance as a high opportunity cost versus returns they imagined were available through stock market investments. A number of investment firms answered that market's desire by offering mutual fund shares. The public sank dollars into a new breed of mutual fund called money market funds. Securities firms (such as Merrill Lynch) and fund operators (such as

---

[18]"Hancock to Acquire Tucker Anthony at Up to $47 Million," *Wall Street Journal*, 15 April 1982, p. 16.
[19]Sources of factual data on the insurance industry were *1983 Life Insurance Factbook*, American Council of Life Insurance, Washington, D.C., 1983, and S.S. Hubner and Kenneth Black, Jr., *Life Insurance*, 9th ed., Prentice Hall, Inc., Englewood Cliffs, N.J., 1976.
[20]For data on the top ten insurance companies, see Exhibit 2.

Fidelity) invested billions of dollars in low-risk securities offering record levels of income. Banks began offering certificates of deposit (CDs) with very high returns. The insurance industry found itself fighting not only for new business but to retain the reserves that they already held.

To grow and, indeed, to survive, traditional insurance institutions like John Hancock found themselves forced to compete with higher-yielding instruments offered by the federal government, municipal governments, and brokerage houses.

JOHN HANCOCK SUBSIDIARIES, INC.

In 1980, the structure of the John Hancock Company was changed to incorporate the existence of ten subsidiaries in the form of a downstream holding company (see Exhibit 3). Table 2 describes the products and services offered by the subsidiaries. Selective financial data on the parent company and the subsidiaries can be found in Exhibits 4 and 5.

Stephen Brown, executive vice president of Financial Operations of the John Hancock Mutual Life Insurance Company and president and chief executive officer of John Hancock Subsidiaries, Inc., had worked for the Hancock for twenty-two years when he became president of the Holding Company in 1981. Brown, offered the following explanation on the origins of the Holding Company and its operations. Initially when the individual companies were started (the first in 1968), they became part of an existing department of the company. For example, Hanseco, which offered a line of casualty insurance, operated as a part of the marketing department and was expected to attract more revenue to the company by giving insurance agents a larger package of securities to offer. At that time the major objective of a new addition was synergy, or as Brown described it, "putting more dollars in the agency force." Profit and growth were secondary.

In January 1980, when the Holding Company (John Hancock Subsidiaries, Inc.) was established, management was charged with the responsibility of overseeing the subsidiary companies and reporting to the board of directors of the Life Company. As control mechanisms, the Holding Company was to submit to the board quarterly financial statements and yearly presentations on its overall strategy. In addition, various board committees on organization, finance, compliance, conflict of interest, and auditing could also ask for reports. The individual

subsidiaries submitted strategic plans to the board of the Holding Company. In 1980 the objectives for the subsidiaries had become first profit followed by growth and then synergy, and the subsidiaries were expected in the long run to return 15 percent on investment. Brown noted that before this time "profit and return in investment" were not commonplace expectations in the company.

In Brown's view, the major reasons for changing the structure to a holding company were for tax purposes (some subsidiaries were profitable and others were not) and to form more consistent planning and control systems throughout the subsidiaries. Although there were some in the company who felt that various departments should continue to control the subsidiaries, the outcome of the restructuring, according to Brown, was that "there are now clear controls in place with the subsidiaries operating autonomously from day to day."

Each subsidiary has its own board of directors. The Holding Company decides on the directors and reviews the minutes of meetings. Major capital requirements and any significant change in the type of business performed by a subsidiary also requires approval by the Holding Company. Personnel selection and compensation are left completely to the subsidiaries. Subsidiaries are welcome, but not required, to use the staff facilities at the Life Company (for example, EDP, accounting, public relations). Brown stated that, on the average, he visits the subsidiaries once a month. With the major objectives of profitability, growth, and synergy clearly stated, the approach used to run the subsidiaries is, according to Brown, "Now, go do it!"

Brown commented on the future of the John Hancock:

> *Profit and return on investment were not common words in the company. In the long run I see us adopting GAAP instead of statutory accounting and defining profit centers throughout the Life Company as we do in the Holding Company. This is a step toward becoming in the long run a stock company where we can purchase with stock as opposed to cash and offer stock incentives to management and tie a bonus to profits and growth. If in the long run this is where we are headed, the only way to do it is the profit center concept.*

The addition of the Holding Company in 1980, along with the different systems used to measure performance, added a new dimension to the John

Exhibit 2 *Assets of Insurance Companies*

Company	Dollar Amount of Total Assets[a]
Prudential	66,707,209
Metropolitan Life	55,731,371
Equitable Life of NY	40,285,559
Aetna Life	28,551,098
New York Life	22,549,386
John Hancock	21,710,494
Travelers	17,440,305
Conn General	15,660,054
Teachers Ins & Ann	13,519,897
Northwestern Mutual	13,252,835

Source: *Best's Insurance Management Reports,* October 1983.
[a]Figures do not include assets of subsidiaries.

Hancock and its way of operating. This became clear as people discussed the changes that had taken place inside the Hancock over the past sixteen years and the future in the changing the financial services industry.

STRUCTURE, CULTURE, AND SYSTEMS

A major focus in the company was the fact that two different entities operate under the name John Hancock Mutual Life Insurance Company. Furthermore, two distinct cultures evolved as a result of defining the subsidiaries as profit centers in 1980 and evaluating them based on profit and return on investment. That change in structure and systems in essence created a new way of operating and, to some extent, a new breed of manager.

Phyllis Cella was president and chief executive officer of Hanseco, a subsidiary spawned in 1971 from within the Hancock and staffed originally with Hancock employees. The expressed purpose of starting Hanseco was to provide products for the Hancock agents. In 1983, Hanseco had approximately $750 million in assets under its management. Up until 1980 it had operated within the Hancock structure. Cella described some of the thinking that went on inside Hanseco as the subsidiary grew. In the beginning,

Hanseco was run according to the Hancock style, and we were all on the Hancock payroll. As we got bigger and began to understand our own business, we began to change that. Having grown up in it you learn how to deal with it, but you also understand how time consuming it is and that you don't always get the answer you

want because it is a bureauracy. Even before the Holding Company offically was formed, we saw ourselves as running a company that was now different from and, in our own minds, separate from the John Hancock, even though we were still on the John Hancock payroll. In our minds the paycheck was the only connection. When the world turned [introduction of the subsidiary structure] and the primary objective now became profit, it strengthened the fact that you really are a completely separate entity—it has now been blessed—and you are your own employer.

In 1984 Hanseco had its own payroll that was processed not on the John Hancock computers but by the First National Bank of Boston. The subsidiary set its own salaries and had its own retirement plan. According to Cella, the attitude at Hanseco was "If I can get it cheaper downtown, then I'm going to do that—it's my bottom line. There are still people in the organization that don't understand or accept the fact that maybe we will buy their services—but maybe we won't. There is no question that there now exist two different cultures."

Hanseco's fortieth-floor offices are a modular arrangement as opposed to the traditional open concept of the Hancock. Cella's office was on the outside corner of the glass building, overlooking the Charles River and the Boston Common. She remarked that she had consciously chosen the modular design and had had to fight for it.

Once you get a taste of it [the profit center concept], I don't think it would be possible to go back and work in the other framework—not at this level or an officer level. Partly because of

Exhibit 3 *John Hancock Mutual Life Insurance Company: Organization Chart (Effective April 1, 1983)*

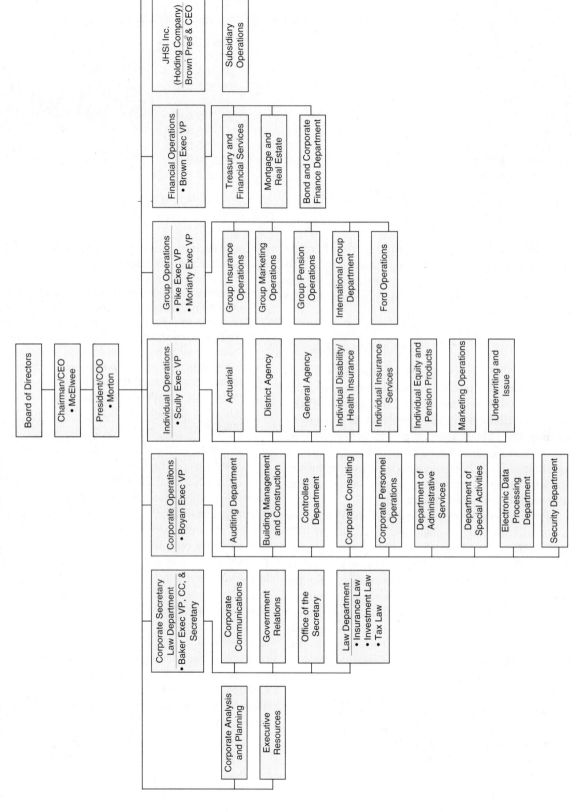

Table 2 *Products and Services of John Hancock*

Subsidiaries of John Hancock Mutual Life Insurance Company (JH)

- *John Hancock International Services S.A., Brussels, Belgium*
  1968 Incorporated in Belgium. Established to enable the International Group Department of John Hancock to perform the international employee benefit services expected by multinational companies that participate in the John Hancock International Group Program (IGP).
- *Maritime Life Insurance Co., Halifax, Nova Scotia*
  1969 Acquired by JH. Reports to Life Company through JH Subsidiaries, Inc. for management reporting purposes. Offers a full range of life insurance products in Canadian markets.
- *John Hancock Servicos Internacionais S/C, Ltda., Sao Paulo, Brazil*
  1973 Organized in Brazil. Established to enable IGP to deliver the same financial results to clients with subsidiaries in Brazil as in all other IGP countries and to enable funds to be transferred out of Brazil.
- *John Hancock Variable Life Insurance Co., Boston*
  1979 Incorporated in Massachusetts. Provides a vehicle for John Hancock agents to sell individual variable life and universal life insurance products.
- *John Hancock Overseas Finance N.V., Curacao, Netherlands Antilles*
  1982 Incorporated in Netherlands Antilles. Raises funds outside the United States and lends such funds to John Hancock and its affiliates.
- *John Hancock Subsidiaries, Inc., Boston*
  1979 Incorporated in Delaware; commenced business in 1980. A downstream holding company organized to provide a means of centralizing the reporting responsibility for the following subsidiaries as a group to coordinate their financial planning and the development of unified policies and strategies.

Subsidiaries of John Hancock Subsidiaries, Inc. (JHSI)

- *Herbert F. Cluthe and Co., Springfield, NJ*
  1968 Acquired by JH.
  1980 Acquired by JHSI. Develops total financial plans and group and pension programs for business and trade associations.
- *John Hancock Advisers, Inc., Boston*
  1968 Incorporated in Delaware.
  1980 Acquired by JHSI. Manages the portfolios of six open-end investment companies: John Hancock Growth Fund, Inc.; John Hancock US Government Securities Fund, Inc.; John Hancock Bond Fund, Inc.; John Hancock Tax-Exempt Income Trust; John Hancock Cash Management Trust; and John Hancock Tax-Exempt Cash Management Trust, shares of which are sold by its subsidiary broker-dealer, John Hancock Distributors, Inc.
- *John Hancock Realty Services Corp., Boston*
  1968 Incorporated in Delaware.
  1980 Acquired by JHSI. Invests in income producing real estate; provides commercial real estate brokerage, mortgage placement and servicing, and appraisal services through its subsidiary, John Hancock Real Estate Finaance, Inc. Operations are conducted nationwide through a series of regional offices.

Table 2 *continued*

- *Profesco Corporation, New York*
  1968 Acquired by JH.
  1980 Acquired by JHSI. A nationwide organization of franchised specialists providing complete financial services to the professional and business communities.
- *Hanseco Insurance Co., Boston*
  1971 Incorporated in Delaware.
  1980 JH ownership transferred to JHSI. In addition to providing a vehicle for John Hancock agents to sell personal lines of Sentry Insurance, the company is actively involved in the reinsurance business through three wholly owned subsidiaries.
- *Hancock/Dikewood Services, Inc., Albuquerque, NM*
  1979 Incorporated in Massachusetts.
  1980 Acquired by JHSI. Provides data processing and systems analysis services to health care providers. The company also offers a full range of management services to health maintenance organizations and associations.
- *John Hancock Financial Services, Inc., Boston*
  1980 Incorporated in Delaware. Provides equipment leasing and financing (tax- and nontax-oriented) and related financial services to the agricultural, professional, and general commercial markets on a national scale.
- *Independence Investment Associates, Inc., Boston*
  1982 Incorporated in Delaware. Provides investment management and advisory and counseling services, principally to pension funds and other institutional investors.
- *John Hancock Venture Capital Management, Inc., Boston*
  1982 Incorporated in Delaware. Serves as general partner and manager of the John Hancock Venture Capital Fund, a limited partnership with $148 million of committed capital.
- *Tucker Anthony Holding Corp., Main Offices: Boston and New York*
  1982 Incorporated in Delaware. A holding company offering through its subsidiary Tucker Anthony & R. L. Day, Inc., a broad range of financial services, including stocks and bonds, money management, corporate finance, and tax-advantaged investments.

Exhibit 4 *John Hancock Companies—Assets Under Management ($ in Millions)*

	1972	1973	1974	1975	1976	1977	1978	1979	1980	1981	1982	1983
General account	$10,377	$10,737	$11,232	$12,071	$13,098	$14,101	$15,212	$16,207	$17,263	$17,824	$18,336	$18,708
Separate account	818	710	591	730	898	937	1,016	1,111	1,377	1,448	1,754	2,066
Guaranteed benefit separate account	0	0	0	0	0	0	0	0	121	671	1,633	2,766
Subsidiaries (estimated)[a]	283	488	462	633	708	838	1,014	1,269	1,625	2,365	5,400	6,013
Pension advisory accounts	0	0	0	0	19	24	83	133	161	203	269	398
Total assets under management	$11,478	$11,935	$12,285	$13,434	$14,723	$15,900	$17,325	$18,720	$20,547	$22,511	$27,392	$29,951

Source: John Hancock Mutual Life Insurance Company Annual Reports
[a]Subsidiary assets are net of Hancock parent equity holdings and contain estimated components.

Exhibit 5A *Consolidated Summary of Operations and Changes in Policyholders' Contingency Reserves (John Hancock Mutual Life Insurance Company and Subsidiary)*

	Year Ended December 31 (in millions)		
	1983	1982	1981
Income			
Premiums, annuity considerations, and pension fund contributions	$2,489.5	$2,573.4	$2,435.6
Investment income	1,818.1	1,668.1	1,491.2
Separate account capital gains (losses)	118.4	132.9	(106.9)
Other	(346.1)	(562.6)	(552.5)
	4,079.9	3,811.8	3,267.4
Benefits and Expenses			
Payments to policyholders and beneficiaries:			
Death benefits	513.3	447.0	405.1
Accident and health benefits	423.9	444.5	496.4
Annuity benefits	182.9	25.0	11.6
Surrender benefits	248.9	90.1	79.1
Matured endowments	15.2	11.6	11.3
	1,384.2	1,018.2	1,003.5
Additions to reserves to provide for future payments to policyholders and beneficiaries	1,560.2	1,599.3	1,187.6
Expenses of providing service to policyholders and obtaining new insurance:			
Field sales compensation and expenses	308.9	292.5	285.6
Home office and general expenses	310.6	279.0	262.5
State premium taxes	30.5	32.2	30.2
Payroll and miscellaneous taxes	27.6	25.2	22.7
	3,622.0	3,246.4	2,792.1
Net gain before dividends to policyholders and federal income taxes	457.9	565.4	475.3
Dividends to policyholders	390.5	326.7	314.2
Federal income taxes	36.0	70.1	50.2
	426.5	396.8	364.4
Net gain	31.4	168.6	110.9
Net capital gain or loss and other adjustments	(52.6)	(50.2)	40.4
Less amounts allocated for:			
Increase (decrease) in valuation reserves	(1.2)	(1.2)	1.2
Additional provision for prior years' federal income taxes		13.9	30.0
Other adjustments	16.0	7.0	15.8
Increase (decrease) in policyholders' contingency reserves	(36.0)	98.7	104.3
Policyholders' contingency reserves at beginning of year	1,002.8	904.1	799.8
Policyholders' contingency reserves at end of year	$ 966.8	$1,002.8	$ 904.1

Exhibit 5B *Consolidated Statement of Financial Position (John Hancock Mutual Life Insurance Company and Subsidiary)*

	Year Ended December 31 (in millions)	
	1983	1982
Assets		
Bonds	$ 6,551.5	$ 6,590.2
Stocks:		
Preferred or guaranteed	190.6	197.1
Common	431.3	361.1
Investment in affiliates	342.5	319.4
	964.4	877.6
Mortgage loans on real estate	6,542.0	6,527.3
Real estate:		
Company occupied	161.4	148.6
Investment properties	636.2	530.6
	797.6	679.2
Policy loans and liens	2,041.2	1,890.4
Cash items:		
Cash in banks and offices	40.0	12.4
Temporary cash investments	558.8	789.8
	598.8	802.2
Premiums due and deferred	388.8	341.1
Investment income due and accrued	362.8	344.3
Other general account assets	−460.9	283.7
Assets held in separate accounts	−4,832.1	3,386.8
Total assets	$23,540.1	$21,722.8
Obligations		
Policy reserves	$11,659.7	$11,442.2
Policyholders' and beneficiaries' funds	4,596.4	4,649.3
Dividends payable to policyholders	429.0	359.5
Policy benefits in process of payment	161.2	99.3
Other policy obligations	161.6	148.3
Indebtedness to affiliate	74.7	74.4
Commercial paper outstanding	72.6	
Mandatory securities and other asset valuation reserves	389.3	272.3
Federal income and other accrued taxes	109.5	148.8
Other general account obligations	101.9	158.1
Obligations related to separate account business	4,817.4	3,367.8
Total obligations	22,573.3	20,720.0
Policyholders' contingency reserves		
Special contingency reserve for group insurance	92.6	87.8
General contingency reserve	874.2	915.0
Total contingency reserves	966.8	1,002.8
Total obligations and contingency reserves	$23,540.1	$21,722.8

the size—we still have only 225 employees but are growing every day—but partly because of the need. We all participate very heavily in this organization—all of the officers. We have eight officers, so it is not hard to get eight people together, hammer things out, let everyone have his say, have everyone really go at it, and wide open. How do you do that in the Hancock? You don't—it is impossible. It is much more fun here. A bigger challenge, a lot more sleepless nights than you ever had in the other big organization, but you cannot match the excitement and satisfaction of it and the gratification when it works.

Although officers of the Life Company were quite aware of the differences, some, like Frank Irish, vice president corporate analysis and planning, viewed the subsidiaries "as indistinguishable from the parent company from the point of view of management control. Standards should be applied equally to subsidiaries and parent company. A lot of my efforts have been designed to achieve this goal, and I think we are close to that."

In response to the issue of transforming units of the Life Company into profit centers, Irish went on to say: "I can only say that we are very seriously considering it. We obviously can. We know we can." He also had some doubts, however, as to whether the change would accomplish what the Hancock wanted and if, in fact, that change was consistent with their policyholders. "When managing a participating insurance business you are not supposed to be profit maximizing—so why have a profit center concept. There is a conflict."

Phyllis Cella felt as Steve Brown did: "Theoretically, they [the units of the Life Company] ought to be profit centers and have a bottom line." There was some concern, however, from a practical point of view as to the difficulty of actually getting to the bottom line of some of the units within the Life Company that really do not have income.

There was also some concern among middle managers within the Life Company concerning the somewhat different nature of the business conducted within the Holding Company and the way the Holding Company managers were being compensated. As Irish commented:

What is at this point different about the subsidiaries is their attitude toward things like personnel policies, tenure, compensation, that sort of thing. Not only have they been decentralized, but in theory the subsidiary personnel are

working in a more highly rewarded more risky business than the parent company. . . . I'm not sure how top management views it—and I usually know top management. I know how many middle managers view it—very critically. They are paid better and have more freedom and have greater opportunities in management. . . . That's how some people view it, and it's a problem we are going to have to work with. I don't know what the answer is. . . . The other side is that you are generally dealing with kinds of operations where you need risk takers. . . . I think the problem is perhaps made worse by the obvious fact that, despite the statements about profit responsibility, some of the subsidiaries have not produced an adequate rate of return.

A related issue was the Hancock's financial restructuring to a stock company. Although this issue was much broader, it related directly to the existing culture within the Hancock. As noted previously, Steve Brown saw the Hancock taking on, in the long run, the structure of a stock company. On that particular issue, Frank Irish pointed out that the thinking had been dominated in the past by having to generate capital internally and that that way of doing things takes away certain possibilities in the way of financial dealings. However, "the good aspect is that we do not have a bunch of people looking over our shoulders asking for quarterly earnings."

Irish went on to say that there are other advantages and disadvantages to both forms of business. Some feel mutual companies have more leeway in pricing their products. By adjusting the dividends, mutual companies may more closely reflect the actual cost of the service provided than their stock company counterparts. Stock companies are constrained to charge whatever the market will bear to achieve the highest possible level of profit for their stockholders.

As insurance companies extend themselves into broader areas of financial service, there is a tendency for firms to make use of holding companies for the management of their subsidiaries. Stock companies typically employ upstream holding companies. An upstream holding company is perched at the top of a corporate organization. The shareholders own it and it owns the subsidiaries. Mutual companies are constrained to use downstream holding companies. A downstream holding company is positioned midway down the corporate hierarchy and is wholly or partially owned by the mutual company. Because the parent mutual company is governed by state insurance laws, the management of a downstream holding company is often more complex than that of an upstream holding company.

As noted earlier, a stock company can raise capital by selling stock. A mutual company does not have this equity option. It may earn revenue from its operations, receive income from its investments, and acquire debt. A stock company may use its stock to acquire other organizations and in merger situations. Frank Irish contends that many of the older and larger mutual companies were able to experience immense growth because at their outset they were not pressured by shareholders to achieve high levels of profitability. Instead, management chose to pursue growth as the company's main objective.

It is possible for a mutual company to convert into a stock company and vice versa. Both processes are complicated, time consuming, and expensive. Conversion from a mutual company to a stock company would typically require the calculation of a policyholder's share of the company and transference of that share to shares of stock. In some instances a stock company, usually motivated by the fear of a takeover, may attempt to mutualize. This conversion would require approval by the company's board, the state insurance commissioner, the stockholders, and the policyholders. All the stock must be purchased and canceled by the company before it can mutualize. According to the *1983 Life Insurance Fact Book*, "In the past 16 years, five companies have converted from the status of a mutual company to a stock company and two stock companies have converted to mutual."[21]

Phyllis Cella commented on moving from a mutual to a stock company:

> *I think that it is essentially a good idea, because then the whole company has to have a bottom line. Right now mutuals do have a net gain from operations. A stock company has a very different attitude and culture because they*

> *have the stockholder that wants a rate of return. But just doing it is not the answer. Just because you become a stock company doesn't suddenly make everything perfect. The old culture is still there.*

THE FUTURE

Given the recent announcement of a merger agreement with Buckeye Financial Corporation and the 1982 purchase of Tucker Anthony in addition to the other ten subsidiaries, the Hancock took some major steps toward competing in the FSI. The strategic thrust behind such moves was that they would result in synergies along such dimensions as offering more products for the sales force, developing multiple service relationships with individual customers, and management synergy—they "knew how to manage financial services."

A major question, however, for Frank Irish, among others, was, "Can you really expect, once you have developed all of these capabilities, that any large percentage of your customers is going to come to you for all of them? We don't know. We are intensely aware of the question and have to be prepared to jump both ways. I hate to say that about strategic questions, but sometimes it is true."

To attract customers in this way, others felt that the Hancock would have to act differently than it had in the past. In the past, when the company started something it stuck with it and never gave up. The major question now appeared to be that if the time comes when the financial services dimension is not working, can the company change the way it functioned rapidly enough and bow out.

There had also been some thought given to management needs in the future based on the changing nature of the company and the industry. Currently, top management at the parent company was to a large degree made up of people who had risen to those positions from actuarial backgrounds. Frank Irish noted:

> *New technical types are coming in who are not actuaries and they are going to become*

---

[21]*1983 Life Insurance Factbook.* The American Council of Life Insurance, Washington, D.C., 1983, pp. 88-89. Of the seven companies that converted, the Council has identified six. Those converting from mutual to stock were: National Heritage Life Insurance (1966), Brookings International Life Insurance (1966), Viking Life Insurance (1972), West States Insurance Company (1973), and Equitable Beneficial Mutual Life Insurance Company (1977). Farmers and Traders Life Insurance converted from stock to mutual in 1974.

stronger and stronger. Market research and that sort of thing is going to bring in a whole host of specialists who maybe once would have been actuaries but are no longer going to be. There once was a time when actuaries were the only technical people around (besides lawyers). That is a day we are well rid of as far as I'm concerned.

Phyllis Cella looked at the question of future management needs somewhat differently:

I think what we need more of is what I would call businessmen. We do not have enough people who know what it is like to take a business risk and not come out with an actuarial model that has 900 assumptions. They can't function unless they do it all with numbers, always having to prove that everything is lovely.

Although the move to the profit center concept in the Holding Company was a conscious choice, there still remained the question of how to measure similarly the performance of the various units within the parent or life company. "We don't know of any mutual company that knows how to do this yet—learn with the learner! It is going to be an interesting experience," remarked Jack McElwee.

For E. James Morton, president and chief operations officer and vice chairman of the board, the question of measuring performance in the life company was at the heart of what he considered one of the Hancock's major problems. What had been done in the past could not be readily identified as bottom line. They essentially had no measures of profit and inconsistent measures of growth. Size as indicated by assets under management had also become difficult to measure. According to Morton: "We have always had some kind of measures that we have tried to be tough about. But I'm not sure they have been the right ones and the ultimate kinds of measures. And they haven't been the kinds of measures that you can really compensate people on."

Morton had some reservations about moving to the profit center concept. He noted that at times they had the feeling that they were a generation behind and that the profit center idea was becoming outmoded. He referred to management journals that indicated that managers spent too much time worrying about short-term results, thus sacrificing long-term objectives.

Part of the problem of moving to the profit center concept was the method of accounting used in mutual life insurance companies. Morton felt, however, that another big piece of the problem was attitude.

Maybe the attitude was not so bad in the days when all we were was a mutual life insurance company being operated with the primary purpose to supply insurance at cost to our policyholders. But now that we are trying to compete in a broader financial services industry we can't do that anymore. We have to operate with the same kinds of efficiencies as our competition.

Morton felt that they had to change the way management and essentially all of the employees of the company look at what the objectives are.

If we do that, we are going to benefit our policyholders a lot more than perhaps we have in the past. We will be forced to cut costs, run things efficiently, be market driven, and expand the base that expenses can be spread over, resulting in lower consumer costs. We think we are headed in the right direction. But that is not to say that for the first 100 years things were done the wrong way. The times have changed.

Demutualizing, or moving to a stock company, is a very complex issue because of having to deal with fifty state insurance commissions and agreeing on whether a mutual company has equitably treated its existing policyholders. For Jack McElwee, it was also a complex issue but one that he related to the future environment of the Hancock.

A lot of people feel that it is too complex, but you can't possibly afford to feel that way. If the reality of the future is that only a corporation which is the form of a stock company will be able to survive, then you'd better find a way to be a stock company, or at least have all the legal and regulatory characteristics that a stock company has.

Even though the future of the FSI is questionable, there should also be all kinds of opportunities. McElwee noted that capitalizing on those opportunities means "managing ourselves properly. That's what this exercise is all about—it's called management."

Jim Morton expanded on the role of the John Hancock in the FSI:

I am not sure what one-stop financial shopping means. What we hope to do is attract clients. If we attract a client in one piece of the organization, we hope to make that client a target for the other pieces of the organization. I think it would be unrealistic to think that there are going to be a lot of people that get all their financial services from us. We want to see a lot of cross-selling. We want to have plenty of clients in all the sectors and hopefully the rest will take care of itself.

Morton felt that to succeed in the FSI, the important step is to fill out the product line. He went on to say, "That is why we so badly need a bank. If we can't buy the bank, let's find that out in a hurry because we have to make other arrangements. There is no way we can be a large financial services organization without offering banking services. If you can't do it by owning a bank, you have to do it some other way."

Morton went on the discuss the future of the John Hancock:

We want to end up with an organization that when people look at it they say, "That's a financial services organization." And if you ask the man on the street, "What is the John Hancock?" he will say that it is a financial services organization where I can go to do almost anything. I can buy stocks and bonds, house insurance, securities, and tax shelters. I can also get a mortgage for my house and banking services. Furthermore, I get a statement on everything once a month . . . that is what we would like to be in 1990, and I think we have a reasonably good chance of doing it. There will be maybe fifty large financial organizations at that time and that is the list we want to be on. In order to do that we have to internally become customer driven, profit oriented, entrepreneurial, and all those good things you are supposed to be if you are a healthy, growing business. We know what we need to do. The trick is to do it.

It was also clear to Jim Morton that in the next five to ten years the composition of the businesses of the Hancock is also going to change. The assets in the nontraditional ventures are going to become bigger than those in the traditional ventures. According to Morton, "If we succeed in buying the bank that is another billion dollars of assets. Clearly, the nontraditional ventures are where the growth is."

To complicate management tasks in the environment of an evolving FSI, McElwee also had to deal with what he considered an intriguing question, namely, "What is beyond the financial services industry?" To this end he recently put together a study group focusing on the time frame of 2025 and these major questions: "What are the directions in which the Hancock should move?""To what extent do those directions influence what we do in the way of financial services today?"

THE SOUTHLAND CORPORATION

Formulating an Acquisition Strategy

Kenneth W. Olm, George G. Eddy, and James B. Thomas
University of Texas at Austin

There are a number of specific brand names on the market that have become synonymous with all brands of a type of good or service. For example, many speak of photocopying as "Xeroxing" or refer to any of the myriad brands of facial tissue as "Kleenex." This use of the specific company or brand name when referring to the generic type is usually the result of a company pioneering the product or service, sustained marketing, and an emphasis on quality.

Appropriately added to this limited list of "generic-specific" goods and services is the world's largest chain of convenience stores—7-Eleven, a division of Southland Corporation.

BACKGROUND

The contemporary concept of the neighborhood convenience store originated on the ice docks of Dallas, Texas, in the summer of 1927. Joe Thompson, then a director of Southland Ice Company, made two decisions that summer that would eventually change a small ice company into, as the president of a present-day rival store chain expresses, ". . . one of the great retailing operations of our time." First, to improve business volume, Thompson decided to remain open 16 hours a day, seven days a week. Next, he began to stock a variety of grocery items on the ice dock allowing late-hour customers to purchase every-day products such as bread, milk, and eggs.

The success of those decisions led Thompson, by then president of Southland, to expand to other store sites. Soon thereafter, on the advice of a local

advertising firm, Thompson renamed the new stores "7-Eleven" as the hours of operation were from 7:00 AM to 11:00 PM.

Incorporated under Texas law in 1961, Southland Corporation operations as of May 31, 1982, included 7,323 7-Eleven company-owned stores in 42 states, the District of Columbia, and Canada. Additionally, 2,231 7-Eleven stores were operated by area licensees in Australia, Hong Kong, Japan, Taiwan, Canada, and certain areas of the United States. Southland operations also included a chain of auto parts stores, sandwich production centers, dairy processing and distribution facilities, specialty chemicals processing, and ice production, among other expanding ventures.

Since 1978, Southland has sustained an average annual rate of growth for net sales of 21.7 percent. The net addition of new stores during that same period has averaged 142 stores per year. Southland is considered the undisputed leader in the convenience store industry with more stores than its next seven competitors combined. From a small ice company in 1927, Southland grew to the the tenth largest retailer in the United States in 1982.

STRUCTURE AND OPERATIONS

In addition to the 7,323 stores in the US and Canada operating principally under the service mark 7-Eleven, Southland operations also include 77 Gristedes and Charles & Co. food stores and sandwich shops in the New York City area; four merchandise distribution centers, six sandwich production centers; dairy distribution under 11 regional brand names; and manufacturing and distribution of specialty chemicals, ice, and safes. Exhibit 1 gives a breakdown of the subsidiaries and divisions of Southland that service the convenience stores. Exhibit 2 displays the percent of stores serviced by these Southland units.

Southland also has interests in 81 stores in Mexico and Sweden and operates 332 confectionary, tobacco, and food stores and six 7-Eleven stores in the United Kingdom.

Finally, Southland operations include 37 Super-Eleven, multipump, self-service gasoline outlets; 283 Chief Auto Parts stores; and a gasoline purchasing and distribution network.

To oversee these various operations, Southland is organized into four operating segments. The Stores Group, managing the bulk of Southland's operations, is the nation's largest operator and franchiser of convenience stores.

The Dairies Group is a major processor of dairy products that are distributed to all 50 states, the District of Columbia, and many parts of Canada. The group operates 21 processing plants and 73 distribution centers while supplying approximately 59 percent of the total dairy requirements of 6,328 7-Eleven stores, including milk, ice cream, cultured products, juice, and other related products.

The Special Operations Group includes the Chemical Division—which manufactures a broad selection of food ingredients and specialty chemicals, Southland Food Labs (a unit of the Chemical Division), and Tidel Systems—which manufactures money-handling equipment used in retail operations.

The Gasoline Supply Division is a central procurement and distribution group providing gasoline to over 60 percent of the 2,979 7-Eleven stores selling gasoline in the first quarter of 1983. Additionally, the division wholesales gasoline to outside customers, which accounted for a large portion of the division's earnings in 1982.

Exhibit 3 gives the breakdown of revenues and operating profits by group. Exhibit 4 is a financial summary of Southland Corporation and its subsidiaries. Exhibit 5 is a five-year consolidated statement of earnings for years 1978–1982.

STORE PROFILE

7-Eleven stores are extended-hour stores that generally remain open every day of the year. As a policy, the stores are open 24 hours a day. However, in certain areas state or local law may limit the hours of operation as well as the sale of beer, wine, and gasoline.

Typical stores contain approximately 2,400 square feet, carry over 3,000 items, and are modeled to have easily recognizable façades. Corporate policy is flexible to allow for regional preferences in product mixes and layout design. Although most items sold are nationally or locally advertised brands, Southland makes available to its stores a variety of private label products. Most items are distributed through four distribution centers which supply 4,870 stores with approximately 50 percent of their merchandise excluding gasoline.

Prices on most items at each store are generally higher than local supermarkets. However, there is an emphasis on competitively pricing products that attract customers such as milk, case beer, and gasoline. Based on the total dollar volume of purchases, the percentages of store sales breakdown is shown in Exhibit 6.

GASOLINE RETAIL SALES

Though many consider it a relatively recent addition to the 7-Eleven product line, gasoline sales actually began at Southland convenience stores in Joe Thompson's original 7-Eleven stores in the late 1920s. However, by the early 1930s the pumps proved to be unsuccessful and were removed.

John and Jere Thompson—Southland's current CEO and president respectively—revisited the idea of 7-Eleven gas sales in 1963. Together with the help of a friend, Sam Susser (since early 1981 the vice-president for petroleum products), the Thompsons, including youngest brother Jodie, began to experiment with self-service gasoline at a number of 7-Eleven locations around the country. The next ten years saw marginal results as the days of 30 cent per gallon gas allowed little mark-up and self-service gas was banned in many areas of the country. Indeed, by 1972 only 200 stores in the 7-Eleven chain had pumps.

Business began to boom in the mid-1970s after the 1973 Arab Oil Embargo tripled gasoline prices. As bargain hunters began to flock to 7-Eleven stores for their gasoline needs, revenue from gasoline sales for the average store jumped over 300 percent between 1974 and 1976. By 1978, gasoline sales accounted for 13.4 percent of total store

Exhibit 1 *Subsidiaries and Divisions Servicing Convenience Stores*

Name	Categories of Merchandise
Dairies	Dairy and related products
Adohr Farms—California	
Bancroft—Wisconsin	
Cabell's—Texas	
Embassy—Maryland	
Harbisons—Pennsylvania	
Knowlton's—Texas	
Merritt Foods—Missouri	
Midwest Farms—Tennessee	
Oak Farms—Texas	
Specialty Products—Texas	
Velda Farms—Florida	
Wanzer—Illinois	
Reddy Ice	Ice
Southland Chemical	Store supplies and syrups
Southland distribution centers	Tobacco products
	Groceries
	Nonfoods
	Soft drinks
	Baked goods
	Candy
	Other food items
	Health and beauty aids
Southland food centers	Sandwiches
	Other food products
	Syrup
The Stanford Agency	Advertising
Tidel Systems	Safes
Gasoline Supply Division	Gasoline

Exhibit 2 *Internal Integration Percent 7-Eleven Stores Served by Other Southland Divisions and Subsidiaries*

	% Stores
Dairies	88
Reddy Ice	18
Gasoline	38
Distribution centers	68
Tidel	100
Chemical[1]	80

[1]Products supplied by Chemical Divisions are used indirectly.

Exhibit 3 *Revenue and Operating Profit by Operating Segment (in Millions)*

	1982	1981	1980	1979	1978
Revenues					
Stores	5,708.1	5,114.5	4,294.1	3,453	2,748
Dairies	584.8	566.5	533.7	472.5	388.4
Special Operations	164.9	140.2	122.3	112.5	55
Gas Division[1]	1,255.8	103.3	—	—	—
Operating Profits					
Stores	224.9	219.9	174.4	143.3	140
Dairies	12.5	13.3	15.3	9.7	6.1
Special Operations	(3.1)	(9.5)	(3.1)	7.4	5.6
Gas Division	27.0	3.0	—	—	—

[1] Formed in December 1981.

sales—$355 million. Just four years earlier, Southland's percentage of sales from gasoline was only 2.7 percent or approximately $35 million. This phenomenal growth is only matched by the growth over the next four years—1978–1982. As Exhibit 6 shows, by the end of 1982 Southland had sales in gasoline that exceed $1.34 billion or over 25 percent of total sales. This made Southland the largest independent retailer of gasoline in the nation.

What made this growth happen? Southland adopted a marketing technique that was quite simple: 7-Eleven gas prices are matched with the lowest gasoline prices in the stores' areas. In addition, at each 7-Eleven store gasoline is treated as an incremental expense. There is virtually no overhead for gasoline beyond installation, since each store is selling over 3,000 other items. Nor are extra employees needed since the regular cashier collects the money and turns the pump on and off from the store counter.

Gross income from gas sales averaged about $42,800 per store in 1982. It is also estimated that the availability of gasoline alone in all stores has led to the generation of additional sales of other products as more than 30 percent of 7-Eleven customers also make extra purchases when purchasing gasoline. Exhibit 7 shows how these revenues impacted total corporate revenue from 1978 to 1982.

DISTRIBUTION AND SUPPLY

During the mid-1970s, procuring gasoline for a 7-Eleven was handled at the district level. As more installations were added and gasoline sales continued to grow, procurement activities were moved first to the zone level, then to the division level, then to the regional level, and finally, under the direction of newly employed Sam Susser, to the corporate level. In December 1981, the Gasoline Supply Division was formed to centrally serve the almost exponentially growing gasoline procurement and distribution needs of Southland.

Under the supervision of Susser, the division turned from previously fragmented procurement practices to a highly centralized, streamlined operation. The division began to purchase refined petroleum products (regular, unleaded, and premium unleaded gas and diesel fuel) in bulk from brokers and also from independent refiners and major oil companies. These products were then resold on the wholesale market. The division began to engage in day-to-day purchases and sales for forward deliveries by means of pipeline tenders and other purchasing practices used in the industry. Indeed, a significant portion of the division's sale and purchase activities by 1982 was accomplished through product exchanges at nearly 130 exchange points, thereby assuring rock-bottom distribution costs.

In turn, customers who purchase products from Southland are located close to the division's eight pipeline terminals which by year-end 1982 provided approximately 23 million gallons of storage capacity in locations adjacent to pipelines. These terminals also facilitate the arrangement of product exchanges. Susser continued to procure exchange points and terminals through the first half of 1983 realizing that the effective participation in the exchange market requires the ability to purchase in bulk, to maintain available supply and storage facilities, and the ability to deliver the products quickly to the customer.

Exhibit 4 *Financial Summaries: The Southland Corporation and Subsidiaries*

	1982	1981	1980	1979	1978
Operations[1,3]		(dollars in thousands, except per share data)			
Net sales	$6,756,933	$5,693,636	$4,758,656	$3,856,222	$3,076,532
Other income	25,450	40,524	23,949	19,837	13,562
Total revenues	6,782,383	5,734,160	4,782,605	3,876,059	3,090, 094
Increase over prior year	18.28%	19.90%	23.39%	25.43%	21.40%
Net earnings	108,051	92,860	76,506	81,251	56,213
Increase over prior year	16.36%	21.38%	(5.84)%	44.54%	26.07%
Per revenue dollar	1.59%	1.62%	1.60%	2.10%	1.82%
Return on beginning shareholders' equity	17.65%	17.03%	15.62%	22.05%	17.30%
Pro forma earnings[2]	108,051	92,860	76,506	66,383	59,473
Increase over prior year	16.36%	21.38%	15.25%	11.62%	26.71%
Assets Employed[1,3]					
Working capital	85,867	135,626	174,966	147,057	125,313
Current ratio	1.16	1.27	1.44	1.46	1.46
Property, plant and equipment					
including capital leases (net)	1,159,337	963,865	854,010	838,796	677,284
Depreciation and amortization	121,701	100,831	89,847	79,111	67,724
Total assets	1,842,584	1,672,171	1,496,242	1,367,575	1,134,476
Capitalization[1,3]					
Long-term debt	386,304	320,918	312,535	326,893	261,461
Capital lease obligations	196,676	213,585	224,753	226,257	211,342
Shareholders' equity	703,348	612,221	545,282	489,721	368,473
Total capitalization	1,286,328	1,146,724	1,082,570	1,042,871	841,276
Shareholders' equity					
to total capitalization	54.68%	53.39%	50.37%	46.96%	43.80%
Per Share Data (Notes 1, 3, 4)					
Primary Earnings	3.02	2.61	2.16	2.43	1.75
Earnings assuming full dilution	2.94	2.54	2.10	2.35	1.70
Pro forma primary earnings[2]	3.02	2.61	2.16	1.99	1.85
Pro forma earnings					
assuming full dilution[2]	2.94	2.54	2.10	1.93	1.79
Cash dividends	.77	.70	.62	.52	.42
Shareholders' equity at year-end	19.48	17.23	15.37	13.82	11.46
Other Data					
Cash dividends	27,657	24,859	21,511	17,382	13,628
Dividends as a % of prior year					
net earnings	29.78%	32.49%	26.47%	30.92%	−30.56%
Stock dividends	—	—	3%	3%	3%
Average shares outstanding[4]	35,772,689	35,513,515	35,460,071	33,411,394	32,116,432
Average diluted shares[4]	36,970,068	36,899,129	36,875,263	34,901,913	33,624,874
Market price range[4]					
High	31 1/2	23 3/8	19 1/2	20 1/8	21 1/8
Low	17	13 5/8	11 3/8	15 3/4	13 1/2
Year-end	25 7/8	21 1/8	13 5/8	18 5/8	16 7/8
Number of shareholders	7,532	7,336	8,429	8,708	8,627
Number of employees	49,900	49,600	46,800	44,300	37,000

[1] The years 1978 through 1980 have been restated to reflect the 1981 changes in accounting for vacation pay.
[2] Earnings data for the year 1978 has been restated to reflect the 1979 change in accounting for investment tax credits.
[3] The years 1980 and 1981 have been restated to reflect the 1982 change in accounting for foreign currency translation. The effect on years prior to 1980 was not material.
[4] Adjusted for stock dividends and January 1983 stock split.

Exhibit 5 *Consolidated Statement of Earnings–1978–1982*

	1982	1981	1980	1979	1978
	(dollars in thousands, except per share data)				
Revenues:					
Net sales	$6,756,933	$5,693,636	$4,758,656	$3,856,222	$3,076,532
Other income	25,450	40,524	23,947	19,837	13,562
	$6,782,383	$5,734,160	$4,782,605	$3,876,059	$3,090,094
Cost of sales and expenses:					
Cost of goods sold, including buying and occupancy expenses	5,350,453	4,454,774	3,689,679	2,930,693	2,311,024
Selling, general and administrative expenses	1,174,886	1,050,073	901,888	781,768	619,519
Interest expense	27,390	24,539	23,841	18,746	15,804
Imputed interest expense on capital lease obligations	21,345	23,048	22,496	21,490	19,325
Contributions to employees' savings and profit sharing plan	19,568	16,965	13,558	13,304	11,714
	$6,593,642	$5,569,399	$4,651,462	$3,766,001	$2,977,386
Earnings before income taxes	188,741	164,761	131,143	110,058	112,708
Income taxes	80,690	71,901	54,637	44,472	55,611
Net earnings	$ 108,051	$ 92,860	$ 76,506	$ 65,586	$ 57,097
Net earnings per share, after adjustment for the January 31, 1983 stock split:					
Primary	$ 3.02	$ 2.61	$ 2.16	$ 2.43	$ 1.75
Fully diluted	$ 2.94	$ 2.54	$ 2.10	$ 2.35	$ 1.70
Net earnings per share, unadjusted primary		3.98	3.22	2.94	2.83
Fully diluted		3.86	3.13	2.85	2.74

Exhibit 6 *Estimated Percent Convenience Store Sales*

	1982	1981	1980	1979	1978
Gasoline	25.3	25.3	23.0	17.2	13.4
Tobacco products	13.1	12.1	12.3	12.9	13.4
Beer/wine	11.9	11.7	11.7	12.4	12.9
Groceries	10.8	11.5	12.4	12.6	12.9
Soft drinks	9.8	10.0	10.1	10.3	10.9
Nonfoods	8.7	8.1	8.0	8.7	9.4
Dairy products	5.9	6.3	6.7	8.4	8.9
Other food items	5.0	5.2	5.6	6.2	5.5
Candy	3.9	4.0	4.0	4.3	4.7
Baked goods	3.0	3.2	3.4	3.8	4.6
Health/beauty aids	2.6	2.6	2.8	3.2	3.4
Total	100.0	100.0	100.0	100.0	100.0

Exhibit 7 *7-Eleven Gasoline Sales*

	1982	1981	1980	1979	1978
Sales (millions)	$1,341.1	$1,195.4	$912.9	$569.3	$355.0
Gallons (millions)	1,155.7	956.4	792.9	675.5	617.3
Number of stores	2,827	2,517	2,246	2,107	1,857
Gross profit (cents per gallon)	$.062	$.076	.086	.091	.037

OUTLOOK

As with other petroleum operations, many different factors affect the operations of the division. These include the availability of refined petroleum products, activities of foreign-producing countries (OPEC especially), federal taxation and regulations, and conservation of customers. To minimize the adverse effect of these factors, Southland attempted to integrate further backward by shopping for reserves in the ground. In the spring of 1982 Southland backed MESA Petroleum's move to take over Cities Service by agreeing to buy $500 million of the combined companies' crude reserves if the bid succeeded. The MESA bid did not succeed and Southland continued to search for large reserves that could act as a hedge against the needs required for future retail sales.

MARKETING POSITION

As of May 1983, Southland was the largest nonproducing retailer of gasoline in the United States. 7-Eleven stores are the nation's largest vendor of candy bars, canned beer, and *Playboy* magazine. This is the only major chain of convenience stores that received permission from the Coca-Cola Company to sell "Coke" alongside Pepsi at the soda fountain. Approximately 7 million customers a day walk through the doors of all the 7-Eleven stores and nearly 3.2 million gallons of gas are purchased each day of the week from those stores selling gasoline for net gasoline sales of $1,341 billion in 1982.

Gasoline sales from 1978 to 1982 have increased on the average of approximately 41 percent a year. All indications are that growth in gasoline sales will continue, albeit at a lesser rate. The tremendous retailing clout of the growing chain of well-located retail stores can only help that growth, provided adequate supplies can be assured at competitive prices. Accordingly, the unresolved strategic question of the Thompson Brothers and Sam Susser remained: How does Southland best assure adequate supplies of gasoline at competitive, and therefore, profitable prices to maximize the potential gain from its marketing position?

THE SOUTHLAND CORPORATION

Implementing an Acquisition Strategy

Kenneth W. Olm, George G. Eddy, and James B. Thomas
University of Texas at Austin

John P. Thompson, chairman of Southland Corporation, and Armand Hammer, chairman of Occidental Petroleum Corporation, jointly announced on July 1, 1983, the signing of a definitive agreement, subject to stockholder approval, for the purchase by Southland of all of the capital stock of CITGO Petroleum Corporation, the refining, marketing, and transportation subsidiary of Cities Service Company from Occidental Petroleum Corporation for approximately 9.3 million shares of Southland stock plus cash for inventory items of approximately $650 million.

Though impressive in its scope, Southland's acquisition was hardly a surprise to most analysts. Indeed, the almost exponentially growing gasoline procurement and distribution needs of Southland since the late 1970s virtually dictated a strategy of gaining long-term control over the sources of Southland's most rapidly increasing product category—gasoline. Gasoline sales from 1978 to 1982 increased on the average of 40.9 percent a year culminating in net gas sales at year end 1982 of $1.34 billion from the nearly 3.2 million gallons of gas purchased each week at Southland's convenience stores around the country. Refer to Exhibit 1 for a five-year summary of gasoline sales. An additional $542.6 million was realized by Southland from sales at wholesale to outside customers. As early as 1975, Southland ranked eighth among the nation's nonproducing, nonrefining retailers of gasoline. However, by the end of 1982, Southland had propelled itself to the top of the list of independent gasoline sellers with more than twice the market share of its closest rival.

Southland's initial implementation of a long-term strategy to control the source of gasoline began in the early 1980s with the acquisition of various pipeline terminals and the purchase or lease of other petroleum product exchange points. By the end of 1982, Southland holdings included eight pipeline terminals providing approximately 23 million gallons of storage capacity and nearly 130 exchange points which accounted for a significant portion of Southland's gasoline purchase and sale activities at the wholesale level. Southland had grown literally overnight from relying on a few long-term purchase and exchange contracts to engaging in day-to-day purchases and sales for forward deliveries by means of pipeline tenders and other purchasing practices used in the industry.

In early 1982, a top executive group at Southland composed of John, Jere, and Jodie Thompson (chairman, president, and executive vice president, retail, respectively), and Sam Susser (newly hired vice president for Petroleum Products) were in agreement that the current gasoline procurement methods were, for the present, keeping pace with Southland's ever-increasing demand for finished petroleum products. However, they were determined that whenever the opportunity presented itself to acquire petroleum reserves or refinery capacity at bargain prices and thus to position the company for the future, they would take action. The number of gallons of gasoline sold at 7-Eleven stores had risen 20.6 percent between 1980 and 1981 and 20.9 percent for 1981–1982, as is shown in Exhibit 1. A conserva-

Exhibit 1 *7-Eleven Gasoline Sales*

	1982	1981	1980	1979	1978
Sales (millions)	$1,341.1	$1,195.4	$ 912.9	$ 569.3	$ 355.0
Gallons (millions)	1,155.7	956.0	792.9	675.5	617.3
Number of stores	2,827	2,517	2,246	2,107	1,857
Gross profit (cents per gallon)	$ .062	$ .076	$.086	$.091	$.037
Sales increase in gallons over previous year (millions)	199.7	163.1	116.7	58.2	—
Percentage increase in gallons sold over previous year	20.9%	20.6%	14.7%	9.4%	—

tive 20 percent annual growth rate was expected through 1986, indicating that demand for retail gasoline at Southland pumps would rise from 1.155 billion gallons at year end 1982 to 2.39 billion gallons in 1986—a forecasted growth of 107 percent in four years.

From the beginning, Southland had developed a gasoline marketing technique that was really quite simple—7-Eleven gasoline prices were matched with the lowest gasoline prices in a given store's area. This was made possible by Southland's purchasing practices that assured rock-bottom wholesale prices and self-service at delivery. But as with other petroleum operations, Southland faced many different factors that could suddenly weaken its current strong position. These factors included variations in the availability of refined petroleum products, activities of foreign oil producers (especially OPEC), federal regulations (including import restrictions), subsidies to refineries, and the buying habits of its customers. If the marketplace were to change appreciably by 1986, Southland could be vulnerable, given its projected needs and its reliance on easily available low-cost finished products from established US-based refineries.

Accordingly, the top executive group recognized that if the opportunity were to be presented to it at the right price, the group would reach out and grasp that opportunity. Thus, a strategy of gaining control over a source of gasoline supply that would prove adequate through the 1980s, both in quantity and in price, was informally agreed upon by the three Thompson brothers and Sam Susser.

THE HUNT FOR A SOURCE

Southland's top management had talked with certain refiners about the advantages of backward integration to gain better control of supplies. It had approached Valero Corp. about buying one-half interest in the Saber refinery, a new residual treatment refinery at Corpus Christi, Texas, scheduled to be completed in mid-1983. However, no serious negotiations to purchase ensued.

In the spring of 1982, Southland discussed a financial commitment with MESA Petroleum to support MESA's move to acquire Cities Service by tentatively agreeing to buy $500 million of the combined companies' crude reserve if the bid succeeded. In essence, the tentative agreement was that Southland offered $500 million in credit to MESA if certain conditions were met. However, a subsequent counterbid by Cities Service to acquire MESA and an attempt by Gulf Oil to merge with Cities Service brought a halt to the hostile takeover by MESA. MESA withdrew with a substantial profit from the sale of their Cities Service stock but no acquisition to share with Southland.

As early as the fall of 1982, Southland had discussed a proposal with several major oil companies to buy some of the stations owned by each company in one region. Southland would, under the proposal, install 7-Elevens on the sites and sell the majors' gasoline. Again the discussions were never pursued to completion of a deal.

In late 1982 the Thompsons and Susser, having monitored and appraised the MESA/Cities Service takeover battle, and then the Gulf/Cities Service takeover battle, began to formulate a Southland offer to acquire only the refinery, marketing, and transportation (RMT) businesses of Cities Service. Cities Service had requested that Southland submit an offer to purchase RMT of Cities Service so that Cities could thwart Occidental.

Southland executives (the Thompsons and Susser) were very interested in the possibility of acquiring the RMT portion of Cities Service (later to be separately organized as CITGO). The small staff of acquisitions specialists were put to work running computer models of what could be expected by Southland if the company were to acquire and operate CITGO. A continuing effort for nearly six months was carried on by the three-person staff attached to the treasurer's office. Susser was encouraged when the results of the acquisition analysis confirmed his judgment about the acquisition.

A critical meeting occurred on a Sunday afternoon in July 1982 in Susser's home with the acquisition analysts and Jodie and Jere Thompson present. While they were reviewing the results of the latest computer-modeling projections, this concern evolved: "Should Southland be getting into a 'foreign' business like this?" Finally, Jodie, the youngest of the Thompson brothers, turned to his next eldest brother, Jere, and asked: "If we were a private company, rather than public, would we go ahead with the deal?" Jere, president of Southland, replied, "Yes. It's an excellent deal. It's an opportunity to acquire assets real cheap, and it's an excellent opportunity to position the company for the future." Later, John, chairman and chief executive officer, agreed and the decision was made to prepare an offer to Cities Service.

The offer was formulated with the assistance of Ray Stancil, an expert consultant in refinery operation, plus the usual backup staff from the legal, accounting, and treasury offices.

Susser's efforts to develop and present an acquisition offer to Cities Service seemed to reach a dead end when members of the executive group received a telephone message on their private plane while en route to deliver the offer. The message reported that the Occidental deal was made with Cities Service and all other negotiations were immediately terminated.

However, a few months later Occidental offered to sell RMT to anyone interested. Susser again began to formulate an offer that would serve as a basis for making a deal with Occidental. The acquisition staff (Frank Gangi, treasurer, and D.

Urbel and R. Bohn, assistant treasurers) prepared the latest iterations of the model for operating CITGO for Susser's examination. Susser then reviewed the various scenarios with Clark Matthews, chief financial officer, Ray Stancil, refinery operations consultant, and the Thompson brothers. Where the cash was going to come from was not a serious issue since the credit of Southland was excellent, and any bank loan necessary would be well collateralized with the fixed assets and inventories of CITGO.

WHAT WAS TO BE ACQUIRED

CITGO was organized as a Delaware corporation during the first quarter of 1983. It owns and operates what was formerly the RMT division of Cities Service. CITGO's businesses can be grouped into three operations:

1. Refining of crude oil into a wide range of petroleum products
2. The marketing on both the wholesale and retail levels of their petroleum products
3. The transportation of both crude oil and petroleum finished products through CITGO's ownership interest in (or operation of) a crude oil gathering system, a common carrier crude oil pipeline system, and various crude oil and finished product pipeline companies. These operations are briefly described below.

The Refinery

The refinery, located in Lake Charles, Louisiana, with direct access to the Southwest, is the tenth largest in the United States based upon its 1983 crude oil throughput capacity of 330,000 barrels per operation day (BPSD). It was originally constructed in 1944 to produce aviation gasoline and has undergone frequent expansion and modernization. The refinery completed an expansion project in 1982 which included a new catalytic reformer, at a cost of $120 million. An additional $320 million expansion and upgrading program which consisted of a 2,000 ton per day coker, a 30,000 BPSD hydrocracker and an associated off-site project was underway. This program was designed to increase the refinery's finished product flexibility and its ability to process heavy, high sulphur content (sour) crude, which is significantly less expensive than the lighter, lower sulphur (sweet) crudes, which the refinery primarily processed in the past. Both types of crude were delivered to the plant by pipelines from the Gulf of Mexico and by tankers which carried crude from Mexico and Venezuela. As part of the refinery operations, Southland would also acquire 65 percent interest in a lubricants refinery ranked as the sixth largest of its kind in the United States. Exhibit 2 illustrates the product output of the refinery.

Refined Product Demand

Southland's special committee, assisted by the acquisitions department staff, concluded that the combined refined product requirements of Southland and CITGO were expected to increase the demand for the refinery's products. Exhibit 3 shows Southland's and CITGO's historical gasoline requirements and the estimated combined needs.

Southland expected that the combined gasoline requirements of Southland and CITGO should permit the refinery to operate (upon completion of the coker and hydrocracker projects) at nearly 100 percent of its effective utilization level—a unique situation in the industry. At 265,000 barrels per day, Southland would be in control of a major source of supply in the industry.

Marketing Operations

CITGO's marketing operations include both wholesale and retail marketing of petroleum products for motor vehicles and for commercial, residential, and industrial use. Exhibit 4 shows the breakdown of sales by types of customers.

CITGO's retail marketing operation sells refined products through 990 retail outlets in 25 states. In April 1983, a management contract was entered into with Sears, Roebuck & Co. to sell motor fuels at Sears' outlets under the Sears brand name. This will increase the number of states in which retail operations will sell products to 35.

The wholesale operations had approximately 350 customers who sell branded CITGO products through more than 4,000 retail outlets. No one customer accounted for more than 5 percent of sales.

Distribution/Transportation Operations

CITGO customers were taking delivery of refined products from approximately 168 pipeline terminals of which CITGO wholly or partially owned 32.

Where it was more economical, other methods of transporting products were utilized by CITGO. These included 39 tractors, 79 trailers, 27 aircraft refuelers, and 251 rail cars by the end of 1982.

CITGO also owned and operated, through a subsidiary, a 1,200-mile crude oil gathering and transportation network and had interests in four other pipeline systems which total more than 370 miles. Through another subsidiary, CITGO owned shares in several crude oil and refined product carrier systems with aggregate mileage of over 14,000 miles.

THE NEGOTIATIONS

Southland's top executive team began in late 1982 to formulate a purchase agreement to place before its stockholders by mid-1983. Southland hired Dean Witter Reynolds, with Ed Wells as the lead person, to assist in the negotiations. Wells had completed negotiations for four similar transactions and Susser had high respect for his ability. Susser, along with the Thompsons, decided to get assistance for their negotiating team by hiring Bob Strauss, a Dallas-based attorney and prominent Democratic party figure, in addition to Ed Wells, the investment banker. Working closely with Cities Services staff, who in March 1983 employed Goldman Sachs & Co. to prepare a confidential analysis of their RMT operation, Southland management formulated terms and conditions of the offer to Occidental as noted below.

Southland agreed to purchase all outstanding and issued stock of CITGO. Southland would issue to Cities Service approximately 9.3 million shares of Southland stock (exactly 20 percent of total outstanding stock at closing date) with a current value of $325 million. Southland also agreed to purchase $310 million of refined product inventories, approximately $300 million in crude oil and other inventories, and approximately $30 million for other miscellaneous current assets. Southland would also need to expend approximately $200 million to complete the funding for the modernization of the refinery. Exhibits 5A and 5B provide summary statements of the pro forma treatment of the acquisition under the purchase method of accounting and selected financial data on CITGO for five years.

Other agreements included a "standstill" agreement with two major stockholders and "control" persons, Armand Hammer, chairman of

Exhibit 2 *Product Output of CITGO Refinery (000's Barrels per Day)*

	Five Months Ended May 31, 1983	Years Ended December 31,				
		1982	1981	1980	1979	1978
Product output						
Gasoline						
Regular	36.1	62.2	65.5	85.7	91.2	109.0
Unleaded	69.7	65.2	54.0	62.0	68.5	54.0
Super unleaded	13.9	4.9	.3	—	—	—
Total	119.7	132.3	119.8	147.7	159.7	163.0
Distillates						
Kerosene	—	—	—	(1.1)	0.8	3.6
Diesel and no. 2 fuel oil	34.3	43.9	44.4	42.3	53.4	57.8
Jet and turbine	30.1	26.0	27.9	32.0	29.9	25.2
Total	64.4	69.9	72.3	73.2	84.1	86.6
General refinery products	42.4	43.4	38.6	46.3	43.6	48.8
Total products[1]	226.5	245.5	230.7	267.2	287.4	298.4
Rated crude capacity	320.0	320.0	291.0	291.0	291.0	268.0
Actual crude run	208.0	213.3	208.8	237.7	259.5	256.2
% crude capacity utilization	65.0	66.6	71.8	81.7	89.2	95.6
% recovery on crude	102.8	102.8	102.5	102.7	102.9	103.0

[1] Includes products from intermediate feedstocks.

Exhibit 3 *Gasoline Requirements (000's of Barrels per Day)*

	Five Months Ended May 31, 1983	Year Ended December 31, 1982
Southland		
Retail	90.0	79.7
Wholesale	18.9	23.9
	108.9	103.6
CITGO		
Retail	38.7	40.7
Wholesale	101.0	100.5
	139.7	141.2
Combined		
Retail	128.7	120.4
Wholesale	119.9	124.4
	248.6	244.8

Exhibit 4 *Product Sales by Type of Customer*

| | Five Months Ended May 31, 1983 | | Year Ended December 31, | | | |
| | | | 1982 | | 1981 | |
	Amount[1]	%	Amount	%	Amount	%
Distributors/resellers	983.7	57.8	2,343.5	58.4	2,393.1	61.8
Retail marketing	246.4	14.5	625.7	15.6	553.7	14.3
Airlines and government	241.9	14.2	560.8	14.0	470.0	12.1
Other	230.5	13.5	483.1	12.0	458.8	11.8
Total	1,702.5	100.0%	4,013.1	100.0%	3,875.6	100.0%

[1]Millions of gallons.

Exhibit 5A *Pro Forma Condensed Combined Balance Sheet*

March 31, 1983
(dollars in thousands)

	Southland	CITGO	Pro Forma Adjustments	Pro Forma Combined
Assets				
Current assets				
Cash and short-term investments	$ 18,866	$ 4,024	$ 12,744	$ 35,634
Accounts and notes receivable	183,873	337,562	—	521,435
Inventories	281,079	66,202	561,798	909,079
Deposits and prepaid expenses	37,762	748	—	38,510
Investment in properties	82,600	—	—	82,600
Materials and supplies	—	27,700	—	27,700
Total current assets	604,180	436,236	574,542	1,614,958
Investments in affiliates	29,714	12,295	19,410	61,419
Property, plant and equipment	1,057,207	765,611	(502,016)	1,320,802
Capital leases	165,785	—	—	165,785
Other assets	36,736	1,936	(1,936)	36,736
	$1,893,622	$1,216,078	$ 90,000	$3,199,700
Liabilities and Shareholders' Equity				
Current liabilities				
Commercial paper	$ 38,324	$ —	$ —	$ 38,324
Notes payable to bank	17,945	—	—	17,945
Accounts payable and accrued expenses	463,944	331,646	82,721	878,311
Income taxes	25,889	—	—	25,889
Long-term debt due within one year	11,828	1,000	—	12,828
Capital lease obligations due within one year	15,594	—	—	15,594
Total current liabilities	573,524	332,646	82,721	988,891
Deferred taxes and credits	26,235	5,526	(1,000)	30,761
Long-term debt	385,823	1,000	—	386,823
Capital lease obligations	194,891	—	—	194,891
Working capital and construction loan	—	—	618,279	618,279
Minority interest in subsidiary	—	10,406	—	10,406
Home office accounts with				
Cities Service Company	—	866,500	(866,500)	—
Shareholders' equity—Southland	713,149	—	256,500	969,649
	$1,893,622	$1,216,078	$ 90,000	$3,199,700

Exhibit 5B   CITGO Petroleum Corporation: Selected Financial Data (Historical)

	Three Months Ended March 31, (Unaudited)		Year Ended December 31, (Dollars in Thousands)			(Unaudited)	
	1983	1982	1982	1981	1980	1979	1978
Results of operations							
Sales and operating income	$1,206,765	$1,291,240	$5,420,320	$5,501,997	$4,891,143	$3,794,970	$2,850,875
Net income (loss)[1,2]	45,673	(14,059)	59,268	7,247	107,232	86,098	65,544
Financial position (at end of period)							
Total assets	$1,216,078	$1,057,762	$1,284,268	$1,212,251	$1,073,176	$ 902,360	$ 769,773
Noncurrent obligations							
Note payable to Cities Service Company	—	11,900	9,902	11,900	12,600	13,300	—
Notes payable to affiliate	—	11,484	11,446	11,446	11,506	10,062	—
Note payable to bank	1,000	2,000	1,000	2,000	3,000	4,000	5,000

[1]Net income for the first quarter of 1983 and for the year 1982 included $46 million and $37 million, respectively, attributable to sales of LIFO inventories accumulated in prior years at lower costs.

[2]Net income for 1981, 1980, and 1979 included profits realized on certain crude oil supply transactions, prior to crude oil price decontrol in January 1981, in amounts of approximately $10 million, $82 million and $55 million, respectively. Subsequent to decontrol and elimination of pricing tiers and the crude oil entitlements program, the economies associated with such transactions were no longer available.

Occidental and David M. Murdock, a director of Occidental. The agreement provided that Occidental could not acquire more than the 20 percent of Southland stock involved in the acquisition nor could Hammer and Murdock personally own any Southland shares. The voting rights of Occidental under the agreement were essentially nullified as voting was to be in accordance with a majority of Southland's board of directors or holders of stock other than Occidental's 20 percent holding. Restrictions were also placed on Occidental's disposition of Southland shares.

During preliminary discussions with Hammer, the dominant figure at Occidental, and Bob Abboud, the president of Occidental, Bob Strauss asked Bob Abboud what he was asking for CITGO. According to observers, the Abboud reply was "$800 million for ½ of the deal." To that Strauss remarked "Bob (Abboud), the Thompsons sell milk and baloney, and they know the difference between the two." The real negotiations then commenced with the three Thompson brothers and Sam Susser (with supporting legal and treasury people on the sidelines) on one side, and Hammer and Abboud, plus key staff from Occidental and Cities Service, on the other side. The only major actor not present was the second major stockholder in Occidental, Murdock.

In the preliminary negotiations in January, 1983, Hammer stated that he wanted cash for inventories and stock of Southland for fixed assets. Of major importance to Southland was the execution of a purchase agreement that would provide access to approximately 75,000 BPD of crude oil from both Cities Service and Occidental. Southland could then use the available crude oil supply directly for the refinery or for trading in the wholesale marketplace for more readily available crude. Thereafter, the question was to decide how much for each.

The final negotiations were held on the top floor of the Southland building in North Dallas. After many hours, a tentative agreement was reached at 2:00 AM. A letter of intent was signed by the principals two days later in Los Angeles. Before the letter was signed, each Southland board member was polled for approval. The definitive agreement was subject to ratification by the stockholders of Southland.

The total cash (in addition to the stock of Southland) required for the purchase of the CITGO

shares was expected to be approximately $575 million. Southland intended to borrow this amount from a bank syndicate immediately before the closing and to repay most of the loan after closing from funds obtained by Southland from CITGO by means of dividends declared and paid to the sole stockholder. Other capital expansion and supplemental working capital monies needed were to be arranged through a term loan from a commercial bank syndicate subject to a $900 million maximum. Southland would not be a party to the loan but rather CITGO would sign the agreement. The lead bank in the loan agreement was most likely to be a Dallas-based bank already serving Southland.

OUTLOOK

The addition of 7-Eleven sales, Southland wholesale marketing, and Cities product volumes meant that the refinery could be operated at 100 percent of normal operating capacity after acquisition. Further cost reductions were expected as a result of the modernization program at the refinery which would enable it to operate mainly on cheaper sour crudes. It was estimated that use of the sour crudes instead of the higher-priced sweet crudes would, by 1985, produce revenues that would be nearly $2 per barrel greater than 1983 and that the cost saving margin would be on the order of $5 to $7 per barrel.

Petroleum Analysis, Ltd., an independent consulting firm, estimated that by 1985, Southland could realize a pretax income in excess of $150 million from CITGO. That estimate is in sharp contrast to the $8 million loss expected in the first year of operation. Exhibit 6 provides additional detail of those estimated by Petroleum Analysis, Ltd.

STOCKHOLDERS' VOTE

The management of Southland Corporation, a majority of the board of directors, and a majority of stockholders had to be convinced that the deal was good for Southland for each group to vote in favor of the acquisition. In essence, the stockholders had to be confident that Southland could effectively manage the newly acquired CITGO assets, especially the complex refinery. Even though many refineries were believed to be operating at breakeven or loss positions in 1982 and 1983, it was forecasted that CITGO would be profitable because of (1) effective modernization, (2) high-volume utilization because of the assured market for end products, and (3) the readily available discounted price of sour crude to be used in the refinery.

Shutdowns of inefficient refineries during 1981 and 1982 reduced domestic capacity for refining by approximately 1.6 million barrels per day.

The sustained, albeit modest, economic recovery being seen through 1983 should have a positive impact on the demand for all petroleum products. This improvement in demand as well as the anticipated easy availability of some crudes (especially sour) along with the overall reduction in refinery capacity should continue to improve profit margins for Southland through the 1980s.

Exhibit 6 *Southland's Estimated Annualized Income (in Millions of Dollars)*

	Sept. 1983 Basis	Jan. 1985 Basis
Revenue	2,753	3,028
Crude	2,368	2,422
Gross margin	385	606
Operating expense	253	314
DDA	34	32
Interest	108	108
Pretax income	(8)	152
Income tax	—	70
Investment tax credit	37	—
Net income	29	82

Source: Petroleum Analysis, Ltd.

TURNER BROADCASTING SYSTEM, INC. (A AND B)

Neil H. Snyder
University of Virginia

TED TURNER: ENTREPRENEUR

In 1962, at age 24, Ted Turner faced some very difficult decisions—more difficult, in fact, than most people, including businesspeople, ever face. His father committed suicide and left an outdoor (billboard) advertising business that was $6 million in debt and short of cash. Rejecting the advice of the company's bankers who believed Turner was too inexperienced to run the company, he chose not to sell the firm, but instead, to build it. Immediately, he sold some of the company's assets to improve its cash position, refinanced its debt, renegotiated contracts with customers, hired new salespeople, and literally turned the company around. By 1969, the company's debt was paid off, and in 1970, having secured the future of Turner Advertising, Ted Turner purchased Channel 17, an Atlanta independent/UHF television station. Although Channel 17 is widely recognized today as a profitable business, in 1970 it was two years old, losing $50,000 per month, and competing in a market dominated by three firmly rooted network stations in Atlanta.

Recently, due in large measure to his phenomenal financial success, journalists have begun to explore Ted Turner, the man. Below are excerpts from a *Wall Street Journal* article:

Associates of broadcaster Ted Turner like to retell the story of his victory in a 1979 yachting race because they think it says it all about the man.

Mr. Turner's boat, Tenacious, battled 40-foot waves whipped by 65-knot winds in the Irish Sea to win the Fastnet race. Of the 306 boats that started the race, only 87 finished, and in one of ocean racing's greatest tragedies, 19 sailors drowned.

After his extraordinary display of skill and courage, Mr. Turner at dockside callously reminded his somber British hosts that in the 16th century the Spanish Armada ran into similar trouble. "You ought to be thankful there are storms like that," he said, "or you'd all be speaking Spanish.". . .

The flamboyant Southerner, called a visionary by some and a buffoon by others, seems a bit of both. Widely referred to as "Terrible Ted" and "The Mouth of the South," he has been charged with hypocrisy for preaching family values and then appearing drunk in public, and for criticizing the networks' TV "garbage" while boasting to Playboy *magazine that he has photographed nude women. . . . .*

Friends and colleagues attribute both Mr. Turner's successes and his excesses to a personality riddled with contradictions. "Ted is a brilliant person," says Irwin Mazo, a former Turner accountant, "but he also borders on egomania." Although he often talks hard-line conservatism, Mr. Turner seems genuinely concerned about pet liberal issues like overpopulation, world hunger and nuclear proliferation. He presides over a major news organization but says he limits his newspaper reading to glances at USA Today *and the Atlanta papers' sports section. He professes to admire the courtly values of the Old South yet often treats his senior executives like servants.*

The conflicting sides are cemented by an overwhelming tenacity. "He competes in everything he does," says Jim Roddey, a former

Turner executive and sailing buddy who has known him for 25 years. "He sails like he conducts business—it's all or nothing." Indeed, when he saw an Atlanta Braves game-night promotion threatened by lack of participants, he jumped into the contest: He rolled a baseball around the infield with his nose and emerged with blood streaming from forehead to chin.

That incident, his friends say, demonstrates both Mr. Turner's love of publicity and his willingness to sacrifice his dignity in his drive to win. . . .

Mr. Turner was thrust into the business world more than 20 years ago, when his father committed suicide immediately after selling most of the family billboard business. Then 24 years old, Mr. Turner challenged the would-be buyers and regained control of the company. "He could have lost it all," recalls Mr. Mazo, the accountant. But then as apparently now, says Mr. Mazo, "Ted is willing to put all his chips on the table and roll the dice."

In 1970, with the billboard business reestablished, Mr. Turner gambled next on buying a floundering Atlanta UHF television station. In 1976, he transformed it into one of the nation's most profitable stations by having its signal bounced off a satellite and into the nation's cable-TV systems. He channeled Turner Broadcasting's profits from the superstation into a round-the-clock news service dubbed Cable News Network. Five years later, as CNN approaches profitability, Mr. Turner is looking for a new challenge.

Throughout, Mr. Turner's revolutionary moves have been scoffed at by the broadcasting establishment, just as brokers now are scoffing at his CBS takeover bid. Even Turner confidants have been skeptical about his moves. "He's made about $500 million and at least $400 million of that was on deals I told him not to do," chuckles Mr. Roddey, the former Turner executive who admits to advising the company to stick with billboards. . . .

Mr. Turner's management technique isn't any more conventional. "He's not a manager," says Mr. Roddey. "He's not hands-on. He always used to tell me I was getting bogged down in the details, like making the payroll."

But the volatile executive is "a very tough guy to work for," says Reese Schonfeld, the first president of CNN, who left after a dispute with Mr. Turner over hiring and firing. "I've seen him abuse a lot of people. Once you let him humiliate you, he'll walk all over you." Mr.

Schonfeld says Mr. Turner has a habit of ordering his senior executives to fetch drinks for him.

Not all Turner employees have such gripes. Lower-level workers at CNN, housed in the basement of Turner Broadcasting's Atlanta headquarters, say their encounters with Mr. Turner are infrequent and non-confrontational. But life in Turner's executive suite looks stressful: In June 1983, for example, when Mr. Bevins was 36, he was struck by a heart attack while in Mr. Turner's office. Mr. Bevins declines to discuss the incident. . . .

In recent years, however, both Mr. Turner and his company have toned down. Aides say the change began when Mr. Turner began to realize that obtaining control of a network might someday be within his grasp. He began to position himself for an eventual combination, they say.

For Mr. Turner, that meant dropping off the interview trail and scaling down his public excesses. He repeatedly declined to be interviewed for this story, for instance. While hardly prim these days, "he's become more discreet," says one longtime Turner employee. And with age, his friends say, has come a dose of maturity. "Lately he talks a lot about world peace, nuclear war, improving the environment," says Gary Jobson, tactician aboard many of Mr. Turner's winning yachts. (Wall Street Journal, April 19, 1985, pages 1 and 6)

Turner's perspective on business is interesting to say the least. He is quoted as saying,

I don't think winning is everything. It's a big mistake when you say that I think trying to win is what counts. Be kind and fair and make the world a better place to live, that's what's important. . . . I think the saddest people I've ever met were people with a lot of wealth. If you polled 90 percent of the people and asked them what they want most, most would want to be millionaires. I'll tell you, you've got to be one to know how unimportant it is. . . . I'm blessed with some talents. I've made a lot of money, more than I ever thought I would. . . . But if I continue to be successful, I would like to serve my fellow man in some way other than doing flips at third base. . . . People want leadership, somebody to rally around, and I want to be a leader. (Atlanta Constitution, January 8, 1977)

CREATING A NETWORK: WTBS, THE SUPERSTATION

WTBS is the pioneer of the SuperStation concept. Owned and operated by the Turner Broadcasting

System Inc., it is an independent UHF television station, Channel 17 in Atlanta, Georgia, whose signal is beamed via satellite to television households nationwide. Ted Turner, TBS president and chairman of the board, purchased Channel 17 in January 1970. By merging the then Turner Communications Corporation with Rice Broadcasting, he gained control of the television outlet, which became WTCG, flagship station of the Turner Communications Group.

Realizing that WTCG's programming could be made available by satellite to millions of television viewers throughout the country, Turner originated the SuperStation concept. In short, the "SuperStation" is a reworking of the traditional television network concept, in which one station acts as original programming supplier for a multiplicity of distant cable markets. On December 16, 1976, WTCG made history, as its signal was beamed to cable systems nationwide via a transponder on RCA's Satcom I satellite. Satcom I was replaced by Satcom III-R in January 1982 and by Galaxy I in January 1985.

In 1979, the Turner Communications Group was renamed Turner Broadcasting System Inc., and, to reflect this change, the WTCG call letters became WTBS. The company estimates that, as of February 29, 1984, WTBS was beamed into approximately 75% of US cable homes and 35% of US television homes.

WTBS broadcasts 24 hours per day, acquiring its programming primarily from film companies, syndicators of programs that have run successfully on television networks, and its sports affiliates. WTBS currently has available 4,100 film titles for its programming needs, the majority of which are available for multiple runs. In addition, approximately 500 titles are under contract and will become available for programming purposes in the future. Approximately 23% of the purchased programming has been obtained from Viacom International, Inc. and 17% from MCA. WTBS has not obtained more than 10% of its purchased programming needs from any other single supplier, and approximately 1,900 hours of programming broadcast on WTBS during 1983 were produced internally, or under contract. WTBS plans to produce more programs internally in the future.

WTBS derives revenue from the sale of advertising time, and advertising prices depend on the size of WTBS' viewing audience and the amount of available time sold. Since February 1981, the A. C. Nielsen Company has been measuring the audience level of WTBS for use by the company and its advertisers. The demand for advertising time on cable television is significantly lower than that for advertising time on the three major networks because of the relatively small size of the cable network audiences and the fact that cable has not penetrated significantly in many of the major urban markets. The board of directors of TBS anticipates that the continued growth of the cable television (CATV) industry, particularly in the major urban markets, will result in increased demand on the part of advertisers.

The revenues of WTBS also include amounts obtained from "direct response" advertising, which represent fees received by the company for the sale of products it promotes by advertisement. The company broadcasts advertisements for the products during unsold advertising time, and the products are ordered directly by viewers through the company by mail or telephone. WTBS collects a fee for each order. In 1983, these fees amounted to 6.6% of total advertising revenues for WTBS.

Advertising time for WTBS as well as the company's cable news services is marketed and sold by the company's own advertising sales force consisting of approximately 101 persons located in sales offices in New York, Chicago, Detroit, Los Angeles, and Atlanta.

According to the *Wall Street Journal* (April 19, 1985):

> It's hard to laugh at Mr. Turner's operations now, or at least the WTBS operation. His superstation, one of the nation's most popular cable services, now beams a steady diet of sports, movies and reruns into almost 34 million US households, or about 84% of all homes equipped for cable.

It has revolutionized the cable-television business, says Ira Tumpowsky, a Young & Rubicam Inc. senior vice president who oversees the agency's cable-TV buying. "He's the person who moved cable from a reception industry to a marketing industry," the advertising executive says.

TBS Sports

In January 1976, TBS acquired the Atlanta Braves professional baseball club, and on December 29, 1976, the Atlanta Hawks professional basketball club was acquired. Although both teams have consistently lost money, they have provided TBS with excellent sports programming, and the Atlanta Braves, "America's Team," have a national following. TBS aired 150 Braves games and 41 Hawks games in 1984.

Along with a full schedule of Atlanta Braves baseball and Atlanta Hawks basketball, TBS Sports offers NCAA basketball, NBA basketball, NCAA football, Southeastern Conference football, and a variety of special sports presentations. For example, TBS Sports telecast the NASCAR circuit's Richmond 400, college football's Hall of Fame Bowl, and World Championship Wrestling during 1984.

Recently, baseball Commissioner Peter Ueberroth persuaded Ted Turner to make annual payments to other major-league teams if he continued to broadcast Braves games across the nation over his cable-station. Turner has agreed to make these payments, totaling more than $25 million according to the *Wall Street Journal* (April 19, 1985), into a central fund for five years. This agreement is a compromise. Ueberroth had wanted to end nationwide cable broadcasts of baseball games, since they were hurting the profits of teams in other cities. Ueberroth is reported to have said that superstations are the most serious problem facing professional baseball (*Richmond Time Dispatch*, Jan. 28, 1985).

Ted Turner is said to be as creative with his sports franchises as he is with TBS. For example, the *Wall Street Journal* (April 19, 1985) concluded that

> even in the stodgy game of baseball, Mr. Turner has displayed some business acumen. The Atlanta Braves franchise that he bought in 1976 was mired in mediocrity. Mr. Turner beefed up its farm system, paid top dollar to lure stars from elsewhere, and transmitted across the nation practically every game the team played. Average attendance at Braves' home games last year was 21,834, triple the figure for 1975. The Braves are widely considered pennant contenders this season.

In baseball, as in his other businesses, Mr. Turner has managed to outrage both his employees and his peers. Mr. Turner once tried to demote a slumping star to the minor leagues. At another point, he named himself manager of the team. Such antics led to a collision with the then-commissioner of baseball, Bowie Kuhn, and to Mr.

Turner's temporary suspension from the game. According to one biography, Mr. Turner pleaded with Mr. Kuhn: "I am very contrite. I would bend over and let you paddle my behind, hit me over the head with a Fresca bottle."

CNN

Through its subsidiary Cable News Network, Inc. (CNN), which began broadcasting on June 1, 1980, TBS provides a 24-hour news programming service which is available to CATV systems throughout the United States and in some foreign countries. The programming includes comprehensive reporting of domestic and international news, sports, business and weather, plus analysis, commentary, and reports by its staff of experts and investigative reporters. CNN obtains news reports from its bureaus in various US and foreign cities. Each of these bureaus is equipped to provide live reports to CNN's transmission facility in Atlanta thereby providing the capability for live coverage of news events around the world. In addition, news is obtained through wire services, television news services by agreement with television stations in various locations worldwide, and from free-lance reporters and camera crews.

CNN employs over 160 journalists, executives, and technicians. The news channel was initially received by 193 CATV systems serving approximately 1.7 million subscribers. As of December 31, 1983, 4,278 CATV systems serving approximately 25.1 million subscribers received CNN's programming.

According to the *Wall Street Journal* (April 19, 1985):

> During its five years of losses, CNN has grown to become the nation's most popular cable service, available in some 32 million homes. And this year, the company indicates, CNN should move into the black. Though still not an equal of the high-powered network news operations, CNN is nipping at their heels, and doing it on a bargain-basement budget.
>
> CNN is weak on features says Jim Snyder, News vice president of Post-Newsweek Stations Inc., the broadcasting division of the Washington Post Co., but it covers breaking news "as well as anybody." A recent Washington Journalism Review assessment of the channel carried the headline "CNN Takes Its Place Beside the Networks."

CNN Headline News

CNN offered another 24-hour news service to cable operators effective December 31, 1981. Referred to as CNN Headline News (CNN HN), this service utilizes a concise, fast-paced format, programming in half-hour cycles throughout the day. CNN HN employs approximately 225 people, and its start-up required the construction and furnishing of a studio facility and additional transmitting facilities. The resources and expertise of CNN is utilized by CNN HN for accumulation of news material. Its revenues are derived from the sale of advertising on CNN HN and from fees charged for the syndication of CNN HN directly to over-the-air television and radio stations.

The number of cable homes receiving the CNN HN signal increased from approximately 5,400,000 in October 1983 to approximately 9,100,000 as a direct result of TBS' agreement to acquire CNN HN's major cable news competitor (The Satellite News Channel). Despite this increase in cable homes, TBS executives do not expect CNN HN to be profitable in 1984.

Cable Music Channel

On October 26, 1984, TBS launched its own brand of video-clip programming to compete with MTV. The Cable Music Channel started with 2.5 million households, about half the expected subscriber count company executives had predicted. However, by November 30, 1984, the Cable Music Channel's title and affiliate list was sold to MTV Networks Inc. for $1.5 million in cash and advertising commitments at a loss of $2.2 million. Cable Music Channel President/TBS Executive Vice President Robert Wussler acknowledges that operator resistance was largely responsible. "We didn't get the homes and we weren't about to get 3 or 5 million homes. We surveyed the field, felt we had a good product, but the industry obviously embraced MTV, the future in terms of acquiring subs was bleak and we felt strongly that this was our best course of action" (*CableVision*, December 10, 1984).

KEY EXECUTIVES AND OWNERSHIP

Ted Turner is aided by highly qualified, experienced men. Robert J. Wussler, executive vice president, had 21 years of experience with CBS, including his appointment as president of the CBS sports division, before joining TBS in August 1981.

William C. Bevins, Jr. is vice president of finance, secretary, and treasurer as well as a director of the company. Previously, he was affiliated with Price Waterhouse for ten years, most recently as senior manager.

Henry L. (Hank) Aaron has been vice president-director of player development for the Atlanta Braves since 1976, and the vice president of community relations and a director of the company since 1980. He was previously a professional baseball player with a total of 28 years of experience in professional sports, and he holds the world's record for the most home runs hit by a professional baseball player.

Burt Reinhardt became president of CNN in 1982 and a director of CNN in 1983. He was employed by the company in 1979 and was instrumental in organizing CNN. Previously, he served as executive vice president of UPI Television News and executive vice president of the Non-Theatrical and Educational Division of Paramount Pictures.

Gerald Hogan joined the company in 1971 and served as general sales manager of WTBS from 1979 until 1981. He became senior vice president of Turner Broadcasting Sales, Inc. in 1982.

Henry Gillespie joined TBS in 1982 as chairman of the board of Turner Program Services, Inc. Prior to that, he served as president of Columbia Pictures Television Distribution and president of Viacom Enterprises.

J. Michael Gearon has been a director of the company, president of Hawks Management Company, and general partner of Atlanta Hawks, Ltd., operator of the Atlanta Hawks professional basketball team, since 1979. He previously owned a real estate brokerage and development firm in Atlanta, Georgia.

Ownership Philosophy

Currently, Ted Turner owns 86% of the common shares outstanding. Exhibit 1 presents TBS common stock ownership of selected individuals. Most of the stockholders besides Turner and his family are either directors or executive officers of TBS.

FINANCIAL ISSUES

Debt Philosophy

TBS is a highly leveraged company that emphasizes the building of asset values. Presently, the company has a $190 million revolving credit

---

Exhibit 1 *Common Stock Ownership*

Name of beneficial owner	Amount	Percent of Class
R. E. Turner	17,579,922	86.2%
William C. Bevins, Jr.	20,000	0.1%
Peter A. Dames	98,910	0.5%
Karl Eller	1,000	—
Tench C. Coxe	128,285	0.6%
J. Michael Gearon	31,500	0.2%
Martin B. Seretean	20,800	0.1%
William C. Bartholomay	210,700	1.0%
Allison Thornwell, Jr.	215,912	1.1%
All directors and officers as a group (27 persons)	18,421,489	90.4%

Source: 1984 Annual 10-K Report of Turner Broadcasting System.

agreement extending until 1987, and $133 million of this credit line has been borrowed. Concerning long-term debt, the company has incurred debt restructuring fees which it expenses as interest based on the weighted average of the principal balance outstanding throughout the term of the agreement. The company paid restructuring fees of $3,650,000 during 1983, and the balance due at year end is classified as current and long term in accordance with the payment terms of the agreements.

Under terms of its 1983 debt agreement, the company is limited with regard to additional borrowings, cash dividends, and acquisition of the company's common stock. TBS is also required, among other things, to maintain minimum levels of working capital and to meet specified current ratio requirements. It is important to note that the company was not in compliance with certain restrictive covenants of its loan agreement on December 31, 1983. TBS received waivers of these restrictions from lenders; accordingly, the amounts due have been classified in accordance with the original terms of the agreement.

Owner's Equity

Characteristic of firms in the growth stage of the business life cycle, TBS has experienced mostly negative earnings since its inception (see Exhibit 2). Most of its losses have resulted from the high start-up costs associated with the divisions that have been created in the past ten years. Exhibit 3 shows balance sheet information for the years 1977 to 1983.

Working Capital

During 1983, the company was unable to generate

sufficient cash flow from operations to meet its needs. Working capital deficits were primarily funded through short-term credit lines and financing agreements with vendors, program suppliers, and others during the first three quarters of the year. A large percentage of cash outflow resulted from the debt restructuring fees.

TBS faces several uncertainties that could arise out of normal operations that might require additional cash. However, management feels that the current financing program will be adequate to meet the company's anticipated needs. In the unlikely event that these uncertainties do materialize and require cash in excess of the anticipated amounts, because of limitations in existing loan agreements, there is no assurance that the company can obtain additional borrowings which might be needed to meet these excess needs.

Dividend Policy

TBS has not paid a cash dividend since 1975. In view of the unavailability of funds to the company and restrictions in its loan agreements against any dividend payments, it is not anticipated that dividends will be paid to holders of its common stock in the foreseeable future.

Capital Structure

Presently, 97% of TBS' capital structure consists of long-term debt. In the fourth quarter of 1984, TBS was considering a public offering to raise $125 million to pay off its bank debt. The company planned to use a combination of ten-year notes, stocks, and warrants to raise the capital. Based on preliminary plans, the offering would boost the number of shares outstanding from the current 20.3 million to 22.2 million, reducing the percentage of shares held by Turner from 87% to 79%.

INDUSTRY AND COMPETITION

The dramatic increase in the number of alternative sources of television broadcasting has led to a measurable drop in the audience shares of the three major networks. Consequently, there is a great deal of pressure for change in the television industry. Pay and ad-supported cable, independent broadcast stations, and videocassettes are all seen as contributing to the decline. In the next decade, it is believed that television entertainment may shift toward a broader range of outlets including ad hoc and regional networks, pay-per-view networks, and more reasonably priced videocassette recorders.

Networks

Although television audience viewing is growing, the big three networks are concerned about the decline in their audience shares and about when the decline will stop. The availability of syndicated programs is becoming scarce as new broadcasters race to buy up existing shows. However, networks have an advantage in this competition because of their programming expertise and facilities. Exhibit 4 shows how precipitous the decline in network television audience share was between 1975 and 1976 and 1981 and 1982.

Independents

Independent television stations have experienced phenomenal growth in the past 15 years. In 1971, there were 65 independent broadcasters serving 30 markets in the United States with losses of $24 million. In 1980, 179 independent stations served 86 markets with profits of $158 million. This growth can be largely attributed to the FCC's financial interest rule which prohibits the big three networks from syndicating programs that they originally aired and from owning any financial interest in programming produced by others. The independents thus have been able to compete against the networks by airing former network hit shows at key times during the day, including prime time.

Cable

The cable industry is in the midst of a gigantic building boom which can be attributed to two advances. First, there was an increase in the number of channels picked up by cable operators from 12 to 54. Second, in 1975, Home Box Office (HBO) started sending its signal via satellite and other stations, including WTBS, followed and were able to easily attain national distribution for their cable programming.

The fall 1984 Cable Study Report conducted by Mediamark Research, Inc. found that the median age of pay television subscribers was 35.2 years with an average yearly income of $29,879. *Cablevision,* the trade magazine of the cable industry, projects that the percentage of pay television subscribers will jump from 23% of the population in 1984 to 27% in 1986. Most of the cable industry's profits will be invested in the wiring of additional homes, particularly those in major urban areas. The high costs associated with wiring these areas had kept cable operators out previously. Now, cities represent more than four-fifths of the potential market.

Ad-Supported Cable

With the emergence of cable television as a national delivery system, many media people became excited about a concept called "narrowcasting." Narrowcasting consists of the programming of one particular type of entertainment (e.g., ESPN—a sports channel) that enables a programmer to target his audience and thus attract specific advertisers at higher rates. Although several narrowcasting networks exist, their success has been very limited because of the lack of quality programming. Dave Martin, vice president for broadcasting at Campbell-Ewall said, "Narrowcasting allows an advertiser to take advantage of a specific opportunity. . . . If it works, though, there is nothing on the mass level that will parallel the opportunity of true narrowcasting to a target audience." Another good example of successful narrowcasting is Music Television (MTV). Narrowcasting is not the only form of ad-supported cable. Stations such as WTBS in Atlanta, WGN in Chicago, and WOR in New York have been successful with their broad-based programming.

Exhibit 2 *Turner Broadcasting System: Historical Common Size Income Statement (Dollars in Thousands)*

	1977		1978		1979		1980		1981		1982		1983	
Revenue														
Broadcasting	19,573	51.9%	23,434	62.1%	27,789	73.7%	35,495	65.0%	55,329	58.2%	96,647	58.3%	136,217	60.7%
Cable production	0	0.0%	0	0.0%	0	0.0%	7,201	13.2%	27,738	29.2%	49,708	30.0%	65,169	29.0%
Sports	6,706	17.8%	8,181	21.7%	7,395	19.6%	9,211	16.9%	8,840	9.3%	16,263	9.8%	21,401	9.5%
Management fees	1,782	4.7%	2,094	5.6%	2,285	6.1%	2,473	4.5%	2,835	3.0%	2,717	1.6%	1,462	0.7%
Other	738	2.0%	134	0.4%	252	0.7%	230	0.4%	305	0.3%	306	0.2%	283	0.1%
Total revenue	28,799	76.3%	33,843	89.7%	37,721	100.0%	54,610	100.0%	95,047	100.0%	165,641	100.0%	224,532	100.0%
Cost of expenses														
Cost of operation	12,767	33.8%	13,219	35.0%	16,997	45.1%	35,124	64.3%	49,036	51.6%	81,187	49.0%	105,695	47.1%
S, G, & admin.	10,729	28.4%	12,736	33.8%	14,460	38.3%	25,218	46.2%	37,067	39.0%	60,343	36.4%	80,722	36.0%
Amortization film contracts	1,178	3.1%	1,571	4.2%	2,290	6.1%	2,803	5.1%	4,010	4.2%	7,497	4.5%	8,674	3.9%
Amort: player/other contracts	1,556	4.1%	1,599	4.2%	1,508	4.0%	1,210	2.2%	0	0.0%		0.0%		0.0%
Depreciation of property, plant, and equipment	934	2.5%	1,037	2.7%	1,222	3.2%	2,172	4.0%	3,469	3.6%	4,182	2.5%	4,706	2.1%
Interest expense/amort. debt.	1,291	3.4%	1,323	3.5%	2,098	5.6%	4,437	8.1%	9,673	10.2%	13,084	7.9%	14,383	6.4%
Other	1,251	3.3%	0	0.0%	0	0.0%	0	0.0%	0	0.0%	0	0.0%	0	0.0%
Total costs and expenses	29,706	78.8%	31,485	83.5%	38,575	102.3%	70,964	*129.9%	103,255	108.6%	166,293	100.4%	214,170	95.4%
Income (loss) from operation	-907	-2.4%	2,358	6.3%	-854	-2.3%	-16,354	-29.9%	-8,208	-8.6%	-652	-0.4%	10,362	4.6%
Equity loss- limited partners	-1053	-2.8%	-1,225	-3.2%	-2,014	-5.3%	-2,905	-5.3%	-5,215	-5.5%	-2,698	-1.6%	-3,350	-1.5%
Income before gains or dispos.	-1960	-5.2%	1,133	3.0%	-2,868	-7.6%	-19,259	-35.3%	-13,423	-14.1%	-3,350	-2.0%	7,012	3.1%
Gain on disposition of prop.	0	0.0%	395	1.0%	312	0.8%	15,694	28.7%	0	0.0%	0	0.0%	0	0.0%
Income bef. tax and extra. items	-1,960	-5.2%	1,528	4.1%	-2,556	-6.8%	-3,575	-6.5%	-13,423	-14.1%	-3,350	-2.0%	7,012	3.1%
Provision (benefit) for taxes	-728	-1.9%	669	1.8%	-1,060	-2.8%	200	0.4%	0	0.0%	0	0.0%	0	0.0%
Income bef. extra. items	-1,232	-3.3%	860	2.3%	-1,496	-4.0%	-3,775	-6.9%	-13,423	-14.1%	-3,350	-2.0%	7,012	3.1%
Gain on prepayment of debt	0	0.0%	343	0.9%	0	0.0%	0	0.0%	0	0.0%	0	0.0%	0	0.0%
Net income (loss)	-1,232	-3.3%	1,203	3.2%	-1,496	-4.0%	-3,775	-6.9%	-13,432	-14.1%	-3,350	-2.0%	7,012	3.1%

Exhibit 3 Turner Broadcasting System: Historical Common Size Balance Sheet (Dollars in Thousands)

	1977		1978		1979		1980		1981		1982		1983	
Current assets														
Cash	1,351	3.6%	154	0.4%	342	0.9%	489	0.9%	504	0.5%	538	0.3%	594	0.3%
Accounts receivable	3,537	9.4%	4,951	13.1%	6,322	16.8%	10,662	19.5%	18,868	19.9%	25,728	15.5%	34,186	15.2%
Less: allow for doubt. accts.	431	1.1%	547	1.5%	415	1.1%	793	1.5%	1,164	1.2%	1,997	1.2%	2,418	1.1%
Net accounts receivable	3,106	8.2%	4,404	11.7%	5,907	15.7%	9,869	18.1%	17,704	18.6%	23,731	14.3%	31,768	14.1%
Prepaid expenses	1,250	3.3%	563	1.5%	585	1.6%	552	1.0%	1,086	1.1%	1,378	0.8%	2,177	1.0%
Notes payable—S-T	0	0.0%	0	0.0%	0	0.0%	0	0.0%	0	0.0%	0	0.0%	0	0.0%
Curr port. def. prog. prod. cost.		0.0%		0.0%		0.0%		0.0%		0.0%	2,490	1.5%	2,660	1.2%
Film contract rights—current	1,128	3.0%	2,055	5.4%	2,570	6.8%	2,521	4.6%	3,495	3.7%	4,516	2.7%	12,163	5.4%
Other current assets	1,359	3.6%	528	1.4%	644	1.7%	1,591	2.9%	1,433	1.5%	2,585	1.6%	2,305	1.0%
Total current assets	8,194	21.7%	7,704	20.4%	10,048	26.6%	15,022	27.5%	24,222	25.5%	35,238	21.3%	51,667	23.0%
Film contract rights	3,193	8.5%	5,632	14.9%	7,537	20.0%	5,660	10.4%	9,464	10.0%	15,633	9.4%	26,057	11.6%
Inv. in limited partnerships	1,000	2.7%	2,578	6.8%	2,480	6.6%	2,027	3.7%	900	0.9%	1,900	1.1%	1,633	0.7%
Net prop., plant, and equipment	6,543	17.3%	7,784	20.6%	13,381	35.5%	26,647	48.8%	28,698	30.2%	67,555	40.8%	71,505	31.8%
Notes receivable—L-T	1,146	3.0%	404	1.1%	514	1.4%	920	1.7%	0	0.0%	0	0.0%	0	0.0%
Deferred program prod costs	0	0.0%	0	0.0%	0	0.0%	0	0.0%	0	0.0%	4,460	2.7%	11,432	5.1%
Deferred charges	0	0.0%	0	0.0%	0	0.0%	0	0.0%	9,623	10.1%	6,585	4.0%	13,926	6.2%
Net contract rights	6,165	16.3%	4,947	13.1%	3,628	9.6%	2,784	5.1%	2,084	2.2%	1,583	1.0%	1,246	0.6%
Intangible assets	0	0.0%	0	0.0%	0	0.0%	0	0.0%	0	0.0%	0	0.0%	25,567	11.4%
Other assets	1,624	4.3%	1,349	3.6%	1,696	4.5%	958	1.8%	1,970	2.1%	2,232	1.3%	2,805	1.2%
Total assets	27,865	73.9%	30,398	80.6%	39,284	104.1%	54,018	98.9%	76,961	81.0%	135,186	81.6%	205,838	91.7%
Current liabilities														
Accounts payable	2,043	5.4%	2,615	6.9%	1,351	3.6%	2,079	3.8%	3,926	4.1%	7,548	4.6%	6,954	3.1%
Accrued expenses	0	0.0%	0	0.0%	1,752	4.6%	7,196	13.2%	11,152	11.7%	16,750	10.1%	22,551	10.0%
Deferred income	0	0.0%	0	0.0%	216	0.6%	700	1.3%	2,226	2.3%	7,220	4.4%	7,083	3.2%
Short-term borrowings	0	0.0%	0	0.0%	0	0.0%	17,907	32.8%	42,783	45.0%	49,924	30.1%	0	0.0%
Long-term debt—current	5,411	14.3%	4,910	13.0%	6,642	17.6%	8,430	15.4%	3,005	3.2%	4,266	2.6%	14,473	6.4%
Obligation-film RTS (current)	0	0.0%	0	0.0%	2,704	7.2%	2,456	4.5%	3,465	3.6%	5,613	3.4%	11,317	5.0%
Debt restructure fees (current)	0	0.0%	0	0.0%	3,344	8.9%	0	0.0%	2,253	2.4%	3,000	1.8%	3,650	1.6%
Income taxes payable	0	0.0%	0	0.0%	0	0.0%	163	0.3%	0	0.0%	0	0.0%	0	0.0%
Total current liabilities	7,454	19.8%	7,525	19.9%	16,009	42.4%	38,931	71.3%	68,810	72.4%	94,321	56.9%	66,028	29.4%

	$	%	$	%	$	%	$	%	$	%	$	%	$	%
Long-term debt	15,968	42.3%	16,329	43.3%	14,158	37.5%	9,825	18.0%	7,165	7.5%	42,802	25.8%	122,404	54.5%
Unfunded pension cost	283	0.8%	283	0.8%	283	0.8%	283	0.5%	283	0.3%		0.0%		0.0%
Deferred income taxes	1,076	2.9%	1,980	5.2%	918	2.4%	918	1.7%	2,834	3.0%		0.0%		0.0%
Deferred income	0	0.0%	0	0.0%	0	0.0%	0	0.0%	1,313	1.4%	646	0.4%	562	0.3%
Debt restructure fees payable	0	0.0%	0	0.0%	0	0.0%	0	0.0%	4,207	4.4%	3,000	1.8%	650	0.3%
Obligations—emp. contracts	0	0.0%	0	0.0%	1,410	3.7%	2,221	4.1%	2,560	2.7%	3,442	2.1%	5,201	2.3%
Obligations—film rights	0	0.0%	0	0.0%	3,631	9.6%	2,662	4.9%	3,943	4.1%	7,379	4.5%	13,959	6.2%
Other liabilities	0	0.0%	0	0.0%	0	0.0%	0	0.0%	0	0.0%	1,097	0.7%	7,507	3.3%
Total liabilities	24,781	65.7%	26,117	69.2%	36,409	96.5%	54,840	100.4%	91,115	95.9%	15,2687	92.2%	216,311	96.3%
Common stock, PAR .125	1,024	2.7%	1,024	2.7%	2,663	7.1%	2,663	4.9%	2,663	2.8%	2,663	1.6%	2,663	1.2%
Capital in excess	1,541	4.1%	1,572	4.2%	291	0.8%	602	1.1%	1,508	1.6%	1,508	0.9%	1,508	0.7%
Retained earnings (deficit)	1,095	2.9%	2,298	6.1%	802	2.1%	-2,973	-5.4%	-16,396	-17.3%	-19,746	-11.9%	-12,734	-5.7%
	3,660	9.7%	4,894	13.0%	3,756	10.0%	292	0.5%	-12,225	-12.9%	-15,575	-9.4%	-8,563	-3.8%
Less shares of stock—treasury		0.0%		0.0%		0.0%		0.0%		0.0%	-474	-0.3%	-754	-0.3%
Notes rec.—sales of CS—treas.		0.0%		0.0%		0.0%		0.0%		0.0%	-1,452	-0.9%	-1,156	-0.5%
Treasury stock	-576	-1.5%	-613	-1.6%	-881	-2.3%	-1,114	-2.0%	-1,929	-2.0%	-1,926	-1.2%	-1,910	-0.9%
Total stockholders' equity	6,744	17.9%	9,175	24.3%	6,631	17.6%	-530	-1.0%	-26,379	-27.8%	-17,501	-10.6%	-10,473	-4.7%
Total liabilities and stockholders' equity	31,525	83.6%	35,292	93.6%	43,040	114.1%	54,310	99.5%	64,736	68.1%	135,186	81.6%	205,838	91.7%

Exhibit 4 *Decline in Network TV Audience*

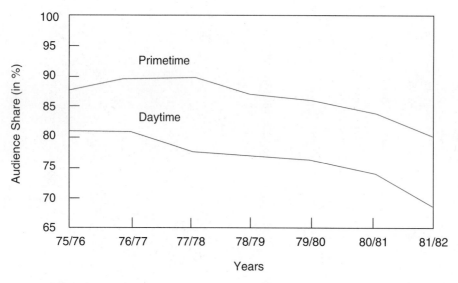

Source: Needham Harper Steers, based on data from A. C. Nielsen

Pay Television

Pay television has been the leader in the cable industry, and it is currently experiencing significant change. Most of the change is being introduced by motion picture companies that are trying to become more directly involved in pay television. For example, Columbia Pictures teamed up with Time, Inc., parent of HBO, and CBS in an attempt to grab a large share of the pay TV market and to become involved in pay-per-view (PPV) television. PPV requires a subscriber to pay an additional fee to view certain major programs. Thus far, most PPV has not been profitable because of the high prices viewers must pay for the programs.

A major threat to large pay television systems comes from smaller private delivery systems. For example, SMATV is a private system that picks up cable signals using a satellite disk and sends the signal via cable to a group of apartment houses, hotels, or clusters of private homes. SMATV has been extremely effective in urban areas previously ignored by other cable systems. This system does not offer the potential, however, of other systems such as MDS (multipoint distribution system) or DBS (direct broadcast satellite).

FCC Rulings

Television broadcasting is subject to the jurisdiction of the Federal Communications Commission (FCC) under the Communications Act of 1934, as amended. Among other things, FCC regulations govern the issuance, term, renewal, and transfer of licenses which must be obtained by persons to operate any television station. The FCC's recent proposal to repeal its network syndication and financial interest rules is strongly supported by the three major networks. Currently, the networks cannot syndicate their own programs, nor can they have a financial interest in programs produced by others. This rule prevents the networks from making money from their shows in syndication. Independent television stations, on the other hand, have grown substantially under this rule because of their ability to air former hit shows.

Independent broadcasters argue that repeal of the financial interest rule will increase the possibility of the networks' monopolizing and withholding off-network, syndicated, prime-time entertainment programming. However, CBS, NBC, and ABC contend that this possibility would not materialize, since the networks have neither the incentive nor the opportunity to discriminate against the independents.

To make the television industry more competitive, the FCC is preparing to adopt a plan to expand the 7-7-7 rule to the 12-12-12 rule. Currently, television station owners are allowed to own only seven AM and seven FM radio stations in addition to seven television stations. This limitation was adopted in the 1950s to encourage program diversity in the marketplace. Under the new plan, media companies would be allowed to own as many as 12 television stations only if the audience reach of the stations does not exceed 25% of the national viewing audience. This plan would eventually result in an increase in the number of television station owners capable of competing with the three major broadcast networks.

Another important issue facing the FCC concerns the reexamination of the fairness doctrine, the 35-year-old requirement that broadcasters cover "controversial issues" and air contrasting views. FCC Chairman Mark S. Fowler says that "the government shouldn't be the one to decide what's fair and what isn't" (*Business Week*, May 7, 1984). However, defenders of the fairness doctrine counter that the airwaves are a scarce public resource that must be protected from abuse. Under Fowler's administration, the FCC has continued to expand its deregulatory efforts by abolishing regulations and relaxing rules that restrict regional concentration and multiple ownership of broadcast stations. "These are the areas where the agency must regulate, but in the choice between competition and regulation, competition is far better for the consumer," says Fowler (*Business Week*, May 7, 1984).

The Changing Landscape of Competition

Clearly, competition in the home entertainment industry in general, and television in particular, is changing. VCRs are the hottest items going. Exhibit 5 shows how rapidly factory sales of VCRs have risen since 1982. Exhibit 6 shows that firms competing in the cable industry have made significant progress over the past 20 years "wiring" homes in our nation. Finally, Exhibit 7 shows how rapidly sales of videocassette tapes have increased. There can be no doubt that the landscape of competition is changing.

OUTLOOK FOR THE FUTURE

The future of the cable industry is still bright. According to Robert J. Wussler, executive vice president of TBS, "I don't think the momentum is out of the game, although I certainly think the bloom is off the rose. But all you have to do is come to a couple of cable conventions and see that there's still enough money around and there are still enough young people around to execute all the ideas people can dream up. No, there's still a lot of momentum around, even if it's not the gold rush" (*Broadcasting*, December 12, 1983). Wussler believes broadcasting in general has hit a plateau or is shrinking. Due to the rise of independents, cable, direct broadcast satellites, videocassette recorders, and our various life-styles, he does not believe broadcasting is becoming more powerful. According to Wussler, broadcasters do not need to worry about getting bigger again, but instead they must worry about getting smaller and about how they are going to manage being smaller. As for cable industry growth, Wussler does not see many limitations. Although it is a tough business to get into today because it requires a lot of capital and there are channel capacity problems, the future is bright.

If the cable industry continues to grow and superstations proliferate, TBS will face more competition. According to the *Wall Street Journal* (April 19, 1985), some industry observers have questioned whether Turner Broadcasting could hold up if superstation imitators proliferated beyond the handful now operating. But Bonnie Cook, an analyst for J. C. Bradford & Co. in Nashville, dismisses that notion. She believes that anybody can transform a television station into a superstation, but cable systems can carry only a limited number of channels. Thus, it is unlikely that the number of superstations will increase dramatically.

Television broadcasting is changing. In early 1985, Capital Cities Communications, Inc. purchased ABC, and in April 1985 Ted Turner made a move to acquire CBS for $5.4 billion including no cash. This acquisition attempt attracted praise, criticism, and ridicule. According to the *Wall Street Journal* (April 19, 1985),

> Mr. Turner has long broadcast his drive to run a network. Some associates contend that this desire became almost an obsession after Capital Cities Communications Inc. last month agreed to acquire American Broadcasting Cos. CBS thus was seen as Mr. Turner's last chance, because RCA, the parent of NBC, was probably too big to be taken over.
>
> William C. Bevins Jr., the financial vice president of Turner Broadcasting, denies that the

Exhibit 5 *Factory Sales in Billions of Dollars*

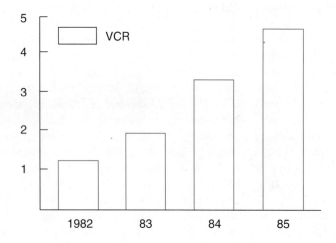

Source: Electronic Industries Association figures for 1985 are projected; appeared in the *Richmond Times-Dispatch,* July 5, 1985.

Exhibit 6 *Homes with Cable TV (in Millions, Rounded) (Figures are as of Jan. 1, except for 1985, when May statistics were used.)*

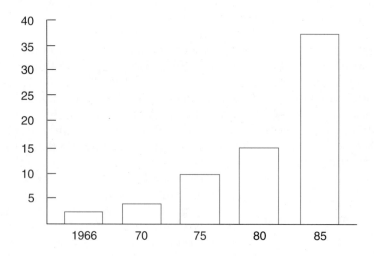

Source: National Cable Television Association using Arbitron estimates for 1985; appeared in the *Richmond Times-Dispatch,* July 4, 1985.

Exhibit 7 *Sales to Dealers in Millions of Units*

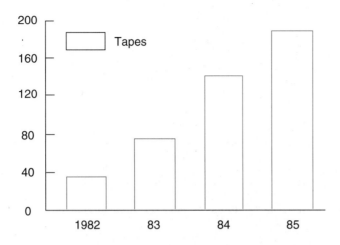

Source: Electronic Industries Association figures for 1985 are projected; appeared in the *Richmond Times-Dispatch*, July 5, 1985.

ABC acquisition move forced Mr. Turner's hand. But he concedes that the transaction 'certainly crystallized where the various regulatory agencies stood and that the timing was propitious.'

The package offered by Turner, which is reputed to be made up primarily of junk bonds, is presented in Exhibit 8.

CBS rejected Turner's offer as inadequate and took steps to prevent a takeover. Andy Rooney, a regular on the television program "60 Minutes," had this to say about Turner's offer,

Ted Turner, the Atlanta, Ga., money operator, yachtsman and baseball team owner, has applied to the Federal Communications Commission for its approval of his scheme to take CBS away from its present owners. He has offered CBS stockholders a grabbag of what are known on Wall Street as "junk bonds" for their shares in CBS. . . .

*I offer my services in trying to locate a new anchorman for the CBS Evening News and someone else to do pieces at the end of "60 Minutes" because if Ted Turner takes over CBS, I doubt very much that Dan Rather will want his job and I know darn well I won't (*Richmond Times Dispatch*, April 25, 1985).*

On May 7, 1985, TBS announced a first quarter loss of $741,000, compared with a $5.3 million loss a year earlier.

AN ABORTED TAKEOVER ATTEMPT

For many years, Ted Turner's interest in acquiring a major television network was widely known. Finally in late April 1985, Ted Turner made his move and announced his intention to purchase CBS, a goal that seemed unattainable since CBS is 17 times bigger than TBS. In preparation for this action, CNN had been offered for sale to the three major networks in 1981. CBS offered $250 million and NBC $200 million. One of Turner's stipulations about the sale of CNN was that he was to be paid in stock. When the networks realized that this deal would make Turner the largest single stockholder of the company acquiring CNN, they promptly withdrew their offers. As recently as March 1985, Turner was still trying to entice CBS into a deal that would enable Turner to gain control of CBS in a friendly manner, but his attempts failed. Undaunted, Ted Turner, together with the aid of E. F. Hutton & Co., made an offer to the shareholders of CBS to gain control of the network by exchanging debt for stock in a hostile takeover attempt.

Turner's plan was to acquire 73% of CBS's 30 million outstanding shares of stock (5% more than the 67% required by New York State for the merger to take place). To do this, TBS would have had to borrow heavily and offer a variety of high-risk debt securities in exchange for the CBS stock. At

Exhibit 8 *Turner Broadcasting System's Package for CBS (For Each of CBS's 30 Million Shares, Turner Offers the Following Package)*

Type of Security	Face Value
$46 of 15% 7-year senior note	$46.00
$46 of 15½% 15-year senior debenture	46.00
$10.31 of 5-year Series A zero coupon note	5.00
$11.91 of 6-year Series B zero coupon note	5.00
$15.90 of 8-year Series C zero coupon note	5.00
$18.38 of 9-year Series D zero coupon note	5.00
$30.00 of 16¼ 20-year senior subordinated debenture	30.00
1 share of $2.80 preferred	16.50
0.75 share of Class B common	16.50
Total	$175.00[a]

Source: Wall Street Journal, April 19, 1985.

[a]This is the face value of the offer for each CBS share. Analysts say there isn't any way of currently evaluating the market value of the package because the issues don't yet exist.

the time of the offer, CBS's net worth was estimated at $7.6 billion, or $254 a share. The face value of Turner's offer was for $175 a share in securities, but estimates of the market value of the offer ranged from $155 to $130 a share.

Besides TBS stock, the other securities offered to CBS shareholders were low-quality, high-risk junk bonds paying 15% interest or higher and zero coupon bonds which require the payment of the principal and interest in a lump sum at maturity. Zeros would have allowed Turner to borrow $600 million and pay nothing until 1990. In addition, each share of TBS offered to CBS shareholders would have had only ¹⁄₁₀ of a vote. Thus, Turner would have maintained control of 73% of the voting rights in TBS stock.

If Turner's offer had been accepted, he would have acquired the broadcast network and four of the five CBS owned and operated television stations. Turner had planned to sell one station, the CBS records group, the CBS publishing group, ratio stations, and various other holdings for $3.1 billion and to apply the proceeds from these sales to the debt. Selling off these pieces of CBS would have reduced the total cost of the deal from $7.6 billion to $4.5 billion. Exhibit 9 presents a financial summary of the offer to CBS.

From the perspective of CBS stockholders, the proposed offer would result in the exchange of a $3 per year CBS dividend for $21.71 in interest and preferred stock dividends from TBS. Although the offer sounds very appealing, Wall Street analysts expressed concern about the security of the TBS assets.

The CBS Response

To ward off the hostile takeover attempt, CBS had several alternatives. One option was to find a "white knight," a more suitable and friendly merger partner. Another possibility, and the one preferred by CBS directors, was to increase its debt and buy back its own stock. By raising additional debt, CBS would make its acquisition by Turner even riskier, because the combined debt of CBS and TBS after the merger would virtually guarantee failure. Additionally, the stock repurchase would leave fewer shares available for purchase by Turner.

Subsequently, CBS purchased 6.4 million shares of its stock, roughly 21% of the shares outstanding, at a cost of $960 million. The price paid by CBS for the stock was $40 per share in cash, plus $110 per share in senior notes at 10 ⅞% interest due to mature in 1995. A "poison pill," a maneuver designed to make CBS an unattractive takeover target in the future, was added by the placing of limits on the amount of debt CBS can carry. The plan also included the sale of $123 million in new convertible preferred shares to institutional investors.

To prevent the repurchase plan, Turner filed a suit against CBS accusing its directors of a breach of fiduciary duty. The complaint alleged that the board was motivated by self interest and that it was attempting to insulate the CBS shareholders from Turner's offer. On July 30, both the FCC and a federal judge in Atlanta ruled that the board had acted in a fair and reasonable manner and in the best interest of the company. Lacking sufficient cash to compete with the CBS stock repurchase offer and lacking the ability to wage a proxy battle, these rulings ended any hope Ted Turner had of gaining control of CBS.

Repercussions

TBS reported that it lost $6.7 million on revenues of $99.3 million in the second quarter of 1985. In total, the takeover attempt cost TBS $18.2 million. According to *Newsweek*, it may have been worth it to Turner just to be in the spotlight for a few weeks (*Newsweek*, April 29, 1985).

The cost of the failed merger attempt to CBS was very high. It purchased approximately 21% of its stock at a cost of $960 million. Since the takeover attempt ended, CBS has had serious financial difficulties and several members of its top management group have been dismissed.

Exhibit 9 *A Summary of the Offer Made by Ted Turner to Acquire CBS*

	Face Value	Estimated Market Value
Interest bearing "junk bonds"[a]	$122.00	$105.00
Zero coupon notes[b]	20.00	19.00
TBS stock[c]	16.50	15.00
−1 share preferred		
¾ share class B common		
Total	$175.50	$150.00

Estimated total market value of offer—$4.5 billion

[a]15% senior notes due 1992; 15.5% senior debenture due 2000; 16.25% senior subordinated debenture due 2005.
[b]Four series with maturity range 1990–1994 with effective interest rate of 15%.
[c]One share preferred $2.64.

THE WORLD TIRE INDUSTRY IN 1989

Briance Mascarenhas and Jun Y. Park
Rutgers University

After acquiring Firestone in 1988 for $2.6 billion, Bridgestone openly declared its intention to wrest world leadership from Western rivals. Bridgestone's acquisition of America's Firestone could bring dramatic change in the United States and Europe. Japanese auto manufacturers will be turning out some 1.3 million cars a year by 1991 in America and will need 6.5 million new tires. The Firestone acquisition gave Bridgestone five North American plants supplying about 40% of North American vehicles built by Ford and 21% of those built by General Motors (GM). Further, Firestone had plants in Portugal, Spain, France, and Italy and 4% of the market in Europe, where Bridgestone had virtually none. The acquisition also provided Bridgestone with plants in Argentina, Brazil, and Venezuela.

OVERALL INDUSTRY TRENDS

In the early 1980s, the tire industry suffered from a recession and compounded its problems by giving customers more durable products. Eliminating overcapacity involved the loss of tens of thousands of jobs, mostly in Europe and North America, and disappearance of dozens of small independent producers, mostly swallowed up by industry majors. Concentration has risen to where 85% of industry sales is held by just six large producers—Goodyear, Michelin, Bridgestone, Continental, Pirelli, and Sumitomo—up from 80% just five years ago. As a result of consolidation, independent major US companies, (see Table 1) which previously controlled more than a third of the world tire industry's sales, now account for only a quarter and have been overtaken by both the Europeans and Japanese.

Surviving players have seen their customer, the vehicle industry, bounce back lately. Altogether, more than $6 billion in new investment for at least 20 new plants and plant modernizations was announced or already undertaken by leading players. Nearly a quarter of this new investment was announced by Bridgestone alone. All this new capacity, however, may start coming on stream just when the world's car markets may enter the next cyclical downturn, beginning possibly in 1990. World car production was expected to be around 45 million units by the turn of the century, compared with 34 million in 1988 and 30 million in 1983. World car population was expected to be over 549 million compared with 369 million in 1985.

Several factors would affect long-term survival. One factor was an international presence to take advantage of currency shifts and to be close to the worldwide main customer, the motor vehicle industry. A second factor was taking part in an accelerating and expensive technology race in both product development and production. Third, increasing vertical integration into retailing was important. In supplying the original equipment market (vehicle manufacturers), tire producers earned little more than prestige initially. However, consumers usually replaced tires with original brands. Fourth, lower margins made achieving economies of scale more important.

Table 1 *Major Players of the World Tire Industry*

	Market Share of World Tire Industry (%)
Goodyear	20
Michelin	18
Bridgestone	16
Continental	8
Pirelli	6
Sumitomo	6
Uniroyal-Goodrich	6
Yokohama Rubber	4
Toyo Tire & Rubber	2
Others	14
Total	100

Source: Financial Times.

PRODUCT AND PROCESS INNOVATIONS

The appendix details the history of tires. Michelin sold the first steel-belted radials for cars in 1948, starting a worldwide industry revolution. Michelin's original idea was to improve mileage on front-wheel drive Citroen cars, which were quickly wearing out their front tires.

The most obvious change to tires in the last 10 to 15 years is that they have become much fatter. Making the cross-section of a tire wider relative to its height was already known to sharpen steering response and increase cornering grip. The tire became less shock absorbent, however; all the potholes and bumps were felt. Pirelli scored a big success in the mid-1970s with its (low-profile) high-performance radials for fast and sporty cars. With careful attention to design, materials, and tread pattern, it combined high-speed grip and handling of racing tires of the 1960s with acceptable ride comfort. High-performance tires wear out sooner, increasing replacement demand relative to ordinary radial tires.

The trend to wider, high-speed tires was strengthening. Nearly 50% of all new cars were expected to be fitted with high-speed tires by 1990 and their replacement demand would rise accordingly, to around 40% of all summer tire replacement sales. For example, European sales of speed-rated tires had risen from 22 to 32 million units in the past three years and were forecasted to reach 38 million by 1991. In West Germany, lack of legal speed limits on major highways dictated an especially high standard of tire quality and performance, and success there provided considerable international prestige.

All manufacturers produced high-performance tires in 1988, though, in Europe Pirelli remained that product's leader. Michelin, Pirelli, and Goodyear were supplying high-performance tires as original equipment to cars, such as the Saab 9000 and Alfa Romeo 164, well ahead of their availability on the replacement market. And Japanese manufacturers (especially Bridgestone) have become very active in the high-performance sector. Bridgestone spent an estimated $20 million developing a 17-inch tire for the Porsche 959, capable of almost 200 mph. The tire facilitated monitoring tire air pressures through a dashboard gauge. Bridgestone's reward was 100% of the original equipment business before Porsche's traditional supplier, Dunlop, came up with a suitable tire.

The tire industry also believes that, eventually, carmakers and their customers will want to rid themselves of the risk of having to change a wheel at the roadside and thus of the spare tire itself. In Germany, the Continental Group devised a "run-flat" tire concept called CTS (for Conti Tyre System), which permitted driving on a punctured tire for 70 miles at speeds up to 50 mph. Daimler-Benz was to offer CTS as an option on its new SI sports car. However, not all carmakers were convinced that a run-flat tire necessarily required a unique wheel, as CTS does. Many were waiting for a system with a wheel compatible with standard tires.

Major manufacturers were also designing tires with automatic production in mind. For example, Pirelli was making, on automatic machinery of its own design and manufacture, a wide range of car and truck tires, including high-performance tires. And Uniroyal-Goodrich had developed a computer simulator of tire noise which permitted analyses of different tread patterns without having to actually cut a tread pattern—a time-consuming process that delayed product development.

MAJOR REGIONAL MARKETS

The North American Region

North America accounted for 41% of global passenger tire demand and 25% of truck tire demand in 1987. Car sales in the North American market, which plummeted to 8.7 million in 1982, rose to over 12 million in 1985 and 1986 and were more than 11 million units in 1988. Commercial vehicle sales were also buoyant.

Original equipment tire prices in 1987 declined by around 0.5% after Michelin agreed to sell to GM at lower prices to increase its share of the original equipment market. Other companies followed suit and original equipment tire prices were expected to be even lower for 1989.

The main players in North America have existed for generations, but their faces have changed in the past three years (see Tables 2&3). The names still sound as American as apple pie—Armstrong Rubber Co., Firestone, General Tire—but only Goodyear, Uniroyal-Goodrich, and smaller Cooper Tire remained in American hands. The rest have been snapped up by foreign competitors seeking a tire manufacturing foothold in the important North American market (see Table 4).

The first to go was Dunlop, bought two years ago by Japan's Sumitomo Rubber Industries. In 1987 General Tire was acquired by West Germany's Continental. Then, Bridgestone bought Firestone in May 1988, and one month later Armstrong was acquired by the Italian Pirelli Group. If Sir James Goldsmith had his way, even Goodyear would have been in foreign hands. The large tire company took on a $3.5 billion debt load at the end of 1986 to fend off a hostile takeover attempt by the Anglo-French financier. Two other US manufacturers may be subject to offers, Uniroyal-Goodrich and Cooper Tire and Rubber Company.

As Japanese automotive manufacturers increase their share of the US market, sales of the Japanese tire manufacturers are likely to follow. However, citing deteriorating quality and service by Firestone over time, GM suspended all orders to Firestone after its acquisition by Bridgestone, in favor mostly of Michelin, Goodyear, and General Tire (owned by Continental).

The Western Europe Region

Record car sales (of close to 13 million) in Western Europe were expected in 1989 for the fourth year in a row, and commercial vehicles sales made a spectacular recovery from an early-1980s severe recession. Europe would officially become a wide-open market in 1992. Though some firms already operate as if the European Community is a single market, 1992 would see more competition from imports, adding pressure on prices.

Western Europe's car population may rise from 120 million in 1985 to 166 million by the year 2000. While demand for tires exceeded supply in 1988, some manufacturers insisted that it was not enough to justify investment levels. Others, like Continental and Pirelli, argued that they were investing significant amounts anyway for maintenance and upgrading. The sector in which investment in Western Europe was heavy, however, was for high-performance car and truck tires. These products were sold on performance first—roadholding, handling, ride, and durability—and price second. Their share of the car original equipment market was growing fast in a region which has probably the world's most sophisticated and demanding drivers.

Within the total market, about a 5% share was taken by various Commission for Economic Corporation (COMECON) and Asian countries, imports from which were concentrated in "commodity" vehicle or bicycle tires at the lower-price end of the replacement tire market. Ironically, much of this East Bloc production, which showed signs of increasing penetration into Western Europe, resulted from earlier technology transfers from West European producers like Pirelli.

The European market was dominated by Michelin, Continental, and Pirelli, while Goodyear and Firestone were strongly represented. The Japanese were represented by Sumitomo through the acquisition of Dunlop and more recently by Bridgestone through the acquisition of Firestone.

Table 2 *US Market Share: Passenger Tires*

	%
Goodyear	30
Uniroyal-Goodrich	17
Firestone	14
Michelin	11
Continental (General Tire)	9
Sumitomo/Dunlop	5
Bridgestone	2
Pirelli	1
Total	89

Source: Business Week estimates.

Table 3 *Consumption of Tire Products in Selected Countries ('000 Tons)*

	United Kingdom	West Germany	Italy	Japan	United States	India
1986						
3 quarter	35.1	64.5	34.0	209.8	340.1	43.7
4 quarter	41.1	68.0	40.0	215.0	370.6	41.5
1987						
1 quarter	41.7	76.5	41.8	213.2	393.0	39.6
2 quarter	42.3	67.7	45.0	221.0	389.0	42.7
3 quarter	36.2	68.2	35.1	224.5	380.6	43.4
4 quarter	42.7	73.5	45.0	245.7	393.6	48.4
1988						
1 quarter	46.5	—	45.0	239.8	—	—
2 quarter	45.3	—	—	250.9	—	—

Table 4 *Acquisitions in Tire Industry*

	Acquiring Company	Acquired Company
1988	Pirelli	Armstrong
	Bridgestone	Firestone
	Michelin	Goodrich's aircraft tire business
1987	Continental	General Tire
1986	Sumitomo	Dunlop
	Uniroyal	Goodrich
1985	Continental	Semperit
1979	Continental	Uniroyal in Europe

Unlike the United States, Western Europe had not seen continuous major new manufacturing plants by the Japanese automotive manufacturers. Nissan was producing in Spain and the United Kingdom and Honda had links with the Rover Group. Yet with more regional integration in 1992, Japanese manufacturers may find setting up plants more attractive.

The Asian-Pacific Region

While tire makers seemed intent on moving into the Asian-Pacific region, the market did not look promising. Demand was linked to car production and use in the region. In southeast Asia, rates of car ownership and production were relatively low but spectacular rises were not expected. Notable exceptions to this picture were Japan and South Korea, but their markets for tires were dominated by domestic manufacturers.

Japanese companies were able to grow with little threat from outside, thanks to close, stable ties with the country's automobile makers. Japanese car manufacturers, for example, stubbornly refused to buy foreign tires for decades even if superior to domestic ones. Even today, as Japan faces intense outside pressure to open its markets to imports, foreign tires are mainly being put on cars for export.

Japanese carmakers' reluctance to buy foreign parts was partly due to their practice of not stocking components but ordering them to be delivered precisely at the time needed for assembly. Foreign tire manufacturers have been put at a disadvantage by this "just-in-time" delivery method pioneered by Toyota. The highly contorted Japanese distribution system has also limited retail sales.

Helped by the dollar's depreciation and by efforts to defuse trade tensions, however, tire exports to Japan from the United States increased 2.9 times to about 2.07 million units between January and June 1988, compared with the same period the prior year, while those from Korea leaped by 86.8%. Michelin accounted for over half of Japanese tire imports, and the company was making considerable efforts to maintain its position with a joint venture with Okamoto. However, in a highly competitive environment imports would do well to reach 10% of the market.

The Korean tire industry was dominated by several domestic manufacturers such as Aamyang Tire and Hankook Tire, which have been protected by extraordinarily high tariffs for imports, averaging 40% of importing costs. With their automotive industry flourishing, South Korean tire manufacturers would become important factors in the world market. Three companies—Kumho, Hankook Tire, and Wuon Poong—were planning to export to Japan and to increase their market shares in the United States.

MAJOR COMPETITORS

Goodyear

As recently as 1986, Goodyear Tire and Rubber's leadership of the world tire industry was accepted unquestioningly. Then came financier Sir James Goldsmith's hostile takeover bid and Goodyear has since had its back to the wall. Victory came at a very high price for which Goodyear, in 1988, was still paying. The company had to borrow $2.6 billion to fund the stock buy-back which allowed Goldsmith to ride off into the sunset with a $90-million-plus profit in his saddlebags.

Mercer, Goodyear's CEO, was not just infuriated by the direct dollar cost of repelling the would-be acquirers: the raid sharply reversed Goodyear's diversification out of what had been heavy dependence on the viciously competitive, low-margin world tire business into oil and gas, pipelines, aerospace, and property. Most of these businesses were subsequently sold to reduce the debt burden, although some 23% of Goodyear's expected sales of around $10 billion in 1988 still came from other activities, like chemicals.

Although Goodyear was profitable in 1988, balance sheet weakness was a severe constraint. Until the ratio of long-term debt to equity improved, either by a reduction in debt or an increase in shareholders' funds, the company would find borrowing difficult.

Goodyear and 65-year-old Mercer continued to put a brave face on events, despite a slide in profits in 1988. Goodyear had 33% of the original equipment market in North America—where 40% of all the world's tires were purchased—and 27% of the replacement market. In October 1988, Goodyear reported nine-month earnings of $293.7 million, or $5.13 a share, down from $603.9 million, or $9.78 a share, in the same period the previous year. It largely blamed sharply higher raw materials costs, a less favorable sales mix, and higher pension costs.

After some early post-raid cutbacks, Goodyear resumed a relatively high level of both research and development spending and capital investment, over $270 million and $665 million, respectively. Despite Bridgestone's rapid rise from being a producer whose products were still being treated contemptuously by its Western rivals in the late 1970s, Mercer maintained that Bridgestone's technology base was still not broad enough to depose either Goodyear or Michelin.

As part of its recovery strategy, Goodyear simplified its structure into two divisions, tires and general products, to control global operations which included nearly 50 tire plants in 30 countries. It invested in new tire plants and plant modernizations, not just in the United States but in Canada, Korea, Greece, and Turkey. Apart from a $110 million Korean plant, where 3 million radial car tires a year were to be made, Goodyear strengthened its presence in Japan. Its shares had been traded on the Tokyo exchange since 1988, and it deputed a corporate vice president full-time to Tokyo with the aim of drumming up more original equipment business. It supplied tires to Hyundai of Korea and to Nissan, Mazda, Toyota, and Isuzu, although these were from Goodyear's European plants and were installed only on products being exported by Japanese vehicle makers. In the United States, one notable investment was the doubling of capacity, to 12,000 units a day, for high-performance car tires at Lawton, Oklahoma—almost the only sector of the US car tire market growing rapidly (8% per year in an otherwise almost static market). Goodyear claimed to dominate this segment in 1988, with more than 85% of the original equipment market and nearly 33% of the replacement market.

Unlike secrecy-obsessed Michelin, which felt it was more advanced than competitors and wanted to keep breakthroughs to itself, visitors had normally been welcomed at Goodyear's tire factories in Europe, the United States and Japan. Goodyear adopted tight security at its plant at Lawton, Oklahoma, however, where a prototype of the minimally-manned-type factory of the future was developed.

The US automotive industry exported little to the major markets of Western Europe and Japan. At the same time, the domestic market for original equipment tires was declining, thanks to the growing share of the US vehicle market accounted for by imports (mainly from Japan and Western Europe).

Michelin

Michelin invented the radial tire and has regularly invested about 5% of annual sales in research and development. After going through a particularly difficult restructuring in the early 1980s after the second oil shock, Michelin's tire production rose by about 40%. At the same time, its overall work force was reduced by about 25,000 to 117,000, underlying sizable productivity gains during the past seven years.

Michelin has adopted a long-term, step-by-step strategy to international expansion. The first step was to consolidate the group's traditional European base. Western Europe, which absorbed about 30% of world car tire production, accounted for 66% of Michelin's passenger car tire sales in 1988. It also accounted for 55% of the company's truck tire business.

The second step was to expand dramatically in the North American market, where Michelin invested about $1 billion since the early 1970s. The group was planning to invest a further $500 million in the United States and Canada to strengthen its position there, which accounted for 27% of Michelin's annual car tire sales in 1988. North America, which represented nearly 25% of the world truck tire market, also accounted for about 33% of Michelin's annual truck tire sales in 1988.

As part of a third stage in its international expansion, the French group negotiated three important joint-venture tire production agreements in South Korea, Thailand, and Japan. In 1987, a joint venture was set up with Wuon Poong, South Korea's third largest manufacturer and with Siam Cement in Thailand. The third joint venture was with Okamoto of Japan.

The French group has also undertaken a new strategic expansion into the aerospace sector by announcing plans to buy the aircraft tire business of Goodrich. The deal was expected to turn Michelin into the world's second largest supplier of aircraft tires after Goodyear.

All these operations reflect the expansionary mood of the French tire group, which even went to the rescue of Epeda-Bertrand Faure, a French diversified manufacturer of car seats threatened by a hostile raid by Valeo, a French car components concern under management control of Mr. Carlo de Benedetti, the Italian businessman. Michelin's intervention in the takeover battle reflects Francois Michelin's personal commitment to a solid sense of traditional industrial ethics when a growing number of French enterprises have been shaken by a new breed of French corporate raiders and financiers.

Through the early 1980s, the Michelin group incurred substantial losses, leading to a severe erosion of shareholders' funds and a massive increase in debt. Its position improved in 1987, but shareholders' funds were low and debt was high. Thanks to firm control of costs and lower interest payments, however, Michelin was profitable from 1985 through 1987 when net income rose by over 20%. Michelin's heavy debt, however, was likely to preclude major new projects.

Bridgestone

Bridgestone dominated the market for tires in Japan with an emabarassingly high market share of almost 50%. It profited from Japanese vehicle makers' preference for buying locally.

Bridgestone was slow to respond to overseas expansion of the Japanese vehicle industry. It bought its first US plant from Firestone in 1983 and later established a second factory. But it won a small share of the market: the main suppliers to Japanese vehicle plants in North America were US producers.

The rise in the value of the yen from 1985 increased the need to establish production overseas. Opportunities for increasing sales, especially exports, declined. Indeed, Bridgestone's sales of tires over the five years to the end of 1987 were virtually unchanged.

The need to build an international presence quickly pushed Bridgestone toward an approach to Firestone, the US company it knew best. Initially, it wanted a partnership—to be secured by buying 75% of Firestone's tire business—but was forced into a takeover by a counterbid from Pirelli. The Firestone acquisition brought Bridgestone a strong presence in North America and Europe to set alongside its position in Japan.

In 1986, Bridgestone exported 2.5 million tires to the United States, all for the replacement market. The company was attempting to double its US sales network from 2,500 outlets to approximately 5,000, which it hoped to achieve by around 1990. Bridgestone's approach to the US market was somewhat different from other Japanese tire makers in that it initially targeted the $7.3 billion replacement tire

market, placing only secondary emphasis on original equipment supply. But Bridgestone might not stay out of the original equipment business for long, with a factory less than 10 miles from Smyrna, Tennessee, home of Nissan (USA).

About $1 billion of investment was scheduled in the North American tire business, principally for expanding output at Firestone factories in Wilson, North Carolina, by 30% and in Joliette, Quebec, by 40%. Firestone's network of 1,500 Master Care car service centers were also to be increased by 300. More than 100 Bridgestone staff, specializing in production, research, and development, were to be seconded to Firestone to help raise product quality and productivity.

Some $300 million was scheduled for tire operations elsewhere, mainly in Europe, including a 30% expansion at a factory in Burgos, Spain. Bridgestone brand tires would be produced for the first time in Europe.

Shortly after the Firestone deal was completed, the company bolstered its position in a fourth area—Africa and the Middle East—by signing a joint venture for tire production in Turkey. Meanwhile at home, Bridgestone was not planning any significant capacity increases, but it might transfer low-margin production to other Asian countries where wage costs were lower.

As it challenged its Western rivals head-on, Bridgestone placed heavier emphasis on technology than it did in the 1970s when it was a latecomer to radial tires. The relation of Bridgestone tires with Porsche (the West German sports-car maker) for its 959 model, one of the world's fastest production cars, is an example. In 1987, Porsche approved Bridgestone tires for use on all of its cars. Bridgestone tires began to be perceived as equal to, or even better than, Europe's best and also won original equipment contracts from Audi (for the new V8). Technology that first saw the light of day in the special Porsche 959 tire was subsequently incorporated in many other Bridgestone high-performance tires.

Unlike Goodyear and Michelin, Bridgestone at the end of 1987 was financially strong. The company's revenue had shown little growth, but it had remained consistently profitable, and in 1987, pretax margins rose to over 10%. Profitability was helped by falling costs for import raw materials due to an appreciating yen, which were not passed on to customers in lower prices. Before acquiring

Firestone, Bridgestone was financially strong enough to cope with any market proposition. The $2.6 billion paid for Firestone seemed high for a group with shareholders' funds of $1.2 billion. However, Bridgestone's cash flow, excluding Firestone, was almost $500 million, and any strain on the balance sheet was likely to be eliminated soon. And from a financial viewpoint, Bridgestone with Firestone was in an even stronger position.

Continental

Continental's $650 million takeover of General Tire of the United States in 1987 placed the West German tire producer to the head of the pack of large companies chasing the three world market leaders: Goodyear, Michelin, and Bridgestone. In earlier expansion moves, Continental acquired the European operations of US Uniroyal in 1979, followed by the acquisition of Semperit, the Austrian tire maker. Continental had also strengthened its position significantly in the retail distribution network through a purchase of the large dealer and vulcanizer, H. Maurer.

Through the takeover of General Tire, Continental acquired a strong position in the original equipment market, supplying 17.5% of the US needs of GM, 12% of Ford's, and 40% of Nissan's.

Continental was also hopeful that its new run-flat tires, which allowed motorists to continue driving with a punctured tire, would enter production next year. Continental also believed different types of tires could be used on the front or back wheels of cars to produce better road handling, depending on which set of wheels provided power or weather conditions. For example, motorists in snow-bound Austria swapped tires seasonally.

Despite ambitious investments and the acquisitions, Continental had managed to strengthen its finances and increased its equity to debt ratio by some 40% since 1983. The group still had some way to go, however, having barely matched the average profitability of the world's biggest tire makers during the mid-1980s.

Apart from acquisitions in West Europe and the United States, Continental had reached cooperation agreements with companies in Scandinavia, Gisved and Viking, and in India, Modi, involving transfers of its technology. More importantly, it entered into agreements with Yokohama and

Toyo, the two Japanese tire producers ranked eighth and ninth in terms of worldwide sales, involving exchange of know-how and production of Continental's tires in Japan.

Continental also supplied some tires from Europe to Japanese carmakers. Around 20% of Japanese cars exported to Europe and around 3.5% of all cars produced in Japan are equipped with the Continental Group's tires.

Pirelli

Having itself fended off an attempted takeover by the considerably smaller Yokohama tire group of Japan, Pirelli was left smarting in 1988 when Bridgestone outbid Pirelli for Firestone. Bridgestone thus thwarted Pirelli's bid to leapfrog Continental and Bridgestone to become the world's third largest tire manufacturer, behind Goodyear and Michelin. That Pirelli then went on to pay $190 million—only one-tenth the size of its unsuccessful bid for Firestone—for much smaller US producer, Armstrong Tires, was seen by many as just partial and temporary compensation for losing Firestone.

The acquisition of Armstrong, however, gave Pirelli the American foothold it long sought. Armstrong, the nation's sixth largest tire producer, which had operating income of about $20 million on sales of $469 million in 1987, had virtually no presence in the original equipment market but a strong position in the replacement market. For example, it had a long-standing agreement to supply Sears with private-label tires. Armstrong was also the second largest producer of tires for farm machinery behind Goodyear.

Some observers reasoned that before long Pirelli would make fresh moves as part of the concentration of the world tire business. Pirelli officials said they also had talks with Uniroyal-Goodrich.

Pirelli has had a global strategy of sorts at least since 1971, when it joined with the British tire maker Dunlop. While that might have been a good merger (in the sense that the two companies complemented each other), it was not a merger made good. The partners split up in 1981 after arguments about different methods of accounting.

The Italians learned some lessons from that failure. One was that to be a global firm they would have to pull together their two separate tire operations: the domestic business based in Milan and the international division in Basel. Pirelli makes almost as many tires in Brazil as it does in Italy and has factories in 16 countries. Only by 1985 had the company integrated these two parts through a new central management company. Despite this rationalization, Pirelli's hierarchy is complicated, the sort that blunt Americans instinctively dislike. The company does not produce consolidated accounts, and its chairman, Leopoldo Pirelli, sits at the center of a web of old men, old money, and old cronies who still control much of the Italian private sector.

Pirelli's rivals have formed themselves into camps of opinion as to precisely what might happen next. One camp argues that Continental and Pirelli should logically join forces. Such a formidable combination would take the group not just ahead of Bridgestone/Firestone in turnover terms, but treading hard on the heels of joint industry leaders Goodyear and Michelin as well. Another camp suggests that Pirelli might opt instead to go after Uniroyal-Goodrich with sales of $2 billion (itself the product of yet another merger), the last of the major US groups seen as vulnerable to a further takeover bid.

Acquisitions will certainly be made easier by Pirelli's consolidation of its tire operations into one new Dutch company, Pirelli Tire Holding BV, which can float a substantial issue. Such an arrangement provides more managerial autonomy, given its relocation away from the Italian industrial-political heartland, and financial flexibility. Pirelli was also less constrained on the financial front after three years of increasing profitability.

Pirelli's profits continued to rise with manufacturing improvements and with a product strategy exploiting premium, "high-tech" sectors of the market. Such tires have proved a major asset to companies that have acquired good reputations for them, competition being based on technology more than prices allowing much better margins than those prevailing at the "commodity" end. Growth of premium tires should also prevent major price wars.

Though Pirelli was a supplier of original equipment tires on some high-performance Japanese cars, it had yet to develop a strategy for the Far East, where car output was growing at an extremely rapid rate in countries like South Korea and Japan. The company had, however, secured a toehold in the potentially vast Chinese market in the form of supplying equipment and technical know-how for a total of three car and truck plants with combined capacity of around 300,000 units a year.

Sumitomo

As recently as 1985, Sumitomo Rubber was an also-ran in the world tire market, ranking twelfth with mostly Japanese sales plus some exports. In 1988, due to the Dunlop Tire acquisition for $450 million and earlier purchases of three of British Dunlop's units in Europe, Sumitomo has suddenly leapfrogged into sixth place worldwide.

Dunlop's linkup with well-financed Sumitomo converted the company into a serious contender in the original equipment market. Dunlop obtained capital resources to modernize its aging tire plants in Buffalo and Huntsville, Alabama.

Sumitomo benefited from its overseas acquisition in two ways. First, by providing local production in the world's two most important markets—North America and Western Europe—it offset the yen's appreciation. Sumitomo Rubber looked to take advantage of long-standing ties with the Japanese auto industry. Second, lower costs on imported raw materials served to increase profit margins on domestic production.

Uniroyal-Goodrich

Uniroyal-Goodrich was a joint venture consummated in 1986 by the two companies. Uniroyal was taken private in 1985 following an attempted takeover by investor Carl Icahn. The firm was relatively stronger in the original equipment market as a supplier to GM but weaker in the replacement business. Goodrich, in contrast, was stronger in the replacement tire market, though its marketing was questioned. Goodrich had been active in product development, including tubeless tires, radial tires, and performance tires. Goodrich sold its tire interests to Uniroyal, retaining, as part of the deal, stock warrants to buy as much as 7% of Uniroyal-Goodrich's stock. Uniroyal-Goodrich did not meet expectations as as a joint concern due to difficulties in integrating manufacturing and management activities. Further, the firm was heavily dependent on GM, which itself was experiencing a decline in US market share. In 1988, Uniroyal-Goodrich was not publicly traded and had no plants outside the United States nor contracts to supply Japanese manufacturers in the United States.

BIBLIOGRAPHY

Anatomy of a Japanese takeover. *Business Month* 129 (June 1987): 46–48.

Japan vs. Europe: Firestone may be just the appetizer. *Business Week.* March 21, 1988:62–63.

Michelin, Goodyear market share to rise sharply with GM in Firestone phase-out. *Wall Street Journal.* August 6, 1988:4.

Pirelli to buy Armstrong from Armtek. *New York Times.* April 19, 1988:D5, col 14.

The tyre industry in West Germany and its market. *E.I.U. Rubber Trends.* March 1989:24–41.

Tire tracks to America. *Automotive Industries.* 168 (January 1988):56–57.

Trends in the development of tires and vehicles. *Rubber World.* 196(June 1987):18–34.

Wheels within wheels. *The Economist.* 306(March 12, 1988):62–64.

World rubber trends and outlook. *E.I.U. Rubber Trends.* December 1988:2–19.

The New Encyclopaedia Britannica. 15th ed., vol. 10. Encyclopaedia Britannica, Inc.

APPENDIX[1]

The first patent for a pneumatic tire, taken out by Robert William Thomson in England in 1845, showed a nonstretchable outer cover and an inner tube of rubber to hold air. Although a set of Thomson's "aerial wheels" ran for 1,200 miles on an English brougham, the same inventor's solid-rubber tires were more popular; and thus, for almost half a century, air-filled tires were forgotten. The growing popularity of the bicycle in the latter half of the nineteenth century revived interest in tire design, and in 1888 John Boyd Dunlop, a veterinary surgeon of Belfast, obtained patents on a pneumatic tire for bicycles. Pneumatic tires were first applied to motor vehicles by the French rubber manufacturer Michelin & Cie. For over 60 years, pneumatic tires had inner tubes to contain the compressed air and outer casings to protect the inner tubes and provide traction. Since the 1950s, however, puncture-sealing, tubeless tires have been standard equipment on most new automobiles.

In the early 1970s, there were three main types of tubeless tires: the conventional bias-ply, the belted bias-ply, and the belted radial-ply. The ply of a tire refers to the way in which the cords in the inner carcass or foundation structure are laid. The cords in a bias-ply tire are laid at an angle of about 55 degrees to the wheel axle, and the cords in successive layers (two or four) cross one another; in a radial-ply tire, the cords run parallel to the axle. The cords in conventional and "old-style" bias-ply tires are either rubberized fabric or, as in the other two types, nylon, rayon, or polyester. In the bias-ply belted tires, the belts, which encircle the tire between the thread and the plies, are fiberglass, whereas the radial-ply belted tires have steel wire-mesh belts.

Belted-bias tires are more expensive than conventional tires, but they are reputed to give about 20% longer tread life, to have better resistance to blowouts, to reduce stopping distance in braking, and to provide increased gasoline mileage. Although their use required minor adjustments by automobile manufacturers, in the early 1970s they were increasingly supplanting the older type in the United States, while in Europe radial tires were already standard equipment. Radial tires provide better steering characteristics and less rolling resistance than the bias-ply tires, they run cooler, are safer in bad weather, and are said to give considerably more mileage. They are more expensive than bias-ply tires, have a slightly hard riding quality, and require substantial modifications of the suspension system on the cars on which they are used.

Snow tires, having an extra-deep tread, are reputed to have 50% more pulling ability than regular tires on loosely packed snow and nearly 30% more on glare ice. In stopping on glare ice, however, snow tires have no advantage over regular tires; tire chains or studded tires are best for ice surfaces. Studded tires usually have about 100 studs tipped with tungsten carbide which contact the road as the tire rotates. Because of the damage they are said to cause road surfaces, they are prohibited in certain localities. Research and development in the early 1970s aimed at a stud tire that would meet this objection.

---

[1]*Source: The New Encyclopaedia Britannica*, vol. 10.

THE BRIDGESTONE-FIRESTONE STORY

John J. Nevin, Bridgestone Corporation

On March 17, 1988, the board of directors of The Firestone Tire & Rubber Company unanimously approved a merger agreement with Bridgestone Corporation of Japan, the terms of which provided that Bridgestone would purchase all of Firestone's outstanding common stock for $80 per share or a total of $2.6 billion. The Bridgestone-Firestone merger, which involved the largest acquisition in history of a US manufacturer by a Japanese corporation, was approved a few weeks later by 99.4% of the votes cast at a special meeting of Firestone's shareholders.

Two hours before Firestone's board gathered for its March 17 meeting, Akira Yeiri, Bridgestone's president, came to my office where I verbally assured him that Bridgestone would have the full support of Firestone's management if the merger was completed and handed him a letter requesting that Bridgestone submit a formal offer to acquire Firestone. Without those verbal assurances and that letter, Bridgestone would not have proceeded with its planned tender offer. I can make that statement without equivocation, because Akira Yeiri came to my office on March 17, 1988 as a respected and valued friend, not as a stranger. Our personal relationship and the relationship between the companies we represented had begun more than seven years earlier.

In September 1980, about ten months after I joined Firestone and a few weeks after I became the company's chief executive officer, I requested a meeting with Bridgestone's management to explore the possibility of Bridgestone's purchasing a Firestone tire plant in LaVergne, Tennessee, or establishing a Bridgestone-Firestone joint venture that would own and operate the facility. That request led to many other meetings in the years that followed, most of which were also requested by Firestone. Those meetings provided the senior executives of the two companies with opportunities to develop personal relationships and exchange views on the extensive changes that were then taking place in the world's tire markets.

Despite the fact that it was neither unfriendly nor precipitous, the Bridgestone-Firestone merger has generated some negative reactions in both the United States and Japan. In this country, it has been criticized by those who consider it to be another threatening example of the "Buying of America" by foreigners made possible by a "cheap" dollar. Interestingly, in Japan, it has been criticized by those who believe that Bridgestone paid too much to acquire Firestone.

I believe that the Bridgestone-Firestone merger was a carefully reasoned response to change in the competitive environment that had radically altered the world's tire markets during the years that preceded it. In my opinion, merging the two companies was the most viable and, perhaps, the only course of action that could have made it possible for both Bridgestone and Firestone to accomplish strategic objectives that each had developed separately but that, nonetheless, proved to be totally compatible.

THE CHANGING COMPETITIVE ENVIRONMENT

When I joined Firestone in December 1979, the major US tire manufacturers were completing a decade during which they had invested huge amounts of capital to convert much of their production from bias-ply to radial tires. Radial tires, which were developed in Europe by Michelin, often provide over 40,000 miles of useful life compared with the 12,000 to 15,000 miles offered by the bias-ply tires they have replaced. In addition, radials offer roll resistance characteristics that add importantly to the fuel economy of cars and trucks equipped with them. Finally, tires throw tiny pieces of rubber into the atmosphere as they wear out, so the more durable radials provide significant environmental advantages.

For many years, Goodyear, Firestone, Uniroyal, General Tire, and Goodrich supplied over 75% of the tires sold in North America. The remaining 25% was supplied by a number of smaller domestic manufacturers, most of which concentrated on producing private-label tires for the replacement market. Competition from foreign tire manufacturers did not become significant on this continent until the late sixties when Michelin launched a major effort to increase sales of its steel-belted radials in the North American market and began supporting that effort by constructing eight tire manufacturing plants in the United States and Canada.

The eight plants Michelin constructed in North America required capital expenditures of about $1.5 billion, but those investments made it possible for Michelin to successfully invade tire markets that had long been dominated by US manufacturers. Today, Michelin is the leading supplier of original equipment and replacement radial tires for medium and heavy trucks in North America and one of the leading suppliers of radial tires for passenger cars and light trucks. Goodyear responded to the Michelin challenge by spending over $3 billion on new plant and equipment during the seventies and early eighties, most of which was required to establish fully competitive radial tire engineering and manufacturing capabilities in North America. The other major US tire producers also responded to that challenge, but with varying levels of vigor and with far less success.

The initial effect that the shift from bias-ply to radial tires had on US tire manufacturers was to weaken their balance sheets, because most of them found it necessary to borrow the funds needed to finance the conversion. Very soon thereafter, it began to have an adverse affect on income statements as they found it necessary to accept the costs of closing dozens of bias-ply tire plants that had become obsolete.

The conversion to radials, however, has also had very significant long-term effects on tire companies in the United States and elsewhere in the world for it has required tire manufacturers to support ongoing research, engineering, and product development efforts in their laboratories and offices far more extensive than those that had been needed to maintain production of the less sophisticated bias-ply tires; and it has required the installation and maintenance of more expensive process and material control programs at the plant level to assure production of a quality product. In addition, the widespread acceptance of the more durable radials has reduced sales opportunities in the higher margin tire replacement markets and has, therefore, increased the extent to which tire companies must rely on lower margin supply contracts with manufacturers of new cars and trucks to sell the tires their plants produce.

US TIRE INDUSTRY RESTRUCTURING

By the end of the seventies, it was clear that the capital markets did not believe that the massive investments the US and European tire companies were making to convert production from bias-ply to radial tires were likely to produce worthwhile rewards for investors.

Between the end of 1969 and the end of 1979, the Standard & Poore's 400 Index, which measures changes in the average of the stock prices of large US companies competing in a wide variety of industries, rose 19%. During that period, Uniroyal's stock dropped 79%; Firestone's dropped 65%; Goodyear's dropped 58%; and Goodrich's stock fell 40%. GenCorp's stock rose 16% during the period only because it was far more diversified than the other US tire companies and less dependent on the tire industry for future sales and profits. (See Exhibit 1.)

The situation was no better in Europe. Between the end of 1969 and the end of 1979, Michelin's stock fell 47% and Dunlop's fell 70%, while the Paris and London indexes were gaining 14% and 2%. In West Germany, Continental's stock fell 70%, while the Frankfurt Index lost only 17%. (See Exhibit 2.)

The dismal performance of their common stocks during the seventies left the major US tire

Exhibit 1 *Major US Tire Companies' Changes in Common Stock Prices*

	Year End		
	1969	1979	Change
Firestone	$ 25.56	$ 8.88	(65)%
Goodyear	30.75	12.88	(58)
Goodrich	32.75	19.63	(40)
GenCorp	18.38	21.25	16
Uniroyal	19.88	4.25	(79)
Standard & Poore's 400 Index	101.50	121.00	19

Exhibit 2 *Major European Tire Companies' Changes in Common Stock Prices*

	Year End		
	1969	1979	Change
Michelin (Francs)	1,559	828.	(47)%
Paris Index	100.0	113.6	14
Dunlop (Pence)	182.	54.	(70)%
London Index	407.4	414.2	2
Continental (DM)	150.	45.	(70)%
Frankfurt Index	866.9	715.7	17

companies very vulnerable to unfriendly takeovers in the eighties and that vulnerability led to an almost total restructuring of the US tire industry during the years that immediately preceded the Bridgestone-Firestone merger. In 1983, Goodrich was forced to defend itself against a takeover threat by repurchasing a large block of its stock that had been acquired by Carl Icahn. In early 1985, Carl Icahn acquired about 10% of Uniroyal's stock and Uniroyal's management then took the company "private" and established a partnership with Goodrich that merged their previously separate tire businesses. As part of a management-led restructuring program, Goodrich sold its interest in the partnership with Uniroyal and withdrew completely from the tire industry in 1987.

In 1986, Goodyear blocked an unfriendly takeover threat from Sir James Goldsmith by repurchasing about 50% of its common stock and selling most of its non-tire businesses to repay part of the debt it had accumulated to do so. In 1987, GenCorp responded to an uninvited tender offer from a partnership affiliated with AFG Industries by repurchasing about 50% of its common stock and implementing a restructuring program that

resulted in the sale of its tire business to Continental Gummi Werke A. G. of West Germany.

Firestone, too, was an attractive takeover target during the eighties. In 1981, a firm controlled by the Tisch brothers acquired almost 3 million shares of Firestone's stock and, a year later, a group reportedly associated with Carl Icahn acquired over 500,000 shares, but neither accumulation resulted in a tender offer. In addition, in late 1983, a respected investment firm that specializes in friendly leveraged buy-outs invited Firestone's management to participate in an effort to acquire the company by offering $27.50 per share or a total of $1.3 billion for all of Firestone's outstanding stock. The proposal anticipated that the new owners would terminate Firestone's salaried pension plan and use about $300 million of excess pension plan funds to repay a portion of the acquisition-related debt.

Firestone's senior management advised the company's board that it was not interested in participating in an effort to take Firestone "private," but Firestone terminated its salaried pension plan about a year later so that the excess funds could not be used to help finance an unfriendly takeover effort. In addition, Firestone entered the equity markets frequently during the 1982–1988 period to repurchase a total of about 50% of its outstanding stock in order to enhance shareholder wealth and make Firestone's stock less attractive to opportunistic investors.

FIRESTONE RESTRUCTURING

From its founding in 1900 until the mid-seventies, Firestone's history was one of almost uninterrupted revenue growth and sustained profitability. In 1976, however, the profits of Firestone's North American tire business began to deteriorate sharply as the company found it increasingly difficult to recover the cost of converting some bias tire plants to radial tire production and impossible to find profitable markets for the output of other bias tire plants that were too old to ever be converted. Overseas, Firestone's tire operations in Switzerland, Sweden, the United Kingdom, and Australia had begun to incur losses that, within a few years, would become so severe it would prove necessary to liquidate those businesses.

During the same period, Firestone experienced several tire quality problems, the most serious of which led to the widely publicized 1978 recall in North America of over 13 million Firestone 500 steel-belted radials. In addition, an SEC investigation was settled in 1976 when Firestone signed a consent order that enjoined it from using corporate funds for unlawful political contributions in the United States or unlawful payments to foreign government officials. In 1978, the company's chief financial officer was sentenced to a federal prison after pleading guilty to five counts of criminal indictment involving fraud; and, in 1979, Firestone, itself, entered a guilty plea to criminal charges in a federal tax case. By the end of 1979, those product quality and corporate governance failures had resulted in the filing of consumer class action and other lawsuits seeking over $2 billion in damages from The Firestone Tire & Rubber Company.

During the 1977–1979 period, Firestone's efforts to cope with its business and legal problems resulted in negative cash flows of $392 million. By the end of 1979, the company's debt exceeded $1 billion and represented over 70% of equity. Firestone's cash and cash equivalents amounted to only $92 million at that time; but the company was still hemorrhaging cash at a rate of $250 million annually.

Early in 1980, Firestone's board and management decided that action would have to be taken immediately to reduce the company's debt and strengthen its balance sheet. In March 1980, Firestone announced that it would close seven of its seventeen North American tire plants. The seven plants were then operating at about 50% of capacity and were being used, in large part, to produce low-profit bias-ply tires for private-label customers. Sharply curtailing such sales made it possible for the company to raise about $200 million in cash by liquidating the inventories and receivables required to support them. Firestone obtained an additional $200 million by selling a plastics business to Occidental in early 1981. Those actions, combined with the effects of rigorous cost and inventory reduction programs, made it possible to strengthen the company's balance sheet very substantially. By the end of 1981, Firestone's debt had been reduced to $639 million and its cash and cash equivalents had been increased to $378 million. (See Exhibit 3.)

During most of its history, Firestone had sought to compete in each of the major segments of the North American tire market by manufacturing and marketing tires for passenger cars and light trucks, for heavy trucks, for off-the-road construction and mining vehicles, and for agricultural equipment. By 1980, however, it was clear that Firestone no longer had the financial resources necessary to pursue so all-encompassing a competitive strategy. Since passenger car and light truck tires accounted for about 38 million of 41 million tires Firestone was selling in 1980, the company's management decided to focus efforts to improve North American tire profits on programs designed to strengthen Firestone's position as a manufacturer and marketer of those tires. It was that decision that led Firestone to seek a meeting with Bridgestone in September of 1980.

During the middle seventies, Firestone had completed construction of a medium and heavy truck radial tire plant in LaVergne, Tennessee, and had introduced a new truck tire called the Transteel Radial that did not come close to meeting customer expectations. As a result of its inability to demonstrate that its truck tires met competitive reliability and durability standards, Firestone was unable to sell more than half of the

Exhibit 3 *Tire and Related Capital Investment: Major US Tire Manufacturers, 1980–1984*

	Average Annual Investment	Percent of Sales
Goodyear	$293	40%
Firestone	185	52
Uniroyal	30	30
Goodrich	43	32
General	39	38

tires the LaVergne plant was capable of producing in 1980. Bridgestone's North American sales of radial truck tires, that it was then importing from Japan, about equaled Firestone's at that time. As a result, there was reason to believe that Bridgestone might consider participating in a joint venture that would own and operate the LaVergne plant or consider purchasing the facility and using the capacity that was not needed to meet Bridgestone's North American requirements to produce Firestone-branded radial truck tires that Firestone would agree to purchase and resell to its dealers.

Before joining Firestone, I had been employed for several years in the television industry as Zenith's chairman and had had the opportunity to meet and spend considerable time with Akio Morita of Sony. Since I had never met Bridgestone's chairman, Kanichiro Ishibashi, I telephoned Mr. Morita in September of 1980 to ask his advice as to how I might best approach Bridgestone. Mr. Morita responded by suggesting that I provide him with a summary of Firestone's proposal that he could pass it on to Mr. Ishibashi, whom he described as a close friend. As a result of a series of meetings that might have been very difficult to arrange without Mr. Morita's help, Bridgestone purchased the LaVergne plant and began supplying radial truck tires to Firestone in early 1983.

The closing of seven bias-ply tire plants in 1980, the sale of plastics business in 1981, and the sale of the LaVergne radial tire plant in 1983 represented only the beginning of the restructuring programs that Firestone found it necessary to implement in its tire and diversified products business during the eighties. In North America, the restructuring subsequently led to the closure or sale of five additional tire plants and to the di-

vestiture of diversified products businesses that produced plastics, beverage containers, foam products, automotive seat belts, truck wheels, and a variety of other products. Overseas, it led to the sale of all or most of Firestone's equity positions in tire manufacturing affiliates located in Chile, Costa Rica, Ghana, India, Japan, Kenya, South Africa, Thailand, and the Philippines.

Firestone used about $450 million of the cash generated by restructuring programs in the early eighties to finance stock repurchase programs; but it used significantly more to fund investments that were critically needed to modernize the company's tire manufacturing plants. During the 1980–1984 period, Firestone's tire and related capital investments averaged $185 million annually or 5.2% of sales. Goodyear's capital investments during that period exceeded Firestone's in total, but were significantly below Firestone's as a percent of sales. The tire-related capital investments of the other major US tire companies were very substantially below Firestone's both in total and as a percent of sales. (See Exhibit 3.)

The extensive capital investment programs produced important productivity and quality gains in Firestone's US and Canadian tire plants but they did not produce satisfactory or sustainable profit improvements. In 1980, Firestone's North American tire businesses reported an operating loss of $46 million. It reported operating profits of $85 million in 1981, $73 million in 1982, and $144 million in 1983. In 1984, however, its operating profits fell to $8 million.

As the profits from the company's North American tire businesses declined during 1984, the finance committee of Firestone's board of directors met regularly to consider the question of to what extent the disappointing earnings should trigger a

Exhibit 4 *Firestone's North American Operating Profit: Tire and Related Businesses, 1980–1984*

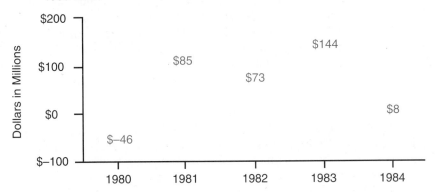

change in the company's competitive strategy. That question was by no means an overreaction for about 60% of Firestone's assets or a total of over $1.5 billion was invested in the company's US and Canadian tire businesses at that time, and Firestone had earned an average of only $75 million annually or about 5% before taxes on those assets during the 1981–1984 period. (See Exhibit 4.)

Opportunistic investors could have paid a significant premium to acquire Firestone during 1984 and could then have very profitably liquidated it, because the company's common stock was then trading in the $16 to $18 range, which represented only 55% to 65% of its book value. Firestone's finance committee concluded from its deliberations in 1984 that the interests of Firestone's shareholders would not be served if their stock were purchased at prices that made opportunistic investors wealthy and that the interests of Firestone's employees would not be served if the businesses in which they worked were liquidated. The committee also concluded, however, that Firestone would remain vulnerable to takeover and liquidation until it had both resolved the profit problems in its North American tire businesses and convinced investors it had done so. Finally, the committee concluded that the competitive strategy Firestone was then pursuing in the tire industry was not likely to accomplish either of those objectives in the foreseeable future.

The sharp decline in Firestone's North American tire profits during 1984 had been caused primarily by the drop in unit revenues. Radial tires that sold at an average of about $70 in the United

States in 1979 sold for about $55 in 1984. To some extent, the 20% price drop was attributable to a determination on the part of domestic tire producers to fully utilize the radial manufacturing capacity they had put in place at such great cost during the seventies. In addition, a strong dollar had made it possible for Japanese, Korean, and Taiwanese producers to enter the North American market and force domestic producers to meet aggressive price competition from imports.

There was little reason to believe in 1984 that Firestone could significantly improve its North American tire profits in the near term, because additional reductions in fixed costs would have significantly reduced the company's technical and manufacturing capabilities and it did not then appear likely that price competition in the tire markets of North America would soon abate.

There was even less reason to believe that Firestone could reduce its vulnerability to takeover and liquidation in 1984 by convincing the capital markets that its future as an independent tire manufacturer offered attractive opportunities for investors. Despite its strong competitive positions in the European and North American tire markets, Michelin reported after-tax losses of about $1.2 billion during the 1981–1984 period. Between the end of 1969 and the end of 1984, Michelin's common stock declined 52% in value, while the Paris Index gained 95%. Goodyear was profitable during the early eighties, but the price of its common stock declined 15% during the 1969–1984 period, while the S&P 400 Index rose 84%. Despite the strength of its brand name and its leadership position among the world's tire companies, Goodyear's common stock was trading at less than book value at the end of 1984.

Those considerations led Firestone's finance committee to conclude that the interests of the company's shareholders and employees would not be served if Firestone continued to pursue a "go-it-alone" tire strategy and that conclusion led the company's board to authorize its chairman to initiate discussions with other major tire manufacturers, to determine their interest in seeking economies of scale in the world's tire markets by establishing joint ventures that would combine some or all of Firestone's tire businesses with theirs or by purchasing some or all of Firestone's tire-related assets.

It was Bridgestone, of course, that Firestone approached first in its efforts to find a partner or a buyer.

THE JOINT VENTURE AND SUBSEQUENT MERGER

When I first met with its management to discuss the LaVergne, Tennessee, plant sale in 1981, Bridgestone had long been Japan's leading tire company, and its tires, which accounted for about 50% of all sales in Japanese original equipment and replacement markets, had established reputations for design and manufacturing excellence that were fully consistent with the company's corporate motto, "Serving Society with Products of Superior Quality." During the seventies, Bridgestone's sales had increased fourfold from slightly under $500 million to over $2 billion annually and its profits had increased fivefold from under $20 million to over $100 million annually. At the end of 1979, Bridgestone's corporate debt of $293 million represented less than 50% of equity and the company's balance sheet showed cash and cash equivalents of $337 million. Between the end of 1969 and the end of 1979, the price of its common stock had increased 296% and had outperformed even the Tokyo Index, which had risen 156%.

When I went to Tokyo in December 1984, Bridgestone's radial tire plants were still operating at capacity, supplying tires to an export-driven Japanese automobile industry. Its bias-tire plants were still being fully utilized, meeting demand in an extremely high-profit margin Japanese replacement market that, without foreign competition, was shifting very, very gradually to radial tires.

Bridgestone, however, was a tire company with an uncertain future at the end of 1984. The performance of its common stock, which had dropped 1% during the previous five years while Tokyo Index gained 99%, reflected investor awareness that Bridgestone's past successes and current strengths were concentrated in Japanese original equipment and replacement tire markets that it already dominated and that were likely to grow little, if at all, in the years to come.

By the end of 1984, import quotas and cost considerations had led the major Japanese automobile companies to begin building car and truck assembly facilities in the United States and Canada and it was apparent that Bridgestone would soon either have to establish substantial manufacturing capabilities in North America or lose the ability to supply millions of tires to its Japanese original equipment customers. The location of new car and truck manufacturers is the major determinant of a tire manufacturer's original equipment sales opportunities, because the bulk and weight of tires relative to their value make it difficult for the sellers to recover the costs of shipping them long distances in price-sensitive original equipment supply contracts, and because vehicle manufacturers are usually unwilling to accept the risks of car and truck assembly interruptions that might result from long tire supply pipelines.

In addition, the post-war surge in demand that had caused the number of cars and trucks in service in Japan to grow very rapidly during the sixties and seventies had been largely met by late 1984, and there was little reason to believe that the vehicle population in Japan would increase significantly in the future. Replacement tire sales opportunities are determined primarily by the number of cars and trucks in service. It was clear, therefore, that Bridgestone would soon find it necessary to either sharply increase sales of its tires in the North American and European tire replacement markets with large car populations or face severe long-term economies of scale disadvantages relative to competitors with more global marketing capabilities. At the conclusion of the December 1984 meeting in Tokyo, Bridgestone's management agreed to study Firestone's proposals and respond at a later date. In April 1985 when Akira Yeiri and I met again in San Francisco, however, he advised me that Bridgestone's strategic planning was not yet complete and that he was not, therefore, in a position to enter into discussions of possible joint ventures or major asset purchases.

During the year that followed the April 1985 meeting in San Francisco, a number of developments suggested that efforts by major world tire companies to establish global competitive capabilities might be accelerating. Sumitomo, Japan's second largest tire company, had purchased six tire plants and rights to the Dunlop brand name in Europe in 1983, but had acquired only a minority position in Dunlop's tire business in the United States and Canada at that time. By early 1986, however, it was understood that Sumitomo would soon establish an ability to compete in the tire markets of Japan, Europe, and North America by acquiring control of the former Dunlop tire business in the United States and Canada. In addition, Michelin and Goodyear had by then announced plans to significantly expand their tire manufacturing capabilities in Southeast Asia.

In July 1986, I met again with Bridgestone's management in Tokyo, where I leaned that Bridgestone was still not prepared to consider major joint ventures or acquisitions. During the course of that meeting, however, I concluded that Bridgestone would find it difficult to build a closer relationship with Firestone until Firestone completed what a Bridgestone executives described as the "retrenchment and rationalization actions" that were still required in Firestone's North American tire business. I left the Tokyo meeting convinced that Bridgestone wanted no part in a joint venture whose early history would involve plant closures and layoffs in the United States and Canada.

In June and December 1986, I met with Francois Michelin and several of his most senior associates in Paris where Group Michelin expressed considerable interest in the possibility of offering Michelin-branded tires for sale in Firestone's company-operated retail outlets. By that time, Firestone's MasterCare store system, with sales approaching $1 billion annually, had become one of the largest marketers of automotive services in the United States and accounted for about 50% of Firestone-brand replacement tire sales in this country. Marketing Michelin tires was attractive to Firestone, because the appeal of its 1,500 MasterCare outlets was limited by the fact that they offered only Firestone tires. Michelin also expressed considerable interest in acquiring some or all of Firestone's Latin American tire operations.

The parties agreed, however, that because both Michelin and Firestone had strong competitive positions in North America and Europe, the purchase of Firestone plants by Michelin or joint ventures in those markets might be challenged successfully on antitrust grounds. As a result, the discussions ended in January 1987 with Firestone agreeing to give continuing consideration to the possibility of joint ventures or asset sales in Latin America.

In February 1987, I met Leopoldo Pirelli in London to explore possible joint ventures or asset sales with Pirelli S.p.A., Italy's largest tire company. In that meeting, however, Pirelli's management proved unwilling to include many of Firestone's North American tire businesses in the joint venture that it was then proposing, and Firestone subsequently advised Pirelli by letter that it was not interested in considering a limited joint venture. About two weeks before the October 1987 stock market crash, I met again with Leopoldo Pirelli in New York, where he expressed an interest in considering the purchase of Firestone's worldwide tire businesses for a cash price that would approximate book value. That possibility was not pursued immediately, however, because after the crash Firestone had entered the US equity markets again to repurchase stock and would have been required to publicly disclose discussions of possible joint ventures and Pirelli felt that public disclosure of what it regarded to be exploratory discussions would have been inappropriate.

In November 1987, Firestone's management had every reason to believe that its discussions with Bridgestone, Michelin, and Pirelli had been terminated or indefinitely suspended, but that proved not to be the case. On December 18, 1987, in response to a request from Bridgestone, I agreed to meet again with Akira Yeiri in Honolulu on January 14, 1988.

During the next two weeks, in response to similar requests, I agreed to meet again with Francois Michelin on January 29 in Paris and with Leopoldo Pirelli again on February 8 in New York. It was an announcement by Continental Gummi Werke A.G. of West Germany and its recently acquired General Tire subsidiary in the United States that gave new life to the seemingly moribund joint venture discussions.

On December 14, 1987, Continental/General announced an agreement with Toyo Tire and Rubber Company and Yokohama Rubber Company of Japan providing that the parties would establish a joint venture in the United States to manufacture radial truck and bus tires; that Toyo and Yokohama would produce tires in their Japanese plants for Continental/General; and that Continental/General would produce tires in their North American plants for Toyo and Yokohama. The agreement provided Continental/General with access to Japan's tire markets and gave Toyo and Yokohama vastly improved access to North American tire markets.

A few months before the Continental/General announcement, Firestone closed two plants that had been used primarily to manufacture bias-ply tires for medium and heavy trucks and for off-the-highway vehicles. The closures, which completed the restructuring of Firestone's North American tire businesses, made it possible for Bridgestone or any other prospective joint venture partner to participate in the benefits the restructuring programs had produced without accepting the adverse political and employee relations risks associated with ongoing plant closures and layoffs. The magnitude of the facility utilization and productivity gains produced by Firestone's restructuring programs are indicated by the fact that Firestone had required fourteen of its seventeen tire plants to produce the 38 million passenger and light truck tires it sold in North America in 1980. By late 1987, however, Firestone was in a position to support sales of 31 million passenger and light truck tires with only five North American plants. (See Exhibit 5.)

The restructuring programs also produced important gains in product quality. In 1985, Firestone earned GM's SPEAR 1 quality award at its Wilson plant. As a passenger and light truck tire supplier to GM, only Michelin earned that award before Firestone did. By 1986, each of Firestone's North American tire plants had earned Ford Motor Company's coveted Q-1 quality award. In 1987, Firestone's performance as a high-quality supplier was a major factor in its selection as the sole tire source for GM's Saturn program. In the same year, Firestone's Wilson and Decatur plants earned Nissan's Supplier Quality Achievement award. Firestone was the only tire supplier to be so honored by Nissan in 1987.

Finally, the restructuring programs significantly upgraded Firestone's tire-marketing capabilities. In 1980, sales of low-margin tires to private-label customers accounted for almost one-third of the 38 million passenger and light truck tires that Firestone sold in North America. In 1987, private-label customers accounted for less than 10% of Firestone's 31 million units. Firestone's sales of original equipment and branded replacement tires increased from slightly below 26 million units to slightly above 28 million units during the 1980–1987 period. (See Exhibit 6.)

When we met on January 14 in Honolulu, Akira Yeiri told me that Bridgestone was prepared to purchase all of Firestone's tire manufacturing operations in North America or acquire a majority position in a joint venture that would own and manage Firestone's global tire operations. Firestone chose the second alternative, because it would provide Bridgestone and Firestone with competitive capabilities in Japan, North America, Europe, and Latin America; eliminate potential conflicts in the use of the Firestone brand name; and avoid orphaning the men and women in Firestone's international tire business. On February 7, I met again with Akira Yeiri in Los Angeles, where we reached agreement in principle with respect to a possible Bridgestone-Firestone joint venture. I gave Mr. Yeiri a somewhat detailed summary of my understanding of the agreements we had reached and on February 12, I received a letter from him advising me that my understanding of those agreements was consistent with his.

On February 16, 1988, Firestone's board carefully considered the merits of possible joint ventures with Bridgestone, Michelin, or Pirelli. In terms of shareholder interests, the board concluded that the firm Bridgestone financial proposal was at least as attractive as any agreement that might subsequently be negotiated with Michelin or Pirelli. It also concluded that, because there were essentially no overlaps in Bridgestone and Firestone tire-related activities anywhere in the world, a joint venture with Bridgestone was less likely to result in merger-related plant closures, layoffs, or antitrust challenges than would an agreement with Michelin or Pirelli.

On February 16, 1988, Bridgestone and Firestone publicly announced their intention to form a joint venture that would own and operate Firestone's tire business in North America and elsewhere in the world. The plan anticipated that Firestone would retain sole ownership of its diversified products and US automotive service retailing

---

Exhibit 5 *Firestone's United Sales and Production Facilities: Passenger and Light Truck Tires, North America (Million of Units/Numbers of Plants)*

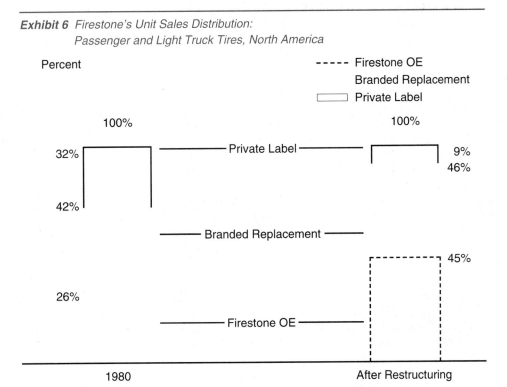

Unit Sales   Plants

38

31

14

5

1980   After Restructuring

Exhibit 6 *Firestone's Unit Sales Distribution: Passenger and Light Truck Tires, North America*

Percent   ----- Firestone OE
                                               Branded Replacement
                                               ☐ Private Label

100%   100%

32%   ——— Private Label ———   9%
                                                               46%
42%

                    ——— Branded Replacement ———

26%   45%

                    ——— Firestone OE ———

1980   After Restructuring

activities and that Firestone would receive about $1,250 million in cash for the 75% interest in the joint venture that would be assumed by Bridgestone. Firestone's common stock was trading at about $30 per share immediately prior to the joint venture announcement and the total market value of the company at that time approximated $900 million. About three weeks after the planned Bridgestone-Firestone joint venture was announced, however, Pirelli announced a $58 per share tender offer for all of Firestone's outstanding stock.

The unexpected Pirelli tender offer made it impossible for Bridgestone and Firestone to implement the joint venture agreement and gave Firestone's board and management only ten days to decide whether to respond to the tender offer by negotiating the sale of the company to Pirelli at a price at or above $58 per share, by encouraging Bridgestone to outbid Pirelli, or by seeking financing for a management-led leveraged buy-out that would take Firestone "private."

I had learned of the Pirelli tender offer on Sunday evening March 6 and after reviewing it with Firestone's outside directors by telephone, I was able to notify Bridgestone's management in Tokyo, where it was Monday morning. In subsequent discussions, Firestone advised Bridgestone that if Bridgestone was satisfied with the financial terms associated with the original tire-related joint venture, Firestone was confident that it could provide information on its diversified products and retailing businesses that would justify a Bridgestone offer for Firestone's stock significantly above the $58 Pirelli tender offer. Bridgestone responded with its successful $80 per share offer on March 17, 1988.

CONCLUSION

The February 1988 announcement of the originally planned Bridgestone-Firestone tire joint venture was greeted with an enthusiasm that in some cases approached euphoria by the men and women working in Firestone's domestic and international tire operations. Firestone had employed 107,000 persons at the end of 1979, but employed only 53,500 at the end of 1987 and the company's tire businesses had been the most severely affected by the restructuring-related plant closures and layoffs. Because they knew that there was very little overlap in Bridgestone and Firestone tire operations in North America, Europe, Asia, or Latin America, the employees working in Firestone's tire-related activities understood that their jobs would be far more secure and would offer significantly greater career opportunities in the planned joint venture than they would in continued "go-it-alone" Firestone efforts to compete in the world's tire markets.

The March 1988 announcement of the Bridgestone-Firestone merger was equally well received by the employees of Firestone's diversified products activities and retail store system. Although Firestone had divested many of its diversified product companies during the eighties, it had retained synthetic rubber, natural rubber, and car and truck air spring businesses that benefited from technical support provided by scientists in the company's research organization who are recognized leaders in rubber and polymer chemistry. The merger, of course, removed any doubts about whether that support would continue.

In addition, since Bridgestone did not produce synthetic rubber, the merger provided the Firestone facilities that produced those materials the opportunity to supply them to Bridgestone's plants in the United States and elsewhere in the world. In the case of air springs, the merger combined Bridgestone's strong position in the Japanese market with Firestone's dominant position in North America to create a powerful new competitive entity. Finally, the merger provided the opportunity to sell Bridgestone-branded tires in Firestone's automotive service and tire retailing outlets and thus increase their appeal to US customers.

Within Firestone, the favorable initial reactions to the merger were bolstered during the days that followed its announcement by the fact that Akira Yeiri immediately took the time to meet with large groups of the company's employees in Chicago and Akron to assure them that they were valued and respected partners in an organization with substantial opportunities for future growth. During the months that followed, Mr. Yeiri traveled extensively to deliver the same message to men and women working in Firestone plants, offices, and laboratories located in France, Italy, Spain, Canada, and several cities throughout the United States. Bridgestone executives never talked about having "acquired" Firestone. They talked, instead, about a "merger" or about a "partnership" and they do so with a sincerity that is convincing.

Additional evidence of Bridgestone's confidence in the future of the merged Bridgestone-Firestone organization became available in November 1988 when the managements of the previously separate companies announced jointly that they planned to invest a total of about $1.5 billion in Firestone's tire, diversified products, and Master-Care automotive service businesses over a period of about three years. The plan anticipated that over $1 billion would be spent to develop and install state-of-the-art tire manufacturing processes in Firestone's domestic and international tire plants and prepare them to produce Bridgestone-branded tires. The capital program also provided funds to expand Firestone's synthetic rubber businesses and to establish a new plant in the United States that would manufacture air springs for passenger cars.

During 1980, Firestone's common stock traded at prices below $7 a share and, at the end of 1987, it traded at $31.50 per share. It is apparent, therefore, that Bridgestone's $80 per share tender offer, in March 1988, produced very substantial benefits for Firestone's stockholders. It is also clear, in my opinion, that Bridgestone's decision to spend $2.6 billion to purchase Firestone's tire, diversified products, and automotive service retailing business and to invest an additional $1.5 billion to modernize and expand them have produced important job security and career opportunity benefits for Firestone's employees. Finally, I believe that the combination of Bridgestone's and Firestone's technical resources will produce important benefits for the merged organization's customers in the years to come.

I also believe that the merger will produce significant benefits for the shareholder, employee, and customer constituencies that Bridgestone's management is obligated to serve. In fact, I would argue that the Bridgestone-Firestone merger provided Bridgestone with what may have been the only course of action that would have permitted it to protect its historical position in the tire industry and achieve its longer-term objective of becoming a leader among the world's tire manufacturers.

In late 1984, when Bridgestone and Firestone executives held their first discussion of joint ventures in Tokyo, a US dollar was worth about 250 yen. By the end of 1987, the dollar's value approximated 125 yen. The increase in the yen's value led Japan's automobile manufacturers to accelerate and expand their efforts to establish manufacturing capabilities in the United States and Canada and confronted Bridgestone with a significantly

increased threat of sharply reduced original equipment tire sales opportunities if it failed to establish manufacturing capabilities in North America very quickly. The increase in the yen's value also made it difficult or impossible for Bridgestone to export tires from Japan and sell them profitably in North America and European replacement markets.

In addition, when Firestone and Bridgestone representatives met in July 1986 in Tokyo, there was very little foreign competition in Japan's tire replacement markets. Shortly thereafter, however, Michelin announced a plan to form a joint venture in South Korea with the capacity to produce 5 million tires annually, most of which would be exported to Japan. About a year later, Michelin announced the establishment of a joint venture in Japan, itself, that would produce about 5 million tires annually. Shortly thereafter, Goodyear obtained approval to build a tire plant in South Korea that would also be used to produce tires for export to Japan.

Those events threatened Bridgestone with substantial reductions in its original equipment and export tire sales volumes and with the prospect of significantly lower profit margins from sales in Japan's tire replacement markets. If Bridgestone had failed to react to those threats, it might have been forced to settle for a long-term role as a bit player in the world's tire markets. If it had reacted on a "go-it-alone" basis, it would have required a decade or more to construct tire plants overseas, mobilize organizations that could manage them, and establish the Bridgestone brand name in markets in which it was not widely recognized or accepted.

The globalization of tire manufacturing and the restructuring of the US tire industry neither began nor ended with the Bridgestone-Firestone merger announced in March 1988. Armstrong, a US tire company that had long been a major producer of agricultural tires and a supplier of private-label passenger car tires to Sears, was purchased by Pirelli in May 1988. Mohawk, a smaller US tire producer, was purchased by Yokohama Rubber in October 1989. In May 1990, Group Michelin acquired the Uniroyal-Goodrich tire business.

In the March-April 1989 issue of the *Harvard Business Review*, Kenichi Ohmae, who heads McKinsey's office in Tokyo, began an article titled, "The Global Logic of Strategic Alliances," with the statement:

Companies are just beginning to learn what nations have always known: in a complex, uncertain world filled with dangerous opponents, it is best not to go it alone. Great powers operating across broad theaters of engagement have traditionally made common cause with others whose interests ran parallel with their own. No shame in that. Entente—the striking of an alliance—is a responsible part of every good strategist's repertoire. In today's competitive environment, this is also true for corporate managers.

During the past two decades, the tire markets of the world have been radically altered by the introduction of a new technology and the emergence of sophisticated new foreign competitors. In response to those changes in the competitive environment, both Bridgestone and Firestone concluded that "striking an alliance" would better serve their interests than would continued efforts to "go it alone." In my opinion, such alliances will become increasingly more frequent and, hopefully, increasingly less controversial as the economies of the world become more interrelated and more interdependent in the years to come.

UNION CARBIDE CORPORATION

Industrial Plant Accident in Bhopal, India: Responsibility of the Multinational Corporation

Paul Shrivastava
Bucknell University

In the middle of the night on December 3, 1984, J. Mukund, the factory manager of the Union Carbide (India) Limited pesticide plant in Bhopal, was awakened by a telephone call from the night-shift supervisor informing him that an accident had occurred at the plant causing a large amount of methyl isocyanate gas to leak out from the underground storage tanks. The lethal gas was causing havoc in the plant neighborhoods, injuring and killing untold numbers of people as they tried to escape the area. Within a short time, Mukund had driven to the plant and initiated damage control and emergency procedures. He telephoned the company headquarters in Bombay, which in turn notified divisional offices in Hong Kong, and the parent company headquarters in Danbury, Connecticut. Within a few hours, news of the disaster had reached all key personnel in the company. The worst corporate crisis in history had just hit Union Carbide Corporation.

The morning of December 4, 1984, found death strewn over the stunned Bhopal city. Bodies and animal carcasses lay on sidewalks, streets, and railway platforms, and in slum huts, bus stands, and waiting halls. Thousands of injured victims streamed into the city's hospitals. Doctors and other medical personnel struggled to cope with the chaotic rush, knowing neither the cause of the disaster nor how to treat the victims. Groping for anything that might help, they treated immediate symptoms by washing their patients' eyes with water and then soothing their burning with eyedrops; they gave the victims aspirins, inhalers, muscle relaxants, and stomach remedies to provide temporary relief. Before the week was over, nearly 3,000 people had died. More than 300,000 others had been affected by exposure to the deadly poison. About 2,000 animals had died, and 7,000 more were severely injured. The worst industrial accident in history was over. But the industrial crisis that made the city of Bhopal international news had just begun.

The impact of the disaster on Union Carbide Corporation was devastating. At the time of the accident, in 1984, Union Carbide had sales revenues of $9.5 billion, net income of $323 million, and total assets of $10.5 billion. Three years later, the sales revenues had fallen to $6 billion, assets had shrunk to about $6.5 billion, and shareholders' equity fell from $4.9 billion to under $1 billion. This drastic reduction in size occurred without a single penny being paid in compensation to victims of the disaster.

During these turbulent three years, the company's financial survival was threatened more than once. First, in 1985, a few months after the disaster, Carbide stock price plunged from about $48 a share to about $33 a share. At the depressed price, speculators and arbitrageurs acquired large amounts of the company stock. On August 14, 1985, the GAF Corporation announced that it had acquired a significant stake in Carbide and would try to take it over. Samuel Heyman, chairman of GAF, said he would sell off Carbide units that contributed about 40% of its revenues. With the money from those sales (estimated by GAF to be $4.5 billion), he would settle the Bhopal victims' claims. This immediately put the company in play in the takeover game. This was followed by frantic bidding and counterbidding wars between GAF and Union Carbide management.

Six months later, GAF gave up its takeover attempt, but only after Carbide management had been maneuvered into a radical financial restructuring. The restructuring involved selling off 25% of the most profitable assets of the company, closing several marginally profitable plants, and laying off about 4,000 people.

After more than four years of legal proceedings and acrimonious and contentious charges and countercharges, a settlement was reached in early February 1989 between the government of India and Union Carbide. The agreement called for Union Carbide to pay $470 million. The agreement resolves all outstanding issues and claims by any and all parties against Union Carbide. The Supreme Court of India, in settling the claim, did not address the issue of who was to blame for the accident. Also as part of the settlement, the Indian Supreme Court ordered dismissal of all criminal charges and other civil suits in India against Union Carbide.[1]

In the years since the accident, a great deal has happened and yet a great deal remains unchanged. Union Carbide went through the shock of a long, drawn-out hostile takeover battle which left the company severely battered, highly leveraged, and financially constrained. The accident also attracted worldwide attention to the broad scope of hazards associated with industrial accidents in general, and those in the Third World in particular. Although this accident was the most severe in history, it was by no means unique.

Large-scale industrial accidents have created crises for corporations and the public regularly throughout this century. Since the beginning of this century, there have been 28 major industrial accidents in fixed facilities in the free world. These accidents do not include transportation accidents, such as airliner crashes or train derailments. These accidents have occurred in both industrialized countries as well as developing countries. In the United States, the explosion of a ship with a cargo of ammonium nitrate caused the deaths of over 530 people in Texas City in 1947. In 1948, the

explosion of confined dimethyl ether in Ludwigshafen, Germany, killed nearly 250 people. In 1970, an accident at an underground railway construction site in Osaka, Japan, killed 92 people. In 1984, accidents in Mexico City and Cubatao, Brazil, killed about 500 people each.

Major industrial accidents can occur anywhere—in industrialized as well as developing countries, in small as well as large organizations, in the public as well as the private sectors. Accidents such as, Bhopal, Chernobyl, and the NASA Challenger explosion have fundamentally changed the public's awareness of the technological hazards facing society. They have highlighted the very limited scope of our knowledge about these hazards and the extreme inadequacy of our ability and resources to cope with such major accidents.

Another sad realization to emerge out of the Bhopal case is that four years after the accident and despite an apparent settlement, the case is still mired in courts and there is no solution in sight for the victims. None of the victims have received a single penny in compensation for damages. While Union Carbide Corporation and the government of India fight in the courts, the plight of the victims largely goes unnoticed. The survivors of those who died remain desperately poor and destitute with no alternative means of supporting themselves. Those who were partially or totally disabled suffer from a lack of adequate medical care and rehabilitation, loss of employment, and financial hardships. One thing is certain, many more will die before seeing justice done, and those who live long enough to see the courts resolve the case may not have much time left to make use of the compensation they eventually receive in any settlement.

ISSUES FOR ANALYSIS

The Bhopal case raises a number of important issues concerning public disclosure of potential hazards, appropriate technology transfers to developing countries, corporate responsibility and liability for overseas plant safety, and the role of host country governments in direct foreign investments. In addition, it highlights the importance of

[1]Sanjay Hazarika, Bhopal payments set at $470.0 million for union carbide, *New York Times*, February 15, 1989, p. 1. See also, Union Carbide agrees to settle all Bhopal litigation for $470.0 million in pact with India's Supreme Court," *Wall Street Journal*, February 15, 1989, p. A-3.

developing expeditious and equitable systems for resolving postaccident conflicts and payment of compensation to victims.

1. What are the responsibilities of multinational corporations for their overseas operations, especially in developing countries, to ensure that these plants are operated safely with regard to workers, communities, and the environment? Can companies adopt a single uniform safety standard for all their plants around the world?
2. To what extent did Union Carbide Corporation (US) and its Indian subsidiary exercise due care in this regard? What more could each of them have done to ensure plant safety?
3. How should environmental and safety concerns be incorporated in strategies for technology transfer to developing countries?
4. How can multinational corporations (MNCs) control the safety performance of their overseas operations?
5. To what extent can majority of other forms of ownership be used to ascertain the liability of various parties in case of major industrial accidents?
6. How do issues 3, 4, and 5 apply to the Bhopal case?
7. What should be the responsibility of government in ensuring plant safety? To what extent should government agencies be held responsible for losses to human lives and property? What should be done if such responsibility is poorly or inadequately discharged?
8. How do the issues raised in item 7 apply to the government of India, the state government of Madhya Pradesh, and the local city government agencies in Bhopal?
9. What criteria should be used in determining compensation to victims? What kinds of compensation systems should be designed to ensure speedy and fair compensation? How much compensation can Union Carbide pay without going bankrupt?
10. Which country's courts should be responsible for handling cases involving multicountry accidents and liability disputes, and why? What role can the International Court of Justice play in this regard?
11. To what extent and under what circumstances are courts an appropriate forum for resolving international liability cases? What alternative forms of dispute resolution mechanisms can be recommended?
12. What corporate and business policies should firms adopt in order to minimize the occurrence of major accidents? How can they trade off between the expense of being safe versus cutting costs to be competitive?
13. What ethical issues does the Bhopal case raise? What ethical standards should be applied in making corporate policies regarding the case?
14. In light of Bhopal-type disasters, how should corporate responsibility toward environmental protection and worker and community safety change? What additional actions should corporations undertake voluntarily that were not warranted before Bhopal?

UNION CARBIDE CORPORATION (UCC)

The organizational context of this accident may be understood by examining the position of the Bhopal plant in the overall business of Union Carbide Corporation. In 1984, Union Carbide Corporation (UCC) was the seventh largest chemical company in the United States with total assets of $10.51 billion and sales approaching $10 billion. It owned or operated businesses in 40 countries and employed over 33,000 people worldwide. Its main product lines included dry cell batteries, chemicals, industrial gases, specialty alloys, and agricultural products.

The early 1970s were a turbulent period for the chemical industry and Union Carbide. The highly cyclical chemical industry became even more volatile because of oil price fluctuations during the early 1970s. The oil embargo created an artificial shortage of petrochemicals and related products and sent their prices skyrocketing. In 1973 and 1974, UCC's sales grew at unprecedented rates of 21% and 35% respectively. This created an upbeat mood at the company, and an aggressive program of growth and expansion was started. Capital expenditure increased annually until 1975. In 1975, the company got the first of a series of jolts. While its sales increased 6% over 1974, world recession triggered by the 1973 oil embargo reduced demand, resulting in a decline in sales and total employment. Inflation caused reductions in net earnings and led to cost-cutting measures and strategic reorientation. The company outlined three strategies: first, to strengthen its position in businesses with a good future and in areas where it had a strong market position; second, to withdraw from businesses which did not meet Carbide's criteria for financial performance; and third, to shift the business mix to include a greater proportion of performance products (e.g., Sevin and Temik pesticides). It also decided to diversify into related and unrelated businesses, and identified the areas of health, food products, environment, and energy as its future focus. The company estimated that about 60% of its business in 1975 was in growth categories, and it planned to allocate about 80% of its capital expenditure from 1975 to 1979 on these growth businesses. Specifically, pesticides and other agricultural products were considered as having high growth potential, whereas old and mature chemical businesses were considered to be less desirable.

In 1976, Congress passed the Toxic Substances Control Act, placing more stringent requirements on the corporation's chemical businesses. Union Carbide set up a new corporate-level Health, Safety, and Environmental Affairs Department to ensure compliance with the new act and centralize internal administration.

The year 1977 saw a change in the top management of Union Carbide. W. S. Sneath took over as chairman of the company, and Warren Anderson became the new president. Together they restructured Carbide's business portfolio and started divesting some of its businesses. These decisions resulted in divestiture of over a billion dollars worth of assets over the next four years, including Carbide's petrochemical business in Europe and the entire medical business, in which the company had developed a number of new products.

In 1979, Union Carbide once again benefited from the steep oil price hike by OPEC. Sales jumped 17% and earnings jumped 41%, and the total number of employees reached an all-time high of 115,763. In the 1980s, Union Carbide continued to refocus its portfolio of businesses away from chemicals and concentrated on industrial gases and batteries. It had divested almost three dozen business units and product ventures in the late 1970s to dilute its chemical operations in the United States. This was done in acknowledgment of increasing competition in the chemicals industry and lackluster financial performance of the company during the past decade.

In 1982, Warren Anderson took over as chairman while Alec Flamm became president. The early 1980s were a period of declining performance. Sales dropped, earnings declined, capital expenditures and working capital were reduced, maintenance expenditures were cut back, assets were stripped, and employment level was curtailed. These trends are apparent in the financial figures presented in Tables 1, 2, and 3.

UNION CARBIDE (INDIA) LTD.

Union Carbide (India) Limited (UCIL) was incorporated in Calcutta under the name of Eveready Company (India) Ltd. on June 20, 1934. Its name was changed to National Carbon Company (Ltd.) and then to Union Carbide (India) Ltd. in December 1959. The company's most important product is dry cells (batteries). In 1984, more than 50% of the company's revenues came from this product. But over the years, as its product lines in batteries, chemicals, and plastics matured, the company sought out new markets to maintain its growth.

The industries UCIL entered were typically technology- and capital-intensive. They catered to mass markets and required large-scale production and technically skilled labor. Most often, UCIL would enter industries still in their early stages of development and gain a dominant market position by using the superior technology of its parent company. One such industry was pesticides. In the 1960s, large-scale use of agricultural pesticides was promoted by the Indian government as part of its "green revolution" campaign to modernize agriculture. Pesticides quickly became popular among farmers, and their use tripled between 1956 and 1970.

The Agricultural Products Division was established in 1969. It developed carbaryl (Sevin) using methyl isocyanate (MIC) as the active agent for a range of pesticides. The Bhopal plant also began operating in 1969. It was located on the north side of Bhopal, about two miles from the railway station and bus stand—the hub of local commercial and transportation activities. Since the plant was initially used only for formulation (the mixing of different stable substances to create pesticides), it did not pose a grave danger to surrounding areas. In 1974, however, it was granted an industrial license to manufacture pesticides and began production of both Sevin and MIC in 1977. While

Table 1 *Selected Financial Data for Union Carbide Corporation*

	1984[a]	1983[b]	1982[c]	1981	1980
	Dollar Amounts in Millions (Except per Share Figures)				
From the income statement					
Net sales	$9,508	$9,001	$9,061	$10,168	$9,994
Cost of sales	6,702	6,581	6,687	7,431	7,186
Research and development expense	265	245	240	207	166
Selling, administrative, and other expenses	1,221	1,243	1,249	1,221	1,152
Depreciation	507	477	426	386	326
Interest on long-term and short-term debt	300	252	236	171	153
Other income (expense)—net	77	120	162	164	41
Nonrecurring charge—closing of facilities	—	241	—	—	—
Income before provision for income taxes	390	82	385	916	1,052
Provision for income taxes	227	(10)	58	258	360
Income before extraordinary charge and cumulative effect of change in accounting principle	341	79	310	649	673
Extraordinary charge	(18)	—	—	—	—
Cumulative effect of change in accounting principle for ITC	—	—	—	—	217
Net income	323	79	310	649	890
Income per share before extraordinary charge and cumulative effect of change in accounting principle	4.84	1.13	4.47	9.56	10.08
Extraordinary charge per share	(0.25)	—	—	—	—
Cumulative effect per share of change in accounting principle for ITC	—	—	—	—	3.28
Net income per share[c]	4.59	1.13	4.47	9.56	13.36
From the balance sheet (at year end)					
Working capital	1,548	$1,483	$1,747	$ 2,147	$2,124
Total assets	10,518	10,295	10,616	10,423	9,659
Long-term debt	2,362	2,387	2,428	2,101	1,859
Total capitalization	7,962	7,999	8,305	8,018	7,282
UCC stockholders' equity	4,924	4,929	5,159	5,263	4,776
UCC stockholders' equity per share	69.89	69.95	73.54	76.74	70.90
Other data					
Funds from operations—sources	$ 964	$ 708	$715	$ 1,172	$1,211
Dividends	240	240	235	224	206
Dividends per share	3.40	3.40	3.40	3.30	3.10
Shares outstanding (thousands at year end)	70,450	70,465	70,153	68,582	67,367
Market price per share—high	65¼	73⅞	61	62⅛	52½
Market price per share—low	32³⁄₄	51	40⅛	45¼	35¼
Capital expenditures	670	761	1,179	1,186	1,129
Number of employees (at year end)	98,366	99,506	103,229	110,255	116,105
Selected financial ratios					
Total debt/total capitalization (at year end)	33.7%	34.0%	33.9%	30.3%	29.9%
Net income/average UCC stockholders' equity	6.6%	1.6%	6.0%	12.9%	15.3%[b]
Net income + minority share of income/average total capitalization	4.5%	1.4%	4.3%	9.1%	10.6%[b]
Dividends/net income	74.3%	303.8%	75.8%	34.5%	30.6%[b]
Dividends/funds from operations—sources	24.9%	33.9%	32.9%	19.1%	17.0%

[a]Amounts for 1982 and subsequent years reflect the adoption of Statement of Financial Accounting Standards No. 52.
[b]Net income in these ratios excludes the nonrecurring credit for the cumulative effect of the change in accounting principle for the investment tax credit (ITC).
[c]Net income per share is based on weighted average number of shares outstanding during the year. *Funds from operations—sources* includes income before extraordinary charge and noncash charges (credits) to income before extraordinary charge. *Total debt* consists of short-term debt, long-term debt, and current installments of long-term debt. *Total capitalization* consists of total debt plus minority stockholders' equity in consolidated subsidiaries and UCC stockholders' equity.

Table 2. *Consolidated Statement of Income and Retained Earnings for Union Carbide Corporation*

	Millions of Dollars (Except per Share Figures) Year Ended December 31		
	1984	1983	1982
Net sales	$9,508	$9,001	$9,061
Deductions (additions)			
Cost of sales	6,702	6,581	6,687
Research and development	265	245	240
Selling, administrative, and other expenses	1,221	1,243	1,249
Depreciation	507	477	426
Interest on long-term and short-term debt	300	252	236
Other income—net	(77)	(120)	(162)
Nonrecurring charge—closing of facilities	—	241	—
Income before provision for income taxes	590	82	385
Provision for income taxes	227	(10)	58
Income of consolidated companies	363	92	327
Less: Minority stockholders' share of income	39	32	36
Plus: UCC share of income of companies carried at equity	17	19	19
Income before extraordinary charge	341	79	310
Extraordinary charge	(18)	—	—
Net income	323	79	310
Retained earnings at January 1	4,509	4,670	4,595
	4,832	4,749	4,905
Dividends declared	240	240	235
Retained earnings at December 31	$4,592	$4,509	$4,670
Per share			
Income before extraordinary charge[a]	$ 4.84	$ 1.13	$ 4.47
Extraordinary charge[a]	$ (0.25)	$ —	$ —
Net income[a]	$ 4.59	$ 1.13	$ 4.47
Dividends declared	$ 3.40	$ 3.40	$ 3.40

[a]Based on 70,478,524 shares (70,347,418 shares in 1983 and 69,305,609 shares in 1982), the weighted average number of shares outstanding during the year.

Table 3. *Consolidated Balance Sheet for UCC*

	Millions of Dollars at December 31	
	1984	1983
Assets		
Cash	$ 28	$ 46
Time deposits and short-term marketable securities	68	72
	96	118
Notes and accounts receivable	1,512	1,460
Inventories		
Raw materials and supplies	468	473
Work in process	409	421
Finished goods	669	616
	1,546	1,510
Prepaid expenses	152	157
Total current assets	3,306	3,245
Property, plant, and equipment	11,131	10,708
Less: Accumulated depreciation	4,748	4,426
Net fixed assets	6,383	6,282
Companies carried at equity	288	300
Other investments and advances	139	121
Total investments and advances	427	421
Other assets	402	347
Total assets	$10,518	$10,295
Liabilities and stockholders' equity		
Accounts payable	$ 470	$ 492
Short-term debt	217	240
Payments due within one year on long-term debt	104	91
Accrued income and other taxes	124	114
Other accrued liabilities	843	825
Total current liabilities	1,758	1,762
Long-term debt	2,362	2,387
Deferred credits	1,119	865
Minority stockholders' equity in consolidated subsidiaries	355	352
UCC stockholders' equity		
Common stock		
Authorized—180,000,000 shares		
Issued—70,600,810 shares (70,567,283 shares in 1983)	756	755
Equity adjustment from foreign currency translation	(419)	(333)
Retained earnings	4,592	4,509
	4,929	4,931
Less: Treasury stock, at cost—150,579 shares (101,784 shares in 1983)	5	2
Total UCC stockholders' equity	4,924	4,929
Total liabilities and stockholders' equity	$10,518	$10,295

these developments occurred inside the company, the pesticide industry underwent major changes. Many small manufacturers entered the industry as formulators. They were less capital intensive and served small market niches.

The Bhopal plant was the key manufacturing facility of the Agricultural Products Division of the company. At the time of the accident in December 1984, Union Carbide (India) Limited was the twenty-first largest company in India. Of UCIL shares, 50.9% were owned by Union Carbide Corporation, New York. Remaining shares were held by individuals and institutions in India.

The company manufactured a wide range of products including agricultural products, chemicals and plastics, marine products, battery products, and special metals and .gases. It had five operating divisions. In addition, it owned majority interest in a joint venture—the Nepal Battery Company Limited.

UCIL was a well-respected company in India. It was considered a good business customer and a responsible and desirable employer. The company worked closely with local, state, and central government agencies to promote the government's family planning and other social programs. It thus developed strong contacts in the government. This excellent relationship with the government facilitated company-government interactions at many levels of operations. The company was easily able to get government permissions for dealing with a variety of operating issues. For example, the parent company was allowed to retain 51% of the stock in the Indian company, even after the revised Foreign Exchange Regulations Act (FERA) required foreign companies to hold less than 40% of a domestic (Indian) company's stock.[2] On another occasion, the company was able to get Bhopal government's objection to its site overruled by the state government.[3]

UCIL had 32.58 million outstanding shares. Of these, 16.58 million shares (50.89%) were held by Carbide Corporation, USA, the holding company. The company had issued and subscribed share capital of Rs.325.83 million and accumulated

reserves and surplus of Rs.293.89. In 1983, company revenues were Rs.2100 million [$1 US = rupees (Rs) 12.8 in 1984], excluding products used internally and valued at Rs.540 million. It reported profit before taxes of Rs.148 million, and profit after taxes and Investment Allowance Reserves of Rs.87 million. It declared a dividend of Rs.1.50 per share. Net worth per share was Rs.19.02, and earnings per share were Rs.2.86. The company employed over 10,000 people, of whom nearly 1,000 earned incomes of over Rs.3,000 per month, making the company one of the best-paying employers in India.[4]

UCIL Management and Organization

UCIL was managed by an 11-member board of directors, with Keshub Mahindra, a well-known industrialist, as chairman. The vice chairman was J. B. Law, who also served as the chairman of Union Carbide Eastern, Inc., Hong Kong. V. P. Gokhale served as the managing director (chief executive) of the company. He took this position on December 26, 1983 and was responsible for overall management of the company. A mechanical engineer by training, he had been with the company since 1959. Each of the five operating divisions were headed by a vice president reporting to the managing director. Each division was a profit center, organized internally on a functional basis.

Management of the Agricultural Products Division was characterized by frequent changes in top management. During the past 15 years, it had eight different division heads. Many of them came from nonchemical businesses of the company. Discontinuity in top management created frequent changes in internal systems and procedures and uncertainty for managers. Many of the more talented managers, particularly those trained in the United States for operating the MIC plant in 1980, had left the company by 1984.[5]

Operations

The company had 13 manufacturing facilities located in major Indian cities such as Bombay,

---

[2]City of death, *India Today,* December 31, 1984, p. 2.

[3]Ward Morehouse and Arun Subramanyam, *The Bhopal Tragedy.* New York: Council on International and Public Affairs, 1986, pp. 18, 32.

[4]Union Carbide Corporation and Union Carbide (India) Limited, annual reports, 1983, 1984.

[5]Personal interviews with the author.

Calcutta, Madras, Hyderabad, Bhopal, and Srinagar. Production technologies used in these facilities were modern and supplied by the parent corporation. For example, the Bhopal facility contained plants to manufacture methyl isocyanate and to formulate MIC-based pesticides. The company operated 20 sales offices and sold through a network of 3,000 dealers, who in turn sold to 249,000 retailers all over India. It had dominant market share in its main product (batteries) and was a significant competitor in other product lines, including pesticides, carbons, special metals, chemicals, and plastics. Differences in product lines, marketing philosophies, and operations made each division distinct and independent. For example, the Battery Division operated through a network of distributors and dealers and advertised intensively. The Agricultural Products Division sent distributors to geographic areas where customers (private farmers) were concentrated. Promotion involved programs for farmers aimed at educating them about the usefulness of pesticides.

INDUSTRIAL ENVIRONMENT IN BHOPAL AND INDIA

Bhopal is the capital of the state of Madhya Pradesh and the most centrally located city in India. It has a good agricultural and forest base and two large lakes that ensure a steady supply of water to the city. The government controls the most important segments of the local economy. It is the largest employer, the largest producer, and the largest consumer. More than 90% of India's productive industrial resources are controlled directly or indirectly by agencies of the city, state, and central (federal) governments. Virtually all service organizations are nationalized, including banks, insurance companies, postal and telephone systems, radio and television stations, energy production and distribution, railways, airlines, intercity bus service, medical services, and education.

Urbanization and industrialization in Bhopal were not integrated with rural development of hinterlands. Agricultural production in rural areas was stagnant, while the state's population grew at a rate of more than 2% per year. These conditions forced the rural unemployed to seek work in urban areas—turning Bhopal into a rapidly growing

urban area. Bhopal's population grew from 102,000 in 1961 to 385,000 in 1971, and to 670,000 in 1981—a growth rate almost three times the average for the state and for the nation as a whole.

Migrants from rural areas were hardly equipped to deal with the difficulties of urban life. In 1971, almost two-thirds of the migrants were unemployed. Of these, half had not completed high school and 20% were totally illiterate. Bhopal's rapidly rising population, coupled with high land and construction costs, caused a severe housing shortage in the city. Government efforts to build housing resulted, for the most part, in the construction of expensive dwellings. Unable to afford housing, many migrants became squatters, illegally occupying land and creating slums and shantytowns. Most of these slums cropped up around industrial plants and other employment centers. Slum dwellers served as a pool of cheap labor for industry, construction, offices, and households seeking domestic help. By 1984, Bhopal had 156 slum colonies, home for nearly 20% of the city's population. Two of them—Jaya Prakash Nagar and Kenchi Chola—were located across the street from Union Carbide's plant, even though the area was not zoned for residential use.

In 1974, UCIL was granted an industrial license by the central government to manufacture, rather than simply formulate, pesticides. By 1977, UCIL had begun producing more sophisticated and dangerous pesticides in which carbaryl was the active agent. Component chemicals such as methyl isocyanate were imported from the parent company in relatively small quantities. Within a short period of time, however, the pesticides market became very competitive. Fifty different formulations and more than 200 manufacturers came into existence to serve small, regional market niches. Increased competition forced manufacturers to cut costs, improve productivity, take advantage of economies of scale, and resort to "backward integration" (that is, not only formulate the final products but manufacture the raw materials and intermediate products as well).

While competitive pressures were mounting, widespread use of pesticides declined. Agricultural production peaked in 1979, declined severely in 1980, and then recovered mildly over the next three years. Weather conditions and harvests during 1982 and 1983 were poor, causing farmers to cut costs temporarily by abandoning the use of pesticides. As a result of reduced demand, the pesticides industry became even more competitive in the early 1980s. The expansion and underutilization of production capacity, coupled with a decline in agricultural production, further fueled competition.

During this period of industry decline, UCIL decided to backward integrate into the domestic manufacture of MIC. Until this time, MIC was imported in small drums and did not need to be stored in great quantities. In 1979, the company expanded its Bhopal factory to include facilities that manufactured five pesticide components, including MIC. Using this strategy, UCIL hoped to exploit economies of scale and save transportation costs. Manufacture of MIC required the establishment of a new hazardous plant and storage facility for MIC. More specifically, this arrangement required MIC to be stored in three large underground tanks with a capacity of about 60 tons each. This made the plant much more hazardous than it had been before.

Municipal authorities in Bhopal objected to the continued use of the UCIL plant at its original location. The city's development plan had earlier designated the plant site for commercial or light industrial use, but not for hazardous industries. With the addition of the MIC facility, this plant had clearly become a hazardous industry. However, at the behest of UCIL, the central and state government authorities overruled the city's objections and granted approval of the backward integration plan.

THE ACCIDENT AND ITS POSSIBLE CAUSE

At the core of any industrial crisis is a triggering event. In Bhopal, the triggering event was the leakage of a toxic gas, MIC, from storage tanks. Human, organizational, and technological failures in the plant paved the way for the crisis that ensued. The events leading to the accident are murky, which is not unusual when major accidents like the one in Bhopal occur. Moreover, the attributable causes of such accidents become highly contentious because of their impact in establishing culpability and payment of damages to the victims.

MIC is a highly toxic substance used for making carbaryl, the active agent in the pesticide

Sevin. It is also very unstable and needs to be kept at low temperatures. UCIL manufactured MIC in batches and stored it in three large underground tanks until it was needed for processing. Two of the tanks were used for MIC that had met specifications, while the third stored MIC that had not met specifications and needed reprocessing.

The Plant

A schematic layout of the storage tanks and various pipes and valves involved in the accident is shown in Figures 1 and 2. MIC was brought into storage tanks from the MIC refining still through a stainless steel pipe that branched off into each tank (see Figure 2). It was transferred out of storage by pressurizing a tank with high-purity nitrogen. Once out of storage, MIC passed through a safety valve to a relief-valve vent header, or pipe, common to all three tanks. This route led to the production reactor unit. Another common line took rejected MIC back to storage for reprocessing and contaminated MIC to the vent-gas scrubber for neutralizing. Excess nitrogen could be forced out of each tank through a process pipe that was regulated by a blow-down valve. Though they served different purposes, the relief-valve pipe and the process pipe were connected by another pipe, called the jumper system. This jumper system had been installed about a year before the accident to simplify maintenance.

Normal storage pressure, maintained with the aid of high-purity nitrogen, was 1 kilogram per square centimeter (kg/sq cm). Each storage tank was equipped with separate gauges to indicate temperature and pressure, one local and the other inside a remote control-room. Each tank also had a high-temperature alarm, a level indicator, and high- and low-level alarms.

The safety valve through which MIC passed on its way to the Sevin plant operated in conjunction with a mediating graphite rupture disk, which functioned like a pressure cooker—holding the gas in until it reached a certain pressure, then letting it out. The rupture disk could not be monitored from a remote location. Checking it required frequent manual inspection of a pressure indicator located between the disk and the safety valve.

The plant had several safety features. The vent-gas scrubber was a safety device designed to

Figure 1. *Schematic Layout of Common Headers of MIC Storage Tanks*

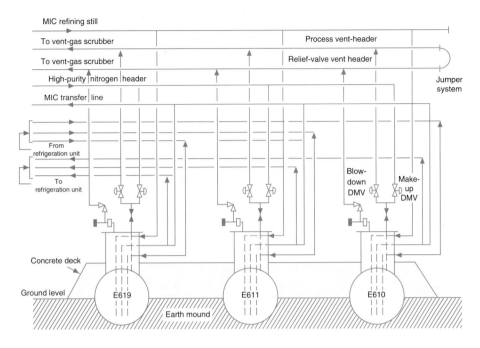

Source: Union Carbide (India) Ltd., *Operating Manual Part II: Methyl Isocyanate Unit* (Bhopal: Union Carbide (India) Ltd., February 1979).

Figure 2. *MIC Storage Tank*

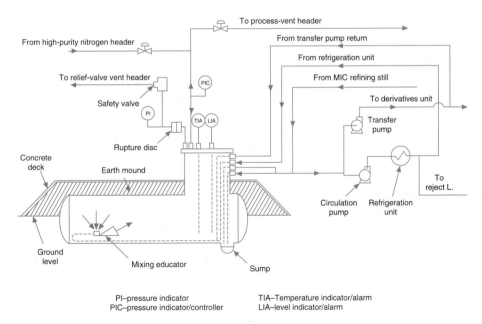

PI–pressure indicator
PIC–pressure indicator/controller
TIA–Temperature indicator/alarm
LIA–level indicator/alarm

Source: Bhopal Methyl Isocyanate Incident Investigation, Team Report (Danbury, Conn.: Union Carbide Corporation, March 1985).

neutralize toxic exhausts from the MIC plant and storage system. Gases leaving the tank were routed to this scrubber, where they were scrubbed with a caustic soda solution and released into the atmosphere at a height of 100 feet or routed to a flare. The gases could also be routed directly to the flare without going through the scrubber. The flare tower was used for burning normally vented gases from the MIC section and other units in the plant. Burning would detoxify the gases before venting them into the atmosphere. However, the flare was not designed to handle large quantities of MIC vapors. A few weeks before the accident, the scrubber was turned off to a standby position.

Two additional features of the plant were relevant for safety. The first was a refrigeration system, used to keep MIC at low temperatures, particulary in the summer when the ambient air could reach temperatures as high as 120°F. However, the refrigeration system was shut down in June of 1984, and its coolant was drained for use in another part of the plant, thus making it impossible to switch on the refrigeration system during an emergency. The second important feature was a set of water-spray pipes that could be used to control escaping gases, overheated equipment, or fires.

A Chronology of Events

The last batch of MIC manufactured before the accident was produced between October 7 and October 22, 1984. At the end of the manufacturing cycle, one storage tank, called tank E610, contained about 42 tons of MIC, while the second tank, E611, contained about 20 tons. After the MIC production unit was shut down, parts of the plant were dismantled for maintenance. The flare tower was shut down so that a piece of corroded pipe could be replaced. On October 21, nitrogen pressure in tank E610 dropped from 1.25 kg/sq cm, which was about normal, to only 0.25 kg/sq cm. Because the first storage tank lacked sufficient pressure, any MIC needed in the manufacturing process was drawn from the other tank—E611. But on November 30, tank E611 also failed to pressurize because of a defective valve. Plant operators attempted to pressurize tank E610 but failed, so they temporarily abandoned it and, instead, repaired the pressure system in tank E611.

In the normal course of operation, water and MIC react with each other in small quantities in the plant's pipes, creating a plastic substance called trimer. Periodically, the pipes were washed with water to flush out all the trimer that had built up on pipe walls. Because the mixture of water and MIC was so volatile, the pipes were normally blocked off with a physical barrier, known as a slip blind, to prevent the water from going into the storage tank.

On the evening of December 2, the second-shift production superintendent ordered the MIC plant supervisor to flush out several pipes that led from the phosgene system through the MIC storage tanks to the scrubber. Although MIC unit operators were in charge of the flushing operation, insertion of the slip blind was the responsibility of the maintenance supervisor, a position that had been eliminated several days earlier, and no worker had yet been given responsibility for inserting the slip blind. The flushing operation began at 9:30 PM. Because several bleeder lines, or overflow devices, downstream from the flushing were clogged, water began to accumulate in the pipes. Many of the valves in the plant were leaking, including one that was used to isolate the lines being flushed, so water rose past that valve and into the relief-valve pipe. When the operator noticed that no water was coming out of the bleeder lines, he shut off the flow, but the MIC plant supervisor ordered him to resume the process. The relief-valve pipe was about 20 feet off the ground, causing the water to flow downhill toward tank E610. First it flowed through the jumper system to the process pipe. From that pipe, which is normally open, the water flowed to the blow-down valve, which should have been closed. However, the blow-down valve is part of the system used to pressurize the tank with nitrogen—the same tank whose pressurization system had not been working for weeks. It is possible that this valve had been inadvertently left open or was not sealed properly.

With the blow-down valve open, about 1,100 pounds of water flowed through another isolation valve, normally left open, and entered tank E610, where it began to react with the MIC being stored there. At 10:45 PM, a change of shift took place. At 11 PM, Suman Dey, the new control-room operator, noticed that the pressure in tank E610 was 10 pounds per square inch (psi), well within the operating range of 2 to 25 psi. One-half hour later, however, a field operator noticed a leak of MIC near the scrubber. Workers inspected the MIC structure and found MIC and dirty water coming out of a branch of the relief-valve pipe, on the downstream side of the safety valve. They also found that another safety valve, called the process-safety valve, had been removed, and the open end of the relief-valve pipe had not been sealed for flushing. They informed the control room about this. By 12:15 AM, Dey saw that the pressure in tank E610 had risen to between 25 and 30 psi and was still rising. Within 15 minutes, it showed a reading beyond 55, which was the top of the scale.

Dey ran to the tank. He heard a hissing sound from the safety valve downstream, indicating that it had popped. Local temperature and pressure gauges showed values beyond their maximums of 25°C (77°F) and 55 psi. Dey heard loud rumbling and screeching noises from the tank and felt heat radiating from it. He went back to the control room and tried to switch on the scrubber, which had been in a standby mode since the last MIC manufacturing run. But Dey's instruments indicated that the caustic soda, the neutralizing agent used in the scrubbers, was not circulating within the scrubber. In the meantime, field operators saw a cloud of gas gushing out of the stack.

Supervisors notified the plant superintendent, who arrived immediately, suspended operation of the MIC plant, and turned on the toxic-gas alarm to warn the community around the plant. A few minutes later the alarm was turned off, leaving only the in-plant siren to warn workers inside the plant. Operators turned on the firewater sprayers to douse the stack, the tank mound, and the relief-valve pipe to the scrubber. Because of low water pressure, the water spray did not reach the gases, which were being emitted at a height of 30 meters. The supervisors tried to turn on the refrigeration system to cool the tanks, but since the coolant from the system was drained, the refrigerator could not work. The safety valve remained open for two hours. A mixture of gases, foam, and liquid escaped at a temperature in excess of 200°C (close to 400°F) and a pressure of 180 psi.

Because the plant was so close to the slums, many thousands of people were affected by exposure to this lethal mixture. Nearly 3,000 people died, although the exact number would never be

fully determined. A few months after the accident, the Indian government officially put the death toll at 1,754. But various sources suggest a wide range of higher figures, and the best conclusion one can draw is that the death toll was probably close to 3,000. Thousands more were harmed in some way, many of whom experience illnesses that linger to this day. More than 2,000 animals were killed, and environmental damage was considerable. Bhopal was not equipped to handle an accident of this magnitude. Hospitals and dispensaries could not accommodate the flow of injured victims; likewise, government officials and registered mortuaries could not keep up with the certification and burial of the dead.

There were many reasons for discrepancies in death toll figures. There was no systematic method to certify and accurately count the dead as they were discovered or brought to government hospitals and cremation or burial grounds. For the first three days after the accident, all available medical personnel were engaged in caring for the injured. Few people were left to care for the dead, register them, perform inquests and autopsies, issue death certificates, or arrange for systematic disposal of bodies.

Dead bodies piled up, one on top of another, in the only city morgue and in temporary tents set up outside of it. Many bodies were released to relatives for disposal without death certificates. Bodies were buried or cremated at unregistered facilities. Graves and funeral pyres registered as single burial units were made to accommodate many corpses because of worker and material shortages. Many people ran from Bhopal and died on roads outside the city and were buried or cremated by the roadside.

THE LONG-TERM HEALTH EFFECTS

The long-term health consequences of exposure to MIC and other toxic gases remain largey unknown and are the subject of considerable controversy in scientific and medical circles. They are likely to be far more serious than originally anticipated.

The most serious permanent damage among the injured was in the respiratory tract. Many victims died of edema (fluid in the lungs). MIC also damaged mucus membranes, perforated lung tissue, inflamed lungs, and caused secondary lung infections. Many survivors could not be employed because they suffered from bronchitis, pneumonia, asthma, and fibrosis and were physically unable to work. Long-term epidemiological studies have been hampered by unwillingness of various government agencies in charge of medical studies to share their data with outsiders. It was expected that this data would be produced in courts as medicolegal evidence. However, even four years after the accident, no comprehensive study of health effects of the disaster was available.

ECONOMIC AND SOCIAL DISRUPTION

The accident did tremendous damage to the local economic and social structures. In addition to the shutdown of the UCIL plant, two mass evacuations—the first at the time of the accident, the second during a fear-ridden "scare" two weeks later—led to the closure of factories, shops, commercial establishments, business and government offices, and schools and colleges. These closures, and labor scarcity resulting from death and injury, disrupted essential services and civil supplies. Establishments that remained open had few employees and few clients.

Estimates of business losses ranged from $8 million to $65 million. The closure of the Union Carbide plant alone eliminated 650 permanent jobs and approximately the same number of temporary jobs—jobs that were particularly important to the local economy because Union Carbide paid high wages. The plant shutdown also dismantled a $25 million investment in the city, which had provided secondary employment to about 1,500 persons. State and local governments lost untold thousands of dollars in taxes. The city, the nation, and the entire developing world suffered a loss of business potential because the accident damaged Union Carbide's business image.

To make matters worse, relief efforts following the accident distorted prices and the availability of goods. At one point, almost 50% of the city's population was receiving free grain from the government. This caused grain prices to decline and labor prices to increase abnormally.

ENVIRONMENTAL CONSEQUENCES

Damage to plant and animal life, while equally devastating, was not studied systematically because most available resources were deployed for mitigat-

ing human losses. Animal deaths probably exceeded 2,000 and included cows, buffaloes, goats, dogs, cats, and birds, although official government records put the figure at only 1,047. About 7,000 animals were given therapeutic care. Postmortems on farm animals suggested the possible presence of an undetected toxin, lending credence to the view that cyanide poisoning was involved. MIC exposure destroyed standing vegetation in surrounding areas. Of 48 plant species examined after the accident, 35 were affected to some degree, and 13 appeared free from damage.

LEGAL PROCEEDINGS

On hearing about the accident, Union Carbide called an emergency meeting of its top executives to develop a crisis management plan. It rushed some medical supplies and teams to Bhopal. Chairman Warren Anderson himself rushed to Bhopal to oversee relief and help to victims. Upon arrival, he was immediately arrested by the local police and confined at the Union Carbide Guest House. After a few hours and the intervention of the central government, he was released and flown to New Delhi. He returned to the United States without making any headway on the relief mission. On the contrary, his visit and arrest served to create the ferociously adversarial mood that governed the subsequent relations between the company and the government of India.

Government agencies mounted a massive relief and rehabilitation effort to deal with the disaster. However, given their limited resources and the vast magnitude of the accident, they were barely able to give first aid treatment to victims. The government made interim relief payments of $80 to $800 to help victims tide over their immediate financial needs. Once the immediate crisis subsided, however, relief efforts lost their intensity. Since then, government agencies have been criticized in the local press for their indifference and insensitivity to the plight of victims.

CONSEQUENCES FOR UNION CARBIDE

The accident threatened Union Carbide's very survival. In its aftermath, the company was subject to worldwide humiliation. The day after the accident, the Bhopal plant was shut down and local managers were arrested on criminal charges. When Union Carbide's chairman, Warren Anderson, and UCIL's top management rushed to Bhopal, they too were arrested. The company's reputation came under intense attack by the news media worldwide.

The Bhopal accident triggered a series of sanctions and protests against Union Carbide all over the world. Public interest and activist groups initiated a variety of grass-roots campaigns against the company. In Breziers, France, where Union Carbide used MIC made in the United States to make pesticides, the local community objected to reopening the plant after it was shut down following the Bhopal accident. In Rio de Janeiro, Brazil, the state government decreed that MIC could not be produced, stored, or transported within the state. In Scotland, despite a local unemployment rate of 26%, the city of Livingston rejected Union Carbide's proposal to set up a plant to manufacture toxic gases.

During this period of scrutiny and backlash, several accidents occurred at Union Carbide in US plants and deepened the company's crisis. On March 28, 1985, the chemical mesityl oxide leaked from the Institute, West Virginia, plant, sickening eight people in a nearby shopping mall. Then, on August 11, 1985, another chemical, aldicarb oxyme, leaked from a storage tank at the same plant, injuring 135 people, 31 of whom were admitted to local hospitals. Two days later, another leak occurred at a sister plant in Charleston, West Virginia. Although no one was injured, the leak was highly publicized and spawned further investigations into company operations. Investigations also revealed that 28 major MIC gas leaks had occurred at the Institute, West Virginia, plant during the five years preceding the Bhopal accident. One of them occurred just a month before the Bhopal leak, releasing 14,000 pounds of an MIC/chloroform mixture into the atmosphere.

LEGAL CONSEQUENCES

Soon after the accident, lawyers from the United States arrived in Bhopal, formed partnerships with Indian lawyers, and started arranging to represent victims in multimillion-dollar personal injury lawsuits against Union Carbide. The chronological development of the legal ramifications of the accident is shown in Table 4. Union Carbide was not the only party taken to court.

Many victims also sued the government of India, charging it with negligence in allowing the disaster to occur. Some lawsuits pointed out the delays, incompetence, and corruption involved in relief efforts. Others argued that government was partly responsible because it had allowed Union Carbide to locate and operate the hazardous facility, and because it had legalized the slums around the plant early in 1984. Critics faulted the government for failing to act on the recommendation of its own Labor Department, which had urged a safety investigation at the plant, and for failing to prepare for the possibility of an emergency at the plant.

In March 1985, the Indian government passed a law conferring on itself sweeping powers to represent victims in the lawsuit and to manage all aspects of registering and processing legal claims. The following month it filed a lawsuit in the United States, charging Union Carbide with liability in the deaths of 1,700 persons, the personal injury of 200,000 more persons, and property damages.

Union Carbide Corporation developed a multilayered defense strategy. First, it argued that the suits should be dismissed from US courts because the accident happened in India, victims were mostly Indians, and most material evidence and witnesses were in India. It also suggested that Indian law and compensation standards should be applied in determining victim compensation in this case. The government of India countered this argument, saying that US courts were an appropriate forum for the case because the parent company was a US corporation. This claim was supported by private victim lawyers, who were interested in keeping the case in the United States where they could legally represent victims. The battle over the correct forum for trial of cases extended over several months. During this time, Carbide began negotiating an out-of-court settlement of the case with the government of India and the private lawyers. The government of India had bestowed on itself all rights to represent the victims. It did not accept the role of private lawyers in the case. These lawyers had also lost legitimacy in the eyes of the victims and the world media because of the insensitive way they had descended upon Bhopal to sign up clients after the accident. They had obtained clients by running newspaper advertisements with affidavit forms attached, which the

Table 4 *Developments in Lawsuits Against Union Carbide*

December 1984 and January 1985	Over 45 suits filed against Carbide in various state and federal courts; 482 personal injury suits filed against UCIL in Bhopal; a $1 billion representative suit filed in Bhopal against UCIL and UCC; a suit in India's Supreme Court against UCIL and the government of India and Madhya Pradesh. Federal suits against UCC consolidated for pretrial proceedings in the Federal Court of the Southern District of New York under Judge J. F. K. Keenan.
March-April 1985	The Bhopal Gas Leak Disaster (Processing of Claims) Ordinance, 1985 passed by Indian Parliament conferring on the government of India powers to secure claims arising out of the disaster. Government of India files parens patriae action against UCC.
May 1985	UCC offers $5 million for relief, to be deducted from payment of final settlement. It attaches stringent accounting requirements and demands detailed information on victims' health.
July 1985	UCC moves to dismiss cases against it on forum non conveniens grounds.
Through 1985	Out-of-court negotiations
March 1986	Union Carbide and private victim lawyers reach a tentative settlement of $350 million for compensation. Government of India is not party to this settlement and rejects it as absurdly low.
May 1986	Judge Keenan rules on the forum issue sending the case to be tried in Indian courts.
August 1986	Government of India refiles case in Bhopal District Court.
April 1987	Judge Deo of the Bhopal Court revives the attempt to bring about a settlement.
December 1987	Bhopal Court orders UCC to pay to victims $270 million in interim payment. UCC appeals.
April 1988	Madhya Pradesh High Court upholds the Bhopal Court ruling, but reduces amount to $190 million.
February 14, 1989	Supreme Court of India orders a settlement of the case whereby Union Carbide agrees to pay $470 million as full and final settlement of all claims arising out of the accident and subsequent litigation. The court also dismisses all criminal and civil charges then pending in India against the company and its executives.

victims could fill out and mail back to the lawyers' respective offices. Some of them never even met their clients or discussed with them the nature or extent of the damages. Their main interest was in the extremely lucrative attorney fees that were likely to result from the case if it were decided in an American court.

Judge J. F. K. Keenan, the presiding judge in this case, attempted to balance the power of the opposing parties in order to keep them negotiating, but was not very successful. For example, in April 1985, the court ordered Union Carbide to pay immediately $5 million for interim relief, deductible from the final settlement amount. But the government of India refused to accept the money, saying the corporation had imposed "onerous conditions" on its use. The court was unable to give away the money for seven months because the litigants could not agree on a plan for using it. This delay was embarrassing for all parties because, all the while, media reports detailed the woefully inadequate relief being provided to the victims.

Initial negotiations led to Union Carbide's offer in August 1985 of about $200 million to be paid out over 30 years for a total and final settlement of the case. The government rejected the offer without explanation. Two detailed estimates of damage made public in 1985 suggested that the compensation to the victims should range from $1 billion to $2 billion.

In late March 1986, *The New York Times* reported that a tentative settlement of $350 million had been reached between Union Carbide and the private lawyers. The lawyers had a strong economic motive for settling the case early, because if the case was moved to India, they would loose all their fees, which amounted to millions of dollars. But the Indian government's attorneys had not been involved in the negotiations, and they once again rejected the offer as absurdly low. Indeed, even if the agreement were sanctioned by the court, it would be virtually impossible to implement without the cooperation of the government, which was the only party with access to the information and administrative procedures needed to distribute the compensation money fairly.

In May 1986, Judge Keenan ruled on the forum issue, deciding to send the case to India for trial. In so doing, he imposed three conditions on Union Carbide. First, the corporation had to submit itself to the jurisdiction of Indian courts. Second, Carbide had to agree to satisfy any judgments rendered by Indian courts through due process. And third, the company had to agree to submit to discovery under the US law, which allowed more exploration of company-held information than Indian laws did. This last condition was appealed by Union Carbide, which requested the court to make discovery under US law a reciprocal condition and impose it on the government of India, too.

Union Carbide's second line of defense was to argue that it was not legally liable for the accident. It said that the parent company was not responsible for the accident, because the plant in which it occurred was designed, constructed, owned, and operated by the Indian company Union Carbide (India) Ltd. It argued that the parent company had no control over its Indian subsidiary in matters of day-to-day operations. It suggested that the "corporate veil" between parent and subsidiary prevent it (the parent) from controlling the causes of the accident. Thus, it blamed the accident on the Indian company, which had total assets of only about $80 million. The government of India argued against this position on the basis of Union Carbide's 51% ownership of its subsidiary, and on the legal doctrine of strict liability. This doctrine says that as long as the source of damage or injury originates within a facility owned by a company, the company is strictly liable for the damages, regardless of whose fault led to the accident. The acceptability and applicability of this doctrine was contested by Union Carbide.

Finally, the company argued that the accident was caused by sabotage. It said that a disgruntled employee had deliberately poured a large quantity of water into the MIC tank to cause the runaway reaction. However, it did not provide the identity of the saboteur. It argued that since the parent company was not in control of the day-to-day operations of the Indian subsidiary, it should not be held liable for the accident. This issue was being debated in courts in India even four years after the accident.

DRIVE TOWARD A SETTLEMENT: THE UNSETTLED FATE OF VICTIMS

As the case moved slowly through the court system in the United States, and then in India, the pressure on both parties to reach an out-of-court settlement increased. The government of India wanted a settlement to prevent political backlash from the dissatisfied victims. UCC wanted a settlement to shake off the legal liability and protect its assets. The differences in their motives and objectives, and the backlash from the lawsuits, kept them from reaching a settlement even four years after the accident.

The board of directors of Union Carbide decided to sell assets of the company and distribute to shareholders the net pretax sale proceeds above the net book value of the businesses. In 1985, the company divested about $2 billion worth of assets. In early 1986, it sold its battery division to Ralston Purina for $1.42 billion and announced intentions of selling its home and automative products division for $800 million. It later sold its corporate headquarters building for $345 million and its agricultural chemicals business for $575 million.

These divestitures alarmed the Indian government. It asked the Bhopal court to bar the company from stripping assets, paying dividends, or buying back debt until a review ensured that these activities would not disadvantage the victims. The company was able to have the injunction lifted by agreeing to maintain at least $3 billion in assets, which could be used to settle the Bhopal claims.

In the Bhopal District Court, the Indian government had demanded $3 billion as compensation for damages. In April 1987, the district judge, M. W. Deo, suggested that the company make an interim relief payment of $4.6 million and urged the litigants to reach an agreement on the final amount of the settlement. In August 1987, the company agreed to distribute the $4.6 million interim aid and a few months later offered about $500 million as a final settlement amount. This money was to be paid over a 30-year period. The net present value of this amount was not different from the earlier offer made by the company. The offer was rejected by the government.

Frustrated by the unyielding positions of both sides and the increasing complexity of the litigation, Judge Deo ordered Union Carbide to pay $270 million as interim aid to victims in December 1987. This money was to be placed with the commissioner of claims named by the Indian govern-

ment. He suggested that this amount be distributed to victims as follows: $15,500 per death, $8,000 per severe injury, and lesser amounts for remaining victims.

Union Carbide appealed this interim payment on the grounds that it amounted to "a judgment and decree without trial." The issue was moved up to the High Court in Jabalpur. The High Court Judge S. K. Seth in April 1988 upheld the order of the lower court but reduced the interim relief amount from $270 to $190 million. He also said that it was not necessary to hold a trial to determine damages to thousands of victims. He suggested that $7,800 should be paid to families of those killed or injured seriously, $3,900 be paid to those injured less seriously, and $1,050 to those with minor injuries.

One problem with implementing this order was the incomplete medicolegal documentation for determining which victims were injured seriously, less seriously, and in a minor way. A more serious problem, as previously stated, was that Union Carbide refused to pay.

Unfortunately for the victims, even the Indian Supreme Court may not be the final arbiter of this case. Even after the Supreme Court rules on it, the judgment must be implemented in the United States. There is the possibility of the case being appealed in the United States. Even four years after the accident, the compensation issue was no closer to being resolved in the legal system. In the meantime, the victims who are poor and unable to work because of their medical conditions continue to die of their ailments and malnourishment.

In light of the agonizing plight of the victims, the issue of who is responsible becomes a crass legalistic exercise. Union Carbide argues that the accident was caused by sabotage by a disgruntled employee. But it refuses to reveal the identity of the saboteur. It also claims that despite its 51% ownership of the Indian subsidiary, it did not control the Indian operation. Hence, it should not be held legally liable for damages. The Indian government argues that since the accident occurred at the company's premises, the company is liable for all damages accruing out of it. There are few legal doctrines and legal precedents available to decide a case as complex as this one. Legal experts estimate that the case could continue in courts for many more years. Settling the case out of court is the legal, moral, and ethical challenge facing the company and the Indian government.

BIBLIOGRAPHY

Abraham, Martin. *The Lessons of Bhopal: A Community Action Resource Manual on Hazardous Technologies.* International Organization of Consumer Unions (IOCO), September 1985.

Alder, Steven J. Carbide plays hardball. *The American Lawyer,* November 1985.

Bang, Rani, and Mira Sadgopal. *Effects of the Bhopal Disaster on Women's Health.* Study Report. SEWA, Bhopal, February 1985.

Bivens, Terry. Union Carbide expected to pay out $500 million. *The Journal of Commerce,* December 13, 1984.

Boffey, Phillip. Bhopal's doctors given high praise. *New York Times,* December 18, 1984.

—————. Few lasting health effects found among Indian gas-leak survivors. *New York Times,* December 20, 1984.

De Grazia, Alfred. *A Cloud Over Bhopal.* The Kalos Foundation, Bombay, 1985.

Diamond, Stuart. The Bhopal disaster (4-article series). *New York Times,* January 28, 29, 30, and February 3, 1985.

Everest, Larry. *Behind The Poison Cloud—Union Carbide's Bhopal Massacre."* Chicago: Banner Press, 1986.

GOMP (Government of Madhya Pradesh) Treatment Arrangements Made for the Affected Cases of the Poisonous Gas That Leaked Out From the Union Carbide Factory on December 2-3, 1984. Internal memo prepared by the Directorade of Health Services, Bhopal, December 1984.

Kurzman, Dan. *A Killing Wind: Inside Union Carbide and the Bhopal Catastrophe.* New York: McGraw-Hill Book Co., 1987.

McFadden, Robert D. India disaster: chronicle of a nightmare. *New York Times,* December 10, 1984, pp. A1–A6.

Report on Scientific Studies on the Factors Related to Bhopal Toxic Gas Leakage. Report Results from Studies, December 1985.

Rogers, W. P. *Report to the President by the Presidential Commission on the Space Shuttle Challenger.* Washington, D.C., 1986.

Shrivastava, Paul. *Bhopal: Anatomy of a Crisis.* Cambridge, Mass: Ballinger Publishing Company, 1987.

Suffering, Sidney C. *Bhopal: Its Setting, Responsibility and Challenge.* New Delhi: Ajanta, 1985.

Union Carbide Corporation. *Operational Safety Survey, CO/MIC/SEVIN Units, Union Carbide India Ltd., Bhopal Plant.* South Charleston, WV, 1982.

Union Carbide (I) Ltd. *Action Plan-Operational Safety Survey, May 1982.* Bhopal, India, October 5, 1982, and June 7, 1983.

Union Carbide Corporation and Union Carbide (I) Limited, annual reports, 1980 to 1985.

Varadaragan, S., et al. *Report on Scientific Studies on Factors Related to Bhopal Toxic Gas Leakage.* New Dehli Council—Scientific and Industrial Research, December 1985.

Weir, David. *The Bhopal Syndrome: Pesticides, Government, and Health.* San Francisco: Sierra Club Books, 1987.

Weisman, Steven. Medical problems continue in Bhopal. *New York Times,* March 31, 1985.

—————. Doctors in India disagree on drug. *New York Times,* April 10, 1985.

CASE
28

YKK ZIPPERS

Hideo Ishida
Hitotsubashi University

YKK—Yoshida Kogyo K. K. (meaning Yoshida Industries, Ltd.)—was the biggest manufacturer of zippers in the world and Japan's leading producer of aluminum sashes. Around 1960, YKK opened its first overseas plant, and as of April 1974 its 27 overseas subsidiary plants turned out zippers in 22 countries, employing more than 3,700 foreign employees and with some 140 Japanese on overseas assignment. Reflecting the management philosophy of Tadao Yoshida, founder and president of the company, management of YKK overseas subsidiaries was quite unique, particularly in the field of personnel policies and practices.

COMPANY BACKGROUND

YKK's main products were metal and plastic zippers and building materials such as aluminum sashes; of its 1973 sales of about Y100 billion, aluminum building materials accounted for Y60 billion and zippers Y40 billion. [Y=yen.] The company's zippers held more than 90 percent of the domestic market, and combined with exports and overseas production of Y32 billion, they accounted for a quarter of the world market. Exhibit 1 shows the company's sales growth since 1965.

YKK, based in Tokyo and with a total capital stock of Y5.6 billion, had five plants in Japan; its two main plants—Ikuji and Kurobe plants—were located in Toyama Prefecture facing to the Japan Sea. It employed about 11,000 workers, 45 percent of whom were women.

The origin of YKK went back to San-S Company, which was established by Tadao Yoshida in 1934 in Nihonbashi, Tokyo. After a zipper plant with 100 workers during its peak years had been burnt down in an air raid, Yoshida established Yoshida Kogyo K. K. in 1945 in his native town Uozu in Toyama Prefecture and started again to produce zippers. In 1950, YKK imported from the United States new machinery that automatically put zipper teeth on tapes. This investment enabled the company to hold an overwhelming position in the domestic market and since then the company paid unceasing interest to the development of its own technology.

In the late 1950s, YKK completed the construction of the large-scale Ikuji plant in Kurobe City, Toyama Prefecture, and starting with plant exports to India, undertook construction of overseas plants. Up to the early 1960s, YKK's overseas plants were only in the countries of Southeast Asia, Oceania, and South America. Then in 1964 it started zipper production in advanced industrial countries with the opening of a plant in New York and one in the Netherlands. Currently the company has 11 plants in the United States, and on the other side of the Atlantic it has plants in the Netherlands, Britain, France, West Germany, Italy, Spain, and Belgium. The list of YKK's overseas subsidiaries is shown in Exhibit 2.

Two factors made YKK's production system uniquely integrated as a zipper manufacturer: its continuous production methods from processing of raw materials—aluminum and copper alloys in one hand and spinning, weaving, and dyeing of raw cotton on the other—to assembling of various components into finished products, and its machine

Exhibit 1 YKK (Yoshida Kogyo K.K.)—Growth of Sales, 1965–1974

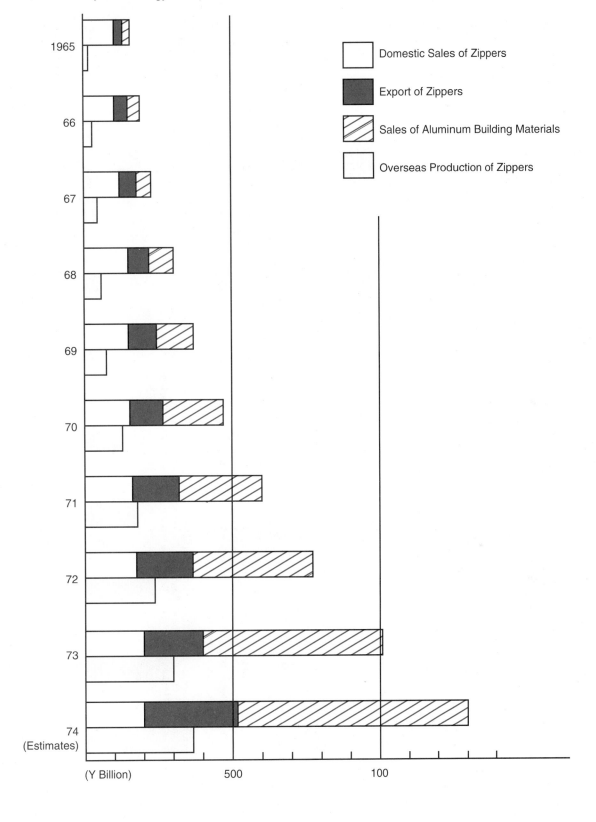

Exhibit 2 *YKK (Yoshida Kogyo K.K.)—Overseas Subsidiaries (as of April 1974)*

Company	Country	Location of Main Office	Established in	Type of Ownership	Number of Establishments	Type of Establishments	Number of Employees		
							Local Nationals	YKK Expatriate	Total
YKK Zipper (USA) Inc.	United States	New Jersey	Aug. 1960	Fully Owned	15	Office, Plant	190	32	222
Union Yoshida Industries Corp., Ltd.	Thailand	Bangkok	Apr. 1962	Joint Venture	1	Office, Plant	672	3	675
Malayan Zips Sdn., Bhd.	Malaysia	Johore Bahru	Jun. 1963	Joint Venture	2	Office, Plant	181	3	184
Slidefast (NZ) Ltd.	New Zealand	Auckland	Dec. 1963	Joint Venture	1	Office, Plant	51	0	51
Yoshida De Costa Rica Ltda.	Costa Rica	San Jose	Dec. 1963	Joint Venture	1	Office, Plant	181	2	183
Yoshida (Nederland) B. V.	Holland	Sneek	May 1964	Fully Owned	3	Office, Plant	76	4	80
YKK Zipper (WI) Ltd.	Trinidad	Port of Spain	Apr. 1965	Joint Venture	1	Office, Plant	83	1	84
Taiwan Zipper Co., Ltd.	Taiwan	Chung Li	May 1965	Joint Venture	2	Office, Plant	925	5	930
YKK Zipper Co. (Hong Kong) Ltd.	Hong Kong	Kowloon	Sep. 1966	Fully Owned	2	Office, Plant	175	7	182
YKK Fasteners (UK) Ltd.	England	London	Mar. 1967	Fully Owned	3	Office, Plant	180	12	192
Yoshida (France) S. A. R. L.	France	Paris	Dec. 1967	Fully Owned	5	Office, Plant	77	10	87
Yoshida (Deutschland) G. m. b. H.	West Germany	Monchengladbach	Dec. 1967	Fully Owned	7	Office, Plant	68	12	80
YKK Zipper Co. (Canada) Ltd.	Canada	Montreal	Jun. 1968	Fully Owned	4	Office, Plant	64	10	74
YKK Australia Pty., Ltd.	Australia	Sydney	Jun. 1968	Joint Venture	2	Office, Plant	56	3	59
Yoshida De El Salvador	El Salvador	San Salvador	Dec. 1968	Joint Venture	1	Office, Plant	135	2	137
Yoshida-Fossanese S. p. A.	Italy	Vercelli	Jan. 1969	Joint Venture	6	Office, Plant	99	8	107
YKK Zipper (S'pore) Private Ltd.	Singapore	Juron	Dec. 1969	Joint Venture	1	Office, Plant	88	2	90
Yoshida Espanola S. A.	Spain	Barcelona	Feb. 1971	Joint Venture	3	Office, Plant	18	4	22
N. V. Yoshida (Belgium) S. A.	Belgium	Gent	Apr. 1971	Joint Venture	1	Office, Plant	9	1	10
YKK Zipper (Middle East) S. A. L.	Lebanon	Beirut	Aug. 1971	Joint Venture	1	Office, Plant	5	2	7
YKK Indonesia Zipper Co., Ltd.	Indonesia	Djakarta	Jan. 1972	Joint Venture	1	Office, Plant	155	3	158
YKK-Belding, Inc.	United States	Atlanta	May 1972	Joint Venture	3	Office	6	1	77
YKK Industries (USA) Inc.	United States	Macon	Jan. 1973	Fully Owned	1	Plant	155	11	166
Hong Kong Ing Kwok Investments	Hong Kong	Hong Kong	Apr. 1973	Fully Owned	1	Office	2	1	3
YKK Export, Inc.	United States	New Jersey	May 1973	Fully Owned	1	Office	4	1	5
Hong Kong Ing Kwok Industrial Co., Ltd.	Hong Kong	Hong Kong	Sep. 1973	Fully Owned	1	Plant	53	2	55
Yoshida Brasileira Industria e Commercio LTDA.	Brazil	Sao Paulo	Apr. 1974	Fully Owned	1	Office, Plant			
					(71)		(3,711)	(142)	(3,853)

In addition to the above overseas subsidiaries, YKK had technical assistance arrangements with the following seven companies in five countries: Korea Zipper Co., Ltd. (Korea, Seoul), Union Fastener Corporation (Pty.) Ltd. (South Africa, Johannesburg), Ecuadorian Agency For Foreign Firms (Ecuador, Guayaquil), Satco, Inc. (Philippines, Quezon), United Fastener Corporation (Philippines, Quezon), Pagasa Industrial Corporation (Philippines, Quezon), Manufacture Bao Ly (Combodge, Phonom-penh).

shop in Kurobe with 1,200 engineers and mechanics and about 1,700 machine tools, which developed and produced almost all machinery used in the company's production facilities, including its overseas plants. It was said that the machine shop turned out 15,000 zipper and zipper parts machines every year.

INTERVIEW WITH PRESIDENT YOSHIDA

After finishing the course of a senior primary school and helping his eldest brother's small shop in his native town, Tadao Yoshida went to Tokyo, where he found a job as a clerk of chinaware dealer and was sent to Shanghai for purchasing porcelain. When Yoshida started his own business in 1934 at the age of 25, he had only two employees: Kiichi Yoshikawa and Toshio Takahashi, currently executive vice presidents of YKK. Hisamatsu Yoshida, elder brother of president Yoshida, works for the company as senior executive vice president. President Yoshida spends the first half of a month in the Tokyo head office and the second half in the factory in Toyama. In February 1974, the case writer had an interview with Yoshida.

Case writer: I should like to know what the underlying principle of the management of YKK.

President: My business philosophy is based on the concept of the "cycle of goodness." Since my boyhood, I was very fond of reading biographies of great men and when I read a biography of Andrew Carnegie, I was deeply inspired by his "unless you render profit or goodness to others you cannot prosper." I was deeply impressed and inspired. At the same time I wondered if and how I could do as he had said. Gradually I came to believe that it is not good to make money without working so hard as to sweat and that to buy things other people made when their prices fall down and sell them over to others when their prices go up is nothing but a rake-off. What is important is to make things by yourself. What is the most precious in man, I believe, is the ability to create something tangible out of nothing. By means of creativeness, man can make his life richer and can gain lots of profits. Now suppose that we succeed in reducing the cost of a certain product to Y50 while other companies make the same product for Y100. Then, we will return two-thirds of the balance or the cost saved to consumers and related industries, and we will

retain the remaining one-third to ourselves, which we will use as much as possible for future investments. This is my idea of profits. Savings make the difference between human beings and animals. Inventiveness and savings are the two indispensable wheels for human progress. I would dare say that those people who made money without toiling but just through rising prices in a concerted way, as you have seen recently, are committing a sin against society. Some people are said to have earned as much as Y100 million by merely buying and selling stocks of the companies for which they are not working. In my view point, this is a result of one of the shortcomings of capitalism. As I cannot favor speculative mentality to make money by means of stocks of companies which are not of your own, YKK does not put its stocks on the market; we are trying to give YKK stocks to YKK employees as much as possible. As we can not afford to pay our workers as much as we wish, we make them our shareholders so that they can get dividends and enjoy a better life. Because our employees have a sense of responsibility to the company performance as shareholders of YKK and try to work hard and exercise their creativeness, YKK can make products with better quality at smaller costs. The 40 years of history of our company is a history of realizing the idea of cycle of goodness in this way.

From last year to this year, costs of our raw materials went up more than 50 percent, and some of them as much as 200 percent. Even if we had boosted prices of our products by 50 percent, our competitors could not have competed against us and we could have earned profits amounting to hundreds of million yen. But we did not. We did increase our prices last year, but we made our utmost efforts to make our price hike as small as possible. As a result, we decided to squeeze this year's production cost on an assumption that we could have purchased raw materials Y10 billion less than what we actually paid. Even with this, we will not go into red. We can rely on our own excellent production facilities. Our investments since the "Nixon shock" alone amount to Y80 billion. But our wages have not been on the high side in the country and some of our people wanted larger price increases and bigger bonuses. I admonished them and reminded them making money by buying things at low prices and selling them at high prices is not compatible with YKK's principle, because that money is not earned by our own efforts and toils. I told them that the now was the time for the YKK group to exert itself to serve society better by keeping prices as low as possible even if we were to use up the last bit of our stockpile. I also told them, "Situations are very bad, we cannot deny it. We are now, so to speak, in winter. But for YKK the winter will be crisp and clear. We need not to be miserable because we are sure that at this time next year we will be able to get raw materials more cheaply and abundantly. Let's prepare ourselves, therefore, for a new spring when we can offer society newly developed materials and products." I believe this is the way to contribute to society. YKK achieved its present position as the world's largest zipper manufacturer because we were and are aiming to serve society.

YKK investments made in the past years amounted to Y190 billion—some Y160 billion in Japan and Y30 billion in foreign countries, including our plant in Kurobe which is unique in the world. We are confident that our products are of the best quality and the cheapest in the world. It is because we not only produce zippers and zipper parts, but also we develop and produce machinery used in our factories all over the world.

Case writer: I heard you have a lot of registered patents.

President: Yes, but I do not remember the exact number; it must be somewhere between 400 and 500. To obtain a patent is not so difficult as people imagine. You have only to have a new idea for producing goods by a new method, by means of new materials, or by saving of, for example, electricity or fuel consumption. Everywhere around us find many things to be improved. I wonder why experts or specialists fail to take notice of them.

Case writer: YKK is one of few Japanese companies that started producing overseas as early as the early 1960s and has successfully expanded its foreign operations since then, isn't it?

President: Now YKK has about 30 plants throughout the world. It is just like seeing seeds spread over the soil by wind and developing into a forest. But YKK in the United States, in the Netherlands, in Britain, and so on are not Japanese companies. They have their roots deep in the soil of the countries where they are operating. When I send our employees on foreign assignments, I always tell them, "As you

are going to work, for instance in Britain, try to get acclimated with local conditions and to behave as the British do. You are Japanese— you can do nothing about it. But try to be good citizen in your new community. Respect their manners, customs, and traditions even when you may find them strange or funny. Do not forget to contribute your share to the progress of the local economy and welfare; remember that if you do not render services to your new community, you will neither be accepted by them nor succeed."

Overseas I hope to distribute YKK stocks to employees as we do in Japan as soon as possible. But we must be careful in doing so in foreign countries. They could sell YKK stocks at a good price. Once we have distributed stocks among local employees, they, as shareholders, have legitimate rights to keep or sell their stocks. If they want to sell them, we can do nothing about it. Suppose that our employees in the United States sold their stocks to some of our American competitors. If the competitors come to see our plants, we cannot refuse them. Or, if some competitors obtained a certain amount of stocks and wanted to sit on our board of directors, we could not do anything but to accept them. The question is how we can give employees a sense of participation in the management of their company as worker-shareholder; and how we can prevent stocks distributed among our local employees from being sold to outsiders. If and when we can find a solution to this problem, gradually we will carry out our stock-sharing plan in our subsidiaries abroad.

I always tell my local employees, "Make your best efforts in your work since all of you have ability and opportunities for advancement to directors, whether you work in an office or in a warehouse or a factory." When I visit our plants abroad, the first person I speak to is a warehouse or a delivery worker. I tell them, "You are doing a very important job for your company. And when you make a delivery to plants or offices of our customers, you will find there one or two small things that can be easily improved but to which no one has ever paid attention. Then, put forward your suggestions to them. They will appreciate your attentiveness and suggestions. They will realize that you are different from the ordinary delivery person. Thus, you will win good reputation among them and they will come to listen to what you tell them. And then, you will be entitled to join *our sales staff." Some of them were moved by my words to tears; some would blush with joy. They would tell me that they would work for YKK as long as they could. It is surprising to find that in the United States and in European countries, as well as in developing countries, there exists too wide a gap between executives and workers to allow effective communication. I cannot help feeling that workers in these countries sell themselves for daily or monthly wages. In this respect, the situation in Japan is much better than in other countries.*

I remember one episode. It was when I visited our plant in the United States for the first time. After I had finished my business there, I was going to leave for Canada. It was Saturday. To my surprise, many workers of the plant came to see me off. "Why didn't you go out with your folk? This is Saturday. Or, do you have something to tell me?" I said. They told me that they had been deeply impressed by my speech, which I made the day before, because they had never heard such inspiring remarks, and they decided to come to see me off. However lofty and noble an idea one may have, it is only pie in the sky unless we translate it into practice. So, we are giving serious consideration to a stock-sharing plan in our overseas companies. At the beginning of this type of plan, foreign employees will agree not to let their shares go at any price. But since they are not accustomed to our way of thinking, avarice may make them change their mind. Even in YKK there were some employees who did not want to have YKK stocks which we offered them and some others who sold their shares to people other than YKK people. And some portion of our stocks are held by outsiders. Today our employment increases more rapidly than our issued stocks. Therefore, we now must ask our older worker-shareholders to transfer their stocks to new comers upon their retirement, or at the time of capital increase we ask them to turn over a part of their right for new stocks to younger employees so that as many employees as possible can participate in the stock-sharing plan.

Case writer: *What is striking about your company is that, unlike other Japanese firms, many of YKK overseas subsidiaries are producing goods in North America and in Europe.*

President: *In advanced countries there are fewer restrictions and we can do our business with more satisfaction than in developing countries, where we are required to tie up with local*

partners. From the view point of YKK management principles, local partners tend to be obstacles rather than partakers. Many of them lack the willingness to consider about betterment of employees. More often than not, they are eager to let employees work for wages as low as possible and to put all the profits into their pockets. When establishing joint ventures in Southeast Asian countries, most of the Japanese companies go into business with Chinese residents with whom they have dealings. But in many cases, that choice turns out to be the cause of failure. I always recommend those people who seek joint venture partners to choose nationals of the host country. If you have overseas Chinese as your partners, it can lead to local people boycotting your company. People of many Southeast Asian countries seem to have a feeling that they have been economically oppressed for a long time by Chinese merchants. They tend to think, therefore, that the Japanese come into their country to exploit them hand in hand with the Chinese living in their country. You should not forget that every country has its own nationalism. It is all right to have a Chinese manager in the sales department, but management of factories should be put in hands of a local national. Unlike commercial business, a manufacturing company must have its roots deep in the soil of the host country. You cannot pull it out easily, even if you come to face unforseen and unfavorable situations. A factory is like a bridge; once you have built one at a certain place, you cannot move it to another place for many years to come. In many cases, local businessmen are short of money and are not good at doing business. But we must think in long-run terms and help them in financing and transferring technical and management know-how.

Case writer: *The personnel administration policies of YKK subsidiaries all over the world seem to have some common features. Can I understand that this means that you think all human beings are the same throughout the world?*

President: *Yes, you are right. That is why we encourage local employees to participate in management. In the management system prevalent in Japan, you must wait for ten or fifteen years before you are a department manager and an additional five or ten years to be a member of top management. If we tell our local employees to wait as their Japanese counterparts do just because it is the Japanese way,* *they will not be fully persuaded. In our overseas companies, therefore, we promote capable employees of two or three years service to the level of department manager or temporary members of the board of directors. Because we do not fully understand their abilities and character, they sit at the table of board of directors for one-term and are replaced by other candidates in the next term. We are hoping that in this way we can develop them into good executives.*

Case writer: *What do you think are the most important requirements of Japanese managers, especially of general managers of your overseas subsidiaries?*

President: *Well, as a matter of fact, we do not, or shall we say, we cannot afford to give much attention to that matter. They are sent to their international assignments without any special preparations and training. To speak frankly, a person is sent to a new post of general manager of an overseas company without well-advanced notice and goes right to work visiting new customers one after another. Because these managers are not specially trained for their new assignments abroad, we may have complaints from our foreign customers that a new general manager could not fully understand what they told him over the phone. If I could find in our company some people who could act in my place, I would happily send such people abroad. But I cannot, and I will not be able to. Although our international assignees are to develop their capability still further, and they have to deepen their understanding of the basic philosophy of YKK, they have very valuable assets: their youthfulness. They should work diligently fully utilizing their vitality. I always tell them, "You are to be pioneers of the country where you are going to work. You are expected to work not only for our company but also for the benefits of your host country. You should have pride that you are doing a task that may make your name written in the history of that country."*

Case writer: *Among local employees there will be some who will not agree to or be skeptical of your philosophy, and other workers will listen to what they tell them.*

President: *In these days, even in Japan, you cannot expect to find simply honest people any more. Almost all people are slightly tainted with the socialist ideology. In the past 40 years our company was exposed to one crisis after another and every time we overcame difficul-*

ties and unified our strength. The only way to win trust of our foreign employees, therefore, is to put into practice what we are telling them, however trite or seemingly insignificant that may be. We do not hope to have only good workers. I think that all the workers of our company joined us led by a certain bondage which is invisible to us. We must treat them kindly and it is our duty to make good workers of them. They are just like transplanted trees; it takes time before they are accustomed to new environments.

The basis of management philosophy of YKK should not be changed. But when my son and his colleagues assume responsible positions in the company, it will reflect their own value judgments and will be slightly different from what it is. Similarly, our principle idea must take different forms from country to country. Management philosophy must have flexibility to adapt itself to different times and different countries. Through this process, we can make it closer to the ideal one.

MANAGEMENT PRACTICE—STOCK-SHARING PLAN AND BOARD OF DIRECTORS MEETING

As it was Yoshida's policy, YKK stocks were not listed on the stock markets. About 2,100 shareholders who were YKK directors, employees, and their families held 68 percent (Y3,790 million) of the company's issued capital of Y5,600 million, and about one-third of the issued capital (Y1,710 million) was held by employees below the director level. At the time of capital increase, shareholder-employees were encouraged to give up their rights for new stocks so that nonshareholder-employees might get some stocks. But the number of employees increased faster than capital and there were many employees who had no stocks. Par value of the stock was Y10,000 and its dividend rate was 18 percent. Thirteen percent of monthly wages and 10 percent of summer bonuses and 50 percent of winter bonuses were deposited in the company's savings account through payroll reductions. Annual bonuses amounted to more than 5.5 month's pay.

The board of directors met once a month in Ikuji Plant in Toyama Prefecture. But more than 100 people sat at the meeting table because the meeting comprised managers and union representatives as well as directors. Some rank-and-file workers also attended the meeting by turns. This was the pattern of the YKK board meeting since the company's establishment. When the size of the company had been small, all the employees had attended the meeting. At the board meeting any participant, regardless of position, could express opinions. The board meeting was regarded as a "forum for education" and a useful means of permeating the company's operating philosophy throughout the organization. Wage increases and size of bonuses were determined not through collective bargaining but over the table of the board meeting. The labor union of YKK was independent, not affiliated with any regional or national unions. The average age of male workers was 27 years and of female workers 21 years. The average annual income from labor of the former was Y2,100,000 and of the latter Y1,400,000. The wage packet of YKK did not include elements of educational backgrounds, and a worker with a large family could live in a large house that was provided by the company. The company began to feel the impacts of labor shortage, but its turnover was lower than that of other companies. According to Mr. Morino, chief of the labor relations section in Ikuji plant, "It takes ordinary employees three to five years to fully grasp the meaning of the 'cycle of goodness.'"

RELATIONS BETWEEN PARENT COMPANY AND OVERSEAS SUBSIDIARIES

The overseas operations division in the YKK main office handled such matters as selection of plant location, plant construction, and communication with overseas subsidiaries. On the other hand, the overseas operations section in the main factory located in Toyama Prefecture dealt with problems related to technology and production facilities to be incorporated in overseas plants and training of engineers to be sent abroad.

Hideo Hirata, director and manager of the overseas operations division, explained, "Over all direction and supervision of this division is maintained by President Yoshida. Most of our production facilities in developing countries were opened at the request of our agents in those countries. What is most important for us in advanced countries with larger markets is to meet demands promptly for various types of zippers—different in materials, colors, sizes, etc. So we started local production. Our policy of overseas operations is to establish fully owned companies wherever possible. Our competitive edge in international markets, particularly in the markets of advanced countries, comes from research and development efforts made in our main factory. Our sales policy is to sell our products directly to our customers without relying on intermediaries."

The directors meeting in February was called "joint meeting of directors" because about 300 managers and directors of all subsidiaries and branches of the YKK group here and abroad were invited to attend the meeting to review annual production-sales plans. The joint meeting was held for three days. On the first day, representatives of all offices and factories expressed their views for about three minutes each. At the suggestion of Yoshida, each speaker prepared charts for his presentation. Annual plans were reviewed and discussed on the second day, and exchange of views on specific problems of each office and factory was held on the third day. In 1973, Yoshida invited to the joint meeting not only Japanese managers but also local executives of overseas subsidiaries and said, "Witnessing this meeting, you will understand, I hope, the sources from which comes out greatness of YKK as a worldwide enterprise. . . . You do not need to be stingy with the travel expenses to this meeting. Working hard, you can easily earn as much money. But I want you to remind that what is more valuable than money is people, people who work hard. We must assume it our duty to bring up each one of our workers in the way a worker should go." National managers of YKK subsidiaries in Australia, West Germany, and Hong Kong attended the 1974 joint meeting. Some 20 foreign workers who were staying in Japan as trainees also attended the meeting.

Considerably detailed information was transmitted from the parent company to overseas subsidiaries. From abroad, annual financial statements, monthly reports of productions, sales, stock, and personnel as well as special reports on specific topics and occasional letters were sent to the main office. Communication through telephone and telex was also quite often regardless of expenses.

YKK had no written evaluation criteria of its subsidiaries performance. Evaluation was usually made on the basis of market share, growth rate of sales, and profits. But what was most important for general manager was to achieve the annual target set for each company at the joint meeting of directors. YKK aimed at sales profit of 7 to 8 percent both for domestic and overseas operations. The general manager of each subsidiary was enpowered to manage in his own way, and whenever any serious problems arouse in his company, he came to the main office to discuss how to solve them, or managers of the parent company went to that company to adjust policies and annual target to the changing conditions. If they found the problems were too tough to be tackled by the general manager, they replaced him with new one.

EXPANSION OF YKK OPERATIONS IN EUROPE

Seijiro Nishizaki, deputy manager of overseas operations division, had been in Europe for five years from 1964, at first involved in construction and management of the plant in the Netherlands (which was YKK's first in Europe) and then developing and implementing plans for opening new plants in other European countries. In 1963, YKK had more than 85 percent of the domestic market and its exports accounted for about 30 percent of its sales. In 1963, however, rapid growth of the company slackened and its export ratio to total production dropped to less than 20 percent. Nishizaki, chief of plant export section at that time, left Japan for Europe to study if it was possible for YKK to start production in Europe.

"At that time no Japanese firms had factories in Europe," he recalled of those days. "And since I had never been in sales and did not know where and how to proceed with my research, I visited governmental agencies of each country I went to and asked them offhandedly how favorable they considered the investment climate in their country. The Dutch government was most enthusiastic about our plan and was kind enough to introduce me to responsible people in its industrial development area. After visiting five or six places in the area, I found Sneek was most eager to attract foreign investment and its location, buildings to let for plants, and housing conditions were better than other places. In retrospect, I think we were lucky to find a small city like Sneek, whose population at that time was only less than 20,000. Unlike in large cities which had many large companies and factories, YKK was very visible and impressive in a modest city like Sneek and people of the city from the mayor on down dealt with us most favorably."

When Nishizaki returned from his European survey tour, he was unexpectedly appointed as general manager of a YKK subsidiary to be established in the Netherlands. In March 1964, four months after the appointment, he left for his new assignment with two assistants and started to set up a new company. He was 32 years old. Before leaving Japan he told president Yoshida that if YKK was to succeed in Europe, it must develop the most suitable nylon zippers to meet local demand, and in view of the wage difference between European countries and Japan, it also must make more labor-saving machinery than that currently used in Japan. Yoshida said, "Leave it to me. I will handle these problems." And he added, "If our project in Europe does not go well, I as well as you are to blame: both of us will appologize for it before the board meeting." Mr. Doguchi who went to the Dutch plant with Nishizaki as an engineer at the age of 23 and who was promoted to the plant manager reminisced, "We left Japan with a grim resolution. We told ourselves that we would not come back alive to Japan unless we succeed. We were like kamikaze pilots."

The first big problem Nishizaki faced on his new assignment was that of distribution channels. A Dutch importer-dealer had been given sole right to sell YKK products in the Netherlands and he demanded an extravagant compensation fee for revision of the contract. At this outrageous demand, Nishizaki decided to sell all the products of the new Dutch plant in West Germany because the plant had been originally established with the ultimate purpose of penetrating into markets of the European Community countries. This decision proved to be successful and they could have confidence that they could go along without relying on agents in European markets. This confidence also played an important role in developing the successful sales strategy of other subsidiaries to be established in the coming years in other European countries. From 1964 to 1965, YYK developed the market in West Germany and set up a plant there; during the period of 1966–1967, it expanded the French market and opened a plant; in 1967–1968, the company went into the Italian market and built a plant in the country. In each case, YKK expanded its operations in the same pattern: develop a national market, reinvest profits coming from the market in the form of establishing a branch office, incorporate the branch office into corporation so that it might engage in production operations, and then open a factory. In 1969–1970, YKK concentrated its efforts in developing the British market. Except in Britain, YKK subsidiaries in West Germany, France, Italy, Belgium, Spain, and Switzerland were established jointly by YKK and Yoshida (Nederland) B. V. "We could easily get approval from the governments of these countries because new companies were not soley established by a Japanese firm," Nishizaki explained. "At the outset, our production costs had been considerably high, but we could gradually succeed in reducing the average cost by making most of the imported materials from Japan, and we could afford to spare money for better setup of factories and training of our employees. When we found an approach employed in one country to be successful, we applied it in another country. But since conditions vary from one country to another in Europe, sometimes we failed. In short, we had a series of trials and errors and we had always to try to attune our policies with different business environments."

Nishizaki explained relations with local employees in the following way: "At that time, when machinery arrived from Japan, I was the first to do unpacking. It happened that a visitor came to see me while I was doing this job. He told me that he wanted to see a manager and I told him I was a manager. 'No, I want to see the general manager,' said he. When I told him I was the general manager, he looked askance at me for a while. Office staff, when and if they did not have pressing work, helped factory hands, and factory workers in turn lent delivery personnel a hand when they had time to spare. This was our way of doing business. While Europeans were infected with class prejudice, we made no attempt to differentiate ourselves from local employees. This attitude was uncommon in European countries where people were accustomed to find their own place in one of social stratum. But local employees responded favorably to our idea that all those working in our company were in the same set."

This case writer asked Nishizaki, "You did not adapt yourselves to the local ways of dealing with people. Was it because you were confident of your policies?" "No, we were not," he replied. "On the contrary, we were deeply worried over the matter. If we had been specially trained and well versed in the policies and procedures of personnel administration in foreign subsidiaries, we might have acco-

modated ourselves to local conditions. But we lacked such sort of expertise. We made up our minds, therefore, to deal with our employees with sincerity, which we understand is communicable among all human beings. And since the number of our employees was rather small, it was easier for us to make them understand our policies."

Except for anonymous letters saying, "We shall never forget about Indonesia (a former Dutch colony that was occupied by Japan during the Second World War)," Yoshida (Nederland) B. V. did not have any unleasant or serious problems vis-à-vis the local community. At the occasion of President Yoshida's visit to the Dutch plant in 1965, the company had its first bus trip as a token reward to employees for service. Before long, the number of employees became too big for one bus but too small for two buses and management decided to invite employees' families or friends on the bus trip. Three or four companies in Sneek started bus trips for their employees. Yoshida (Nederland) B. V. was popular in the local community and experienced no difficulty in recruitment, despite general labor shortage in the country. The cities of Sneek and Kurobe became sister-cities in 1970 and have been pursuing closer friendly relations.

RELATIONS WITH LOCAL COMMUNITIES

Because YKK's aim of opening overseas plants was to "serve the local community," all the profits of each subsidiary were reinvested in the country where it was operating. Yoshida used to tell the people who were going to be sent abroad, "Do not mix with the other Japanese working abroad. Avoid joining Japanese associations over there unless you find difficulties in doing business without being a member of such associations. Try to learn the language of the country where you are going to work. Do not teach local employees Japanese."

Every year YKK invited about 2,000 people from all over the world to a two-week tour in Japan during which they visited the YKK Toyama factory, Kyoto, and Nikko. Most of these foreign visitors were customers of the YKK group, and some of them were public officials (such as mayor), journalists, and financial people of the city where one of YKK subsidiary was located. A small number of local employees also joined the tours; for example, a team from the US was comprised of 150 customers and other related people plus 10 local employees, and another team from Britain consisted of 100 customers and 10 local employees. The cost of this program was paid by each of the overseas subsidiaries, and the parent company paid for expenses of receptions and so on. At the Toyama factory both directors and workers accorded foreign visitors a cordial welcome, showed them round production facilities to their satisfaction, and had several occasions to make or renew acquaintance with each other. The purpose of the visitation program was to let customers, community leaders, and local employees of each overseas subsidiary understand fully how YKK was operating in its main factory. According to one executive of the parent company, "The program has proved to be far more effective in promoting customer relations and in building up better corporate image than newspaper advertising."

In addition to the visitation program, YKK had training programs for local employees in Japan; there were always many foreign employees receiving engineering training in the factories of the parent company for a period of two to six months. To make their stay in Japan as comfortable as possible, the company built a special dormitory for them, but they could spend a lot of time with Japanese workers on the job as well as on Sundays and holidays—going out, for instance, on picnics together. Both visitation and training programs in Japan were considered as very useful means for infusing into foreign workers YKK management policies and their application.

Because all of the general managers of YKK overseas companies were in their 30s, from time to time they requested the parent company to send over someone from top management to negotiate with or to attend some special ceremonies held by local customers, financial institutions, and governmental bodies. On the other hand, top management of the parent company, from the president on down, intended to visit overseas companies as often as possible on such occasions as opening of a new plant.

YKK also had the Overseas Training Tour Program for employees of the parent company. Each year, 200 to 300 employees chosen by drawing from workers with more than three years of service were sent to countries in Southeast Asia, Europe, and North America. Furnished by the company with personal expenses and a suit, as well as round-trip air tickets, they visited YKK plants, exchanged good wishes with local employees, and made sight-seeing trips.

PERSONNEL POLICY

YKK had a Japanese way of personnel management in its overseas subsidiaries. Hirata, manager of overseas operations division, said on this point: "I think we should take a fresh look at the Japanese way of management. Management philosophy of YKK is based on a belief that all human beings, in spite of differences in races, customs, and so on, have many things in common. I must admit that I am wondering if our local workers understand what we tell them of our policies as the Japanese workers do. But if they think there is something with which they can have sympathy or something challenging to them, we should be satisfied with them. We are sure that we can keep our policy effective even when we have 300 or 500 employees in each of our plants. If not, we had better to leave management in the hands of the locals. "By promoting our employees to responsible positions regardless of their educational backgrounds and not making any distinctions between factory workers and office staff, we are challenging customary employees relations. But the results come up to our expectations: our approach gives our workers incentives for work. Company trips by bus with employees and their families are also effective. Since many of our overseas plants are located in industrial development areas which are generally abundant in labor force, and since we try to keep our wage level higher than the average of the community, we can attract good workers."

Several overseas subsidiaries of YKK began to have local top management: three in the United States, one in Canada, Britain, Belgium, and Italy, and one "proxy director" in West Germany, France, and the Netherlands.

This case writer asked, "It seems to me that most of overseas subsidiaries of Japanese companies do not recruit the elites of the host countries. How about your company?" To this question Nishizaki replied, "Neither do we. If we were in an industry that must start its overseas operations with large-scale production, it might be possible for us to employ elite people on our staff. But our strategy of overseas operations is to start small and to grow gradually commensurate with our local market development. Accordingly, our recruitment policy is to hire young people with potential and willingness to work hard, rather than people well educated and trained, and to train and develop them within our own organization such as the training programs in Japan. And the local elites tend to ask from the start for their own rooms with carpets and their own secretaries. I think that our recruiting and training policies will remain the same even when our overseas companies grow much bigger than they are now."

EXPATRIATE POLICY

All the general managers and plant managers sent from YKK to its subsidiaries abroad were in their 30s. Most of the general managers would have been at the level of section chief of a sales department of the parent company had they been in Japan. All the plant managers in European operations were engineers graduated from senior high school and had been supervisors or foremen before they were sent abroad. Candidates for overseas assignments were selected on the basis of individual performance (technical skills, sales skills, and administrative skills, etc.), personality and character, and aptitude to unfamiliar surroundings. Language skills were considered as "secondary requirement" and had no significance in selecting plant managers and engineers.

According to Hirata, "What is the most important is whether he is good or not as an individual human being. In other words, whether he can be accepted as a representative of YKK. However fluent in foreign languages and competent as a manager he may be, he can not be qualified for overseas assignments unless he understands fully the spirit of YKK. And he must not be reserved. Our overseas managers are sent to their new assignments without much orientation and training. But since they are young, they are rich in vitality and flexibility in their thought and action. Because our president always encourages them by telling them, 'Do not be afraid of two or three misfires,' they can freely exercise their own initiative and potentialities. And in most cases, this resulted in satisfactory achievements."

Salaries of the Japanese managers abroad were decided by the parent company and they included what would be equivalent to the average annual bonuses they would receive on their domestic assignments. Their bonuses as well as pay raise were supposed to full reflect performance of their own company; their bonuses ranged from 1.5 to 3 months' pay according to results for the year, and

extra bonuses were given to the managers of the companies with excellent records. Even when the good results of a company were solely credited to the general manager of the company, all of its Japanese managers were given bigger bonuses.

Performance evaluation of each subsidiary was made according to its growth rate of sales, market share, profits, and so on. Differences of business and economic environments, relations with employees, and the local community were also taken into consideration.

Having worked on overseas assignments, average managers received higher salaries than people working in the home country with comparable performance records. This was justified by the reason that "while managers in the home country have lots of people who are willing to support them or listen to their complaints when they face to difficult situations, overseas managers do not have such people around them. On the other hand, the latter have greater opportunities to excercise their own initiative and creativity as a manager. Consequently, they have greater chances for growth as an individual as well as a manager. When they come back to Japan, they usually are in an abstract state of mind for a while, but as they adjust themselves again to Japanese surroundings, they have favorable influence over people working with them. The company, too, can rely on them."

When Nishizaki returned to Japan in 1969 after his five-year assignment in the Netherlands, the president said, "I will give you a special bonus." That special bonus turned out to be Y3,500,000, far surpassing his expectation. And since then, it has become customary for the company to give a special bonus to people coming back from overseas assignments.

YKK FASTENERS (UK)

The United Kingdom imposed a high rate of tariffs on imported zippers. YKK, therefore, established YKK Fasteners (UK) Ltd. in London in 1967 as a sales company. The company aimed to enter the British markets with zippers produced in YKK Hong Kong by taking advantage of preferential tariffs between the United Kingdom and Hong Kong. But business records of the new company were far from being satisfactory, because delivery from Hong Kong took too much time to satisfy the British customers and because the products of the Hong

Kong plant fell short of meeting varied demands of the British market.

In 1969, Takahashi was appointed as general manager of YKK (UK). He reshuffled supply channels to secure prompt delivery and completed a new plant in Runcorn, investing Y1,000 million. After the production of the new plant was well under way, the company started to show remarkable results; annual sales rose from Y800 million in 1972 to Y2,100 million in 1973, which accounted for 28 percent of the British market. YKK (UK) had 30 employees (5 Japanese) in the London office and 160 employees (5 Japanese) in the Runcorn plant.

Takahashi said about management practice of YKK (UK): "I had only to follow faithfully what president Yoshida always tells us. Since the size of the company as well as mores here were different from what we were accustomed in Japan, I had to modify our management practice slightly. But the fundamental policies remain the same. I have invented nothing new in our way of doing business here. If you yourself are not fully convinced of the basic philosophy of YKK, your management practice reveals lacks of confidence and cannot be consistent. But fortunately, I had been under the guidance of Mr. Yoshida for more than 10 years. So, even in these unfamiliar surroundings I do not have any doubt of our management policies and I can behave here as naturally as I did in the home country."

The Runcorn plant of YKK (UK) was located in an industrial development area near Liverpool where one could get from London by a two-hour trip on an express train. Liverpool, which had been the center of British shipbuilding and woolen industries, suffered industrial decline and consequently increasing unemployment. The area was also known for its frequent industrial strife. This case writer visited the Runcorn plant in April 1973. Then 60 percent of 100 factory workers were women. The Runcorn plant was the biggest of all the YKK plants in Europe, and about 45 percent of its raw materials were provided from local suppliers.

Mr. Minami, plant manager said: "YKK decided to set up a plant in this area because the government was eager to attract foreign investments to develop this area. We were well aware that there had been a lot of labor disputes in this area. But I do not think this means that this area has nothing to offer; every place has its bright side. For instance, the unemployment rate in this area is the highest in

this country. So, we can hire good workers without much difficulty. If we were located in an area where every company wants to go, we would have much difficulty in securing our work force. Every location has its advantages as well as disadvantages." Runcorn was not far from London, which was a major market for zippers. Covered by the government's incentive development plan, Runcorn could provide well-developed utilities and housing; the area also offered some tax incentives, for example, a three-year tax credit for investments. All of these factors were taken into account in deciding the location of a plant of YKK (UK).

Labor Problems

Minami, who was 36 years old, had been in India supervising the construction of a plant which had been the first plant export of YKK. He said on labor problems in the area: "I am still not very familiar with British labor problems. Some Japanese once warned me and said, 'If you knew anything about the history of the British labor movement, you could not help being very cautious in dealing with workers here.' The valor of ignorance? Perhaps they are right. In spite of many industrial development measures provided by the government, such as tax credits for investments and subsidies for promoting employment, investments in manufacturing industries in this area are not growing so rapidly. This, I think, is mainly due to rampant labor management disputes in this area. One Englishman told me that he would prefer keeping his on banking deposits which would pay good interest rates to investing the in manufacturing just to be put out of business by work stoppages. While nt was still under construction, there was a labor dispute which dragged on for one month. A newspaper reported on our project of coming into this area and said that we were bold enough to set up a plant in an area where strikes were an everyday occurrence. As we were the first Japanese company making products in this country and as we had a problem over our labor union soon after our operations started here, our plant drew so much public attention that a TV station reported what we were doing. In a sense, we could get our existence here advertised for nothing."

Soon after the operation of the Runcorn plant was under way, representatives of the General Union came to the plant and brought workers together in the cafeteria to persuade them to join the union. At that time, there were about 60 workers and half of them joined the union. As a countermeasure, management expressed its intention to cut the company's wage rates to the prevailing union rates. At a meeting with employees, Minami asked them why they wanted to be a member of the union. To this question, they replied that they had a feeling that the plant manager would not listen to grievances brought to him by representatives of employees and that they needed some protection in case of being discharged. And he explained to them, "Management is willing to observe the established rules in your country. But since we are not yet well versed in your practices and customs, we must try to learn from you. But do not make unreasonable demands. We are convinced that interests of management and employees are compatible and our way of management is based on that conviction and aims to make both the company and employees prosperous." According to him, all the union members of the company spontaneously got out of the union within three months.

Soon after that, an unregistered union was organized in the company and it had a meeting with management once a month. At the meeting, representatives of employees and management exchanged requests or suggestions with each other.

When this case writer asked Minami what was the most difficult problem he had ever had, he replied: "I think that most serious problems are still to come. What was very trying and embarrassing, but which was beyond our control, were strikes of related industries. Last winter we were affected by the strikes in the steel industry and electricity company. We were often vexed by strikes in cotton yarn companies, packaging companies, and construction industries."

With regard to possible problems in the years to come, he said: "We must be prepared to deal with new types of labor-management problems which will arise when our employment expands to 200 or 300. But as we have been operating in our own way since the time when we had only a small number of employees, labor-management situations in our company in the future will not be as serious as those in other companies in this country."

Working Conditions

Many workers of the Runcorn plant were married women and young men in their 20s, the average wage for women was £18 a week and for men £25. The wage packet was made up of wage based on job, performance, length of service, and piece-work pay. In England there was no bonus system similar to that prevailing in Japan: the bonus was a special payment paid at the time of Christmas which amounted to a week's pay. YKK (UK) paid a Christmas bonus equal to one month's pay and increased wages by 10 to 15 percent annually.

Working hours of the company were forty hours per week, five days per week, and workers got a ten-minute tea-time at 10:00 AM. and 3:00 PM. Sometimes, Japanese managers worked on Saturdays. Since there were few workers who came to work by their own cars, the company provided commuting buses at reduced fares for its workers.

When this case writer visited the plant, he saw young male workers with long hair playing football at lunch time in an open space in front of the plant office. Seeing them enjoy the game, Minami said, "As we have a piece of spare land, I am telling them that we will make a football field for them. I also encourage them to have their own football team so that they may have a chance to make a playing tour to Japan. They find the idea very exciting."

The company recruited most employees through a public employment service office, but it was rather difficult to find able young men. Minami had a feeling that workers in this country were brought up as people of the lower classes, but that they were "straight side" in their thinking and behavior. He also sensed that British managers in general were eager to give orders to their subordinates but not so eager to work hard themselves. In YKK (UK), too, the most diligent and capable workers were found among specialists and members on the middle-management level. Turnover rate of workers was low but "5 percent of the bottom" was always new.

Labor Practices

"Did you find anything difficult to understand about British labor practices?" asked this case writer and Minami replied: "Not particularly. If there is something which is difficult for us to understand, it is because we see the matter from a viewpoint of Japanese customs. If we can put the matter in the right place of the traditional and social context of this country, we can understand why such and such a thing is taken for granted here."

British workers seemed to the Japanese managers not to be neat and cooperative enough: operators did not clean up their machines when their work was over—that was to be done by sweepers, not by themselves; truck drivers did not help to load or unload their cargoes—the union forbade them to do so. Carrol, the only woman clerical worker in the factory, could type and operate teleprinters. When Minami said, "We do not need a typist nor a teleprinter in this office for the moment. I want you instead to serve tea to visitors as well as to do the assignments we give," she indignantly said, "I have never been treated in such a rude way." Minami told this case writer, "No demarcation in this plant. All of us must aim to be 'generalists' tackling any kind of jobs. When our company grows larger, we will need 'division of labor,' but for the moment if this small factory is to survive, we must help each other." And he added, "In this factory, there is no organization as it should be. Layers and steps are not necessary in a modest factory with less than 100 workers. I told them to bring to me all the problems and complaints they have. And I am working with them just a member of a team."

Minami's staff was composed of Mr. D'Arcy who was assistant plant manager, Carrol, and a young Japanese who dealt with outside relations and communications with the parent company. Another Japanese was engaged in sales and the remaining two Japanese were engineers.

Relations with the Local Community

In industrial Runcorn there were about 100 factories. Local employers were going to set up an employers' association of the district and they invited Minami to join it. Some English managers asked him seriously to teach them the Japanese way of management, and he said to them, "You have your own established way, and it is we who are trying to learn your method." A factory in Yorkshire which supplied YKK (UK) with cotton yarn had many Indian workers. "We have no intention to employ Indian workers," said Minami. "It is not because of racial prejudice but because we are here to serve this country and its people. To depend on Indian workers, which may cause less labor problems, means that we have failed in dealing with British workers." When Minami took this case writer to lunch by his Ford car, the case writer observed that it was amazing to see so many Japan-ese cars in European cities. Minami said, "It is against YKK policy to use a Japanese car when you are on overseas assignments."

Every year YKK (UK) invited to Japan for a two-week tour about 100 customers (mainly garment manufacturers) and leaders of the local community such as the chairman of county council, mayor, and officials working on industrial development programs, as well as 10 YKK employees, 5 of whom come from the Runcorn plant. The program in Japan consisted of visiting YKK factories, meeting top management of the parent company, and sight-seeing in Kyoto and Nikko. Employees themselves elected candidates as participants in the visitation program to Japan and management selected final participants, taking their years of service into consideration. In addition to this program, the company sent three employees every year to the parent company for a period of from one to two months for the purpose of training and infusing them with the basic principles of YKK. No male employees who had training in Japan left the company. Some women employees quit after the training in Japan but they had their own special reasons for quitting.

Conversation with D'Arcy

When this case writer's interview at the plant was over, Minami asked D'Arcy, assistant plant manager, to take the case writer to the Liverpool Station by car. During the 30-minute ride to the station, he was kind enough to answer several questions. D'Arcy had worked for a British automobile factory before he joined YKK (UK).

> **Case writer:** *Why did you change your job?*
> **D'Arcy:** *Because they staged strikes so often in automobile industries.*
> **Case writer:** *Why do you think there are so many strikes in your country?*
> **D'Arcy:** *As far as automobile factories are concerned, workers are doing tedious and uninspiring jobs. So they feel, I think, that they are doing something important when they stage strikes.*
> **Case writer:** *Do you find any difference between the behavior of Japanese managers and that of British managers?*
> **D'Arcy:** *A great deal of difference. Japanese managers, for instance, do not hesitate to go and stay on the factory floor while English managers will never do such sort of things.*

Case writer: In your opinion, which way do British workers prefer?
D'Arcy: It is difficult to answer that question. But I myself like the Japanese way better.

On the way to the station, D'Arcy indicated the factories of well-known companies located in the industrial estate and pointed to a two-storied flat and said, "That is the apartment house in which the Japanese managers of YKK (UK), including the Minamis, live." That was a modest apartment house built by the local government. Seeing that, the case writer remembered Minami's words, "Some local people told me 'Managers should live in better quarters,' but I do not mind such a thing."

Personnel Administration

In October 1971 president Yoshida visited the Runcorn plant. According to Takahashi, general manager of YKK (UK), "For ordinary British employees, managers are 'great men' and the president of the head office is almost 'a man of noble rank.' But when Mr. Yoshida visits a facotry, he deals with employees frankly and considerately, and they are impressed by his unaffected manner. They can tell whether he is making a speech as a matter of form or if he really has something to tell them and he really wants to communicate with them." It was said that Yoshida sang a love song currently popular among young Japanese to YKK (UK) employees at a party.

"What is important for us," said Takahashi, "is to observe local customs without abandoning our basic principles. It is better, I think, to refrain from stressing the Japanese way of doing as long as it does not affect our business seriously." One of the company's principles in the field of sales was to pay attention to the needs of modest customers, like dressmakers, and internally, to take good care of those workers doing chores in a factory or warehouse. In England, a worker who started as a warehouse worker was expected to remain a warehouse worker, and a salesman was expected to relish his career as a salesman, and a blue-collar worker was rarely promoted to a white-collar position. But YKK (UK) held a view that all workers are equal and treated all its employees on the same basis and offered ample opportunities for advancement to any capable workers. To cite a few examples: an able salesman who had worked for

the company for three years was appointed as the director in charge of sales activities; a warehouse keeper with ingenuity was promoted to salesman; a driver with four years service became a sales assistant.

Sometimes the company's customary practices of personnel administration caused some troubles. When management decided to bring in a time clock in one office, an elderly employee was opposed to it and said, "You want to have a time clock because you do not trust us. We do not need a time clock in the office." Takahashi retorted, "Would it be quite proper to say that it is all right to have a time clock in the factory but it is a sign of mistrust to have one in the office? I do not think it makes sense. I want to see that office workers are treated in the same way as factory workers."

So far, YKK (UK) had never employed university graduates. Its policy was to "cultivate virgin soil" rather than rely on "ready-made" people. Management was well aware, however, that as the company would expand and its activities would diversify, they would find it necessary to recruit specialists in such areas as public relations, accounting, and so forth. They also felt that university graduates would want to have managerial positions from the start. But if necessity compelled them, and if they could find promising candidates, they would employ some university graduates in the future.

Relations with the Parent Company

Takahashi said, "Perhaps the only thing the parent company has decisive power over in the affairs of our company is treatment of me." Each overseas subsidiary had considerable autonomy in doing its business: each company had freedom and responsibility in selecting its product mix and in pricing. As for the treatment of Japanese employees on overseas assignment, the parent company made its suggestions, but general managers were responsible for the final decision over their subordinates. According to the policy of YKK, all the profits of its overseas subsidiaries were reinvested in the countries where they were operating. The only policy applied to investments in production facilities of a subsidiary was to "put into investments as much money as the general manager deems to be necessary." Therefore, the parent company rarely modified the investment plans that were developed by the subsidiaries. "But we are well aware that if we make up a slipshod plan, we will be criticized by the parent company," said Takahashi. "According to our past records, however, we can fairly say that companies whose operations are going well have more investment plans than others. We can also say that companies with larger investments proved to be more successful than others."

The main reports of overseas subsidiaries to the parent company were annual financial statements, monthly sales reports, and annual plans (sales ordering, financing, and production facilities). Each subsidiary's annual plans were submitted to and reviewed at the "joint meeting" in February where general managers of all the subsidiaries met with top management of the parent company. This case writer asked Takahashi if he had any idea of how the performance of his company was evaluated by the parent company. He said that the evaluation would be made on the basis of sales records, appropriate rate of profits, employee relations, and popularity in the local community. As for the latter two, he added, "If we have some troubles with them, the staff of the parent company becomes aware of them before long because we have many visitors from the parent company and because there are a lot of occasions when our own employees go to Japan." In conclusion, Takahashi said, "I am happy to say that the parent company takes a long outlook in evaluating our overall performance. If you have good records for one or two years, they take it calmly. But three or four years later, you will understand that they accurately measure and reward your contribution." (See the appendix.)

YOSHIDA (FRANCE)

When this case writer visited the Lille plant of Yoshida (France), in April 1973, it had been in operation for only six months. Lille, which one can reach in two hours from Paris by a north-bound express train, was the third largest industrial city in France located in a region near the border dividing France and Belgium. The plant of Yoshida (France) was in an industrial development area adjacent to the city of Lille. In the Paris office of the company there were 6 Japanese including Mr. Furuya, general manager, and 20 French employees, and in the Lille plant there were 3 Japanese and 31 French workers (of whom 19 were men.)

The company was established around the end of 1967. Government approval could be obtained without much difficulty because situations at that time were different from today's and because the company was established as a sales unit by Yoshida (Nederland). For the first two or three years of its existence, Yoshida (France) limited its activities to sales operations, and it was only in 1970 that it started production in a small service plant in the suburbs of Paris. In October 1972 the Lille plant started its operation. But before "the first Japanese plant in France" could be put well underway, the company had had many serious difficulties. Since the French government was very cautious of accepting foreign capital, the company had to spend much time going through the necessary formalities and fulfilling the requirements. Although the company had originally been approved by the government to engage in sales and production activities, when it applied to the government for approval of financing the plant construction with money which would be introduced from Japan in the form of capital increase and loans, it had to draw up a plan with specified figures on production, sales, funds, and employees for the five years to come and submit it to the Foreign Investment Council. The application was kept pending. The company modified the plan again and again and obtained approval at the third application. By that time, plant construction was almost completed. If the actual production volume topped the figure in the plan, the government would intervene and demand explanations. To avoid this kind of trouble, the company modified the plan so that production realized might not outnumber the planned figure. But the government found such a figure too ambitious and demanded the company reduce production. Nevertheless, Yoshida (France) had been making fair progress in its sales. According to Furuya, "If there were not so many government restrictions, I would take greater pleasure in doing business in this country than in any other country."

A Japanese View on French Workers

The three Japanese working in the Lille plant were the plant manager, Doguchi, and two engineers. Before he was appointed to the present position, Doguchi had been plant manager of the Sneek plant of Yoshida (Nederland). To Japanese managers, French workers' views on the company seemed to be quite different from Japanese workers'. French employees worked for their own individual welfare, but not for the organizations to which they belonged. When management said, "We want you to make the maximum efforts to make a profit this year. If we can go into the black, you will have a bonus," they replied, "Profits are what the company is to be concerned with. We have nothing to do with it." "But if the company can make progress," said the manager, "it enables us to make your living improved." "Well, if we want better pay," said employees with a shrug of the shoulders, "we'll go where we can get what we want to have." The Japanese managers had a feeling that French businessmen aimed to keep a certain level of profits rather than to pursue bigger profits and that French workers would stop working harder once they achieved a certain level of affluence.

In France, workers were given two paid holidays a month and it was customary for them to accumulate holidays and to have a one-month summer vacation—spending all the 24 annual paid holidays at once with four weekends during the month. The Lille plant was closed from July 15 to August 15 and the office in Paris was closed for one or two weeks during the period. But the Japanese of the company had a vacation of only one week. They would say, "When other people are on vacation, you can deal with a lot of work which remains to be done without being disturbed with routine tasks." In the summer vacation period, the building where the Furuyas lived would become almost empty; even the concierge left for vacation and a part-time gardener took his place. During summer vacation, almost all the employees of the Paris office left the city, while about half of the employees of the Lille plant left the city. Ordinary French workers wanted to have as large a vacation and salary as possible while they made a clear distinction between their company and their individual life. The Japanese managers felt that they could do nothing about it except to accept it.

Human Relations

Doguchi, plant manager, told the case writer, "Europeans have different views of things from ours. But this does not mean that they and we are completely different. If we have prejudgment or suspicion of them, we can't get along with them. They find delightful what we Japanese find delightful: what we don't like, neither do they. Even if our way of thinking is different, we can communicate with them if we have good faith." Furuya put it in the following way, "Whichever country you may go to, you are coming in contact with human beings. If you don't lack sincerity in dealing with them, you won't rouse their antipathy. What is important is to enjoy things together as well as to work together. President Yoshida always insists, 'When in a foreign country, never do anything as Japanese by yourselves.' Because we have been in constant touch with our employees, they have so far been willing to do what we tell them to do, even when we ask them to do something quite difficult or troublesome."

In the plant, Doguchi and two Japanese engineers often helped workers to load delivery packages on trucks. In the Paris office, too, when they had a large shipment, the entire office from the general manager down worked together. When a newcomer watched the scene, he would say saucer-eyed, "But this is a work to be done by stockmen!" Both in the office and factory, a morning meeting was held on Monday. In the factory, the plant manager transmitted orders or messages from the management at the meeting and workers expressed their views or made suggestions.

Furuya and Doguchi invited the case writer to have lunch in the employee cafeteria of the factory where all the people had the same food supplied from a nearby restaurant. Lunch cost 6 francs and the company paid 3 francs. Mr. Carpro, chief of the sales section and the only employee in the factory who could speak English, sat next to the case writer. Carpro said, "Last year I went to Japan with our customers. That was my first visit to Japan. Unfortunately, I could not see almost anything I wanted to see myself because I was so busy in interpreting. I do hope to visit your country again." When lunch with beer was over, the Japanese managers started to play table-tennis with employees in the cafeteria. In Paris, complying with its employees wishes, the company changed a room in the office into a cafeteria, where all the people in the office including Japanese managers had lunch. But eventually employees started to have lunch outside and only the Japanese and French managers still had lunch in the cafeteria.

In the Lille plant, "YKK Bar" opened when the day's work was over. Workers chatted with Japanese managers for half an hour or so drinking beer for half a franc. This habit of YKK employees was rather unusual among French workers who wanted to go home soon after the day's work was over. From time to time, the company organized such reacreational activities as picnics, hikes, and dances. This year they had a plan to make a one-day bus trip to the Netherlands together with employees' families.

Working Conditions

Workers of YKK Lille factory worked 40 hours in a five-day week. The factory started at 8:30 AM and most of the workers were in by 8:15. In northern France some people still worked half a day on Saturday and workers of YKK came to the factory on Saturdays when they were asked to do so. Management saw to it that wages of the company were "always a bit ahead of those of the companies in the area." The minimum wage was regulated at 4.75 francs an hour but the company paid men from 6 to 6.5 francs and women 5.5 francs. In France wages were mostly determined according to kinds of jobs. But YKK (France) took length of service into consideration in determining wages because "even if a worker continued the same kind of job, he or she contributes to the growth of the company nonetheless."

In December 1972, as things went pretty well in the year, the company paid a Christmas bonus equal to one-month's pay. Because it was customary for companies in France to pay a Christmas bonus of one-month's wage to white-collar employees and one week's wage to blue-collar workers, the workers of the Lille plant were very pleased to get such an unexpected amount. The Japanese managers, too, were happy and proud because they could put into practice what they always said to their employees: "If your company goes better, your life will get better." Some companies with good working conditions gave a bonus of one-week's pay before summer vacation. Doguchi asked Furuya to do the same thing in the company. Furuya agreed to do so and added, "If our sales tops so and so francs, we will have a party at a restaurant to reward our employees' services."

Workers of nearby factories went out on strikes from time to time. The employees of YKK (France) were interested in the labor union, and one day representatives of the leftist union in the district came to the factory in the hope of organizing its employees. Management of the company were confident, however, that even if a labor union was organized in the company managers would not have serious problems with the union because they had already established good employees relations.

Japanese Managers

When Furuya was appointed to the general manager of YKK (France), he was chief of a sales section of the parent company, and this was his first overseas assignment. When he left Japan, Yoshida encouraged him, "You have been in our company for ten years. Now it is the time for you to exercise your potentialities as you like in France."

"Just think of his entrusting management of the subsidiary in France with such a stripling like me," said Furuya, "How bold he is! Almost intrepid, I would say. I must meet his expectation all the more because he trusts me. . . . In the area of investment projects, too, we can do as we like as far as our projects make sense. Recently we had applied to the parent company for bringing in one of the newest type of plastic injection machines in our plant. Mr. Yoshida thought over the application a little but he approved it. Our plant will be the first to have such type of machines in all the YKK overseas factories. . . . Yes, you can say that we have complete autonomy."

Neither Furuya nor Doguchi could speak French well. "Well, sometimes we feel ashamed not to speak French well when we meet young men of Japanese trading companies who just arrived here from Japan and speak French so well," said Furuya. "In order to get an overseas company acclimated to local conditions, we managers must overcome the language barriers. But our approach is to learn the language through direct contacts with the local national rather than going to school to learn it. One advantage of our approach is that it forces us to mingle with our employees. They come to know that we are really trying to make ourselves understood and they are sympathetic, and then it is their turn to make efforts to make themselves understood to us. We are trying to make up for the lack of communication resulting from insufficient language skills through direct contacts with employees in recreation periods as well as in work time. Fortunately, we have had no serious troubles so far from language problems." When Furuya had important visitors or some important letters to write, he relied on a Japanese interpreter who worked on a part-time basis.

The period during which YKK employees are on foreign assignments had been about five years, but recently it was extended to ten years. Furuya said, "I hope young men of YKK will work hard on overseas assignments for a period of ten years. But as for engineers, I would rather send them back home after about three years." Doguchi recently went back to Japan for about four weeks with his family but he said, "I was surprised to find that I did not feel quite at home while I was staying in Japan."

Unionization and Human Relations

In June 1973, a labor union was organized in the Lille plant. Two of the four union officials elected belonged to the Communist-led Confederation Generale du Travail (CGT). But because some errors were found in the election process, the election of the union officials was held over again and no CGT members were elected this time. At the outset, the union counted about ten CGT members but gradually that was reduced to five. According to Doguchi, "It seems that they became tuned into our thinking and found it useless to pay a union fee of 10 francs to CGT. Our union is friendly with management because its members already know well what we are doing for them."

As his words show, management of the company was optimistic about labor-management relations. At the beginning, the workers of the Lille plant had been skeptical of what management had been telling them. They used to say, "We admit that what our managers tell us is really wonderful. But we also know that many French employers also tell their workers wonderful things but that they do not put them into practice. We wonder if our Japanese managers can do what they tell us." "By the time when we had been here for a little more than one year, we could feel that our words started to be taken at their face value by our employees," recalled Doguchi. "At Christmas party in 1973, many of them told me that they would trust us because we

had done as we had told them. We are confident of our management philosophy. What is vital is to put it into practice."

For the year-end bonus, the employees of the Paris office got from one to two months' pay according to appraisal of individual performance, and one employee received two months' pay. In the Lille plant, the size of the bonus ranged from one month to one and a half months' pay and it was determined on the basis of attendance, work efficiency and "earnestness." Three workers qualified for the biggest bonus in the plant. When the plant manager personally explained to one worker why he thought she deserved such a reward, she was moved to tears.

At the beginning, the company's turnover rate was rather high, but gradually the rate dropped and few employees quit the company recently. Furuya stopped unloading packages but Doguchi still helps workers in the storehouse from time to time. They found that if managers help workers too often, the workers seem to have a feeling that there is something wrong with their work or that their own jobs are being taken away.

Training and Development of Employees

Development of French managers went on as management expected. There were three promising employees in the Paris office and two in the Lille plant. In the plant, Carplo who had been the chief of the sales section when the case writer had visited was promoted to assistant plant manager. In the office, a 28-year-old employee, who was a graduate of a commercial high school and who was never late for nor absent from work and stayed late every day, was advanced to chief of the accounting section. The three in the office worked late and sometimes the Japanese managers could not leave the office because they were still working. The Japanese manager said about them, "These people who are to be advanced to the managerial level do a lot of work. They are different from others." Loyalty to the company as well as sense of responsibility and diligence were important elements in deciding promotion and pay raise.

Because French office workers could not get a pay raise unless they acquired some new qualification, most of them tended to draw a line around their own jobs and hated to teach others how they did their jobs. In order to change this tendency, Furuya often said to them, "I know you work very hard and very well. But one who has some expertise or skills should teach and transfer them to others. In so doing, you can cultivate your own leadership. I promise you that you will have a pay raise if you can teach others what you know, even if you do not obtain another new qualification."

POLICY DOCUMENTS

HOW TO ANALYZE
POLICY DOCUMENTS

In most policy courses, the case method is used as a vehicle for illustrating text material and applying classroom learning to actual business situations. It serves as a basis for class discussion and a method for developing your ability to analyze and solve complex business problems. The case method promotes group interaction and enriches learning.

One of the major purposes of the case method is development of your decision-making skill and analytical ability. Specifically, the case study is designed to encourage independent thinking in identifying major issues and attacking problems. It also helps develop your oral and written communication skills when you articulate and defend your position.

CASE ANALYSIS

You will gain most from case analysis if you are prepared for the task. Read and study the text and materials assigned for case discussions, participate in team activities, and write the case analysis. Prepare for class discussion and independent analysis by following these three steps:

Step 1: Understand the Case

1. Read through the case rapidly to determine the general nature of the case.
2. Reread and note the background of the company—its size, product/market, organization, and brief history.
3. Study external and internal factors affecting the company's performance.
4. Understand the operations of important functions and personnel.
5. Study tables, figures, exhibits, and financial statements.

Step 2 Case Analysis.

1. Identify missing information and facts to be researched from outside sources.
2. Compute ratio analysis and trend analysis to study the company's financial position.
3. Pinpoint internal strengths and weaknesses and external opportunities and threats.
4. Study resource expenditures concerning R&D, capital, and facilities.
5. Define the central issues (major constraints and critical problems) and comment on ongoing strategies.

Step 3 Conclusions and Recommendations

1. Restate critical problems and propose solutions.
2. Recommend the choice of strategic alternatives, and provide justification for them.
3. State future resource needs and means for their development. Examine implementation issues.
4. Consider contingency plans.
5. Rethink the salient points and jot down questions for class discussion.

CLASS DISCUSSION AND PRESENTATION

Class discussion can follow a variety of methods: the question/answer dialogue led by the instructor, the open discussion and critique; and team presentation. A well-conducted discussion encourages class interaction, sharing, and self-discovery. Self-discovery is an important goal that enables students to discover the true meaning of conceptual ideas, subtle facts and fine points, and means to obtain consensus. Students learn other people's viewpoints, information, and value judgments. Remember, most cases do not have a single right or wrong answer. All solutions should be subjected to critical scrutiny.

SOURCES OF INFORMATION ON CASES

In analyzing case studies that involve company policy documents, outside research is often necessary. Not only is case material limited, but outside information published at the time of case writing is very relevant to the situation. You may want to consult some of the following sources:

1. Industrial sources:
   a. *U. S. Industrial Outlook,* published annually by the Department of Commerce, with five-year projections
   b. Annual Report on American Industry, published by *Forbes*—a compilation of statistics by industry and company
   c. *Fortune's Directories* on the 500 largest US corporations, second largest 500, and 200 foreign
   d. *Industry Survey,* published quarterly by Standard and Poor's Corp.

2. Company information:
   a. *Moody's Manual of Investments,* containing a brief history of each company, its operations, and five-year financial statements
   b. Standard and Poor's *Corporation Records,* providing company statistics

3. Trade association sources:
   a. A good source on an individual industry's status and trends. Consult, for example, Aerospace Industries Association of America, American Petroleum Institute, Air Transport Association of America

4. Sources for ratio analysis:
   a. *Dun's Review,* published annually in September–December issues by Dun and Bradstreet, Inc.
   b. *Annual Statement Studies,* published by Robert Morris Associates—useful for small business firms
   c. *Almanac of Business and Industrial Financial Ratios,* published by Prentice-Hall

AMERICAN EXPRESS TRAVEL RELATED SERVICES COMPANY

Building A Twenty-first Century Company: The Next Ten Years

Welcome to Marrakech and to the fourth Travel Related Services Senior Management Meeting. It's great to see our management from around the world together in this wonderful tourism Mecca.

I enjoy these meetings tremendously. As most of you know, they serve two distinct objectives. First, it is critical in our decentralized worldwide organization to get our senior management group together to share ideas and reaffirm our goals. Second, and equally important, we all benefit greatly from the opportunity to get better acquainted with each other.

My topic today is building a twenty-first century company. As a famous scientist once said, "We should all be concerned about the future because we will have to spend the rest of our lives there."

The speeches and breakout sessions are designed to be provocative—to help us stretch our minds and think about our business in unconventional and new ways. Travel Related Services is at an exciting juncture in its history. My hope is that we can use this meeting to continue building a strong foundation into the 1990s.

1977: MASSIVE COMPETITIVE ONSLAUGHT

Oliver Wendell Holmes, the famous American jurist, once said, "To understand what is happening today or what will happen in the future, I look back."

So before looking into the future, I'd like to spend a few minutes talking about where we've been over the past decade, where we are today and, most importantly, what we have learned from our past experiences.

As I started to think back on TRS in 1977, I thought it would be interesting to reread some of the speeches and planning documents from that year. I wanted to see what was keeping us up at night back then.

Well, not too surprising, in the "Marrakeches of 1977," we were talking a lot about a massive competitive onslaught.

Our competitors were Visa, Mastercard and Eurocard in Europe, Middle East, and Africa. Citicorp had just acquired Carte Blanche and Bank America was still a powerful factor in payment systems around the world. The American banks were expanding their card bases at a rapid rate. On the other hand, European banks promoted Eurocard primarily to keep US cards out of their market. There were ominous rumblings about banks going into the travellers cheque business and about Citicorp paying interest on its Travellers Cheques.

We were also talking a great deal about maturity in our various product lines. Some people thought we were about to hit a wall in terms of new card acquisition and the doomsday predictors were beginning to suggest that smart cards, debit cards, and other electronic instruments were going to replace our "antiquated" paper-intensive payment systems.

Sound familiar? Yes, growing competition and market maturity: the same devils we face today. In fact, the same dual threats all leader companies face constantly—whether it's IBM, McDon-

---

[1]Note: This speech was delivered by Louis V. Gerstner, Jr., Chairman, American Express Travel Related Services Company, Inc., in 1987. Reprinted with permission.

ald's, Coca-Cola, or Sony. The answer, in all instances, is constant self-renewal.

PHENOMENAL GROWTH SINCE 1977

Now let's look at the Travel Related Services Company today, relative to where it was ten years ago.

- Most analysts project that by year end, TRS net income will exceed $690 million (see Chart 1). That is up from $132 million in 1977 and represents an average growth rate of 18 percent per year over the past ten years. (By the way, none of the other companies I mentioned—IBM, Coca-Cola, Sony, or McDonald's—matches this record.)
- By the end of 1987, we expect to have more than 26 million Cardmembers, nearly two and one-half times the Card base in 1977 (see Chart 2). And we will have 2 million Service Establishments, more than six times the number ten years ago.
- Our overall sales performance during the past decade has been equally impressive; discount business is projected to be seven times the 1977 level.
- Travellers Cheque sales will hit $19 billion—not bad for a business that some people thought we should sell—and Travel sales will reach $3 billion, five times the sales level a decade ago (see Chart 3).

And now two other measures we don't look at as often as the prior numbers—but of critical strategic importance.

- We have doubled the number of Travel Service Offices to more than 1,500 offices worldwide and during the past ten years have launched 12 new local currency cards, bringing the current total to 29 (see Chart 4).
- And of course, it takes more people to run a bigger business. By year end 1987, the TRS work force will have tripled, to more than 44,000 employees worldwide (see Chart 5).

Our growth in all respects has been phenomenal. On its own, TRS net income today ranks fifth among the 50 largest diversified financial companies. Many of the people in this room have contributed to this outstanding record of success. Collectively, we can take great pride in what we have achieved.

The critical question, though, is why have we been successful? What has been the basis of our successful self-renewal—despite the howls of maturity and increased competition of 1977?

TRS PRINCIPLES: CODE FOR SUCCESS

In fact, the reasons we have achieved this spectacular growth record have been identified and codified in the TRS principles which were first outlined in our TRS senior management meeting in Bermuda in 1985. These principles, which do not change despite changing competitive, economic, or regulatory environment, codify the essence of our success.

I want to take a few minutes now to highlight these principles again. They're not only extremely relevant as we look back, but will be even more important as we look forward.

First, *the marketplace is the driving force behind all we do.*

Implicit in this statement is the overriding belief that our efforts must be directed at meeting the needs of our customers, rather than in our own preconceived notions of what businesses we want to be in and how we want to be in them.

Central to this principle is also the desire to segment our markets and to appeal to the needs and mindsets of these subsegments with targeted products and services. This marketplace orientation enables us to anticipate and create trends, rather than simply following them when they emerge.

The past decade is full of extraordinary cases of TRS marketing genius: Travel Management Services, Platinum Card, Optima Card, Cause-Related Marketing, the "Membership" campaign, split billing in Latin America, the Gift Cheque, expansion of Card acceptance into retail and health care industries and year-end summaries. In other words, we erased maturity by constantly redefining and expanding our markets. As we work to the future, this marketing leadership must thrive and expand.

The second principle upon which our business success is based is *outstanding customer service is both our greatest competitive strength and our overriding commitment.*

The past decade has seen us rise up from an also-ran to a leader in the field of quality service. Led by our Chairman Jim Robinson's constant commitment and prodding, we have built a competitive weapon that is at the heart of our success. American Express has had a century-long tradition

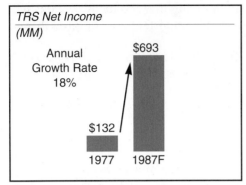

Chart 1

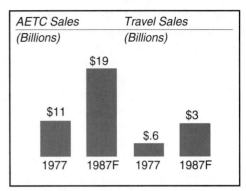

Chart 3

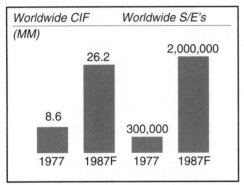

Chart 2

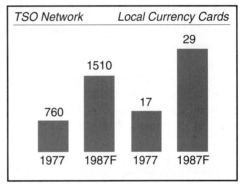

Chart 4

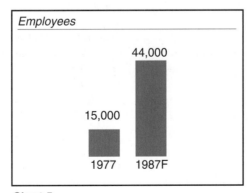

Chart 5

of being a home away from home—a security blanket for travelers across the world. On top of that rich tradition and image, we built a sophisticated quality assurance program unmatched by any company in the service world. We can be proud of that decade of accomplishment.

Nevertheless, time and competitors march on. As we look to the future, we must reawaken our strongest creative energies in this area. A new burst of self-renewal is critical in this basic principle of our success.

The third principle is that *nothing we ever do should undermine our prestige, top-of-the-line position.*

Perhaps in no other area has the importance of adhering to fundamental principles been more evident than here. Constantly over the past decade—and particularly the past three to four years—we have been sorely tempted to trade down: sell or rent our precious Cardmember list, offer discounts on our products, and so forth. Without this clearly stated principle—and without senior management commitment to it—we would have succumbed.

Instead, we come out of the decade with a powerful upscale positioning, refreshed and renewed by innovative programs such as "Membership Has Its Privileges," the Platinum Card, and Consul Clubs.

Before we leave this area, I want to say one more thing on positioning. We've finally gotten over the false dilemma of whether our core Card positioning was one of "prestige" or "value." In today's world, our Card must not only have a prestigious image, but also deliver real value to the customer. The two are totally linked and both are part of our core product positioning. Inherent in any relevant, modern definition of "prestige" is "value." We must never forget this.

The fourth principle is that *productivity, derived from intelligently applied technology and human insight, is a constant objective.*

We don't talk about this one very much—except perhaps at budget time—but it has been critical to our past success.

For example, effective management of operating costs over the past decade has resulted in after-tax profits of $415 million from Card and $80 million from Travellers Cheques. Without these savings, TRS's cumulative growth rate over this period would have been 15 percent instead of 18 percent.

Given the low margins in all of our businesses, it goes without saying that productivity gains will always be vitally important to our growth and profitability.

The fifth principle states that *entrepreneurial instincts and practices dominate our managerial approach.*

When we started the decade, I must confess, we were not risk takers. We studied things to death and were bound up in organizational rigidity and rivalry. While we still seem to run into pockets of bureaucratic mummification, we have come a long way. We take risks easier—big ones like Platinum Card, Optima Card, or Japan—and smaller ones like New York Woman, asset management products in Hong Kong, and a service establishment price test.

We constantly and consciously shake up the organization to ensure our focus is external and responsive to the market place. In the US for example, the Card division lost Corporate Card—gained Travellers Cheques—lost T/C, gained consumer financial services—lost consumer financial services—added merchandise services and then lost merchandise services, and so forth.

International has gone through no less than five reorganizations in ten years. We bought FDR, sold it, bought it back. I know that organizations are difficult for some people, but they are absolutely necessary to preserve our entrepreneurial environment.

Innovation and entrepreneurial behavior must be reinforced with performance-based compensation. Again, under Jim Robinson's leadership (and aided a bit by the arrival of Shearson Lehman Brothers), compensation and capital building opportunities in TRS have exploded in the past decade.

To make sure that this entrepreneurial environment continues, we will continue to pay for outstanding performance. We will reward our innovators and prudent risk takers because we know how essential they are to victory in a very competitive marketplace.

Our sixth principle is that we *manage our day-to-day competitive battles within the context of a clear strategic vision.*

Much of our success over the past decade can be attributed to this principle. By having a clear vision of who we are and where we want to be, we were able to avoid overreacting to short-term tactical actions by our competitors.

Instead, we established true long-term strategies and commitments—whether it was TMS,

Japan, building Data Based Services, or refusing to yield our position in T/C. In each of these cases as well as others, we funded massive, multiyear efforts and readily absorbed short-term costs.

As part of this long-term commitment, we focused our dollars and management resources on basic product enhancements like 24-hour refunds, Enhanced Country Club Billing, and 24-hour Card customer service. These programs resulted in giving us real, long-lasting competitive advantage. Today, new threats like affinity cards and banking cartels in EMEA continue to tempt us to react with short-term promotional Band-Aids, rather than longer-term strategic solutions.

It will be a challenge to all of us to keep our visions clear, our commitments firm, and to find those products and programs that keep us out in front and give us true competitive leverage.

The seventh principle in the TRS company is that *we believe in active corporate citizenship because it is good for our company, our employees, and the communities in which we operate.*

The many programs like Cause-Related Marketing, foundation and cultural grants, and our employee loan program are highly visible demonstrations of both my and Jim Robinson's commitment to this principle.

In the past decade, TRS established itself as a pioneer in combining philanthropic activities with broader business goals. We led the way and now everyone is following us. This commitment to good corporate citizenship is central to being a market leader and therefore will always be a priority for us.

The last principle is fundamental to all the rest: *Outstanding, dedicated people make it all happen.*

Ten years ago, we were committed to having the best-quality people. But we didn't have the right programs in place to make this commitment a reality.

Since then, we've instituted worldwide management development programs like the Graduate Management Program and the Internal Management Program, the TRS management curriculum, Great Performers, and the Management Incentive Programs. These programs, together with a renewed commitment from senior management, have been enormous contributors to our success.

These are the eight TRS principles which have been key to our growth in the past decade. We must never forget what has made us successful. On some level, the more things change, the more they stay the same. No matter what the world looks like or how our businesses evolve, these principles will always be the key to keeping TRS on top.

A TRUE WORLDWIDE ECONOMY WILL EMERGE

Now let's look to the future. Of course, there is no way I can cover the entire spectrum of what the world will be like in the 1990s. Nor is predicting the future ever an exact science. So, given those caveats, let me just describe a few projections and then concentrate on how these developments may impact TRS.

Although many of these trends have been described in a US context, they also apply to most of the developed countries in the world today.

First, over the next decade we will have a true worldwide economy, with countries becoming highly interdependent upon each other. Despite current difficulties, there will be open trade and greater parity in share of economic wealth among regions in the world.

Japan will continue to rise in importance as a worldwide economic force. Europe will see a resurgence in economic stability and strength, and the Pacific Basin, including countries like Korea, Hong Kong, and Australia, will continue to grow at a faster pace than much of the rest of the world.

Travel Related Services will be in an excellent position to operate in this evolving international economy. As a company operating in more than 150 countries, we will be able to provide our customers with access to markets throughout the world. And we're well on our way to establishing a strong market presence in key overseas markets like Japan and Germany.

Nevertheless, we will need to achieve two milestones over the next two to three years: first, a greater balance of investment focus between the US and the rest of the world; second, worldwide systems that support customers on a truly global basis.

1990S—A DECADE OF CHANGES

The 1990s will also be a decade of tremendous demographic and psychographic changes. These changes will have a profound effect on the overall economic, political, and social environment.

Let me highlight a few of the major demographic changes:

- Explosive growth in minority and economically disadvantaged population segments will result in a widening schism in societies. As the middle class declines, we will move toward a world of have and have-nots. Highly visible symbols of wealth will be taboo and prestige and status will be very low key.
- Women will continue to enter the work force in great numbers, creating an even larger group of families with dual incomes. This group will have more money than time and will create a tremendous demand for hassle-free services.
- The population will continue to age and overall population growth will slow down. This will create enormous retraining needs and put increasing demands on underfinanced retirement and health care systems. The so-called "baby bust" could create a skilled labor shortage. On a more positive side, this aging population will be richer, will have more time, and is likely to be willing to spend more to enjoy their life-style.

There will also be significant psychographic changes among consumers.

In an era where everything changes so quickly, consumers will lean toward well-known brands and companies with experience and heritage. They will want old values and old-fashioned quality from their products.

Consumers will develop a highly sophisticated awareness that high quality is more efficient and more economical in the long run. They will buy less, but will buy better-quality goods and services. They will look for real value for their dollar. Trendy items will not sell. Low price alone won't sell.

Quality will no longer be a point of difference: It will be the ticket of entry.

Consumers in the 1990s will think of themselves very much as individuals. They will resist being viewed as a typical mass consumer. As a result, the consumer will look for a club he or she wants to join in every brand decision—and will be attracted to products that set him apart from the masses. Of course, if he perceives that the club is getting too big, he might just look for a new club to join.

These demographic and psychographic changes will raise many new challenges for us, both internally with employees and externally with customers.

Let's look first at our employees. With a vastly reduced supply of skilled workers, we'll need to make sure TRS is a very good place to work. We'll need to consider innovative benefit programs, retraining programs, and flexible work schedules.

Over the past decade, we have done much to improve our management work force. An equal amount of attention must be spent on our clerical work force in the years ahead. This is an urgent and compelling need. Done well, it could be a major competitive weapon.

And, in this next decade, what will be needed to continue our history as a market-driven company?

Clearly, TRS will need to segment its markets and understand the needs, attitudes, and behaviors of the largest and most influential population groups—the mature market, the aging baby boom, and the new youth market.

NEW PRODUCTS: SENIOR CITIZEN CARDS?

We will want to tailor products for these groups, like offering a senior citizen card or special travel club, and adapt our marketing to talk to them with messages that will be meaningful.

In a have and have-not world, everyone will want to sell to the same limited group of affluent people. In order to obtain the greatest share of this group's expenditures and assets, TRS must have the highest-quality products and deliver the best service. In other words, everyone will be after our market—we must protect and build our high ground—there can be no slippage in our positioning and service standards.

Everything suggests that our customers will still be willing to pay a premium price if we deliver real value. This value may be defined by that "extra" measure of service, that "unique" product feature. But whatever it is, it must be tangible, deliverable, and meet a specific customer's needs.

"Membership Has Its Privileges" must be more than just an advertising campaign. It must be an encompassing philosophy that is pervasive in everything we do. To be real, it must be restrictive—and we must respect those restrictions—even at the cost of short-term gains.

American Express' image of experience and reliability will not only enable us to retain the tremendous brand loyalty we enjoy, but also to sell new products to our customer bases and deepen our relationships with them.

ERA OF THE S/E

And while we are on the subject of customers, let me talk for a moment about service establishments. The next five years must be the era of the Service Establishment.

To become genuine business partners with service establishments, we will need immediately to do three things.

First, use technology to provide superior service at every point of contact, including authorization, settlement, and reporting. Implicit in the automation required to deliver these service levels will be an evolution toward much faster speed of pay.

Second, develop unique and innovative marketing programs which either solve a real industry need (like the new restaurant liability insurance in the US) or deliver profitable customers. For years we've built our selling story to business partners around the concept of "Plus Business." In the same way that we have redefined and reenergized the concept of "prestige" for Cardmembers, we need to breathe new life into "Plus Business." The delivery of good customers remains a very powerful reason for any establishment to want to be our business partner.

Third, we must commit to real investment on the Service Establishment side of the business by pouring our productivity gains into exciting Service Establishment programs.

TECHNOLOGY: A FULL PRIORITY

The third future trend I want to discuss is that technological development and automation will be pervasive and critical.

The world will be increasingly linked together electronically. As electronic networks create new distribution channels, products and services will be able to be purchased more easily in the home and at the workplace.

Technology will bring the end of mass marketing. There will be fewer standardized products. Customer databases will be highly personalized. This will give marketers the ability to market to highly targeted segments. However, it may also make privacy much more of a concern.

Technology and automation are likely to have the greatest single impact on TRS businesses in the next decade. They are likely to affect dramatically both our economics and how we operate. And critically, if we don't manage technology properly, we could lose some of our competitive leverage.

Perhaps the greatest risk in an electronic world is the potential to lose control of our product definition and customer interface. For example, if we don't control what data are collected at the point of sale, we may not be able to offer Enhanced Country Club Billing—or even offer our services at all.

Technology also has the ability to alter drastically many of our products' basic functionality. For example, this may be the decade that "smart cards" and interactive video finally take off. We can't afford not to be in the forefront of any technological research and development that directly affects our businesses. It is critical that these technologies be delivered according to our specifications and not our competitors'.

At the same time, technology and its impact on competitive cost structures and service delivery mechanisms will continue to fuel an enormous opportunity for us in Data Based Services, and we intend to take advantage of that.

And finally, technology and automation will raise many human resources issues. Our people will need constant training and retraining. And, as technologies like artificial intelligence take much of the thinking out of certain jobs, we will need to develop new ways of attracting and motivating large groups of our employees.

Technology is an area where we can't lose. It deserves our full priority and is the basis for the heavy investment we are making in the strategic business systems project now underway.

Whatever disagreement there is on specific future trends, there is total agreement that the rate of change will accelerate and the degree of change will sharpen as we approach the year 2000.

This means that our organization must remain entrepreneurial, flexible, and responsive. We can't afford to be locked into organizational structures or units which prohibit us from anticipating the opportunity and going after it aggressively. We must have people in TRS who can adapt and meet the challenges that change creates.

ORGANIZATIONAL CHALLENGES

Let me talk a bit about organization because it is a subject I have been mulling over in my mind a great deal lately.

I don't see any pressing problems, or for that matter, compelling alternatives to our current approach. But let me just touch on two organizational concerns that I believe are strategic and critical in determining our future success.

The first revolves around our clearly defined and clearly correct strategy of broadening our relationship with Cardmembers through the sale of financial and other products. This is an exciting and already proven opportunity for us. However, it brings a host of serious organizational issues. These include:

- "The tail wagging the dog" problem. This emerges as we create a host of insurance companies, mutual fund complexes, and credit granting institutions, all of whom begin to set agendas of their own. Instead of being "franchise enhancers" to the basic Card product line, they seek to become independent profit centers. At that point, the conflicts erupt like mushrooms—conflicts over credit standards, product access, list access, and so on. We then face that most crucial of all business strategy questions: What business are we in in? Are we a card business or a diversified financial services company?

- This then leads to a further issue: span of control. I believe we need the undivided attention of brilliant, committed entrepreneurial teams to build a dominant Card base in eight to ten countries in the next five years. Can those managers do that with maniacal focus and, at the same time, start or buy and then manage three new financial businesses, plus Travel and Travellers Cheques and perhaps Data Based Services? I don't think so. The evidence of the last ten years is crystal clear. Every time we wanted to build a new Card-related business it languished until we pulled it away from the basic Card business—TMS, Merchandise, Publishing and Leasing are just the most obvious examples. Yet when we pull these businesses away we are back to my first problem—namely, the tail wagging the dog. So you see, it is not an easy problem to address. Let me conclude, however, with one overriding observation:

Great businesses succeed because they are reduced to a simple, concentrated focus. Complexity always brings inertia, bureaucracy, and marketing clumsiness.

Let me quickly turn to my second strategic organizational concern. I'm afraid it is equally subtle and vexing. Once again, it starts with a strength—in this case, our decentralized organizational approach.

Over the past decade, we have vastly decentralized TRS. Freedom to act on the local level has been a keystone of our success. Obviously, we centralized strategy and policy as well as those functions that require worldwide standards and/or offer significant economies of scale. It is a good approach and we should continue with it. However, decentralization in our company, as well as in other companies who follow this practice, fosters a dangerous and unfortunate disease. I call it the "lonesome cowboy" syndrome or "I'd rather do it myself."

Managers develop an attitude that only they and their subordinates can or should be involved in their business. They see it as a sign of weakness on their part or interference on their bosses' part if involvement from above takes place. The cost of this practice is, of course, gigantic. Instead of bringing to bear the enormous collective expertise, wisdom, and experience of our great organization on our problems and opportunities, some of our managers operate as small industrial proprietorships.

So one of the things I am going to be concerning myself about in the next few years is the concept of partnership in TRS. How can we maintain the best of our decentralized approach while adding the best of a true partnership environment? What does partnership mean?

It means, first of all, a collective sense of responsibility for the whole. It means trust—trust in each other. It means sharing of talents willingly to get a task done without the asker or the giver even thinking about turf issues. In essence, it means recognizing that your boss and your peers are your best resources for getting a job done.

It means, as a boss, that your main job is to help your subordinates succeed. It means closer, more collegiate relationships between line and staff. It means defining success for our managers not as producing self-contained victories but as the ability to bring to bear all of American Express' resources on a manager's specific set of responsibilities. It means less fretting about why my boss is involved in my business and more collaboration across hierarchical lines.

We need to do a lot more of this collaboration in TRS: in S/E relationships, in problem solving, in people managing.

TRS IN 1997: LARGE IN SIZE, SCOPE

Now, if we keep to our principles, what will we look like in ten years?

Given our strengths and our clear strategic vision, there is every reason to believe that TRS will be an enormous company in 1997, both in size and scope.

- For example, our projections show that with an average annual growth rate of 15 percent over the next ten years, TRS could make nearly $3 billion in net income—equal to that of General Motors today (see Chart 6).
- We could have 62 million cards and 6 million S/Es (see Chart 7).
- Discount business could reach $300 billion; T/C sales could reach $43 billion—greater than Mobil Oil's sales today. And Travel sales could hit $10 billion (see Chart 8).
- We are likely to make nearly $700 million in businesses other than Card, T/C, and Travel. This is equal to all of TRS net income today.
- We will have 78,000 employees, or enough to fill the Roman Coliseum twice.

And, if our businesses grow to these sizes, we will have:

- Authorization requests of more than 3 billion, or close to 1 percent of all the telephone calls made in the US in 1987 terms.

- Nearly 2 billion ROCS, which if laid end to end would stretch two-thirds of the way to the moon.
- Telephone service volume of 50 million calls. This means that a customer's call will be answered and resolved every 1.58 seconds, 24 hours a day, 365 days a year.

It seems inconceivable that we could ever be this big, this diverse, and this complex, but, who would have thought in 1977 that we'd ever be where we are today?

To conclude, let me summarize what I've said today:

First, we're in for another decade of exhilarating, roller-coaster change. There is no question the future will be vastly different than what we see today.

Second, to succeed in that environment, we will need an ever present capability of self-renewal—we must be change agents and constantly anticipate, create, and embrace change.

Third, we must adhere with extraordinary commitment to the principles of our business. They are our road map in this unparalleled landscape of change.

And finally, we have an extraordinary group of people in this company—restless people, risk takers—people who are always self-critical. I hope we are always self-critical. I hope we are always resisting the arrogance and hubris of leadership and success.

If we do all these things, we will achieve all we talked about today and have a lot of fun doing it.

I want to thank everyone for the last decade and look forward to working with all of you in the next decade.

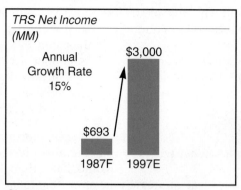

Chart 6

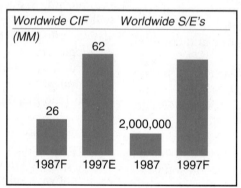

Chart 7

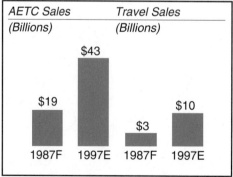

Chart 8

CHATEAU STE MICHELLE

Corporate Strategy and Business Plan, 1982–1991

CORPORATE MISSION

Chateau Ste Michelle will enhance long-term corporate profits by capturing and maintaining a significant share of the premium-priced table wine market. This effort will be accomplished through the development of premium vineyards and the production of world-class wines. In addition, we will deploy a superior trained sales force and develop a strong distributor network in key markets. Once distribution is established and we have sufficient product availability, we will develop consumer preference through high-quality marketing and selected advertising programs.

CORPORATE OBJECTIVES

1. Create high consumer awareness and support for all Chateau Ste Michelle products among the premium wine consumers in key markets expected to represent 80% of our sales volume.
2. Develop a well-planned, flexible, and highly responsive marketing program tailored to the needs of local, regional, national, and international markets.
3. Explore, plan, and develop tangential business opportunities which directly enhance our ability to achieve our corporate objectives (e.g., retail shop, winery, restaurant, etc.) and avoid and/or divest of all extraneous projects which do not directly contribute to attainment of corporate mission (e.g., dessert and berry wines).
4. Develop a strong distributor network capable of meeting or exceeding our growth demands.
5. Develop a top-quality, well-trained national sales force.
6. Manage overall operations in a manner which assures excellent long-term financial returns as measured by return on assets.
7. Develop and maintain highly motivated, cost-conscious, quality-oriented personnel.
8. Produce annually 1 million cases of top-quality premium-priced wine while continuing to expand both vineyard and wine production operations to allow for growth to a minimum of 2 million cases of wine per year by 1991.
9. Develop 5,000 acres of vineyards in eastern Washington capable of producing premium varietal grapes that can compete in quality with the finest grapes grown anywhere in the world.

*Reprinted with permission.

Chateau Ste Michelle Sales History (20-Year Sales History and Forecast—Table Wine Sales Only)

Year	Dollar Volume	Cases
1973	$ 160,000	16,000
1974	220,000	19,600
1975	570,000	27,400
1976	1,149,000	48,400
1977	2,219,000	88,400
1978	3,850,000	135,800
1979	6,004,000	207,400
1980	6,096,204	168,217
1981	6,760,179 (94%)*	204,326 (86%)*
Forecast		
1982	$10,566,000 (87%)	297,000 (80%)
1983	17,153,000 (94%)	477,000 (86%)
1984	26,402,000 (95%)	680,000 (89%)
1985	36,543,000 (94%)	900,000 (87%)
1986	45,672,000 (92%)	1,071,000 (82%)
1987	54,674,000 (89%)	1,234,000 (76%)
1988	63,963,000 (87%)	1,375,000 (72%)
1989	74,952,000 (84%)	1,554,000 (66%)
1990	86,441,000 (79%)	1,763,000 (59%)
1991	97,112,000 (75%)	1,937,000 (54%)

*Percentages represent Chateau Ste Michelle label.

INDUSTRY DATA AND TRENDS

For the seventeenth consecutive year, wine sales have increased in the US. There was slow and orderly growth in the 36 years between the end of Prohibition and 1969, but between 1970 and 1980 the wine industry exploded. Consumption increased from 267 million gallons to 476 million and is projected to exceed 1 billion by 1990 (see Table 1).

In 1960 Americans consumed twice as much dessert-aperitif wine as table wine. By 1980 dessert-aperitif wines had declined to a 9% share of the market while table wines grew to a 75% share. The only other wine category to have shown healthy growth is the sparkling wine category. Although sparkling wine has not increased its market share, it has held its own in a booming table wine market with actual volume increasing 50% in the last five years.

Table 2 shows market share of different types of wines. The dominant table wine category, 75% is American-made table wine and 25% is imported. As table 3 shows, almost all of the American wine is coming from California and its share of the market continues to increase.

This explosion is not just a passing fad; it is supported by fundamental factors in our society.

The US currently ranks 31st among nations in per capita consumption of wine (see Table 4).

Every other major wine-producing country in the world consumes three to twelve times more wine than does the US on a per capita basis. Because of our historical roots in Protestant temperance and the resultant prohibition laws, our country was slow to develop the cultural maturation of fine wine appreciation. But once established, like all great cultural movements it will not be easily extinguished. Indeed, as we shall see shortly, the demographics of new consumers read like a profile of the future leaders of this country. They represent the best-educated, highest-incomed, professional young people of our society. These are the people who are creating the trends that will set the standards for tomorrow's world. For these reasons there is little disagreement with the forecast for continued dramatic growth. The standard accepted forecast is that wine consumption will continue to increase at an 8% compounded annual rate for the next 10 years. No other beverage category is expected to increase at this rate. The next two fastest growing categories, beer and soft drinks, are projected to increase at a 4% rate and spirits are projected to remain flat.

Table 1 *Total US Wine Market by Type, 1960–1990 (Millions of Gallons)*

Wine Type	1960	1970	1975	1980	Estimated 1981	1985	1990
Table	53	133	214	359	391	590	972
Dessert	87	74	67	45	42	35	28
Vermouth	7	10	10	9	9	9	9
Sparkling	4	22	20	30	30	39	49
Special natural	12	28	57	33	28	23	18
Total	163	267	368	476	500	696	1,076
Compound growth rate*		5.0%	6.6%	5.3%	. . .	8.0%	9.1%

*All rates are five-year intervals except 1970 which is ten.

Table 2 *Total Wine Shares by Type (Figures in Percents)*

Wine Type	1970	1975	1976	1977	1978	1979	1980	1981 (est)
Table	50%	58%	61%	66%	71%	73%	75%	77%
Dessert	28	18	16	14	12	11	10	9
Vermouth	4	3	3	2	2	2	2	2
Sparkling	8	6	6	6	6	6	6	6
Special natural	10	15	14	11	9	8	7	6
Sales volume	267	368	376	400	430	444	476	500

Table 3 *Table Wine by Origin (Millions of Gallons)*

Origin	1970	1976	1977	1978	1979	1980	1981
California	95	160	183	203	223	249	276
Other states	17	22	22	19	23	18	15
Italy	4	18	24	39	43	54	62
France	7	10	12	14	13	11	11
Germany	3	9	10	14	12	12	12
Portugal	4	6	6	6	6	6	6
Spain	2	5	4	5	4	5	5
Other	0	2	2	3	3	3	4

Table 4 *Wine Consumption in the US*

Date	Gallons (Millions)	Per Capita Adults (Gallons)	Consumer Expenditure (Millions)
1981 (est)	500.0	3.15	$6,670
1980	471.8	3.04	5,939
1979	439.1	2.94	5,242
1978	418.0	2.83	4,573
1977	389.7	2.69	3,941
1976	371.8	2.59	3,575
1975	361.6	2.58	3,286
1970	341.8	2.09	1,748
1960	158.1	1.46	751
1950	135.0	1.38	551
1940	87.1	1.03	260
1930	32.7	.42	90

In 1980 an important milestone was reached. For the first time ever, wine sales surpassed those of distilled spirits (see Table 5).

And while beer volumes are still much larger than those of wine, there has nevertheless been a steady narrowing of the gap between wine and beer's share over the past 10 years (see Table 6).

As was noted in Table 3, states other than California are actually losing share of market—a trend that is expected to continue according to most wine industry spokespersons. This begs the question as to where the projected increases in volume will come from. We know that there are many countries hoping to unload their surpluses in the US (Italy, France, Argentina, and Australia to name just four), and certainly more grapes can be grown in central California. The combination of these two factors will certainly handle the growing demand for the nonpremium wines, but what about the premium wines? There is little premium viticultural land left in California and what exists is prohibitively priced ($20,000 to $30,000 per acre). France, Italy, and Germany have planted their best land centuries ago and already the high demand for those truly premium wines allows for prices which are out of most people's range. So we still ask, where will the premium wine come from?

Few people outside the United States Tobacco (UST) organization fully understand and appreciate the phenomenon taking place in Washington state. There are currently 8,000 acres of vinifera grape vines planted in the state. There is an estimated additional 50,000 acres suitable to premium wine grapes. This acreage tends to be widely scattered in small holdings. The next 10 years will see many small new wineries coming to Washington to produce those premium wines which will always be in high demand. One of the pleasing aspects of this is that virtually all the vinifera table wine produced in Washington is being made from premium grapes. There is no inexpensive table wine produced in Washington. Consequently Washington, unlike California, will be known only for its premium wines and in the future may actually overtake California's reputation as a producer of extraordinary wines. This can only serve to create further awareness and demand for Chateau Ste Michelle wines. And given our headstart, it is unlikely that anyone can remove us from the position of Washington's premier winery.

COMPETITIVE WINERIES

To understand the working dynamics of the wine industry, it is important to appreciate the positioning that has taken place in the past few years.

Wine is a highly image-intensive product. Perhaps no other arena except designer clothes and fragrances carries as much intense consumer status imagery as does wine. For this reason, brand positioning becomes critical. Moving up or down the scale from, for example, premium to super-premium will not necessarily effect cost of sales but it can greatly affect profits. The following are the five wine classifications now being used within the industry along with their projected growth rates:

Table 5 *Spirits and Wine Sales (Millions of Gallons)*

	1970		1975		1976		1977		1978		1979		1980		1981 (est)	
	Vol	%	Vol	%	Vol	%	Vol	%	Vol	%	Vol	%	Vol	%	Vol	%
Spirits	388	59	446	55	434	54	440	52	470	52	473	52	455	49	450	47
Wines	267	41	368	45	376	46	400	48	430	48	444	48	476	51	500	53

Table 6 *Beer and Wine Sales (Millions of Gallons)*

	1970		1975		1976		1977		1978		1979		1980		1981 (est)	
	Vol	%	Vol	%	Vol	%	Vol	%	Vol	%	Vol	%	Vol	%	Vol	%
Beer	4,037	93	4,588	92	4,666	92	4,901	92	5,118	92	5,304	92	5,419	91	5,530	91
Wines	267	7	368	8	376	8	400	8	430	8	444	8	476	9	500	9

- Economy: Gallo's Carlo Rossi—the leader in this category. These are the price sensitive, generic jugs. Growth is estimated at 15% or more compounded annually.
- Popular: The position of the standard Gallo, United Vintners, and Taylor California Cellars wines. All are attempting to move up into the premium category as this category is perceived to be flat.
- Premium: Almaden, Inglenook, Paul Masson, Farron Ridge, Gallo varietals—projected to have continued rapid growth at 15% annually
- Super-premium: Mondavi, Wente, Sterling, Beaulieu, and Chateau Ste Michelle—growth rate projected to continue at 8% to 9%.
- Small estate: Reserve wine, Stag Leap, Heitz, and Schamsberg—growth rate is projected by the industry to be generally flat unless the laws change which would allow sales by mail. This category, unlike the others, does not necessarily reflect superior quality but rather lower quantity, therefore rarer wines.

The most significant trend in table wine sales during the past decade has been the unprecedented growth in consumption of white table wine. Shipments of white table wine in 1980 were 190 million gallons compared to 9 million gallons in 1960. White wine now has 57% of the total table wine market. This share has grown from 24% in 1970 when it was the least favored segment. The acceptance of white table wine as a cocktail has certainly expanded the traditional image pattern for white wine (at the expense of traditional spirit- or vermouth-based cocktails).

Over the past five years table wine has grown at 12% per year. White table wines within the same category during that period grew at over 24% per year. Red table wines have shown serious signs of weakness during the latter part of the decade. Rosé has shown more resilience. Although white wine has shown tremendous growth, and red wine appears static, the growth of red wines in the super-premium sector of the market is substantial. Industry forecasts suggest that 60% of super-premium wine volume is red wine. Therefore, red wines will continue to play a major role in the development of the wine industry, in addition to the development of the Northwest as a well-accepted viticultural region.

Two other major trends have continued to interest the wine community. The first of these is the introduction of low calorie or "light" wines. To date these wines are targeted at the 1.5-liter, high-volume, mass market. While wine purists shun the product and pass it off as another fad, there is evidence that like the "light" or diet categories in other beverages (beer and soft drinks), the light wines will eventually represent a 10% to 15% share of market.

The second interesting trend is the continued growth of Italian wines in the US. It is important to note that almost all of this growth is attributed to the Lambrusco's, a slightly carbonated sweet wine.

Table 7 Table Wine Sales—All Origins (Millions of Gallons)

	1960	(%)	1970	(%)	1975	(%)	1976	(%)	1977	(%)	1978	(%)	1979	(%)	*Est.* 1980	(%)	1981	(%)
Red	39	(74)	64	(50)	88	(44)	88	(40)	96	(37)	97	(34)	90	(29)	94	(27)	97	(25)
White	9	(17)	31	(24)	64	(32)	76	(35)	101	(39)	134	(47)	159	(50)	190	(54)	223	(57)
Rosé	5	(9)	33	(26)	49	(26)	54	(25)	60	(24)	67	(19)	66	(21)	70	(19)	70	(18)
	53	(100)	128	(100)	201	(100)	218	(100)	257	(100)	288	(100)	315	(100)	354	(100)	391	(100)

This wine appeals to the youth market and serves as an entry-level product with more legitimacy than the old "pop" wines. There is some evidence that this category is peaking and will follow the path of sangrias which were the big fad in the mid-1970s.

1981 was another strong year for major American vintners. But the big story of the year was the continued success of Taylor California Cellars and E. & J. Gallo. Both attribute their growth to aggressive marketing and large advertising budgets (see Table 8). Gallo's growth is perhaps the most spectacular considering its high share of market and the fact that growth came while it was repositioning almost all of its table wine lines *upward*.

Table 9 shows that although there is dynamic growth in sales of the top 10 wineries, the market share that they hold has remained relatively stable over the past decade. This is a good sign for the industry as it displays the competitive success of the premium and super-premium wineries in the US.

There is a lack of specific brand information in this industry due to the number of privately held companies and the varying methods of retailing required by each state, all which make tracking difficult. In addition, wineries are not required to divulge how their bulk sales are broken down and many of the super-premium wineries have either premium jugs or second 750-ml brands included in their line.

Table 10 (drawn from California depletion reports) represents our best estimates of the volume of wine in super-premium labels; thus, although Beringer is the largest of the super-premium wineries, Mondavi is the brand leader in the super-premium category. An estimated 40% of super-premium wine sales come from brands in the top 20. The super-premium wineries continue to be the wine industry's most dynamic segment. Although relatively insignificant when compared to the volumes of the top 10, the super-premiums represent a unique segment which will determine the future of the American wine industry. For it is from this category that wine writers and other wine experts find the wines to write and talk about. As new consumers develop an interest in wines, they are led into this arena of wine enjoyment. Once exposed to the pleasures of fine wine, few ever retreat.

BUSINESS PLAN

The first five corporate objectives [listed previously] are all within the purview of the marketing department and sales department and will be addressed in the first section of the business plan, which is the marketing plan. The next two objectives (six and seven) are the shared responsibilities of every department but can most appropriately be dealt with in the finance and administration section. Finally, the last two objectives (eight and nine) are primarily production objectives and will be discussed in that section. The previous section has set forth concisely and objectively the environment in which Chateau Ste Michelle must operate. The marketing plan grew out of an in-depth analysis of that environment while utilizing the corporate objectives as a backdrop from which to view each strategy.

MARKETING PLAN

Distribution

As was evidenced by the market analysis in the previous section, virtually every market is unique in terms of state laws, attitudes toward premium wines, awareness of Washington state wines, preference of imported versus domestic, per capita consumption, life-styles, trade practices, and distributor relations. For this reason, it is necessary to

Table 8 *Selected Large US Wineries (Millions of Gallons)*

Producer	Volume (gallons)	Change 1980/1981 (%)	Market Share (%)	Cumulative Share (%)
1. E. & J. Gallo	133.0	12.7	23.8	23.8
2. United Vintners	48.6	−9.1	11.3	35.1
3. Taylor California Cellars	25.3	53.8	4.3	47.3
4. Almaden	30.9	−1.4	7.9	43.0
5. Paul Masson	18.3	13.4	4.0	51.3
6. Guild	11.1	−9.0	3.2	54.5
7. Sebastiani	8.7	−11.5	2.6	57.1
8. C. Mondavi/Krug	4.8	3.0	1.3	58.4
9. Christian Brothers	4.5	−3.9	1.1	59.5
10. Beringer/L.H.	4.0	31.2	1.1	60.6

Table 9 *Cumulative Volume and Share of 10 Largest Table Wine Wineries*

(Millions of Gallons)

	1970	1975	1976	1977	1978	1979	1980	1981 (est)
Sales	94	167	170	181	190	208	231	276
Share (%)	63	65	62	61	58	60	61	61

Table 10 *Top Premium Wineries*

	Volume of Premium Priced Wines in Cases	Total Volume 1980 (000's cases)	Growth Potential
1. Mondavi	350	1,300	Med
2. Korbel	300	300	Med
3. Wente	285	718	Med
4. Beaulieu Vineyard	280	558	Med
5. Mirassou	280	280	Med
6. Souverain	230	503	Med
7. Beringer	250	1,473	High
8. Sonoma	235	468	Med
9. Martini	235	324	Low
10. Fetzer	204	204	Med
11. Monterey	195	393	High
12. Chateau Ste Michelle	175	300	High
13. San Martin	155	311	Med
14. Domain Chandon	128	128	High
15. Parducci	125	249	Low
16. Chateau Ste Jean	120	120	Med
17. Rutherford Hill	100	100	Low
18. H. Kornell	75	75	Low
19. Lawrence	74	74	Low
20. Simi	73	73	Low
21. Sterling	68	68	Low
22. Concannon	56	56	Med
23. Buena Vista	53	53	Low

develop a specific marketing strategy for each market. This section will not go into each market in detail but address only the general strategy.

We have divided our domestic sales regions into primary, secondary, and tertiary markets. A fourth category, international, will be treated separately. A primary market will sell 40,000 cases in 1982 and have the potential to grow significantly from that base. Our strategy stated simply is to create as many primary markets as possible over the next decade. In primary markets we can afford to place our own salespeople; we can design promotions that are tailored to local needs, we can advertise, wine sample, run special events, and make frequent trade visits to survey, motivate, or plan. In addition, we become important to distributors and retailers and thus have a degree of clout in the market. We can dictate where we are placed on the shelf, how displays are used, what wine list we go on, and so on. The problem, of course, is just the opposite with small markets. It becomes difficult to impossible to influence a market when one can't justify salespeople, advertising, promotions, or trade visits.

Our Farron Ridge brand is an example of how we will implement this strategy. We recently released Farron Ridge throughout Washington state. Currently, the supply exceeds the demand. Our Oregon, Idaho, and Montana brokers are begging for the brand as are various California distributors. We could exhaust our supply tomorrow by opening new markets. Instead, we are working within the state to build the brand. We do not want retailers and distributors to become disenchanted with the brand because of out of stocks. At the same time we are teaching our distributors to develop the brand. As quantities increase we will begin opening new markets. The brand must be important to every one who is selling it—something that won't happen if we spread it too thin.

Secondary markets will sell 5,000 cases in 1982. A secondary market must show immediate potential growth opportunities.

Tertiary markets are those currently doing at least 500 cases and offering long-term potential. These markets will be looked at and worked on selectively so as to elevate them to secondary or primary status. Some will be weeded out and others will be added. In most of these markets, our products are too sparsely distributed to justify a major marketing commitment. We cannot justify tailoring merchandising programs or assigning our full-time salespeople. The following is the current list of primary, secondary, and tertiary markets.

- Primary markets (40,000 cases): Seattle, Washington (except Seattle), Southern California.
- Secondary markets (5,000 cases): Connecticut, Illinois, New York (metro), northern California, Northwest (except Washington), Washington, D.C.
- Tertiary Markets (500 cases): Colorado, Florida, Georgia, Maryland, Massachusetts, Michigan, Minnesota, New Jersey, New York (except NYC), Ohio, Pennsylvania, Texas.

International. The marketing strategy for international is straightforward. We recognize the future potential of international markets and the obvious benefits we can derive from their successful penetration, but we wish to be cautious in our approach. We would not enter a new market anywhere without fully investigating the capability of the broker or distributor to properly handle and distribute our product. A recent French introduction in this country may never recover from the damage done when one wine writer wrote a national column about a bad bottle he received. We must approach these highly sophisticated and potentially profitable markets in Europe and Asia with great caution. Because of the inherent difficulties in exporting wines to major wine-producing nations and the more immediate need to fully penetrate the US market, it is felt that we should approach all export opportunities from a test market standpoint. For this reason, the marketing department has assumed responsibility to thoroughly research all export recommendations and closely monitor results. In this early exploratory stage it is important that we establish good, workable, policies and procedures. In this regard we are currently working with a Japanese restaurant chain to test market products in the country; our Los Angeles distributor is working with a European broker to test our wines in Switzerland and Germany; and another independent broker has taken certain products to England to test market.

Chain Accounts. Possibly the greatest opportunity that exists for Chateau Ste Michelle is in the arena of chain supermarkets. Already on the West Coast it is common to see super-premium wines displayed in supermarkets. This situation exists nowhere else in the country, partly because consumers have not yet made super-premium wines a part of their daily consumption, but mostly because distributors and chain wine buyers have not been educated to the opportunity. It has not been in the interest of other super-premium wineries to foster this education because they have not had sufficient supply of wines and they have been fearful of the negative image they might create if their brand becomes associated with mass marketing. Chateau Ste Michelle could become the leader in this area by being the first super-premium winery with a tailor-made supermarket sales program. The nucleus of this program would be built around a national accounts sales manager and a specially designed chain store audiovisual program that would educate distributors and buyers to the exciting profit potential of selling fine wines in supermarkets.

Goals.

1. Table 11 shows 1981's actual sales, 1982 sales goals, and projected goals for 1983, 1986, and 1991 for all key markets for Chateau Ste Michelle varietal wines only.

2. New markets will be added to the key market list only after an exhausting review of distributor capabilities, market potential, and product availability.

3. Products will be made available on a selected basis to those nonkey markets when special opportunities or situations arise. It is always intended that 20% of Chateau Ste Michelle products will be sold to nonkey markets.

4. A market sales analysis will be conducted monthly and distributor analysis will be conducted biannually for all key markets.

5. Markets will be divided into six regions plus international. By 1983 all regional sales managers will be appointed. In addition, any market area with 15,000 cases or more will be staffed with a sales representative.

6. By 1984 we will hire a national accounts manager to service opportunities in the airlines, chain restaurants, and hotels.

7. We will work with and explore the possibility of providing a major Japanese restaurant chain with appropriate line of Chateau Ste Michelle products; by September 1982 we will provide a recommendation to the executive committee.

8. Marketing will review results of past shipments to the United Kingdom and West Germany and contact Los Angeles distributors and report on success of negotiations with European importers.

9. Marketing will formalize a policy for export market exploration—policy to be available no later than January 1, 1983. We want to gain sufficient experience in this very important area of distribution before we approach the UST International Department for support.

10. We will develop a new label for export to Canada (Chateau Ste Michelle is an infringement of a Canadian winery trademark and cannot be used in that country) as Canada is clearly our single best export opportunity if we had the right products. Canadian export plan is to be prepared by mid-1983.

11. We will develop by October 1982 a total chain supermarket sales program complete with audiovisual presentations, literature, special luncheon presentations, and so on, which will be carried across the country to markets that allow supermarket wine sales.

Resource and Responsibility.

Goal 1: It will be the joint responsibility of sales and marketing to forecast sales and set projected sales goals. This will be done on a yearly basis prior to business plans and budgets, and they will be periodically reviewed. With the coming computer capabilities, no additional manpower is required.

Goal 2: New-market analysis will be the joint responsibility of sales and marketing. A formal review will be approved by executive committee before new distributors are taken on. No new resources required.

Goal 3: Sales analysis will be the responsibility of marketing with input from sales; whereas distributor analysis will be conducted by sales with input from marketing. Sales and distributor analyses will require computer assistance and periodic trade visits. Existing travel budgets are deemed sufficient.

Goals 4 and 5: Regional sales managers and national accounts manager will be appointed by the vice president of sales. Regional sales managers currently exist in three regions. Three more will be required by 1983. In addition, we currently require additional sales representatives in both the Seattle and southern California markets. These additional people are not budgeted for 1982 but should be added

Table 11 *Chateau Ste Michelle Projected Case Sales by Market*

	Actual 1981	Forecast 1982	Projected 1983	Projected 1986	Projected 1991
Primary					
Seattle	47,000	58,000	80,000	105,000	115,000
Washington (except Seattle)	44,000	50,000	85,000	100,000	105,000
Southern California	20,000	32,000	50,000	100,000	115,000
	111,000	140,000	215,000	305,000	335,000
Secondary					
Connecticut	1,980	3,000	8,000	15,000	20,000
Illinois	1,675	3,000	12,000	35,000	45,000
New York (metro)	2,000	5,000	15,000	25,000	40,000
Northern California	9,000	12,000	25,000	12,000	60,000
Northwest (except Washington)	10,500	12,000	30,000	50,000	60,000
Washington, D.C.	2,350	5,000	10,000	15,000	20,000
	27,505	40,000	100,000	190,000	245,000
Tertiary					
Colorado	1,800	3,000	10,000	28,000	30,000
Florida	895	2,000	8,000	32,000	40,000
Georgia	0	500	3,000	13,000	15,000
Maryland	0	500	3,000	12,000	13,000
Massachusetts	1,500	2,000	6,000	25,000	30,000
Michigan	600	750	3,000	15,000	20,000
Minnesota	500	750	2,000	8,000	10,000
New Jersey	1,300	2,000	6,000	15,000	20,000
New York (except NYC)	650	1,000	5,000	15,000	20,000
Ohio	1,000	1,500	3,000	10,000	15,000
Pennsylvania	1,850	2,500	7,000	20,000	25,000
Texas	2,600	3,000	10,000	30,000	30,000
	12,695	19,500	66,000	223,000	268,000
Other markets	11,469	37,000	25,000	180,000	212,000
All markets—total case sales	162,669	236,500	407,000	898,000	1,060,00

by October 1982 and treated as a budget variance so they can be on board and productive by January 1983.

Goals 6 through 9: The responsibility of international will be that of the marketing department while in this exploratory stage.

Second-labels (Farron Ridge)

Farron Ridge represents the winery's first second-label. From the beginning, it was decided that the brand should have its own identity and not compromise Chateau Ste Michelle's image. The major marketing premise supporting this brand is the knowledge that we can produce a better 1.5-liter table wine at a cheaper cost than the competition.

The demand for sophisticated wines at everyday prices has caused the premium 1.5-liter market to become the fastest-growing segment of the US domestic table wine industry.

The entry of Farron Ridge into this market was a logical direction for the company to take for a number of reasons.

- The market is viable and profitable.
- It provides an outlet for wines that are not accepted as super-premium varietals but nevertheless are of high quality.
- It reduces corporate risk by having more than one viable brand.
- This brand helps develop the reputation of the Northwest as a quality viticultural region.

Farron Ridge was launched statewide at the end of 1981 and has subsequently been given to Alaska as a developmental brand as well as being test marketed in Eugene, Oregon (a student town), to examine its potential for 21- to 26-year-old consumers.

On April 1, 1982, a new 4-liter pack was launched to sell as a house brand in on-sale accounts. Little profit will be made with this package but it is intended to serve as a sampling program for Farron Ridge. The introductory price ($19 a case) has given the brand a competitive opportunity as a house wine in restaurant accounts (though still higher priced than most house wines).

Packaging and pricing flexibility has enabled the brand to react quickly to changing market conditions. Our next bottling of the brand will see a significant packaging change. The case of Bordeaux-styled bottles and flint glass for the rosé are

expected to communicate higher quality and thus benefit the brand.

Just as the image of the brand is improving, so will the wine. Currently only 10% of the wine is produced from our own vineyards, by 1984 100% will be from our own vines. Most of the purchased grapes do not compare in quality to those that come from our own vineyards.

We have planned two promotional periods during the coming year. Promotional materials with price incentives have been designed to build distribution and trial.

Consideration for a Canadian introduction is to be reviewed in the coming year and the possible introduction of Farron Ridge varietal wines in a 750-ml package will be considered as a developmental project for the brand in coming years.

The brand is poised for further growth in 1983; the product is good and was well received in tastings. Continuous enological development will ensure that the product quality remains very high.

By 1990 we have the potential, with advertising support, to sell over 200,000 cases of this wine through national distribution. As will be discussed in the New Products section of this plan, we have not yet determined that Farron Ridge is the only direction for us to take in generating this additional growth.

The brand has a great many positive attributes. It is good-quality wine made from premium varietals from a premier viticultural region, and it will become an important brand for the company.

Goals.
1. To achieve sales of 60,000 cases by the end of 1982
2. To establish long-term brand awareness so as to achieve minimum case sales of 230,000 by 1990 (See Table 12.)
3. To ensure adequate product supply in all markets and to release the brand only into new markets as sufficient product becomes available
4. To reinforce the benefits of Northwest viticulture through the brand communications.

Resource and Responsibility. It will be the duty of the marketing department to plan and execute all programs related to brand promotion.

Pricing

The brands have been priced to maximize profit; however, it is also recognized that this image-sen-

Table 12 *Farron Ridge and Other Second-Labels Projected Case Volume (000's)*

State	1982	1983	1984	1985	1986	1987	1988	1989	1990	1991
Seattle	48	50	51	66	75	86	97	113	123	136
Washington	10	13	15	22	25	29	32	37	42	46
Oregon	1	3	5	11	13	14	17	21	25	34
Alaska	1	2	3	6	7	8	10	13	16	18
Idaho				5	7	9	11	15	19	23
Montana				4	5	6	8	9	11	13
Total Farron Ridge	60	68	74	114	132	152	175	208	236	270
Additional cases*	___	___	___	___	59	140	210	315	479	620
Total cases					191	292	385	523	715	890

*As discussed in the New Products section, we will not commit those additional cases to Farron Ridge until we have studied the alternatives.

sitive product must be priced high to be considered of true merit by most consumers. Due to the large volumes of many of the Chateau Ste Michelle wines we will be producing in the next five years, we cannot always charge top of the line prices that would protect our prestigious image. The company has designed a four-tier pricing strategy for Chateau Ste Michelle wines.

Specialty Items. Products like the Chateau Reserve label and the sparkling wine will be used for the ad hoc release of wines of unique quality (e.g., Ice Wine, 1976 Cabernet, etc.). This range of wines will be priced against the most expensive small-estate wines of California. Both the price and the packaging will reflect the high quality of Chateau Ste Michelle wines.

Cabernet Sauvignon and Chardonnay. These wines have been priced higher than the rest of the range and will serve as our flagship products. The quality image of these two varieties will establish the quality of the rest of the range.

Strategically, these two varieties will keep pace with Cabernets and Chardonnays of major super-premium competitors.

Fume Blanc, Merlot, Gewurztraminer, and Muscat Alexandria. These products represent our middle range of pricing. They will be priced to be comparable to the better super-premium wines in their respective category; however, individual prices may rise or fall depending on the quality characteristics of each variety's vintage.

Chenin Blanc, Grenache Rosè, Johannesberg Riesling, Rosè of Cabernet, and Semillon Blanc. These products are the Chateau Ste Michelle volume items. The range has been competitively priced for volume sales in order to induce trial and repeat purchase.

In addition to the Chateau Ste Michelle pricing strategy, second-labels have and will be developed which require their own pricing strategy. The only second-label currently offered by Chateau Ste

---

Current Pricing

	Wholesale Case Price	Recent Retail Price per Bottle
Specialty Products		
1976 Private Reserve Cabernet (magnum)	$89.50	$30.50
1978 Private Reserve Cabernet (750 ml)	91.00	15.50
1976 Sparkling wine	136.00	23.00
1980 White Riesling	46.00	8.00
Flagship		
Cabernet Sauvignon	50.00	8.70
Chardonnay	52.00	9.00
Middle Range		
Fume Blanc	41.00	7.20
Merlot	40.00	7.00
Gewurztraminer	37.50	6.60
Muscat Alexandria	38.00	6.70
Volume Items		
Johannesberg Riesling	34.25	6.05
Chenin Blanc	30.50	5.50
Rosé of Cabernet	27.50	4.95
Grenache Rosé	27.50	4.95
Semillon Blanc	30.50	5.50
Second Labels		
Farron Ridge (1.5 liter)	14.65	4.99

Michelle is the Farron Ridge brand (this assumes that the dessert and berry wines will be sold or otherwise discontinued).

Farron Ridge is a price-point product. It competes in the premium 1.5 table wine category with other brands that all sell in the narrow $4 to $6 price range. Farron Ridge is currently pegged in the middle of this price range.

Goals.
1. A pricing survey will be conducted monthly to determine competitive relationships for all brands.
2. Quarterly pricing meetings will be held between sales, marketing, and finance to review existing prices in light of sales history, perceived product quality, and profit margins.
3. All new products will be reviewed prior to release for possible price adjustments.
4. The pricing strategy described above will be reviewed yearly. Certain products like White Riesling are currently priced dearly due to limited availability. As availability increases, this product may be moved to a lower tier to stimulate sales. Conversely, other products like Mer-

lot and Semillon are currently priced lower than their value due to low demand caused by low awareness of these specific varieties. If, as we predict, these varieties become popular, the pricing will move up dramatically.

Resource and Responsibility. Accomplishment of the above goals will be the responsibility of the marketing department with support from finance and sales. No additional manpower is required.

New Products

Consistent with the goals of selling 2 million cases of wine per year and maximizing our financial returns, we will continue pursuit of new product opportunities.

We recognize that quantity and quality are considered by serious wine consumers to be inversely correlated, and we also know that wine writers need new and unique products about which to write. More importantly, we need the prestige image that is created by specialty products like private reserve, late harvest, select blends, and so forth. Thus, we will always endeavor to create small quantities of new, interesting wines from every vintage. These products, because of their combination of uniqueness, quality, and scarcity, command high prices, high praise, and high prestige for the winery that can create them.

In addition, it is important to maintain our flexibility in planning ways to utilize future grape increases. We know there is going to be a wine market for our projected increases. We have yet to determine how we can most profit from those wines. At this point we would prefer to protect our options rather than lock in on arbitrary sales goals for specific brands. Stated succinctly, we don't wish to commit to a million cases of Farron Ridge that will sell at approximately $20 per case in 1991 if, for the sake of example, the possibility exists for only 300,000 Farron Ridge, 200,000 cases of additional premium-priced Chateau Ste Michelle, and 500,000 cases of a proprietary label of high-priced Chardonnay. In addition, we believe that the thousands of additional unplanted vineyard acres could be converted into specially designated vineyards each with its special labels or proprietary name. We know, for example, that we can produce, although with some difficulty, possibly the world's best rosé. The opportunity to sell the world's finest or most expensive rosé is one we may eventually pursue. Our success in producing great sparkling wines is already well documented and the exciting growth in the champagne market has been noted previously. The obvious future opportunity to capitalize on this market is being carefully studied.

In conjunction with our new product strategy is the recognition that our first commitment is to develop the Chateau Ste Michelle brand. We do not wish to get sidetracked from this ambitious goal. New products will be scrutinized from this priority perspective.

Goals.

1. During 1982 and all future harvests, the enology department will explore opportunities to produce a limited quantity of Ice Wine.
2. From the 1982 harvest, enology will attempt to produce a private reserve Chardonnay.
3. Using the 1982 harvest, enology will explore blends of Semillon and Sauvignon Blanc for a special release Sauterne-styled white wine.
4. Each year every attempt will be made by enology to produce a limited quantity of late harvest or Botrytis Riesling.
5. Enology, viticulture, and marketing will set up an ad hoc committee by July 1982 to periodically review opportunities for specialty products.
6. The winery will produce an average 4,000 cases of sparkling wine per year for purposes of creating a high-price, prestigious showcase product.
7. Limited bottlings of Private Reserve Cabernet, and when possible Merlot, will be planned each year assuming availability of quality grapes.
8. Marketing will continue to examine market segmentation and competition in order to consider new product launches.

Resource and Responsibility. All of the above goals can be accomplished with existing resources and within the framework of existing budgets. The responsibility will be primarily that of the enology department with the cooperation and support of viticulture and marketing.

Promotion and Merchandising

We must build awareness of Washington state as a premium viticultural region and Chateau Ste Michelle as a top-quality, super-premium brand. This needs to happen at every level: distributors, retailers, and consumers. Most wine consumers outside of the Northwest have no knowledge of the fact that great wines are being produced in Washington. Fewer yet have ever heard of Chateau Ste Michelle. This problem will become critical in 1983 when we attempt to double sales in most of our key markets.

Given a limited marketing budget, the most effective tools we have to correct our awareness problem are in promotion and merchandising. Because of differences in brand development, distribution laws, trade practices, distributor organizations, and consumer and market patterns, it is necessary to consider each market individually when planning promotions. Each key market has a promotion calendar specifically designed to its needs. This section will not deal with individual markets, just the marketing tools.

Point of Sale. The development of top-quality point of sale (POS) material is a key task for the marketing group. There is little distinction in wine packaging and literally hundreds of brands exist in most retail accounts, therefore, in-store merchandising becomes critical. We must improve in-store visibility if we are to secure better placement, induce consumer trial, and create repeat purchase. POS material must be available in varying types and sizes to adapt to the needs of each market. The types of POS material currently being produced include display bins, large display signs, small cut case cards, shelf talkers, wobblers, bottle neckers, posters, price signs, generic pieces, restaurant table tents, consumer opinion brochures, and so on. In all cases it is critical that our POS material be an expression of our commitment to quality. Not only is this the message we wish to convey to the consumer, but it assures that the materials will be properly used by the retailer. The abuse of POS materials by distributors and retailers is a constant problem which quality pieces help to overcome.

Audiovisual. The company has recently purchased equipment to make audiovisual presentations. They allow for effective sales presentations. Two presentations have already been developed and others are planned.

Merchandising Cycles. Distributors and retailers plan their promotion calendar at least six months in advance. It is, therefore, important that Chateau Ste Michelle plan its merchandising cycles early. Merchandising material and sales literature must be prepared and shipped well in advance of the promotion period.

Price Incentives. The offering of special price discounts during the merchandising cycles has become institutionalized in the wine industry. Unless we offer substantial price incentives most markets will not respond to our promotions. At this stage we are more interested in using promotions to gain distribution and increase trial. In later years promotions will be designed to move volume. Each year we will offer selected price discounts during six merchandising cycles. Price discounts will range from $3 to $6 per case. Both the distributor and retailer will be encouraged to contribute additional dollars to the discount. In markets where the product is so sparsely distributed as to not significantly benefit from price discounts, the distributor will be encouraged to use the monies as sales incentives for the sales force.

In-store Tastings. Where the law permits, we will explore the effectiveness of an in-store tasting program. Basically we will use trained demonstrators provided by the distributor to sample products in key accounts that agree to heavily merchandise the brand. We envision this as an ongoing program in key developing markets.

Retail Tastings. In our key markets we will conduct retailer tastings designed to familiarize the trade with the brand in hope of obtaining better placement. In the past, retailer tastings have been very effective in improving the brand's distribution. Literature and sales kits will be available to reinforce key attributes of the presentation.

Gift Packs. Gift packs are an important sales tool. Gift packs stimulate trial and create additional facings within the store during peak seasons. We are currently researching the most effective types of gift packs in the market.

Distribution Drives. Most distributors handle 15 to 30 lines of wine and have great latitude in which wines get placed in each account. Once a base level of distribution is established, distribution drives are useful in stimulating increased placements. It is necessary to work independently with each distributorship in order to determine the most effective incentives to be offered in the drive.

Goals.

1. A marketing plan and promotion calendar will be developed for all key markets each year with specific sales goals and objectives. The plan will be available for distributors to review by the third week of November in the prior year of implementation.

2. In addition to existing audiovisual presentations, marketing will develop a chain store presentation by August 1982 (no super-premium winery has ever aggressively gone after chain supermarket accounts; this provides a unique opportunity for Chateau Ste Michelle). Also, we will develop a slide-show sales presentation for the 1983 promotional calendar. This will be continued every year if successful.

3. Marketing is working to develop a permanent library of POS materials for every wine variety and every potential retail requirement. By the end of 1982 a POS inventory will exist for Farron Ridge, Cabernet, Merlot, Muscat, Rosé of Cabernet, Grenache Rosé, Johannesberg Riesling, and Semillon. In addition, we will have available display bins, table tents, retail handouts, posters, and numerous information pieces and fact sheets. A special room has been con-

structed in the Woodinville warehouse to properly store and ship all materials.

4. Marketing and sales will implement at least six national promotional programs every year. The following lists the promotional calendar for 1982:

Month	Promotional Item	Discount
February	Cabernet	$3 per case
	Merlot	$3 per case
	Muscat	$4 per case
April	Rosé of Cabernet	$5 per case
	Grenache Rosé	$5 per case
June	Johannesberg Riesling	$4 per case
July	Semillon Blanc	$4 per case
October	Cabernet	$4 per case
	Merlot	$4 per case
	Gift packs	
November	Johannesberg Riesling	$3 per case
	Grenache Rosé	$3 per case
	Gift packs	
December	Semillon Blanc	$3 per case
	Merlot	$3 per case
	Gift packs	

In addition, there will be a Washington state program for Farron Ridge Rosé in May and for the entire Farron Ridge line in September. Both promotions are designed to increase facings and obtain floor displays.

5. Distribution drives are being conducted in key markets with special incentive programs set up for the top sales performers. Those markets participating include Los Angeles, Chicago, Connecticut, and New York.

Resources and Responsibility. Responsibility of designing promotions and merchandising tools rest with the marketing department with input from sales. The cost of incentives and materials will vary from year to year depending on quantity and type of wine being promoted.

Advertising

The rapid rate and magnitude of growth for Chateau Ste Michelle in the next few years necessitates the immediate development of significant con-

sumer demand. This will not happen if all we do is stack product on retail floors. We must advertise to establish the brand in certain key markets. Advertising a super-premium wine requires a special finesse, as super-premium wines are assumed to be in short supply. The advertising must not destroy the mystique of rarity that one associates with fine wines. Although advertising dollars are limited, we are fortunate in that we can target in on a very small specific audience. (Remember, 2% of the population is drinking 50% of all wines.) Because of the specific demographics, upscale print, FM radio, and possibly select local TV will be the primary media considerations.

Goals.
1. By June 1983 we will begin test market advertising. Marketing will work with our ad agencies to develop and test various ad formats. It is estimated that $50,000 will be required for productions and $100,000 for test market media.
2. By fall 1983 we will begin select market advertising directed toward specific programs. Cost is estimated at $300,000.

Resources and Responsibility. Advertising will be budgeted through 1991 at $3 per case, weighted toward the early years where the need is greatest. Marketing requires no additional manpower as most of the activity will be shouldered by an ad agency.

Packaging

Research has demonstrated that packaging is one of the key elements influencing purchase decision of premium wines. The winery places great importance on quality packaging and has strategically decided to continue to upgrade packaging as volume increases. This is the opposite of what most wineries do as they grow larger. Upgrading our packaging to reflect the quality associated with small-estate bottled wines will help minimize the negative implications of being considered a large winery.

Goals.
1. In 1982 we will begin putting all of our red wines and our most expensive white wines in high-quality punt glass bottles, thus creating a high-status package.
2. Beginning in 1982 back labels for wines aged in

wood will be overprinted at the time of bottling with enological data concerning the wine's analysis. Only the smallest wineries offer this information, which is highly sought after by serious consumers.

3. The winery has embarked on an ongoing program of upgrading packaging components and quality control procedures.

Resources and Responsibility. The actual responsibility of obtaining packaging components rests with the purchasing agent who will work with marketing and production to determine quality standards. The cost of punt bottles and special labels will be recovered in the pricing of those products. The quality control program is expected to save the company money over the long term.

Public Relations and Communications

The successful development of a top-quality premium reputation is of paramount importance to the long-term success of Chateau Ste Michelle. No other consumer product receives as much critical analysis and written assessment as does wine. Most serious wine consumers search for information to evaluate the wines before they purchase. This information comes from myriad sources: books, magazines, newspaper wine columns, newsletters, wine clubs and associations, wine festivals, restaurant critics, radio and television programs, and so forth.

Americans' increasing thirst for wine is exceeded only by their fascination for wine information. This provides an opportunity for well-prepared public relations material that can significantly impact the wine opinion leaders.

Millions of dollars are spent annually by domestic wineries in creating and maintaining their consumer and trade images. Some wineries have virtually built their entire image by nonadvertising programs.

Currently, only California and Europe are accepted by most consumers as fine-wine-producing areas. Advertising and public relations have been most effective in building this consumer awareness and loyalty. Nationally, there is low consumer demand for wines produced in Washington. The wine consumer is not unwilling, just uninformed. We have a double task—to convince the buyer that good wines are being made in Washington and that Chateau Ste Michelle is the finest among them. We have a unique advantage

in that if we turn consumers on to Washington viticulture we have by extension turned them on to Chateau Ste Michelle, as we represent 90% of the wine shipped out of state. Wine enthusiasts are always experimenting and searching out new wines. If public relations programs are effectively prepared and executed, this enthusiast can be significantly impacted to our advantage.

For the most part, Washington's identity as a wine-producing state is one of a white-wine-producing area because of our early successes with Johannesberg Riesling and Chenin Blanc. To enjoy the status of a truly premium domestic winery, Chateau Ste Michelle must also be accepted as a producer of high-quality red wines, particularly Cabernet Sauvignon. The use of industry opinion leaders can often be more effective than advertising in this effort. Third-party testimony by the wine experts can make the story of Washington viticulture and Chateau Ste Michelle excellence highly believable. Wine writers can print commentary which we could never say about ourselves with credibility. Fortunately, these writers need a constant supply of high-quality public relations material for their very existence.

Communication Goals.

1. Develop high consumer awareness of Washington viticulture in general and Chateau Ste Michelle in particular.

2. Establish Chateau Ste Michelle as a producer of world-class red and white wines.

3. Position Chateau Ste Michelle with selected highly respectful competitors.

4. Develop a national and international wine awards record.

5. Position Chateau Ste Michelle nationally as the voice of Washington wine making.

6. Use public relations as a supportive marketing tool to reach brand objectives.

7. Develop and/or maintain strong media relationships in key markets.

The following are some of the specific actions that will be taken to accomplish the above goals.

Publishing of a Chateau Ste Michelle Trade/Consumer Newsletter. For 1982 a consultant firm has been retained to publish two issues of a newly designed newsletter featuring articles designed to build credibility for Washington's viticulture region and for the excellence of Chateau Ste Michelle. A large trade, media, and consumer mailing list exists as a base for its distribution. Additionally, each wholesale distributor will be supplied copies for key customers.

Press Release Program. An active press release program will be initiated in 1982, delivering releases to a core group of 390 wine writers every other month. The releases will be coordinated with wine release schedules, promotional programs, and significant events. Multiple copies of releases will be sent to wholesale distributors to maintain effective communication and provide a merchandise piece for salespeople.

Sample Program. A national wine writers' sample program will be initiated in 1982, delivering wines to a group of 45 to 50 wine writers. Samples will be packaged and sent with descriptive literature on a schedule to coincide with a wine's release, a promotional program, or an award announcement.

Society of Wine Educators. The Society of Wine Educators is a national organization of wine instructors offering classes at the informal, community, adult education, and university levels. During 1982, factual information, promotional and descriptive literature, and audiovisual programs will be sent or offered to this group of instructors.

Les Amis du Vin. This is an international organization for wine appreciation with headquarters in Washington, D.C.; it publishes a national wine magazine. The national director and editor will be scheduled to visit the winery to prepare material for an article. Our sales representative in Washington, D.C. will maintain close contact with the national officers to arrange local and other major market presentations.

Consumer Tasting Events. A major effort in 1982 will be to enter several consumer-oriented wine festivals and tasting events. These are particularly effective when Chateau Ste Michelle enters traditionally "California only" events and is the only representative from any other viticultural region. The tastings help to establish Chateau Ste Michelle's preeminence in the Washington wine industry and build the national acceptance of Washington viticulture.

The following tasting events have already been scheduled: Walt Disney World Annual Wine Festival—Chateau Ste Michelle is the only non-California winery invited to attend; Seattle Wine Institute Tasting—wine tasting event for 1,500 people;

Connecticut World Wide Wines Annual American Wine Festival—sponsored by Chateau Ste Michelle's Connecticut wholesale distributor; and Washington, D.C. International Wine and Food Exposition—A three-day consumer/retailer show.

PRODUCTION

The relative youth of Washington viticulture has necessitated that the company build from scratch the technology, vineyard, and production facilities needed to become a 2-million case winery by the end of the decade. Table 13 shows the capacity of our winery facilities and Tables 14 and 15 show existing and future vineyard acreage by variety.

Our production operations are designed for flexibility, thereby maximizing wine quality and profit opportunities. Our vineyard operations accommodate our product lines in that we use the same basic grape varieties for both Chateau Ste Michelle and our second-labels, employing selection techniques which optimize quality at each level. It is our intent that the grapes produced for our primary labels (i.e., Chateau Ste Michelle) and our secondary labels (i.e., Farron Ridge) be interchangeable. The winery at Paterson, however, will actually consist of two separate facilities with somewhat different technologies. (For example, Chateau Ste Michelle has small fermentors, is committed to small-lot processing, and uses dejuicing tanks. Farron Ridge will be structured with larger fermentors, will use continuous process, and will use inclined dejuicers). The two operations are separate but interconnected; if necessary, wine can be moved from one to the other.

Vineyards for each line of wines will be the same, basic, premium varieties, but Farron Ridge will be cropped at a higher level. Cropping levels can be controlled by viticultural practices, so a given vineyard plot can be modified to produce at a level consistent with either product line.

Rapid growth of our business continues to require emphasis in three areas: capital investment, personnel administration, and quality control. The following sections briefly address each of these three topics.

Capital Investment

Our capital development plan is mature and now in the final stages of implementation, with the exception of our vineyard planting. No major

Table 13 *Winery Capacity Data for Premium Wine Production (000's)*

Winery	Startup	Gallons Storage and Fermentation (except Redwood)	Gallons Redwood	Gallons Oak Cooperage	Case Through Put
Woodinville	1976	1,212	0	383	390
Grandview	1978	232	365	48	150
Paterson (1st stage)	1982	1,730	120	609	460
Paterson (2nd stage)	Beginning in 1984	2,530	417	0	1,000

Table 14 *Chateau Ste Michelle Acreage Summary*

Variety	No. 3	No. 4	No. 6	No. 8	No. 10	Total
Cabernet Sauvignon	10	—	—	189	154	353
Chardonnay	—	—	—	52	240	292
Chenin Blanc	9	—	—	—	313	322
Gewurztraminer	—	—	42	—	44	86
Grenache	—	4	11	121	198	334
Merlot	3	—	23	—	30	56
Muscat Blanc	—	—	—	56	30	86
Pinot Noir	9	—	23	—	—	32
Sauvignon Blanc	—	52	—	—	198	250
Semillon	11	—	7	—	149	167
White Riesling	26	11	—	162	420	619
Total	68	67	106	582	1,776	2,598

Table 15 *Farron Ridge Acres by Planting Year*

Variety	Actual 1981	Projected 1984	Projected 1985	Projected 1986	Total
Merlot	56	0	120	120	296
Chardonnay	0	120	120	0	240
Chenin Blanc	91	120	120	0	331
Semillon Blanc	93	120	120	138	471
White Riesling	0	120	120	240	480
Total	240	480	600	498	1,818

changes are anticipated in this plan. We are "fine-tuning," to be sure, our facility and equipment decisions to maximize the benefits of the latest technology, meet our cost objectives, and adapt to related production demands.

The planting cycle has been altered due to the disease problem of verticillium wilt. Verticillium wilt is a soil-born fungus that has infected a number of vines at vineyard no. 10. The incidence of the disease is sufficiently severe such that we have deferred further planting until the results of our research project on verticillium demonstrate that it is prudent to proceed. At the same time we are investigating the alternative of planting existing undeveloped acreage at vineyard no. 10. This is subject to soil test assuring that no verticillium is present in the undeveloped acreage.

Verticillium in grapes is rare, and the lack of history on its treatment has made the research effort more difficult. The research committee is chaired by Dr. Richard Manning, vice president research for US Tobacco and the research team is headed by Dr. Wade Wolfe, acting vineyard operations manager and research viticulturist, and Donna Hirschfeld, Chateau Ste Michelle's staff plant pathologist.

The current plans, as reflected in both the marketing plan and financial statements, are to begin planting again by 1984.

Goals.
1. The capital plan for the new winery in Paterson will proceed on schedule and the facility will be operational by September 1982.
2. Our research goal is to contain and eliminate the verticillium problem such that we can begin planting again by spring 1984. Five hundred acres will be planted each year in 1984, 1985, and 1986. In 1983 we will plant 200 acres, assuming site selection is approved.
3. Research is ongoing to determine optimal grape-growing techniques relating to such issues as site selection, cropping techniques, trellising techniques, irrigation practices, harvest schedules, variety selection and other viticultural factors.

Resource and Responsibility. All capital investments are provided for in existing approved budgets. It is the responsibility of production to properly plan and control this expenditure.

Personnel

Manpower is in a stage of developmental planning, preparatory to a significant buildup to man our new plant. Again, we have not deviated materially from our previous organizational plans. Our wine-making staff is increased in size and will be selectively increased again to correspond to the manning requirements of the new plant. The addition of an independent quality control function represents a significant and very desirable change to support orderly growth without loss of quality. Availability of high-quality, experienced personnel in all areas (wine making, cellar work, bottling, warehousing and transportation, quality control, and laboratory and viticulture) appears to be excellent. Administration manpower plans reflect a need for selected additional personnel to provide for necessary administrative controls and data management.

As we grow, administrative control becomes increasingly important. We have and are continuing to develop a more precise organization structure with well-defined job descriptions. Procedures are becoming more detailed and extensive. More stringent controls are being implemented in areas like purchasing, research, quality control, and accounting. The transition from a smaller less structured and controlled organization is not without its difficulties, but it is a necessary step. To help make this transition we are increasing employee communication in our effort to keep people informed and to clarify the demands in this highly disciplined, controlled environment.

Goals.
1. Establish, coordinate, and implement administrative procedures in personnel, purchasing, security, and other administrative areas.
2. Add responsible, quality-oriented personnel to handle complex data processing, recording, and accessibility requirements.

Resource and Responsibility. Personnel additions will be hired by production management on an as-needed basis and are covered in existing budgets. Organization procedures will be the joint responsibility of the executive committee.

Quality Control

Quality begins in the vineyards. We have a proven viticultural area and are the technological leaders in the region in viticultural practices related to the special soil and climatic conditions. Our knowledge of the influence of micro-climates on different grape varieties has allowed us to continue to grow and purchase grapes of optimum quality. We feel that, long range, our fruit quality will be second to none in the country. We have continued our practices of a small winery, which impact on fruit quality.

Our maximum fermentation size for Chateau Ste Michelle will be 12,000 gallons, which allows individual lots of wine to be separately treated according to their special requirements. All fermentors are jacketed for precise temperature control during fermentation.

In addition, we are adding a new quality control function which will have the responsibility of establishing, monitoring, and enforcing rigorous quality standards from incoming fruit to bottled product. These standards will include chemical analysis, hygiene and sanitation, and organoleptic evaluation. Quality control will function both cooperatively with and independently from the wine-making function.

It is our belief that both our experience in wine-making technology and the intensive emphasis to be placed on quality control measures will result in continuing improvements in our high-quality product lines.

Goals.
1. Establish and staff a quality control organization in time to have personnel on board and trained prior to opening the Paterson facility in September 1982.
2. Realign the enological staff to assure optimal coordination of quality control and enological functions while maintaining the independence of quality control.

Resource and Responsibility. Production will hire a competent, well-trained quality control manager by July 1. Production will staff the labs with quality control technicians by August 1982.

FINANCIAL ASSUMPTIONS

The accompanying tables and projections are based on certain broad assumptions and should be reviewed in that context. It is recognized that the dynamic nature of the wine industry coupled with the dramatic growth of Chateau Ste Michelle will require that our strategy be reviewed and adjusted at regular intervals. The assumptions used for this forecast are the following:

1. Five percent (5%) annual inflation index is assumed for both sales and nonfixed expenses.
2. Gross margin is based on current gross margin. Estimated effect of raw material mix of purchased grapes and Chateau Ste Michelle grapes has been factored into the increased margin for later years.
3. The first two years operating costs of a new vineyard are capitalized. Starting in the third year, the vineyard produces a small crop and the operating budget is no longer capitalized. The harvested crop from the vineyard increases each year until approximately the seventh year at which point the vineyard becomes fully producing. Vineyard operating costs, however, remain relatively constant for all years. To get a reasonable matching of costs to quantity harvested, industry convention calls for a diminishing portion of the operating costs to be written off to period costs in the third through the sixth years of operation. In the ten-year plan, it has been estimated that the Chateau Ste Michelle vineyard operating costs are approximately $1,400 an acre in 1982 dollars. Of this $1,400 per acre, approximately $300 per acre represents fixed costs. The difference of $1,100 was indexed at the 5% inflation rate. Fixed costs were added back and used to determine the addition to fixed assets and related depreciation. For years three through six, the period cost portion was included in other income and expense. The Farron Ridge vineyards were treated in an identical manner with the exception that operating costs per acre were estimated to be $1,250 in 1982 dollars with $250 per acre in fixed costs.
4. Depreciation lives on addition were estimated to be: vineyard equipment—7 years, winery equipment—20 years, vehicle equipment—3 years, and grape growing equipment—25 years. The year 1982 was used for a base depreciation with estimated depreciation on inflation adjusted additions added to this base. For replacements, it was assumed that the depreciation related to the original cost was already included in the 1982 base. Therefore,

only the depreciation attributable to the inflation-caused increase was added to the base.

5. Other income and expense includes both an estimated write-off of excess plant capacity and a write-off of partially bearing vineyards. Interest expense includes the Farron Ridge portion of the interest attributable to the debt assumed on the buy-out of the farm.

6. The December 31, 1981 balance sheet was restated to exclude the effects of farming operations.

7. Sales estimates were produced by the marketing department and reconciled with production information.

8. Direct and department expenses were based on both the estimated effects of inflation on current level expenses and any known increases for staffing, marketing needs, and so on.

9. Investment tax credit was assumed to be 10% of total equipment purchases. The federal tax rate was computed at 46% of total pretax earnings. (No state income tax in Washington.)

10. Accounts receivable is assumed to be $\frac{1}{12}$ of total annual sales.

11. Preharvest cost is the December 31, 1981 balance indexed at the estimated inflation rate and adjusted by estimated increases caused by a higher level of winery and vineyard operations.

12. AP and other liabilities are estimated to be 7% of total assets.

13. Long-term debt includes the effects of increased Farron Ridge plantings on farmland purchased via the assumption of existing debt.

14. Case price is the current price indexed at the estimated inflation rate.

15. Cash is assumed to always be in a negative balance. This is caused by outstanding checks which have not cleared our zero balance account as set up by US Tobacco.

16. The following assumptions were made about the amount and percentages of purchased grapes for the 10-year plan.

Table 16 Chateau Ste Michelle Proforma Income Statement ($000 Omitted)

	1982	1983	1984	1985	1986	1987	1988	1989	1990	1991
Sales revenue	11,203	18,217	26,895	36,085	44,000	51,495	58,962	67,637	76,409	82,793
Cost of sales	5,659	9,078	13,111	17,213	20,376	23,446	26,399	29,840	33,939	36,922
% of sales	50.5	49.8	48.7	47.7	46.3	45.5	44.8	44.1	44.4	44.6
Gross margin	5,544	9,139	13,784	18,872	23,624	28,049	32,563	37,797	42,470	45,871
% of sales	49.5	50.2	51.3	52.3	53.7	54.5	55.2	55.9	55.6	55.4
Operating expenses	3,224	6,352	8,750	11,162	13,005	14,337	15,885	17,605	19,420	21,296
% of sales	28.8	34.9	32.5	30.9	29.6	27.8	26.9	26.0	25.4	25.7
Operating margin	2,320	2,787	5,034	7,710	10,619	13,712	16,678	20,192	23,050	24,575
% of sales	20.7	15.3	18.7	21.4	24.1	26.6	28.3	29.9	30.2	29.7
Other income (expense)	(2,278)	(2,447)	(1,534)	(1,034)	(2,199)	(2,386)	(2,459)	(1,690)	(1,041)	(365)
% of sales	−20.3	−13.4	−5.7	−2.9	−5.0	−4.6	−4.2	−2.5	−1.4	−0.4
Profit (loss) before tax	42	340	3,500	6,676	8,420	11,326	14,219	18,502	22,009	24,210
% of sales	0.4	1.9	13.0	18.5	19.1	22.0	24.1	27.4	28.8	29.2
Fed tax (Net of ITC)	(740)	(48)	1,362	2,928	3,421	4,845	6,325	8,436	10,103	11,116
% of sales	−6.6	−0.3	5.1	8.1	7.8	9.4	10.7	12.5	13.2	13.4
Profit (loss) after tax	782	388	2,138	3,748	4,999	6,481	7,894	10,066	11,906	13,094
% of sales	7.0	2.1	7.9	10.4	11.4	12.6	13.4	14.9	15.6	15.8

*The above information excludes farming operations.

Table 17 Chateau Ste Michelle Proforma Balance Sheet ($000 Omitted)

	1982	1983	1984	1985	1986	1987	1988	1989	1990	1991
Assets										
Cash	(380)	(399)	(418)	(441)	(464)	(486)	(509)	(536)	(562)	(589)
Accounts receivable	934	1,518	2,241	3,007	3,667	4,291	4,914	5,636	6,367	6,899
Inventory	12,237	17,783	24,307	28,811	32,954	35,630	37,706	38,709	38,202	36,932
Preharvest cost	762	777	866	964	1,105	1,268	1,446	1,630	1,793	1,971
Total current	13,553	19,679	26,996	32,341	37,262	40,703	43,557	45,439	45,800	45,213
Plant, prop. and equip. accum.	48,323	51,920	56,336	60,452	67,904	73,672	76,651	77,979	78,244	78,553
Less deprec.	5,566	8,042	10,751	13,790	17,245	21,174	25,323	29,453	33,475	37,500
Net plant, prop. and equip.	42,757	43,878	45,585	46,662	50,659	52,498	51,328	48,526	44,769	41,053
Total assets	56,310	63,557	72,581	79,003	87,921	93,201	94,885	93,965	90,569	86,266
Liabilities and Equity										
Interco. loan	48,537	54,953	61,273	63,218	66,426	64,351	57,742	47,339	32,431	15,438
AP and other liabilities	3,942	4,449	5,081	5,530	6,154	6,524	6,642	6,578	6,340	6,039
Long-term debt	1,109	1,045	979	1,259	1,346	1,850	2,131	1,612	1,456	1,353
Stockholders' equity	2,722	3,110	5,248	8,996	13,995	20,476	28,370	38,436	50,342	63,436
Total liabil. and stockholders' equity	56,310	63,557	72,581	79,003	87,921	93,201	94,805	93,965	90,569	86,266
Net income after tax	782	388	2,138	3,748	4,999	6,481	7,894	10,066	11,906	13,094
Net income/total assets (return on total assets)	1.4	0.6	2.9	4.7	5.7	7.0	8.3	10.7	13.1	15.2

*The above information excludes farming operations.

CRAIN'S NEW YORK BUSINESS

The Vision

Crain's New York Business is the business newspaper of New York. It is a weekly publication packed with information about New York: the business people, the market, the industries, and the companies. It is informative, entertaining, provocative, fair—but above all, interesting and useful. It has its finger on the pulse of the most vibrant city in America.

Crain's brings something new, something needed, something essential to New York. Others cover New York as part of a global village; *The New York Times* and *The Wall Street Journal* focus on the 200 or 300 largest companies. *Crain's* covers New York as a small town, providing information our readers can't get anywhere else. It writes about the people who bring new stores to Madison Avenue, the developers who change the skyline, the producers behind Broadway, the business people who make the town tick.

As a result, *Crain's New York Business* is essential to all those doing business here. It is a tool with which people can make money by finding out about who is expanding and who's leaving town, by investing in the interesting companies it spotlights, by making contact with the movers and the shakers on the rise.

Its readers are people interested in the business and economy of New York. That primarily means business people; especially people who run their own companies and need to have wide knowledge of real estate, banking, professions, etc. But the paper also appeals to anyone with an interest in the business climate and what business people are doing. Some examples: development

directors, college presidents, accountants, lawyers, and economists.

Its focus is primarily the city of New York. But *Crain's* reports on the surrounding areas when developments in those suburbs affect the city and its businesses. For example, the burgeoning development along the Jersey Shore is as much a New York story as it is a Jersey story.

New York is at once a sprawling, international business center and an intensely provincial, gossipy town. Our opportunities lie in both areas.

WHAT WE DO

What we do is threefold: we cover the market, we cover the big companies in a new way, and we cover the thousands of businesses no one else cares about.

The market: think of this as real estate, retailing, advertising. We write about neighborhoods that are hot and those that are not. We care about who is building what, and whether it is renting. We write about what stores are selling in New York. We write about the latest local advertising campaigns to hit the TV stations.

The big companies: We write about these companies as New York institutions. When Mobil and Penney leave New York, we look into the real estate left behind. When Macy's goes private, we write about the expected changes in operations in New York stores and in the headquarters staff. We won't follow Citicorp to South Africa, but we watch every move with the branch system in New York. (The only thing we avoid is merger and

---

*Reprinted with permission of Crain's New York Business, 220 East 42nd Street, New York, NY 10017.

acquisition stories involving giant companies, stories the *Times* and the *Journal* beat to death.)

The other companies: One of our greatest strengths is that we cover hundreds of companies no one else writes about. Elsewhere, publicly held companies with $300 million in sales could expect to be written about at least five times a year in the local papers and business journals. Here they are lucky to get the naming of a new president in the *Times*. This is our bread and butter. We cover these companies, and as we grow we will cover more and more.

Interestingly, more than any other Crain city book, *Crain's New York Business* has emerged as an investment vehicle, a place to find the small but attractive stocks no one else touches. Not only Wall Street types but readers with a couple of thousand dollars to invest find lots of possibilities in *Crain's*.

All this adds up to a product that informs readers about what is going on around them and one that tells them about developments they can use to make money.

HOW WE DO IT: THE ELEMENTS

These are the components of *Crain's New York Business*.

1. **Scoops, scoops and scoops:** We want our readers to feel compelled to grab us first thing Monday morning so they're not behind the news. And we want the market's newsmakers—particularly sources sitting on big stories—to know that *Crain's* will jump at reliable tips and pursue such stories wholeheartedly.

    This means that we are aggressive, willing to jump on tips and to report and report and report them until we know whether the information is true or not. One anecdote: We wrote a story about a Queens retailer of large men's clothes that planned to expand to 13 stores in the metropolitan area; the day the paper appeared he received 13 calls. These stories send the message that to know what's going on, you have to read *Crain's*. It is important to remember that scoops are the cream of the information spread throughout the paper which people can't get anywhere else: promotions, real estate transactions, etc.

2. **Personality stories:** An increasingly important part of the *Crain's* mix is the personality story.

More than any other city, New York is a people town. We want to profile the people who are making business work—or not work—in New York. But personality means more. We emphasize personality as a way to tell stories. Even our non-personality stories search out the people and their traits that bring otherwise routine business stories to life.

3. **Company stories:** This element was explained before, but companies are the heartbeat of New York. We don't do these stories like many daily newspapers. We search for the winners and losers, the hot and the passe. And we go beyond the surface. Every *Crain's* company profile searches out analysts, competitors, consultants, and even consumers to test the company's strategy. Every such story tries to get into the business to find the unusual source or telling anecdote that illustrates the pitfalls or opportunities a company faces. We favor publicly held companies or names with wide consumer appeal, but we do any company when tension makes an interesting story.

4. **Offbeat stories:** Call them what you will (pacing, offbeat, soft business stories). These are pure voyeurism stories. They are fun, entertaining, gee-whiz pieces (gee, I didn't know that).

5. **Special sections:** A key ingredient of *Crain's* is the special section each week, whether a real estate story, a financial story or a how-to Take-Out section. These stories often include crucial charts ranking companies, professions, etc.

6. **Big stories:** More and more as we grow, *Crain's New York Business* will become known for the big story, the story that will step back and take apart an issue, a company, a city.

HOW WE DO IT: THE STYLE

A *Crain's New York Business* story must be lively, anecdotal, filled with trenchant detail and other illustration.

A *Crain's* story must take a point of view, based on through reporting. It will say that a company is doing well or poorly and why. It will convey, as much as possible, the truth of a situation rather than what people say about it. But it will be fair: fair in that it will be based on thorough, resourceful, and persistent reporting. Fair in that the opposing view will be given a fair airing in the story.

A *Crain's* story is always searching for the angle: the information that allows us to interpret developments in a new light, the fresh approach that makes a well-worn story come alive.

Crain's stories emphasize photography—bright, lively, aggressive images that help give our book a personality and a focus on people.

Here are three reporters' views about what this means:

Patrick: A *Crain's* story is not meant to be a story of record. It is, however, one that will get to the heart of the matter, leaving out extraneous matter. It is specific and local, but also sophisticated in that it explains the subject's place in the world (read: business, field, profession, milieu).

In most cases, we tell a story through a strong character. We look for one person or thing to embody the theme of the story. And we are critical in our reporting. We are not restrained by conventional journalism etiquette of daily newspapers. To us, the essential facts, not all the facts, are what matter.

We want scoops whenever possible. We look at where a person or story might be heading. We make predictions based on expert opinions. We stretch in hopes of being provocative yet reliable.

We are the loud-mouthed, too-smart second cousin who won't shut up at the dinner table, pesky but with something to say.

Joan: A *Crain's New York Business* story should be something a business person can read on the No. 4 train between 86th Street and Fulton Street and come away with insight into news developments in the city's business. If they read it first in *Crain's,* that's all for the best, but even scoops should have the how and why a weekly can and should offer.

Every story, but particularly those that are not "hard news," should also have a "voice" that comes from the writer. This doesn't mean the overall tone can't be set by the paper. I think *Crain's* does set a tone of its own, one that's a little irreverent and breezier than most business publications. It pokes the reader, by raising questions about strategies, pointing out risks, and setting events in the larger context of what's going on any given industry and, indeed, in the city in general.

While it's preferable that each story begin with a news peg, we can offer "second day" interpretation or a "what really happened" angle on recent news events reported first elsewhere. The details

we provide should always be our own. There should be enough of of them to make the article entertaining, but not overwhelming either on the side of dryness or description.

Numbers are vital and should always be presented with some analysis, not just as "well, here's the bottom line, folks."

Crain's should be a money-making tool, but not one more chore piled on an executive's cluttered desk. Descriptions of personalities and surroundings should add color to a story, but news of restructuring, expansion, acquisition plans, and the like should be stressed because it's information readers can use to fill their own pockets. The questions we raise should relate in some ways to all business people or even all New Yorkers. We can cover big stories that way, and yet smaller ones with a real local slant can succeed because they tell of something familiar to a large audience.

Linda: The best *Crain's* story is indeed one with lots of drama, with lots of potential winners and losers.

Thinking back, there are two kinds of stories I like that stick in my mind. One involves taking a news event and going deeper to give it a new twist. The second type explains the problems facing New York institutions that most people take for granted, but don't know very much about, businesswise. The idea is to target and write about these high-profile institutions when they're facing a challenge or crisis. Examples of these two varieties of stories are Betty's piece on the coke-snorting CEO of Iroquois Brands, Patrick's story on the *Daily News,* and Joan's Elizabeth Arden story. Even in a New York-oriented *Crain's,* I think Betty's piece on the Connecticut guy would fly.

I agree, finally, that these stories work best when there is a point of view, when they're written from an obvious standpoint. That's something I grow more comfortable with as I understand and know my beat better.

REFOCUSING

From its inception, *Crain's New York Business* has covered business in a broadly defined New York metropolitan market that encompasses 12 counties. Anyone who lives and does business in the area knows there is an enormous amount of interaction within the market. The New York/New Jersey real estate border wars are an important part of the news nearly every week. And companies that specialize in business services reach across all segments of the market to serve clients.

Nonetheless, the size of the market means it is difficult to make a mark. To improve the impact of *Crain's New York Business,* we intend to focus in on New York City and to cover the surrounding areas as they relate to the city.

The concept is "inside out." That means we will cover what's going on in New York and what's going on outside New York as it relates to New York. The first part is self-evident. We will cover the city in impressive detail. We will cover New York City companies wherever they go in the region and sometimes the nation.

The second is illustrated by examples: (1) we will cover Zeckendorf's move to Jersey, just as we covered Hartz's move to Queens. (2) we will cover the big New Jersey banks, because they are acquisition targets for New York banks (and that's our angle); (3) we will cover regional companies that have a strong city presence; we would cover Tofutti, even though it's based in Rahway, NJ.

We will no longer cover: (1) Regina, the Rahway, NJ, vacuum cleaner company, because its products are national in scope; (2) North Fork, the Suffolk County bank that's moving into Nassau. (We wouldn't cover it until it moves into the city or becomes the target of a takeover bid by a New York bank); (3) The revival of Hempstead, LI.

We will continue to run agate from the broader region (earnings, on the move, pulse). But the stories that go with that material will emphasize New York companies.

THE WISH LIST

The week of May 4 was an auspicious one for *Crain's New York Business.* Late in the week we broke a story about the city's proposed package of business tax incentives designed to help keep companies in New York. Our work prompted the city to unveil the program sooner then it wanted to and may have prevented the city from making an end run around opposition. The story was also a watershed in our relationship with the city, prompting city officials to sit up, take notice, and work harder to communicate with us.

On Monday of that same week we published a story on New York stores that focused on extremely tiny niches. The story, uncovering odd, amusing retailers, was the first fruit of our new emphasis on offbeat stories and profiles. Our reporters have tackled these new stories enthusiastically and creatively, adding a new dimension to the book. And it seems clear from reaction to stories like the Stanley Steingut profile and the oddest restaurant dishes piece that readers appreciate the new touch.

Since that week it has become increasingly clear to us that we need to maintain our additional focus on both the government-business beat and feature, offbeat stories. That insight sets the stage for what we need to make *Crain's New York Business* better.

Space: The space issue is crucial for us because even at our present staff level, we're simply not giving our readers enough to pick from. We need more story starts so that we get both more depth and breadth in our coverage of areas that are of most interest to readers. We'd like to be guaranteed between 18 and 20 editorial pages an issue, excluding TakeOuts. That translates to an editorial hole of 1,200 to 1,350 inches.

We'd use some of that space expanding what we already do. Sometimes our number of back-of-the-book story starts is as small as six, and we often give short shrift to such important elements as calendar, which many readers comb regularly, earnings, and on the move.

Added space means more people in on the move and pictures; it means more earnings of companies that can't get coverage anywhere else; it means more calendar events in New York City; and it means many more short stories (four- to six-inch stories) that often provide lots of useful information.

We believe the columns and standing features we're currently running should remain, with the probable exclusion of the Broadway theater listings.

But we'd like to go beyond just adding depth to the book—we also want more breadth. And that is where new positions will be useful.

Government/Business Reporter: The first would be a new beat reporter to cover New York City, New York state and state regulatory agencies, and their relationship to business. It's clear from our New York's New Crisis series that this is an area only covered sporadically by local dailies. Their City Hall reporters have a much broader beat to cover and often let business-related stories pass by as they focus on city corruption or other sexy issues for their diverse readership.

We are already doing these stories. Recently, we looked at Drexel's move to Jersey and what it meant for the city's outerborough program. In the previous issue, we looked at competition between Westchester and Fairfield counties for New York City companies, the city's squad to catch sales tax cheaters, and the fight over economic development zones. Need I say more?

There are two ways to proceed. A new reporting position would provide the greatest benefit. But we could carve out a position from the current staff. That would have risks, however. We would eliminate much of our flexibility that derives from having 1½ general assignment reporters (one reporter concentrates on professions but has some available time) and an editorial assistant who writes one story every other week.

Feature Page: The second proposal involves a page and a person. We propose the creation of an open, four-color page inside the book. This would be a "signature page, a destination page" and would be composed of some of the following elements: Bob Lape's restaurant review; New York, New York; a soft business story; a standing fact modeled on *New York* magazine (e.g., the cost of limousines these days).

We would continue to run such stories up front. But this page would provide a place in the book for people interested but not obsessed with business. It would give the book more variety while maintaining the *Crain's* attitude and business-oriented view of New York.

To handle such a page, we would want a senior editing position, probably "assistant managing editor/features." This person would edit the feature page, write and edit feature stories and personality pieces, and help out on the editing desk as needed.

DONALDSON, LUFKIN & JENRETTE

Code of Business Ethics

INTRODUCTION

Since Donaldson, Lufkin & Jenrette was founded in 1959, our firm has consistently adhered to the highest ethical standards in the conduct of all aspects of our business. Thus, the basic moral and ethical values set forth in this Code of Business Ethics (the Code), which was initially published in 1981 and has been periodically revised, reflects the manner in which the firm has operated from its inception.

As President and Chief Executive Officer, I assume responsibility for the overall implementation of this Code. In turn, I require each supervisor to accept responsibility for its implementation in his or her area of supervision, and I require each employee to honor its provisions. The Code applies to all of us employed by DLJ, which for this purpose includes Donaldson, Lufkin & Jenrette, Inc. and its subsidiaries.

I urge each of you, no matter how long or how short a time you have been employed by DLJ, to study this newly revised Code and to review it periodically. Abiding by its letter and its spirit is important to individual success at DLJ and to our collective success as a firm. [John S. Chalsty, *president and chief executive officer*, September 1986]

COMPLIANCE WITH LAWS

Donaldson, Lufkin & Jenrette will transact its business in compliance with all laws of the United States and all countries in which it does business.

APPEARANCE OF IMPROPRIETY

Because DLJ's reputation and good name are our most important assets and because the firm is often judged by the conduct of its people, DLJ employees must avoid not only actual impropriety but also the appearance of impropriety.

CONFLICT OF INTEREST

A conflict of interest exists when an employee's financial or other interests are inconsistent with the interests of DLJ's clients or of DLJ. Employees should avoid conflicts of interest as well as the appearance of conflicts of interest.

In addition to the policies set forth in DLJ's "restricted list" memorandum (See *Memorandum on Security Transactions for Accounts of DLJ, DLJ Personnel and DLJ Clients*), the following policies cover specific situations which can give rise to a conflict of interest.

Interests in Other Businesses

During their employment by DLJ, professional employees should devote all their business time, attention, and skill to the business and interests of DLJ. No employee should invest in, participate in, assist, or enter into any consulting or employment relationship with any present or prospective business competitor, supplier, or present or prospective client of DLJ without the written permission of the Chief Executive Officer. This prohibition applies even though the area of assistance may be unre-

---

*Reprinted with permission.

lated to DLJ's business. Permission need not be obtained, however, for passive investments in the stock of a public company if the investment does not exceed 5% of the company's outstanding stock, or for investments in tax shelters. Where permission is given for employees to hold outside directorships or consulting relationships, any fees paid as a result of such directorships or consulting relationships must be turned over to DLJ.

No employee may compete with DLJ by selling or leasing or offering to sell or lease services or products similar to services or products offered by DLJ. Employees should not take personal advantage of a business opportunity that may be of interest to DLJ without first offering that opportunity to DLJ in accordance with the procedure set forth in the "restricted list" memorandum.

To avoid circumventing the restrictions applicable to DLJ employees, family members of DLJ employees occupying the same residence as the employees should not have more than a 5% investment in, or any type of *extraordinary* consulting or employment relationship with, any present or prospective business competitor, supplier, or client of DLJ without the written permission of the Chief Executive Officer. While written permission of the Chief Executive Officer is not required where family members of DLJ employees have *ordinary* consulting or employment relationships with present or prospective business competitors, suppliers, or clients of DLJ, our employees should be particularly sensitive in such situations to the provisions of this Code of Ethics relating to the protection of DLJ's confidential information.

Family

DLJ employees may not purchase services or products for DLJ from their family members, or from business organizations with which they or their family are associated, without first obtaining written permission from the Chief Executive Officer.

Accepting Gifts and Entertainment from Third Parties

DLJ employees and members of their immediate families may not accept significant gifts, discounts, or other favored personal treatment from any person associated with a present or prospective client, competitor, or supplier of DLJ.

Providing Gifts and Entertainment

Employees may not give money or gifts of significant value to a present or prospective DLJ client, competitor, or supplier in order to gain a business advantage for DLJ. Favors and entertainment may be given to present or prospective clients, competitors, and suppliers at DLJ expense only when all the following conditions are met:

- They are consistent with accepted business practice.
- They are of limited value and cannot be construed as a bribe or payoff.
- They do not violate any applicable law or generally accepted ethical standards.
- Public disclosure of the facts will not embarrass DLJ.

Employees must not pay commissions or other compensation which would directly or indirectly benefit employees, family members, or associates of present or prospective DLJ clients, competitors, or suppliers.

INTEGRITY OF DLJ ASSETS AND INFORMATION

DLJ's assets consist of more than corporate funds and office furniture and supplies. Our assets include valuable ideas, business plans, and other information about DLJ's business. Employees should respect all of DLJ's assets as they would their own.

Confidential Information

Employees should not divulge to unauthorized persons, either during or after their term of employment, any information of a confidential nature connected with the business of DLJ or any of its clients or affiliates. Examples of confidential information include:

- Business information, such as client lists, markets, and development plans
- Personnel information, such as job title, level, duties, skills, or salary
- Any information disclosure of which could adversely affect the interest of DLJ or its clients

Accurate Reporting

Most employees report data of some kind in connection with their job. All reporting of information should be a fair presentation of the facts. Some forms of inaccurate reporting are illegal (e.g., listing a fictitious expense on an expense account or petty cash voucher or reporting overtime hours not actually worked).

Records Management

DLJ has established various programs providing for the retention, protection, and disposition of corporate records. These programs should be carefully adhered to.

Public Statements

All public statements, oral as well as written, about Donaldson, Lufkin & Jenrette or its business must be accurate and complete. Such statements should summarize the relevant facts, not make general pronouncements which could be interpreted in different ways.

Financial information and information related to DLJ's future performance may be released only by the President or Chief Financial Officer. All inquiries from financial analysts or brokers should be referred to the Chief Financial Officer.

Communications with News Media

With the exception of the Chief Executive Officer, no employee should discuss any aspect of DLJ's business activities or internal operations with the news media without prior coordination with the Director of Public Relations. Discussions with the news media relating to general market conditions, industry overviews (other than overviews of the securities industry), or opinions on specific companies or securities need not be coordinated with the Public Relations Department so long as such discussions are permissible under DLJ's "restricted list" memorandum and under other policies established by supervisory personnel for the employee's business area.

PAYMENT PRACTICES

Foreign Corrupt Practices Act

The Foreign Corrupt Practices Act, which applies to domestic practices as well as those outside the United States, imposes several restrictions on payment and accounting procedures. DLJ could be fined up to $1,000,000 and individual employees could be imprisoned for up to five years and fined $10,000 for violation of the Act or of the rules outlined in this section.

Questionable Payments

No payment, promise of payment, or offer of payment of anything of value may be made if there is a reasonable suspicion that it will be given to any foreign official, employee of a foreign government, or foreign political party or party official. Neither DLJ nor its employees shall make gifts of substantial value or provide entertainment beyond that customarily extended in ordinary commercial transactions. Any foreign government restrictions on the receipt of gifts or entertainment must be strictly observed.

However, small facilitating payments to persuade foreign clerical personnel to perform acts that they are otherwise legally required to perform may be permissible in certain circumstances. Before such payments can be made, employees must make certain that such payments do not contravene local laws but are a customary business practice. For example, a customs official may demand payment to speed the processing of documents. All facilitating payments must be properly documented and recorded. If a facilitating payment exceeds $50, prior written permission should be obtained from the Legal and Compliance Department.

Business and Accounting Practices

Employees shall at all times comply with DLJ's accounting rules and internal control policies. These rules and policies include the following prohibitions:

- No false or misleading entries shall be made in DLJ's books or records.
- No payment on DLJ's behalf shall be made without adequate supporting documentation or for any purpose other than as described in the documentation.
- No undisclosed or unrecorded DLJ account or fund shall be established for any purpose.
- No DLJ resources shall be used for any unlawful or improper purpose, whether or not disclosed.

In general, all transactions should be conducted so as to be recorded and traceable in the normal course of business.

Political Contributions

DLJ, as a corporate entity, is prohibited by law from making political contributions to candidates for federal office and is restricted in the political contributions it may make to candidates for state office. DLJ is, however, permitted to sponsor political action committees which may contribute to both federal and state candidates. DLJ sponsors one political action committee—the DLJ Better Government Fund which contributes to candidates for federal, state, and local office. It is DLJ's policy to encourage employees to participate in the political action committee. To the extent DLJ employees become personally involved in political activity, such involvement must be on their own time and at their own expense.

TRADE REGULATIONS

DLJ believes in vigorous and energetic competition. However, this competition must be accomplished within the framework of trade regulation and antitrust laws. All DLJ employees should be sensitive to and uphold the spirit and letter of antitrust legislation.

Federal Law.s

In the United States there are four primary trade regulation or antitrust laws:

- The Sherman Act, which prohibits contracts, combinations, or conspiracies in restraint of trade (e.g., price-fixing by competitors) and prohibits monopolizing (or attempting to monopolize) any part of trade or commerce. (Most violations of the Sherman Act are felonies and may be punishable by prison terms of up to three years for individuals and fines of up to $1,000,000 for corporations and $100,000 for individuals.)
- The Clayton Act, which among other things, limits certain exclusive dealing agreements and generally prohibits arrangements for "tying" products or services
- The Robinson-Patman Act, which prohibits discrimination in prices or services provided to purchasers of items of like grade and quality where there is injury to competition

- The Federal Trade Commission Act, which prohibits, in general terms, any unfair methods of competition and unfair or deceptive acts or practices

Laws of Other Countries

Most countries have enacted some form of trade regulation law. Countries such as Canada, West Germany, France, Japan, and Australia have enacted legislation covering all aspects of trade regulation and have been very aggressive in enforcing such laws.

Specific Prohibitions

Generally, any action taken either individually or in combination with others, which is predatory toward a competitor or which by nature restrains competition raises the possibility of violation of one or more antitrust laws.

The following rules, which should be strictly adhered to, prohibit activities that might give rise to possible antitrust violations:

- No employee shall discuss the possibility of an arrangement or understanding with competitors or potential competitors concerning prices, products, or services.
- No employee shall, in any joint ventures with competitive organizations, discuss anything but the specific transactions involved.
- No employee shall, when participating in industry associations, meetings, or similar group conferences, discuss prices or other competitive policies or practices.
- No employee shall discuss with others the possibility of an understanding not to deal with a particular customer or supplier, or an agreement or understanding obligating DLJ's clients to deal exclusively with DLJ or not to purchase the goods or services of a competitor.

RELATIONSHIPS WITH SUPPLIERS

All DLJ employees are expected to use common sense, good judgment, and the highest level of integrity in their relationships with suppliers of materials and services. Prime consideration should be given to DLJ's interests in developing and enhancing mutually productive long-term relationships.

All bids and quotations shall be evaluated on the basis of the price and quality of the product or service to be provided, as well as the financial stability of the supplier. The required quality and service need not be sacrificed solely for the sake of a lower price.

No employee shall suggest or imply that a supplier obtain goods or services from DLJ in return for DLJ's agreeing to buy from that supplier. Of course, DLJ may otherwise attempt to market its services and products to suppliers.

RESPONSIBILITY FOR IMPLEMENTATION

Each employee with supervisory duties is expected to discharge the responsibilities of his or her position at DLJ in full compliance with this Code of Business Ethics and shall make this Code known to all personnel under his or her direction.

Any infraction of applicable law or of this Code will subject an employee to disciplinary action. In addition, disciplinary measures will apply to any supervisor who directs or approves of such action, or who has or should have knowledge of it and does not act promptly to correct it.

Of practical necessity, the Code leaves most factual situations to the individual judgment of each employee. Whenever a question arises as to ethical standards, it is the responsibility of each employee to raise the question with his or her supervisor, who should, if necessary, discuss the matter with the officer in charge of the business unit affected. If that officer is uncertain as to how to treat the matter, he or she will ask the Legal and Compliance Department to resolve the issue. An exception to the forgoing procedures would be any situation which involves questionable conduct on the part of an employee's supervisor. In that case, the employee should promptly raise the issue with the Legal and Compliance Department.

If for any reason an employee is not fully satisfied after having approached his or her supervisor with a matter involving ethical standards, the employee is also encouraged to take the matter to the officer in charge of the business unit in which he or she works. Thereafter, if dissatisfaction remains, the employee should go directly to the Legal and Compliance Department.

CONCLUSION

Donaldson, Lufkin & Jenrette's reputation for integrity is perhaps unsurpassed in the more than a quarter century of our corporate existence. Despite the enormous growth of the firm during this period, we are confident that the sound judgment and personal standards of ethics of our people will allow us to continue this record.

Nothing contained in the Code constitutes a contract of employment. Neither the Code nor any part of the Code should be construed by any employee or prospective employee of DLJ as creating an express or implied contract of employment or continued employment with DLJ. Circumstances will obviously require that the Code be changed from time to time. Consequently, DLJ reserves the right to modify the Code as it deems appropriate and revisions will be distributed to employees.

ERNST & WHINNEY

And *Results*: They Go Together

As E&W continues to grow, we face an ever increasing challenge of communicating to our people the firm's fundamental philosophy and guiding principles. Accordingly, we have prepared this Statement of Firm Philosophy expressing our commitment to quality—in our services to clients, in our people—in everything we do.

This Statement should influence and guide our everyday actions—whether it be recommending accounting principles, providing tax advice, or assisting a client in the installation of a new management information system. Our future success depends on how well we live up to our Philosophy.

We are proud of our Philosophy, and you may share it with those who express an interest in the fundamental principles that guide our firm. [R. J. Groves, chairman, October 1986]

STATEMENT OF FIRM PHILOSOPHY

Ernst & Whinney is an international organization of professionals committed to the highest level of *quality service*—delivered by quality people. Our long tradition of providing technical excellence through teamwork responsive to clients' needs and expectations—and doing so to the very best of our ability—requires that our single focus be on quality in everything we do. We know that our commitment to quality will result in

- Personal satisfaction and opportunity for professional growth for every member of our organization
- Attracting and retaining clients of the highest caliber

- A fair return to reward our people and reinvest in future growth

We demonstrate our commitment to *quality service* by

- Accepting engagements to provide objective solutions to business challenges within our realm of expertise—accounting and auditing, tax, management consulting, and related business advisory services
- Maintaining independence in fact and appearance in all attest engagements and avoiding conflict of interest in all engagements
- Designing, maintaining, and enhancing worldwide methodologies that are innovative and technologically advanced and that provide consistency in the way we deliver similar services
- Organizing, staffing, and managing engagements to provide for appropriate levels of technical competence, experience, supervision, and review.
- Providing consultation resources within the firm to assist in resolving issues
- Undertaking reviews of selected engagements and practice units to assure compliance with professional standards and our quality control policies and procedures
- Recognizing our obligation to the public as well as our clients
- Providing our full range of services locally, nationally, and internationally, coordinated by a local client service executive
- Conducting engagements in accordance with applicable professional standards

*Reprint with permission.

- Accepting and maintaining relationships with clients whose concern for reputation and integrity is similar to our own
- Maintaining professional fee arrangements that are fair and commensurate with the value of services rendered

We afford equal opportunity to all our people to enhance their careers and to reach the highest level within the firm commensurate with their ability. We demonstrate our commitment to *quality people* by recruiting, developing, and retaining people who

- Maintain the highest level of integrity in fulfilling their responsibilities
- Maintain the confidentiality of client information

- Maintain objectivity in performing their assigned responsibilities and independence in fact and appearance in all attest engagements
- Participate in training and counseling offered by the firm to enhance their personal and professional knowledge and skill
- Seek engagements that offer them challenge and opportunities for personal and professional growth
- Value the sense of accomplishment that comes from meeting or exceeding client expectations and personal standards of excellence
- Participate in professional and other organizations that serve appropriate public purposes
- Dedicate themselves to providing the best quality service possible

ABC COMPANY

Organization and Policy Guide

INTRODUCTION TO THE POLICY VOLUME

Introduction

The ABC Company has adopted an organization and management concept of decentralization based on the principle that decisions concerning business activities should be made as close to the operating level as practicable. Under this concept, managers closest to a business have been delegated the responsibility and authority to make decisions, exercising their own knowledge, initiative, judgment, and inventiveness to the maximum extent possible with minimum mandatory directives. Managers are limited only by necessary minimum reservations of authority on specific items having broad company significance, which have been specifically defined and withheld by higher management. Most published guidance is designed to release initiative and encourage individuals to think, decide, and take action in the balanced best interest of all who benefit from the company's growth.

Definition

In order to channel management effort toward achievement of the company's balanced best interest, it is necessary to define those specific items of common purpose which have reservations of authority or where mandatory courses of action are required. Definitions of common purpose among components having common interests are embodied in what are usually termed "policies." In this context, a policy may be defined as follows:

> *A policy is a definition of common purposes for organization components or the company as a whole in matters where, in the interest of achieving both component and overall company objectives, it is necessary that those responsible for implementation adhere to a uniform course of action*

The classification and communication of common purposes throughout the company is accomplished by two types of policy documents: company policy statements and company management policies. The basic difference between the two is that company management policies contain certain organizationally derived reservations of authority while the company policy statements do not have such reservations. Other distinguishing characteristics are as follows:

Company Policy Statements

- Enduring statements of beliefs, aims, ideals
- Tendency toward broad societal orientation
- Basic purposes usually can be achieved without further reservations of authority
- Generally not subject to change because of inflation or changes in organization structure, nomenclature, etc.
- Statements may be communicated externally

Company Management Policies

- Frequently employ compliance assurance mechanisms

- Management control orientation
- Achievement of basic purpose requires consistent, uniform, and frequently mandatory courses of action
- Subject to more frequent revision due to inflation, changes in organization structure, nomenclature, etc.
- Relevant mainly for internal audience

Company policy statements and company management policies together comprise the ABC "Company Policies" and as such require review and approval of the corporate executive office prior to issuance. It is intended that company policies be few in number, text be kept to a minimum, and be fully communicated to facilitate understanding and compliance by all officers and managers throughout the company. All officers and managers are responsible for knowing, understanding, adhering to, and being able to interpret the provisions of subjects about which the company has a policy and also for ensuring that employees in their component understand and support policies that are directly applicable to their individual work and relationships.

Policy Development

The origin of a company policy may be anywhere in the company, although most policies originate in one of the corporate components.

A proposed policy will be sponsored by one or more of the members of the corporate executive council throughout the policy development process. The executive management staff procedure for formulating a new or revised policy provides more detailed information on the policy development process.

The corporate executive council assures that approved policies support overall company objectives and assigns responsibility for corporate guidance, counsel, and compliance assurance for applicable policies to the appropriate corporate component.

Executive management staff is responsible for overall administration of the company policy system, including responsibility for issuing procedures for developing, reviewing, and obtaining approval for all company policies. Executive management staff, in addition to having responsibility for publication and distribution of company policies, is also responsible for developing and implementing the process whereby policies are periodically subjected to intensive review by the assigned sponsor, including cost/benefit analyses of pertinent compliance assurance mechanisms.

Policy Implementation

When functional procedures or bulletins are considered necessary to implement company policies, they will be developed by the appropriate corporate component for distribution to, and use by, functional personnel responsible for the detailed implementation of policy provisions.

Functional procedures or bulletins provide detailed guidance on implementation of company policies but should not contain compliance requirements which are beyond the scope and intended purpose of the approved policy. Accordingly, functional procedures or bulletins with mandatory courses of action will require the same corporate and operating component reviews as the policies they supplement.

Applicability

A great deal of thought and work goes into the development of company policies and they are not issued until they reflect the varied interests of the many businesses and people who will be affected.

Affiliates should take advantage of this development work where the guidance contained in a particular company policy closely approximates affiliate company requirements and local circumstances.

While company policies have been developed primarily for application within the United States, they obviously state principles which are applicable for guidance of management on a worldwide basis.

STANDARDS OF CONDUCT IN TRANSACTIONS WITH THE UNITED STATES GOVERNMENT

Need for Policy

ABC Company maintains certain policies to guide its employees with respect to standards of conduct expected in areas where improper activities could damage the company's reputation and otherwise result in serious adverse consequences to the company and to employees involved. The purpose of this policy is to affirm, in a comprehensive statement, required standards of conduct and practices with respect to transactions with the United States government. In this area even the appearance of impropriety can erode public confidence in the company and in the government procurement process.

An employee's actions under this policy are significant indications of the individual's judgment and competence. Accordingly, those actions constitute an important element in the evaluation of the employee for position assignments and promotion. Correspondingly, insensitivity to or disregard of the principles of this policy will be grounds for appropriate management disciplinary action as provided in this policy.

Statement of Policy

It is the objective of the ABC Company to excel as a responsible and reputable supplier to the United States government. In furtherance of that objective, no employee shall, in connection with any transaction with the United States government, engage in any conduct in violation of law or otherwise inconsistent with the standards of honesty and integrity necessary to achieve that objective.

Specifically, but without limiting the standards of conduct required by this policy, scrupulous attention must be given to the following areas:

1. Many contracts with the United States government require that only those costs properly allocated to the contract may be reimbursed by the government. Any intentional allocation of costs to a government contract contrary to the contract provisions or related regulations are prohibited by this policy. Such mischarging may result, for example, from the improper execution of employee time cards, charging nonsupportable overhead costs, incorrectly classifying costs, or shifting of costs between contracts.

2. In the negotiation of certain contracts with the United States government cost and pricing data must be submitted to the government before any award and there must be a certification that the cost or pricing data submitted is current, accurate, and complete. Such disclosures and certifications are obligations imposed by statute. Obviously, this is an area where special care must be exercised. Any nondisclosure or certification in violation of this statute is prohibited by this policy.

3. How business is obtained and conducted with the United States government are also sensitive areas.

Company Policy 20.4 on business practices specifically prohibits improper payments or gratuities in connection with any governmental activity. Additionally, that policy provides that when a governmental agency has published policies with respect to the acceptance of entertainment, gifts, or other business courtesies by employees of that agency, such policies shall be respected by ABC personnel. Many agencies of the United States government have strict standards in this area which their employees must follow. It is also expected that company personnel will respect the United States government's conflict of interest regulations regarding the hiring and the activities of present or former United States government employees.

Company Policy 20.5 on compliance with the antitrust laws specifically directs, among other things, that no employee shall enter into any understanding or agreement with a competitor in violation of the Sherman Act. Obviously, Policy 20.5 flatly prohibits any collusive arrangements in selling or bidding to the United States government.

Violations of the Policy.

1. Violations of the policy will be grounds for discharge or other disciplinary action, adapted to the circumstances of the particular violation.

2. Disciplinary action will be taken, not only against individuals who authorize or participate directly in a violation of the policy, but also against:

   a. Any employee who may have deliberately failed to report a violation, as required by the policy;

   b. Any employee who may have deliberately withheld relevant and material information concerning a violation of this policy; and

   c. The violator's managerial superiors, to the extent that the circumstances of the violation reflect inadequate leadership and lack of diligence.

Responsibility and Authority

Management Responsibility. Each manager is responsible for taking timely action to secure compliance with the policy, including the taking of prompt remedial action when required. Each manager will be expected to consult with assigned company legal counsel concerning applicable legal requirements.

Department and division general managers will be responsible for maintaining regular educational programs, with the assistance of counsel, for familiarizing personnel with requirements applicable to doing business with the United States government. They will also be responsible for identifying other areas of sensitivity and concern in the government contracting area. This includes responsibility for determining whether individuals or firms should be retained to assist the company in connection with government business. Any individuals or firms so retained must be selected on the basis of their competence, integrity, and the absence of any real or apparent conflicts of interest.

Corporate Compliance Oversight. A Government Contract Compliance Review Board will be established at the corporate level. Initially, it will consist of the senior vice president—finance, the senior vice president—corporate relations staff, the senior vice president and general counsel, and the senior vice president—executive management staff. The principal responsibility of the Government Contract Compliance Review Board will be to inquire into reports of violations of this policy.

The Government Contract Compliance Review Board will designate an individual as an ombudsman to whom employees may directly report any information concerning violations of the policy.

The Government Contract Compliance Review Board will have available to it any company resources necessary to discharge its responsibilities under this policy. The company's corporate audit staff will also develop an audit program for compliance with this policy.

The ombudsman will be promptly advised by operating components of the following:

- Any external allegations (whether by an individual or government agency) that there has been any fraud, false statements, false claims,

or any other violation of law in connection with company contracts with the United States government

- Any report received in an operating component from an employee pursuant to the provisions of this policy relating to employee reported violations
- Any other violation of this policy which component management regards as potentially significant

The ombudsman will also be advised of the results of the corporate audit staff's audits for compliance with this policy.

The Government Contract Compliance Review Board will meet at least monthly with the ombudsman to review all compliance issues which have come to the attention of the ombudsman and will recommend any action necessary to satisfactorily resolve these matters. The Government Contract Compliance Review Board will report as required to the chairman of the board.

Employee Reported Violations.

1. Any employee who is requested to engage in any activity which the employee believes would be contrary to this policy will promptly report such information to the appropriate level of management or directly to the designated ombudsman.

2. Any employee who acquires information that gives the employee reason to believe that any other employee is engaged in conduct prohibited by this policy, or that any other person or firm representing the company is engaged in such conduct, will similarly promptly report such information in the manner provided in paragraph 1.

3. Any manager receiving a report under paragraph 1 or 2 will promptly investigate the matter and take timely remedial or other action as warranted under the provisions of this policy. Such manager will also promptly report the matter to higher management and to the ombudsman.

Policy Review Process. At least annually, each division general manager and each general manager reporting directly to a group executive or sector executive will review with direct reports and such other employees as the manager may select, compliance with the policy in component operations.

The general manager will report the results of these reviews to the officer to whom the general manager reports. The officers ultimately responsible for the various segments of the company's business will report the results of these annual reviews to the Government Contract Compliance Review Board.

Contracts with Local and State Government

Operating components are expected to develop procedures for following practices consistent with this policy in transactions with local and state governments in the United States.

HEWLETT-PACKARD

Statement of Corporate Objectives

THE ORGANIZATIONAL FRAMEWORK FOR OUR OBJECTIVES

The achievements of an organization are the result of the combined efforts of each individual in the organization working toward common objectives. These objectives should be realistic, should be clearly understood by everyone in the organization, and should reflect the organization's basic character and personality.

If the organization is to fulfill its objectives, it should strive to meet certain other fundamental requirements.

First, there should be highly capable, innovative people throughout the organization. Moreover, these people should have the opportunity—through continuing programs of training and education—to upgrade their skills and capabilities. This is especially important in a technical business where the rate of progress is rapid. Techniques that are good today will be outdated in the future, and people should always be looking for new and better ways to do their work.

Second, the organization should have objectives and leadership which generate enthusiasm at all levels. People in important management positions should not only be enthusiastic themselves, they should be selected for their ability to engender enthusiasm among their associates. There can be no place, especially among the people charged with management responsibility, for half-hearted interest or half-hearted effort.

Third, the organization should conduct its affairs with uncompromising honesty and integrity. People at every level should be expected to adhere to the highest standards of business ethics, and to understand that anything less is totally unacceptable. As a practical matter, ethical conduct cannot be assured by written policies or codes; it must be an integral part of the organization, a deeply ingrained tradition that is passed from one generation of employees to another.

Fourth, even though an organization is made up of people fully meeting the first three requirements, all levels should work in unison toward common objectives, recognizing that it is only through effective, cooperative effort that the ultimate in efficiency and achievement can be obtained.

It has been our policy at Hewlett-Packard not to have a tight military-type organization, but rather to have overall objectives which are clearly stated and agreed upon, and to give people the freedom to work toward those goals in ways they determine best for their own areas of responsibility.

Our Hewlett-Packard objectives were initially published in 1957. Since then they have been modified from time to time, reflecting the changing nature of our business and social environment. This booklet represents the latest updating of our objectives. We hope you find them informative and useful. [David Packard, *chairman of the board*; Wilbur Hewlett, *director emeritus*; John Young, *president and chief executive officer*, October 1986]

---

*Reprint with permission.

PROFIT

Objective: To achieve sufficient profit to finance our company growth and to provide the resources we need to achieve our other corporate objectives.

In our economic system, the profit we generate from our operations is the ultimate source of the funds we need to prosper and grow. It is the one absolutely essential measure of our corporate performance over the long term. Only if we continue to meet our profit objective can we achieve our other corporate objectives.

Our long-standing policy has been to reinvest most of our profits and to depend on this reinvestment, plus funds from employee stock purchases and other cash flow items, to finance our growth.

Our level of business varies from year to year, reflecting changing economic conditions and varying demands for our products. To deal with these changes, it is important that we be consistently profitable. When our business grows slowly, our profits allow us to accumulate cash reserves for the periods of rapid growth that require more capital to finance. We rely primarily on profits and the cash reserves to fund the growth of our ongoing operations, using debt when special requirements arise.

Meeting our profit objective requires that we design and develop each and every product so that it is considered a good value by our customers, yet is priced to include an adequate profit. Maintaining this competitiveness in the marketplace also requires that we perform our manufacturing, marketing and administrative functions as economically as possible.

Profit is not something that can be put off until tomorrow; it must be achieved today. It means that myriad jobs be done correctly and efficiently. The day-to-day performance of each individual adds to—or subtracts from—our profit. Profit is the responsibility of all.

CUSTOMERS

Objective: To provide products and services of the highest quality and the greatest possible value to our customers, thereby gaining and holding their respect and loyalty.

HP's view of its relationships with customers has been shaped by two basic beliefs. First, we believe the central purpose of our business—the reason HP exists—is to satisfy real customer needs. Second, we believe those needs can be fully satisfied only with the active participation and dedication of everyone in the company.

The essence of customer satisfaction is a commitment to *quality*, a commitment that begins in the laboratory and extends into every phase of our operations. Products must be designed to provide superior performance and long, trouble-free service. Once in production, these products must be manufactured at a competitive cost and with superior workmanship.

Careful attention to quality not only enables us to meet or exceed customer expectations, but it also has a direct and substantial effect on our operating costs and profitability. Doing a job properly the first time, and doing it consistently, allows us to employ fewer assets, reduces our costs, and contributes significantly to higher productivity and profits.

Providing innovative, reliable products is a key element in satisfying customer needs, but there are other important elements as well. HP offers many different products to many different customers, and it is imperative that the products recommended to a specific customer are those that will best fulfill the customer's overall, long-term needs. This requires that our field salespeople, operating individually or in well-coordinated teams, work closely with customers to determine the most appropriate, effective solutions to their problems. It requires, as well, that once a product is delivered, it be supported with prompt, efficient services that will optimize its usefulness.

Our fundamental goal is to build positive, long-term relationships with our customers, relationships characterized by mutual respect, by courtesy and integrity, by a helpful, effective response to customer needs and concerns, and by a strong commitment to providing products and services of the highest quality.

FIELDS OF INTEREST

Objective: To participate in those fields of interest that build upon our technology and customer base, that offer opportunities for continuing growth, and that enable us to make a needed and profitable contribution.

Our company's growth has been generated by a strong commitment to research and development in electronics and computer technology. That growth has been accomplished in two ways—first, by providing a steady flow of new products to markets which we already serve, and second, by expanding into new areas that build upon our existing technology and customer base.

Our first products were electronic measuring instruments used primarily by engineers and scientists. In time, we extended our range of measurement expertise to serve the areas of medicine and chemical analysis. Recognizing our customers' needs to gather and use large quantities of measurement data, we developed a small family of computers which later evolved into a broad line of computer and computer-based products, including associated software.

By combining and effectively applying its expertise in both measurement and computation, HP is able to serve the growing needs for high-performance business, manufacturing and design systems, test and measurement instrumentation, and medical and analytical products.

The basic purpose of our business is to provide products and services that help our customers develop and use better information to improve their personal and business effectiveness. We recognize that some customer information needs may require an industry-specific application where HP has little expertise. For that reason, our design goal is to provide highly functional, interactive hardware and software that can be easily assembled by HP, customers or other organizations to solve specific needs.

Within its broad fields of interest, HP has ample opportunities to pursue a variety of businesses. In evaluating those opportunities, we choose those that have strong links to our existing technology and customer base. In addition, we evaluate those businesses on the basis of their profit potential, long-term stability, our ability to make a distinguishing *contribution,* and their likelihood of generating the cash flow needed to continue HP's tradition of self-financing.

GROWTH

Objective: To let our growth be limited only by our profits and our ability to develop and produce innovative products that satisfy real customer needs.

How large should a company become? Some people feel that when it has reached a certain size there is no point in letting it grow further. Others feel that bigness is an objective in itself. We do not believe that large size is important for its own sake; however, for at least two basic reasons, continuous growth in sales *and* profits is essential for us to achieve our other objectives.

In the first place, we serve a dynamic and rapidly growing segment of our technological society. To remain static would be to lose ground. We cannot maintain a position of strength and leadership in our fields without sustained and profitable growth.

In the second place, growth is important in order to attract and hold high-caliber people. These individuals will align their future only with a company that offers them considerable opportunity for personal progress. Opportunities are greater and more challenging in a growing company.

OUR PEOPLE

Objective: To help HP people share in the company's success which they make possible; to provide employment security based on their performance; to ensure them a safe and pleasant work environment; to recognize their individual achievements; and to help them gain a sense of satisfaction and accomplishment from their work.

We are proud of the people we have in our organization, their performance, and their attitude toward their jobs and toward the company. The company has been built around the individual, the personal dignity of each, and the recognition of personal achievements.

Relationships within the company depend upon a spirit of cooperation among individuals and groups, and an attitude of trust and understanding on the part of managers toward their people. These relationships will be good only if employees have faith in the motives and integrity of their peers, managers, and the company itself.

On occasion, situations will arise where people have personal problems which temporarily affect their performance or attitude, and it is important that people in such circumstances be treated with sympathy and understanding while the problems are being resolved.

HP selects and manages its businesses with a goal of providing long-term employment for its people and opportunities for personal growth and development. In return, HP people are expected to meet certain standards of performance on the job, to adjust to changes in work assignments and schedules when necessary, and to be willing to learn new skills and to apply them where most critically needed. This flexibility is particularly important in our industry where rapid technological change and intensifying worldwide competition compel us all to continually seek better ways to do our jobs.

Another objective of HP's personnel policies is to enable people to share in the company's success. This is reflected in a pay policy and in employee benefit programs that place us among the leaders in our industry.

There is also a strong commitment at HP to the concept of equal opportunity and affirmative action, not only in hiring but also in providing opportunities for advancement. Advancement is based solely upon individual initiative, ability, and demonstrated accomplishment. Since we promote from within whenever possible, managers at all levels must concern themselves with the proper development of their people, and should give them ample opportunity—through continuing programs of training and education—to broaden their capabilities and prepare themselves for more responsible jobs.

The physical well-being of our people has been another important concern of HP's since the company's founding. With the growing complexity and diversity of our research and manufacturing processes, we must be especially vigilant in maintaining a safe and healthful work environment.

We want people to enjoy their work at HP and to be proud of their accomplishments. This means we must make sure that each person receives the recognition he or she needs and deserves. In the final analysis, people at all levels determine the character and strength of our company.

MANAGEMENT

Objective: To foster initiative and creativity by allowing the individual great freedom of action in attaining well-defined objectives.

In discussing HP operating policies, we often refer to the concept of "management by objective." By this we mean that, insofar as possible, each individual at each level in the organization should make his or her own plans to achieve company objectives and goals. After receiving managerial approval, each individual should be given a wide degree of freedom to work within the limitations imposed by these plans, and by our general corporate policies. Finally, each person's performance should be judged on the basis of how well these individually established goals have been achieved.

The successful practice of "management by objective" is a two-way street. Management must be sure that each individual understands the immediate objectives, as well as corporate goals and policies. Thus a primary HP management responsibility is communication and mutual understanding. Conversely, employees must take sufficient interest in their work to want to plan it, to propose new solutions to old problems, to stick their necks out when they have something to contribute. "Management by objective," as opposed to management by directive, offers opportunity for individual freedom and contribution; it also imposes an obligation for everyone to exercise initiative and enthusiasm.

In this atmosphere it is important to recognize that cooperation between individuals and coordinated efforts among operating units are essential to our growth and success. We are a *single* company whose strength is derived from mutually helpful relationships among units that may be geographically dispersed but are closely linked through common technologies, customers, goals and objectives.

It is important, as well, for everyone to recognize there are some policies which must be established and maintained on a companywide basis. We welcome recommendations on these companywide policies from all levels, but we expect adherence to them at all times.

CITIZENSHIP

Objective: To honor our obligations to society by being an economic, intellectual, and social asset to each nation and each community in which we operate.

All of us should strive to improve the environment in which we live. As a corporation operating in many different communities throughout the world, we must make sure that each of these communities is better for our presence. This means identifying our interests with those of the community; it means applying the highest standards of honesty and integrity to all our relationships with individuals and groups; it means enhancing and protecting the physical environment, building attractive plants and offices of which the community can be proud; it means contributing talent, time, and financial support to worthwhile community projects.

Each community has its particular set of social problems. Our company must help to solve these problems. As a major step in this direction, we must strive to provide worthwhile employment opportunities for people of widely different backgrounds. Among other things, this requires positive action to seek out and employ members of disadvantaged groups, and to encourage and guide their progress toward full participation at all position levels.

As citizens of their community, there is much that HP people can and should do to improve it— either working as individuals or through such groups as churches, schools, civic or charitable organizations. In a broader sense, HP's "community" also includes a number of business and professional organizations, such as engineering and scientific societies, whose interests are closely identified with those of the company and its individual employees. These, too, are deserving of our support and participation. In all cases, managers should encourage HP people to fulfill their personal goals and aspirations in the community as well as attain their individual objectives within HP.

At a national level, it is essential that the company be a good corporate citizen of each country in which it operates. Moreover, our employees, as individuals, should be encouraged to help find solutions to national problems by contributing their knowledge and talents.

The betterment of our society is not a job to be left to a few; it is a responsibility to be shared by all.

J.C.PENNEY COMPANY, INC.

Statement of Business Ethics

The JCPenney Company's Statement of Business Ethics goes back to the founding of the Company. It's significant that James Cash Penney's first store was named The Golden Rule. To "do unto others as you would have them do unto you" has been called the foundation of morality.

The final principle of The Penney Idea, developed by the Penney partners in 1913, reads "To test our every policy, method and act in this wise: 'Does it square with what is right and just?'"

Our unique heritage is both an aid to us and a challenge. It's helpful to have principles to guide us which have been in existence and enunciated for so many years. At the same time, we have more to live up to. More is expected of us and we expect more of ourselves.

As a result, our "code" may seem more demanding than that of many other companies, including some of those companies with which we do business.

This booklet on our business ethics offers nothing new in basic content. Every principle here is part of our official written policy. What we have here is a clarification of our policy, distributed to Penney Associates so we may know what our Company expects of us. We are asked to sign a certificate that we have received and read this booklet and are, and will continue to be, in compliance with the Statement of Business Ethics of J. C. Penney Company, Inc.

On a more personal note, I would like to take this opportunity to recognize the high moral and ethical standards of Penney Associates. Since 1902,

the people of JCPenney have had the right to feel proud of themselves both individually and collectively. I'm sure we all agree we want this tradition to continue. [William R. Howell, chairman of the board, JCPenney Company, Inc.]

THE SPIRIT OF THIS STATEMENT

This Statement of Business Ethics was written under the direction of a committee charged with the responsibility by Penney's chairman of the board. It went through many drafts. A key stage in the development was a series of discussions of the various versions in manuscript form. In fact, this introduction itself has been included in response to suggestions made at the discussion meetings.

Before publication and distribution, drafts of this statement were read and discussed by over 2,000 Penney management Associates. This statement reflects a great many of their suggestions. To the extent of practicality, this statement is the work of the people who are asked to follow it. This developmental process is very appropriate for an organization which has always recognized that the Company is its people.

In the 1986 update, several new examples have been added to further illustrate the application of the principles which guide our business. These examples include material from previously issued Interpretive Bulletins.

Periodically the Business Ethics Committee will publish revisions, updates, or further illustrations that will help all Associates guide their busi-

---

*Reprinted with permission.

ness conduct. Recertification (signing a new Certificate of Compliance) will generally not be part of this process since the original signature confirms that each such Associate will continue to comply with the principles as they are expressed from time to time.

In the year 1913, six Penney partners including James Cash Penney and Earl C. Sams met in a hotel room in Salt Lake City to develop a set of principles to guide them in the management and operation of Golden Rule Store Company. The statement which resulted was called "The Original Body of Doctrine." Later the name was changed to "The Penney Idea."

The Penney Idea

1. To serve the public as nearly as we can to its complete satisfaction.
2. To expect for the service we render a fair remuneration, and not all the profit the traffic will bear.
3. To do all in our power to pack the customer's dollar full of value, quality, and satisfaction.
4. To continue to train ourselves and our associates so that the service we give will be more and more intelligently performed.
5. To improve constantly the human factor in our business.
6. To reward the men and women in our organization through participation in what the business produces.
7. To test our every policy, method, and act in this wise: "Does it square with what is right and just?"

Many Shared Responsibilities

When we discuss the Penney Associates' responsibility to the Company, and vice versa, it is always in the context that the Associates are the Company. Our responsibility is to each other, and to ourselves. The leadership of the Company is as responsible to Penney Associates as the Associates are to their leaders.

As representatives of JCPenney, we are also responsible to the public or, more precisely, to several publics. These include our customers, our stockholders, our suppliers, and the many local communities in which we conduct our business.

In the largest sense, we are responsible both to our heritage and to our future, to the people who preceded us in the Company and to those who will follow us. We are responsible to, and for, our reputation.

Purpose of the Statement

In light of the vast and growing extent of our activities, the Company has recognized the need to provide Associates with some practical guidelines to the business conduct which is expected of us. Over the years, official written policies have been adopted in a number of significant areas to assist Penney Associates in fulfilling their responsibilities. This booklet restates some of the more important policies relating to situations which you may encounter in the performance of your duties.

As a Company, we are accustomed to spelling out our work responsibilities or job descriptions. This document is a similar effort to communicate our standards of ethics. The principles set forth here are applicable to all Penney Associates at all levels of Company operations, including its subsidiaries and divisions, wherever located. It is important to comply with these principles to ensure our ability to perform our obligations fairly and honestly and to protect against corporate or personal liability or adverse public comment.

There are three major sections to the statement—Compliance with Laws, Conflicts of Interest, and Preservation of Company Assets. Because of the requirement for accuracy and thorough coverage, the language of the document sometimes tends to become more legalistic than intended. The "spirit" of the statement is not legalistic. It is people oriented, as befits a Company of people.

The Certificate of Compliance

The mere act of producing a statement on business ethics is not enough. There is the further obligation of assuring that the standards of conduct are communicated to and agreed upon by those who are asked to follow them.

In the back of the statement is a Certificate of Compliance. The signing of this certificate signifies that the Associate has read the statement, is in compliance with it, but that in doing so understands that it is not a guarantee of continued employment which, in fact, the Associate or the Company can end at any time for any reason.

Each Associate is expected to realize that this statement does not constitute an employment contract which in any way is designed to limit his or her freedom, or the Company's, to respond to situations in a flexible manner which recognizes each person as an individual. In fact, no one except the officer of the Company with corporate responsibility for personnel is authorized to enter into employment agreements on behalf of JCPenney with its Associates, and then only in writing.

In discussions of earlier drafts, several variations of this question were asked: "Suppose I'm not sure if I'm in compliance with everything in the statement. What should I do then?"

The answer is simply—*ask*. There is virtually no problem or potential problem which cannot be resolved with the exchange of ideas and understanding.

Communication and Disclosure Are the Keys

It isn't possible to describe the infinite variety of situations to which our policies apply. We urge and, in fact, expect you to bring any questions concerning this statement or its application to the attention of appropriate supervisory personnel, such as a unit manager or department head. Many times, what appears to be prohibited may, under certain circumstances, be sanctioned by disclosure and approval. No set of principles can eliminate the need for human judgment.

Communication and disclosure are not only part of the program; they are the key components, and the foundation for the free and open working environment which has always characterized our Company.

COMPLIANCE WITH LAW

The Official JCPenney Policy Statement. Each Associate of the Company, while acting on behalf of the Company, shall comply with all applicable governmental laws and regulations.

The Purpose of the Policy. More and more, our activities are subject to a variety of federal, state, and local laws and regulations. Penney Company policy has always been to comply with all applicable laws and regulations in the conduct of its business. Accordingly, no Associate should take, or permit to be taken, any action on behalf of the Company which he or she knows, or reasonably should know, violates any applicable governmental law or regulation.

Discussion. Our Company policy statement is, simply, "we will obey the laws," certainly the starting point for any business conduct. It's been said that "the law is a floor". We have to do much more than just obey the laws, although very obviously, we can do no less. Violation of the laws can result in both corporate and personal liability.

At the same time we recognize that we are not all lawyers. We cannot know all the laws which may apply. Nor can we understand all aspects of the laws which apply. We are expected, however, to take certain common-sense precautions. The first and most important is—when in doubt, ask. The section entitled "Procedures for Questions and Reports" explains how you should go about it.

Maintenance of Books, Records, and Accounts

The results of operations of our Company must be recorded in accordance with the requirements of law and generally accepted accounting principles. It is Company policy, as well as a requirement of law, to maintain books, records, and accounts which, in reasonable detail, accurately and fairly reflect the business transactions and disposition of assets of the Company. In order to carry out this policy and assure compliance with applicable laws, no Associate should take, or permit to be taken, any action in a manner whereby the Company's books, records, and accounts would not accurately, fairly and completely reflect the action taken. No false or misleading entries should be made in any books or records of the Company for any reason, and no fund, asset or account of the Company may be established or acquired for any purpose unless such fund, asset, or account is accurately reflected in the books and records of the Company. No corporate funds or assets should be used for any unlawful purpose.

Antitrust

Broadly speaking, the antitrust laws regulate the competitive conduct and dealings of business. Penalties for violation can lead to extremely serious consequences for both the Company and the individuals involved. A complete description of the antitrust laws is beyond the scope of this document. However, it should be noted that any activity with a competitor or supplier in restraint of trade, such as price fixing, is illegal. Such activities with suppliers as discriminatory pricing, terms, promotional allowances, services, and facilities may violate the antitrust laws. This does not mean, of course, that we cannot and should not negotiate hard in all areas with our suppliers.

Product Safety

Products sold by the Company must not only meet all applicable safety standards set by law, they must also meet our often more stringent Company standards. It is Company policy not to handle knowingly any defective product and to minimize as much as possible hazards from products which inherently entail some risks. The reputation and success of our Company has been built upon the performance of our products. Our customers have a right to expect that our products will not endanger their health or safety in any way.

Advertising

Advertising used by the Company is legally required to be true and not deceptive in any manner. All product claims must be substantiated by supporting data before they are made. We must be careful to assure that the Penney customer is not disappointed by claims for our products which are not supported by performance. The purpose of our advertising has always been to emphasize the quality of our products and the fairness of our prices. We believe that a properly informed customer will be a loyal Penney customer.

Political Activities

The impact of government on business in our society continues to grow. The Company and its Associates have a legitimate interest in the composition of our state, local and federal governments and in the laws which prescribe the ways business should be conducted. This is, however, an extremely sensitive area. There are laws on the federal, state, and local levels which govern the involvement of the Company and its Associates in political activities. Corporate payments of cash, merchandise, or services in connection with political activities are generally either illegal or strictly regulated by law. Regulated activities include the support of, or opposition to, candidates for public office; contributions in support of, or opposition to, initiatives or referenda; and contributions, gifts, or honoraria to government officials. All proposed payments or donations or services in any of these areas must be reviewed in advance and approved in writing by the designated representatives of the Government Relations Department and the Legal Department. Failure to obtain the requisite approvals can lead to embarrassment and serious problems for the Company and its Associates.

Securities Laws

The securities laws and rules of the securities exchanges affect a wide variety of the Company's activities. No Associate may engage in, or permit any other Associate to engage in, any activity on behalf of the Company which he or she knows, or reasonably should know, is prohibited by the securities laws. Examples include the following: No false, misleading or deceptive statements may be made in connection with the purchase or sale of any security or in any report filed with the Securities and Exchange Commission, or distributed to any financial analyst or stockholder. Improper or premature disclosure of confidential information to outsiders or Associates who do not require the information to perform their jobs must be avoided. In addition, no Associate may trade in securities of the Company when he or she has knowledge of material events affecting the Company which have not been made public.

Personnel Related Laws

The Company's operations and procedures, as they relate to Associates (their wages, hours, working conditions, and other terms and conditions of employment) reflect the importance the Company places on fair and equitable treatment of all Associates and conform in every respect to federal, state, and local laws.

The employment relationship is increasingly controlled and regulated by legal requirements. For example, laws such as the Age Discrimination Act, the Civil Rights Act, the Fair Credit Reporting Act, the Fair Labor Standards Act, the Equal Pay Act, the National Labor Relations Act, and a variety of similar state acts cover all or nearly all aspects of the employment relationship. Violations of these laws can result in corporate and individual liability. Employment laws dealing with sexual harassment even create liability on the part of the Company for Associate dealings with employees of suppliers. It's not possible in this statement to list all the laws which apply, or to furnish specific guidance. Such guidance is provided in the Digest of Personnel Laws which should be supplemented, as required, by the Regional Personnel Relations attorneys, Division Personnel Relations attorneys, or Corporate Personnel Relations in the New York Office, as appropriate.

CONFLICTS OF INTEREST

The Official JCPenney Policy Statement. Each Associate of the Company shall avoid any activity, interest, or relationship with non-Company persons or entities which would create, or might appear to others to create, a conflict with the interests of the Company.

The Purpose of the Policy. To assure that all Company Associates, at all levels, wherever located, are able to perform their duties and exercise their judgments on behalf of the Company without impairment, or the appearance of impairment, by virtue of a non-Company activity, interest, or relationship.

Discussion. Associates should avoid the development of any relationships or participation in any transaction involving a possible conflict, or appearance of conflict, between the interest of the Company and the personal interest of the Associate.

While we wish to preserve the privacy of our Associates and their right to conduct their personal affairs without interference, a full and timely disclosure of the facts is necessary to avoid problems. The determination as to whether there is a conflict, or appearance of a conflict, is to be made by the Company and not the Associate involved. In appropriate circumstances where the facts are known, and if there is no illegal or unethical conduct involved, the Company could consent to the proposed activity even though a conflict of interest may exist.

Gifts, Loans, Entertainment

Commercial bribery is illegal and the payment or receipt of any business-related bribe is prohibited. An Associate should not, directly or indirectly, accept gifts of cash or anything else of value from anyone having or seeking business with the Company, other than non-cash gifts of nominal value generally used for promotional purposes by the donor.

Participation in business-related functions, in-

cluding the acceptance of lunches or other meals on occasion, is a normal and permissible business practice. However, care must be exercised to ensure that they are necessary and that their value and frequency are not excessive under all the applicable circumstances.

Other forms of entertainment or "outings," such as dinners, theater tickets, golf dates, fishing or hunting trips, may be accepted only if it is practicable for the Associate to reciprocate at an appropriate time. In those cases where reciprocation does not seem possible, but the Associate believes it is in the Company's interest to attend, he or she should get the agreement of appropriate supervisory personnel such as a unit manager or a department head.

Associates should not accept loans from any persons or entities having or seeking business with the Company except recognized financial institutions at normal interest rates for individual borrowers prevailing at the time of borrowing. In discussing personal financing with banks, no Associate should state or imply that the bank's response will in any way affect its relationship with the Company. The Company's business relationships with financial institutions are not to be utilized to influence in any way personal loans to Associates.

In summary, nothing should be accepted which could impair, or appear to impair, an Associate's ability to perform his or her Company duties or to exercise his or her judgment in a fair and unbiased manner. A divided loyalty will invariably create serious problems for the Company and its Associates.

Examples of situations that might be encountered by Penney Associates are presented here to help clarify the Conflicts of Interest Statement and its applications.

Example A. A supplier of the Company invites an Associate with whom he or she does business, and the Associate's spouse, to have dinner at the supplier's home. The Associate does not wish to turn down this invitation because it helps to build a good working relationship and the Associate intends to reciprocate at a later date.

Analysis of Example A. The Associate would be permitted to accept this invitation because of the intention to reciprocate. If reciprocation did not appear practicable, the invitation could be accepted only with the approval of the Associate's unit manager or department head.

Example B A manager whose store places a significant amount of advertising in a local newspaper is given two tickets covering all expenses for a week's trip to the Bahamas. These trips are made available by a local newspaper to all major advertisers in the area and are well attended.

Analysis of Example B. A conflict of interest would exist if the store manager or other member of store management used the tickets personally. However, if the tickets are in fact a "discount earned" through advertising space or frequency and if they are used as prizes for a store contest or promotion, then it would be in the Company's interest to accept and no conflict would exist.

Example C. An Associate has been invited by a supplier to attend a two-day seminar which is held in a resort area. This meeting is a combination of business and pleasure but it is regarded in its particular area as being the most important meeting of the year.

Analysis of Example C. The Associate would be permitted to attend this meeting with the approval of his or her unit manager or department head. Attendance at such meetings, even though they may appear to be attractive from the entertainment point of view, are necessary or desirable at times in order that Associates remain current in their areas of responsibility for the Company.

Example D An Associate attends a luncheon given by a local supplier, at the supplier's expense, for some of its more important accounts, with the approval of the Associate's manager. During the course of the luncheon, nominal door prizes are given, based on the number of invitations to the luncheon. The Associate wins one of the nominal prizes.

Analysis of Example D. The Associate may accept the prize. Since the door prize was nominal and was not geared to influence or to appear to influence the decision of the Associate with respect to purchasing the supplier's goods and since the Associate was attending the luncheon with the permission of his or her manager a conflict of interest would not result from accepting the prize.

Interest in Other Businesses and Organizations

An Associate should not have any direct or indi-rect interest in, or relationship to, any transaction to which the Company is or will be party if such interest or relationship might influence, or appear to influence, that Associate in the performance of Company duties. Associates should not have any interest, financial or otherwise, in any competitor or supplier of the Company, which could influence the Associate's objectivity or independence of judgment in performing his or her duties or could otherwise create a conflict of interest.

Interest in Competitors

A Competitor of the Company is any organization which sells goods or services similar to any of those offered for sale by the Company. Under this definition, it is the type of goods or services sold, and not the manner of sale, which determines another organization's status as a competitor. Accordingly, the fact that goods or services are not marketed through traditional types of retail stores, but, for example, out of one's home, is not relevant. An Associate should not have any direct or indirect interest in, or relationship with, any competitor of the Company if such interest or relationship might influence, or appear to influence, that person in the performance of his or her Company duties. For these purposes, prohibited interests or relationships with respect to competitors include selling, recruiting, distribution, or similar activities, whether conducted out of the Associate's home or otherwise.

Example A. A newly employed Associate has worked for a major competitor of the Company and during the course of that previous employment has acquired shares of stock which amount to a very small percentage of the outstanding stock of the competitor. A question has arisen as to whether ownership of that stock will constitute a conflict of interest.

Analysis of Example A. Ownership of stock in a competitor will not be deemed a conflict of interest if both of the following conditions exist: (1) the stock is publicly traded, and (2) the amount owned by the Associate and his or her "relatives" (as defined in this booklet) does not exceed one-tenth of 1% of the amount outstanding.

Example B. A Company store manager proposes to buy a substantial number of shares of stock of a corporation formed to operate a women's apparel shop. The shop will be located in a shopping center which also contains a Penney store, and will carry similar merchandise.

Analysis of Example B. A conflict of interest would exist. The apparel shop is a competitor because of its location and because of the merchandise it carries. In addition, the proposed purchase of stock by the Associate does not meet the guidelines described in the Analysis of Example A above.

Example C. A general merchandise manager sells casualty and life insurance for a major insurance company on a part-time basis (i.e., after work and on weekends).

Analysis of Example C. A conflict of interest may exist. Part-time work for an insurance company may be deemed to be a conflict of interest because the Company sells life and casualty insurance through its Financial Services Division. Accordingly, an Associate should notify his or her department head or superior of the activity. The Associate's department head, in conjunction with the director of insurance, will determine whether the Associate's activity is competitive with any Company insurance operations and, accordingly, whether a conflict of interest exists.

Interest in Suppliers

A supplier is one who furnishes or offers to furnish goods or services of any kind to the Company. It is Company policy to select a supplier on the basis of price, quality, and performance. An Associate must avoid financial or other involvement with a supplier with whom he or she does or is likely to do business. Such involvement might appear to cause the Associate to select a supplier for reasons other than price, quality, and performance.

Example A. A buyer of consumer electronics in the Merchandise Department contemplates purchasing 100 shares of X corporation, which is listed on the New York Stock Exchange, for a long-term investment. X corporation is one of three manufacturers from whom the Company buys consumer electronics, and this buyer is currently involved in the decision as to whether to select X corporation to supply a new line of merchandise.

Analysis of Example A. A conflict of interest would exist in this situation because ownership of the stock might influence, or appear to influence, the Associate in his or her decision-making process. A conflict generally would exist where an

Associate's duties or position would enable him or her to influence the decision as to whether the Company should acquire goods, services, supplies, properties, or facilities from an organization in which the Associate has an interest.

Example B. A buyer of soft goods receives a recommendation from a broker to purchase 100 shares of the common stock of Y corporation. The buyer knows that Y corporation is a supplier of tools which the Company sells through its catalog. Moreover, the buyer of soft goods is generally aware of the fact that the Company has a high regard for the merchandise manufactured by Y corporation. The buyer of soft goods is not, however, in a position to influence the Company's transactions with Y corporation.

Analysis of Example B. Ownership of an interest in Y corporation should not create a conflict for the buyer of soft goods in this situation because his or her Company duties do not involve any relationship with Y corporation and the buyer is not able to influence transactions with Y corporation.

Example C. An Associate has dealings with a sales representative of Z corporation in the performance of his or her duties for the Company. The Associate is asked by the sales representative to join the representative and five other individuals in a partnership formed to own income-producing real property.

Analysis of Example C. This situation involves a conflict of interest. Any non-Company business relationship with a representative of a supplier creates an appearance of a conflict if the Associate's Company duties involve dealings with, or decisions relating to the use of, that supplier.

Example D. An Associate owns a 5% interest in a partnership, ABC Associates, which owns and operates a shopping center with space suitable for the Company. This Associate supervises a number of other Associates who are engaged actively in seeking space for a Penney store in the same area in which the ABC Associates shopping center is located. The Associate must approve a recommendation as to the location of the store.

Analysis of Example D. A conflict of interest exists in this situation because the supervisor is in a position where ownership of the partnership interest could influence the approval of the recommendation or influence the decision of Associates reporting to the supervisor.

Example E. An Associate has been invited to join the board of directors of a bank.

Analysis of Example E. To guard against conflict or the appearance of conflict, Associates are advised to check with the Treasurer's Department before going on the board of a bank.

Indirect Interests and Relationships

Direct interests and relationships of Associates have been described and illustrated in the preceding pages. With respect to indirect interests and relationships, there are three general rules to follow. First, an Associate should not be in a position to make or influence a decision relating to the Company's engaging in business with a relative of the Associate. Second, an Associate should not be in a position to derive an indirect benefit from a Company transaction involving a relative. Third, an Associate should disclose any situation in which a relative has an interest in a competitor or supplier or in any Company transaction. For these purposes, "relative" should be construed to include the Associate's spouse and any relative who resides with the Associate. When other relatives are involved—including sons and daughters and their spouses; parents; brothers and sisters and their spouses; and other "in-laws"—Associates should protect themselves against the appearance of conflict by reporting the situation to their supervisors.

Example A. An Associate is assigned to direct a special project to examine a certain area of the Company's business. A part of the project will involve the hiring of a consulting firm to advise on a specific aspect of the project. The Associate, having a high regard for a consulting firm in which the Associate's brother-in-law has an interest, contemplates hiring that firm to do the necessary work.

Analysis of Example A. A conflict of interest could exist in this situation because the interest of the Associate's relative in the firm selected by the Associate to supply services to the Company might appear to have influenced the Associate in his or her decision-making process. In this example, the relationship should be disclosed to the Associate's supervisor who might ask others to share in the decision.

Example B. A buyer of housewares has a son who works for a manufacturer of apparel which is a major supplier of the Company.

Analysis of Example B. A conflict of interest does not exist under these particular circumstances. If, however, the buyer were to be transferred to the department which included the merchandise supplied by the son's employer, the situation would have to be disclosed to the Associate's supervisor.

Example C. The spouse of a store personnel manager has a 25% interest in a local employment agency, but the spouse does not participate in the day-to-day management of the business. The personnel manager decides on the extent to which the store uses that employment agency to fill open positions.

Analysis of Example C. Even though the personnel manager does not deal with the spouse in the use of the agency, there is still a conflict of interest because the income the spouse receives from the agency might influence the personnel manager in the performance of his or her Company duties.

Example D. A store manager's spouse contemplates purchasing with his or her own funds an interest in a warehouse which the Company leases.

Analysis of Example D. A conflict of interest would exist in this instance even though the store manager has no connection with the warehouse because he or she would have an indirect interest which might be adverse to the Company's interest as a lessee of the building.

Example E. A relative of an Associate has a small ownership interest in a competing business located in the same market area as that in which the Associate works.

Analysis of Example E. All situations in which a relative of an Associate has an ownership or employment interest in a competing business should be disclosed even if the Associate was not involved in establishing that business.

Example F. The spouse of a management Associate sells Avon cosmetics and merchandise to friends and neighbors. The Associate has asked whether this type of activity would constitute an "indirect interest" in a competitor.

Analysis of Example F. Not all part-time work for other companies that sell or distribute products of the types sold in Penney stores would represent a conflict of interest. The focus of review is, to some degree, on the extent of the merchandise offering of the other company, and, to a greater degree, on the extent to which the Associate becomes involved in promoting the sale of the products of that other company. For instance, if the spouse of a store management Associate sold products for Avon in the Associate's neighborhood without any involvement by the Associate, it generally would not represent a conflict of interest.

However, a potential conflict, or appearance of conflict, could develop in the case of companies (such as Amway) which market a broad range of merchandise through catalogs or door-to-door selling and which encourage participation by the Associate in the relative's sales or other activities. The participation is encouraged in a variety of ways, such as by attending the relative's distribution activities. In these situations, the assortment of merchandise offered, and the involvement of the Associate, can result in a conflict or the appearance of a conflict.

In all these cases, the determination of whether or not a particular situation is or is not a conflict is not a simple one. Accordingly, Associates are required to disclose each such situation for review.

Example G. An Associate has noted an exception on the Certificate of Compliance, and received an indication that his or her spouse's activities for a competitor do not represent a conflict of interest. The spouse has asked other Penney spouses to work with him or her in the approved activity.

Analysis of Example G. Associates are expected to avoid the appearance of conflicts as well as actual conflicts. Thus, the spouse of an Associate should not solicit other Associates as customers, or recruit other Associates or relatives of other Associates as potential dealers/distributors for competitors, even where these activities are carried on outside the Company's facility. Similarly, there is a conflict of interest or the appearance of a conflict if the relative of an Associate conducts any business for a competitor within a Penney store or other Company facility.

Example H. The spouse of an assistant buyer has been hired by Sears Roebuck in a managerial capacity. Prior to that the spouse worked for non-retail firms.

Analysis of Example H. No conflict exists if the situation does not influence or give the appearance of influencing the decisions of the assistant buyer. Thus, if the activities of the spouse involve work totally different from that which the Associate performs at the Company, there should be no conflict.

However, if the spouse is a buyer for Sears assigned to the same general merchandise areas, that situation should be reported. While situations in which the spouse of an Associate is performing related activities for a competitor such as Sears do not necessarily involve a conflict of interest, it is only through reporting the matter that an Associate can avoid any misunderstanding about his or her intent.

Example I. The spouse of a senior merchandise manager (whose responsibilities include stationery) just became a distributor for a well-known greeting card company. The spouse plans to conduct that business from a special room in their home.

Analysis of Example I. The criteria as to permissibility of conduct are the extent of the merchandise offering made by the spouse's firm and the extent to which the Associate becomes involved in lending support to the spouse's activities. In this case, there is the appearance of a possible conflict only because of the merchandise line responsibilities of the senior merchandise manager. The situation should be disclosed and a determination made taking into account the two criteria.

Example J. The son of an Associate was hired on a temporary basis for summer employment by a company which performs services for Penney. The Associate is responsible for choosing and negotiating the contract with the service company.

Analysis of Example J. A conflict of interest could exist in this situation since the Associate is responsible for choosing the service company. The employment of the son, even on a temporary basis, could influence the Associate's decision and, accordingly, the situation should be disclosed to the Associate's supervisor.

Example K. A buyer uses his or her position to induce a representative of a supplier to develop a non-marital, intimate relationship with him or her.

Analysis of Example K. The Company could well be liable if the buyer threatened the representative with a potential loss of business in this situation.

Even assuming that the relationship evolves into one welcomed by both parties, it creates the appearance of a conflict and can create an actual conflict if the relationship influences the Associate's business judgment.

This type of conduct shall not be allowed to

play a role in any business decision. While the Company does not want to interfere with Associates' privacy, Associates must ensure that their conduct does not compromise in any way the Company's legitimate business interests.

Use of Company Information

An Associate should not use for personal benefit information concerning any aspect of the Company's business or information acquired as a result of his or her relationship with the Company. Moreover, such information should not be disclosed to any other person or entity except as required in the performance of Company duties or as expressly authorized by the Company. An Associate can be held liable to the Company for any benefit gained from improper use of such information or any damages sustained by the Company as a result of improper disclosure of such information.

Example A. An Associate learns as a result of his or her duties with the Company that D corporation is about to announce a major breakthrough which should greatly increase the value of D corporation's stock. The Associate purchases 500 shares of D corporation before the news becomes public and also tells a friend about it.

Analysis of Example A. The Associate in this situation would be using Company information improperly in two ways. First, the Associate would be using information acquired solely as a result of his or her relationship to the Company for personal benefit. Second, the Associate would be disclosing to another person who is not a Company Associate needing the information for the proper performance of Company duties, information which had not been previously disclosed to the public. Such disclosure may also constitute a violation of the Securities Exchange Act of 1934.

Example B. An Associate's neighbor is planning to go into the business of selling radios, televisions, and other household appliances. The Associate obtains certain Company manuals relating to this aspect of the Company's business and gives them to the neighbor without the Company's permission.

Analysis of Example B. The Associate in this situation has made an improper use of Company information by giving the neighbor Company manuals which the Associate acquired solely as a result of his or her relationship with the Company. These manuals had been prepared for the Company's own use and contain information that had been developed through large expenditures of time and money.

Example C. An Associate with access to Company financial information discusses non-public information with a stockbroker in anticipation of trading stock in the Company.

Analysis of Example C. A conflict of interest would exist in addition to possible violations of federal securities laws. The conflict would arise from discussing confidential Company information with someone other than as required in performance of Company duties or as expressly authorized by the Company.

Example D. An Associate uses Company information to develop a mailing list for his or her spouse's business.

Analysis of Example D. A conflict of interest would exist. The conflict would arise from using confidential Company information for personal gain.

Example E. An Associate shares his or her password to help a fellow Associate, who has forgotten his, to gain access to the system.

Analysis of Example E. This sharing of the password would violate the Statement of Business Ethics. Company procedures require that Associates must maintain the confidentiality of their own password.

Diversion of Corporate Opportunity

An Associate should not appropriate to himself or herself, nor divert to any other person or entity, a business or financial opportunity which the Associate knows, or reasonably could anticipate, the Company would have an interest in pursuing.

Example A. An Associate overhears a conversation at a Company meeting to the effect that the Company is about to look for a new store site in a certain town. The Associate immediately calls an old friend, who now lives near that town, and relays the information. The friend forms a corporation which acquires a suitable site. The Company subsequently purchases that site from the corporation formed by the Associate's friend.

Analysis of Example A. This situation involves a diversion of corporate opportunity even though the Associate did not gain personally. The Associate has diverted to another an opportunity which belonged to the Company.

Presentation/Honorarium Guidelines

This subject includes the making of presentations (i.e., giving a talk, participating in a panel discussion or seminar, teaching a course, writing an article or book, and the like) and the possible acceptance of an honorarium or other compensation in connection with such presentation. The Company has no concern with any presentation or honorarium not related to work activities.

Any activity falling into the category of those described above must be discussed in advance of acceptance with the Associate's department head or other appropriate supervisory personnel. The supervisor will decide whether further approval is required and if so, make application for such approval.

Legal Department clearance is required in cases where (1) the sponsor of the presentation has an existing or potential relationship (including competitive relationship) with the Company or (2) the department head or supervisor believes the presentation could disclose confidential, proprietary or sensitive information of, or relating to, the Company.

Public Relations clearance is required in cases where presentations involving the Company are likely to be picked up by the media.

When the presentation involves written material, such as a speech or magazine article, the Legal and/or Public Relations Department have the option of approving a proposed presentation on condition that the final text be cleared prior to its delivery or publication.

If, using the above criteria, it is the judgment of the department head or supervisor that Legal or Public Relations approval is not required, he or she will make the decision. In this case, the presentation will generally be approved so long as it is prepared and performed on the Associate's own time and without the use of Company facilities. If Company time or facilities are involved in the preparation and/or performance, the department head or supervisor will take into account the value of the presentation to Company interests and grant permission at his or her discretion.

An honorarium is "a payment as to a professional person for services on which no fee is set." Generally, honorariums are modest payments, not intended as compensation.

An Associate's department head or supervisor may determine whether, and the extent to which, acceptance and retention of an honorarium or other compensation is permissible.

Example A. An Associate who has been offered an honorarium of $100 to make a talk wonders if the dollar amount fits the definition of "honorarium."

Analysis of Example A. The definition of "honorarium" in dollar terms is relative. For instance, an honorarium paid to a senior officer for a major presentation might be three times that paid to an Associate who makes a ten-minute speech and conducts a short question and answer period. In general, any amount over $100 would seem to require approval for the Associate to retain it.

Example B. A store manager has been invited to conduct a special two-day mid-week operations program for a local fashion school. The store manager will receive a fee of $500 from the school.

Analysis of Example B. Participation might even be encouraged. But certainly the district manager should be notified. The district manager, perhaps in conjunction with the regional office, will determine whether Company information is to be used, whether review by Public Relations or Legal Department is necessary, and whether the Associate can retain the acceptance of the honorarium.

Example C. A furniture buyer whose avocation is collecting Early American antiques is asked to make a short speech to a community historical society, and because he or she is recognized as an amateur authority, to evaluate the authenticity and worth of some pieces belonging to members of that group.

Analysis of Example C. This is not the kind of talk or activity which is intended to be covered by these guidelines. It is not anticipated that any Company clearance would be necessary, but normal business judgment would dictate that the Company name not be used in this context.

Holding Public Office

The Company encourages Associates to become

involved in the political process on their own time. Company policy does not in any way restrict an Associate's right to participate personally in political activities or to use personal funds for political purposes. However, in the case of an Associate holding public office, whether elective or appointive, the potential for conflict of interest, or the appearance of conflict, must be taken into account as in the following examples.

Example A. An Associate who has been active in parent-teacher activities has received a request to run for a position of member on the local school board. The school board generally meets in the evenings or weekends and occasionally requires other minor commitments of time during the day.

Analysis of Example A. The holding of a position such as school board member does not result in a conflict of interest in the normal situation. It may be advisable to review this matter with the appropriate unit manager or department head with respect to the amount of the time that will be required. In most cases, the Company encourages this type of community service.

Example B. An Associate in a district office has been offered an appointment to a county planning board. This board has the authority and responsibility to rule on the issuance of permits for the construction of shopping centers and other commercial developments in that county.

Analysis of Example B. The Associate must obtain specific approval of the district manager to accept this appointment because a conflict or the appearance of conflict would arise in the event the Company were to seek authorization for commercial development from the planning board. The decision regarding the Associate would require consideration of Company plans and the degree to which the Associate could be insulated from the appearance of conflict through abstention from the deliberations of the board.

Example C. A store manager, due to his or her past community involvement, is asked to consider running for mayor of the town in which the manager's store is located. The position is deemed to be part time.

Analysis of Example C. The store manager holding the office of mayor could find himself or herself in conflict with the best interests of the Company. In fulfilling his or her duties, the manager could become involved with licenses, permits, inspections, or other governmental functions on which the town and Company positions would differ. In the event the town is not within the business area of the store, the conflicts of interest might not exist, but the manager should review the decision with his or her district manager.

Example D. A store Associate is asked to serve on the campaign committee of a state senatorial candidate in the role of campaign treasurer, or the Associate wishes to become a candidate himself or herself. Either of these activities also includes raising campaign contributions.

Analysis of Example D. Company policy does not restrict the right of an Associate to participate in the political process or to make personal political contributions. However, the Company prohibits the use of Company facilities (e.g., telephones, copying machines, mailing lists) or personnel (e.g., secretarial help) for this purpose and prohibits political activities during work hours. Such activities must be restricted to the use of an Associate's personal resources and facilities. An Associate who requests an extended leave of absence for the purposes of engaging in political activities should disclose this fact to his or her supervisor when seeking approval. This is because there are potential restrictions against the payment of benefits (e.g., continuation of participation in benefit plans) by corporations in such circumstances which should be reviewed prior to the beginning of the leave period.

PRESERVATION OF COMPANY ASSETS

The Official JCPenney Policy Statement. Each Associate of the Company shall comply with Company procedures to preserve the assets of the Company and shall not create situations which unwarrantedly may harm the reputation of the Company or create financial liability.

The Purpose of the Policy. To assure that the assets of the Company are acquired, used, and disposed of for the benefit of the Company and its stockholders, and not for the personal enrichment of its Associates.

Discussion. In addition to the principles described in this booklet the Company has adopted certain internal control procedures which have been designed to assure that the Company receives reasonable direct or indirect value for the acquisition, use, or disposition of its assets. No corporate funds or assets should be used for any unlawful purpose. In addition, no Associate should appropriate or make available to others any Company property for a non-Company purpose. Each Associate must be familiar with the procedures applicable to his or her responsibilities and must be sure that they are followed, particularly in connection with the acquisition, use, or disposition of Company assets. Associates should recognize that Company assets are not only physical or tangible items (such as Company funds, supplies, or computer and telephone networks), but also include intangibles (such as the ideas, concepts, or inventions which associates develop in the course of, or related to, their work for the Company; or the data and information which associates have access to as a result of their work responsibilities). Associates who are in a supervisory role also must require compliance on the part of those whom they supervise. Three examples are set forth as guidelines for Associates.

Example A. An Associate, in a rush to complete his or her work before leaving on a business trip, authorizes the payment of supplier's invoice without following the prescribed Company procedures for approving invoices for payment.

Analysis of Example A. This conduct would involve a violation of the Statement of Business Ethics. Company procedures require that invoices be approved only by certain designated Associates. Each is required to determine that the Company, in accordance with applicable Company procedures, has received or will receive full value in terms of cost, quantity and quality and that accurate supporting documentation is available.

Example B. A buyer of women's fashion goods and his or her family have been invited to attend a formal wedding of their neighbor's daughter. The buyer has recently received a gown as a sample from one of the Company's suppliers, which the buyer brings to his or her daughter. The sample gown was given to the Company free of charge.

Analysis of Example B. A violation of the Statement of Business Ethics would exist in this situation because Company procedures require that samples not returned to the supplier be disposed of by the Company.

Example C. A computer programmer working in systems and data processing has as a hobby the restoration of antique automobiles. Over the course of numerous weekends, the Associate invented a cruise control system for automobiles. The Associate's invention was conceived and developed after working hours and does not have any relationship to the Associate's work responsibilities for the Company. All equipment and facilities used in developing this invention belong to the Associate. The Associate had signed the Company's Associate Invention Agreement.

Analysis of Example C. According to the Associate Invention Agreement, inventions or innovations conceived or devised by Associates are an asset of the Company when they either (1) arise out of or are suggested by work performed by an Associate for the Company, (2) result from the Associate's use of Company time, facilities, equipment, or supplies, or (3) arise out of or are suggested by the Associate's use of Company information or trade secrets or other confidential information of the Company. When an Associate invention is deemed an asset of the Company, the Associate must assign the invention to the Company. In this example, however, none of the required criteria have occurred. Accordingly, the Associate is the sole owner of the invention.

Further information concerning Associates' rights and obligations regarding inventions and innovations is explained in the "Statement of Revised Inventions Policy," the Associate's Invention Agreement, and the Company Policy on Inventions, Innovations, and Like Developments.

PROCEDURES FOR QUESTIONS AND REPORTS

Through clarification of policy and the citing of specific examples, this booklet has sought to explain the basic JCPenney principles of business ethics. Obviously, however, it has not been possible to cover the infinite variety of situations to which the policies apply. For this reason, the Company has established the Business Ethics Committee to advise and assist Associates on matters relating to the interpretation of business ethics. The committee consists of the general counsel, the director of auditing, the controller, the director of corporate personnel, the director of public affairs, and the director of catalog.

In most instances, Associates should bring

questions concerning the policies described in this booklet to the attention of appropriate supervisory personnel (such as a unit manager or department head) who may in turn refer matters of policy interpretation to the Business Ethics Committee. Examples of matters to be handled in this manner include reports of possible violations of Company policy, whether involving the Associate or other Associates.

It is recognized, however, that there may be some cases in which the Associate should bring a matter directly to the attention of members of management who have been delegated the responsibility for dealing with matters of business ethics. These cases would involve non-routine matters affecting the overall reputation of the Company, such as possible violations which could (1) reflect on the integrity of management or financial books, records, or accounts, or (2) result in a significant loss or penalty to the Company or any of its subsidiaries or divisions, or (3) endanger life, health, or safety.

In any of these cases, Associates are requested to bring such information directly to the attention of the general counsel (mailing address: 1301 Avenue of the Americas, New York, NY 10019), who will refer those matters requiring advice and assistance relating to the interpretation of business ethics to the Business Ethics Committee as a whole.

Any questions specifically relating to the interpretation of laws or regulations and their applicability to the operations of the Company or any subsidiary or division of the Company should be referred to the Legal Department, except that questions relating to compliance with personnel related laws should be brought to the attention of the Corporate Personnel Relations Department.

VERIFICATION AND CERTIFICATION FOR COMPLIANCE

Inserted in this final section of the Statement of Business Ethics is a Certificate of Compliance which all management Associates (and those non-management Associates designated by their unit managers or department heads as being in sensitive positions) are required to fill out and sign.

Every Penney Associate should comply with the principles contained in this booklet to avoid any impairment, or appearance of impairment, of his or her ability to perform Company duties, as well as to avoid liability for the Company or for the Associate involved, or possible adverse comment.

This statement is intended to be a positive document. It must be recognized, however, that this statement is more than an expression of desire that certain ideals be observed. Accordingly, Associates should be aware that failure to comply with the principles described in this booklet, including the disclosure requirements, may result in termination of employment. Such termination, under certain circumstances, may have additional significant financial implications for management profit-sharing level Associates. These additional implications may include, for example, termination of unexercised stock options under the terms of the applicable stock option plan and failure to earn an award under the terms of the Performance Unit Plan.

Certificate of Compliance

All JCPenney management Associates (and those non-management Associates designated by their unit managers or department heads as being in sensitive positions) are required to fill out and sign this Certificate of Compliance. In the event you are not now in compliance, or are not certain, you should discuss the matter with your unit manager or department head and attach a memorandum to your certificate explaining the situation.

I certify that I have received and read the booklet setting forth personnel and policy guidelines connected with the Statement of Business Ethics of JCPenney Company, Inc. I certify that I understand and accept the statements contained therein and that as of this date I am in compliance, and will continue to comply with, the policies set forth in the booklet, and all future revisions, except to the extent described in the attached memorandum of exceptions.

Signature: _____ Date: _____

Please print or type name, department, or other area of responsibility, and unit number.

Name: _____

Department: _____

Unit Number: _____

Social Security Number: _____

☐ I have attached a memorandum of exceptions to this Certificate.
__ If hired in the current year please fill-in date of hire.
__ Please check here if this Certificate covers an Associate in a non-management position.

J. P. MORGAN AND COMPANY
Auditing Department Function/Organization

FUNCTION OF THE AUDITING DEPARTMENT

The function of the Auditing Department on a worldwide basis is defined in the following mission statement presented by the auditor to the Audit Committee of the board of directors.

The mission of the Auditing Department is to assist the board of directors and management of J. P. Morgan and Co. Incorporated and its subsidiaries (JPM) in the effective discharge of their responsibilities. In order to successfully fulfill this objective, the Auditing Department has been charged with three major functions:

1. Assure management that the controls they believe are in place are adequate and functioning.
2. Act as consultants to management in the independent evaluation of new or existing products and procedures.
3. Develop individuals who can be effective throughout the organization.

This mission statement will address each major function in detail.

ASSURE MANAGEMENT THAT THE CONTROLS THEY BELIEVE ARE IN PLACE ARE ADEQUATE AND FUNCTIONING

In order to provide this assurance, the Auditing Department is responsible for maintaining a comprehensive program of continuous independent examinations and evaluations of the adequacy and effectiveness of the internal control systems and related operating procedures. The program recognizes that the control systems and procedures are not ends in themselves. The effectiveness of these systems and procedures can only be measured in terms of management objectives and the constraints imposed by JPM's operating environment.

Auditing's function does not relieve management of its primary responsibility to develop and maintain sound internal control systems and related operating procedures. The department cannot prevent possible loss due to fraud. However, it can determine that adequate controls are in place and are complied with to such a degree to help minimize loss due to recurring fraud.

The scope of the program should provide the board of directors and management with reasonable assurance that

- transactions are executed in accordance with their design and authorization;
- corporate and customer assets are properly safeguarded;
- underlying financial reporting systems (including computer applications) are reliable and accurate;
- applicable laws, regulations and sound fiduciary principles are complied with; and
- all material weaknesses in controls have been reported to the proper levels and corrective action has been taken or management or the board of directors has assumed the risk of not taking corrective action.

---

*Reprinted by permission of the Auditor of J. P. Morgan & Co. Incorporated, July 1988.

The results of the regular examinations are summarized in reports directed to management and reflect Auditing's opinion on the adequacy and efficiency of the systems of internal control and related operating procedures, and the degree of compliance therewith. In addition, periodic reports reflecting audit scope and status are rendered to the Audit and Examining committees of the board of directors. The department coordinates its efforts with those of the external auditors in the achievement of this function.

ACT AS CONSULTANTS TO MANAGEMENT IN THE INDEPENDENT EVALUATION OF NEW OR EXISTING PRODUCTS AND PROCEDURES

The Auditing Department assumes a consultative role in monitoring product development, emerging technology, and overall business trends as they relate to Morgan as a means to help identify potential exposure and risk to management. In addition, the Auditing Department is available to management to consult with regarding existing products and procedures in order to devise means of enhancing efficiency of operations.

The Auditing Department further contributes to the quality of innovation at Morgan by evaluating new or existing products and procedures and communicating any suggested improvements or areas of concern to Morgan management.

DEVELOP INDIVIDUALS WHO CAN BE EFFECTIVE THROUGHOUT THE ORGANIZATION

The Auditing Department, by the very nature of the functions it performs, is an excellent training ground for individuals at all levels. Rotation on a variety of audit assignments provides the individual with a broad based exposure to the business of Morgan, specialized technical training, as well as training in general business and interpersonal skills. This training places an emphasis on the ability to identify risk and build a system of control to effectively contain that risk and to work with user departments as a cohesive unit to mitigate risks to the bank.

The Auditing Department further provides the individual with the opportunity to develop unique evaluative, analytical, and decision-making skills which management has come to value. After an initial commitment, the Auditing Department can place the individual into a position in another area of Morgan where talents and abilities developed will be utilized to the fullest extent or the individual can advance within Auditing.

NATIONAL WESTMINSTER BANK USA

The NatWest Way: Our Values, Mission, and Commitment to Quality

THE STATEMENT OF VALUES

The Statement of Values provides the philosophical foundation for all we do. It is our credo, our system of fundamental beliefs.

As National Westminster Bank USA we share values which both support our Mission Statement and commit us to excellence in fulfilling the needs of our customers, the communities we serve, our parent organization, and ourselves.

Customers

Our customers are the foundation of our business. We listen to their needs and respond in a manner which is timely, straightforward, and courteous. We earn our future with them through leadership in quality and service.

Communities

The prosperity and well-being of the communities in which we live and work are fundamental to our long-term success. Therefore, we commit to serve them by providing leadership and support which enrich the overall quality of life.

Parent

The National Westminster Bank Group has entrusted us with capital and its good name. We commit to invest these resources prudently, to earn a superior return and to work in partnership with our parent to enhance its worldwide stature.

Ourselves

We, the employees, are the strength of the bank and the source of its character. We work together to foster an open environment where trust and caring prevail. Pride and enjoyment come from commitment, leadership by example and accomplishment. We encourage personal growth and ensure opportunity based upon performance.

We recognize our individual responsibility to uphold these values, and in turn to enhance the bank's reputation, which is rooted in integrity, achievement, and quality.

THE MISSION STATEMENT

The Mission Statement is the strategic translation of the Statement of Values. It is more specific, converting the value system into goals and programs.

Mission

As the principal banking vehicle of the NatWest Group in the United States, our mission is to serve the overall marketing and operational requirements of the group in this country. In doing so, we achieve profitable growth and an enhanced reputation.

To fulfill this mission we must continue to see ourselves not as a full-service, across-the-board competitor of the largest money-center banks in every market, but rather as a significant competitor in what we regard as our core businesses. In addi-

---

*Reprinted with permission.

tion, we must continue to develop the considerable potential for synergy that exists with our parent, in international markets as well as in this country.

Customers

We are in four core businesses. In each of these core markets two fundamental precepts apply: our commitment to relationship banking and the essential responsibility of our support units to provide high-quality, low-cost service.

Consumer

In this market, an area of traditional strength, we seek a stable and increasing source of core deposits that can be invested at an acceptable spread. We are relatively well positioned for this with a sizable branch network, including offices in some key locations in New York City and substantial coverage in the desirable suburban counties surrounding it.

We will compete not by attempting to gain market share through the introduction of product breakthroughs, but by offering superior personal service, coupled with a competitive line of both deposit and consumer credit products introduced in a timely manner.

Commercial lending and deposit responsibility for companies with sales of up to $10 million is an important element of our consumer business. Commercial business adds a significant dimension to what was formerly a purely retail approach and is aimed at enabling us to use our branch system more efficiently.

Middle Market

The middle market continues to be one of the natural markets for NatWest USA. By our definition, it consists of companies with annual sales ranging between $10 million and $250 million, located primarily within a 100-mile radius of New York City, as well as companies on a selective basis throughout the country wherever we can serve them effectively. We compete by meeting the credit needs of customers in a responsive and flexible manner, and by bringing specialty services—particularly trust, treasury, cash management, and trade finance—to middle-market companies in a more effective way than do other major banks.

Corporate

Together with our parent, we have developed a rational and effective way for the group to approach the enormous corporate market on a national basis. NatWest PLC is responsible for multinational companies and for servicing certain specialized-industry customers on behalf of London. Other than these, NatWest USA is responsible for the national market. We address this on a niche basis, both as to industry and geography, through our network of regional offices. Here again, our specialized support services—cash management, trust, treasury, and trade finance—play a key role in our ability to compete effectively against money-center as well as regional banks.

International

While we will continue to service the well-established and profitable public and quasi-public sectors, our mission in international is to increasingly concentrate on activities that more directly serve the offshore needs of our domestic customer base. These are principally credit and non-credit transactions that facilitate foreign trade.

Further, we will continue to build on our strengths in correspondent banking, and from that base expand selectively into private sector lending if margins are acceptable. Our areas of particular expertise are Latin America and the Far East. In Europe, we utilize the capabilities of our parent to a greater extent. Our international strategy reflects, in a complementary way, our role within the worldwide coverage of the NatWest Group.

Communities

We derive business and our profits from the communities in which we operate. Therefore, we acknowledge a responsibility to invest in those communities to keep them vigorous and attractive. This goes beyond mere compliance with the Community Reinvestment Act. It involves active participation by our staff, as well as direct financial support.

Parent

Because we have been entrusted with our parent's name, we have a responsibility to enhance its reputation in all we do, as well as to achieve a superior financial return.

We expect to achieve this year—two years ahead of schedule—the 60-basis-point return on assets (ROA) goal set forth in the original 1981 Mission Statement. Our new goal is 70 basis points by 1988. In comparing our performance, we continue to regard Bank of New York, Irving Trust, Marine Midland, and European American Bank as our peers.

Our quality effort is directly related both to achieving our new ROA goal and to enhancing the reputation of our parent.

Ourselves

The internal environment we seek, as outlined in the Statement of Values, rests on a set of strategies, policies, and programs that are fundamental in our bank:

- An uncompromising insistence on quality people
- A pay-for-performance policy which has application bankwide as well as individually
- A standard of excellence in communications
- A lean organizational structure, free of redundant staff layers, to encourage individual initiative and decision making
- A willingness by supervisors and managers to be judged on how well they foster the desired environment in their areas

QUALITY PROGRAM

Quality represents the everyday expression of our value system. It is the means by which we carry out the strategies and achieve the goals set forth in the Mission Statement.

The bank's commitment to quality is thoroughgoing and long term. It is how we intend to differentiate ourselves and, at the same time, achieve a cost advantage over our competitors. In addition, customers are willing to pay a premium for high-quality services.

Customers

The everyday things we do to better serve customers are obvious, but they bear repeating. These actions apply to everyone because, even where there is no direct customer contact, everything we do is related to serving customers:

- We listen to our customers to determine their needs and then attempt to fill those needs.
- We respond in a thoughtful, professional, and timely manner.
- We deliver our products and services error free and in a consistent manner.
- We price our products and services fairly.
- We are always respectful and courteous.
- We do our work in essential staff areas as cost-effectively as possible, because we invest our principal resources in customer-driven activities.

Communities

In all our community activities we seek to reflect the bank's commitment to quality and excellence while helping others.

This is a dimension of our job that goes beyond day-to-day duties. It involves community service: giving generously to United Way, donating blood, taking leadership roles in significant community organizations.

We furnish substantial community support on the corporate level as well. Our contributions budget has grown each year and provides major funding for education, health care, community welfare, and the arts. In addition, we have chosen to direct significant portions of our corporate communications budget to sponsorship of quality arts projects.

Parent

Superior quality in everything we do is the only way to meet the dual responsibility we have to our parent of enhancing its reputation and meeting our financial goals.

High-quality work is key to enhancing the NatWest name. But it is also critical to achieving our new financial goal, because we must do this by improving margins rather than by expanding assets. Quality banking involves several things:

- Wider lending and investing spreads
- Increased fee and service-charge income, which can be expected if we deliver quality products consistently
- Expanded demand deposits
- Higher credit quality, resulting in lower credit costs and fewer non-performing loans and charge-offs
- Reduced tax liability

An additional element that enhances our reputation as a quality institution and ensures that we achieve our goals is consistent prudence both in the extension of credit and in our asset/liability management activities.

Ourselves

The competence, dedication, and hard work of our staff are the essential ingredients in our success. We need quality people. Therefore, we are very selective in hiring and take training and promotion from within very seriously.

We closely monitor salary and benefit trends and seek to be fully competitive, increasing compensation levels in relation to those of our peers as the performance of the bank improves. On an individual level, we reward according to contribution.

We have developed a variety of programs to improve communication: an expanded News-Beam, staff and management bulletins, staff meetings, special surveys, and the like. We constantly seek new ways to increase communication at all levels of the bank.

We encourage leadership by example, creating an environment that is caring, trusting, fair, and enjoyable.

By doing quality work, each of us contributes directly to achieving the bank's goals. In the process, we also foster a stimulating work environment and enhance our individual well-being.

NCR

Directional Strategy

The following summary outlines NCR's fundamental thoughts about its business, including the products and services the company sells and the markets and customers the company serves.

NCR DIRECTIONAL STRATEGY

The company has focused its resources on achieving a rate of revenue growth higher than the industry average while maintaining above-average profitability and a conservative balance sheet. Our efforts to achieve these objectives are reflected in the fundamental way we think about our business: *"offering a product set."*

This approach to the marketplace is summarized as follows:

> *Sell the largest practical volume of products identified with the product set by addressing all markets and customers for whom the products are suitable.*

Our strategic emphasis is on selling the largest volume of products into all applicable markets. This requires focusing on the scope of our current and future products and services by concentrating on achieving higher market shares in our current target markets and by penetrating new markets.

Over time, a company with this business view would effectively penetrate all applicable markets, as portrayed in Illustration 1, resulting in high volume for its products in the product set. High volume, in turn, would result in cost-effective manufacturing, higher yield from development spending, and more effective marketing programs.

This view is in contrast to that of a company that thinks of its business as "serving a customer set" within a limited number of vertical target markets. The objective of this approach is to sell as many products as possible to these defined customer sets, and this, in turn, shapes its product development programs accordingly.

A company with this business view tends to grow by adding more and more products, as portrayed in Illustration 2. However, as the number of products grows, the number of market segments does not. In addition, products become more specialized for the applicable market segments and are generally sold in low volumes, making economies of scale difficult to achieve.

NCR BUSINESS FOCUS

Product Focus

At its most general level, NCR's product set is as follows:

- Industry-specific workstations
- General-purpose workstations
- Multi-user computer systems
- Large computer systems
- Communication processors
- Synergistic products and services

NCR derives approximately half of its revenue from computer/processor systems and the other half from workstations. Our product lines are well positioned for revenue growth since they address fast-growing segments: networked workstations and distributed processing systems.

---

*Reprinted with permission of NCR Corporation.

Illustration 1

Offering a Product Set

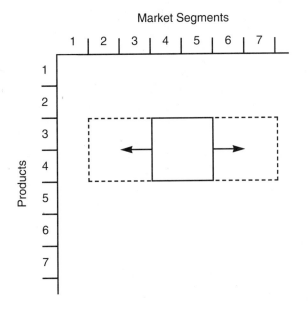

Illustration 2

Serving a Customer Set

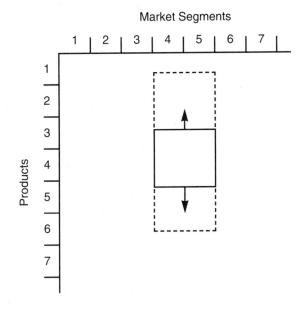

Market Focus

The products and services within NCR's product set are directed at two of the fastest growing environments:

- Transaction processing: Where individual transactions are processed so databases can be updated and maintained. Examples include grocery check-out and automated banking systems.
- Office information: Where information is gathered, processed, communicated, stored, and retrieved. Example applications include word processing, electronic mail, accounts receivable, and inventory control.

In both areas, we emphasize systems designed to be operated by people whose main job is other than data processing, such as a sales clerk in a department store or an assembler in a factory. In some instances, the operator will be our customer's customer.

On a vertical market basis, NCR derives more than half of its revenue from the retail and banking industries. We enjoy a significant market share with the products and services from our industry-specific workstation product lines, and we are recognized as market leaders. The opportunity for growth in these two industries for NCR remains significant.

In addition to increasing our position in these two very important markets, it is our strategy to address other markets for which our products are suitable. These other applicable markets provide us with sizable opportunities since they represent three-fourths of the information processing industry's expenditures for the type of products in our product set.

NCR STRATEGIC EMPHASIS

NCR's directional strategy of "offering a product set" has important implications on marketing, product development, and technology selection.

Marketing

The success of "offering a product set" rests upon our ability to sell the largest practical volume of our products to all applicable markets. To achieve this, we need to focus on the following areas.

Account Management. We care about our total relationship with our customers. Each ac-count is managed by an individual who is responsible for servicing its total needs, calling on other resources within the company as required.

Selling Motion. NCR employs two basic selling techniques to successfully implement its directional strategy: "solutions in detail" and "tools."

"Solutions in detail" selling focuses on the application; hardware and systems software are secondary. NCR has specialized for decades in selling "solutions in detail," based on application packages for specific businesses.

"Tools" selling focuses on selling all levels of hardware and systems software for others to integrate into business solutions.

- In direct tools sales, end users integrate and write the application software.
- In indirect tools sales, third parties integrate and/or write applications for our products.

Specialization. The "solutions in detail" selling motion requires a different body of knowledge on the part of the NCR representative than the "tools" selling motion. Therefore, we specialize our selling efforts by:

- Markets: NCR's sales people act as business and systems consultants for defined customer groups.
- Products: NCR's sales people are the product experts, and, in many cases, they are also specialized by products within markets.

The account managers can bring together other market and product specialists as needed to service their accounts.

Sales Channels. To succeed in selling to all markets and customers for whom our products are suitable, we must sell our products through multiple sales channels. This approach will allow us to reach all applicable markets. While NCR's primary sales channel is direct sales, additional channels help NCR sell to customers who may not be reached through direct sales. Examples of third-party sales channels include: OEMs (original equipment manufacturers), VARs (value-added resellers), distributors, and dealers.

These channels do not replace the direct selling effort, but complement it by extending our market coverage. They help NCR get new business by reaching additional market segments.

Application Software Availability. To successfully penetrate a wide range of markets, NCR needs to offer system solutions. This means application software for our products must be readily available. NCR will make sure software is available through third-party developers; will encourage customers to write their own software; and, on a selected basis, will develop software internally.

In our marketing efforts, successful implementation of NCR's directional strategy rests upon good account management, implementing both "solutions in detail" and "tools" selling motions, specialization, the use of third-party channels of distribution, and the availability of application software for our offerings.

Products and Technology

In order to sell our products successfully into all applicable markets, it is important that we develop flexible products and systems which can be easily integrated by customers and third parties at the appropriate levels. In order to achieve such product and system flexibility, we need to focus on the following:

- Incorporate leading-edge technology into our offerings.
- Converge to a common set of platforms, as appropriate.
- Use industry standards, wherever practical.
- Implement "open systems" architecture so NCR systems can be expanded and non-NCR devices can be added easily.
- Provide advanced communications capabilities to link heterogeneous systems, whether NCR or non-NCR.

Strategic emphasis on these points will provide the high-volume production needed to reduce manufacturing costs and increase the yield from our development investments.

SUMMARY

NCR's product, service, and marketing directions include a solid family of product lines and emphasize a diverse customer base. The success of our company is the cumulative result of all NCR people working together to satisfy customers' expectations for the highest standards of excellence in all NCR products and services.

SEARS, ROEBUCK AND CO.

Our Corporate Vision

Sears, Roebuck and Co., a family of diversified businesses, is the leader in providing and distributing quality products and services to consumers. We will engage in those commercial opportunities that leverage the distinctive capabilities of our existing businesses.

We are committed to our most valued asset, our reputation for integrity.

We dedicate ourselves to the principle that serving the customer is of prime importance.

We strive to provide our shareholders with a foundation for consistent and profitable investment-growth. Our attractiveness to investors will be enhanced by the additional value created through our family of companies' coordinated activities.

We will manage ourselves as strong, decentralized business groups reporting to the chairman of the board. In their commitment to further objectives consistent with approved plans and the overall direction of the corporation, our groups will be supported by an efficiently structured corporate organization.

We will be a low-cost provider, managing with efficiencies of scale, building upon a foundation of competitive cost advantages, and maximizing the productivity of resources which contribute directly to serving our customers.

We will allocate resources among our enterprises based upon an evaluation of their long-term relative profitability and the financial goals established by the corporation. We will maintain an overall capital structure which is stable, cost efficient, and which provides an appropriate balance between financial leverage and business risk.

We will develop and distribute proprietary products and services when our reputation and skills add value and provide the opportunity to achieve greater profitability.

Our commitment to strategic planning is integral to managing our businesses and thinking long term.

We will be a leader in developing innovative applications of proven technology.

We will provide all employees—regardless of their sex, race, age, religion, disability, or ethnic background—with an environment in which to maximize their potential and their contribution to our success, and we will see that they share in that success in meaningful ways.

We will faithfully fulfill our social and citizenship responsibilities.

We will communicate with customers, employees, shareholders, governments, and the general public with the company's traditional devotion to integrity in order to enhance our reputation, advance company goals, and clarify company policy and activities.

STRATEGIC FOCUS INITIATIVES

The corporate vision describes the philosophies and operating principles which guide each of our business groups. The vision also provides a foundation for the company's strategic focus, which is the consumer. The most important aspect of the collective strength of the entities comprising Sears, Roebuck and Co. is value creation. Sears' ability to create value is enhanced by our distinct competitive advantages: our reputation for integrity, an extensive consumer franchise, a complementary range of distribution channels, and our stability in the mar-

---

*Reprinted with permission of Sears, Roebuck and Co..

ketplace. The lifeblood of the company is value creation through new initiatives that strengthen our long-term relationships with consumers. Examples of initiatives, driven by the corporate goals highlighted below, are fully developed in the following pages. These initiatives actively demonstrate how Sears is creating value for the consumer. Management is providing an environment to ensure successful execution of these initiatives and to foster the development of new ones as we continue to pursue our strategic direction. By taking care of our customers' needs, we can enjoy profitable growth while working to achieve maximum return on invested capital.

Reaffirming Our Commitment to Service Excellence

Each of our businesses is committed to providing the customer with the best possible service. Taking care of the customer is a major reason for our existence. Being responsive to what the customer wants in a friendly, courteous, and efficient manner is the key to our success.

Achieving Cost Efficiency without Compromising Value

We will strive to have the lowest costs where our commitment to service, excellence, and value creation will not be compromised. We are determined to provide unsurpassed value for our customers and shareholders.

Developing Products and Services

For more than 100 years, Sears' success has been directly related to its ability to anticipate and meet the needs of the consumer. This ability has also enabled the company to extend its leadership into financial services through the development of innovative products and services.

Expanding, Strengthening, and More Effectively Sharing Distribution Channels

Sears provides special opportunities for each of our companies to combine their resources to develop new products and services while increasing effectiveness of existing distribution channels. As a result, each of our businesses is stronger than it would be as an individual company.

REAFFIRMING OUR COMMITMENT TO SERVICE EXCELLENCE

It's our commitment to service excellence—not only in terms of standing behind the products we sell, but by being responsive to what the customer wants—that will ensure our success. Reinforcing our overall standards of customer service, fostering customer trust, providing convenience and meaningful guarantees, are examples of how we are meeting this commitment.

Merchandise Group

One of today's most vital consumer needs is time—for family, friends, and relaxation—especially among two-income households. Sensitive to this trend, the Merchandise Group has initiated a program to enhance service for purchasers of home appliances and home entertainment products. Now in virtually all Sears markets, the program includes evening and Saturday deliveries; removal of old appliances; expanded hours at repair centers, and day-ahead scheduling and call-ahead notification for deliveries, installation, and service. The program serves as a prototype for similar efforts being developed for other product lines.

Allstate Insurance Group

Service excellence has always been the focus of "The Good Hands People." Allstate's product is a promise—the peace of mind of its policyholders. And this unique buyer/seller relationship creates many opportunities for Allstate to foster and expand customers' trust. Products, processes, and procedures are constantly refined to enhance Allstate's ability to serve the consumer, to provide products to more people in more places than ever before, and to empower front-line employees to deliver quality service more effectively. For example, a 1987 claim department reorganization placed Allstate's claim-service delivery closer to the marketplace with renewed customer focus. In addition, planned focus group meetings with customers across the country help Allstate determine how to serve them better.

Dean Witter Financial Services Group

"Discover Excellence" is the name of a formal, comprehensive effort to distinguish Discover Card on the basis of service. In 1987, the program was significantly broadened. For example, training of customer service representatives was intensified and quarterly polling of card members and merchants implemented. The results: higher efficiency and excellent customer satisfaction rankings. Reflecting this, in 1987, operations personnel received 5 million customer telephone inquiries and resolved 95% at the point of contact.

Similarly, on the day after Thanksgiving, 67,471 voice authorization calls—more than double normal "busy" volume—were answered on average in 2.6 seconds and handled conclusively in well under a minute.

Coldwell Banker Real Estate Group

In a bold move to meet the formidable challenge of its "Expect the Best" philosophy, the Coldwell Banker Residential Group introduced its 18-point best-seller marketing services guarantee which promises specific marketing services will be delivered or the listing contract can be terminated. The company has two objectives in developing the guarantee: first, to demonstrate the level of quality and service represented by its Expect the Best promise; and second, to provide home sellers with peace of mind by incorporating a meaningful termination provision in the guarantee. Expect the Best highlighted several services introduced in 1987 to give the customer a comprehensive home seller's package.

ACHIEVING COST EFFICIENCY WITHOUT COMPROMISING VALUE

A challenge Sears is meeting on many fronts is that of achieving cost efficiency without compromising value or service. One example is gathering timely and accurate data on sales to gain greater control of inventory while reducing transaction time for the customer. Also, sophisticated training programs are at the root of efforts to provide the best values in the marketplace.

Merchandise Group

New bar-code reading at point of purchase will provide better customer service and greater control of inventory through improved information gathering. Using a retail-oriented system called the "3 of 9 Code Symbology," laser pen scan-

ners at the checkout register will read sales and inventory information faster and more accurately. The new system allows all Merchandise Group suppliers to attach bar-coded tags to goods at the manufacturing site—saving in-store time and costs now required for receiving and pricing merchandise. Overall, this leading-edge technology means faster transaction time for customers and more current and accurate data on sales and inventory.

Allstate Insurance Group

The company is continually testing and implementing cost-containment programs that are sustainable programs that will strike a balance between costs and customers' needs. Allstate's goal is not merely to reduce expenses, but also to achieve maximum return on every investment. One example of this philosophy is Allstate's problem-solving "Growth Teams," a participative management process that allows groups of employees from various disciplines to find new opportunities for enhanced customer relations, growth, profit, and savings. Another program involves participation by Allstate managers in the strategic planning process for their markets.

Dean Witter Financial Services Group

The Consumer Markets Division traditionally has maintained one of the most competitive cost structures on Wall Street. This key discipline guided its growth plans in recent years and has produced measurable benefits. Today, Consumer Markets has the third-largest sales force in the industry and profit margins more favorable than many of its competitors. Additional benefits should accrue in the future, with margins improving as account executives gain experience. To help account executives as well as their branch managers continually build their skills, Consumer Markets offers professional development programs designed to be among the most comprehensive in its industry. In 1987, 60% of the sales force and most branch managers participated in these programs.

Coldwell Banker Real Estate Group

Homart's strategy to provide the best value in the marketplace for its customers is exemplified by its Texas development of The Parks at Arlington. A 700,000-square-foot regional mall anchored by

Sears, Mervyn's, and Dillard's, The Parks at Arlington was designed to provide an appealing and efficient shopping facility. For its construction, Homart used a new light-weight frame which reduced its structural costs by $500,000. Construction of the tenth regional shopping center developed in Texas by Homart was accomplished on a budget planned to provide value to both retailers and shoppers.

DEVELOPING PRODUCTS AND SERVICES

The ability to meet customer needs for quality products and services has been a key factor in the company's leadership positions in both merchandising and financial services. Innovative business relationships with Disney and McDonald's demonstrate Sears' ability to design and market products which have exceptional customer appeal. Innovative approaches to meet customer needs are a hallmark of the company's financial services businesses as well.

Merchandise Group

Business relationships with some of America's premier companies are bringing appealing new products to Sears customers. Last November, Sears signed an unprecedented 10-year agreement with the Walt Disney Company to develop a wide variety of exclusive Sears/Disney marketing ventures. For example, a special line of products will be codesigned with Disney. Also, Sears will have the exclusive right to develop and sell products featuring the Disney characters from new feature-length animated films or re-releases. Sears and McDonald's launched the McKids line of children's apparel. Its phenomenal success has resulted in plans to test mall boutiques highlighting the McKids merchandise.

Allstate Insurance Group

The ability to grow is largely dependent on the ability to reach new markets—and Allstate continues to expand its reach. In personal lines, a new auto policy targeted at three distinct markets, and prices to reflect individual risk, will allow agents to offer coverage to more potential customers. In addition, the product Allstate Advantage, offers a discount to qualified customers who have both Allstate auto and home-owners insurance. The Allstate Indemnity Company's new emphasis targets drivers who find it difficult to secure conventional insurance because of exotic cars, inexperience, or individual driving records. This product presents a marketing alternative for the Allstate agent and excellent growth potential for the company. It helped boost Allstate in indemnity premium volume by about 50% during 1987.

Dean Witter Financial Services Group

Responsiveness to customers' varied investment preference has helped make Dean Witter one of America's leading money managers. New products introduced in 1987 included the Government Securities Plus Fund, which invests in long- and intermediate-term treasury securities and financial derivatives; Cornerstone IV, the first interbank world currency fund available to US investors; Allstate Municipal Income Trust, a diversified portfolio consisting principally of investment quality long-term bonds; and the High Income Advantage Trust, which seeks high income from lower-rated or unrated securities. In response to customers' increasing interest in conservative, income-oriented investments, new products for 1988 include a fund that invests in the utilities industry and a government securities fund.

Coldwell Banker Real Estate Group

During 1987, the Commercial Group paved the way for personal and family trust officers to invest assets under their management in real estate. Through the unique Coldwell Banker Real Estate Partnership for Personal Trust I, the company plans to meet the requirement of personal trust managers with an investment product tailored to their needs. The partnership plans to offer shares to financial institutions which in turn will place the shares in their trusts. Assets of the partnership are planned to be invested in high-quality commercial real estate. Formed and administered by Coldwell Banker Capital Management Services, the Partnership for Personal Trust I is regarded as an innovative advancement in customized real estate investments.

EXPANDING, STRENGTHENING, AND MORE EFFECTIVELY SHARING DISTRIBUTION CHANNELS

A primary goal of the company's diversification has been the creation of value through the interaction of our businesses. Major avenues for company growth are being opened by the development and expansion of channels through which customers may be offered a broader array of products and services. These distribution channels are being created within each business group as well as between and among the groups.

Merchandise Group

Extending its reach to consumers and broadening its assortments of merchandise through strategic acquisitions, the group acquired two specialty retailers in recent months: Eye Care Centers of America, Inc. in 1987—operator of 41 optical superstores, and Pinstripes Petites, Inc. in 1988—a chain of 25 women's apparel units. Emphasizing convenience and selection, Eye Care units offer one-hour prescription service and a full range of family eyewear products in Arizona, California, Louisiana, New Mexico, and Texas. Pinstripes Petites markets career and weekend apparel for petite sizes through mall stores clustered in Chicago, Detroit, Minneapolis, Washington, D.C., and New England. Along with internally developed ventures, the acquisition of these two successful businesses signals Sears active expansion into speciality retailing.

Allstate Insurance Group

Allstate's growth can be attributed partly to its increasing number of distribution systems. New sales avenues opened in all lines of insurance resulted in about 6,000 new producers, bringing the total number of producers selling Allstate products to approximately 56,000. Existing channels expanded as well. More than 1,000 agent locations were added during the year. Sales of Allstate Life products through Dean Witter account executives increased 166% last year. Also, Allstate's Direct Marketing Center, one of the largest financial services mailers in the country, distributed an average of 1 million pieces every work day during 1987, while Allstate Enterprises Teleservices completed more than 1.5 million telephone calls.

Dean Witter Financial Services Group

Since Dean Witter account executives began selling Allstate annuities in 1984, annual premiums received for proprietary insurance products have risen nearly twelvefold, to $721 million in 1987. The Allstate-Dean Witter relationship continues to strengthen and expand, leveraging this success. Collaborative efforts on new products, such as the Dean Witter Growth & Income Annuity, begin at the design stage. Once a prototype is jointly developed, Dean Witter account executives provide feedback to help Allstate shape a final product. After the launch, Dean Witter insurance coordinators work with account executives to enhance the sales effort. In all, the Dean Witter-Allstate relationship has produced five life and annuity insurance products and more than $12 billion in premiums over four years.

Coldwell Banker Real Estate Group

A major strength of the Coldwell Banker Residential Group on a national level is its ability to integrate and meet all consumer real estate needs. Coldwell Banker can locate and finance a home in one process that includes the origination of mortgages through the Sears mortgage chain. This allows Coldwell Banker to provide consistently competitive mortgage products through a servicing and funding system which is responsive to its sales associates and home buyers' needs. In 1987, Coldwell Banker originated over $1.1 billion in Sears mortgages for its customers. Coldwell Banker also plans to begin offering selected Allstate products and services in 1988, further expanding Sears family distribution channels.

News from Sears, Roebuck and Co.

Sears, Roebuck and Co. today announced a series of actions designed to increase shareholder value and unveiled strategic plans for its merchandising and consumer financial services businesses.

Key elements of the corporate strategy, approved yesterday by the company's board of directors, were spelled out by Edward A. Brennan, chairman and chief executive officer. They include:

- Plans to sell Sears Tower. The corporate headquarters for Sears, Roebuck and Co. will continue to be located in Sears Tower. Sears Merchandise Group, with 8,000 employees in its administrative, buying, and marketing offices, will relocate to smaller, less costly facilities over the next several years.
- Divestiture of the Commercial Division of Coldwell Banker Real Estate Group, redirection of the Allstate Business Insurance Division, and strengthening of Dean Witter's commitment to consumer-driven activities.
- Repurchase in the open market of up to 40 million shares of Sears common stock, or approximately 10 percent of its 380 million shares outstanding, by mid-1989.
- An aggressive new marketing plan featuring a transition to everyday low pricing in its 825 retail stores and its catalogs.
- Implementation of an intense cost-cutting program at all levels of the organization.
- Rapid expansion of its "store of superstores" concept.

Sears also announced that non-recurring charges of $425 million after-tax will be taken in the fourth quarter as a result of expenses related to inventory reassortment and liquidation, anticipated office relocation expense, and other organizational changes.

In addition, Sears said it will adopt FAS 96, relating to accounting for income taxes, this year. As a result of this change, it will report additional non-recurring net income of approximately $340 million in 1988. The additional income is attributable to the reduction in the amount of deferred taxes payable in 1989 and subsequent years as a result of the 1986 Tax Act.

Pending completion of the asset sales, Brennan said, the share repurchase will be financed from working capital and from capital redeployed from several of the company's operations. Additional funding will come from capital released by continuation of the company's program to securitize its credit card receivables, he said.

The actions to lower costs and redeploy assets, he said, "will enable Sears to compete more effectively and profitably in its merchandising, insurance, financial services, and real estate businesses."

"We are acutely aware of investors' desires for improved returns and enhanced share value," Brennan said, "and over the past year we have thoroughly evaluated all strategic and financial alternatives available to the company. These alternatives have been reviewed not only with regard to shorter-term valuation objectives, but also giving consideration to the longer-term needs of our customers and 526,000 employees, the financial strength of our company, and fulfillment of Sears long-term strategic potential.

"During the past several years, we have laid the groundwork for a balanced, integrated consumer merchandising and financial network. Dean Witter's rapidly growing and profitable business based on the sale of Allstate annuities and the recent swing to profitability—somewhat ahead of previous expectations—of the Discover Card operations, gives testimony to the enormous potential which lies ahead. In short, we believe that each of our major divisions contributes to the strength of our integrated network."

Noting that Sears has been meeting the needs of American consumers for 102 years, Brennan said:

"As America has changed through the years, Sears has changed. This applies to merchandise and services—most recently, in financial services. The revenues from Allstate, Dean Witter, and Coldwell Banker, when combined with credit revenues of Sears Merchandise Group, represent approximately 50 percent of the company's consolidated revenues. From time to time comments have been made that Sears is experimenting in financial services. It is clear from looking at the numbers that financial services are an integral part of Sears past, present, and obviously, its future."

POSITIONING OF FINANCIAL SERVICES

In financial services, Brennan said, Sears strategy is to strengthen consumer operations and sell or reposition those that are not directly consumer oriented. The Coldwell Banker Commercial Division and the Allstate group life and health insurance business will be sold. With the refocusing of the Allstate Business Insurance Division and Dean Witter's consumer-driven activities, he said, Sears businesses will be better able to fully share in the company's customer base of 68 million households.

Allstate will refocus its business insurance division to provide broadened growth opportunities for its Northbrook agents and Allstate employee agents in the local commercial market. Allstate will reduce its premium writings in the national accounts market.

Brennan said Allstate and Dean Witter have built a significant business by coordinating the development, packaging, and sale of creative investment-oriented products. Annuities, which are created by Allstate and sold by Dean Witter account executives, have grown into a major business with revenues in excess of $1.0 billion in the

last 12 months. Significant expansion opportunities lie ahead for selling investment products by combining the resources of Allstate with the distribution power of Dean Witter, he said.

As a long-term strategy, Dean Witter will aggressively pursue its commitment to the individual investor by significantly increasing its account executive force from the current level of 7,600, Brennan said. The Dean Witter organization, which currently manages more than $37 billion of assets, has a leadership position in packaged products, particularly mutual funds. It will also focus on building investment banking product origination to serve all its clients, especially in municipal and equity securities. This strategy will generate significant growth but will not require the capital commitment or have the risks associated with the institutional fixed-income business, Brennan said.

"The Discover Card has exceeded our expectations," he said. "We are delighted with its performance and look forward to reaching its goal of being the largest and most profitable bank credit card in the nation." The number of Discover Card holders should increase from 26 to 40 million and receivables should exceed $15 billion within five years, he added.

Coldwell Banker Real Estate Group will continue to profitably build an integrated residential brokerage business that will include Sears Mortgage Corporation, which will be transferred from Dean Witter effective January 1, 1989. Coldwell Banker's market share of residential home sales in the nation has grown from 1 percent in 1981 to 11 percent this year.

Homart Development Co. will continue its real estate development programs, Brennan said, which assure Sears retail stores the best available locations and are a key source of value creation for the corporation. The use of funds from outside investors will free up substantial capital for Sears core consumer businesses.

Regarding the planned sale of Sears Tower, Brennan said Coldwell Banker, Dean Witter, and Goldman Sachs would be involved in the transaction.

SUPPLEMENTAL INFORMATION

Sale of Sears Tower

Following the sale of Sears Tower, Sears Merchandise Group will move its headquarters offices to less costly space as part of its low-cost provider strategy. "We have a strong desire to remain in the Chicagoland area," Brennan said, "but such a major move requires examination of many factors."

Everyday Low Pricing

Everyday low pricing will be implemented in Sears retail stores and catalogs in the months ahead. In the near term, the company has planned much stronger promotional activities to reduce inventories and boost sales.

"Retailers across the nation have relied increasingly on frequent sales events in recent years," Brennan said. "Such frequent sales promotions result in unpredictable inventory flows, warehousing needs, excessive price marking, and other promotional costs.

"We believe the results of everyday low pricing will be greater volume at an acceptable margin," he said. "With less emphasis on the time-consuming tasks related to special sales, we will be able to direct more staffing toward serving the customer.

"Our customers have told us that they would prefer outstanding values every day instead of waiting for sales. We believe everyday low pricing is an idea whose time has come," Brennan said.

Merchandise Group Expansion

Sears retail stores will move as rapidly as possible to become a "store of superstores," reflecting increased consumer preference for dominant assortments of merchandise, including broader selections of name brand products. Initial results from Sears prototype "Brand Central" home appliances and home electronics are very positive,

Brennan said, and other category-dominant superstore plans are nearing completion. One of the first will be an automotive superstore, which is now being tested.

Other key elements of the merchandise group strategy, Brennan said, include catalogs and direct marketing, product services, and specialty stores.

Establishing the catalog operation as a distinct business and separating it from the retail operation was an important step in the new direction being implemented.

Sears appliance service business will be greatly expanded, offering repairs for all major national brands in addition to Sears Kenmore. "We look for this business to provide tremendous growth in sales and profits in the years ahead," Brennan said.

Sears Specialty Merchandising Division will continue to evaluate opportunities for further acquisitions in growth industries or those which, when combined with Sears current strengths, will make it a dominant player, he added.

The use of SearsCharge cards is being tested in selected Western Auto stores, Brennan noted, offering further opportunities for growth. Western Auto was acquired by Sears earlier this year.

Financial Policy

Sears said that it would establish a net after-tax reserve of $10 million to cover the cost of calling its 8 percent sinking fund debentures due 2006 on April 1, 1989 at 103.72 percent of the principal amount and $7\frac{7}{8}$ percent sinking fund debentures due 2007 on February 1, 1989 at 103.939 percent of the principal amount. The company said it expects to issue a formal notice of call in the near future.

The company said Dean Witter and Goldman Sachs will comanage the repurchase of Sears stock.

NYNEX

The NYNEX Vision: How We Plan to Win in the Global Information Marketplace

MESSAGE FROM THE CHAIRMAN

NYNEX is a different corporation today than it was when we began business on January 1, 1984.

We've added new companies . . . and put the NYNEX name on office doors from Boston to Los Angeles—from London to Hong Kong. And though our networks remain a vital component of our overall strategy, we've branched out from what once was our main business—telecommunications.

The obvious question on the minds of both industry observers and our employees is: Why? Why change a business that has worked so well for so many years? Why acquire new companies, create new organizations, or restructure those we already have?

The most important reason is that technology has created a truly global marketplace which presents NYNEX with an entirely new set of opportunities than those we faced 20, 10, or even 5 years ago.

Today's customers require a range of products and services that go beyond what we've traditionally provided. And as the needs of customers grow and change, we too must make adjustments to better meet those needs.

We're making those adjustments. Today we have an even clearer vision of the directions we must take in order to grow our success. To respond to the dynamics of our changing markets we've reexamined our mission and our business strategies. In addition we've crystalized and articulated the values I believe we must instill in ourselves as a corporation and as individuals if we're to succeed in meeting the challenges that lie ahead.

The NYNEX vision sets high standards, some of which we're closer to achieving than others. Quite rightly then, the vision does not reflect what we are today as a corporation. Rather, it conveys the essence of what we're striving to become.

This booklet spells out the NYNEX vision— our mission, our values, our direction, and our strategies. These are the precepts that must drive our efforts—and our decisions—as we work to meet the varied and changing needs of today's Information Age customers. [A. C. Staley]

OUR MISSION:

Our mission is evolving, just as all parts of our business are evolving. And while the shift in our mission is by no means dramatic, it reflects a clearer understanding of the directions we have to move in to grow our success.

NYNEX is a collection of businesses with a common focus—the *global information industry.* This is our mission:

- To be a leader in the global information industry
- To know and capture the full potential of our targeted markets as a family of companies
- To anticipate and meet customer requirements for quality solutions at competitive prices
- To develop and fully utilize the capabilities of all NYNEX people

---

*Reprinted with permission.

- To be a profitable company with steady earnings growth

BUSINESS DIRECTION

NYNEX is a global company because our customers do business in a global marketplace. Being a global company says something about our perspective as a business. Having a global strategy does not necessarily imply that our companies must have international operations. But it does mean we must position ourselves carefully in strategic information markets and prepare to manage the changes that come from a constantly shifting global business environment.

NYNEX is targeting markets in selected segments of the global information industry.

Careful targeting and selection are key elements of our strategy. The global information marketplace offers a tremendous range of opportunities to grow NYNEX. Although our resources make us a world-class player, we can't possibly compete in all of the many information industry markets. So at NYNEX we're carefully targeting those markets where we have or can obtain the skills and resources needed to maintain a position of leadership.

What's more, we select markets with healthy growth and solid earnings potential.

Broadly speaking, NYNEX is evolving to meet the needs of customers in three segments of the industry: information transport, information management, and information content.

The *information transport* segment includes businesses that transport and distribute information in all its forms—voice, data, image, and text—using a variety of transmission media. These businesses provide technically advanced network-based products and services such as public, private, and hybrid networks; basic and enhanced network services; and associated hardware and software.

NYNEX companies in the *information management* segment provide expertise and tools that help customers put information to work. In other words, they help customers use information to make smarter business decisions more quickly, and improve operational efficiency. Businesses in this segment offer software-based applications, computer systems, systems integration, and professional services such as consulting.

The *information content* segment includes businesses that create, collect, and package information from a variety of both internal and external sources. NYNEX companies in this segment provide value-added market information and database products and services for advertisers, buyers, and marketers.

While these three segments focus on customers outside NYNEX, we have a fourth segment which exists primarily to support and enhance the success of all NYNEX's businesses. This segment is *business services.*

Companies in this segment may participate on a limited basis in external markets to develop the competitive capabilities and cost structures that will best serve the NYNEX family.

Every NYNEX business is expected to be a leader in its chosen markets. Segments will build off common skills, knowledge, systems, sales, image, values, and training. When appropriate, segments will team together to provide customer solutions not possible alone. However, they will not depend on each other for success. In some markets, for instance, it will make sense to build on our network capabilities. In others it won't.

Moreover, not one of the segments is constrained by geography. Every segment has the opportunity to compete in the global arena—if this is identified as the correct strategy for that business.

And as trade barriers and regulatory constraints relax over time, those opportunities will become more and more prevalent.

How will we allocate our limited resources among the four segments? We'll continue to make investments that ensure quality service to our customer base. At the same time, we'll seek opportunities to increase value to share owners.

OUR GOALS AND STRATEGIES

Our mission requires that we do these things well:

- Satisfy our customers
- Protect and grow our revenues
- Use our resources wisely
- Gain the freedom to compete freely and fairly in our chosen markets
- Foster employee excellence

- Create shareholder wealth

To help us achieve these goals, we've devised the following strategies:

Marketing Strategies

Understand and meet customer needs. To achieve our mission we must focus on the customer. We need to develop relationships with our customers, learn their needs, and meet their expectations with quality products and services.

Provide excellent customer service. Quality service is a top priority. Service standards are developed not only according to appropriate measurements, but also with respect to customer expectations and perceptions of service.

Seek competitive freedom. Changes in customer needs, the marketplace, and technology demand relief from the traditional regulatory and legislative constraints on our industry. We must find creative solutions that provide greater marketing freedom, pricing flexibility, and earnings latitude.

Stimulate network usage. Revenues will increase by stimulating usage of existing services, especially measured use of the network. If we market existing products and services well, we'll earn higher returns without incurring significant new expenses.

Introduce new products and services. To serve untapped market segments, fill product gaps in existing segments, and take advantage of new technology, we must continually seek new opportunities to create, package, manage, and distribute information.

Increase our expertise in data technology. Customers today require increasingly sophisticated products and services to meet their information needs. To remain competitive, we must enhance our data technology capabilities, including processing, networking, and software. We must become one of the most knowledgeable companies in the global information industry.

Research and Development Strategies

Invest in research and development. NYNEX recognizes the need to maintain a technological advantage and has taken steps to ensure access to emerging technologies. In addition to Bellcore, we look to our Science & Technology Center to provide the technological capability to meet changing market demands. Where appropriate, we encourage and form partnerships with suppliers to respond to market needs by developing products and services on a proprietary basis. We also seek out and foster relationships with selected academic research facilities.

Focus on applications. NYNEX research and development activities focus on the application of emerging technologies and on the timely development of products and services that best meet customer needs.

Build an effective information infrastructure. Technological advances will benefit NYNEX internally as well. It is essential that we develop efficient and coordinated management information systems and extend their use throughout the NYNEX family of companies.

Human Resources Strategies

Attract and retain high-quality employees with the skills and diversity to bring about continual business growth.

Foster a partnership with employees that provides the opportunity, the training, and the resources to attain the full potential of the individual and the corporation.

Build an equitable work environment. Develop and implement personnel policies that promote openness and equity in the workplace.

Implement competitive benefit and compensation programs throughout NYNEX that foster the achievement of corporate goals.

Recognize and reward performance. Establish recognition and reward programs that enhance the total quality concept and encourage employees to reach beyond the norm.

Financial Strategies

Exceed share owner expectations. Our specific financial goal is to achieve sustainable earnings growth which places NYNEX in the top quartile of its peers. To do so, we must focus on growth in existing as well as new businesses.

Use assets more productively. All our markets should be profitable. The growth of earnings and profitability requires more efficient and effective use of existing assets.

Manage selective growth. Sustained earnings

growth is essential to pursue new ventures. Funding of new business opportunities is based on long-term expectations of profitability, earnings growth potential, degree of risk, and other strategic criteria.

Shape our balance sheet. Capitalization—the mix between debt and equity—should continue to reflect the composite of our business risks.

Image Strategies

Focus on the family. Position NYNEX as a leading competitor in the global information industry. Market NYNEX as a family of companies providing solutions that meet the information management and communications needs of customers.

Communicate commitment to quality and value. Demonstrate our continuing corporate and individual commitment to quality and value in everything we do.

Be a leader on the issues. Where appropriate, influence the positions of key stakeholders in the public policy debate on issues critical to NYNEX.

Be socially responsible. Contribute to the educational, social and economic growth of the communities where we live and work.

OUR VALUES

Our values are statements of our desire to improve, change, and strike a balance in all the areas we care about. They are not statements of where we see ourselves today. They're statements about the kind of business we're striving to become.

Customer Satisfaction

Driven by a commitment to anticipate and meet customer needs, NYNEX is a worldwide family of companies that strives to be the best. We focus on the customer in everything we do. We offer innovative products and services. We satisfy customer needs better than our competition.

Quality, defined as meeting agreed upon customer requirements, is inherent in all that we do. We are committed to providing all our customers, inside and outside NYNEX, with superior products and excellent service. We enter only those markets that we believe we can serve well.

Respect for Employees

The skills, creativity, dedication, and productivity of NYNEX people are key to achieving a competitive edge. Our people make a difference on a winning team and are proud to work for NYNEX.

Our goal is to create a challenging work environment that recognizes cultural diversity, offers equal opportunity in all areas of employment, values and treats everyone with dignity and respect, and encourages all employees to contribute their best.

We strive for an environment of openness and trust that enables employees to communicate, innovate, and take risks. Employees are given training and developmental opportunities that enable them to make the most of their abilities. Management listens to employee concerns and suggestions. Individual contributions are recognized. Pay and promotions are based on merit.

Ethical Behavior

We maintain the highest ethical standards in all our business dealings. Corporate and personal integrity are not sacrificed in pursuit of business objectives.

Corporate Citizenship

We foster an environment of educational, cultural, and economic growth, lend our effort and support to worthy causes, and encourage employee participation in community affairs.

Fiscal Responsibility

Meeting our corporate objectives requires maintaining steady earnings growth and sound financial health.

A WINNING FORMULA

NYNEX has come a long way. We hold a strong and respected position in the global information industry. And as the industry grows and evolves, we'll continue to grow and evolve with it. Nothing about our business can be static.

Our mission continues to reflect the dynamic nature of the marketplace we serve. Our values and our strategies must be communicated and understood so we can build on the many opportunities we choose to pursue.

The only way to truly win in the global information game is by putting these principles to work . . . each of us . . . together . . . continuously. Winning is not a sometime thing. It's an all-the-time thing. You don't win by doing things right once in a while; you win by doing them right all the time.

We know what it's going to take for NYNEX to win. Now, it's a matter of putting that knowledge to work.

TOUCHE ROSS

Human Resource Initiatives: A First Look

For the past three years, we have worked to build the firm's profitability and capital base, putting together cash reserves that will allow us to invest in the future. We have met these goals. It is now time to move boldly into the next stage of our strategic plan—gaining a sustained competitive advantage through a human resource renaissance.

The human resource initiatives announced in this brochure represent a major shift in direction. They include new programs for developing leadership and management skills, building a new sense of collegiality throughout the firm, improving benefits, offering an increased array of lifestyle options, creating more opportunities for staff development, stepping up our efforts to recruit high-talent people, and communicating better with staff, nationally and in our practice offices.

I believe these initiatives will attract and retain the people who can fuel an explosive growth in our firm, creating exciting new career opportunities for all who want them. The result will be a different firm: not the biggest, nor simply the best, but the most valuable professional partnership in the world. I want your help to reach this goal.

Getting there will not be easy, and it will take time. Indeed, I might describe our challenge as a relay race. As a firm, we are in the race for the long haul, with each of you an important member of a team that includes firm management, the partners, staff, and even the newest recruit. I intend to run my leg of the race. When the baton is passed to you, will you take it and do your part? I am confident that you will.

I want to stress that the material outlined here represents a beginning—it is the first look at a comprehensive set of new initiatives that we have already started to put in place and that will continue to evolve over the next few years. You will hear more about each of these programs as they are introduced to the firm.

In a very real sense, you have an opportunity to influence the directions we take. Please take the time to read this brochure, talk with your colleagues, and think about what you can contribute to implementing our human resource initiatives. I think you will agree, the best is yet to come. [Edward A. Kangas, managing partner of the firm]

COLLEGIALITY

New initiatives, including skill-building and training efforts for partners and staff, will lay the foundation for the staff's full participation as colleagues in our practice:

- Creating an environment in which Touche Ross professionals have significant access to information and the opportunity to influence the decision makers
- Sharing with all professional staff information about national, local, and departmental plans and results
- Instituting a national orientation program for all new hires
- An Office Managing Partner development series—ongoing since 1987
- Multifunction departmental Partner in Charge

---

*Reprinted with permission.

meetings that focus on building the skills for collegial management—first session, September 1988

- Annual Leadership Development Conferences designed for new managers and conducted by the senior leadership of the firm—initiated in the fall of 1987
- A common framework of basic human resource practices, designed to create a collegial environment in every office
- Development and retention programs in each of the functions—D&R task forces active in audit, tax, and management consulting

BENEFITS

Comprehensive benefit programs have been expanded to include:

- A new dental plan
- An improved medical plan
- Flexible spending accounts, using pre-tax dollars to pay for selected health and dependent-care expenses
- Expanded eligibility for the 401(k) tax-deferred savings and investment plan
- An improved retirement program
- An annual benefits statement

STAFF DEVELOPMENT

New programs will demonstrate our continuing commitment to staff development:

- Establishing a Touche Ross Development Center, located at the Scottsdale Conference Resort in Arizona—under construction
- A policy of promoting staff based on capability and readiness, rather than on time in grade
- Developing alternative career paths, including a new position of Principal and a series of positions in Tax Accounting Service Centers
- A pilot program to support graduate education for qualified staff
- A comprehensive set of programs to build personal skills, including sales training, leadership development, and counseling
- More substantial national and local office programs for Touche Ross alumni
- A new approach to outplacement that will provide significant assistance to staff who leave the firm after reaching the manager/senior consultant level, or higher

LIFE-STYLE

New programs meet the life-style needs of our people:

- In the first five years of employment: a third week of vacation for all professional staff; A sick leave/vacation incentive program for all support staff
- A national mortgage assistance program with easy access that will provide 90 percent mortgages at competitive rates
- A national child-care referral program
- A part-time employment policy to provide an alternative for career continuation

RECRUITING

Significantly enhanced recruiting efforts will meet our goal of recruiting a greater share of top students each year:

- A national intern program, including a firmwide meeting led by the senior management of the firm—begins summer of 1988
- Regional student leadership conferences for top students
- New programs for the recruitment of talented liberal arts and MBA candidates
- A professional case study seminar program for college juniors and seniors
- The Trueblood Subscription Series, a program for regular dissemination of case studies for use in classroom teaching
- A new program of firm-sponsored and funded faculty research support
- Significantly improved communication vehicles—including publications and videos—for recruits and faculty
- Significantly increased presence of the chairman, managing partner, and senior leadership of the firm on the nation's top-40 campuses

STAFF COMPENSATION

Compensation policies will help Touche Ross attract and retain the best staff:

- A firmwide compensation methodology that moves compensation decisions to the office level; allows the office to respond effectively to competition for top people; addresses the issue of salary compression resulting from increases in entry-level pay

- More differentiation in starting salaries
- Increased differentiation in compensation adjustments based on performance

STAFF COMMUNICATION

Communication programs will inform colleagues about developments in the firm:

- National communications addressed directly to the staff
- Slides, videos, and other materials to support local office staff meetings
- Questionnaires, field interviews, and audience response systems at meetings to evaluate the impact of our new initiatives

UNITED STATES COAST GUARD

Commandant's Long-range View

INTRODUCTION

Purpose. The purpose of this instruction is to disseminate the Commandant's Long-range View, a policy document revised and issued biennially.

Background. The Commandant's Long-range View is the initial document in the Coast Guard's planning process. Although not a plan in itself, it provides broad policy guidance to be used throughout the service as a foundation for the formulation of planning documents. Several key terms should be defined.

The scenario presented in the Long-range View is the Commandant's assessment and evaluation of the setting in which the Coast Guard will be operating during the next 15 years. The challenges to be faced within that setting may be operational, administrative, or budgetary in nature and are of sufficient impact as to require early consideration.

Objectives are statements of what we will be trying to accomplish, that is, how we will meet the challenges presented in the established scenario. Defining objectives is the first and most important step in developing the structure and focus of the organization.

Policies, for the purpose of this document, are broad governing principles or guidelines indicating courses of action for achieving the established objectives. They are not "rules" per se, but instead allow for flexibility in dealing with the dynamics of the scenario, unexpected budgetary constraints, and technological advances.

Plans are the documents used to set forth a strategy for implementing the Commandant's established policies. Planning involves defining causal relationships, developing and evaluating alternatives, and deciding upon an appropriate course of action. Plans are developed in response to the Commandant's Long-range View and provide a recommended course of action for achieving the objectives within the established policy framework.

Discussion. The Long-range View is intended to facilitate the planning process by providing the Commandant's sense of the direction the Coast Guard must take over the next 15 years.

Establishing a scenario that identifies the factors most likely to influence the Coast Guard in the future is a formidable task. Predicting the effects of those factors is even more difficult. Nevertheless, program planners must carefully consider the objectives and policy guidance resulting from such projections in preparing short- and mid-range planning documents. Such documents must not only be responsive to near-term requirements but should also contribute to the achievement of long-range objectives.

The Long-range View is divided into two major parts. The Overview briefly describes the scenario and sets forth the Commandant's direction for addressing it. In Policy Guidance, specific issues are discussed and policy is provided to serve as a focal point for use in developing plans.

Action. The Commandant's Long-range View will serve as a basis for the preparation of Coast Guard planning documents. Minor deviations to accommodate unforeseen changes in the operating environment are expected. Suggestions and com-

---

*Reprinted with permission.

ments concerning significant changes in direction, alternative approaches, or additional areas of emphasis are welcome. [P. A. Yost, Admiral, US Coast Guard]

OVERVIEW

Purpose

- To present the Commandant's sense of the future environment in which the Coast Guard will operate
- To provide broad guidelines that will serve as frames of reference for policy implementation
- To provide policy guidance that is sufficiently specific to be of immediate use and relevance to program managers' resource management decisions

The Scenario

The nation's maritime regions hold the potential for great benefit to this and future generations. The wise use of the sea affects the national security, transportation needs, economy, food resources, energy and raw materials needs, international leadership, and the quality of the environment of the people of the United States. As a time-proven provider of marine- and maritime-related services, the Coast Guard's future will be influenced by specific national needs as they develop. The effectiveness with which we respond to these national needs will be determined in large part by our accuracy in anticipating these needs and our ability to respond appropriately.

Increased ocean use has led to a significant increase in the need for maritime law enforcement. The growing abuse of illegal drugs in the US has increased illegal importation of these drugs from abroad. While the Coast Guard's effective maritime law enforcement has been one of the key market factors that caused drug traffickers to change their emphasis from waterborne smuggling of marijuana to air smuggling of cocaine, the Coast Guard will be required to respond to the drug threat in its role as the primary law enforcement agency on, over, and under the high seas.

Similarly, the nationally growing recognition of the military capabilities and nature of the Coast Guard have led to a new awareness of the Coast Guard's military role and a redefinition of our relationship with the Navy. Our recently developed Maritime Defense Zone responsibilities, which include wartime operational command of forces assigned to coastal and harbor defense and port security, and our participation in the NAVGARD Board have solidified the Coast Guard position in the national defense establishment. Specifically, our unique expertise in several coastal mission areas including small-boat operations is increasingly becoming a vital strategic part of US defense planning.

While sea piracy has existed since the beginning of maritime commerce, the *Achille Lauro* and other recent incidents illustrate that terrorist activity has expanded into this arena. Passenger vessels, hazardous cargoes, and offshore production facilities should be considered terrorist targets. Coupled with the threat of increased terrorist activity is the potential for violent confrontation over political activity involving the oceans. The Coast Guard expects the majority of maritime incidents to be low-intensity conflicts. In general, political activism affecting maritime issues has substantially increased and in either a violent or non-violent format can be expected to impact both the conduct of maritime operations and national ocean policies. Our need to be responsive to maritime terrorism is coupled with our enhanced role in the nation's maritime defense. We will emphasize the war-fighting capabilities of our personnel. Coast Guard hardware will be compatible with our military mission.

Much of our cutter fleet, aircraft, and boats have been or are scheduled to be replaced with new, highly capable equipment. Our new ships and aircraft have a higher standard of habitability, and some are equipped with modern sensor and data processing equipment which should significantly enhance our productivity. Other sensors are being developed to update existing equipment. We have developed a new, more efficient system for acquiring major systems.

The Coast Guard is recognized as the preeminent organization in the world for its safety of life mission. We will maintain our emphasis on our lifesaving role and will continue to seek improvement in our performance by exploiting advanced technology.

The commercial importance of the waters surrounding the territorial regions of the US has grown substantially in recent years and is expected to continue through the end of the century. The oceans are a major transportation conduit—not only for cargo and passengers, but also for pipelines and cables. Transportation will remain the single most valuable commercial aspect of ocean use and the basis of our need to maintain uninterrupted sea lines of communication. In addition, the abundance of marine resources ranging from hard minerals to thermal gradients will lead to increased investment and development. The challenges that accompany the diversity of ocean use include maintaining defense responsiveness, protecting the resources, ensuring the safety and security of people and property, suppressing illegal activities, and balancing resource development with environmental protection.

Factors that will significantly influence the range of decisions the Coast Guard must make in the future are the cost and availability of energy. In the near term, increased energy conservation has reduced demand growth and, along with increased production, has lowered prices. This lessens the demand for substantially increased US outer continental shelf oil and gas exploration. However, as traditional oil fields are depleted, and if the availability of foreign oil is again limited by political and economic factors, discovery of new and alternative energy sources close to home will increase in importance and raise concerns as to the interrelationships of varied marine activities along our coasts. In addition, energy considerations will have important industrial, commercial, and political implications, both domestically and internationally.

The large federal deficit combined with tax reform initiatives have placed increased emphasis on controlling the level of federal expenditures. Issues raised by policymakers that could change the way the Coast Guard does business include defederalization of certain functions, contracting certain operations to private firms, and user fees. In addition, the need to control spending will force the Coast Guard to continually review its operations to improve productivity and assure operational efficiency. It could lead to a reduction of services in certain areas.

In examining ways to meet the challenges ahead, all alternative actions must be considered. These may include initiating and implementing new activities, redirecting the emphasis on existing programs, continuing to participate in governmental task forces (assuming the leadership role when appropriate), and assisting state and local agencies, volunteer groups, and private industry in solving national problems. We will not seek to acquire inappropriate new missions, that is, those in which it is not reasonably clear that our unique blend of expertise and multimission facilities make us the most efficient and effective federal agency for the mission. We will pursue defederalization of our non-defense missions where it will save money and make sense and, where appropriate, will turn over those missions to the private sector. We are pursuing defederalizing some short-range aids to navigation functions, certain commercial vessel safety inspections, and operation of some Vessel Traffic Services facilities. We will provide leadership in international maritime issues.

The increased density and variety of maritime activities, plus the gradual expansion of our region of responsibility—exemplified by the establishment of the Exclusive Economic Zone (EEZ) and our responsibilities in the Maritime Defense Zone (MDZ)—will increase the demands in many program areas. Demands for services in other areas, such as inspection of US merchant ships, can be expected to decline because we are actively pursuing third-party delegation of the activity. Accomplishing our objectives within the tighter budgetary climate will require ingenuity and resourcefulness. We will need to prioritize our activities and review our performance rigorously to ensure that we are accomplishing our key missions as effectively as possible. We are constantly reassessing our operations and organization to allow maximum effectiveness and flexibility. These improvements have established the framework on which we can build the future.

PREMISES

- We will remain an integrated, single organizational body within the Department of Transportation.
- We will continue to be an Armed Force of the United States.
- We will continue to serve as a model for many foreign navies, particularly in the Third World, because of our heritage and versatility.
- We will carry out our responsibilities for the Maritime Defense Zone.
- We will continue to be this nation's primary law enforcement agency in, on, and over the high seas.

- We will maintain our long-standing role as the federal authority on matters of marine safety and facilitation.
- We will continue to be an operational service, using a variety of multimission cutters, aircraft, boats, and shore facilities to execute a broad range of responsibilities.

POLICY GUIDANCE ON SPECIFIC LONG-RANGE ISSUES

This section of the Commandant's Long-range View offers observations and sets forth policy guidance on specific issues. The issues may apply to a single operating or support program, more than one program, or a future issue that may develop into a Coast Guard program.

The material is presented in two sections. Leadership/Administration provides forecasts and guidance in various categories dealing with internal organizational efficiency and effectiveness: human resources, member and dependent support, professionalism, command and managerial skills, financial management and fiscal integrity, user fees and privatization, capital resources, research and development, information resource management, information security, and internal organization. Coast Guard Objectives provides forecasts and guidance specific to the seven formal Coast Guard objectives that guide our operations including vessel, aircraft, and shore facility activity and standard-setting, licensing, certification, and other regulatory activities (Not included in this book).

Section 1: Leadership/Administration

Human Resources. While the Coast Guard has traditionally relied upon a large recruiting pool of persons aged 18 to 24, certain factors will cause reliance on new recruitment to change. The total number of persons in the 18 to 24-year age group peaked in 1982 after more than two decades of growth and will decline from 30.3 million in 1982 to an estimated 23.2 million in 1995 when the number in this age group is expected to level off. In the United States, the number of teenagers was exceeded by the number of persons over 65 for the first time in July of 1985. The net result will be that during the present decade the number of persons 18 to 24 years of age actively participating in the

work force will decline from 21.6 million to an estimated 19.1 million, with a further decrease anticipated in the 1991–1995 period. This decline in the traditional recruiting pool will require innovative approaches to personnel resource management in order to minimize the number of people required from this age group through increased retention, productivity improvements, increased employee services such as counseling, and expanded use of technology to reduce and simplify workloads. It will be necessary to continually prioritize our missions and activities as well as carefully examine proposals for new or expanded missions to assure that we can meet our challenges successfully.

The increasing participation of women in the work force will mitigate the impact of this decline to some extent. The increase of women as a percentage of the work force will have a significant effect upon Coast Guard personnel practices. It will mean not only more women employed by the Coast Guard in both military and civilian roles but also more two-career families in the Coast Guard. This will mean that more reenlistment and mobility assignment decisions will be affected by consideration of the family's total income as opposed to only the military spouse's salary. The Coast Guard will be tasked with designing programs to meet the needs of displaced spouses or accommodating the increasing number of two-career families in the assignment process.

The proportion of minority personnel in military service will increase, reflecting both their higher birthrate and the employment opportunities offered by the Coast Guard. Increased recruiting of minorities will also help offset the decline in the total number of youth in the work force.

The aging of the US population as reflected by the decline in the number of teenagers will also be evident through increasing work force participation of older Americans. Coupled with the increasing health and life expectancy of older Americans is the question of the future of the federal civilian and military pension systems, for which many reforms are being proposed. Should reform of the retirement systems include increasing the qualifying age for retirement benefits, the Coast Guard's work force will become increasingly older. Changes in the military pension system will affect the pyramid of officers and will mean more time in grade and fewer promotions for officers. Services for an older work force will include expanded health and wellness programs, productivity improvements to accommodate older, less physically capable workers, and greater flexibility in assignments.

A factor that will require adjustment is the slower personnel turnover rates currently being experienced. We expect the current high military reenlistment rate to remain so. With reenlistment rates rising, the military Coast Guard work force has become more stable. This may reduce the number of new recruits needed. Slower turnover for civilians is the result of the numerical decline in the federal non-Department of Defense (DOD) work force which has substantially reduced opportunities for transfer elsewhere within the federal establishment.

We have placed increased emphasis on training our people to increase efficiency. Our training programs will continue to emphasize increased productivity as a way of assuring that our resource requests are supportable in the tightening budgetary climate.

We are always attuned to the need to adapt our recruitment, retention, and training programs to assure the highest quality of leadership obtainable in our personnel.

Policy Guidance

- We will continue to offer a wide range of opportunities for minorities and women that will enhance their promotion and retention rates.
- We will continue our active commitment to equal opportunity for all members of the Coast Guard without regard to race, color, national origin, sex, and religion.
- We will emphasize our efforts to include handicapped personnel among our civilian employees.
- An understanding of and commitment to the Coast Guard's Human Relations Policy and concerns will be a prerequisite for advancement and retention of all supervisory personnel.
- We will constantly tailor our recruitment, promotion, and employee assistance programs to assure a work force that meets the needs of the Coast Guard.
- We will continue to foster the development of strong leadership in our personnel.

Member and Dependent Support. Permanent change of station (PCS) moves are expensive for the Coast Guard and burdensome for our personnel, particularly for the growing number of two-career families. To the extent that it is practicable, we will seek to reduce the number of PCS moves, to minimize the disruptions associated with them, and to provide more comprehensively for the financial impacts of PCS moves.

Changing life-styles and increased expectations for habitability of housing, personal privacy, and leisure time have affected the Coast Guard's housing and personnel policies. We have made continued adjustments in our housing plant. Our policy is to assure that service in the Coast Guard provides families the maximum time together consonant with requirements for shipboard and remote duty. Continued variations in life-styles, such as smaller families, two-career families, and an increased number of grown children living with parents, make flexibility in housing alternatives more important than in the past. In order to be responsive to such trends in life-style, leased housing becomes a better long-term alternative than construction of Coast Guard-owned housing. Coast Guard-owned housing, however, will still be required where the local community cannot provide adequate affordable housing.

We must also consider the needs of our single personnel. Living conditions aboard ships have been improved in recent years to help meet crew members' needs for rest and relaxation. In spite of this improvement, the Coast Guard does not consider even its modern ships as adequate housing for bachelor personnel in port during off-duty hours. Likewise, high-density, open-bay barracks are no longer acceptable for single personnel. A combination of construction programs, leased quarters, payment of quarters allowance, and certain statutory changes have been initiated to correct this situation and will be carried forward to the extent permitted by resource constraints.

Unaccompanied personnel will be housed in the local community when housing market conditions permit. Newly arrived non-rated unaccompanied personnel, however, will be berthed aboard in order to ensure their proper orientation to the Coast Guard, the unit, their work, and the environment.

We must help our members cope with the stresses that accompany military life. Drug and alcohol addiction have become major factors in every aspect of American society, including the military. We will continue to assist those who seek help with their problems while maintaining the integrity of our work force. Growing evidence of the impact of life-style on health and productivity, combined with rapidly growing costs for health care and disability compensation, will make fitness an important factor in personnel costs, as well as an important factor in the welfare and morale of each member.

Management of the Coast Guard's member and dependent support programs will continue to improve, relying more upon the Coast Guard's own resources and less on DOD resources. We should strive to provide our members and their dependents a quality of life consistent with their status as dedicated professionals.

Policy Guidance

- We will provide for the full range of needs of Coast Guard members and their dependents at all levels of our organization.
- We will minimize PCS moves to the extent that it can be accomplished in consonance with the needs of the service.
- We will provide adequate living space, privacy, and furnishings for our single personnel.

Professionalism. The Coast Guard is a professional, military, seagoing service operating multimission vessels, aircraft, and shore facilities to meet a wide range of public service requirements, national interests, and goals. One of the great strengths of the Coast Guard has been the background of seagoing experience and knowledge of the maritime arena in the officer corps and senior enlisted ranks. For example, the Coast Guard has long been recognized as the expert in small-boat operations. Historically, the Coast Guard has been characterized by the cost-effectiveness of its operations and the ability to move quickly and effectively into new missions or to provide new points of focus in traditional ones. New emphasis on our defense operations mission and responsibility for the MDZ will require us to place a higher priority on the warfare skills of our officers and enlisted personnel. We will maintain sufficient breadth and depth in our force structure to respond to changing national needs.

Commercial vessel safety, port and environmental safety, deepwater port safety, and vessel traffic management are examples of facilitation and regulatory functions that require the expertise gained through sea duty, but in turn do not provide experience at sea. Duty in cutters provides the necessary first-tour seagoing experience for personnel in subsequent shoreside assignments.

There will be a continuing need to focus on the career development of personnel. Innovative approaches to rating management, training, and sea/shore rotational assignments will be necessary to assure professional development.

Our reserve forces and the Coast Guard Auxiliary provide a wealth of experience and expertise, and we anticipate increasing opportunities to utilize their services to augment our regular personnel. They also serve as an important source of familiarization and assistance in local maritime affairs.

Law enforcement demand throughout the remainder of the century will require us to hone the law enforcement skills of our personnel.

Policy Guidance

- We will stress performance of missions that develop operational expertise and we will consider defederalizing those functions that will not decrease our ability to perform our appropriate roles in the maritime and defense readiness arenas.
- We will vigorously pursue new initiatives to enhance officer and enlisted professionalism in the Coast Guard.
- We will stress development of warfare skills of our uniformed members in order to enhance our defense readiness mission.
- We will take increased advantage of the skills and capabilities of our reserve and auxiliary personnel and facilities to meet our increasing demands and to provide locale-specific expertise.
- We will emphasize training that provides job-specific skills.
- We will enhance program-specific training for such missions as law enforcement and defense operations to ensure the multimission capability of Coast Guard people.

Command and Managerial Skills. As the United States moves to exploit the resources of the sea in new ways, our role in the formulation of ocean policy will increase because of our acknowledged expertise in marine safety, resource protection, facilitation of transportation, and responsibility for the MDZ. This will add to the existing requirements for political, economic, scientific, and military skills and an in-depth understanding of federal government operations among our headquarters, area, and district staffs and our operating personnel. These requirements will continue to influence education, training, and assignment of officers, petty officers, and civilians to command or management positions.

The constraints on federal expenditures will require increased productivity as well as enhanced management skills to accomplish our goals within stable or reduced Coast Guard budgets. Examples of productivity improvements include increased automation, contracting of services which can be performed effectively and at lower cost by the private sector, and ensuring that decisions are made by the lowest competent level and are not subjected to unnecessary review levels. Our efforts will focus on reducing our personnel-intensive functions through technological improvements, particularly through increased communications and automated data processing (ADP) applications.

Recognition of accomplishments, whether of an individual or a team, is an important component of effective leadership. Internal recognition within the service builds morale and increases confidence in abilities. Public recognition of Coast Guard activities builds pride in the service, resulting in higher levels of motivation and enhanced retention. All command levels should emphasize development of public relations and media contact skills and should establish systems to regularly evaluate unit operations and individual performance to ensure that high performers are recognized promptly and visibly.

Policy Guidance

- We will adjust the focus of our personnel system as necessary to develop and maintain needed expertise in command and leadership skills.
- We will continue to seek opportunities to recognize outstanding performance by our military and civilian employees.

Financial Management and Fiscal Integrity. The Coast Guard, in concert with the rest of the federal government, will undergo an extended period of financial review and reprioritization. The emphasis will be on operational and administrative efficiencies. The advent of user fees will require refinements in our record-keeping system in order to avoid litigation about our fee schedule.

Equally important will be our ability to analyze our activity from a financial perspective. These capabilities are directly contingent upon two factors: (1) a cadre of trained financial managers and (2) the ADP systems required for fast retrieval and analysis of data.

In light of severe resource constraints, the Coast Guard must become more efficient in employing its personnel for preventive and enforcement activities. The Coast Guard's role will broaden through becoming the coordinator and overseer of preventive and enforcement activities of all parties involved in the port complex, that is, state and local governments, third parties, owners, and operators. The Coast Guard will establish cooperative relationships with these other entities in order to avoid duplication of activities where third parties have the capability and desire to ensure an appropriate level of safety and where there are no conflicts of interest. Wherever this can be done, Coast Guard activities will be limited to spot checks to ensure compliance and occasional inspections for the purpose of maintaining Coast Guard proficiency and reserve training for mobilization readiness.

Policy Guidance

- We will maintain/improve development training for our line financial managers and analysts.
- We will improve efficiency in the supply, procurement, and financial management areas, including application of developing computer technology.
- Field commanders will endeavor to share or recognize the prevention and enforcement activities of third parties, owners, operators, and state or local government agencies.

User Fees and Defederalization. The desire to reduce the size of the annual federal budget deficit will increase the probability of revenue enhancements, particularly user fees and efforts to reduce federal costs by defederalizing the performance of certain federal activities. User fees are generally a preferred means of revenue enhancement since they more directly impact upon actual program beneficiaries rather than the population as a whole. The implementation of user fees can be expected to result in a reduction in the demand for certain services currently performed by the Coast Guard or increased pressure to privatize some of them.

Policy Guidance

- The Coast Guard will continue to support charging of user fees for certain services.
- The Coast Guard will review its operations to assure that it maintains its capability to fulfill its statutory obligations.
- The Coast Guard will maintain its capability to contribute to the national defense.
- The Coast Guard will review alternative means of providing its services where appropriate to assure best use of government resources.

Capital Resources. In 1986 the Coast Guard established a new Office of Acquisition to improve internal planning and management of major systems acquisitions.

The major capital investment programs undertaken in recent years include the acquisition of 270 medium-endurance cutters (WMEC), patrol boats (WPB), medium-range search aircraft (HU-25A), short-range recovery helicopters (HH-65A), ice-breaking tugs (WTGB), polar icebreaker (WAGB) replacements, the 378 high-endurance cutter (WHEC) fleet rehabilitation and modernization (FRAM), the 180 buoy tender (WLB) Service Life Extension Project (SLEP), and the 210 WMEC mid-life maintenance availability (MMA). We are also equipping our aircraft with a variety of sensor equipment. Programs to replace the medium-range recovery helicopter (MRR), the oceangoing (WLB) and coastal (WLM) buoy tenders, and the motor lifeboat (MLB) capabilities are underway. These can be expected to pay valuable dividends in the form of increased mission capabilities, reduced maintenance workload, and improved working and living conditions. Future capital investments must take full advantage of technological advances to improve productivity in mission performance. Any decision to make major improvements in our existing ships and aircraft is likely to entail some short-term reduction in availability during the transition period.

Policy Guidance

- We will improve our planning and coordination for major systems acquisition.
- We will vigorously pursue capital investments that will improve our productivity and operational capabilities.
- We will invest in support systems only when such investment will result in increased pro-

ductivity or necessary improvement in the quality of life for our people. Quality of life includes the ability to perform assigned tasks as effectively and safely as possible.

- We will incorporate integrated logistics support concepts into our planning for systems acquisitions.
- We will tailor user requirements and specifications where possible to utilize off-the-shelf systems in satisfying our operational missions and safety needs.
- We will seek commonality with DOD hardware where appropriate.

Research and Development. Basic scientific research will remain the responsibility of organizations such as the National Science Foundation. We will continue to monitor closely and, where indicated, participate in R&D work undertaken by the Navy, Maritime Administration (MARAD), National Oceanic and Atmospheric Administration (NOAA), academia and industry; however, our own Research, Development, Test and Evaluation (RDT&E) program will focus primarily on problems unique to Coast Guard operations. We will continue our emphasis on innovative projects that offer potentially high payoffs, even when accompanied by significant levels of risk.

Policy Guidance

- We will concentrate our RDT&E emphasis in the areas of interest where no similar effort is being undertaken and where the potential for high payoff to Coast Guard programs exist.
- We will undertake projects with high levels of risk within RDT&E rather than within other support or operating programs.

Information Resources Management. Effective use of information technology (automated data acquisition and processing, telecommunications, and data communications) has the potential for real productivity and performance gains in the Coast Guard. The capability to integrate automatic remote sensing and automated data processing systems will be particularly valuable for law enforcement, military readiness, port and environmental safety, and waterways management. It will also improve our ability to contribute to the quality of life and to meeting human needs through a wide range of personnel support functions. The

Coast Guard must have a comprehensive plan to move from manually prepared incident and periodic statistical reports toward a database system for information management and decision support. Changes will be necessary in the training system to provide qualified personnel to support our information resources management efforts.

The Coast Guard lacks the capability at present to transmit video sensor data in real time from the sensor to the operational commander or other decision maker. The Coast Guard will acquire such a capability, which will improve mission effectiveness by reducing delays in response time for missions which rely on video sensor data input.

One of the primary areas of emphasis will be the application of command, control, and communications (C3) to improve personnel productivity. There will be increased automation of vessel operations, including engine rooms, which will reduce the number of personnel that would otherwise be required to operate the Coast Guard.

We need to recognize rapid technological advances in the information arena. The Long-range View covers four+ generations of hardware/software at the current rate of change. Systems designs will have to consider these factors to facilitate and economize upgrades.

Policy Guidance

- We will prepare and maintain a comprehensive plan for implementation of database-oriented teleprocessing for Coast Guard information management. In those areas where it is reasonably clear that the resulting improvement in productivity or operating/management capability will outweigh the costs, we will actively pursue this implementation.
- We will follow a complementary strategy for the development of automated systems which (1) are user friendly, manageable, and productive, (2) tie to various databases, and (3) make aggregate information available for summary review to support policy making and operational decisions. These systems will emphasize integrated planning, shared facilities, standard equipment, public access data networks, high response rates, and user chargeback/responsibility.

Information Security. Coast Guard sensitive information, both classified and unclassified, is a resource that must be protected. The amount of sensitive information we process will increase. The increased ability of adversaries to intercept or sabotage Coast Guard sensitive information poses a great threat to our operational effectiveness. We will intensify efforts to provide adequate protection to databases and communication links. Changes may be necessary in the training system to provide qualified personnel to support the protection of Coast Guard information.

Innovations in the area of command, control, and communications will continue to have an important effect on the Coast Guard's capability to perform its missions effectively.

The need for secure communications will increase significantly in order to meet Coast Guard responsibilities in the MDZ and the conduct of law enforcement.

Current emergency locator transmitters procedures require periods of radio silence to avoid compromising the presence and location of patrol vessels. This limitation reduces the opportunity for an exchange of information, and may even create an information void that can foil successful mission accomplishment. To overcome these limitations, the Coast Guard will acquire the capability to provide voice and data communications, including ship/ship, ship/shore, or air/surface, without permitting detection of our units by non-friendly monitoring units, thus avoiding a compromise of our presence or location. A significant obstacle to communication automation at present is the inability to switch traffic between secure and non-secure circuits. This limitation will be overcome, and the labor intensiveness of the communications relay function will be reduced.

In December 1985, National Security Decision Directive (NSDD) number 201 was signed by the President, outlining policy with respect to National Security Emergency Preparedness (NSEP) Telecommunications Funding. The policy directed that the implementation and recurring costs for national level NSEP telecommunications programs, that is, those which benefit multiple federal departments, agencies, or entities, be shared on a pro-rata basis determined by each agency's share of NSEP communications requirements beginning in fiscal year 1988. Development costs for national level NSEP telecommunications programs will be funded by an executive agent.

To meet its responsibilities under the National Security Communications Policy Plan, the Coast Guard will develop or ensure that it meets requirements for access to the Nationwide Emergency Telecommunications Systems (NETS), Commercial Network Survivability (CNS) program, and the Commercial Satellite Survivability (CSS) program. It will require increasing Coast Guard capabilities in mobility, connectivity, interoperability, restorability, redundancy, system hardness, and security of its communications systems.

Policy Guidance

- Security will be a basic element of comprehensive management information plans.
- We will increase our capability to secure or protect sensitive information systems throughout the service.
- The ability to protect Coast Guard information must satisfy both wartime and peacetime needs.
- The Coast Guard will take active steps to assure the availability of telecommunications services that will enhance the effectiveness of its forces in times of war or national emergency.

Coast Guard Internal Organization. We operate in a dynamic environment in which new responsibilities arise while existing ones may expand, contract or, in rare cases, disappear. The Coast Guard will continually review its organization and consolidate and reorganize as necessary to meet changes in technology, to improve productivity, and to respond to budget cuts. Any reorganization will be conducted in line with our general organizational policies of maintaining unity of command, organizational integrity, appropriate span of control, and of delegating decision-making authority as close as possible to the point at which action is taken. Recent examples of this are the establishment of the Office of Acquisition, the reorganization of the Office of Operations, merger of the Offices of Merchant Marine Safety and Marine Environment and Systems, provision of a new flag officer for the Third District, the regionalized recruiting function, and recent district reorganizations of MSOs and Groups.

Policy Guidance

- We will continually review our organization for streamlining, consolidation, and the like to gain management efficiency and effectiveness.
- We will minimize disruption to ongoing programs if reorganization becomes necessary.

READINGS

READING 1

THE CHANGING SHAPE OF THE STRATEGIC PROBLEM

H. Igor Ansoff
The European Institute for Advanced Studies in Management

Management is the creative and error-correcting activity that gives the firm its purpose, its cohesion, and assures satisfactory return on the investment. Thus, it can be said that the essence of management is creation, adaption, and coping with change. Seen from the viewpoint of general management, there are two basic types of change. One is the fluctuations in the operating levels and conditions: in sales, profits, inventory, labor force, budgets, productive capacities, etc. This kind of change expands and contracts the activities of the firm, but leaves the nature of the firm intact. The other type transforms the firm: its products, its markets, its technology, its culture, its systems, its structure, its relationships with governmental bodies. I shall refer to this second type as the *strategic change.*

It is the need for strategic change that caught the attention of management in the mid-1950s and led to today's pervasive concern with strategy.

Strategy is a concept which is useful for perceiving the underlying patterns of managerial activity. It is also useful for giving guidance to the enterprise-transforming work. But it is a synthetic concept in the sense that strategies ascribed to organizations are frequently not perceived or made explicit by managers who pursue them.

Strategy is a type of solution to a problem, but not the problem itself. The problem that gave rise to this particular type of solution was a product/technology mismatch between the firm and its newly turbulent markets. But strategy was not the only tool used by firms to extricate themselves from their predicament.

Since the time of the original application of strategy to the task of transforming the firm, the underlying problem has undergone enormous changes. Whereas the original mismatch was at the interface with the environment, today it is the interiors of many enterprises that are mismatched to the surrounding turbulence. Whereas the original external mismatch was with the market environment, today there are additional mismatches with socio-political, ecological, and resource environments. Whereas the speed of environmental change was such as to permit a deliberate formulation and execution of strategy, in many situations today strategic surprises do not give sufficient warning to permit advanced strategic planning.

While the problem has been undergoing all these changes, much of the study and research in the field of strategy has been focused on understanding and elaboration of the originally perceived problem. Given the size and the extent of the changes that are taking place, it is necessary to ask to what extent the knowledge gained to date is applicable to the new dimensions of the strategic problem.

This paper suggests that this knowledge is only partially applicable and that further understanding must be sought on several levels. First, on the level of content, in addition to the product/market/technology strategy, content and understanding now must be given to social, political, and resource strategies. Second, the assumption of search for growth, which underlies the original concept of product/market strategy, needs to be modified to accommodate conditions of limited and zero

Reprinted with permission of the author.

841

growth. Third, the assumption, ever present in most research on strategy, that the problem starts in the market place, and that all other considerations are derivatives from the product/market strategy (i.e., "structure follows strategy") must be replaced by a question: where does the enterprise-transforming problem start? Does it start with limited external resources, with a particular configuration of internal capabilities; does it start with a zero growth assumption, or with redefining the *raison d'être* of the firm in society? In most cases, we shall probably find that it does not start in any of these places, that it can no longer be solved by a unidirectional flow of logic from the market to technology, to structure, to resources, to social posture. Instead, it needs to be solved by a procedure which involves multidirectional flows and feedbacks.

Finally, on the abstract level, we need to reexamine the usefulness of the concept of strategy as a decision heuristic for choosing the external interface with the environment, formulated through anticipation of trends in the environment. The concept must be reexamined in the context of large multinational firms where it is already evident that the concept of strategy as a style level heuristic is giving way to multiple-level strategy concept. The concept must also be reexamined in situations in which anticipation is impossible and strategic surprise is likely. I would predict that use of the traditional action strategy ("in which direction do we change the firm's position in the environment") will be increasingly supplemented, and sometimes replaced, by a flexible configuration strategy ("how do we configure the resources of the firm for effective response to unanticipated surprises").

To summarize, both the concepts and the content of today's understanding of strategy are now largely responsive to the problem as it existed in the 1950s. Since the problem has changed fundamentally, the concepts must be redefined and enriched.

A useful way to approach this task is to start by tracing the historical evolution of the strategic problem. This is the aim of this paper. We shall proceed in three steps. First, we shall construct a historical scenario of the evolution of the firm's environment. In constructing the scenario we shall try to mirror the complex historical reality, without attempting to organize it. Second, we shall identify several underlying patterns of evolution which are observable in the evolutionary process. Third, we

shall combine these patterns to describe the evolution and the future of the strategic problem.

The Industrial Revolution. Modern business history starts in the United States roughly in the 1820–1830s. First, construction of a network of canals, and then of a nationwide railroad system, triggered a process of economic unification, of the country. A stream of basic inventions—the steam engine, the cotton gin, the Bessemer steel process, the vulcanization of rubber, etc.—provided a technological base for a rapid industrial takeoff. Technological invention proceeded alongside the social invention of one of the most successful and influential organizations in history—the business firm.

By 1880–1900 a modern industrial infrastructure was in place. It unified the country into an American common market. The firm emerged as a privileged and central instrument of social progress. This period, which became known as the *Industrial Revolution,* was one of extraordinary strategic turbulence. The early industrial entrepreneurs devoted most of their energies to creating modern production technology, surrounding it with organizational technology, and staking out their market shares. The concept of competition, as it is known today, did not begin to evolve until the 1880s. The earlier concept was to dominate or absorb the competitor rather than meet him head-on in the market place. Thus modern marketing, as we know it today, was yet to be developed.

The Mass-production Era. From 1900 on, focus shifted to developing and consolidating the industrial structure created during the Industrial Revolution. This new period which lasted until the 1930s has been named the *Mass-production Era.* As the name suggests, the focus of industrial activity was on elaborating and perfecting the mechanism of mass production which progressively decreased the unit cost of products. The concept of marketing was straightforward and simple: the firm which offered a double standard product at the lowest price was going to win. This was succinctly summarized in the phrase of Henry Ford I, who, in response to a suggestion in favor of product differentiation, responded to his sales people: "Give it [the Model T] to them in any color so long as it is black."

There were many problems to be solved, but worrying about strategic challenges was not one of them. The industrial lines were well drawn and most offered promising growth opportunities. The inducement to diversify into new environments appealed only to the most adventurous firms. A majority were satisfied with their own growth prospects. It was obvious that the steel companies were in the "steel industry," automobile companies in the "automotive industry," etc. As a result, the focus of managerial attention was focused inward on the efficiency of the productive mechanism. The result was a set of managerial perceptions, attitudes and preferences which later came to be known as a "production mentality."

On the political front, the business sector was well protected against outside interference. Political and social controls were minimal. Government "interference" with the free enterprise was infrequent. When needed, the government could be expected to provide a protectionist economic policy. When business flagrantly transgressed social norms, government reacted by limiting freedoms of business action, such as anti-trust or anti-price collusion legislation. But these were occasional events; most of the time the boundary of the business environment remained inviolate. The business of the country was business. It was this sense of the centrality of the business sector that led "Engine Charlie" Wilson, a president of General Motors, to say: "What is good for General Motors is good for the country."

Mass-marketing Era. For the first thirty years of the century, success went to the firm with the lowest price. Products were largely undifferentiated and the ability to produce at the lowest unit cost was the secret to success. But toward the 1930s the demand for basic consumer goods was on the way toward saturation. With "a car in every garage and a chicken in every pot" the increasingly affluent consumer began to look for more than basic performance. Demand for Model-T types of products began to flag.

In the early 1930s, General Motors triggered a shift from production to a market focus. The introduction of the annual model change was symbolic of a shift of emphasis from standard to differentiated products. By contrast to the earlier "production orientation," the new secret to success began to shift to a "marketing orientation." Mr. Ford, having tried to replace a standard Model T with a standard Model A, was forced to follow the multi-model suit of General Motors. Promotion, adver-tising, selling, and other forms of consumer influence became priority concerns of management.

The shift to the marketing orientation meant a shift from an internally focussed, introverted perspective to an open, extroverted one. It also meant a transfer of power from production-minded to marketing-minded managers. Internal conflicts and power struggles were a frequent outcome. But, beyond power struggles, managers resisted the shift because it required costly, time-consuming, and psychologically threatening acquisition of new skills and facilities, development of new problem-solving approaches, changes in structure, in systems, and acceptance of new levels of uncertainty about the future.

In process industries and in producer durable industries, the marketing concept was slow to penetrate. When confronted with saturation, firms in such industries frequently settled for stagnating growth under a production orientation, rather than undertake the pains of a shift to the marketing outlook. It was not until after World War II that many of these industries were propelled by new technologies, first into a belated marketing orientation and, soon thereafter, into the higher turbulence of the Post-industrial Era.

Consumer industries and technologically intensive producer industries were early in embracing the marketing orientation. An overswing frequently occurred: marketing began to dominate operations at the expense of the production efficiency. As a compensation for the overswing, a "total marketing concept" emerged which balanced the conflicting demands of marketing and production. Such balanced sharing of priorities gradually emerged and is still to be found in most progressive firms.

The Mass-production Era greatly enhanced the marketing turbulence of the environment. The enterprise-changing strategic activity, which subsided during the mass-production period, was also enhanced but less drastically. In technology-based industries, new product development became an important activity early in the century. An historical milestone was the establishment of intra-firm research and development laboratories in companies such as Du Pont, Bell Telephone, General Electric, a step which institutionalized innovation within the firm.

In low-technology consumer industries the advent of the annual model change generated a demand for incremental product improvements, better packaging, cosmetic appeal, etc. But, with significant exceptions, the change in products and markets was evolutionary, rather than revolutionary. Focus on current markets and products dominated the concern with future profit potential.

During the Industrial Era, most of the major changes in the environment originated from leading aggressive firms which established the style and the pace of progress. Thus, with considerable justification, business could claim to control its own destiny. To be sure, business initiative sometimes produced an invisible chain of adverse consequences which led to periodic "loss of control," such as recurring recessions. But these were viewed as the price of competitive freedom well worth paying for "blowing off" of "economic steam" to enable progress to resume. These periodic "surprises" were seen as an exception in an otherwise surprise-free world.

The Post-industrial Era. From the mid-1950s, accelerating and cumulating events began to change the boundaries, the structure, and the dynamics of the business environment. Firms were increasingly confronted with novel unexpected challenges which were so far-reaching that Peter Drucker called the new era an *Age of Discontinuity*. Daniel Bell labeled it the *Post-industrial Era*—a term we shall adopt for our discussion. Today change continues at a pace which makes it safe to predict that the current escalation of turbulence will persist for at least another ten to fifteen years. It is harder to predict whether beyond this time horizon, the acceleration will persist or (what is more probable) whether the environment will settle down to absorbing and exploiting the accumulated change.

To an outside observer business problems of the Industrial Era would appear simple by comparison to the new turbulence. The manager's undivided attention was on "the business of business." He had a willing pool of labor (so long as the wage was right), and he catered to a receptive consumer. He was only secondarily troubled by such esoteric problems as tariffs, monetary exchange rates, differential inflation rates, cultural difference, and political barriers between markets.

Research and development was a controllable tool for increased productivity and product improvement. Society and government, though increasingly on guard against monopolistic tendencies and competitive collusion, were essentially friendly partners in promoting economic progress.

But managers inside firms had found the problems of the era very complex, challenging, and demanding. Outside the firm, the manager had to fight constantly for market share, anticipate customers' needs, provide timely delivery, produce superior products, price them competitively, and assure the retention of customer loyalty. Internally, he had to struggle constantly for increased productivity through better planning, more efficient organization of work, and automation of production. Continually, he had to contend with union demands and still maintain the level of productivity, retain his competitive position on the market, pay confidence-inspiring dividends to stockholders, and generate sufficient retained earnings to meet the company's growth needs.

Thus, it was natural for busy managers to treat the early Post-industrial signs in much the same way they had treated periodic economic recessions. Inflation, growing governmental constraints, dissatisfaction of consumers, invasion by foreign competitors, technological breakthroughs, changing work attitudes—each of these changes was at first treated as a distraction from "the business of business," to be weathered and overcome within a basically sound preoccupation with commercial marketing and operations.

Just as in the earlier shift from production to the marketing orientation, the shift to a Post-industrial orientation is still unrecognized or resisted in many firms, because it introduces new uncertainties, threatens a loss of power, and requires new perceptions and new skills. The resistance to change frequently leads to a gap between the behavior of a firm and the imperatives of the environment. The firm continues to focus on marketing and disregards the technological and political changes, continues to rely on past precedents when experience is no longer a reliable guide to the future. Managerial attitudes are well summed up by a popular French saying: "plus ca change, plus c'est la même chose."[1]

---

[1] The more it changes, the more it is the same.

But it is not the "même chose." The underlying cause of the new change is society's arrival at a new level of economic affluence. The Mass-production Era was a drive to meet the basic physical comfort and safety needs of the population. The Mass-marketing Era lifted the aspirations from comfort and safety to a drive for affluence. The Post-industrial Era is the arrival of affluence.

Satisfaction of survival needs and growth in discretionary buying power change consumer demand patterns. Industries that served the basic needs in the Industrial Era reach saturation. These industries do not necessarily decline, but their growth slows down. New industries emerge that cater to the affluent consumer—luxury goods, recreation, travel, services, etc.

Technology fundamentally affects both supply and demand. Massive wartime investment in research and development spawns new technology-based industries on the one hand, and brings about obsolescence in others. Internal to the firm, fueled by technological progress, the "R&D Monster" acquires a dynamic of its own, which spawns unasked-for products, increases the technological intensity of the firm, and directs the firm's growth thrusts independently and sometimes in spite of the aspirations of the management.

The arrival of affluence casts doubt on economic growth as the main instrument of social progress. Social aspirations shift away from "quantity" to "quality" of life. Industrial bigness increasingly appears as a threat both to economic efficiency through monopolistic practices, and to democracy through "government-industrial" complexes. Large enterprises are challenged on their immoral "profiteering" tendencies, lack of creativity, and their failure to enhance efficiency while increasing size. Acquisition of other firms is challenged because it is seen to destroy competition. Studies are prepared for dismemberment of giant firms. The growth ethic, which had provided a clear guiding light to social behavior, begins to decline. "Zero growth" alternatives are advanced, but without a clear understanding of how social vitality is to be retained when growth stops.

Realignment of social priorities focuses attention on the negative side-effects of profit-seeking behavior: environmental pollution, fluctuations in economic activity, inflation, monopolistic practices, "manipulation" of the consumer through artificial obsolescence, blatant advertising, incomplete disclosure, and low-quality after-sale service. All these effects begin to appear to be too high a price to pay for the laissez-faire conditions of "free enterprise."

The firm is now assumed to be able not only to maintain affluence under stringent constraints (which only twenty years ago would have been considered fundamentally subversive and socially destructive), but also to undertake "social responsibility." Thus, one of the consequences of affluence is the loss of social centrality for the institution that created it.

Having "filled their bellies," individuals begin to aspire to higher levels of personal satisfaction both in their buying and in their working behavior. They become increasingly discriminating—increasingly demanding "full disclosure" about their purchases, demanding "post-sales" responsibility from the manufacturer, unwilling to put up with ecological pollution as a by-product. They begin to lose faith in the wisdom of management and its knowledge of "what is good for the country." They challenge the firm directly through "consumerism" and put pressure on government for increased controls.

Within the firm, the traditional solidarity of the managerial class begins to disintegrate. Middle managers begin to reject the role of working for the exclusive benefit of the shareholders. The traditional aspiration of every manager to become the president of the firm is not shared by the new generation, which wants the firm to become more socially responsive, and to offer opportunities for individual self-fulfillment on the job. Thus managers begin with the interest of technocracy rather than with those of the top management, or the shareholders.

As another result of affluence, developed nations turn their attention to social problems that remained unsolved while the focus was on economic growth: social justice, poverty, housing, education, public transportation, environmental pollution, and ecological imbalance. The private sector is now called upon to perform a twofold role: (1) to restrain and remove its problem-causing activities (such as pollution), and (2) to take responsibility for positive social progress.

New demands for social services create potential new markets, but they are not easy to serve because they have remained previously unattended precisely because they were inherently unprofitable.

Thus, socio-political transactions with the environment which lay dormant during the Industrial Era acquire a life-or-death importance to the firm. They become important as a source of information and opportunities for new commercial activities, as a source of new social expectations from the firm, and as a source threatening constraints on the commercial activity.

At first glance, the turbulence in the Post-industrial environment may appear as a return to days of the Industrial Revolution. But today's turbulence is much more complex. In the earlier era, creation of marketable products and of the markets was the major concern of the entrepreneurs. They dreamed grandly and had the genius and the energy to convert dreams into reality. But their priorities were almost wholly entrepreneurial. Having created the business sector, they often lacked the motivation and the capability to settle for the job of competitive exploitation of their creations. Other managers, no less talented but less visionary and more pragmatic, replaced them and began to elaborate and perfect the production mechanism of the firm and to realize growth and profit. Later, marketeers injected new vitality in the environment.

Thus, the industrial environment up to the 1950s was a "sequential" one. In succeeding periods the key to success shifted; managerial preoccupation with the previous priority also shifted to the next one.

But in the 1970s, the new priorities do not replace, but rather, add to the previous ones. Competition is not slackening, but intensifying as a result of internationalization of business, scarcities of resources, and acceleration of technological innovation. Production and distribution problems are growing bigger and more complex. And to these are added concerns with technological breakthroughs, with obsolescence, with structural changes in the economy and in the market, and in the firm's relations to government and society. Thus, entrepreneurial concerns come on top of, and not in exchange for, the historical preoccupation with competition and production.

To summarize briefly, during the past twenty years, a major escalation of environmental turbulence has taken place. For the firm it has meant a change from a familiar world of marketing and production to an unfamiliar world of strange technologies, strange competitors, new consumer attitudes, new dimensions of social control and, above all, a questioning of the firm's role in society.

PATTERNS IN COMPLEXITY

In the preceding sections we have explored, in a discursive fashion, the complex and multifaceted nature of the changing business environment. In this section we identify several regular patterns in the flow of change.

One such pattern is shown in Exhibit 1, which presents a historical perspective of the challenges to the firm, along four dimensions, shown at the left of the exhibit. The upper two are the historically important commercial dimensions, and the lower two are the newly important socio-political dimensions.

As Exhibit 1 shows, prior to the 1950s the socio-political environment of the firm was quiescent, and the commercial challenges were focused on exploiting the firm's historical market position.

Between 1950 and 1970 the focus began to shift to regeneration of growth potential for the reasons listed in the Exhibit. It is during this period that the problem of strategy was recognized and formulated by a number of business firms.

The solution developed by these firms, which became known as *strategic planning*, was an essentially optimistic one. Confronted, on the one hand, with saturation of growth in their historical industries, and, on the other hand, with new technologies and new growth fields, firms sought to revitalize their historical growth and to diversify into new industries. The optimism of this approach rested on two assumptions. The first was that the initiative in the interaction with the environment belonged to the firm, and that the firm was the master of its own destiny. The second assumption was that the environment was predictable enough to enable the firm to plan its response to change in advance of the event.

These assumptions were consistent with the experience of the previous fifty years of the century. But the right-hand column of the Exhibit shows the historical experience no longer applies. The firm is rapidly losing much of its control over the environment. Part of this loss is caused by the increasingly stringent controls and regulations. Another part is due to the new interconnectedness and complexity of environment which make it increasingly difficult for the firm to foresee conse-

Exhibit 1 *Environmental Changes in a Historical Perspective*

Dimensions of challenge	1900	1930	1950	1970	1990
Products-Markets-Technology	–Basic demand	–Differentiated demand –Product-line expansion –Market expansion –Incremental evolution of technology		–Saturation of demand –Technological turbulence –Multinational markets –Government markets –Leisure markets –Technology created industries	–Loss of control over environment –Socio-political impact on market behavior –Strategic surprises –Constraints on growth –Constraints on resources –Socialist markets –Developing country markets
Geographic perspective	–Nation-state	–Developed nations			–Socialist and third world
Internal environment	–"Honest day's work for fair day's pay"	–Enrichment of work –Local participation			–Redesign of work –Participation in strategic decision
	–Management by authority	–Management by consensus			–Management by conflict
External socio-political environment	–Laissez faire	–Loss of social immunity –Consumerism –Pressures for social responsibility –Reaction to "pollution" –Reaction to business power			–New ideological raison d'être: –Socialism –Neocapitalism

quences of its own action, and also to anticipate key events and initiatives by others. Increasingly, positive growth strategies of the firm must be accompanied, and sometimes superseded by defensive *survival strategies* which guard the firm against environmental controls and surprises.

As the lower part of the right-hand column shows, the 1970s also extended the firm's strategic concern beyond its product/technology interface with the markets. The new concerns are with the design of the internal environment of the firm, with assuming a new set of responsibilities with respect to the environment, and with establishing a new basis of social legitimacy for the firm. In response to these concerns, concepts of *capability strategy*, of *social responsibility strategy*, and of *political strategy* have begun to emerge.

Another historical pattern is illustrated in Exhibit 2, which shows managerial responses to the challenges of Exhibit 1. The transition from the production orientation of the first thirty years of the century to the subsequent marketing orientation was accompanied by a shift of managerial focus from efficiency of internal operations to effective marketing in the environment. After the 1950s the pendulum began to swing back to center, to sharing of managerial attention between internal and external preoccupations.

But as the lower part of Exhibit 2 shows, the complexity of the new internal and external concerns is now higher than ever. From concerns with effective marketing, the external concerns have expanded to product innovation, multinational expansion, and diversification into new industries. From a focus on efficient mass production, the internal concerns are shifting to redesign of work, to providing for needs and aspirations of the human beings, and to managing the firm as a political (rather than consensual) environment.

Within the perspective of Exhibits 1 and 2, the original concept of product/market strategy appears as only one component of a much broader concept. We might call it *enterprise strategy*, which is needed to integrate and relate the new dimensions of the strategic problems.

A third historical pattern is illustrated in Exhibits 3 and 4 where the evolution of strategies which firms used in their response to changing turbulence is shown. Exhibit 3 shows the *competitive strategies* which firms have used to gain success in the market place. It is to be noted that the

progression from left to right was not one of replacement, but of proliferation. Today all of the strategies in Exhibit 3 can be found in use.

Exhibit 4 shows the evolution of the entrepreneurial strategies—the product/market/technology configuration of the firm. Again the process has been one of proliferation and most of the strategies shown can be found in practice today.

The erosion of the earlier optimistic assumption of predictability of the environment is illustrated in Exhibit 5, which shows the historical trend of predictability. The Exhibit shows that there is a growing incidence of events which are novel to the firm (e.g., petroleum scarcity, stagflation, disappearance of the work ethic, etc. etc.), which cannot be predicted in terms specific enough and far enough in advance to permit deliberate "set piece" response through periodic organization-wide strategic planning.

Exhibit 6 presents yet another pattern. This is the evolution of formal management systems which firms developed over the years to help them cope with problems of increasing complexity. (The names of most of the systems up to the 1970s will be familiar to the reader.)

The three horizontal lines in Exhibit 6 represent important barriers in the historical development of systems. The first barrier, crossed early in this century, was a transition from a historical backward-looking to a future-oriented, forward-looking perspective. The series of forward-looking systems that followed this crossing shared an underlying assumption about the environment. This was that the basic structure of the environment remained unchanged and that the variables and the models which adequately explained the past were usable for prediction of the future. In this sense of the word, all of these systems were *extrapolative.*

The second barrier was crossed when past models became inadequate for prediction. The succeeding management systems, such as strategic planning, attempt to analyze the new variables and new relationships which will determine both future demand and the future performance.

The third barrier is presently being crossed in response to the progressive loss of predictability. New systems are emerging which permit the firm to respond rapidly with developing events and to surprises. As such systems emerge, the traditional distinction between systems and structure will dis-

Exhibit 2 *Evolution of Managerial Response*

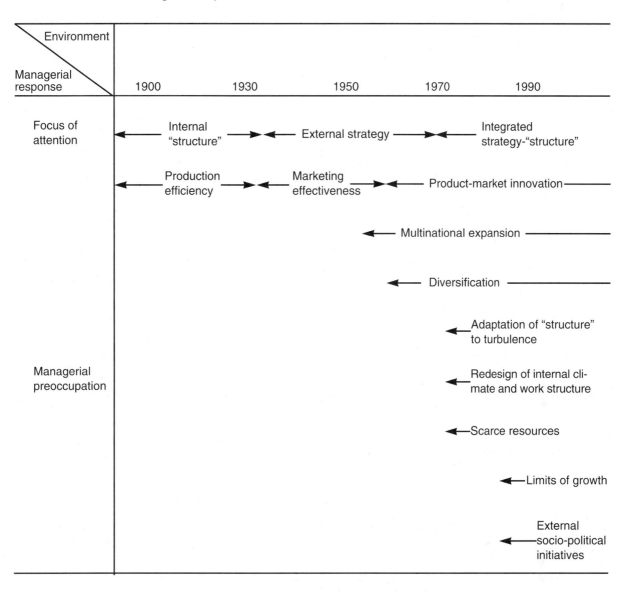

Exhibit 3 *Evolution of Competitive Strategy*

1900	1930	1950	1970

Price competition

    Market share

           Product differentiation

              Artificial obsolescence

                    Consumer manipulation

                        Affluence and leisure

                            Truth in advertising

                              Ecological benefits

                              Resource
                                conservation

Exhibit 4 *Evolution of Entrepreneurial Strategies*

1900	1930	1950	1970	1990

Product rationalization

  Backward integration

    National expansion

        Rounding of product line

         Technological evolution

           Annual model change

             Diversification

             Multinational expansion

            Technology substitution

                Forward integration

                Life-cycle balance

                  Vulnerability balance

                  Third-world expansion

                    Resource invulnerability

                  Recycling

                  Surprise preparedness

Exhibit 5 *Decreasing Predictability of the Future*

Characteristic	1900	1930	1950	1970	1990
Familiarity of events	← Familiar →	← Extrapolation of experience →	←	Discontinuous but related to experience →	← Discontinuous and novel
Rapidity of change	← Slower than firm's response →	Comparable to firm's response →	← Shorter than firm's response		
Visibility of future	← Recurring →	← Forecastable by extrapolation →	←	Predictable threats and opportunities →	← Partially predictable — weak signals
					← Unpredictable surprises

Exhibit 6 *Evolution of Management Systems*

Environment	1900	1930	1950	1970	1990
Recurring	• Systems and procedures manuals	• Financial control			
Forecastable by extrapolation		• Short-term budgeting	• Capital budgeting • Management by objectives • Long-range planning		
Predictable threats and opportunities				• Periodic strategic planning • Periodic strategic management	
Partially predictable "weak signals"				• Issue analysis • Real time strategic management	
Unpredictable surprises				• Surprise management	

appear, and *preparedness* strategies (which deal with flexible configurations of resources) will replace the historical *action strategies* (which deal with selection of an action response).

EVOLUTION OF THE STRATEGIC PROBLEM

The previous discussion can be summarized by tracing the evolution of the strategic problem from the middle of this century until the present. As Exhibit 7 illustrates, this evolution has been rapid. The problem confronting the firm today is much more complex and richer in content than it was in the 1950s. As Exhibit 8 illustrates, the prospects are for a further increase in complexity. (In both figures the word "strategy" is used in a general sense to mean a "solution-guiding heuristic.")

As Exhibit 7 shows, the strategic problem of the 1950s was to decide "what business are we in?" This meant finding a profit-producing match between the products/technology of the firm and the needs of the market. Internal capabilities of the firm were seen as important, but essentially invariant characteristics in this process. The idea was to find a strategy which took advantage of the strengths of the firm and avoided its weaknesses. This reflected the optimism about the environment which was discussed earlier. The firm perceived itself as the center of a Ptolemean universe which it could understand and control. As the sketch at the top of Exhibit 7 shows, changes in strategy generated needs for changes in capabilities, but these were largely increases in size of the firm, such as the need for additional capacity, capital, personnel, etc., rather than changes in the basic configuration of the firm.

Exhibit 7 also shows that resources needed from the external environment were viewed as derivative from strategy; and resource availability was seen as unlimited. This perception was well captured in a contemporary business phrase, "We'll find the money for any right opportunity that comes along."

The second sketch in Exhibit 7 shows that capability is becoming a major concern by the 1970s. Many firms have difficulties in finding attractive growth opportunities which match their strengths and weaknesses. Other firms find that new strategies do not work until the "structure" (managerial skills, rewards, structure, systems, and organiza-

tional values and information) was adjusted to support the new strategy. A new understanding of this "strategy-structure" relationship was provided by Chandler (1962) in his classic book, *Strategy and Structure.* This new perception was that transformation of the internal configuration and capabilities was just as much a part of the strategic problem as finding a new viable product/market strategy for the firm. When a firm enters "a new kind of business" it cannot succeed unless it develops an appropriate "new kind of capability." Further, the new perception is that "structure" need not follow strategy; frequently, the reverse sequence is preferable.

In the mid-1970s another major dimension of complexity surfaces in the strategic problem. This is the increasingly frequent scarcity of strategic resources. Although the particular manifestations come from different directions, such as cost of petroleum, cost of money, or shortage of non-ferrous metals, the underlying phenomenon is a strategic resource scarcity.

Resource scarcity makes it necessary to plan not only the "front" interface with the market but also the "rear" interface with the sources of supply. It also makes problematic the traditional flow of strategic planning from opportunities to the resources. For firms which are severely resource-constrained the reverse flow of planning has become a two-way feedback process in which the "front" and the "rear" strategies must be reconciled.

The lower sketch in Exhibit 7 demonstrates the state of the strategic problem which is already a reality in Europe, and which is expected by leading US managers to become an American reality in the 1980s. It reflects the increasing importance of the socio-political variables in the life of the firm. As the preceding discussion has indicated, two new important dimensions of strategy are added. One is the *strategy* of socio-political relations with the society outside the firm, and the other is the strategy for structuring and managing the internal work within the firm. Both introduce power structure and power dynamics as key determinants of strategic behavior.

Exhibit 8 suggests the "ultimate" shape of the strategic problem which includes all of the key variables which have been discussed in the preceding pages. Two new problems are added to the preceding stage. One, shown in the upper left part, is acceleration of change to a point which makes the "conventional" concept of strategy inapplica-

Exhibit 7 *Evolution of Strategic Problem*

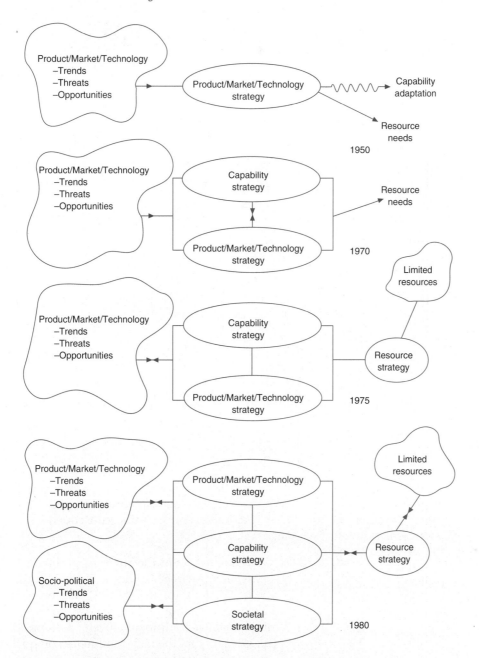

Exhibit 8 *The "Ultimate" Strategic Problem*

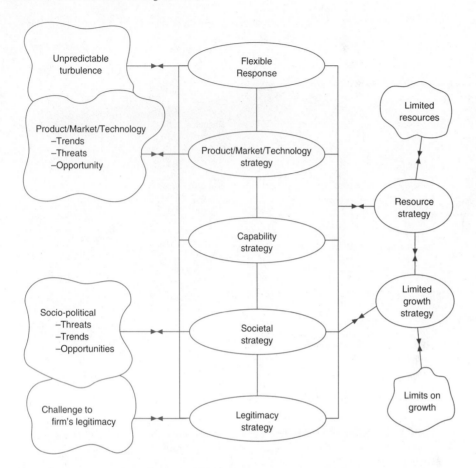

ble in situations in which the speed of change is greater than the speed of strategic response, or, to put this differently, the environment is not sufficiently predictable to permit timely action strategy formulation.

The other new problem is likely to come from society's refusal to continue accepting the historical unlimited "growth ethic" as a legitimate mode of business behavior.

IMPLICATIONS FOR RESEARCH

The general implication from the preceding discussion is that researchers seeking to understand the current and emerging strategic challenges will need to deal with a problem which contains many more variables and has a much more complex structure and dynamics than the problems of the 1950s. Each reader can interpret this general impli-

cation for consequences for his own focus of interest. Below several of these consequences are suggested:

1. Whatever aspect of the strategic problems he treats, the researcher needs to check its validity in the light of the 1970s–1980s problem scope. For example, research on goals and objectives has traditionally been based on the assumption that the major influences on goals were to be found within the firm ("control of its own destiny" hypothesis). The 1970–1980s perception suggests that the goals *and* objectives are going to be increasingly influenced by extra-firm influences. Research on goals also has traditionally been based on the assumption of ideological uniformity within the firm. But already, in Europe, the powerful internal constituencies are ideologically polar-

ized, and differences of ideology and realities of power must be taken into account.

2. Much of the research on strategy has focused on logically rational strategic decision-making. The implied hypothesis was that reasonable decisions will induce reasonable compliant response. The introduction of socio-political variables challenges this assumption. As a result, separation of strategic decision-making from strategic implementation becomes artificial. For understanding of strategy we need to shift the focus from the problem of *strategy formulation* to the level of *strategic response* as evidenced by behavior in the environment.

3. The historical preoccupation with product/market/technology strategies must be broadened to include the other types of "strategy" shown in Exhibits 7 and 8. Their unique nature needs to be understood, and they must be related to each other. This means the traditional model built on the assumption of one critical contact point with the environment must be enlarged to handle multiple and distinctive critical contact points. The traditional conception of strategy as one level heuristic problem must be expanded to allow multilevel strategies, hierarchically related to one another.

4. Finally, practically all of literature has focused on strategies of action in the external environment. Concepts of "strategy of structure" now need to be developed.

In recent years, unlike many other fields of inquiry into management, the strategic problem has been unique as a "problem that wouldn't stand still." On the one hand, this has greatly complicated the problems of the researcher and placed him in danger of providing obsolete understanding and obsolete solutions. On the other hand, the rapid change in the shape of the problem gives the researcher an opportunity to develop insights which are new and current to managers, instead of providing a stream of refinements on solutions to well-understood problems, as is done in much of the management science literature.

Exhibit 9 *Generalized Contributor Group Interaction between the Firm and Its Environment*

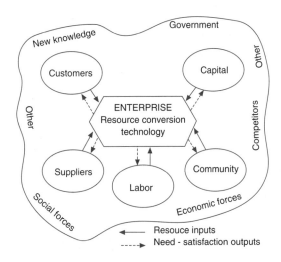

WHY SOME FACTORIES ARE MORE PRODUCTIVE THAN OTHERS

Robert H. Hayes and Kim B. Clark
Harvard University

The battle for attention is over. The time for banging drums is long past. Everyone now understands that manufacturing provides an essential source of competitive leverage. No longer does anyone seriously think that domestic producers can outdo their competitors by clever marketing only—"selling the sizzle" while cheating on quality or letting deliveries slip. It is now time for concrete action on a practical level: action to change facilities, update processing technologies, adjust work-force practices, and perfect information and management systems.

But when managers turn to these tasks, they quickly run up against a stumbling block. Namely, they do not have adequate measures for judging factory-level performance or for comparing overall performance from one facility to the next. Of course, they can use the traditional cost-accounting figures, but these figures often do not tell them what they really need to know. Worse, even the best numbers do not sufficiently reflect the important contributions that managers can make by reducing confusion in the system and promoting organizational learning.

Consider the experience of a US auto manufacturer that discovered itself with a big cost disadvantage. The company put together a group to study its principal competitor's manufacturing operations. The study generated reams of data, but the senior executive in charge of the activity still felt uneasy. He feared that the group was getting mired in details and that things other than managerial practices—like the age of facilities and their location—might be the primary drivers of performance. How to tell?

Similarly, a vice president of manufacturing for a specialty chemical producer had misgivings about the emphasis his company's system for evaluating plant managers placed on variances from standard costs. Differences in these standards made comparisons across plants difficult. What was more troubling, the system did not easily capture the trade-offs among factors of production or consider the role played by capital equipment or materials. What to do?

Another manufacturer—this time of paper products—found quite different patterns of learning in the same departments of five of its plants scattered across the United States. Although each department made much the same products using similar equipment and materials, they varied widely in performance over a period of years. Why such differences?

Our point is simple: before managers can pinpoint what's needed to boost manufacturing performance, they must have a reliable way of ascertaining why some factories are more productive than others. They also need a dependable metric for identifying and measuring such differences and a framework for thinking about how to improve their performance—and keep it improving. This is no easy order.

These issues led us to embark on a continuing, multiyear study of 12 factories in 3 companies (see the appendix for details on research methodology). The study's purpose is to clarify the variables that influence productivity growth at the micro level.

The first company we looked at, which employs a highly connected and automated manufacturing process, we refer to as the Process Company. Another, which employs a batch approach based on a disconnected line-flow organization of work, we refer to as the Fab (fabrication-assembly) Company. The third, which uses several different batch processes to make components for sophisticated electronic systems, is characterized by very rapid changes in both product and process. We refer to it as the Hi-Tech Company. All five factories of the Process Company and three of the four factories of the Fab Company are in the United States (the fourth is just across the border in Canada). Of the three factories belonging to the Hi-Tech Company, one is in the United States, one in Europe, and one in Asia.

In none of these companies did the usual profit-and-loss statements—or the familiar monthly operating reports—provide adequate, up-to-date information about factory performance. Certainly, managers routinely evaluated such performance, but the metrics they used made their task like that of watching a distant activity through a thick, fogged window. Indeed, the measurement systems in place at many factories obscure and even alter the details of their performance.

A FOGGED WINDOW

Every plant we studied employed a traditional standard cost system: the controller collected and reported data each month on the actual costs incurred during the period for labor, materials, energy, and depreciation, as well as on the costs that would have been incurred had workers and equipment performed at predetermined "standard" levels. The variances from these standard costs became the basis for problem identification and performance evaluation. Other departments in the plants kept track of head counts, work-in-process inventory, engineering changes, the value of newly installed equipment, reject rates, and so forth.

In theory, this kind of measurement system should take a diverse range of activities and summarize them in a way that clarifies what is going on. It should act like a lens that brings a blurry picture into sharp focus. Yet, time and again, we found that these systems often masked critical developments in the factories and, worse, often distorted management's perspective.

Each month, most of the managers we worked with received a blizzard of variance reports but no overall measure of efficiency. Yet this measure is not hard to calculate. In our study, we took the same data generated by plant managers and combined them into a measure of the total factor productivity (TFP)—the ratio of total output to total input (see the appendix for more details on TFP).

This approach helps dissipate some of the fog—especially because our TFP data are presented in constant dollars instead of the usual current dollars. Doing so cuts through the distortions produced by periods of high inflation. Consider the situation at Fab's Plant 1, where from 1974 to 1982 output fluctuated between $45 million and $70 million—in nominal (current dollar) terms. In real terms, however, there was a steep and significant decline in unit output. Several executives initially expressed disbelief at the magnitude of this decline because they had come to think of the plant as a "$50 million plant." Their traditional accounting measures had masked the fundamental changes taking place.

Another advantage of the TFP approach is that it integrates the contributions of all the factors of production into a single measure of total input. Traditional systems offer no such integration. Moreover, they often overlook important factors. One of the plant managers at the Process Company gauged performance in a key department by improvements in labor hours and wage costs. Our data showed that these "improvements" came largely from the substitution of capital for labor. Conscientious efforts to prune labor content by installing equipment—without developing the management skills and systems needed to realize its full potential—proved shortsighted. The plant's TFP (which, remember, takes into account both labor and capital costs) improved very little.

This preoccupation with labor costs, particularly direct labor costs, is quite common—even though direct labor now accounts for less than 15% of total costs in most manufacturing companies. The managers we studied focused heavily on these costs; indeed, their systems for measuring direct labor were generally more detailed and extensive than those for measuring other inputs that were several times more costly. Using sophisticated barcode scanners, Hi-Tech's managers tracked line operators by the minute but had difficulty identifying the number of manufacturing engineers in the same department. Yet these engineers accounted for 20% to 25% of total cost—compared with 5% for line operators.

Just as surprising, the companies we studied paid little attention to the effect of materials consumption or productivity. Early on, we asked managers at one of the Fab plants for data on materials consumed in production during each of a series of months. Using these data to estimate materials productivity gave us highly erratic values.

Investigation showed that this plant, like many others, kept careful records of materials purchased but not of the direct or indirect materials actually consumed in a month. (The latter, which includes things like paper forms, showed up only in a catchall manufacturing overhead account.) Further, most of the factories recorded materials transactions only in dollar, rather than in physical, terms and did not readily adjust their standard costs figures when inflation or substitution altered materials prices.

What managers at Fab plants called "materials consumed" was simply an estimate derived by multiplying a product's standard materials cost—which itself assumes a constant usage of materials—by its unit output and adding an adjustment based on the current variation from standard materials prices. Every year or half-year, managers would reconcile this estimated consumption with actual materials usage, based on a physical count. As a result, data on actual materials consumption in any one period were lost.

Finally, the TFP approach makes clear the difference between the data that managers see and what those data actually measure. In one plant, the controller argued that our numbers on engineering changes were way off base. "We don't have anything like this level of changes," he claimed. "My office signs off on all changes that go through this place, and I can tell you that the number you have here is wrong." After a brief silence, the engineering manager spoke up. He said that the controller reviewed only very large (in dollar terms) engineering changes and that our data were quite accurate. He was right. The plant had been tracking all engineering changes, not just the major changes reported to the controller.

A CLEAR VIEW

With the foglike distortions of poor measurement systems cleared away, we were able to identify the real levers for improving factory performance. Some, of course, were structural—that is, they involve things like plant location or plant size, which lie outside the control of a plant's managers. But a handful of managerial policies and practices consistently turned up as significant. Across industries, companies, and plants, they regularly exerted a powerful influence on productivity. In short, these are the managerial actions that make a difference.

Invest Capital

Our data show unequivocally that capital investment in new equipment is essential to sustaining growth in TFP over a long time (that is, a decade or more). But they also show that capital investment all too often reduces TFP for up to a year. Simply investing money in new technology or systems guarantees nothing. What matters is how their introduction is managed, as well as the extent to which they support and reinforce continual improvement throughout a factory. Managed right, new investment supports cumulative, long-term productivity improvement and process understanding—what we refer to as "learning."

The Process Company committed itself to providing new, internally designed equipment to meet the needs of a rapidly growing product. Over time, as the company's engineers and operating managers gained experience, they made many small changes in product design, machinery, and operating practices. These incremental adjustments added up to major growth in TFP.

Seeking new business, the Fab Company redesigned an established product and purchased the equipment needed to make it. This new equipment was similar to the plant's existing machinery, but its introduction allowed for TFP-enhancing changes in work flows. Plant managers discovered how the new configuration could accommodate expanded production without a proportional increase in the work force. These benefits spilled over: even the older machinery was made to run more efficiently.

In both cases, the real boost in TFP came not just from the equipment itself but also from the opportunities it provided to search for and apply new knowledge to the overall production process. Again, managed right, investment unfreezes old assumptions, generates more efficient concepts and designs for a production system, and expands a factory's skills and capabilities.

Exhibit 1 shows the importance of such learning for long-term TFP growth at one of Fab's plants between 1973 and 1982. TFP rose by 96%. Part of this increase, of course, reflected changes in utilization rates and the introduction of new technology. Even so, roughly two-thirds (65%) of TFP growth was learning-based, and fully three-fourths of that learning effect (or 49% of TFP growth) was related to capital investment. Without capital investment, TFP would have increased, but at a much slower rate.

Such long-term benefits incur costs; in fact, the indirect costs associated with introducing new equipment can be staggering. In Fab's Plant 1, for example, a $1 million investment in new equipment imposed *1.75 million* of additional costs on the plant during its first year of operation! Had the plant cut these indirect costs by half, TFP would have grown an additional 5% during that year.

Everyone knows that putting in new equipment usually causes problems. Everyone expects a temporary drop in efficiency as equipment is installed and workers learn to use it. But managers often underestimate the costly ripple effects of new equipment on inventory, quality, equipment utilization, reject rates, downtime, and material waste. Indeed, these indirect costs often exceed the direct cost of the new equipment and can persist for more than a year after the equipment is installed.

Here, then, is the paradox of capital investment. It is essential to long-term productivity growth, yet in the short run, if poorly managed, it can play havoc with TFP. It is risky indeed for a company to try to "invest its way" out of a productivity problem. Putting in new equipment is just as likely to create confusion and make things worse for a number of months. Unless the investment is made with a commitment to continual learning—and unless performance measures are chosen carefully—the benefits that finally emerge will be small and slow in coming. Still, many companies today are trying to meet their competitive problems by throwing money at them—new equipment and new plants. Our findings suggest that there are other things they ought to do first, things that take less time to show results and are much less expensive.

Reduce Waste

We were not surprised to find a negative correlation between waste rates (or the percentage of rejects) and TFP, but we were amazed by its magnitude. In the Process plants, changes in the waste rate (measured by the ratio of waste material to total cost, expressed as a percentage) led to dramatic operating improvements. As Exhibit 2 shows, reducing the percentage of waste in Plant 4's Department C by only one-tenth led to a 3% improvement in TFP, conservatively estimated.

The strength of this relationship is more surprising when we remember that a decision to boost the production throughput rate (which ought to raise TFP because of the large fixed components in labor and capital costs) also causes waste ratios to increase. In theory, therefore, TFP and waste percent should increase together. The fact that they do not indicates the truly powerful impact that waste reduction has on productivity.

Get WIP Out

The positive effect on TFP of cutting work-in-process (WIP) inventories for a given level of output was much greater than we could explain by reductions in working capital. Exhibit 3 documents the relationship between WIP reductions and TFP in the three companies. Although there are important plant-to-plant variations, all reductions in WIP are associated with increases in TFP. In some plants, the effect is quite powerful; in Department D of Hi-Tech's Plant 1, reducing WIP by one-tenth produced a 9% rise in TFP.

These data support the growing body of empirical evidence about the benefits of reducing WIP. From studies of both Japanese and American companies, we know that cutting WIP leads to faster, more reliable delivery times, lowers reject rates (faster production cycle times reduce inventory obsolescence and make possible rapid feedback when a process starts to misfunction), and cuts overhead costs. We now know it also drives up TFP.

The trouble is, simply pulling work-in-process inventory out of a factory will not, by itself, lead to such improvements. More likely, it will lead to disaster. WIP is there for a reason, usually for many reasons; it is a symptom, not the disease itself. A long-term program for reducing WIP must attack the reasons for its being there in the first place:

Exhibit 1 *Capital Investment, Learning, and Productivity Growth in Fab Company's Plant 2 (1973–1982)*

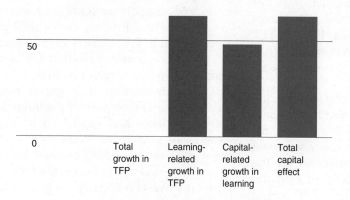

These estimates are based on a regression analysis of TFP growth. We estimated learning-related changes by using both a time trend and cumulative output. The capital-related learning effect represents the difference between the total learning effect and the effect that remained once capital was introduced into the regression. The total capital effect is composed of a learning component and a component reflecting technical advance.

Exhibit 2 *Impact of Waste on TFP in Process Company Plants*

Plant/ Department	Average Waste Rate	Effect on TFP of a 10% Reduction in Waste Rate	Degree of Uncertainty*
1-C	11.2%	+1.2%	.009
2-C	12.4	+1.8	.000
3-C	12.7	+2.0	.000
4-C	9.3	+3.1	.002
5-C	8.2	+0.8	.006

* The probability that waste rate reductions have a zero or negative impact on TFP.

Exhibit 3 *Impact of Work-in-process Reductions on TFP*

Company	Plant/ Department	Effect on TFP of a 10% Reduction in WIP	Degree of Uncertainty*
Hi-Tech	1-A	+1.15%	.238
	1-B	+1.18	.306
	1-C	+3.73	.103
	1-D	+9.11	.003
Process	1-H	+1.63%	.001
	2-H	+4.01	.000
	3-H	+4.65	.000
	4-H	+3.52	.000
	5-H	+3.84	.000
Fab	1	+2.86%	.000
	2	+1.14	.000
	3	+3.59	.002

*The probability that work-in-process reductions have a zero or negative impact on TFP.

erratic process yields, unreliable equipment, long production changeover and set-up times, ever-changing production schedules, and suppliers who do not deliver on time. Without a cure for these deeper problems, a factory's cushion of WIP is often all that stands between it and chaos.

REDUCING CONFUSION

Defective products, mismanaged equipment, and excess work-in-process inventory are not only problems in themselves. They are also sources of confusion. Many things that managers do can confuse or disrupt a factory's operation: erratically varying the rate of production, changing a production schedule at the last minute, overriding the schedule by expediting orders, changing the crews (or the workers on a specific crew) assigned to a given machine, haphazardly adding new products, altering the specifications of an existing product through an engineering change order (ECO), or monkeying with the process itself by adding to or altering the equipment used.

Managers may be tempted to ask, "Doesn't what you call confusion—changing production schedules, expediting orders, shifting work crews, adding or overhauling equipment and changing product specifications—reflect what companies inevitably have to do to respond to changing customer demands and technological opportunities?"

Our answer to this question is an emphatic, No! Responding to new demands and new opportunities requires change, but it does not require the confusion it usually creates. Much of our evidence on confusion comes from factories that belong to the same company and face the same external pressures. Some plant managers are better than others at keeping these pressures at bay. The good ones limit the number of changes introduced at any one time and carefully handle their implementation. Less able managers always seem caught by surprise, operate haphazardly, and leapfrog from one crisis to the next. Much of the confusion in their plants is internally generated.

While confusion is not the same thing as complexity, complexity in a factory's operation usually produces confusion. In general, a factory's mission becomes more complex—and its focus looser—as it becomes larger, as it adds different technologies and products, and as the number and variety of production orders it must accommodate growth. Although the evidence suggests that complexity harms performance, each company's factories were too similar for us to analyze the effects of complexity on TFP. But we could see that what managers did to mitigate or fuel confusion within factories at a given level of complexity had a profound impact on TFP.

Of the sources of confusion we examined, none better illustrated this relationship with TFP than engineering change orders. ECOs require a change in the materials used to make a product, the manufacturing process employed, or the specifications of the product itself. We expected ECOs to lower productivity in the short run but lead to higher TFP over time. Exhibit 4, which presents data on ECO activity in three Fab plants, shows its effects to be sizable. In Plant 2, for example, increasing ECOs by just ten per month reduced TFP by almost 5%. Moreover, the debilitating effects of ECOs persisted for up to a year.

Our data suggest that the average level of ECOs implemented in a given month, as well as the variation in this level, is detrimental to TFP. Many companies would therefore be wise to reduce the number of ECOs to which their plants must respond. This notion suggests, in turn, that more pressure should be placed on engineering and marketing departments to focus attention on only the most important changes—as well as to design things right the first time.

Essential ECOs should be released in a controlled, steady fashion rather than in bunches. In the one plant that divided ECOs into categories reflecting their cost, low-cost ECOs were most harmful to TFP. More expensive ECOs actually had a positive effect. The reason: plant managers usually had warning of major changes and, recognizing that they were potentially disruptive, carefully prepared the ground by warning supervisors, training workers, and bringing in engineers. By contrast, minor ECOs were simply dumped on the factory out of the blue.

Value of Learning

If setting up adequate measures of performance is the first step toward getting full competitive lever-age out of manufacturing, identifying factory-level goals like waste or WIP reduction is the second. But without making a commitment to ongoing learning, a factory will gain no more from these first two steps than a one-time boost in performance. To sustain the leverage of plant-level operations, managers must pay close attention to—and actively plan for—learning.

We are convinced that a factory's learning rate—the rate at which its managers and operators learn to make it run better—is at least of equal importance as its current level of productivity. A factory whose TFP is lower than another's, but whose rate of learning is higher, will eventually surpass the leader. Confusion, as we have seen, is especially harmful to TFP. Thus the two essential tasks of factory management are to create clarity and order (that is, to prevent confusion) and to facilitate learning.

But doesn't learning always involve a good deal of experimentation and confusion? Isn't there an inherent conflict between creating clarity and order and facilitating learning? Not at all.

Confusion, like noise or static in an audio system, makes it hard to pick up the underlying message or figure out the source of the problem. It impedes learning, which requires controlled experimentation, good data, and careful analysis. It chews up time, resources, and energy in efforts to deal with issues whose solution adds little to a factory's performance. Worse, engineers, supervisors, operators, and managers easily become discouraged by the futility of piecemeal efforts. In such environments, TFP lags or falls.

Reducing confusion and enhancing learning do not conflict. They make for a powerful combination—and a powerful lever on competitiveness.

Exhibit 4 *Impact of Engineering Change Orders on TFP in Three Fab Company Plants*

Plant	Mean Level of ECOs per Month	Number of ECOs in Lowest Month	Number of ECOs in Highest Month	Effect on TFP of Increasing Number of ECOs from 5 to 15 per Month
1	16.5	1	41	−2.8%
2	12.2	2	43	−4.6
3	7.0	1	19	−16.6

A factory that manages change poorly, that does not have its processes under control, and that is distracted by the noise in its systems learns too slowly, if at all, or learns the wrong things.

In such a factory, new equipment will only create more confusion, not more productivity. Equally troubling, both managers and workers in such a factory will be slow to believe reports that a sister plant—or a competitor's plant—can do things better than they can. If the evidence is overwhelming, they will simply argue, "It can't work here. We're different." Indeed they are—and less productive too.

'Where the Money Is'

Many companies have tried to solve their data-processing problems by bringing in computers. They soon learned that computerizing a poorly organized and error-ridden information system simply creates more problems: garbage in, garbage out. That lesson, learned so long ago, has been largely forgotten by today's managers, who are trying to improve manufacturing performance by bringing in sophisticated new equipment without first reducing the complexity and confusion of their operations.

Spending big money on hardware fixes will not help if managers have not taken the time to simplify and clarify their factories' operations, eliminate sources of error and confusion, and boost the rate of learning. Of course, advanced technology is important, often essential. But there are many things that managers must do first to prepare their organizations for these new technologies.

When plant managers are stuck with poor measures of how they are doing and when a rigid, by-the-book emphasis on standards, budgets, and exception reports discourages the kind of experimentation that leads to learning, the real levers on factory performance remain hidden. No amount of capital investment can buy heightened competitiveness. There is no way around the importance of building clarity into the system, eliminating unnecessary disruptions and distractions, ensuring careful process control, and nurturing in-depth technical competence. The reason for understanding why some factories perform better than others is the same reason that Willie Sutton robbed banks: "That's where the money is."

APPENDIX: RESEARCH METHODS

There are three basic approaches for identifying the effects of management actions and policies on factory-level productivity: first, a longitudinal analysis, which looks at a single factory over a long time; second, a cross-sectional analysis, which compares the performance (at the same time) of two or more factories that make similar products and have similar manufacturing processes; and third, a combined approach, which collects several years' worth of data for factories having a variety of structural characteristics and uses statistical analysis to identify the effects of what managers do. We have used all three methods.

For each factory, we gathered data on a monthly basis for at least one-and-a-half years and usually for more than five. In several cases, we were able to track performance over a nine-year period; in more than half the cases, our data go back to the factory's start-up. To our knowledge, this is the first attempt to explore in such depth the sources of productivity growth at the factory level in the United States, and our data base is the most comprehensive yet compiled.

We developed our central performance measure, total factor productivity, by first calculating each factory's monthly partial factor productivities—that is, by dividing its output in turn by labor, materials, capital, and energy (for both outputs and inputs, we used 1982 dollars to eliminate the impact of inflation). To calculate a factory's total monthly output, we multiplied the quantity of each of the products it made in any month by that product's 1982 standard cost. To estimate labor input, we relied on total hours of work in each major employee classification (direct labor, indirect labor, and so forth); to estimate capital input, we used the book value of assets adjusted for inflation; and to estimate materials input, we deflated the dollar values of materials consumption by a materials price index based on 1982 dollars.

We then combined these partial measures into an index of overall total factor productivity (TFP). Because of the large fixed component in capital as well as labor cost, each factory's TFP is quite sensitive to changes in production volume and to the timing of major capital investments. To separate the movements in TFP linked to changes in production capacity from those linked to changes in operating efficiency, we included an estimate of capacity utilization in all regression analyses.

Exhibit 5 shows the quite different productivity experience at the Process Company's five plants. Hi-Tech's plants enjoyed rapid growth in output and productivity, but some of the Process and Fab plants had declining productivity and (in one case) declining output. All the Hi-Tech plants learned at a very high rate, although productivity growth in the early months was anything but fast or smooth, and some plants seemed to learn faster than others. Moderate growth and learning characterized the Fab Company's plants 2, 3, and 4; at Plant 1, however, volume declined, and TFP growth was flat or negative during much of the time we studied it.

This disparity in performance is not limited to comparisons across companies. Even within a company, productivity growth differed significantly across plants—even where each produced identical products and faced the same market and technological conditions. We cannot explain these differences by reference to technology, product variety, or market demands—they have to do with management.

Once we developed the data on TFP, we discussed each factory's results with its management. Some of the anomalies we found resulted from errors in the data provided us; others were caused by certain events (the advent of the deer-hunting season, for example, or a year-end peak in purchased materials). We made no attempt to relate monthly TFP figures to managerial variables until each factory's managers understood our method of calculating TFP and agreed that the patterns we found fairly represented their factory's behavior.

After developing credible TFP estimates, we had to identify and measure those managerial policies that might have an impact on TFP. Exhibit 6 lists these policies and describes the measures we used to capture them.

Using multiple linear regression analysis, we first examined the effect of these policy variables on TFP in the same factory over time. Early findings, coupled with discussions with a number of managers, suggested that the simple ratios and averages we were using did not adequately capture the phenomena we were trying to understand. Actions like overhauling older equipment, training workers, and implementing an engineering change order are similar in nature to investments—that is, they will likely cause short-term inefficiencies. To test the long-term effects of such actions, we included lagged variables, which allowed us to estimate the effect on TFP of management actions taken in previous months.

Other management activities may have little effect on productivity unless they are held at a certain level for several months. Boosting the amount spent on maintaining equipment, for example, does not do much if sustained for only one month. In these cases, we looked at the relationship between TFP and a five-month moving average of relevant management variables.

For still other activities—a profound change, say, in production rates—it matters greatly if the change is highly unusual or is part of a pattern of widely fluctuating rates. For each of these variables, we examined the relationship between TFP and the variable's average absolute deviation (using the five-month moving average as the estimated mean value for the variable).

A last, brief note about the importance of combining statistical analysis with ongoing field research. We found immense value in discussing our findings with the managers involved. We expected, for example, that equipment maintenance and workforce training would share a positive relationship to productivity growth. Our plant data, however, revealed a consistently negative relationship: high expenditures on maintenance and training, even in lagged forms, generally were associated with *low* TFP. When we talked about this with plant managers in all three companies, we discovered that they used maintenance and training as *corrective* measures. That is, they boosted maintenance in response to equipment problems; when the problems were solved, they reduced it. By themselves, the data would not allow us to separate corrective from preventive maintenance, or even from the costs of modifying or rebuilding equipment.

Exhibit 5 *Productivity at Process Company Plants*

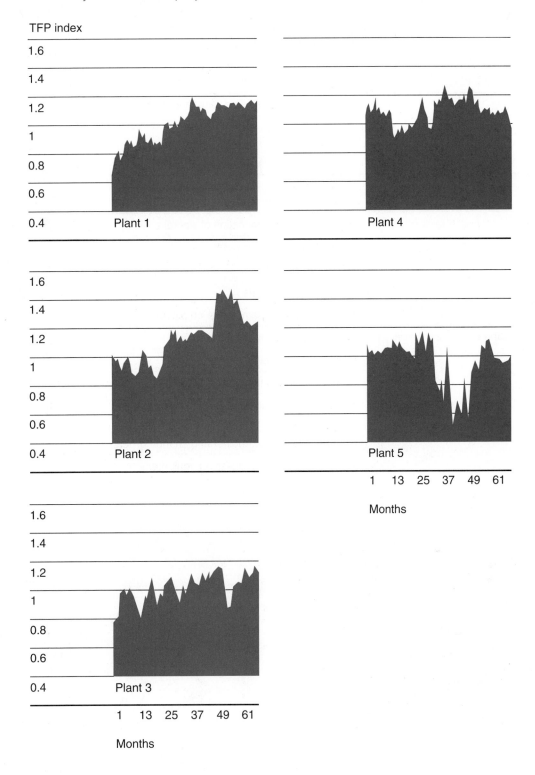

Exhibit 6 *Managerial Policies*

Policy Category	Indicators
Equipment	Average age of equipment
	Average maintenance expense as a percentage of equipment book value
Quality	Process waste; yield as a percentage of total input materials
	Intermediate and final reject rates
	Customer return rates
Inventory	Work-in-process as a percentage of total materials or production cost
Work force	Average age and education of workers
	Hours of overtime per week
	Absenteeism rate
	Hiring and layoff rates
	Average hours of training per employee
Policies affecting confusion	Fluctuations in production volume
	Number of product types produced
	Number of production orders scheduled
	Number of schedule changes as a percentage of number of production orders scheduled
	Number and type of engineering change orders
	Introduction of new processing equipment

GENERIC STRATEGIES: TOWARD A COMPREHENSIVE FRAMEWORK

Henry Mintzberg
McGill University

INTRODUCTION

Almost every serious author on the "content" side of the strategic management field (what we prefer to call the "positioning school"), not to mention strategy consulting "boutique," has his, her, or its own list of strategies commonly pursued by different organizations. The problem is that these lists almost always either focus narrowly on special types of strategies or else aggregate arbitrarily across all varieties of them. It is as if the proverbial apples and oranges were either reduced to Valencia, Jaffa, and Delicious, or else enlarged to include pumpkins, baseballs, and elephants. Thus, on one hand we have the strategies of build, hold, harvest and withdraw associated with the Boston Consulting Group's growth share matrix, and on the other hand the following list from the Arthur D. Little Company (as reported by Hax and Majluf, 1984:23):

Backward Integration
Development of Overseas Business
Development of Overseas Facilities
Distribution Rationalization
Excess Capacity
Export/Same Product
Forward Integration
Hesitation
Initial Market Development
Licensing Abroad
Complete Rationalization
Market Penetration
Market Rationalization
Methods and Functions Efficiency

New Products/New Markets
New Products/Same Market
Production Rationalization
Product Line Rationalization
Pure Survival
Same Products/New Markets
Same Products/Same Markets
Technological Efficiency
Traditional Cost Cutting Efficiency
Unit Abandonment

In 1965, Igor Ansoff (p. 109) proposed a matrix of four strategies (in fact first presented by Johnson and Jones, 1957) that became quite well known, as follows:

	Present Product	New Product
Existing Mission	Market Penetration	Product Development
New Mission	Market Development	Diversification

But this was hardly comprehensive. Fifteen years later, Michael Porter (1980) introduced what became the best-known list of "generic strategies": cost leadership, differentiation, and focus. But the Porter list covered only business-level strategies, and even there can be regarded as incomplete (as we shall argue later). Indeed, it is interesting to note that while Ansoff focused on *extensions* of business strategy, Porter, fifteen years later, focused on *identifying* business strategy in the first place. In fact, elsewhere in his 1980 book Porter did discuss what to Ansoff were strategies of extension, but he labeled these "strategic decisions" and explicitly precluded them from being considered strategies. As he noted in his 1985 book, ". . . acquisition and vertical integration are not strategies but means of achieving them" (p. 25). Even "build, hold, and harvest are the results of a generic strategy, or recognition of the inability to achieve any generic strategy" (p. 25) To Porter, "the centerpiece of a firm's strategic plan should be its generic strategy" (p. 25), namely one of his three.

To us, however, such distinctions seem arbitrary, the result of presuming some a priori hierarchy, that certain "strategies" are inevitably more important than others. In fact, Richard Caves, who supervised Porter's doctoral thesis, took a position similar to ours (and in so doing labeled Porter's "strategic decisions" as "strategies"):

> The standard of taxonomy of corporate strategies has proved fruitful, but is certainly incomplete. For instance, the alternative strategies available to firms directly competing in a given market often seem to differ in many ways other than the extent of their diversification and vertical integration. We must determine what other families of strategic choices are widely represented in industrial markets, what conditions lead firms to select them, and what consequences they hold for firms' organization and market behavior. (1980:89)

In this paper, we seek to delineate in an orderly fashion the "families" of strategies widely represented in organizations in general. In other words, we wish to develop a comprehensive typology, a single logical framework, of generic strategies. We wish to draw on all the lists, where appropriate, but only for possible candidates which we wish to incorporate into one comprehensive framework.

Many popular lists of strategies distinguish corporate from business level strategies, the former concerned with identifying the core mission(s) or business(es) of the organization in the first place, the latter with how each of these is pursued. Functional-level strategies, in marketing, purchasing, manufacturing, etc. are sometimes also identified below business level strategies. We believe this breakdown is far too limited. There is a need to distinguish within so-called corporate strategies the identification of a core business in the first place from the extension of that core business to other businesses, related and unrelated. Furthermore, we believe that business strategies need to be divided into those that describe the core business and those that elaborate the core business. Moreover, we believe that there is the need for a category of strategies that seeks to reconceive the organization's business or overall portfolio of businesses (in effect, perceiving a corporate strategy in business strategy terms).[1] We shall therefore focus on five levels of the content of strategy, making generous use of graphics in their presentation:

A. First we shall consider *locating* the core business, which will be shown as a single node— one circle—in a matrix of circles. (Note that we use the word "business" as a substitute for "mission": the framework is not meant to exclude non-profit organizations.)

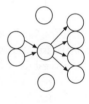

B. Second, we shall consider *distinguishing* the core business, by looking inside that circle.

C. Third, we shall take up *elaborating* the core business, considering how the circle may be enlarged or developed in various ways.

D. Fourth, we shall consider *extending* the core business, leading the circle to link up with other circles (other businesses).

---

[1]There is also a need to distinguish so-called "institutional" or "collective" strategies (we prefer the label "political"), but we shall restrict our discussion here to strategies of a competitive nature.

E. Fifth, we shall consider *recon-ceiving* the (core) business(es), in effect changing or combining the circles.[2]

In keeping with the spirit of the positioning school, we present these five as a logical hierarchy.[3] We do not believe this is necessarily the way strategies develop in organizations, however, and shall present evidence elsewhere on how various strategies can drive others. But there is a certain logic to this flow, at the very least for purposes of exposition as well as for maintaining a link with the traditional literature.

Before proceeding with our discussion of the content of strategy, we wish to provide a list of what appear to be their most common characteristics. Each strategy can be pursued more or less comprehensively, more or less quickly, more or less uniquely, and just plain more or less, among other characteristics. The list that appears in Table 1 was developed by combining strategy characteristics that can be found in various places in the literature. It is separated into conditions that concern stability and those that deal with strategic change. Sometimes these characteristics are presented as content strategies, as in the example of the "low growth" strategies of "no change" or "retreat" in Christensen et al. (1987:124) "No change" from what? "Retreat" from what? are the natural questions. We believe this only confuses a sufficiently confusing subject, and so have tried to be careful not to mix characteristics and content of strategies (although, we will be clear, some of the content strategies are inextricably linked with particular characteristics).

A Note on the Label "Generic"

While many authors use the label "generic" with respect to any common identifiable strategy, Porter reserves it for overall strategies, in effect, integrated clusters of strategies rather than single ones. For example, he describes a whole set of specific strategies under the heading of "cost leadership." Thus, our use of the label in the former sense—for individual strategies—may cause some confusion, especially given the popularity of Porter's work. We do so, however, in the firm belief that this is where the label belongs—at the most basic level of disaggregation.

In fact, in doing this, we may not even be violating the effect (if not the intention) of Porter's work, since his own "generic strategies" are identified not as aggregates per se, but by the leading strategy in the cluster (*cost* leadership, differentiation, focus). Indeed, the following quotation from Porter suggests that he himself sees the generic strategies as single rather than clusters: "The generic strategy specifies the fundamental approach to competitive advantage a firm is pursuing, and provides the context for the actions to be taken in each functional area" (1985:25). Moreover, when we discuss strategies that characterize the business, our level B, the one wherein Porter's generic strategies lie, we find ourselves also, necessarily, discussing clusters in terms of single leading strategies.[4]

LOCATING THE CORE BUSINESS

Jay Galbraith (1983) has proposed a helpful starting point for the identification of an organization's

---

[2]It is interesting to note how different communities tend to concentrate on these different levels. Locating the business is the concern largely of government and university economists who work with SIC codes and the like; strategic management and marketing people to some extent as well as some industrial organization economists concerned with industry concentration, are most interested in characterizing the core business; the marketing people are especially interested in the strategies of elaboration, and the international business people in the geographic dimension of this; transactional cost economists such as Oliver Williamson are especially interested in extending strategies, as are some strategic management people; and the reconceiving strategies have captured the attention recently of a few of the leading edge thinkers in strategic management (notably Porter, with his 1985 discussion of "horizontal" strategy).

[3]As Abell and Hammond claim, for example, about identifying one aspect of distinguishing the core business: ". . . in spite of the chicken and egg relationship between business definition and other strategic decisions, *a definition of the business and its segmentation logically precedes all other strategic decisions*" (1979:391; italics added).

[4]Of course, those who conceive a strategy as an integrated perspective rather than as a clustered set of positions may not accept this distinction in the first place. But that has not generally been the orientation of the positioning school authors, whose predisposition toward strategic positon has caused them to study individual strategies on the one hand, and integrated strategies as clusters of particular strategies on the other.

Table 1 *Generic Characteristics of Strategies*

	Description (with Examples)
Characteristic: Stable	
Amount	How big (e.g., size of expansion), how frequent (e.g., product line proliferation versus product line extension), how strong (e.g., extent of price differentiation), etc.
Quality	How well, how carefully (e.g., extent of quality differentiation)
Comprehensiveness	How all encompassing (e.g., completeness of vertical integration), how dedicated (e.g., proportion of market segments covered)
Commitment[1]	How committed as opposed to hedged or opportunistic, also degree of irreversibility as opposed to flexibility, "rifle" versus "shotgun," "go for broke" as opposed to "test the water" (e.g., vertical integration versus diversification, acquisition versus joint venture), also presence of "critical mass" (e.g., product line proliferation)
Originality	How unique or novel as opposed to generic (e.g., differentiation by design versus by price), also how customized as opposed to standardized and how contemporary or fashionable as opposed to traditional
Riskiness	How risky (e.g., unrelated versus related diversification)
Offensiveness	How confrontative, aggressive, or proactive as opposed to reactive, how offensive or preemptive as opposed to defensive (e.g., market penetration versus niche), how oriented to monopolize or defeat as opposed to cooperate or retreat (e.g., takeover versus joint venture)
Overtness	How direct as opposed to indirect, overt or explicit as opposed to covert or implicit (e.g., differentiation by quality versus by image)
Interrelatedness	How linked as opposed to loosely coupled or disconnected (e.g., vertical integration versus related and unrelated diversification, product bundling versus unbundling)
Characteristic: Dynamic	
Changefulness	How increased as opposed to maintained or decreased (e.g., market elaboration versus market consolidation, acquisition versus divestment), how improved as opposed to weakened (e.g., differentiation by quality versus harvesting)
Speed	How fast (e.g., sudden divestment)
Pace[2]	How regular as opposed to sporadic or paused[2] (e.g., steady expansion versus periodic acquisition or holding pattern)
Position	How early as opposed to late, leader as opposed to follower (e.g., first mover, fast second, late entry)
Convergence	How convergent as opposed to divergent, open ended as opposed to closed ended (e.g., consolidation versus diversification)

[1]In this regard, Rumelt (1981: see also Johansen and Edey, 1981) draws on population biology to contrast "r" strategists, encompassing those species that produce many offspring with little commitment in any one in the hope that some will survive (e.g., ants, wild grass, oysters), with "k" strategists, those species that commit heavily to a very few offspring (e.g., great apes, oak trees).
[2]Melin (1983:23) refers to this as a "hibernation strategy."

strategy, a graphical means to locate its essential function, or core business, in a basic industry as well as to find its particular stage of operations. Galbraith in fact sees these two as interlinked: industries have natural sequences of stages and organizations within them may operate along a number of them, but favoring one as its "center of gravity"—the stage at which it focuses its attention, in a sense where its collective mind lies. Thus, in Figure 1, we see his depiction of the "supply stages in an industry chain" in general, followed by the examples of various firms at different centers of gravity of the "paper" industry.

While making use of Galbraith's basic idea, we choose to differ with him on the assumed relationship between industry and stages. Papermaking certainly relies on the input of timber, but it also makes use of sulfur. Moreover, why should Weyerhauser be called a paper company more than, say, a lumber company, or Procter and Gamble a paper company more than a detergent company or a personal care company? While it is true, for example, that the aluminum producers use bauxite as their primary material and produce ingot which they fabricate into a host of end products in one dominant chain, many other "industries" draw on a variety of more or less equally important inputs and diffuse other outputs widely so that it makes less sense to talk about a single chain than it does a network within it. In this respect, the "industry" becomes a junction in the network, a "node" if you like where inputs and outputs meet. Thus, for us the focal stage of operations (the node) *is* the industry.[5]

Figure 2 shows the network for a hypothetical manufacturer of canoes, an example we shall draw on throughout this discussion. Here there is no clear chain, just the "industry"—the fabrication of canoes—surrounded by a range of inputs and outputs. The inputs can come from a variety of "industries" in their own right—the fiberglass, Kevlar, plastics, aluminum, and wood industries among others, perhaps even the birchbark and spruce gum industries. Likewise, the outputs go to another variety of "industries"—the sporting goods retail indus-

try, the summer camp industry, the government parks industry, the fur trapping industry, and so on.

Add up all these "industries" and we get, not successive strips of Galbraith's chains, but a *matrix* of core businesses (each designated by a circle in Figure 2), with all kinds of interconnections between them. The figure shows the canoe business as described above overlaid on such a matrix.

The question then arises: how to characterize any particular circle within the diagram in general terms, in other words, how to describe our first level of the location of the core business in terms of generic strategies.

The vertical dimension in our diagram distinguishes industry sectors in the classic sense, in terms of the basic products and services provided, while the horizontal dimension relates to classic stages in the basic production and distribution processes. We can more easily find generic labels for the latter than the former.

Strategies of Stage of Operations

Traditionally, industries have been categorized according to stage of operations more or less as follows:

Primary industries:	extracting raw materials
Secondary industries:	processing raw materials (largely into "commodities")
Tertiary industries:	fabricating parts assembling final products transportation wholesale distribution retail distribution financial services professional services government services other services

More recently, it has become popular simply to distinguish upstream and downstream industries, one closer to the raw material end, the other closer to the final consumer. Galbraith emphasizes this distinction, noting that the two differ on "the factors for success, the lessons learned by managers, and the organizations used."

---

[5]Individual firms may, of course, integrate backward or forward in the network, so that they operate at various nodes, although Galbraith may be right that only one typically constitutes their center of gravity. Here we shall assume the single node; in section D we shall consider such integration.

Figure 1 *Locating a Core Business in an Industry Chain (According to Galbraith, 1983:65, 68)*

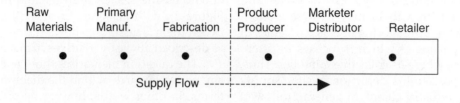

"Supply stages in an industry chain."

"Examples of five paper companies operating at different centers of gravity."

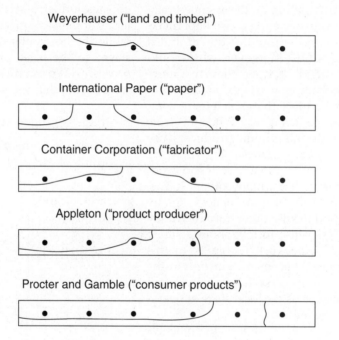

The upstream stages add value by reducing the variety of raw materials found on the earth's surface to a few standard commodities. The purpose is to produce flexible, predictable raw materials and intermediate products from which an increasing variety of downstream products are made. The downstream stages add value through producing a variety of products to meet varying customer needs. The downstream value is added through advertising, product positioning, marketing channels, and R&D. (p. 65)

Upstream industries tend to be technology and capital intensive rather than people intensive, more concerned with process than with product innovation, more oriented to standardizing out-

puts in convergent ways than to segmenting them in divergent ways, more inclined to search for advantage through low costs than through high margins and to favor sales push over market pull (pp. 65–66). All this means that our (A) strategies of locating a core business can drive our (B) strategies of distinguishing a core business.

In presenting these upstream and downstream locations as generic strategies, we prefer to add a midstream category as well.

Upstream Business Strategy. As shown in the little figure, the flow of product is divergent (even though the product itself may converge on standardized forms). In other words, all kinds of uses are sought for the

Figure 2 *Locating a Core Business as a Node in a Matrix of Industries*

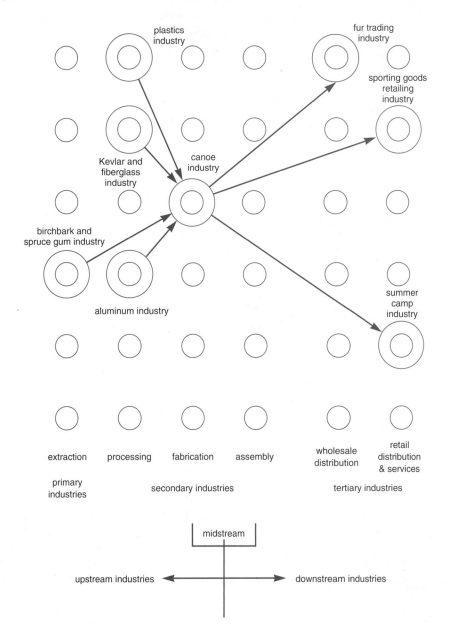

basic upstream product; Galbraith (1983:66) uses the example of Intel, whose 1981 annual report cover showed 10,000 uses of the commodity semiconductors. The same would apply to the manufacturer of Kevlar, whose basic concern is to uncover and promote an increasing variety of uses of its basic material, not just canoes and tires and bulletproof vests, but perhaps auto bodies and arrows, etc.

Midstream Business Strategy. Here the organization sits at the neck of an hourglass, drawing a variety of inputs into a single production process out of which flows the product to a variety of users, much as we characterized the general canoe business.

Downstream Business Strategy. Here a wide variety of inputs converge into a narrow funnel. Sporting goods stores (in Canada) buy canoes, and hockey sticks and pucks and snowshoes and moccasins and thermal underwear and hundreds if not thousands of other items from dozens of different "industries," all to be pushed through a single channel to their shivering retail customers.

Strategies of Industry

Horizontally (in our diagram at least), the development of a compact system of generic labels proves far more difficult, simply because so many factors are involved in the identification of an industry that the number of possible ones grows beyond reasonable limit.

Abell and Hammond (1979:391–392; see also Abell, 1980) claim that a basic business can be defined by the *markets* served (the demand side of the equation) and the *products* or *services* provided (the supply side). Together these encompass three dimensions: *who* is served (the customer group, as in the outdoorsman industry), *what* need is being satisfied (the customer function, as in the recreation or the racing industry), and *how* that need is being satisfied (the technological dimension, as in the canoe industry). Any unique combination of these may be taken to constitute a business. Obviously, in any contemporary developed economy, that can be a large number indeed, and one that grows larger every day. We have the canoe business and the calligraphy business, the prune business and the petrochemical business, health care and hotels, revenue collection and rainwear, energy and engines. The list seems endless, as do the criteria for definition.

Further compounding the problem is that change continually renders the boundaries between "industries" arbitrary. Diverse products get bundled together so that two industries become one ("Try our Kevlar canoe and get three free hours of white-water instruction"), while traditionally bundled products get separated so that one industry becomes two ("We make only the shell; gunnels and thwarts are made in the next town"). And the concept of industries get redefined, narrowed or broadened, so that boundaries become even more vague (canoes, chainsaws, and flannel shirts become the "outdoors" industry, stock brokerage, real estate, banking, insurance, etc. become the "financial services" industry). The fact that "competitors often choose dissimilar definitions of the business and do not compete from the same perspective . . . makes it difficult to define market boundaries" (Abell and Hammond, 1979:401).

Economists in government and elsewhere of course spend a great deal of time trying to pin these things down, via SIC codes and the like. But we have no intention of getting caught up here in what seems to us like chasing a set of papers that have scattered in a gale, with the categorizers having to run in every direction, or perhaps better metaphorically, trying to slice a bowl of loose gelatin into definitive sections. Perhaps the basic problem reflects the fact that the analysts are trying to fix what the strategists are trying to change: competitive advantage often comes from reconceiving the definition of an industry. That makes boundary definition at best historical, at worst arbitrary.

Of course, this criticism applies to all sets of generic strategies. They identify what strategists have already converged upon, at least the less creative strategists who have followed the lead of same innovator. Only when a novel strategy becomes copied several times can it be recognized as "generic." It might, of course, be argued that creative strategists innovate within the contexts of existing generic categories (being "upstream" hardly limits strategic creativity). In any event, none of this helps in the particular problem of trying to develop a typology of generic strategies of industry definition. We therefore close with the conclusion that the first step in the identification of an organization's strategy can be conceived simply as to locate the core business on a two-dimensional matrix, the state of the operating process (as categorized earlier) and the basic product-market configuration.

DISTINGUISHING THE CORE BUSINESS

Having located the circle that identified the core business, the next step is to open it up—to define the distinguishing characteristics that enable an organization to achieve competitive advantage and so to survive in its own context. Porter refers to these as "the determinants" of relative competitive position within an industry" (1985:1), most other writers simply as "business strategy." We like to think of it also as competitive *posture*.

The Functional Strategy Areas

This second level of strategy can encompass a whole host of strategies in the various functional areas. Considering an organization in "general systems theory" notions, these can be shown in terms of a flow model, as in Figure 3, consisting of input "sourcing" strategies, throughput "processing" strategies, led by "design" strategies, and output "delivery" strategies, all reinforced by a set of "supporting" strategies.

It has been popular of late to describe organizations in this way, especially since Porter built his 1985 book around the "generic valve chain," reproduced in Figure 4. Our figure differs from Porter's in certain ways. Because he places his major emphasis on the flow of physical materials (for example, referring to "inbound logistics" as encompassing "materials handling, warehousing, inventory control, vehicle scheduling, and returns to suppliers"), he shows procurement and human resource management as support activities, whereas by taking more of a general systems theory orientation, we show them as inputs, among the sourcing strategies. Likewise, he considers technology development as support whereas we

consider it as part of processing.[6] In fact, Porter's description would relegate research and development and engineering (not to mention human resources and purchasing) to staff rather than line activities, a place that would certainly be disputed in a great many manufacturing firms.

An initial effort by us to delineate generic strategies for each of these functional areas was abandoned as overwhelming: there would simply be too many possible strategies, a great number of them industry-specific. That is perhaps why most strategy content authors either avoid trying to delineate generic functional strategies altogether, or else present haphazard lists that hardly cover the subject.[7] It is true, of course, that certain functional strategies have become commonly generic across all kinds of industries, for example, tight credit or debt financing, private label marketing, skimming pricing, just-in-time inventory. But such a list could become endless. Accordingly, rather than focusing on functional strategies, we shall describe ones of a broader nature at the business level, noting however that these not only drive functional strategies, but, as we shall see, are also driven by them.

In describing the strategies that distinguish the core business, we take our lead from Porter's "generic strategies." But in so doing, we once again take issue with some major aspects of his classification scheme, seeking to develop a tighter typology.

Cost Leadership Versus Price Differentiation

We follow Porter in distinguishing *focus* or *scope* from the other business level generic strategies. Scope pertains to market definition—how the organization perceives its markets, the inside looking out so to speak, corresponding to the marketing people's concentration on market segmentation. Porter's other two generic strategies describe

---

[6]Among the reasons Porter gives for doing this is that such development can pertain to "outbound logistics" or delivery as well as processing. While true, it also seems true that far more technology development pertains to operations than to delivery, especially in the manufacturing firms that are the focus of Porter's attention. Likewise, he describes procurement as pertaining to any of the primary activities, or other support activities for that matter. But in our terms that does not make it any less an aspect of sourcing on the inbound side.

[7]Acknowledgment must, however, be given here to the noble effort of Cannon back in the 1960s to delineate functional strategies for the typical large manufacturing firm (1968:103–263). It is by far the best effort we have come across, including many excellent examples. But it nevertheless remains limited, and in fact it appears to have had virtually no influence on the subsequent literature. The citation index suggests the futility of such efforts. The Cannon text was cited only a total of 26 times in the eighteen years since its publication, never more than three times in a year, and only one or two times a year since 1982.

Figure 3 *Functional Strategy Areas, in Systems Terms*

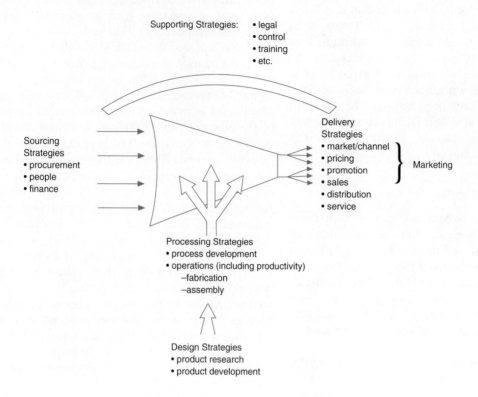

Figure 4 *Porter's "Generic Value Chain" (1985:37).*

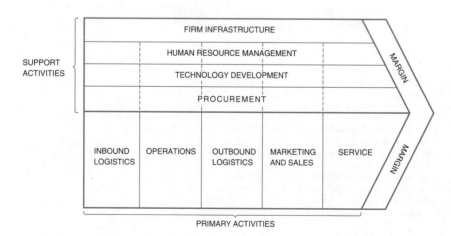

aspects of the firm itself, in one case the *differentiation* of its product or service offerings, in the other its tendency to concentrate on minimizing costs (which he calls *cost leadership*).

We believe, however, that cost leadership is better identified as *price differentiation* (by which we mean pricing below the competition). If, as Porter argues, the intention of a generic strategy is to seize competitive advantage, then cost leadership per se does not do this. Rather, its natural consequence does: to use cost leadership to underprice the competition and thereby attract buyers. The whole thrust of the positioning school is to identify strategy as a viable position in a marketplace, and cost reduction has nothing per se to do with the marketplace. Our view is that price differentiation naturally drives the functional strategy of cost reduction just as product differentiation naturally drives the functional strategy of product quality or product innovation, which are the means to achieve it. (To be consistent with his label of cost leadership, Porter would have had to label what he calls differentiation "product leadership.")

Because Porter's labels have become so widely used, our departure from them should be justified carefully. We propose to do so further by using Porter's own words and examples.

A "cost leadership" strategy could, of course, be pursued to increase margins while simply meeting the prices of competitors. That would justify the label Porter gives to it. Such strategies do exist, but we suspect they are restricted largely to commodity products (upstream) where prices are more or less fixed. Otherwise, we believe that cost leadership strategies not only provide no competitive advantage per se (do nothing in the marketplace), but in fact actually undermine competitive advantage. That advantage must therefore be recovered in another way, and the obvious way is price differentiation.

Consider how Porter describes cost leadership: selling "a standard, or no frills, product" (1985:13), "vigorous pursuit of cost reductions," "avoidance of marginal customer accounts," "cost minimization in areas like R & D, service, sales force, advertising," "designing products for ease in manufacturing"; overall, "low cost relative to competitors becomes the theme running through the entire strategy" (1980:35,36). All good for the cost side of the ledger. But hardly the basis for attracting customers, that is, for sustaining competitive advantage. "A business unit's strategy is the route to competitive advantage that will determine its performance," claims Porter (1985:25). But what advantage *in the marketplace* is there to cutting costs? Why should the customers care? Something is obviously missing.

Porter argues that "if a firm can achieve and sustain overall cost leadership, then it will be an above-average performer in its industry provided it can command prices at or near the industry average" (1985:13). But what would enable it to command such prices? On what basis would any customer beat a path to its door? If no other competitor had any advantage—in other words, if the product was a pure commodity—then our cost leader would be no worse off than anywhere else. But no better off either.

Porter continues: "A cost leader cannot ignore the basis of differentiation." Its products must be "perceived as comparable or acceptable by buyers," otherwise "a cost leader will be forced to discount prices well below competitors' to gain sales" (p. 13). In other words, price differentiation *may* have to follow cost leadership, implied almost as a necessary evil. (Indeed, Porter goes on to say that price reductions "may nullify the benefits of [the] favourable cost position.") But how can the cost leader achieve the necessary product comparability, how can it maintain "parity or proximity in the bases of differentiation relative to its competitors," as Porter says it must (p. 13), without getting "stuck in the middle" (to use his own term)? In fact, alongside these comments Porter provides examples of two firms that "fell into [the] trap" of not being able to sustain parity in differentiation; Texas Instruments which was forced to exit the watch industry (although, as it happens, it set out to be a price differentiator as well) and Northwest Airlines which had to upgrade its services in order to compete.

The fact is that the differentiation likely to result from cost leadership is negative: less service, lower quality, fewer features, fewer options. Price differentiation then becomes not the fallback position, not even the derivative strategy, but the very raison d'être for the overall generic strategy. What attracts the customers is the price; cost reductions simply makes low pricing a viable strategy. The customers pay less, they get less, and the firm hopefully makes more money.

Porter implicitly acknowledges the relationship between cost leadership and price differentiation further down on the same page of his 1985 book. "Proximity in differentiation means that the price discount necessary to achieve an acceptable market share does not offset a cost leader's cost advantage and hence the cost leader earns above average returns" (p. 13). Porter says nothing else about pricing in his discussion of cost leadership in this book (pp. 12–14), and hardly anything at all in general in the equivalent discussion of his 1980 book (pp. 35–37), only that the strategy "may require . . . aggressive pricing" (p. 36).[8] But the example he uses to close that discussion conveys the message. It is about the firm Harnischfeger that, starting with a 15 percent market share in the crane industry, redesigned its product for inexpensive manufacture. As a result its market share grew to 25 percent. But it was not the cost leadership strategy that did that: the key was that the company dropped its prices by 15 percent. The general manager of the division in question tells by example what Porter fails to tell by concept:

> *We didn't set out to develop a machine significantly better than anyone else but we did want to develop one that was truly simple to manufacture and was priced, intentionally, as a low cost machine. (1980:37, quote from* Business Week*).*

Thus we conclude that price differentiation must be the driving force behind cost leadership, especially downstream. If Porter's generic strategies are to be defined by their leading elements, as he seems to want them to be, then his first one should be called price differentiation.[9]

Two Basic Dimensions of Business Strategy

Thus we are left with two basic dimensions of business strategy, differentiation on the one hand, scope on the other. In both cases, we wish to develop a concise typology of generic strategies.

In considering differentiation at large, we believe that this dimension needs more systematic disaggregation than Porter provides. He does list forms of differentiation. But we believe there is the need for delineation of fundamental generic types of differentiation. We also believe that scope should be broken down into a set of basic generic strategies not discussed in Porter's work.[10]

Thus we develop our typology of generic business-level strategies in two parts: first, a set of increasingly extensive strategies of differentiation, shown on the face of our circle, which identify what is fundamentally distinct about a business in the marketplace, as perceived by its customers, and, second, a set of decreasingly extensive strategies of scope, shown as a third dimension that converts our circle into a cylinder, that identify what markets the business is after, as perceived by itself.

Strategies of Differentiation

As is generally agreed in the positioning school literature (although sometimes only implicitly), an organization distinguishes itself in a competitive marketplace by differentiating itself in some way—by acting to distinguish its products and services from those of its competitors. We take this to mean that all competitive advantage amounts to one form or another of differentiation, hence, this becomes the fundamental basis of every business-level strategy, and therefore fills the face of the circle we have used to identify the core business.

An organization can differentiate its offerings in more or less substantial ways. It can, for example, design them to be better or different, or it can simply act only to have them perceived that way. Maytag has long invested in producing products that would last longer and require less service, while a few years ago, a number of the detergent companies thought they could capture market share (for a few days at least) by stuffing towels in their boxes. And Smirnoff Vodka is reported (in Smith et al., 1972:259) to have gained market share by *raising* its price: that apparently enhanced its image!

---

[8]Under the section on "buyer selection and strategy," Porter does write that "the firm with a low-cost position can sell to powerful, price sensitive buyers and still be successful" (1980:119).

[9]One recent article does in fact define a differentiated product as one that "is perceived by the customer to differ from its competition on any physical or nonphysical product characteristic including price" (Dickson and Ginter, 1987:4).

[10]It is ironic that a work so characterized by lists should be questioned here for lack of systematic lists. But in his 1980 book, for example, Porter ends his list of "approaches" to differentiation with the phrase "or other dimensions" (p. 37). It is at this level that concise "generic" typologies are critical, in our view.

Below we show on the face of the circle what we believe to be the six major forms of differentiation, each of which is discussed briefly.

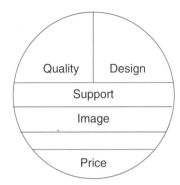

Differentiation by Price. The most basic way to differentiate a product (or service; for convenience we shall assume service under product from here on) is simply to charge a lower price for it. All things being equal, or not too unequal, some people at least will always beat a path to the door of the cheaper product.

Price differentiation may be used with a product undifferentiated in any other way—in effect, a standard design, perhaps a commodity. The producer simply absorbs the lost revenue, or makes it up through a higher volume of sales or a position of cost leadership. But other times, backing up price differentiation is a strategy of design intended to create a product that is intrinsically cheaper. It may be cheaper to produce (IKEA sells its furniture unassembled to save handling costs; the customer does the assembling, as a kind of reverse of the strategy of support differentiation discussed below). Or the product itself may be cheaper, produced more quickly and less carefully or perhaps of components that are themselves of lower quality (thinner, of lower grade, etc.). Sometimes this amounts to shoddiness—fooling the customer into thinking that he or she is getting a bargain (the toy that breaks on the way home)—but other times it amounts to a reasonable tradeoff, as in those firms that produce cheap fiberglass canoes for consumers who do not need the strength for rapids or do not care about the quality of the finish.

Differentiation by Image. Marketing is sometimes used to feign differentiation where it does not otherwise exist (say, by labeling an ordinary canoe "rapidbuster" and painting it with teeth on the front). An image is created for the product, or to use the words of Ian Macmillan, a "psychological position" is preempted in the mind of the customers (1983:19). While General Motors was advertising "Wouldn't you really rather own a Buick?", it was being challenged successfully in the courts for interchanging components between its cheaper and more expensive automobiles. Smirnoff, as noted earlier, differentiated its Vodka by upping the price and so enhancing the image (among some people at least) while filling the bottles with the same old stuff.

A great deal of advertising of consumer products has, from the looks of things, had to do with this essentially artificial form of differentiation: seeking to create perceived differences for products that were in fact not different at all. But under image differentiation we also include cosmetic differences to the product that do not enhance its performance in any serious way, for example, putting fins on an automobile or a fancier package around yogurt. (Of course, if it is the image that is for sale, in other words if the product is intrinsically cosmetic, as say in designer jeans, then cosmetic differences would have to be described as design differentiation.) Dickson and Ginter (1987) point out that the economist Chamberlain noted the possibilities of differentiation "real or imagined" back in 1933 (p. 2), the latter labeled "pseudodifferentiation" by Lancaster (p. 3).[11]

Differentiation by Support. More substantial, yet still having no effect on the product itself, is to differentiate on the basis of something that goes alongside the product, some basis of support. This might be called peripheral differentiation, or simply support differentiation. It may have something to do with selling the product (such as special credit or twenty-four-hour delivery), servicing the product (such as exceptional after-sales service, as in "free repair if you can find a way to put a hole in our super ABS canoe"), or providing a related

---

[11]They also note a tendency in economics to overemphasize image differentiation: ". . . among many economists 'product differentiation' has become a disparaging term used to describe what is 'judged' to be manipulation and/or for wasteful competitive strategy" (p. 8).

product or service alongside the basic one (paddling lessons with your canoe). The support may be included with the product (as in the ABS repair) or sold alongside it (charging for the paddling lessons). *Bundling* has become the popular label for the former.

In a paper entitled "Marketing Success through Differentiation—of Anything," Theodore Levitt has argued the interesting point that "there is no such thing as a commodity" (1980:83). His basic point is that no matter how difficult it may be to achieve design differentiation for some products, there is always a basis to achieve another substantial form of differentiation, notably of the support kind. (He is *not* arguing the case for image differentiation.) Levitt's argument is built on the point that "to the potential buyer, a product is a complex cluster of value satisfactions" (p. 84), not just intrinsic in the product itself. For example, the buyer of sheet steel "specifies much more than the steel itself. It also demands certain delivery conditions and flexibilities, price and payment conditions, and reordering responsiveness" (p. 85). Thus, in addition to the "generic product," there is the "expected product," including delivery, terms, support efforts, and new ideas that come along with it; the "augmented product" which includes things the customer never thought about (such as canoeing lessons with the canoe); and the "potential product," including other things to hold the customer (such as a free newsletter on new canoeing routes). In other words, often "it is the *process*, not just the product, that is differentiated" (p. 90).

Differentiation by Quality. Finally, on top of our circle come, in our view, the two most extensive bases for differentiation, each having to do with substantial differences in the product or service itself. One has to do with its quality, the other with unique features of its design.

Quality differentiation has to do with features of the product that make it better—not different, just better. In other words, the product does not do anything that competing products cannot do, it just does them with (a) greater reliability, (b) greater durability, and/or (c) superior performance. In the first case, the product does what it is supposed to do, arriving without defects and not breaking down soon after: in the second, it keeps doing so for long periods of time; and in the third, it does so better or faster or whatever one expects of it.

Canoes made of ABS offer all three to white-water enthusiasts: they are vitually indestructible and moreover slide over the rocks on which other canoes tend to stick. Russell Miller used to custom make canoes in Niagara Falls, Ontario. A quality differentiator, he produced for this author a Kevlar canoe of especially light weight so that he could pick mushrooms while portaging his canoe with the other arm. The finish was also excellent. But this canoe, otherwise, looks, loads, and paddles more or less like all those canoes mass produced of fiberglass. Maytag washing machines are known to last longer, Toyota automobiles to arrive with fewer defects and to need less subsequent servicing, Marks and Spencers fabrics to be more durable, and Singapore Airlines to provide more seating space. Simmonds' (1972, 1973) reference to "performance maximizing strategies" would seem to fit here, in contrast to his "cost minimizing strategies" (price differentiation) and "sales maximizing strategies" (probably one of the other forms of differentiation, notably image or support).

It is, of course, image that matters to the quality differentiator—a claim that can in fact be made, and will, for all the forms of differentiation—but here the image is created and sustained by what the producer does in producing the product, not just in marketing it. And in a world in which price differentiation seems to reign supreme—driven not just by standardization in design but by a "bottom line" mentality that is prepared to exploit anything for short-term gain—real quality differentiation can be a major sustainable competitive advantage. As Tom Peters likes to note in his corporate revival meetings, there are companies that "differentiate" themselves by serving those customers who like to get what they pay for!

Differentiation by Design. Last but certainly not least is differentiation on the basis of design—offering something that is truly different, that breaks away from the "dominant design" if there is one, to provide unique features. Miller might choose to offer a 16-foot Kevlar canoe that folds into the backpack for easy portaging through the Canadian woods (though we are not at liberty to reveal our design here). While everyone else was making cameras whose pictures could be seen next week, Edwin Land went off and made one whose pictures could be seen in the next minute. Of course, design differentiation need not be so ambitious. At the other extreme may be cosmetic differentiation for a cosmetic product (some twist in designer jeans). Further along are the modifications or variations in dominant designs (Piná Colada yogurt, a sixteen *and a half* foot canoe), including the upgrading of products. The truly reconceived products (yogurt ice cream, Land's Polaroid camera, the folding canoe) sometimes evoke a complete reconception of an industry with all its standard recipes, although this gets us into the realm of our fifth level of generic strategy, to be discussed later.

Undifferentiated Products. To have no basis for differentiation is a strategy too, indeed by all observation a common one, and in fact one that may be pursued deliberately. Hence we have left a blank space in our circle, just above price differentiation, for those organizations whose offerings are truly undistinguished (except perhaps in their scope, as we shall discuss below). Given enough room in a market, and a management without the skill or the will to create something novel, there can be place for copycats. One need only visit the corner supermarket or gas station or, all too often read the local newspaper. In ecological systems, after all, each species is differentiated, but there is little differentiation within a species. Thus, Ford seemed to pursue a strategy of undifferentiation for several decades after World War II, happy to follow in the shadow of General Motors and pick up a smaller market share. Later Burger King "McDonaldized" itself, offering "Whoppers" in place of "Big Macs." Such strategies are, of course, most likely to be found in commodity markets, although Levitt eloquently makes the case that they need not.

Differentiation Strategies by Functional Area

A few final points on differentiation are in order here. First we wish to return to the question of leading strategies and the relationship between differentiation and the functional strategies. We have argued that, in the spirit of the positioning school, business strategies should first be defined in terms of some basis of differentiation, in other words some basis by which the essential products and/or services of the organization are distinguished in the marketplace. We have proposed five of these—by price, image, support, quality, and design (as well as by nothing at all). Note that each of these is based on some different function of the product—

how much it costs, what image it projects, what comes along with it, how well it performs, and what unique things it can do. It follows that each of these strategies is rooted primarily in some functional area, some element in the chain of activities. The associated functional area strategy thus becomes the leading strategy behind the particular strategy of differentiation, and the other functional area strategies follow, as derivatives.

- The price differentiation strategy evokes above all cost-reduction strategies, all along the chain of operations but probably most significantly in *processing* (using economies of scale and experience curve effects and making associated investments in process R&D), followed by product design strategies (use of standardized and interchangeable components, rationalized designs, etc.), and then perhaps sourcing strategies (cheaper materials) and delivery strategies (using mass of channels of distribution, etc.).
- The image differentiation strategy obviously evokes strategies of *delivery* above all, especially in the marketing areas of advertising and promotion to create the image, supported perhaps by higher pricing and higher status forms of physical distribution.
- The support differentiation strategy concerns support activities that pertain directly to the product; these may come under the function of processing (when they deal with some related product, such as software for a computer manufacturer), but probably more likely came under the *delivery* functions of promotion and distribution or the *support* function itself (when they pertain to an auxiliary area such as after-sales service for an appliance maker).
- The quality differentiation strategy evokes strategies in the *processing* area primarily, in how the product is produced, also perhaps in product development in terms of how it is designed in the first place, commonly also in *sourcing* in terms of quality of its raw materials and components, and perhaps also in delivery in terms of the care with which the product is brought to the point of sale (and indeed delivered to the customer after that, and then assembled or installed if necessary).
- The design differentiation strategy obviously evokes activities above all in the functional area of *design*—product R&D—which may of

course have derivative implications for the other areas of functional strategy as well.

One final point. Differentiation has to be perceived by the customer to have any meaning. To be differentiated, as we just noted, means to be different. But if the customer does not know it, for all practical purpose it does not exist. Trees that fall in the forest *do* make noise, in terms of causing vibrations in the atmosphere, but if no one hears it, the noise has no social meaning. Likewise, differentiation that is not perceived in the marketplace has no strategic meaning. This draws attention to the delivery functions of marketing, since even the serious forms of differentiation require some management of the image of the product. But we prefer to view this more broadly: the image is managed substantively not only by promoting it but also by providing the basis for it, believing in it, and carrying out *every* function with an eye toward it.

Let us now turn to generic business strategies *of* the customer, ones that exist strategically only when they are perceived by the *producer*.

Scope Strategies

Our second of the two dimensions of business strategy, to distinguish the core business, has to do with the *scope* of the products and services offered, in effect the extents of the markets in which they are sold. Scope encompasses what the marketing people like to call segmentation, although we shall describe that as but one aspect of scope, even if the most important one.

Scope Versus Differentiation. As Wendell Smith pointed out in a classic article published in 1956 entitled "Product Differentiation and Market Segmentation as Alternate Marketing Strategies," the two concepts are quite different, though "closely related (perhaps even inseparable)" (p. 4). Scope is essentially a demand-driven concept, taking its lead from the market—what exists out there. As Smith characterized segmentation, it "is *disaggregative* in its effects and tends to bring about recognition of several demand schedules where only one was recognized before" (1956:5); later he added that it "consists of viewing a heterogeneous market . . . as a number of smaller homogenous markets" (p. 6). Differentiation, in contrast, is a supply-driven concept, rooted in the nature of the product—what is offered to the market. It "is con-

cerned with the bending of demand to the will of supply . . . an attempt to shift or to change the scope of the demand curve" (p. 5). Of course, business takes place at the intersection of the two. Indeed, Smith uses a metaphor that exactly reverses our display of these two strategies: "The differentiator seeks to secure a layer of the marketing cake, whereas one who employs market segmentation strives to secure one or more wedge-shaped pieces" (p. 5). A different cut of the same idea!

Ironically, differentiation, by concentrating on the product offered, adopts the perspective of the customer: as we have just noted, differentiation only takes on strategic importance when it exists in the mind of the customer—in terms of some perceived characteristic of the product that adds value for the user. And scope, by focusing on the market served, adopts the perspective of the producer: it exists only in the collective mind of the organization—in terms of how markets are defined and disaggregated. (Smith refers to it as "essentially a merchandising strategy" [p. 6]).

Smith believes that while these two strategies can be applied simultaneously, they are more likely to be used in sequence. "In one sense, segmentation is a momentary or short-term phenomenon" that can result in market "redefinition," which itself "may result in a swing back to differentiation" (p. 5). Writing in the same *Journal of Marketing* thirty-one years later, however, in an article with almost the exact title as that of Smith, Dickson and Ginter (1987) point out in reviewing sixteen "contemporary marketing textbooks" that five describe product differentiation as an "alternative" to market segmentation and eleven as a "complement or means of implementing" a market segmentation (and three of them "limit product differentiation to only nonphysical product characteristics") (p. 1). Dickson and Ginter address the issue themselves through a kind of graphical analysis and conclude:

> . . . *a strategy of product differentiation does not require the existence of market segments . . . but may be used in conjunction with market segmentation strategy when segments are perceived to exist . . . [moreover] a strategy of segment development is feasible only when product differentiation either already exists or is an accompanying strategy. Within this framework, product differentiation and market segmentation are clearly not alternative*

management strategies. A product differentiation strategy can be pursued with or without a market segmentation strategy, but [not vice-versa] (p. 9).

Porter uses the term "scope" in his 1985 book, alongside "focus", although he restricted himself to the latter term in his 1980 book. That change reflects the fact that while in 1980, only narrow scope was acknowledged, in other words focus (what we shall later label a niche strategy), broad as well as narrow scope were discussed in the 1985 book. This is perhaps best reflected in the matrices Porter presented in the two books, reprinted here in Figure 5. The first shows focus in a "particular segment only", but in an unclear relationship with his other two generic strategies of cost leadership and differentiation. The second shows scope more clearly as a second dimension of a 2 × 2 matrix of business-level strategies, oriented to a "broad" or "narrow target" alongside either cost leadership or differentiation. (The other dimension could have been labeled "differentiation" instead of "competitive advantage", or at least "differentiation forms of competitive advantage", had Porter described cost leadership as price differentiation.)[12]

Categorizing Scope. Any market can be defined in an infinite number of ways. Put another way, segmentation is a creative act, and so is continually subject to redefinition (much as we argued for industry itself). Coke began with just plain coke, available at the fountain and then in bottles. Then followed a wide variety of sizes and shapes of bottles and cans, glass and plastic, steel and aluminum. Now there is new Coke, Classic Coke, Diet Coke, Caffeine Free Coke, Cherry Coke, and a few combinations of these, with perhaps soon to come all the remaining permutations and combinations (Diet Classic Cherry Coke With or Without Caffeine?). Each one is supposed to tap its own market segment (imagined if not real, for a segment is after all just a perceived pattern of buying behavior). Note that here product design seems to have been

for purposes of segmentation. In our opinion, this would constitute design differentiation only when the producer seeks to make its product unique in some way. Put another way, segmentation deals with generic *types* of products (with respect to markets, or else just the market themselves), whereas differentiation deals with the *characteristics* of products that make them distinct. Thus product *variety* is a dimension of scope, not differentiation.

Abell and Hammond, in their marketing textbook identify six bases to engage in "creative segmentation":

What
- benefits does the customer seek?
- factors influence demand?
- functions does the product perform for the customer?
- are important buying criteria?
- is the basis of comparison with other products?
- risks does the customer perceive?
- services do customers expect?

How
- do customers buy?
- long does the buying process last?
- do various elements of the marketing program influence customers at each stage of the process?
- do customers use the product?
- does the product fit into their life style or operation?
- much are they willing to spend?
- much do they buy?

Where
- is the decision made to buy?
- do customers seek information about the product?
- do customers buy the product?

When
- is the first decision to buy made?
- is the product repurchased?

---

[12]By extending scope in his 1985 book to vertical integration and diversification (pp. 53–54, e.g., "industry scope" as "the range of related industries in which the firm competes with a coordinated strategy"), Porter in our opinion extends it too far, combining strategies that differ in kind (even if they do all deal with the "scope" of an organization's activities). We prefer to restrict scope strategies to Porter's categories of product varieties and buyers served, including geographical areas ("segment scope" and "geographical scope") while reserving vertical integration and industry diversification for another level of strategy.

Figure 5 *From Focus to Scope in Porter's Book*

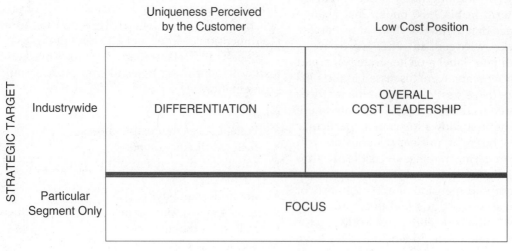

STRATEGIC ADVANTAGE

	Uniqueness Perceived by the Customer	Low Cost Position
Industrywide	DIFFERENTIATION	OVERALL COST LEADERSHIP
Particular Segment Only	FOCUS	

STRATEGIC TARGET

Porter's 1980 Matrix of "Generic Strategies" (p. 39)

COMPETITIVE ADVANTAGE

	Lower Cost	Differentiation
Broad Target	1. Cost Leadership	2. DIfferentiation
Narrow Target	3A. Cost Focus	3B. Differentiation Focus

COMPETITIVE SCOPE

Porter's 1985 Matrix of "Generic Strategies" (p. 12)

Why

- do customers buy?
- do customers choose one brand as opposed to another?

Who

- are the occupants of segments identified by previous questions?
- buys our product, and why?
- buys our competitors' products, and why? (1979:49–50)

Within each of these, of course, the possibilities of slicing up any serious market are endless, limited only by the imagination of those doing the slicing. In canoes, for example, we have customers who want to race, fish, shoot rapids, deliver furs, relax on lakes; those who want to do the latter for an afternoon or a week, alone or en family, independently or with a recreational camp, in the wilderness or near the city, in the Florida Everglades or on Baffin Island; and who themselves are tall, short, strong, weak, poised, awkward, experienced, inexperienced, optimistic, pessimistic, and on and on.[13] And that is just canoes; imagine contemplating all the market segments for lighting fixtures!

Accordingly, it makes no sense to develop generic strategies of segmentation, at least outside of marketing texts that have chapters on end to devote to the subject. (Even these, to the extent that they succeed, risk putting blinders on their readers and thereby making them vulnerable to competitors with peripheral vision.) But it does make sense to develop a generic classification of an organization's scope in terms of how narrowly or comprehensively it competes, and to what extent it relies on segmentation. In fact, a comment by Dickson and Ginter reinforces this approach: "Market segmentation [considered "as a form of research analysis directed at identification of, and allocation of resources among market segments"] is seen as a way of *viewing* the market rather than defined as a management strategy. The purpose of such an analysis is to provide a foundation for market segmentation strategy" (1987:3). Thus, in a sense, we skip the exercise of segmenting in order to focus on the strategies associated with segmentation.

For visual convenience, we show scope below as a third dimension on our circle, converting it into a cylinder.

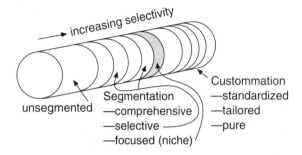

Later, in fact, we shall distinguish visually two aspects of this third dimension, (a) the disks of the cylinder to represent the variety and range of products offered, (b) with arrows eminating from the cylinder to represent the variety and range of markets served, as shown in another figure below.

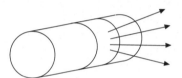

As indicated on our first diagram, the generic strategies of scope to be discussed here include, in order of increasing selectivity, unsegmented, segmented, whether comprehensive or selective, niche (which will be considered separately), and three levels of customization (standardized, tailored, and pure) which we consider to be the limiting cases of market segmentation.

Unsegmentation Strategy. "One size fits all": the Ford Model T, aluminum ingot, table salt. In fact, it is difficult to think of any product today that is not segmented in some way. There must be a package of designer table salt available somewhere, and the salt people must surely talk about

---

[13]Lest anyone consider any of these criteria frivolous, remember that the weak want lightweight Kevlar canoes for portaging, the pessimistic or the awkward flotation along the outer sides to minimize the chances of tipping.

salt to enhance flavor as opposed to salt to keep wintering Montrealers from breaking their necks on the city's famous outdoor stairways.

What the unsegmented strategy really means then is a relatively blind eye to segmentation: the organization tries to capture a wide swath of the market with a basic configuration of the product. The market is perceived of as one big segment or chunk, a mass of indistinguishable buyers who take the product as it comes. Typical would be general products, likely delivered through mass channels (such as discount department stores) supported by general advertising (such as hit TV shows). In Quebec, Cadorette sells its basic 16-foot fiberglass canoe to recreational camps and government parks, to flat-water and white-water paddlers, out for a week and an afternoon, optimistic and pessimistic, poised and awkward (within reason at least). The white-water fanatics wouldn't be caught dead in one—they go for the Old Town Royalex canoes without keel. But many a Quebecer who never knew any better (myself included) has had a great time shooting rapids in one of these Cadorettes. It's not exactly in the class of aluminum ingot, but this "dominant design" has become a kind of commodity product in the Quebec canoes business.

Segmentation Strategy. The possibilities for segmentation are, as already noted, limitless, as are the possible degrees. We can, however, distinguish a range of this, from simple segmentation (three basic sizes of paper clips) to hyperfine segmentation, in which customers in a segment can almost be counted on one's fingers and toes (some designer clothing, Kevlar racing canoes).

But of more practical use for our purposes is the organization's stand vis-à-vis the segments, assuming a number of these have been identified. First are those organizations that seek to be *comprehensive*—to serve all segments. Department stores are typical of this, in offering a full line of products, each in its own department. So too are the large cigarette manufacturers that produce every conceivable form, length, taste, and strength of cig-

arette. Alfred Sloan (1963) taught the automobile business how to segment, to cover the entire range of price and status; Renault in France has pursued this strategy aggressively since the late 1950s, proliferating not only basic models but every conceivable permutation and combination within each.

Second are those organizations that seek to be *selective,* targeting carefully only certain segments—such as Ewert's Fiberglass of Bemidji, Minnesota that produces only four models, the "Autumn Blend Camoflage," with "molded-in earth tone colors" for families, the "Square Back Ricer" for harvesting wild rice and trapping," the "Square Back Sports Boat" for the "avid fishermen, waterfowler, and big game hunter," and the 26-foot "North Canoe" whose "textured surface . . . exactly simulate[s] the prized winter birch bark" (*Canoe* magazine, *1988 Buyer's Guide,* p. 41, and no kidding!). Subaru does this in the American automobile business, with its few basic models, two or three sizes of family cars, a sporty truck ("the brat"), and one sports car, most available in four-wheel drive. Likewise McDonald's might be considered to target very specific segments of the fast food business (though very large ones).

Finally there are those organizations that *focus* on a single segment, a strategy more often called *specialization* or *niche.* This one is important enough to merit its own discussion.

The Niche Strategy. Just as the panda bear has found its biological niche in the consumption of bamboo shoots, so too has Mouve Canoes of Staughton, Wisconsin found its market niche in the fabrication of 10- to 13-foot solo canoes. Likewise Porsche pursues a niche strategy in its production of expensive, high-performance sports cars. Porter's third generic strategy, which he calls "focus" in the 1980 book, is in fact the niche strategy: "focusing on a particular buyer group, segment of the product line, or geographic market" (1980:38).[14] To Porter, the key is to serve "a particular target very well" either through cost leadership or differentiation or both (1980:38).

As Porter suggests, an organization can specialize on a variety of bases—by product (solo

---

[14]Curiously, Porter only uses the term niche in that book, briefly, in his discussion of declining industries ("create or defind a strong position in a particular segment," p. 267), not in his discussion of fragmented or emerging industries, where we would expect niche strategies to be most common.

canoes), by customer or channel (wild rice harvesting), by geographic area (Baffin Island). It can, of course, specialize by functions having nothing to do with scope per se, for example, by technology (as do anteaters in the biological world, though that of course manifests itself as a "market" segment too!).

In Quebec, most canoe manufacturers in fact fit the category of geography, selling essentially undifferentiated products (the "dominant-design" 16-foot all purpose canoe) in a geographical niche. And that seems to be the single most common strategy in use today, though not so recognized in the literature of strategic management. The vast majority of retailers and providers of other services, even many producers of primary and secondary products, seem to be distinguished only by the fact that they provide their highly standardized offerings in a unique place, a geographical niche. We call them the "local producers"—the corner grocery store, barber shop, and gas station, the municipal hospital, performing arts center, and rock radio station, the regional bottling plant, supermarket chain, and cement producer, even the national accounting firm, government tax collection agency, and Red Cross office. All tend to follow "industry" recipes to the letter, providing them to their particular community.

One final point on niche strategies. While some strategies are clearly more niche-like than others, all strategies are in some sense of this nature. That is to say, a strategy is characterized as much by what it excludes as by what it includes. No organization can be all things to all people (though some try), just as no biological species can live off the environment in general. The all-encompassing strategy is no strategy at all. Thus, to facilitate survival, every real strategy deposits the organization that pursues it into a particular segment of the overall environment—in ecological terms, into its own niche (Starbuck and Dutton, 1973:21).

Customizing Strategies. Customization too has been a neglected subject in the literature of strategic management. As we have pointed out elsewhere (Lampel and Mintzberg, 1987), a generic logic has driven this field (no less evident in our own discussion to

this point), based on the assumption of aggregation: that standardized products are promoted to aggregated sets of customers (however segmented these may be). But there also exists out there a good deal of customization: products or services that in one way or another are oriented to one single customer.[15] Such customization is, of course, the limiting case of segmentation: disaggregation of the market to the point where each customer constitutes a unique segment. And customization also constitutes a form of differentiation, since the product is always distinguished by some characteristic desired by that customer.

Pure customization, in which the product is developed from scratch for each customer, is of course an expensive proposition. That is not to say that it does not exist: a surprising amount of activity in fact fits this category, at least where the customer is able to pay—the architecturally designed house, the company headquarters' building, the special purpose machine or instrument, the Olympic organizing committee, the Apollo moon project. If we look back at our value chain diagram of functional strategies (Figure 3), we can describe pure customization as infiltrating the entire chain: the product is not only delivered in a personalized way, not only assembled and even fabricated to order, but is also designed for the individual customer in the first place.

Less ambitious but probably more common is what we call *tailored customization:* a basic design is modified to the customer's needs or specifications. Here, in other words, the needs of the customer project back not so much to the design stage of the operating chain as to the fabrication stage. This author in fact plies the lakes and rivers of Quebec in just such an example, his canoe tailored to order by Mr. Miller, our Ontario craftsman: Miller used the classic Chestnut Prospector mold but in this case laid up the Kevlar differently above and below the water line to produce an especially lightweight canoe. A certain amount of clothing has, of course, always be so tailored, as has some house construction. But new forms of machinery have recently opened this strategy up to all kinds of new products: rugs woven to customer designs, prostheses modified to fit the bone joints of each patient, and so on.

---

[15]The rest of this section is based largely on the Lampel and Mintzberg (1987) paper.

What we call *standardized customization* encompasses individualized final products assembled from standard components—exactly what happens when most people buy a stereo system or visit the Harvey's chain in Canada where you can specify ketchup, mustard, relish, tomatoes, and/or onions etc. on your hamburger. The customer as an individual penetrates to the assembly process but not beyond, not into basic fabrication, let alone design. The components are all standardized. As in the case of these hamburgers, or automobiles that may be ordered in a similarly customized way, the final product may be built around a standardized central core, with each element added from a set stock of peripheral components. Here, in other words, the product is customized, but from a circumscribed set of choices. (Don't try to get a Rolls Royce emblem on your Volvo, or pumpkin relish on your Harvey's hamburger). Advances in computer-aided design and manufacturing (CAD, CAM) will doubtlessly cause a proliferation of standardized customization, as well as tailored customization, at the expense of fully standardized market segmentation on the one end and, paradoxically, pure customization on the other. Much as in the case of the bumper stickers some people put on their cars, consumers shall be distinguished by their categories, not by their individuality.

Before leaving the issue of scope, we should note that because there are so many dimensions of scope, organizations can naturally pursue mixed strategies, for example, a niche strategy on one dimension and a comprehensive segmentation strategy on another. For example, Porter discusses the "global focus" strategy, which "targets a particular segment of the industry in which the firm competes on a worldwide basis" (1980:294), say to be the world supplier of featherweight racing canoes. (Of course, the same applies to differentiation strategies, except that this is often by necessity: to be differentiated on one dimension may mean to be undifferentiated on certain others, such as high quality at the expense of low price. These interrelationships among the various forms of differentiation and scope would make for an interesting analysis.)

ELABORATING THE CORE BUSINESS

 Given a core business with a particular competitive posture, in terms of differ-

entiation and scope, we now come to the question of what strategies of a generic nature are available to develop and extend that core mission. We shall present these on three levels, the first to do with the elaboration of the core business itself, the second with the extension of the core business (elaboration beyond its basic industry), and the third to do with the reconception (or reconfiguration) of the core business or set of businesses, including their reintegration. It should be noted that all of the strategies we shall present are ones of change: they are all defined by some shift from the core mission and/or posture. But the strategies themselves are static (as are all strategies, by definition), in the sense that they represent, not the process of change but the final consequences of it.

By using core mission and competitive posture as our starting points, we seem to be making the assumption that organizations grow in some simple linear sequence: first they identify a core business, then they develop a posture to compete in it, later they elaborate that business, within its own boundaries and eventually beyond before finally reconceiving it. This certainly seems to be one common progression: entrepreneurs, for example, generally found not just focussed but niche businesses, not conglomerates. Diversification generally takes place only after the core business market has been extensively exploited. But there are no less certainly all kinds of other progressions, many quite common. Thus, our order of presentation should be taken less as a declaration of one definitive pattern than as one for conceptual convenience. Even for an organization that begins its life in, say, a variety of businesses, an understanding of its strategies (if not their evolution) would seem to be facilitated by seeking to locate each business first and then to look inside each to understand its competitive posture before considering the interrelationships among them.

One last point before we consider these strategies. All are presented initially on the expansion side—penetration, product development, acquisition, and so on. Again this is in keeping with our sequence (and with the proactive orientation of the positioning school), but again this is only for conceptual convenience. As we shall subsequently discuss, each of these strategies has a downside equivalent—contraction, product consolidation, divestment, and so on.

Given a core business, an organization can

elaborate it in a number of ways. It can develop its product offerings within that business (adding white-water canoes to the existing line of flat-water ones), it can develop its market via new segments or new channels (selling canoes as status symbols to be worn atop automobiles, promoting them through BMW dealers) or via new geographical areas (selling them to the Inuit, or to the Japanese to make gigantic flower arrangements—a new market segment too, we might add), or it can simply push the same products more vigorously through the same markets. These are, of course, Igor Ansoff's four strategies mentioned at the outset, as presented in his well-known matrix in 1965:

	Existing Product	New Product
Existing Market	Penetration Strategies	Product Development Strategies
New Market	Market Development Strategies	Diversification Strategies

(from Ansoff, 1965: 109, with minor modifications[16])

The strategies labeled on the matrix are the ones we shall discuss below under elaborating the core mission, except for the case of new products in new markets, which because it seems to constitute a diversification beyond the core business, is more appropriately considered in the next section. (Of course, that need not always be true: a producer of large canoes for trappers who introduces a new line of smaller canoes for racers has entered a new market with a new product yet remains in the canoe business. But we have no need to discuss such combined strategies here apart from our consideration of the component strategies that make them up.)

Penetration Strategies

Penetration strategies work from a base of existing products and existing markets: the object of the exercise is to penetrate the market by increasing the organization's share of it. This may be done by straight expansion or by the takeover of existing competitors; conversely, the firm can reduce its market share through a so-called harvesting strategy.

Expansion Strategy

Trying to expand sales with no fundamental change in product or market (Miller getting on the phone and calling the subscribers of *Canadian Geographic* to drum up sales for handcrafted canoes) is at one and the same time the most obvious thing to do and perhaps the most difficult. For, at least in a relatively stable market, it means extracting market share from others, and that logically leads to increased competition.

Nevertheless, perhaps as a reflection of the lack of imagination in much of this field, in both scholarship and practice, simple penetration strategies have had a lot of attention in recent years. Based on the belief that higher market share is per se more profitable, a view vigorously promoted in the 1970s by the Boston Consulting Group and the PIMS project, though now in question, firms have been implored to "buy" market share by expanding production and increasing advertising, pushing harder through existing sales channels to enlarge the size or the frequency of purchases, and so on. ("Trying again" is another such strategy, as when the Disney Studio rereleased *Snow White and the Seven Dwarfs*.)

This strategy, however, by often having no real basis in competitive advantage, can prove to be an expensive failure. It is sustainable competitive advantage that brings market share and then profits, not aggressively throwing money at a problem. "The . . . riskiest way to attack a leader is through pure spending, without reconfiguration or redefinition . . . without [doing] anything differently or better than the leader, but simply [overwhelming] the leader with resources or with a greater willingness to invest" (Porter, 1985:528).

Leaders, of course, seem to have a natural competitive advantage in size per se. IBM sells more computers in part because if the purchasing agent buys anyone else's computer and it goes

---

[16]As noted earlier, Johnson and Jones first presented this matrix (in more elaborate form) in a 1957 article (p. 52). Also Chandler mentions product and market development strategies in his 1962 book *Strategy and Structure* (p. 42).

wrong *he* gets blamed; if he buys IBM, *it* gets blamed. Likewise, Air Canada tends to get called first for a flight from Montreal to Toronto because it has more flights to begin with. But the important point is that *being* there is different from *getting* there. Dominance is fine to explain *being* there and (within reason) for *staying* there; competitive advantage is necessary for *getting* there, also usually for *leaving* there (upward, at least).

We show the expansion strategy as an expanding circle with an expanding arrow emanating from it to indicate that not only do the sales increase (in an unsegmented manner, hence the single arrow), but all functions must expand to provide and support the increased output.

Takeover Strategy

There is, of course, one way to expand market share without upsetting the competitive balance, and that is to acquire competitors. Miller takes over Grumman, just to get its canoe business, of course. This sometimes goes under the label of "horizontal" acquisition, although we have no idea what makes it geometrically "horizontal." Hence we prefer to label it the *takeover* strategy. (Competitive takeovers may, of course, result in product or market development as well; Miller gets a share of the US canoe market in the bargain, plus the capability to produce aluminum canoes, not to mention fighter aircraft.)

Harvesting Strategy

The opposite of an expansion strategy is obviously a contraction strategy, sometimes referred to as one of "retrenchment." But it is difficult to conceive of a practical opposite to buying market share. Who would want to sell or reduce market share per se, in a non-segmented way? (Doing so in a segmented way, for example, by culling out infrequent buyers or lopping off low-margin products, is the negative equivalent of market or product development, not expansion.) Likewise, one does not generally sell part of a homogeneous business to competitors. (Selling it all—called "divestment"—or else liquidating the business is the obvious alternative, but since that takes the

organization out of the industry altogether, it is considered the opposite of diversification, and so is discussed later.)

One strategy that we believe amounts to contraction, however, is the *harvesting* strategy, made popular in the 1970s in the lower left-hand quadrant of the BCG growth-share matrix. The way to deal with the "cash cows"—high shares of low-growth businesses—was to harvest them. The mixing of the metaphors may have been an indication of the dubiousness of the strategy, since to harvest a cow could be a quick way to kill it (even to harvest a field without regard for sowing was a formula for failure, especially when neighbors planted newer strains). But harvesting many firms nonetheless did, which essentially meant exploiting a set position, for example, by cutting back on investment or service.[17] What this amounted to was a cost-cutting strategy, and assuming the harvesters were not inclined to cut on price—since offering bargains was hardly the way to milk a dominant market share—the logical result had to be contraction of the business, until it was eventually sold or liquidated (Porter, 1980:269). Schoeffler of PIMS in fact defined harvesting as "the attempt to 'sell' market position by trading increased short-term earnings for a diminished market share" (1972:6; see also Feldman and Page, 1985:79–80, who address the issue of whether or not this amounts eventually to outright withdrawal). Thus harvesting might be labeled an emergent (unintended) strategy of contraction.

Market Development Strategies

Here we simply distinguish market elaboration strategies from market consolidation strategies.

Market Elaboration Strategies. Promoting existing products in new markets—in effect broadening the scope of the business by finding new market segments, perhaps served by new channels—is an obvious strategy to pursue. Creative market segmentation not only isolates new ways to view existing customers; it also identifies whole new groups of customers. A firm selling branded products might go after the private label market. Miller might try selling to fur trappers or

---

[17]Porter (1980:269) also mentions reducing the variety of products and channels and eliminating small customers, both of which are, again, negative forms of product and market development.

the Inuit, or he might try to have his canoes become the latest status symbols among top executives by having *Fortune* do a photo spread on them.

Product *substitution* is a particular case of the market elaboration strategy. Here uses for the product are promoted that enable it to substitute for another product, as in our example of canoes for Japanese flower arrangements. Sometimes, of course, the manufacturer may have to engage in product or process research to enable the charge to be made (as was necessary in the switch from steel to aluminum cans).

Market Consolidation Strategies. The inverse of market expansion is market consolidation, reducing the number of segments. But this is not just a strategy of failure, to be adopted by organizations in trouble. Given the common tendency to proliferate market segments, it makes sense for the healthy organization to rationalize market segments periodically, to purge the excesses. Thus, we would expect to see these two opposite strategies of market development appearing commonly in sequential cycles, a phase of proliferation to expand followed by one of consolidation to clean house.

Market consolidation, or "countersegmentation" as Kotler and Singh (1981:41) refer to it, can be just as creative an exercise as market segmentation—indeed it is often one of discovering or inventing new segments, but in this case to identify those worth dropping, or else attending to at the expense of others. Organizations may look for the slow payers, the low margin customers (that famous 80 percent that contributes only 20 percent of the profits), the infrequent buyers, the ones who require too much heavy advertising or too much service, and so on.

Geographic Expansion Strategies

An important form of market development can be geographic expansion—carrying the existing product offering to new geographical areas, whether the next block, the next town, the rest of the country, other countries, or across the world.

The so-called "global" strategy would seem to fit here, leaving aside the fact that the label often reflects a first world chauvinism that views the United States, Western Europe, and Japan as the globe—what amounts in our terms to *selective* geographic segmentation (not to mention selective

perception). But this often seems to be a strategy of international rationalization—of locating different business functions in different places but selling the same family of products across various markets. In other words, the strategy of geography expansion can amount to more than product development when organizations diffuse not only their markets but also their functions—from delivery, production, and design, back to sourcing—across geographical areas. The IKEA furniture company, for example, a classic international rationalizer, designs in Scandinavia, sources significantly in Eastern Europe, and markets in Western Europe and North America. This is another reason, aside from its intrinsic importance, why we present the geographic expansion strategies independently of the market development ones. It also explains why we represent these strategies by expansion of our business strategy circle: that can be taken to signify that all functional aspects of strategy expand.

It should be noted that there are also incomplete forms of geographic expansion, short of complete commitment (the latter known as the strategy of *direct investment*). In the words, an organization can find intermediate forms of commitment to a new geographic area. An *exporting* strategy stops short of expanding anything beyond the marketing function, while a *licensing* or *franchising* strategy enables the organization to create an equivalent production function in a new place without making costly investments; a *joint venture* strategy provides a midpoint between full investment and simple licensing. (We shall return to these intermediate auxiliary strategies in the next section, under our discussion of acquisition strategies.)

Product Development Strategies

Here we can distinguish a simple product extension strategy from a more extensive product line proliferation strategy, and their counterparts, product line rationalization.

Product Extension Strategy. Offering new or modified products in the same basic business is another obvious way to elaborate a core business. You start with cornflakes, add bran flakes and rice crispies, and before you know it you have every permutation and combination of the edible grains, in every practical shape, with additives of sugars, dried fruits, colors, and chemicals of supposedly edible sorts. This may amount to differentiation by design, if the results are new distinctive products, or it may not, if standard products are added to the line, resulting in no more than a strategy of increased scope through segmentation.

Often this strategy amounts to marginal modifications in existing products, variations on a theme of the dominant design, as we saw earlier in the example of the various kinds of Coca-Cola.

> *One of the least imaginative strategies of a manufacturer, distributor, or retailer in an expanding or highly competitive market is to increase the product line by relatively minor or subtle variation in style, size, flavor, grade, packaging, brand name or price level. . . . the proliferation is . . . often due to over-sensitivity to new competitive items or the clamoring of salesmen and distributors for additional choices. (Cannon, 1968:117)*

Pearce (1982:25) offers a list of various ways in which new product features can be developed, including modifications in odor, shape, sound, etc., magnifications or minifications (for example, to make the product stronger or smaller), substitutions (of ingredients, etc.), rearrangements of layouts, and so on.

Alternately, an organization can add wholly new products that may be standard to its industry but are nevertheless new to itself. Miller in Niagara Falls can, for example, add a line of kayaks, then rowboats, power boats, yachts, and finally ocean liners. This example was, of course, judiciously chosen to make the point that where one industry ends and another begins can be perfectly arbitrary, a matter of degree more than kind. Is Miller to be described as being the canoe business (as we have been doing), the recreational boat business, the "floating business," or the "thrills business"? It all depends, obviously, on how you define an industry, and that can be both a creative and a delusory act. There is no formula to tell where the product extension strategy ends and the industry diversification strategy begins. We shall return to the issue later to make the point that pinning down an industry can be like pinning down the wind.

Product Line Proliferation Strategy. This is a product development strategy that is intended to end up with comprehensive product segmentation—the complete coverage of a given business.

Our canoe firm seeks to sell every conceivable type of canoe—all the lengths, materials, shapes, keels (or lack of them), weights, floatations, and so on—if not kayaks, yachts, and ocean liners. A retail store seeks to upgrade to a department store, so that everything becomes available under one roof; three airlines merge in Canada to provide comprehensive coverage of all the major routes; Du Pont offers its nylon "in more than a thousand different 'put-ups'," each tailored for use in a different end product, such as women's hosiery, parachutes, and nylon-reinforced rubber tires (Corey, 1975:126). All this is done to ensure that customers need never look elsewhere to fulfill their needs. As Ohmae notes for the electrical equipment business, "ordinarily, an engineer who is designing circuitry reaches for the thickest catalog with the broadest product selection" (1982:111).

One variation of this worth noting is the product line *fortification* strategy: plugging holes in an existing line, say by offering 15-foot canoes between 14- and 16-foot ones to preempt competitors from making inroads in the organization's territory.

Product Line Rationalization Strategies. Again the opposite of extension or proliferation is rationalization or simplification: products are culled, the range of products thinned to get rid of unprofitable excesses or overlaps. McNichols (1983:106) refers to this as "segment retreat": backing into segments where the organization can best protect its markets.

Cannon distinguishes two strategies in this regard, "product-line simplication," which involves the streamlining of the range of product offering, and "product elimination," which is "the drastic pruning of major product types" (1968:117). They became necessary because product line proliferation can result in "'tired' brands or slow movers which drain working capital and profits" (p. 117). But the streamlining or pruning that then becomes necessary can, of course, be done more or less carefully: organizations can simply cut what do not seem to produce the highest profits, or they can redesign their product ranges to encompass more highly integrated lines of fewer overall products. Again we might expect cycles of product extension and rationalization, at least in businesses (such as cosmetics or textiles) predisposed to proliferation in their product lines.

EXTENDING THE CORE MISSION

Now we come to strategies designed to take organizations beyond their core business, strategies that in effect extend the mission. This can be done in so-called vertical or horizontal ways, as well as combinations of the two.

"Vertical" means backward or forward in the operating chain (that is, to businesses that either supply or are supplied by the core business); the strategy is known formally as "vertical integration." But why this has been designated vertical, as if raw materials are down below and finished products up above, is difficult to understand, especially since this particular flow, and the operating chain itself, are almost always drawn horizontally![18] Hence we shall just use the term "chain integration."

"Horizontal" diversification (its own geometry no less evident), which we shall call just plain diversification, refers to encompassing within the organization other, parallel businesses, not in the same chain of operations, whether *related* or *unrelated*, and whether *acquired* or *developed internally*.

We shall discuss the strategies of business extension in three groups: first chain integration, second diversification, related and unrelated as well as various ways in which they can be achieved (forms of entry and ownership), and finally combinations of the two.

 ## Chain Integration Strategies

Organizations can extend their operating chains forward or backward, or more accurately, downstream or upstream, encompassing within their own operations the activities of their customers on the delivery end or their suppliers on the sourcing end. In effect, they choose to "make" rather than to "buy" or sell. More formally, "Vertical integration is the combination under a single ownership of two or more stages of production or distribution (or both) that are actually separate" (Buzzel, 1983:92). Miller enters the canoe tripping business, running tours to the Northwest Territories (in its canoes, of

course), or he buys out Du Pont's Kevlar operations to supply himself with some of the raw materials that make up his canoes.

Our diagram depicts chain integration in two ways, one as encompassing a circle in the downstream chain, the other as an arrow going out to include a supplier upstream. The former is meant to depict chain integration by internal development (creating his own tripping operation), the other by acquisition (of Du Pont's Kevlar operation). For convenience, we shall discuss these two strategies under diversification, although that discussion applies equally to chain integration. Also to be discussed there are intermediate forms of control, such as licensing and franchising (e.g., of downstream outlets for canoe rentals) or joint ventures and long-term contracts (e.g., with a Dutch tulip manufacturer to supply the Japanese flower arrangers). Of course, looked at the other way, these strategies enable the organization to exercise some control over sourcing or delivery without necessarily owning them. Thus, Harrigan refers to them as "quasi-integration," and includes among them "cooperative ventures, minority equity agreements, loans or land guarantees, prepurchase credits, specialized logistical facilities, or understandings concerning customary arrangements" (1985a:78).

Of additional interest here is that beside partial control can be partial integration of the upstream source or the downstream market. Sometimes referred to as a strategy of *tapered* integration (e.g., Harrigan, 1985a:78–79; Porter, 1980:319–320), this involves the buying of some of the inputs or the selling of some of the outputs on the open market, independent of the relationship between the two businesses that have been integrated in the operating chain. In other words, either the additional business or the core business is not fully captive to its partner at the next stage of the operating chain: it can also deal with outside suppliers or customers. But as this can amount to some combination of chain integration and diversification strategies, we shall return to it when we discuss the combinations of the two.

---

[18]See, for example, Porter's value chain (1985:37) or Galbraith's depiction of the product flow (1983). Indeed, we set out to draw the flow of product vertically on paper (at least bottom to top, even if on a flat surface), with the raw materials coming out of a round earth, but it just did not look right, presumably because once extracted, with the exception of the occasional elevator, these materials are processed and sold along the horizontal surface of the earth.

Impartition Strategy

The label *impartition* has been promoted by Pierre-Yves Barreyre of the University of Grenoble (Barreyre, 1984; Barreyre and Carle, 1983) to describe the strategy opposite of chain integration.[19] Essentially the organization decides to buy what it previously made, or (we can add) sell what it previously transferred.

Impartition may be a form of *de*integration (not disintegration!) when the firm gets rid of an activity upstream or downstream in its basic chain of operations. But as the Barreyre and Carle discussion makes clear, it may also amount to the elimination of a function intrinsic to the core business itself, related to sourcing or delivery or any other activity for that matter. Thus, Barreyre and Carle note that virtually any activity can be imparted, from advertising and after-sales-services to personnel training, engineering design, data processing, even financing (as in factoring) or manufacturing itself (as in NASA's contracting out the production of its rockets). Only general management must remain if an "organization" is to merit that label (p. 5) ". . . at one extreme, we know firms [that] buy ideas from the outside, farm out production, and have distribution done by independent partners" (p. 5).

Diversification Strategies

Diversification refers to the entry into some business, not in the same chain of operation but nevertheless possibly related to some distinctive competence or asset of the core business itself. *Related* (sometimes *concentric*) diversification is the label used when the relationship exists (shown by the encompassing circle in our diagram), *unrelated* (sometimes *conglomerate*) diversification when it does not (shown by the separate arrow coming down). Of course, relatedness can also reside in the eyes of the beholder: with a little imagination, relations can be found between any two businesses (and, in fact, some perpetrators of what appear to be the purest forms of conglomerate diversification have used a great deal of imagination, not so much to conceive their acquisitions initially as to justify them later). If Mr. Miller bought,

say a pencil company, someone might easily define him as being in the consumer products business, or the wood processing business, or perhaps even the "hard surfaces folowing over soft" business.

> *If you believe the text of the countless corporate annual reports, just about anything is related to just about anything else! But imagined synergy is much more common than real synergy. GM's purchase of Hughes Aircraft simply because cars were going electronic and Hughes was an electronics concern demonstrates the folly of paper synergy. Such corporate relatedness is an ex post facto rationalization of a diversification undertaken for other reasons (Porter, 1987:54).*

Diversification can be discussed in terms of its basis, its degree, and its means. We shall begin with its basis—related or unrelated.

Related Diversification Strategies. Related diversification is based on some common competence or asset. (The *Random House Dictionary* defines "concentric" as "having a common center.") In other words, there is evident potential synergy between the new business and the core one, based on a common facility (Miller producing Kevlar doghouses in the off-season), a common asset (the railroad becoming a real estate developer over its downtown tracks), a common channel (selling a "complementary product," such as paddles, through the channel used to distribute canoes), a common skill (3M using its bonding competences gleaned from Scotch Tape, etc. to develop "Post-it" notepads), even a common opportunity (as in the next bench syndrome at Hewlett-Packard, where the instrumentation needs of colleagues became the basis for developing certain new products).

Porter (1985:323–324) makes the important distinction between relatedness that is based on some functional or managerial skills across the different businesses, as in Philip Morris using its marketing capabilities to promote the sales of Miller beer, and relatedness of businesses that actually "share activities in the value chain" (p. 323), for example, different products sold by the same sales forces. He refers to the former as "intangible," the

---

[19]Barreyre and Carle (1983:1) point out that the French word *impartition* appears to have no equivalent in English.

latter as "tangible relationships," noting that the two represent "fundamentally different" forms of synergy (p. 325).

It should be emphasized here that no matter what its basis, every related diversification is also fundamentally an *unrelated* one, as many diversifying organizations have discovered to their regret. That is, no matter what basis *is* common to the new business, many other bases *are not* common at all. Accordingly, our circles should really be joined as below.

That, of course, is why the strategy is called "diversification": the two businesses are fundamentally diverse. Even such a seemingly insignificant change as the diversification from supermarket retailing to soft goods discount retailing can fail when the obvious similarities (wheeling carriages through aisles stocked with merchandise which is then passed through check-out counters) can be undermined by subtle differences in merchandising (styling, product obsolescence, etc.; see Mintzberg and Waters, 1982). Because of this, and because organizational distinctive competences often prove far narrower than any of the actors could have imagined, diversification almost inevitably proves to be a tricky business indeed.

On the other hand, some of the most dramatic successes in business have resulted from multiple synergies that themselves being synergistic have propelled an organization far beyond the capabilities of its competitors. Jelinek, for example, discusses the early dramatic success of Texas Instruments as resulting from "a dual competence, in both the new electronics field and in the mechanical, a rare combination in those early days of electronics" (1979:54).

Unrelated Diversification. Unrelated diversification is, of course, based on no specific strength or competence, by definition (Miller going from canoes to nail polish, though he did apply red finishes to canoes). But arguments have been put forward, most notably by Williamson (1975, 1985), that conglomerate diversification does have a *gen-*

eral basis of justification, in the ability of the divisionalized structures that arose to deal with it to move capital among the various businesses more efficiently than do capital markets, and to exercise more effective control over those businesses than would the various boards of directors of independent firms. The argument, in effect, is that this form of diversification is justified by the skills of general corporate management.

We disagree with this conclusion profoundly, both in and of itself and for its implication for society, and have argued our case elsewhere (Mintzberg, 1979:414–430). Essentially we do not find conglomerate diversification and its structural counterpart of pure divisionalization any more efficient at all: as we argued there at length, it suppresses innovation, discourages risk taking, and dampens initiative, encouraging overall bureaucratization and strategic lethargy and sometimes promoting unethical behavior. If capital markets and boards of directors do not function efficiently, society would be better off ensuring that they do rather than allowing resources to become so concentrated instead.

Others, such as Porter (1987), have presented complementary arguments, namely that there has to be some tangible basis to link different businesses together—some specific synergy beyond the ability of general "professional managers." And there is, in fact, evidence that related diversification, however tricky itself, generally proves more profitable than the conglomerate variety. Going into any business just because you believe that you are a smarter manager or better able to move money around seems to have proved the trickiest proposition of all.

Degree of Diversification. The degree of diversification has had some attention in the literature, particularly in two widely cited doctoral dissertations of the 1970s carried out at the Harvard Business School (Wrigley, 1970; Rumelt, 1974). Firms were categorized as being in a *single* business (95 percent of sales), a *dominant* business (accounting for more than 70 percent of their sales), or else sufficiently diversified so that no one business dominated to that degree, whether the mix of businesses was related or unrelated.

Strategies of Entry and Control

Here we consider the means of diversification (or

chain integration), the basis on which the organization moves into the new business and seeks to control what it ends up with.

Most commonly, this is divided into *internal* development strategies (sometimes "start-up," although this implies a conscious effort to enter a new business as opposed to seizing an inadvertent opportunity) and *acquisition* strategies (or so-called "merger" strategies, although given that one firm usually takes over the other, the label seems inappropriate). In other words, an organization can enter a new business by developing it itself, from nothing, or by buying an organization already in that business. We show each in our theme diagram on diversification, internal development by the circle growing out from the core business to envelope the new business, acquisition by an arrow coming out of the core business to connect to the new but already established one.

It is generally believed that the dimensions of relatedness and entry are independent of each other, in other words, as shown by the matrix below, how an organization enters a business is quite independent of how related that business is to its own operations. An organization can grow a related or unrelated business, or acquire either. In one important respect, however, we disagree fundamentally, and indicate so by how we have filled in the matrix. In effect, we argue that there is no such a thing as a related diversification by acquisition, nor an unrelated one by internal development, at least at the outset. Put the other way, every diversification by internal development is initially related, every one by acquisition initially unrelated.

aspect of the internal operations of the existing business. If a Miller employee, in the process of trying to cut gunnels, invents a new type of saw, that may become the basis for a whole new business. But it grew initially out of an activity or a skill that was intrinsic to the existing business. Later, of course, it may grow unrelated, as the new business establishes its operating autonomy. This is depicted below.

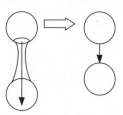

Likewise, every diversification by acquisition brings together two businesses that are unrelated in actual fact, even if the potential relationship is perfectly obvious. Miller may buy Cadorette, which makes canoes that look (if do not perform) like his own, but on the day after the purchase, the two firms have nothing whatsoever to do with each other in any tangible sense: they share no employees, no materials, no skills, no assets. It may take only a few days to begin forging the obvious links, but those links must be forged, as we show below (either by drawing the skill, asset, or whatever out of the acquired firm or else by imposing the link directly).

Means of Diversification

	internal development	acquisition
related	happens naturally at the outset	(takes time at best)
unrelated	(may happen later)	natural status at the outset

Basis of Diversification

Every diversification by internal development is initially related because it grew out of some

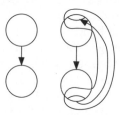

The point may seem trivial, but the fact that so many related acquisitions have come to grief suggests that organizations might do well to take it into account—to recognize that forging links between large, established organizations is in fact seldom quick or simple. This is one major reason why the literature of management is so obsessed with "culture" at the moment, the word for that host of intangible factors that makes true integration of different organizations so difficult.

Over time, of course, the acquisition may become fully related, while the internal development may become totally unrelated. Marathon Realty began as a real estate arm to exploit the rights of way of the Canadian Pacific Railroad; eventually the two businesses grew to have little to do with one another. Ironically, the same became true of this firm's airline. One railroad that took seriously Levitt's (1960) concept of being in the "transportation" business found it irrelevant: in 1987 it in fact sold its airline. The acquiring airline then set out to integrate this and another acquired airline as well as itself into a single line called Canadian Airlines International. At this initial writing, a few days after the announcement, few doubt that this acquisition will eventually result in complete integration, although the route to it may not be easy.

Both internal development and acquisition involve complete ownership and formal control of the new business. But there are a host of other strategies that involve only partial ownership and/or control. (In fact, these are really structures, in that they describe organizational arrangements for achieving product-market strategies. But they are decided upon like strategies and are generally viewed as part and parcel of the strategic moves of diversification as well as chain integration, and often geographic expansion as well.) Table 2 summarizes these strategies under three headings, full ownership and control (acquisition and internal development, as already discussed), partial ownership and control, and partial control without ownership.

Partial ownership and control may involve simple a equity position less than complete, ranging from *majority* to *minority*. It may also involve more complex partnership arrangements, such as *joint ventures*, where each partner contributes certain skills or assets (such as Miller molding the Kevlar doghouses and Dr. Ballards promoting and distributing them). Joint venture strategies have in fact received a great deal of attention in the positioning school literature of recent years (especially Harrigan, 1985b, 1986, 1987). *Turnkey* arrangements are also partnerships of sorts, except temporary ones—one partner exercises full control until the facility is built and then turns it over to the other.

Partial control without direct ownership can be achieved in a number of ways. *Licensing* is a strategy for allowing some sort of asset—say the rights to a new product—to be used by others for a fee. Lacking the production know-how, Miller might logically license Stanley to produce its new saws, and then sit back and cash the checks rather than having to learn a new business. *Franchising* is similar, except that here the organization designs a whole system of operations and controls which is then, in effect, licensed out. Since this usually happens downstream, at the retail level, franchising really often amounts to a partial form of chain integration. Likewise *long-term contracting* usually takes place along the operating chain, as for example when an automobile company arranges to take the full production of a parts supplier (which then becomes, in effect, captive). Such a strategy is also common in the case of private label producers.

Combined Integration-Diversification Strategies

Among the most interesting are those strategies that combine chain integration with business diversification, sometimes leading organizations into whole networks of new businesses.

First a word on the distinction between these two strategies is in order. While that is certainly clear in theory, there are times when it is difficult to make in practice. When a supermarket chain expands into the shopping center business or into bread baking, can we call this upstream integration or related diversification? The answer is not obvious and can depend not only on how the organization enters the new business, but on what goes on in the heads of the managers who make the decision. Diversification or integration, it sometimes turns out, exist fundamentally in the mind of the beholder.

In the supermarket chain we studied (Mintzberg and Waters, 1982), the bread baking move was clear enough. Used initially to supply the stores, it was upstream integration. But the move into shopping centers was less evident. Shopping center management is a kind of wholesale service business, quite different from supermarkets, although supermarkets, of course, constitute a key element in shopping centers. So the move into that business looked to be related diversification. But in fact the intention behind the move tells another story, and ultimately positions it elsewhere. When

Table 2 *Strategies of Entry and Control*

Full ownership and control	Internal development
	Acquisition
Partial ownership and control	Majority, minority
	Partnership, including:
	joint venture
	turnkey (temporary control)
Partial control without ownership	Licensing
	Franchising
	Long-term contracting

the first shopping center came to Montreal, Steinberg's (the chain) was asked to bid on putting stores in it. Its chief executive, Sam Steinberg told us that at the time he'd be "damned" if he'd settle for one store in four; the only way to realize the growth he wanted in his traditional business was to control those shopping centers himself. That way he could get most of the supermarkets. Since he owned the necessary land, and he found the means of financing, he was able to do it. In other words, Steinberg's entered the new business fundamentally to protect its traditional one. In that sense, what it did has to be described as upstream chain integration. Over time, however, the shopping center business became an important activity in its own right, as well as the basis for diversification into various other forms of retailing, while the bakery (before it was sold off recently) soon began to sell off excess bread to other stores and ended up selling more on the open market than to its sister retail operation! Thus, both examples of chain integration *became,* in part at least, forms of business diversification.

Below we discuss three types of combined integration-diversification strategies—labeled by-product, linked, and crystalline—which are really three stages of increasing elaboration of the combination.

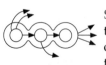 **By-Product Diversification Strategy.** Selling off excess bread to other food stores is an example of *by-product* diversification; so is the commerical marketing of an airline's maintenance services, the development of land over a railroad's urban tracks, the selling off of chemicals that result from an aluminum firm's smelting process or even of cargo space in its empty trucks

on their return hauls. The actual figures for Alcoa in this regard, circa 1969, are shown in Figure 6. As the examples make clear, the by-product may be literally so—a spinoff of a production process—or else it may relate to some function, resource, asset, or whatever else that becomes available as a result of the core operating process. Either way, the new activity amounts to a form of market development at some intermediate point in the operating chain, in effect into a related though peripheral business treated largely as an additional delivery function.

The word by-product means, of course, that the sales are secondary. The firm is committed to its traditional chain of operations, but nevertheless is willing to exploit certain peripheral opportunities that naturally present themselves. Also, of course, what is considered peripheral can change too. Steinberg's was reportedly offered the McDonald business for Canada; had it accepted, supermarket operations would today likely be the peripheral business. These things do happen, but seemingly more common is the growth of the by-product activity into a (related) diversified business in its own right. This is what happened to both Canadian Pacific and Steinberg's in the real estate business, which became important self-standing entities (the former especially unrelated, as noted earlier). As shown in the figure below, the by-product arrows converge to create new circles—free standing, even if related, businesses.

Figure 6 *By-product and End Product Sales of Alcoa in 1969 (From Rumelt, 1974, p. 21; Prepared from Data in Company's Annual Reports.)*

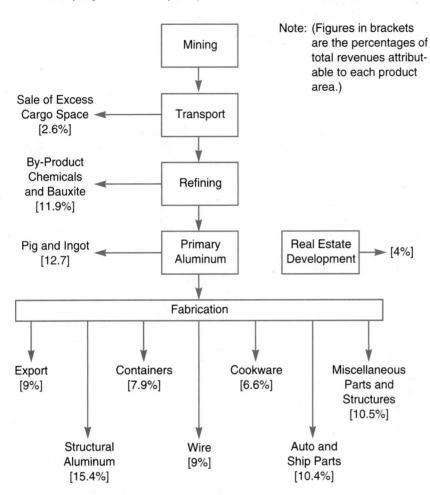

Figure 7 contrasts a purely integrated operating chain (a), with by-product diversification (b), followed by the full move to related product diversification (c), where what is transferred internally may no more important than what is sold on the open market, as for example in the relationships among various divisions of the General Electric Company.[20]

Linked Diversification Strategy. *Linked* diversification naturally extends by-product diversification. One business simply leads to another, whether integrated "vertically" or diversified "horizontally." The organization pursues its operating chain upstream, downstream, sidestream; it exploits preproducts, end products, and by-products of its core products as well as of each other. What emerges is a network of integration and diversification, linked in all kinds of vertical, horizontal, and lateral ways with the original core business—the place where all this began. Miller decides to market paddles, and from there goes into all manner of sporting equipment; he back integrates into Kevlar, and uses that to make radial tires and bulletproof vests; from there he's into three-piece suits, sports cars, and eventually the world.

As we shall consider more carefully below, in his 1983 article, Jay Galbraith built on the idea of the "center of gravity," the focal function of the organization in the operating chain no matter how integrated or diversified it may be (e.g., engineering design in a Hewlett-Packard). To Galbraith, therefore, linked diversification means diffusing that center of gravity, "operating at different centers of gravity in those new industries" (1983:70).

We can show linked diversification in different ways. Galbraith's example of Union Camp moving from paper to woodlands (upstream integration) and to chemicals (by-product of paper-

making) and then downstream in both chemicals and wood products, is shown superimposed on his framework in Figure 8. In Figure 9, we show the linked diversification of the Steinberg firm on a time scale, with integration above the line and diversification below it. Essentially the firm integrated upstream (there is no downstream for a retail chain) for a number of years, into warehousing, real estate, food manufacturing, etc., and then began to diversify in related ways, mostly into other forms of retailing, using its shopping center position as a base. This development is repeated in the form of the diagram we have been using in this discussion in Figure 10, to show the various diagonal or lateral aspects of a combined integration-diversification strategy.

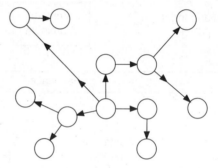

Crystalline Diversification Strategy. Push the previous discussion to the limit, and it becomes difficult and perhaps irrelevant to distinguish integration from diversification, core activities from peripheral activities, closely related businesses from distantly related ones. What were once clear links in a few chains now metamorphose into what looks like a form of crystalline growth, as business after business gets added literally right and left as well as up and down. Hence we propose the label *crystalline diversification strategy*. In effect, the organization becomes a vigorous product developer, the extreme from of what Miles and Snow (1978) call a "prospector", or to Prahalad, the pursuer of a

---

[20]The bread example shows that chain integration can also lead to by-product diversification and then to related diversification. In a sense, certain forms of integration appear to be the counterpart to by-product diversification, as when a firm integrates backward to supply *itself* with a necessary but peripheral input. The following quotation from a Texas Instruments executive provides such an example that in fact grew to related diversification, presumably via by-product diversification.

When we went to the digital processing of information, we made our own computers, because in the mid-1950s, nobody made what we needed—so we made our own. We've very often done this, and that acquired skill gradually allowed us to move on into another field, that became larger than the original purpose had been (in Jelinek, 1979:63).

Figure 7 *From Integration to Diversification via the By-product Strategy (Adapted from Mintzberg, 1979:404).*

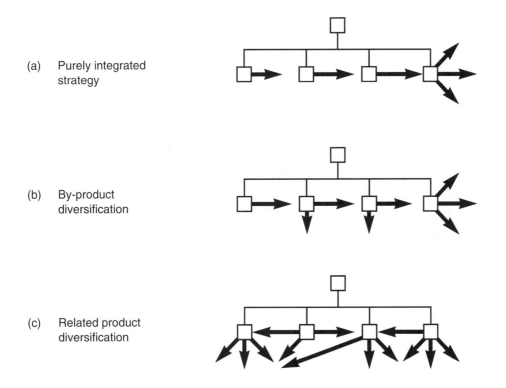

(a)   Purely integrated
       strategy

(b)   By-product
       diversification

(c)   Related product
       diversification

Figure 8 *Linked Diversification in Terms of Galbraith's Operating Chain — the Case of Union Camp (from Galbraith, 1983:70).*

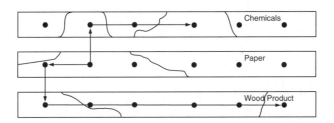

Figure 9 Linked Diversification on a Time Scale—the Case of Steinberg (from Mintzberg and Waters, 1982:490).

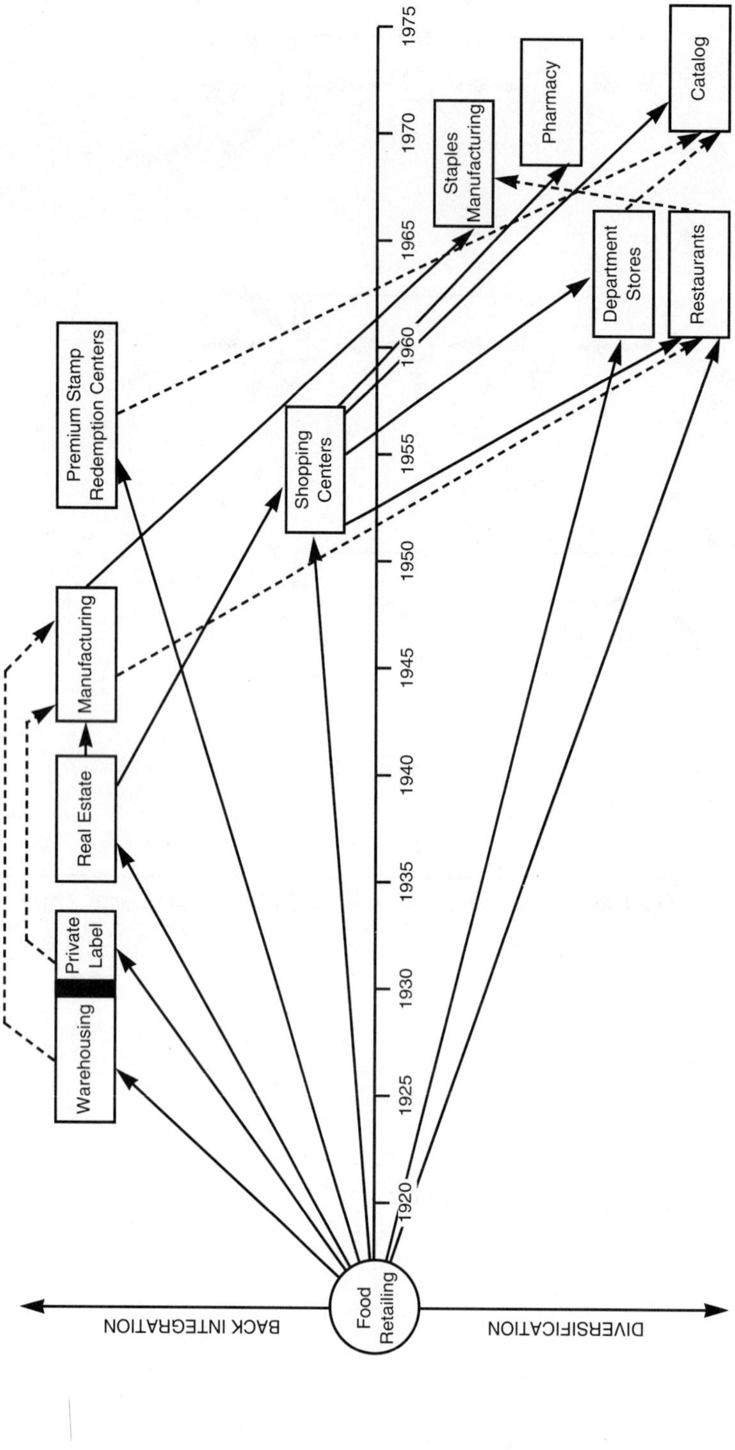

Figure 10 *Steinberg's Linked Diversification in Terms of our Theme Diagram*

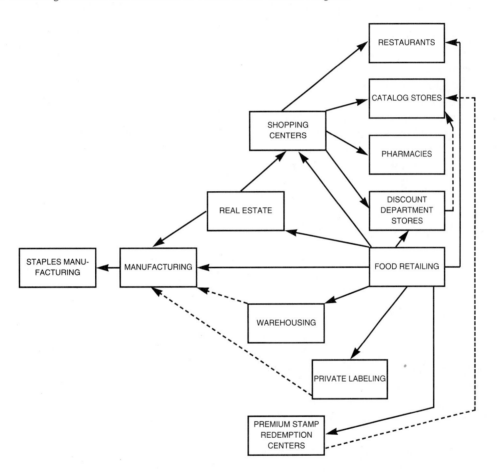

"cascading" strategy.[21] Normann has likewise written of "centrifugal diversification from an established business idea" (1977:146).

The organization here is less concerned with what official business it is in than with pursuing business opportunities through its competences, wherever they happen to take it. Figure 11 shows Rumelt's depiction of the elaboration of the products of the Carborundum Company from 1949 to 1969, through two snapshot views of those years.

In such crystalline diversification, the organization's competences are, in fact, critical, for that is how the businesses tend to be related, at least initially: the strategy is generally one of internal development, as one experience leads to another, based on a core skill. Thus, for example, "95 percent of 3M's revenue comes from products using coating and bonding technologies" (Galbraith, 1985:17). For Hewlett-Packard, the core strength seems to have been engineering, largely related to instrumentation, while for Procter and Gamble, it appears to have been a powerful marketing capability as well as an uncanny knack to come up with the right innovation in product development. Of course, we cannot conclude that the organization with a successful strategy of crystalline diversification does not know what business it is in; its business simply defies traditional SIC codes. It is defined by the core skill being exploited.

Withdrawal Strategies

Finally there are the strategies that reverse all those of diversification: organizations cut back on the businesses they are in. "Exit" has been one popular label for this; we prefer *withdrawal* as the opposite of diversification, just as contraction is the opposite of expansion. Sometimes organizations choose to *shrink* their activities. They cancel long-term licenses and close down joint ventures, cease to sell by-products, eliminate links with other businesses, reduce their crystalline networks. Other times they abandon or *liquidate* businesses (the opposite of internal development), or else they *divest* them (the opposite of acquisition).

The divestment strategy, especially of unrelated businesses (or at least ones that have become increasingly unrelated to the core business), has become a popular one of late, a reflection presumably of the excesses of diversification. Organizations have discovered that it literally pays to know what business you are in, that mindless (or more exactly concept-less) diversification can be a costly exercise because the justification for an organization generally remains, as always, some *distinctive* competence. Managing "professionally," or moving money around, without any sense of the business being managed, has not proved to be a sufficiently critical factor for success, except in rare cases of brilliant leaders who somehow manage to hold agglomerations together personally. Even then, the bright but more ordinary managers who follow them often seem to have no idea how to manage the legacies they inherit. Eventually, therefore, many are forced to pursue strategies of withdrawal, paring the businesses down to a more manageable set, more comprehensible and so more amenable to workable strategic management.

But there remains another set of strategies that can be pursued in this and other situations, strategies that require more imagination.

RECONCEIVING THE BUSINESS

It may seem strange to end a discussion of strategies of ever more elaborate development of a business with ones involving reconception of the business. But in an important sense, this is one logical sequence: after the core business has been identified, distinguished, elaborated, and extended, there often follows the need not just to consolidate it but also to redefine it and reconfigure it—in essence, to reconceive it.

As they develop, some organizations manage to maintain sight of their essence—their distinctive competences and the resulting strategic definition of their business. But many do not: through all the waves of expansion, integration, diversification, etc., they lose a sense of themselves. Then reconception becomes the ultimate form of consolidation: rationalizing not just excesses in product offerings or market segments or even new businesses, but all of these things together and more— the essence of the entire strategy. Organizations add a good deal of strategic baggage over time, just as individuals do in their private lives; periodic

---

[21]In presentation transparencies, C. K. Prahalad, University of Michigan, circa 1986.

Figure 11 *Crystalline Diversification in the Carborundum Company 1949–1969 (from Rumelt, 1974:17, 19, as Prepared from Data in the Company's Annual Report).*

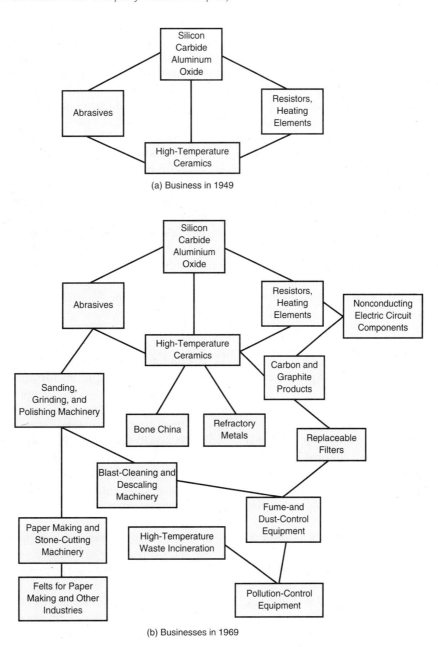

(a) Business in 1949

(b) Businesses in 1969

housecleaning is often in order for both. That should involve not just throwing out the junk, but also rethinking and recombining what is left behind. Thus, in a sense, reconception becomes the highest level of strategy, and perhaps also the most demanding one: finding ways to redefine and reconfigure the basic business of the organization.

Just a few years ago, the literature on strategy had almost nothing to say about the issue of reconception. The notion persisted until quite recently that organizations could develop and expand simply by adding new businesses. Related diversification was beginning to be recognized as superior to unrelated diversification, but what that really meant—beyond the linking of some basic function, product line, asset, competence, or whatever—remained largely unexplored. Today, although we have a long way to go, at least the issues are being considered: how to reconceive an existing business for competitive advantage, how to knit different businesses into some integrated whole, how to shift the focal attention of management for one stage or one business to another or to several. Here we shall discuss these three types of reconception strategies (although the distinctions among them, as we shall note, appear fuzzy at the margins): redefining the core business, recombining the different businesses, and relocating the organization's core.

○──▶◇ Business Redefinition Strategies

A business, as Abell (1980) has thoughtfully pointed out, may be defined in a variety of ways— by the function it performs, the market it serves, the product it produces. All businesses have popular conceptions. Some are narrow and tangible, such as the paper clip or canoe business. Others are broad and vague, such as the so-called transportation or financial services businesses, and this can range to the ethereal, such as the business of reducing function.

All of these, no matter how tangible, are ultimately concepts that exist only in the minds of actors and observers (recorded, perhaps, in the files of the government bureaucracies as well). It therefore becomes possible, with a little effort and imagination, to redefine a business. What we mean by business definition strategies are ones that reconceive the core business itself, and so change how it is conducted. Adding a line of white-water

canoes to flat-water ones keeps Miller in the "canoe" business; adding a line of paddles may too. But when snowshoes are added, he may have entered the "recreational transportation" business, and with deck chairs, the definition may have to be broadened to the "leisure-time" business. But if the chairs and snowshoes are made of Kevlar, like the canoes, then maybe he has moved into the "Kevlar molding" business.

For economists and government lawyers intent on categorizing things, pinning down businesses can be an elusive act, like pinning down the wind. But for businessmen who must worry about satisfying customers, motivating employees, and coming out at year-end with more revenues than expenses, where one business begins and another ends should be of less concern than should playing with business definitions to stimulate the creative use of competitive advantage. In other words, while the boundaries of the organization may be a problem for the analysts, they are a strategic variable for the strategists, the most creative of whom use the boundaries to their advantage. (Of course, this is true of generic strategies in general, that while the uninspired organizations slot comfortably into one generic strategy or another, the most creative ones recombine or invent new ones to their competitive advantage.)

Thus business redefinition strategies are fundamentally creative ones. There is no rule for developing them, no formula, because in essence they are designed to change the rules, to dispense with the accepted formula in favor of new ways to think about a business. If it had been done before, it would not constitute a reconception.

Timex changed the rules when it redefined the watch as an inexpensive, utilitarian, almost throw-away item rather than a piece of cherished jewelery that happened to be worn on the wrist. That had implications for channels (drugstores as opposed to jewelers), for pricing (low prices, low markups), for manufacture (more highly automated, far less costly production processes), for sourcing and advertising, and for almost every other conceivable function of the watch business. Likewise, IKEA redefined one important segment of the furniture business: it ships its products unassembled to stores that look like showrooms in one part and supermarkets in another; customers pick packages of dining room tables or whatever off the shelves, wheel them in oversized carriages to conveyor belts where they check them out as if they were cans of peas; they then borrow roof racks or else rent trucks at the store to take their furniture home where they assemble it according to the instructions and with the tools provided in the package.

In such cases, although the new concept may originate in one function or activity, virtually every function in the operating chain is eventually affected. Indeed this is so almost by definition, because otherwise a strategic change would not merit the label of business redefinition. The essence of the strategy is to use some dramatic innovation to play with the very conception of the business from beginning to end in order to gain competitive advantage.

McMillan refers to the business redefinition strategy as "reshaping the industry infrastructure" (1983:18), while Porter calls it "reconfiguration" (1985:519–523), although his notion of product *substitution* (pp. 273–314) could sometimes also constitute a form of business redefinition. A well known case of this occurred when Howard Head remade the ski industry by substituting metal for wood; another example took place when containers were introduced to enable railroads to recapture some of the business they lost to trucking.

In some work in progress with Lampel, we are developing some notions of how creative strategists can play with "product spaces." They can, of course, simply *expand* the product space, as when McDonald's added the breakfast Egg McMuffin alongside its regular lunch and dinner products. They can *shift* the product space, as Timex did in the watch business. Then they can *split* the product space, say by opening a fast food chain of cheese blintze restaurants alongside the more conventional hamburger and chicken ones. They can *usurp* the product space by doing things better, as did Toyota against the American automobile makers through higher quality combined with lower prices (cost leadership and differentiation, without getting caught in the middle, another way to break the rules). They can also *create* the product space in the first place, as did Apple with the personal computer or Xerox with the photocopying machine. Later they can *recreate* the product space, by changing the nature of the business, as did Sears when it provided stock brokerage services in its department stores. And finally they can *recombine* the product space, say by bundling two

separate products together, as in the linking of real estate services with stock brokerage. While some of the less ambitious of these may amount simply to forms of product or market development, or design differentiation, etc., the more creative and far reaching, especially as we move down the list, bring us into the realm of business redefinition.

Business Recombination Strategies

As Porter notes, through the waves of diversification that swept American business in the 1960s and 1970s, and the resulting attention to the distinctions between corporate and business strategy and all the SBU and growth-share matrix paraphernalia that accompanied it, "the concept of synergy has become widely regarded as passé"—a "nice idea" but one that "rarely occurred in practice" (1985:317–318). Businesses were elements in a portfolio to be bought and sold, or, at best, grown and harvested. Deploring that conclusion, Porter devotes three chapters of his recent book to "horizontal strategy," which we prefer to call (given our problems with the geometry of this field) *business recombination* strategies. These are efforts to recombine different businesses in some tangible sense, at the limit to reconceive various businesses as one business. In Porter's terms, this means to coordinate explicitly the activities of "distinct but interrelated business units," "based on competitive advantage, not on financial considerations or stock market perceptions. . . . Horizontal strategy—not portfolio management—is thus the essence of corporate strategy" (pp. 318, 319).

Businesses can be recombined tangibly or only conceptually. Since Theodore Levitt published his famous "Marketing Myopia" article in 1960, it has become evident that businesses can easily change their strategic definitions—redefine themselves conceptually. By a stroke of the pen, railroads could be in the transportation business and ball-bearing manufactures in the function-reduction business. It all amounted to a kind of *intellectual* diversification—diversifying how managers *thought* about the business (or at least claimed they did). Realizing some practical change in behavior proved another matter, however. Some firms could do nothing different and still gloat in the loftiness of their business definition. After all, you didn't have to do anything more than produce ball bearings to be in the function reduction business. Others could at least take the reconception seriously, diversifying from railroads into trucking, shipping, and air transport, if not taxicabs. The Canadian Pacific Railroad was one that did, and decades later, as already noted, it found itself with virtually no synergy between its major "transportation" components, the railroad and the airline, and recently divested the latter. Writing an idea on a piece of paper proved far simpler then realizing the tangible synergies required to weld different activities into a single "business." In practical fact then, there may never have been a "transportation" business.

But when there is some substantial basis for combining different activities, the business recombination strategy can be very effective. There *is* a "coating and bounding" business because 3M has been able to draw on common technical capabilities to create one, just as there is a "personal care" business because Procter and Gamble could so draw on its common marketing and innovating capabilities. Of course, you will find no "personal care" business in the SIC codes, only a soap and cleaning compounds business, a toilet preparations business, etc. But if the label fits, and helped one firm to comprehend itself and so to bound what might otherwise have been uncontrolled product proliferation, so much the better for it.[22] Whether there is also a "financial services" business remains to be seen: firms such as Sears, Merrill Lynch, and American Express are betting there is, but so far the results seem to be mixed. Our guess is that in the end there will be something more than the brokerage or real estate or banking businesses, but something less than the financial services business. Experimentation—emergent strategy—will decide what "business" will result.

So far we have discussed synergies that are real enough but not concrete, closer to what Porter calls "intangible relationships," based on common skills (1985:324). But as he notes, there are also synergies based on shared activities in the value chain,

more tangible in nature. Most concrete is the increasingly popular strategy of *bundling*, where complementary products are sold together, for a single price, say two paddles with the purchase of one canoe, or investment included with protection in the purchase of "whole life" insurance. Of course, *unbundling* can emerge as an equally viable strategy, such as selling "term" insurance free of any investment obligation.

While these are rather obvious examples, bundling and unbundling can be creative acts too, capable of shifting the basis of competition. People Express unbundled a number of airline services (such as baggage handling) to save the money of its thrifty passengers, while at the time of this writing, SAS is bundling with its flights the ground services of transportation to and from its hotels as well as check-in there to save the time of its well-heeled passengers.

Porter devotes a chapter of his 1985 book to "complementary products"—"the opposite of substitutes, because the sale of one promotes the sale of another" (p. 416). Beside bundling, he considers such strategies as simply offering the "full range" and "cross-subsidization" (as when retailers use loss leaders to attract customers). Carried to their logical extreme, these concrete recombination strategies lead to a "systems view" of the business, where all products and services are conceived to be tightly interrelated. Cannon, in fact, back in 1968 (pp. 125–129) discussed such system strategies at some length, showing at one point how the perception of products in systems terms can lead into the business redefinition strategy (through the example of the Carborundum Company that, by so viewing its market for abrasives, redefined its mission as the removal of metal, which apparently led to "dramatic" differences for it [p. 128]).

Core Relocation Strategies

Finally we come full circle by closing the discussion where we began, on the location of the core busi-

---

[22]Our suspicion, we should note, is that such labels usually emerge after the fact, as the organization seeks a way to rationalize its diversification that has already taken place. In effect, the strategy is emergent (Mintzberg, 1987), as we saw in the case of Steinberg's that groped for an explanation through several annual reports until it finally hit upon the label of the "total marketing package" to describe its use of various forms of retailing to exploit its shopping center position (Mintzberg and Waters, 1982). The firm, incidentally, has since sold off most of its nonsupermarket retailing businesses as well as its manufacturing businesses, choosing instead to broaden its geographic and service scope in its traditional business.

ness. An organization, in addition to having one or more strategic positions in a marketplace, tends to have what Jay Galbraith (1983, 1985) calls a single "center of gravity," some conceptual place where is concentrated not only its core skills but also its cultural heart. For example, Galbraith describes Procter and Gamble as focusing virtually all its efforts on "branded consumer products," each "sold primarily by advertising to the homemaker and managed by a brand manager" (1985:13). The firm finds its center of gravity downstream in the marketing function.

But as changes in strategic position take place, in all the ways we have been describing, shifts can also take place in this center of gravity, often, we suspect, pulled more in emergent fashion by position shifts than pushed in a deliberate way by conceptual thinking.

The center of gravity, of course, reflects strategy more as perspective than as position (Mintzberg, 1987), so changes in it should probably be considered as moving beyond the strict confines of the traditional strategy content literature (the positioning school). But for completeness and even though "there has been virtually no work done on center of gravity changes" (Galbraith, 1983:72), this final strategy merits inclusion in our discussion here.

We believe four distinct forms are possible in the shift in the center of gravity of an organization's perspective. First it can shift *along the operating chain,* upstream or downstream, as with Miller focusing his attention on the business of producing Kevlar or of running canoe trips. The examples available suggest the latter is far more common. General Mills represents one well-known example of a downstream shift in center of gravity, "from a flour miller to a related diversified provider of products for the homemaker"; eventually the company sold off the flour milling operation altogether (Galbraith, 1983:76).

Second, important center of gravity shifts can also take place, not just between different stages of a business, but *between functions* of the business more proximate to one another. For example, as an industry shifts from an excess of demand to an excess of supply, influence and so center of gravity can shift from the manufacturing function to that of marketing. Similarly, a good deal of publicity was given in recent years to Hewlett-Packard's efforts to shift from an engineering to a marketing orientation in order to enhance its fortunes in the computer business.

A third core relocation strategy is the shift to a *new business,* whether or not at the same stage of the operating chain, as in Miller moving over to become a manufacturer of vests. Such shifts can be awfully demanding, simply because industries are cultures too. Each has its own tangible ways of doing things, in the form of various "receipes" (Gringer and Spender, 1979), as well as particular ways of thinking about things, in the form of various mindsets. This can include which functions in the operating chain are given emphasis, and how.

In his discussion of center-of-gravity shifts, Galbraith does not acknowledge this third type. This is based on his belief that a parallel shift to a new business at the some stage of the operating chain is more natural and so easier to effect. "Strategic changes that do not involve changes in the center of gravity [in the first sense] . . . are easier to implement and historically have been more successful" because "each stage of an industry has different success factors . . . the organization and its management are shaped by the lessons learned at their stage in an industry" (1985:8–9,4). We are less comfortable with such a blanket conclusion, however, because of the factors that can be associated with specific changes in a business. For example, shifting from the toy business to the detergent business hardly sounds simple, even though the center of gravity of both may be focused on the marketing activities in the delivery stage.

Even the seemingly minor shift from supermarket retailing to discount department store retailing caused difficulties for the Steinberg chain (Mintzberg and Waters, 1982). The two businesses looked awfully similar—same displays, same carriages, same check-out counters, etc. But the merchandising proved quite different: styling counts more for a T-shirt than for a can of tuna fish, and perishability proves a different issue for designer jeans than for iceberg lettuce. More trivial still was the National Film Board's shift from documentary filmaking for theatres and library distribution to documentaries for television series (Mintzberg and McHugh, 1985). Everything seemed the same—the technology, the skills, the subject matter; only the physical screen was obviously different. What tripped up the shift was the simple fact of regularity: this filmmaking agency could not sustain its creativity on a weekly basis. Thus, distinctive competences often prove to be narrow indeed; in this case they focused on the *creative* application of film making skills, and that was not possible every Tuesday at 8 PM.

Some discussion of the difficulties of relocating centers of gravity between businesses appears in, of all places, the literature of sociology (e.g., Sills, 1957). Under the heading of "goal succession," really in our terms mission or business succession, it deals with how not-for-profit organizations cope with the need for sudden shifts in their core missions because of failure or success. Well-known is Sills's discussion of the Foundation for Infantile Paralysis, which ran the successful "March of Dimes" campaign. It was so successful in fact that it raised much of the money that helped Jonas Salk develop the vaccine that eradicated the disease. Faced with that success, the foundation had to relocate its core mission—in simpler terms, it had to find another reason to exist—and that proved a long and difficult process. Of course, when an organization is able to do so gradually, while its old business continues, the shift is likely to be far less agonizing.

Our fourth and final form of core relocation strategies is not to *a* new business but to several, around a *core theme,* in effect the reorientation from a single process or product to a broader concept. Miller might broaden his perspective to be in the recreational business, much as Procter and Gamble went from the soap business to the personal care business, or ITT and Litton Industries of the 1960s went from a core business to business in general, as a portfolio. Ironically, the latter is probably easier to effect (if not to sustain), since it involves simply acquiring a whole series of businesses with little regard for synergies, the management having to concern itself only with applying a set of financial controls and mechanisms to move money around. No *distinctive* competences need be managed. Indeed the central management is characterized more by what it must unlearn than what it must learn, namely not to interfere in specifics of

running a business, for after all, the shift is one of *de*focus rather than focus. But as we have noted in several places in our discussion, viable strategic definition normally requires more than that, and the recent tendencies to consolidate the conglomerates—in effect to relocate the central core around some *tangible* theme—suggests that *distinctive* competence does matter after all.

This brings us to the end of our discussion of generic strategies—our loop from locating a business, to distinguishing it, elaborating it, extending it, and then reconceiving it, and finally relocating it. Table 3 summarizes all the generic strategies we have introduced in the five categories.

Having delineated all these strategies, the next obvious question becomes: Which strategies are pursued where? What are the conditions under which each of these strategies is used? Unfortunately, the evidence so far available on this issue is very uneven. A few strategies have been investigated empirically at great length and some have been the subject of a good deal of conceptual speculation. This is especially true of diversification and somewhat less so of chain integration; some work has also been done on certain forms of differentiation and on the particular scope strategy of niche. But other important generic strategies have had hardly any serious attention (while some seemingly less important ones, such as joint ventures, have been the subject of a good deal of research). Just as we need to have a comprehensive framework of generic strategies, so too do we need more systematic investigation of the consequences of the different strategies that make it up.

We close this paper by reiterating the warning that while a framework of generic strategies may help an organization to think about positioning itself, use of this as a pat list may put it at a disadvantage against competitors that develop their strategies in more creative ways.

Table 3 *The Framework of Generic Strategies*

A. Locating the Core Business: —Stage Strategies
                                                Upstream strategies
                                                Midstream strategies
                                                Downstream strategies
                                              —Industry Strategies

B. Distinguishing the Core Business: —(Business Strategy Areas
     Sourcing strategies
     Processing strategies
     Delivery strategies
     Design strategies
     Supporting strategies)
     —Differentiation Strategies
     Price differentiation strategies
     Image differentiation strategies
     Support differentiation strategies
     Quality differentiation strategies
     Design differentiation strategies
     Undifferentiated strategies
     —Scope Strategies
     Unsegmentation strategy
     Segmentation strategy
     (comprehensive, selective)
     Niche strategy
     Customizing strategies
     (pure, standardized, tailored)

C. Elaborating the Core Business: —Penetration Strategies
     Expansion strategy
     Takeover strategy
     Harvesting strategy
     —Market Development Strategies
     Market elaboration strategies
     (including substitution)
     Market consolidation strategies
     —Geographic Expansion Strategies
     —Product Development Strategies
     Product extension strategy
     Product line proliferation strategy
     Product line rationalization strategy

D. Extending the Core Business: —Chain Integration Strategies
     Upstream, downstream integration strategies
     Tapered integration strategies
     Impartition strategy
     —Diversification Strategies
     Related diversification strategies
     Unrelated diversification strategies
     Internal development strategies
     Acquisition strategies
     (majority, minority ownership, other arrangements including
     partnerships [joint venture and turnkey], franchising, licensing, long-term
     contracting)
     —Combined Integration-Diversification Strategies
     By-product diversification strategy

continued

Table 3 *continued*

Linked diversification strategy
Crystalline diversification strategy
—Withdrawal Strategies
Shrinkage strategies
Liquidation strategy
Divestment strategy

E. Reconceiving the Business: —Business Redefinition Strategies
—Business Recombination Strategies
(including conceptual and tangible, bundling and unbundling)
—Core Relocation Strategies
Upstream or downstream shift strategy
Functional focus shift strategy
New business shift strategy
Core theme shift strategy
No focus shift strategy

REFERENCES

Abell, D. F., *Defining the Business: The Starting Point of Strategic Planning* (Prentice Hall, 1980)

Abell, D. F., and Hammond, J. S., *Strategic Market Planning: Problems and Analytical Approaches* (Prentice Hall, 1979)

Ansoff, H. I., *Corporate Strategy: An Analytic Approach to Business Policy for Growth and Expansion* (McGraw-Hill, 1965)

Barreyre, P. Y., *The Concept of "Impartition" Policy in High Speed Strategic Management* (Working Paper, Institut d'Administration des Entreprises, Grenoble, 1984)

Barreyre, P. Y., and Carle, M., *Impartition Policies: Growing Importance in Corporate Strategies and Applications to Production Sharing in Some Worldwide Industries* (Paper presented at Strategic Management Society Conference, Paris, 1983)

Cannon, J. T., *Business Strategy and Policy* (Harcourt, Brace, 1968)

Caves, R. E., Industrial Organization, Corporate Strategy, and Structure *Journal of Economic Literature* (March 1980:64–92)

Chandler, A. D. Jr., *Strategy and Structure: Chapters in the History of the Industrial Enterprise* (The M.I.T. Press, 1962)

Christensen, C. R., Andrews, K. R., Bower, J. L., Hammermesh, R. G. and Porter, M. E., *Business Policy: Text and Cases* (Richard D. Irwin, Sixth Edition, 1987)

Corey, E. R., Key Options in Market Selection and Product Planning *Harvard Business Review* (September–October 1975:119–128)

Dickson, P. R. and Ginter, J. L., Market Segmentation, Product Differentiation, and Market Strategy *Journal of Marketing* (April 1987:1–10)

Feldman, P. and Page, A. L., Harvesting: The Misunderstood Market Exit Strategy, *The Journal of Business Strategy* (Spring 1985:79–85)

Galbraith, J. R., Strategy and Organization Planning *Human Resource Management* (1983:63–77)

Galbraith, J. R., Types of Strategic Changes (Working Paper, 1985)

Grinyer, P. H. and Spender, J. C., *Turnaround: The Fall and Rise of the Newton Chambers Group* (Associated Press, 1979)

Harrigan, K. R., *Strategic Flexibility: A Management Guide for Changing Times* (Lexington Books, 1985a)

Harrigan, K. R., *Strategies for Joint Ventures* (Lexington Books, 1985b)

Harrigan, K. R., *Managing for Joint Ventures Success* (Lexington Books, 1986)

Harrigan, K. R., *Joint Ventures: A Mechanism for Creating Change* (Paper presented at Strategic Management Society Conference, Boston, 1987)

Hax, A. C. and Majluf, N. S., *Strategic Management: An Integrative Perspective* (Prentice Hall, 1984)

Jelinek, M., *Institutionalizing Innovation* (Praeger, 1979)

Johansen, D. C. and Edey, M. A., How Ape Became Man: Is It a Matter of Sex? *Science* (April 1981:45–49)

Johnson, S. C. and Jones, C., How to Organize for New Products *Harvard Business Review* (May–June 1957:49–62)

Kotler, P. and Singh, R., Marketing Warfare in the 1980s *Journal of Business Strategy* (Winter 1981:30–41)

Lampel, J. and Mintzberg, H., Customizing Strategies . . . and Strategic Management (Working Paper, McGill University, Montreal, 1987)

Levitt, T., Marketing Myopia *Harvard Business Review* (July–August 1960:45–56)

Levitt, T., Marketing Success through Differentiation—of Anything *Harvard Business Review* (January–February 1980:83–91)

MacMillan, I. C., Preemptive Strategies *Journal of Business Strategy* (Fall 1983:16–26)

McNichols, T. J., *Policy-Making and Executive Action* (McGraw Hill, 1983)

Melin, L., Implementation of New Strategies and Structures (Paper presented at Strategic Management Society Conference, Paris, 1983)

Miles, R. E. and Snow, C. C., *Organizational Strategy, Structure, and Process* (McGraw-Hill, 1978)

Mintzberg, H., *The Structuring of Organizations* (Prentice Hall, 1979)

Mintzberg, H., Crafting Strategy *Harvard Business Review* (July–August 1987:66–75)

Mintzberg, H. and McHugh, A., Strategy Formation in an Adhocracy *Administrative Science Quarterly* (1985:160–197)

Mintzberg, H. and Waters, J. A., Tracking Strategy in an Entrepreneurial Firm *Academy of Management Journal* (1982: 265–499)

Normann, R., *Management for Growth* (Wiley, 1977)

Ohmae, K., *The Mind of the Strategist* (McGraw-Hill, 1982)

Pearce, J. A., Selecting Among Alternative Grand Strategies *California Management Review* (Spring 1982:23–31)

Porter, M. E., *Competitive Strategy: Techniques for Analyzing Industries and Competitors* (Free Press, 1980)

Porter, M. E., *Competitive Advantage: Creating and Sustaining Superior Performance* (Free Press, 1985)

Porter, M. E., From Competitive Advantage to Corporate Strategy *Harvard Business Review* (May–June 1987:43–59)

Rumelt, R. P., *Strategy, Structure, and Economic Performance* (Harvard University, 1974)

Rumelt, R. P., How Important is Industry in Explaining Firm Profitability? (Working paper, UCLA, 1981)

Sills, D. L., *The Volunteers* (Free Press, 1957)

Simmonds, W. H. C., A New Classification of Industry and Its Uses (Working Paper, National Research Council of Canada, 1972)

Simmonds, W. H. C., Toward an Analytical Industry Classification *Technological Forecasting and Social Change* (1973:375–385)

Sloan, A. P., *My Years at General Motors* (Doubleday, 1963)

Smith, W. R., Product Differentiation and Market Segmentation as Alternative Marketing Strategies *Journal of Marketing* (July 1956:3–8)

Smith, G. A., Christensen, C. R., Berg, N. A., and Salter, M. S., *Policy Formulation and Administration* (Richard D. Irwin, Sixth Edition, 1972)

Starbuck, W. H. and Dutton, J. M., Designing Adaptive Organizations *Journal of Business Policy* (Summer 1973:21–28)

Williamson, O. E., *Markets and hierarchies: Analysis and Antitrust Implications* (Free Press, 1975)

Williamson, O. E., *The Economic Institutions of Capitalism: Firms, Markets, Relational Contracting* (Free Press, 1985)

Wrigley, L., Divisional Autonomy and Diversification (Doctoral Thesis, Harvard Business School, 1970)

STRUCTURE IS NOT ORGANIZATION

Robert H. Waterman, Jr., Thomas J. Peters, and Julien R. Phillips
McKinsey & Company

*Diagnosing and solving organizational problems means looking not merely to structural reorganization
for answers but to a framework that includes structure and several related factors.*

The Belgian surrealist René Magritte painted a series of pipes and titled the series *Ceci n'est pas une pipe*: this is not a pipe. The picture of the thing is not the thing. In the same way, a structure is not an organization. We all know that, but like as not, when we reorganize what we do is to restructure. Intellectually all managers and consultants know that much more goes on in the process of organizing than the charts, boxes, dotted lines, position descriptions, and matrices can possibly depict. But all too often we behave as though we didn't know it; if we want change we change the structure.

Early in 1977, a general concern with the problems of organization effectiveness, and a particular concern about the nature of the relationship between structure and organization, led us to assemble an internal task force to review our client work. The natural first step was to talk extensively to consultants and client executives around the world who were known for their skill and experience in organization design. We found that they too were dissatisfied with conventional approaches. All were disillusioned about the usual structural solutions, but they were also skeptical about anyone's ability to do better. In their experience, the techniques of the behavioral sciences were not providing useful alternatives to structural design. True, the notion that structure follows strategy (get the strategy right and the structure follows) looked like an important addition to the organizational tool kit; yet strategy rarely seemed to dictate unique structural solutions. Moreover, the main problem in strategy had turned out to be execution: getting it done. And that, to a very large

extent, meant *organization*. So the problem of organization effectiveness threatened to prove circular. The dearth of practical additions to old ways of thought was painfully apparent.

OUTSIDE EXPLORATIONS

Our next step was to look outside for help. We visited a dozen business schools in the United States and Europe and about as many superbly performing companies. Both academic theorists and business leaders, we found, were wrestling with the same concerns.

Our timing in looking at the academic environment was good. The state of theory is in great turmoil but moving toward a new consensus. Some researchers continue to write about structure, particularly its latest and most modish variant, the matrix organization. But primarily the ferment is around another stream of ideas that follow from some startling premises about the limited capacity of decision makers to process information and reach what we usually think of as "rational" decisions.

The stream that today's researchers are tapping is an old one, started in the late 1930s by Fritz Roethlisberger and Chester Barnard, then both at Harvard (Barnard had been president of New Jersey Bell). They challenged rationalist theory, first—in Roethlisberger's case—on the shop floors of Western Electric's Hawthorne plant. Roethlisberger found that simply *paying attention* provided a stimulus to productivity that far exceeded that induced by formal rewards. In a study of workplace hygiene, they turned the lights up and got an expected productivity increase. Then to validate their results they turned the lights down. But something surprising was wrong: productivity went up again. Attention, they concluded, not working conditions per se, made the difference.

Barnard, speaking from the chief executive's perspective, asserted that the CEO's role is to harness the social forces in the organization, to shape and guide values. He described good value-shapers as *effective* managers, contrasting them with the mere manipulators of formal rewards who dealt only with the narrower concept of *efficiency*.

Barnard's words, though quickly picked up by Herbert Simon (whom we'll come back to later), lay dormant for thirty years while the primary management issues focused on decentralization and structure—the appropriate and burning issue of the time.

But then, as the decentralized structure proved to be less than a panacea for all time, and its substitute, the matrix, ran into worse trouble, Barnard's and Simon's ideas triggered a new wave of thinking. On the theory side, it is exemplified by the work of James March and Karl Weick, who attacked the rational model with a vengeance. Weick suggests that organizations learn—and adapt—very slowly. They pay obsessive attention to internal cues long after their practical value has ceased. Important business assumptions are buried deep in the minutiae of organizational systems and other habitual routines whose origins have been long obscured by time. March goes further. He introduced, only slightly facetiously, the garbage can as an organizational metaphor. March pictures organizational learning and decision making as a stream of choices, solutions, decision makers, and opportunities interacting almost randomly to make decisions that carry the organization toward the future. His observations about large organizations parallel Truman's about the presidency: "You issue orders from this office and if you can find out what happens to them after that, you're a better man than I am."

Other researchers have accumulated data which support this unconventional view. Henry Mintzberg made one of the few rigorous studies of how senior managers actually use time. They don't block out large chunks of time for planning, organizing, motivating, and controlling as some suggest they should. Their time, in fact, is appallingly

but perhaps necessarily fragmented. Andrew Pettigrew studied the politics of strategic decision and was fascinated by the inertial properties of organizations. He showed that organizations frequently hold onto faulty assumptions about their world for as long as a decade, despite overwhelming evidence that it has changed and they probably should too.

In sum, what the researchers tell us is: "We can explain why you have problems." In the face of complexity and multiple competing demands, organizations simply can't handle decision making in a totally rational way. Not surprisingly, then, a single blunt instrument—like structure—is unlikely to prove the master tool that can change organizations with best effect.

Somewhat to our surprise, senior executives in the top-performing companies that we interviewed proved to be speaking very much the same language. They were concerned that the inherent limitations of structural approaches could render their companies insensitive to an unstable business environment marked by rapidly changing threats and opportunities from every quarter—competitors, governments, and unions at home and overseas. Their organizations, they said, had to learn how to build capabilities for rapid and flexible response. Their favored tactic was to choose a temporary focus, facing perhaps one major issue this year and another next year or the year after. Yet at the same time, they were acutely aware of their peoples' need for a stable, unifying value system— a foundation for long-term continuity. Their task, as they saw it, was largely one of preserving internal stability while adroitly guiding the organization's responses to fast-paced external change.

Companies such as IBM, Kodak, Hewlett-Packard, GM, Du Pont, and P&G, then, seem obsessive in their attention to maintaining a stable culture. At the same time, these giants are more responsive than their competitors. Typically, they do not seek responsiveness through major structural shifts. Instead, they seem to rely on a series of temporary devices to focus the attention of the entire organization for a limited time on a single priority goal or environmental threat.

SIMON AS EXEMPLAR

Thirty years ago, in *Administrative Behavior*, Herbert Simon (a 1977 Nobel laureate) anticipated several themes that dominate much of today's thinking about organization. Simon's concepts of "satisficing" (settling for adequate instead of optimal solutions) and "the limits of rationality" were, in effect, nails in the coffin of economic man. His ideas, if correct, are crucial. The economic man paradigm has not only influenced the economists but has also influenced thought about the proper organization and administration of most business enterprises—and, by extension, public administration. Traditional thought has it that economic man is basically seeking to maximize against a set of fairly clear objectives. For organization planners the implications of this are that one can specify objectives, determine their appropriate hierarchy, and then logically determine the "best" organization.

Simon labeled this the "rational" view of the administrative world and said, in effect, that it was all right as far as it went but that it had decided limits. For one, most organizations cannot maximize—the goals are really not that clear. Even if they were, most business managers do not have access to complete information, as the economic model requires, but in reality operate with a set of relatively simple decision rules in order to *limit* the information they really need to process to make most decisions. In other words, the rules we use in order to get on with it in big organizations limit our ability to optimize anything.

Suppose the goal is profit maximization. The definition of profit and its maximization varies widely even within a single organization. Is it earnings growth, quality of earnings, maximum return on equity, or the discounted value of the future earnings stream—and if so, at what discount rate? Moreover, business organizations are basically large social structures with diffuse power. Most of the individuals who make them up have different ideas of what the business ought to be. The few at the top seldom agree entirely on the goals of their enterprise, let alone on maximization against one goal. Typically, they will not push their views so hard as to destroy the social structure of their enterprise and, in turn, their own power base.

All this leaves the manager in great difficulty. While the research seems valid and the message of complexity rings true, the most innovative work in the field is descriptive. The challenge to the manager is how to organize better. His goal is organization effectiveness. What the researchers are saying is that the subject is much more complex than any of our past prescriptive models have allowed for. What none has been able to usefully say is, "OK, here's what to do about it."

THE 7-S FRAMEWORK

After a little over a year and a half of pondering this dilemma, we began to formulate a new framework for organizational thought. As we and others have developed it and tested it in teaching, in workshops, and in direct problem solving over the past year, we have found it enormously helpful. It has repeatedly demonstrated its usefulness both in diagnosing the causes of organizational malaise and in formulating programs for improvement. In brief, it seems to work.

Our assertion is that productive organization change is not simply a matter of structure, although structure is important. It is not so simple as the interaction between strategy and structure, although strategy is critical too. Our claim is that effective organizational change is really the relationship between structure, strategy, systems, style, skills, staff, and something we call superordinate goals. (The alliteration is intentional: it serves as an aid to memory.)

Our central idea is that organization effectiveness stems from the interaction of several factors—some not especially obvious and some under-analyzed. Our framework for organization change, graphically depicted in the exhibit [Figure 1], suggests several important ideas:

- First is the idea of a multiplicity of factors that influence an organization's ability to change and its proper mode of change. Why pay attention to only one or two, ignoring the others? Beyond structure and strategy, there are at least five other identifiable elements. The division is to some extent arbitrary, but it has the merit of acknowledging the complexity identified in the research and segmenting it into manageable parts.

- Second, the diagram is intended to convey the notion of the interconnectedness of the variables—the idea is that it's difficult, perhaps impossible, to make significant progress in one area without making progress in the others as well. Notions of organization change that ignore its many aspects or their interconnectedness are dangerous.

Figure 1 A New View of Organization

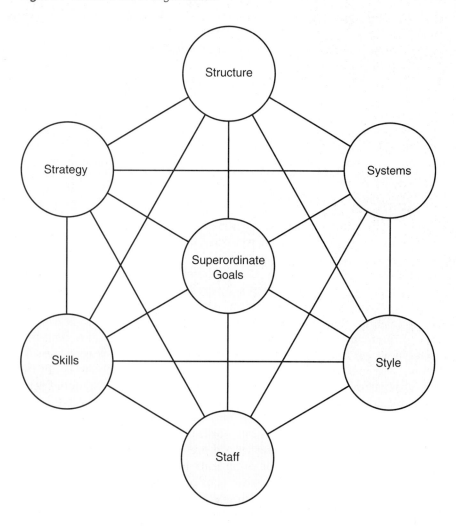

- In a recent article on strategy, *Fortune* commented that perhaps as many as 90 percent of carefully planned strategies don't work. If that is so, our guess would be that the failure is a failure in execution, resulting from inattention to the other S's. Just as a logistics bottleneck can cripple a military strategy, inadequate systems or staff can make paper tigers of the best-laid plans for clobbering competitors.
- Finally, the shape of the diagram is significant. It has no starting point or implied hierarchy. A priori, it isn't obvious which of the seven factors will be the driving force in changing a particular organization at a particular point in time. In some cases, the critical variable might be strategy. In others, it could be systems or structure.

Structure

To understand this model of organization change better, let us look at each of its elements, beginning—as most organization discussions do—with structure. What will the new organization of the 1980s be like? If decentralization was the trend of the past, what is next? Is it matrix organization? What will "Son of Matrix" look like? Our answer is that those questions miss the point.

To see why, let's take a quick look at the history of structural thought and development. The basic theory underlying structure is simple. Structure divides tasks and then provides coordination. It trades off specialization and integration. It decentralizes and then recentralizes.

The old structural division was between production and sales. The chart showing this was called a functional organization. Certain principles of organization, such as one-man/one-boss, limited span of control, grouping of like activities, and commensurate authority and responsibility, seemed universal truths.

What happened to this simple idea? Size—and complexity. A company like General Electric has grown over a thousandfold in both sales and earnings in the past eighty years. Much of its growth has come through entry into new and diverse businesses. At a certain level of size and complexity, a functional organization, which is dependent on frequent interaction among all activities, breaks down. As the number of people or businesses increases arithmetically, the number of interactions required to make things work increases geometrically. A company passing a certain size and complexity threshold must decentralize to cope.

Among the first to recognize the problem and explicitly act on it was Du Pont in 1921. The increasing administrative burden brought about by its diversification into several new product lines ultimately led the company to transform its highly centralized, functionally departmental structure into a decentralized, multidivisional one. Meanwhile, General Motors, which has been decentralized from the outset, was learning how to make a decentralized structure work as more than just a holding company.

However, real decentralization in world industry did not take place until much later. In 1950, for example, only about 20 percent of the Fortune 500 companies were decentralized. By 1970, 80 percent were decentralized. A similar shift was taking place throughout the industrialized world.

Today three things are happening. First, because of the portfolio concept of managing a business, spun off from General Electric research (which has now become PIMS), companies are saying, "We can do more with our decentralized structure than control complexity. We can shift resources, act flexibly—that is, manage strategically."

Second, the dimensions along which companies want to divide tasks have multiplied. Early on, there were functional divisions. Then came product divisions. Now we have possibilities for division by function, product, market, geography, nation, strategic business unit, and probably more.

The rub is that as the new dimensions are added, the old ones don't go away. An insurance company, for example, can organize around market segments, but it still needs functional control over underwriting decisions. The trade-offs are staggering if we try to juggle them all at once.

Third, new centralist forces have eclipsed clean, decentralized divisions of responsibility. In Europe, for example, a company needs a coherent union strategy. In Japan, especially, companies need a centralized approach to the government interface. In the United States, regulation and technology force centralization in the interest of uniformity.

This mess has produced a new organization form: the matrix, which purports, at least in concept, to reconcile the realities of organizational complexity with the imperatives of managerial control. Unfortunately, the two-dimensional matrix model is intrinsically too simple to capture the real situation. Any spatial model that really did capture it would be incomprehensible.

Matrix does, however, have one well-disguised virtue: it calls attention to the central problem in structuring today. That problem is not the one on which most organization designers spend their time—that is, how to divide up tasks. It is one of emphasis and coordination—how to make the whole thing work. The challenge lies not so much in trying to comprehend all the possible dimensions of organization structure as in developing the ability to focus on those dimensions which are currently important to the organization's evolution—and to be ready to refocus as the crucial dimensions shift. General Motors' restless use of structural change—most recently the project center, which led to their effective downsizing effort—is a case in point.

The General Motors solution has a critical attribute—the use of a temporary overlay to accomplish a strategic task. IBM, Texas Instruments, and others have used similar temporary structural weapons. In the process, they have meticulously preserved the shape and spirit of the underlying structure (e.g., the GM division or the TI Product Customer Center). We regularly observe those two attributes among our sample of top performers: the use of the temporary and the maintenance of the simple underlying form.

We speculate that the effective "structure of the eighties" will more likely be described as "flexible" or "temporary"; this matrix-like property will be preserved even as the current affair with the formal matrix structure cools.

Strategy

If structure is not enough, what is? Obviously, there is strategy. It was Alfred Chandler who first pointed out that structure follows strategy, or more precisely, that a strategy of diversity forces a decentralized structure.[1] Throughout the past decade, the corporate world has given close attention to the interplay between strategy and structure. Certainly, clear ideas about strategy make the job of structural design more rational.

By "strategy" we mean those actions that a company plans in response to or anticipation of changes in its external environment—its customers, its competitors. Strategy is the way a company aims to improve its position vis-à-vis competition—perhaps through low-cost production or delivery, perhaps by providing better value to the customer, perhaps by achieving sales and service dominance. It is, or ought to be, an organization's way of saying: "Here is how we will create unique value."

As the company's chosen route to competitive success, strategy is obviously a central concern in many business situations—especially in highly competitive industries where the game is won or lost on share points. But "structure follows strategy" is by no means the be-all and end-all of organization wisdom. We find too many examples of large, prestigious companies around the world that are replete with strategy and cannot execute any of it. There is little if anything wrong with their structures; the causes of their inability to execute lie in other dimensions of our framework. When we turn to nonprofit and public-sector organizations, moreover, we find that the whole meaning of "strategy" is tenuous—but the problem of organizational effectiveness looms as large as ever.

Strategy, then, is clearly a critical variable in organization design—but much more is at work.

Systems

By systems we mean all the procedures, formal and informal, that make the organization go, day by day and year by year: capital budgeting systems, training systems, cost accounting procedures, budgeting systems. If there is a variable in our model that threatens to dominate the others, it could well be systems. Do you want to understand how an organization really does (or doesn't) get things done? Look at the systems. Do you want to change an organization without disruptive restructuring? Try changing the systems.

A large consumer goods manufacturer was recently trying to come up with an overall corporate strategy. Textbook portfolio theory seemed to apply: Find a good way to segment the business, decide which segments in the total business portfolio are most attractive, invest most heavily in those. The only catch: Reliable cost data by segment were not to be had. The company's management information system was not adequate to support the segmentation.

Again, consider how a bank might go about developing a strategy. A natural first step, it would seem, would be to segment the business by customer and product to discover where the money is made and lost and why. But in trying to do this, most banks almost immediately come up against an intractable costing problem. Because borrowers are also depositors, because transaction volumes vary, because the balance sheet turns fast, and because interest costs are half or more of total costs and unpredictable over the long term, costs for various market segments won't stay put. A strategy based on today's costs could be obsolete tomorrow.

One bank we know has rather successfully sidestepped the problem. Its key to future improvement is not strategy but the systems infrastructure that will allow account officers to negotiate deals favorable to the bank. For them the system *is* the strategy. Development and implementation of a superior account profitability system, based on a return-on-equity tree, has improved their results dramatically. "Catch a fish for a man and he is fed for a day; teach him to fish and he is fed for life": The proverb applies to organizations in general and to systems in particular.

Another intriguing aspect of systems is the way they mirror the state of an organization. Con-

---

[1]Alfred D. Chandler, Jr., *Strategy and Structure: Chapters in the History of the American Industrial Enterprise* (Cambridge, Mass.: MIT Press, 1962).

sider a certain company we'll call International Wickets. For years management has talked about the need to become more market oriented. Yet astonishingly little time is spent in their planning meetings on customers, marketing, market share, or other issues having to do with market orientation. One of their key systems, in other words, remains *very* internally oriented. Without a change in this key system, the market orientation goal will remain unattainable no matter how much change takes place in structure and strategy.

To many business managers the word "systems" has a dull, plodding, middle-management sound. Yet it is astonishing how powerfully systems changes can enhance organizational effectiveness—without the disruptive side effects that so often ensue from tinkering with structure.

Style

It is remarkable how often writers, in characterizing a corporate management for the business press, fall back on the word "style." Tony O'Reilly's style at Heinz is certainly not AT&T's, yet both are successful. The trouble we have with style is not in recognizing its importance, but in doing much about it. Personalities don't change, or so the conventional wisdom goes.

We think it important to distinguish between the basic personality of a top-management team and the way that team comes across to the organization. Organizations may listen to what managers say, but they believe what managers do. Not words, but patterns of actions are decisive. The power of style, then, is essentially manageable.

One element of a manager's style is how he or she chooses to spend time. As Henry Mintzberg has pointed out, managers don't spend their time in the neatly compartmentalized planning, organizing, motivating, and controlling modes of classical management theory.[2] Their days are a mess—or so it seems. There's a seeming infinity of things they might devote attention to. No top executive attends to all of the demands on his time; the median time spent on any one issue is nine minutes.

What can a top manager do in nine minutes? Actually, a good deal. He can signal what's on his mind; he can reinforce a message; he can nudge

people's thinking in a desired direction. Skillful management of his inevitably fragmented time is, in fact, an immensely powerful change lever.

By way of example, we have found differences beyond anything attributable to luck among different companies' success ratios in finding oil or mineral deposits. A few years ago, we surveyed a fairly large group of the finders and nonfinders in mineral exploration to discover what they were doing differently. The finders almost always said their secret was "top-management attention." Our reaction was skeptical: "Sure, that's the solution to most problems." But subsequent hard analysis showed that their executives *were* spending more time in the field, *were* blocking out more time for exploration discussions at board meetings, and *were* making more room on their own calendars for exploration-related activities.

Another aspect of style is symbolic behavior. Taking the same example, the successful finders typically have more people on the board who understand exploration or have headed exploration departments. Typically they fund exploration more consistently (that is, their year-to-year spending patterns are less volatile). They define fewer and more consistent exploration targets. Their exploration activities typically report at a higher organizational level. And they typically articulate better reasons for exploring in the first place.

A chief executive of our acquaintance is fond of saying that the way you recognize a marketing-oriented company is that "everyone talks marketing." He doesn't mean simply that an observable preoccupation with marketing is the end result, the final indication of the company's evaluation toward the marketplace. He means that it can be the lead. Change in orientation often starts when enough people talk about it before they really know what "it" is. Strategic management is not yet a crisply defined concept, but many companies are taking it seriously. If they talk about it enough, it will begin to take on specific meaning for their organizations—and those organizations will change as a result.

This suggests a second attribute of style that is by no means confined to those at the top. Our proposition is that a corporation's style, as a reflec-

[2]Henry Mintzberg, "The Manager's Job: Folklore and Fact," *Harvard Business Review,* July/August 1975: 49–61.

tion of its culture, has more to do with its ability to change organization or performance than is generally recognized. One company, for example, was considering a certain business opportunity. From a strategic standpoint, analysis showed it to be a winner. The experience of others in the field confirmed that. Management went ahead with the acquisition. Two years later it backed out of the business, at a loss. The acquisition had failed because it simply wasn't consistent with the established corporate culture of the parent organization. It didn't fit their view of themselves. The will to make it work was absent.

Time and again strategic possibilities are blocked—or slowed down—by cultural constraints. One of today's more dramatic examples is the Bell System, where management has undertaken to move a service-oriented culture toward a new and different kind of marketing. The service idea, and its meaning to AT&T, is so deeply embedded in the Bell System's culture that the shift to a new kind of marketing will take years.

The phenomenon at its most dramatic comes to the fore in mergers. In almost every merger, no matter how closely related the businesses, the task of integrating and achieving eventual synergy is a problem no less difficult than combining two cultures. At some level of detail, almost everything done by two parties to a merger will be done differently. This helps explain why the management of acquisitions is so hard. If the two cultures are not integrated, the planned synergies will not accrue. On the other hand, to change too much too soon is to risk uprooting more tradition than can be replanted before the vital skills of the acquiree wither and die.

Staff

Staff (in the sense of people, not line/staff) is often treated in one of two ways. At the hard end of the spectrum, we talk of appraisal systems, pay scales, formal training programs, and the like. At the soft end, we talk about morale, attitude, motivation, and behavior.

Top management is often, and justifiably, turned off by both these approaches. The first seems too trivial for their immediate concern ("Leave it to the personnel department"), the second too intractable ("We don't want a bunch of shrinks running around, stirring up the place with more attitude surveys").

Our predilection is to broaden and redefine the nature of the people issue. What do the top-performing companies do to foster the process of developing managers? How, for example, do they shape the basic values of their management cadre? Our reason for asking the question at all is simply that no serious discussion of organization can afford to ignore it (although many do). Our reason for framing the question around the development of managers is our observation that the superbly performing companies pay extraordinary attention to managing what might be called the socialization process in their companies. This applies especially to the way they introduce young recruits into the mainstream of their organizations and to the way they manage their careers as the recruits develop into tomorrow's managers.

The process for orchestrating the early careers of incoming managers, for instance, at IBM, Texas Instruments, P&G, Hewlett-Packard, or Citibank is quite different from its counterpart in many other companies we know around the world. Unlike other companies, which often seem prone to sidetrack young but expensive talent into staff positions or other jobs out of the mainstream of the company's business, these leaders take extraordinary care to turn young managers' first jobs into first opportunities for contributing in practical ways to the nuts-and-bolts of what the business is all about. If the mainstream of the business is innovation, for example, the first job might be in new-products introduction. If the mainstream of the business is marketing, the MBA's first job could be sales or product management.

The companies who use people best rapidly move their managers into positions of real responsibility, often by the early- to mid-thirties. Various active support devices like assigned mentors, fast-track programs, and carefully orchestrated opportunities for exposure to top management are hallmarks of their management of people.

In addition, these companies are all particularly adept at managing, in a special and focused way, their central cadre of key managers. At Texas Instruments, Exxon, GM, and GE, for instance, a number of the very most senior executives are said to devote several weeks of each year to planning the progress of the top few hundred.

These, then, are a few examples of practical programs through which the superior companies manage people as aggressively and concretely as others manage organization structure. Considering people as a pool of resources to be nurtured, developed, guarded, and allocated is one of the many ways to turn the "staff" dimension of our 7-S framework into something not only amenable to, but worthy of practical control by senior management.

We are often told, "Get the structure 'right' and the people will fit" or "Don't compromise the 'optimum' organization for people considerations." At the other end of the spectrum we are earnestly advised, "The right people can make any organization work." Neither view is correct. People do count, but staff is only one of our seven variables.

Skills

We added the notion of skills for a highly practical reason: It enables us to capture a company's crucial attributes as no other concept can do. A strategic description of a company, for example, might typically cover markets to be penetrated or types of products to be sold. But how do most of us characterize companies? Not by their strategies or their structures. We tend to characterize them by what they do best. We talk of IBM's orientation to the marketplace, its prodigious customer service capabilities, or its sheer market power. We talk of Du Pont's research prowess, Procter & Gamble's product management capability, ITT's financial controls, Hewlett-Packard's innovation and quality, and Texas Instruments' project management. These dominating attributes, or capabilities, are what we mean by skills.

Now why is this distinction important? Because we regularly observe that organizations facing big discontinuities in business conditions must do more than shift strategic focus. Frequently they need to add a new capability, that is to say, a new skill. The Bell System, for example, is currently striving to add a formidable new array of marketing skills. Small copier companies, upon growing larger, find that they must radically enhance their service capabilities to compete with Xerox. Meanwhile Xerox needs to enhance its response capability in order to fend off a host of new competition. These dominating capability needs, unless explicitly labeled as such, often get lost as the company "attacks a new market" (strategy shift) or "decentralizes to give managers autonomy" (structure shift).

Additionally, we frequently find it helpful to

label current skills, for the addition of a new skill may come only when the old one is dismantled. Adopting a newly "flexible and adaptive marketing thrust," for example, may be possible only if increases are accepted in certain marketing or distribution costs. Dismantling some of the distracting attributes of an old "manufacturing mentality" (that is, a skill that was perhaps crucial in the past) may be the only way to insure the success of an important change program. Possibly the most difficult problem in trying to organize effectively is that of weeding out old skills—and their supporting systems, structures, etc.—to ensure that important new skills can take root and grow.

Superordinate Goals

The word "superordinate" literally means "of higher order." By superordinate goals, we mean guiding concepts—a set of values and aspirations, often unwritten, that goes beyond the conventional formal statement of corporate objectives.

Superordinate goals are the fundamental ideas around which a business is built. They are its main values. But they are more as well. They are the broad notions of future direction that the top management team wants to infuse throughout the organization. They are the way in which the team wants to express itself, to leave its own mark. Examples would include Theodore Vail's "universal service" objective, which has so dominated AT&T; the strong drive to "customer service" which guides IBM's marketing; GE's slogan, "Progress is our most important product," which encourages engineers to tinker and innovate throughout the organization; Hewlett-Packard's "innovative people at all levels in the organization"; Dana's obsession with productivity, as a total organization, not just a few at the top; and 3M's dominating culture of "new products."

In a sense, superordinate goals are like the basic postulates in a mathematical system. They are the starting points on which the system is logically built, but in themselves are not logically derived. The ultimate test of their value is not their logic but the usefulness of the system that ensues. Everyone seems to know the importance of compelling superordinate goals. The drive for their accomplishment pulls an organization together. They provide stability in what would otherwise be a shifting set of organization dynamics.

Unlike the other six S's, superordinate goals don't seem to be present in all, or even most, organizations. They are, however, evident in most of the superior performers.

To be readily communicated, superordinate goals need to be succinct. Typically, therefore, they are expressed at high levels of abstraction and may mean very little to outsiders who don't know the organization well. But for those inside, they are rich with significance. Within an organization, superordinate goals, if well articulated, make meanings for people. And making meanings is one of the main functions of leadership.

CONCLUSION

We have passed rapidly through the variables in our framework. What should the reader have gained from the exercise?

We started with the premise that solutions to today's thorny organizing problems that invoke only structure—or even strategy and structure—are seldom adequate. The inadequacy stems in part from the inability of the two-variable model to explain why organizations are so slow to adapt to change. The reasons often lie among our other variables: systems that embody outdated assumptions, a management style that is at odds with the stated strategy, the absence of a superordinate goal that binds the organization together in pursuit of a common purpose, the refusal to deal concretely with "people problems" and opportunities.

At its most trivial, when we merely use the framework as a checklist, we find that it leads into new terrain in our efforts to understand how organizations really operate or to design a truly comprehensive change program. At a minimum, it gives us a deeper bag in which to collect our experiences.

More importantly, it suggests the wisdom of taking seriously the variables in organizing that have been considered soft, informal, or beneath the purview of top management interest. We believe that style, systems, skills, superordinate goals can be observed directly, even measured—if only they are taken seriously. We think that these variables can be at least as important as strategy and structure in orchestrating major change; indeed, that they are almost critical for achieving necessary, or desirable, change. A shift in systems, a major retraining program for staff, or the generation of top-to-bottom enthusiasm around a new superordinate goal could take years. Changes in strategy and structure, on the surface, may happen more quickly. But the pace of real change is geared to all seven S's.

At its most powerful and complex, the framework forces us to concentrate on interactions and fit. The real energy required to redirect an institution comes when all the variables in the model are aligned. One of our associates looks at our diagram as a set of compasses. "When all seven needles are all pointed the same way," he comments, "you're looking at an *organized* company."

THE COMPETITIVE ADVANTAGE OF NATIONS

Michael E. Porter
Harvard University

National prosperity is created, not inherited. It does not grow out of a country's natural endowments, its labor pool, its interest rates, or its currency's value, as classical economics insists.

A nation's competitiveness depends on the capacity of its industry to innovate and upgrade. Companies gain advantage against the world's best competitors because of pressure and challenge. They benefit from having strong domestic rivals, aggressive home-based suppliers, and demanding local customers.

In a world of increasingly global competition, nations have become more, not less, important. As the basis of competition has shifted more and more to the creation and assimilation of knowledge, the role of the nation has grown. Competitive advantage is created and sustained through a highly localized process. Differences in national values, culture, economic structures, institutions, and histories all contribute to competitive success. There are striking differences in the patterns of competitiveness in every country; no nation can or will be competitive in every or even most industries. Ultimately, nations succeed in particular industries because their home environment is the most forward-looking, dynamic, and challenging.

These conclusions, the product of a four-year study of the patterns of competitive success in ten leading trading nations, contradict the conventional wisdom that guides the thinking of many companies and national governments—and that is pervasive today in the United States. (For more about the study, see Insert 1 "Patterns of National Competitive Success.") According to prevailing thinking, labor costs, interest rates, exchange rates, and economies of scale are the most potent determinants of competitiveness. In companies, the words of the day are merger, alliance, strategic partnerships, collaboration, and supranational globalization. Managers are pressing for more government support for particular industries. Among governments, there is a growing tendency to experiment with various policies intended to promote national competitiveness—from efforts to manage exchange rates to new measures to manage trade to policies to relax antitrust—which usually end up only undermining it. (See Insert 2 "What Is National Competitiveness?")

These approaches, now much in favor in both companies and governments, are flawed. They fundamentally misperceive the true sources of competitive advantage. Pursuing them, with all their short-term appeal, will virtually guarantee that the United States—or any other advanced nation—never achieves real and sustainable competitive advantage.

We need a new perspective and new tools—an approach to competitiveness that grows directly out of an analysis of internationally successful industries, without regard for traditional ideology or current intellectual fashion. We need to know, very simply, what works and why. Then we need to apply it.

Insert 1 *Patterns of National Competitive Success*

To investigate why nations gain competitive advantage in particular industries and the implications for company strategy and national economies, I conducted a four-year study of ten important trading nations: Denmark, Germany, Italy, Japan, Korea, Singapore, Sweden, Switzerland, the United Kingdom, and the United States. I was assisted by a team of more than 30 researchers, most of whom were natives of and based in the nation they studied. The researchers all used the same methodology.

Three nations—the United States, Japan, and Germany—are the world's leading industrial powers. The other nations represent a variety of population sizes, government policies toward industry, social philosophies, geographical sizes, and locations. Together, the ten nations accounted for fully 50% of total world exports in 1985, the base year for statistical analysis.

Most previous analyses of national competitiveness have focused on single nation or bilateral comparisons. By studying nations with widely varying characteristics and circumstances, this study sought to separate the fundamental forces underlying national competitive advantage from the idiosyncratic ones.

In each nation, the study consisted of two parts. The first identified all industries in which the nation's companies were internationally successful, using available statistical data, supplementary published sources, and field interviews. We defined a nation's industry as internationally successful if it *possessed competitive advantage relative to the best worldwide competitors.* Many measures of competitive advantage, such as reported profitability, can be misleading. We chose as the best indicators the presence of substantial and sustained exports to a wide array of other nations and/or significant outbound foreign investment based on skills and assets created in the home country. A nation was considered the home base for a company if it was either a locally owned, indigenous enterprise or managed autonomously although owned by a foreign company or investors. We then created a profile of all the industries in which each nation was internationally successful at three points in time: 1971, 1978, and 1985. The pattern of competitive industries in each economy was far from random: the task was

to explain it and how it had changed over time. Of particular interest were the connections or relationships among the nation's competitive industries.

In the second part of the study, we examined the history of competition in particular industries to understand how competitive advantage was created. On the basis of national profiles, we selected over 100 industries or industry groups for detailed study, we examined many more in less detail. We went back as far as necessary to understand how and why the industry began in the nation, how it grew, when and why companies from the nation developed international competitive advantage, and the process by which competitive advantage had been either sustained or lost. The resulting case histories fall short of the work of a good historian in their level of detail, but they do provide insight into the development of both the industry and the nation's economy.

We chose a sample of industries for each nation that represented the most important groups of competitive industries in the economy. The industries studied accounted for a large share of total exports in each nation: more than 20% of total exports in Japan, Germany, and Switzerland, for example, and more than 40% in South Korea. We studied some of the most famous and important international success stories—German high-performance autos and chemicals, Japanese semiconductors and VCRs, Swiss banking and pharmaceuticals, Italian footwear and textiles, US commercial aircraft and motion pictures—and some relatively obscure but highly competitive industries—South Korean pianos, Italian ski boots, and British biscuits. We also added a few industries because they appeared to be paradoxes: Japanese home demand for Western-character typewriters is nearly nonexistent, for example, but Japan holds a strong export and foreign investment position in the industry. We avoided industries that were highly dependent on natural resources: such industries do not form the backbone of advanced economies, and the capacity to compete in them is more explicable using classical theory. We did, however, include a number of more technologically intensive, natural-resource-related industries such as newsprint and agricultural chemicals.

The sample of nations and industries offers a rich empirical foundation for developing and testing the new theory of how countries gain competitive advantage. The accompanying article concentrates on the determinants of competitive advantage in individual industries and also sketches out some of the study's overall implica-tions for government policy and company strate-gy. A fuller treatment in my book, *The Competitive Advantage of Nations,* develops the theory and its implications in greater depth and provides many additional examples. It also contains detailed descriptions of the nations we studied and the future prospects for their economies.

—**Michael E. Porter**

Insert 2 *What Is National Competitiveness?*

National competitiveness has become one of the central preoccupations of government and industry in every nation. Yet for all the discussion, debate, and writing on the topic, there is still no persuasive theory to explain national competitiveness. What is more, there is not even an accepted definition of the term "competitiveness" as applied to a nation. While the notion of a competitive company is clear, the notion of a competitive nation is not.

Some see national competitiveness as a macroeconomic phenomenon, driven by variables such as exchange rates, interest rates, and govern-ment deficits. But Japan, Italy, and South Korea have all enjoyed rapidly rising living standards despite budget deficits; Germany and Switzerland despite appreciating currencies; and Italy and Korea despite high interest rates.

Others argue that competitiveness is a func-tion of cheap and abundant labor. But Germany, Switzerland, and Sweden have all prospered even with high wages and labor shortages. Besides, shouldn't a nation seek higher wages for its work-ers as a goal of competitiveness?

Another view connects competitiveness with bountiful natural resources. But how, then, can one explain the success of Germany, Japan, Switzerland, Italy, and South Korea—countries with limited natural resources?

More recently, the argument has gained favor that competitiveness is driven by government poli-cy: targeting, protection, import promotion, and subsidies have propelled Japanese and South Kore-an auto, steel, shipbuilding, and semiconductor industries into global preeminence. But a closer look reveals a spotty record. In Italy, government intervention has been ineffectual—but Italy has experienced a boom in world export share second only to Japan. In Germany, direct government intervention in exporting industries is rare. And even in Japan and South Korea, government's role in such important industries as facsimile machines, copiers, robotics, and advanced materials has been modest; some of the most frequently cited exam-ples, such as sewing machines, steel, and ship-building, are now quite dated.

A final popular explanation for national com-petitiveness is differences in management prac-tices, including management-labor relations. The problem here, however, is that different industries require different approaches to management. The successful management practices governing small, private, and loosely organized Italian family com-panies in footwear, textiles, and jewelry, for exam-ple, would produce a management disaster if applied to German chemical or auto companies, Swiss pharmaceutical makers, or American aircraft producers. Nor is it possible to generalize about management-labor relations. Despite the common-ly held view that powerful unions undermine competitive advantage, unions are strong in Ger-many and Sweden—and both countries boast internationally preeminent companies.

Clearly, none of these explanations is fully sat-isfactory; none is sufficient by itself to rationalize the competitive position of industries within a national border. Each contains some truth; but a broader, more complex set of forces seems to be at work.

The lack of a clear explanation signals an even more fundamental question. What is a "competi-tive" nation in the first place? Is a "competitive" nation one where every company or industry is competitive? No nation meets this test. Even Japan has large sectors of its economy that fall far behind the world's best competitors.

Is a "competitive" nation one whose exchange

rate makes its goods price competitive in international markets? Both Germany and Japan have enjoyed remarkable gains in their standards of living—and experienced sustained periods of strong currency and rising prices. Is a "competitive" nation one with a large positive balance of trade? Switzerland has roughly balanced trade; Italy has a chronic trade deficit—both nations enjoy strongly rising national income. Is a "competitive" nation one with low labor costs? India and Mexico both have low wages and low labor costs—but neither seems an attractive industrial model.

The only meaningful concept of competitiveness at the national level is *productivity*. The principal goal of a nation is to produce a high and rising standard of living for its citizens. The ability to do so depends on the productivity with which a nation's labor and capital are employed. Productivity is the value of the output produced by a unit of labor or capital. Productivity depends on both the quality and features of products (which determine the prices that they can command) and the efficiency with which they are produced. Productivity is the prime determinant of a nation's long-run standard of living; it is the root cause of national per capita income. The productivity of human resources determines employee wages; the productivity with which capital is employed determines the return it earns for its holders.

A nation's standard of living depends on the capacity of its companies to achieve high levels of productivity—and to increase productivity over time. Sustained productivity growth requires that an economy continually *upgrade itself*. A nation's companies must relentlessly improve productivity in existing industries by raising product quality, adding desirable features, improving product technology, or boosting production efficiency. They must develop the necessary capabilities to compete in more and more sophisticated industry segments, where productivity is generally high. They must finally develop the capability to compete in entirely new, sophisticated industries.

International trade and foreign investment can both improve a nation's productivity as well as threaten it. They support rising national productivity by allowing a nation to specialize in those industries and segments of industries where its companies are more productive and to import where its companies are less productive. No nation can be competitive in everything. The ideal is to deploy the nation's limited pool of human and other resources into the most productive uses. Even those nations with the highest standards of living have many industries in which local companies are uncompetitive.

Yet international trade and foreign investment also can threaten productivity growth. They expose a nation's industries to the test of international standards of productivity. An industry will lose out if its productivity is not sufficiently higher than foreign rivals' to offset any advantages in local wage rates. If a nation loses the ability to compete in a range of high-productivity/high-wage industries, its standard of living is threatened.

Defining national competitiveness as achieving a trade surplus or balanced trade per se is inappropriate. The expansion of exports because of low wages and a weak currency, at the same time that the nation imports sophisticated goods that its companies cannot produce competitively, may bring trade into balance or surplus but lowers the nation's standard of living. Competitiveness also does not mean jobs. It's the *type* of jobs, not just the ability to employ citizens at low wages, that is decisive for economic prosperity.

Seeking to explain "competitiveness" at the national level, then, is to answer the wrong question. What we must understand instead is the determinants of productivity and the rate of productivity growth. To find answers, we must focus not on the economy as a whole but on *specific industries and industry segments*. We must understand how and why commercially viable skills and technology are created, which can only be fully understood at the level of particular industries. It is the outcome of the thousands of struggles for competitive advantage against foreign rivals in particular segments and industries, in which products and processes are created and improved, that underpins the process of upgrading national productivity.

When one looks closely at any national economy, there are striking differences among a nation's industries in competitive success. International advantage is often concentrated in particular industry segments. German exports of cars are heavily skewed toward high-performance cars, while Korean exports are all compacts and subcompacts. In many industries and segments of industries, the competitors with true international competitive advantage are *based in only a few nations*.

Our search, then, is for the decisive characteristic of a nation that allows its companies to create and sustain competitive advantage in particular fields—the search is for the competitive advantage of nations. We are particularly concerned with the determinants of international success in technology- and skill-intensive segments and industries, which underpin high and rising productivity.

Classical theory explains the success of nations in particular industries based on so-called factors of production such as land, labor, and natural resources. Nations gain factor-based comparative advantage in industries that make intensive use of the factors they possess in abundance. Classical theory, however, has been overshadowed in advanced industries and economies by the globalization of competition and the power of technology.

A new theory must recognize that in modern international competition, companies compete with global strategies involving not only trade but also foreign investment. What a new theory must explain is why a nation provides a favorable *home base* for companies that compete internationally. The home base is the nation in which the essential competitive advantages of the enterprise are created and sustained. It is where a company's strategy is set, where the core product and process technology is created and maintained, and where the most productive jobs and most advanced skills are located. The presence of the home base in a nation has the greatest positive influence on other linked domestic industries and leads to other benefits in the nation's economy. While the ownership of the company is often concentrated at the home base, the nationality of shareholders is secondary.

A new theory must move beyond comparative advantage to the competitive advantage of a nation. It must reflect a rich conception of competition that includes segmented markets, differentiated products, technology differences, and economies of scale. A new theory must go beyond cost and explain why companies from some nations are better than others at creating advantages based on quality, features, and new product innovation. A new theory must begin from the premise that competition is dynamic and evolving; it must answer the questions: Why do some companies based in some nations innovate more than others? Why do some nations provide an environment that enables companies to improve and innovate faster than foreign rivals?

—**Michael E. Porter**

HOW COMPANIES SUCCEED IN INTERNATIONAL MARKETS

Around the world, companies that have achieved international leadership employ strategies that differ from each other in every respect. But while every successful company will employ its own particular strategy, the underlying mode of operation—the character and trajectory of all successful companies—is fundamentally the same.

Companies achieve competitive advantage through acts of innovation. They approach innovation in its broadest sense, including both new technologies and new ways of doing things. They perceive a new basis for competing or find better means for competing in old ways. Innovation can be manifested in a new product design, a new production process, a new marketing approach, or a new way of conducting training. Much innovation is mundane and incremental, depending more on a cumulation of small insights and advances than on a single, major technological breakthrough. It often involves ideas that are not even "new"— ideas that have been around, but never vigorously pursued. It always involves investments in skill and knowledge, as well as in physical assets and brand reputations.

Some innovations create competitive advantage by perceiving an entirely new market opportunity or by serving a market segment that others have ignored. When competitors are slow to respond, such innovation yields competitive advantage. For instance, in industries such as autos and home electronics, Japanese companies gained their initial advantage by emphasizing smaller, more compact, lower capacity models that foreign competitors disdained as less profitable, less important, and less attractive.

In international markets, innovations that yield competitive advantage anticipate both domestic and foreign needs. For example, as international concern for product safety has grown, Swedish companies like Volvo, Atlas Copco, and AGA have succeeded by anticipating the market opportunity in this area. On the other hand, innovations that respond to concerns or circumstances that are peculiar to the home market can actually retard international competitive success. The lure of the huge US defense market, for instance, has diverted the attention of US materials and machine-tool companies from attractive, global commercial markets.

Information plays a large role in the process of innovation and improvement—information that either is not available to competitors or that they do not seek. Sometimes it comes from simple investment in research and development or market research; more often, it comes from effort and from openness and from looking in the right place unencumbered by blinding assumptions or conventional wisdom.

This is why innovators are often outsiders from a different industry or a different country. Innovation may come from a new company, whose founder has a nontraditional background or was simply not appreciated in an older, established company. Or the capacity for innovation may come into an existing company through senior managers who are new to the particular industry and thus more able to perceive opportunities and more likely to pursue them. Or innovation may occur as a company diversifies, bringing new resources, skills, or perspectives to another industry. Or innovations may come from another nation with different circumstances or different ways of competing.

With few exceptions, innovation is the result of unusual effort. The company that successfully implements a new or better way of competing pursues its approach with dogged determination, often in the face of harsh criticism and tough obstacles. In fact, to succeed, innovation usually requires pressure, necessity, and even adversity: the fear of loss often proves more powerful than the hope of gain.

Once a company achieves competitive advantage through an innovation, it can sustain it only through relentless improvement. Almost any advantage can be imitated. Korean companies have already matched the ability of their Japanese rivals to mass-produce standard color televisions and VCRs; Brazilian companies have assembled technology and designs comparable to Italian competitors in casual leather footwear.

Competitors will eventually and inevitably overtake any company that stops improving and innovating. Sometimes early-mover advantages such as customer relationships, scale economies in existing technologies, or the loyalty of distribution channels are enough to permit a stagnant company to retain its entrenched position for years or even decades. But sooner or later, more dynamic rivals will find a way to innovate around these advantages or create a better or cheaper way of doing things. Italian appliance producers, which competed successfully on the basis of cost in selling midsize and compact appliances through large retail chains, rested too long on this initial advantage. By developing more differentiated products and creating strong brand franchises, German competitors have begun to gain ground.

Ultimately, the only way to sustain a competitive advantage is to *upgrade it*—to move to more sophisticated types. This is precisely what Japanese automakers have done. They initially penetrated foreign markets with small, inexpensive compact cars of adequate quality and competed on the basis of lower labor costs. Even while their labor-cost advantage persisted, however, the Japanese companies were upgrading. They invested aggressively to build large modern plants to reap economies of scale. Then they became innovators in process technology, pioneering just-in-time production and a host of other quality and productivity practices. These process improvements led to better product quality, better repair records, and better customer-satisfaction ratings than foreign competitors had. Most recently, Japanese automakers have advanced to the vanguard of product technology and are introducing new, premium brand names to compete with the world's most prestigious passenger cars.

The example of the Japanese automakers also illustrates two additional prerequisites for sustaining competitive advantage. First, a company must adopt a global approach to strategy. It must sell its product worldwide, under its own brand name, through international marketing channels that it controls. A truly global approach may even require the company to locate production or R&D facilities in other nations to take advantage of lower wage rates, to gain or improve market access, or to take advantage of foreign technology. Second, creating more sustainable advantages often means that a company must make its existing advantage obsolete—even while it is still an advantage. Japanese auto companies recognized this; either they would make their advantage obsolete, or a competitor would do it for them.

As this example suggests, innovation and change are inextricably tied together. But change is an unnatural act, particularly in successful companies; powerful forces are at work to avoid and defeat it. Past approaches become institutionalized in standard operating procedures and management controls. Training emphasizes the one correct way to do anything; the construction of specialized, dedicated facilities solidifies past practice into expensive brick and mortar; the existing strategy takes on an aura of invincibility and becomes rooted in the company culture.

Successful companies tend to develop a bias for predictability and stability; they work on defending what they have. Change is tempered by the fear that there is much to lose. The organization at all levels filters out information that would suggest new approaches, modifications, or departures from the norm. The internal environment operates like an immune system to isolate or expel "hostile" individuals who challenge current directions or established thinking. Innovation ceases; the company becomes stagnant; it is only a matter of time before aggressive competitors overtake it.

THE DIAMOND OF NATIONAL ADVANTAGE

Why are certain companies based in certain nations capable of consistent innovation? Why do they ruthlessly pursue improvements, seeking an evermore sophisticated source of competitive advantage? Why are they able to overcome the substantial barriers to change and innovation that so often accompany success?

The answer lies in four broad attributes of a nation, attributes that individually and as a system constitute the diamond of national advantage, the playing field that each nation establishes and operates for its industries. These attributes are:

1. Factor conditions. The nation's position in factors of production, such as skilled labor or infrastructure, necessary to compete in a given industry.
2. Demand conditions. The nature of home-market demand for the industry's product or service.
3. Related and supporting industries. The presence or absence in the nation of supplier industries and other related industries that are internationally competitive.
4. Firm strategy, structure, and rivalry. The conditions in the nation governing how companies are created, organized, and managed, as well as the nature of domestic rivalry.

These determinants create the national environment in which companies are born and learn how to compete. (See the diagram [Figure 1] "Determinants of National Competitive Advantage.") Each point on the diamond—and the diamond as a system—affects essential ingredients for achieving international competitive success: the availability of resources and skills necessary for competitive advantage in an industry; the information that shapes the opportunities that companies perceive and the directions in which they deploy their resources and skills; the goals of the owners, managers, and individuals in companies; and most important, the pressures on companies to invest and innovate. (See the Insert 3 "How the Diamond Works: The Italian Ceramic Tile Industry.")

When a national environment permits and supports the most rapid accumulation of specialized assets and skills—sometimes simply because of greater effort and commitment—companies gain a competitive advantage. When a national environment affords better ongoing information and insight into product and process needs, companies gain a competitive advantage. Finally, when the national environment pressures companies to innovate and invest, companies both gain a competitive advantage and upgrade those advantages over time.

Factor Conditions. According to standard economic theory, factors of production—labor, land, natural resources, capital, infrastructure—will determine the flow of trade. A nation will export those goods that make most use of the factors with which it is relatively well endowed. This doctrine, whose origins date back to Adam Smith and David Ricardo and that is embedded in classical economics, is at best incomplete and at worst incorrect.

In the sophisticated industries that form the backbone of any advanced economy, a nation does not inherit but instead creates the most important factors of production—such as skilled human resources or a scientific base. Moreover, the stock of factors that a nation enjoys at a particular time is less important than the rate and efficiency with which it creates, upgrades, and deploys them in particular industries.

The most important factors of production are those that involve sustained and heavy investment and are specialized. Basic factors, such as a pool of labor or a local raw-material source, do not constitute an advantage in knowledge-intensive industries. Companies can access them easily through a global strategy or circumvent them through technology. Contrary to conventional wisdom, simply having a general work force that is high school or even college educated represents no competitive advantage in modern international competition. To support competitive advantage, a factor must be highly specialized to an industry's particular needs—a scientific institute specialized in optics, a pool of venture capital to fund software companies. These factors are more scarce, more difficult for foreign competitors to imitate—and they require sustained investment to create.

Nations succeed in industries where they are particularly good at factor creation. Competitive advantage results from the presence of world-class institutions that first create specialized factors and then continually work to upgrade them. Denmark has two hospitals that concentrate in studying and treating diabetes—and a world-leading export position in insulin. Holland has premier research institutes in the cultivation, packaging, and shipping of flowers, where it is the world's export leader.

What is not so obvious, however, is that selective disadvantages in the more basic factors can prod a company to innovate and upgrade—a disadvantage in a static model of competition can become an advantage in a dynamic one. When there is an ample supply of cheap raw materials or abundant labor, companies can simply rest on these advantages and often deploy them inefficiently. But when companies face a selective disadvantage, like high land costs, labor shortages, or the lack of local raw materials, they *must* innovate and upgrade to compete.

Implicit in the oft-repeated Japanese statement, "We are an island nation with no natural resources," is the understanding that these deficiencies have only served to spur Japan's competitive innovation. Just-in-time production, for example, economized on prohibitively expensive space. Italian steel producers in the Brescia area faced a similar set of disadvantages: high capital costs, high energy costs, and no local raw materials. Located in Northern Lombardy, these privately owned companies faced staggering logistics costs due to their distance from southern ports and the inefficiencies of the state-owned Italian transportation system.

Figure 1 Determinants of National Competitive Advantage

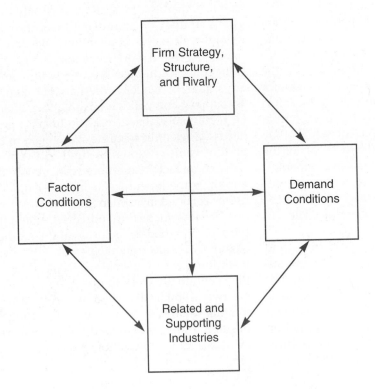

Insert 3 How the Diamond Words: The Italian Ceramic Tile Industry

In 1987, Italian companies were world leaders in the production and export of ceramic tiles, a $10 billion industry. Italian producers, concentrated in and around the small town of Sassuolo in the Emilia-Romagna region, accounted for about 30% of world production and almost 60% of world exports. The Italian trade surplus that year in ceramic tiles was about $1.4 billion.

The development of the Italian ceramic tile industry's competitive advantage illustrates how the diamond of national advantage works. Sassuolo's sustainable competitive advantage in ceramic tiles grew not from any static or historical advantage but from dynamism and change. Sophisticated and demanding local buyers, strong and unique distribution channels, and intense rivalry among local companies created constant pressure for innovation. Knowledge grew quickly from continuous experimentation and cumulative production experience. Private

ownership of the companies and loyalty to the community spawned intense commitment to invest in the industry.

Tile producers benefited as well from a highly developed set of local machinery suppliers and other supporting industries, producing materials, services, and infrastructure. The presence of world-class, Italian-related industries also reinforced Italian strength in tiles. Finally, the geographic concentration of the entire cluster supercharged the whole process. Today foreign companies compete against an entire subculture. The organic nature of this system represents the most sustainable advantage of Sassuolo's ceramic tile companies.

THE ORIGINS OF THE ITALIAN INDUSTRY

Tile production in Sassuolo grew out of the earthenware and crockery industry, whose history traces back to the thirteenth century. Immediately after World War II, there were only a handful of ceramic tile manufacturers in and around Sassuolo, all serving the local market exclusively.

Demand for ceramic tiles within Italy began to grow dramatically in the immediate postwar years, as the reconstruction of Italy triggered a boom in building materials of all kinds. Italian demand for ceramic tiles was particularly great due to the climate, local tastes, and building techniques.

Because Sassuolo was in a relatively prosperous part of Italy, there were many who could combine the modest amount of capital and necessary organizational skills to start a tile company. In 1955, there were 14 Sassuolo area tile companies; by 1962, there were 102.

The new tile companies benefited from a local pool of mechanically trained workers. The region around Sassuolo was home to Ferrari, Maserati, Lamborghini, and other technically sophisticated companies. As the tile industry began to grow and prosper, many engineers and skilled workers gravitated to the successful companies.

THE EMERGING ITALIAN TILE CLUSTER

Initially, Italian tile producers were dependent on foreign sources of raw materials and production technology. In the 1950s, the principal raw materials used to make tiles were kaolin (white) clays. Since there were red- but no white-clay deposits near Sassuolo, Italian producers had to import the clays from the United Kingdom. Tile-making equipment was also imported in the 1950s and 1960s: kilns from Germany, America, and France; presses for forming tiles from Germany. Sassuolo tile makers had to import even simple glazing machines.

Over time, the Italian tile producers learned how to modify imported equipment to fit local circumstances: red versus white clays, natural gas versus heavy oil. As process technicians from tile companies left to start their own equipment companies, a local machinery industry arose in Sassuolo. By 1970, Italian companies had emerged as world-class producers of kilns and presses; the earlier situation had exactly reversed: they were exporting their red-clay equipment for foreigners to use with white clays.

The relationship between Italian tile and equipment manufacturers was a mutually supporting one, made even more so by close proximity. In the mid-1980s, there were some 200 Italian equip-

ment manufacturers; more than 60% were located in the Sassuolo area. The equipment manufacturers competed fiercely for local business, and tile manufacturers benefited from better prices and more advanced equipment than their foreign rivals.

As the emerging tile cluster grew and concentrated in the Sassuolo region, a pool of skilled workers and technicians developed, including engineers, production specialists, maintenance workers, service technicians, and design personnel. The industry's geographic concentration encouraged other supporting companies to form, offering molds, packaging materials, glazes, and transportation services. An array of small, specialized consulting companies emerged to give advice to tile producers on plant design, logistics, and commercial, advertising, and fiscal matters.

With its membership concentrated in the Sassuolo area, Assopiastrelle, the ceramic tile industry association, began offering services in areas of common interest: bulk purchasing, foreign-market research, and consulting on fiscal and legal matters. The growing tile cluster stimulated the formation of a new, specialized factor-creating institution: in 1976, a consortium of the University of Bologna, regional agencies, and the ceramic industry association founded the Centro Ceramico di Bologna, which conducted process research and product analysis.

SOPHISTICATED HOME DEMAND

By the mid-1960s, per-capita tile consumption in Italy was considerably higher than in the rest of the world. The Italian market was also the world's most sophisticated. Italian customers, who were generally the first to adopt new designs and features, and Italian producers, who constantly innovated to improve manufacturing methods and create new designs, progressed in a mutually reinforcing process.

The uniquely sophisticated character of domestic demand also extended to retail outlets. In the 1960s, specialized tile showrooms began opening in Italy. By 1985, there were roughly 7,600 specialized showrooms handling approximately 80% of domestic sales, far more than in other nations. In 1976, the Italian company Piemme introduced tiles by famous designers to gain distribution outlets and to build brand name awareness among consumers. This innovation drew on another related industry, design services, in which Italy was world leader, with over $10 billion in exports.

SASSUOLO RIVALRY

The sheer number of tile companies in the Sassuo-lo area created intense rivalry. News of product and process innovations spread rapidly, and companies seeking technological, design, and distribution leadership had to improve constantly.

Proximity added a personal note to the intense rivalry. All of the producers were privately held, most were family run. The owners all lived in the same area, knew each other, and were the leading citizens of the same towns.

PRESSURES TO UPGRADE

In the early 1970s, faced with intense domestic rivalry, pressure from retail customers, and the shock of the 1973 energy crisis, Italian tile companies struggled to reduce gas and labor costs. These efforts led to a technological breakthrough, the rapid single-firing process, in which the hardening process, material transformation, and glaze-fixing all occurred in one pass through the kiln. A process that took 225 employees using the double-firing method needed only 90 employees using single-firing roller kilns. Cycle time dropped from 16 to 20 hours to only 50 to 55 minutes.

The new, smaller, and lighter equipment was also easier to export. By the early 1980s, exports from Italian equipment manufacturers exceeded domestic sales; in 1988, exports represented almost 80% of total sales.

Working together, tile manufacturers and equipment manufacturers made the next important breakthrough during the mid- and late 1970s: the development of materials-handling equipment that transformed tile manufacture from a batch process to a continuous process. The innovation

reduced high labor costs—which had been a substantial selective factor disadvantage facing Italian tile manufacturers.

The common perception is that Italian labor costs were lower during this period, than those in the United States and Germany. In those two countries, however, different jobs had widely different wages. In Italy, wages for different skill categories were compressed, and work rules constrained manufacturers from using overtime or multiple shifts. The restriction proved costly: once cool, kilns are expensive to reheat and are best run continuously. Because of this factor disadvantage, the Italian companies were the first to develop continuous, automated production.

INTERNATIONALIZATION

By 1970, Italian domestic demand had matured. The stagnant Italian market led companies to step up their efforts to pursue foreign markets. The presence of related and supporting Italian industries helped in the export drive. Individual tile manufacturers began advertising in Italian and foreign home-design and architectural magazines, publications with wide global circulation among architects, designers, and consumers. This heightened awareness reinforced the quality image of Italian tiles. Tile makers were also able to capitalize on Italy's leading world export positions in related industries like marble, building stone, sinks, washbasins, furniture, lamps, and home appliances.

Assopiastrelle, the industry association, established trade-promotion offices in the United States in 1980, in Germany in 1984, and in France in 1987. It organized elaborate trade shows in cities ranging from Bologna to Miami and ran sophisticated advertising. Between 1980 and 1987, the association spent roughly $8 million to promote Italian tiles in the United States.

—**Michael J. Enright and Paolo Tenti**

The result: they pioneered technologically advanced minimills that require only modest capital investment, use less energy, employ scrap metal as the feedstock, are efficient at small scale, and permit producers to locate close to sources of scrap and end-use customers. In other words, they converted factor disadvantages into competitive advantage.

Disadvantages can become advantages only under certain conditions. First, they must send companies proper signals about circumstances that will spread to other nations, thereby equipping them to innovate in advance of foreign rivals. Switzerland, the nation that experienced the first labor shortages after World War II, is a case in point. Swiss companies responded to the disadvantage by upgrading labor productivity and seeking higher value, more sustainable market segments. Companies in most other parts of the world, where there were still ample workers, focused their attention on other issues, which resulted in slower upgrading.

The second condition for transforming disadvantages into advantages is favorable circumstances elsewhere in the diamond—a consideration that applies to almost all determinants. To innovate, companies must have access to people with appropriate skills and have home-demand conditions that send the right signals. They must also have active domestic rivals who create pressure to innovate. Another precondition is company goals that lead to sustained commitment to the industry. Without such a commitment and the presence of active rivalry, a company may take an easy way around a disadvantage rather than using it as a spur to innovation.

For example, US consumer-electronics companies, faced with high relative labor costs, chose to leave the product and production process largely unchanged and move labor-intensive activities to Taiwan and other Asian countries. Instead of upgrading their sources of advantage, they settled for labor-cost parity. On the other hand, Japanese rivals, confronted with intense domestic competition and a mature home market, chose to eliminate labor through automation. This led to lower assembly costs, to products with fewer components and to improved quality and reliability. Soon Japanese companies were building assembly plants in the United States—the place US companies had fled.

Demand Conditions. It might seem that the globalization of competition would diminish the importance of home demand. In practice, however, this is simply not the case. In fact, the composition and character of the home market usually has a disproportionate effect on how companies perceive, interpret, and respond to buyer needs. Nations gain competitive advantage in industries where the home demand gives their companies a clearer or earlier picture of emerging buyer needs, and where demanding buyers pressure companies to innovate faster and achieve more sophisticated competitive advantages than their foreign rivals. The size of home demand proves far less significant than the character of home demand.

Home-demand conditions help build competitive advantage when a particular industry segment is larger or more visible in the domestic market than in foreign markets. The larger market segments in a nation receive the most attention from the nation's companies; companies accord smaller or less desirable segments a lower priority. A good example is hydraulic excavators, which represent the most widely used type of construction equipment in the Japanese domestic market—but which comprise a far smaller proportion of the market in other advanced nations. This segment is one of the few where there are vigorous Japanese international competitors and where Caterpillar does not hold a substantial share of the world market.

More important than the mix of segments per se is the nature of domestic buyers. A nation's companies gain competitive advantage if domestic buyers are the world's most sophisticated and demanding buyers for the product or service. Sophisticated, demanding buyers provide a window into advanced customer needs; they pressure companies to meet high standards; they prod them to improve, to innovate, and to upgrade into more advanced segments. As with factor conditions, demand conditions provide advantages by forcing companies to respond to tough challenges.

Especially stringent needs arise because of local values and circumstances. For example, Japanese consumers, who live in small, tightly packed homes, must contend with hot, humid summers and high-cost electrical energy—a daunting combination of circumstances. In response, Japanese companies have pioneered compact, quiet air-conditioning units powered by energy-saving rotary compressors. In industry after industry, the tightly constrained requirements of the Japanese market have forced companies to innovate, yielding products that are *kei-haku-tan-sho*—light, thin, short, small—and that are internationally accepted.

Local buyers can help a nation's companies gain advantage if their needs anticipate or even shape those of other nations—if their needs provide ongoing "early-warning indicators" of global market trends. Sometimes anticipatory needs emerge because a nation's political values foreshadow needs that will grow elsewhere. Sweden's long-standing concern for handicapped people has spawned an increasingly competitive industry focused on special needs. Denmark's environmentalism has led to success for companies in water-pollution control equipment and windmills.

More generally, a nation's companies can anticipate global trends if the nation's values are spreading—that is, if the country is exporting its values and tastes as well as its products. The international success of US companies in fast food and credit cards, for example, reflects not only the American desire for convenience but also the spread of these tastes to the rest of the world. Nations export their values and tastes through media, through training foreigners, through political influence, and through the foreign activities of their citizens and companies.

Related and Supporting Industries. The third broad determinant of national advantage is the presence in the nation of related and supporting industries that are internationally competitive. Internationally competitive home-based suppliers create advantages in downstream industries in several ways. First, they deliver the most cost-effective inputs in an efficient, early, rapid, and sometimes preferential way. Italian gold and silver jewelry companies lead the world in that industry in part because other Italian companies supply two-thirds of the world's jewelry-making and precious-metal recycling machinery.

Far more significant than mere access to components and machinery, however, is the advantage that home-based related and supporting industries provide in innovation and upgrading—an advantage based on close working relationships. Suppliers and end-users located near each other can take advantage of short lines of communication, quick and constant flow of information, and an ongoing exchange of ideas and innovations. Companies have the opportunity to influence their suppliers' technical efforts and can serve as test sites for R&D work, accelerating the pace of innovation.

The illustration of "The Italian Footwear Cluster" [Figure 2] offers a graphic example of how a group of close-by, supporting industries creates competitive advantage in a range of interconnected industries that are all internationally competitive. Shoe producers, for instance, interact regularly with leather manufacturers on new styles and manufacturing techniques and learn about new textures and colors of leather when they are still on the drawing boards. Leather manufacturers gain early insights into fashion trends, helping them to plan new products. The interaction is mutually advantageous and self-reinforcing, but it does not happen automatically: it is helped by proximity, but occurs only because companies and suppliers work at it.

The nation's companies benefit most when the suppliers are, themselves, global competitors. It is ultimately self-defeating for a company or country to create "captive" suppliers who are totally dependent on the domestic industry and prevented from serving foreign competitors. By the same token, a nation need not be competitive in all supplier industries for its companies to gain competitive advantage. Companies can readily source from abroad materials, components, or technologies without a major effect on innovation or performance of the industry's products. The same is true of other generalized technologies—like electronics or software—where the industry represents a narrow application area.

Home-based competitiveness in related industries provides similar benefits: information flow and technical interchange speed the rate of innovation and upgrading. A home-based related industry also increases the likelihood that companies will embrace new skills, and it also provides a source of entrants who will bring a novel approach to competing. The Swiss success in pharmaceuticals emerged out of previous international success in the dye industry, for example; Japanese dominance in electronic musical keyboards grows out of success in acoustic instruments combined with a strong position in consumer electronics.

Firm Strategy, Structure, and Rivalry. National circumstances and context create strong tendencies in how companies are created, organized,

Figure 2 *The Italian Footwear Cluster*

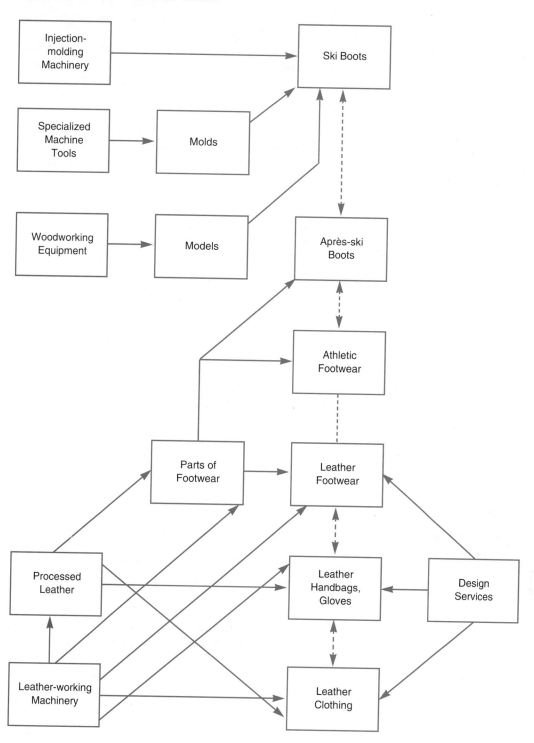

and managed, as well as what the nature of domestic rivalry will be. In Italy, for example, successful international competitors are often small or medium-sized companies that are privately owned and operated like extended families; in Germany, in contrast, companies tend to be strictly hierarchical in organization and management practices, and top managers usually have technical backgrounds.

No one managerial system is universally appropriate—notwithstanding the current fascination with Japanese management. Competitiveness in a specific industry results from convergence of the management practices and organizational modes favored in the country and the sources of competitive advantage in the industry. In industries where Italian companies are world leaders—such as lighting, furniture, footwear, woolen fabrics, and packaging machines—a company strategy that emphasizes focus, customized products, niche marketing, rapid change, and breathtaking flexibility fits both the dynamics of the industry and the character of the Italian management system. The German management system, in contrast, works well in technical or engineering-oriented industries—optics, chemicals, complicated machinery—where complex products demand precision manufacturing, a careful development process, after-sale service, and thus a highly disciplined management structure. German success is much rarer in consumer goods and services where image marketing and rapid new-feature and model turnover are important to competition.

Countries also differ markedly in the goals that companies and individuals seek to achieve. Company goals reflect the characteristics of national capital markets and the compensation practices for managers. For example, in Germany and Switzerland, where banks comprise a substantial part of the nation's shareholders, most shares are held for long-term appreciation and are rarely traded. Companies do well in mature industries, where ongoing investment in R&D and new facilities is essential but returns may be only moderate. The United States is at the opposite extreme, with a large pool of risk capital but widespread trading of public companies and a strong emphasis by investors on quarterly and annual share-price appreciation. Management compensation is heavily based on annual bonuses tied to individual results. America does well in relatively new industries, like software and biotechnology, or ones where equity funding of

new companies feeds active domestic rivalry, like specialty electronics and services. Strong pressures leading to underinvestment, however, plague more mature industries.

Individual motivation to work and expand skills is also important to competitive advantage. Outstanding talent is a scarce resource in any nation. A nation's success largely depends on the types of education its talented people choose, where they choose to work, and their commitment and effort. The goals a nation's institutions and values set for individuals and companies, and the prestige it attaches to certain industries, guide the flow of capital and human resources—which, in turn, directly affects the competitive performance of certain industries. Nations tend to be competitive in activities that people admire or depend on—the activities from which the nation's heroes emerge. In Switzerland, it is banking and pharmaceuticals. In Israel, the highest callings have been agriculture and defense-related fields. Sometimes it is hard to distinguish between cause and effect. Attaining international success can make an industry prestigious, reinforcing its advantage.

The presence of strong local rivals is a final, and powerful, stimulus to the creation and persistence of competitive advantage. This is true of small countries, like Switzerland, where the rivalry among its pharmaceutical companies, Hoffmann-La Roche, Ciba-Geigy, and Sandoz, contributes to a leading worldwide position. It is true in the United States in the computer and software industries. Nowhere is the role of fierce rivalry more apparent than in Japan, where there are 112 companies competing in machine tools, 34 in semiconductors, 25 in audio equipment, 15 in cameras—in fact, there are usually double figures in the industries in which Japan boasts global dominance. (See the table [Table 1] "Estimated Number of Japanese Rivals in Selected Industries.") Among all the points on the diamond, domestic rivalry is arguably the most important because of the powerfully stimulating effect it has on all the others.

Conventional wisdom argues that domestic competition is wasteful: it leads to duplication of effort and prevents companies from achieving economies of scale. The "right solution" is to embrace one or two national champions, companies with the scale and strength to tackle foreign competitors, and to guarantee them the necessary resources, with the government's blessing. In fact,

Table 1 *Estimated Number of Japanese Rivals in Selected Industries*

Air conditioners	13
Audio Equipment	25
Automobiles	9
Cameras	15
Car Audio	12
Carbon Fibers	7
Construction Equipment*	15
Copiers	14
Facsimile Machines	10
Large-scale Computers	6
Lift Trucks	8
Machine Tools	112
Microwave Equipment	5
Motorcycles	4
Musical Instruments	4
Personal Computers	16
Semiconductors	34
Sewing Machines	20
Shipbuilding†	33
Steel‡	5
Synthetic Fibers	8
Television Sets	15
Truck and Bus Tires	5
Trucks	11
Typewriters	14
Videocassette Recorders	10

Sources: Field interviews; *Nippon Kogyo Shinbun, Nippon Kogyo Nenkan,* 1987; Yano Research, *Market Share Jitan,* 1987; researchers' estimates.

*The number of companies varied by product area. The smallest number, 10, produced bulldozers. Fifteen companies produced shovel trucks, truck cranes, and asphalt-paving equipment. There were 20 companies in hydraulic excavators, a product area where Japan was particularly strong.

†Six companies had annual production exports in excess of 10,000 tons.

‡Integrated companies.

however, most national champions are uncompetitive, although heavily subsidized and protected by their government. In many of the prominent industries in which there is only one national rival, such as aerospace and telecommunications, government has played a large role in distorting competition.

Static efficiency is much less important than dynamic improvement, which domestic rivalry uniquely spurs. Domestic rivalry, like any rivalry, creates pressure on companies to innovate and improve. Local rivals push each other to lower costs, improve quality and service, and create new products and processes. But unlike rivalries with foreign competitors, which tend to be analytical and distant, local rivalries often go beyond pure economic or business competition and become intensely personal. Domestic rivals engage in active feuds; they compete not only for market share but also for people, for technical excellence, and perhaps most important, for "bragging rights." One domestic rival's success proves to others that advancement is possible and often attracts new rivals to the industry. Companies often attribute the success of foreign rivals to "unfair" advantages. With domestic rivals, there are no excuses.

Geographic concentration magnifies the power of domestic rivalry. This pattern is strikingly common around the world: Italian jewelry companies are located around two towns, Arezzo and Valenza Po; cutlery companies in Solingen, West Germany and Seki, Japan; pharmaceutical companies in Basel, Switzerland; motorcycles and musical instruments in Hamamatsu, Japan. The more localized the rivalry, the more intense. And the more intense, the better.

Another benefit of domestic rivalry is the

pressure it creates for constant upgrading of the sources of competitive advantage. The presence of domestic competitors automatically cancels the types of advantage that come from simply being in a particular nation—factor costs, access to or preference in the home market, or costs to foreign competitors who import into the market. Companies are forced to move beyond them, and as a result, gain more sustainable advantages. Moreover, competing domestic rivals will keep each other honest in obtaining government support. Companies are less likely to get hooked on the narcotic of government contracts or creeping industry protectionism. Instead, the industry will seek—and benefit from—more constructive forms of government support, such as assistance in opening foreign markets, as well as investments in focused educational institutions or other specialized factors.

Ironically, it is also vigorous domestic competition that ultimately pressures domestic companies to look at global markets and toughens them to succeed in them. Particularly when there are economies of scale, local competitors force each other to look outward to foreign markets to capture greater efficiency and higher profitability. And having been tested by fierce domestic competition, the stronger companies are well equipped to win abroad. If Digital Equipment can hold its own against IBM, Data General, Prime, and Hewlett-Packard, going up against Siemens or Machines Bull does not seem so daunting a prospect.

THE DIAMOND AS A SYSTEM

Each of these four attributes defines a point on the diamond of national advantage; the effect of one point often depends on the state of others. Sophisticated buyers will not translate into advanced products, for example, unless the quality of human resources permits companies to meet buyer needs. Selective disadvantages in factors of production will not motivate innovation unless rivalry is vigorous and company goals support sustained investment. At the broadest level, weaknesses in any one determinant will constrain an industry's potential for advancement and upgrading.

But the points of the diamond are also self-reinforcing: they constitute a system. Two elements, domestic rivalry and geographic concentration, have especially great power to transform the diamond into a system—domestic rivalry because it

promotes improvement in all the other determinants and geographic concentration because it elevates and magnifies the interaction of the four separate influences.

The role of domestic rivalry illustrates how the diamond operates as a self-reinforcing system. Vigorous domestic rivalry stimulates the development of unique pools of specialized factors, particularly if the rivals are all located in one city or region: the University of California at Davis has become the world's leading center of wine-making research, working closely with the California wine industry. Active local rivals also upgrade domestic demand in an industry. In furniture and shoes, for example, Italian consumers have learned to expect more and better products because of the rapid pace of new product development that is driven by intense domestic rivalry among hundreds of Italian companies. Domestic rivalry also promotes the formation of related and supporting industries. Japan's world-leading group of semiconductor producers, for instance, has spawned world-leading Japanese semiconductor-equipment manufacturers.

The effects can work in all directions: sometimes world-class suppliers become new entrants in the industry they have been supplying. Or highly sophisticated buyers may themselves enter a supplier industry, particularly when they have relevant skills and view the new industry as strategic. In the case of the Japanese robotics industry, for example, Matsushita and Kawasaki originally designed robots for internal use before beginning to sell robots to others. Today they are strong competitors in the robotics industry. In Sweden, Sandvik moved from specialty steel into rock drills, and SKF moved from specialty steel into ball bearings.

Another effect of the diamond's systemic nature is that nations are rarely home to just one competitive industry; rather, the diamond creates an environment that promotes *clusters* of competitive industries. Competitive industries are not scattered helter-skelter throughout the economy but are usually linked together through vertical (buyer-seller) or horizontal (common customers, technology, channels) relationships. Nor are clusters usually scattered physically; they tend to be concentrated geographically. One competitive industry helps to create another in a mutually reinforcing process. Japan's strength in consumer electronics, for example, drove its success in semiconductors toward the memory chips and integrated circuits these products use. Japanese strength in laptop computers, which contrasts to limited success in other segments, reflects the base of strength in other compact, portable products and leading expertise in liquid-crystal display gained in the calculator and watch industries.

Once a cluster forms, the whole group of industries becomes mutually supporting. Benefits flow forward, backward, and horizontally. Aggressive rivalry in one industry spreads to others in the cluster, through spin-offs, through the exercise of bargaining power, and through diversification by established companies. Entry from other industries within the cluster spurs upgrading by stimulating diversity in R&D approaches and facilitating the introduction of new strategies and skills. Through the conduits of suppliers or customers who have contact with multiple competitors, information flows freely and innovations diffuse rapidly. Interconnections within the cluster, often unanticipated, lead to perceptions of new ways of competing and new opportunities. The cluster becomes a vehicle for maintaining diversity and overcoming the inward focus, inertia, inflexibility, and accommodation among rivals that slows or blocks competitive upgrading and new entry.

THE ROLE OF GOVERNMENT

In the continuing debate over the competitiveness of nations, no topic engenders more argument or creates less understanding than the role of the government. Many see government as an essential helper or supporter of industry, employing a host of policies to contribute directly to the competitive performance of strategic or target industries. Others accept the "free market" view that the operation of the economy should be left to the workings of the invisible hand.

Both views are incorrect. Either, followed to its logical outcome, would lead to the permanent erosion of a country's competitive capabilities. On one hand, advocates of government help for industry frequently propose policies that would actually hurt companies in the long run and only create the demand for more helping. On the other hand, advocates of a diminished government presence ignore the legitimate role that government plays in shaping the context and institutional structure surrounding companies and in creating

an environment that stimulates companies to gain competitive advantage.

Government's proper role is as a catalyst and challenger; it is to encourage—or even push—companies to raise their aspirations and move to higher levels of competitive performance, even though this process may be inherently unpleasant and difficult. Government cannot create competitive industries; only companies can do that. Government plays a role that is inherently partial, that succeeds only when working in tandem with favorable underlying conditions in the diamond. Still, government's role of transmitting and amplifying the forces of the diamond is a powerful one. Government policies that succeed are those that create an environment in which companies can gain competitive advantage rather than those that involve government directly in the process, except in nations early in the development process. It is an indirect, rather than a direct, role.

Japan's government, at its best, understands this role better than anyone—including the point that nations pass through stages of competitive development and that government's appropriate role shifts as the economy progresses. By stimulating early demand for advanced products, confronting industries with the need to pioneer frontier technology through symbolic cooperative projects, establishing prizes that reward quality, and pursuing other policies that magnify the forces of the diamond, the Japanese government accelerates the pace of innovation. But like government officials anywhere, at their worst Japanese bureaucrats can make the same mistakes: attempting to manage industry structure, protecting the market too long, and yielding to political pressure to insulate inefficient retailers, farmers, distributors, and industrial companies from competition.

It is not hard to understand why so many governments make the same mistakes so often in pursuit of national competitiveness: competitive time for companies and political time for governments are fundamentally at odds. It often takes more than a decade for an industry to create competitive advantage; the process entails the long upgrading of human skills, investing in products and processes, building clusters, and penetrating foreign markets. In the case of the Japanese auto industry, for instance, companies made their first faltering steps toward exporting in the 1950s—yet did not achieve strong international positions until the 1970s.

But in politics, a decade is an eternity. Consequently, most governments favor policies that offer easily perceived short-term benefits, such as subsidies, protection, and arranged mergers—the very policies that retard innovation. Most of the policies that would make a real difference either are too slow and require too much patience for politicians or, even worse, carry with them the sting of short-term pain. Deregulating a protected industry, for example, will lead to bankruptcies sooner and to stronger, more competitive companies only later.

Policies that convey static, short-term cost advantages but that unconsciously undermine innovation and dynamism represent the most common and most profound error in government industrial policy. In a desire to help, it is all too easy for governments to adopt policies such as joint projects to avoid "wasteful" R&D that undermine dynamism and competition. Yet even a 10% cost saving through economies of scale is easily nullified through rapid product and process improvement and the pursuit of volume in global markets—something that such policies undermine.

There are some simple, basic principles that governments should embrace to play the proper supportive role for national competitiveness: encourage change, promote domestic rivalry, stimulate innovation. Some of the specific policy approaches to guide nations seeking to gain competitive advantage include the following:

Focus on Specialized Factor Creation. Government has critical responsibilities for fundamentals like the primary and secondary education systems, basic national infrastructure, and research in areas of broad national concern such as health care. Yet these kinds of generalized efforts at factor creation rarely produce competitive advantage. Rather, the factors that translate into competitive advantage are advanced, specialized, and tied to specific industries or industry groups. Mechanisms such as specialized apprenticeship programs, research efforts in universities connected with an industry, trade association activities, and, most important, the private investments of companies ultimately create the factors that will yield competitive advantage.

Avoid Intervening in Factor and Currency Markets. By intervening in factor and currency markets, governments hope to create lower factor costs or a favorable exchange rate that will help companies compete more effectively in international markets. Evidence from around the world indicates that these policies—such as the Reagan administration's dollar devaluation—are often counterproductive. They work against the upgrading of industry and the search for more sustainable competitive advantage.

The contrasting case of Japan is particularly instructive, although both Germany and Switzerland have had similar experiences. Over the past 20 years, the Japanese have been rocked by the sudden Nixon currency devaluation shock, two oil shocks, and, most recently, the yen shock—all of which forced Japanese companies to upgrade their competitive advantages. The point is not that government should pursue policies that intentionally drive up factor costs or the exchange rate. Rather, when market forces create rising factor costs or a higher exchange rate, government should resist the temptation to push them back down.

Enforce Strict Product, Safety, and Environmental Standards. Strict government regulations can promote competitive advantage by stimulating and upgrading domestic demand. Stringent standards for product performance, product safety, and environmental impact pressure companies to improve quality, upgrade technology, and provide features that respond to consumer and social demands. Easing standards, however tempting, is counterproductive.

When tough regulations anticipate standards that will spread internationally, they give a nation's companies a head start in developing products and services that will be valuable elsewhere. Sweden's strict standards for environmental protection have promoted competitive advantage in many industries. Atlas Copco, for example, produces quiet compressors that can be used in dense urban areas with minimal disruption to residents. Strict standards, however, must be combined with a rapid and streamlined regulatory process that does not absorb resources and cause delays.

Sharply Limit Direct Cooperation among Industry Rivals. The most pervasive global policy fad in the competitiveness arena today is the call for more cooperative research and industry consortia. Operating on the belief that independent research by rivals is wasteful and duplicative, that collaborative efforts achieve economies of scale, and that individual companies are likely to underinvest in R&D because they cannot reap all the benefits, governments have embraced the idea of more direct cooperation. In the United States, antitrust laws have been modified to allow more cooperative R&D; in Europe, mega-projects such as ESPRIT, an information-technology project, bring together companies from several countries. Lurking behind much of this thinking is the fascination of Western governments with—and fundamental misunderstanding of—the countless cooperative research projects sponsored by the Ministry of International Trade and Industry (MITI), projects that appear to have contributed to Japan's competitive rise.

But a closer look at Japanese cooperative projects suggests a different story. Japanese companies participate in MITI projects to maintain good relations with MITI, to preserve their corporate images, and to hedge the risk that competitors will gain from the project—largely defensive reasons. Companies rarely contribute their best scientists and engineers to cooperative projects and usually spend much more on their own private research in the same field. Typically, the government makes only a modest financial contribution to the project.

The real value of Japanese cooperative research is to signal the importance of emerging technical areas and to stimulate proprietary company research. Cooperative projects prompt companies to explore new fields and boost internal R&D spending because companies know that their domestic rivals are investigating them.

Under certain limited conditions, cooperative research can prove beneficial. Projects should be in areas of basic product and process research, not in subjects closely connected to a company's proprietary sources of advantage. They should constitute only a modest portion of a company's overall research program in any given field. Cooperative research should be only indirect, channeled through independent organizations to which most industry participants have access. Organizational structures, like university labs and centers of excellence, reduce management problems and minimize the risk to rivalry. Finally, the most useful cooperative projects often involve fields that touch a number of industries and that require substantial R&D investments.

Promote Goals That Lead to Sustained Investment. Government has a vital role in shaping the goals of investors, managers, and employees through policies in various areas. The manner in which capital markets are regulated, for example, shapes the incentives of investors and, in turn, the behavior of companies. Government should aim to encourage sustained investment in human skills, in innovation, and in physical assets. Perhaps the single most powerful tool for raising the rate of sustained investment in industry is a tax incentive for long-term (five years or more) capital gains restricted to new investment in corporate equity. Long-term capital gains incentives should also be applied to pension funds and other currently untaxed investors, who now have few reasons not to engage in rapid trading.

Deregulate Competition. Regulation of competition through such policies as maintaining a state monopoly, controlling entry into an industry, or fixing prices has two strong negative consequences: it stifles rivalry and innovation as companies become preoccupied with dealing with regulators and protecting what they already have; and it makes the industry a less dynamic and less desirable buyer or supplier. Deregulation and privatization on their own, however, will not succeed without vigorous domestic rivalry—and that requires, as a corollary, a strong and consistent antitrust policy.

Enforce Strong Domestic Antitrust Policies. A strong antitrust policy—especially for horizontal mergers, alliances, and collusive behavior—is fundamental to innovation. While it is fashionable today to call for mergers and alliances in the name of globalization and the creation of national champions, these often undermine the creation of competitive advantage. Real national competitiveness requires governments to disallow mergers, acquisitions, and alliances that involve industry leaders. Furthermore, the same standards for mergers and alliances should apply to both domestic and foreign companies. Finally, government policy should favor internal entry, both domestic and international, over acquisition. Companies should, however, be allowed to acquire small companies in related industries when the move promotes the transfer of skills that could ultimately create competitive advantage.

Reject Managed Trade. Managed trade represents a growing and dangerous tendency for dealing with the fallout of national competitiveness. Orderly marketing agreements, voluntary restraint agreements, or other devices that set quantitative targets to divide up markets are dangerous, ineffective, and often enormously costly to consumers. Rather than promoting innovation in a nation's industries, managed trade guarantees a market for inefficient companies.

Government trade policy should pursue open market access in every foreign nation. To be effective, trade policy should not be a passive instrument; it cannot respond only to complaints or work only for those industries that can muster enough political clout; it should not require a long history of injury or serve only distressed industries. Trade policy should seek to open markets wherever a nation has competitive advantage and should actively address emerging industries and incipient problems.

Where government finds a trade barrier in another nation, it should concentrate its remedies on dismantling barriers, not on regulating imports or exports. In the case of Japan, for example, pressure to accelerate the already rapid growth of manufactured imports is a more effective approach than a shift to managed trade. Compensatory tariffs that punish companies for unfair trade practices are better than market quotas. Other increasingly important tools to open markets are restrictions that prevent companies in offending nations from investing in acquisitions or production facilities in the host country—thereby blocking the unfair country's companies from using their advantage to establish a new beachhead that is immune from sanctions.

Any of these remedies, however, can backfire. It is virtually impossible to craft remedies to unfair trade practices that avoid both reducing incentives for domestic companies to innovate and export and harming domestic buyers. The aim of remedies should be adjustments that allow the remedy to disappear.

THE COMPANY AGENDA

Ultimately, only companies themselves can achieve and sustain competitive advantage. To do so, they must act on the fundamentals described above. In particular, they must recognize the central role of innovation—and the uncomfortable truth that innovation grows out of pressure and challenge. It takes leadership to create a dynamic, challenging environment. And it takes leadership to recognize the all-too-easy escape routes that appear to offer a path to competitive advantage, but are actually short-cuts to failure. For example, it is tempting to rely on cooperative research and development projects to lower the cost and risk of research. But they can divert company attention and resources from proprietary research efforts and will all but eliminate the prospects for real innovation.

Competitive advantage arises from leadership that harnesses and amplifies the forces in the diamond to promote innovation and upgrading. Here are just a few of the kinds of company policies that will support that effort:

Create Pressures for Innovation. A company should seek out pressure and challenge, not avoid them. Part of strategy is to take advantage of the home nation to create the impetus for innovation. To do that, companies can sell to the most sophisticated and demanding buyers and channels; seek out those buyers with the most difficult needs; establish norms that exceed the toughest regulatory hurdles or product standards; source from the most advanced suppliers; treat employees as permanent in order to stimulate upgrading of skills and productivity.

Seek Out the Most Capable Competitors as Motivators. To motivate organizational change, capable competitors and respected rivals can be a common enemy. The best managers always run a little scared; they respect and study competitors. To stay dynamic, companies must make meeting challenge a part of the organization's norms. For example, lobbying against strict product standards signals the organization that company leadership has diminished aspirations. Companies that value stability, obedient customers, dependent suppliers, and sleepy competitors are inviting inertia and, ultimately, failure.

Establish Early-warning Systems. Early-warning signals translate into early-mover advantages. Companies can take actions that help them see the signals of change and act on them, thereby getting a jump on the competition. For example, they can find and serve those buyers with the most anticipatory needs; investigate all emerging new buyers or channels; find places whose regulations foreshadow emerging regulations elsewhere; bring some outsiders into the management team; maintain ongoing relationships with research centers and sources of talented people.

Improve the National Diamond. Companies have a vital stake in making their home environment a better platform for international success.

Part of a company's responsibility is to play an active role in forming clusters and to work with its home-nation buyers, suppliers, and channels to help them upgrade and extend their own competitive advantages. To upgrade home demand, for example, Japanese musical instrument manufacturers, led by Yamaha, Kawai, and Suzuki, have established music schools. Similarly, companies can stimulate and support local suppliers of important specialized inputs—including encouraging them to compete globally. The health and strength of the national cluster will only enhance the company's own rate of innovation and upgrading.

In nearly every successful competitive industry, leading companies also take explicit steps to create specialized factors like human resources, scientific knowledge, or infrastructure. In industries like wool cloth, ceramic tiles, and lighting equipment, Italian industry associations invest in market information, process technology, and common infrastructure. Companies can also speed innovation by putting their headquarters and other key operations where there are concentrations of sophisticated buyers, important suppliers, or specialized factor-creating mechanisms, such as universities or laboratories.

Welcome Domestic Rivalry. To compete globally, a company needs capable domestic rivals and vigorous domestic rivalry. Especially in the United States and Europe today, managers are wont to complain about excessive competition and to argue for mergers and acquisitions that will produce hoped-for economies of scale and critical mass. The complaint is only natural—but the argument is plain wrong. Vigorous domestic rivalry creates sustainable competitive advantage. Moreover, it is better to grow internationally than to dominate the domestic market. If a company wants an acquisition, a foreign one that can speed globalization and supplement home-based advantages or offset home-based disadvantages is usually far better than merging with leading domestic competitors.

Globalize to Tap Selective Advantages in Other Nations. In search of "global" strategies, many companies today abandon their home diamond. To be sure, adopting a global perspective is important to creating competitive advantage. But relying on foreign activities that supplant domestic capabilities is always second-best solution. Innovating to offset local factor disadvantages is better than outsourcing; developing domestic suppliers

and buyers is better than relying solely on foreign ones. Unless the critical underpinnings of competitiveness are present at home, companies will not sustain competitive advantage in the long run. The aim should be to upgrade home-base capabilities so that foreign activities are selective and supplemental only to over-all competitive advantage.

The correct approach to globalization is to tap selectively into sources of advantage in other nations' diamonds. For example, identifying sophisticated buyers in other countries helps companies understand different needs and creates pressures that will stimulate a faster rate of innovation. No matter how favorable the home diamond, moreover, important research is going on in other nations. To take advantage of foreign research, companies must station high-quality people in overseas bases and mount a credible level of scientific effort. To get anything back from foreign research ventures, companies must also allow access to their own ideas—recognizing that competitive advantage comes from continuous improvement, not from protecting today's secrets.

Use Alliances Only Selectively. Alliances with foreign companies have become another managerial fad and cure-all: they represent a tempting solution to the problem of a company wanting the advantages of foreign enterprises or hedging against risk, without giving up independence. In reality, however, while alliances can achieve selective benefits, they always exact significant costs: they involve coordinating two separate operations, reconciling goals with an independent entity, creating a competitor, and giving up profits. These costs ultimately make most alliances short-term transitional devices, rather than stable, long-term relationships.

Most important, alliances as a broad-based strategy will only ensure a company's mediocrity, not its international leadership. No company can rely on another outside, independent company for skills and assets that are central to its competitive advantage. Alliances are best used as a selective tool, employed on a temporary basis or involving noncore activities.

Locate the Home Base to Support Competitive Advantage. Among the most important decisions for multinational companies is the nation in which to locate the home base for each distinct business. A company can have different home bases for distinct businesses or segments. Ultimately, competitive advantage is created at home: it is where strategy is set, the core product and process technology is created, and a critical mass of production takes place. The circumstances in the home nation must support innovation; otherwise the company has no choice but to move its home base to a country that stimulates innovation and that provides the best environment for global competitiveness. There are no half-measures: the management team must move as well.

THE ROLE OF LEADERSHIP

Too many companies and top managers misperceive the nature of competition and the task before them by focusing on improving financial performance, soliciting government assistance, seeking stability, and reducing risk through alliances and mergers.

Today's competitive realities demand leadership. Leaders believe in change; they energize their organizations to innovate continuously; they recognize the importance of their home country as integral to their competitive success and work to upgrade it. Most important, leaders recognize the need for pressure and challenge. Because they are willing to encourage appropriate—and painful—government policies and regulations, they often earn the title "statesmen," although few see themselves that way. They are prepared to sacrifice the easy life for difficulty and, ultimately, sustained competitive advantage. That must be the goal, for both nations and companies: not just surviving, but achieving international competitiveness.

And not just once, but continuously.

FORMULATING STRATEGY ONE STEP AT A TIME

James Brian Quinn
Dartmouth College

In many companies, strategy changes do not come about as most people imagine. Strategy often evolves one step at a time, in response to various internal pressures and external events.

Like many others observing formal planning practice over the last decade, I became increasingly disturbed by three major tendencies:

1. Planning activities in major enterprises often became bureaucratized, rigid, and costly paper-shuffling exercises divorced from actual decision processes. In many organizations, their primary impacts were:

- To expand the scope of capital and operational budgeting procedures;
- To extend formal performance measurements to new activity areas; and thus
- To achieve greater central control over operations.
- Instead of stimulating creative options, innovation, or entrepreneurship, formal planning often became just another aspect of controllership—and another weapon in organizational politics.

2. Most important strategic decisions seemed to be made outside the formal planning structure, even in organizations with well-accepted planning cultures. This tendency was especially marked in highly entrepreneurial or smaller enterprises. But, as one closely observed well-managed large companies over extensive time periods, it became increasingly apparent that this might well be a characteristic of good management practice, and not an abrogation of some immutable principle.

3. Much of the management literature and technique associated with planning seemed increasingly bent on developing ever more sophisticated models of a system that was not working the way the model builders thought it was—or should be—operating. In fact, various purported "normative" approaches to planning began to appear highly questionable, if not actively destructive, in many instances.

These were unnerving, although not very systematic, observations. Consequently, I undertook a more careful study of how several large companies actually did arrive at their strategic changes and how this fitted into accepted formal planning and management concepts.[1]

---

[1]This study was jointly sponsored by the Associates Program of the Amos Tuck School of Business Administration and Centre d'Etudes Industrielles, Geneva, Switzerland, and was published by Dow Jones Irwin in 1980. Some ten companies were selected for study based on the following criteria: (1) They had to be large (multiple billion dollar) companies. (2) They had to either be undergoing important strategic changes or have recently completed such shifts. (3) They had to allow sufficient access to top levels to obtain desired data. (4) They had to be balanced among several different industry characteristics: consumable goods, basic processes, high technology, or consumer-durable industries. Both industries and companies were purposely chosen to represent a variety of technologies, time horizons, and national versus international dimensions. (5) Finally, the sample had to include at least two companies meeting these criteria in each industry.

continued

FORMAL PLANNING—JUST A BUILDING BLOCK

My data suggest that when well-managed major organizations make significant changes in strategy, the approaches they use frequently bear little resemblance to the rational-analytical systems so often described in the planning literature. This literature clearly states what factors should be included in a formally designed strategy[2] and precisely how to analyze and relate these factors step by step.[3] Many articles have described in some detail how to apply this "formal planning approach" to strategy formulation for specific businesses.[4] Its main elements include:

- Analyzing one's own internal situation: strengths, weaknesses, competencies, problems;
- Projecting current product lines' profits, sales, investment needs, and the like into the future;
- Analyzing selected external environments and opponents' actions for opportunities and threats;

- Establishing broad goals as targets for subordinate groups' plans;
- Identifying the gap between expected and desired results;
- Communicating planning assumptions, goals, and policies to the divisions;
- Generating proposed plans from subordinate groups with more specific target goals, resource needs, and supporting detail;
- Occasionally asking for special studies of alternatives, contingencies, or longer-term opportunities;
- Reviewing and balancing lower-level plans and summing these for corporate needs;
- Developing long-term budgets presumably related to plans;
- Assigning implementation of plans to specific groups; and
- Monitoring and evaluating performance for emphasis presumably against plans, but usually against budgets.[5]

(Footnote 1 continued)

    The following companies generously cooperated: General Mills, Inc., and Pillsbury Company (consumable products); Exxon Corporation and Continental Group (basic processes); Xerox Corporation and Pilkington Brothers, Ltd. (advanced technology); General Motors Corporation, Chrysler Corporation, and Volvo AB (consumer durables). Texas Instruments, Inc., participated on a special basis.

    Within each company, I tried to interview at least ten of the persons most involved in the strategic changes studied. Before interviews, I conducted an extensive survey of secondary source data about each company. I used a standardized typed sheet of questions to guide each respondent and to insure adequate and comparable coverage. Respondents were asked to trace through how—to their knowledge—strategic change had actually come about in their company.

[2]M.L. Mace, "The President and Corporate Planning," *Harvard Business Review*, Jan.-Feb. 1965, pp. 49–62; W.D. Guth, "Formulating Organizational Objectives and Strategy: A Systematic Approach," *Journal of Business Policy*, Autumn 1971, pp. 24–31; K. J. Cohen and R.M. Cyert, "Strategy: Formulation, Implementation, and Monitoring," *The Journal of Business*, July 1973, pp. 349–367; G.J. Skibbins, "Top Management Goal Appraisal," *International Management*, July 1974, pp. 41–42; F. Goronzy and E. Gray, "Factors in Corporate Growth," *Management International Review* No. 4-5, 1974, pp. 75–90; and W.E. Rothschild, *Putting It All Together: A Guide to Strategic Thinking* (New York: AMACOM, 1976).

[3]J.T. Cannon, *Business Strategy and Policy* (New York: Harcourt, Brace & World, 1968); G.A. Steiner, *Top Management Planning* (New York: Macmillan, 1969); R.L. Katz, *Management of the Total Enterprise* (Englewood Cliffs, NJ: Prentice-Hall, 1970); E.K. Warren, *Long-Range Planning, The Executive Viewpoint* (Englewood Cliffs, NJ: Prentice-Hall, 1966); R.L. Ackoff, *A Concept of Corporate Planning* (New York: Wiley-Interscience, 1970); H.J. Ansoff, "Managerial Problem-Solving," *Journal of Business Policy*, Autumn 1971, pp. 3–20; E.C. Miller, *Advanced Techniques for Strategic Planning* (New York: American Management Association, 1971); R.F. Vancil and P. Lorange, "Strategic Planning in Diversified Companies," *Harvard Business Review*, Jan.-Feb. 1975, pp. 81–90; R.F. Vancil, "Strategy Formulation in Complex Organizations," *Sloan Management Review*, Winter 1976, p. 1–18.

[4]These include W.J. MacGinnitie, "How to Design a Strategic Planning System," *Best's Review, Property/Liability Insurance Edition*, May 1973, pp. 198–112; F.E. deCarbonnel and R.G. Dorrance, "Information Sources for Planning Decisions," *California Management Review*, Summer 1973, pp. 42–53; C.H. Springer, "Strategic Management in General Electric," *Operations Research*, Nov.-Dec. 1973, pp. 1177–1182; M.E. Salveson, "The Management of Strategy," *Long Range Planning*, Feb. 1974, pp. 19–26; and C. Holloway and G.T. Jones, "Planning at Gulf—A Case Study," *Long Range Planning*, April 1975, pp. 27–39.

[5]K.J. Cohen and R.M. Cyert, note 2 *supra*, critique each step in a similar series in some detail.

Some Definitions

Since the words "strategy," "objectives," "goals," "policy," and "programs" may have different meanings to individual readers or to various organizational cultures, I have tried to use certain definitions consistently throughout this article. For clarity—not pedantry—these are set forth below:

- A *strategy* is the pattern or plan that integrates an organization's major goals, policies, and action sequences into a cohesive whole. A well-formulated strategy helps marshal and allocate an organization's resources into a unique and viable posture based upon its relative internal competencies and shortcomings, anticipated changes in the environment, and contingent moves by intelligent opponents.

- *Goals* (or objectives) state what is to be achieved and when results are to be accomplished. But they do not state how the results are to be achieved. All organizations have multiple goals existing in a complex hierarchy, from "value objectives," which express the broad value premises toward which the company is to strive, through "overall organizational objectives," which establish the intended nature of the enterprise and the directions in which it should move, to a series of less permanent goals which define targets for each organizational unit, its subunits, and finally all major program activities within each subunit. Major goals—those which affect the entity's overall direction and viability—are called strategic goals.

- *Policies* are rules or guidelines that express the limits within which action should occur. These rules often take the form of contingent decisions for resolving conflicts among specific objectives. For example: "Don't use nuclear weapons in war unless American cities suffer nuclear attack first" or "Don't exceed three months' inventory in any item without corporate approval." Like the objectives they support, policies also exist in a hierarchy throughout the organization. Major policies—those that guide the entity's overall direction and posture or determine its viability—are called strategic policies.

- *Programs* specify the step-by-step sequence of actions necessary to achieve major objectives. They express how objectives will be achieved within the limits set by policy. They insure that resources are committed to achieve goals, and they provide the dynamic track against which progress can be measured. Those major programs that determine the entity's overall thrust and viability are called strategic programs.

Strategic decisions are those that determine the overall direction of an enterprise and its ultimate viability in light of the predictable, the unpredictable, and the unknowable changes that may occur in its most important environments.

When well developed, formal planning in sample companies was one of many important building blocks in a continuously evolving structure of analytical and political events that combined to determine overall strategy.[6] But for good reasons, strategy in these companies tended to emerge in ways that differed quite markedly from this prescribed methodology. The full strategy was rarely written down in any one place. The processes used to arrive at the total strategy were typically fragmented, evolutionary, and largely intuitive. Although one could frequently find embedded in these processes some fragments of very refined formal strategic analysis, the overall corporate strategy tended to evolve as internal decisions and external events flowed together to create a new consensus for action among key members of the top management team. In well-run organizations, managers proactively guided these streams of actions and events incrementally toward strategies embodying many of the structural principles of elegant formal strategies. But for reasons to be explained shortly, top executives rarely designed their overall strategies—or even major segments of them—in the formal planning cycle of the corpora-

tion. Instead they used a series of incremental processes which built strategies largely at more disaggregated levels and then integrated these subsystem strategies step by step for the total corporation. The rationale behind this kind of incremental strategy formulation was so powerful that it—rather than the "formal systems planning" approach so often espoused—seemed to provide an improved normative model for strategic decision making.

THE POWER-BEHAVIORAL APPROACH

Also recognizing that the formal systems approach suffered some extreme limitations, another school has provided important insights on many of the crucial psychological, power, and behavioral relationships that vitally affect strategy formulation. Among other things, this group's research has enhanced understanding about the multiple goal structures of organizations,[7] the politics of strategic decisions,[8] executive bargaining and negotiation processes,[9] satisficing in decision making,[10] the role of coalitions in strategic management,[11] and the practice of "muddling" in large-scale decision-

---

[6]W.K. Hall, "Strategic Planning Models: Are Top Managers Really Finding Them Useful?" *Journal of Business Policy*, Winter 1972/1973, pp. 33–42, supports the concept that formal planning models are just one element in a political commitment process.

[7]H.A. Simon, "On the Concept of Organizational Goals," *Administrative Science Quarterly*, June 1964, pp. 1–2; P. Diesing, "Noneconomic Decision-Making," in M. Alexis and C.Z. Wilson, eds., *Organizational Decision Making* (Englewood Cliffs, NJ: Prentice-Hall, 1967), pp. 185—200; C. Perrow, "The Analysis of Goals in Complex Organizations," *American Sociological Review*, Feb. 1961, pp. 854–866; P. Georgiou, "The Goal Paradigm and Notes Towards a Counter Paradigm," *Administrative Science Quarterly*, Sept. 1973, pp. 291–310.

[8]R.M. Cyert, H.A. Simon, and D.B. Trow, "Observation of a Business Decision," *The Journal of Business*, Oct. 1956, pp. 237–248; J.M. Pfiffner, "Administrative Rationality," *Public Administration Review*, Summer 1960, pp. 125–132; J.L. Bower, "Planning Within the Firm," *The American Economic Review*, May 1970, pp. 186–194; A. Zaleznik, "Power and Politics in Organizational Life," *Harvard Business Review*, May-June 1970, pp. 47–60; R.A. Bauer and K.J. Gergen, eds., *The Study of Policy Formation* (New York: Free Press, 1968); G.T. Allison, *Essence of Decision; Explaining the Cuban Missile Crisis* (Boston: Little, Brown 1971); A.M. Pettigrew, "Information Control as a Power Resource," *Sociology*, May 1972, pp. 187–204.

[9]R.M. Cyert and J.G. March, *A Behavioral Theory of the Firm* (Englewood Cliffs, NJ: Prentice-Hall, 1963); L.R. Sayles, *Managerial Behavior: Administration in Complex Organizations* (New York: McGraw-Hill, 1964); J.L. Bower, note 8 *supra*; E.E. Carter, "The Behavioral Theory of the Firm and Top-Level Corporate Decisions," *Administrative Science Quarterly*, Dec. 1971, pp. 413–428; J. Pfeffer, G.R. Salancik, and H. Leblebici, "The Effect of Uncertainty on the Use of Social Influence in Organizational Decision Making," *Administrative Science Quarterly*, June 1976, pp. 227–245; R.E. Miles and C.C. Snow, *Organizational Strategy, Structure, and Process* (New York: McGraw-Hill, 1978).

[10]J.G. March and H.A. Simon, *Organizations* (New York: John Wiley, 1958); H.A. Simon, note 7 *supra*; R.M. Cyert and J.G. March, note 9 *supra*.

[11]W.H. Riker, *The Theory of Political Coalition* (New Haven: Yale University Press, 1962); R.M. Cyert and J.G. March, note 9 *supra*; W.D. Guth, "Toward a Social System Theory of Corporate Strategy," *The Journal of Business*, July 1976, pp. 374–388.

making situations, especially in the government.[12] Unfortunately, many power-behavioral studies have been conducted in experimental settings far removed from the realities of actual strategy formulation. Others have concentrated solely on human dynamics, power relationships, or formal organizational processes, and ignored the ways in which systematic data analysis shapes and often determines crucial aspects of strategic decisions. And few have offered much normative guidance for the strategist.

COMBINING APPROACHES

My data suggest that:

- A synthesis of various power-behavioral and formal-analytical approaches more closely approximates the processes major organizations use in changing their strategies;
- This synthesis has a normative validity beyond any other approach taken alone; and
- Managers seemed to consciously integrate both formal-analytical and power-behavioral practices to improve both the quality of the decisions made and the effectiveness of their implementation.

Although the processes top executives used appeared at first to be disjointed or "muddling," they embodied a strong internal logic that seemed consistent between companies and among action sequences within individual companies. Upon analysis, this logic appeared to embrace many central elements of both the "formal systems planning approach" and the "power-behavioral approach." My observations suggested that:

- Effective strategies tended to emerge from a series of strategic formulation subsystems.[13] Each subsystem involved a somewhat different set of players, information needs, and time imperatives. Each attacked a specific issue of corporate-wide importance (like product-line positioning, technological innovation, product diversification, acquisitions, divestitures, government-external relations, major reorganizations, or the concern's international posture) in a disciplined way.[14] Yet, for good reasons, optimum strategies within each subsystem tended to demand incrementalism and opportunism in their formulation.
- The logic patterns underlying formulation of effective strategies for each "subsystem" were so powerful that they could serve as normative approaches for creating these key components of strategy in large organizations.[15] Yet the timing imperatives and internal pacing parameters of each subsystem rarely matched the precise needs of other simultaneously active strategic subsystems.
- Because each subsystem had its own cognitive[16] and process limits,[17] its strategies tended to be arrived at incrementally. Consequently, the total enterprise's strategy—which had to

---

[12]C.E. Lindblom, "The Science of 'Muddling Through,'" *Public Administration Review,* Spring 1959, pp. 79–88; D. Braybrooke and C.E. Lindblom, *A Strategy of Decision: Policy Evaluation as a Social Process* (New York: Free Press of Glencoe, 1963); H.E. Wrapp, "Good Managers Don't Make Policy Decisions," *Harvard Business Review,* Sept.-Oct. 1967, pp. 91–99.

[13]C.E. Lindblom, "The Science of 'Muddling Through,'" note 12 *supra,* suggests this disaggregation occurs in part because the administrator cannot be consistent in all aspects of policy or realize all the implications of even one policy thoroughly.

[14]A. Newell and H.A. Simon, *Human Problem Solving* (Englewood Cliffs, NJ: Prentice-Hall, 1972), also note that when faced with complex unstructured decisions, executives tend to break them down into subdecisions to which more routinized or understood decision procedures can be applied.

[15]J.G. March and H.A. Simon, note 10 *supra,* at 169, note the need to break large decisions into more familiar "action programs" that are "only loosely coupled together" in an "approximating fragmented" decision process.

[16]J.G. March and H.A. Simon, "Cognitive Limits on Rationality," in *Organizations,* note 10 *supra,* and C.E. Lindblom, *The Policy-Making Process* (Englewood Cliffs, NJ: Prentice-Hall, 1968), note that the incremental manager is a shrewd, resourceful problem solver, wrestling bravely with a universe he is wise enough to know is too big for him.

[17]Not the least of these is executive time, as H. Mintzberg, *The Nature of Managerial Work* (New York: Harper & Row, 1973), notes: the top manager is a "juggler" who must constantly make small decisions whether or not he is ready for them.

deal with the interactions of all the subsystem strategies—was also arrived at by an approach most appropriately described as "logical incrementalism."

- In the hands of a skillful manager, such incrementalism was not "muddling." It was a purposeful, effective, proactive[18] management technique for improving and integrating both the analytical and behavioral aspects of strategy formulation. And it was compatible with the best practices recommended by both decision and power-behavioral theorists.

"HARD" VS. "SOFT" DATA DECISIONS

Methodologies for analyzing certain "hard data" decisions (e.g., on product-market segmentation, plant location, make-lease-or-buy options, financial access and capital costs, or internal financial allocations) have been extensively covered in the analytical literature about business strategies.[19] However, executives in the sample repeatedly identified other "soft" changes as having at least as much importance in shaping their concern's overall strategic postures. Most often cited during the study were changes in the company's:

- Degree of diversification (whether induced internally or through acquisitions);
- Approach to divisional controls and divestitures;
- Overall organizational structure or basic management style;
- Relationships with government or other external interest groups;
- International posture and relationships with foreign governments;
- Innovative capabilities or personnel motivations as affected by growth;
- Worker and professional relationships reflect-

ing changed social expectations and values;
- Past or anticipated capacity to deal with its technological environment.

When executives were asked to describe the processes through which their companies had arrived at their new postures vis-á-vis each of these critical domains, several important points emerged. First, few of these issues lent themselves to quantitative modeling techniques or perhaps even formal financial analysis. Second, successful companies essentially used a different "subsystem" (see Exhibit 1) to formulate strategy for each major class of strategic issue—including market segmentation, capital access, and capital cost and other strategies—yet these "subsystems" were quite similar among companies even in very different industries. Third, no single formal analytical process could handle all of these strategic variables simultaneously on a planned basis. Why?

PRECIPITATING EVENTS

Often external or internal events over which managements had essentially no control would precipitate urgent, piecemeal, interim decisions which inexorably shaped the company's future strategic posture.[20] One clearly observed this phenomenon in the decisions forced on General Motors by the 1973–1974 oil crises,[21] the shift in posture pressed upon Exxon by sudden nationalizations, and the dramatic opportunities allowed Haloid (Xerox) Corporation[22] and Pilkington Brothers, Ltd.,[23] by the unexpected inventions of xerography and float glass.

No organization—no matter how brilliant, rational, or imaginative—could possibly foresee the timing, severity, or even the nature of all such precipitating events. In this sense, they were truly unknowable. Analyses from earlier formal planning

[19]See H.I. Ansoff, *Corporate Strategy: An Analytic Approach to Business Policy for Growth and Expansion* (New York: McGraw-Hill, 1965); R.L. Katz, *Cases and Concepts in Corporate Strategy* (Englewood Cliffs, NJ: Prentice-Hall, 1970); S. Schoeffler, R.D. Buzzell, and D.F. Heany, "Impact of Strategic Planning on Profit Performance," *Harvard Business Review,* March-April 1974, pp. 137–145; B.D. Henderson, *Henderson on Corporate Strategy* (Cambridge, MA: Abt Books, 1979).
[20]W.D. Guth, note 2 *supra*, also notes this phenomenon.
[21]J.B. Quinn, *General Motors Corporation,* copyrighted © case, 1979. Amos Tuck School of Business Administration, Dartmouth College.
[22]J.B. Quinn, *Xerox Corporation (A),* copyrighted case © 1972. Amos Tuck School of Business Administration, Dartmouth College.
[23]J.B. Quinn, *Pilkington Brothers, Ltd.,* copyrighted © case, 1977, Amos Tuck School of Business Administration, Dartmouth College.

Exhibit 1 *Strategies Form in Subsystems (Involving Different People, Skills, Goals, Information, Timing Imperatives)*

Overall
Organizational
Structure
Subsystem

Government
External
Relations
Subsystem

Capital Access
and Cost
Subsystem

Product Line
Positioning
Subsystem

Technology
Internal
Growth
Subsystem

BUT

Annual Planning
Strength-Weakness
Opportunities-Threats
Goals
Programs
Alternatives
Contingencies

Acquisition
Diversification
Subsystem

International
Posture
Subsystem

Employee
Relations
Subsystem

Causes
Better Communications
Extends Time Horizons
Involves Lower Levels
Confirms Commitments Made
Helps Evaluate Budgets/Plans
Forces Executives from Daily Focus
Protects Long-term Commitments
Helps Sum and Balance Commitments
Encourages Horizon-scanning Studies
Activates a High-level Planning Gadfly
Teaches Executives about Future Impact of Decisions
Provides a Vehicle for Negotiating Operating Goals
Coordinates Tactical, Divisional, Corporate, Strategic Plans
Etc.

cycles might contribute greatly by broadening the information base available (as in Exxon's case), extending the options considered (Haloid-Xerox), creating shared values to guide decisions in consistent directions (Pilkington), or building up resource bases, management flexibilities, or active search routines for opportunities whose precise nature could not be defined in advance (General Mills, Pillsbury).[24] But specific events could not be forecast and planned for in their entirety. When such events did occur, there might not be time, resources, or information enough to undertake a full formal strategic analysis of all possible options and their consequences. Yet, early decisions made under stress conditions often meant new thrusts, precedents, or lost opportunities that were difficult to reverse later. And these decisions became key elements in the enterprise's future strategic posture.

Recognizing this, top executives usually consciously tried to deal with precipitating events in an incremental fashion. Early commitments were kept broadly formative, tentative, and subject to later review. In some cases, neither the company nor the external players could understand the full implications of alternative actions. All parties wanted to test assumptions and have an opportunity to learn from and adapt to the others' responses. For example:

> I was in the office of the president of Esso France in 1968 when the country was suddenly shut down by political rioting and turmoil, and it appeared a major revolution might be possible. Our discussions were interrupted several times by announcements that various activist groups had taken over one or another of Esso's facilities. Instead of ending our conversation to take some action, the president quietly said, "Right now we must merely find out what is going on. Then we must wait until the situation clarifies enough to know what to do." It took several days to clarify the demands of the activists, to understand the forces at play, to participate effectively in coalitions, and to assess the management team's capabilities for running operations.

Even when a crisis atmosphere tended to shorten time horizons and make decisions more urgently goal-oriented, effective executives consciously tried to keep their options open until they understood how the crisis would affect their constituencies and their own power bases. Further information and political support had a value, and incrementalism often helped to buy this at a low price—as General Motors did in its step-by-step responses to the conflicting demands of the oil and environmental pressures of 1971–1976.[25] To improve both the informational content and the process aspects of decisions surrounding precipitating events, logic dictates and practice affirms that they should be made incrementally, as late as possible consistent with the information available and needed.[26] But crisis decisions do not provide the essential rationale for incrementalism.

HOW A STEP-BY-STEP APPROACH WORKS

Incrementalism occurs for good reasons in many other strategic contexts. In addition to improving the quality of information available for strategic decisions, conscious incrementalism helps in several important process dimensions:

- Coping with the varying lead times and sequencing arrangements demanded by interacting subsystems and individual major decisions that have specific time constraints;
- Overcoming political and emotional barriers to change; and
- Creating the personal and organizational awareness, understanding, acceptance, and commitment needed to implement strategies effectively.

Effectively formulated strategies deal with the timing imperatives and interactions among each of these processes simultaneously. Since executives can never completely control the timing or pacing of all interrelated factors, they move forward incrementally, integrating the four (informational,

[24]J.B. Quinn and M. Jelinek, *General Mills, Inc.*, copyrighted © case, Amos Tuck School of Business Administration, Dartmouth College, 1978; J.B. Quinn and M. Jelinek, *Pillsbury Company*, manuscript in preparation.

[25]See J.B. Quinn, note 21 *supra.*.

[26]R.M. Cyert and J.G. March, note 9 *supra;* J. Marschak, "Toward an Economic Theory of Organization and Information," in R.M. Thrall, C.H. Coombs, and R.L. Davis, eds., *Decision Processes* (New York: John Wiley, 1954).

Innovation

Neither the potential producer nor user of a completely new product or process (like xerography or float glass) can fully conceptualize its ramifications without interactive testing. Yet the positioning of such innovations in the marketplace can affect the strategic posture of both the innovating company and its entire industry. Both buyer and seller benefit from procedures that purposely delay decisions and allow mutual feedback and learning. Consequently, some companies, like IBM or Xerox, have formalized the concept into "phased program planning systems" for major new innovations. They make concrete decisions only on individual phases (or stages) of new product developments, establish interactive testing procedures to learn how the customer uses or abuses the product, and postpone final configuration commitments until the latest possible moment. As a result, many of their new products occupy a quite different strategic position than initial strategic analyses might have suggested. Such interactive adjustments in early product-positioning strategies are common in smaller company situations where added information is vital to survival. For example, Howard Head's first metal skis became "cheaters" for learning skiers, rather than high-performance racing skis.[27] And Haloid's first xerographic devices were used primarily to make offset masters.[28] Both product positions "learned from the marketplace." And both entry positions significantly affected the viability and initial strategic postures of these companies in their industries.

One of the greatest potential errors in managing technical programs is to freeze plans too soon. One should consciously manage innovative programs to allow adoption of the latest available technical solutions and adaptation toward the customers' most current perceived needs. Consequently, the entire innovation process should be designed for high levels of feedback and interactive learning between the marketplace, outside technical sources, and internal development teams.[29] Logic dictates that information from this exchange be introduced into the development process as long as possible—until truly fixed commitments must be made for plants, buildings, or major equipment. Early commitment to PERT charts or detailed schematic diagrams essentially assumes that no new knowledge will be discovered during the development process, no new inventions will occur, and no new design concepts will be worthwhile. Frequently this becomes a destructive and self-fulfilling prophecy.

Highly adaptive learning interactions with outside information sources and strong incentives to use the information attained are among the primary reasons why high-morale smaller companies (like Intel or KMS Fusion, Inc.)[30] can so often outdesign larger electronics companies (like Fairchild or RCA) or huge planned bureaucracies (like the American and Russian atomic energy establishments). Innovative larger companies like IBM, Bell Telephone Laboratories, and United Technologies have learned to institutionalize such incremental learning processes for their own benefit.

Diversification

Strategies for diversification, either through R&D or acquisitions, provide excellent examples of how "formal-analytical" and "power-behavioral" processes may be integrated incrementally in successful strategic formulation. The formal-analytical steps needed for successful (internal or acquisition) diversification are well documented.[31] These include:

---

[27] *Head Ski Company, Inc.*, copyrighted © case, 1967, President and Fellows of Harvard College.

[28] J.B. Quinn, note 22 *supra*.

[29] J.B. Quinn, "Technological Innovation, Entrepreneurship, and Strategy," *Sloan Management Review*, Spring 1979, pp. 19–30, develops the rationale in more detail.

[30] J.B. Quinn, *KMS Industries*, copyrighted © case, 1976, Amos Tuck School of Business Administration, Dartmouth College.

[31] M.L. Mace and G.G. Montgomery, Jr., *Management Problems of Corporate Acquisitions* (Boston: Division of Research Graduate School of Business Administration, Harvard University, 1962); J.B. Quinn and J.A. Mueller, "Transferring Research Results to Operations," *Harvard Business Review*, Jan.-Feb. 1963, pp. 49–66.

- Clarifying the overall objectives of the corporation;
- Setting forth broad goals for the diversification program within these overall objectives;
- Defining specific criteria that acquisitions or developments should meet;
- Systematically searching out new product or acquisition candidates;
- Setting priorities for pursuing these;
- Evaluating specific candidates in technical, operational, and financial terms;
- Pricing acquisition deals or controlling R&D projects for adequate returns;
- Planning the integration of new divisions or lines into the enterprise; and
- Implementing their integration and following up to see that intended yields are realized.

However, the precise directions that R&D may project for the company can only be understood step by step as scientists uncover new phenomena, make and amplify discoveries, build prototypes, reduce concepts to practice, and interact with users during product introductions. Similarly, only as each acquisition is sequentially identified, investigated, negotiated for, and integrated into the organization can one predict its ultimate strategic impact on the total enterprise. The acquisition and development of Richmond Corporation by Continental Group provides a classic example.

A step-by-step approach is clearly necessary to guide and assess the proper timing and strategic fit of each major internal or external diversification candidate.[32] The ultimate strategic impact of a diversification program will be determined by how all its pieces blend together—a fact that cannot really be determined until at least the key pieces are known and are in place. For example:

> *General Mills very carefully laid out the criteria for its (1969 era) acquisition program in the classic manner. Out of this came two thrusts. One was to expand in food-related fields. The other was to develop new growth centers based on General Mills' skills at marketing to the homemaker. The informal feeling was that*

the great majority of resources should go to food-related areas. Almost the reverse occurred. Over the next five years General Mills invested something like $450 million in new businesses, and most were not closely related to foods. Because of external factors beyond the control of the company, the corporation had a good selection of candidates in nonfood areas, and few in food-related fields. As a result, by 1973, General Mills had diversified into a dazzling array of new areas from creative crafts to fine clothing, with high impact on its total strategic posture. This strategy was shaped by the nature and sequencing of opportunities available. And it was logical that this should be the case.[33]

Incremental processes are also required to manage the crucial psychological and power shifts that ultimately determine a program's overall direction and consequences. These processes help unify both the analytical and behavioral aspects of diversification decisions. They create the broad conceptual consensus, the risk-taking attitudes, the organizational and resource flexibilities, and the adaptive dynamism that determine both the timing and direction of diversification strategies. Most important among these processes are:

- *Generating a genuine top-level psychological commitment to diversification.* General Mills, Pillsbury, and Xerox all started their major diversification programs with broad analytical studies and goal-setting exercises designed both to build top-level consensus around the need to diversify and to establish the general directions for diversification. Without such action, top-level bargaining for resources would have continued to support only more familiar (and, hence, apparently less risky) old lines, and this could have delayed or undermined the entire diversification endeavor.
- *Consciously preparing to move opportunistically.* Organizational and fiscal resources must be built up in advance to exploit candidates as they randomly appear. And a "credible activist" for ventures must be developed and backed by someone with commitment power.

---

[32]R.F. Vancil and P. Lorange, "Strategic Planning in Diversified Companies," *Harvard Business Review,* Jan.-Feb. 1975, pp. 81–90, also note that formal strategic planning is inappropriate beyond setting broad guidelines for acquisition planning.

[33]J.B. Quinn and M. Jelinek, *General Mills, Inc.,* note 24 *supra.*

All successful acquirers among the companies studied created the potential for "profit-centered" divisions within their organi-zational structures, strengthened their financial controllership capabilities, took action to create low-cost capital access, and maintained the shortest possible communication lines from the "acquisition activist" to the resource-committing authority. All these actions integrally determined which diversifications actually would be made, the timing of their accession, and the pace at which they could be absorbed.

- *Building a "comfort factor" for risk taking.* Perceived risk is largely a function of one's knowledge about a field. Hence, well-conceived diversification programs anticipated a trial-and-error period during which top managers were likely to reject early proposed fields or opportunities until they had analyzed enough trial candidates to "become comfortable" with an initial selection. Early successes tended to be "sure things" close to the companies (real or supposed) expertise. After a few successful diversifications, managements tended to become more confident and to accept more candidates—farther away from traditional lines—at a faster pace. The way this process was handled affected both the direction and pace of the actual program.
- *Developing a new ethos.* If new divisions were more successful than the old—as they should be—they attracted relatively more resources and their political power grew. Their most effective line managers moved into corporate positions, and slowly the company's special competency and ethos changed. Finally, the concepts and products that once dominated the company's culture might decline in importance and even disappear. Acknowledging these ultimate consequences to the organiza-

tion at the beginning of a diversification program would clearly have been impolitic, even if the strategic manager both desired and could have predicted the probable new ethos. These philosophical shifts had to be handled adaptively,[34] as opportunities presented themselves and as individual leaders and power centers developed.

Each of the above management processes interacted with other subsystem decisions (and with the random appearance of diversification candidates) to affect action sequences, elapsed time, and ultimate results in unexpected ways.[35] Complexities were generally so great that few diversification programs ended up as initially envisioned. Consequently, wise managers recognized the limits to systematic analysis in diversification and used formal planning:

- To establish general goals and criteria for their diversification program;
- To help build the "comfort levels" executives needed for risk taking; and
- To help guide the program's initial directions and priorities.

They then modified these flexibly, step by step, as new opportunities, power centers, or developed competencies merged to create new potentials.

Reorganizations

Major reorganizations provide another example of how "logical incrementalism" can integrate formal-analytical and power-behavioral processes in formulating strategy. It is well recognized that organizational changes are integral parts of most significant strategic changes. In general, the observation is that "organization follows strategy."[36] My data showed, however, that major reorganizations themselves sometimes constituted the central element of a strategy change. Sometimes they preceded and/or precipitated a new strategy, and

---

[34]R. Normann, *Management for Growth* (trans. by N. Adler) (New York: John Wiley, 1977), describes this as an interactive learning process, adjusting both goal perceptions and the relevancy of options incrementally as new information and psychological commitments develop.

[35]J.G. March, J.P. Olsen, S. Christensen, et al., *Ambiguity and Choice in Organizations* (Bergen, Norway: Universitetsforlaget, 1976), also note that the sequence in which decisions are made often determines the nature of this final outcome.

[36]A.D. Chandler, *Strategy and Structure: Chapters in the History of the Industrial Enterprise* (Cambridge, MA: M.I.T. Press, 1962); D.R. Daniel, "Reorganizing for Results," *Harvard Business Review,* Nov.-Dec. 1966, pp. 96–104.

sometimes they helped to implement a strategy. But like most other important strategic decisions, macroorganizational moves were typically handled incrementally *and* outside of the formal planning process. Why?

Their effects on personal or power relationships precluded discussion in the open forums and reports of formal planning. In addition, major organizational changes had timing and sequencing imperatives (or "process limits") all their own. In making any significant shifts, top executives had to think through the new roles, capabilities, and probable individual reactions of the many principals affected. Perhaps they had to wait for the promotion or retirement of valued colleagues before consummating a change. They then frequently had to bring in, train, or test new people for substantial periods before they could staff key posts with confidence.

During such testing periods, top executives might substantially modify their original concepts of the entire reorganization as individuals' potentials, performance, personal drives, and relationships with other team members developed. Because this chain of evaluations could affect the career development, power, affluence, and self-image of so many, top executives tended to keep close counsel in their discussions. They negotiated individually with key people and made final commitments as late as possible in order to obtain the best possible matches between people's capabilities, personalities, and aspirations in their new roles. Rarely, if ever, did all these events come together at one convenient time, particularly at the moment annual plans were due. Instead, top executives moved opportunistically, step by step, selectively leading people toward a broadly conceived organizational goal which was constantly modified and rarely articulated in detail until the last important psychological and structural pieces fit together.

Major organizational moves might define entirely new strategies that the guiding executive could not fully foresee at the outset. For example:

At General Mills, General Rawlings and his team of outside professional managers actively redefined the company's problems and opportunities in ways the prior management could not have foreseen. Because of the new values these individuals brought with them, various divisions which had been the core of the company's product line were divested. Once these divestitures were made, the funds released were used for acquisitions, thus automatically increasing the visibility and power of the new controllership-financial group which had been brought in by General Rawlings. Similarly, with fewer large divisions competing for funds, the Consumer Foods Group rapidly increased in its importance. This ultimately led to a choice between these two groups' leaders for the next chairmanship of the company—and hence for control over the corporation's future strategy.[37]

In such situations, executives might be able to predict the broad direction but not the precise nature of the ultimate strategy that would result from an organizational change. In some cases, the rebalance of power and information relationships became the strategy, or at least its central element. In others, organizational shifts were primarily means of triggering or implementing new strategic concepts or philosophies. But in all cases, major organizational changes created unexpected new stresses, opportunities, power bases, information centers, and credibility relationships that affected both previous plans and future strategies in unanticipated ways.[38] Effective reorganization decisions, therefore, should allow for testing, flexibility, and feedback. Hence, they should—and, from my observations, usually do—evolve incrementally. With so many "unknowables" involved in major reorganizational changes, incrementalism—working toward a broadly and flexibly conceived framework—was the dictated logic. Such incrementalism, properly managed, allowed the integration of a full range of "formal-analytical," "power-behavioral," and "process-timing" considerations.

---

[37]J.B. Quinn and M. Jelinek, *General Mills, Inc.,* note 24 *supra.*
[38]The Pilkington experience was typical. Despite careful planning, the reorganization strategy overdecentralized and the "polo" at the center had to be recorrected. The addition of professional managers, while necessary, unintentionally changed the values of the company, resulting in the use of more formal plans and controls, the isolation of workers from owners, the willingness of workers to strike, and a shift in reward systems, and so on.

Other Instances

One could continue to detail how incrementalism fits each of the subsystems outlined in Exhibit 1. But a few more sample observations will make the essential points:

- In governmental-external relations, companies were dealing with very large-scale forces, mostly beyond their direct control. Data tended to be very soft, often could be only subjectively sensed, and might be costly to quantify. The possible responses of individuals and groups to different stimuli were often very difficult to determine in advance. Yet their power relative to the company was likely to be very high and the diversity in their potential modes of attack was so great that it was physically impossible to lay out probabilistic decision diagrams that would have much meaning. Results were unpredictable and error costs extreme. Hence, the best intended and most rational seeming strategies could be converted into disasters unless they were thoroughly and interactively tested.

- International strategies encountered the same diversity and power of outside forces. Only now, these were multiplied by the number of nations involved and the complex interactions of interests within and among various nations. Most multinationals have learned to their regret that they must interactively test their strategies within each nation with great care. And they must consciously avoid rigid policies for their worldwide operations. Because of the power and unknowability of external forces, successful companies operating multinationally tended to develop significant components of their strategies in a testing-interactive mode that consciously delayed final commitments until relevant forces and reactions could be incrementally assessed.

- Divestiture strategies also required incrementalism. Top executives often found they had to reinforce vaguely felt concerns with detailed data, build up key managers' "comfort levels" about new issues, achieve participation in and commitment to decisions, and move opportunistically to make actual changes. In many cases, the precise nature of the divestiture decision was not clear at the outset. Executives might make seemingly unrelated personnel shifts or appointments to change the values set of critical groups. Or they might initiate staff studies or assessments to generate awareness or to evaluate possible options. Then they might wait for a crucial retirement, an economic change, a crisis, or an attractive offer before determining the final handling of a complex situation. Their final solution and timing might bear little relationship to their original concept of divestiture. Yet, the resulting decisions could affect the whole future strategic posture of the company.

In my observed companies, each such subsystem had its own pacing parameters, which were different from those in other subsystems. As they made or approved key decisions within each subsystem, top managers tried intuitively to integrate their projected actions into a cohesive whole. However, the imperatives of a given moment might easily drive any one subsystem out of synchronization with others. Examining and maintaining the potential meshing of the various subsystems with ongoing operating commitments was one of the main functions of formal corporate planning. Integrating these to form a total corporate strategy was a highly intuitive consensus-oriented process that seemed to occur largely in the minds of individual executives as they interacted with their peers.

APPLYING THE CONCEPT TO FORMAL PLANNING

All companies in the study did have some form of formal planning procedure embedded in their management direction and control systems. But such formal planning systems did not formulate the corporation's central strategy. Perhaps the most important contributions of these corporate planning systems were actually in the "process" (rather than the decision) realm:

- They created a network of information that would not have otherwise been available;
- They periodically forced operating managers to extend their time horizons and see their daily decisions in a larger framework;
- They required rigorous communications about goals, strategic issues, and resource allocations;
- They systematically taught managers about the future so they could better intuitively calibrate their own short-term or interim decisions;

- They often created an attitude about and a "comfort factor" concerning the future (i.e., managers felt less uncertain about the future and consequently were more willing to make commitments that extended beyond short-term horizons); and
- They often stimulated longer-term "special studies" which could have high impact at key junctures for specific strategic decisions.[39]

In most cases, even formal planning was actually a part of an incremental process. Although individual staff planners might identify potential problems and develop management's awareness of them during interim discussions and presentations, the annual planning process itself was rarely (if ever, in the study) the initiating source of really new key corporate issues or radical departures into entirely different product/market realms. These almost always came from the kind of precipitating events, special studies, or subsystem formulations described above. Annual planning was almost always dominantly a "bottom-up" process which—by its very nature—meant that those making proposals had a limited perspective on total corporate needs or resources. And they had defined "turfs" or domains they tended to defend or extrapolate within strongly felt limits. The result tended to be incremental movement, not new major corporate thrusts.

Formal annual planning was typically merely the point at which earlier strategic decisions were confirmed—in the guidelines or instructions issued from the top or in the goals negotiated with subordinate groups. Annual planning, to a large extent, provided the interface between strategic and tactical decisions. As such, planning was the sine qua non of all decentralization. Without codifying agreed-upon goals, commitments, patterns, and action sequences, operating managers could not coordinate their tactics toward longer-term objectives. Nevertheless, most of the important strategies represented in annual plans were determined in processes separate from the annual planning itself. And most were generated in the types of incremental processes described above.

Occasionally, however, some top managers did attempt very broad assessments of their company's total posture. For example:

Shortly after becoming CEO of General Mills, James McFarland decided that his job was "to take a very good company and move it to greatness," but that it was up to his management group, not himself alone, to decide what a great company was and how to get there. Consequently, he took some thirty-five of the company's highest managers away for a three-day management retreat. On the first day, after agreeing to broad financial goals, the group broke up into units of six to eight persons. Each unit was to answer the question "What is a great company?" from the viewpoints of stockholders, employees, suppliers, the public, and society. Each unit reported back at the end of the day, and the whole group tried to reach a consensus through discussion. In the succeeding two days, the group assessed (1) the company's strengths and weaknesses relative to the defined posture of "greatness" and (2) how to move the company toward a "great company." These provided the broad outlines of the strategy of the McFarland era at General Mills.

Yet, even such major endeavors were only portions of a total strategic process. Values and organizational relationships that had built up over decades stimulated or constrained alternatives. Precipitating events, acquisitions, divestitures, external relations, and organizational subsystems developed important segments of each strategy incrementally. Even then, strategies articulated left key elements to be defined as new information became available, politics permitted, or particular opportunities appeared. Major product thrusts, conceived strategically, proved impractical or unsuccessful. Actual strategy, therefore, evolved as each company overextended, consolidated, made errors, and rebalanced various thrusts over time. And it was both logical and expected that initial, broadly conceived strategies would be reshaped in light of subsequent information and realities.

---

[39]These are a bit different from the usual lists of benefits assessed for planning (W.B. Schaffir, "What Have We Learned about Corporate Planning?" *Management Review*, Aug. 1973, pp. 19–26), but they were repeatedly confirmed by top executives—rather than planners. They are amplified in *id.*, Ch. V.

HOW A STRATEGY EMERGES

Successful executives in my study linked together and brought order to a series of strategic processes and decisions spanning years. At the beginning of the process, it was literally impossible to predict all the events and forces that would shape the future of the company. The best that executives could do was to forecast the forces most likely to impinge on the company's affairs and the ranges of their possible impact. Executives then attempted to build a resource base and a corporate *posture* that was so strong in selected areas that the enterprise could survive and prosper despite all but the most devastating events. They consciously selected market/technological/product segments that the concern could "dominate" given its resource limits, and placed some "side bets"[40] in order to decrease the risk of catastrophic failure or to increase the company's flexibility for future options.

They then proceeded incrementally to handle urgent matters, to start long-term sequences whose specific future branches and consequences were perhaps murky, to respond to unforeseen events as they occurred, to build on successes, and to brace up or cut losses on failures. When properly managed, this was a proactive change process—rather than a reactive one as some have suggested.[41] Executives constantly reassessed the future, found new congruencies as events unfurled, and blended the organization's skills and resources into new balances of dominance and risk aversion as various forces intersected to suggest better—but never perfect—alignments. The process was dynamic, with neither a real beginning nor end. Exhibit 2 shows in simplified form some of the interacting ways in which the strategy of Pilkington Brothers, Ltd., emerged around various subsystem flows over a period of some twenty-five years.

Integrating All the Elements

How did top executives integrate these subsystem strategies into a cohesive whole? Since each major subsystem operated at a different pace, it was likely to be at an entirely different stage of problem definition, awareness building, preliminary conceptualization, experimentation, consensus creation, specificity, commitment, or implementation at any given moment. Consequently, except at the level of broad principles, there was no way to set forth the total enterprise strategy in a way which instantaneously covered all areas. The overall strategy could never be truly complete in detail. Even if all the subsystems did actually come into place at any one moment, logic dictated that the strategy begin to mutate and shift almost immediately as new data and events began to impinge on it. In fact, my data indicated that it may even be dangerous to believe that one can realistically first formulate a detailed total strategy and then implement it. Too many experiences suggest this approach can build up rigidities, noncommitment, or opposition forces that are positively counterproductive.

Instead of seeking ultimate specificity in their overall strategies, effective executives in my study accepted much ambiguity. They sought sufficient definition and balance to keep major subsystem thrusts from getting out of control and to keep the organization from working at cross purposes. They tried to design the overall strategy in enough detail to encourage people in the right directions and to avoid disruptions. But they consciously avoided overspecifics which might impair the flexibility or commitment needed to exploit further information or new opportunities. Both subsystem and overall strategies remained broad enough to accommodate and deal with a wide range of possible futures. Yet, to be effective, these strategies had to form a cohesive whole. How did executives achieve needed coordination?

At each stage of the strategy's development, effective executives constantly tried to visualize what new patterns might exist among the emerging strategies of various subsystems. As each subsystem strategy became more apparent, both its executive team and top-level groups consciously tried to project its implications for the total enter-

---

[40]H.I. Ansoff, *Corporate Strategy: An Analytic Approach to Business Policy for Growth and Expansion* (New York: McGraw-Hill, 1965), details the need for internal and external flexibilities. J.L. Bower, "Planning Within the Firm," *The American Economic Review,* May 1970, pp. 186–194, notes that executives place diversifying side bets to reduce their personal risk as well as the corporate risk.

[41]H.I. Ansoff, "The Concept of Strategic Management," *Journal of Business Policy,* Summer 1972, pp. 2–7.

Exhibit 2 *Simplified Strategy Flows — Pilkington Brothers, Ltd.*

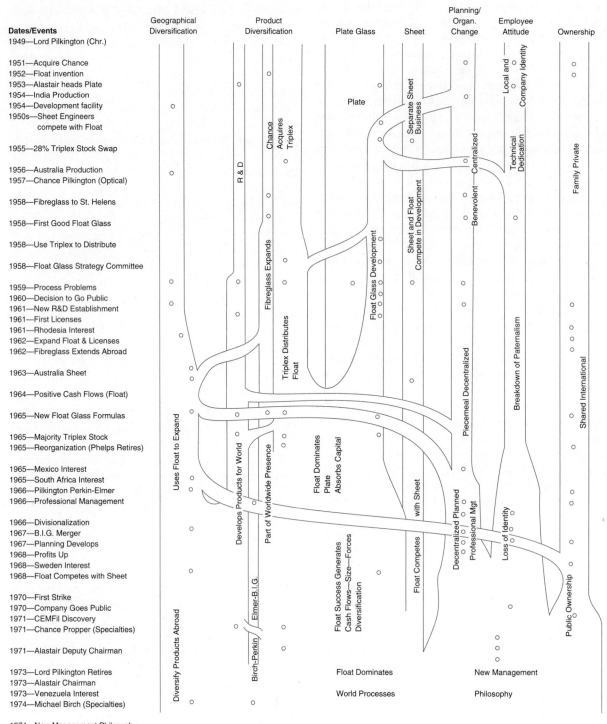

NEW STRATEGIC POSTURE

Diagram of Pilkington Brothers, Ltd., strategy development showing how separate subsystems develop independently yet interrelate and flow together for final strategic posture as an innovative, decentralized, professionally managed, publicly held, worldwide, diversified glass products company. Cross relations vastly simplified for diagram.

prise and to stimulate queries, support, and feedback from those involved in other interrelated strategies. Effective top executives saw that the various teams generating subsystem strategies had overlapping members. They required periodic updates and reviews before higher-echelon groups that could bring a total corporate view to bear. They used formal planning processes to interrelate and evaluate the resources required, benefits sought, and risks undertaken vis-à-vis other elements of the enterprise's overall strategy. Some used scenario techniques to help visualize potential impacts and relationships. Others utilized complex forecasting models to understand better the basic interactions between subsystems, the total enterprise, and the environment. Still others consciously used specialized staffs, "devil's advocates," or "contention teams" to make sure that all important aspects of their strategies received a thorough evaluation.

All of these more formal methodologies helped. But the real integration of all the components in a total enterprise's strategy eventually took place only in the minds of individual top executives. Each executive might legitimately perceive the intended balance of goals and thrusts differently. Some of these differences might be openly expressed as issues to be resolved when new information became available. Other differences might remain unstated, hidden agendas to emerge at later dates. Still others might be masked by accepting so broad a statement of intention that many different views could be brought toward a seeming consensus—while a more specific statement might be outright divisive. Nevertheless, effective strategies did achieve a level of understanding and consensus sufficient to focus action. Top executives actively managed the incremental processes within each subsystem to create the underlying bases for consensus. But the strategic consensus one could observe for the total enterprise appeared much more like a giant river system, constantly in flux and flow with many more or less discrete tributaries contributing to its strength. The system's central thrust and general dimensions might be reasonably clear. But its specific boundaries and important currents were rarely perceivable in their totality at any given moment.

Managing the Process

How does one manage such continuous, flowing, consensus-building processes? More complete answers can be found in another article of mine and in my book.[42] But space may allow some glimpses of the most relevant processes. Perhaps the most articulate short explanation is quoted below.

> *Typically you start with a general concern, vaguely felt. Next, you roll an isssue around in your mind until you think you have a conclusion that makes sense for the company. Then you go out and sort of post the idea without being too wedded to its details. You then start hearing the arguments pro and con, and some very good refinements of the idea usually emerge. Then you pull the idea in and put some resources together to study it so it can be put forward as more of a formal presentation. You wait for "stimuli occurrences" or "crises," and launch pieces of the idea to help in these situations. But they lead toward your ultimate aim. You know where you want to get. You'd like to get there in six months. But it may take three years, or you may not get there at all. And when you do get there, you don't know whether it was originally your own idea—or somebody else had reached the same conclusion before you and just got you on board for it. You never know. The president would follow the same basic process, but he could drive it much faster than an executive lower in the organization.*

Because of differences in organizational form, management styles, and the content of individual decisions, no single paradigm can hold for all strategic decisions.[43] But management of the most complex strategic decisions tends to involve certain broad process steps, briefly outlined below. The reader will recognize the parallels with various "phase theorems"[44] about decision making.

---

[42]See J.B. Quinn, note 1 *supra*, and "Managing Logical Incrementalism," paper submitted for publication.

[43]O.G. Brim, D. Glass, et al., *Personality and Decision Processes; Studies in the Social Psychology of Thinking* (Stanford, CA: Stanford University Press, 1962).

[44]E. Witte, "Field Research on Complex Decision-Making Processes—The Phase Theorem," *International Studies of Management & Organization,* Summer 1972, pp. 156–182.

But the actual process is much more multiphased and complex in political-behavioral term than such theorems generally indicate.

The following steps were typical in proactively managed strategic processes:

- *Leading the formal information system* was a conscious part of strategic management. Rarely did the earliest signals for strategic change come from the company's formal horizon-scanning, planning, or reporting systems. Instead, needs for the major strategic changes were initially perceived or sensed as "something you felt uneasy about," "inconsistencies," or "anomalies" between the enterprise's current posture and some general perception of its future environment. Proactive managers purposely established multiple credible internal and external sources to obtain objective information about their enterprise and its surrounding environments. They consciously used these networks to short-circuit all the careful screens their organizations built up "to tell the top only what it wanted to hear." They actively searched beyond their organization's established information systems, deeming the latter to be too historical or extrapolative to pinpoint needed basic changes in time.

- *Amplifying understanding* was often necessary either to avoid too rapid a problem definition or response—as in GM's initial reactions to air depollution pressures—or to develop more convincing evidence or greater organizational support to stimulate effective action. Far from accepting the first satisfactory (satisfying) solution—as some have suggested executives do—successful change managers seemed to consciously generate and consider a broad array of alternatives. They used multiple information sources to critique one another, to add objectivity, and to flush upward various potential solutions the best brains in and outside the organization might have to offer. In fact, they often delayed adopting the first satisfactory solution, even if it seemed attractive. They wanted to avoid being the prime supporter of a losing idea or having the organization attack or slavishly adopt "the boss's solution" and having to change it as more evidence became available. Before backing a particular solution, they often sought additional objective data to

argue effectively against preconceived ideas or blindly followed past practices. All this frequently required consciously delaying decisions.

- *Building awareness* might be essential when key players did not have enough information or psychological stimulation concerning specific issues, variables, or options to voluntarily change their past action patterns, or even to investigate options creatively. At early stages, top strategic managers might not feel committed to any specific solution. Hence, while tapping the "collective wit" of the organization, they wanted to prevent irreconcilable opposition, emotional overcommitment, or organizational momenta they could not control. And they did not want to prematurely threaten existing power centers that might kill any potential changes before potential supporters really knew what was at stake and could bring broader interests to bear. At this stage, management processes involved were rarely directive. Instead they were likely to consist of studying, challenging, questioning, listening, perhaps generating options, but purposely avoiding commitments.

- *Changing symbols* was often necessary when managers wanted to signal the organization that certain types of changes were coming, even when specific solutions might not be in hand. Knowing they could not communicate directly with the thousands who would carry out the strategy, some executives purposely undertook highly visible symbolic actions that wordlessly conveyed complex messages they could never have communicated as well—or as credibly—in verbal terms. For example, when GM's top management agreed, if it was necessary, to buy up the whole aluminum capacity of the United States to lighten their cars, engineers began to feel the downsizing program would receive the support it needed. Top management's response was probably more symbolic than real, but it had a galvanizing effect. Organizations often needed such symbolic moves—or decisions regarded as symbolic—to signal the coming of a new strategy or to build credibility behind one in its initial stages. And such actions tended to be more forceful than any rhetoric.

- *Legitimizing new viewpoints* often caused

planned delays. Top managers might consciously create discussion forums and allow slack time for their organizations to talk through threatening issues, work out the implications of new solutions, or gain in an improved information base that would permit new options to be evaluated objectively in comparison with more familiar—hence, apparently less risky—alternatives. In many cases, strategic concepts that were strongly resisted at first gained acceptance and positive commitment simply by the passage of time, when executives did not exacerbate hostility by pushing them too fast from the top. Many top executives consciously planned such "gestation periods" and found that the concept itself was made more effective by the resulting feedback.

- *Tactical shifts and partial solutions* typically preceded a total new strategic posture. Early problem resolutions were likely to be partial, tentative, or experimental. Beginning moves often appeared as mere tactical adjustments in the enterprise's existing posture. The guiding executive tried to carefully maintain the enterprise's ongoing strengths while shifting its total posture incrementally—at the margin—toward new needs. Executives themselves might not yet have perceived the full nature of the strategic shift they had begun. They could still experiment with partial new approaches without risking the viability of the total enterprise. Their broad early steps could still legitimately lead to a variety of different success scenarios.

- *Broadening political support* for emerging new thrusts through consultative processes and discussion forums was frequently an essential and consciously proactive step. Committees, task forces, or retreats tended to be favored mechanisms. By selecting the committee's chairman, membership, timing, and agenda, the guiding executive could largely influence and predict a desired outcome, yet force other executives toward a consensus. Nevertheless, the executive still maintained complete control over these "advisory" processes through his various influence and veto potentials. In addition to facilitating smooth implementation, many managers reported that interactive consensus building also improved the quality of the strategic decisions themselves and helped achieve posi-

tive and innovative assistance when things otherwise would have gone wrong.

- *Overcoming opposition* was almost always necessary. Executives tried to get key people behind their concepts whenever possible, to co-opt or neutralize serious opposition if necessary, or to find zones of indifference where the proposition would not be disastrously opposed. Best of all, they sought "no-lose" situations that would activate all important players positively toward a common goal. Successful executives tended to honor legitimate differences in views concerning major directions and noted that initial opponents often shaped new strategies in more effective directions and became supporters as new information became available. But strong-minded executives sometimes disagreed to the point where they had to be moved to positions of less influence or stimulated to leave. And timing could dictate the necessity for very firm top-level direction at key junctures.

- *Structuring flexibility* was essential to deal with the "unknowables" in the total environment. Because one could not predict the precise form or timing of all possible important threats and opportunities, the essence of contingency planning was to anticipate the possible range of likely changes in the environment, to build resource "buffers" that allowed the organization to respond flexibly to these, to build emotional commitments among "credible activists" who would be motivated to take advantage of specific opportunities as they occurred, and to shorten the decision lines from such persons to the top for the most rapid possible system response. Consciously designed flexibility was an essential aspect of proactive, incremental strategic management.

- *Trial balloons and systematic waiting* were often necessary to stimulate major change. Thus, a strategist might proactively launch trial concepts like McColough's "architecture of information" or Spoor's "Super Box" in order to attract options and concrete proposals. Usually these trial balloons were phrased in very broad contextual terms. Without making a commitment to any specific solution, the executive could activate the organization's creative abilities. This approach kept the manager's own options open until substantive alternatives could be evaluated against one another and against concrete current realities. It prevented practical line managers from rejecting a strategic shift because they were forced to compare what they only saw as "paper options" against well-defined and urgent current needs.

- *Creating pockets of commitment* was essential for entirely new strategic thrusts. The executive might encourage exploratory projects toward each of several possible options. Initial projects might be kept small, partial, or ad hoc, not forming a comprehensive program or seeming to be integrated into a cohesive strategy. The guiding executive might merely provide broad goals, a proper climate, and flexible resource support, without being identified with specific projects. In this way, the executive could avoid escalating attention to any one solution too soon or losing personal credibility if it failed. But he could stimulate those which led in observed directions, set higher hurdles for those that did not, or quietly have them killed by someone two levels below. Once small teams were activated on new strategic thrusts, they tended to become committed to them, thus providing pockets of support deep within the organization. Yet, top managers could delay their final decisions on a total thrust until the last moment, thus obtaining the best possible match between the company's psychological commitments and changing market needs.

- *Crystallizing focus* was essential at critical points in the process. For reasons noted, guiding executives might purposely keep early goal statements vague and commitments broad and tentative. But as these executives saw consensus emerging around key thrusts, they might use their prestige or position to push or crystallize a particular formulation. Despite adhering to the rhetoric of specific goal setting, most executives were careful not to state new strategic goals in too concrete terms until they had carefully built consensus among key players. They feared they might prematurely centralize the organization, preempt interesting options, provide a common focus for otherwise fragmented opposition, or cause the organization "to do something stupid" to carry out a stated commitment.

- *Managing coalitions* was essential at this point.

Individual top executives might legitimately perceive problems, opportunities, or probabilities differently based upon their particular experiences and vantage points. Hence, there was no objectively "right answer" in strategic formulation. In an organization with dispersed power, the central power figure was the one who could maneuver top-level coalitions toward acceptable solutions most key people could support energetically and creatively. As comfort levels and polities within the top group built around various needed specific decisions, the guiding executive began to consciously seek out a combination of features—within his conception of a more complete solution—that the most influential and credible parties would live with and actively support. The result was a stream of partial decisions on specific strategic issues, evolving toward a broader consensus acceptable to the top executive and the most important power centers.

- *Formalizing commitment* was now possible. As each major thrust came into final focus, the guiding executive would insure that one or more persons felt responsible for its execution. If it was an entirely new vector for the enterprise, top executives often wanted more than mere accountability for its success—they wanted genuine commitment from its leaders. Hence, they sought to empower a "champion" to take over such thrusts.

- *Continuing dynamics and eroding consensus* were final stages in the strategic change process. Once the organization had arrived at its new consensus, guiding executives had to move immediately to insure that this, too, did not become inflexible. The most effective executives, therefore, purposely continued the change process, constantly introducing new faces and stimuli at the top. They consciously began to erode the very strategic thrusts they might have just created—a very difficult but essential psychological and management task.

While various process phases—for both subsystems and overall enterprise strategies—generally flowed in the sequence represented, the stages were by no means orderly or discrete. (See Exhibit 3.) It would be improper to assume that any executive consciously managed the process through all its phases linearly. Although executives did man-

Exhibit 3 Some Typical Process Steps in Logical Incrementalism (Highly Simplified to Help Visualize a Few Basic Relationships)

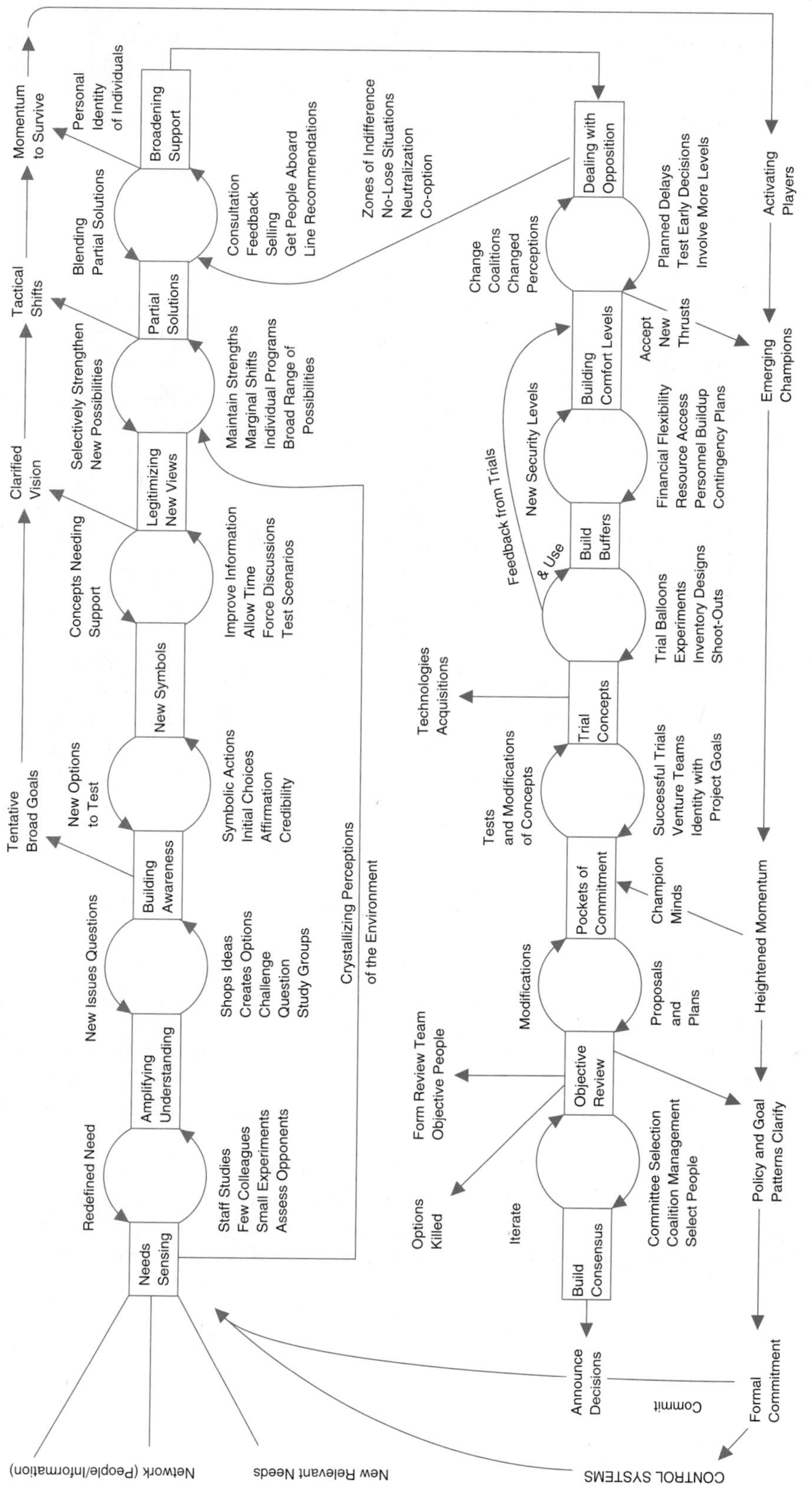

age individual steps proactively, any single decision might well involve numerous loops back to
earlier stages as unexpected issues were encountered. Similarly, decision times might become
extremely compressed and require short-circuiting
leaps forward if major crises suddenly appeared.

The decision process for each strategic subsystem moved from the selection of broad targets, to
general routes, to specific pathways, to initial commitment, to short tactical adaptations—until the
subsystem strategy became complete or was reshaped to new goals. The total strategic process
was anything but linear. Integrating all the subsystem strategies was a groping, cyclical process that
often circled back upon itself, encountered interruptions and delays, and rarely arrived at clear-cut
decisions at any one point in time. The strategy's
ultimate development involved a series of nested
partial decisions (in each subsystem) interacting
with other partial decisions in all subsystems and
the total resource base available. Pfiffner[45] has aptly
described the process as "like fermentation in bio-
chemistry, rather than an industrial assembly line."

Nevertheless, the total pattern action—though
highly incremental—did not remain piecemeal in
well-managed organizations. It required constant,
conscious reassessment of the total organization, its
capacities, and needs as related to its surrounding
environments. And it required a continual attempt
by top managers to integrate these actions into an
understandable, cohesive whole. How did this integrative function operate? Several quotes suggest
how a single organization approached the issue.

• The president of General Motors (Estes) said:
  "We try to give them the broad concepts we
  are trying to achieve. We operate through
  questioning and fact gathering. Strategy is a
  state of mind you go through. When you think
  about a little problem, your mind begins to
  think how it will affect all the different elements in the total situation. Once you have had
  all the jobs you need to qualify for this position, you can see the problem from a variety of
  viewpoints, but you don't try to ram your conclusions down people's throats. You try to persuade people what has to be done and provide
  confidence and leadership for them."

• J.N. Stuart, director of GM's marketing staff,
  said: "No one has written down strategic
  objectives. But these are well understood
  throughout the organization. The decision
  process tends to work within these broad concepts. And the concept itself is molded by a
  series of incremental decisions made in
  response to particular opportunities or problems. The inputs and weightings used in these
  decisions vary widely. But the sum of these
  decisions and ideas represents the strategy. It
  is not a one man, one vote system. Certain
  people with greater expertise will wield a
  heavier vote on an issue. And people will
  defer to the most persuasive person. The strategy of GM may not even exist in the mind of
  one man. I certainly don't know where it is
  written down. It is simply transmitted in the
  series of decisions made."

• Another General Motors executive said: "Formal meetings [on subsystem strategies] make
  sure that everything gets looked at. One is
  forced to listen to a complete rationale. We get
  clear cost estimates and a thoroughly worked
  out plan for a given subject. Everyone feels
  more comfortable about decisions after they
  have been discussed in a broadly based form.
  More importantly, the line people know how
  we are planning to get where we are going.
  The more they understand this, the more they
  know what to do on their own as the program
  progresses."

• Still another General Motors executive said:
  "For the most part policy simply evolves. In
  meetings, people say things that do or don't
  hold up to argument. Slowly everyone begins
  to sort out a sensible position from all of this.
  . . . We may write this position into testimony
  or a speech writer may put it into a draft
  speech for one of our corporate officers. After
  an initial review by the principal, we will circulate the draft to all the appropriate staffs for
  comment. . . . The top people are very open to
  critiques of this sort. The ideas tend to flush
  upward so the top level can adopt them as
  they see a consensus emerging. If there is a
  major policy question, the executive may take

[45]J.M. Pfiffner, "Administrative Rationality," *Public Administration Review,* Summer 1960, pp.
125–132.

the statement to the Executive Committee for comment or approval. Mr. Murphy will nearly always comment on any important issue."

Building Coalitions

Coalition management also lay at the heart of most controlled strategy developments.[46] Top managers recognized that they were at the confluence of innumerable pressures from stockholders, environmentalists, government bodies, customers, suppliers, distributors, producing units, marketing groups, technologists, unions, special issue activists, individual employees, ambitious executives, and so on, where knowledgeable people of goodwill could easily disagree on proper actions. In response to changing pressures and coalitions among these groups, the top management team constantly formed and reformed its own coalitions on various decisions representing different members' values concerning the particular issues at hand.[47]

Most major strategic moves would tend to assist some interests—and executives' careers—at the expense of others. Consequently, each set of interests could serve as a check on the others and thus help maintain the breadth and balance of strategy.[48] To avoid significant errors, some managements tried to insure that all important polities had representation or access at the top.[49] And the guiding executive group might continuously adjust the number, power, or proximity of these access points as needed to maintain desired balance and focus.[50] These delicate adjustments represented a source of constant negotiations and implied bargains among the leadership group. And control over the balance of forces these inter-ests could bring to bear was perhaps the ultimate control top executives had in guiding and coordinating their companies' strategies.

Establishing, Measuring, and Rewarding Key Thrusts

Few individual executives or top management teams could keep the full dimensions of a complex strategy in mind as they dealt with the continuously changing flux of urgent issues they faced. Consequently, effective strategic managers constantly sought to distill out a few (six to ten) "central themes" that would help draw several diverse efforts together into a common cause.[51] Once identified, these helped maintain focus and consistency in the strategy. They made it easier to both discuss and monitor intended directions. Ideally, these themes would be converted into a "matrix" of strategic "thrusts" cutting across formal divisional plans and dominating other ranking criteria within the divisions. These thrusts could in turn serve as the basis for strategic performance measurement, control, and reward systems. Unfortunately, few companies were able to implement such a complex planning and control system without undue rigidities. Texas Instruments came as close as any company studied. The following short description suggests how one company simultaneously integrated both "formal analytical" and "power-behavioral" considerations using the approximate process sequences of Exhibit 3. Other companies followed this general sequence both in subsystems and at overall corporate levels.

In the late 1970s a major nation's largest bank named as its new president and CEO a man

---

[46]R. James, "Corporate Strategy and Change—The Management of People," monograph, University of Chicago (1978), does an excellent job of pulling together the threads of coalition management at top organizational levels.

[47]R.M. Cyert and J.G. March, *A Behavioral Theory of the Firm*, (Englewood Cliffs, NJ: Prentice-Hall, 1963), p. 115.

[48]C.E. Lindblom, "The Science of 'Muddling Through,'" *Public Administration Review*, Spring 1959, pp. 79–88, notes that every interest has a "watchdog" and that purposely allowing these watchdogs to participate in and influence decisions creates consensus decisions all can live with. Similar conscious access to the top for different interests can now be found in corporate structures.

[49]A. Zaleznik, "Power and Politics in Organizational Life," *Harvard Business Review*, May-June 1970, pp. 47–60.

[50]L.R. Sayles, *Managerial Behavior: Administration in Complex Organizations* (New York: McGraw-Hill, 1964), pp. 207–217, provides an excellent view of the bargaining processes involved in coalition management.

[51]H.E. Wrapp, "Good Managers Don't Make Policy Decisions," *Harvard Business Review*, Sept.-Oct. 1961, pp. 91–99, notes the futility of a top manager trying to push a full package of goals.

with a long and successful career, predominantly in domestic operating positions. The bank's chairman had been a familiar figure on the international stage and was due to retire in three to five years. The new CEO, with the help of a few trusted colleagues, his chief planner, and a consultant, first tried to answer the question "If I look ahead seven to eight years to my retirement as CEO, what would I like to leave behind as the 'hallmarks' of my leadership? What accomplishments would define my era as having been successful?" He distilled these to the following: (1) to be the country's number one bank in profitability and size without sacrificing the quality of its assets or liabilities; (2) to be recognized as a major international bank; (3) to substantially improve the image, public perception, and employee identity of the bank; (4) to maintain progressive policies that prevent unionization; (5) to be viewed as a skillful, professional, well-controlled bank with strong planned management continuity; (6) to be clearly identified as the country's most professional corporate finance bank, with a strong base in the country but with foreign and domestic operations growing in balance; (7) to have women in top management and achieve full utilization of the bank's female resources; (8) to have a tighter, smaller headquarters with a more rationalized, decentralized structure.

The CEO brought back to the corporate offices the head of his overseas divisions to be COO and a member of the small line Executive Committee, which ran the company's affairs. The CEO discussed his personal views concerning the bank's future with this group and individually with several of his group VPs. Then, to arrive at a cohesive set of corporate goals, the Executive Committee investigated the bank's existing strengths and weaknesses (again with consultants' assistance) and extrapolated its existing growth trends seven to eight years into the future. The results of this exercise quickly highlighted that the bank's foreseeable growth would require: (1) that the whole bank's structure be reoriented to make it a much stronger force in international banking; (2) that the bank must decentralize operations much more than it ever had; (3) that the bank find or develop "at least 100" new top-level specialists and general managers within a few years; (4) that it reorganize around a "four bank" principle (i.e., an international, a commercial, an investment, and a retail bank) with entirely new linkages forged between these units; (5) that these linkages and much of its

new international thrust should probably be built on the bank's expertise in certain industries that were the primary bases of its parent country's international trade; and (6) that the bank's profitability must be improved across the board, but especially in its diverse retail banking units.

To develop more detailed data for specific actions and to further develop consensus around needed moves, the CEO commissioned two consulting studies: one on the future of the bank's home country, the other on changing trade patterns and relationships worldwide. As these studies became available, the CEO allowed an ever wider circle of top executives to critique the studies' findings and share in their insights. Finally, the CEO and Executive Committee were willing to draw up and agree to a statement of some ten broad goals (quite parallel to the CEO's original goals but enriched in flavor and detail). By then, some steps were already underway to implement specific goals, for example, the "four bank" concept. But the CEO wanted further participation of his line officers in the formulation of the goals and the strategic "thrusts" they represented across the whole bank. By now a year and a half had gone by, but there was widespread consensus of the top management group on major goals and directions.

The CEO then organized an international conference of some forty top officers of the bank and had a background document prepared for this meeting, containing: (1) the broad goals agreed on; (2) the "ten major thrusts" the Executive Committee thought were necessary to meet these goals; (3) the key elements needed to back up each thrust (one to one and a half pages per thrust); and (4) a summary of the national and economic analyses the thrusts were based on. The forty executives had two full days to critique, question, improve, and clarify the ideas in this document. Small work groups of line executives reported their findings and concerns directly to the Executive Committee. At the end of the meeting, the Executive Committee "tabled" one of the major thrusts for further study, agreed to refine wording for some of the bank's broad goals, and modified details of the major thrusts in line with expressed concerns.

The CEO then announced that within three months each line officer would be expected to submit his own statement of how his unit would contribute to the major goals and thrusts agreed on. Once these unit goals were dis-

cussed and negotiated with the appropriate top executive group, the line officers would develop specific budgetary and nonbudgetary programs showing precisely how their unit would carry out each of the major thrusts in the strategy. The COO was asked to develop measures both for all key elements of each unit's fiscal performance and for performance against each agreed-upon strategic thrust within each unit. As these came into place, it became clear that the old organization had to be aligned behind these new thrusts. The CEO had to substantially redefine the COO's job, deal with some crucial internal political pressures, and place the next generation of top management in the line positions supporting each major thrust. The total process from concept formulation to implementation of the control system would span some three to four years, with new goals and thrusts emerging flexibly as external events and opportunities developed.

CONCLUSIONS

In recent years, there has been an increasing chorus of discontent concerning corporate strategic planning. Many managers are concerned that despite elaborate strategic planning systems, costly staffs for this purpose, and major commitments of their own time, their most elaborate strategies never get implemented. These executives and their companies have generally fallen into the classic trap of thinking about strategy formulation and implementation as separate sequential processes. They have relied on the awesome rationality of their formally derived strategies and the inherent power of their positions to cause their organizations to respond. When this does not occur, they become bewildered, if not frustrated and angry. Instead, successful managers who operate with logical incrementalism build the seeds of understanding, identity, and commitment into the very processes that create their strategies. By the time the strategy begins to crystallize and focus, pieces of it are already being implemented. Through their strategic formulation processes, they have built a momentum and psychological commitment into the strategy that cause it to flow toward flexible implementation. Constantly integrating the simultaneous incremental processes of strategy formulation and implementation is the heart of effective strategic management.

LINKING COMPETITIVE STRATEGY AND SHAREHOLDER VALUE ANALYSIS

Alfred Rappaport

Strategy valuation is not merely a measurement technique that is applied after the strategy formulation process is completed. Its real power lies in the way it can be integrated throughout the strategy formulation effort.

Management has been coming under increasing pressure to select and implement strategies that will create value for shareholders. This pressure has intensified recently as a result of some converging trends. First, there has been a growing recognition that traditional accounting measures, such as earnings per share, are not reliably linked to increasing the value of the company's stock price. Couple this with the pervasive threat of corporate takeover, for which incumbent management's best defense is a higher stock price, and it comes as no surprise that increasing shareholder value has become the driving force for the current corporate restructuring movement.

Yet among publicly held companies, there has been great uncertainty within management about how to identify and select strategies that will create value for shareholders. Fortunately, a relatively straightforward approach does exist for estimating the shareholder value created by a business strategy, and an increasing number of major companies have begun to use this "strategy-valuation" method.

Strategy valuation is not merely a measurement technique that is applied after the strategy formulation process is completed. Its real power lies in the way it can be integrated throughout the strategy formulation effort. The technique of strategy valuation can be applied even in the earliest stages of strategy formulation; for example, it can help establish criteria for strategy selection by identifying which financial factors have the greatest effect on value creation in a business.

This article will begin with a discussion of the rationale for the shareholder-value approach. Next, the process of strategy valuation will be explained. Then, the discussion will focus on how to integrate strategy valuation with the strategy-formulation process, using the well-known competitive-analysis framework developed by Professor Michael Porter of Harvard.

RATIONALE FOR SHAREHOLDER VALUE APPROACH

Business strategies should be judged by the economic returns they generate for shareholders, as measured by dividends plus the increase in the company's share price. As management considers alternative strategies, those expected to develop the greatest sustainable competitive advantage will be those that will also create the greatest value for shareholders.

The "shareholder-value approach" estimates the economic value of an investment (e.g., the shares of a company's strategies, mergers and acquisitions, and capital expenditures) by discounting forecasted cash flows by the cost of capital. These cash flows, in turn, serve as the foundation for shareholder returns from dividends and share-price appreciation.

The reason why management should pursue this objective is comparatively straightforward. Management is often characterized as balancing the interest of various corporate constituencies, such as employees, customers, suppliers, debtholders, and stockholders. As Treynor[1] points out, the company's continued existence depends on a financial relationship with each of these parties. Employees want competitive wages. Customers want high quality at a competitive price. Suppliers and debt-holders have financial claims that must be satisfied with cash when they fall due. Stockholders as residual claimants of the firm look for cash dividends and the prospect of future dividends that is reflected in the market price of the stock.

If the company does not satisfy the financial claims of its constituents, it will cease to be a viable organization. Employees, customers, and suppliers will simply withdraw their support. Thus, a going concern must strive to enhance its cash-generating ability. The ability of a company to distribute cash to its various constituencies depends on its ability to generate cash from the operation of its businesses, and on its ability to obtain any additional funds needed from external sources.

Debt and equity financing are the two basic external sources. The company's ability to borrow today is based on projections of how much cash will be generated in the future. Borrowing power and the market value of the shares both depend on a company's cash-generating ability. The market value of the shares directly impacts the second source of financing, that is, equity financing. The higher the share price for a given level of funds required, the less dilution will be borne by current shareholders. Therefore, management's financial power to deal effectively with corporate claimants also comes from increasing the value of the shares. Treynor, a former editor of the *Financial Analysts Journal*, summarizes this line of thinking best:

> *Those who criticize the goal of share value maximization are forgetting that stockholders are not merely the beneficiaries of the corporation's financial success, but also the referees who determine management's financial power.[2]*
>
> *Any management—no matter how powerful and independent—that flouts the financial objective of maximizing share value, does so at its own peril.[3]*

STRATEGY VALUATION

In today's fast-changing, often bewildering business environment, formal systems for strategic planning have become one of top management's principal tools for evaluating and coping with uncertainty. Corporate board members are also showing increasing interest in ensuring that the company has adequate strategies and that these are tested against actual results. While the organizational dynamics and the sophistication of the strategic planning process vary widely among companies, the process almost invariably culminates in projected (commonly five-year) financial statements.

This accounting format enables top managers and the board of directors to review and approve strategic plans in the same terms that the company uses to report its performance to shareholders and the financial community. Under current practice, the projected financial statements, particularly projected earnings-per-share performance, commonly serve as the basis for judging the attractiveness of the strategic or long-term corporate plan.

The conventional accounting-oriented approach for evaluating the strategic plan does not, however, provide reliable answers to such basic questions as:

- Will the corporate plan create value for shareholders? If so, how much?
- Which business units are creating value and which are not?
- How would alternative strategic plans affect shareholder value?

The essential purpose of the planning *process* is to provide managers with a systematic framework for thinking strategically and thereby shaping the future of their businesses. It is important to emphasize that qualitative strategic thinking, based on judgments and even intuition, and the discipline of analytic and quantitative analysis, are neither mutually exclusive nor contradictory. To the contrary, they are complementary. Ultimately, it is necessary to translate qualitative, and, it is hoped, creative strategic analysis into plans that specify resources required and expected rates of

---

[1] J.L. Treynor, "The Financial Objective in the Widely Held Corporation," *Financial Analysts Journal*, March-April, 1981.

[2] *Id.* at 71.

[3] *Id.* at 69.

return. All of this is best summarized, perhaps by a comment attributed to President Eisenhower: "Plans are nothing, planning is everything."

Consider two basic beliefs: first, that businesses can create shareholder value by superior planning; second, that managers are particularly motivated in the current climate of corporate takeovers by the knowledge that "capitalism offers no refuge for companies that don't maximize their value."

The basic valuation parameters or *value drivers* are sales growth rate, operating profit margin, income tax rate, working capital investment, fixed capital investment, cost of capital, and value growth duration.

Operating decisions, such as product mix, pricing, promotion, advertising, distribution, and customer service level, are impounded primarily in three value drivers—sales growth rate, operating profit margin, and income tax rate. *Investment* decisions, such as increasing inventory levels and capacity expansion, are reflected in the two investment value drivers—working capital and fixed capital investment. The cost of the capital value driver is governed not only by business risk but also by management's *financing* decisions; that is, the question of the proper proportions of debt and equity to use in funding the business, as well as appropriate financing instruments. The final value driver, value growth duration, is management's best estimate of the number of years that investments can be expected to yield rates of return greater than the cost of capital.

The first valuation component, cash flow from operations, is determined by operating and investment value drivers along with the value growth duration. The second component, the discount rate, is based on an estimate of cost of capital. Recall that discounting cash flow from operations yields corporate value. To obtain shareholder value, the final valuation component—debt—is deducted from corporate value. Shareholder value creation, in turn, serves as the foundation for providing shareholder returns from dividends and capital gains.

THE COMPETITIVE ANALYSIS FRAMEWORK

Strategy formulation typically entails analyzing the attractiveness of the industry and the position of the business vis-à-vis its competitors. The analysis then seeks to understand how alternative strategies might affect industry attractiveness and the competitive position of the business. In contrast, strategy valuation involves an estimation of the economic value created by alternative strategies. Successful planning requires sound analysis for *both* formulating business strategies and valuing strategies.

While there is no shortage of "systematic frameworks" for strategy formulation, none has had a greater impact during the past few years than the competitive strategy framework developed by Michael E. Porter in his seminal work, *Competitive Strategy*. Porter presents a framework for first assessing industries and competitors, and then formulating an overall competitive strategy.[4] The core of Porter's framework is the analysis of the five competitive forces that drive industry structure, and thereby drive the long-run rates of return that firms in an industry can expect to earn.

The five competitive forces—threat of new entrants, threat of substitute products, bargaining power of buyers, bargaining power of suppliers, and rivalry among current competitors—reflect the fact that current competitors determine only a part of the competitive setting. Customers, suppliers, potential entrants, and substitute products also affect competitive structure, and thereby affect industry and individual company rates of return. The relative importance of the five forces differs by industry and may well change over time. For example, the impressive return achieved during the 1970s by leading computer time-sharing companies was recently disrupted by a substitute technology. The advent of microcomputers coupled with the steadily declining cost of mainframe computers has led to a significantly decreased demand for time-sharing services.

For those not familiar with the framework, a detailed discussion of the five competitive forces and their structural determinants can be found in Porter's *Competitive Strategy*, Chapter 1. For purposes here, it is important to establish that the five competitive forces govern shareholder return because they influence prices, quantities sold,

[4]M.E. Porter, *Competitive Strategy* (1980).

costs, investment, and the riskiness of firms in an industry. These variables, in turn, are the building blocks for the value-driver determinants of shareholder value. Specifically, price and quantity determine sales growth. The operating profit margin is affected by costs relative to prices, and quantities sold. Investment is divided into two essential value drivers—working capital and fixed capital investment. Finally, risk is conditioned by management's investment choices, and its capital structure or financing policy.

Consider the relationship between Porter's five competitive forces and the value drivers. The *threat of new entrants* into an industry depends on the barriers to entry. The higher the barriers, the lower the threat of new entrants. The height of entry barriers depends on factors such as economies of scale, product differentiation, switching costs, capital requirements, and government policy.

Economies of scale refer to the decrease in unit product costs as volume per period increases. Scale economies represent an important barrier because potential entrants are forced either to enter at a large scale, and therefore with a large investment, or to face a competitive cost disadvantage. The firm with scale economies in purchasing, manufacturing, distribution, and research enjoys cost advantages that can benefit three value drivers—operating profit margin, working capital investment, and fixed capital investment.

A second barrier to entry is product differentiation, which can be accomplished by exceptional customer service, advertising, and actual product differences. Differentiation affects the sales growth and operating profit margin value drivers by the higher prices that firms can charge. These higher prices are likely to be offset to some extent by the cost associated with differentiation activities, such as customer service. Similar analysis for the conceptual linking of each of the five competitive forces and their structural determinants to value drivers can be performed. For present purposes, the essential link between Porter's competitive forces and value drivers has been established.

Recall that strategy formulation involves assessing the attractiveness of the industry and the firm's competitive position within the industry. Porter's five competitive forces provide an eco-

nomically sound, systematic framework for analyzing industry attractiveness. Regardless of the relative attractiveness of an industry, firms in the same industry will often perform very differently. The wide range of performance within an industry underlines the necessity of understanding the firm's position within the industry.

Differences in firm performance within an industry may be driven by differences in chosen strategies. These strategies, in turn, can materially affect the relative attractiveness of the industry. Competitors may exercise different strategic options in areas such as product quality, technology, vertical integration, cost position, service, pricing, brand identification, and channel selection. IBM, for example, with its low-cost position, excellent service, and distribution network, continues its dominance of the computer industry. Auditing, on the other hand, is being viewed increasingly as a commodity by price-sensitive corporate buyers. The "Big 8" public accounting firms have largely responded with price cutting and cost-containment in their audit practice, and increased investment in their management consulting practice. The economic attractiveness of the public accounting industry has been affected adversely by these structural changes.

Once a company's planners assess industry structure and its competitive position in the industry, the focus shifts to translating this knowledge into a *competitive advantage*. Porter describes competitive advantage as follows:

> Competitive advantage grows out of value a firm is able to create for its buyers that exceeds the firm's cost of creating it. Value is what buyers are willing to pay, and superior value stems from offering lower prices than competitors for equivalent benefits or providing unique benefits that more than offset a higher price. There are two basic types of competitive advantage: cost leadership and differentiation.[5]

LINKING STRATEGY VALUATION TO VALUE CHAIN ANALYSIS

Porter proceeds to develop the value chain as a tool to identify the two types of competitive advantage mentioned above—cost leadership and

---

[5] *Id.* at 3.

differentiation. In contrast to five-forces analysis, which focuses on an entire industry, value-chain analysis is oriented to a specific business within the industry. Porter views a business as a "collection of activities that are performed to design, produce, market, deliver, and support its product." Disaggregating a firm into its strategically relevant activities enables the manager to understand both the behavior of costs, and the possible bases for differentiation. Competitive advantage potential can then be assessed by examining essential differences among competitor value chains.

The link between competitive strategy analysis using value chains and the cash flows fundamental to the shareholder-value approach to valuing business strategies is shown in Exhibit 1. To derive cash flow from operations, we begin with sales. Operating expenses are then deducted. Major classes of operating expenses for a typical manufacturing business are shown for each of the five primary activities. This activity-oriented classification scheme has important advantages over conventional accounting classifications, which often merge costs involving several activities or, in other cases, may separate costs that properly belong to a single activity. Strategic alternatives are essentially based on scenarios involving trade-offs within an activity or between activities, and therefore are assessed more easily by an activity-based financial information system than by conventional accounting systems.

After subtracting income taxes from operating profit, one arrives at operating profit after taxes. To convert this amount to a cash basis, depreciation and other noncash expenses deducted as part of operating expenses are added back. Investments in working capital and fixed capital, which are classified by activities, are then deducted to arrive at cash flow from operations. These cash flows, when discounted by the appropriate cost of capital, serve as the essential basis for valuing businesses and the value created by their strategies. Exhibit 1 thus establishes the link between value chains and the value drivers—sales growth rate, operating profit margin, income tax rate, working capital investment, fixed capital investment, and cost of capital—which are the essential building blocks of the shareholder-value approach to valuing business strategies. The Porter value-chain framework enables management to project value driver esti-

mates more systematically and therefore more confidently.

Exhibit 2 summarizes the relationship between competitive analysis and strategy valuation as outlined in this section. The Porter competitive-analysis framework provides a powerful aid to strategic thinking. The shareholder-value approach, on the other hand, evaluates the chosen strategies to see whether they are in fact likely to create a sustainable competitive advantage.

INTEGRATING STRATEGY VALUATION WITH THE COMPETITIVE-ANALYSIS PROCESS

As shown in Exhibit 2, the competitive-analysis process involves three basic steps: to assess industry attractiveness, to evaluate a business's competitive position within an industry, and to identify sources of competitive advantage. In this section, these steps are discussed. In addition, the integral relationship between competitive-strategy variables and the financially oriented value drivers underlying strategy valuation is demonstrated.

Industry Attractiveness and Business-Risk Assessment

The fundamental purpose of industry-attractiveness analysis is to gauge the value creation potential of each of the industries in which the company competes. Identifying competitive risk is a key consideration in industry-attractiveness analysis. Industry-attractiveness analysis using Porter's five-forces framework is particularly useful for assessing risk.

Total risk is the sum of the unsystematic or firm-specific risk (which can be eliminated largely by investing in a diversified portfolio) and systematic or market risk (which cannot be avoided). Since firm-specific risk can be eliminated, investors can expect to be rewarded only for bearing market risk. When viewed from the manager's perspective, total risk is often characterized as *business risk* plus *financial risk*. Business risk is the uncertainty inherent in business operations, and may be measured by the variability of cash flows. Financial risk represents the additional risk borne by common stockholders as a result of the introduction of fixed obligations such as debt and preferred stock in the capital structure. As financial

Exhibit 1 *Link Between Value Chain and Cash Flows*

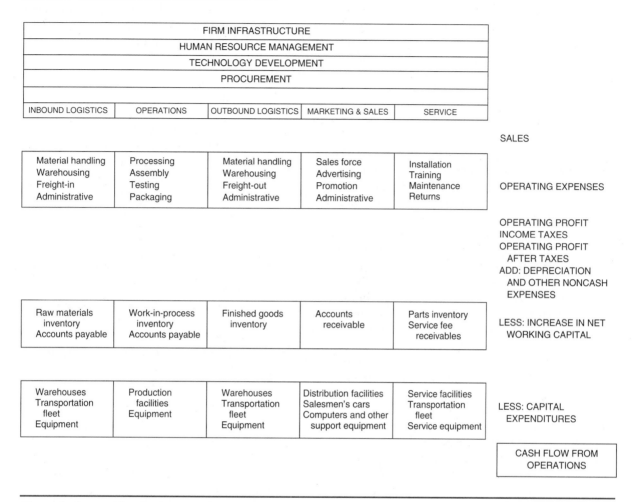

Figure 2 *Competitive Analysis and Strategy Valuation*

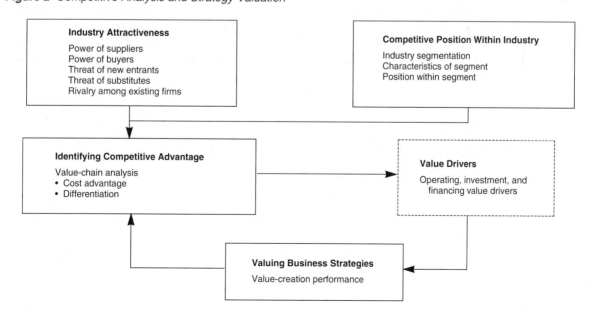

leverage increases, so does the variability of cash flows available for shareholders, because these flows are subordinate to the contractually fixed interest payments. In effect, the risk inherent in operations—business risk—is now spread over a smaller equity base, thus increasing the risk for each share.

While strategies that increase business risk probably will increase a firm's systematic risk as measured by its beta coefficient, a part of the increased business risk will generally be unsystematic or firm-specific, and therefore can be eliminated by diversification. Thus, methods that establish cost of capital or hurdle rates based on business unit or corporate cash flow variability essentially include diversifiable risk as well as the systematic component of risk. This, in turn, leads to higher hurdle rates than those demanded by investors who require compensation based on systematic market risk only.

Two observations are pertinent here. First, under some circumstances, determining a business's cost of equity by its systematic risk may understate the risk assumed by shareholders because bankruptcy costs are not taken into account. Assuming that the bankruptcy losses associated with one stock are only partially offset by gains in other stocks held in a diversified portfolio, then the higher the probability of a business going bankrupt, the greater will be investors' concern with *total risk* rather than just systematic risk. As a consequence, investors will demand a higher rate of return for the manager's focus on cash flow variability of the business (total risk approach) rather than cash flow variability relative to the overall market or economy (systematic risk approach). This is perhaps explained by the fact that, unlike well-diversified shareholders, managers, who typically have most of their wealth (stock, stock options, future compensation) linked to the firm, cannot easily balance the risk of business unit or company failure against other risks in their portfolio. Thus, managers view bankruptcy or failure with substantially greater concern than well-diversified shareholders, and this aversion to risk may well manifest itself in overly high hurdle rates for risky projects and strategies.

Keeping the foregoing discussion in mind,

one is ready to examine how the five-forces approach to industry-attractiveness analysis facilitates the assessment of business risk. Business risk depends on a variety of factors, some of the more important of which include:

- *Demand variability.* The more stable the demand for a firm's products, other things held constant, the lower its business risk.
- *Sales price variability.* Firms in which products are sold in highly volatile markets are exposed to more business risk than similar firms in which output prices are more stable.
- *Ability to adjust output prices for changes in input prices.* Some firms are better able to raise their own output prices when input costs rise. The greater the ability to adjust output prices, the lower the degree of business risk, other things held constant. This factor becomes increasingly important during the 1970s and 1980s because of inflation.
- *Input price variability.* Firms in which input prices are highly uncertain are exposed to a high degree of business risk.
- *The extent to which costs are fixed: operating leverage.* If a high percentage of a firm's costs are fixed, and hence do not decline when demand falls off, then it is exposed to a relatively high degree of business risk.[6]

Exhibit 3 shows which of Porter's five competitive forces principally impact each of the above business risk factors. The first three business risk factors jointly determine the variability of the sales-growth value driver. When we add the other two business factors, input-price variability and operating leverage, we have the factors that affect the variability of the operating profit margin value driver. Operating leverage establishes the trade-off between two value drivers—fixed capital investment and operating profit margin. Each of the business risk factors, of course, affects the cost of capital value driver.

The principal competitive forces that affect the first four business risk factors are apparent. The fifth business risk factor, operating leverage, deserves a comment. The economic trade-off between variable and fixed costs is influenced by the bargaining power of suppliers. For example, a

[6]E.F. Brigham and L.C. Gapenski, *Intermediate Financial Management* (1985), p. 214.

Figure 3 *Impact of Competitive Forces on Business Risk Factors*

Business Risk Factor	Principally Impacted by
Demand variability	Threat of substitute products Threat of new entrants
Sales price variability	Bargaining power of buyers Rivalry among existing firms
Ability to adjust prices	Bargaining power of buyers
Input price variability	Bargaining power of suppliers
Operating leverage	Bargaining power of suppliers Rivalry among existing firms

business wishing to become the low-cost producer in the industry will examine carefully the labor versus fixed-capital-investment trade-off. Rivalry also impacts operating leverage. More precisely, the current level of operating leverage within the industry may affect rivalry. For example, high levels of operating leverage create substantial pressure for firms to operate at high levels of capacity that are often achieved by price cutting. Operating leverage thus can have an important effect on business risk not only in its own right but also because of its impact on sales-price variability.

At the conclusion of the industry-attractiveness analysis, insights into the following questions should have been developed:

- How attractive is the industry as a whole?
- Which factors are generally most critical for creating value in this industry?
- How sensitive is the value of various companies in this industry to changes in key factors?
- How might individual entities and the industry as a whole be affected by changes in industry structure, by the competitive and general economic environment, and by other pressures?

COMPETITIVE POSITION AND VALUE CREATION POTENTIAL

The second basic step in competitive analysis is to evaluate the business unit's competitive position within the industry. The business unit may find itself in a very attractive industry, but a poor competitive position may nonetheless seriously limit its value-creation potential. The reverse is

also true; a strong competitive position in a lackluster industry can lead to excellent shareholder value prospects.

As Porter points out, whereas industry attractiveness reflects factors over which the firm has minimal control, differences in firm performance and competitive position can be driven by differences in chosen strategies. By its choice of strategy, a firm can change its relative position within its industry, thereby making the industry more or less attractive *for the firm*. Industries are not, however, homogeneous. Segments of a single industry may have very different structures as reflected in differences in the behavior of the five competitive forces. Competitive position must be analyzed in the context of the industry segment in which the business chooses to compete. Industry segmentation thus becomes an essential part of the competitive-analysis process. It is a prerequisite for determining what part of an industry a business should serve as well as how to compete within the chosen segment.

Once a business unit has properly identified its industry segment and the firms competing in that segment, it can continue its data gathering and analysis of competitive position with substantially greater confidence. The analysis should yield insights into questions such as:

- What appear to be the relative strengths and weaknesses of the competitors in the relevant industry segment?
- How might a company respond to a competitor's strategy, and how would a retaliatory strategy affect the company?

- How well will a competitor be able to pursue its apparent strategy given its current competitive position, cost structures, and available funding?
- How might individual competitors and the industry as a whole be affected by changes in industry structure, the competitive and general economic environment, and other pressures?

COMPETITIVE ADVANTAGE AND SUSTAINABLE VALUE CREATION

Industry-attractiveness analysis, along with an assessment of the business unit's position within its industry segment, provides the background for the third step in competitive analysis—the identification of competitive advantage. Estimating the shareholder-value-creation potential of strategies is a theoretically sound and practical means of evaluating the absence or presence of competitive advantage. More precisely, *sustainable value creation* (i.e., developing long-run opportunities to invest above the cost of capital) is the ultimate test of competitive advantage. The value chain is a robust tool for identifying competitive advantage. Moreover, as shown previously, there is a direct link between value-chain analysis and the cash flow forecasts required for estimating the value created by business unit strategies.

Because the most rewarding value-creating strategies emerge from exploiting a *sustainable* competitive advantage, it becomes important not only to identify how competitive forces can yield competitive advantage for the business, but also to predict the relative stability of these forces. Without consideration of the dynamics of the five competitive forces over time and their impact on the value chains, the business may find that it has developed a strategy with short-term rather than sustainable competitive advantage. In some industries, there are changes in the relationships among skills embodied in its value chain, strategies, and competitive forces shaping industry structure.

Any strategy designed to promote competitive advantage must, in the final analysis, meet the test of sustainable value creation. The value-creation process in turn depends on the translation of competitive dynamics into forecasts of value drivers. Thus, competitive advantage, whether driven by cost leadership or differentiation, involves a number of supporting strategies which affect each of the value drivers and collectively yield the best value-creation prospects. To illustrate, Exhibits 4 and 5 present some relevant tactics, classified by their impact on value drivers, for cost leadership and differentiation approaches to competitive advantage.

Cost leadership (Exhibit 4) is attained by controlling costs (by controlling scale, learning, and capacity utilization), and reconfiguring the value chain (i.e., developing more efficient ways to design, produce, distribute, or market the product). The reduction of services at ticket counters and gates, during the flight, and for baggage handling by the no-frills airlines such as People Express, is an excellent example of reconfiguring value chains. Differentiation (Exhibit 5), which seeks to provide something both different from competitors and valuable to the buyer, calls for a set of supporting tactics that are clearly distinct from those appropriate for a cost leadership strategy. These differences in supporting tactics will be reflected in forecasts for each of the value drivers. For example, value creation is ordinarily very sensitive to even small changes in operating profit margin. In the cost leadership case, the key to achieving target margins is likely to be effective cost control, while for the differentiation strategy the critical focus is more likely to be on the firm's ability to command a premium price.

Regardless of how a firm plans to achieve a competitive advantage, it is essential that management become familiar with the trade-offs between various value drivers. Below are some illustrative questions germane to cost leadership and then to differentiation strategies:

Cost Leadership
- Do the labor savings justify the productivity-motivated capital expenditures?
- Are the tight controls on inventory levels offset by reduced customer service and consequent loss of revenue?
- Can a less restrictive accounts receivable policy lead to increased market penetration and greater scale economics?
- Would increasing the sales growth rate also lead to an increase in financial risk which would result from debt financing the growth?
- If increased growth is due principally to lower selling prices, will cost savings improve oper-

ating profit margin sufficiently to justify the growth strategy?

Differentiation

- Does the premium price justify the costs of product features and other costs required to differentiate the product or service?
- Is the cost of maintaining inventory levels to ensure the highest service level necessary to attract and maintain buyers willing to pay the premium price?
- Is the cost of granting liberal credit terms necessary to attract and maintain buyers willing to pay the premium price?

- What would be the impact on sales growth and operating profit margin of a selling price reduction aimed at capturing a larger market share?

By integrating strategy valuation into every stage of the competitive-analysis effort, the strategic planner can expand the range of strategic alternatives to be considered, and thereby select strategies that will enable the company to gain a competitive advantage as measured by sustainable value creation.

Figure 4 *Cost-Leadership Strategy and Supporting Tactics Classified by Value Drivers*

Value Drivers	Tactics Supporting Cost Leadership Strategy
Sales growth rate	• Maintain competitive prices • Pursue market share opportunities to gain scale economies in production, distribution, etc. • Achieve relevant economies of scale for each of the value activities
Operating profit margin	• Introduce mechanisms to improve the rate of learning (e.g., standardization, product design modifications, improved scheduling) • Search for cost-reducing linkages with suppliers based on supplier's product design, quality, packaging, order processing, etc. • Search for cost-reducing linkages with channels • Eliminate overhead that does not add value to the product • Minimize cash balance
Working capital investment	• Manage accounts receivable to reduce average number of days outstanding • Minimize inventory without impairing required level of customer service • Promote policies to increase utilization of fixed assets
Fixed capital investment	• Obtain productivity-increasing assets • Sell unused fixed assets • Obtain assets at least cost (e.g., lease vs. purchase) • Target an optimal capital structure
Cost of capital	• Select least-cost debt and equity instruments • Reduce business risk factors in manner consistent with strategy

---

Figure 5 *Differentiation Strategy and Supporting Tactics Classified by Value Drivers*

Value Drivers	Tactics Supporting Differentiation Strategy
Sales growth rate	• Command a premium price • Pursue growth in market segments in which buyer is willing to pay premium for differentiation • Choose combination of value activities that create the most cost-effective means of differentiating (e.g., by lowering buyer's cost and risk and by raising performance)
Operating profit margin	• Eliminate costs that do not contribute to buyer needs • Minimize cash balance
Working capital investment	• Link accounts receivable policy to differentiation strategy • Maintain inventory level consistent with differentiating level of service • Obtain best terms with suppliers for accounts payable • Invest in specialized assets that create differentiation
Fixed capital investment	• Purchase assets for optimal utilization • Sell unused fixed assets • Obtain assets at least cost (e.g., lease vs. purchase) • Target an optimal capital structure
Cost of capital	• Select least-cost debt and equity instruments • Increase differentiation and thereby make demand less dependent on general economy

Strategic Management

by

Paul Shrivastava

INDEX

STRATEGIC MANAGEMENT

by

Paul Shrivastava